The Achievement of
AMERICAN CRITICISM

Representative Selections from
Three Hundred Years of
American Criticism

Selected By

CLARENCE ARTHUR BROWN
Marquette University

WITH A FOREWORD BY
HARRY HAYDEN CLARK

THE RONALD PRESS COMPANY ⋅ NEW YORK

PN
99
US
B7

Library of Congress Catalog Card Number: 54–6962

PRINTED IN THE UNITED STATES OF AMERICA

FOR MY MOTHER AND FATHER

PREFACE

This volume is the first to offer representative selections of American literary criticism from its beginnings up to and including contemporary criticism. It is designed as a text in literary criticism courses and as a supplementary volume in the study of American literature.

The selection of the individual essays has been guided primarily by the extent to which each essay is (1) representative of the critical theory and method of its author; (2) an elucidation of the critical background of the period in which it was written; and (3) a significant contribution to an understanding of the growth of American literary theory and of American literature. The essays are presented in a historical framework—in terms of the various periods and literary movements that have characterized the growth of American writing. Some of this material is here available in book form for the first time; much has previously appeared only in books or periodicals that are now scarce and long out of print.

An attempt has been made to balance the types of critical essays represented: evaluations of the work of major American poets and prose writers; statements of literary theory by American poets and writers of fiction; expositions of critical standards and methods by important literary critics; and studies of the relation between the writer and his age, his society, and his traditions.

In the selection of essays, emphasis has been placed upon American criticism from the beginnings to the close of the nineteenth century because it is this period which has never adequately been covered by an anthology and because the critical essays of this period are less accessible to the student than are those of the present century. A number of selections have been included, however, to illustrate the development and main trends of modern criticism.

The introductions aim to show the conditions under which literary criticism developed in America, the problems with which it was concerned, and the development of its methods and standards, from the earliest critical writings of the Puritans to the present time. Critical and literary theory has been presented only in its general outlines, but sufficient analysis of each writer and of the background of each period is provided so that the student may be able to read the essays with an understanding of the author's general critical theory and the relationship of the essay to the period in which it was written. For those who are interested in a more extensive study of the development of American criticism, the critical introductions have been documented and the critical essays have been annotated.

The essays in this volume have been selected not to illustrate any particular thesis or taste of the editor but to offer as impersonal a survey of the field of American criticism as the scholarship of the editor and the physical limitations of a single volume would permit.

I wish to thank Rev. Virgil Roach, S.J., Dean of the College of Liberal Arts, Marquette University, and Professor Jerome W. Archer, Director of the Department of English, for the reduction of my teaching load and for the provision of clerical assistance without which the preparation of this book would not have been possible. To Rev. Edward J. Drummond, S.J., Dean of the Graduate School, and to Professor Victor M. Hamm of the Department of English, I am indebted for reading portions of the manuscript and for providing criticism and information by which this book has benefited.

I wish to thank Professor Harry Hayden Clark of the University of Wisconsin for his essay which appears in print for the first time as the Foreword to this book, and for the suggestions he has offered concerning the book itself. The Marquette University Library and the Milwaukee Public Library have been particularly helpful in extending to me more than the usual privileges. To Mr. John W. Rathbun, my research assistant during the preparation of the book, I owe a debt of gratitude which greatly exceeds the adequacy of this acknowledgment to express.

CLARENCE ARTHUR BROWN

Milwaukee, Wisconsin
March, 1954

ACKNOWLEDGMENTS

Grateful acknowledgment is made to the following authors, publishers, and individuals whose courtesy in granting permission to reproduce these essays has made the collection possible:

Appleton-Century-Crofts, Inc., for "On the Nature of Poetry" and "On the Value and Uses of Poetry" from the *Prose Writings of William Cullen Byrant*, edited by Parke Godwin.

R. P. Blackmur, for "The Craft of Herman Melville: A Putative Statement" from *The Expense of Greatness*, Arrow Editions. Copyright 1940 by Richard P. Blackmur.

Doubleday and Company, Inc., for "The Novel with a 'Purpose'" from *The Responsibilities of the Novelist* by Frank Norris, copyright 1901, 1902, 1903 by Doubleday and Company, Inc.; for Preface to 1855 edition of *Leaves of Grass* and "A Backward Glance O'er Travel'd Roads," Preface to *November Boughs* by Walt Whitman, copyright 1924 by Doubleday and Company, Inc.

E. P. Dutton and Co., Inc., for "The Critical Movement in America" from *Sketches in Criticism* by Van Wyck Brooks, copyright 1932 by E. P. Dutton and Co., Inc.

Darrah More Fine, for "Criticism" from *Shelburne Essays, Seventh Series* by Paul Elmer More, Houghton Mifflin Company, 1910.

Harcourt, Brace and Company, Inc., for "The New Criticism" from *Creative Criticism and Other Essays* by J. E. Spingarn, copyright 1931 by J. E. Spingarn; for "Hamlet and His Problems" and "The Metaphysical Poets" from *Selected Essays: 1917–1932* by T. S. Eliot, copyright 1932 by Harcourt, Brace and Company, Inc.

Harper and Brothers, for the essay "Fenimore Cooper's Literary Offences" from *In Defense of Harriet Shelley and Other Essays* by Mark Twain, copyright 1918 by the Mark Twain Company, copyright 1945 by Clara Clemens Samossoud; for the selection from the essay "What Paul Bourget Thinks of Us" from *In Defense of Harriet Shelley and Other Essays* by Mark Twain, copyright 1897 by Harper and Brothers, copyright 1926 by the Mark Twain Company.

Harvard University Press, for "The Prayse of Eloquence" by Michael Wigglesworth, reprinted by permission of the publishers from Samuel Eliot Morison, *Harvard College in the Seventeenth Century*, copyright 1936 by The President and Fellows of Harvard College.

Houghton Mifflin Company, for chap. xi from *The Masters of Modern French Criticism* by Irving Babbitt, copyright 1912 by Houghton Mifflin Company; for "The Poet" from *Essays, Second Series* by Ralph Waldo Emerson, copyright 1883 by Houghton Mifflin Company; for the Preface to *The House of the Seven Gables* and the Preface to *The Blithedale Romance* by Nathaniel

Hawthorne, copyright 1883 by the Houghton Mifflin Company; for "Realism in Literature" and "On Whitman" from *Over the Tea Cups* by Oliver Wendell Holmes, copyright 1892 by Houghton Mifflin Company; for "The Function of the Poet" and "The Imagination" from *The Function of the Poet and Other Essays* by James Russell Lowell, copyright 1920 by Houghton Mifflin Company; for "What Is Poetry?" from *The Nature and Elements of Poetry* by Edmund Clarence Stedman, copyright 1892 by Houghton Mifflin Company.

Mildred Howells and John Mead Howells, for selections from *Criticism and Fiction* by William Dean Howells, copyright 1891 by Harper and Brothers.

Alfred A. Knopf, Inc., for "The American Novel" reprinted from *Prejudices: Fourth Series* by H. L. Mencken by permission of Alfred A. Knopf, Inc. Copyright 1924 by Alfred A. Knopf, Inc.

Isabel Garland Lord and Constance Garland Doyle for "Local Color in Art" and "The Local Novel" from *Crumbling Idols* by Hamlin Garland (Stone & Kimball, 1894), copyright by Hamlin Garland, 1894.

The Macmillan Company, for "The Art of Fiction" from *Partial Portraits* by Henry James, copyright 1888 by Henry James; for "Impressionism and Appreciation" from *Studies and Appreciations* by Lewis E. Gates, copyright 1900 by The Macmillan Company.

The Ronald Press Company, for "Modern Criticism" by Cleanth Brooks, printed as a Foreword to *Critiques and Essays in Criticism*, selected by Robert Wooster Stallman, copyright 1949 by The Ronald Press Company.

Charles Scribner's Sons, for "Remy de Gourmont" reprinted from *Unicorns* by James G. Huneker, copyright 1917 by Charles Scribner's Sons, 1945 by Josephine Huneker; used by permission of the publishers; for "Preface to *The Ambassadors*" reprinted from Volume XXI of *The Novels and Tales of Henry James*, copyright 1909 by Charles Scribner's Sons, 1937 by Henry James; used by permission of the publishers; for "The Elements and Function of Poetry" reprinted from *Interpretations of Poetry and Religion* by George Santayana, copyright 1900 by Charles Scribner's Sons, 1927 by George Santayana; used by permission of the publishers.

The Viking Press, Inc., for "Reality in America" from *The Liberal Imagination* by Lionel Trilling, copyright 1940, 1946, and 1950 by Lionel Trilling; reprinted by permission of The Viking Press, Inc.

Edmund Wilson for "The Historical Interpretation of Literature" from *The Triple Thinkers* by Edmund Wilson, Oxford University Press, Revised Edition, 1948. Copyright 1938, 1948 by Edmund Wilson.

CONTENTS

ix

PART II

THE AESTHETICS OF ROMANTICISM

CONTENTS

PART III

REALISM AND AESTHETICISM

PART IV

TRENDS IN MODERN LITERARY CRITICISM

FOREWORD

WHY IS LITERARY CRITICISM IN AMERICA WORTH STUDYING?

by Harry Hayden Clark

Howells remarks that in America we must read or we "barbarize." This, he says, is because, having less than Europe has of great architecture or great painting, books represent America's chief passport to mankind's great heritage of twenty-five centuries of ethical and artistic experience, whose availability for guidance and enjoyment constitutes one of man's chief distinctions from the animal or the barbarian, limited to his own paltry experience. And yet it is doubtless true that books mean little to the *majority* of Americans, even those who have leisure to read, because they have had little training in sensitive and perceptive response to what books have to offer, or they have *thought* little about the matter in contrast merely to reading emotionally. In the largest sense, the study of literary criticism is our best way of increasing the kind of sensitive "awareness" which Henry James prized in the gifted reader: it opens up all kinds of vistas of increased enjoyment and of appraisal. For the critic is like an older and wiser brother who has already served his apprenticeship and is eager to help us; or, to change the figure, the critic is a kind of "catalyzer" whose function in part is to provoke a reaction between the book and the reader. As James remarks, "To lend himself, to project himself and steep himself, to feel and feel till he understand and to understand so well that he can say, to have perception at the pitch of passion and expression as embracing as the air, to be infinitely curious and incorrigibly patient, and yet plastic and inflammable and determinable, stooping to conquer and serving to direct—these are fine chances for an active mind, chances to add the idea of independent beauty to the conception of success. Just in proportion as he is sentient and restless, just in proportion as he reacts and reciprocates and penetrates, is the critic a valuable instrument." While novels and dramas are usually concrete and limited to action, criticism translates these into abstract meaning and human significance. And the best criticism is in itself literature, with all its beauty of organization, emotional appeal, and rich play of thought. Indeed, it should be emphasized that while the average person doubtless reads merely with his feelings, sopping up only the emotional atmosphere of a book, reading diverse critical estimates of such a book sharpens our wits and trains us to read perceptively and so is creative in provoking us to use not only our feelings but our *minds*, to compare and to contrast, and to arrive by a creative act of our own at a *reasoned* and logically defensible interpretation or appraisal.

II

Perhaps some disappointment among those seeking the help of criticism has been caused by not distinguishing between the different kinds so that one can secure the kind for which one has a particular need. For criticism includes many approaches, and each has many advantages. Roughly speaking, one may divide criticism into four general kinds—the historical or explanatory; expository or textual interpretative; impressionist; and judicial or evaluative criticism. (In practice, of course, a given critical essay usually includes a bit of all four kinds, although one can generally classify it by finding where the principal emphasis is placed.)

The historical or explanatory critic is primarily concerned with showing how a given book came into being, with what influences produced it, but he may do this in at least three different ways: by limiting his inquiry to the author's own life; or by including that in a broader study of how the book was inspired by the author's time, place, and race; or by showing how it unfolds out of the author's expressed intention. Sainte-Beuve was the major spokesman of the first, and Taine of the second. As regards biographical criticism, it is usually thought that Hawthorne's own early solitude and sense of social maladjustment led him to brood on the "psychology" of a man in such a plight until this became the master theme in his major works. And the vitality and balance of *The Rise of Silas Lapham* doubtless owe much to the fact that Howells had himself come from a log cabin to "make his way" to the heights of Boston's cultured society and had brooded on the problems involved in the adjustment of two families of very diverse origins and tastes. Taine's *History of English Literature* (1864) greatly broadened Sainte-Beuve's approach and helped to ally the study of literature to social and intellectual history, and to give historical criticism a factual dignity and seriousness of purpose. As Lewis Gates remarks, compared to the subjective Romanticists' "dilettante experiments on their senses and emotions" and their "paltry juggling with fine phrases," such objective historical criticism "as Taine's is as healthy as sea air." One of the fascinations of such criticism is that it is concerned with the dynamics of change set in a firm contexture of chronology: one is dealing with explanations (for example, of the transition from romanticism to realism) in terms of cause and effect and not merely in terms of loose or appreciative description. Barrett Wendell's very influential *Literary History of America* (1900) was partly influenced by Taine, but the most impressive continuator of Taine (in a more sophisticated way) is V. L. Parrington in his richly stimulating *Main Currents of American Thought*. This approach to books as influenced by their time and place and race can be readily turned around so that the successive authors may be studied as "spokesmen" of their people. This kind of criticism is perhaps more useful for undergraduate survey courses and for those who wish to get a broad and stimulating preliminary view, in contrast to the more intensive analyses associated with graduate study.

If Taine's approach seems inadequate in its deterministic neglect of many authors' variable individualities and its neglect of purely aesthetic or formal analysis, one may turn to another general kind of explanatory criticism, to that concerned with the author's distinctively individual aesthetic aims or theories as a guide to interpreting his practice, his artistry. For example, to understand "The Raven," one ought to study Poe's revelation of how he conceived and developed the poem step by step, as told in his "Philosophy of Composition." Such historical criticism encourages a nonpartisan understanding not only of how the poem was created but (in this case at least) of what the author intended it to mean. For he says he began it not as an expression of subjective grief but as an exercise in the technique of expressing the mood he regarded as most aesthetic; and contrary to those who would center the poem's meaning on a faith in immortality and hope (cf. C. Alphonso Smith, for instance), Poe says that the Raven's refusal to be driven away is "emblematical of *Mournful and Never-ending Remembrance*," for "my soul from out that shadow that lies floating on the floor/ Shall be lifted—nevermore." The writer's craftsmanship can also be better understood by studying Hawthorne's notebook ethical axioms as the cores from which he bodied forth concretely many of his stories. Thus if Hawthorne the artist aimed to make an abstract idea (such as egotism being a bosom serpent) concrete, to dramatize it in terms of flesh and blood characters in conflict, the function of the interpreter is to reverse the creative process and to turn the concrete back into the abstract idea from which it developed. Such historical criticism not only illuminates Hawthorne's central idea in a given story but also enables us to appreciate the skill with which he elaborated his stories so as to give each an impressive unity, usually illustrated by a stream-lined focus on one brilliant symbol. Thus pride leading to wilful and then retributive social isolation is illustrated by the haughty Lady Eleanor who says "I wrapped myself in pride as a mantle," a scarlet cloak which symbolized her ostentatious elevation above her associates and which (by being the means of introducing smallpox germs and spreading an epidemic) united her in deadly sympathy with others and punished her. And the "germ" of "Ethan Brand," together with Bliss Perry's fascinating illustration of this kind of historical criticism in "Hawthorne at North Adams," showing how painfully he traveled and jotted down concrete facts, casts a flood of light on this story of a man who starved his heart (as a symbol of brotherly sympathy) to feed his brain until as the body of the suicide burns in the brick-kiln his heart is found to be marble, silhouetted against the red flames. Thus all the episodes and characters drawn from Hawthorne's observations taken from the notebooks come to a focus on this lurid and unforgettable symbol—the marble heart. Henry James's elaborate prefaces to each of his twenty-six volumes of his "New York Edition" in conjunction with his *Notebooks* containing the cores of his stories, early trial-plots, etc., are priceless in helping us to enter into his creative process and to appreciate his highly calculated artistry—such as his plan of having "seven lamps" (reflector-friends) illuminate the character, from different angles, of his heroine of *The Awkward Age*. In short, such a critical approach guards us against distortions of meaning derived from the reader's lack of sympathy or his demand for something which the author never intended to provide; and it is especially useful in a practical way to those who wish to become themselves creative writers, for the master takes us behind the scenes and illustrates step by step and stroke by stroke precisely how and why he attained his ends.

This leads us logically to a second major kind of criticism, the expository, devoted primarily to describing the texture of a given book within itself, the relation of the parts to the whole, what the parallel plots are if there are any, and how the images or figures are used to illuminate the theme. Such criticism may be concerned with the relation of the *ideas* within the book or with matters of *form* or prosody. For example, Shakespeare scholars make *Henry IV,* Part 1 more meaningful by showing how, within the conventional dramatic form, the characters are arranged in terms of contrasts to embody and illustrate five or six different concepts of Honor, from Hotspur's involving headstrong physical prowess to Falstaff's ironical view that Honor is but a word. And Poe's "Fall of the House of Usher" takes on a deftly patterned beauty if one studies it not only in the light of his five "laws" of the short story including finality and the focus on "one pre-established design" but also in the light of the images of several houses successively treated—from the physical house or building, to the family or "House of Usher," to Usher's diseased body as the house of his mind, to his eventually deranged mind itself ("The Haunted Palace" in "thought's dominion"), all five being united at last in destruction as lightning dissolves them all in the tarn and the reader's burning curiosity is quenched in "finality" illustrating the fulfillment of his last narrative or structural "law." Often one can discover purposeful parallels which greatly enhance the deeper meaning of the work. Thus Robert B. Heilman's perceptive study of "The Unity of King Lear" analyzes the play's two parallel plots focused on the filial ingratitude of children, shows that "Lear and Gloucester are, in terms of structure, not duplicates, but complements, Lear being active and Gloucester passive"; that "to be the father of Goneril is to create a symbol of the evil brought forth from oneself"; that the play is full of "ironic reversals" as when the evil children destroy each other—a magnificent symbol of the self-destructiveness of their kind of world; and that *Lear* is thus a tragedy "in which the externalized conflict exactly corresponds to the war within the soul—whether the begetting is an affirmation and an imposition of error or a Gloucester-like acquiescence in worldly imperfections." Even the pointing out of simple parallels often adds to the beauty of a poem, as when George Sherburn shows how Gray's "Elegy" is constructed in such a way that the evocation of the approaching evening of a day parallels the theme of the approaching night of life. How many people have memorized this poem without noticing this important structural plan! F. O. Matthiessen, Newton Arvin, Howard Vincent, and others have raised *Moby Dick* to great heights of suggestiveness calling attention to Melville's "linked analogies" and complex images used as symbols, some of which Lawrence Thompson thinks are used ironically and not without "triple talk." Henry Nash Smith has recently shown how much, even in the prosaic "literature of knowledge" such as "The Federalist Papers," a close study of the emotional associations aroused by each of the images selected to refer to the Constitution and to the Articles of Confederation helps us to understand precisely how the authors managed to achieve the persuasive "slant" they sought, to convert their readers to their scale of value-judgment, and to give their work aesthetic appeal which has helped *The Federalist Papers* to survive in the struggle for existence with other controversial literature expressing similar general ideas. For if history is essentially denotative and usually coldly factual, literature is at its best connotative; by means of carefully chosen images associated with what we love or fear the author stirs our emotions in preconceived directions, just as a stone dropped into still waters sends out concentric ripples. Emerson based much of his work on the doctrine of correspondence, the idea that the "laws of physics translate the laws of ethics," and Henry James said that a novel should begin with a picture and end with an idea. It is in accord with the general tradition of earlier American criticism that many of our most suggestive critical essays in recent years should have begun with a study of imagery as the key to all sorts of ramifying meanings and the management of aesthetic appeal.

Such semitechnical analyses of textures are not likely to outmode entirely a third kind of criticism, the impressionistic or personal. In this kind of criticism someone of fine sensitivity whose views we respect stands between the book and the reader and attempts by his gusto (or disgusto) to arouse the reader's interest in the book. Thus Hazlitt, revolting from neoclassic "criticism by rules," tells us that "Mrs. M's conversation is as fine cut as her features, and I like to sit in the room with that sort of coronet face. What she said leaves a flavor, like fine green tea. H-'s is like champagne, and N-'s like anchovy sandwiches." And Hazlitt gives us the flavor of the criticism of his fellow-impressionist, Charles Lamb: "But with what a gusto would he describe his favorite authors, Donne, or Sir Philip Sidney, and call their most crabbed passages *delicious!* He tried them on his palate as epicures taste olives, and his observations had a *smack*, in them, like a roughness on the tongue." Lowell's *Fireside Travels*, by no means exclusively literary criticism, illustrates how his apprenticeship in the tradition of the familiar bookish Lamb-like essay helped to give his later criticism the charm associated with a rich and appealing individuality, carrying his learning lightly, capricious and full of unexpected confidences, eager to make his delight in good things contagious. Howells's *My Literary Passions, Heroines of Fiction,* and *My Literary Friends* (including "My Mark Twain") illustrates the same delightful ease and shared delight in presenting authors in their habit as they lived. And Bliss Perry's essays *In Praise of Folly*, especially on the occasion of Emerson's "American

Scholar," illustrate the mastery of rich impressionism buttressed by sound knowledge. Probably more than scholars devoted to technicalities realize, many indifferent students have been first inspired to read by contact with one of these inspired impressionists whom they admired first as a *man* with very human and many-sided interests, who seemed to be taking them into his confidence in the warmth of his cozy fireside! And such criticism is perhaps most likely to result in being literature in its own right, with variety, color, surprises, and the charm of a zestful personality stamped upon it. Lamb, or Howells's "My Mark Twain," is likely to outlive dozens of ponderous superscholarly volumes of the PMLA!

Finally, fourth, there is the kind of criticism which does not primarily explain historically, interpret the text, or try to make subjective enthusiasm contagious, but which addresses itself to the sober and weighty task of appraising ultimate values in ethics or artistry. Such a judicial approach obviously involves critical criteria or "yardsticks" for measurement, and the reader should try to find out at once, in reading such criticism, precisely what the yardsticks are, for not all critics are as honest as Mr. Parrington was in confessing his at the start. Historians such as Charles Beard emphasized that even in reading narrative history one should always ascertain the writer's "frame of reference," his personal background, associations, prejudices and preferences, for these almost always influence what he has chosen to include and to exclude. Of the more frequent patterns of ideas used as judicial yardsticks are those associated with ancient classicism (Plato and Aristotle), the Christian tradition (dualism, etc.), democracy (laissez faire or regulatory?), Marxism (materialistic determinism, the inevitable coming of the proletarian revolution, class-hatred, etc.), and the New Humanism. (On the Marxian, see E. R. A. Seligman's temperate *Economic Interpretation of History*, 1907, along with Bernard Smith's *Forces in American Criticism*, 1939, in connection with criticism of it by Morris Cohen in the *Journal of the History of Ideas* in 1940; on the Humanistic approach, see Norman Foerster's *Toward Standards*, 1928, especially the last chapter. If the Freudian approach, associated with biographical criticism, is now considered common enough to warrant an additional category, see Frederick J. Hoffman's *Freudianism and the Literary Mind*, 1945, and the *Columbia Dictionary of Modern European Literature*, 1947, edited by Horatio Smith, pp. 651–57.) This is hardly the place to presume to evaluate evaluations, but one might suggest that in considering a given yardstick it is important to be sure before attempting over-all value-judgment that the precise historical meaning of the book in question is clear and accurate, for otherwise any evaluation will be faulty, and it is important to find a system of evaluation which takes into account all sides of human nature (cf. the question of free will vs. fatalism) and which provides for a proper consideration of literature's dual heritage of *both* ideas and form or beauty, preferably organically related. If too narrow a yardstick is chosen, it is likely to militate not only against strict justice of appraisal but against our enjoyment of diverse books which have something to offer us in diverse moods and for diverse needs. On the other hand, reading different or opposite appraisals often sharpens one's wits, stimulates one to renewed study of the book appraised, and increases the self-reliance of mature readers.

III

In distinctively *American* literary criticism two problems may be singled out as having aroused special interest. The first involves the consequences of democratic freedom of discussion. Without any politically established church, monarchical control, or rigidly enforced Party-Line such as that of Moscow, our critics have been free to debate every side of every issue and our books still read have had to survive in a genuine "struggle for existence" amid conflicting interests. The "interests" behind each critical essay or review, however, ought to be ascertained and weighed before the reader gives his full assent. For reviews (out of which critical essays or books usually grow) are of course solicited or accepted by periodicals which are owned or operated by partisan groups to further partisan purposes. There is nothing sinister about this, as long as the facts are known; it is part of our democratic belief in free debate and free competition. But readers of reviews and criticism ought to know the facts—i.e., what interests are back of them. It is of course comparatively easy to understand the coloration of religious parochial periodicals, and many politically sponsored periodicals are candid about their bias. But more careful investigation is needed in the case of those periodicals or individuals who pretend to be eclectic or omniscient. The relation of religious and literary tastes and standards is a fascinating subject of investigation, especially *why* Unitarianism should have had such a powerful influence (cf. *The Christian Examiner* and the *Unitarian Review*) much out of proportion to the number of its adherents as contrasted with adherents of other religious sects. Why were most of our major writers, from Bryant through Holmes and Longfellow, Unitarians? How did Unitarian assumptions color their literary theories and the criticism accepted by Unitarian periodicals? Until recently there has been little attention to the way in which political partisanship has "slanted" criticism. Dorothy Waples' *The Whig Myth of James Fenimore Cooper*, published by The Yale Press in 1938, suggests what might be done in the way of studying the history of criticism of other individual authors in the light of conflicting political issues. (Miss Waples concludes that Cooper was roughly aligned with the Jacksonian or Democratic party at least in their attack on banks and commercialism, and that *The Whig Review* and other Whig spokesmen deliberately were "out to get him." Dispassionate literary criticism was apparently very infrequent during that era.) And more comprehensive and stimulating is Dr. John Stafford's well-documented monograph, *Literary Criticism of "Young America, A Study in the Relationship of Politics and Literature, 1837–50"* (1952). This shows that if the Whigs had their literary critics, the Democrats had equally partisan critics also, such as W. A. Jones, who was sponsored by *The United States Magazine*

and Democratic Review (edited by O'Sullivan, Hawthorne's close friend)
opposed to *The Whig Review*. In an article in the PMLA Dr. Stafford
has shown that even the clerical H. N. Hudson's criticism of Shakespeare was mainly motivated by a political desire to use Shakespeare as
an arsenal for lambasting a faith in the common man. Later on, *Shakespeare from an American Point of View*, 1882, by George Wilkes, who
influenced Walt Whitman, also presented a full-length interpretation
biased because of Shakespeare's alleged lack of democratic sympathy. Thus
in the very complex matter of tracing the critical history of America's reaction to the multitude of English, German, French, and other foreign
authors, the political biases of our critics, and the conjunction of publication dates with political campaigns and political crises are worthy of close
attention. We need to guard against the assumption, too prevalent, that
criticism is written in a vacuum by men of Olympian detachment! However, taking such matters into account, it is likely that on the whole American criticism will show a long process of trial-and-error endeavor to win-
now and sift those European ideas which can be fruitfully adapted to
our new environment and changing social and economic conditions. The
interplay of all these variable factors is important in reading the history
of American criticism. With the possible exception of Australia, perhaps
no other country has developed criticism in such a complex setting, and
this offers the adventurous reader a challenge.

The second situation distinctive in American criticism has been the
debate from the Revolution to the present as to whether we ought to
favor and try to develop a criticism and literature uniquely national and
cut off from traditionalism and from English and Continental literatures.
Details of the long controversy in which most of our critics engaged in
part at least have been studied by such scholars as William Ellery Sedgwick, Benjamin Spencer, Nanette M. Ashby, J. C. McCloskey, R. W.
Bolwell, Ralph T. Flewelling, Earl L. Bradsher, and Howard M. Jones.
By nationalism different critics meant different things, such as the use of
American landscape for settings; the contrast between American political
institutions or ideas and those of Europe, regarded as less favored; use
of European settings and ideas (as in Cooper's *Bravo* and *Headsman*)
as inferior to American ideas; emphasis on American dialects and the ver-
nacular as contrasted to "Oxford English"; the use of Locke's *tabula rasa*
theory along with the environmentalism of French *philosophes* such as
Raynal, to whom Crèvecoeur dedicated his *Letters from an American
Farmer*, whom he regarded as a new man because rooted in a new soil;
or the use of Darwin's evolutionary ideas associated now with the idea of
progress and involving man as adapted to a new environment and thus
different from the European, as in Edward Eggleston's frontier books. Of
all the different compromises between nationalism and universalism proposed, those of Longfellow (and his Harvard successor, Lowell) and the
Platonic Emerson seem most fruitful, especially in these days of the
United Nations' ideal. Longfellow's early expressions of literary theory
called for a mild nationalism and he devoted many poems to national

heroes and scenes, but eventually in 1849 in *Kavanagh* he concluded that "Nationality is a good thing to a certain extent, but universality is better." And he worked out a most interesting program to integrate his work as professor (translating foreign masterpieces such as the Italian *Divine Comedy*) with our social and political need of assimilating many diverse immigrant races. His work helped to give the downtrodden immigrants a sense of their great racial and cultural heritage, and also it helped to teach the more condescending "upper-class" Americans (such as S. F. B. Morse with his "nativist" prejudices against Catholics from foreign lands) to be more tolerant and sympathetic, and to see the long-range advantages of the "melting-pot" concept. "As the blood of all nations is mingling with our own," said Longfellow, "so will their thoughts and feelings finally mingle in our literature. We shall draw from the Germans, tenderness; from the Spaniards, passion; from the French, vivacity, to mingle more and more with our English solid sense. And this will give us universality, so much to be desired." In his "Arsenal of Springfield" Longfellow suggested that if half the money America spent on armaments were spent on an educational program of this sort to redeem the human mind from the "error" (of prejudice between nations and races), wars might be eliminated. Longfellow's successor, Lowell, after his early nationalism, developed much the same approach to literature and criticism, with a similar stress eventually on Dante and universality of appeal as a criterion.

Emerson had said in "The American Scholar" (1837) that we had listened too long to "the courtly voices of Europe" and he disliked the abuse of books by mere antiquarians concerned only with the otherness of past ages. But his more mature essay on "History" develops the Platonic theme that mankind's "mind is one, and nature is its correlative," and that consequently our main concern should be with the unchanging One, the characteristics which men in all ages have in common, rather than with the changing Many, the localistic idiosyncrasies which make men different and antagonistic. A great book being an organic expression of a man who has risen above the uniqueness of himself and his age to the plane of "the universal mind," Emerson valued not so much an antiquarian quest of the mutable particulars of literary or social history as the perception of the extent to which a book reveals "the universal mind," "the law for man," in contrast to local manifestations of "the law for thing" which "doth the man unking." (These "two laws" were for Emerson, in contrast to the monists and naturalists, "not reconciled.") Thus he has no hostility toward the past when it is "rightly used," when it is subjected to "creative reading," when (genius being "a larger imbibing of the common heart") "the great poet makes *us* feel our *own* wealth," and *we* are "born into the great, the universal mind." In common with spokesmen of the Christian tradition, he finds that a "dualism is always present," and he is aware of "the eternal distinction between the soul and the world, aware that a founding of life upon the stream of sensation," upon "one condition of nature, namely motion," results in "uneasiness" and despair. Unlike the materialists from his time to Moscow today,

Emerson as a dualist would found our life as a people upon that "which
changes not, which ranks all sensations and states of mind," upon a
democratic self-reliance not Byronic but a "reliance on God himself," God
being the Universal (not the national) Mind. As a dualist he urges that
we should "not take counsel of flesh and blood but of the law, alive and
beautiful, which works over our heads and under our feet. Pitiless, it
avails for our success when we obey it, and for our ruin when we con-
travene it." To Emerson determinism (such as Taine used to explain
literature in terms of distinct races and nations and places) was "a sty of
sensualism." In his essay on "The Poet" (1844, eleven years before Whitman's *Leaves of Grass*) Emerson included what seemed a very adequate
clarion call for the nationalistic celebration of the American scene: "We
have yet had no genius in America, with tyrannous eye, which knew the
value of our incomparable materials, and saw, in the barbarism and materialism of the times, another carnival of the same gods whose picture
he so much admires in Homer . . . Our log-rolling, our stumps and
their politics, our fisheries, our Negroes, and Indians, our boats and our
repudiations, the wrath of rogues and the pusillanimity of honest men,
the northern trade, the southern planting, the western clearing, Oregon,
and Texas, are yet unsung. Yet America is a poem in our eyes; its ample
geography dazzles the imagination, and it will not wait long for metres."

But if Emerson thought our poets should begin with the American
scene, he thinks they should use this only as a *means* of vividly bodying
forth the great unseen spiritual laws that are universal and unite all races.
Thus he says "things admit of being used as symbols, because nature (the
American scene) is a symbol, in the whole and in every part." From his
point of view limiting poetry merely to a physiological description of this
scene would be an acknowledgment of the bankruptcy of the poetic imagination, a falling short of the more important half of the poet's true
function. Emerson of course welcomed Whitman, and his poems such as
"Passage to India" no doubt came near to fulfilling Emerson's ideal in its
combination of the celebration of current American events (such as join-
ing the Atlantic and the Pacific by the Union Pacific) and his more "universal" interpretation that such achievements of engineers would effect
"the marriage of continents," effect world peace so that man could enjoy
his immortal spirituality. In reading criticism of our later spokesmen, it is
well to keep in mind the yardsticks of such major critics of our Golden
Day, involving a harmonious reconciliation of nationalism *and* universalism, of individualism *and* brotherhood.

PART I

THE ORIGINS OF AMERICAN
CRITICAL THEORY

THE PURITANS[1]

LITERATURE arrived late in America. The immensely practical purpose
of gaining a living from the new land and living a life devoted primarily
to spiritual realities pre-empted the possibility of any strictly creative writing. It was in New England, under the Puritans, that the first literary
efforts of value took place. But their value today lies largely in the depicting of the Puritan consciousness: the problems, habits, and manners which
occupied their lives. English writing naturally dictated the forms for
American writing; the times were not propitious for the severing of cultural
ties.[2] And so New England prayed and worked, its lyrical voice the moralistic poem and its conscience the sermon.

The first writing in America that we can call critical is, in many respects,
not critical at all. This is the preface to the *Bay Psalm Book,* the first book
published in America. Between the years 1640 and 1752, New England's
famous biblical paraphrase passed through twenty-seven editions. In the
preface, written by Richard Mather, are given the reasons for the manner
of translation:

> If therefore the verses are not always so smooth and elegant as some
> may desire or expect; let them consider that Gods Altar needs not our
> pollishings: Ex.20. for we have respected rather a plain translation,
> than to smooth our verses with the sweetness of any paraphrase, and
> so have attended Conscience rather than Elegance, fidelity rather than
> poetry, in translating the hebrew words into english language. . . .

The writer, here, is aware of the problems arising out of the paraphrasing
of God's Word within the restrictions of metre, and accuracy and clarity
are more dominant as motives than the poetic quality of the work.

While the Puritans have left a surprising number of comments on the
art of writing, and a few essays, it is obvious that they did not, as a group,
think of literature from primarily an aesthetic point of view. There is a
constant preoccupation with the problem of how poetry and prose can be
made more useful to the causes of religion, history, or controversy. Most

[1] An excellent introduction to Puritan literary theory and literary criticism may be
found in *The Puritans,* by Perry Miller and Thomas H. Johnson (New York, 1938),
pp. 545–51 and 665–68. There is a bibliography on literary theory, pp. 820–21.
General studies of the period include Perry Miller, *The New England Mind* (New
York, 1939); Samuel E. Morison, *Builders of the Bay Colony* (Boston, 1930); Kenneth B. Murdock, *Literature and Theology in Colonial New England* (Cambridge,
1949); Moses C. Tyler, *A History of American Literature During the Colonial
Period, 1607–1765* (New York, 1878); and Thomas Wright, *Literary Culture in
Early New England, 1620–1730* (New Haven, 1920).
[2] Elizabeth Cook, in *Literary Influences in Colonial Newspapers, 1704–1750* (New
York, 1912), emphasizes the interest shown in English writers during this period.

frequently, comments on literature, and on literary style and technique, are therefore somewhat incidental to a broader purpose. Literature was never considered as mere enjoyment or as an end in itself.

The Puritans, however, were far from being devoid of literary sensibilities.[3] Early Puritan writers were almost all college graduates with classical backgrounds, well trained in the humanistic tradition.[4] They are to be regarded as essentially carrying on the medieval and Elizabethan traditions of rhetorical theory which had characterized English universities during the Renaissance. This would be particularly true of the Puritan ministry with its dual emphasis upon the Bible and upon the advancement of learning.

Typical of this tradition is Michael Wigglesworth's essay, *The Prayse of Eloquence* (1650), which was intended to make ministers more effective in their sermons through the art of rhetoric. "Eloquence," he says, "overturns . . . and carries them down with the irresistible stream of its all controlling power." Wigglesworth praises eloquence because it is an art which gives new strength and vitality to the truth. His interest is utilitarian, but it is utilitarian in the finest sense of the word. Art is considered as not being restricted to one class of men, say the poets, but it is regarded as being universal in its service to truth and in making that truth prevail. Hence, that art was considered best which was clear, convincing, and appropriate.[5]

A plain style, which was at the same time eloquent, was therefore much in favor among the Puritans. Governor Bradford in his preface to *Of Plimmoth Plantation* (ca. 1650) indicates that he is going to write "in a plain style; with singular regard unto the simple truth in all things." [6] The Puritans usually rejected imagery which served merely to delight and favored that which served to make the truth more easily understood. Anything which appealed too strongly to the senses was regarded as a danger to the concentration on what must be grasped by the reason. Good writing was to teach; its method was to make direct, clear, and persuasive what man most needed to know. Mather Byles's essay on style (1745) reflects this preference for the plain style in its attack upon bombast.

In poetry, the traditions of the Puritans were Renaissance and Elizabethan. Although the Bible always remained supreme, the Puritans felt that the classical poets had much to offer in the achievement of virtue in life. That classical poets, orators, and historians were sources of wisdom that could be drawn upon for purposes of illustration, they had on no

[3] See Kenneth Murdock, "The Puritan Tradition in American Literature," in *The Reinterpretation of American Literature*, ed. by Norman Foerster (New York, 1928), chap. v.

[4] A good discussion of Puritan humanism can be found in Samuel E. Morison, *Harvard College in the Seventeenth Century* (Cambridge, 1936), particularly chaps. vii and viii.

[5] An interesting study of Wigglesworth as an artist is F. O. Matthiessen, "Michael Wigglesworth, a Puritan Artist," *New England Quarterly*, I (1928), 491–504.

[6] See Eugene F. Bradford, "Conscious Art in Bradford's *History of Plymouth Plantation*," *New England Quarterly*, I (1928), 133–57.

less an authority than Peter Ramus.[7] While it is clear that the Puritans did not cut themselves off from the tradition of poetic art, it is also true that they made such use of it as they considered most fitting. It is, on the whole, the ethical, the moral import of poetry which appealed to the Puritan mind. Poetry was not merely to delight; thus, to the Puritans, the subject matter of poetry was regarded as being of the highest consequence. While the Puritans did not develop a conscious poetic theory, it is nevertheless true that they display a considerable awareness of the art. This awareness, however, was always a secondary consideration. Matter counted for more than manner. Hence, their criticism is primarily judicious in nature and only secondarily concerned with aesthetics.

Poetry, like prose, was considered as an art to serve God and truth. Of Michael Wigglesworth, Cotton Mather wrote in his funeral sermon, *A Faithful Man, Described and Rewarded* (1705), "And that yet he might more *Faithfully* set himself to do Good, when he could not Preach he *Wrote* several Composures, wherein he proposed the edification of such Readers as are for plain Truths, dressed up in a *Plain Meeter*." Poets were thus encouraged to search for profitable learning and doctrine which would teach great precepts when incorporated with the pleasing manner of poetry. Richard Mather indicated that poetry was employed in the *Bay Psalm Book* the better to honor God, and Edward Taylor chose poetry better to express his love for Christ.

While the Puritans were keenly aware of the poet's high calling, they were just as aware of the danger for them which lay in poetry of a too highly impassioned nature or which dealt with fable rather than with truth. Cotton Mather, writing in the *Manuductio ad Ministerium* (1726) concerning poetry and style, warns: "Be not so set upon poetry as to be always poring on the passionate and measured pages. Let not what would be sauce rather than food for you engross all your application." He condemns Homer, in part, for his fables; and Ovid entirely for his impassioned pages.

Mather, himself, was an immensely learned man; his library in this period was one of the largest the colonies had yet seen assembled. He sees poetry as a means of cultural, as well as moral, enrichment if it exhibits skill and high seriousness in handling its theme; and, with the Bible, recommends Homer and particularly Virgil as fit for cultivation. The conception of poetry as a learning or a moral philosophy was a heritage of the Renaissance and of the metaphysical poets.

As the eighteenth century in America progressed, the Puritans, in their literary thought, reflected English trends. They were gradually becoming

[7] French Protestant logician, martyr in the St. Bartholomew massacre. Morison, in *Harvard College in the Seventeenth Century*, calls him a major influence on the Puritans, particularly as revealed in the severely logical structure of Puritan sermons. Assuming that a simple and comprehensible order permeated the universe, Ramus attempted to reflect this in his logic, which was simple, clear-cut, and direct. It is interesting to speculate on the extent of this influence in the formation of the Puritan preference for a "plain" style. That Ramus did not hesitate to draw upon rhetoric and classical scholarship to reinforce his system of logic, and to illustrate his arguments, undoubtedly provided Puritan writers with good authority to do likewise.

more conscious that style was an important consideration in writing and that a consciousness of it should not be concealed. Writing in 1726, Mather reacts against such acute sensitivity to style:

> The blades that set up for critics . . . appear to me, for the most part, as contemptible as they are a supercilious generation. For indeed no two of them have the same style; and they are as intolerably cross-grained, and severe in their censures upon one another, as they are upon the rest of mankind. . . .

As for the conflict between the Ciceronian and Senecan styles, he sees no justice in the controversy:

> However, since every man will have his own style, I would pray that we may learn to treat another with mutual civilities and condescensions. . . . I wonder what ails people, that they can't let Cicero write in the style of Cicero, and Seneca write in the (much other!) style of Seneca, and own that both may please in their several ways. . . .

Mather is more tolerant in his attitude toward the interests of poetry and style than were his forebears. The emphasis is still upon matter, "uplifted" matter, but the sign is implicit of things to come. His comments are undoubtedly among the most enlightened of the colonial period.[8]

As the Puritan era drew toward a close, the work of Puritan writers displayed an increasing catholicity of taste and an urbanity of tone that stands in sharp contrast with the narrower and more utilitarian quality of earlier Puritan attitudes toward literature. In his Preface to the *Poetical Meditations* (1725) of Roger Wolcott, John Bulkley writes that "what is properly call'd *Wit* is what, as I take it, makes the *Accomplish'd Poet*." His definition of wit as "a ready Assemblage of Ideas, or a putting those together with quickness & variety wherein there can be found any *Congruity* or *Resemblance*; or to speak more plain, an aptness at Metaphor and Allusion," echoes what had become a commonplace of English neoclassical criticism. Although still implying that a good style is one which is plain and which has utility, Mather Byles's satire on style (1745) possesses a literary self-consciousness and a polish which more nearly resembles the eighteenth century periodical essay than any Puritan writing which had preceded it.

NEOCLASSICISM

By the end of the first half of the eighteenth century, Puritanism as a specific religious force in America had pretty much run its course. There were to be strong manifestations of its spirit remaining in the New Eng-

---

[8] Although Mather did not understand blank verse, he was one of the first to defend its use. See his Preface to *Psalterium Americanum* (Boston, 1718), his attempted blank verse translation of the Psalms. For an extended study of Mather see Barrett Wendell, *Cotton Mather: The Puritan Priest* (New York, 1891, 1926), a sympathetic study written by a "Genteel" critic. See also Kenneth Murdock, *Selections from Cotton Mather* (New York, 1926).

land consciousness, but its organizational feature declined, revived for a short time under the impact of the thunderous fire of Jonathan Edwards, then further declined into the twilight.[9] During the latter part of the seventeenth century and the first half of the eighteenth, new methods and ideas from Europe were exerting an increasingly strong influence upon the American mind. Under the impact of such forces as the methods and ideas of the new science, particularly those of Newton,[10] and of thinkers like Descartes, Locke, Voltaire, Shaftesbury, and Diderot, a new attitude toward life had slowly formed which finds its expression now in such terms as the Age of the Enlightenment and the Age of Reason. That no sharp dividing line between the two periods can be drawn seems obvious. The emphasis upon logic, and upon reason, which had characterized Puritan literary theory and practice forms a connecting link between the two ages although for the new age there existed no background of dogmatic theology such as Calvinism had furnished for the Puritan mind.[11]

Possessed of a keen and discerning wit, extraordinarily concerned with manifold problems that could be solved under the scrutiny of reason and experiment, Benjamin Franklin, more than anyone else, serves as a representative of the American enlightenment.[12] While none of his writing specifically concerns itself to any degree with literary criticism, it does afford a penetrating insight into some of the more general attitudes toward literature which prevailed during the period and which tended to make the eighteenth century in America somewhat different from the period in England.

Writing to the young artist Charles Willson Peale, soon after the Revolution, Franklin expressed the opinion that "The arts have always traveled westward, and there is no doubt of their flourishing hereafter on our side of the Atlantic." Franklin's use of "hereafter" is significant, since he felt that while the fine arts were necessary to a refined society, they had little place in a young nation seeking to establish itself. On another occasion he wrote:

> All things have their season, and with young countries as with young men, you must curb their fancy to strengthen their judgment. . . . To America, one schoolmaster is worth a dozen poets, and the invention of a machine or the improvement of an implement is of more importance than a masterpiece of Raphael. . . . Nothing is good or beautiful but in the measure that it is useful. . . .

[9] A pertinent study of the decline of Puritanism is in *Transitions in American Literary History*, ed. by Harry H. Clark (Durham, N. C., 1954): see chap. xiv, Clarence H. Faust's "Why Puritanism Declined."

[10] See Harry H. Clark, "The Influence of Science on American Ideas, from 1775 to 1809," *Trans. Wisconsin Academy Sciences, Arts, and Letters*, XXV (1944), 305-49.

[11] Olive M. Griffiths, *Religion and Learning: A Study in English Presbyterian Thought from the Bartholomew Ejections (1662) to the Foundation of the Unitarian Movement* (Cambridge, Eng., 1935) is an excellent study of the steps of development whereby Calvinism became Unitarian rationalism, a parallel movement to the New England Puritan development which is much illuminated by comparison.

[12] A recent critical biography of Franklin is Carl Van Doren, *Benjamin Franklin* (New York, 1938).

An indication of Franklin's attitude toward at least one function of literature may be had from reading his *Idea of the English School* (1751):

> . . . Let it then be required of them to give an Account . . . of the *Intention* of the Writer, or the *Scope* of the Piece, the Meaning of each sentence, and of every uncommon Word. . . . Where the Author has us'd an Expression not the best, let it be pointed out; and let his Beauties be particularly remarked to the youth. . . . Let such Lessons for Reading be chosen, as contain some useful Instruction, whereby the Understandings or Morals of the Youth, may at the same Time be improv'd.

With reference to prose style, Franklin's model is, of course, Addison's *Spectator*. Students should be taught "to express themselves clearly, concisely, and naturally, without affected Words or high-flown Phrases."

What Franklin has to say about John Kitel's elegy in *Dogood Papers*, No. VII (1722) is, from the point of view of neoclassical poetic theory, entirely justified. Franklin's position is that New England poetry is made by poets with the best of intentions but with little instruction in how to govern Fancy with Reason. His recipe for the making of a New England funeral elegy is one of the most delightful parodies to be found in his work.

Like Franklin, George Washington declared "that only arts of a practical nature would for a time be esteemed," and added that the genius of the country was scientific rather than imaginative. Even as to the drama, which he loved as he did music, Washington's judgment, like that of his age, was practical. He regarded it as primarily "a chief refiner," and said that it would "advance the interest of private and political virtue . . . and have a tendency to polish the manners and habits of society."

No one of the early statesmen expected to see the rise of a class whose profession would be the arts. Thomas Jefferson wrote to a friend that "Every man is engaged in some industrious pursuit." And on another occasion, he wrote "Literature is not yet a distinct profession with us. Now and then a strong mind arises, and at intervals of leisure from business emits a flash of light. But the first object of young societies is bread and covering."

Jefferson offered an insight into the concern of the age with the practical service that letters might render, when he wrote, concerning the Declaration of Independence, that he sought "not to find out new principles, or new arguments, never before thought of, not merely to say things which had never been said before; but to place before mankind the common sense of the subject in terms so plain and firm as to command their assent. . . . Neither aiming at originality of principle or sentiment, nor yet copied from any previous writing, it was intended to be an expression of the American mind."

That these statesmen would be concerned with the arts to any considerable degree could hardly be expected in a period of such radical growth and change. Yet Franklin had formulated an aesthetic principle concern-

Locke and Hume, he was particularly attracted to Kames's identification of aesthetic and moral perceptions as the activities of an "internal sense," common to all men, immediate in its judgments and therefore independent of elaborate reasoning processes:

> Upon a sense common to the species, is erected a standard of taste, which without hesitation is apply'd to the taste of every individual. This standard, ascertaining what actions are right and what wrong, what proper and what improper, hath enabled moralists to establish rules for our conduct from which no person is allowed to swerve. We have the same standard for ascertaining in all the fine arts, what is beautiful or ugly, high or low, proper or improper, proportioned or disproportioned. And here, as in morals, we justly condemn every taste that swerves from what is thus ascertained by the common standard.[18]

In his examination of "human nature" based upon this "sense common to the species," Kames discovered certain aesthetic principles many of which were carried over into the criticism of the period in England and America and which can be seen in the criticism of Trumbull. Beauty, according to Kames, results from proper proportion, uniformity, order, and simplicity. Trumbull criticizes Richardson's *Clarissa* for its lack of proportion and probability as well as for its objectionable morality.[19]

The emphasis that Kames placed upon simplicity and clarity perhaps has some bearing on Trumbull's being one of the earliest critics to attack the extremes of eighteenth century "poetic diction." In the *Essay on the Use and Advantages of the Fine Arts* (1770) which Trumbull delivered as his Master's oration at Yale, he attacks extreme examples of "poetic diction" and praises Gray and Goldsmith for "this long lost style of simplicity."[20] He also criticizes, on another occasion, romantic poetry for its lack of clarity which "leads astray the mind from the object, or renders the descriptions often pompously obscure."

Since Kames considered beauty an absolute, based "upon a sense common to the species," he favored, as did the neoclassicists, a generalized approach to literature, the representative rather than the individual, the typical rather than the particular. Hence, the subjective, the introspective, is to be avoided, as Trumbull indicates in his criticism of the excessive subjectivity of Moore and Wordsworth. Likewise, individual and immoderate emotions are not to be expressed. Trumbull criticizes Byron not only for moral reasons but for expressing passion and feeling. Coleridge, he

[18] For a more complete exposition of Kames's theory see Helen W. Randall, "The Critical Theory of Lord Kames," *Smith College Studies in Modern Languages*, XXII (1941), 1-147; William Charvat, *The Origins of American Critical Thought* (Philadelphia, 1936), chap. iii, "Scottish Sources." Charvat has noted at least thirty-one American editions of Kames. For the influence of Kames on Trumbull, see Leon Howard, "Yale College, 1763-78," and "John Trumbull," in *The Connecticut Wits*. See also the unpublished dissertation by Warren A. Guthrie, *The Development of Rhetorical Theory in America, 1635-1850* (Northwestern, 1940).
[19] Alexander Cowie, "John Trumbull Glances at Fiction," *American Literature*, XII (1940), 69-75.
[20] Leon Howard, *The Connecticut Wits*, p. 47, states that "the ideas in his Master's *Essay* were taken bodily from Lord Kames's *Elements of Criticism*."

ing the practical arts when he wrote that "Nothing is good
but in the measure that it is useful," thus anticipating the tw
tury's theory of functional art. For the eighteenth century
there could be no arbitrary distinction made between the fine a
useful arts, for the practical arts were considered to have bea
successfully achieved their ends.[13]

Although the "Connecticut Wits" are known today only to
of American literature, they are important in any study of the i
life and the literary pretensions of the late eighteenth and early
centuries.[14] Two of the group in particular, John Trumbull and
Dwight, are representative of the trends of literary theory and c
the period.[15]

Neoclassicism, with its emphasis upon rule and propriety, w
the strongest factors in molding the critical theory of Trumbull, a
to reinforce the emphasis that Puritanism had placed upon dec(
morality. In both theory and practice, neoclassicism implied conf
certain laws which governed "correctness" in writing. It is a comi
that American writers in this period were culturally dependent u
land, which meant that for Trumbull the "laws" were those end
Pope, and the models of "correctness" were such poets as Pop(
Prior, Goldsmith, and Gray; in prose such writers as Swift, Addi
Johnson. As a true neoclassicist, he valued decorum, formality
certain degree of elegance and polish in diction. In poetry, he
order and design, and he admired strength and conciseness in versi
He condemns Wordsworth and Crabbe for having "sought origin
attempting to dignify by verse objects the most vulgar and disgustir
for lacking restraint and craftsmanship, terming their effects "disc
and "unnatural." Similarly, he did not approve of blank verse bec
its "Too near resemblance to Prose," and its "diffusion and prolixity

A second influential factor in the period which influenced Tr
was the philosophical background of the Scottish "common-sense"
particularly the critical and aesthetic tradition of Kames.[17] As Tr
was a defender of religious orthodoxy and feared that the elaborate a
tion of reason in metaphysics would lead only to scepticism as it

[13] See Constance Rourke, *The Roots of American Culture* (New York, 19.
[14] General studies of the Connecticut Wits are Leon Howard, *The Con*
Wits (Chicago, 1943), and Vernon L. Parrington, *The Connecticut Wits*
York, 1926).
[15] An excellent critical biography of Trumbull is Alexander Cowie, *John Tru*
Connecticut Wit (Chapel Hill, N. C., 1936). For a discussion of Trumbu
critic see Alexander Cowie, "John Trumbull as a Critic of Poetry," *New E*
Quarterly, XI (1938), 773-93, and "John Trumbull Glances at Fiction," *An*
Literature, XII (1940), 69-75. A recent critical biography of Dwight is Cha
Cunningham, *Timothy Dwight* (New York, 1942). There is an unpublishe
sertation on *Timothy Dwight, Man of Letters* by Lewis E. Buchanan (Wisc
1940).
[16] Most of the critical writing of Trumbull exists only in manuscript form a
the "Tyler Papers" in the Cornell University Library. Extensive quotations are
in Cowie's "John Trumbull as a Critic of Poetry," and "John Trumbull Glan(
Fiction."
[17] Henry Home, Lord Kames, *Elements of Criticism* (3 vols.; Edinburgh, 17

thinks, wrote "as though a poetical Bedlam was about to be erected on the summit of Parnassus."

The true function of literature, Trumbull thinks, as did the neoclassicists, is "to enoble the soul, purify the passions, and give the thoughts a better turn . . . to add dignity to our sentiments, delicacy and refinement to our manners." Pope he considers to be the supreme example of what fine art should be.[21] As a neoclassicist, he particularly admires the art and craftsmanship of Pope; and in a discussion of prosody which he wrote for Noah Webster's *Grammatical Institute of the English Language* (1785) he attempts to point out the possibilities of the heroic couplet as it had been used by Pope. Though a little critical of such excesses of neoclassicism as "poetic diction," pedantry, and servile imitation, Trumbull did not wish to change the movement but merely reform it.

Like that of Trumbull, the literary criticism of Timothy Dwight is in the neoclassical tradition and is strongly moral and judicious in nature. Like Trumbull, he criticizes fiction because it demands nothing but "the luscious indulgence of fancy," and contributes nothing to the mental or spiritual integration of the reader. Moreover, it does not aid him to face the sober truth and realities of life, since fiction is improbable and untrue— a distorted view of life. He adheres generally to neoclassical ideals. In style he prefers "preciseness, directness, simplicity," and in poetry he prefers the style of Pope.

Like Trumbull, Dwight, when young, reacted against the authority of neoclassical rules and the reverence for literary models. As with Trumbull, Dwight's early antagonism came in a large measure as a result of the influence of Kames.[22] In a Master's essay delivered at Yale in 1772, *A Dissertation on the History, Eloquence, and Poetry of the Bible*, Dwight defended the practices of the Hebrew writers, who did not follow neoclassical rules:

> Unincumbered by critical manacles, they gave their imaginations an unlimited reign . . . and in every period, snatched the grace which is beyond the reach of art. . . .
> "But" says the Critic "they don't describe *exactly according to our rules.*" True sir; and when you can convince me that *Homer* and *Vergil* from whom you gather those rules, were sent into the world to give Laws to all other authors; when you can convince me that every beauty of fine writing is to be found, in its highest perfection, in their works, I will allow the beauties of the divine writers to be faults.

In the fourth number of "The Friend" (1789), a series of periodical essays in the manner of Addison and Johnson which Dwight wrote for the *New Haven Gazette and the Connecticut Magazine*, the influence of Kames and the Scottish "common-sense" school can again be seen. There is, according to Dwight, too much worship of authority for its own sake.

[21] A valuable study of American criticism relating to Pope is Agnes M. Sibley, *Alexander Pope's Prestige in America, 1725-1835* (New York, 1949).
[22] See Leon Howard, *The Connecticut Wits*, "Timothy Dwight," pp. 79-111.

He uses Aristotle as his example and indicates that Aristotle did not make rules but suggested means to produce poetry as it was then being written. If Aristotle had lived after Milton, if he could have read or seen the tragedies of Shakespeare, then his rules concerning the epic and tragedy would have been entirely different and we today would be imprecating Homer and not Milton. Criticism builds upon criticism in the eternal quest for perfection:

> As criticism, like the science of healing, forms all its precepts from facts, the more numerous the collection of facts is, the fairer opportunity is furnished for reducing it to the standard of truth. Milton and Shakespeare have added, every original genius adds, to the stock of critical ideas, and exhibits means of pleasure, the knowledge of which is true criticism.

Dwight is one of the earliest writers to urge the use of American materials and to advocate freedom for the American writer from European tradition and authority.[23] While much of his revolt against authority is derived from Kames, his desire to promote an American literature and to defend it against the attacks of British critics must also be considered as an influential factor. In his *Travels, in New-England and New-York* (4 vols.; New Haven, 1821–22), he devotes much space to the inhabitants, institutions, manners, morals, and natural scenery of the New England countryside which he considers materials for literature. Irritated by attacks of British critics upon American literary efforts, he discusses reasons why America was inferior to Britain in its literature. He cites all of the factors contributing to this American deficiency: the energetic life of a new country, the scarcity of libraries, the lack of a literary tradition, the easy access of English writings, etc.[24]

Not only did Dwight, in his literary criticism, urge the development of an American literature which was national in character, but, like other eighteenth century critics, he wished it to be moral and utilitarian in purpose. He wrote in the Preface to his own *The Conquest of Canaan* (1785) that it was "A Fable related by a Poet, in order to raise the Admiration, and inspire the Love of Virtue . . ." In the Preface to *Greenfield Hill* (1794), he wrote that its purpose is "to contribute to the innocent amusement of his countrymen, and to their improvement in manners, and in economical, political, and moral sentiments."

The early criticism of both Dwight and Trumbull illustrates their revolt against the authority of neoclassical rules and the use of models while both

[23] For further information concerning the early development of literary nationalism in America, there is valuable material in C. W. Cole's unpublished dissertation, *The Beginnings of Literary Nationalism in America* (George Washington, 1935). Also see E. K. Brown, "The National Idea in America Criticism," *Dalhousie Review,* XIV (1934), 133–47.

[24] Cf. Timothy Dwight, *Remarks on the Review of Inchiquin's Letters* (Boston, 1815), a key document in the beginnings of American literary criticism and the development of a national literature. Both in the *Travels* and in the *Remarks,* Dwight accounts for literature in terms of its milieu, an early example of the historical point of view in criticism.

remain essentially neoclassical in their discussion and practice of literary techniques. Later in life, both reacted and became defenders of authority and of the Federalism and religious orthodoxy which dominated the period.

One of the most distinguished literary journals of the first decade of the nineteenth century was the Philadelphia *Portfolio* under the editorship of Joseph Dennie.[25] A "literary lawyer," he brought to the criticism of literature a shrewd and penetrating intellect; sensitive and able, he was one of the few serious literary critics of the period.

Apparently less influenced by the aesthetics of the Scottish school than any other critic of the time, Dennie was centrally neoclassical in his literary preconceptions. His love of balance, order, clarity, and proportion, as well as his urbane and witty style, can be seen in an article on Gothicism which appeared in the *Portfolio* in 1803. He reflected typical neoclassical standards of judgment in criticizing the Gothicism which was beginning to become fashionable in America. Writers like Radcliffe and Monk Lewis, he thought, see nothing of value unless it holds corpses, bandits, horrible descriptions:

> It is a misrepresentation to state that the whole world resembles Bunyan's valley of the shadow of death. It is mischievous to exhibit such a false picture. It enfeebles the mind. . . . Instead of thus wantonly weakening the mind, by directing its attention to ghastly illusions, to "horrible shadows, and unreal mockery," we should adopt the discipline of the Poet.

Dennie was violently hostile to French and American "infidelity" and equalitarian democracy, and his political and social prejudices frequently dominate his criticism. He was inclined to be of the opinion that deism and democracy, opposed to everything that Federalism stood for, were in large measure responsible for the sad state of American taste. He upheld the authority of English culture, and bitterly opposed the use of Americanisms and the growth of the new language. All of these prejudices are operative in his criticism of Franklin:[26]

> He was the founder of that Grubstreet sect, who have professedly attempted to degrade literature to the level of vulgar capacities, and debase the polished and current language of books, by the vile alloy of provincial idioms, and colloquial barbarism, the shame of grammar, and akin to any language, rather than English. He was one of our first jacobins, the first to lay his head in the lap of French harlotry; and prostrate the Christianity and honour of his country to the deism and democracies of Paris.

Of Philip Freneau, on the other hand, Dennie apparently thought much, although in matters of political beliefs the two were at opposite poles. The

[25] For a general study of Dennie and his associates, see Milton Ellis, *Joseph Dennie and His Circle: A Study in American Literature from 1792–1812* (Austin, Texas, 1915).
[26] A more extensive study is Lewis Leary, "Joseph Dennie on Benjamin Franklin: A Note on Early American Literary Criticism," *Pennsylvania Magazine of History and Biography*, LXXII (1948), 240–46.

fact that he did adjust himself to this difficulty and recognize the worth of Freneau's better poems is a tribute to his critical acumen and his ability, on occasion, to rise above issues. In a review of Freneau's poems published in 1807, Dennie praises Freneau for his sympathy to nature, his affection, force, simplicity, clarity, and an ability to incorporate original subject matter in essentially timeless verse. On the other hand, in the criticism of Freneau's satires some of the same prejudices appear that were present in his criticism of Franklin:

> Our author has, in a very desultory manner, rambled from subject to subject, but satire appears to be his favourite one. Here, however, we cannot, in general, praise him. He is far from being elegant in the choice of his language, which is, for the most part, downright railing. . . . His subjects also, which are local, have lost much of their interest.

In the prospectus for the *Portfolio*, which he founded in 1801, Dennie stated very clearly the premise from which his literary criticism was to be written when he said that "We will not strive to please the populace at the expense of their quiet by infusing into every ill-balanced and weak mind a jealousy of rulers, a love of innovation, an impatience of salutary restraint." [27] Although prejudiced at times, on many occasions Dennie proved himself the most perceptive critic of the early years of the nineteenth century. In spite of his neoclassical principles, he was one of the first American critics to recognize Wordsworth, praising some of the less philosophical aspects of the *Lyrical Ballads*. The greater part of his criticism reveals him, however, to be an ardent neoclassicist, preoccupied with matters of form and taste, and elegance and polish of diction.

THE TRANSITION TO ROMANTICISM [28]

When American romantic tendencies are considered in the light of the European movement, such phases as the appreciation of nature, the democratic spirit, and the antiquarian mood have clear reference to the American scene. However, certain phases of romanticism were rejected in America because of a conservatism stemming from, among other sources, religious

---

[27] See Ellis Oberholtzer, *A Literary History of Philadelphia* (Philadelphia, 1906).
[28] Since the complexity of this period renders treatment of it here of necessity cursory, for a more complete study see W. B. Cairns, *On the Development of American Literature from 1815 to 1833* (Madison, Wis., 1898); William Charvat, *The Origins of American Critical Thought: 1810–1835* (Philadelphia, 1936); Harry H. Clark, "Literary Criticism in the *North American Review*, 1815–1835," *Trans. Wisc. Academy Sciences, Arts, and Letters*, XXXII (1940), 299–350; Howard L. Flewelling, *Literary Criticism in American Periodicals, 1783–1820*, unpublished dissertation (Michigan, 1931); Arthur E. Jones, *A Study of Literary Criticism in America, 1742–1820*, unpublished dissertation (Syracuse, 1950); Leon Howard, "Changing Contradictions in the Late Eighteenth Century"; Merrill Heiser, "Why Neo-classicism Declined"; and G. H. Orians, "Why Romanticism Arose," in *Transitions in American Literary History*, ed. by Harry H. Clark (Durham, N. C., 1954); Robert E. Streeter, *Critical Ideas in the North American Review, 1815–1865*, unpublished dissertation (Northwestern, 1943).

orthodoxy, Scottish common-sense philosophy, and Federalism. Romantic extremes found little genuine response among American literary critics, particularly the sensual phase of the European romanticism. The purely subjective phases of romanticism were strongly modified by objective standards in conduct and criticism. The aesthetic phase, which sought to erect a standard of pure Beauty, led most Americans, who had traditionally emphasized the didactic function of literature, to reject it.

American emphasis upon common sense, deriving from the Scottish school, led to a distrust of romantic weakness, self-pity, and absurdity. Though Byron's poetic genius was admired by American critics, his moody, melancholy heroes were not, on the whole, accepted.[29] In American criticism, reaction to the Gothic romance, based upon the adherence of American critics to the principles of Scottish common-sense realism, led to insistence upon probability in all realms, an insistence which strongly modified tendencies toward the highly romantic and unusual. The influence of the Scottish rhetoricians tended to retard the acceptance of Wordsworthian simplicity in diction.

The background factors which prepared for the reception of romantic concepts and led to the gradual attenuation of neoclassicism are complex and diverse. One of the most obvious influences on American criticism was the British periodicals. Professor Mott points out that there were American editions of the *Quarterly Review*, the *New Monthly Magazine*, the *Foreign Quarterly*, and, most important, the *Edinburgh Review*.[30] In addition to the spreading of the influence of British critical methods and standards, the popularity of British periodicals also influenced American criticism indirectly by leading to a vast enlargement of American periodicals, including the establishment of the influential *North American Review* and the *Southern Review*.

A second factor in the period was the continuing influence on American criticism of the Scottish rhetoricians, Lord Kames, Hugh Blair,[31] and Archibald Alison,[32] and the closely allied Scottish common-sense philosophers, Thomas Reid, Dugald Stewart, and Thomas Brown.[33] Since the Scottish rhetoricians reacted against the authority of neoclassical historical literary principles in favor of the determination of principles of taste based upon the experience of men, there is already implicit in their theory a tendency to move away from strict rationalism in the direction of the concept of taste as being intuitive. There is, of course, much late neoclassical literary opinion reflected, particularly in Kames and Blair. Blair, for example, in the third lecture of *Lectures on Rhetoric and Belles Lettres* defines

[29] See William Ellery Leonard, *Byron and Byronism in America* (Boston, 1905).
[30] Frank L. Mott, *A History of American Magazines* (Cambridge, 1938), Vol. I, p. 131.
[31] *Lectures on Rhetoric and Belles Lettres* (Edinburgh, 1783). Charvat, *The Origins of American Critical Thought*, p. 31, states that Blair's book was the standard text for courses in rhetoric in American colleges where a large majority of American critics were trained.
[32] *Essays on the Nature and Principles of Taste* (Edinburgh, 1790).
[33] See James McCosh, *The Scottish Philosophy* (New York, 1875), and I. W. Riley, *American Philosophy—The Early Schools* (New York, 1907).

the man of correct taste as he who "estimates with propriety the comparative merit of the several beauties which he meets with in any work of
genius; refers them to their proper classes; assigns the principles, as far as
they can be traced, whence this power of pleasing flows; and is pleased
himself precisely in that degree in which he ought, and no more." As
William Charvat has pointed out, "The lack of joyously appreciative
criticism in America before 1830 cannot be surprising in the light of such
doctrines." [34] The entire emphasis of Blair is on correctness and propriety
of diction and style; and, through his pervasive influence in America, he
did much to retard the adoption of a romantic idiom. Like Kames's, his concept of the function of literature was a didactic one—that it should "make
some useful impression on the mind."

The Scottish aesthetician who had the greatest influence on the development of a romantic criticism was Archibald Alison, whose *Essays on the
Nature and Principles of Taste* was published in 1790. Unlike Kames and
Blair, his concept of the emotion of beauty was based upon the principle of
the association of ideas which he derived in large measure from David
Hartley.[35] According to Alison, the emotion of beauty is the result of the
ideas which are associated with objects by the human imagination—for example, the emotion of beauty which might result from viewing a pleasant
landscape would not be caused so much by qualities immediately perceptible in the landscape itself, but rather by the train of agreeable ideas
with which it is associated by the imagination of the viewer. This concept of the emotion of beauty is of great importance, since, while Alison
stressed that the principle of association was universal in terms of a given
society (i.e. that all members of a society would have the same associations
with the same objects), he had to grant that it was also subjective (i.e. that
individuals could have associations which the society as a whole might not
have), an admission which added great impetus to the development of
the concept of subjectivity which is a central factor in romanticism.[36]

The associational principle was influential in American critical theory
not only through the work of Alison, and through Jeffrey's review of Alison's work in the widely read *Edinburgh Review,* but also through its influence on the theory and work of Wordsworth, who was an important
force in the American transition to romanticism.[37] It was such a strong and

---

[34] Charvat, *The Origins of American Critical Thought,* p. 46.
[35] For a convenient exposition of Hartley's theories, see Arthur Beatty, *William
Wordsworth, His Doctrine and Art in Their Historical Relations* (Madison, Wis.,
revised, 1927). Also see Howard C. Warren, *A History of the Association Psychology*
(New York, 1921).
[36] For a study of associationism in literary criticism in the late eighteenth century,
see Gordon McKenzie, *Critical Responsiveness: A Study of the Psychological Current
in Later Eighteenth Century Criticism* (Berkeley, Cal., 1949). Also see Walter J.
Ong, "Psyche and the Geometers: Aspects of Associationist Critical Theory," *Modern
Philology,* XLIX (1951), 16–27.
[37] Arthur Beatty states that Wordsworth "very clearly . . . began his literary
criticism as an adherent of the school of taste as it is represented by such writers as
David Hartley, Lord Kames, Sir Joshua Reynolds, Hugh Blair, Archibald Alison, and
Erasmus Darwin," and that he followed Hartley and Alison in the associationist
principles from which he derived his concept of nature as teacher.

widespread influence that it was a dominant force in American criticism from 1815 to 1835, particularly in the leading periodical, the *North American Review*.[38] Many of its characteristic attitudes and ideas were influential in the development of romanticism in American critical theory. There was a growing skepticism concerning the neoclassical notion that men have a common nature toward which works of art should be directed. There was an increasing concentration of interest upon the effect of literature on the reader. There was a conviction that the essence of literature resides in its ability to kindle the imagination,[39] leading it on to independent activity, which, according to Alison, is the following out of associated ideas. This resulted in a plea for enthusiasm in art which stands in sharp contrast to the restraint and correctness which the analytical approach to literature of Kames and Blair fostered.

The belief that beauty results from the stirring up of a chain of clearly apprehended ideas led to the conclusion that mere "correctness" and "technique" while important were not enough, that great literature could not be divorced from expression of mind. This insistence upon intellectual conceptions as well as beauty of form and expression influenced the critics' attitude toward morality and art. Alison is very specific on this point, stating that the associations that nature awakens in man lead directly to "religious sentiment."

Because associations, by their very nature, are established in the individual's previous experience as well as in the accumulated experience of a given society and age, associationism fostered a keen interest in the past— in whatever would act to enrich the associations of a literary work and hence improve its quality.[40] As G. H. Devereux pointed out in his review of Bulwer's *The Last Days of Pompeii*, [41] the use of a setting drenched with rich historical associations is one of the most successful ways of stirring the imagination of the reader. In dealing with the present, the writer finds associations incompletely fixed or entirely absent.

Associationism was one of the strongest forces in the advocacy of American literary nationalism.[42] Because of this insistence upon the desirability of subject matter for literature which would be rich in associations for the reader, it was only natural that American critics, already stirred by patriotic motives following the War of 1812 and whetted by British attacks upon American literature, would advocate the use, for literary material, of the American scene which held such rich associations for Americans with the bravery and high ideals of the struggle for independence. As John Knapp points out, "In part, we love our country because our minds seem to have been furnished from its surface, and because our most natural and vivid

---

[38] See Streeter, *Critical Ideas in the North American Review, 1815–1865*. For a contemporary tribute to associationism, see Samuel Gilman, "Brown's Philosophy of Mind," *North American Review*, XIX (1824).

[39] Cf. E. T. Channing, "On Models in Literature," *North American Review*, III (1816), a plea for greater imagination and less imitation in literature.

[40] This is what Henry James later was to call "density" in literary materials.

[41] *North American Review*, XL (1835).

[42] See Robert E. Streeter, "Association Psychology and Literary Nationalism in the *North American Review*," *American Literature*, XVII (1945), 243–54.

ideas are inseparable from pictures which have it for their groundwork." [43] Mere description of the American scene, however, was not enough; it must be associated with significant intellectual and moral qualities of man, as Knapp indicates, since beauty was not an intrinsic quality of the natural scene. William H. Prescott attributed to natural associations whatever beauty artificial objects might possess.[44] F. W. P. Greenwood praises Wordsworth because he chooses only those materials which "call forth pleasant associations." [45]

The general tendencies of associationism as an influence in the transition to romanticism in American criticism were its weakening of fixed standards of taste; its enthusiasm for naturalness, for an appeal to the simple and spontaneous associations of man; its hostility toward poetic diction; its broadening of the artist's scope; and its moral idealism.[46]

Another strong factor in the development of American criticism during this period of transition was the rise of historical criticism. As early as 1803, Samuel Miller in *A Brief Retrospect of the Eighteenth Century* employed the historical approach in pointing out how neoclassicism was slowly but perceptibly giving way before changing conditions of time and place. He sees that cultures are essentially organic and must be studied in terms of their internal relationships. He considers it a "great improvement" that the eighteenth century connected "the progress of literature, science, arts, and manners, with the chain of civil and military transactions." And he goes on to say that "national events are often connected with the current of literary, moral, and religious opinions; and . . . much knowledge of one is frequently fitted to elucidate the other." He praises Bishop Lowth's publication in 1753 of his *Hebrew Poetry* and Herder's *Spirit of Hebrew Poetry*, both written from the historical point of view.

It was, however, the Schlegels and Madame de Staël who were the strongest influence on the American critics' historical and national study of literature. Friedrich Schlegel's *Lectures on the History of Literature, Ancient and Modern* appeared in America in translation as early as 1818. A. W. Schlegel's *Lectures on Dramatic Art and Literature* appeared in an English edition on the American market soon after 1815. William Charvat states that "by 1833 he was universally acknowledged one of the foremost living critics." [47] The Schlegels exerted great influence on ro-

---

[43] *North American Review*, VII (1818).

[44] Cf. "Essay Writing," *North American Review*, XIV (1822), and "Novel Writing," *ibid.*, XXV (1827).

[45] "Wordsworth's Poems," *North American Review*, XVIII (1824).

[46] Most critics did not favor superimposition of didactic comment upon a poem or story; instead they favored a particular circumstance, or scene of nature, as the expression of a moral idea. Cf. Dana, "The Sylphs of the Seasons," *North American Review*, V (1817), and Prescott, "Essay Writing," who states "a good moral purpose may be effected, although no direct moral precept is inculcated."

[47] *Op. cit.*, p. 61. Also see Scott H. Goodnight, *German Literature in American Magazines Prior to 1846* (Madison, Wis., 1907); H. C. Goddard, "German Literature in New England in the early 19th. Century," in *Studies in New England Transcendentalism* (New York, 1908); and H. S. Jantz, "German Thought and Literature in New England, 1620–1820," *Journal English and Germanic Philology*, XLI (1942), 1–45.

mantic criticism in fostering antiquarianism, spiritual and mystical doctrines, romantic theories of style and diction, organic concepts of the nature of art, and literary nationalism.

In addition to spreading the reputation of the Schlegels through her work on German literature, De l'Allemagne,[48] Madame de Staël was extremely influential in her own right on the development of historical criticism in America. Her Influence of Literature on Society, which was published in three cities in America in 1813, is a sociological and historical study, attempting to establish the intimate relationship between literature and society.[49] In the preface to A Treatise on Ancient and Modern Literature, she states that "The object of the present work is to examine what is the influence of Religion, of Manners, of Laws, upon Literature; and reciprocally how far Literature may affect Laws, Manners, and Religion." Howard Mumford Jones has assembled a multitude of reviews from 1813 on, showing how much these ideas of Madame de Staël were respected by American critics.[50]

Herder was a pioneer in viewing literature as having evolutionary roots in environment, time, and race. His Spirit of Hebrew Poetry, which was translated by James Marsh in 1833 and reviewed by George Ripley in the Christian Examiner in 1835, was another significant influence on American historical criticism, since it was argued by Ripley that if Holy Scriptures were so conspicuously conditioned by race, place, and time of the Hebrews other writers might be illuminated by the same approach. George Bancroft's article on "Herder's Writings," in the North American Review in 1825 is also revealing of Herder's reception by American critics.[51] The amount of historical criticism of foreign and ancient literature which appeared in such periodicals as the North American Review, the American Quarterly, the Portfolio, and the American Quarterly Review testifies to the rapid rise of historical criticism in America during this period.[52]

With associationism, the theory of the importance of milieu, developed by Madame de Staël, the Schlegels, and Herder, afforded intellectual support to eager nationalists. It encouraged the use of historical criticism, the study of literary works as products of the conditions in which their creators lived. Writers turned to the theory of milieu and thus helped create an intellectual background in which literary nationalism was almost taken for

[48] See Emma G. Jaeck, Madame de Staël and the Spread of German Literature (New York, 1915).

[49] Although this theory of the sociology of literature is frequently regarded as a modern idea, especially by such "sociological critics" as V. F. Calverton and Granville Hicks, it actually was popularized as early as Herder's Ideen zur Philosophie der Geschichte der Menschheit (1784–1791).

[50] America and French Culture, 1750–1848 (Chapel Hill, N. C., 1927), and Ideas in America (Cambridge, 1944). Also see R. C. Whitford, "Mme. de Staël's Literary Reputation in America," Modern Language Notes, XXXIII (1918), 476–80.

[51] See Russell B. Nye, "George Bancroft, Early Critic of German Literature," Modern Language Notes, LVIII (1943), 128–30.

[52] Francis Gallaway in Reason, Rule, and Revolt in English Classicism (New York, 1940) states that the rise of historical literary criticism was more important than Scotch associationism in upsetting neoclassicism.

granted.[53] Many reviewers relied most heavily on the idea that good writing expresses an era and a place as well as an individual creating spirit.[54]

It was not until 1829, when James Marsh published Coleridge's *Aids to Reflection* in Burlington, Vermont, that Coleridge and Kantian philosophy became influential in the beginnings of New England transcendentalism.[55] Coleridge stressed the importance of reason and intuition, emphasized the immanence of divinity in nature and in man, and believed that poetry should be ideal and generic. In the introduction to his edition, Marsh wrote "that reason includes both the logical faculty and intuition." It was not, however, until much later that Coleridge was widely accepted by American critics, perhaps due to the abiding influence of Scottish common-sense philosophy and its reaction against mysticism and unintelligibility.[56]

Throughout the period of the transition to romanticism, neoclassicism remained as a lingering influence tending to modify the extremes of romanticism. The criticism of fiction in this period is especially marked by the neoclassicism of the Scottish common-sense school. Like Trumbull and Dennie prior to 1815, the critics still reacted strongly against improbability, excessive sentimentalism, and immorality in fiction, and insisted upon a close relationship between fiction and the realities of life. While ideas which are typically neoclassical appeared from time to time in the period, they did not appear consistently enough to challenge seriously the associationist aesthetic or the historical point of view in criticism.[57]

Representative of those critics who applied the associationist theory in their literary nationalism is John Knapp. In an article, "National Poetry," which appeared in the *North American Review* in 1818, he urges the exploitation by poets of the nation's birth throes not only for reasons of national pride but for the value of the associations which this subject matter would hold for the reader: "Would it not, moreover, the more lastingly preserve the memory of those actions which afford noble instruction, are exemplars of men's ability to be greatly virtuous, and kindle in others an honourable ambition . . . ?"

---

[53] For additional material concerning literary nationalism, see Harry H. Clark, "Nationalism in American Literature," *University of Toronto Quarterly*, II (1933), 492–519; John C. McCloskey, "The Campaign of Periodicals After the War of 1812 for National American Literature," *Publications Modern Language Association*, L (1935), 262–73; William E. Sedgwick, "The Materials for American Literature: A Critical Problem of the Early Nineteenth Century," *Harvard Studies and Notes in Philology and Literature*, XVII (1935), 145–62; and his unpublished dissertation, *The Problem of American Literature as Seen by Contemporary Critics* (Harvard, 1935).

[54] Cf. Longfellow's "Old English Romances," *North American Review*, XXXVII (1833), and "Defence of Poetry," *ibid.*, XXXIV (1832).

[55] See Marjorie H. Nicolson, "James Marsh and the Vermont Transcendentalists," *Philosophical Review*, XXXIV (1925), 28–50.

[56] Cf. F. H. Hedge, "Coleridge," *Christian Examiner*, XIV (1833).

[57] Among the reviews which are predominantly neoclassical in their point of view are Franklin Dexter, "Fine Arts," *North American Review*, XXVI (1828); A. H. Everett, "Lord Byron's Poems," *ibid.*, XX (1825); George Bancroft, "Value of Classical Learning," *ibid.*, XIX (1824); and Jared Sparks, "John Brainard's Poems," *ibid.*, XXI (1825).

Reflecting the rising romanticism in poetic theory, Knapp considers the elements of poetry to be chiefly strong passions and great interests which are derived from the associations which man has with his environment:

> If men's minds are influenced by the scenes in which they are conversant, Americans can scarcely be denied a claim to be inspired with some peculiar moral graces, by their grand and lovely landscapes. But, moreover, it is beneficial to connect our best intellectual associations with places in our own land.

One of the best critics of the period is Richard H. Dana. One of the first Americans to know and to appreciate Coleridge, he reflects almost all of the central aspects of Coleridge's theory: organic unity, exalted imagination, poetry as the supreme intellectual activity, idealism, the literary critic as a man of high intellect and extensive knowledge, suggestive language to stir the imagination, and power of condensation. One of the most significant reviews of the period is his review of "Hazlitt's English Poets," written in 1819. Concerning the task of the critic who sets out to write on the English poets, he says:

> . . . these surely are subjects deserving our attention, and require an intellect of more power and variety to comprehend, than those are well aware of, who hold poetry to be a matter of mere amusement, and all that is connected with it, a very light thing. The man who would do this well, must have a wide taste; and be trammeled by no narrow systems or schools. . . . He should have an imagination which can group and fill out, and give the lights and shades to the scanty materials left us, with the distinctness of a picture. . . . He must not mistake simplicity for weakness, nor frankness for coarseness.

Reflecting the reaction of the period against Pope,[58] Dana writes that he "never touches the heart, and never fires the passions, nor bursts with a glory over our heads. He is witty and sensible, and often moralizes well, but these do not constitute poetry." He criticizes Pope because everything "is put down directly before us, by a kind of visible, manual accumulation, or set immediately opposite to something else by a laboriously ingenius antithesis." Concerning Pope's language, Dana establishes his criticism on the basis of the associationist aesthetic: "Pope had no more idea of a poetical language than a Frenchman. His words are never pictures, nor are there ever any poetical attachments or associations connected with them. They move you no more than the sing-song of his metre." He sums up by saying "As Pope is denied imagination, Mr. Hazlitt would give him fancy; we should rather allow him ingenuity."

Dana reserves his highest praise for Wordsworth, as might be expected in view of his romantic tendencies. He speaks of Wordsworth as possessing "powers of description unsurpassed by any poet of his age," and says that "he has such an air of plain truth in telling his stories and giving the characters of those he is speaking of,—puts into the mouths of his person-

[58] See Agnes M. Sibley, *Alexander Pope's Prestige in America, 1725–1835* (New York, 1949); and Leon Howard, "The American Revolt Against Pope," *Studies in Philology*, XLIX (1952), 48–65.

ages sentiments so very simple, though elevated, and makes his scenery so like that which we see every where, that we lose the impression while reading him, that we are taken out of the world and reality into the regions of imagination and poetry." He praises Wordsworth's versification which is for "the most part filled with varied harmony," and his diction which is simple and unornamented.[59] Dana also praises Coleridge's criticism of Wordsworth, for his "criticism, in his 'Life and Opinions,' upon Mr. Wordsworth, has more good taste and philosophy in it, than any that has been written upon Mr. Wordsworth, or any other man in modern times." In his praise of Wordsworth and Coleridge, in his Coleridgean concept of poetry, in his preference for a diction that was simple, concrete, and rich in associations, Dana was ten years ahead of his contemporaries.[60]

Beginning to publish prolifically as the first quarter of the nineteenth century was drawing to a close, John Neal, like Dana and Knapp, heralds the coming of romanticism in American criticism. One of the most unusual figures in American literature, Neal published in 1823 a novel, *Randolph,* which deservedly ranks as one of the strangest productions of American fiction. It is of interest today largely for the literary criticism which it contains and which is apparently completely irrelevant to the story. Some of this criticism is among the most interesting to appear prior to the work of the major critics of romanticism. Writing on the state of the American novel in his day, he criticizes its lack of development:

> There is no class of literature, which may be made to have; nay which *has*, in reality, such an influence—upon society; and, if a man, who had the strength and vividness, of a dramatist, and a poet, were called upon to reflect and to choose, that mode of writing, which would be most likely, if he were truly powerful, to give him the widest theatre for a display of that power, it is my deliberate opinion that he would choose a *novel*;—and yet, in whose hands do we find this body of our literature?—In the feeble of heart—and the faint of spirit—the gossiping and childish.

Interested, as were most of the critics of the period, in the problem of a national literature, Neal is hopeful that "The time is rapidly approaching, when, it will be enough to sell a work, if it be called American." "We are," he says, "getting to feel a national pride; and men are already beginning to put in their title pages, 'by an American!' . . ."

Thoroughly romantic in his conception of poetry, his is perhaps one of the earliest pleas in American criticism for a "free" verse:

> Poetry is the naked expression of power and eloquence. But, for many hundred years—poetry has been confounded with false musick—measure and cadence—the soul with the body—the thought with the lan-

---

[59] In a review of Pollok's *Course of Time* in 1828, Dana wrote: "The ornamental terms are well-nigh used up, and the poet nowadays must trust almost solely to the happy combination of the simplest words. . . . But the simple terms of our language never can grow old."

[60] See Annabel Newton, *Wordsworth in Early American Criticism* (Chicago, 1928); Norman Foerster, "Wordsworth in America," *Studies in Philology*, XXVI (1929), 85–95; and Leon Howard, "Wordsworth in America," *Modern Language Notes*, XLVIII (1933), 359–65.

guage—the manner of speaking, with the mode of thinking. The secondary qualities of poetry have been mistaken for the primary ones.

He considers poetry to be "the natural language of every human heart when it is roused—or inflamed," and he states "that rhyme, or blank verse, or *regular* rhythm, is altogether as artificial, unnatural and preposterous a mode of expression, for the true poet; as the use of a foreign idiom, or foreign phrase, is to the true home-bred man."

Anticipating Whitman, Neal writes "What I call poetry has nothing to do with art or learning. It is a natural musick—the musick of woods and waters; not that of the orchestra." [61] As Poe later was to develop the same theory, Neal holds that a poem could be too long: "Could you possibly hold out to read any poem, by the greatest poet that ever lived, which should contain as many words, as one of the Waverly novels?" The reader would, he continues, "In the confusion of such a beautiful and confounding exhibition of power and brightness . . . retain no distinct impression at all." [62]

Erratic thought at times characterized his work; yet for the most part Neal's critical judgments have stood the test of time. There is a keenness, a sharpness of critical vision, which marks his best work that belies the obscurity into which his name has fallen. Poe was later to consider him "at all events second among our men of indisputable genius." [63]

The transition from classicism to romanticism in the period can be seen in the transformation of Washington Irving, the classicist, to Irving, the romanticist, although in some matters of literary theory and judgment he was always to show decidedly neoclassical preferences. [64]

In his reviews of Edwin C. Holland and Robert Treat Paine, written and published in 1814 while Irving was editor of the *Analectic Magazine,* his insistence upon neoclassical standards is revealed in his rather sharply critical dissection of some of these writers' "grand poetical figures and effects," and in his advice to Holland to refrain from publishing so profusely and to spend more time on the perfection and polish of his style and diction.

In almost all of Irving's literary criticism, there is a strong emphasis upon technique and style—upon order and form—which characterized neoclassical critical theory. At one time he wrote: "I wish, in everything I do, to write in such a manner that my productions may have something to recommend them, which is very evanescent; something, if I dare to use the phrase, of classic merit, i.e., depending upon style, etc., which gives a

[61] See Joseph J. Rubin, "John Neal's Poetics as an influence on Whitman and Poe," *New England Quarterly,* XIV (1941), 359–62.

[62] *Blackwood's Magazine,* which followed Schlegel, advised poets to limit their poems to one hundred and fifty lines. Cf. Margaret Alterton, *Origin of Poe's Critical Theory* (Iowa City, 1925).

[63] For Neal's criticism of American writers, see *American Writers: A Series of Papers Contributed to Blackwood's Magazine* (1824–1825), edited by Fred L. Pattee (Durham, N. C., 1937).

[64] A detailed study of Irving and his times is Stanley T. Williams, *The Life of Washington Irving* (2 vols.; New York, 1935); useful for European sources and Irving's contacts abroad is Henry A. Pochmann's introduction to *Washington Irving: Representative Selections* (New York, 1934).

production some chance for duration beyond the mere whim and fashion of the day."

Like other critics of the period, Irving was influenced by the rise of historical criticism. His essays on James I, "A Royal Poet," and on Shakespeare, "Stratford-on-Avon," which appeared in *The Sketch Book* in 1820 are attempts to see the work of James and Shakespeare in terms of its historical background. In the essay, "A Royal Poet," Irving reveals his affinities with neoclassicism in applying such critical standards as purity and grace of style and diction, moral purpose, poetic artifice, refined and exquisite delicacy of taste and sentiment.

By 1839, when he published "Desultory Thoughts on Criticism," Irving as a literary critic was obviously more sympathetically inclined toward romanticism. His reviews written about this time reveal him to be in many ways similar to his concept of the American critic developed in this essay as a romantically sympathetic interpreter whose main function should be to point out "beauties and excellencies" of a writer's work: "Give me the honest bee, that extracts honey from the humblest weed, but save me from the ingenuity of the spider, which traces its venom even in the midst of a flower-garden." While his attitude became more sympathetic, his conception of what he considered good literature to be was still biased somewhat by neoclassical principles. His own literary taste manifested itself in his preference among the romantics for those, like Byron and Moore, who were more strongly influenced by the eighteenth century, as opposed to such other romantic poets as Wordsworth and Shelley. It was, perhaps, with Wordsworth in mind that he wrote the following passage in one of his diaries: "There is an endeavor among some of the writers of the day to introduce into poetry all the common colloquial phrases and vulgar idioms. . . . Now the language of poetry cannot be too pure and choice. Poems are like classical edifices, for which we seek the noblest materials."

Irving did not possess a systematic theory concerning literary criticism, and his critical reviews reveal him using his own highly sensitive taste rather than any set standards as his basis for literary judgment. He came to thoroughly dislike the profession of the literary critic, and he adopted an increasingly sympathetic attitude toward our national literature: "Seriously speaking, however, it is questionable whether our national literature is sufficiently advanced to bear this excess of criticism; and whether it would not thrive better if allowed to spring up, for some time longer, in the freshness and vigor of native vegetation." Perhaps it was because of this and because of his own sympathetic, impressionistic approach to literary criticism that Irving's critical essays do not reveal any striking critical abilities.

In a period when many American literary men, including Irving, still revered the Augustans and were hesitant to approve Wordsworth and Coleridge, William Cullen Bryant [65] began his career as a literary critic

[65] The standard biography of Bryant is Parke Godwin, *A Biography of William Cullen Bryant, with Extracts from His Private Correspondence* (2 vols.; New York, 1883). A good critical analysis is Tremaine McDowell's Introduction to *William Cullen Bryant: Representative Selections* (New York, 1935).

with his essay "On the Use of Trisyllabic Feet in Iambic Verse," [66] which was in close accord with his own poetic practices of freeing himself from Augustan regularity and exploring with romantic delight the varied resources of meter. "The meter for which I have been contending," he wrote, "has often been censured and ridiculed. The utmost favour which it has, at any time, to my knowledge, received from the critics, is to have been silently allowed—no one has openly defended it." Again, in reviewing Solyman Brown's *An Essay on American Poetry* in 1818, he condemned the "balanced and wearisome regularity" of the American Augustans which "allows just as much play and freedom to the faculties of the writer as a pair of stilts allows to the body."

Bryant's was our earliest systematic study of the nature of poetry, and the views which he held were, in the main, romantic.[67] From his early "Lectures on Poetry," which were delivered in 1826, to the end of his career, he consistently defined poetry in the same terms: imagination, feeling, originality, morality, and simplicity. The romantic faith in originality was a major premise in Bryant's theory. The idea that poetry, like painting, is an imitative art, he sharply denied. In his lecture "On Originality and Imitation," he stated that the copying of models of poetic composition is wrong, since poetry is an art and as such speaks the language of experience to man in an original way. The mind of genius, it is true, is "formed by the labors of others," but poetic excellence must be sought after in the entire intellectual realm, not limited as, for instance, the "puerile followers of Pope were limited."

That poetry is a suggestive art dealing primarily with the imagination and the emotions as well as the intellect was another premise of his theory. But with critics who limit poetry solely to the exercise of the imagination Bryant disagreed. The "great spring of poetry" is emotion and its true office is "to touch the heart." Not only must the poet appeal to the imagination and to the human heart, but also Bryant never doubted that the poet should teach "direct lessons of wisdom" and should have as his chief aim to perfect the moral character of his readers.

Wordsworth was the strongest influence on Bryant, who in turn was responsible, in part at least, for the increased interest in Wordsworth during the third decade of the century. The publication of Wordsworth's *Poetical Works* in Boston in 1824, and the changed attitude of the *North American Review* toward Wordsworth, can be attributed in some measure to Bryant and his influence. When, in 1825, Bryant left Great Barrington and the law for New York and joint editorship of the *New-York Review* and later the *United States Review*,[68] those periodicals reflected the pervasive influ-

---

[66] According to Godwin, Bryant began writing this essay in 1811 although it was not published until 1819 when it appeared in the *North American Review*.

[67] For a study of the influence of classicism and neoclassicism on Bryant, see John P. Pritchard, *Return to the Fountains* (Durham, N. C., 1942), pp. 13–25.

[68] See C. I. Glicksberg, "Bryant and the United States Review," *New England Quarterly*, VII (1934), 687–701.

ence of Wordsworth which soon spread in the magazines of the Knicker-bockers.[69]

Wordsworth's influence on Bryant's criticism can be seen most strongly in his conception of poetry as "that art which selects and arranges the symbols of thought in such a manner as to excite it the most powerfully and delightfully," and in his emphasis upon the importance of emotion in poetry: "The most beautiful poetry is that which takes the strongest hold of the feelings . . ." Also, like Wordsworth, Bryant insisted that one of the greatest uses of poetry is "the exhibition of those analogies and correspondences which it beholds between the things of the moral and of the natural world."

Second only to the influence of Wordsworth on Bryant was the influence of the Scottish tradition, particularly the associationist aesthetic of Alison.[70] Like Alison, he emphasized the "moral associations" that people have with nature which "act like a spell upon the imagination and awaken it to greater activity." He conceived the associations that man has with nature as leading to the religious sentiment: "There are a purity and innocence in the appearances of Nature that make them refuse to be allied to the suggestions of guilty emotion. . . . They cannot be studied without inducing the love, if they fail of giving the habit, of virtue." And he questioned, "Is there any one for whom the works of Nature have no associations but such as relate to his animal wants?"

Bryant, like most critics of the day, exhibited a strong tendency toward neoclassicism in his criticism of fiction. In a review, written in 1825, of Catherine Sedgwick's *Redwood*, he praised this novel of manners because it dealt with contemporary society as most people knew it. Reacting against the extremes of Gothicism, he favored an imagination which was cultivated and regulated. He felt that fiction should reflect typical American life which, with its great sectional differences, offered many opportunities for the novelist.[71] He favored simplicity; and, like the Scottish critics, was suspicious of "ingenious casuistry and labored sophistry," which "may confuse and puzzle the understanding."

These basic premises of Bryant's poetic theory reveal themselves as the standards of judgment in his criticism which tended on the whole to be judicious in nature. It was this same moralistic Bryant who condemned Byron for "indecency and blasphemy" and at the same time praised that extravagant romantic, James Gates Percival, for "the reckless intoxication with which this author surrenders himself to the enchantments of that multitude of glorious and beautiful images that come crowding upon his mind." His critical writings clearly reveal the cultural sources from which he drew his essential principles. One perceives in his criticism some of the best of the sentiments of "gentility."

[69] For a study of this group, see the introduction to Kendall B. Taft's *Minor Knickerbockers* (New York, 1947).
[70] See William Palmer Hudson, "Archibald Alison and William Cullen Bryant," *American Literature*, XII (1940), 59–68, for a study of Bryant's early knowledge of the theories of Alison.
[71] This is one of the early statements of the principle that was to become the guiding point of view with writers of local color fiction.

William Ellery Channing, one of the leading literary figures of the period, is representative not only of the transition to romanticism but also of the developing complex of ideas which was to culminate in Emersonian transcendentalism.[72] Like Emerson, he was interested mainly in broad, general aspects of literature, its relationship to religion, to man, to nature, and to the nation, rather than in the analysis and criticism of specific literary works. As a review of a lecture delivered by C. J. Ingersoll before the American Philosophical Society in Philadelphia in 1823, Channing's "Remarks on National Literature" appeared in the *Christian Examiner* in 1830. Reacting against the materialism of Ingersoll, the review reveals Channing's idealism and his conception of the moral and social function of literature.

Influenced strongly by Wordsworth and the associationist conception of nature as a moral force and teacher of man, Channing stresses that "Poetry is useful by touching deep springs in the human soul . . . by breathing out and making more intelligible, the sympathy which subsists between the mind and the outward universe; by creating beautiful forms of manifestations for great moral truths." As Alison and Wordsworth had done, Channing stresses the close relationship between poetry and religion: "Are we asked, then, to what impulse or power we look for a higher literature than has yet existed? We answer, to a new action or development of the religious principle." With the optimism of American Unitarianism, he adds that literature written from such an impulse "will still be pervaded by a healthful cheerfulness, and will often break forth in tones of irrepressible joy, responsive to that happiness which fills God's universe." Conceiving of a moral point of view as a creative principle in great literature, Channing's criticism is representative of the development in this period of the moral idealism which was to characterize romantic aesthetics and which was to stand in such sharp contrast with the aesthetic theories of Poe.

Familiar with the work of Madame de Staël and the Schlegels,[73] Channing conceives of literature as "the expression of a nation's mind in writing." Like them, he believes that men must learn to perceive the beauties of alien literatures as expressions of particular nations, societies, and times: "We earnestly recommend to our educated men a more extensive acquaintance with the intellectual labors of continental Europe. Our reading is confined too much to English books, and especially to the more recent publications of Great Britain. In this we err. We ought to know the different modes of viewing and discussing great subjects in different nations."

Likewise, considering an American literature as being the product of its environment, Channing expresses the belief "that a literature, springing up in this new soil, would bear new fruits, and, in some respects, more precious fruits than are elsewhere produced." He sees that the great and unique characteristic of American society is the democracy that prevails

---

[72] See Arthur I. Ladu, "Channing and Transcendentalism," *American Literature*, XI (1939), 129-37. For a modern estimate of Channing, see Robert E. Spiller, "A Case for W. E. Channing," *New England Quarterly*, III (1930), 55-81.

[73] See Elizabeth P. Peabody, *Reminiscences of Rev. William Ellery Channing* (Boston, 1880).

here, that "our position favors a juster and profounder estimate of human nature," since "Man is not hidden from us by so many disguises as in the Old World." A truly American literature, reflecting the national mind, should therefore deal primarily with man and "the essential equality of all human beings."

The work of Dana, Bryant, and Channing represents the best and most liberal literary criticism of the period.

Of the many significant trends in American criticism during the period of the transition to romanticism, the change from the static uniformitarianism of neoclassicism to the relativism of historical criticism was most fruitful in causing the revolt from the neoclassical theory and practice of eighteenth century England. This resulted in the turn from a mechanistic criticism, from criteria regarded as universally valid and absolute, to a criticism that conceived of a literary work as organic, and to criteria regarded as historically relative to the author's race, place, and time.

Influential in the rise of historical criticism were Madame de Staël, Friedrich Schlegel, and the biblical criticism of Herder; the popularity of Scottish thinkers, particularly Alison, who stressed the importance of the readers' associations; the application, by such historians as William H. Prescott and John Lothrop Motley, of the methods of history to literary criticism; the growth of nationalism which interested critics in the relation between literature and the nation; the increasing number of studies of Shakespeare relating him to his age; [74] the turn from the mechanism of Newton in science to concepts of growth and change fostered by biological and geological studies; and the antiquarianism stimulated by the popularity of the work of Sir Walter Scott.

Trends in the criticism of the period also involved the change from the didactic and moralistic, the harshly judicial, to the ideal of sympathetic criticism; from a preoccupation with form and finish to a concern for their unity with the ideas and spirit of a literary work; from an emphasis on satire to enforce conformity to society to a stress on sentiment or lyricism; from rationalism to emotion and intuition; from a concept of imitation or traditionalism to one which valued originality; and from a concern with the universal or abstract to the particularized and concrete.[75]

During this period of transition, American criticism, for the first time, exhibited a surer grasp of literary principles and a more mature attitude toward art. It began increasingly to concern itself with such fundamental questions as the nature and function of literature and its relationships to the artist, to morality, to the nation, and to life. These are the questions that came to be discussed more and more frequently by the ever increasing number of literary critics as American literature matured during the years dominated by the aesthetics of romanticism.

[74] See Van R. Westfall, *American Shakespearean Criticism, 1607–1865* (New York, 1939), and Robert P. Falk's unpublished dissertation, *Representative American Criticism of Shakespeare, 1830–1885* (Wisconsin, 1940).

[75] I am indebted in my discussion of the trends in American criticism to a forthcoming study by Harry H. Clark, "Changing Trends and Criteria in American Literary Criticism, 1800–1840."

The Puritans: Critical Essays

RICHARD MATHER

THE PREFACE TO THE BAY PSALM BOOK [1]
(1640)

THE SINGING of Psalmes, though it breath forth nothing but holy harmony, and melody: yet such is the subtilty of the enemie, and the enmity of our nature against the Lord, & his wayes, that our hearts can finde matter of discord in this harmony, and crotchets of division in this holy melody. -for- There have been three questions especially stirring concerning singing. First. what psalmes are to be sung in churches? whether Davids and other scripture psalmes, or the psalmes invented by the gifts of godly men in every age of the church. Secondly, if scripture psalmes, whether in their owne words, or in such meter as english poetry is wont to run in? Thirdly. by whom are they to be sung? whether by the whole churches together with their voices? or by one man singing alone and the rest joyning in silence, & in the close saying amen.

Touching the first, certainly the singing of Davids psalmes was an acceptable worship of God, not only in his owne, but in succeeding times. . . .

As for the scruple that some take at the translation of the book of psalmes into meeter, because Davids psalmes were sung in his owne words without meeter: wee answer- First. There are many verses together in several psalmes of David which run in rithmes (as those that know the hebrew and as Buxtorf [2] shews *Thesau.* pa. 629.) which shews at least the lawfullnes of singing psalmes in english rithmes.

Secondly. The psalmes are penned in such verses as are sutable to the poetry of the hebrew language, and not in the common style of such other bookes of the old Testament as are not poeticall; now no protestant doubteth but that all the bookes of the scripture should by Gods ordinance be extant in the mother tongue of each nation, that they may be understood of all, hence the psalmes are to be translated into our english tongue; and is in our english tongue wee are to sing them, then as all our english songs (according to the course of our english poetry) do run in metre, soe ought Davids psalmes to be translated into meeter, that soe wee may sing the Lords songs, as in our english tongue soe in such verses as are familiar to an english eare which are commonly metricall: and as it can be no just offence to any good conscience, to sing Davids hebrew songs in english words, soe neither to sing his poeticall verses in english poeticall metre: men might as well stumble at singing the hebrew psalmes in our english tunes (and not in the hebrew tunes) as at singing them in eng-

[1] *The Whole Book of Psalmes* (Cambridge, 1640).
[2] Johannes Buxtorf (1564–1629), German Hebrew scholar and author of *Thesaurus Grammaticus Linguae Sanctae Hebraeae* (1629).

lish meeter, (which are our verses) and not in such verses as are generally
used by David according to the poetry of the hebrew language: but the
truth is, as the Lord hath hid from us the hebrew tunes, lest wee should
think our selves bound to imitate them; soe also the course and frame (for
the most part) of their hebrew poetry, that wee might not think our selves
bound to imitate that, but that every nation without scruple might follow
as the grave sort of tunes of their owne country songs, soe the graver sort
of verses of their owne country poetry.

Neither let any think, that for the meetre sake wee have taken liberty
or poeticall licence to depart from the true and proper sence of Davids
words in the hebrew verses, noe; but it hath beene one part of our religious care and faithfull indeavour, to keepe close to the originall text. . . .

For although wee have cause to bless God in many respects for the
religious indeavours of the translaters of the psalmes into meetre usually
annexed to our Bibles, yet it is not unknowne to the godly learned that
they have rather presented a paraphrase then the words of David translated according to the rule 2 *chron.* 29. 30. and that their addition to the
words, detractions from the words are not seldome and rare, but very
frequent and many times needles, (which we suppose would not be approved of if the psalmes were so translated into prose) and that their variations of the sense, and alterations of the sacred text too frequently, may
iustly minister matter of offence to them that are able to compare the
translation with the text; of which failings, some iudicious have oft complained, others have been grieved, wherupon it hath bin generally desired, that as wee doe inioye other, soe (if it were the Lords will) wee
might inioye this ordinance also in its native purity: wee have therefore
done our indeavour to make a plaine and familiar translation of the psalmes
and words of David into english metre, and have not soe much as presumed to paraphrase to give the sense of his meaning in other words; we
have therefore attended heerin as our chief guide the originall, shunning
all additions, except such as even the best translators of them in prose
supply, avoiding all materiall detractions from words or sence. . . .

As for our translations, wee have with our english Bibles (to which next
to the Originall wee have had respect) used the Idioms of our owne tongue
in stead of Hebraismes, lest they might seeme english barbarismes.

Synonimaes wee use indifferently: as *folk* for *people*, and *Lord* for
Iehovah, and sometime (though seldome) *God* for *Iehovah*; for which
(as for some other interpretations of places cited in the new Testament)
we have the scriptures authority ps. 14. with 53. Heb. 1. 6. with psalme
97. 7. Where a phrase is doubtfull wee have followed that which (in our
owne apprehension) is most genuine & edifying:

Somtime wee have contracted, somtime dilated the same hebrew word,
both for the sence and the verse sake: which dilatation wee conceive to be
no paraphrasticall addition no more then the contraction of a true and full
translation to be any unfaithfull detraction or diminution: as when wee
dilate *who healeth* and say *he it is who healeth;* soe when wee contract,
those that stand in awe of God and say *Gods fearers.*

Lastly. Because some hebrew words have a more full and emphaticall signification then any one english word can or doth somtime expresse, hence wee have done that somtime which faithfull translators may doe, *viz.* not only to translate the word but the emphasis of it. . . .

As for all other changes of numbers, tenses, and characters of speech, they are such as either the hebrew will unforcedly beare, or our english forceably calls for, or they no way change the sence; and such are printed usually in an other character.

If therefore the verses are not alwayes so smooth and elegant as some may desire or expect; let them consider that Gods Altar needs not our pollishings: Ex. 20. for wee have respected rather a plaine translation, then to smooth our verses with the sweetnes of any paraphrase, and soe have attended Conscience rather then Elegance, fidelity rather then poetry, in translating the hebrew words into english language, and Davids poetry into english meetre; that soe wee may sing in Sion the Lords songs of prayse according to his owne will; untill hee take us from hence, and wipe away all our teares, & bid us enter into our masters ioye to sing eternall Halleluiahs.

MICHAEL WIGGLESWORTH

THE PRAYSE OF ELOQUENCE [1]
(1650)

How SWEETLY doth eloquence even inforce trueth upon the understanding, and subtly convay knowledge into the minde be it never so dull of conceiving, and sluggish in yeelding its assente. So that let a good Oratour put forth the utmost of his skill, and you shall hear him so lay open and unfould, so evidence and demonstrate from point to point what he hath in hand, that he wil make a very block understand his discourse. Let him be to giue a description of something absent or unknown; how strangely doth he realize and make it present to his hearers apprehensions, framing in their mindes as exact an idea of that which they never saw, as they can possibly have of any thing that they have bin longest and best acquainted with. Or doth he take upon him to personate some others in word or deedes why he presents his hearers not with a lifeless picture, but with the living persons of those concerning whom he speaks. They see, they hear, they handle them, they walk they talk with them, and what not? Or is he to speak about such things as are already known? Why should he here discourse after the vulgar manner, and deliver his mind as a cobler would doe: his hearers might then have some ground to say they knew as much as their oratour could teach them. But by the power of eloquence ould truth receivs a new habit. though its essence be the same yet its visage is so altered that it may currently pass and be accepted as a novelty. The same verity is again and again perhaps set before the same guests but drest and disht up after a new manner, and every manner season'd so well that the intellectuall parts may both without nauseating receiv, and so oft as it doth receiv it still draw some fresh nourishing virtue from it. So that Eloquence giues new luster and bewty, new strength, new vigour, new life unto trueth; presenting it with such variety as refresheth, actuating it with such hidden powerful energy, that a few languid sparks are blown up to a shining flame.

And which is yet more: Eloquence doth not onely reviue the things known but secretly convay life into the hearers understanding rousing it out of its former slumber, quickning it beyond its naturall vigour, elevating it aboue its ordinary conception. There are not onely objects set before it, but ey's (after a sort) giuen it to see these objects in such wise as it never saw. Yea it is strengthened as to apprehend that which is taught it, so of it self with enlargment to comprehend many things which are not made known unto it. Hence it comes to pass that after the hearing of

[1] This selection is reprinted from Samuel E. Morison, *Harvard College in the Seventeenth Century* (Cambridge, 1936).

a wel-composed speech livelily exprest the understanding of the Auditor is so framed into the mould of Eloquence, that he could almost goe away and compose the like himself either upon the same or another subject. And whats the reason of this? why his mind is transported with a kind of rapture, and inspired with a certain oratoric fury, as if the oratour together with his words had breathed his soul and spirit into those that hear him.

These and the like effects hath Eloquence upon the understanding. But furthermore 'tis a fit bait to catch the will and affections. For hereby they are not onely layd in wait for, but surprized: nor onely surprized but subdued; nor onely subdued, but triumphed over. Yet Eloquence beguil's with such honesty, subdues with such mildness, triumphs with such sweetness: that here to be surprized is nothing dangerous, here to be subject is the best freedom, this kind of servitude is more desireable than liberty. For whereas our untractable nature refuseth to be drawn, and a stiff will scorn's to be compel'd: yet by the power of wel-composed speech nature is drawn against the stream with delight, and the will after a sort compelled with its owne consent. Altho: for a time it struggle and make resistance, yet at length it suffer's it self to be vanquish't, and takes a secret contentment in being overcome.

In like manner, for the affections. Look as a mighty river augmented with excessiue rains or winter snows swelling above its wonted channel bear's down banks and bridges, overflows, fields and hedges, sweeps away all before it, that might obstruct its passage: so Eloquence overturn's, overturn's all things that stand in its way, and carrys them down with the irresistible stream of its all controuling power. Wonderful it were to speak of the severall discoverys of the power in severall affections: wonderfull but to think in generall, how like a blustering tempest it one while driues before it the raging billow's of this troubled Ocean: how other whiles (as though it had them in fetters) it curb's and calm's the fury at a word. And all this without offering violence to the party's so affected; nay with a secret pleasure and delight it stirs men up to the greatest displeasure and distast. Doth it affect with grief? why to be so grieved is no grievance. doth it kindle coales, nay flames of fiery indignation? why those flames burn not, but rather cherish. doth it draw tears from the eys? why even tears flow with pleasure. For as is wel sayd by one upon this point In omni animi motu etiam in dolore est quaedam jucunditas.[2] So potently, so sweetly doth Eloquence command, and of a skilfull oratour in point of the affections that may be spoken really, which the Poet affirmeth fabulously of Aeolus god of the winds. . . .

But I need instance no more. some of you I hope will by this time assent unto what has bin hitherto prov'd that Eloquence is of such useful concernment and powerfull operation. But methinks I hear some still objecting. 'Tis very true Eloquence is a desirable thing, but what are we the better for knowing its worth unless we could hope our selues to attain it? It is indeed a right excellent indowment but 'tis not every ca-

[2] "In all motions of the spirit, even in sorrow, there is some pleasure."

pacity, nay scarce one of a hundreth that can reach it. How many men of good parts do we find that yet excel not here? Cicero indeed, a man in whom vast understanding and naturall fluent facility of speech con-spire together; no marvail if he make judges weep and princes tremble. But to what purpose is it for a man of weak parts and mean abilitys to labour after that which he is never like to compass? Had we not as good toss our caps against the wind as weary out our selves in the pursuit of that which so few can reach to?

An. To these I would answer first, the reason why so few attain it is because there [are] few that indeed desire it. hence they run not as if they ment to win, they pursue not as if they hop't to overtake. But 2ly let me answer them with Turner's words upon this very argument Negligen-tiam nostram arguit, qui cum non possimus. quod debemus, optimus, nolumus quod possimus, benè.[3] we cannot do what we would therefore will not doe what we may. This savours of a slouthfull sistem. Because we cannot keep pace with the horsemen, shall we refuse to accompany the footmen? Because we cannot run, shall we sit down and refuse to goe? we cannot reach so far as our selues desire and as some others it may be attain, shall we not therefore reach as far as our endeavours may carry us? Because we cannot be Oratores optimi, do we content our selues to be Oratores Pessimi?

And as for those that have most excell'd in this kind, whence had they their excellency? they did not come declaming into the world: they were not born with orations in their mouths: eloquence did not sit upon their lips whilest they lay in their cradles: neither did they suck it in from their mothers brests. But if you examine the matter you shall find that by incredible paines and daly exercise, they even turn'd the cours of nature into another channel, and cut out a way for the gentle stream of Elo-quence, where naturall impediments seem'd altogether to deny it passage: thereby effecting as much as another could bragg, viam aut inveniam aut faciam:[4] Eminent in this respect is the example of the two best oratours that fame has brought to our ears. Of Cicero, who when he had naturally a shrill, screaming, ill-tun'd voyce rising to such a note that it indanger'd his very life: yet by art and industry he acquired such a commendable habit, as none with ease could speak more sweetly than he. And Demos-thenes, though he were naturally of a stammering tongue crasy-body'd and broken-winded, and withall had accustom'd himself to a jetting un-comely deportment of his body, or some part of it at least: when to con-clude he had scarce any part of an oratour, saue onely an ardent desire to be an oratour: yet by his indefatigable paines he so overcame these naturall defects, as that he came to be reputed prince of the Graecian Eloquence. Though this was not gotten without some further difficulty and seeming vain attempts. Insomuch as he was severall times quite discouraged, and

[3] The quotation is from Robert Turner's *Orationes Septemdecim* (1602): "It argues our negligence since we are not able at best to do that which we ought, we do not wish to do well what we could."
[4] "I shall either find a way or make one."

once threw all aside, dispairing ever to become an oratour because the people laught at his orations. yet notwithstanding being heartned to it again by some of welwillers, he never left striving till he had won the prize.

Go too therefore my fellow-students (for to you I address my speech, my superiours I attempt not to speak to, desiring rather to learn of them more of this nature, but) to you giue me leav to say: Let no man hereafter tel me I despair of excelling in the oratoricall faculty, therefore 'tis bootless to endeavour. Who more unlike to make an oratour than Demosthenes except it were one who had no tongue in his head? yet Demosthenes became orator optimus. Tell me not "I have made trial once and again, but find my labour fruitless." Thou are not the first that hast made an onset, and bin repelled; neither canst thou presage what renew'd endeavours may produce. Would you then obtain this skill? take Demosthenes his course; gird up your loines, put to your shoulders, and to it again, and again, and agen, let nothing discourage you. Know that to be a dunce, to be a stammerer, unable to bring forth three or four sentences hanging well together, this is an easy matter: but to become an able speaker, hic labor, hoc opus est.[5] Would you haue your orations pleas, such as need not be laught at? why follow him in that also. Let them be such as smell of the lamp, as was sayd of his. Not slovenly I mean, but elaborate, diurnam industriam et nocturnis lucubrationibus elaboratae,[6] such as savour, of some paines taken with them. A good oration is not made at the first thought, nor scarce at the first writing over. Nor is true Eloquence wont to hurry it out thick and threefould, as if each word: were running for a wadger: nor yet to mutter or whisper it out of a book after a dreaming manner, with such a voyce as the oratour can scantly heare himself speak; but to utter it with lively affection, to pronounce it distinctly with audible voyce.

But I shall burden your patience no further at the present. Those and the like vices in declaming that are contrary to Eloquence, were the chief motives that drew me first into thoughts of this discourse. But I see I cannot reach at this season to speak of them particularly. wherefore with your good leav and gods assistance I shall rather treat of them at another opportunity. . . .

[5] "This the labor, this is the work."
[6] "industry by day, and by night ceaseless toil."

JOHN BULKLEY

PREFACE TO WOLCOTT'S POETICAL MEDITATIONS [1]
(1725)

THE BUISY and restless Soul of Man which in all Ages has been Fruitful in *Many Inventions,* as it has been greatly disserviceable to the Good and Comfort of Humane Life by the Discovery of things Prejudicial to it; so at the same time may we not say, has made some Compensation by the Invention of others of a Proportionable Advantage and Benefit. It were easy by a detail of some of the many Useful Arts found out by Man to give Evidence of this, but it must Suffice at Present, to Instance in one only, *viz.* That *Art of Writing* or Expressing all Sounds, and Consequently the Conceptions of our Minds, by a *Few Letters Variously Disposed or Plac'd,* the Commodity or Profit of which to Mankin'd is so Various & Extensive as not to be easily accounted for. This Art is Stiled by One *Admirandarum Omnium inventionum humanarum Signaculum. i.e.* The Wonder or Master-piece of all Humane Inventions: And how deservedly is it so, whether we Speak with Reference to the *Strangeness* or the *Benefit* of it? How Strange is it that by the Various Disposition of so *Few Letters* as Our *Alphabet* contains, *all Sounds* should be express'd, and thereby all the Conceptions or Ideals of our Minds! And as for the *Commodity* of it; not to mention others, from hence it comes to pass that we are Furnish'd with so much Useful History, which bringing into our View both Persons and Things most distant from us in time and place, does greatly delight and entertain us, and at the same time Instruct or Teach and Furnish us with a main part of our most useful Knowledge.

In the Early Ages of the World, before this most certain way of Communicating the Knowledge of things was found out; other *Mediums* were made use of for that end, the Principal of which seems to have been Representative *Symbols* or *Hieroglyphicks,* which way or Method of Communication every one knows still Obtains among many *Unletter'd Nations* in the World. But this as its very uncertain on the Account of that great Variety of *Interpretations* such *Symbols* are liable to, and as the Misconstruction of them, its reasonable to think, has been none of the least Prolifick Fountains of the *Heathen Mythology,* by which the Antient & True Tradition of the First Ages of the World has been so much Corrupted and Alter'd, so is now out of use with such Nations, as among whom the *Use of Letters* has been Introduced. I said above that to this we are Debtors for the useful History we are Furnish'd with: and I must observe on

[1] Roger Wolcott (1679–1767) was prominent in public affairs and became chief justice of the Supreme Court, and governor of Connecticut. His *Poetical Meditations* was published in New London in 1725.

this Occasion that there are two ways in which those who have Oblig'd us with it, according to their different Genius and Humours, have Improv'd this Noble Invention in Composing the Historys they have put into our Hands; that some therein have Confin'd themselves to *Poetical Numbers* and *Measures*, others not so restricting themselves, have Written in *Prose*, which last in latter Ages has been the more common way. That a considerable part, especially of our more *Ancient History*, is delivered to us in the former of these ways, is known to most that are not Strangers to Books, a considerable part of the Writings both of the *Latin* and *Greek* Poets what are they but *Poemata Historica?* . . .

. . . I have premis'd this in way of *Apology* for the manner in which this *Worthy Person* has given us the *Ensuing History*, in Composing which he has Diverted some of his *Leisure Hours*. And from hence tis evident he has for a Precedent some of the most *Antient History*, and has trod in the steps of many of the most Eminent *Sages*, and earliest *Writers* History gives us any Knowledge of, who have taken that same way to raise up Monuments to, and eternize the Names and Actions of their Admired *Heroes*.

Its undoubtedly true that as the Minds of Men have a very different *Cast, Disposition* or *Genius* leading to & accomplishing for very differing Improvements, so generally speaking, those are the most Accomplished to make a Judgment on any Performance that have by Nature a Genius Leading to and Accomplishing for the same: And it being so, and withal there being none among the *whole number of Mortals* less furnish'd for a Performance of this Nature *than my self,* I may well be excus'd in Omitting the part of a *Censor* or *Judge* upon it, further than to say that the Intelligent Reader will herein discern an uncommon *Vigour* of *Mind,* considerable *Reading,* and see reason to say, that herein we have a *Specimen* what good parts cultivated with a laudable Ambition to Improve in Knowledge will do, tho' not Assisted with those Advantages of *Education* which some are favoured withal.

Some there are that have remark't, That the *Accomplish'd Poet* and the *Great Man* are things seldom meeting together *in one Person,* Or that its rare those Powers of Mind that *make* the one, are found *United* with those that Constitute the other. And perhaps it may be a Truth which for the main holds true. For whereas what is properly call'd *Wit,* (which is no other than a ready Assemblage of Ideas, or a putting those together with quickness & variety wherein there can be found any *Congruity* or *Resemblance;* or to speak more plain, an aptness at Metaphor and Allusion) is what, as I take it, makes the *Accomplish'd Poet;* exactness of Judgment, or Clearness of reason (which we commonly and truly say makes *the Great Man*) on the other hand lies in an Ability of Mind nicely to distinguish its Ideas the one from the other, where there is but the least difference thereby avoiding being misled by Similitude, and by Affinity to take one thing from another. And the process of the Mind in these two things being so *contrary* the one to the other, tis not strange if they are Powers not ever *United* in the same Subject, yet this notwithstanding, all must say, this is not a Remark that universally and without exception will hold true; but that how contrary and inconsistent soever the process of the mind in the exercise of these two Powers may seem to be, yet there are *Instances* wherein they are United in a Wonderful Measure: And many Men in whom we find a great deal of *Pleasantry* or *Wit*, are notwithstanding very *Judicious* and *Rational*. And tho' Modesty forbids me to say this of the *Author*, yet this I shall venture to say, *viz*. That whatever may be said in Commendation of this Performance by the Accomplished for a Judgment upon it; yet that there will not that Honour be done him thereby, as I conceive may with a great deal of Truth and Justice otherwise.

COTTON MATHER

From MANUDUCTIO ad MINISTERIUM [1]
(1726)

OF POETRY AND STYLE

POETRY, whereof we have now even an *Antediluvian* piece in our hands, has from the beginning been in such request, that I must needs recommend unto you some acquaintance with it. Though some have had a soul so unmusical, that they have decried all verse as being but a meer playing and fiddling upon words; all versifying, as if it were more unnatural than if we should chuse dancing instead of walking; and rhyme, as if it were but a sort of morisce-dancing with bells: yet I cannot wish you a soul that shall be wholly unpoetical. An old Horace has left us an art of poetry, which you may do well to bestow a perusal on. And besides your lyric hours, I wish you may so far understand an epic poem, that the beauties of an Homer and a Virgil may be discerned with you. As to the moral part of Homer, it is true, and let me not be counted a Zoilus [2] for saying so, that by first exhibiting their gods as no better than rogues, he set open the flood-gates for a prodigious inundation of wickedness to break in upon the nations, and was one of the greatest apostles the devil ever had in the world. Among the rest that felt the ill impressions of this universal corrupter, (as men of the best sentiments have called him,) one was that overgrown robber, of execrable memory, whom we celebrate under the name of Alexander the Great; who by his continual admiring and studying of his Iliad, and by following that false model of heroic virtue set before him in his Achilles, became one of the worst of men, and at length inflated with the ridiculous pride of being himself a deity, exposed himself to all the scorn that could belong to a lunatic. And hence, notwithstanding the veneration which this idol has had, yet Plato banishes him out of a common-wealth, the welfare whereof he was concerned for. Nevertheless, custom or conscience obliges him to bear testimonies unto many points of morality. And it is especially observable, that he commonly propounds prayer to heaven as a most necessary preface unto all important enterprizes; and when the action comes on too suddenly for a more extended supplication, he yet will not let it come on without an ejaculation; and he never speaks of any supplication but he brings in a gracious answer

[1] The *Manuductio ad Ministerium* was intended as a handbook for divinity students. In it Mather discusses philosophy, literature, science, and languages. The book was published in Boston in 1726.

[2] Zoilus (*ca.* 400–320 B.C.) was a Greek critic notorious for his vehement and spiteful attacks on Homer.

to it. I have seen a travesteering high-flier, not much to our dishonour, scoff at Homer for this; as making his actors to be like those whom the English call dissenters. . . .

. . . Nevertheless, it is observed, that the Pagans had no rules of manners that were more laudable and regular than what are to be found in him. And some have said, it is hardly possible seriously to read his works without being more disposed unto goodness, as well as being greatly entertained. To be sure, had Virgil writ before Plato, his works had not been any of the books prohibited. But then, this poet also has abundance of rare antiquities for us: and such things, as others besides a Servius, have imagined that they have instructed and obliged mankind, by employing all their days upon. Wherefore if his Aeneid, (which though it were once near twenty times as big as he has left it, yet he has left it unfinished,) may not appear so valuable to you, that you may think twenty-seven verses of the part that is the most finished in it, worth one and twenty hundred pounds and odd money, yet his Georgics, which he put his last hand to, will furnish you with many things far from despicable. But after all, when I said, I was willing that the beauties of these two poets might become visible to your visive faculty in poetry, I did not mean that you should judge nothing to be admittable into an epic poem, which is not authorized by their example; but I perfectly concur with one who is inexpressibly more capable to be a judge of such a matter than I can be; that it is a false critic who, with a petulant air, will insult reason itself, if it presumes to oppose such authority.

I proceed now to say, that if (under the guidance of a Vida) [3] you try your young wings now and then to see what flights you can make, at least for an epigram, it may a little sharpen your sense, and polish your style for more important performances; for this purpose you are now even overstocked with patterns, and—*Poemata passim,* you may, like Nazianzen,[4] all your days make a little recreation of poetry in the midst of your painful studies. Nevertheless, I cannot but advise you. Withhold thy throat from thirst. Be not so set upon poetry, as to be always poring on the passionate and measured pages. Let not what should be sauce, rather than food for you, engross all your application. Beware of a boundless and sickly appetite for the reading of the poems which now the rickety nation swarms withal; and let not the Circaean cup intoxicate you. But especially preserve the chastity of your soul from the dangers you may incur, by a conversation with muses that are no better than harlots: among which are others besides Ovid's Epistles, which for their tendency to excite and foment impure flames, and cast coals into your bosom, deserve rather to be thrown into the fire, than to be laid before the eye which a covenant should be made withal. Indeed, not merely for the impurities which they convey, but also on some other accounts; the powers of darkness have a library among us, whereof the poets have been the most numerous as well as the most

[3] Marco Girolamo Vida (1490–1566), Italian critic and epic poet.
[4] St. Gregory Nazianzen (329–389), Bishop of Sasima (in the Eastern Church) and devoted to literary studies.

venemous authors. Most of the modern plays, as well as the romances, and novels and fictions, which are a sort of poems, do belong to the catalogue of this cursed library. The plays, I say, in which there are so many passages that have a tendency to overthrow all piety, that one, whose name is Bedford,[5] has extracted near seven thousand instances of them, from the plays chiefly of but five years preceding; and says awfully upon them, They are national sins, and therefore call for national plagues; and if God should enter into judgment, all the blood in the nation would not be able to atone for them. How much do I wish that such pestilences, and indeed all those worse than Egyptian toads, (the spawns of a Butler,[6] a Brown,[7] and a Ward,[8] and a company whose name is legion!) might never crawl into your chamber! The unclean spirits that come like frogs out of the mouth of the dragon, and of the beast; which go forth unto the young people of the earth, and expose them to be dealt withal as the enemies of God, in the battle of the great day of the Almighty. As for those wretched scribbles of madmen, my son, touch them not, taste them not, handle them not: thou wilt perish in the using of them. They are the dragons, whose contagious breath peoples the dark retreats of death. To much better purpose will an excellent but an envied Blackmore feast you, than those vile rhapsodies (of that *Vinum daemonum*)[9] which you will find always leave a taint upon your mind, and among other ill effects, will sensibly indispose you to converse with the holy oracles of God your Saviour.

But there is, what I may rather call a parenthesis than a digression, which this may be not altogether an improper place for the introducing of.

There has been a deal of a-do about a style; so much, that I must offer you my sentiments upon it. There is a way of writing, wherein the author endeavours that the reader may have something to the purpose in every paragraph. There is not only a vigour sensible in every sentence, but the paragraph is embellished with profitable references, even to something beyond what is directly spoken. Formal and painful quotations are not studied; yet all that could be learnt from them is insinuated. The writer pretends not unto reading, yet he could not have writ as he does if he had not read very much in his time; and his composures are not only a cloth of gold, but also stuck with as many jewels as the gown of a Russian ambassador. This way of writing has been decried by many, and is at this day more than ever so, for the same reason that, in the old story, the grapes were decried, that they were not ripe. A lazy, ignorant, conceited set of authors, would persuade the whole tribe to lay aside that way of writing, for the same reason that one would have persuaded his brethren to part with the incumbrance of their bushy tails. But however fashion and humour may prevail, they must not think that the club at their coffeehouse

---

[5] See *The Evil and Danger of Stage Plays* (1706) by Arthur Bedford.
[6] Samuel Butler (1612–1680), who wrote *Hudibras* (1663–1668), the famous satire on Puritanism.
[7] Thomas Brown (1663–1704), English satirist who wrote coarse and abusive satires against the Puritans.
[8] Edward Ward (1667–1731), author of *Hudibras Redivivus* (1705).
[9] "wine of evil spirits."

is all the world; but there will always be those, who will in this case be governed by indisputable reason: and who will think that the real excellency of a book will never lie in saying of little; that the less one has for his money in a book, it is really the more valuable for it: and the less one is instructed in a book, and the more superfluous margin and superficial harangue, and the less of substantial matter one has in it, the more it is to be accounted of. And if a more massy way of writing be ever so much disgusted at this day, a better gust will come on, as will some other thing, *quae jam cecidere*.[10] In the mean time, nothing appears to me more impertinent and ridiculous than the modern way (I cannot say, rule; for they have none!) of criticising. The blades that set up for critics, I know not who constituted or commissioned them!—they appear to me, for the most part, as contemptible as they are a supercilious generation. For indeed no two of them have the same stile; and they are as intolerably cross-grained, and severe in their censures upon one another, as they are upon the rest of mankind. But while each of them, conceitedly enough, sets up for the standard of perfection, we are entirely at a loss which fire to follow. Nor can you easily find any one thing wherein they agree for their stile, except perhaps a perpetual care to give us jejune and empty pages, without such touches of erudition (to speak in the stile of an ingenious traveller) as may make the discourses less tedious, and more enriching to the mind of him that peruses them. There is much talk of a florid stile obtaining among the pens that are most in vogue; but how often would it puzzle one, even with the best glasses, to find the flowers! And if they were to be chastised for it, it would be with much the same kind of justice as Jerom was,[11] for being a Ciceronian. After all, every man will have his own stile, which will distinguish him as much as his gait: and if you can attain to that which I have newly described, but always writing so as to give an easy conveyance unto your ideas, I would not have you by any scourging be driven out of your gait; but if you must confess a fault in it, make a confession like that of the lad unto his father while he was beating him for his versifying.

However, since every man will have his own stile, I would pray that we may learn to treat one another with mutual civilities and condescensions, and handsomely indulge one another in this as gentlemen do in other matters.

I wonder what ails people that they cannot let Cicero write in the stile of Cicero, and Seneca write in the (much other!) stile of Seneca; and own that both may please in their several ways.—But I will freely tell you, what has made me consider the humourists that set up for critics upon stile as the most unregardable set of mortals in the world, is this! Far more illustrious critics than any of those to whom I am now bidding defiance, and no less men than your Erasmus's and your Grotius's,[12] have taxed the

---

[10] "which now to cut short."

[11] St. Jerome (*ca.* 340–420), scholar of the Church, maker of the Latin version of the Bible known as the Vulgate.

[12] Desiderius Erasmus (1466?–1536) was a famous Dutch humanist and theologian. Hugo Grotius (1583–1645) was a Dutch statesman and humanist.

Greek stile of the New Testament with I know not what solecisms and barbarisms; and how many learned folks have obsequiously run away with the notion! whereas it is an ignorant and an insolent whimsey which they have been guilty of. It may be (and particularly by an ingenious Blackwall,[13] it has been) demonstrated, that the gentlemen are mistaken in every one of their pretended instances; all the unquestionable classics may be brought in to convince them of their mistakes. Those glorious oracles are as pure Greek as ever was written in the world; and so correct, so noble, so sublime is their stile, that never any thing under the cope of Heaven, but the Old Testament, has equalled it.

[13] Anthony Blackwall (1674-1730), classical scholar and author of *The Sacred Classics* (1725).

MATHER BYLES

[AN ESSAY ON STYLE][1]

(1745)

As ONE great Design of many of the Entertainments in our *Magazine*,
is to cultivate *polite* Writing, and form and embellish the Style of
our ingenious Countrymen: So, Instead of a Preface to this Volume,
we ask Leave to give the following Piece of *Criticism*.

> *Clamorem immensum tollit, quo pontus et omnes*
> *Intremuere undae, penitusque exterrita tellus*
> *Italiae, curvisque immugiit Aetna cavernis.*
>
> Virg. Aeneid.[2]

There have been innumerable Authors, from *Aristotle's Rhetorick* to
Longinus's Treatise of the Sublime, and from thence down to the Compiler
of our modern *Horn-book,* who have written Introductions to the Art of
Polite Writing. Every one that can just distinguish his Twenty Four Letters sets up for a Judge of it; as all who are able to flourish a Goose's Quill,
pretend to be Masters of that Secret. The noblest Productions have given
Birth to many a supercillious Caveller; Cricticks of all Sizes and Dimensions have nibled round the divinest Pages; and Ignorance and Conceit
have endeavoured to shake down the most beautiful Structures, in order to
build themselves a Reputation out of the Ruins. A superiour Genius,
though he seems to kindle a wide Horizon of Light all about him, and is
admired by the understanding Part of Mankind, yet he must expect to be
the Occasion of a great many Absurdities, with which the unknowing and
envious will strive to satyrize him: As the Sun scatters Day through a
whole Frame of Worlds, but yet may, in some particular Spots, raise a
Fog, or hatch a Nest of Vermin. To conclude, the Science of correct Writing having been a Subject exhausted by so many able Hands, and seeing
all the Rabble of Scriblers are such indisputable Proficients in it; not to
mention my own Incapacity for such an Undertaking; I shall not be so
vain as to offer my Thoughts upon it: But I shall apply my Labours at
this Time, to an Ornament of a contrary Nature, which is a Theme intirely
New, Namely, *The Art of writing Incorrectly.*

This, I take it, is a Work that I am excellently well qualified for, and I
doubt not but to convince the World that I am a perfect Master of my
Subject. In the Prosecution of this useful Design, I shall show the Excel-

[1] Published in *The American Magazine and Historical Chronicle,* January, 1745.
[2] "Then he utters a roar so loud that the sea and the surges tremble together with
fear, and Italy's heart is affrighted, while Mount Aetna reechoes the roar from deep
winding caverns." (*Aeneid,* III, 672-74.)

lency of Incorrect Writing in general; I shall lay open the several Artifices, by which a Man of competent Abilities, may, with proper Application, attain to a tolerable Degree of Perfection in it; I shall produce pertinent Examples from Writers of undoubted Eminence in that improving Science: And in the last place, I may possibly address the World with a very pathetick Exhortation, to follow the Instructions which I shall give them, in order to accomplish themselves in the Art of Incorrect Writing. In short, I intend to entertain the Publick, with a regular Criticism upon Nonsense.

Authors of this Kind may be divided into two Classes, generally known under the Denomination of the *Bombastick* and the *Grubstreet*.[3] The latter of these Characters is easily attained, provided a Man can but keep himself from thinking, and yet so contrive Matters, as to let his Pen run along unmolested over a Sheet of White Paper, and drop a convenient Quantity of Words, at proper Intervals on it. A Person who is acquainted with this Secret, may, with great Facility and Composure of Mind, furnish himself with a comfortable Stock of Reputation, as often as he finds it requisite. This he might do, as without any Ruffle to his own Tranquility, so neither would it prove the least Disturbance to his Readers: For while he flow'd along with that unmeaning Softness, every one within the Warble of his Accents would undoubtedly dissolve away in a supine Indolence, and, (as a late Musical Author of this Species has very tenderly expressed it) be *hush'd into lulling Dreams*.

I shall, perhaps, dedicate some future Essay to the Incouragement of these worthy Gentlemen, but at this Time I intend to consider those my ingenious Fellow-Labourers, who deviate into the contrary Extream; I mean the Admirers of Bombast and Fustian.

These Writers, to avoid the Imputation of low and flat, blow up every Subject they take in Hand beyond its natural Dimensions; and nothing will please them that is not big and boisterous, wild and irregular. They wonderfully delight in Noise and Clamour; a Rattle of Words, and an Extravagance of Imagination, they look upon as the Perfection of Rhetorick; and are Transported beyond themselves, at the Tumult and Confusion that bellows through a Hurricane of Nonsense. In short, that which Men of this Turn applaud as the Masterpiece of good Writing, differs from the *true Sublime*, as a Boy's artificial Kite, wadling among the Clouds at the End of a Skein of Pack-thread, does from the natural Flight of an Eagle, towering with steddy Pinions up the Sky, and bearing full upon the Sun.

If this false Taste prevails amongst us, we shall quickly prove such a Generation of Blusterers, that our Country will resemble the Cave of Aeolus, where the Winds make their general Rendezvous, and battel and clash together in an eternal Din and Uproar. For my own Part, I look upon it to be the Duty of every one, as far as in him lies, to lend his Assistance in banking out this Inundation of Sound, which, if it finds a clear Passage, will not fail to overwhelm us in a Deluge of Folly and Absurdity.

[3] A London street much inhabited by needy, inferior, hack writers.

A Friend of mine who writes in this exorbitant Style, Mr. *Richard Stentor* by Name, shall be the Hero of the present Essay. Mr. *Stentor* as to his exterior Figure, is one of the portliest Mortals that have flourished in our World, since *Goliah* over-top'd the *Philistian* Army. He is moderately speaking, Nine Foot high, and Four in Diameter. His Voice is not unlike the Roar and Rapidity of a Torrent foaming down a Mountain, and reverberated amongst the neighboring Rocks. The Hurry of Vociferation with which he drives along in the Heat of an Argument, imitates the Thunder of a Cartload of Stones poured out upon a Pavement. He was educated in a Ship of War, and one would imagine he learnt the Notes of his Gamut, from the various Whistlings of a Tempest thro' the Rigging of his Vessel. I was once so unadvised as to offer my Dissent from one of his Opinions; but I had better have held my Tongue: He turned upon me, and rung me such a Peal of Eloquence, that had I not made off with the greatest Precipitation, would have gone near to have stun'd, and made me deaf all my Days. Nay, I have cause to think my Hearing has been never the better for it to this Moment.

This is a short Description of his external Accomplishments; as to the Qualifications of his Mind, they will be best perceived, by a Transcript I shall here make, from an Oration he formerly composed in *Praise* of *Beacon Hill*. I must inform my Readers, that it was conceived as he stood upon the Summit of that little Mount, one Training-Day, when, as he has since owned to me, the Drums and Musquets assisted his Inspiration, and augmented and deepend the Rumbling of his Periods. It begins in the following Manner—

> *The gloriously-transcendent, and highly-exalted Precipice, from which the sonorous Accents of my Lungs resound with repeated Echoes; is so pompous, magnificent, illustrious, and loftily-towering, that, as I twirle around my Arm with the artful Flourish of an Orator, I seem to feel my Knucles rebound from the blew Vault of Heaven, which just arches over my Head. I stand upon an amazing Eminence that heaves itself up, on both sides steep and stupendous! high and horrendous! The spiry* Teneriffe, *the unshaken* Atlas, *or Olympus divine and celestial, when compared to this prodigious Mountain, sink to Sands, and dwindle to Atoms. It is deep-rooted in its ever-during Foundations, firm as the Earth, lasting as the Sun, immoveable as the Pillars of Nature! I behold from this awful and astonishing Scituation, the concave Expanse of uncreated Space, stretch itself above: and the Land and Ocean below, spreading an Infinitude of Extension all about me. But what daring Tropes and flaming Metaphores shall I select, O aspiring Beacon! to celebrate Thee with a suitable Grandeur, or exalt thee to a becoming Dignity? How does it shoot up its inconceivable Pinnacle into the superior Regions, and blend itself with the cerulian circum-ambient Aether! It mocks the fiercest Efforts of the most piercing Sight, to reach to its impenetrable Sublimities. It looks down upon the diminish'd Spheres; the fixt Stars twinkle at an immeasurable Distance beneath it; while the Planets roll away, unperceived, in a vast, a fathomless Profound!* * * * * *

By this little Quotation from Mr. *Stentor's* Panegyrick on Beacon Hill, my Reader will in some Measure be able to judge of his Manner of thinking, and expressing himself. It appears plainly that he heaps his Subject with improper and foreign Thoughts; that he strains those Thoughts into the most unnatural and ridiculous Distortions; and, last of all, that he clouds them with so many needless supernumerary Epithets, as to fling the whole Piece into this unaccountable Huddle of Impertinence and Inconsistency. *Richard* is mighty fond of great sounding Words, and, let his Topick be what it will, he has perpetual Recourse to them upon all Emergencies. He once took it in his Head to be in Love, and wrote a Poem to his Mistress on that delicate Passion: But instead of the gentle Flow of Harmony which any one would reasonably have expected, and which is indeed essential to Compositions of that Kind, his Numbers stalked along as sturdy and outragious as in any other of his Performances. I my self counted in Fifty Six Lines of it, three *Celestials,* eight *Immortals,* eleven *Unbounds,* six *Everlastings,* four *Eternities,* and thirteen *Infinites;* Besides *Bellowings, Ravings, Yellings, Horrors, Terribles, Rackets, Hubbubs,* and *Clutterings,* without Number. But what pleased me the most of any of my Friend's Compositions, was, *A Poetical Description of a Game at Push-pin.* Sure, thought I, when I read the Title, there can be nothing very loud and impetuous upon so trivial a Matter as This. How I was surprized out of my mistake, my Reader will in some Measure conceive, when he understands that the first Distich of the Poem runs thus,

> *Rage, fire, and fury in my bosom roll,*
> *And all the gods rush headlong on my soul.*

He then proceeded to compare the Pins to two Comets, whose Heads, as he expressed it, enlightned the boundless Desarts of the Skies with a bloody Glare, and threw behind them the ruddy Volumes of their tremendous Trains, into the tractless Wastes of Immensity. When the Pins met in the Progress of the Game, for a Similitude, he supposed the two Continents to be tossed from their Foundations, and encounter, with a direful Concussion, in the midst of the briny *Atlantick*: or rather, *says he,* as if two Systems of Worlds, Suns, Planets and all, should be hurled resistless one against another, and dash a horrible *Chaos,* from the general Ruins of Matter, and Wrecks of a whole Universe. He concluded the Poem with the following Lines, which I look upon to be the most finished Pattern of this Sort of Productions, that I have any where met with; whether I consider, the Uncouthness of the Language, the Ruggedness of the Style, or the Disproportion and Extravagance of the Images. Speaking of the Pins he says,

> *The Bars of Brass, harsh-crashing, loud resound,*
> *And jarring discords rend th' astonish'd ground.*
> *So when aloft dire hurricanes arise,*
> *And with horrendous shatterings burst the skies,*
> *Dread ghastly terrors drive along in crowds,*

And hideous thunder howls amongst the clouds;
Eternal whirlwinds on the ocean roar,
Infinite earth-quakes rock the bounding shore.

I shall conclude these Remarks upon Bombast, with an Observation which I ought in Justice to make, in favour of those who fall into it; *viz. That no Person can be a considerable Proficient this way, who has not a good Share of natural Powers and Abilities.* Hence, when we see a Young Man delivering himself in this warm Manner, he is to be regarded as a good *Genius* run wild, for want of Cultivation from Study, and the Rules of Art: And it follows, that should such a juvenile Writer, take proper Methods to improve his Mind, in innuring himself to a close Way of Reasoning, and by conversing with the best Authors, however defective he might be in this Particular at first, he would in the End make a chaste and excellent Writer. Thus it happened to the immortal *Virgil,* whose divine *Aeneid* once shot itself into so great a Luxuriance, as to be near twenty Times as Large as it appears at this Day. As his Imagination cooled by Years, and his Judgment ripened, and hasted on to Maturity, his Style dropped the false Glare of Ornaments, and shone with an equal Purity and Elegance; His Thoughts learned to proportion themselves to his Subject, and cast themselves into that exact Symmetry of Arrangement and Disposition, in which they now charm us; And, in a word, a new Beauty began to dawn in every Line of that exquisite Work which consecrates his deathless Fame to the Admiration of all Posterity.

Critical Essays of Neoclassicism

BENJAMIN FRANKLIN

DOGOOD PAPERS, NO. VII [1]
(1722)

IT HAS BEEN the Complaint of many Ingenious Foreigners, who have travell'd amongst us, *That good Poetry is not to be expected in* New-England. I am apt to Fancy, the Reason is, not because our Countrymen are altogether void of a Poetical Genius, nor yet because we have not those Advantages of Education which other Countries have, but purely because we do not afford that Praise and Encouragement which is merited, when any thing extraordinary of this Kind is produc'd among us: Upon which Consideration I have determined, when I meet with a Good Piece of *New-England* Poetry, to give it a suitable Encomium, and thereby endeavour to discover to the World some of its Beautys, in order to encourage the Author to go on, and bless the World with more, and more Excellent Productions.

There has lately appear'd among us a most Excellent Piece of Poetry, entituled, *An Elegy upon the Much Lamented Death of Mrs.* Mehitebell Kitel, *Wife of Mr.* John Kitel *of* Salem, *Etc.* It may justly be said in its Praise, without Flattery to the Author, that it is the most *Extraordinary* Piece that was ever wrote in *New-England.* The Language is so soft and Easy, the Expression so moving and pathetick, but above all, the Verse and Numbers so Charming and Natural, that it is almost beyond Comparison.

> The Muse *disdains* *
> *Those Links and Chains,*
> *Measures and Rules of Vulgar Strains,*
> *And o'er the Laws of Harmony a Sovereign Queen she reigns.*

I find no English Author, Ancient or Modern, whose Elegies may be compar'd with this, in respect to the Elegance of Stile, or Smoothness of Rhime; and for the affecting Part, I will leave your Readers to judge, if ever they read any Lines, that would sooner make them *draw their Breath* and Sigh, if not shed Tears, than these following.

> *Come let us mourn, for we have lost a*
> *Wife, a Daughter, and a Sister,*
> *Who has lately taken Flight, and*
> *greatly we have mist her.*

* Watts. [Franklin's note.]
[1] This is the seventh of a series of essays published by Franklin under the pseudonym of "Dogood" in the *New England Courant* in Boston. It is one of his earliest published writings.

In another place,

> Some little Time *before she yielded up her Breath,*
> *She said, I ne'er shall hear one Sermon more on Earth.*
> *She kist her Husband* some little Time *before she expir'd,*
> *Then lean'd her Head the Pillow on, just out of Breath*
> *and tir'd.*

But the Threefold Appellation in the first Line

> —*a Wife, a Daughter, and a Sister,*

must not pass unobserved. That Line in the celebrated *Watts,*

> Gunston, *the Just, the Generous, and the Young,*

is nothing Comparable to it. The latter only mentions three Qualifications of *one* Person who was deceased, which therefore could raise Grief and Compassion but for *One.* Whereas the former, (*our most excellent Poet*) gives his Reader a Sort of an Idea of the Death of *Three Persons,* viz.

> —*a Wife, a Daughter, and a Sister,*

which is *Three Times* as great a Loss as the Death of *One,* and consequently must raise *Three Times* as much Grief and Compassion in the Reader.

I should be very much straitened for Room, if I should attempt to discover even half the Excellencies of this Elegy which are obvious to me. Yet I cannot omit one Observation, which is, that the Author has (to his Honour) invented a new Species of Poetry, which wants a Name, and was never before known. His muse scorns to be confin'd to the old Measures and Limits, or to observe the dull Rules of Criticks;

> Nor Rapin *gives her Rules to fly, nor* Purcell
> Notes to Sing.
> Watts.

Now 'tis Pity that such an Excellent Piece should not be dignify'd with a particular Name; and seeing it cannot justly be called, either *Epic, Sapphic, Lyric,* or *Pindaric,* nor any other Name yet invented, I presume it may, (in Honour and Remembrance of the Dead) be called the *Kitelic.* Thus much in the Praise of *Kitelic Poetry.*

It is certain, that those Elegies which are of our own Growth, (and our Soil seldom produces any other sort of Poetry) are by far the greatest part, wretchedly Dull and Ridiculous. Now since it is imagin'd by many, that our Poets are honest, well-meaning Fellows, who do their best, and that if they had but some Instructions how to govern Fancy with Judgment, they would make indifferent good Elegies; I shall here subjoin a Receipt for that purpose, which was left me as a Legacy, (among other valuable Rarities) by my Reverend Husband. It is as follows,

A Receipt *to make* a New-England
Funeral Elegy

For the Title of your Elegy. *Of these you may have enough ready made to your Hands; but if you should chuse to make it your self, you must be sure not to omit the words* Aetatis Suae, *which will Beautify it exceedingly.*

For the Subject of your Elegy. *Take one of your Neighbours who has lately departed this Life; it is no great matter at what Age the Party dy'd, but it will be best if he went away suddenly, being* Kill'd, Drown'd, or Frose to Death.

Having chose the Person, take all his Virtues, Excellencies, &c. and if he have not enough, you may borrow some to make up a sufficient Quantity: To these add his last Words, dying Expressions, &c. if they are to be had; mix all these together, and be sure you strain them well. Then season all with a Handful or two of Melancholy Expressions, such as, Dreadful, Deadly, cruel cold Death, unhappy Fate, weeping Eyes, *&c. Have mixed all these Ingredients well, put them into the empty Scull of some* young Harvard; *(but in Case you have ne'er a One at Hand, you may use your own,) there let them Ferment for the Space of a Fortnight, and by that Time they will be incorporated into a Body, which take out, and having prepared a sufficient Quantity of double Rhimes, such as* Power, Flower; Quiver, Shiver; Grieve us, Leave us; tell you, excel you; Expeditions, Physicians; Fatigue him, Intrigue him; *&c. you must spread all upon Paper, and if you can procure a Scrap of Latin to put at the End, it will garnish it mightily; then having affixed your Name at the Bottom, with a* Moestus Composuit, *you will have an Excellent Elegy.*

BENJAMIN FRANKLIN

From IDEA OF THE ENGLISH SCHOOL [1]
(1751)

. . . SOME short Pieces, not exceeding the Length of a *Spectator,* to be given this Class as Lessons (and some of the easier *Spectators* would be very suitable for the Purpose.) These Lessons might be given over Night as Tasks, the Scholars to study them against the Morning. Let it then be required of them to give an Account, first of the Parts of Speech, and Construction of one or two Sentences; this will oblige them to recur frequently to their Grammar, and fix its principal Rules in their Memory. Next of the *Intention* of the Writer, or the *Scope* of the Piece; the Meaning of each Sentence, and of every uncommon Word. This would early acquaint them with the Meaning and Force of Words, and give them that most necessary Habit, of Reading with Attention.

The Master then to read the Piece with the proper Modulations of Voice, due Emphasis, and suitable Action, where Action is required; and put the Youth on imitating his Manner.

Where the Author has us'd an Expression not the best, let it be pointed out; and let his Beauties be particularly remarked to the Youth.

Let the Lessons for Reading be varied, that the Youth may be acquainted with good Stiles of all Kinds in Prose and Verse, and the proper Manner of reading each Kind. Sometimes a well-told Story, a Piece of a Sermon, a General's Speech to his Soldiers, a Speech in a Tragedy, some Part of a Comedy, an Ode, a Satyr, a Letter, Blank Verse, Hudibrastick, Heroic, &c. But let such Lessons for Reading be chosen, as contain some useful Instruction, whereby the Understandings or Morals of the Youth, may at the same Time be improv'd. . . .

. . . to *form their Stile,* and even to take Care that the Stops and Capitals are properly disposed, is the Part of the *English* Master. The Boys should be put on Writing Letters to each other on any common Occurrences, and on various Subjects, imaginary Business, &c., containing little Stories, Accounts of their late Reading, what Parts of Authors please them, and why; Letters of Congratulation, of Compliment, of Request, of Thanks, of Recommendation, of Admonition, of Consolation, of Expostulation, Excuse, &c. In these they should be taught to express themselves clearly, concisely, and naturally, without affected Words or high-flown Phrases . . .

[1] Philadelphia, 1751.

JOHN TRUMBULL

AN ESSAY ON THE USE AND ADVANTAGES OF THE FINE ARTS [1]
(1770)

No SUBJECT can be more important in itself, or better suited to the present occasion, and the exercises of this day, than the Use and Advantages of the fine Arts, and especially those of Polite Literature. These studies are perhaps too much undervalued by the public, and neglected by the youth in our seminaries of science. They are considered as meer matters of trifling amusement, and despised in comparison with the more solid branches of Learning.

The knowledge of Languages, Mathematics, Metaphysics and Philosophy, undoubtedly deserves to engage the attention of the greatest Genius. For skill in these sciences, the World (while the world remains) will revere the memory of a Bacon, a Newton, and a Locke. But when they are carried beyond a certain point; when they are of no advantage to the common purposes of life; when they are employed upon questions which human Reason can never with certainty determine, they degenerate into meer speculations of amusement, and become no farther valuable, than as they serve to enlarge the mind, clear the understanding, and entertain us in the hours of leisure from the important avocations of business. The Geometrical labours for the Quadrature of the Circle, the Metaphysical controversies about the Existence of matter, and the Essence of Spirit, though a field for the display of genius, in what are they more interesting to mankind than the contentions of Antiquaries about the genuineness of a medal, or the disputes of Commentators about the various readings of their antient manuscripts?

Let us consider the advantages which arise to the world from the study of the liberal Arts.

Mankind in the present state, are extremely liable to be led away by mean and sordid vices, to be attached to the low enjoyments of sense, and thus degraded almost to a level with the brutal creation. As that unceasing thirst for happiness, which is the universal spring of action, must have some object for its gratification; the Divine Being, to raise us above these low desires, hath implanted in our minds a taste for more pure and intellectual pleasures. These pleasures have their source in the fine Arts, and are more especially found in the elegant entertainments of polite Literature. They ennoble the soul, purify the passions, and give the thoughts a better turn. They add dignity to our sentiments, delicacy and refinement to our

[1] Delivered at the Commencement, New Haven, September 12, 1770. Published in pamphlet form, New Haven, 1770.

57

manners. They set us above our meaner pursuits, and make us scorn those low enjoyments, which perhaps we once esteemed as the perfection of human felicity. I appeal to all persons of judgment, whether they can rise from reading a fine Poem, viewing any masterly work of Genius, or hearing an harmonious concert of Music, without feeling an openness of heart, and an elevation of mind, without being more sensible to the dignity of human nature, and despising whatever tends to debase and degrade it?

These are the delights, which humanize the soul, and polish away that rugged ferocity of manners, which is natural to the uncultivated nations of the world.

In every land, in every age, at the time when the unconquered spirit of freedom, joined with that laudable ambition, which fires the soul to heroic deeds; hath raised the nation to the highest pitch of glory, the fine Arts have been studiously cultivated, and have shined forth with peculiar lustre. For Learning and Glory walk hand in hand through the world. A savage People, before the dawn of literature, may indeed be terrible in arms: but being stained with the blood of cruelty, tarnished with that wild barbarity, which degrades courage into brutality, they never attain to the summit of renown; and either sink unnoticed into oblivion, or leave to posterity a name more infamous for barbarism, than famed for heroic atchievements. While every voice celebrates the bravery of an Alexander, a Scipio, a Caesar, and a Marlborough; who remembers the savage fierceness of the lion-hearted Richard; or what mouth is opened in the praise of that scourge of Asia, the Persian Nadir?

The same ardour of ambition, the same greatness of thought, which inspires the Warrior to brave danger in the conquering field, when diffused among a people will call forth Genius in every station of life, fire the imagination of the Artist, and raise to sublimity the aspiring Muse.

Look into the annals of antiquity. View the Grecians at the aera of learning and politeness, when the fine Arts were carried to their highest glory, when the whole nation were encouragers of science, and every person a judge of literature; when by greatness of genius, correctness of taste and refinement of manners, they rendered themselves famous throughout the world, and patterns of imitation to all posterity. Then was the time that Greece produced those Heroes that astonished Europe and Asia with the sound of their victories; then was the time that Athens, Sparta and Thebes gave laws to the world. And could a Nation fail of rising to the highest pitch of fame, when animated with the thundering eloquence of Demosthenes and Pericles, fired to warlike deeds by the martial muse of Homer, and warmed with those noble sentiments which inspire the productions of Aeschylus, Euripides and Sophocles?

The glory of Arts and Arms sunk in Greece and rose again with renewed lustre in Hesperia. Rome distinguished herself for literature, even from the first dawn of her greatness. In her early days, while her unpolished manners bore too near a resemblance to the rough virtues of Sparta, she could boast an Ennius, the boldness of whose thoughts even Virgil himself did not disdain to imitate. Then flourished Accius, Naevius, Pacuvius, those famed dramatic poets, with the bold and spirited Lucilius, the father of the Roman satire. But these writers have sunk into the dark grave of oblivion, and left behind only some small traces of their fame. Then appeared the rough genius of Plautus, the milder elegance of Terence, and the soft muse of Catullus: Then the polished Lucretius, so distinguished for all the graces of poetic expression, that Virgil evidently borrowed from his writings, his style, versification and manner of description. In the mean time Eloquence rose to the highest perfection at Rome. Be Cicero a witness, whose praise is unnecessary, whether as an orator, a patriot, or a philosopher.

But see Rome attains to the summit of greatness. The world submits to her sway. Satiated with the spoils of victory, she sits unmolested on the throne, and diffuses the mild blessings of peace. Then flourish the names dearest to fame, the glories of the Augustan age: The majestic Muse of Virgil, the second who dared attempt the dignity of the epic song; the polished elegance of Horace, graced with the sounding lyre, and armed with the keen sword of satire; the strong and sportive imagination of Ovid; the soft elegiac strains of Tibullus and Propertius; and the historic grandeur of Livy. The world is conscious of their fame. Their characters need not be illustrated by the tedious impertinence of praise.

The Glory of Rome faded by a gradual decay. The Muse still shone, though with tarnished lustre, in the tragedies of Seneca, the satires of Juvenal and Persius, and the heroic poems of Lucan, Statius, Claudian, and Silius Italicus. History produced the nervous, the manly Tacitus; and Philosophy could still show her Seneca and Pliny. Till at length Tyranny usurped the dominion, and Barbarism overspread the land of Italy.

For a nearer instance of the trophies of the liberal Arts, let us view the state of Russia in the last century. In a cold unpolished land, deep-sunk in the shades of savage ignorance, a Monarch rises, who moved with compassion for his subjects, fired with love of glory, and endowed with a soul superior to the age, forms a project of civilizing his country. He sails to other lands, imports the rudiments of the arts, and affords both by precept and example the utmost encouragement to genius. The Nation raises herself from the dust, repels her enemies, extends her borders, leads forth her conquering armies, and now threatens the total subversion of the Ottoman empire.

Britain alone can claim the glory of an equality with Greece and Rome. There for two centuries the Arts have flourished with almost unabated lustre: And the slightest reflection will inform us that this period is by far the most celebrated in the British history. In the glorious reign of Elizabeth, there arose a Spenser, unequalled in all the pleasing charms of luxuriant description; whose fancy transports us to fairy land, and brings us acquainted with a shadowy race, the beings of his own creation. Then a Shakespear, the matchless genius of the drama; endowed with the most noble extravagance of imagination, the strongest powers of humour, the sovereign command of the passions, and the keenest inspection into all the mazes of the human soul. To these succeeded the unbridled wit of Cowley, the soft graces of Waller, and the various grandeur of all-accomplished Dryden.

Then with the united charms of every Muse, appeared the immortal
Milton; who with the greatest force of natural genius, assisted by all the
aids of art, and by the noble descriptions of the inspired writers, hath produced a Poem, almost as much superior to Homer's, in sublimity of conception, as it is in the greatness of its subject:

> A Genius universal as his theme,
> Astonishing as Chaos, as the bloom
> Of blowing Eden fair, as Heav'n sublime.
>   Thomson

After a short eclipse in the luxurious reign of Charles II, the reviving
Arts shone forth with superior brightness in the prosperous days of William
and Anne; while the victorious Marlborough bore Britain's thunder on
her foes, and made Europe tremble at the sound of his arms. Then flourished the polished muse of Addison, who revived in England the classic
elegance of the Augustan age; whose works, adorned with the highest
sublimity of sentiment, and the nicest delicacy of thought, filled with easy
humour which points the ridicule at vice, (while they afford instruction
and entertainment of the noblest kind to every reader,) may boast as their
greatest honour and distinguished excellence, that they are peculiarly calculated to please and improve the fairest part of the creation.

Then arose a Swift, the friend of virtue, the scourge of folly, and the
terror of vice; unequalled for manly sense, liveliness of fancy, the powers
of wit and humour, and the severest poignancy of satire. Happy, had not
his mind, soured with disappointment in the earliest views of his ambition,
too often endeavoured by the grossest indelicacy of description to debase
the dignity of human nature; and indulged a spirit of misanthropy, which
clouds his best productions, and while we admire the force of his Genius,
bids us detest the sentiments of his heart. What age shall forget the undying fame of Pope! Whether in pleasing strains he paints the beauties of
nature; mourns with the softest notes of elegiac verse; or with moral rapture
unfolds all the principles and passions of the human soul: Whether in
sportive lays he displays the foibles of the gentler Sex; impales vice and
dulness on the point of satire; or holding up the glass of translation, reflects with unabated light the glories of the Maeonian song.

For the power of describing the beauties of rural scenes, and copying
the different appearances of nature, what writer can vie with the pleasing
Thomson! The liveliness of his paintings, his sublime morality, and his
delicacy of thought justly raise him to the highest rank of genius.

Nor must we forget the unaffected ease of Gay and Prior, the spirited
wit of Congreve, the delicate fancy of Parnelle, the dramatic powers of
Otway, Southern and Rowe, the cervantic humour of Arbuthnot, with the
pointed satire and strong imagination of Young. These writers will convey
the English glory to the most distant ages of posterity.

Polite Letters at present are much on the decline in Britain; not through
a scarcity of authors, or want of encouragement from the public; but by
reason of that luxurious effiminacy, which hath caused a decay of genius,

and introduced a false taste in writing. Their Men of learning are infected with pedantry. They are great admirers of antiquity and followers in the path of servile imitation. They sacrifice ease and elegance to the affectation of classic correctness, fetter the fancy with the rules of method, and damp all the ardour of aspiring invention. While the men of Genius (who are at present a distinct class of writers) in contempt of the critic chains, throw off all appearance of order and connection, sport in the wildest sallies of imagination, and adopt the greatest extravagance of humour, which too often sinks to buffoonery, or is soured with the malevolence of satire.

America hath a fair prospect in a few centuries of ruling both in arts and arms. It is universally allowed that we very much excel in the force of natural genius: And although but few among us are able to devote their whole lives to study, perhaps there is no nation, in which a larger portion of learning is diffused through all ranks of people. For as we generally possess the middle station of life, neither sunk to vassalage, nor raised to independance, we avoid the sordid ignorance of peasants, and the unthinking dissipation of the great. The heroic love of Liberty, the manly fortitude, the generosity of sentiment, for which we have been so justly celebrated, seem to promise the future advancement and established duration of our glory. Many incidents unfortunate in themselves, have tended to call forth and sustain these virtues. Happy, in this respect, have been our late struggles for liberty! They have awakened the spirit of freedom; they have rectified the manners of the times; they have made us acquainted with the rights of mankind; recalled to our minds the glorious independance of former ages, fired us with the views of fame, and by filling our thoughts with contempt of the imported articles of luxury, have raised an opposition, not only to the illegal power, but to the effeminate manners of Britain. And I cannot but hope, notwithstanding some dangerous examples of infamous defection, that there is a spirit remaining in these Colonies, that will invariably oppose itself to the efforts of usurpation and perfidy, and forbid that Avarice should ever betray us to Slavery.

This Land hath already begun to distinguish itself in literature. It is peculiarly famed for the study of Theology; and though too much infested with the short-lived productions of controversy, can boast of some Divines, who however inelegant in style and expression, have perhaps never been excelled in depth of thought and profoundness of reasoning. Our late writers in the cause of liberty have gained the applause of Europe. Many elegant essays have been produced in the style of wit and humour; nor hath Poetry been entirely uncultivated among us. The encouragement, which is given to the Arts and Sciences, affords a prospect of our future glory.

[Trumbull has here appended a poem giving a prospect of
the future glory of American literature.]

TIMOTHY DWIGHT

From THE FRIEND, NO. IV [1]
(1789)

AMONG THE prejudices which are entertained by the mind, none has a more powerful influence, than reverence for the opinions and practices of those who have lived before us. This prejudice reaches all classes of men, and extends its dominion over every method of thinking and acting. Great men observe, and laugh at it, in the conduct of little ones; every sect perceives it in every other sect; and every individual, in the conduct of every other. In agriculture, at least in this country, it decides every practice; in the mechanical arts, in the liberal arts, and even in science, it has a very extensive influence. Thus the nature of the subject to be considered, or pursued, is little attended to, the force of arguments, pleaded in vain; and men live not by reason, but by precedent. This folly has been often exploded by philosophy, and caricatured by satire; yet its power, either in extent or degree, is little abated. The reason is obvious: every man sees the defect in another, but not in himself; and while he wonders that his neighbors are so deaf to reasoning, and so slow of reformation, never reflects that himself is equally diseased, and equally needs the benefit of the cure.

The man, who, upon his shoulders, carried weekly to the mill, a stone of sufficient weight to balance a bushel of wheat, and who refused to rid himself of the burden, because his father and grandfather had carried the same stone, forty years, before him; was, in the eye of reason, a less ridiculous object than the person, who is voluntarily burdened with a load of errors and follies, because others, who have preceded him, chose to carry them. Yet we daily see multitudes, whose shoulders are humped higher than their heads, laughing heartily at the awkward figure, their fellow Hudibrasses make around them.

Homer, some thousand years since, with great force and beauty, formed the Iliad, an epic, or narrative poem. It was the first poem of the kind, and written with the first degree of human abilities. Accordingly, the pleasure it gave mankind was very great, and the praises they heaped upon it were without measure. Aristotle, a shrewd and curious investigator, examined the structure of this poem, and the Odyssey, and having satisfied himself what were the means of the pleasure they afforded, ventured to form, from the practice of Homer, general rules for the conduct of the epic poem. From the tragedies of Sophocles and Euripides, regarded by their countrymen with similar applause, he formed other rules for the conduct of tragedy. This code of criticism has partly escaped the depreda-

[1] From *The American Museum*, V, Philadelphia, 1789.

tions of time, and is now a law less disputed, even by most persons of taste, than either of the two fundamental rules of moral rectitude. Had these three poets been moderns—had Milton written Paradise Lost, when the Iliad was written, and the best tragedies of Shakespeare been exhibited on the Athenian stage, Aristotle would doubtless have consulted their writings, for the source of the pleasure derived from them, and formed his maxims of criticism on their authority. How different a system would these events have produced; and how many rules would have then been received, with the same implicit faith, with which every age has now swallowed their opposites? Many of Aristotle's present laws would then have been considered as the lunacies of Zoilus.[2] All epic poems must have had an unfortunate issue; all tragedies five acts; and the inferior parts been written in prose. A chorus would have been railed at as a modern absurdity; simplicity of plot been deemed the effusion of dullness; and a new cluster of great ancients moved down the tide of ages, with undisputed glory and perfection. The dispute would then have been, whether the Iliad and Aeneid were entitled to the name of epic poems; and whether their fortunate issues were not such a trespass on the established rules of criticism, as to preclude them from a rank in this high class of productions. Homer's machinery would have been the grossest of all absurdities; and the wonder of all men of taste would have been excited, at the groveling relish of such persons as were capable of enduring in dignified performances, the heathen mythology. Thus the face of the critical world would have been essentially altered, and the propriety of every maxim would have been as questionless as of those, at present adopted.

To those persons who never questioned the authority of the received system of criticism, these remarks will appear ill founded; for the prejudice above mentioned, which produced their implicit faith in it, will prevent them from discerning their propriety. In the view of candour, the justice of them will scarcely be doubted. Yet how much of the common reverence for Aristotle, for all the ancients, and for many of the moderns, will the acknowledgment of them destroy?

I would not here be understood to condemn the generality of precepts in the present critical code, or to think disrespectfully of its author. Aristotle was an excellent, a wonderful critic, for the advantages he possessed; and many of the acknowledged critical maxims are undoubtedly just. But Aristotle's ideas of criticism were taken from a few performances: and had he lived in the present age, with the same independence of mind, he would have altered many of them for the better. As criticism, like the science of healing, forms all its precepts from facts, the more numerous the collection of facts is, the fairer opportunity is furnished for reducing it to the standard of truth. Milton and Shakespeare have added, every original genius adds, to the stock of critical ideas, and exhibits means of pleasure, the knowledge of which is true criticism. Hence criticism will advance towards a higher perfection, as the varieties of the human mind open new views of poetical objects, and peculiarity of genius furnishes new springs and meanderings

[2] Greek critic notorious for his attacks on Homer.

of delight. The stock of poetical images is as infinite, as the diversities of infinite workmanship, in the natural and moral creation; and the modes of exhibiting them as various, as the endlessly various modes of perception in intelligent beings. All these constitute the field of criticism, and concerning them all just and valuable remarks in the progress of things will probably be made.

A few specimens of the influence of the above prejudice, on this branch of human knowledge may perhaps be advantageously subjoined to these observations.

The question, whether Paradise Lost, the Jerusalem Delivered,[3] and various other poems, are epic poems, has often agitated the critical world. To decide this question with propriety, or even at all, one would naturally imagine it necessary to have previously decided the nature of the epic poem. Yet this article is hitherto totally undecided. It has indeed been often defined, but that definition has been as often contested. It would be not a little surprising—if any human folly were surprising—to see grave and learned men seriously and warmly debate, whether a poem belongs to a certain class, before they have agreed upon the characteristics of that class.

The word epic signifies merely narrative, and according to its plain meaning, every narrative poem is epic. But the phrase epic poem has been appropriated to such narrative poems, as concerned a dignified subject, were written in an elevated style, and contained noble images, and interesting sentiments. In this sense, also, the poems referred to are as truly epic, as any hitherto written. But if an epic poem must be exactly like the Iliad, Odyssey, or Aeneid, or if it must rehearse the actions of a warrior, Paradise Lost will be excluded from the number.

The truth is, such is the reverence for Homer and Virgil, and such the submission to Aristotle's idea of this subject, that in deciding this question, we recur to Aristotle's ideas of that example, and not to the nature of the subject at large, nor to any definite principles of our own. Thus a single specimen is, by this prejudice, erected into a class, and while we make that a species, as a logician would say, which is no more than an individual of that species, in endeavouring to reduce other individuals of the species to the exact characteristic of that individual, an article necessarily impossible—we debate much with ourselves, and with others, where a little freedom of mind would at once dispel the cause of our doubts.

Indeed the general applause given to Paradise Lost, has almost forced the reluctant critics of the present age to silence, on this subject: but it has been long and warmly contested by eminent writers, and is even now scarcely reduced to a certainty.

Pastoral poetry has also suffered from this prejudice, in the highest degree. Theocritus, a Sicilian, wrote a number of pastoral poems of a particular character. Virgil copied after him, with less nature, and more art. From their examples, pastoral poetry has been defined; and to their modes of writing, succeeding pastoral writers have been limited. Hence a

[3] The *Gerusalemme Liberata*, Italian epic by Torquato Tasso (1544–1595).

poem, however abounding in rural images and ideas, and however unadorned in its style, is denied the name, because it is not copied from
Virgil, or Theocritus, as if all the scenes of rural life were not pastoral
subjects, and all the pleasing modes of exhibiting them to the mind in
verse, did not belong to this species of poetry.

The misfortunes of this mode of judging are great. Writers are fettered
by it within such limits, as to prevent every genuine adventure of genius,
and degraded to the humble character of copyers; and readers are precluded from that diversity of pleasure rationally to be expected from the
perpetually variegated rovings of imagination. Poems, by the manner of
forming them, are necessitated to be stale and trite, and innumerable
beauties of nature are locked up from the enjoyment of mankind. From
this prejudice arose most of that sterility and tastelessness, complained of
in the pastorals of Pope, pardonable in a youth of sixteen, but foolishly
defended by the author when grown to manhood, and more foolishly
praised by doctor Warburton.[4]

In our own happy state of society, disjointed from the customs and
systems of Europe, commencing a new system of science and politics, it
is to be ardently hoped, that so much independence of mind will be
assumed by us, as to induce us to shake off these rusty shackles, examine
things on the plan of nature and evidence, and laugh at the grey-bearded
decisions of doting authority. There is ever a propensity in the mind, when
forming a class, species, or genus, to form it from the knowledge of a few
individuals. Hence it is of necessity imperfectly formed, and all conclusions based upon it, must be erroneous. This is the great imperfection
of theories and systems, and the chief cause of their failure in a practical
application; classes ought never to be erected but from the knowledge of
many individuals belonging to them, and to be accurately just from the
knowledge of all. Perhaps even with this knowledge, they would be constituted with difficulty in the poetical world. Most poems are of such a
nature as to blend and harmonize, in several characteristics, with the kinds
bordering on them; and can be no more exactly limited or separated than
the hues of the rainbow.

For these reasons every definition intended to be just on this subject,
ought to be general and liberal; nature ought to be consulted in preference
to Aristotle; and other approved writers, as well as Homer and Virgil, Sophocles and Theocritus. On this plan, the wings of genius would be no
longer clipped, and its flight, taking the natural direction, and using the
natural strength of opinion, would be free and elevated; on this plan, the
writer who produced pleasing selections of images and sentiments from
the widely extended and endlessly diversified paradise of nature, would
be assured of regaling the taste of his readers; and on this plan, Goldsmith's
Deserted Village would hold the first rank in pastoral poetry, and Paradise
Lost be clearly seen to be superior to every other epic production.

[4] William Warburton (1698-1779), English critic, editor of Shakespeare, and
Bishop of Gloucester.

JOSEPH DENNIE

[ON THE GOTHIC IN LITERATURE] [1]
(1803)

WITH THE punctuality of a merchant, I shall now perform the promise made in my last speculation. I then took occasion to review and to reprove the fantastic romances of the eighteenth century. To shew some of their operations upon nervous, timid, and indeed, upon all exquisitely organized systems, shall be the business of this sermon. In my digressive manner, a few topics, slightly connected with the main design, will be started; and may possibly add to the amusement of the reader, though they will hardly improve his logic.

If, as the farmers say, 'my memory serves me,' Dr. Beattie [2] has somewhere cautioned youthful readers of sensibility to beware of immoderately indulging in the perusal of such works as the Night Thoughts of Young. This judicious Scotchman assigns an excellent reason for his rule. For he adds that books, which present sometimes false, and always gloomy views of life, and which wear out the mind by a constant succession of horrors, must ultimately prove pernicious. For terrific and mournful images are, from their very nature, striking; and, to men of strong fancy, easily adherent. Hence, in times of grief and sickness, and even amid the common calamities and cares of life, such images will rise, and, in a 'long, unbroken, funeral train,' will continually pass before our distracted eyes. One of the most useful and necessary of our virtues is Fortitude; a companion, in the season of distress, absolutely necessary to enable the fretful impatience of our nature to tolerate its woes. But when, from our habits of reading and thinking, spectres, demons, Melancholy, Sorrow, black cares, and 'sights unholy,' are present with us, Fortitude flies away. We mistake the phantoms of Imagination for the ills of life. The poison of Romance tips every arrow from the quiver of Fate; and we fall victims, not so much to the fever in our veins, or to the poverty of our coffers, as to the despondency of our thoughts, and to the 'giant of Despair.'

In the works of Mrs. Radcliff, [3] and of all her imitators, mournfull or horrible description predominates. The authors go out of the walks of Nature, to find some dreadful incident. Appalling noises must be created. Ghosts must be manufactured by dozens. A door is good for nothing, in the opinion of a romance writer, unless it creak. The value of a room is

---

[1] From the Port Folio, III (1803), 226.

[2] James Beattie (1735–1803), Scottish poet and philosopher of the "common-sense" school, whose most influential work was the Essay on the Nature and Immutability of Truth (1770).

[3] Mrs. Ann Radcliffe (1764–1823), English author, writer of Gothic novels. Her most famous work is The Mysteries of Udolpho (1794).

much enhanced by a few dismal groans. A chest full of human bones is twice as valuable as a casket of diamonds. Every grove must have its quiet disturbed, by the devil, in some shape or other. Not a bit of tapestry but must conceal a corpse; not an oak can grow, without sheltering banditti. Now, in real life, examined in any age, or in any country, we cannot find such a series, such a combination of horrible events, as the romance writers display in almost every page. All their knights are 'knights of the Doleful Countenance.' Fortunately for mortals, though there is much misfortune, and much evil here, yet every object is not covered with a pall. There are objects less sable to our eyes than the coffin. It is a misrepresentation to state that the whole world resembles Bunyan's valley of the shadow of death.[4] It is mischievous to exhibit such a false picture. It enfeebles the mind. It induces a habit of melancholy; it strengthens frantic fear, a passion remarkable, according to Collins,[5] for beholding 'appalled the unreal scene.' Instead of thus wantonly weakening the mind, by directing its attention to ghastly illusions, to 'horrible shadows, and unreal mockery,' we should adopt the discipline of the Poet,

> That superstition mayn't create
> And club its ills with those of fate,
> I many a notion take to task,
> Made by dreadful its vizor mask,
> Since optic Reason shews me plain,
> I dreaded spectres of the brain.

If I had a friend of exquisite sensibility, whose irritable nerves vibrated like the chords of music, I would lock up Mrs. Radcliff's novels from his morbid curiosity. I would not suffer him to turn pale at the thoughts of any of her ghosts. He should 'laugh and shake in Rabelais' easy chair.' He should not walk in any of her galleries, nor abide in any of her courts. I would address him then in words of the sensible Green.[6]

> Love not so much the doleful knell,
> And news the boding night birds tell;
> Nor in imprest remembrance keep
> Grim tap'stry figures wrought in sleep;
> Nor rise to see, in antique hall,
> The moonlight monsters on the wall;
> And shadowy spectres darkly pass,
> Trailing their sables o'er the grass.

A hypochondriac would be as much injured by the perusal of the woeful romance, as by a denial of air and exercise. He would fancy, like Don Quixote, that his sick chamber was a castle. He would mistake his nurse for a witch; and call his apothecary 'Montoni.' He would convert his phials into 'vials of wrath' and poison, and insist that his pill box was made of 'gloomy pine or black larch wood.'

[4] The reference is to John Bunyan's (1628–1688) The Pilgrim's Progress (Part I, 1678; Part II, 1684).
[5] William Collins (1721–1759), English poet.
[6] Joseph Green (1706–1780), American poet and satirist.

JOSEPH DENNIE

From FRENEAU'S POEMS [1]
(1807)

THERE IS nothing with which the inhabitants of the United States have been so much reproached, as the little encouragement given by them to the Belles Lettres. No traveller, or Journalist, can mention us without making this charge; and even they who kindly endeavour to apologize for our defects, for the most part find our excuse in a poverty of genius, or negation of intellect with which nature has cursed our unhappy land; and for which, they think, as her operations were beyond our control, we should rather be excused than condemned.

If foreigners, however, would take the trouble to view the scenes which we present to their observation, they could not avoid seeing, at a glance, why the works of fancy or imagination are less attended to than the crudest political theories, or the dryest details of mercantile calculation.

In this country, though, perhaps, a moderate competency is more general than in any other part of the world, large fortunes are rare, and the youth released from college, immediately applies himself to some business or profession, to which he finds it necessary to devote an assiduous attention in order to obtain a proper rank in society; and thus a period of life is passed in close application to business, in which, otherwise, a taste for polite literature would have been either formed or fixed; and the lustre of that eye is extinguished, which else, perhaps, had rolled "in a fine frenzy" of poetick inspiration. Youthful leisure, which *alat formetque poetam*,[2] is almost unknown to us. How many of the English poets have felt—I might, indeed, ask, how few have not felt the *res augusta domi?*[3] And when the poverty of their bards is so common as even to be proverbial, in a nation, the birthright of whose numerous nobility and gentry it should be to foster the Muses; shall we be reproached if, as fortune here is within the reach of every man of talents, he forsake the barren steeps of Parnassus for the rich lowlands of domestick comfort and independence? In popular governments, eloquence has justly been called the road to wealth and power, and our foes themselves will not deny that in the United States it is a well beaten one, and that some of our oratours might safely challenge a comparison with the most exalted names which Europe could oppose to them. The literature encouraged by us is solid and useful, and although it may not have the fragrance of the flower-garden, it assuredly has the fruitfulness of the harvest field.

[1] From the *Port Folio*, IV, Series 2 (1807), 251–53, 258–59, 313–15, 349–52.
[2] "nourishes and forms poets."
[3] "the august things of the home."

Among the few in this country who have wandered from "the main road of business" to stray in the paths of poesy, is Philip Freneau, who, as I have been informed, was born in New-Jersey, educated at Princeton College, and, with a singular versatility of character, has been alternately a commander of a ship, and an editor of a newspaper. A volume of this gentleman's poems, "printed at the press of the authour," is now before me, and as I think it much deserving of attention, I shall devote some pages to an examination of it. . . .

Freneau very seldom attuned his lyre to love, and in his works we find none of those "fabled tortures, quaint and tame," so common in the writings of the amatory poets. The following stanzas conclude an address, in a seaman's phrase, to a "scornful lady;" and although the threat of Time punishing the fair one for her cruelty is very common, yet the introduction of this personage in the last line is certainly very uncommon:

> Ah, Celia, what a strange mistake,
> To ruin thus for ruin's sake;
> Thus to delude us, in distress,
> And quit the prize you should possess.
>
> Years may advance with silent pace,
> And rob that form of ev'ry grace;
> And all your conquest be repaid
> By—Teague O'Murphy, and his spade.

In many passages he evinces a capacity for the pathetick; but in general passes rapidly to other sensations. The following lines are not unlike some written by Cowper on seeing a favourite grove of trees cut down:

> Inspir'd at the sound, while the *name* she repeats,
> Wild fancy conveys me to Hudson's retreats—
>
> At sweet recollection of juvenile dreams,
> In the groves and the forests that skirted his streams!
>
> How often with rapture those streams were survey'd,
> When, sick of city, I flew to the shade!
>
> How often the bard and the peasant shall mourn
> Ere those groves shall revive, and those shades shall
> return!

And again, with a happy allusion to one of the emblems of Time:

> But days such as these were too happy to last;
> The *sand of felicity settled too fast!*

The lines to his dog are an affectionate recollection of that faithful animal, and all who read them will remember the days of their boyhood.

How oft in the year shall I visit your grave,
Amid the lone forest that shadows the wave!
How often lament, when the day's at its close,
That a mile from my cot is your place of repose!

Ah here (I will say) in this path he has run;
And there stands a tree where a squirrel he won;
And here, in this spot where the willow trees grow,
He dragg'd out a rabbit that lurk'd in the snow.

Speaking of the battle of Eutaw springs, his language is both pathetick and forcible, and the epitaph on those who were slain in the action, is, at once, beautifully simple and comprehensive:

Ah! had our friends that led the fray
Surviv'd the ruins of that day,
We should not mix our joy with pain,
Nor, sympathizing, now complain.

Strange! that of those who nobly dare
Death always claims so large a share!
That those of virtues most refin'd,
Are soonest to the grave consign'd!

But fame is theirs—and future days
On pillar'd brass shall tell their praise;
Shall tell—when cold neglect is dead—
"*These* for their country fought and bled."

Freneau has given several translations and imitations from the Latin and French. The conclusion of the sixteenth ode of the second book of Horace,

On me a poor and small domain,
With something of a poet's vein,
Kind fate bestow'd—*and share of pride*
To spurn a scoundrel from my side.

is extremely indignant, and expresses the very sensations of the Prince of lyrick poets:

————Mihi parva rura, et
Spiritum Graiae tenuem camenae
Parca non mendax dedit, et malignum
    Spernere vulgus.

The address to a Jug of Rum is very much in the manner of Swift, who with all his power of condensing his expression, could not afford us a better example of the *multum in parvo* than the following:

Here only by a cork control'd,
And slender walls of earthen mould,
In all the pomp of death repose
The seeds of many a bloody nose;
The chattering tongue, the horrid oath,
The fist for fighting nothing loth,
The passion which no words can tame,
That bursts, like sulphur, into flame;
The nose carbuncled, glowing red,
The bloated eye, the broken head;
The tree that bears the deadly fruit
Of murder, maiming, and dispute;
Assault that Innocence assails,
The images of gloomy jails,
The giddy thought, on mischief bent,
The midnight hour in riot spent:
All these within this jug appear,
And Jack, the hangman, in the rear!

Falconer, Captain Thompson,[4] and Freneau have shown that the Muses may be induced to accommodate themselves to the boisterous habits of a sailor's life, and sing as melodiously on board a ship, as on Parnassus. Aeschylus was, at the same time, a poet and a sailor. Homer, Virgil, Appolonius Rhodius,[5] and others, with the maritime adventures of their respective heroes, describe the vessels on board of which they were embarked: these, however, with little rigging, and of simple structure required no great art to introduce, with a description of all their parts, into poetry, in comparison with the complex machinery of modern navigation. When, a soldier was at once, by a mandate of his officer, transformed into a sailor, and a general, upon stepping on board a galley, became an admiral: now, years are necessary to acquire a requisite knowledge of the science of directing a ship, as well as of the language spoken on board it, which is perfectly unintelligible to a landsman; and which some of our best writers have in vain endeavoured to use. Shakspeare's "Lay her a-hold!" and Dryden's "Veer starboard sea and land," would be understood neither at sea nor on shore. Falconer first wrote a nautical poem in nautical language, and his work may justly be termed classical in a new department of poetry.

Sannazarius,[6] stepping out of the beaten path of pastoral, wrote his Piscatory Idylls; but this required little invention, and although they talked of mullets, tunnies, oysters, &c. the language and sentiments of his fishermen, and the language and sentiments of the shepherds of the pastoral bards, who have all servilely imitated each other in committing so great an outrage on nature, as to cause rivers to weep and rocks to groan whenever some country wench was supposed to be in an ill humour. . . .

[4] William Falconer (1732-1769), British poet and sailor, author of *The Shipwreck* (1762). Just who Captain Thompson was is not clear.
[5] Appolonius Rhodius (*ca.* 260 B.C.), Greek scholar and epic poet.
[6] Iacopo Sannazzaro (*ca.* 1456-1530), Italian poet, author of the *Arcadia* (1504).

Too many criticks judge of the excellence of a poet by the length of his pieces. Freneau, measured by this scale, would not rank high; for he never detains his reader long on one subject. He, in too many places, shows a disrespect for the pulpit, which deserves to be highly censured; but although we touch, with much reverence, in whatever is connected with that guardian of our happiness both here and hereafter, we cannot avoid smiling at the odd association in the stanzas on the crew of a certain vessel several of whom happened to be of the same name with celebrated clergymen.

> In life's unsettled, odd career
> What changes every day appear
>   To please, or plague the eye;
> A goodly brotherhood of priests
> Are here transformed to swearing beasts
>   That heaven and hell defy.
>
> Here Bonner, bruised with many a knock,
> Has chang'd his surplice for a frock;
>   Old Erskine swabs the decks:
> And Watts, that once such pleasure took
> In writing hymns, here turn'd a cook,
>   No more shall sinners vex.
>
> Here Burnet, Tillotson, and Blair,
> With Jemmy Hervey, curse and swear;
>   Here Cudworth mixes grog;
> Pearson the crew to dinner hails,
> A graceless Serlock trims the sails,
>   And Bunyan heaves the log.

Our authour has, in a very desultory manner, rambled from subject to subject, but satire appears to be his favourite one. Here, however, we cannot, in general, praise him. He is far from being elegant in the choice of his language, which is, for the most part, downright railing: and this we do not think sufficiently justified by the examples of the ancient satyrists, the vulgarity of whose expressions affords no favourable ideas of their own manners. His subjects also, which are local, have lost much of their interest; and we are unwilling to recall the recollection of feuds long past. In the phrase of the aborigines, the tomahawk is buried, and we wish not to dig it up. It is the more to be regretted, that Freneau wasted so much of his time in this manner, as he has convinced us that he is capable of better things. . . .

Having thus rambled through Freneau's Poems, with a spirit of no illiberal criticism, it may not be amiss to mention our regret at the authour, in several places giving us cause to censure him for principles, which in this country, are rarely in union with genius. Providence, while she permits the pest of Jacobinism [7] to range at large among us, has kindly

[7] Extreme radical movement in politics deriving its name from the society of French revolutionists organized in 1789 and who were associated with the Reign of Terror.

shown her in her foulest colours; she displays no elegance of form, no fascination of manners, no persuasion of eloquence, but rude and deformed, is equally disgusting to the spirit of philosophy and to the eye of taste.

We have mentioned some causes of the little encouragement given to our bards; but we confidently look forward to a time not distant, when we may say, in the words of Cicero: *Rudem enim esse omnino in nostris poetis, aut inertissimae signitiae est, aut fastidii delicatissimi. Mihi quidem nulli satis eruditi videntur, quibus nostra ignota sunt.*[8]

[8] "For, in the case of our own poets, to be altogether crude, is either a matter of extreme laziness, or one of a very delicate fastidiousness. To me, indeed, none of them seem to be sufficiently learned; to them all our things are unknowns."

Critical Essays of the Transition to Romanticism

JOHN KNAPP

NATIONAL POETRY [1]
(1818)

THERE HAS lately arisen a spirit of inquiry concerning the events that took place, and the characters that flourished in our country, from the beginning of its settlement by Europeans, until our establishment as an independent nation. A desire has also been publicly expressed, that men of letters would employ themselves in searching and collecting works and writings, which any wise contributed to the changes in our condition, or which commemorate their various causes.

In the annals of every country, there is an era, in which the people have been pre-eminently actuated by public spirit and enterprising virtue, and the writer is to be honoured, who stays a nation's decline, by holding up to view just and attractive representations of them, through successive ages. If we would perpetuate the race of national benefactors, of those who will encounter dangers and hardships, and labour with their minds and hands, for the promotion of public prosperity and honour and harmony, we must be just to the deceased; we must acquaint ourselves with their worthy deeds and sufferings, and take delight in the recital of their praises. This would not fail to create a higher estimation of posthumous fame among all classes, and an inciting thirst for it among the more generous. A taste of this kind is compatible only with pure and disinterested pursuits; since no one can desire to be mentioned by those whose judgment is without fear or flattery,—and such are all mankind in regard to the dead,—unless his life shall have been deserving and honourable. Some persons, it is confessed, appear to have coveted a brief renown for acts of baseness and inhumanity:—But who is he, of human beings, that can listen complacently to the voice of solemn futurity proclaiming its reproaches over his sepulchre? The general decay of this ennobling anticipation of the regards of after ages is an undoubted fore-runner of national decline; but the cultivation and growth of it must ever exalt the sense of honour, and multiply the good, the industrious and the valiant.

The rank a people take among nations is not measured by its population, wealth and military power, or even by the excelling wisdom of its government, merely, but often by the number of its distinguished individuals of former ages,—and often by the superiority of its men of letters. The regrets of Sallust,[2] on account of the earlier Romans, are well known. The higher renown which they, in his opinion, had merited, was obscured by the glory of the Greeks, solely because partial fortune had granted in-

[1] Published in the *North American Review*, VII (1818).
[2] Roman historian, 86–34 B.C.

genious writers to the latter, and denied them to the former.—'Sed quia provenêre ibi magna scriptorum ingenia, per terrarum orbem Atheniensium facta pro maximis celebrantur; ita eorum qui ea fecêre, virtus tanta habetur, quantum verbis ea potuêre extollere proeclara ingenia. At populo Romano nunquam ea copia fuit, quia prudentissimus quisque negotiosus maxime erat. Ingenium nemo sine corpore exercebat. Optimus quisque facere quam dicere; sua ab aliis benefacta laudari, quam ipse aliorum narare malebat.' *³ It is superfluous to add, that this country may look for lasting distinction to its achievements and characters;—that these will have existed in vain, with regard to posterity, unless some gifted author shall record them in a language and manner suited to their sublime import.

It may be of use to consider, whether the poetical form of writing is not the most calculated to accomplish the object recommended. Is it not the best means to acquaint the greater portion of our population with the most memorable acts, to make them familiar in their mouths, and the associates of their favourite thoughts and fancies? Would it not, moreover, the most lastingly preserve the memory of those actions which afford noble instruction, are exemplars of men's ability to be greatly virtuous, and kindle in others an honourable ambition; and at the same time exhibit and tend to perpetuate the characteristic feelings and habits in which all these originated?

The times may be fruitful of events, and men may abound, whose deeds deserve to be kept in remembrance forever; but their country will receive only a transient glory, and after ages be ignorant or hear of them without due interest, unless the record be made vital with a poet's enthusiasm. Histories and memorials that detail them are precious to the learned, for they may know in what part of our accumulated libraries to find them. Just so may contracts and title deeds be brought to light, for whomsoever it may concern, by such as are disposed to resort to the registry. But what is it that dwells in the minds of the learned and unlearned,—giving them pleasures that are common and connecting,—and which spontaneously occurs to afford a moral association to every transaction they may be engaged in or witness,—in comparison with those deep and cherished sentiments which were first infused by the recitals of heroic verse? Whatever we have learnt under pleasing emotions is constantly recurring to our thoughts. If we have heard noble actions described in language that charmed our ears, and filled us with transport, shall we not be fonder of reflecting on them and their similitudes; and will they not tend more to give a bias to our dispositions, than if they were related only for the fact's sake, with dry precision and circumstance? None can be blind to the in-

---

* Bellum Catilinarium. [Knapp's note.]

³ "But because great skills of writers arose there, the deeds of the Athenians are celebrated throughout the world as being among the greatest. Consequently the valor of those who performed them is esteemed as being as great as those outstanding artists could extoll them by their words. But such a skill was never available to the Roman people, for every sage was thoroughly occupied with some business. No one exercised his skill except in some bodily manner. Every one of our best men preferred to do rather than to narrate; he preferred to have his exploits praised by others rather than himself to narrate those of other men."

valuable uses or the dignity of history. Yet how few among the more numerous ranks of the community derive from it any thing to influence their feelings or inform their understandings? It boots nothing what things have happened, if men have no delight in thinking of them. The events and characters, which have distinguished the eras of England are, indeed, well known to the British people, but it is Shakspeare, who has made it a pleasurable thing to be told of them.

It can hardly be doubted, that the American revolution might afford subjects to employ the poet, with success and glory, limited only by his talents. The materials it would furnish are infinite, its characters innumerable, and the scenery of its places full of beauty and grandeur. All ranks of the community took part in it; every station of life was reached by its agitations. The hopes and fears of the remote cultivator and *woodsman*, no less than the busy townsman, the concerns of lovers, their plans for connubial welfare, the prouder calculations of men of property and station, all were at the mercy of the times. Above all, the crisis was brought upon them by their resolute adherence to principles esteemed just.

It is in such periods, that the soul is transformed, and acquires energies unimagined in tamer ages. What calls into motion all our inward powers, those diviner faculties which are proof of our immortality, like the occurrences of perilous and calamitous times? What men are great like those, who have passed through scenes of general distress, and perplexity, and change, and mighty, but almost despaired of deliverance?

When such a union of interests and feelings exists, as binds together all orders and conditions of men; when the hopes and fears, joys and misfortunes, in which we fluctuate, equally toss and swell the bosoms of unnumbered fellow-beings, the sensations and capacities of every individual are mysteriously magnified. A providential interposition seems to work in us a change, so that we can endure and perform what we could not before have passed through in imagination only, without agony of spirit; and at the same time it yields us solemn pleasures of no earthly nature. The soul, perceiving a more congenial quality in outward things, comes forth into full dominion, thoughtless of its garment of flesh, as if to anticipate its disembodied state. So much superior are the enjoyments bestowed by the predominance of this immortal part of us, to those more connected with our animal nature, that the rudest of mankind, who have once been conscious of them, are not only ever fond of the recollection, but often disposed to renew the dangers and commotions, to which they had owed the transient expansion of their faculties.

But, to be thus moved, we need not pass through these dangers ourselves,—there is efficacy in language for the production of equal excitement. Personal experience is not requisite to him whose intelligence may be quickened through sympathies, which the appealing voice of poetry can touch. It is enough and more than enough for the poet, that in times long elapsed, men and elements have contended and wrought overthrow. His materials already abound,—the ravages of armies, plots of the ambitious, assemblies of men with anxious countenances and agitated hearts;—all past ages have endowed him with their ruins and their glories. Say not, that words are of the substance of air. The words of the poet are like the breath of life to him that hears them worthily. They dilate the intellectual frame, and match it to high and vast contemplations:—they call up our whole humanity, and again soothe the troubled affections into a mild, but never lifeless calm.

But, though the elements of poetry are chiefly strong passions and great interest, and consist not with feeble emotions, yet are the tender affections essential in its composition. The poem that does not abound in themes of kind humanity, in the vicissitudes of friendship and love, in scenes and images of innocent joy and pastoral simplicity;—in the soft bird-like music, as well as the trumpet notes of its verses,—cannot be the lasting favourite of any people. These gentle but impressive incidents were copiously supplied by the situation and habits of our population. Even those who were engaged in the most arduous operations, the civil and military heroes of the times, were involved in the various fortunes, and often romantic adventures of heart-formed connexions. Unlike the European military, who, on entering their armies and fleets, like the monk on entering his convent, separate themselves from all domestic interest and feelings, the American soldiery retained in the fort and field every concern and sympathy of the fireside and neighbourhood. Our females, indeed, came not out among them, girt with shining armour, like Artemisia of the Leonidas, Clorinda and Gildippe of the Jerusalem Delivered, or the Maid of Orleans. There were some, however, as private memoirs tell us, who caught the zeal of martial enterprise, and performed deeds, that might, with slight poetic aid, be managed to equal the exploits of those antique heroines. But the poet need not enlist them in his service. Females, that follow the camp in modern wars, scarcely expect the notice of the muses.—Yet our matrons and sisters were exposed to the dangers and often heard the tumult of the contest; for the march of armies was by their own doors, and the battle field not seldom on their patrimonial hills and plains. An acquaintance with such scenes was not, however, an object of their curiosity or ambition.—They also partook in the civil agitations, for the fortunes and rank in life of both the retired and forward depended also on political measures; and they could not but sympathise with their connexions and friends, who were delegated to councils of government, and returned to their families fraught with the anxieties and hopes and resolves of freemen under proscription.

These circumstances will give animation to local descriptions, of which the poetical uses are obvious. If we take any glory in our country's being beautiful and sublime and picturesque, we must approve the work which reminds us of its scenery by making it the theatre of splendid feats and heartmoving incidents. If men's minds are influenced by the scenes in which they are conversant, Americans can scarcely be denied a claim to be inspired with some peculiar moral graces, by their grand and lovely landscapes. But, moreover, it is beneficial to connect our best intellectual associations with places in our own land. In part, we love our country because our minds seem to have been furnished from its surface, and because our most natural and vivid ideas are inseparable from pictures which have it for their groundwork. The places which we have long frequented are the props of our memory:—it fails, and the mind misses its fulness of ideas, when we are absent from them. It is no idle forecasting to consider, whether, in the course of providence, it may not be necessary for this nation to avail itself of the full strength and operation of its patriotic attachments and principles.

Important uses will undoubtedly accrue from the labours of the antiquary and historical collector. They have already attested that the lives and adventures of our predecessors comprehend things interesting to the scholar and philosopher, as well as the patriot. The poet and sentimentalist would no longer lament the want of human incident, if informed by them of the numberless trials and achievements which have marked every league of our unmeasured country. There is no necessity, in our travels through it, to recollect the stories and romances and heroic exploits, which have signalized transatlantic regions of similar localities and features. We need but inquire, and we shall seldom fail, wherever the place, to hear some story that will either touch the heart or lift it with strong emotion.

But it may be questioned, whether the modern origin of the transactions and personages designed for celebration, would not defeat the plans of the poet. The antiquity of our compatriots does not extend to two hundred years; and men are now alive, who may have conversed with the children of those who first arrived on our shore. This circumstance, it is apprehended, would cut off the poet from what has ever been esteemed his peculiar province. It denies him space to employ any of those magnificent beings, the kin of gods, which glorify the times anterior to the date of annals. As it requires a misty atmosphere to elevate into view the distant island and promontories, which are ordinarily intercepted by the curve of the globe, so is the obscurity of remote time deemed necessary to exhibit the fields of romance and poetry, and their wonder-working inhabitants. It is conceded that history may appeal to our admiration, and secure a passionate interest, although the matters it relates should be of recent occurrence. Herodotus [4] recounted the wars of the Greeks with the Persians in the famed Olympic Assembly, where not a few attended who had been engaged in them, and great numbers who had learnt the principal facts from heroes whose funeral rites they had just performed. He did not, however, refrain from inserting many fables and marvellous traditions, which had doubtless obtained belief in that age. Most of these appear to have been related with the view to expose their untruths or absurdity, and so correct the credulity of the people by the remarks and arguments he subjoined. But they nevertheless had the effect of heightening the interest and ornament of the story. A work under the denomination of history, abounding with similar embellishment, would scarcely be approved at the present day. Yet, for the purposes of moral instruction, as well as enter-

[4] Greek historian, 484?–425? B.C.

tainment, things real may, without offence, be modified and take their form from the hand of an author not strictly historical; and it is best to leave this to the poet. Characters and events drawn wholly from the imagination, may charm for a moment; but nothing will permanently interest, that is wholly without the sphere of human duties and experience. Traditions and fables are however necessary to poetry. Men delight in listening to them, no less than to recorded truth. In all countries, men have fancied that their first progenitors were empowered to hear the voice of gods and enjoy the personal society of immortals. Therefore, though obscure and susceptible of contradictory meanings, traditions do not cease to be reverenced; for they seem to have proceeded from that favoured ancestry, and to owe to sacrilegious time the loss of what would make them consistent and plain. The poet may interpret them, and illustrate and enlarge their influence upon national character.

A country is undeniably the more endeared by the multitude of its tender and heroical tales and memoirs, fabulous as well as authentic. Let us then not slight even its barbarian annals. Let us not only revisit the dwellings of the European settler exposed to savage incursions, and every variety of affecting vicissitude; but let us hasten to acquaint ourselves with the earlier native. Let us hasten;—for already has the cultivator levelled many a monumental mound, that spoke of more than writings might preserve. Already are the lands cleared of their heaven-planted forests, once hallowed by the visits of the Wakon bird, before she ascended into other regions, indignant at the approach of a race, who knew not the worship of nature. Already are the hills surmounted, and the rocks violated by the iron hammer, which the Indian regarded with distant awe, as the barriers of his 'humble heaven.'—And why should not these vast and magnificent regions have been the haunts of majestic spirits, such as imbodied themselves with mist, and shaped them from the clouds, so as to be seen of heroes and bards of other days? Our tall, dense forests are fitter for the mysterious abodes of the shadowy powers, and our hills lead farther into the sky;—our mountains present a firmer pathway through the clouds, for the descent of the rushing hosts that deign a concern for the affairs of mortals. In every place, wherever we rest or walk, we may feel, in fancy, the animating spirit, declared by ancient philosophers and poets to pervade the stupendous frame of nature;—we may feel its life-breathing motions, perceive its immortal complacency in the gleamings which break from out the hill-side and the plain; and listen to its supernatural promptings.

RICHARD HENRY DANA

From HAZLITT'S ENGLISH POETS [1]
(1819)

THE STUDY of the works of the older English poets, along with what we can learn of their character and that of mankind in their day—the history of the religion, laws, superstitions and customs, under which they were born,—the unperceived but ever working influences of these on their passions and cast of thought,—the vastness and variety which were given to their imaginations by the strange mixture of ignorance, wild conjecture and bold adventure,—the moral effect of the open simplicity, the close and keen cunning, of the tenderness and hard brutality, of the exquisite delicacy, and what we, sometimes falsely, and again truly, call the vulgarity of those days,—surely are subjects deserving our attention, and require an intellect of more power and variety to comprehend, than those are well aware of, who hold poetry to be a matter of mere amusement, and all that is connected with it, a very light thing. The man who would do this well, must have a wide taste; and be trammeled by no narrow systems or schools. He must have a sure taste for the minutest beauties, nor pass them over because they may be surrounded by deformities. He should have an imagination which can group and fill out, and give the lights and shades to the scanty materials left us, with the distinctness of a picture. He must love old books even as Southey does, who says he should be miserable without them—that they are to him, what old pictures are to a painter. He must do more,—he must love a long story, and not count it labour lost, so it end well, though it has carried him, "from hence to Eartham." He must have a relish for the quaint and grotesque, without becoming quaint or grotesque himself. He must not mistake simplicity for weakness, nor frankness for coarseness. He must understand and love nature with all his heart, through all her varieties. Not only with her beauties, but even with the harsh and uncouth he must have poetical associations which shall give them a hold upon his imagination. He must have an ear like Cowper's to which the noise of a goose in a barn yard was pleasant, though he confesses he should not care to have the bird hung up in a cage in his parlour. But in all this, let him beware of affectation. Hypocrisy in the love of nature is as fatal as in religion. There are some who read old authors and affect to despise the new. They are satisfied with nothing since the days of Milton, and would not have been satisfied with him had they lived then. They want the sanction of posterity for their admiration, and affect to speak lightly of living men whose praises will be upon the tongues of

[1] The *North American Review*, VII (1819).

those who come after them. Of this number may be considered the writer before us, of whom it is quite time that we said something.

This work is divided into eight lectures.—The introductory one is on poetry in general; the three following on six only of the older poets ending with Pope, and bringing us to the middle of the volume; and the remaining four, first taking up Thompson and Cowper, close with criticisms on the living poets. Though Mr. Hazlitt has not gone into the subject with that fulness with which we have just intimated that it should be considered, nor followed down the poetry of his country through its changes, as perhaps connected with and brought about by the alterations in society, nor wrought into his work old anecdote, which could be put to uses as instructive as entertaining,—we would still make no objection to his book had he carried out his own plan. But from aught we can learn from Mr. Hazlitt, Chaucer and Spenser, Shakspeare and Milton, Dryden and Pope, were about all the poets that lived from the days of the heptarchy to the end of Queen Anne. We should not care to have a lecture devoted to Pierce Plouman, but we did expect to meet with the names, and something more than the names, of Ben Jonson, Beaumont and Fletcher, Otway and Allan Ramsay,[5] (the Gentle Shepherd) who certainly are not so out of date that one need fear being thought pedantic should he venture to talk upon them. If Mr. Hazlitt knows any thing about them, or has the good taste to relish their beauties, he might have found much in Surrey, Wyatt, Drayton, Browne, P. Fletcher, Daniel, Donne and others, whom we need not name, as they are easily turned to, which he could have pointed out to his readers as well worth their looking into. The inferior order among the old poets differ from the moderns of the same class in having amidst all their lameness and dulness, beauties choice enough to repay us for the toil of our search. As to his omissions among the modern poets, we have little to censure, with the exception of Beattie,[6] and let us add Hogg,[7] with all his inequalities. Had he stopt short of the living poets, he would have left us with more favourable impressions of his taste, and what is of more worth, of his good feelings. But of this, by and by.

[POPE]

It is not because Pope has chosen to write so much upon manners and fashions,—upon what is called the artificial, that many nowadays deny that he is strictly a poet. No matter what the subject, a poetical mind will work its character into it. Shakspeare is a poet every where and in all companies. Whether he argues or moralizes, is witty or sentimental, there is a poetical atmosphere over him, and all that belongs to him takes a tone from it. The same thing may be said (we speak generally) of Cowper, Burns, and Crabbe. Pope never touches the heart, and never fires the passions, nor

[5] Thomas Otway (1652–1685) was an English Restoration dramatist. Allan Ramsay (1686–1758) was a Scottish editor of ballads, song writer, and dramatist. His most popular success was the pastoral drama *The Gentle Shepherd* (1725).
[6] James Beattie (1735–1803), Scottish poet.
[7] Thomas Hogg (1792–1862), English poet and friend of Shelley.

bursts with a glory over our heads. He is witty and sensible, and often moralizes well, but these do not constitute poetry, though they may all in their turn serve as materials for it to work upon. He is very gay upon fashionable follies, and exceeding dexterous in setting out a toilet; but he associates these with no poetical images or impressions, and never sends the mind abroad by suggestions to any thing in nature. Even in art, one thing is not, as it were, hinted by another, but is put down directly before us, by a kind of visible, manual accumulation, or set immediately opposite to something else by a laboriously ingenious antithesis. He is always sprightly, however, and it is quite enlivening to see him so briskly at work. The things are well arranged, and there is quite a gay show of ladies and beaux, powdered heads and craped cushions, fans and ruffles, cards and tea-cups, all sorts of essences, washes and perfumery, too, till the senses nigh ache at it. Now though this is very well so far as it goes, we cannot allow that it does more than touch upon the borders of poetry. Nor do we think it easy to see in it much of good taste; we mean a taste that would discriminate nicely in better things.

As Pope is denied imagination, Mr. Hazlitt would give him fancy; we should rather allow him ingenuity. His Rape of the Lock is cited. A good deal of it is parody, the machinery borrowed, and the beings used in it are as old as our language, but have been described much better many times before. Drayton's Nymphidia is a good instance of the combination of the ludicrous and poetical, to explain our meaning. Take as a closer instance, the fairies in Midsummer-Night's Dream fanning the moon-beams from the eyes of honest Bottom with the wings of painted butter-flies—warring with bats—all their offices and their language, bring before you little poetical beings, of forms as delicate as the soft air they play in. They are not tied up to the leading object and kept close about it, as in Pope, but are seen playing among flowers and silver dewdrops, or just coming into sight through the moonlight, with some trophy of their skill and spirit. Yet the main purpose is never forgotten, or unnecessarily de-layed.

But the English Moralist, as he is called, has produced one poem, at least, in which Mr. Hazlitt thinks 'the tears shed are drops gushing from the heart: the words are burning sighs breathed from the soul of love.' And can Mr. Hazlitt come from reading the old poets, or those of this day, and take up the Epistle of Eloisa to Abelard, and feel his eye moisten or his heart move? We are angry with no man for his bad taste, but it is something more serious when he can come directly before the face and eyes of the Lady and Gentleman auditors of the Surrey Lectures, with an intimation of the grossest sort, and in language so warm upon a poem that no man would dare to write at this day. In this instance, as in most others, bad morals taint the taste, and Pope has contrived to produce a work as marked for false passion and false sentiment, as it is for the disgust-ing nature of the subject. It is not made up of sudden bursts of passion, breaking upon us with a fearful power, and then sinking us in grief till we "pour out our hearts like water." General reflections are continually brought in, remarkable for nothing but their being perfectly cool and wholly out of place, and apostrophes of Eloisa to herself, her hand, pen, ink, and paper, complaining, very reasonably too, that they should have any thing to do with writing such a letter. If an oyster were supposed to make an address to his shell, for shutting him up, we should be quite as much moved by his speech, we have not the least doubt. There is a perpetual toiling to bring in circumstances antithetically, and the arrangement appears just as obvious as in his once famous parallel between Homer and Virgil, which must give an impassioned cast to the poem, indeed. Here and there we find a passage which comes very nigh to passion, but is ruined by an unmeaning word, or a mighty ingenious conceit. We do not cite the following as an instance.

> "See in her cell sad Eloisa *spread*
> Propt on some tomb, a neighbour of the dead."

We will pass by the word *spread*. There is a great plenty of such indefinite language. She watches "the dying lamps around." A voice from a shrine summons her to prepare for death. She bursts out into the following rhapsody:

> "I come, I come! prepare your roseate bowers,
> Celestial palms, and every-blooming flowers."

This is certainly unequalled, except, perhaps, by the following passage in Windsor-Forest. Pope being almost overcome by his state of violent poetical excitement, cries out,

> "Ye sacred Nine! that all my soul possess,
> Whose raptures fire me, and whose visions bless,
> Bear me, oh bear me to sequestered scenes,
> The bow'ry mazes, and surrounding greens."

Now, Mr. Hazlitt, this will never do in these days. 'Tis a thousand pities that your personal dislike of certain living poets, should so warp your judgment of the dead. Mr. Hazlitt remarks,

> 'His Satires are not in general so good as his Epistles. His enmity is effeminate and petulant from a sense of weakness, as his friendship was tender from a sense of gratitude. I do not like, for instance, his character of Chartres, or his characters of women. His delicacy often borders upon sickliness; his fastidiousness makes others fastidious.' p. 152.

And again speaking of Dryden,

> 'Mac Flecknoe is the origin of the idea of the Dunciad; but it is less elaborately constructed, less feeble, and less heavy. The difference between Pope's satirical portraits and Dryden's appears to be this in a good measure, that Dryden seems to grapple with his antagonists, and to describe real persons; Pope seems to refine upon them in his own mind,

and to make them out just what he pleases, till they are not real characters, but the mere drivelling effusions of his spleen and malice. Pope describes the thing, and then goes on describing his own description till he loses himself in verbal repetitions. Dryden recurs to the object often, takes fresh sittings of nature, and gives us new strokes of character as well as of his pencil.' p. 157.

There is much truth in all this, though it is severely said. There is a want of richness,—an overflowing and heartiness in his satire, which comes of the same defect of mind that is more apparent in his other productions, because satire can do much better without these, and fortunately for Pope, be very entertaining with little or no poetry. He wants the generous abuse of Swift's, or the moral elevation of Young's and Cowper's satire. It is something little and spleeny. Yet it is dexterous, sensible, keen, and shrewd. His weapons are small, but smooth and sharp, and he is perfect master of them. It is withal very entertaining reading when one is in the humour for it.

Mr. Hazlitt remarks upon the wearisome monotony of his versification, and adds, his 'rhymes are constantly defective, being rhymes to the eye instead of the ear, and this to a greater degree, not only than in later, but than in preceding writers.' He gives from the Essay on Criticism no less than a half score of couplets rhyming to the word 'sense.' It is amusing to run them over. Pope had other favourite words, and choice ones too for poetry—such as "survey," "display," and the like. Take samples of a few.

"Here waving groves, a chequer'd scene *display*,
And part admit, and part exclude the day."

"E'en the wild heath *displays* her purple dyes,
And 'mid the desert fruitful fields *arise*."

"New graces yearly like thy works *display*,
Soft without weakness, without glaring gay."

"There at one passage, oft you might *survey*,
A lie and truth contending for the way."

"Heav'n scarce believed the conquest it *survey'd*."

"Stretch'd on the lawn his second hope *survey*
At once the chaser, and at once the prey." &c. &c.

"There *purple* Vengeance bath'd in *gore* retires,
Her weapons blunted and *extinct* her fires."

"Here all its frailties, all its flames *resign*."

"Repent old pleasures, and *solicit* new."

"Unequal task, a passion to *resign*."

"Come with one *glance* of those deluding eyes,
Blot out each bright idea of the skies."

This last is another specimen of the rapturous. The truth is, Pope had no more idea of a poetical language than a Frenchman. His words are never pictures, nor are there ever any poetical attachments or associations connected with them. They move you no more than the sing-song music of his metre. His words are cold abstractions, and there is often a loose, unphilosophical use of them which ought not to be tolerated in prose.

If poetry has a character of its own, and does not mean every thing or nothing to suit Mr. Hazlitt's humour, the way to put at rest Pope's claim to the rank of a poet is to place his best passages by the side of the good ones of the old or living poets. It is quite surprising to see how instantly he is tamed down by it. Take, too, his translation of the Iliad, and compare the best parts with what has been called the bald and naked version of Cowper,—the famous description of night—the meeting of Hector and Andromache,—the description of Polypheme, or indeed any of the better passages of the original, and it will be perfectly clear, how wanting Pope was in the eye or language of a poet.

[SWIFT]

Swift's satire differs from that of Pope, not only in appearing to throw itself off from a full mind without effort, but in its manly character. He seems honestly conscious of his own merits and powers, but does not write like one fretted at their poor rewards. It would rather seem to be the world's heartlessness,—mean selfishness,—its great sin,—and littleness, cheating it into respect, through much bustling and many words, which acting on a mind of large views, hating hypocrisy and longing for the workings of strong passions, had hurt it where it was most sensible, and forced it to find a relief in making a mockery of all it had secretly held most dear. For the disappointments of those feelings which lie deepest, and out of which spring up the wildest beauties of the imagination, will either break down a sensitive mind or turn all that is best in it into bitterness or scorn. It becomes angry with itself for its shortsightedness and folly, and finds its revenge in sneering at the world's weakness and feeling it to be greater than its own. This is not christianity, but, we fear, it is humanity. It becomes evil almost to rankness, yet it may have had its root among some of our highest virtues.

Though it may sometimes be the self-satisfaction of correctness, which censures weakness, still it is not well to confound the one with the other by seeking excuses for errour. Yet in reading of the sufferings and melancholy deaths of the two females who loved Swift with such depth of passion, there presses upon the mind a disposition to find something to extenuate his conduct, and instead of cursing him, we are moved to pity him. He held the world so lightly, that he scorned letting it see what was good in him. He thought it without feeling, was mortified that he should himself feel while in it, and made jest at his own heart and the hearts of others. When in the midst of this coldness and abstraction, he at last met with a being that loved him, it was like coming out of death into life, and that vague but intense desire—which knows not its own purpose—to make sure to ourselves how strong a hold we have in the heart of another, took full possession of him. He went on, little thinking in the outset to what it was leading him, torturing not from cruelty, but because in seeing the sufferings and workings of another, he felt with more and more certainty with what a passion he was loved. Then again the recollection of his estrangement from the world would make him ashamed of what he thought a weakness;—he would throw it from him,—and those who were fitted to open his heart and make him a better man, sunk away under the sufferings that he inflicted on them, and left him alone, dissatisfied with himself and impatient of the world, till the sense of all things was lost to him, and his mind went out in dreary vacuity. It is not for us to judge hardly of a mind that so perishes. What would have been another man's vice, was, perhaps, his disease.

We have been led unwarily from our purpose, and feel little disposition to return to it now. We will make one short remark, however, and that is, that Swift's satire differs from Pope's, and is superior to it, in bringing his scenery and images poetically before you, and in now and then having a picturesque appearance. Some may say that the Dunciad has the same character. It is quite a different thing, and in those parts which probably would be cited, is little else than travesty. We must close here with Swift. We are sorry for it.

[GRAY]

We can hardly believe that Gray's Pindaric Odes are generally given up at present, and we think with him and Beattie, and against the opinion of Mr. Hazlitt, that the Elegy is not his greatest production. We had much rather have written the Bard.[8] It required another and a much higher order of mind. It is a poem of vast and awful conception, and is sustained with terrible energy. There is nothing of conceit in the startling abruptness of the opening, but it is in perfect agreement with the state of superstitious dread, which was the only kind of terrour fitted to move the bold and barbarous minds of that age. The situation of the Bard, and then again of Edward and his army, opens as wild, dark and grand a scene, as ever lay before us. It is not made out by nice delineations, or a multiplying of particulars,—but one or two grand, leading circumstances, told to us in close and energetic and at the same time picturesque language, turn our light imagination into a gloomy and awful region of bare and rough mountains, wandered over by giant forms.

> "Such were the sounds that o'er the crested pride
> Of the first Edward scatter'd wild dismay,

[8] Thomas Gray (1716-1771) published his Pindaric Ode, "The Bard," in 1757.

As down the steep of Snowdon's shaggy side
He wound with toilsome march his long array.
Stout Glo'ster stood aghast in speechless trance:
To arms! cried Mortimer, and couch'd his quiv'ring lance."

It is in vain to say that any other than a mind of lofty poetical conceptions could have so imagined and expressed this. There are instances in
the Bard of the faults we just now mentioned; but all and more than we
have said, or have time to say, is due to it as a whole. To his character and
to his prose writings Mr. Hazlitt has done justice. We have still better
authority to the merits of his letters; for Cowper somewhere says, that
"they have all the wit, without any of the ill nature of Swift's." He is
almost the only man of whom it can be said, his wit alone makes the heart
better.

We should not have said thus much of Gray—and we have been able
to do no more than hint an opinion—were not his situation singularly unfortunate. Those who call themselves of the school of genuine English
poetry, say that he is not of them,—that he wants truth and closeness of
description, for the eye to dwell upon and run over its parts,—that he is too
vague,—that he does not seem to be in love with nature and the character
of his fellow men—that he studied these too little, and books too much.
There is some truth in this, but it is carried too far; and those of the present day, who are so inveterately natural, are in some little danger of put-
ing nature herself to school. They have looked at nature closely, but
rather too much in one aspect, and with a set of feelings and associations
that want variety. And when a mind, without doubt poetical, works in a
way differing from their rules, they shut it out from their number. They
are wrong in this, and we think them far from right in the sweeping
clause of excommunication against Gray, with all his faults. Perhaps, however, this treatment towards him was to be expected from such men. But,
surely, it was a matter of surprise, that those who are not of the vulgar—
who never soil their shoes in muddy lanes or in the wet grass, of a morning—who make mouths at their mother tongue, and have only "fed on
the dainties that are bred in a book,"—should turn their backs upon a man
who was as classical and fastidious as heart could wish—who "spoke scholarly and wisely," and was always in his very best apparel. We can give
no reason for it, unless it was that the true native genius of English poetry
was easily discovered through these disguises. We think it was; and for
this, we like him, and for this he should fare better with the English
school. Though Milton's learning was the occasion of some faults of manner, he had a mind strong enough to bear up under it, and put it all to
use. Gray would have been a better poet had he been less of a scholar.

[WORDSWORTH]

Mr. Wordsworth, with a mind perfectly original, with an imagination
full of forms of beauty and grandeur, and with powers of description un-

surpassed by any poet of this age, has such an air of plain truth in telling his stories and giving the characters of those he is speaking of,—puts into the mouths of his personages sentiments so very simple, though elevated, and makes his scenery so like that which we see every where, that we lose the impression while reading him, that we are taken out of the world and reality into the regions of imagination and poetry,—we are wholly absorbed in what we are about in this new state of things, and deluded into all the earnestness with which the concerns of life affect us. When we read other men, we look at the scenery they are describing, with the sense upon us that it is seen by us through the imagination; but in Wordsworth this is lost, and every thing he shows us appears to the eye with the same distinctness and immediate reality, as if the object itself was directly before us.

It may at first seem strange that the poetical interest should be so deep, where there is so slight a departure from plain experience. It is the change wrought in ourselves that gives it. It is we and the pleasures, the business and desires of life that have been a delusion; we are made to feel a serious concern in what we find in him, and reality itself becomes idle and unimportant. He brings right thoughts and pure wishes into our minds and hearts, clears our dim imaginations, and the poetry of our being becomes its truth. He has formed another creation, but it is one within ourselves— the mountains and valleys, the rivers and plains are the same, and so are the trees and the smaller plants, they are no greener, nor are the clouds passing over them any brighter than before. To our eyes they are the same as when we saw them yesterday; but a new sense is in our hearts, new and delightful relations have grown out from them, running over the earth and twisting themselves about every little thing upon it that has life, and connecting its being with our own. A moral sense is given to all things; and the materials of the earth which seemed made only for homely uses, become the teachers of our minds and ministers of good to our hearts. Here the love of beauty is made religion, and what we had falsely esteemed the indulgence of idle imaginations, is found to have higher and more serious purposes, than the staid affairs of life. The world of nature is full of magnificence and beauty; every thing in it is made to more than a single end. The fruit that nourishes us is fair to the eye, that we may find in it a second and better delight. Lasting and purifying pleasures are awakened within us and happy thoughts and images brought into being. In the luxury of this higher existence, we find a moral strength, and from the riot of imagination comes our holiest calm. It is true that other poets have given this double existence to creation, bestowing a moral and intellectual being upon the material world, but they have done it by hasty suggestions and rapid and short hints, with other purposes in view. Mr. Wordsworth carries us through all its windings,—he touches the strings of our hearts, and the vibration makes us feel that they rest upon and connect themselves with every thing in nature.

If poetry of this kind has peculiar beauties, Mr. Wordsworth must remember that it is but a small class of society that can see or feel them.

He must not be impatient if the larger portion give the name of mysticism to what they were not born to understand. In truth, what one poet sees to be the choicest parts in another, are not what the world at large ever think of turning to. That which is more obvious, and no doubt very good, is what pleases them, and they are gratified with the thought that they have a sense of the whole. Shakspeare is more read than any work except the bible, yet how many understand a tithe of Shakspeare?

No poet since Milton seems so thoroughly imbued with old English and the truly poetical language, as Mr. Wordsworth. There is no affectation in the use of these, or ill sorting of old and modern phrases, but every word comes from him naturally. His versification, though sometimes tame, is for the most part filled with varied harmony. His main fault in his "Excursion" is too much rambling and lengthening out, places, of the sentiments and conversation. A little more compactness in such parts would give them life and energy. This appears to be an accidental, and by no means a frequent fault. Mr. Coleridge's criticism, in his "Life and Opinions," upon Mr. Wordsworth, has more good taste and philosophy in it, than any that has been written upon Mr. Wordsworth, or any other man in modern times. We must except from this, however, his objections to the Pedler. We think that characters enough like him for the purposes of poetry, must have been common in Scotland,—he is in agreement with the scenery, and certainly has an imaginative interest, which it would have been difficult to have given to an accomplished gentleman—a trio of them would have been rather too much.

JOHN NEAL

From RANDOLPH [1]

(1823)

AMERICAN NOVELISTS

OUR NOVELISTS—You have frequently spoken of them, with emphasis. We have no such thing with us.—I know not why it is; but the trade of novel writing has been of late, as if by common consent, relinquished by men of genius and power, to women and children; and if, now and then, a tolerable affair comes out, like these late Scotch novels,[2] all the world seems to run mad after it.—It is surely not well considered, this thing. Is it Stafford? There is no class of literature, which may be made to have; nay which *has*, in reality, such an influence—upon society;—and, if a man, who had the strength and vividness, of a dramatist, and a poet, were called upon to reflect and to choose, that mode of writing, which would be most likely, if he were truly powerful, to give him the widest theatre for a display of that power, it is my deliberate opinion that he would choose a *novel;*—and yet, in whose hands do we find this body of our literature?—In the feeble of heart—and the faint of spirit—the gossiping and childish. Now and then, it is true, a Godwin will break the seals,[3] and invoke the genii to ascend; but it is with an uncertain aim; and as if he were not proud of the office. So too, there is a Maturin [4]—he might do well; but he is haunted by the spirit of Byron, and the devil himself, at the same time. Such men are out of their element—novels might be made, yet, full of distinctness; full of reality, yet carrying the marvellous in every page.

But in our country, there is every thing to discourage a novelist—nothing to incite him. The very name of having written a novel—although the wise and reflecting acknowledge, that no literature hath such an influence upon our language, and manners—none such fascination,—for, in its witchery, it surpasses the stage—and is read, secretly, by them that read nothing else—and them that are not permitted to visit the theatre—and none so wants to be purged and purified—yet the very name of a novel writer would be a perpetual reproach to a man of genius.—Would that some one would arise! and laugh to scorn, the presumption and folly, of this doctrine—and trample it under his feet! What is to prevent him, even in

[1] [New York] 1823.
[2] The novels of Sir Walter Scott (1771–1832).
[3] William Godwin (1756–1836), English political theorist and writer who published his popular and influential novel *Caleb Williams* in 1794.
[4] Charles Robert Maturin (1782–1824), Irish novelist and dramatist who published *Melmoth* in 1820.

America? We have no old castles—no banditti—no shadow of a thousand years to penetrate—but what of that. We have men and women—creatures that God himself hath fashioned and filled with character. And what more do we want? By heaven, Stafford, if I had the power, I would, myself, set about the work, before I slept:—I would take up the tale, with the events of this very day—and I would dare to say, to them that, questioned me.—Lo! here is a proof, that we want no traditions—no antiquity —nothing but tolerable power, to tell you a tale that shall thrill to your marrow—and that too, without borrowing from anybody, or imitating anybody.—You laugh at my enthusiasm. I am sure of it. But why need we go back to the past for our heroes?—There is no such necessity; and he who shall first dare to grapple with the *present*, will triumph, in this country. Remember, my prediction.

Another very serious reason why, whatever were the merit of our writers, we could not enter into competition with the men of Europe is, that we cannot afford to write for nothing; and yet, if we would write for nothing; and *give* the copy right of a novel, for instance, to a publisher, it would still be a perilous adventure to him. Shall I tell you the reason? Our booksellers here can publish your costliest poems, and novels, and dramas, without any expense for the copy-right. You give Byron or Moore five thousand guineas * for a poem; and, in forty days, there will be an American edition published here, for the copy right of which, our publishers have not given a cent. Names will sell anything. We all know that. Here is a poem, for example, of Walter Scott, for sale in Philadelphia, at this moment, called *Hallidon Hill*, which I venture to say, has not been read, by twenty people in the city. And yet, the time was, when the man who should have predicted such a thing, would have been hooted at for a fool, or a madman. Then, Walter Scott was, "the greatest poet in the world."—Now he is not thought of, as a *poet*. Then, he had a name—now, he has no name at all—as a poet. The consequence, you will perceive, of this practice in our country, is, that, until the authors, or publishers of European works, have the wisdom to take out copy-rights in this country, their reputation will be at our mercy; they will be subject to all sorts of bookselling piracy and trick; they will get nothing of the vast profit, that is obtained here, by the sale of their works; and our native authors cannot contend with them for a day; because, it is more profitable for a bookseller, in America, to re-publish established works, of established authors, when the publick in England have already past judgment upon them, and there is therefore no risk in re-publishing them here, than to publish *native works*, though they be made a present of the copy-right.

But will this last forever? No. The time is rapidly approaching, when, it will be enough to sell a work, if it be called American. We are getting to feel a national pride; and men are already beginning to put in their title pages, *"by an American"*—and *"an American Tale"*—words, that, a few years ago, would have been as politick, as "by a Choctaw"—or *"or a Narraganset tale."* (*Randolph*, II, 207.)

* Five thousand guineas!—fudge! [Neal's note.]

POETRY

Will *poetry* itself become extinct. No, never.—You never can put out that light. As well might you hope to blot out the solar system. No: poetry is the "divinity within us." It will be the better understood; and far more devoutly worshipped, when this revolution shall have taken place; when the great, beautiful *thought*, of the anointed among men, shall be disincumbered of words without meaning. Poetry is the naked expression of power and eloquence. But, for many hundred years—poetry has been confounded with false musick—measure and cadence—the soul with the body—the thought with the language—the manner of speaking, with the mode of thinking. The secondary qualities of poetry have been mistaken for the primary ones.

What I call poetry, has nothing to do with art or learning. It is a natural musick—the musick of woods and waters; not that of the orchestra. It is a fine, volatile essence, which cannot be extinguished or confined, while there is one drop of blood in the human heart, or any sense of Almighty God, among the children of men. I do not mean this, irreverently—I mean, precisely, what I say—that poetry is a religion as well as a musick. Nay—it is eloquence.—It is, whatever affects, touches, or disturbs the animal or moral sense of man. I care not how poetry may be expressed, nor in what language, it is still poetry; as the melody of the waters, wherever they may run; in the desert or the wilderness; among the rocks or the grass, will always be melody. It is not artificial musick—the musick of the head —of learning, or of science; but it is one continual voluntary of the heart; to be heard every where—at all times—by day—and by night, whenever men will stay their hands, for a moment, or lift up their heads and listen. It is not the composition of a master; the language of art, painfully and entirely exact; but, it is the wild capricious melody of *nature*—pathetick or brilliant, like the roundelay of innumerable birds whistling all about you, in the wind and water—sky and air; or the coquetting of a river breeze over the fine strings of an Eolian harp—concealed among green leaves and apple blossoms.

All men talk poetry, at some time or other, in their lives; even the most reasonable, cold-hearted, mathematical and phlegmatick; but most of them, without knowing it—and women, yet more frequently, than men: and young children too, talk it, perpetually, when alarmed or delighted. Yet they never talk in rhyme; nay, nor in blank verse. Even the writers of tragedy—the most perverse of God's creatures—do now and then, stumble upon this truth—for, in all their passionate and deepest passages, they do all that they can, to get rid of the foolish restraint of rhythm. And when they do not—they are, to the full, as absurd as the opera-singer—who murders and makes love, by the gamut.

Poetry too, is the natural language of the human heart—its *mother-tongue*; and is, just as naturally resorted to, on any emergency or distress, by the devout—the terrified—the affectionate—the tender-hearted and the loving—the widowed and the afflicted—as a man's native tongue is, when, after having been a great while among strangers, where he has learnt a strange language, good enough for all the common purposes of life—he is called upon, by some signal, and unexpected calamity, to pray aloud; or to cry out, with a broken and bowed spirit, or a crushed heart. Instantly, that man over-leaps all time and space—and, falls down, before the woman that he loves; or his Maker, with the very language that his mother taught him, when he fell upon his little knees, and lisped the dictated prayer after her, syllable by syllable. Just so, it is, with poetry. Prose will do for common people; or, for all the common occasions of life, even with uncommon people. We cannot drive a better bargain, or make a better argument in poetry, than in prose. But strike us here, into our very vitals, with some weapon of fire; and see how instantly a combustion takes place, inwardly—within all of us—flaming at our eyes, and trembling on our tongues, like inspiration. The poetry within us takes fire, and becomes audible and visible.—We might have died, without thinking that we were combustible, but for something that had jarred all our blood, like an earthquake.

I speak of this matter, freely and boldly, because I know that I am competent to speak of it—and fully authorized to bear witness against the mischievous and perverted tendencies, of poetical thought, when it is put, like a beautiful child, or a strong giant, into shackles and gyves; hand-cuffs and pinions. Some men affect to talk about it; and to give rule for it, who never had a poetical idea in their heads. Fools! they might as well learn eloquence from an automaton; or swimming, by seeing other people swim, as how to make poetry, by reading and studying the great masters—and listening to the jackasses, who are called criticks; not one, in a million of whom ever was, or ever will be a poet. Why?—because if a man be a poet, he will lack, nine hundred and ninety nine times out of a thousand, either the judgment; or the moral courage; or the honesty, to criticise boldly; and to speak of poetry as it deserves; and more than that, if he be a *poet*, he will be above the practice of criticism.

My notion, in one word, is—that poetry is the natural language of every human heart, when it is roused—*or* inflamed, or agitated, or affected: and that prose, on the contrary, is the natural language of every human heart, on all other occasions; and that rhyme, or blank verse, or *regular* rhythm, is altogether as artificial, unnatural and preposterous a mode of expression, for the true poet; as the use of a foreign idiom, or foreign phrase, is to the true home-bred man. The Romans affected to talk Greek; the Germans do talk French—as if they were ashamed of their mother language; and so do poets talk in rhyme or blank verse—but, let them all talk ever so beautifully, one can always discover that it is not natural to either of them. They are too Attic—or too provincial—too exact, or too slovenly.

To put this in another light—one example will do more than a volume of abstract reasoning. Could you possibly hold out to read any poem, by the greatest poet that ever lived, which should contain as many words, as one of the Waverly novels? It would be about five or six times as long, as Paradise Lost. If it were the best of poetry, would you not get the sooner tired of it? Assuredly. In the confusion of such a beautiful and confounding exhibition of power and brightness, your senses would lose all their activity: they would reel under it; and retain no distinct impression at all.—It would be like seeing a multitude of beautiful women, at the same moment—in a place, crowded with august personages—innumerable pictures—statuary—delicious musick and fire works.—What would you remember of the whole?—nothing.

How many volumes of prose *do* you read in a year? and how many would you read, if the same things were told in verse! Probably not a hundredth part, as many as you do now; hence the superiority of prose, if one want to convey instruction, or amusement; or obtain reputation, glory, or popularity. (*Randolph,* II, 184.)

WASHINGTON IRVING

EDWIN C. HOLLAND [1]
(1814)

Odes, Naval Songs, and other occasional Poems.
By Edwin C. Holland, Esq., Charleston.

A SMALL volume, with the above title, has been handed to us, with a request that it might be criticised. Though we do not profess the art and mystery of reviewing, and are not ambitious of being either wise or facetious at the expense of others, yet we feel a disposition to notice the present work, because it is a specimen of one branch of literature at present very popular throughout our country, and also because the author, who, we understand, is quite young, gives proof of very considerable poetical talent, and is in great danger of being spoiled.

We apprehend, from various symptoms about his work, that he has for some time past received great honors from circles of literary ladies and gentlemen, and that he has great facility at composition—we find, moreover, that he has written for public papers under the signature of "Orlando;" and above all, that a prize has been awarded to one of his poems, in a kind of poetical lottery, cunningly devised by an "eminent bookseller."

These, we must confess, are melancholy disadvantages to start withal; and many a youthful poet of great promise has been utterly ruined by misfortunes of much inferior magnitude. We trust, however, that in the present case they are not without remedy, and that the author is not so far gone in the evil habit of publishing, as to be utterly beyond reclaim. Still we feel the necessity of extending immediate relief, from a hint he gives us on the cover of his book, that the present poems are "presented merely as specimens of his manner, and comprise but a *very small portion*" of those he has on hand. This information really startled us; we beheld in imagination a mighty mass of odes, songs, sonnets, and acrostics, impending in awful volume over our heads, and threatening every instant to flutter down, like a theatrical snow-storm of white paper. To avert so fearful an *avalanche* have we hastened to take pen in hand, determined to risk the author's displeasure, by giving him good advice, and to deliver him, if possible, uninjured out of the hands both of his admirers and his patron.

The main piece of advice we would give him is, to lock up all his remaining writings, and to abstain most abstemiously from publishing for some years to come. We know that this will appear very ungracious coun-

[1] From the *Analectic Magazine*, III (1814), 242–52.

sel, and we have not very great hope that it will be adopted. We are well aware of the eagerness of young authors to hurry into print, and that the Muse is too fond of present pay, and "present pudding," to brook voluntarily the postponement of reward. Besides, this early and exuberant foliage of the mind is peculiar to warm sensibilities and lively fancies, in which the principles of fecundity are so strong as to be almost irrepressible. The least ray of popular admiration sets all the juices in motion, produces a bursting forth of buds and blossoms, and a profusion of vernal and perishable vegetation. But there is no greater source of torment to a writer than the flippancies of his juvenile Muse. The sins and follies of his youth arise in loathsome array, to disturb the quiet of his maturer years, and he is perpetually haunted by the spectres of the early murders he has perpetrated on good English and good sense.

We have no intention to discourage Mr. Holland from his poetic career. On the contrary, it is in consequence of the good opinion we entertain of his genius, that we are solicitous that it should be carefully nurtured, wholesomely disciplined, and trained up to full and masculine vigor, rather than dissipated and enfeebled by early excesses. We think we can discern in his writings strong marks of amiable, and generous, and lofty sentiment, of ready invention, and great brilliancy of expression. These are as yet obscured by a false, or rather puerile taste, which time and attention will improve, but it is necessary that time and attention should be employed. Were his faults merely those of mediocrity we should despair, for there is no such thing as fermenting a dull mind into anything like poetic inspiration; but we think the effervescence of this writer's fancy will at a future day settle down into something substantially excellent. Rising genius always shoots forth its rays from among clouds and vapors, but these will gradually roll away and disappear, as it ascends to its steady and meridian lustre.

One thing which pleases us in the songs in this collection is, that they have more originality than we commonly meet with in our national songs. We begin to think that it is a much more difficult thing to write a good song than to fight a good battle; for our tars have achieved several splendid victories in a short space of time; but, notwithstanding the thousand pens that have been drawn forth in every part of the Union, we do not recollect a single song of really sterling merit that has been written on the occasion. Nothing is more offensive than a certain lawless custom which prevails among our patriotic songsters, of seizing upon the noble songs of Great Britain, mangling and disfiguring them, with pens more merciless than Indian scalping-knives, and then passing them off for American songs. This may be an idea borrowed from the custom of our savage neighbors, of adopting prisoners into their families, and so completely taking them to their homes and hearts, as almost to consider them as children of their own begetting. At any rate, it is a practice worthy of savage life and savage ideas of property. We have witnessed such horrible distortions of sense and poetry; we have seen the fine members of an elegant stanza so mangled and wrenched, in order to apply it to this country, that our

very hearts ached with sympathy and vexation. We are continually an-
noyed with the figure of poor Columbia, an honest, awkward, dowdy sort
of dame, thrust into the place of Britannia, and made to wield the trident
and "rule the waves," and play off a thousand clumsy ceremonies before
company, as maladroitly as a worthy tradesman's wife enacting a fine lady
or a tragedy queen.

Besides, there is in this a pitifulness of spirit, an appearance of abject
poverty of mind, that would be degrading if it really belonged to the nation. Nay, more, there is a positive dishonesty in it. We may, if we choose,
plunder the bodies of our enemies, whom we have fairly conquered in the
field of battle; and we may strut about, uncouthly arrayed in their garments, with their coats swinging to our heels, and their boots "a world
too wide for our shrunk shanks," but the same privilege does not extend
to literature; and however our puny poetasters may flaunt for a while in
the pilfered garbs of their gigantic neighbors, they may rest assured that
if there should be a tribunal hereafter to try the crimes of authors, they
will be considered as mere poetical highwaymen, and condemned to swing
most loftily for their offences.

It is really insulting to tell this country, as some of these varlets do,
that she "needs no bulwarks, no towers along the steep," when there is a
cry from one end of the Union to the other for the fortifying our sea-
ports and the defence of our coast, and when every post brings us intelligence of the enemy depredating in our bays and rivers; and it is still
more insulting to tell her that "her home is on the deep," which, if it
really be the case, only proves that at present she is turned out of doors.
No, if we really must have national songs, let them be of our own manufacturing, however coarse. We would rather hear our victories celebrated
in the merest doggerel that sprang from native invention, than beg, borrow, or steal from others, the thoughts and words in which to express
our exultation. By tasking our own powers, and relying entirely on ourselves, we shall gradually improve and rise to poetical independence; but
this practice of appropriating the thoughts of others, of getting along by
contemptible shifts and literary larcenies, prevents native exertion, and
produces absolute impoverishment. It is in literature as in the accumulation of private fortune; the humblest beginning should not dishearten;
much may be done by persevering industry or spirited enterprise; but he
who depends on borrowing will never grow rich, and he who indulges in
theft will ultimately come to the gallows.

We are glad to find that the writer before us is innocent of these enormous sins against honesty and good sense; but we would warn him against
another evil, into which young writers, and young men, are very prone
to fall—we mean bad company. We are apprehensive that the companions
of his literary leisure have been none of the most profitable, and that he has
been trifling too much with the fantastic gentry of the Della Cruscan
school, revelling among flowers and hunting butterflies, when he should
have been soberly walking, like a duteous disciple, in the footsteps of the
mighty masters of his art. We are led to this idea from seeing in his poems

the portentous names of "the blue-eyed Myra," and "Rosa Matilda," and
from reading of "lucid vests veiling snowy breasts," and "satin sashes,"
and "sighs of rosy perfume," and "trembling eve-star beam, through some
light cloud's glory seen" (which, by the bye, is a rhyme very much like
that of "muffin and dumpling"), and—

> "The sweetest of perfumes that languishing flies
> Like a kiss on the nectarous morning-tide air."

Now all this kind of poetry is rather late in the day—the fashion has
gone by. A man may as well attempt to figure as a fine gentleman in a
pea-green silk coat, and pink satin breeches, and powdered head, and
paste buckles, and sharp-toed shoes, and all the finery of Sir Fopling Flutter, as to write in the style of Della Crusca.[2] Gifford has long since brushed
away all this trumpery.[3]

We think also the author has rather perverted his fancy by reading the
amatory effusions of Moore; which, whatever be the magic of their imagery
and versification, breathe a spirit of heartless sensuality and soft voluptu-
ousness beneath the tone of vigorous and virtuous manhood.

This rhapsodizing about "brilliant pleasures," and "hours of bliss," and
"humid eyelids," and "ardent kisses," is, after all, mighty cold-blooded,
silly stuff. It may do to tickle the ears of love-sick striplings and romantic
milliners; but one verse describing pure domestic affection, or tender innocent love, from the pen of Burns, speaks more to the heart than all the
meretricious rhapsodies of Moore.

We doubt if in the whole round of rapturous scenes, dwelt on with
elaborate salacity by the modern Anacreon, one passage can be found,
combining equal eloquence of language, delicacy of imagery, and impassioned tenderness, with the following picture of the interview and parting of two lovers:—

> "How sweetly bloomed the gay, green birk,
>   How rich the hawthorn's blossom;
> As underneath their fragrant shade
>   I clasped her to my bosom!
> The golden hours, on angel wings,
>   Flew o'er me and my dearie:
> For dear to me, as light and life,
>   Was my sweet Highland Mary.
>
> "Wi' mony a vow, and locked embrace,
>   Our parting was fu' tender;
> And pledging aft to meet again,
>   We tore oursel's asunder;

[2] The Della Cruscans were a group of insignificant versifiers in Florence during
the late eighteenth century. They were notorious for their fantastic and insipid
manner.

[3] William Gifford (1756–1826), editor of the *Quarterly Review* and bitterly opposed
to radicals and new writers. He was the author of the notorious article on Keats's
Endymion.

> But oh! fell death's untimely frost,
>   That nipt my flower sae early!
> Now green's the sod, and cauld's the clay,
>   That wraps my Highland Mary.
>
> "O pale, pale now those rosy lips,
>   I aft hae kissed sae fondly!
> And closed for aye the sparkling glance
>   That dwelt on me sae kindly!
> And mouldering now in silent dust
>   That heart that lo'ed me dearly!
> But still within my bosom's core
>   Shall live my Highland Mary."

Throughout the whole of the foregoing stanzas we would remark the extreme simplicity of the language, the utter absence of all false coloring, of those "roseate hues," and "ambrosial odors," and "purple mists," that steam from the pages of our voluptuous poets, to intoxicate the weak brains of their admirers. Burns depended on the truth and tenderness of his ideas, on that deep-toned feeling which is the very soul of poetry. To use his own admirably descriptive words,—

> "His rural loves are Nature's sel,
>   Nae bombast spates o' nonsense swell;
>   Nae *snap conceits*, but that *sweet spell*,
>   *O' witchin' love*,
>   *That charm, that can the strongest quell*,
>   *The sternest move.*"

But the chief fault which infests the style of the poems before us, is a passion for hyperbole, and for the glare of extravagant images and flashing phrases. This taste for gorgeous finery and violent metaphor prevails throughout our country, and is characteristic of the early efforts of literature. Our national songs are full of ridiculous exaggeration, and frothy rant and common-place bloated up into fustian. The writers seem to think that huge words and mountainous figures constitute the sublime. Their puny thoughts are made to sweat under loads of cumbrous imagery, and now and then they are so wrapt up in conflagrations, and blazes, and thunders and lightnings, that, like Nick Bottom's hero, they seem to have "slipt on a brimstone shirt, and are all on fire!"

We would advise these writers, if they wish to see what is really grand and forcible in patriotic minstrelsy, to read the national songs of Campbell,[4] and the "Bannock-Burn" of Burns, where there is the utmost grandeur of thought conveyed in striking but perspicuous language. It is much easier to be fine than correct in writing. A rude and imperfect taste always heaps on decoration, and seeks to dazzle by a profusion of brilliant incongruities. But true taste evinces itself in pure and noble simplicity, and a fitness and chasteness of ornament. The Muses of the ancients are described as beautiful females, exquisitely proportioned, simply attired, with

[4] Thomas Campbell (1777-1844), Scottish poet.

no ornaments but the diamond clasps that connected their garments; but were we to paint the Muse of one of our popular poets, we should represent her as a pawnbroker's widow, with rings on every finger, and loaded with borrowed and heterogeneous finery.

One cause of the epidemical nature of our literary errors, is the proneness of our authors to borrow from each other, and thus to interchange faults, and give a circulation to absurdities. It is dangerous always for a writer to be very studious of contemporary publications, which have not passed the ordeal of time and criticism. He should fix his eye on those models which have been scrutinized, and of the faults and excellences of which he is fully apprised. We think we can trace, in the popular songs of the volume before us, proofs that the author has been very conversant with the works of Robert Treat Paine,[5] a late American writer of very considerable merit, but who delighted in continued explosions of fancy and glitter of language. As we do not censure wantonly, or for the sake of finding fault, we shall point to one of the author's writings, on which it is probable he most values himself, as it is the one which publicly received the prize in the Bookseller's Lottery. We allude to "The Pillar of Glory." We are likewise induced to notice this particularly, because we find it going the rounds of the Union,—strummed at pianos, sang at concerts, and roared forth lustily at public dinners. Having this universal currency, and bearing the imposing title of "Prize Poem," which is undoubtedly equal to the "Tower Stamp," it stands a great chance of being considered abroad as a prize production of one of our Universities, and at home as a standard poem, worthy the imitation of all tyros in the art.

The first stanza is very fair, and indeed is one of those passages on which we found our good opinion of the author's genius. The last line is really noble.

> "Hail to the heroes whose triumphs have brightened
>   The darkness which shrouded America's name!
> Long shall their valor in battle that lightened,
>   Live in the brilliant escutcheons of fame!
>   Dark where the torrents flow,
>   And the rude tempests blow,
>   The stormy-clad Spirit of Albion raves;
>   Long shall she mourn the day,
>   When in the vengeful fray,
>   Liberty walked, like a god, on the waves."

The second stanza, however, sinks from this vigorous and perspicuous tone. We have the "halo and lustre of story" *curling* round the "wave of the ocean"; a mixture of ideal and tangible objects wholly inadmissible in good poetry. But the great mass of sin lies in the third stanza, where the writer rises into such a glare and confusion of figure as to be almost incomprehensible.

[5] Robert Treat Paine, Jr. (1773-1811), American poet and one of the leading literary figures of his day.

"The pillar of glory, the sea that enlightens,
　　Shall last till eternity rocks on its base!
The splendor of fame its waters that brightens,
　　Shall follow the footsteps of time in his race!
　　　　Wide o'er the stormy deep,
　　　　Where the rude surges sweep,
　　Its lustre shall circle the brows of the brave!
　　　　Honor shall give it light,
　　　　Triumph shall keep it bright,
　　Long as in battle we meet on the wave!"

We confess that we were sadly puzzled to understand the nature of this ideal pillar, that seemed to have set the sea in a blaze, and was to last "till eternity rocks on its base," which we suppose is, according to a vulgar phrase, "forever and a day after." Our perplexity was increased by the cross light from the "splendor of fame," which, like a foot-boy with a lantern, was to jog on after the footsteps of Time; who it appears was to run a race against himself on the water—and as to the other lights and gleams that followed, they threw us into complete bewilderment. It is true, after beating about for some time, we at length landed on what we suspected to be the author's meaning; but a worthy friend of ours, who read the passage with great attention, maintains that this pillar of glory which enlightened the sea can be nothing more nor less than a light-house.

We do not certainly wish to indulge in improper or illiberal levity. It is not the author's fault that his poem has received a prize, and been elevated into unfortunate notoriety. Were its faults matters of concernment merely to himself, we should barely have hinted at them; but the poem has been made, in a manner, a national poem, and in attacking it we attack generally that prevailing taste among our poetical writers for excessive ornament, for turgid extravagance, and vapid hyperbole. We wish in some small degree to counteract the mischief that may be done to national literature by eminent booksellers crowning inferior effusions as prize poems, setting them to music, and circulating them widely through the country. We wish also, by a little good-humored rebuke, to stay the hurried career of a youth of talent and promise, whom we perceive lapsing into error, and liable to be precipitated forward by the injudicious applauses of his friends.

We therefore repeat our advice to Mr. Holland, that he abstain from further publication until he has cultivated his taste and ripened his mind. We earnestly exhort him rigorously to watch over his youthful Muse; who, we suspect, is very spirited and vivacious, subject to quick excitement, of great pruriency of feeling, and a most uneasy inclination to breed. Let him in the meanwhile diligently improve himself in classical studies, and in an intimate acquaintance with the best and simplest British poets, and the soundest British critics. We do assure him that really fine poetry is exceedingly rare, and not to be written copiously nor rapidly. Middling poetry may be produced in any quantity; the press groans with it, the shelves of circulating libraries are loaded with it; but who reads merely

middling poetry? Only two kinds can possibly be tolerated,—the very good
or the very bad,—one to be read with enthusiasm, the other to be laughed at.

We have in the course of this article quoted him rather unfavorably, but
it was for the purpose of general criticism, not individual censure; before
we conclude, it is but justice to give a specimen of what we consider his
best manner. The following stanzas are taken from elegiac lines on the
death of a young lady. The comparison of a beautiful female to a flower
is obvious and frequent in poetry, but we think it is managed here with
uncommon delicacy and consistency, and great novelty of thought and
manner:—

"There was a flower of beauteous birth,
     Of lavish charms, and chastened dye;
It smiled upon the lap of earth,
     And caught the gaze of every eye.

"The vernal breeze, whose step is seen
     Imprinted in the early dew,
Ne'er brushed a flower of brighter beam,
     Or nursed a bud of lovelier hue!

"It blossomed not in dreary wild,
     In darksome glen, or desert bower,
But grew, like Flora's fav'rite child,
     In sunbeam soft and fragrant shower.

"The graces loved with chastened light
     To flush its pure celestial bloom,
And all its blossoms were so bright,
     It seemed not formed to die so soon.

"Youth round the flow'ret ere it fell
     In armor bright was seen to stray,
And beauty said, her magic spell
     Should keep its perfume from decay.

"The parent-stalk from which it sprung,
     Transported as its halo spread,
In holy umbrage o'er it hung,
     And tears of heaven-born rapture shed.

"Yet, fragile flower! thy blossom bright,
     Though guarded by a magic spell,
Like a sweet beam of evening light,
     In lonely hour of tempest fell.

"The death-blast of the winter air,
     The cold frost and the night-wind came,
They nipt thy beauty once so fair!—
     It shall not bloom on earth again!"

From a general view of the poems of Mr. Holland, it is evident that he has the external requisites for poetry in abundance,—he has fine images, fine phrases, and ready versification; he must only learn to think with fulness and precision, and he will write splendidly. As we have already hinted, we consider his present productions but the blossoms of his genius, and like blossoms they will fall and perish; but we trust that after some time of silent growth and gradual maturity, we shall see them succeeded by a harvest of rich and highly flavored fruit.

WASHINGTON IRVING

DESULTORY THOUGHTS ON CRITICISM [1]
(1839)

"Let a man write never so well, there are nowadays a sort of persons they call critics, that, egad, have no more wit in them than so many hobby-horses; but they'll laugh at you, sir, and find fault, and censure things, that, egad, I'm sure they are not able to do themselves; a sort of envious persons, that emulate the glories of persons of parts, and think to build their fame by calumniation of persons that, egad, to my knowledge, of all persons in the world, are in nature the persons that do as much despise all that, as—a—I'll say no more of 'em!"

Rehearsal.

ALL THE world knows the story of the tempest-tossed voyager, who, coming upon a strange coast, and seeing a man hanging in chains, hailed it with joy as the sign of a civilized country. In like manner we may hail, as a proof of the rapid advancement of civilization and refinement in this country, the increasing number of delinquent authors daily gibbeted for the edification of the public.

In this respect, as in every other, we are "going ahead" with the accelerated velocity, and promising to outstrip the superannuated countries of Europe. It is really astonishing to see the number of tribunals incessantly springing up for the trial of literary offences. Independent of the high courts of Oyer and Terminer, the great quarterly reviews, we have innumerable minor tribunals, monthly and weekly, down to the Pie-poudre courts in the daily papers; insomuch that no culprit stands so little chance of escaping castigation as an unlucky author, guilty of an unsuccessful attempt to please the public.

Seriously speaking, however, it is questionable whether our national literature is sufficiently advanced to bear this excess of criticism; and whether it would not thrive better if allowed to spring up, for some time longer, in the freshness and vigor of native vegetation. When the worthy Judge Coulter, of Virginia, opened court for the first time in one of the upper counties, he was for enforcing all the rules and regulations that had grown into use in the old, long-settled counties. "This is all very well," said a shrewd old farmer; "but let me tell you, Judge Coulter, you set your coulter too deep for a new soil."

For my part, I doubt whether either writer or reader is benefited by what is commonly called criticism. The former is rendered cautious and dis-

[1] From the *Knickerbocker Magazine*, XIV (1839), 175–78.

trustful; he fears to give way to those kindling emotions, and brave sallies of thought which bear him up to excellence; the latter is made fastidious and cynical; or rather, he surrenders his own independent taste and judgment, and learns to like and dislike at second hand.

Let us, for a moment, consider the nature of this thing called criticism, which exerts such a sway over the literary world. The pronoun *we*, used by critics, has a most imposing and delusive sound. The reader pictures to himself a conclave of learned men, deliberating gravely and scrupulously on the merits of the book in question; examining it page by page, comparing and balancing their opinions, and when they have united in a conscientious verdict, publishing it for the benefit of the world: whereas the criticism is generally the crude and hasty production of an individual, scribbling to while away an idle hour, to oblige a book seller, or to defray current expenses. How often is it the passing notion of the hour, affected by accidental circumstances; by indisposition, by peevishness, by vapors or indigestion, by personal prejudice or party feeling. Sometimes a work is sacrificed because the reviewer wishes a satirical article; sometimes because he wants a humorous one; and sometimes because the author reviewed has become offensively celebrated, and offers high game to the literary marksman.

How often would the critic himself, if a conscientious man, reverse his opinion, had he time to revise it in a more sunny moment; but the press is waiting, the printer's devil is at his elbow, the article is wanted to make the requisite variety for the number of the review, or the author has pressing occasion for the sum he is to receive for the article; so it is sent off, all blotted and blurred, with a shrug of the shoulders, and the consolatory ejaculation, "Pshaw! curse it! it's nothing but a review!"

The critic, too, who dictates thus oracularly to the world, is perhaps some dingy, ill-favored, ill-mannered varlet, who, were he to speak by word of mouth, would be disregarded, if not scoffed at; but such is the magic of types; such the mystic operation of anonymous writing; such the potential effect of the pronoun *we*, that his crude decisions, fulminated through the press, become circulated far and wide, control the opinions of the world, and give or destroy reputation.

Many readers have grown timorous in their judgments since the all-pervading currency of criticism. They fear to express a revised, frank opinion about any new work, and to relish it honestly and heartily, lest it should be condemned in the next review, and they stand convicted of bad taste. Hence they hedge their opinions, like a gambler his bets, and leave an opening to retract, and retreat, and qualify, and neutralize every unguarded expression of delight, until their very praise declines into a faintness that is damning.

Were every one, on the contrary, to judge for himself, and speak his mind frankly and fearlessly, we should have more true criticism in the world than at present. Whenever a person is pleased with a work, he may be assured that it has good qualities. An author who pleases a variety of readers, must possess substantial powers of pleasing; or, in other words, intrinsic merits; for otherwise we acknowledge an effect and deny the cause. The reader, therefore, should not suffer himself to be readily shaken from the conviction of his own feelings by the sweeping censures of pseudo-critics. The author he has admired may be chargeable with a thousand faults; but it is nevertheless beauties and excellences that have excited his admiration; and he should recollect that taste and judgment are as much evinced in the perception of beauties among defects, as in a detection of defects among beauties. For my part, I honor the blessed and blessing spirit that is quick to discover and extol all that is pleasing and meritorious. Give me the honest bee, that extracts honey from the humblest weed, but save me from the ingenuity of the spider, which traces its venom even in the midst of a flower-garden.

If the mere fact of being chargeable with faults and imperfections is to condemn an author, who is to escape? The greatest writers of antiquity have, in this way, been obnoxious to criticism. Aristotle himself has been accused of ignorance; Aristophanes of impiety and buffoonery; Virgil of plagiarism, and a want of invention; Horace of obscurity; Cicero has been said to want vigor and connection, and Demosthenes to be deficient in nature, and in purity of language. Yet these have all survived the censures of the critic, and flourished on to a glorious immortality. Every now and then, the world is startled by some new doctrines in matters of taste, some levelling attacks on established creeds; some sweeping denunciations of whole generations or schools of writers, as they are called, who had seemed to be embalmed and canonized in public opinion. Such has been the case, for instance, with Pope, and Dryden, and Addison; who for a time have almost been shaken from their pedestals, and treated as false idols.

It is singular, also, to see the fickleness of the world with respect to its favorites. Enthusiasm exhausts itself, and prepares the way for dislike. The public is always for positive sentiments, and new sensations. When wearied of admiring, it delights to censure; thus coining a double set of enjoyments out of the same subject. Scott and Byron are scarce cold in their graves, and already we find criticism beginning to call in question those powers which held the world in magic thraldom. Even in our own country, one of its greatest geniuses has had some rough passages with the censors of the press; and instantly criticism begins to unsay all that it has repeatedly said in his praise; and the public are almost led to believe that the pen which has so often delighted them is absolutely destitute of the power to delight!

If, then, such reverses in opinion as to matters of taste can be so readily brought about, when may an author feel himself secure? Where is the anchoring-ground of popularity, when he may thus be driven from his moorings, and foundered even in harbor? The reader, too, when is he to consider himself safe in admiring, when he sees long-established altars overthrown, and his household deities dashed to the ground?

There is one consolatory reflection. Every abuse carries with it its own remedy or palliation. Thus the excess of crude and hasty criticism, which has of late prevailed throughout the literary world, and threatened to overrun our country, begins to produce its own antidote. Where there is a multiplicity of contradictory paths, a man must make his choice; in so doing, he has to exercise his judgment, and that is one great step to mental independence. He begins to doubt all, where all differ, and but one can be in the right. He is driven to trust his own discernment, and his natural feelings; and here he is most likely to be safe. The author, too, finding that what is condemned at one tribunal is applauded at another, though perplexed for a time, gives way at length to the spontaneous impulse of his genius, and the dictates of his taste, and writes in the way most natural to himself. It is thus that criticism, which by its severity may have held the little world of writers in check, may, by its very excess, disarm itself of its terrors, and the hardihood of talent become restored.

WILLIAM CULLEN BRYANT

ON THE NATURE OF POETRY [1]
(1826)

IN TREATING of the subject which has been assigned me, it is obvious that it will be impossible for me to compress into four lectures anything like a complete view of it. I am to speak of one of the most ancient of all arts, of the very earliest and most venerable branch of literature—one which even now exists in many countries that have no other; one, which although it has not in every period been cultivated with the same degree of success, has yet in no age of the world ceased to attract a large degree of the attention of mankind. Not only have the writers of poetry been exceedingly numerous—more so, perhaps, than those of any other class—but poetry has shot forth another branch of literature, her handmaid and satellite, and raised up a large body of authors, who speculate upon what the poets have written, who define the elements and investigate the principles of the art, and fix the degrees of estimation in which its several productions should be held. Not only has the poetry of one age been exceedingly different from that of another, but different styles of poetry have prevailed at the same time in different nations, different schools of poetry have arisen in the same nation, and different forms of poetical composition have been preferred by the several writers of the same school. So much poetry has been written, and that poetry has been the subject of so much criticism, so much matter for speculation has been collected, and so many reasonings and theories have been framed out of it, that the subject has grown to be one of the most comprehensive in the whole province of literature.

If I were to treat of either of its great subdivisions—if, for example, I were to attempt its history from its earliest origin, through its various stages, to the present time; if I were to analyze the several forms of poetical composition, or to point out the characteristics of the various kinds of poetry that have prevailed at different periods, or to compare the genius of the most illustrious poets—in either case, I could do little more than pass rapidly over the principal topics. The view would be so brief that it would seem like a dry table of the contents of a large work, and would become tedious from its very brevity. I shall, therefore, in the short course of lectures which I have undertaken, attempt no entire view of the subject assigned to me; but shall only endeavor to select a few of the topics which seem to me among the most interesting, and on which I may imagine that I shall weary you the least.

[1] This was the first of a series of four lectures on poetry which Bryant delivered before the Athenaeum Society in New York in 1826. The lectures were not published until the *Prose Writings*, ed. by Parke Godwin, appeared in New York in 1884.

Of the nature of poetry different ideas have been entertained. The ancient critics seemed to suppose that they did something toward giving a tolerable notion of it by calling it a mimetic or imitative art, and classing it with sculpture and painting. Of its affinity with these arts there can be no doubt; but that affinity seems to me to consist almost wholly in the principles by which they all produce their effect, and not in the manner in which those principles are reduced to practice. There is no propriety in applying to poetry the term *imitative* in a literal and philosophical sense, as there is in applying it to painting and sculpture. The latter speak to the senses; poetry speaks directly to the mind. They reproduce sensible objects, and, by means of these, suggest the feeling or sentiment connected with them; poetry, by the symbols of words, suggests both the sensible object and the association. I should be glad to learn how a poem descriptive of a scene or an event is any more an imitation of that scene or that event than a prose description would be. A prose composition giving an account of the proportions and dimensions of a building, and the materials of which it is constructed, is certainly, so far as mere exactness is concerned, a better imitation of it than the finest poem that could be written about it. Yet who, after all, ever thought of giving such a composition the name of an imitation? The truth is, painting and sculpture are, literally, imitative arts, while poetry is only metaphorically so. The epithet as applied to poetry may be well enough, perhaps, as a figure of speech, but to make a metaphor the foundation of a philosophical classification is putting it to a service in which it is sure to confuse what it professes to make clear.

I would rather call poetry a suggestive art. Its power of affecting the mind by pure suggestion, and employing, instead of a visible or tangible imitation, arbitrary symbols, as unlike as possible to the things with which it deals, is what distinguishes this from its two sister arts. It is owing to its operation by means of suggestion that it affects different minds with such different degrees of force. In a picture or a statue the colors and forms employed by the artist impress the senses with the greatest distinctness. In painting, there is little—in sculpture, there is less—for the imagination to supply. It is true that different minds, according to their several degrees of cultivation, will receive different degrees of pleasure from the productions of these arts, and that the moral associations they suggest will be variously felt, and in some instances variously interpreted. Still, the impression made on the senses is in all cases the same; the same figures, the same lights and shades, are seen by all beholders alike. But the creations of Poetry have in themselves nothing of this precision and fixedness of form, and depend greatly for their vividness and clearness of impression upon the mind to which they are presented. Language, the great machine with which her miracles are wrought, is contrived to have an application to all possible things; and wonderful as this contrivance is, and numerous and varied as are its combinations, it is still limited and imperfect, and, in point of comprehensiveness, distinctness, and variety, falls infinitely short of the mighty and diversified world of matter and mind of which it professes to be the representative. It is, however, to the very limitation of this power of language, as it seems to me, that Poetry owes her magic. The most detailed of her descriptions, which, by the way, are not always the most striking, are composed of a few touches; they are glimpses of things thrown into the mind; here and there a trace of the outline; here a gleam of light, and there a dash of shade. But these very touches act like a spell upon the imagination and awaken it to greater activity, and fill it, perhaps, with greater delight than the best defined objects could do. The imagination is the most active and the least susceptible of fatigue of all the faculties of the human mind; its more intense exercise is tremendous, and sometimes unsettles the reason; its repose is only a gentle sort of activity; nor am I certain that it is ever quite unemployed, for even in our sleep it is still awake and busy, and amuses itself with fabricating our dreams. To this restless faculty—which is unsatisfied when the whole of its work is done to its hands, and which is ever wandering from the combination of ideas directly presented to it to other combinations of its own—it is the office of poetry to furnish the exercise in which it delights. Poetry is that art which selects and arranges the symbols of thought in such a manner as to excite it the most powerfully and delightfully. The imagination of the reader is guided, it is true, by the poet, and it is his business to guide it skilfully and agreeably; but the imagination in the mean time is by no means passive. It pursues the path which the poet only points out, and shapes its visions from the scenes and allusions which he gives. It fills up his sketches of beauty with what suits its own highest conceptions of the beautiful, and completes his outline of grandeur with the noblest images its own stores can furnish. It is obvious that the degree of perfection with which this is done must depend greatly upon the strength and cultivation of that faculty. For example, in the following passage, in which Milton describes the general mother passing to her daily task among the flowers:

> "With goddess-like demeanor forth she went
> Not unattended, for on her as queen
> A pomp of winning graces waited still."

The coldest imagination, on reading it, will figure to itself, in the person of Eve, the finest forms, attitudes, and movements of female loveliness and dignity, which, after all, are not described, but only hinted at by the poet. A warmer fancy, kindling at the delicate allusions in these lines, will not only bestow these attractions on the principal figure, but will fill the air around her with beauty, and people it with the airy forms of the graces; it will see the delicate proportions of their limbs, the lustre of their flowing hair, and the soft light of their eyes. Take, also, the following passage from the same poet, in which, speaking of Satan, he says:

> "His face
> Deep scars of thunder had entrenched, and care
> Sat on his faded cheek—but under brows
> Of dauntless courage and considerate pride
> Waiting revenge; cruel his eye but cast

> Signs of remorse and passion to behold
> The fellows of his crime, the followers rather,
> (Far other once beheld in bliss), condemned
> For evermore to have their lot in pain."

The imagination of the reader is stimulated by the hints in this powerful passage to form to itself an idea of the features in which reside this strong expression of malignity and dejection—the brow, the cheek, the eye of the fallen angel, bespeaking courage, pride, the settled purpose of revenge, anxiety, sorrow for the fate of his followers, and fearfully marked with the wrath of the Almighty. There can be no doubt that the picture which this passage calls up in the minds of different individuals will vary accordingly as the imagination is more or less vivid, or more or less excited in the perusal. It will vary, also, accordingly as the individual is more or less experienced in the visible expression of strong passion, and as he is in the habit of associating the idea of certain emotions with certain configurations of the countenance.

There is no question that one principal office of poetry is to excite the imagination, but this is not its sole, nor perhaps its chief, province; another of its ends is to touch the heart, and, as I expect to show in this lecture, it has something to do with the understanding. I know that some critics have made poetry to consist solely in the exercise of the imagination. They distinguish poetry from pathos. They talk of pure poetry, and by this phrase they mean passages of mere imagery, with the least possible infusion of human emotion. I do not know by what authority these gentlemen take the term poetry from the people, and thus limit its meaning.

In its ordinary acceptation, it has, in all ages and all countries, included something more. When we speak of a poem, we do not mean merely a tissue of striking images. The most beautiful poetry is that which takes the strongest hold of the feelings, and, if it is really the most beautiful, then it is poetry in the highest sense. Poetry is constantly resorting to the language of the passions to heighten the effect of her pictures; and, if this be not enough to entitle that language to the appellation of poetical, I am not aware of the meaning of the term. Is there no poetry in the wrath of Achilles? Is there no poetry in the passage where Lear, in the tent of Cordelia, just recovered from his frenzy, his senses yet infirm and unassured, addresses his daughter as she kneels to ask his blessing?

> "Pray do not mock me;
> I am a very foolish, fond old man,
> Fourscore and upward:
> Not an hour more or less, and to deal plainly
> I fear I am not in my perfect mind."

Is there no poetry in the remorse of Othello, in the terrible consciousness of guilt which haunts Macbeth, or the lamentations of Antony over the body of his friend, the devoted love of Juliet, and the self-sacrificing affection of Cleopatra? In the immortal work of Milton, is there no poetry in the penitence of Adam, or in the sorrows of Eve at being excluded from Paradise? The truth is, that poetry which does not find its way to the heart is scarcely deserving of the name; it may be brilliant and ingenious, but it soon wearies the attention. The feelings and the imagination, when skilfully touched, act reciprocally on each other. For example, when the poet introduces Ophelia, young, beautiful, and unfortunate, the wildness of frenzy in her eye, dressed with fantastic garlands of wild flowers, and singing snatches of old tunes, there is a picture for the imagination, but it is one which affects the heart. But when, in the midst of her incoherent talk, she utters some simple allusion to her own sorrows, as when she says,

"We know what we are, but know not what we may be,"

this touching sentence, addressed merely to our sympathy, strongly excites the imagination. It sets before us the days when she knew sorrow only by name, before her father was slain by the hand of her lover, and before her lover was estranged, and makes us feel the heaviness of that affliction which crushed a being so gentle and innocent and happy.

Those poems, however, as I have already hinted, which are apparently the most affluent of imagery, are not always those which most kindle the reader's imagination. It is because the ornaments with which they abound are not naturally suggested by the subject, not poured forth from a mind warmed and occupied by it; but a forced fruit of the fancy, produced by labor, without spontaneity or excitement.

The language of passion is naturally figurative, but its figures are only employed to heighten the intensity of the expression; they are never introduced for their own sake. Important, therefore, as may be the office of the imagination in poetry, the great spring of poetry is emotion. It is this power that holds the key of the storehouse where the mind has laid up its images, and that alone can open it without violence. All the forms of fancy stand ever in its sight, ready to execute its bidding. Indeed, I doubt not that most of the offences against good taste in this kind of composition are to be traced to the absence of emotion. A desire to treat agreeably or impressively a subject by which the writer is himself little moved, leads him into great mistakes about the means of effecting his purpose. This is the origin of cold conceits, of prosing reflections, of the minute painting of uninteresting circumstances, and of the opposite extremes of tameness and extravagance. On the other hand, strong feeling is always a sure guide. It rarely offends against good taste, because it instinctively chooses the most effectual means of communicating itself to others. It gives a variety to the composition it inspires, with which the severest taste is delighted. It may sometimes transgress arbitrary rules, or offend against local associations, but it speaks a language which reaches the heart in all countries and all times. Everywhere are the sentiments of fortitude and magnanimity uttered in strains that brace our own nerves, and the dead mourned in accents that draw our tears.

But poetry not only addresses the passions and the imagination; it appeals to the understanding also. So far as this position relates to the principles of taste which lie at the foundation of all poetry, and by which its merits are tried, I believe its truth will not be doubted. These principles have their origin in the reason of things, and are investigated and applied by the judgment. True it is that they may be observed by one who has never speculated about them, but it is no less true that their observance always gratifies the understanding with the fitness, the symmetry, and the congruity it produces. To write fine poetry requires intellectual faculties of the highest order, and among these, not the least important, is the faculty of reason. Poetry is the worst mask in the world behind which folly and stupidity could attempt to hide their features. Fitter, safer, and more congenial to them is the solemn discussion of unprofitable questions. Any obtuseness of apprehension or incapacity for drawing conclusions, which shows a deficiency or want of cultivation of the reasoning power, is sure to expose the unfortunate poet to contempt and ridicule.

But there is another point of view in which poetry may be said to address the understanding—I mean in the direct lessons of wisdom that it delivers. Remember that it does not concern itself with abstract reasonings, nor with any course of investigation that fatigues the mind. Nor is it merely didactic; but this does not prevent it from teaching truths which the mind instinctively acknowledges. The elements of moral truth are few and simple, but their combinations with human actions are as innumerable and diversified as the combinations of language. Thousands of inductions resulting from the application of great principles to human life and conduct lie, as it were, latent in our minds, which we have never drawn for ourselves, but which we admit the moment they are hinted at, and which, though not abstruse, are yet new. Nor are these of less value because they require no laborious research to discover them. The best riches of the earth are produced on its surface, and we need no reasoning to teach us the folly of a people who should leave its harvests ungathered to dig for its ores. The truths of which I have spoken, when possessing any peculiar force or beauty, are properly within the province of the art of which I am treating, and, when recommended by harmony of numbers, become poetry of the highest kind. Accordingly, they abound in the works of the most celebrated poets. When Shakespeare says of mercy,

> "it is twice blessed—
> It blesses him that gives and him that takes,"

does he not utter beautiful poetry as well as unquestionable truth? There are passages also in Milton of the same kind, which sink into the heart like the words of an oracle. For instance:

> "Evil into the mind of God or man
> May come and go so unapproved, and leave
> No spot or blame behind."

Take, also, the following example from Cowper, in which he bears witness against the guilt and folly of princes:

> "War is a game which, were their subjects wise,
> Kings should not play at. Nations would do well
> To extort their truncheons from the puny hands
> Of heroes whose infirm and baby minds
> Are gratified with mischief, and who spoil,
> Because men suffer it, their toy—the world."

I call these passages poetry, because the mind instantly acknowledges their truth and feels their force, and is moved and filled and elevated by them. Nor does poetry refuse to carry on a sort of process of reasoning by deducing one truth from another. Her demonstrations differ, however, from ordinary ones by requiring that each step should be in itself beautiful or striking, and that they all should carry the mind to the final conclusion without the consciousness of labor.

All the ways by which poetry affects the mind are open also to the prose-writer. All that kindles the imagination, all that excites emotion, all those moral truths that find an echo in our bosoms, are his property as well as that of the poet. It is true that in the ornaments of style the poet is allowed a greater license, but there are many excellent poems which are not distinguished by any liberal use of the figures of speech from prose writings composed with the same degree of excitement. What, then, is the ground of the distinction between prose and poetry? This is a question about which there has been much debate, but one which seems to me of easy solution to those who are not too ambitious of distinguishing themselves by profound researches into things already sufficiently clear. I suppose that poetry differs from prose, in the first place, by the employment of metrical harmony. It differs from it, in the next place, by excluding all that disgusts, all that tasks and fatigues the understanding, and all matters which are too trivial and common to excite any emotion whatever. Some of these, verse cannot raise into dignity; to others, verse is an encumbrance: they are, therefore, all unfit for poetry; put them into verse, and they are prose still.

A distinction has been attempted to be made between poetry and eloquence, and I acknowledge that there is one; but it seems to me that it consists solely in metrical arrangement. Eloquence is the poetry of prose; poetry is the eloquence of verse. The maxim that the poet is born and the orator made is a pretty antithesis, but a moment's reflection will convince us that one can become neither without natural gifts improved by cultivation. By eloquence I do not mean mere persuasiveness: there are many processes of argument that are not susceptible of eloquence, because they require close and painful attention. But by eloquence I understand those appeals to our moral perceptions that produce emotion as soon as they are uttered. It is in these that the orator is himself affected with the feelings he would communicate, that his eyes glisten, and his frame seems to dilate, and his voice acquires an unwonted melody, and his sentences arrange themselves into a sort of measure and harmony, and the listener is chained in involuntary and breathless attention. This is the very enthusiasm that is the parent of poetry. Let the same man go to his closet and clothe in numbers conceptions full of the same fire and spirit, and they will be poetry.

In conclusion, I will observe that the elements of poetry make a part of our natures, and that every individual is more or less a poet. In this "bank-note world," as it has been happily denominated, we sometimes meet with individuals who declare that they have no taste for poetry. But by their leave I will assert they are mistaken; they have it, although they may have never cultivated it. Is there any one among them who will confess himself insensible to the beauty of order or to the pleasure of variety— two principles, the happy mingling of which makes the perfection of poetic numbers? Is there any one whose eye is undelighted with beautiful forms and colors, whose ear is not charmed by sweet sounds, and who sees no loveliness in the returns of light and darkness, and the changes of the seasons? Is there any one for whom the works of Nature have no associations but such as relate to his animal wants? Is there any one to whom her great courses and operations show no majesty, to whom they impart no knowledge, and from whom they hide no secrets? Is there any one who is attached by no ties to his fellow-beings, who has no hopes for the future, and no memory of the past? Have they all forgotten the days and the friends of their childhood, and do they all shut their eyes to the advances of age? Have they nothing to desire and nothing to lament, and are their minds never darkened with the shadows of fear? Is it, in short, for these men that life has no pleasures and no pains, the grave no solemnity, and the world to come no mysteries? All these things are the sources of poetry, and they are not only part of ourselves, but of the universe, and will expire only with the last of the creatures of God.

WILLIAM CULLEN BRYANT

ON THE VALUE AND USES OF POETRY [1]
(1826)

In my last lecture I attempted to give some notion of the nature of poetry. In the present I intend to examine its value and uses, to inquire into its effects upon human welfare and happiness, and to consider some of the objections that have been urged against an indulgence in its delights. It is of no little consequence that we should satisfy ourselves of the tendency of a class of compositions which forms so large a part of the literature of all nations and times, so that, if it is found beneficial, we may estimate the degree in which it is worthy of encouragement; if pernicious, that we may bethink ourselves of a remedy. In what I have to say on this head I cannot by any means be certain that my partiality for the art will permit me to treat the subject with that coolness of judgment and freedom from prejudice which might be desirable. I only ask your frank assent to whatever may be true in the apology I shall make for it. It is not for my hands to hold the balance in which it is weighed.

I shall consider the influence of poetry on the welfare and happiness of our race in the three points of view in which I placed it in my last lecture—namely, as it addresses itself to the imagination, to the passions, and to the intelligence. As it respects the imagination, I believe the question may be soon and easily disposed of; for, so far as that faculty merely is excited by poetry without taking into account the effect produced on the passions, its activity is an amusement, an agreeable intellectual exercise— no more. A great deal of poetry, doubtless, has no higher object than this, and excites no stronger emotion than that complacency which proceeds from being agreeably employed. This is something in a world whose inhabitants are perpetually complaining of its labors, fatigues, and miseries. It has, however, a still higher value when regarded as in some sort the support of our innocence, for there is ever something pure and elevated in the creations of poetry. Its spirit is an aspiration after superhuman beauty and majesty, which, if it has no affinity with, has at least some likeness to, virtue. We cannot eradicate the imagination, but we may cultivate and regulate it; we cannot keep it from continual action, but we can give it a salutary direction. Certainly it is a noble occupation to shape the creations of the mind into perfect forms according to those laws which man learns from observing the works of his Maker.

[1] This was the second of a series of four lectures on poetry which Bryant delivered before the Athenaeum Society in New York in 1826. The lectures were published in *Prose Writings*, ed. by Parke Godwin (New York, 1884).

There are exercises of the imagination, it must be confessed, of too gross and sordid a nature to be comprised within the confines of any divine art—revellings of the fancy amid the images of base appetites and petty and ridiculous passions. These are the hidden sins of the heart, that lurk in its darkest recesses, where shame and the opinion of men cannot come to drive them out, and which pollute and debase it the more because they work in secrecy and at leisure. Is it not well, therefore, to substitute something better in the place of these, or, at least, to preoccupy the mind with what may prevent their entrance, and to create imaginative habits that may lead us to regard them with contempt and disgust? Poetry is well fitted for this office. It has no community with degradation, nor with things that degrade. It utters nothing that cannot be spoken without shame. Into the window of his bosom who relishes its pleasures, all the world may freely look. The tastes from which it springs, the sentiments it awakens, the objects on which it dwells with fondness, and which it labors to communicate to mankind, are related to the best and most universal sympathies of our nature.

In speaking of the influences of poetry on the happiness of mankind as connected with its effects on the imagination, I have been obliged to anticipate a part of what I had to say in regard to its power over the passions. These two topics, indeed, are closely connected; they may be separated in classification, but it is difficult to speculate upon them separately; for, as I observed in my last lecture, the excitement of the imagination awakens the feelings, and the excitement of the feelings kindles the imagination. It is the dominion of poetry over the feelings and passions of men that gives it its most important bearing upon the virtue and the welfare of society. Everything that affects our sensibilities is a part of our moral education, and the habit of being rightly affected by all the circumstances by which we are surrounded is the perfection of the moral character. The purest of all religions agrees with the soundest philosophy in referring the practice of virtue to the affections. Every good action has its correspondent emotion of the heart given to impel us to our duty, and to reward us for doing it. Now, it is admitted that poetry moves these springs of moral conduct powerfully; but it has sometimes been disputed whether it moves them in a salutary way, or whether it perverts them to evil. This question may be settled by inquiring what kind of sentiments it ordinarily tends to encourage. Has it any direct connection with vice? for, if it has not, the emotions it inspires must be innocent, and innocent emotions are emphatically healthful. Is there any poetry in cruelty? are the vivid descriptions of human and animal suffering it sets before us such as make us to rejoice in that suffering, or even such as leave us unmoved? Is there any poetry in injustice? Is there any poetry in fraud and treachery? The stronger the colors in which the former is painted, the more thoroughly do we detest it; the more forcibly the latter is presented to our minds, the more cordially do we despise it. Has poetry any kindred with covetousness and selfishness? or, rather, are they not a blight, and death itself, to that enthusiasm to which poetry owes its birth? On the other hand, do we not know that poetry delights in inspiring compassion, the parent of all kind offices? Does it not glory in sentiments of fortitude and magnanimity, the fountain of disinterested sacrifices? It cherishes patriotism, the incitement to vigorous toils endured for the welfare of communities. It luxuriates among the natural affections, the springs of all the gentle charities of domestic life. It has so refined and transformed and hallowed the love of the sexes that piety itself has sometimes taken the language of that passion to clothe its most fervent aspiration. It delights to infold not only the whole human race, but all the creatures of God, in the wide circle of its sympathies. It loves to point man to the beginning and end of his days, and to the short and swift passage between; to linger about the cradle and about the grave, and to lift the veil of another life. All moral lessons which are uninteresting and unimpressive, and, therefore, worthless, it leaves to prose; but all those which touch the heart, and are, therefore, important and effectual, are its own. One passion, indeed, is excited by poetry, about the worth of which moralists differ—the love of glory. I cannot stay to inquire into the moral quality of this passion; but this I will say, that, if it be not a virtue, it is frequently an excellent substitute for one, and becomes the motive of great and generous actions. At all events, a regard for the good opinion of our fellow-creatures is so interwoven with our natures, is of so much value to the order and welfare of society, does so much good and prevents so much evil, that I cannot bring myself to think ill of anything that encourages and directs it. None the less, poetry teaches us, also, lessons of profoundest humility. Reverence for that boundless goodness and infinite power which pervade and uphold all things that exist is one of its elements, and is the source of some of its loftiest meditations and deepest emotions. Much as we all glory in the power that is our own, the mind delights quite as naturally to raise its view to power that is above it, and to lose itself in the contemplation of strength and wisdom without bound. The poet who wrote atheist after his name knew not of what manner of spirit he was. He, too, paid a willing and undissembled homage to the Divinity. He called it Nature, but it was the Great First Cause whom we all worship, whatever its essence, and whatever its name.

One of the great recommendations of poetry in that point of view in which I am now considering it is, that it withdraws us from the despotism of many of those circumstances which mislead the moral judgment. It is dangerous to be absorbed continuously in our own immediate concerns. Self-interest is the most ingenious and persuasive of all the agents that deceive our consciences, while by means of it our unhappy and stubborn prejudices operate in their greatest force. But poetry lifts us to a sphere where self-interest cannot exist, and where the prejudices that perplex our every-day life can hardly enter. It restores us to our unperverted feelings, and leaves us at liberty to compare the issues of life with our unsophisticated notions of good and evil. We are taught to look at them as they are in themselves, and not as they may affect our present convenience, and then we are sent back to the world with our moral perceptions cleared and invigorated.

Among the most remarkable of the influences of poetry is the exhibition of those analogies and correspondences which it beholds between the things of the moral and of the natural world. I refer to its adorning and illustrating each by the other—infusing a moral sentiment into natural objects, and bringing images of visible beauty and majesty to heighten the effect of moral sentiment. Thus it binds into one all the passages of human life and connects all the varieties of human feeling with the works of creation. Any one who will make the experiment for himself will see how exceedingly difficult it is to pervert this process into an excitement of the bad passions of the soul. There are a purity and innocence in the appearances of Nature that make them refuse to be allied to the suggestions of guilty emotion. We discern no sin in her grander operations and vicissitudes, and no lessons of immorality are to be learned from them, as there are from the examples of the world. They cannot be studied without inducing the love, if they fail of giving the habit, of virtue. In so far as poetry directly addresses the understanding, it would be preposterous to apprehend any injurious consequences from it, which in my last lecture I said was by means of those moral truths which the mind instinctively acknowledges, and of which it immediately feels the force. The simplicity and clearness of the truths with which it deals prevent any mistake in regard to their meanings or tendencies. They strike the mind by their own brightness, and win its assent by their manifest and beautiful agreement with the lessons of our own experience. It belongs to more subtle and abstruse speculations than any into which poetry can enter, to unsettle the notions of men respecting right and wrong. Ingenious casuistry and labored sophistry may confuse and puzzle the understanding, and lead it through their own darkness to false conclusions; but poetry abhors their assistance. It may be said, however, that the power which poetry exercises over the mind is liable to abuse. It is so, undoubtedly, like all power. Its influences may be, and unquestionably have been, perverted; but my aim has been to show that they are beneficial in their nature, intrinsically good, and, if so, not to be rejected because accidentally mischievous. To confound the abuses of a thing with the thing itself is to sophisticate. Why do not they who set up this objection to poetry talk in the same manner of the common and universal sources of human enjoyment? When you tell them of the element which diffuses comfort through our habitations, when the earth and the air are frozen, and enables us to support life through the inclemency of the season, do they deny its utility, or endeavor to convince you of your error, by pointing you to dwellings laid waste by conflagrations, or by telling you tales of martyrs roasted at the stake? When you speak of the beneficent influences of the sun, why do they not meet you with the scorched and barren deserts of Africa, with diseases born under his heat, the plague of Europe, and the yellow fever of America? When you are simple enough to rejoice in the kind provision of rains for the refreshment of the earth and the growth of its plants, why do they not silence you with stories of harvest and cattle and human beings swept away by inundations? Well, when we are persuaded to part with our hearth-fires, and to refuse the fruits which sunshine and showers have ripened for our sustenance, let us give up poetry. In the mean time, instead of putting it by with scorn, let us cherish it as we do the other gifts of Heaven.

In those works which have met with merited reprehension on account of their pernicious tendencies, it is not of the poetry that the friends of virtue have reason to complain; it is of the foul ingredients mingled with it; it is of the leaven of corruption interspersed with what is in itself pure and innocent. The elements of poetry are the beautiful and noble in the creation and in man's nature; and, so far as anything vicious is mingled with these, the compound is incongruous. Indeed, I am apt to think that those poems which are objectionable on account of their immoral character have won for their authors the reputation of greater powers than they really possessed. The passages of real beauty and excellence which they contain appear the more beautiful and excellent from the contrast they offer to the grossness by which they are surrounded. Those bursts of true feeling, those fine moral touches, those apprehensions of the glory and beauty of the universe, and the language it speaks to the heart of man, delight us there by a certain unexpectedness. Their innocence appears more spotless, their pathos more touching, because such qualities refresh the mind in the midst of its horror and disgust.

The heroic poems of the ancients are said to inspire a sanguinary spirit, the love of war, and an indifference to the miseries of which war is the cause; but I cannot believe that they produce this effect to the extent which many suppose, and, so far as they do produce it, it is from an imperfection in the poetry. Poetry that is unfeeling and indifferent to suffering is no poetry at all. It is but justice, however, to these writers to say that, if they do encourage a fondness for war, it is rather by what they leave undone than what they do. War, like all other situations of danger and of change, calls forth the exertion of admirable intellectual qualities and great virtues, and it is only by dwelling on these, and keeping out of sight the sufferings and sorrows, and all the crimes and evils that follow in its train, that it has its glory in the eyes of men. We do not admire the heroes of Homer because they shed blood and cut throats—any highwayman may do this—but we admire them for the greatness of mind they show in the dreadful scenes in which they are engaged. We reverence that hardy spirit that faces danger without shrinking, and voluntarily exposes the body to pain, for it is a modification of that noble principle which gives birth to all virtue and all greatness—the endurance of present toils and submission to present sacrifices, in order to insure great good for the future. We love, also, to contemplate strong and skilful action of the body, which in the personal combats he describes is prompted and ordered by strong action of the mind, by intense emotion, and clear sagacity. But the purer and gentler spirit of the Father of Verse and the humanizing influences of poetry show themselves strongly in his great works, and set him far in advance of the age in which he wrote. The poet often stops to lament those whom his favorite heroes slew without remorse—old men cut off in the honors of a blameless age, young men in the bloom of their years and the promise of their virtues—and to sympathize with the unavailing and unappeasable sorrow of those to whom they were dear. Nay, it would seem that his mind was ever haunted with a secret sentiment of the emptiness of the very glory he was celebrating, for not only the Odyssey, but the Iliad itself, is full of allusions to the final fate of those who earned renown at the siege of Troy, to their wanderings, their hardships, their domestic calamities, and their violent and unhonored deaths.

I shall close this lecture with an extract from an eloquent writer, who has replied to some other objections that have been raised against poetry in such a manner that I should not feel myself justified in using any other words than his own: "It is objected to poetry," he says, "that it gives wrong views and excites false expectations of life, peoples the mind with shadows and illusions, and builds up imaginations on ruins of wisdom. That there is a wisdom against which poetry wars—the wisdom of the senses, which makes physical comfort the chief good, and wealth the chief interest of life—is not denied; nor can it be denied, the least service which poetry renders to mankind, that it redeems them from the thraldom of this earth-born prudence. But, passing over this topic, it may be observed that the complaint against poetry as abounding in illusion and deception is in the main groundless. In many poems there is more of truth than in many histories and philosophic theories. The fictions of genius are often the vehicles of the sublimest verities, and its flashes often open new regions of thought, and throw new light on the mysteries of our being. In poetry the letter is falsehood, but the spirit is often the profoundest wisdom. And, if truth thus dwells in the boldest fictions of the poet, much more may it be expected in his delineations of life; for the present life, which is the first stage of the immortal mind, abounds in the materials of poetry, and it is the high office of the bard to detect this divine element among the grosser labors and pleasures of our earthly being. The present life is not wholly prosaic, precise, tame, and finite. To the gifted eye it abounds in the poetic. The affections, which spread beyond ourselves and stretch far into futurity; the workings of mighty passions, which seem to arm the soul with an almost superhuman energy; the innocent and irrepressible joy of infancy; the bloom and buoyancy and dazzling hopes of youth; the throbbings of the heart when it first wakes to love, and dreams of a happiness too vast for earth; woman, with her beauty and grace and gentleness and freshness of feeling and depth of affection, and her blushes of purity, and the tones and looks which only a mother's heart can inspire—these are all poetical. It is not true that the poet paints a life which does not exist. He only extracts and concentrates, as it were, life's ethereal essence, arrests and condenses its volatile fragrance, brings together its scattered beauties, and prolongs its more refined but evanescent joys; and in this he does well; for it is good to feel that life is not wholly usurped by cares for subsistence and physical gratification, but admits, in measures which may be indefinitely enlarged, sentiments and delights worthy of a higher being. This power of poetry to refine our views of life and happiness is more and more needed as society advances. It is needed to withstand the encroachments of heartless and artificial manners which make civilization so tame and uninteresting. It is needed to counteract the tendency of physical science, which—being now sought, not, as formerly, for intellectual gratification, but for multiplying bodily comforts—requires a new development of imagination, taste, and poetry to preserve men from sinking into an earthly, material, epicurean life." *

* William Ellery Channing. [*Godwin's note.*] [Parke Godwin edited the *Prose Writings* of Bryant in 1884, the first publication of the lectures on poetry.]

WILLIAM E. CHANNING

REMARKS ON NATIONAL LITERATURE [1]
(1830)

[Review of a Discourse concerning the Influence of America on the Mind; being the Annual Oration delivered before the American Philosophical Society, at the University in Philadelphia, October 18, 1823. By C. J. Ingersoll.] [2]

WE SHALL use the work prefixed to this article as ministers are sometimes said to use their texts. We shall make it a point to start from,—not the subject of our remarks. Our purpose is to treat of the importance and means of a National Literature. The topic seems to us a great one, and to have intimate connections with morals and religion, as well as with all our public interests. Our views will be given with great freedom; and if they serve no other purpose than to recommend the subject to more general attention, one of our principal objects will be accomplished.

We begin with stating what we mean by national literature. We mean the expression of a nation's mind in writing. We mean the production among a people of important works in philosophy, and in the departments of imagination and taste. We mean the contributions of new truths to the stock of human knowledge. We mean the thoughts of profound and original minds, elaborated by the toil of composition, and fixed and made immortal in books. We mean the manifestation of a nation's intellect in the only forms by which it can multiply itself at home, and send itself abroad. We mean that a nation shall take a place, by its authors, among the lights of the world. It will be seen that we include under literature all the writings of superior minds, be the subjects what they may. We are aware that the term is often confined to compositions which relate to human nature and human life; that it is not generally extended to physical science; that mind, not matter, is regarded as its main subject and sphere. But the worlds of matter and mind are too intimately connected to admit of exact partition. All the objects of human thought flow into one another. Moral and physical truths have many bonds and analogies, and, whilst the former are the chosen and noblest themes of literature, we are not anxious to divorce them from the latter, or to shut them up in a separate department. The expression of superior mind in writing we regard, then, as a nation's

---

[1] This essay was first published in the *Christian Examiner* in 1830 as "The Importance and Means of a National Literature." The title and text printed here are from Channing's *Complete Works* (Boston, 1849).

[2] Charles Jared Ingersoll (1782–1862) was a prominent Philadelphia lawyer, author, and congressman. In this *Discourse* he advocated a literature that would satisfy the practical and utilitarian American character.

literature. We regard its gifted men, whether devoted to the exact sciences, to mental and ethical philosophy, to history and legislation, or to fiction and poetry, as forming a noble intellectual brotherhood; and it is for the purpose of quickening all to join their labors for the public good that we offer the present plea in behalf of a national literature.

To show the importance which we attach to the subject, we begin with some remarks on what we deem the distinction which a nation should most earnestly covet. We believe that more distinct apprehensions on this point are needed, and that, for want of them, the work of improvement is carried on with less energy, consistency, and wisdom, than may and should be brought to bear upon it. The great distinction of a country, then, is, that it produces superior men. Its natural advantages are not to be disdained. But they are of secondary importance. No matter what races of animals a country breeds, the great question is, Does it breed a noble race of men? No matter what its soil may be, the great question is, How far is it prolific of moral and intellectual power? No matter how stern its climate is, if it nourish force of thought and virtuous purpose. These are the products by which a country is to be tried, and institutions have value only by the impulse which they give to the mind. It has sometimes been said that the noblest men grow where nothing else will grow. This we do not believe, for mind is not the creature of climate or soil. But were it true, we should say that it were better to live among rocks and sands than in the most genial and productive region on the face of the earth.

As yet, the great distinction of a nation on which we have insisted has been scarcely recognized. The idea of forming a superior race of men has entered little into schemes of policy. Invention and effort have been expended on matter much more than on mind. Lofty piles have been reared; the earth has groaned under pyramids and palaces. The thought of building up a nobler order of intellect and character has hardly crossed the most adventurous statesman. We beg that we may not be misapprehended. We offer these remarks to correct what we deem a disproportioned attention to physical good, and not at all to condemn the expenditure of ingenuity and strength on the outward world. There is a harmony between all our great interests, between inward and outward improvements; and by establishing among them a wise order, all will be secured. We have no desire to shut up man in his own spiritual nature. The mind was made to act on matter, and it grows by expressing itself in material forms. We believe, too, that in proportion as it shall gain intellectual and moral power, it will exert itself with increased energy and delight on the outward creation; will pour itself forth more freely in useful and ornamental arts; will rear more magnificent structures, and will call forth new beauties in nature. An intelligent and resolute spirit in a community perpetually extends its triumphs over matter. It can even subject to itself the most unpromising region. Holland, diked from the ocean,—Venice, rising amidst the waves,—and New England, bleak and rockbound New England, converted by a few generations from a wilderness into smiling fields and opulent cities,—point us to the mind as the great source of physical good, and teach us that, in making the culture of man our highest end, we shall not retard but advance the cultivation of nature.

The question which we most solicitously ask about this country is, what race of men it is likely to produce. We consider its liberty of value only as far as it favors the growth of men. What is liberty? The removal of restraint from human powers. Its benefit is, that it opens new fields for action and a wider range for the mind. The only freedom worth possessing is that which gives enlargement to a people's energy, intellect, and virtues. The savage makes his boast of freedom. But what is its worth? Free as he is, he continues for ages in the same ignorance, leads the same comfortless life, sees the same untamed wilderness spread around him. He is indeed free from what he calls the yoke of civil institutions. But other and worse chains bind him. The very privation of civil government is in effect a chain; for, by withholding protection from property, it virtually shackles the arm of industry, and forbids exertion for the melioration of his lot. Progress, the growth of power, is the end and boon of liberty; and, without this, a people may have the name, but want the substance and spirit of freedom.

We are the more earnest in enlarging on these views, because we feel that our attachment to our country must be very much proportioned to what we deem its tendency to form a generous race of men. We pretend not to have thrown off national feeling; but we have some stronger feelings. We love our country much, but mankind more. As men and Christians, our first desire is to see the improvement of human nature. We desire to see the soul of man wiser, firmer, nobler, more conscious of its imperishable treasures, more beneficent and powerful, more alive to its connection with God, more able to use pleasure and prosperity aright, and more victorious over poverty, adversity, and pain. In our survey of our own and other countries, the great question which comes to us is this, Where and under what institutions are men most likely to advance? Where are the soundest minds and the purest hearts formed? What nation possesses, in its history, its traditions, its government, its religion, its manners, its pursuits, its relations to other communities, and especially in its private and public means of education, the instruments and pledges of a more resolute virtue and devotion to truth, than we now witness? Such a nation, be it where it may, will engage our warmest interest. We love our country, but not blindly. In all nations we recognize one great family, and our chief wish for our native land is, that it may take the first rank among the lights and benefactors of the human race.

These views will explain the vast importance which we attach to a national literature. By this, as we have said, we understand the expression of a nation's mind in writing. It is the action of the most gifted understandings on the community. It throws into circulation through a wide sphere the most quickening and beautiful thoughts which have grown up in men of laborious study or creative genius. It is a much higher work than the communication of a gifted intellect in discourse. It is the mind giving to multitudes, whom no voice can reach, its compressed and selected thoughts in the most lucid order and attractive forms which it is capable of inventing. In other words, literature is the concentration of intellect for the purpose of spreading itself abroad and multiplying its energy.

Such being the nature of literature, it is plainly among the most powerful methods of exalting the character of a nation, of forming a better race of men; in truth, we apprehend that it may claim the first rank among the means of improvement. We know nothing so fitted to the advancement of society as to bring its higher minds to bear upon the multitude; as to establish close connections between the more or less gifted; as to spread far and wide the light which springs up in meditative, profound, and sublime understandings. It is the ordinance of God, and one of his most benevolent laws, that the human race should be carried forward by impulses which originate in a few minds, perhaps in an individual; and in this way the most interesting relations and dependencies of life are framed. When a great truth is to be revealed, it does not flash at once on the race, but dawns and brightens on a superior understanding, from which it is to emanate and to illumine future ages. On the faithfulness of great minds to this awful function, the progress and happiness of men chiefly depend. The most illustrious benefactors of the race have been men who, having risen to great truths, have held them as a sacred trust for their kind, and have borne witness to them amid general darkness, under scorn and persecution, perhaps in the face of death. Such men, indeed, have not always made contributions to literature, for their condition has not allowed them to be authors; but we owe the transmission, perpetuity, and immortal power of their new and high thoughts to kindred spirits, which have concentrated and fixed them in books.

The quickening influences of literature need not be urged on those who are familiar with the history of modern Europe, and who of course know the spring given to the human mind by the revival of ancient learning. Through their writings, the great men of antiquity have exercised a sovereignty over these later ages not enjoyed in their own. It is more important to observe that the influence of literature is perpetually increasing; for, through the press and the spread of education, its sphere is indefinitely enlarged. Reading, once the privilege of a few, is now the occupation of multitudes, and is to become one of the chief gratifications of all. Books penetrate everywhere, and some of the works of genius find their way to obscure dwellings which, a little while ago, seemed barred against all intellectual light. Writing is now the mightiest instrument on earth. Through this the mind has acquired a kind of omnipresence. To literature we then look, as the chief means of forming a better race of human beings. To superior minds, which may act through this, we look for the impulses by which their country is to be carried forward. We would teach them that they are the depositaries of the highest power on earth, and that on them the best hopes of society rest.

We are aware that some may think that we are exalting intellectual above moral and religious influence. They may tell us that the teaching of moral and religious truth, not by philosophers and boasters of wisdom, but by the comparatively weak and foolish, is the great means of renovating the world. This truth we indeed regard as "the power of God unto salvation." But let none imagine that its chosen temple is an uncultivated mind, and that it selects, as its chief organs, the lips of the unlearned. Religious and moral truth is indeed appointed to carry forward mankind; but not as conceived and expounded by narrow minds, not as darkened by the ignorant, not as debased by the superstitious, not as subtilized by the visionary, not as thundered out by the intolerant fanatic, not as turned into a drivelling cant by the hypocrite. Like all other truths, it requires for its full reception and powerful communication a free and vigorous intellect. Indeed, its grandeur and infinite connections demand a more earnest and various use of our faculties than any other subject. As a single illustration of this remark, we may observe that all moral and religious truth may be reduced to one great and central thought, perfection of mind,—a thought which comprehends all that is glorious in the divine nature, and which reveals to us the end and happiness of our own existence. This perfection has as yet only dawned on the most gifted human beings, and the great purpose of our present and future existence is to enlarge our conceptions of it without end, and to embody and make them manifest in character and life. And is this sublime thought to grow within us, to refine itself from error and impure mixture, to receive perpetual accessions of brightness from the study of God, man, and nature, and especially to be communicated powerfully to others, without the vigorous exertion of our our intellectual nature? Religion has been wronged by nothing more than by being separated from intellect; than by being removed from the province of reason and free research into that of mystery and authority, of impulse and feeling. Hence it is that the prevalent forms or exhibitions of Christianity are comparatively inert, and that most which is written on the subject is of little or no worth. Christianity was given, not to contradict and degrade the rational nature, but to call it forth, to enlarge its range and its powers. It admits of endless development. It is the last truth which should remain stationary. It ought to be so explored and so expressed as to take the highest place in a nation's literature, as to exalt and purify all other literature. From these remarks it will be seen that the efficacy which we have ascribed to literary or intellectual influence in the work of human improvement, is consistent with the supreme importance of moral and religious truth.

If we have succeeded in conveying the impressions which we have aimed to make, our readers are now prepared to inquire with interest into the condition and prospects of literature among ourselves. Do we possess, indeed, what may be called a national literature? Have we produced eminent writers in the various departments of intellectual effort? Are our chief resources of instruction and literary enjoyment furnished from ourselves? We regret that the reply to these questions is so obvious. The few standard works which we have produced, and which promise to live, can hardly, by any courtesy, be denominated a national literature. On this point, if marks and proofs of our real conditions were needed, we should find them in the current apologies for our deficiencies. Our writers are accustomed to plead in our excuse our youth, the necessities of a newly settled country, and the direction of our best talents to practical life. Be the pleas sufficient or not, one thing they prove, and that is, our consciousness of having failed to make important contributions to the interests of the intellect. We have few names to place by the side of the great names in science and literature on the other side of the ocean. We want those lights which make a country conspicuous at a distance. Let it not be said that European envy denies our just claims. In an age like this, when the literary world forms a great family, and the products of mind are circulated more rapidly than those of machinery, it is a nation's own fault if its name be not pronounced with honor beyond itself. We have ourselves heard, and delighted to hear, beyond the Alps, our country designated as the land of Franklin. This name had scaled that mighty barrier, and made us known where our institutions and modes of life were hardly better understood than those of the natives of our forests.

We are accustomed to console ourselves for the absence of a commanding literature by urging our superiority to other nations in our institutions for the diffusion of elementary knowledge through all classes of the community. We have here just cause for boasting, though perhaps less than we imagine. That there are gross deficiencies in our common schools, and that the amount of knowledge which they communicate, when compared with the time spent in its acquisition, is lamentably small, the community begin to feel. There is a crying need for a higher and more quickening kind of instruction than the laboring part of society have yet received, and we rejoice that the cry begins to be heard. But, allowing our elementary institutions to be ever so perfect, we confess that they do not satisfy us. We want something more. A dead level of intellect, even if it should rise above what is common in other nations, would not answer our wishes and hopes for our country. We want great minds to be formed among us,— minds which shall be felt afar, and through which we may act on the world. We want the human intellect to do its utmost here. We want this people to obtain a claim on the gratitude of the human race, by adding strength to the foundation, and fulness and splendor to the development, of moral and religious truth; by originality of thought, by discoveries of science, and by contributions to the refining pleasures of taste and imagination.

With these views, we do and must lament that, however we surpass other nations in providing for, and spreading elementary instruction, we fall behind many in provision for the liberal training of the intellect, for forming great scholars, for communicating that profound knowledge, and that thirst for higher truths, which can alone originate a commanding literature. The truth ought to be known. There is among us much superficial knowledge, but little severe, persevering research; little of that consuming passion for new truth which makes outward things worthless; little resolute devotion to a high intellectual culture. There is nowhere a literary atmosphere, or such an accumulation of literary influence, as determines the whole strength of the mind to its own enlargement, and to the manifestation of itself in enduring forms. Few among us can be said to have followed out any great subject of thought patiently, laboriously, so as to know thoroughly what others have discovered and taught concerning it, and thus to occupy a ground from which new views may be gained. Of course, exceptions are to be found. This country has produced original and profound thinkers. We have named Franklin, and we may name Edwards, one of the greatest men of his age, though unhappily his mind was lost, in a great degree, to literature, and we fear to religion, by vassalage to a false theology. His work on the Will throws, indeed, no light on human nature, and, notwithstanding the nobleness of the subject, gives no great or elevated thoughts; but, as a specimen of logical acuteness and controversial power, it certainly ranks in the very highest class of metaphysical writings.[3] We might also name living authors who do honor to their country. Still, we may say we chiefly prize what has been done among us as a promise of higher and more extensive effort. Patriotism, as well as virtue, forbids us to burn incense to national vanity. The truth should be seen and felt. In an age of great intellectual activity, we rely chiefly for intellectual excitement and enjoyment on foreign minds; nor is our own mind felt abroad. Whilst clamoring against dependence on European manufactures, we contentedly rely on Europe for the nobler and more important fabrics of the intellect. We boast of our political institutions, and receive our chief teachings, books, impressions, from the school of monarchy. True, we labor under disadvantages. But, if our liberty deserves the praise which it receives, it is more than a balance for these. We believe that it is. We believe that it does open to us an indefinite intellectual progress. Did we not so regard it, we should value it little. If hereditary governments minister most to the growth of the mind, it were better to restore them than to cling to a barren freedom. Let us not expose liberty to this reproach. Let us prove, by more generous provisions for the diffusion of elementary knowledge, for the training of great minds, and for the joint culture of the moral and intellectual powers, that we are more and more instructed by freedom in the worth and greatness of human nature, and in the obligation of contributing to its strength and glory.

We have spoken of the condition of our literature. We now proceed to the consideration of the causes which obstruct its advancement; and we are immediately struck by one so prevalent as to deserve distinct notice. We refer to the common doctrine that we need, in this country, useful knowledge, rather than profound, extensive, and elegant literature, and that this last, if we covet it, may be imported from abroad in such variety and abundance as to save us the necessity of producing it among ourselves. How far are these opinions just? This question we purpose to answer.

That useful knowledge should receive our first and chief care we mean not to dispute. But in our views of utility we may differ from some who take this position. There are those who confine this term to the necessaries

---

[3] Jonathan Edwards (1703-1758), one of the greatest of the Puritan divines, published his *A Careful and Strict Enquiry Into . . . Freedom of Will . . .* in 1754.

and comforts of life, and to the means of producing them. And is it true that we need no knowledge but that which clothes and feeds us? Is it true that all studies may be dispensed with but such as teach us to act on matter, and to turn it to our use? Happily, human nature is too stubborn to yield to this narrow utility. It is interesting to observe how the very mechanical arts, which are especially designed to minister to the necessities and comforts of life, are perpetually passing these limits,—how they disdain to stop at mere convenience. A large and increasing proportion of mechanical labor is given to the gratification of an elegant taste. How simple would be the art of building, if it limited itself to the construction of a comfortable shelter! How many ships should we dismantle, and how many busy trades put to rest, were dress and furniture reduced to the standard of convenience! This "utility" would work a great change in town and country, would level to the dust the wonders of architecture, would annihilate the fine arts, and blot out innumerable beauties which the hand of taste has spread over the face of the earth. Happily, human nature is too strong for the utilitarian. It cannot satisfy itself with the convenient. No passion unfolds itself sooner than the love of the ornamental. The savage decorates his person, and the child is more struck with the beauty than the uses of its raiment. So far from limiting ourselves to convenient food and raiment, we enjoy but little a repast which is not arranged with some degree of order and taste; and a man who should consult comfort alone in his wardrobe, would find himself an unwelcome guest in circles which he would very reluctantly forego. We are aware that the propensity to which we have referred often breaks out in extravagance and ruinous luxury. We know that the love of ornament is often vitiated by vanity, and that, when so perverted, it impairs, sometimes destroys, the soundness and simplicity of the mind and the relish for true glory. Still it teaches, even in its excesses, that the idea of beauty is an indestructible principle of our nature, and this single truth is enough to put us on our guard against vulgar notions of utility.

We have said that we prize, as highly as any, useful knowledge. But by this we mean knowledge which answers and ministers to our complex and various nature; we mean that which is useful, not only to the animal man, but to the intellectual, moral, and religious man,—useful to a being of spiritual faculties, whose happiness is to be found in their free and harmonious exercise. We grant that there is primary necessity for that information and skill by which subsistence is earned and life is preserved; for it is plain that we must live in order to act and improve. But life is the means; action and improvement the end; and who will deny that the noblest utility belongs to that knowledge by which the chief purpose of our creation is accomplished? According to these views, a people should honor and cultivate, as unspeakably useful, that literature which corresponds to, and calls forth, the highest faculties; which expresses and communicates energy of thought, fruitfulness of invention, force of moral purpose, a thirst for the true, and a delight in the beautiful. According to these views, we attach special importance to those branches of literature which relate to human nature, and which give it a consciousness of its own powers. History has a noble use, for it shows us human beings in various and opposite conditions, in their strength and weakness, in their progress and relapses, and thus reveals the causes and means by which the happiness and virtue of the race may be enlarged. Poetry is useful, by touching deep springs in the human soul; by giving voice to its more delicate feelings; by breathing out, and making more intelligible, the sympathy which subsists between the mind and the outward universe; by creating beautiful forms of manifestations for great moral truths. Above all, that higher philosophy, which treats of the intellectual and moral constitution of man, of the foundation of knowledge, of duty, of perfection, of our relations to the spiritual world, and especially to God; this has a usefulness so peculiar as to throw other departments of knowledge into obscurity; and a people among whom this does not find honor has little ground to boast of its superiority to uncivilized tribes. It will be seen from these remarks that utility, with us, has a broad meaning. In truth, we are slow to condemn as useless any researches or discoveries of original and strong minds, even when we discern in them no bearing on any interests of mankind; for all truth is of a prolific nature, and has connections not immediately perceived; and it may be that what we call vain speculations may, at no distant period, link themselves with some new facts or theories, and guide a profound thinker to the most important results. The ancient mathematician, when absorbed in solitary thought, little imagined that his theorems, after the lapse of ages, were to be applied by the mind of Newton to the solution of the mysteries of the universe, and not only to guide the astronomer through the heavens, but the navigator through the pathless ocean. For ourselves, we incline to hope much from truths which are particularly decried as useless; for the noblest and most useful truth is of an abstract or universal nature; and yet the abstract, though susceptible of infinite application, is generally, as we know, opposed to the practical.

We maintain that a people which has any serious purpose of taking a place among improved communities, should studiously promote within itself every variety of intellectual exertion. It should resolve strenuously to be surpassed by none. It should feel that mind is the creative power through which all the resources of nature are to be turned to account, and by which a people is to spread its influence, and establish the noblest form of empire. It should train within itself men able to understand and to use whatever is thought and discovered over the whole earth. The whole mass of human knowledge should exist among a people, not in neglected libraries, but in its higher minds. Among its most cherished institutions should be those which will ensure to it ripe scholars, explorers of ancient learning, profound historians and mathematicians, intellectual laborers devoted to physical and moral science, and to the creation of a refined and beautiful literature.

Let us not be misunderstood. We have no desire to rear in our country a race of pedants, of solemn triflers, of laborious commentators on the mysteries of a Greek accent or a rusty coin. We would have men explore antiquity, not to bury themselves in its dust, but to learn its spirit, and so to commune with its superior minds as to accumulate on the present age the influences of whatever was great and wise in former times. What we want is, that those among us whom God has gifted to comprehend whatever is now known, and to rise to new truths, may find aids and institutions to fit them for their high calling, and may become at once springs of a higher intellectual life to their own country, and joint workers with the great of all nations and times in carrying forward their race.

We know that it will be said that foreign scholars, bred under institutions which this country cannot support, may do our intellectual work, and send us books and learning to meet our wants. To this we have much to answer. In the first place, we reply that, to avail ourselves of the higher literature of other nations, we must place ourselves on a level with them. The products of foreign machinery we can use without any portion of the skill that produced them. But works of taste and genius, and profound investigations of philosophy, can only be estimated and enjoyed through a culture and power corresponding to that from which they sprung.

In the next place, we maintain that it is an immense gain to a people to have in its own bosom, among its own sons, men of distinguished intellect. Such men give a spring and life to a community by their presence, their society, their fame; and, what deserves remark, such men are nowhere so felt as in a republic like our own; for here the different classes of society flow together and act powerfully on each other, and a free communication, elsewhere unknown, is established between the gifted few and the many. It is one of the many good fruits of liberty that it increases the diffusiveness of intellect; and accordingly a free country is, above all others, false to itself in withholding from its superior minds the means of enlargement.

We next observe—and we think the observation important—that the facility with which we receive the literature of foreign countries, instead of being a reason for neglecting our own, is a strong motive for its cultivation. We mean not to be paradoxical, but we believe that it would be better to admit no books from abroad than to make them substitutes for our own intellectual activity. The more we receive from other countries, the greater the need of an original literature. A people into whose minds the thoughts of foreigners are poured perpetually, needs an energy within itself to resist, to modify this mighty influence, and, without it, will inevitably sink under the worst bondage, will become intellectually tame and enslaved. We have certainly no desire to complete our restrictive system by adding to it a literary non-intercourse law. We rejoice in the increasing intellectual connection between this country and the Old World; but sooner would we rupture it than see our country sitting passively at the feet of foreign teachers. It were better to have no literature than form ourselves unresistingly on a foreign one. The true sovereigns of a country are those who determine its mind, its modes of thinking, its tastes, its principles; and we cannot consent to lodge this sovereignty in the hands of strangers. A country, like an individual, has dignity and power only in proportion as it is self-formed. There is a great stir to secure to ourselves the manufacturing of our own clothing. We say, let others spin and weave for us, but let them not think for us. A people whose government and laws are nothing but the embodying of public opinion, should jealously guard this opinion against foreign dictation. We need a literature to counteract, and to use wisely the literature which we import. We need an inward power proportionate to that which is exerted on us, as the means of self-subsistence. It is particularly true of a people whose institutions demand for their support a free and bold spirit, that they should be able to subject to a manly and independent criticism whatever comes from abroad. These views seem to us to deserve serious attention. We are more and more a reading people. Books are already among the most powerful influences here. The question is, shall Europe, through these, fashion us after its pleasure? Shall America be only an echo of what is thought and written under the aristocracies beyond the ocean?

Another view of the subject is this. A foreign literature will always, in a measure, be foreign. It has sprung from the soul of another people, which, however like, is still not our own soul. Every people has much in its own character and feelings which can only be embodied by its own writers, and which, when transfused through literature, makes it touching and true, like the voice of our earliest friend.

We now proceed to an argument in favor of native literature, which, if less obvious, is, we believe, not less sound than those now already adduced. We have hitherto spoken of literature as the expression, the communication, of the higher minds in a community. We now add that it does much more than is commonly supposed to *form* such minds, so that, without it, a people wants one of the chief means of educating or perfecting talent and genius. One of the great laws of our nature, and a law singularly important to social beings, is, that the intellect enlarges and strengthens itself by expressing worthily its best views. In this, as in other respects, it is more blessed to give than to receive. Superior minds are formed, not merely by solitary thought, but almost as much by communication. Great thoughts are never fully possessed till he who has conceived them has given them fit utterance. One of the noblest and most invigorating labors of genius is to clothe its conceptions in clear and glorious forms, to give them existence in other souls. Thus literature creates, as well as manifests, intellectual power, and, without it, the highest minds will never be summoned to the most invigorating action.

We doubt whether a man ever brings his faculties to bear with their whole force on a subject until he writes upon it for the instruction or gratification of others. To place it clearly before others, he feels the necessity of viewing it more vividly himself. By attempting to seize his thoughts, and fix them in an enduring form, he finds them vague and unsatisfactory to a degree which he did not suspect, and toils for a precision and harmony of views of which he had never before felt the need. He places his subject in new lights,—submits it to a searching analysis, compares and connects with it his various knowledge, seeks for it new illustrations and analogies, weighs objections, and through these processes often arrives at higher truths than he at first aimed to illustrate. Dim conceptions grow bright. Glorious thoughts, which had darted as meteors through the mind, are arrested, and gradually shine with a sunlike splendor, with prolific energy, on the intellect and heart. It is one of the chief distinctions of a great mind that it is prone to rush into twilight regions, and to catch faint glimmerings of distant and unbounded prospects; and nothing perhaps aids it more to pierce the shadows which surround it than the labor to unfold to other minds the indistinct conceptions which have dawned on its own. Even where composition yields no such fruits, it is still a great intellectual help. It always favors comprehensive and systematical views. The laborious distribution of a great subject, so as to assign to each part or topic its just position and due proportion, is singularly fitted to give compass and persevering force of thought.

If we confine ourselves simply to the consideration of style, we shall have reason to think that a people among whom this is neglected wants one important intellectual aid. In this, great power is exerted, and by exertion increased. To the multitude, indeed, language seems so natural an instrument, that to use it with clearness and energy seems no great effort. It is framed, they think, to the writer's hand, and so continually employed as to need little thought or skill. But in nothing is the creative power of a gifted writer seen more than in his style. True, his words may be found in the dictionary. But there they lie disjointed and dead. What a wonderful life does he breathe into them by compacting them into his sentences! Perhaps he uses no term which has not yet been hackneyed by ordinary writers; and yet with these vulgar materials what miracles does he achieve! What a world of thought does he condense into a phrase! By new combinations of common words, what delicate hues or what a blaze of light does he pour over his subject! Power of style depends very little on the structure of copiousness of the language which the writer of genius employs, but chiefly, if not wholly, on his own mind. The words, arranged in his dictionary, are no more fitted to depict his thoughts than the block of marble in the sculptor's shop to show forth the conceptions which are dawning in his mind. Both are inert materials. The power which pervades them comes from the soul; and the same creative energy is manifested in the production of a noble style as in extracting beautiful forms from lifeless stone. How unfaithful, then, is a nation to its own intellect, in which grace and force of style receive no culture!

The remarks now made on the importance of literature as a means of educating talent and genius, we are aware, do not apply equally to all subjects or kinds of knowledge. In the exact or physical sciences, a man may acquire much without composition, and may make discoveries without registering them. Even here, however, we believe that, by a systematic development of his views in a luminous style, he will bring great aid to his own faculties, as well as to others'. It is on the vast subjects of morals and human nature that the mind especially strengthens itself by elaborate composition; and these, let it be remembered, form the staple of the highest literature. Moral truth, under which we include every thing relating to mind and character, is of a refined and subtile, as well as elevated nature, and requires the joint and full exercise of discrimination, invention, imagination, and sensibility, to give it effectual utterance. A writer who would make it visible and powerful, must strive to join an austere logic to a fervent eloquence; must place it in various lights; must create for it interesting forms; must wed it to beauty; must illuminate it by similitudes and contrasts; must show its correspondence with the outward world; perhaps must frame for it a vast machinery of fiction. How invigorating are these efforts! Yet it is only in writing, in elaborate composition, that they are deliberately called forth and sustained, and without literature they would almost cease. It may be said of many truths, that greater intellectual energy is required to express them with effect than to conceive them; so that a nation which does not encourage this expression impoverishes so far its own mind. Take, for example, Shakspeare's Hamlet. This is a development of a singularly interesting view of human nature. It shows us a mind to which life is a burden; in which the powers of meditation and feeling are disproportioned to the active powers; which sinks under its own weight, under the consciousness of wanting energies commensurate with its visions of good, with its sore trials, and with the solemn task which is laid upon it. To conceive clearly this form of human nature, shows indeed the genius of the writer. But what a new power is required to bring it out in such a drama as Shakspeare's; to give it life and action; to invent for it circumstances and subordinate characters, fitted to call it forth; to give it tones of truth and nature; to show the hues which it casts over all the objects of thought! This intellectual energy we all perceive; and this was not merely *manifested* in Shakspeare's work, but, without such a work, it would not have been awakened. His invention would have slumbered, had he not desired to give forth his mind in a visible and enduring form. Thus literature is the nurse of genius. Through this, genius learns its own strength, and continually accumulates it; and of course, in a country without literature, genius, however liberally bestowed by the Creator, will languish, and will fail to fulfil its great duty of quickening the mass amidst which it lives.

We come now to our last—and what we deem a weighty—argument in favor of a native literature. We desire and would cherish it, because we hope from it important aids to the cause of truth and human nature. We believe that a literature, springing up in this new soil, would bear new fruits, and, in some respects, more precious fruits, than are elsewhere produced. We know that our hopes may be set down to the account of that national vanity which, with too much reason, is placed by foreigners among our besetting sins. But we speak from calm and deliberate conviction. We are inclined to believe that, as a people, we occupy a position from which the great subjects of literature may be viewed more justly than from those which most other nations hold. Undoubtedly we labor under disadvantages. We want the literary apparatus of Europe,—her libraries, her universities, her learned institutions, her race of professed scholars, her spots consecrated by the memory of sages, and a thousand stirring associations which hover over ancient nurseries of learning. But the mind is not a local power. Its spring is within itself, and, under the inspiration of liberal and high feeling, it may attain and worthily express nobler truth than outward helps could reveal.

The great distinction of our country is, that we enjoy some peculiar advantages for understanding our own nature. Man is the great subject of literature, and juster and profounder views of man may be expected here than elsewhere. In Europe, political and artificial distinctions have, more or less, triumphed over and obscured our common nature. In Europe, we meet kings, nobles, priests, peasants. How much rarer is it to meet *men*; by which we mean human beings conscious of their own nature, and conscious of the utter worthlessness of all outward distinctions compared with what is treasured up in their own souls. Man does not value himself as man. It is for his blood, his rank, or some artificial distinction, and not for the attributes of humanity, that he holds himself in respect. The institutions of the Old World all tend to throw obscurity over what we most need to know, and that is, the worth and claims of a human being. We know that great improvements in this respect are going on abroad. Still the many are too often postponed to the few. The mass of men are regarded as instruments to work with, as materials to be shaped for the use of their superiors. That consciousness of our own nature which contains, as a germ, all nobler thoughts, which teaches us at once self-respect and respect for others, and which binds us to God by filial sentiment and hope,—this has been repressed, kept down by establishments founded in force; and literature, in all its departments, bears, we think, the traces of this inward degradation. We conceive that our position favors a juster and profounder estimate of human nature. We mean not to boast, but there are fewer obstructions to that moral consciousness, that consciousness of humanity, of which we have spoken. Man is not hidden from us by so many disguises as in the Old World. The essential equality of all human beings, founded on the possession of a spiritual, progressive, immortal nature, is, we hope, better understood; and nothing more than this single conviction is needed to work the mightiest changes in every province of human life and of human thought.

We have stated what seem to us our most important distinction. But our position has other advantages. The mere circumstance of its being a new one gives reason to hope for some new intellectual activity, some fresher views of nature and life. We are not borne down by the weight of antiquated institutions, time-hallowed abuses, and the remnants of feudal barbarism. The absence of a religious establishment is an immense gain, as far as originality of mind is in question; for an establishment, however advantageous in other respects, is, by its nature, hostile to discovery and progress. To keep the mind where it is, to fasten the notions of one age on all future time, is its aim and proper business; and if it happened, as has generally been the case, to grow up in an age of strife and passion, when, as history demonstrates, the church was overrun with error, it cannot but perpetuate darkness and mental bondage. Among us, intellect, though far from being free, has broken some of the chains of other countries, and is more likely, we conceive, to propose to itself its legitimate object, truth,—everlasting and universal truth.

We have no thought of speaking contemptuously of the literature of the Old World. It is our daily nutriment. We feel our debt to be immense to the glorious company of pure and wise minds which in foreign lands have bequeathed us in writing their choicest thoughts and holiest feelings. Still, we feel that all existing literature has been produced under influences which have necessarily mixed with it much error and corruption; and that the whole of it ought to pass, and must pass, under rigorous review. For example, we think that the history of the human race is to be rewritten. Men imbued with the prejudices which thrive under aristocracies and state religions cannot understand it. Past ages, with their great events and great men, are to undergo, we think, a new trial, and to yield new results. It is plain that history is already viewed under new aspects, and we believe that the true principles for studying and writing it are to be unfolded here, at least as rapidly as in other countries. It seems to us that in literature an immense work is yet to be done. The most interesting questions to mankind are yet in debate. Great principles are yet to be settled in criticism, in morals, in politics; and, above all, the true character of religion is to be rescued from the disguises and corruptions of ages. We want a reformation. We want a literature, in which genius will pay supreme if not undivided homage to truth and virtue; in which the childish admiration of what has been called greatness will give place to a wise moral judgment; which will breathe reverence for the mind, and elevating thoughts of God. The part which this country is to bear in this great intellectual reform we presume not to predict. We feel, however, that, if true to itself, it will have the glory and happiness of giving new impulses to the human mind. This is our cherished hope. We should have no heart to encourage native literature, did we not hope that it would become instinct with a new spirit. We cannot admit the thought that this country is to be only a repetition of the Old World. We delight to believe that God, in the fulness of time, has brought a new continent to light, in order that the human mind should move here with a new freedom, should frame new social institutions, should explore new paths, and reap new harvests. We are accustomed to estimate nations by their creative energies; and we shall blush for our country if, in circumstances so peculiar, original, and creative, it shall satisfy itself with a passive reception and mechanical reiteration of the thoughts of strangers.

We have now completed our remarks on the importance of a native literature. The next great topic is, the means of producing it. And here our limits forbid us to enlarge; yet we cannot pass it over in silence. A primary and essential means of the improvement of our literature is, that, as a people, we should feel its value, should desire it, should demand it, should encourage it, and should give it a hearty welcome. It will come if called for; and, under this conviction, we have now labored to create a want for it in the community. We say that we must call for it; by which we mean not merely that we must invite it by good wishes and kind words, but must make liberal provision for intellectual education. We must enlarge our literary institutions, secure more extensive and profound teaching, and furnish helps and resources to men of superior talent for continued laborious research. As yet, intellectual labor, devoted to a thorough investigation and a full development of great subjects, is almost unknown among us; and, without it, we shall certainly rear few lasting monuments of thought. We boast of our primary schools. We want universities worthy of the name, where a man of genius and literary zeal may possess himself of all that is yet known, and may strengthen himself by intercourse with kindred minds. We know it will be said that we cannot afford these. But it is not so. We are rich enough for ostentation, for intemperance, for luxury. We can lavish millions on fashion, on furniture, on dress, on our palaces, on our pleasures; but we have nothing to spend for the mind. Where lies our poverty? In the purse, or in the soul?

We have spoken of improved institutions as essential to an improved literature. We beg, however, not to be misunderstood, as if these were invested with a creating power, or would necessarily yield the results which we desire. They are the means, not causes, of advancement. Literature depends on individual genius, and this, though fostered, cannot be created by outward helps. No human mechanism can produce original thought. After all the attempts to explain by education the varieties of intellect, we are compelled to believe that minds, like all the other products of nature, have original and indestructible differences; that they are not exempted from that great and beautiful law which joins with strong resemblances as strong diversities; and, of consequence, we believe that the men who are to be the lights of the world bring with them their commission and power from God. Still, whilst institutions cannot create, they may and do unfold genius; and, for want of them, great minds often slumber or run to waste, whilst a still larger class, who want genius, but possess admirable powers, fail of that culture through which they might enjoy and approach their more gifted brethren.

A people, as we have said, are to give aid to literature by founding wise and enlarged institutions. They may do much more. They may exert a nobler patronage. By cherishing in their own breasts the love of truth, virtue, and freedom, they may do much to nurse and kindle genius in its favored possessors. There is a constant reaction between a community and the great minds which spring up within it, and they form one another. In truth, great minds are developed more by the spirit and character of the people to which they belong than by all other causes. Thus, a free spirit, a thirst for new and higher knowledge in a community, does infinitely more for literature than the most splendid benefactions under despotism. A nation under any powerful excitement becomes fruitful of talent. Among a people called to discuss great questions, to contend for great interests, to make great sacrifices for the public weal, we always find new and unsuspected energies of thought brought out. A mercenary, selfish, luxurious, sensual people, toiling only to secure the pleasures of sloth, will often communicate their own softness and baseness to the superior minds which dwell among them. In this impure atmosphere the celestial spark burns dim; and well will it be if God's great gift of genius be not impiously prostituted to lust and crime.

In conformity with the views now stated, we believe that literature is to be carried forward, here and elsewhere, chiefly by some new and powerful impulses communicated to society; and it is a question naturally suggested by this discussion, from what impulse, principle, excitement, the highest action of the mind may now be expected. When we look back, we see that literature has been originated and modified by a variety of principles; by patriotism and national feeling, by reverence for antiquity, by the spirit of innovation, by enthusiasm, by scepticism, by the passion for fame, by romantic love, and by political and religious convulsions. Now, we do not expect from these causes any higher action of the mind than they have yet produced. Perhaps most of them have spent their force. The very improvements of society seem to forbid the manifestation of their former energy. For example, the patriotism of antiquity and the sexual love of chivalrous ages, which inspired so much of the old literature, are now seen to be feverish and vicious excess of natural principles, and have gone, we trust, never to return.

Are we asked, then, to what impulse or power we look for a higher literature than has yet existed? We answer, to a new action or development of the religious principle. This remark will probably surprise not a few of our readers. It seems to us that the energy with which this principle is to act on the intellect is hardly suspected. Men identify religion with superstition, with fanaticism, with the common forms of Christianity; and seeing it arrayed against intellect, leagued with oppression, fettering inquiry, and incapable of being blended with the sacred dictates of reason and conscience, they see in its progress only new encroachments on free and enlightened thinking. Still man's relation to God is the great quickening truth, throwing all other truths into insignificance, and a truth which, however obscured and paralyzed by the many errors which ignorance and fraud have hitherto linked with it, has ever been a chief spring of human improvement. We look to it as the true life of the intellect. No man can be just to himself—can comprehend his own existence, can put forth all his powers with an heroic confidence, can deserve to be the guide and inspirer of other minds—till he has risen to communion with the Supreme Mind; till he feels his filial connection with the Universal Parent; till he regards himself as the recipient and minister of the Infinite Spirit; till he feels his consecration to the ends which religon unfolds; till he rises above human opinion, and is moved by a higher impulse than fame.

From these remarks it will be seen that our chief hopes of an improved literature rest on our hopes of an improved religion. From the prevalent theology which has come down to us from the dark ages, we hope nothing. It has done its best. All that can grow up under its sad shade has already been brought forth. It wraps the divine nature and human nature in impenetrable gloom. It overlays Christianity with technical, arbitrary dogmas. True faith is of another lineage. It comes from the same source with reason, conscience, and our best affections, and is in harmony with them all. True faith is essentially a moral conviction; a confidence in the reality and immutableness of moral distinctions; a confidence in disinterested virtue or in spiritual excellence as the supreme good; a confidence in God as its fountain and Almighty Friend, and in Jesus Christ as having lived and died to breathe it into the soul; a confidence in its power, triumphs, and immortality; a confidence, through which outward changes, obstructions, disasters, sufferings, are overcome, or rather made instruments of perfection. Such a faith, unfolded freely and powerfully, must "work mightily" on the intellect as well as on practice. By revealing to us the supreme purpose of the Creator, it places us, as it were, in the centre of the universe, from which the harmonies, true relations, and brightest aspect of things are discerned. It unites calmness and enthusiasm, and the concord of these seemingly hostile elements is essential to the full and healthy action of the creative powers of the soul. It opens the eye to beauty and the heart to love. Literature under this influence, will become more ingenuous and single-hearted; will penetrate farther into the soul: will find new interpretations of nature and life; will breathe a martyr's love of truth, tempered with a never-failing charity; and, whilst sympathizing with all human suffering, will still be pervaded by a healthful cheerfulness, and will often break forth in tones of irrepressible joy, responsive to that happiness which fills God's universe.

We cannot close our remarks on the means of an improved literature without offering one suggestion. We earnestly recommend to our educated men a more extensive acquaintance with the intellectual labors of continental Europe. Our reading is confined too much to English books, and especially to the more recent publications of Great Britain. In this we err. We ought to know the different modes of viewing and discussing great subjects in different nations. We should be able to compare the writings of the highest minds in a great variety of circumstances. Nothing can favor more our own intellectual independence and activity. Let English literature be ever so fruitful and profound, we should still impoverish ourselves by making it our sole nutriment. We fear, however, that at the present moment English books want much which we need. The intellect of that nation is turned now to what are called practical and useful subjects. Physical science goes forward, and, what is very encouraging, it is spread with unexampled zeal through all classes of the community. Abuses of government, of the police, of the penal code, of charity, of poor-laws, and corn-laws, are laboriously explored. General education is improved. Science is applied to the arts with brilliant success. We see much good in progress. But we find little profound or fervid thinking expressed in the higher forms of literature. The noblest subjects of the intellect receive little attention. We see an almost total indifference to intellectual and moral science. In England there is a great want of philosophy, in the true sense of that word. If we examine her reviews, in which much of the intellectual power of the nation is expended, we meet perpetually a jargon of criticism, which shows a singular want of great and general principles in estimating works of art. We have no ethical work of any living English writer to be compared with that of Degerando,[4] entitled "Du Perfectionnement Moral;" and, although we have little respect for the rash generalizations of the bold and eloquent Cousin,[5] yet the interest which his metaphysics awaken in Paris is, in our estimation, a better presage than the lethargy which prevails on such topics in England. In these remarks we have no desire to depreciate the literature of England, which, taken as a whole, we regard as the noblest monument of the human mind. We rejoice in our descent from England, and esteem our free access to her works of science and genius as among our high privileges. Nor do we feel as if her strength were spent. We see no wrinkles on her brow, no decrepitude in her step. At this moment she has authors, especially in poetry and fiction, whose names are "familiar in our mouths as household words," and who can never perish but with her language. Still, we think that at present her intellect is laboring more for herself than for mankind, and that our scholars, if they would improve our literature, should cultivate an intimacy not only with that of England, but of continental Europe.

We have now finished our remarks on the importance and means of an improved literature among ourselves. Are we asked what we hope in this particular? We answer, much. We see reasons for anticipating an increased and more efficient direction of talent to this object. But on these we cannot enlarge. There is, however, one ground of expectation, to which we will call a moment's attention. We apprehend that literature is to make progress through an important change in society, which civilization and good institutions are making more and more apparent. It seems to us that, through these causes, political life is less and less regarded as the only or chief sphere for superior minds, and that influence and honor are more and more accumulated in the hands of literary and thinking men. Of consequence, more and more of the intellect of communities is to be drawn to literature. The distinction between antiquity and the present times, in respect to the importance attached to political life, seems to us striking; and it is not an accidental difference, but founded on permanent causes which are to operate with increased power. In ancient times every thing, abroad and at home, threw men upon the public, and generated an intense thirst for political power. On the contrary, the improvement of later periods inclines men to give importance to literature. For example, the instability of the ancient republics, the unsettled relations of different classes of society, the power of demagogues and orators, the intensity of factions, the want of moral and religious restraints, the

---

[4] Joseph Marie Degerando (1772–1842), French philosopher and statesman, published his *Du Perfectionnement Moral* in 1825.

[5] Victor Cousin (1792–1867), French philosopher and educational reformer.

want of some regular organ for expressing the public mind, the want of precedents and precise laws for the courts of justice,—these and other circumstances gave to the ancient citizen a feeling as if revolutions and convulsions were inseparable from society, turned his mind with unremitting anxiety to public affairs, and made a participation of political power an important, if not an essential, means of personal safety. Again, the ancient citizen had no home, in our sense of the word. He lived in the market, the forum, the place of general resort, and of course his attention was very much engrossed by affairs of state. Again, religion, which now more than all things throws a man upon himself, was in ancient times a public concern, and turned men to political life. The religion of the heart and closet was unknown. The relation of the gods to particular states was their most prominent attribute; and to conciliate their favor to the community, the chief end of worship. Accordingly, religion consisted chiefly in public and national rites. In Rome, the highest men in the state presided at the altar, and, adding to their other titles that of Supreme Pontiff, performed the most solemn functions of the priesthood. Thus the whole strength of the religious principles was turned into political channels. The gods were thought to sustain no higher office than a political one, and of consequence this was esteemed the most glorious for men. Once more, in ancient times political rank was vastly more efficient, whether for good or for evil, than at present, and of consequence was the object of a more insatiable ambition. It was almost the only way of access to the multitude. The public man held a sway over opinion, over his country, perhaps over foreign states, now unknown. It is the influence of the press and of good institutions to reduce the importance of the man of office. In proportion as private individuals can act on the public mind; in proportion as a people read, think, and have the means of expressing and enforcing their opinions; in proportion as laws become fixed, known, and sanctioned by the moral sense of the community; in proportion as the interest of the state, the principles of administration, and all public measures are subjected to free and familiar discussion, government becomes a secondary influence. The power passes into the hands of those who think, write, and spread their minds far and wide. Accordingly, literature is to become more and more the instrument of swaying men, of doing good, of achieving fame. The contrast between ancient and modern times, in the particulars now stated, is too obvious to need illustration, and our great inference is equally clear. The vast improvements which, in the course of ages, have taken place in social order, in domestic life, in religion, in knowledge, all conspire to one result, all tend to introduce other and higher influences than political power, and to give to that form of intellectual effort which we call literature dominion over human affairs. Thus truth, we apprehend, is more and more felt; and from its influence, joined with our peculiar condition and free institutions, we hope for our country the happiness and glory of a pure, deep, rich, beautiful, and ennobling literature.

PART II

THE AESTHETICS OF ROMANTICISM

THE AESTHETICS OF ROMANTICISM [1]

THE RISE of romanticism can be seen in early issues of the *North American Review*. Traditionally, since its founding in 1815, the magazine had been recognized for its conservatism and its expression of late eighteenth-century points of view in literary criticism as well as in politics. During the first years of its career, the *North American* was unfriendly to romanticism—Keats, Shelley, Byron, and Coleridge, among others, were either ignored or attacked. [2] Such men as Jared Sparks, Edward Everett, and others writing in its pages exhibit parallel literary, social, and political prejudices against those who were preaching the unquiet doctrines of romanticism. They stood for arbitrary, authoritarian conventions and proprieties, for "decorum," and for traditional morality and "common sense."

Beginning about 1820, within five years romanticism had succeeded in penetrating the pages of even this highly respectable journal. By the July, 1832, issue, W. H. Prescott, who had been much more conservative in earlier reviews, in an article on "English Literature of the Nineteenth Century," could accuse the eighteenth century of "timidity, sobriety, and artificial . . . elegance," and he could accuse Dr. Johnson of being "strangely insensible to the beauties of sentiment, as well as those of external nature . . . destitute of imagination." [3] On the other hand, Prescott praises highly Wordsworth and his romantic qualities.

It was in this period that the first significant progress was made in the development of a national literature. Nationalism first manifested itself in critical writing and gathered force as the period advanced and as American literature itself became more consciously national. [4] As the nation began to realize its potentialities and its worth, it became increasingly reluctant to accept its previous cultural dependence upon England. There was a gradually developing judicious attitude in criticism toward Ameri-

[1] For more detailed studies of this period, see R. P. Adams, "Romanticism and the American Renaissance," *American Literature*, XXIII (1952), 419–32; Eugene Current-Garcia, *Criticism and the Problem of Literary Expression in a Democratic Society: The Awakening of American Critical Thought, 1835–1850,* unpublished dissertation (Harvard, 1947); Edwin H. Eby, *American Romantic Criticism, 1815–1860,* unpublished dissertation (Washington, 1927); F. O. Matthiessen, *American Renaissance* (New York, 1941); and Robert E. Spiller, "Critical Standards in the American Romantic Movement," *College English*, VIII (1947), 344–52.

[2] See Robert E. Streeter, *Critical Ideas in the North American Review, 1815–1865.* Also see William Ellery Leonard, *Byron and Byronism in America* (Boston, 1905); Julia Power, *Shelley in America* (Lincoln, Neb., 1940); Hyder Rollins, *Keats' Reputation in America to 1848* (Cambridge, 1946); and Anna Whitmer, *American Reaction to the Literary Criticism of Samuel Taylor Coleridge, 1830–1860,* unpublished dissertation (Ohio State, 1939).

[3] For a study of Johnson's reception in America, see Daniel Long's unpublished dissertation, *Dr. Johnson in America* (Illinois, 1939).

[4] See Benjamin T. Spencer, "A National Literature, 1837–1855," *American Literature*, VIII (1936), 125–59.

can literature and a determination to provide an artistic rationale. Bryant's essay on "Early American Verse" in 1818 was a judicious estimate and urged American poets to use the natural beauties of their own country. In 1820, in the second series of *Salmagundi*, James Kirke Paulding, in his article on "National Literature," attacked "servile imitation" and "the ascendenancy of foreign tastes and opinions." Bryant again in 1825 made a further plea for a national literature, and anticipated regionalism in American fiction by pointing out, in his article "American Society as a Field for Fiction," the rich field which existed in the exploitation for artistic purposes of American society, with its diversity and its regional and sectarian peculiarities.

In 1830, one of the most distinguished of the Boston group, William Ellery Channing, offered a cogent formula for creating a genuinely American literature in his "Remarks on National Literature," published in the *Christian Examiner*. Not until Emerson's "The American Scholar" in 1837 was cultural nationalism stated more effectively. From the 1830's on, nationalism became one of the hallmarks of American criticism, culminating in certain passages of Melville's essay on Hawthorne and in Walt Whitman's Preface to the 1855 edition of *Leaves of Grass*.

One of the most important forces in the development of a new and democratic literature in the period was the literary criticism of the group known as "Young America."[5] Publishing in such liberal periodicals as the *Democratic Review*, and including such capable critics as Evert A. Duyckinck, William A. Jones, John L. O'Sullivan, and Parke Godwin, the group was consistently one of the strongest advocates of a democratic national literature, a literature for "the people," as opposed to the *Whig Review*'s advocacy of an aristocratic English literature.[6] Devoted to the younger and more progressive American writers, and generally sympathetic toward New England transcendentalism, the group was instrumental in leading the approval of such new writers as Emerson, Hawthorne, Melville, and the "folk" humorists. The liberal, democratic criticism of the *Democratic Review*, called by Longfellow a "Loco-foco politico-literary system," exerted some influence on such critics as Thoreau, Hawthorne, Whittier, Lowell, Bryant, and Emerson,[7] who were all frequent contributors to the journal.

Having little to say about the element of "art" in literature, the "Young America" critics concentrated rather on such pertinent romantic ideas as the interest in and glorification of the common man, reform, brotherhood,

[5] An excellent study of the criticism of this group is by John Stafford, *The Literary Criticism of "Young America"* (Berkeley, Cal., 1952).

[6] Literary criticism of the Whig opposition centered in such Whig journals as the *New York Review*, the *Whig Review*, and the *Knickerbocker*. Leading Whig critics were E. P. Whipple, Henry Norman Hudson, and Rufus W. Griswold. For interesting studies of Whig bias in criticism, see Dorothy Waples, *The Whig Myth of James Fenimore Cooper* (New Haven, 1938), and John Stafford, "Henry Norman Hudson and the Whig Use of Shakespeare," *Publications Modern Language Association*, LXVI (1951), 649–61. See also Walter Graham, *Tory Criticism in the Quarterly Review, 1809–1853* (New York, 1921).

[7] See Emerson's essay, "The Young American," in *Nature, Addresses, and Lectures* (Boston, 1849).

and freedom. Their concept of the function of literature was utilitarian rather than aesthetic in its primary emphasis.[8] This led in their critical judgments to a preference for Shelley over more conservative English romantics, such as Wordsworth and Coleridge, and, among American writers, to a preference for those whose point of view was sympathetic toward a more liberal, a more democratic American literature.[9] On the other hand, the Whig critics, in the more conservative tradition of Coleridge, were more interested in artistic considerations and tended to approach a work of art as an organic unity rather than from the point of view of its ideas alone.

By 1850, the "Young America" critics had ceased to be influential as a group, although some individual members were to continue to write criticism. While not as significant in the history of the criticism of the period as some of the more conservative romantic critics, like Poe, the group was influential in fostering the growth of a more democratic national literature, in promoting the acceptance of new American writers, and in drawing upon American liberalism in the judgment of literature. In referring to the *Democratic Review* in 1858, Whitman wrote that it was a "magazine of a profounder quality of talent than any since"; and Poe, while not sympathetic toward its point of view, said that "were it not for its ultraism in politics, we should consider the *Democratic Review* the most valuable journal of the day." [10]

With the attempt to foster the growth of a national literature, American criticism of the period is characterized chiefly by its preoccupation with the problem of the relationship between art and morality. That the emphasis which Puritanism had placed upon morality, and which is exhibited in Cotton Mather's comments on poetry in the *Manuductio,* had not disappeared from American critical theory is evidenced by the fact that scarcely a critic, major or minor, would admit to the establishment of purely aesthetic standards of literary theory and judgment. Perhaps one cause of this may be found in the fact that Puritanism itself had contributed to the establishment of a tradition of middle class gentility and morality in literature in the New England which was to provide most of the major arbiters of American taste during the period. To this may be added the influence of the Scottish associationalists' emphasis upon the identification of beauty and the moral sentiment, and Transcendentalism, with its emphasis upon the ideal and its concept of the important function of the poet in society.

[8] For a convenient summary of the connection between the liberal, reforming wing of romanticism and utilitarianism in America, see Merle Curti's section, "The Roots of Reform: Romanticism and Utilitarianism," in *The Growth of American Thought* (New York, 1943). See also Arthur M. Schlesinger, Jr.'s "Jacksonian Democracy and Literature," in *The Age of Jackson* (Boston, 1945).

[9] The critical judgments of William A. Jones, probably the best of the "Young America" critics, are typical. See his "Critics and Criticism of the Nineteenth Century," *Democratic Review,* XV (1844), and in the same issue his "Criticism in America." For a more detailed study of Jones's theories, see John Stafford, "William A. Jones, Democratic Literary Critic," *Huntington Library Quarterly,* XII (1949), 289–302.

[10] See Poe's "The Democratic Review," *Broadway Journal,* II (1845).

Moreover, it is more than just a possibility that literature, and poetry in particular, felt itself on the defensive against the tradition of religious orthodoxy as well as the ever-increasing utilitarianism of an expanding industrial society. Most of the critics of the period stress the moral quality of poetry and its utility to society. Whitman, as late as 1871, indicates the continuity of the tradition when he writes in *Democratic Vistas* of literature "teaching and training men—and, as perhaps the most precious of its results, achieving the entire redemption of woman out of these incredible holds and webs of silliness, millinery, and every kind of dyspeptic depletion." Only Poe, of all the major critics of the period, assails the "Heresy of the Didactic" and establishes purely aesthetic and artistic standards. While romanticism saw the formulation of this close affinity between art and morality, its logical conclusion is in "The Genteel Tradition" of the late Victorian age. Where it reached heights in Lowell, it would descend to a watered-down, somewhat futile imitation in Aldrich, Stedman, and Stoddard.

Turning away from the emphasis of the associationalists upon the psychological reactions of the reader, romantic critics directed their attention instead toward a world of ideal beauty which they considered both the source and standard of great art. Attention was also turned toward the creating spirit of the artist, who served as a link between his material environment and the ideal. Art fulfilled its end only when it reflected the ideal. The *North American Review* after 1835 gave frequent expression of faith in idealism as the philosophical background for aesthetic thought.

Most of the major premises of romantic criticism can be traced to the influence of Coleridge and the Schlegels: that there is an hierarchy of ideal forms which is the source and standard of beauty; that the human imagination (as defined by Coleridge) forms the bridge between the material world and the ideal; that the basic principle of art is the organic unity wherein great art fuses soul and body, thought and expression, content and form;[11] that criticism is an art with its own aims and methods.

One of the earliest statements concerning the ideal as the best subject and ultimate standard for art is to be found in Emerson's essay, "Michael Angelo," which he published in the *North American Review* in 1837. A detailed exposition of this romantic-transcendental attitude toward art was made by S. G. Fisher in his review of a series of aesthetic essays by Horace Binney Wallace in 1855.[12] He quotes Emerson frequently and maintains that art possesses value only in so far as it symbolizes the "invisible order of things." External objects symbolize "invisible spiritual laws" and also provide emblems for the contemplation of the artist. Samuel Osgood, in an essay, "The Real and the Ideal in New England," published in the *North American Review* in 1857, also stresses the idealizing power of poetry as its essential quality.

---

[11] See Craig La Drière, "Organic Form," in *Dictionary of World Literature,* ed. by Joseph T. Shipley (New York, 1943).
[12] "Art, Its Meaning and Method. Essays of Horace Binney Wallace," *North American Review,* LXXXI (1855).

A number of critics offer testimony of the wide acceptance by the period of A. W. Schlegel's idea of the organic unity of an artistic work. Edwin P. Whipple, in a review, "Verplanck and Hudson: Shakespeare's Plays," in the *North American* in 1848, pays tribute to Schlegel as the originator of the concept of organicism. Other reviews which reflect Schlegel's concept are Lowell's "The New Timon," in 1847, and his review of "Browning's Plays and Poems," in the following year. While not as widespread as the influence of Schlegel's work, some attention should be paid to Hegel's *Aesthetik,* with its exposition of the three stages of aesthetic development—symbolism, classicism, romanticism—and the implication that spirit and matter should be blended into an organic living unity in the work of art.[13] That Hegel's work was of some influence in promoting an organic approach to literature can be seen in the criticism of his American disciple, C. C. Everett. In "Ruskin's Last Volume" (1857), "Elizabeth Barrett Browning" (1857), and "Tennyson" (1860), all appearing in the *North American,* Everett applies the principles of Hegel.

Most American critics of the period seem to have been strongly influenced by Coleridge's conception of the imagination as the faculty by which the material forms of the understanding could be brought into relationship with the ideal. Edwin P. Whipple's statement that the "imagination . . . evolves from material objects the latent spiritual meaning," is a thoroughly representative one.[14] This led to a highly subjective, intuitive conception of the creative process which stands in sharp contrast to the rationalistic authoritarianism and the principle of art as imitation which dominated the aesthetics of neoclassicism.

Critics of fiction during the period reflected, for the most part, the same general principles as those who were engaged in the criticism of poetry. The idealizing function of the novelist was stressed by such critics as Cooper, Hawthorne, and Melville. There was much comment concerning the organic unity of the novel. As the years passed, critics insisted more and more firmly that the novel should be regarded as a legitimate work of art, able to attain equal beauty with other literary forms, and therefore to be judged by the same artistic standards.[15] With other critics of the period, critics of fiction emphasized the close affinity between art and morality and expressed the belief that fiction should concern itself with moral problems. Almost all of the critics, however, agreed that the moral element should be fused with the work and should not appear as a superimposed didacticism.

[13] Also current in the period was the Schlegels' distinction between classical and romantic art. The former, ending with Christianity, achieved a mastery of material beauty, while the romantic aimed at a greater spiritual emphasis.

[14] "Wordsworth's Poetical Works," *North American Review,* LIX (1844), 356.

[15] See Edwin P. Whipple, "The Life and Works of Henry Fielding," *North American Review,* LXVIII (1849); and an anonymous review, "A Chapter on Novels," *ibid.,* LXXXIII (1856). A general study is L. P. Leland's unpublished dissertation, *Theories of Fiction in America, 1789–1870* (Ohio State, 1940). Also see A. L. Rabinovitz, "Criticism of French Novels in Boston Magazines, 1830–1860," *New England Quarterly,* XIV (1941), 488–504.

While romantic aesthetics dominated the literary criticism of the period, neoclassicism continued to assert itself in the work of such major figures as Edgar Allan Poe and Oliver Wendell Holmes, and in the reviews of such *North American* critics as Cornelius C. Felton and Francis Bowen, who were both influenced largely by neoclassical and rhetorical ideas. Bowen edited the *North American* from 1843 to 1853, and both contributed frequently throughout the period. Bowen, like Holmes, berated the "mystical nonsense" in the poetry of Emerson and his followers.[16]

Turning to a survey of the major critics of the period, one finds a breadth in romanticism in America and an astonishing diversity of its elements which has often been unappreciated, particularly as it manifests itself in the literary criticism of the period.

It has been customary to speak of James Fenimore Cooper's "non-literary approach," a tendency which has often resulted in an obscuring of the fact that he did have some fairly definite theories concerning the art of the novel which he expressed in his prefaces and introductions.[17] Stressing the right of the writer of romances to "a poetical view" of his subject, Cooper stated, in the Introduction (1850) to *The Pioneers*, a principle of dealing with facts in an imaginative way: "Rigid adhesion to truth, an indispensable requisite in history and travels, destroys the charm of fiction; for all that is necessary to be conveyed to the mind by the latter had better be done by delineations of principles, and of characters in their classes, than by too fastidious attention to originals." Cooper continues that "the incidents of this tale are purely a fiction. The literal facts are chiefly connected with the natural and artificial objects, and customs of the inhabitants. . . . There was no intention to describe with particular accuracy any real character in this book."

In the Preface (1850) to "The Leather-Stocking Tales," Cooper elaborated on this point, emphasizing explicitly the function of the imagination in fiction. Speaking of the character of Leather-Stocking, he writes: "In a physical sense, different individuals known to the writer in early life, certainly presented themselves as models, through his recollections: but in a moral sense this man of the forest is purely a creation." For Cooper, the novel is determined by its "moral" requirements; hence the writer has a perfect freedom in the selection or rejection of details taken from life.

Cooper saw the function of literature as not being an end in itself, but rather as being the expression of national and social ideals. As opposed to

---

[16] See his "Nine New Poets," *North American Review*, LXIV (1847) and "Lowell's Poems," *ibid.*, LXVI (1848). For Felton's neoclassicism, see his "Greek Language and Literature," *ibid.*, XLII (1836).

[17] A valuable study is Arvid Shulenberger's unpublished dissertation, *Cooper's Theory of Fiction: His Prefaces and Their Relation to His Novels* (Chicago, 1951). The standard biography is T. R. Lounsbury, *James Fenimore Cooper* (Boston, 1882). Also see Robert E. Spiller, *Fenimore Cooper: Critic of His Times* (New York, 1931) and his introduction to *James Fenimore Cooper: Representative Selections* (New York, 1936). For Cooper's relations with the *North American Review*, see Gregory L. Paine's "Cooper and the *North American Review*," *Studies in Philology*, XXVIII (1931), 799–809.

the romanticism of Sir Walter Scott, Cooper's theory in this respect is more nearly related to the social criticism of the Victorian novelists, Dickens and Thackeray. Consequently, there is, in Cooper's theory, an emphasis not so much upon aesthetic principles as upon ethical ones. In the Preface (1845) to *Satanstoe*, he wrote: "Every chronicle of manners has a certain value. When customs are connected with principles, in their origin, development, or end, such records have a double importance." Thus, in his theory of fiction, Cooper saw the value of both historical representation of manners and the American scene, which affords the novelist a kind of "local" or "native" realism, and romantic idealism which permits the imaginative representation of moral and ethical values.

While favoring the development of a national literature, Cooper wrote in 1828, in the *Notions of the Americans,* of the obstacles to its development: "There are no annals for the historian; no follies (beyond the most vulgar and commonplace) for the satirist; no manners for the dramatist; no obscure fictions for the writer of romance; no gross and hardy offences against decorum for the moralist; nor any of the rich artificial, auxiliaries of poetry." Those books which, in his estimation, have been best received "are those in which the authors have trusted most to their own conceptions of character and to qualities that are common to the rest of the world." That he did not link a national literature with the use of native materials is obvious from a statement he made a few years later: "A more impudent piece of literary empiricism has never been palmed on the world than the pretension that the American reading public requires American themes."

That Cooper's criticism did, however, carry a strong American political and social bias can be seen in his comment that "these very works of Sir Walter Scott are replete with one species of danger to the American readers; and the greater the talents of the writer, as a matter of course, the greater is the evil. The bias of his feelings, his prejudices, I might almost say his nature, his deference to hereditary rank . . . the deference of mere feudal and conventional laws, which have their origin in force, and are continued by prejudice and wrong." [18] While Cooper's criticism is significant from the point of view of the general aesthetics of fiction, there is little specific criticism of individual works or writers.

From the beginning, much of American criticism had been for the most part ideological, a criticism of ideas largely devoted to argument for or against various social and moral philosophies as expressed in art. Edgar Allan Poe was the first critic of importance to express the aesthetic tradition—to confine himself largely to problems of "form," "design," all of those factors which enter into literary craftsmanship.[19] In this emphasis

[18] For Cooper's comments on Scott, see *Gleanings in Europe: England* (1837).

[19] A recent critical biography of Poe is Arthur H. Quinn, *Edgar Allan Poe* (New York, 1941). See also Killis Campbell, *The Mind of Poe, and Other Studies* (Cambridge, 1933). Studies of Poe's literary criticism include Margaret Alterton, *Origins of Poe's Critical Theory* (Iowa City, 1925); John E. Cooke, *Poe as a Literary Critic,* ed. by N. Bryllion Fagin (Baltimore, 1946); George E. DeMille, "Poe as Critic," *American Mercury,* IV (1925), 433–40; Norman Foerster, *American Criticism* (Boston, 1928), pp. 1–51; David K. Jackson, *Poe and the "Southern Literary Messenger"* (Richmond, Va., 1934); Albert J. Lubell, *Edgar Allan Poe, Critic and Re-*

upon the *rational* in art, in his constant insistence upon "the application
of a rigorous *method* in all forms of thought," Poe demonstrated an affinity
with neoclassicism which set him somewhat apart from the main trends of
the age. That he sought, however, to avoid the conventional rules of neoclassicism as well as romanticism is evident. As early as 1831, when he set
forth his poetic theory in the "Letter to B——" prefacing his own poems,
he emphasized that authority resides in principles contained within the
work of art itself and not in persons, in reason, or in past precedent.

The prospectus prepared by Poe for *The Penn Magazine* contains one
of the best statements of his theory of criticism:[20]

A criticism self-sustained; guiding itself only by the purest rules of Art; analyzing and urging these rules as it applies them; holding itself aloof from all
personal bias; acknowledging no fear save that of outraging the right; yielding
no point either to the vanity of the author, or to the assumptions of antique
prejudice, or to the involute and anonymous cant of the Quarterlies or to the
arrogance of those organized *cliques* which, hanging like nightmares upon
American literature, manufacture, at the nod of our principal booksellers, a
pseudo-public-opinion by wholesale.

Poe brought to his criticism an ability and a set of standards hitherto
unknown in America. He was unique in his stress upon "design," "upon a
strict subordination of the parts to the whole," and in his concern with
Schlegel's "unity or totality of interest." His particular interest in Coleridge's emphasis upon the "value of words" is shown in his detailed criticism of the diction of Simms. His conclusion that Drake and Halleck were
poets not of imagination but of fancy demonstrated again his allegiance
to his master.[21]

Poe's ideals again ran counter to one of the major interests of the day,
cultural nationalism. In an unusually acute analysis of the state of American criticism at the beginning of his essay on Drake's "The Culprit Fay,"
he indicated his concern over the substitution for our earlier subservience
to British standards of a form of provincialism which he feared was even
worse. He declared that "We are becoming boisterous and arrogant in the
pride of a too speedily assumed literary freedom," and urges his readers
not to forget "that *the world* is the true theatre. . . . So far from being
ashamed of the many disgraceful literary failures to which our own
inordinate vanities and misapplied patriotism have lately given birth . . .
we adhere pertinaciously to our original blindly conceived idea, and thus
often find ourselves involved in the gross paradox of liking a stupid book

---

viewer, unpublished dissertation (New York, 1951); E. C. Stedman, "Introduction to the Literary Criticism," *The Works of Edgar Allan Poe* (Chicago, 1894–95),
Vol. VI, xi–xxvi; and Edmund Wilson, "Poe as Literary Critic," *Nation*, 155 (1942),
452–53.

[20] For another elaboration of his critical position, see his "Exordium," *Graham's
Magazine* (January, 1842).

[21] Poe's stress upon "design" and a "strict subordination of the parts to the whole"
is a reflection of Coleridge's organic theory of art. For a study of Coleridge's influence
on Poe, see Floyd Stovall, "Poe's Debt to Coleridge," *U. of Texas Studies in English*,
X (1930), 70–127.

the better, because, sure enough, its stupidity is American." He repeated frequently his attack upon a narrow nationalism and favored limiting "literary criticism to comment upon Art."

He was the first American critic to emphasize that it is impossible to separate literary practice "from the theory which includes it," and to point out that where the practice fails "it is because the theory is imperfect." That he himself followed this principle is obvious from the close relationship which exists between his statement of theory in such essays as "The Poetic Principle" and "The Philosophy of Composition" and his own poetic practice. That Poe did not separate his own theory from his practice as a literary critic is seen in his balanced judgment of Longfellow whom he criticizes for the "too obtrusive nature of his didacticism" as opposed to Poe's own view of poetry as "the rhythmical creation of beauty." In his review of Hawthorne's *Twice-Told Tales*, he judges Hawthorne as a writer of "indisputable genius" according to his own conception of the short story as being based upon "a single effect."

Poe's central artistic and critical standards can be summarized briefly. The end of art is not truth but pleasure. To arouse pleasure, poetry concerns itself with the creation of beauty; not principally the beauty of particular things, but rather "supernal beauty." To create an intense pleasure, a work of art must be brief and must have organic unity, "a single effect." [22] The musical element in poetry is of paramount importance, since it is principally in music that man comes closest to attaining the goal of supernal beauty. While beauty is the sole province of poetry, the prose tale, which, like poetry, is brief and limited to a single effect, may produce other effects—horror, terror, truth.

It is clear that Poe, an aesthete and a craftsman, ran counter in most of his artistic ideals to every major interest of the New England renaissance. In his critical rationalism, in his conception of the function of the critic as being harshly judicial, in his critical criteria of orderly unity and harmony, in his evaluation of the short story in the light of his "five laws" deduced from Hawthorne's practice, and in his constant concern with prosody, structure, finish, and form, Poe's eighteenth-century neoclassical qualities are apparent. The relevance of many of his artistic ideals to contemporary American criticism and poetry lies in their profound attraction for French symbolism which, in turn, derived many of its major principles from Poe. [23]

Poe's concentration of his critical and artistic theories toward a definite end—art for the sake of art—gave his criticism a unity and a sense of direction which is lacking in his chief contemporaries. This is particularly true of the Transcendentalists, of whose critical and artistic theories Emerson may be considered representative. [24]

[22] See G. F. Richardson, "Poe's Doctrine of Effect," *Univ. of California Publications in Modern Philology*, XI (1928), 177–86.

[23] See George Snell, "First of the New Critics," *Quarterly Review of Literature*, II (1946), 333–40.

[24] The standard study of Transcendentalism is H. C. Goddard, *Studies in New England Transcendentalism* (New York, 1908). Also see Perry Miller's introduction

When Margaret Fuller [25] wrote that "the critic must know and be regulated by an absolute invariable principle," she was stating the position from which the critical judgments of Emerson were actually delivered. Emerson demanded a "transcendental criticism." The final judgment of a poem is whether it justifies itself in relation to the hypothetically supreme poem—the ideal poem. And beyond this ideal poem is the Ideal itself, the criterion of all human striving. All works have value only in so far as they catch, for a moment, this Universal Spirit. When Emerson applied this absolute standard to his contemporaries, Poe became "the jingle man," and he asks, "How shall I find my heavenly bread in Tennyson? in Lowell? or in Longfellow?" There are only a few indubitable masters in Emerson's lexicon, and throughout his life he devoted himself to Homer, Plato, Plotinus, Plutarch, Montaigne, Shakespeare, [26] Bacon, and Milton. [27] More recent, he had words of praise for Wordsworth, [28] Coleridge, Goethe, and his favorite Swedenborg.

Coleridge, whom Emerson began reading in 1830, was a major influence on his literary theory. [29] Like Coleridge, he believed that the creative effort begins with the inflow into the artist's mind of ideas from a source beyond himself, with the surrender of will to the Universal Power. In his theory of the imagination as "symbolic sight," as a means of conveying Ideas through symbols and revealing the spiritual latent in material objects, Emerson also was influenced by Coleridge. It was also Coleridge who supplied him with the application of organic form, as opposed to mechanic form, in literature. While Coleridge stressed the architectonic aspect of the principle, the development of a work according to a controlling purpose or design, Emerson more often used the analogy of art to nature in its

to *The Transcendentalists: An Anthology* (Cambridge, 1950). More specialized studies include Clarence F. Gohdes, *The Periodicals of American Transcendentalism* (Durham, N. C., 1931); Henry Pochmann, *New England Transcendentalism and St. Louis Hegelianism* (Philadelphia, 1948); and René Wellek, "The Minor Transcendentalists and the German Philosophers," *New England Quarterly*, XV (1942), 669.

The best brief critical biography of Emerson is George E. Woodberry, *Ralph Waldo Emerson* (New York, 1907). More recent studies include Bliss Perry, *Emerson Today* (Princeton, 1931), and Frederick I. Carpenter's introduction to *Ralph Waldo Emerson: Representative Selections* (New York, 1934). One of the best critical studies is "From Emerson to Thoreau," in F. O. Matthiessen, *American Renaissance* (New York, 1941). Studies of Emerson's criticism include Norman Foerster, *American Criticism*, pp. 52–110; Vivian C. Hopkins, *Spires of Form: A Study of Emerson's Aesthetic Theory* (Cambridge, 1951); and Leah Jordan, *The Fundamentals of Emerson's Literary Criticism*, unpublished dissertation (Pennsylvania, 1945).

[25] See Roland Burton, *Margaret Fuller's Criticism: Theory and Practice*, unpublished dissertation (Iowa, 1941), and H. H. McMaster, "Margaret Fuller as a Literary Critic," *Univ. Buffalo Studies*, VII (1928), 35–100.

[26] See R. P. Falk, "Emerson and Shakespeare," *Publications Modern Language Association*, LVI (1941), 523–43.

[27] See R. C. Pettigrew, "Emerson and Milton," *American Literature*, III (1931), 45–59.

[28] See J. B. Moore, "Emerson on Wordsworth," *Publications Modern Language Association*, XLI (1926), 179–92.

[29] For a more detailed study, see Frank T. Thompson, "Emerson's Indebtedness to Coleridge," *Studies in Philology*, XXIII (1926), 55–76. Also see Vivian C. Hopkins, *Spires of Form*; and F. O. Matthiessen, *American Renaissance*.

principle of organic unity and growth.[30] In his denotation of the eighteenth century as an "arid desert," he indicated that it was Coleridge and Goethe [31] who had to "reinstate men in the Real" through their Kantian distinction between the Reason and the Understanding.

Closely related to his concept of the organic nature of art is Emerson's doctrine of the correspondence between the artist and material nature in the creative process. As a result of this, a successful work will bear the stamp of the world of nature by means of which the artist reveals his understanding of the Universal Spirit which links his soul and natural objects. Besides this organic form which art derives from nature, Emerson also stresses the spiritual aspect of form which is derived by the artist directly from the Divine. It is just such a realization of spiritual form that Emerson sees in the work of Michelangelo.[32] Nature—the world of material objects—assists the artist in objectifying the ideal. The imagination perceives the symbolic nature of things and treats them as representative. This process of objectifying the ideal through the symbols of nature is implied in all poetry, in allegory, in fable, in the use of emblems, and in the structure of language.

Art, for Emerson, is the creation of beauty which, unlike the "supernal beauty" of Poe, is also truth and goodness. All beauty must be organic; modern or romantic art bears the stamp of caprice or chance, according to Emerson. The delight which a work of art affords seems to arise from our recognizing in it the mind that formed nature, again in active cooperation. It is not metres, "but a metre-making argument, that makes a poem,—a thought so passionate and alive, that, like the spirit of a plant or an animal, it has an architecture of its own, and adorns nature with a new thing." The supreme value of poetry is to educate man in order and virtue.

Primarily a critic of poetry, Emerson tended to carry over into the judgment of fiction most of the same principles.[33] While appreciating the strength and charm of Sir Walter Scott, Emerson, criticizing him for not being aware of ideas, claimed that he was lacking in high imagination.[34] Unable to sympathize with what he considered to be the surface realism of Jane Austen, he wrote in his journals in 1861 that her novels "seem to me vulgar in tone, sterile in artistic invention, imprisoned in the wretched conventions of English society, without genius, wit, or knowledge of the world. Never was life so pinched and narrow." He was equally blunt in his criticism of Dickens because "his eye rests always on surfaces."

[30] See Norman Foerster, "Emerson on the Organic Principle in Art," *Publications Modern Language Association*, XLI (1926), 193–208.

[31] For Goethe's influence on Emerson, see Vivian C. Hopkins, "The Influence of Goethe on Emerson's Aesthetic Theory," *Philological Quarterly*, XXVII (1948), 325–44.

[32] See Emerson's article, "Michael Angelo," in the *North American Review*, XLIV (1837).

[33] For a more thorough study of Emerson's criticism of fiction, see J. T. Flanagan, "Emerson as a Critic of Fiction," *Philological Quarterly*, XV (1936), 30–45.

[34] James E. Cabot, *A Memoir of Ralph Waldo Emerson* (Boston, 1895), Vol. I, 240.

Suspicious of most fiction, he objected, as did the neoclassicists, particularly to pessimistic novels, which led him to express his dislike of Hawthorne's work as being too gloomy and melancholy, too introspective and analytical. Justifying the romance on the basis of its idealizing power, Emerson insisted on insight into the Ideal as a criterion of excellence, and instruction in the value of character and morality as a necessary function of fiction.

Emerson quite frequently employed the historical approach as an aid to understanding literature. He shows a considerable awareness of national characteristics, of art's relation to the factors of race, place, and time, in his comments on English, French, and American traits, in his distinction between Eastern, or Persian, poetry and Western, and in his differentiation between the creative powers of Semitic races and Indo-European. During the winter of 1835–36, Emerson gave a series of ten lectures in Boston on English literature. Covering the span of English literature from the Anglo-Saxon through the eighteenth century, these lectures analyzed the interaction of literary genius with qualities of the age. While of use in arriving at a greater comprehension of literature, the historical method, for Emerson, could not account for the nature or function of literature nor could it be used as a criterion of excellence.

The vision of life and art dominating the critical and aesthetic theories of Emerson was characterized, in many respects, by his outspoken dissatisfaction with romanticism as a whole, with the exception of Wordsworth, Coleridge, and Goethe. Turning away from the romanticism of the nineteenth century, and from the "pseudo-classicism" that preceded it, he belongs largely in the tradition of Plato and Plotinus—to whom his debt can hardly be exaggerated.

It is only with great difficulty that one can glean from the voluminous writings of Henry Thoreau any system or pattern of literary criticism.[35] Scattered throughout his works are innumerable criticisms and comments on the theory of literature which, when isolated and gathered together, form an impressive amount yet scarcely represent any systematic development and application of a method of criticism.

Like Emerson, Thoreau held art to be organic; and, like Emerson, most of his analogies concern art and nature.[36] Thoreau recognizes a close correspondence between the poet and nature: "He is another Nature,—Nature's brother. Kindly offices do they perform for one another. Each publishes the

[35] The most useful critical biography is Henry S. Canby, *Thoreau* (Boston, 1939). Also see Bartholow V. Crawford, Introduction to *Henry David Thoreau: Representative Selections* (New York, 1934); Joseph Wood Krutch, *Henry David Thoreau* (New York, 1948); Henry S. Salt, *The Life of Henry David Thoreau* (London, 1896); and Mark Van Doren, *Henry David Thoreau, a Critical Study* (Boston, 1916). Invaluable source material is presented by Thoreau's most intimate friend and a leading literary figure of the day, William Ellery Channing, *Thoreau, the Poet-Naturalist: With Memorial Verses* (Boston, 1873, rev. and enlarged by Frank B. Sanborn, Boston, 1902). The fullest treatment of Thoreau's aesthetic is F. O. Matthiessen's "From Emerson to Thoreau," in his *American Renaissance*.
[36] See F. W. Lorch, "Thoreau and the Organic Principle in Poetry," *Publications Modern Language Association*, LIII (1938), 286–302.

other's truth." And it is the poet who is the true lover of nature and knows best how to use nature: "Is it the lumberman, then, who is the friend and lover of the pine, stands nearest to it, and understands its nature best? . . . No! No! it is the poet; he it is who makes the truest use of the pine."

The poet, for Thoreau, is a man set aside, a man inspired: "He must be something more than natural,—even supernatural." And "When the poet is inspired," he "is stimulated by an *aura* which never even colors the afternoons of common men." Based upon this conception of the poet, Thoreau recognizes two kinds of poetry: "one that of genius, or the inspired, the other of intellect and taste. . . . The former is above criticism, always correct, giving the law to criticism. It vibrates and pulsates with life forever. It is sacred, and to be read with reverence, as the works of nature are studied."

Thoreau would send the poet to nature to discover there beauty and truth, that which is fixed and unchanging. But the poet is not merely to copy nature. Coleridge had pointed out that the artist must not try to make a surface reproduction of nature's details but "must imitate that which is within the thing . . . for so only can he hope to produce any work truly natural in the object and truly human in the effect." Thoreau writes that the poet will make nature "the expression of his thought. He then poetizes when he makes a fact out of nature into spirit."

Thoreau seldom discusses poetic forms. His ideas on this subject flow directly from his concept of literary inspiration and are influenced greatly by his notion that ideal literature must be organic, that the form must be shaped by the artist's intuition. Like Emerson, he saw the correspondence between nature's art and man's, even in the details and trifles. Speaking of "the simplest and most lumpish fungus," he says, "it is so obviously organic and related to ourselves. . . . It is the expression of an idea; growth according to a law; matter not dormant, not raw, but inspired, appropriated by spirit." Likewise in literature, it is the thought, or spirit, that inspires the form: "The nearer we approach to a complete but simple transcript of our thoughts, the more tolerable will be the piece." English literature suffers, Thoreau thinks, because it has never breathed a really free air, and because the wildest forest it has ever known is a greenwood. The real poet would be he who "could impress the winds and streams into his service, to speak for him; who nailed words to their primitive senses, as farmers drive down stakes in the spring."

There is available in the works of Thoreau a collection of singularly interesting and varied literary criticisms.[37] One finds critical observations on everything from the *Laws of Menu* to some lines addressed to a peach tree by one Mr. Heaman Doane, whose name survives probably only because Thoreau thought his work to be "the only specimen of Cape Cod

[37] Among the best studies of Thoreau's literary criticism is the unpublished dissertation of Raymond William Adams, *Henry Thoreau's Literary Theory and Criticism* (North Carolina, 1928).

verse" which he could remember having seen. Some of these observations demonstrate keen critical powers; others are obviously lacking in discrimination. Sprinkled throughout the works, for instance, is lavish praise of Ossian, whom Thoreau often places on a level wth Homer and Virgil. James Russell Lowell, in his critical essay on Thoreau, found this a bitter pill to swallow. On the other hand, Thoreau's essay on Thomas Carlyle is literary criticism of a high order.

In his *Journal* (March, 1861) Thoreau wrote: "You can't read any genuine history—as that of Herodotus or the Venerable Bede—without perceiving that our interest depends not on the subject but on the man,—on the manner in which he treats the subject and the importance he gives it . . . a Shakespeare, for instance—would make the history of his parish more interesting than another's history of the world."

It is from this point of view, "that our interest depends not on the subject but on the man," that Thoreau wrote "Thomas Carlyle and His Works," published in *Graham's Magazine* in 1847. In this, his most ambitious critical work, he tells us that "We have not attempted to discriminate between his works, but have rather regarded them all as one work, as is the man himself." He is primarily interested in the relation between the man and his work and discusses the personal qualities, of humor, style, ideas, which the work reveals and which are revealing in terms of the work. Praising Carlyle for "the richest prose style we know of," Thoreau, however, is mainly interested in the ideas, since style "is something for use, and not to look at." That, like Emerson, Thoreau tended to judge literary work by the quality and degree of insight into truth which it possesses is demonstrated by his most serious objection to Carlyle's work, "that Carlyle indicates a depth,—and we mean not impliedly, but distinctly,—which he neglects to fathom. . . . The universe expects every man to do his duty in his parallel of latitude."

Thoreau's letters contain some of his best criticism. Here he is most relaxed and straightforward, and his criticism takes on an interesting personal tone. In a letter to Emerson, he criticizes Emerson's "Ode to Beauty." The criticism is from the organic point of view, and it is sharp and penetrating. He begins with the form of the poem and finds it utterly unsuited to the matter:

> But I have a good deal of fault to find with your "Ode to Beauty." The tune is altogether unworthy of the thoughts. You slope too quickly to the rhyme, as if that trick had better be performed as soon as possible, or as if you stood over the line with a hatchet, and chopped off the verses as they came out, some short and some long. But give us a long reel, and we'll cut it up to suit ourselves. It sounds like parody. "Thee I knew of old," "Remediless thirst," are some of those stereotyped lines.

Thoreau's criticism of Walt Whitman is unreservedly the most interesting. After having visited him, Thoreau wrote to Harrison Blake: "I am still somewhat in a quandry about him.—feel that he is essentiall strange to me, at any rate; but I am surprized by the sight of him. He is very broad, but, as I have said, not fine. He said that I misapprehended him.

I am not sure that I do. . . ." But his praise for Whitman's poetry was sound and unequivocal:

> I have just read his second edition (which he gave me) and it has done me more good than any reading for a long time. Perhaps I remember best the poems of Walt Whitman an American and the Sun-Down Poem. . . . I have found his poem exhilarating, encouraging. . . .
>
> On the whole it seems to me to be very brave and American, after whatever deductions. I do not believe that the sermons, so called, that have been preached in this land put together are equal to it for preaching.
>
> We ought to rejoice greatly in him. He occasionally suggests something more than human. . . .

There was, however, one fault which he found in Whitman, his sensuality. What is most interesting are Thoreau's ideas of the immorality involved, which he places in the reader, not in the work of art:

> There are two or three places in the book which are disagreeable, to say the least; simply sensual. He does not celebrate love at all. It is as if the beasts spoke. . . . As for its sensuality, it may turn out to be less sensual than it appears,—I do not so much wish that those parts were not written, as that men and women were so pure that they could read them without harm, that is, without understanding them. . . . Of course Walt Whitman can communicate to us no experience, and if we are shocked, whose experience is it that we are reminded of?

This is the temper of Thoreau's literary criticism. It is obvious that the forces influential in his criticism are the same as those revealed in Emerson's: transcendentalism, organic theories of art, and, less influential, the reproductive criticism of Goethe.[38] He was not interested to the degree that Emerson was in historical criticism and preferred more frequently a biographical approach. As Professor Matthiessen pointed out, "He had understood that in the act of expression a man's whole being, and his natural and social background as well, function organically together. He had mastered a definition of art akin to what Maritain has extracted from scholasticism: *Recta ratio factibilium,* the right ordering of the thing to be made, the right revelation of the material."

It is surprising to find that Nathaniel Hawthorne, who was one of the most consciously artistic craftsmen of his age, contributed so little to the literary criticism of the period.[39] With few exceptions, only scattered

---

[38] In the conclusion to his essay on Carlyle, Thoreau writes: "To try him by the German rule of referring an author to his own standard, we will quote the following from Carlyle's remarks on history." Thoreau does not, however, use this approach himself but leaves "the reader to consider how far his practice has been consistent with his theory."

[39] For biographical studies of Hawthorne, see Newton Arvin, *Hawthorne* (Boston, 1929); Henry James, *Hawthorne* (New York, 1879); Randall Stewart, *Nathaniel Hawthorne: A Biography* (New Haven, 1948); and George E. Woodberry, *Nathaniel Hawthorne* (Boston, 1902). For an able analysis of Hawthorne's art and theory, see F. O. Matthiessen, "Hawthorne," in *American Renaissance.* Also see Leland Schu-

critical comments can be found in his works concerning his judgment of other writers. He made fun of the tedious epics of Dwight and Barlow, and he had some praise for the work of Charles Brockden Brown. Bryant, he thought, had done his best work and had gone "to his last sleep, with the Thanatopsis gleaming over him like a sculptured marble sepulchre by moonlight." He had special praise for Emerson and Lowell although he felt that Whittier's muse had been "perversely assigned a battle trumpet." In a short notice which he wrote, Hawthorne indicated that he liked Melville's *Typee* "uncommonly well." Later, he added "I have read Melville's works with a progressive appreciation of the author. No writer ever put the reality before his reader more unflinchingly . . . with depths here and there that compel a man to swim for his life." In a letter to Duyckinck in 1845 concerning Thoreau, he wrote that "the only way, however, in which he could ever approach the popular mind, would be by writing a book of simple observation of nature. . . ." Later, in commenting on *Walden,* he referred to it as one of the few books having "American characteristics." In a review of *Evangeline* in 1847, he placed Longfellow "at the head of our list of native poets. . . ." [40] Among English writers he especially admired Spenser, Milton, and Bunyan, for their rich allegorical significance, and Shakespeare. He also had a relish for the eighteenth-century writers, an undercurrent of whose taste is reflected in his style.[41]

Hawthorne's comments concerning the nature and function of art form a much more substantial body of opinion than do his criticisms of individual writers and works.[42] That Hawthorne considered the highest function of the imagination to be allegorical and symbolic is clear from his designation as "rulers . . . of the imagination" of Spenser, Milton, and Bunyan, whose work relied heavily upon allegory and symbolism. Like Emerson, Hawthorne found this higher symbolic imagination lacking in the surface realism of the contemporary novel, and he was convinced "that the world requires a deeper moral and a closer and homelier truth than is supplied by Scott and Dickens." In *Notes of Travel,* II, Hawthorne wrote "that nature is better, no doubt, but Nature cannot be reproduced on canvas or in print, and the artist's only resource is to substitute something that may stand instead of and suggest the truth."

Conscious of the limitations of a literal realism in the novel, Hawthorne felt "that the highest merit of art is suggestiveness." The artist should strive, as Hawthorne contends in "The Artist of the Beautiful," to achieve "a beauty that should attain to the ideal which Nature has proposed to

bert, *Hawthorne the Artist: Fine-Art Devices in Fiction* (Chapel Hill, N.C.,1944); and Austin Warren, introduction to *Nathaniel Hawthorne: Representative Selections* (New York, 1934). The most recent study is Mark Van Doren, *Nathaniel Hawthorne* (New York, 1949).

[40] See H. H. Hoeltje, "Hawthorne's Review of *Evangeline,*" *New England Quarterly,* XXIII (1950), 232–35.

[41] Also see Harold Blodgett, "Hawthorne as Poetry Critic; Six Unpublished Letters to Lewis Mansfield," *American Literature,* XII (1940), 173–84.

[42] For a valuable exposition of Hawthorne's artistic theories, see F. O. Matthiessen, *American Renaissance.* Also see Charles H. Foster, "Hawthorne's Literary Theory," *Publications Modern Language Association,* LVII (1942), 241–54.

herself in all creatures, but has never taken pains to realize." This beauty, however, like Emerson's, was one which was also truth. For Hawthorne, art and the imagination were not ends in themselves but rather means of "spiritualizing the grossness of this actual life."

In "The Prophetic Pictures" Hawthorne again stresses that true art does not concern itself with the surface of things: "The artist—the true artist—must look beneath the exterior. It is his gift—his proudest, but often a melancholy one—to see the inmost soul, and, by a power indefinable even to himself, to make it glow or darken upon the canvas, in glances that express the thought and sentiment of years." Hawthorne favored poetic idealization as the best method of revealing human character and of illustrating some universal truth. "There is no harm," he wrote, "but on the contrary, good, in arraying some of the ordinary facts of life in a slightly idealized and artistic guise."

Writing in the preface to *The House of the Seven Gables* (1851), Hawthorne distinguishes the Romance, the type he is writing, from the Novel, which he equates with realism:

> The latter form of composition is presumed to aim at a very minute fidelity, not merely to the possible, but to the probable and ordinary course of man's experience. The former—while, as a work of art, it must rigidly subject itself to laws, and while it sins unpardonably so far as it may swerve aside from the truth of the human heart—has fairly a right to present that truth under circumstances of the writer's own choosing or creation.

Hawthorne also pleaded for the right of the artist to create atmosphere, which was so foreign to the literal-minded American public: "If he think fit, also, he may so manage his atmospherical medium as to bring out or mellow the lights and deepen and enrich the shadows of the picture." [43] Hawthorne's stress on the visual affords an interesting comparison with Emerson's belief that sight is the most spiritual of the senses.

In the preface to *The Scarlet Letter* (1850), Hawthorne wrote of the relation between the "actual" and the "imaginary," between the "real" and the "ideal," when, late at night, he sat "in the deserted parlor, lighted only by the glimmering coal-fire and the moon, striving to picture forth imaginary scenes. . . . If the imaginative faculty refused to act at such an hour, it might well be deemed a hopeless case. . . . Glancing at the looking-glass, we behold—deep within its haunted verge—the smouldering glow of the half-extinguished anthracite, the white moonbeams on the floor, and a repetition of all the gleam and shadow of the picture, with one remove further from the actual, and nearer to the imaginative. . . . Thus . . . the floor of our familiar room has become a neutral territory, somewhere between the real world and fairy-land, where the Actual and the Imaginary may meet, and each imbue itself with the nature of the other."

[43] In this connection see Walter Blair's important findings on Hawthorne's use of color-imagery in the *New England Quarterly*, XV (1942), 74-94.

Rather than escapism, Hawthorne views the function of the imaginative and the ideal as that of raising its material to the level of contemplation where it might be freed from accidents and irrelevancies, where it might be disengaged from the "appearance" of things, from a too literal concern with the surface of life.[44] Thus he wrote in the preface to *Rappaccini's Daughter* (1844) that his own fictions "so far as can be discovered, have little or no reference to time or space. In any case, he generally contents himself with a very slight embroidery of outward manners—the faintest possible counterfeit of real life,—and endeavors to create an interest by some less obvious peculiarity of the subject."

Just as Hawthorne defended the right of the romancer to idealize only on condition that he not violate the truth of the human heart, he, like Coleridge, insisted that artistic genius consisted in a union of intellect and heart. He feared that a too exclusive use of intellect would lead to only "a concrete arrangement of crystallizations . . . as cold as they were brilliant." Not a startling effect, intellectually contrived, but a high and beautiful seriousness was the goal of art to Hawthorne: "An innate perception and reflection of truth gives the only sort of originality that does not finally grow intolerable." Hence, the artist, in order to be successful in his art, must pass through "a thorough apprenticeship, both in learning the essentials of the work to be done and in developing the character necessary for any accomplishment."

Although, like most of his contemporaries, he stresses the element of truth and morality in literature, Hawthorne reveals himself to be the true artist and to have avoided the "heresy of the didactic." In conformity with his belief that "the highest merit of art is its suggestiveness," he wrote: "When romances do really teach anything, or produce an effective operation, it is usually through a far more subtle process than the ostensible one. . . . A high truth, indeed, fairly, finely, and skilfully wrought out, brightening at every step, and crowning the final development of a work of fiction, may add an artistic glory, but it is never any truer, and any more evident, at the last page than the first."

It is a matter for some conjecture that Hawthorne was so little affected by the literary modes and aims of nineteenth-century fiction and criticism. His reading seems to have been done chiefly for confirmation of his own principles. Our first artist of the novel, Hawthorne thus consciously dedicated himself to the fulfillment of his aesthetic principles which so impressed his disciple Henry James.

Like Hawthorne, Melville left no manual for writers; and, like Hawthorne, he does not loom large in any survey of the critical writing of the

[44] F. O. Matthiessen, *American Renaissance,* quotes, in this connection, Butcher's comment on the Aristotelian doctrine of how art discovers the universal beneath the particular: "It passes beyond the bare reality given by nature, and expresses a purified form of reality disengaged from accident, and freed from conditions which thwart its development. The real and the ideal from this point of view are not opposites, as they are sometimes conceived to be. The ideal is the real, but rid of contradictions, unfolding itself according to the laws of its own being, apart from alien influences and the disturbances of chance." See p. 264.

period.[45] Pierre, to a large extent, was speaking for Melville when he said, "I write precisely as I please."

Although it would be difficult to regard Melville as a transcendentalist, he came to believe, no less than Emerson, that "Nature is the symbol of spirit." Ahab, in his soliloquy on the whale's skull in *Moby Dick*, is made to exclaim: "O Nature, and O soul of man! how far beyond all utterance are your linked analogies! not the smallest atom stirs or lives on matter, but has its cunning duplicate in mind." Like Hawthorne, Melville regarded the imagination, in its highest symbolic and allegorical function, as the agent mediating between them. This conception of the relation between spirit and matter, and of the function of the imagination in relation to them and to art, precluded for Melville, as it did for Hawthorne, any satisfaction with fiction which strove merely to reproduce the surface details of life with a literal realism. It meant that if art were to retain its organic expression the method of fiction would be allegorical and symbolic, the use of natural fact as spiritual symbol.

Stemming partially from Hawthorne, and bearing a marked resemblance to Hawthorne's prefaces, Melville's own defense of his idealization, his heightening of reality, is to be found in *The Confidence Man* (1857). Protesting against a literalism that appeared to be a dominant attitude of his time in fiction, he found it difficult to understand that "severe fidelity to real life should be exacted by anyone" in a work of fiction:

> And as, in real life, the proprieties will not allow people to act out themselves with that unreserve permitted to the stage; so, in books of fiction, they look not only for more entertainment, but, at bottom, even for more reality than real life itself can show. Thus, though they want novelty, they want nature, too; but nature unfettered, exhilarated, in effect transformed. In this way of thinking, the people in a fiction, like the people in a play, must dress as nobody exactly dresses, talk as nobody exactly talks, act as nobody exactly acts. It is with fiction as with religion; it should present another world, and yet one to which we feel the tie.

Melville seems to have placed comparatively little emphasis on the classic principles of unity and order which form such a central aspect of Poe's theory. He felt that symmetry of form is often impossible to attain, since "Truth uncompromisingly told will always have its ragged edges; hence the conclusion of such a narration is apt to be less finished than an architectural finial." Likewise, he believed that the demand for consistency of character in fiction is far from being true to the higher reality which

[45] Indicative of the current interest in Melville is the number of critical biographies of recent date: Newton Arvin, *Herman Melville* (New York, 1950); Richard Chase, *Herman Melville* (New York, 1949); Leon Howard, *Herman Melville* (Berkeley, Cal., 1951); and William E. Sedgwick, *Herman Melville: The Tragedy of Min.!* (Cambridge, 1944). See also Lewis Mumford, *Herman Melville* (New York, 1929); and Raymond M. Weaver, *Herman Melville: Mariner and Mystic* (New York, 1921). Interpretations of Melville's art and thought can be found in F. O. Matthiessen, "Melville," in *American Renaissance;* and in Willard Thorp, Introduction to *Herman Melville: Representative Selections* (New York, 1938).

fiction attempts to portray: "That fiction where every character can, by reason of its consistency, be comprehended at a glance, either exhibits but sections of character, making them appear for wholes, or else is very untrue to reality."

Particularly illuminating in view of his own propensity for the creation of characters of such magnitude as Ahab and Pierre are Melville's comments concerning "originality" of character:

> Furthermore, if we consider, what is popularly held to entitle characters in fiction to being deemed original, is but something personal—confined to itself. The character sheds not its characteristic on its surroundings, whereas, the original character, essentially such, is like a revolving Drummond light, raying away from itself all round it—everything is lit by it, everything starts to it (mark how it is with Hamlet), so that, in certain minds, there follows upon the adequate conception of such a character, an effect, in its way, akin to that which in Genesis attends upon the beginnings of things.

It is obvious that Melville is again opposing the popular trends of contemporary fiction which demanded many characters of equal development and which conceived of "originality" of character in terms of some trait peculiar to the individual.

Melville himself had a dislike for criticism and commentary, and, with one exception, his efforts in this direction were negligible. In a long critical review, "Hawthorne and His Mosses," which appeared in *The Literary World* in 1850, he attempted to convince American readers that they had in their midst a genuinely great artist, one of "the new and far better generation of writers."

Sensing that, perhaps for the first time, in the work of Hawthorne, American art had achieved a ripeness culminating a long struggle for cultural independence, he praises the maturity of Hawthorne's thought and style and does not hesitate to compare him with Shakespeare, pointing out that "the difference between the two men is by no means immeasurable." "Let America, then," he urges, "prize and cherish her writers; yea, let her glorify them." Pointing out that no writer merits great praise who is not original, and with unmistakable reference to Irving, Melville regrets that "that graceful writer, who perhaps of all Americans has received the most plaudits from his own country for his productions,—that very popular and amiable writer, however good and self-reliant in many things, perhaps owes his chief reputation to the self-acknowledged imitation of a foreign model, and to the studied avoidance of all topics but smooth ones." He concludes that "we want no American Goldsmiths: nay, we want no American Miltons. . . . Let us away with this leaven of literary flunkeyism toward England."

Pondering the question of what constitutes greatness in an artist, Melville notices that often "it is the least part of genius that attracts attention," that "Where Hawthorne is known, he seems to be deemed a pleasant writer, with a pleasant style,—a sequestered, harmless man, from whom any deep and weighty thing would hardly be anticipated—a man who means no meanings." But seeing the same quality in Hawthorne that had so impressed him in Shakespeare, he emphasizes that "there is no man in whom humor and love are developed in that high form called genius; no such man can exist without also possessing, as the indispensable complement of these, a great, deep intellect, which drops down into the universe like a plummet." He is fully aware that no mere technical skill, no superficial imitation of life, was responsible for the artistry of Hawthorne but rather that his greatness, as Shakespeare's, lies in "those deep far-away things in him; those occasional flashings-forth of the intuitive Truth in him; those short, quick probings at the very axis of reality."

A second measure of Hawthorne's greatness Melville finds in the delicate revelation of human nature which characterized his work and which Melville is sure could come only from "such a depth of tenderness, such a boundless sympathy with all forms of being, such an omnipresent love, that we must needs say that this Hawthorne is here almost alone in his generation—at least, in the artistic manifestation of these things." Balancing this "Indian-summer sunlight on the hither side of Hawthorne's soul," Melville also senses "this great power of blackness in him," which "derives its force from its appeals to that Calvinistic sense of Innate Depravity and Original Sin, from whose visitations, in some shape or other, no deeply thinking mind is always and wholly free."

Though it is impressionistic to a considerable degree, there is, however, in Melville's criticism of Hawthorne a judicial standard implied. Great literature must reveal a ripeness, a maturity of thought and style. It must reveal the originality of a "deeply thinking mind" to which must be added "a boundless sympathy," "an omnipresent love." That great literature must possess this union of thought and emotion, a concept which affords an interesting parallel to Hawthorne's insistence on the union of heart and intellect in his conception of the creative artist, is implicit in Melville's comments on Irving.

Melville was aware of an historical point of view in criticism, as is evident from his comment that "Whereas, great geniuses are parts of the times, they themselves are the times, and possess a correspondent coloring," and "that, in his own lifetime, Shakspeare was not Shakspeare, but only Master William Shakspeare of the shrewd, thriving business firm of Condell, Shakspeare & Co., proprietors of the Globe Theatre in London; and by a courtly author, of the name of Chettle, was looked at as an 'upstart crow,' beautified 'with other birds' feathers.'" He also looks upon Hawthorne as being a product of America: "The smell of your beeches and hemlocks is upon him; your own broad prairies are in his soul . . ." And he speculates on "whether there really lurks in him, perhaps unknown to himself, a touch of Puritanic gloom . . ." In the main, however, Melville is not interested in viewing the work of Hawthorne in relation to its age, but rather in seeing it in its relation to the qualities of character from which it originated.

Perhaps the principal contribution of Melville to American criticism, the essay displays a remarkably perceptive judgment of Hawthorne, and a nationalism which, though enthusiastic, is not provincial, since Melville emphasizes that "it is not meant that all American writers should studiously cleave to nationality in their writings; only this, no American writer should write like an Englishman or a Frenchman; let him write like a man, for then he will be sure to write like an American."

John Greenleaf Whittier was not a great literary critic by any standards.[46] In some instances his judgment of his contemporaries was curiously weak—yet it was a weakness shared by other critics of the time. His tendency to overrate such poets as Percival and Brainard is perhaps less damaging when it is considered that Bryant, among others, committed the same error. Much of the critical writing of Whittier was in the form of reviews for newspapers and magazines, and is not available in his collected works.[47]

Like most critics of the period, he tended to subordinate most artistic considerations to moral values. Throughout his career, he praised the moral and the Christian, often without regard to literary merit. Subject, particularly in his early years, to the current English and American romanticisms, he praised the literature of heroism, adventure, and escape— especially Cooper's The Last of the Mohicans. However strong his interest in dominant literary modes of the day, including Gothicism, he never permitted it to offset the strong emphasis upon morality which led him to criticize such poets as Byron and Shelley.

Whittier later turned from this strong early interest in the Gothic and other European literary moods to a concern for the New England locale which was to characterize his work for the rest of his life. Associated with this localism was a literary nationalism which was firm but temperate. In his later years, after devoting himself to the cause of freedom and reform, his criticism advocated a sort of realism, or Quaker "plainness," which led him to oppose the pretentiousness and elegance of the genteel tradition and to admire the homely realism of Burns.

In place of his early fascination for the Gothic which had led him to admire Brockden Brown and Susannah Rowson, he turned to a sort of realism expressed in "the poetry of Home, Nature and the Affections . . . the calm, quiet appreciation of the beautiful in common daily life." Late in life he wrote in his preface to Songs of Three Centuries (1875) praising Bryant's "Thanatopsis" and Dana's Buccaneer with its "terse realism" and pointing out that they "left the weak imitators of an artificial school without an audience. All further attempts to colonize the hills and pastures of New England from old mythologies were abandoned. . . . If we

---

[46] The best biography of Whittier is Samuel T. Pickard, Life and Letters of John Greenleaf Whittier, 2 vols. (Boston, 1894, rev. ed., 1907). Also see Albert Mordell, Quaker Militant: John Greenleaf Whittier (Boston, 1933).

[47] A valuable collection of Whittier's criticism is Edwin H. Cady and Harry H. Clark, Whittier on Writers and Writing: The Uncollected Critical Writings of John Greenleaf Whittier (Syracuse, N.Y., 1950). Also see Clara P. Marcy, The Literary Criticism of John Greenleaf Whittier, unpublished dissertation (Boston, 1946).

no longer have ambitious Columbiads and Conquests of Canaan, we have
at least truth and nature, wit and wisdom, in Bryant's 'Robert of Lincoln,'
Emerson's 'Humblebee,' Lowell's 'Courtin',' and the 'One-Hoss Shay' of
Holmes."

In his conception of the nature of poetic genius, Whittier reflected the
conventional belief of the age that it was a "divine creative faculty." Concerning the nature of art, Whittier likewise reflected current trends in
holding that it was organic, that it was "energy, enthusiasm, beauty, abandonment to the emotions, and . . . spontaneous adaptation of language
and rhythm to their subjects." Regarding the function of literary criticism,
Whittier wrote:

> The true cause of the imbecility of our poetry is found in the dangerous
> encouragement which is given to the light flashes of fancy. . . . It is
> time a more independent Mode of criticism was commenced in this
> country. Most of our literary periodicals are too timid, in fact too de-
> pendent, to give their opinions, with the firmness and regard to truth
> which are necessary. We are becoming effeminate in everything—in our
> habits as well as our literature.

In his method of criticism, Whittier tended to approach the literary
work as an organic unity considering, as he does in his essay on *Evangeline* (1848), the appropriateness of the rhythm, language, and themes to
the general purpose, or "design," of the author. In general, Whittier combines the reproductive and judicial in his criticism, with the latter always
the more pronounced in his work. While not insensitive to literary craftsmanship, he always subordinated it to the moral and humanitarian values
of art. As he wrote of *Evangeline*, "it is not merely a work of art; the pulse
of humanity throbs warmly through it." And he made perfectly clear that a
purely aesthetic love of beauty was not enough. Writing in an essay on
Thomas Paine, which he significantly titles "The Infidel," Whittier pointed
out that Paine "loved the works of God for their exceeding beauty—not
for their manifestation of an overruling intelligence. . . . He perished, a
worshipper of that beauty. . . . There is a moral in his history, which is
full of fearful warning." And he made equally clear, in an essay on Shelley,
that "mere Genius shall never take the precedence of Virtue, in our
estimation."

There is little evidence that points to Whittier as a great critic or to
any of his criticism as possessing a lasting significance. Yet there is value
in its revelation of the development of Whittier himself and in its mirror-
ing of many of the dominant ideas and intentions which inform the literary criticism of his age.

Considering the nature of Longfellow's poetry and the particular qualities of mind that it reveals, it is perhaps not surprising to find that he was
not prominent as a critic.[48] Whenever commenting upon literature, he

[48] The primary biography of Longfellow is still *The Life of Henry W. Longfellow*
by his brother Samuel Longfellow (2 vols., Boston, 1886), supplemented by his
Final Memorials of Henry Wadsworth Longfellow (Boston, 1887), later published

did, however, reveal a sharply defined set of values: homely affection, simple piety, refinement of thought, sentiment, and a love for the remote, strange, and indistinct.

In an early article on Sidney's *Defence of Poesy* (1832), Longfellow is primarily concerned with defending poetry in his own day against the growing utilitarianism of the American people. He stresses, as most critics of the period did, the fact that the fine arts also have utility, that "they will enrich the heart, freight the understanding, and make up the garnered fulness of the mind." Using the example of the Hebrew poets, he points out "that the legitimate tendency of poetry is to exalt, rather than to debase,—to purify, rather than to corrupt," and further, "to give us correct moral impressions, and thereby advance the cause of truth and the improvement of society."

Longfellow, as a critic, is concerned with literature primarily from the historical point of view. Quoting from Schlegel's *Lectures on the History of Literature,* "literature . . . as the aggregate mass of symbols, in which the spirit of an age or the character of a nation is shadowed forth," Longfellow states that "As nations advanced in civilization and refinement, poetry advanced with them. In each successive age, it became the image of their thoughts and feelings, of their manners, customs, and characters; for poetry is but the warm expression of the thoughts and feelings of a people, and we speak of it as being national, when the character of a nation shines visibly and distinctly through it." He continues, pointing out that "Castilian poetry is characterized by sounding expressions, and that pomp and majesty, so peculiar to Spanish manners and character. On the other hand, English poetry possesses in a high degree the charms of rural and moral feeling . . ."

Longfellow views this relationship between poetry and its race, place, and time as one of its highest uses, since "The impressions produced by poetry upon national character at any period, are again re-produced, and give a more pronounced and individual character to the poetry of a subsequent period." An additional use is also related to this character of poetry: "Historic facts are chiefly valuable, as exhibiting intellectual phenomena. And so far as poetry exhibits these phenomena more perfectly and distinctly than history does, so far is it superior to history."

The influence of climate upon literature is stressed by Longfellow in further developing the historical point of view. "As an illustration of the influence of climate on the character of poetry," he writes, "it is worthy of remark, that the English poets excel those of the South of Europe in their descriptions of morning and evening," which he traces to the "rural beauty which pervades the English landscape, and to the long morning

as Vol. III of the *Life.* For an excellent analysis of Longfellow's early life, see Lawrance Thompson, *Young Longfellow, 1807–1843* (New York, 1938). For European influences on Longfellow, see James T. Hatfield, *New Light on Longfellow, with Special Reference to His Relations to Germany* (Boston, 1933); and Orie W. Long, *Literary Pioneers* (Cambridge, 1935). A good, brief critical study is Odell Shepard, introduction to *Henry Wadsworth Longfellow: Representative Selections* (New York, 1934).

and evening twilight of a northern climate." On the other hand, "A love of indolence and a warm imagination are characteristic of the inhabitants of the South. These are natural effects of a soft voluptuous climate."

Closely related to his historical view of literature is his plea for nationalism in American literature: "We repeat, then, that we wish our native poets would give a more national character to their writings. In order to effect this, they have only to write more naturally, to write from their own feelings and impressions, from the influence of what they see around them, and not from any pre-conceived notions of what poetry ought to be, caught by reading many books, and imitating many models."

As did most of the American critics of the period, Longfellow deplores the rather widespread American imitation of Byron and states his belief "that no writer has done half so much to corrupt the literary taste as well as the moral principle of our country . . ." He expresses a much different opinion of Wordsworth "whose pure and gentle philosophy has been gradually gaining the ascendency. . . . The sobriety, and, if we may use the expression, the republican simplicity of his poetry, are in unison with our moral and political doctrines." It is interesting to note Longfellow's use here of the historical conception of literature as a standard of judgment, that a literary work should be suitable to a nation's characteristics.

In an article on "Old English Romances," which appeared in the *North American Review* in 1833, Longfellow also adopts the historical method and comes to the conclusion that the elder English poets are superior to poets of the present and that they have a greater force and clarity of thought. Further illustration of his use of this approach can be found in his review of Hawthorne's *Twice-Told Tales* for the *North American* in 1837 where he considers "One of the prominent characteristics of these tales is that they are national in character."

In this same review Longfellow demonstrates another aspect of his critical theory, that romantic literature should concern itself with the past rather than the present. Closely related to the associationist principle because of its emphasis upon the rich connotations which the distant and the past hold for the imagination, this remained one of the central aspects of Longfellow's aesthetics. He praises Hawthorne's tales because "The author has chosen his themes among the traditions of New England, the dusty legends of 'the good old Colony times, when we lived under a king.' This is the right material for story. . . . The dreary old Puritanical times begin to look romantic in the distance." Advocating themes and settings that are mellowed and remote, he emphasized the effect to be gained by romantic distance whether the locale was native or foreign. As he writes in *Kavanagh* (1849): "They were too near to be clothed by the imagination with the golden vapors of romance; for the familiar seems trivial, and only the distant and unknown completely satisfy the mind."

One of the few changes that occurred in Longfellow's theory or practice was his opinion concerning nationalism in literature. In the twenty-eighth chapter of *Kavanagh*, he writes: "Nationality is a good thing to a certain extent, but universality is better. All that is best in the great poets

of all countries is not what is national in them, but what is universal." [49]
That he had not changed his mind concerning the historical conception
of literature is evidenced in the same passage by his comment that "all
literature, as well as all art, is the result of culture and intellectual refinement."

That Longfellow did not write more criticism than he did is perhaps
owing to the low opinion he held of it. Like Irving, he felt that the practice of criticism had been used by critics in chiefly a faultfinding manner:
"Doubtless criticism was originally benignant, pointing out the beauties
of a work rather than its defects. The passions of men have made it malignant, as the bad heart of Procrustes turned the bed, the symbol of repose,
into an instrument of torture." It is ironical that his own criticism tended,
for the most part, to be historical and judicial rather than appreciative.

In terms of comprehensiveness, Lowell was perhaps the greatest of nineteenth-century critics.[50] While others, like Poe, Emerson, or Whitman,
possessed greater originality and vigor, none could match the distinguished,
well-rounded literary essays of Lowell comprising a critical history extending from Dante to his own age. As Norman Foerster was one of the first
to point out, while Lowell is impressionistic in his criticism, he did possess critical standards that were clearly defined.[51] That he was attracted to
impressionism is evident from such statements as "the critic is to record
his impressions, which may be valuable or not, according to the greater or
less ductility of the senses on which they are made." But Lowell was not
content to remain merely an impressionist, and ultimately did formulate
critical principles involving historical as well as aesthetic and didactic
standards.

Lowell pointed out that historical criticism was necessary not so much
to "explain" but to "understand" an author relative "to his position in the

[49] See James Russell Lowell, "Longfellow's *Kavanagh*: Nationality in Literature,"
North American Review, LXIX (1849).
[50] The best biography of Lowell is Horace E. Scudder, *James Russell Lowell*, 2
vols. (Cambridge, 1901). Also see W. C. Brownell, "Lowell," in *American Prose
Masters* (New York, 1909), pp. 271–335; W. D. Howells, "Studies of Lowell," in
Literary Friends and Acquaintance (New York, 1900), pp. 212–50; and Henry
James, "James Russell Lowell," in *Essays in London and Elsewhere* (New York,
1893), pp. 44–80. A recent study of Lowell's early career is Leon Howard, *Vic-
torian Knight Errant: A Study of the Early Literary Career of James Russell Lowell*
(Berkeley, Cal., 1952). The best brief critical study of Lowell is Harry H. Clark and
Norman Foerster, introduction to *James Russell Lowell: Representative Selections*
(New York, 1947). One of the major estimates of Lowell as a critic is Norman Foer-
ster, "Lowell," in *American Criticism* (Boston, 1928), pp. 111–56. Also see R. D.
Altick, "Was Lowell an Historical Critic?" *American Literature*, XIV (1942), 250–
59; Harry H. Clark, "Lowell's Criticism of Romantic Literature," *Publications Modern
Language Association*, XLI (1926), 209–28; A. L. Lange, "James Russell Lowell as
a Critic," *California University Chronicle*, VIII (1906), 352–64; and J. J. Reilly,
James Russell Lowell as a Critic (New York, 1915).
[51] J. J. Reilly, *James Russell Lowell as a Critic*, contended that Lowell was merely
an impressionist and not a critic. For the opposite point of view, see Norman Foerster's analysis of Lowell as a critic in *American Criticism*. Harry H. Clark in
"Lowell's Criticism of Romantic Literature" also dissents from the view of Lowell
as merely an impressionist, and holds that Lowell's judgments are based on well-
considered literary and philosophic principles.

literary history of his country and the conditions of his generation." [52]
"If," he wrote in his essay on Milton, "Goethe was right in saying that
every man was a citizen of his age as well as of his country, there can be
no doubt that in order to understand the motives and conduct of the man
we must first make ourselves intimate with the time in which he lived." [53]
Again, in the essay on Fielding, he wrote that it is "an established principle of criticism that in judging a man we must take into account the
age in which he lived, and which was as truly a part of him as he of it."
Particularly, he warns, in judging Fielding's morality "we must guard
against falling into the anachronism of forgetting the coarseness of the
age into which he was born and whose atmosphere he breathed." Likewise,
his essay on Spenser, as well as the one on Shakespeare, illustrate his
attempt to "understand" these writers in terms of the Elizabethan age.
Nowhere is the value of this sort of judgment so clearly indicated as in
Lowell's attitude toward the eighteenth century, which he managed to
evaluate more fairly than any other romantic critic. The question he
raises in his essay on Pope is "How much was it possible to make of the
material supplied by the age in which he lived? and how much did he
make of it?" His conclusion is that Pope "had one of the prime qualities
of a great poet in exactly answering the intellectual needs of the age in
which he lived, and in reflecting its lineaments." [54]

Historical judgments, while of great value, are not according to Lowell
final standards of evaluation. In the end, a poet must be judged by his
poetic qualities "absolutely, with reference, that is, to the highest standard,
and not relatively to the fashions and opportunities of the age in which
he lived." It is thus necessary to rise above the historical and seek the
absolute value of a work of art "from the purely literary point of view."
But not only are aesthetic considerations involved in seeking this absolute
value: "I believe we should judge a book rather by its total effect than by
the adequacy of special parts, and is not this effect moral as well as aesthetic?" And again, "moral and aesthetic defects are more nearly related
than is commonly supposed."

Within the sphere of aesthetic judgment, Lowell derived his principles
from the Greeks: "It is the Greeks who must furnish us with our standard of comparison. Their stamp is upon all the allowed measures and
weights of aesthetic criticism." [55] However, Lowell condemned the mere
imitation of classical models:

[52] For a more detailed study of Lowell as an historical critic, see R. D. Altick,
"Was Lowell an Historical Critic?"
[53] For a carefully documented study of the influence of Goethe on Lowell, see
George Wurfl, "Lowell's Debt to Goethe," *Pennsylvania State College Studies*, I
(1936), 1–89.
[54] See Byron D. Murray, *Lowell's Criticism of Dryden and Pope*, unpublished
dissertation (Iowa, 1946).
[55] For the influence of the classics on Lowell's literary theory, see John P. Pritchard,
"Lowell's Debt to Horace's *Ars Poetica*," *American Literature*, III (1931), 259–76,
and "Aristotle's *Poetics* and Certain American Literary Critics," *Classical Weekly*,
XXVII (1934); for the section on Lowell see pp. 89–93.

The model is not there to be copied merely, but that the study of it may lead us insensibly to the same processes of thought by which its purity of outline and harmony of parts were attained, and enable us to feel that strength is consistent with repose, that multiplicity is not abundance, that a thought is none the less profound that the limpidity of its expression allows us to measure it at a glance.

According to Lowell, "The poet, under whatever name, always stands for one thing—imagination." Lowell recognizes three types of imagination: "the plastic," which shapes materials into organic unity; [56] "the expressive," which "represents" the parts of the whole; and the "spiritual," which is intuition. The "spiritual" imagination which images the ideal can be ethical or spiritual. Lowell considered Shakespeare the greatest of poets in ethical imagination while Dante excelled in the spiritual. While the primary criterion in judging a work of art is form, the product of the plastic imagination, since there can be, for Lowell, no art at all without form, the final and highest consideration is the quality of the ethical or spiritual insight. Hence, a poet is great beacuse of "insight, and not for any faculty of observation and description." And it is by virtue of his imagination that he pierces through the temporal to the eternal.

If the significance of poetry does not lie in its observation and description, it must be, as Lowell points out in "The Function of the Poet" (1855), that "The study of literature, that it may be fruitful, that it may not result in a mere gathering of names and dates and phrases, must be a study of ideas and not of words . . ." However, "The first duty of the Muse," he says, "is to be delightful"; and he deplores the tendency "to value literature and even poetry for their usefulness as courses of moral philosophy." He was aware of the purely aesthetic values of a work of art as well as the highest values to be found in the exercise of all faculties of mind and spirit. Poetry, he believed, is the expression of beauty; but, like Matthew Arnold, he believed that beauty should serve as the medium for such ideas as render truth and nobility more dear to man: "The poet is he who can best see and best say what is ideal." [57]

That Lowell had little sympathy for the creative imagination "that is not drawn back to any ethical centre," is evident from his objection to Shelley's subjectivity as being too unique and remote from normal experience. Referring to him as a "mere poet," and as "ineffectual," Lowell criticized Shelley because he "substitutes his own impression of the thing for the thing itself; he forces his own consciousness upon it, and herein lies the root of all sentimentalism." Lowell's objection to romantic subjectivity can also be seen in his comment that Wordsworth lacks universality, that there is "something insular . . . I might say parochial, in his choice of subject and tone of thought," and that he "never saw beyond limits of

[56] For reviews illustrating Lowell's concept of the organic unity of a work of art, see "Disraeli's Tancred," North American Review, LXV (1847), "The New Timon," ibid., LXIV (1847), and "Browning's Plays and Poems." ibid., LXVI (1848).
[57] For a more thorough exposition of Lowell's principles of poetry and criticism, see Ferris Lockwood, "Mr. Lowell's Art-Principles," Scribner's, XV (1894), 186–89.

his own consciousness and experience." He also reacted against the subjectivity of Wordsworth's pantheism: "Great poetry should have breadth as well as height and depth; it should meet men everywhere on the open levels of their common humanity, and not merely on their occasional excursions to the heights of speculation or their exploring expeditions among the crypts of metaphysics." Anticipating Irving Babbitt, he denounced the sentimentalism of Byron, Rousseau, Moore, and Thoreau, among others.[58]

Lowell's creed of criticism is perhaps the best in nineteenth-century American criticism, and yet even Lowell himself wrote in his old age: "I feel that my life has been mainly wasted—that I have thrown away more than most men ever had." The answer is inevitable—the weakness lay not in the creed but rather in the man himself, as many scholars have already pointed out, and as Lowell himself intimated. Drawing upon the resources of the historical, judicial, reproductive, and impressionistic methods of criticism, his own criticism suffers from a lack of system. In spite of this, most of his critical judgments are sound and his influence upon scholarship and literary criticism in America has been deep and abiding.

Completing the "New England Triumvirate," Oliver Wendell Holmes, with his love of common sense, his urbanity, his antipathy toward romantic poets and poetry, stands as one in whom neoclassicism was still the prevailing force.[59] His hatred of disorder and confusion, whether in literature or in life, was evidence of his passion for order and clarity which he felt that science in particular could offer mankind. His life-long devotion to science is reminiscent of eighteenth-century Deism, which looked upon the laws of nature as being a revelation of God. In prose his ideals were those of Addison and Steele; in poetry those of Pope. Moderation, urbanity, and control were qualities he especially prized.

In the prefatory note to "Poetry: A Metrical Essay" (1836), Holmes referred to himself as "a young person trained after the schools of classical English verse as represented by Pope, Goldsmith, and Campbell." This preference for neoclassical principles in poetry characterized Holmes for the rest of his life. While he had at times a moderate admiration for the romantic, he always preferred the "normal," "sunlit" genius:

---

[58] For a more complete study of Lowell's criticism of romanticism, see Harry H. Clark, "Lowell's Criticism of Romantic Literature." Another valuable study is Austin Warren, "Lowell on Thoreau," *Studies in Philology*, XXVII (1930), 442–61.

[59] J. T. Morse, *Life and Letters of Oliver Wendell Holmes*, 2 vols. (Boston, 1896), is a fundamental source book. Mark A. De Wolfe Howe's *Holmes of the Breakfast Table* (New York, 1939) is the most recent and authoritative life. Also valuable is William Lawrence Schroeder, *Oliver Wendell Holmes, An Appreciation* (London, 1909). A good, brief critical study is S. I. Hayakawa, introduction to *Oliver Wendell Holmes: Representative Selections* (New York, 1939). For a study of Holmes's criticism of Wordsworth, Keats, Shelley, Byron and others as reported in the Boston *Transcript* and *Traveller*, see S. I. Hayakawa, "Holmes's Lowell Institute Lectures," *American Literature*, VIII (1936), 281–90. For an analysis of Holmes's theory of poetry, see W. S. Knickerbocker, "His Own Boswell: a Note on the Poetry of Oliver Wendell Holmes," *Sewanee Review*, XLI (1933), 454–66. John P. Pritchard, *Return to the Fountains* (Durham, N.C., 1942), pp. 90–98, contains a study of the classical influences on Holmes.

Just so we have the great sun-kindled, constructive imaginations, and a far more numerous class of poets who have a certain kind of moonlight-genius given them to compensate for their imperfection of nature. Their want of mental coloring-matter makes them sensitive to those impressions which stronger minds neglect or never feel at all.

Holmes's common sense particularly rebelled against transcendentalism and he speaks of "Alcott in speculations, which often led him into the fourth dimension of mental space," and of "Thoreau, the nullifier of civilization, who insisted on nibbling his asparagus at the wrong end." Likewise, Wordsworth's mysticism could not be accepted:

> Wordsworth's "Ode" is a noble and beautiful dream; is it anything more? . . . The cloud of glory which the babe brings with it into the world is a good set of instincts, which dispose it to accept moral and intellectual truths,—not the truths themselves. And too many children come into life trailing after them clouds which are anything but clouds of glory.

The volume, *Ralph Waldo Emerson,* which Holmes did for the American Men of Letters series in 1885 is not perceptive criticism of Emerson. While it is of value in revealing Holmes's neoclassical literary principles, the book is characterized principally by his attempt to present Emerson as a considerably modified transcendentalist and hence to be praised for not going to extremes. That the work can be taken as Holmes's honest criticism of Emerson is doubtful, since he must have felt himself under some obligation to present Emerson from a favorable point of view.

Possessing the neoclassicist's preference for the ancient classics, Holmes could not sympathize with the attempt to establish a distinctively American literature, particularly when the attempt took the form that it did in Whitman. His disapproval of Whitman is largely based upon Whitman's violation of the classical principles of decorum: "He takes into his hospitable vocabulary words which no English dictionary recognizes as belonging to the language. . . . He accepts as poetical subjects all things alike, common and unclean, without discrimination . . ."

Similarly, for its violation of decorum, as well as for its literalism, Holmes disliked the realism of Zola:

> Leave the description of the drains and cesspools to the hygienic specialist, the painful facts of disease to the physician, the details of the laundry to the washerwoman. If we are to have realism in its tedious descriptions of unimportant particulars, let it be of particulars which do not excite disgust.

Reflecting classical literary theory, as well as eighteenth-century neoclassicism, Holmes believed that the poet was inspired: "The poet always recognizes a dictation *ab extra*; and we hardly think it a figure of speech when we talk of his inspiration." While never completely reconciling this theory of inspiration with his rationalism, Holmes continued to think of the poet as one who "trusts to his inner sense."

Like such eighteenth-century writers as Sterne and Goldsmith, Holmes also placed great emphasis, both in literary theory and practice, upon sentiment. But with Holmes, the sentiment is always controlled by principles of decorum and order, and never approaches the expansive, rebellious, individualistic emotions of romanticism.

If Holmes represents the conservatism of the period in his neoclassical affinities and his distaste for romanticism, Walt Whitman represents the radical and the revolutionary heralded by Emerson in "The American Scholar." [60] In spite of Whitman's own admonition, "I am a hell of a critic," his importance in American literary criticism has never been completely realized. Perhaps one reason for this is that he was primarily interested in the theory of literature rather than in the application of this theory to specific writers, though there is even more of this in his works than is commonly realized. Although as Whitman grew older his interest in literary criticism increased, he never considered himself a critic in perhaps the sense that Lowell did.

In a long preface to the 1855 edition of *Leaves of Grass*, Whitman developed a theory of poets and poetry that was not to be substantially changed for the remainder of his life. The spirit of the American poet must respond to his country's spirit, "must incarnate its geography and natural life and rivers and lakes . . . the union . . . free American workmen and workwomen." The greatest poet must express faith in the common people, must be a seer, and must, like Emerson's poet, perceive what is permanent in the flux of things, must "indicate the path between reality and their souls." Whitman, like Emerson, believed that the form of perfect poems is organic and the uniformity shows "the free growth of metrical laws and buds from them as unerringly and loosely as lilacs or roses on a bush. . . . The fluency and ornaments of the finest poems . . . are not independent but dependent." The greatest poet is the complete lover of the universe and his whole purpose is to "tally nature." And like Emerson, Whitman stressed originality, individuality, and self-reliance: "The poems distilled from other poems will probably pass away. The coward will surely pass away." The best poetry shall be "without meter, rhyme, or other ornament" and without other form than that which belongs to the "free growth of organic nature."

[60] Biographical studies of Whitman include Henry S. Canby, *Walt Whitman, An American: A Study in Biography* (Boston, 1943); Bliss Perry, *Walt Whitman: His Life and Work* (Boston, 1906); Newton Arvin, *Whitman* (New York, 1938); Frederik Schyberg, *Walt Whitman*, translated from the Danish by Evie Allison Allen, with an introduction by Gay Wilson Allen (New York, 1951); and Emory Holloway, *Whitman: An Interpretation in Narrative* (New York, 1926). Much valuable information, including some of Whitman's critical comments, can be found in Horace Traubel, *With Walt Whitman in Camden*, 3 vols. (New York, 1906-1914). Briefer critical studies include Gay Wilson Allen, *Walt Whitman Handbook* (Chicago, 1946); Floyd Stovall, *Walt Whitman: Representative Selections* (New York, 1934, rev. 1939); and F. O. Matthiessen, "Whitman," in *American Renaissance*, pp. 517-656. Major studies of Whitman's criticism are Norman Foerster, "Whitman," in *American Criticism*, and Maurice O. Johnson, *Walt Whitman as a Critic of Literature* (Lincoln, Neb., 1938).

Like most romantic critics, Whitman believed that poetry was suggestive and secured its effects largely through indirection. In the preface to the 1876 edition of *Leaves of Grass*, he elaborated: "Poetic style when address'd to the Soul, is less definite form, outline, sculpture, and becomes vista, music, half-tints, and even less than half-tints." The poet of the future must not merely reflect nature but must absorb and spiritualize it, must make "no useless attempt to repeat the material creation," but rather through imagination "project" and "transcend" it. Art must endow the facts of life with a greater and higher reality.

Whitman disparaged the intellectual element in poetry, and even to a certain extent the aesthetic as it had been emphasized by the genteel tradition, and called for a literature "underlying life, religious, consistent with science, handling the elements and forces with competent power, teaching and training men—." In criticizing American poetry, he claimed that most of it had been trivial and imitative, "piano songs and tinkling rhymes." He warned the future poet to beware of too much refinement and conformity, and to trust to his instincts. In style, particularly, he admonished, "Be natural, be natural, be natural!"

Ultimately, Whitman's chief criterion for greatness in literature was its depth of ethical and spiritual insight—its ability to "tally and express nature in its cosmic fullness," for in the final analysis "nature is the only complete and actual poem."

Derived in large measure from the romanticism, and particularly the transcendentalism, of the age, from its evangelicism and its oratory, this in summary fashion is Whitman's literary theory and his standard of literary judgment. In his critical essays, and in shorter statements scattered throughout his works, he applied these criteria at times with unusual acumen. Much of Whitman's literary criticism deals with the literature of England. Viewing literature from the historical point of view, throughout the writings of that country he saw the connecting thread of feudal culture. This culture he found best reflected in the works of Shakespeare, Scott, and Tennyson. Whitman had high regard for Shakespeare as an artist and a true figure of literary excellence. He pointed out, though, that being the great literary representative of the feudal age at its zenith, Shakespeare can in no way be reconciled with democracy or serve as a model for the present day or for the future.[61]

Tennyson, Whitman tells us, continues and stands for the same feudal tradition and is its final great portrayer. "I find it impossible," Whitman wrote, "as I taste the sweetness of those lines, to escape the flavor, the conviction, the lush-ripening culmination, and last honey of decay (I dare not call it rottenness) of that feudalism which the mighty English dramatist painted in all the splendors of its noon and afternoon." While praising Burns for his democracy and his portrayal of common life, Whitman pointed out one great fault which he considers a fatal weakness, "He has,

[61] See Clifton J. Furness, "Walt Whitman's Estimate of Shakespeare," *Harvard Studies and Notes in Philology and Literature*, XIV (1932), 1–33.

moreover, little or no spirituality. This last is his mortal flaw and defect, tried by highest standards."

Whitman seems to have reserved the highest praise in American literature for the four poets he honors in his essay, "My Tribute to Four Poets," Emerson, Longfellow, Bryant, and Whittier. Emerson seemed for a time to Whitman to be the top poet of America, giving way, according to a later judgment, to Bryant. Emerson was "perhaps too perfect, too concentrated," greater as a critic or "a diagnoser," than as a poet, an artist, or a teacher. Though criticizing Emerson, Whitman held him in reverence always and maintained that "the wonderful heart and soul" of Emerson, "present in all he writes, thinks, does, hopes," went a long way toward "justifying the whole literary business."

Longfellow, Whitman felt, was eminent in style and form as a poet, being a poet "of melody, courtesy, and deference" and "a universal poet of women and young people." Unfortunately, from Whitman's standpoint, he lacked American feeling and could probably be best tabbed as a great transitional figure, "reminiscent, polish'd, elegant, with the air of the finest conventional library."

Whitman saw Whittier as a figure grand enough "but pretty lean and ascetic." He accepted the severe moral tone in Whittier's work because it was "wholly, beautifully genuine." In his verses, which proceed with the "measur'd step of Cromwell's old veterans," he saw a kind of excellence. In so far as Whittier's place as a great American poet was concerned, Whitman felt that he was not "universal and composite enough," reflecting only a limited aspect of America's greatness.

Bryant became to Whitman the first-ranking American poet. In contrasting him with Emerson, Whitman said that "Bryant is more significant for his patriotism, Americanism, love of external nature, the woods, the sea, the skies, the rivers, and this at times, the objective features of it especially, seems to outweigh Emerson's urgent intelligence and psychic depth." Bryant's classic discipline, though admired by Whitman, was nevertheless in conflict with his views and Whitman felt that such bonds of formality would have to be broken.

Whether Whitman, when compared with Poe and Lowell, can be regarded as a critic of major importance may be open to question. Perhaps Whitman's criticism is American criticism's most prophetic, if not most perfect, voice in insisting upon the necessity for literature to reflect America—particularly in "its divine average," its democracy: "As I have lived in fresh lands, inchoate, and in a revolutionary age, future-founding . . ."

This period, which was dominated by the aesthetics of romanticism, was one which saw the rapid rise of literary criticism to a position of prominence in American letters; and it was a period which saw the development of several different schools of criticism, with distinctive criteria, of which the following are perhaps the most significant: the formal and judicial criticism best typified by Poe; the criticism of the liberal "Young America" critics such as William A. Jones; the conservative Whig criticism of Edwin P. Whipple and Henry N. Hudson; [62] the transcendentalist critics such as Margaret Fuller, Emerson, and Thoreau; the "sympathetic" criticism of critics such as George Allen; [63] and the historical criticism which manifests itself in the work of many of the major critics of the period.

[62] Representative of Whipple's criticism are "Wordsworth's Poetical Works," *North American Review*, LIX (1844), and "Criticism: Coleridge," *Whig Review*, III (1846). Much of his work is gathered in *American Literature and Other Papers* (Boston, 1887). For Hudson's point of view, see "Festus," *Whig Review*, V (1847), "Whipple's Essays and Reviews," *ibid.*, IX (1849), and his edition of Shakespeare.

[63] See "Reproductive Criticism," *New York Review*, II (1838), and "The Study of Works of Genius," *ibid.*, I (1837). Deriving from Goethe, "sympathetic" criticism consisted of "reproducing, step by step, the creative process of the artist."

Critical Essays of Romanticism

EDGAR ALLAN POE

LETTER TO MR. ——[1]

West Point, ——, 1831.

Dear B——

BELIEVING ONLY a portion of my former volume to be worthy a second edition,—that small portion I thought it as well to include in the present book as to republish by itself. I have therefore herein combined "Al Aaraaf" and "Tamerlane" with other Poems hitherto unprinted. Nor have I hesitated to insert from the "Minor Poems" now omitted whole lines, and even passages, to the end that, being placed in a fairer light and the trash shaken from them in which they were embedded, they may have some chance of being seen by posterity.

It has been said that a good critique on a poem may be written by one who is no poet himself. This, according to *your* idea and *mine* of poetry, I feel to be false—the less poetical the critic, the less just the critique, and the converse. On this account, and because there are but few B——'s in the world, I would be as much ashamed of the world's good opinion as proud of your own. Another than yourself might here observe, "Shakespeare is in possession of the world's good opinion, and yet Shakespeare is the greatest of poets. It appears then that the world judges correctly, why should you be ashamed of their favorable judgment?" The difficulty lies in the interpretation of the word "judgment" or "opinion." The opinion is the world's, truly, but it may be called theirs as a man would call a book his, having bought it; he did not write the book, but it is his; they did not originate the opinion, but it is theirs. A fool, for example, thinks Shakespeare a great poet—yet the fool has never read Shakespeare. But the fool's neighbor, who is a step higher on the Andes of the mind, whose head (that is to say, his more exalted thought) is too far above the fool to be seen or understood, but whose feet (by which I mean his every-day actions) are sufficiently near to be discerned, and by means of which that superiority is ascertained, which *but* for them would never have been discovered,—this neighbor asserts that Shakespeare is a great poet,—the fool believes him, and it is henceforward his *opinion*. This neighbor's own opinion has, in like manner, been adopted from one above *him*, and so, ascendingly, to a few gifted individuals, who kneel around the summit, beholding, face to face, the master-spirit who stands upon the pinnacle.

You are aware of the great barrier in the path of an American writer. He is read, if at all, in preference to the combined and established wit

---

[1] Published as preface to *Poems* (New York, 1831). It is probable that the letter is addressed to Elam Bliss, Poe's publisher.

of the world. I say established; for it is with literature as with law or empire—an established name is an estate in tenure, or a throne in possession. Besides, one might suppose that books, like their authors, improve by travel—their having crossed the sea is, with us, so great a distinction. Our antiquaries abandon time for distance; our very fops glance from the binding to the bottom of the title page, where the mystic characters which spell London, Paris, or Genoa, are precisely so many letters of recommendation.

I mentioned just now a vulgar error as regards criticism. I think the notion that no poet can form a correct estimate of his own writings is another. I remarked before, that in proportion to the poetical talent, would be the justice of a critique upon poetry. Therefore, a bad poet would, I grant, make a false critique, and his self-love would infallibly bias his little judgment in his favor; but a poet, who is indeed a poet, could not, I think, fail of making a just critique. Whatever should be deducted on the score of self-love, might be replaced on account of his intimate acquaintance with the subject; in short, we have more instances of false criticism than of just, where one's own writings are the test, simply because we have more bad poets than good. There are of course many objections to what I say: Milton is a great example of the contrary; but his opinion with respect to the "Paradise Regained" is by no means fairly ascertained. By what trivial circumstances men are often led to assert what they do not really believe! Perhaps an inadvertent word has descended to posterity. But, in fact, the "Paradise Regained" is little, if at all, inferior to the "Paradise Lost," and is only supposed so to be, because men do not like epics, whatever they may say to the contrary, and reading those of Milton in their natural order, are too much wearied with the first to derive any pleasure from the second.

I dare say Milton preferred "Comus" to either—if so—justly.

As I am speaking of poetry, it will not be amiss to touch slightly upon the most singular heresy in its modern history—the heresy of what is called, very foolishly, the Lake School. Some years ago I might have been induced, by an occasion like the present, to attempt a formal refutation of their doctrine; at present it would be a work of supererogation. The wise must bow to the wisdom of such men as Coleridge and Southey, but being wise, have laughed at poetical theories, so prosaically exemplified.

Aristotle, with singular assurance, has declared poetry the most philosophical of all writings; but it required a Wordsworth to pronounce it the most metaphysical. He seems to think that the end of poetry is, or should be, instruction—yet it is a truism that the end of our existence is happiness; if so, the end of every separate part of our existence—everything connected with our existence should be still happiness. Therefore the end of instruction should be happiness; and happiness is another name for pleasure;—therefore the end of instruction should be pleasure: yet we see the above-mentioned opinion implies precisely the reverse.

To proceed: *ceteris paribus*, he who pleases is of more importance to his fellow-men than he who instructs, since utility is happiness, and pleasure is the end already obtained which instruction is merely the means of obtaining.

I see no reason, then, why our metaphysical poets should plume themselves so much on the utility of their works, unless indeed they refer to instruction with eternity in view; in which case, sincere respect for their piety would not allow me to express my contempt for their judgment; contempt which it would be difficult to conceal, since their writings are professedly to be understood by the few, and it is the many who stand in need of salvation. In such case I should no doubt be tempted to think of the devil in "Melmouth," who labors indefatigably through three octavo volumes to accomplish the destruction of one or two souls, while any common devil would have demolished one or two thousand.[2]

Against the subtleties which would make poetry a study—not a passion —it becomes the metaphysician to reason—but the poet to protest. Yet Wordsworth and Coleridge are men in years; the one imbued in contemplation from his childhood, the other a giant in intellect and learning. The diffidence, then, with which I venture to dispute their authority, would be overwhelming, did I not feel, from the bottom of my heart, that learning has little to do with the imagination—intellect with the passions —or age with poetry.

> Trifles, like straws, upon the surface flow,
> He who would search for pearls must dive below,

are lines which have done much mischief.[3] As regards the greater truths, men oftener err by seeking them at the bottom than at the top; the depth lies in the huge abysses where wisdom is sought—not in the palpable palaces where she is found. The ancients were not always right in hiding the goddess in a well: witness the light which Bacon has thrown upon philosophy; witness the principles of our divine faith—that moral mechanism by which the simplicity of a child may over-balance the wisdom of a man. Poetry above all things is a beautiful painting whose tints to minute inspection are confusion worse confounded, but start boldly out to the cursory glance of the connoisseur.

We see an instance of Coleridge's liability to err, in his "Biographia Literaria"—professedly his literary life and opinions, but, in fact, a treatise *de omni scibili et quibusdam aliis*.[4] He goes wrong by reason of his very profundity, and of his error we have a natural type in the contemplation of a star. He who regards it directly and intensely sees, it is true, the star, but it is the star without a ray—while he who surveys it less inquisitively is conscious of all for which the star is useful to us below—its brilliancy and its beauty.

As to Wordsworth, I have no faith in him. That he had, in youth, the feelings of a poet I believe—for there are glimpses of extreme delicacy in

[2] Poe's reference is to *Melmoth*, a prose romance by Charles Robert Maturin (1782–1824), Irish novelist and dramatist, which was published in 1820.
[3] The lines are from the Prologue to *All for Love* by Dryden.
[4] "about everything knowable and certain other things."

his writings—(and delicacy is the poet's own kingdom—his *El Dorado*)—
but they have the appearance of a better day recollected; and glimpses, at
best, are little evidence of present poetic fire—we know that a few strag-
gling flowers spring up daily in the crevices of the avalanche.

He was to blame in wearing away his youth in contemplation with the
end of poetizing in his manhood. With the increase of his judgment the
light which should make it apparent has faded away. His judgment consequently is too correct. This may not be understood,—but the old Goths
of Germany would have understood it, who used to debate matters of importance to their State twice, once when drunk, and once when sober—
sober that they might not be deficient in formality—drunk lest they should
be destitute of vigor.

The long wordy discussions by which he tries to reason us into admiration of his poetry, speaks very little in his favor: they are full of such assertions as this—(I have opened one of his volumes at random) "Of genius
the only proof is the act of doing well what is worthy to be done, and what
was never done before" [5]—indeed! then it follows that in doing what is
un-worthy to be done, or what *has* been done before, no genius can be
evinced; yet the picking of pockets is an unworthy act, pockets have been
picked time immemorial, and Barrington,[6] the pickpocket, in point of
genius, would have thought hard of a comparison with William Wordsworth, the poet.

Again—in estimating the merit of certain poems, whether they be Ossian's or M'Pherson's can surely be of little consequence,[7] yet, in order to
prove their worthlessness, Mr. W_____ has expended many pages in the
controversy. *Tantaene animis?* Can great minds descend to such absurdity? But worse still: that he may bear down every argument in favor of
these poems, he triumphantly drags forward a passage, in his abomina-
tion of which he expects the reader to sympathize. It is the beginning of
the epic poem "Temora." [8] "The blue waves of Ullin roll in light; the
green hills are covered with day; trees shake their dusky heads in the
breeze." And this—this gorgeous, yet simple imagery, where all is alive and
panting with immortality—this, William Wordsworth, the author of "Peter
Bell," has *selected* to dignify with his imperial contempt. We shall see
what better he, in his own person, has to offer. Imprimis:—

> And now she's at the pony's head,
> And now she's at the pony's tail,
> On that side now, and now on this,
> And almost stifled her with bliss—
> A few sad tears does Betty shed,

[5] Poe is quoting from Wordsworth's "Essay, Supplementary to the Preface," 1815.
[6] George Barrington (1755-1840), English poet and dramatist, also a pickpocket.
[7] James Macpherson (1736-1796) published poems purported to be by Ossian, an
early Gaelic poet. When he could produce no original manuscripts of Ossian, the
poems were declared to be false. The ensuing controversy reached major proportions. See *Fragments of Ancient Poetry Collected in the Highlands of Scotland*, which
was published by Macpherson in 1760.
[8] "Temora," an "Ossian" poem which appeared in 1763.

> She pats the pony where or when
> She knows not: happy Betty Foy!
> O, Johnny! never mind the Doctor!

Secondly:—

> The dew was falling fast, the—stars began to blink,
> I heard a voice; it said—drink, pretty creature, drink;
> And, looking o'er the hedge, be—fore me I espied
> A snow-white mountain lamb, with a—maiden at its side.
> No other sheep were near; the lamb was all alone,
> And by a slender cord was—tether'd to a stone.

Now, we have no doubt this is all true; we *will* believe it, indeed, we will, Mr. W———. Is it sympathy for the sheep you wish to excite? I love a sheep from the bottom of my heart.

But there *are* occasions, dear B———, there are occasions, when even Wordsworth is reasonable. Even Stamboul, it is said, shall have an end, and the most unlucky blunders must come to a conclusion. Here is an extract from his preface:—[9]

> Those who have been accustomed to the phraseology of modern writers, if they persist in reading this book to a conclusion (*impossible!*), will, no doubt, have to struggle with feelings of awkwardness; (ha! ha! ha!) they will look round for poetry (ha! ha! ha! ha!) and will be induced to inquire by what species of courtesy these attempts have been permitted to assume that title. Ha! ha! ha! ha! ha!

Yet let not Mr. W——— despair; he has given immortality to a wagon, and the bee Sophocles has eternalized a sore toe, and dignified a tragedy with a chorus of turkeys.[10]

Of Coleridge, I cannot speak but with reverence. His towering intellect! his gigantic power! To use an author quoted by himself, "J'ai trouvé souvent que la plupart des sectes ont raison dans une bonne partie de ce qu'elles avancent, mais non pas en ce qu'elles nient," [11] and to employ his own language, he has imprisoned his own conceptions by the barrier he has erected against those of others. It is lamentable to think that such a mind should be buried in metaphysics, and, like the Nyctanthes, waste its perfume upon the night alone. In reading that man's poetry, I tremble, like one who stands upon a volcano, conscious, from the very darkness bursting from the crater, of the fire and the light that are weltering below.

[9] From the Preface to the *Lyrical Ballads* (1800).
[10] F. C. Prescott in his *Selections from the Critical Writings of Edgar Allan Poe* (New York, 1909) cites Poe's reference to "the bee Sophocles" as interesting evidence that Poe had read A. W. Schlegel's *Lectures on Dramatic Art* in which Sophocles is called the "Attic Bee."
[11] From the *Biographia Literaria*. Coleridge is quoting Leibnitz's *Trois Lettres à M. Remond de Mont-Mort* (1741). The quotation reads: "I have often found that most sects have reason in the most part in what they advance, but not in what they deny."

What is Poetry?—Poetry! that Proteus-like idea, with as many appellations as the nine-titled Corcyra! "Give me," I demanded of a scholar some time ago, "give me a definition of poetry." "Très-volontiers"; and he proceeded to his library, brought me a Dr. Johnson, and overwhelmed me with a definition. Shade of the immortal Shakespeare! I imagine to myself the scowl of your spiritual eye upon the profanity of that scurrilous Ursa Major. Think of poetry, dear B____, think of poetry, and then think of—Dr. Samuel Johnson! Think of all that is airy and fairylike, and then of all that is hideous and unwieldy; think of his huge bulk, the Elephant! and then—and then think of the "Tempest"—the "Midsummer Night's Dream"—Prospero-Oberon—and Titania!

A poem in my opinion, is opposed to a work of science by having, for its *immediate* object, pleasure, not truth; [12] to romance, by having, for its object, an *indefinite* instead of a *definite* pleasure, being a poem only so far as this object is attained; romance presenting perceptible images with definite, poetry with *in*definite sensations, to which end music is an *essential*, since the comprehension of sweet sound is our most indefinite conception. Music, when combined with a pleasurable idea, is poetry; music, without the idea, is simply music; the idea, without the music, is prose, from its very definitiveness.

What was meant by the invective against him who had no music in his soul?

To sum up this long rigamarole, I have, dear B____, what you, no doubt perceive, for the metaphysical poets, *as* poets, the most sovereign contempt. That they have followers proves nothing—

> No Indian prince has to his palace
> More followers than a thief to the gallows.

---

[12] Cf. Coleridge's definition in the *Biographia Literaria*, Chap. XIV: "A poem is that species of composition, which is opposed to works of science, by proposing for its immediate object pleasure, not truth . . ."

EDGAR ALLAN POE

HAWTHORNE'S "TALES" [1]
(1842)

WE SAID a few hurried words about Mr. Hawthorne in our last number,[2] with the design of speaking more fully in the present. We are still, however, pressed for room, and must necessarily discuss his volumes more briefly and more at random than their high merits deserve.

The book professes to be a collection of *tales*, yet is, in two respects, misnamed. These pieces are now in their third republication, and, of course, are thrice-told. Moreover, they are by no means *all* tales, either in the ordinary or in the legitimate understanding of the term. Many of them are pure essays: for example, "Sights from a Steeple," "Sunday at Home," "Little Annie's Ramble," "A Rill from the Town Pump," "The Toll-Gatherer's Day," "The Haunted Mind," "The Sister Years," "Snow Flakes," "Night Sketches," and "Footprints on the Sea Shore." I mention these matters chiefly on account of their discrepancy with that marked precision and finish by which the body of the work is distinguished.

Of the essays just named, we must be content to speak in brief. They are each and all beautiful, without being characterized by the polish and adaptation so visible in the tales proper. A painter would at once note their leading or predominant feature, and style it *repose*. There is no attempt at effect. All is quiet, thoughtful, subdued. Yet this repose may exist simultaneously with high originality of thought; and Mr. Hawthorne has demonstrated the fact. At every turn we meet with novel combinations; yet these combinations never surpass the limits of the quiet. We are soothed as we read; and withal is a calm astonishment that ideas so apparently obvious have never occurred or been presented to us before. Herein our author differs materially from Lamb or Hunt or Hazlitt— who, with vivid originality of manner and expression, have less of the true novelty of thought than is generally supposed, and whose originality, at best, has an uneasy and meretricious quaintness, replete with startling effects unfounded in nature, and inducing trains of reflection which lead to no satisfactory result. The essays of Hawthorne have much of the character of Irving, with more of originality, and less of finish; while, compared with "The Spectator," they have a vast superiority at all points. "The Spectator," Mr. Irving, and Hawthorne have in common that tranquil and subdued manner which I have chosen to denominate *repose*; but, in the case of the two former, this repose is attained rather by the absence of novel combination, or of originality, than otherwise, and con-

[1] Published in *Graham's Magazine*, XX (1842), 298-300.
[2] See *Graham's Magazine*, April, 1842.

sists chiefly in the calm, quiet, unostentatious expression of commonplace thoughts, in an unambitious, unadulterated Saxon. In them, by strong effort, we are made to conceive the absence of all. In the essays before me the absence of effort is too obvious to be mistaken, and a strong under-current of *suggestion* runs continuously beneath the upper stream of the tranquil thesis. In short, these effusions of Mr. Hawthorne are the product of a truly imaginative intellect, restrained, and in some measure repressed, by fastidiousness of taste, by constitutional melancholy, and by indolence.

But it is of his tales that I desire principally to speak. The tale proper, in my opinion, affords unquestionably the fairest field for the exercise of the loftiest talent, which can be afforded by the wide domains of mere prose. Were I bidden to say how the highest genius could be most advantageously employed for the best display of its own powers, I should answer, without hesitation—in the composition of a rhymed poem, not to exceed in length what might be perused in an hour. Within this limit alone can the highest order of true poetry exist. I need only here say, upon this topic, that, in almost all classes of composition, the unity of effect or impression is a point of the greatest importance. It is clear, moreover, that this unity cannot be thoroughly preserved in productions whose perusal cannot be completed at one sitting. We may continue the reading of a prose composition, from the very nature of prose itself, much longer than we can persevere, to any good purpose, in the perusal of a poem. This latter, if truly fulfilling the demands of the poetic sentiment, induces an exaltation of the soul which cannot be long sustained. All high excitements are necessarily transient. Thus a long poem is a paradox. And, without unity of impression, the deepest effects cannot be brought about. Epics were the offspring of an imperfect sense of Art, and their reign is no more. A poem *too* brief may produce a vivid, but never an intense or enduring impression. Without a certain continuity of effort—without a certain duration or repetition of purpose—the soul is never deeply moved. There must be the dropping of the water upon the rock. De Béranger [3] has wrought brilliant things, pungent and spirit-stirring; but, like all immassive bodies, they lack *momentum*, and thus fail to satisfy the Poetic Sentiment. They sparkle and excite, but, from want of continuity, fail deeply to impress. Extreme brevity will degenerate into epigrammatism; but the sin of extreme length is even more unpardonable. *In medio tutissimus ibis.* [4]

Were I called upon, however, to designate that class of composition which, next to such a poem as I have suggested, should best fulfil the demands of high genius—should offer it the most advantageous field of exertion—I should unhesitatingly speak of the prose tale, as Mr. Hawthorne has here exemplified it. I allude to the short prose narrative, requiring from a half-hour to one or two hours in its perusal. The ordinary novel is objectionable, from its length, for reasons already stated in substance. As

[3] Pierre Jean de Béranger (1780–1857), French lyric poet.
[4] "You go most safely in the middle way."

it cannot be read at one sitting, it deprives itself, of course, of the immense force derivable from *totality*. Worldly interests intervening during the pauses of perusal, modify, annul or counteract, in a greater or less degree, the impressions of the book. But simple cessation in reading would, of itself, be sufficient to destroy the true unity. In the brief tale, however, the author is enabled to carry out the fulness of his intention, be it what it may. During the hour of perusal the soul of the reader is at the writer's control. There are no external or extrinsic influences—resulting from weariness or interruption.

A skilful literary artist has constructed a tale. If wise, he has not fashioned his thoughts to accommodate his incidents; but having conceived, with deliberate care, a certain unique or single *effect* to be wrought out, he then invents such incidents—he then combines such events as may best aid him in establishing this preconceived effect. If his very initial sentence tend not to the outbringing of this effect, then he has failed in his first step. In the whole composition there should be no word written, of which the tendency, direct or indirect, is not to the one pre-established design. And by such means, with such care and skill, a picture is at length painted which leaves in the mind of him who contemplates it with a kindred art, a sense of the fullest satisfaction. The idea of the tale has been presented unblemished, because undisturbed; and this is an end unattainable by the novel. Undue brevity is just as exceptionable here as in the poem; but undue length is yet more to be avoided.

We have said that the tale has a point of superiority even over the poem. In fact, while the *rhythm* of this latter is an essential aid in the development of the poem's highest idea—the idea of the Beautiful—the artificialities of this rhythm are an inseparable bar to the development of all points of thought or expression which have their basis in *Truth*. But Truth is often, and in very great degree, the aim of the tale. Some of the finest tales are tales of ratiocination. Thus the field of this species of composition, if not in so elevated a region on the mountain of Mind, is a tableland of far vaster extent than the domain of the mere poem. Its products are never so rich, but infinitely more numerous, and more appreciable by the mass of mankind. The writer of the prose tale, in short, may bring to his theme a vast variety of modes or inflections of thought and expression —(the ratiocinative, for example, the sarcastic, or the humorous) which are not only antagonistical to the nature of the poem, but absolutely forbidden by one of its most peculiar and indispensable adjuncts; we allude, of course, to rhythm. It may be added, here, *par parenthèse,* that the author who aims at the purely beautiful in a prose tale is laboring at a great disadvantage. For Beauty can be better treated in the poem. Not so with terror, or passion, or horror, or a multitude of such other points. And here it will be seen how full of prejudice are the usual animadversions against those *tales of effect,* many fine examples of which were found in the earlier numbers of Blackwood.[5] The impressions produced were wrought

[5] *Blackwood's Magazine,* published in Edinburgh beginning in 1817, was one of the most popular and most influential periodicals in America at this time.

in a legitimate sphere of action, and constituted a legitimate although sometimes an exaggerated interest. They were relished by every man of genius: although there were found many men of genius who condemned them without just ground. The true critic will but demand that the design intended be accomplished, to the fullest extent, by the means most advantageously applicable.

We have very few American tales of real merit—we may say, indeed, none, with the exception of "The Tales of a Traveller" of Washington Irving, and these "Twice-Told Tales" of Mr. Hawthorne. Some of the pieces of Mr. John Neal abound in vigor and originality; but, in general, his compositions of this class are excessively diffuse, extravagant, and indicative of an imperfect sentiment of Art. Articles at random are, now and then, met with in our periodicals which might be advantageously compared with the best effusions of the British magazines; but, upon the whole, we are far behind our progenitors in this department of literature.

Of Mr. Hawthorne's "Tales" we would say, emphatically that they belong to the highest region of Art—an Art subservient to genius of a very lofty order. We had supposed, with good reason for so supposing, that he had been thrust into his present position by one of the impudent cliques which beset our literature, and whose pretensions it is our full purpose to expose at the earliest opportunity; but we have been most agreeably mistaken. We know of few compositions which the critic can more honestly commend than these "Twice-Told Tales." As Americans, we feel proud of the book.

Mr. Hawthorne's distinctive trait is invention, creation, imagination, originality—a trait which, in the literature of fiction, is positively worth all the rest. But the nature of the originality, so far as regards its manifestation in letters, is but imperfectly understood. The inventive or original mind as frequently displays itself in novelty of *tone* as in novelty of matter. Mr. Hawthorne is original in *all* points.

It would be a matter of some difficulty to designate the best of these tales; we repeat that, without exception, they are beautiful. "Wakefield" is remarkable for the skill with which an old idea,—a well-known incident,—is worked up or discussed. A man of whims conceives the purpose of quitting his wife and residing *incognito*, for twenty years, in her immediate neighborhood. Something of this kind actually happened in London. The force of Mr. Hawthorne's tale lies in the analysis of the motives which must or might have impelled the husband to such folly, in the first instance, with the possible causes of his perseverance. Upon this thesis a sketch of singular power has been constructed. "The Wedding Knell" is full of the boldest imagination,—an imagination fully controlled by taste. The most captious critic could find no flaw in this production. "The Minister's Black Veil" is a masterly composition of which the sole defect is that to the rabble its exquisite skill will be *caviare*. The obvious meaning of this article will be found to smother its insinuated one. The moral put into the mouth of the dying minister will be supposed to convey the true import of the narrative; and that a crime of dark dye (having reference to the "young lady") has been committed, is a point which only minds congenial with that of the author will perceive. "Mr. Higginbotham's Catastrophe" is vividly original and managed most dexterously. "Dr. Heidegger's Experiment" is exceedingly well imagined, and executed with surpassing ability. The artist breathes in every line of it. "The White Old Maid" is objectionable, even more than "The Minister's Black Veil," on the score of its mysticism. Even with the thoughtful and analytic, there will be much trouble in penetrating its entire import.

"The Hollow of the Three Hills" we would quote in full, had we space; not as evincing higher talent than any of the other pieces, but as affording an excellent example of the author's peculiar ability. The subject is commonplace. A witch subjects the Distant and the Past to the view of a mourner. It has been the fashion to describe, in such cases, a mirror in which the images of the absent appear; or a cloud of smoke is made to arise, and thence the figures are gradually unfolded. Mr. Hawthorne has wonderfully heightened his effect by making the ear, in place of the eye, the medium by which the fantasy is conveyed. The head of the mourner is enveloped in the cloak of the witch, and within its magic folds there arise sounds which have an all-sufficient intelligence. Throughout this article also, the artist is conspicuous,—not more in positive than in negative merits. Not only is all done that should be done, but (what perhaps is an end with more difficulty attained) there is nothing done which should not be. Every word *tells*, and there is not a word which does *not* tell. * * *

EDGAR ALLAN POE

THE POETIC PRINCIPLE [1]
(1850)

IN SPEAKING of the Poetic Principle, I have no design to be either thorough or profound. While discussing, very much at random, the essentiality of what we call Poetry, my principal purpose will be to cite for consideration some few of those minor English or American poems which best suit my own taste, or which upon my own fancy have left the most definite impression. By "minor poems" I mean, of course, poems of little length. And here in the beginning permit me to say a few words in regard to a somewhat peculiar principle, which, whether rightfully or wrongfully, has always had its influence in my own critical estimate of the poem. I hold that a long poem does not exist. I maintain that the phrase, "a long poem," is simply a flat contradiction in terms.

I need scarcely observe that a poem deserves its title only inasmuch as it excites, by elevating the soul. The value of the poem is in the ratio of this elevating excitement. But all excitements are, through a psychal necessity, transient. That degree of excitement which would entitle a poem to be so called at all cannot be sustained throughout a composition of any great length. After the lapse of half an hour, at the very utmost, it flags—fails—a revulsion ensues—and then the poem is, in effect, and in fact, no longer such.

There are, no doubt, many who have found difficulty in reconciling the critical dictum that the "Paradise Lost" is to be devoutly admired throughout, with the absolute impossibility of maintaining for it, during perusal, the amount of enthusiasm which that critical dictum would demand. This great work, in fact, is to be regarded as poetical, only when, losing sight of that vital requisite in all works of Art, Unity, we view it merely as a series of minor poems. If, to preserve its Unity—its totality of effect or impression—we read it (as would be necessary) at a single sitting, the result is but a constant alternation of excitement and depression. After a passage of what we feel to be true poetry, there follows, inevitably, a passage of platitude which no critical prejudgment can force us to admire; but if, upon completing the work, we read it again, omitting the first book (that is to say, commencing with the second), we shall be surprised at now finding that admirable which we before condemned—that damnable which we had previously so much admired. It follows from all this that the ultimate, aggregate, or absolute effect of even the best epic under the sun is a nullity:—and this is precisely the fact.

[1] Originally delivered as a lecture in 1848–49 and was not published until after Poe's death when it appeared in *Sartain's Union Magazine*, VII (1850), 231–39.

In regard to the "Iliad," we have, if not positive proof, at least very good reason for believing it intended as a series of lyrics; but, granting the epic intention, I can say only that the work is based in an imperfect sense of Art. The modern epic is of the supposititious ancient model, but an inconsiderate and blindfold imitation. But the day of these artistic anomalies is over. If, at any time, any very long poem *were* popular in reality—which I doubt—it is at least clear that no very long poem will ever be popular again.

That the extent of a poetical work is, *ceteris paribus*, the measure of its merit, seems undoubtedly, when we thus state it, a proposition sufficiently absurd—yet we are indebted for it to the Quarterly Reviews. Surely there can be nothing in mere size, abstractly considered—there can be nothing in mere bulk, so far as a volume is concerned—which has so continuously elicited admiration from these saturnine pamphlets! A mountain, to be sure, by the mere sentiment of physical magnitude which it conveys, does impress us with a sense of the sublime—but no man is impressed after *this* fashion by the material grandeur of even "The Columbiad." [2] Even the Quarterlies have not instructed us to be so impressed by it. *As yet*, they have not *insisted* on our estimating Lamartine by the cubic foot, or Pollok by the pound [3]—but what else are we to *infer* from their continual prating about "sustained effort"? If, by "sustained effort," any little gentleman has accomplished an epic, let us frankly commend him for the effort,—if this indeed be a thing commendable,—but let us forbear praising the epic on the effort's account. It is to be hoped that common-sense, in the time to come, will prefer deciding upon a work of Art, rather by the impression it makes—by the effect it produces—than by the time it took to impress the effect, or by the amount of "sustained effort" which had been found necessary in effecting the impression. The fact is, that perseverance is one thing and genius quite another; nor can all the Quarterlies in Christendom confound them. By-and-by, this proposition, with many which I have been just urging, will be received as self-evident. In the mean time, by being generally condemned as falsities they will not be essentially damaged as truths.

On the other hand, it is clear that a poem may be improperly brief. Undue brevity degenerates into mere epigrammatism. A *very* short poem, while now and then producing a brilliant or vivid, never produces a profound or enduring, effect. There must be the steady pressing down of the stamp upon the wax. Béranger has wrought innumerable things, pungent and spirit-stirring; but, in general, they have been too imponderous to stamp themselves deeply into the public opinion, and thus, as so many feathers of fancy, have been blown aloft only to be whistled down the wind.

A remarkable instance of the effect of undue brevity in depressing a poem—in keeping it out of the popular view—is afforded by the following exquisite little serenade:—

[2] Joel Barlow's (1754–1812) patriotic epic.
[3] Lamartine (1790–1869), nineteenth-century French poet many of whose works were lengthy. Robert Pollok (1798–1827), Scottish religious poet whose long poem, *The Course of Time*, appeared in 1827.

"I arise from dreams of thee
    In the first sweet sleep of night,
When the winds are breathing low,
    And the stars are shining bright;
I arise from dreams of thee,
    And a spirit in my feet
Hath led me—who knows how?—
    To thy chamber-window, sweet!

"The wandering airs, they faint
    On the dark, the silent stream;
The champak odors fail
    Like sweet thoughts in a dream;
The nightingale's complaint,
    It dies upon her heart,
As I must die on thine,
    Oh, beloved as thou art!

"Oh, lift me from the grass!
    I die! I faint! I fail!
Let thy love in kisses rain
    On my lips and eyelids pale.
My cheek is cold and white, alas!
    My heart beats loud and fast;
Oh, press it close to thine again,
    Where it will break at last!"

Very few, perhaps, are familiar with these lines—yet no less a poet than Shelley is their author. Their warm, yet delicate and ethereal imagination will be appreciated by all; but by none so thoroughly as by him who has himself arisen from sweet dreams of one beloved to bathe in the aromatic air of a southern midsummer night.

One of the finest poems by Willis [4]—the very best, in my opinion, which he has ever written—has, no doubt, through this same defect of undue brevity, been kept back from its proper position, not less in the critical than in the popular view.

"The shadows lay along Broadway,
    'T was near the twilight-tide—
And slowly there a lady fair
    Was walking in her pride.
Alone walked she; but, viewlessly,
    Walked spirits at her side.

"Peace charmed the street beneath her feet,
    And Honor charmed the air;
And all astir looked kind on her,
    And called her good as fair;
For all God ever gave to her
    She kept with chary care.

[4] Nathaniel Parker Willis (1806–1867), American poet and editor.

"She kept with care her beauties rare
     From lovers warm and true,—
For her heart was cold to all but gold,
     And the rich came not to woo,—
But honored well are charms to sell
     If priests the selling do.

"Now walking there was one more fair—
     A slight girl, lily-pale;
And she had unseen company
     To make the spirit quail:
'Twixt Want and Scorn she walked forlorn,
     And nothing could avail.

"No mercy now can clear her brow
     For this world's peace to pray;
For, as love's wild prayer dissolved in air,
     Her woman's heart gave way!—
But the sin forgiven by Christ in Heaven
     By man is cursed alway!"

In this composition we find it difficult to recognize the Willis who has written so many mere "verses of society." The lines are not only richly ideal, but full of energy, while they breathe an earnestness—an evident sincerity of sentiment—for which we look in vain throughout all the other works of this author.

While the epic mania—while the idea that, to merit in poetry, prolixity is indispensable—has for some years past been gradually dying out of the public mind by mere dint of its own absurdity—we find it succeeded by a heresy too palpably false to be long tolerated, but one which, in the brief period it has already endured, may be said to have accomplished more in the corruption of our Poetical Literature than all its other enemies combined. I allude to the heresy of *The Didactic*. It has been assumed, tacitly and avowedly, directly and indirectly, that the ultimate object of all Poetry is Truth. Every poem, it is said, should inculcate a moral; and by this moral is the poetical merit of the work to be adjudged. We Americans, especially, have patronized this happy idea; and we Bostonians, very especially, have developed it in full. We have taken it into our heads that to write a poem simply for the poem's sake, and to acknowledge such to have been our design, would be to confess ourselves radically wanting in the true Poetic dignity and force; but the simple fact is, that, would we but permit ourselves to look into our own souls, we should immediately there discover that under the sun there neither exists nor *can* exist any work more thoroughly dignified, more supremely noble, than this very poem—this poem *per se*—this poem which is a poem and nothing more—this poem written solely for the poem's sake.

With as deep a reverence for the True as ever inspired the bosom of man, I would, nevertheless, limit in some measure its modes of inculcation. I would limit to enforce them. I would not enfeeble them by dissipation. The demands of Truth are severe; she has no sympathy with the myrtles. All *that* which is so indispensable in Song, is precisely all *that* with which *she* has nothing whatever to do. It is but making her a flaunting paradox to wreathe her in gems and flowers. In enforcing a truth we need severity rather than efflorescence of language. We must be simple, precise, terse. We must be cool, calm, unimpassioned. In a word, we must be in that mood, which, as nearly as possible, is the exact converse of the poetical. He must be blind indeed who does not perceive the radical and chasmal differences between the truthful and the poetical modes of inculcation. He must be theory-mad beyond redemption who, in spite of these differences, shall still persist in attempting to reconcile the obstinate oils and waters of Poetry and Truth.

Dividing the world of mind into its three most immediately obvious distinctions, we have the Pure Intellect, Taste, and the Moral Sense. I place Taste in the middle, because it is just this position which in the mind it occupies. It holds intimate relations with either extreme, but from the Moral Sense is separated by so faint a difference that Aristotle has not hesitated to place some of its operations among the virtues themselves. Nevertheless, we find the *offices* of the trio marked with a sufficient distinction. Just as the intellect concerns itself with Truth, so Taste informs us of the Beautiful, while the Moral Sense is regardful of Duty. Of this latter, while Conscience teaches the obligation, and Reason the expediency, Taste contents herself with displaying the charms:—waging war upon Vice solely on the ground of her deformity—her disproportion—her animosity to the fitting, to the appropriate, to the harmonious—in a word, to Beauty.

An immortal instinct, deep within the spirit of man, is thus, plainly, a sense of the Beautiful. This it is which administers to his delight in the manifold forms, and sounds, and odors, and sentiments, amid which he exists. And just as the lily is repeated in the lake, or the eyes of Amaryllis in the mirror, so is the mere oral or written repetition of these forms, and sounds, and colors, and odors, and sentiments, a duplicate source of delight. But this mere repetition is not poetry. He who shall simply sing, with however glowing enthusiasm, or with however vivid a truth of description, of the sights, and sounds, and odors, and colors, and sentiments, which greet *him* in common with all mankind—he, I say, has yet failed to prove his divine title. There is still a something in the distance which he has been unable to attain. We have still a thirst unquenchable, to allay which he has not shown us the crystal springs. This thirst belongs to the immortality of Man. It is at once a consequence and an indication of his perennial existence. It is the desire of the moth for the star. It is no mere appreciation of the Beauty before us, but a wild effort to reach the Beauty above. Inspired by an ecstatic prescience of the glories beyond the grave, we struggle by multiform combinations among the things and thoughts of Time to attain a portion of that Loveliness whose very elements, perhaps, appertain to eternity alone. And thus when by Poetry— or when by Music, the most entrancing of the Poetic moods—we find ourselves melted into tears, not as the Abbate Gravina [5] supposes through excess of pleasure, but through a certain petulant, impatient sorrow at our inability to grasp now, wholly, here on earth, at once and forever, those divine and rapturous joys, of which *through* the poem, or *through* the music, we attain to but brief and indeterminate glimpses.

The struggle to apprehend the supernal Loveliness—this struggle, on the part of souls fittingly constituted—has given to the world all that which it (the world) has ever been enabled at once to understand and to feel as poetic.

The Poetic Sentiment, of course, may develop itself in various modes—in Painting, in Sculpture, in Architecture, in the Dance—very especially in Music,—and very peculiarly, and with a wide field, in the composition of the Landscape Garden. Our present theme, however, has regard only to its manifestation in words. And here let me speak briefly on the topic of rhythm. Contenting myself with the certainty that Music, in its various modes of metre, rhythm, and rhyme, is of so vast a moment in Poetry as never to be wisely rejected—is so vitally important an adjunct, that he is simply silly who declines its assistance—I will not now pause to maintain its absolute essentiality. It is in Music, perhaps, that the soul most nearly attains the great end for which, when inspired by the Poetic Sentiment, it struggles—the creation of supernal Beauty. It may be, indeed, that here this sublime end is, now and then, attained in fact. We are often made to feel, with a shivering delight, that from an earthly harp are stricken notes which cannot have been unfamiliar to the angels. And thus there can be little doubt that in the union of Poetry with Music in its popular sense we shall find the widest field for the Poetic development. The old Bards and Minnesingers had advantages which we do not possess, and Thomas Moore, singing his own songs, was, in the most legitimate manner, perfecting them as poems.

To recapitulate, then:—I would define, in brief, the Poetry of words as *The Rhythmical Creation of Beauty.* Its sole arbiter is Taste. With the Intellect or with the Conscience, it has only collateral relations. Unless incidentally, it has no concern whatever either with Duty or with Truth.

A few words, however, in explanation. That pleasure which is at once the most pure, the most elevating, and the most intense, is derived, I maintain, from the contemplation of the Beautiful. In the contemplation of Beauty we alone find it possible to attain that pleasurable elevation, or excitement, *of the soul,* which we recognize as the Poetic Sentiment, and which is so easily distinguished from Truth, which is the satisfaction of the Reason, or from Passion, which is the excitement of the Heart. I make Beauty, therefore,—using the word as inclusive of the sublime,—I make Beauty the province of the poem, simply because it is an obvious rule of Art that effects should be made to spring as directly as possible from their causes—no one as yet having been weak enough to deny that the peculiar elevation in question is at least *most readily* attainable in the poem.

[5] Giovanni Vincenzio Gravina (1664-1718), Italian poet and dramatist, author of *Della ragion poetica libri due* (1718).

It by no means follows, however, that the incitements of Passion, or the precepts of Duty, or even the lessons of Truth, may not be introduced into a poem, and with advantage; for they may subserve, incidentally, in various ways, the general purposes of the work; but the true artist will always contrive to tone them down in proper subjection to that *Beauty* which is the atmosphere and the real essence of the poem.

I cannot better introduce the few poems which I shall present for your consideration than by the citation of the "Proem" to Mr. Longfellow's "Waif";

> "The day is done, and the darkness
>   Falls from the wings of Night,
> As a feather is wafted downward
>   From an eagle in his flight.
>
> "I see the lights of the village
>   Gleam through the rain and the mist,
> And a feeling of sadness comes o'er me,
>   That my soul cannot resist:
>
> "A feeling of sadness and longing,
>   That is not akin to pain,
> And resembles sorrow only
>   As the mist resembles the rain.
>
> "Come, read to me some poem,
>   Some simple and heartfelt lay,
> That shall soothe this restless feeling
>   And banish the thoughts of day.
>
> "Not from the grand old masters,
>   Not from the bards sublime,
> Whose distant footsteps echo
>   Through the corridors of Time.
>
> "For, like strains of martial music,
>   Their mighty thoughts suggest
> Life's endless toil and endeavor;
>   And to-night I long for rest.
>
> "Read from some humbler poet,
>   Whose songs gushed from his heart,
> As showers from the clouds of summer,
>   Or tears from the eyelids start;
>
> "Who, through long days of labor,
>   And nights devoid of ease,
> Still heard in his soul the music
>   Of wonderful melodies.
>
> "Such songs have power to quiet
>   The restless pulse of care,
> And come like the benediction
>   That follows after prayer.

> "Then read from the treasured volume
>   The poem of thy choice,
> And lend to the rhyme of the poet
>   The beauty of thy voice.
>
> "And the night shall be filled with music,
>   And the cares, that infest the day,
> Shall fold their tents, like the Arabs,
>   And as silently steal away."

With no great range of imagination, these lines have been justly admired for their delicacy of expression. Some of the images are very effective. Nothing can be better than—

> "the bards sublime,
> Whose distant footsteps echo
> Through the corridors of Time."

The idea of the last quatrain is also very effective. The poem, on the whole, however, is chiefly to be admired for the graceful *insouciance* of its metre, so well in accordance with the character of the sentiments, and especially for the *ease* of the general manner. This "ease," or naturalness, in a literary style, it has long been the fashion to regard as ease in appearance alone—as a point of really difficult attainment. But not so; a natural manner is difficult only to him who should never meddle with it—to the unnatural. It is but the result of writing with the understanding, or with the instinct, that *the tone*, in composition, should always be that which the mass of mankind would adopt—and must perpetually vary, of course, with the occasion. The author who, after the fashion of the "North American Review," should be, upon *all* occasions, merely "quiet," must necessarily, upon *many* occasions, be simply silly, or stupid; and has no more right to be considered "easy," or "natural," than a Cockney exquisite, or than the sleeping Beauty in the wax-works.

Among the minor poems of Bryant, none has so much impressed me as one which he entitles "June." I quote only a portion of it:—

> "There, through the long, long summer hours,
>   The golden light should lie,
> And thick, young herbs and groups of flowers
>   Stand in their beauty by.
> The oriole should build and tell
> His love-tale, close beside my cell;
>   The idle butterfly
> Should rest him there, and there be heard
> The housewife-bee and humming-bird.
>
> "And what if cheerful shouts, at noon,
>   Come, from the village sent,
> Or songs of maids, beneath the moon,
>   With fairy laughter blent?

And what if, in the evening light,
Betrothèd lovers walk in sight
    Of my low monument?
I would the lovely scene around
Might know no sadder sight nor sound.

"I know that I no more should see
    The season's glorious show,
Nor would its brightness shine for me,
    Nor its wild music flow;
But if, around my place of sleep,
The friends I love should come to weep,
    They might not haste to go.
Soft airs, and song, and light, and bloom
Should keep them, lingering by my tomb.

"These to their softened hearts should bear
    The thought of what has been,
And speak of one who cannot share
    The gladness of the scene;
Whose part, in all the pomp that fills
The circuit of the summer hills,
    Is—that his grave is green;
And deeply would their hearts rejoice
    To hear again his living voice."

The rhythmical flow, here, is even voluptuous—nothing could be more melodious. The poem has always affected me in a remarkable manner. The intense melancholy, which seems to well up, perforce, to the surface of all the poet's cheerful sayings about his grave, we find thrilling us to the soul, while there is the truest poetic elevation in the thrill. The impression left is one of a pleasurable sadness. And if, in the remaining compositions which I shall introduce to you, there be more or less of a similar tone always apparent, let me remind you that (how or why we know not) this certain taint of sadness is inseparably connected with all the higher manifestations of true Beauty. It is, nevertheless,

"A feeling of sadness and longing,
    That is not akin to pain,
And resembles sorrow only
    As the mist resembles the rain."

The taint of which I speak is clearly perceptible even in a poem so full of brilliancy and spirit as the "Health" of Edward C. Pinkney:— [6]

"I fill this cup to one made up
    Of loveliness alone,
A woman, of her gentle sex
    The seeming paragon;

[6] Edward C. Pinckney (1802–1828), Maryland lyric poet.

To whom the better elements
    And kindly stars have given
A form so fair, that, like the air,
    'Tis less of earth than heaven.

"Her every tone is music's own,
    Like those of morning birds,
And something more than melody
    Dwells ever in her words;
The coinage of her heart are they,
    And from her lips each flows
As one may see the burdened bee
    Forth issue from the rose.

"Affections are as thoughts to her,
    The measures of her hours;
Her feelings have the fragrancy,
    The freshness of young flowers;
And lovely passions, changing oft,
    So fill her, she appears
The image of themselves by turns,—
    The idol of past years!

"Of her bright face one glance will trace
    A picture on the brain,
And of her voice in echoing hearts
    A sound must long remain;
But memory, such as mine of her,
    So very much endears,
When death is nigh my latest sigh
    Will not be life's, but hers.

"I fill this cup to one made up
    Of loveliness alone,
A woman, of her gentle sex
    The seeming paragon—
Her health! and would on earth there stood
    Some more of such a frame,
That life might be all poetry,
    And weariness a name."

It was the misfortune of Mr. Pinkney to have been born too far south. Had he been a New Englander, it is probable that he would have been ranked as the first of American lyrists by that magnanimous cabal which has so long controlled the destinies of American Letters, in conducting the thing called the "North American Review." The poem just cited is especially beautiful; but the poetic elevation which it induces we must refer chiefly to our sympathy in the poet's enthusiasm. We pardon his hyperboles for the evident earnestness with which they are uttered.

It was by no means my design, however, to expatiate upon the *merits* of what I should read you. These will necessarily speak for themselves.

Boccalini,[7] in his "Advertisements from Parnassus," tells us that Zoilus once presented Apollo a very caustic criticism upon a very admirable book; whereupon the god asked him for the beauties of the work. He replied that he only busied himself about the errors. On hearing this, Apollo handing him a sack of unwinnowed wheat, bade him pick out *all the chaff* for his reward.

Now this fable answers very well as a hit at the critics; but I am by no means sure that the god was in the right. I am by no means certain that the true limits of the critical duty are not grossly misunderstood. Excellence, in a poem especially, may be considered in the light of an axiom, which need only be properly *put* to become self-evident. It is *not* excellence if it requires to be demonstrated as such; and thus, to point out too particularly the merits of a work of Art is to admit that they are *not* merits altogether.

Among the "Melodies" of Thomas Moore, is one whose distinguished character as a poem proper seems to have been singularly left out of view. I allude to his lines beginning: "Come, rest in this bosom." The intense energy of their expression is not surpassed by anything in Byron. There are two of the lines in which a sentiment is conveyed that embodies the *all in all* of the divine passion of Love—a sentiment which, perhaps, has found its echo in more, and in more passionate, human hearts than any other single sentiment ever embodied in words:—

> "Come, rest in this bosom, my own stricken deer,
> Though the herd have fled from thee, thy home is still here;
> Here still is the smile that no cloud can o'ercast,
> And a heart and a hand all thy own to the last.

> "Oh! what was love made for, if 't is not the same
> Through joy and through torment, through glory and shame?
> I know not, I ask not, if guilt's in that heart,
> I but know that I love thee, whatever thou art.

> "Thou hast called me thy angel in moments of bliss;
> And thy angel I'll be, 'mid the horrors of this,—
> Through the furnace, unshrinking, thy steps to pursue,
> And shield thee, and save thee,—or perish there too!"

It has been the fashion, of late days, to deny Moore Imagination, while granting him Fancy—a distinction originating with Coleridge, than whom no man more fully comprehended the great powers of Moore. The fact is that the fancy of this poet so far predominates over all his other faculties, and over the fancy of all other men, as to have induced, very naturally, the idea that he is fanciful *only*. But never was there a greater mistake. Never was a grosser wrong done the fame of a true poet. In the compass of the English language I can call to mind no poem more profoundly, more

---

[7] Trajano Boccalini (1556–1613), Italian satirist. Zoilus was a Greek critic noted for his bitter and spiteful attacks on Homer.

weirdly *imaginative,* in the best sense, than the lines commencing: "I would I were by that dim lake," which are the composition of Thomas Moore. I regret that I am unable to remember them.

One of the noblest—and, speaking of Fancy, one of the most singularly fanciful—of modern poets, was Thomas Hood.[8] His "Fair Ines" had always, for me, an inexpressible charm:—

> "O saw ye not fair Ines?
>   She's gone into the West,
> To dazzle when the sun is down,
>   And rob the world of rest;
> She took our daylight with her,
>   The smiles that we love best,
> With morning blushes on her cheek,
>   And pearls upon her breast.
>
> "O turn again, fair Ines,
>   Before the fall of night,
> For fear the moon should shine alone,
>   And stars unrivalled bright;
> And blessèd will the lover be
>   That walks beneath their light,
> And breathes the love against thy cheek
>   I dare not even write!
>
> "Would I had been, fair Ines,
>   That gallant cavalier
> Who rode so gayly by thy side,
>   And whispered thee so near!
> Were there no bonny dames at home,
>   Or no true lovers here,
> That he should cross the seas to win
>   The dearest of the dear?
>
> "I saw thee, lovely Ines,
>   Descend along the shore,
> With bands of noble gentlemen,
>   And banners waved before;
> And gentle youth and maidens gay,
>   And snowy plumes they wore;
> It would have been a beauteous dream—
>   If it had been no more!
>
> "Alas, alas, fair Ines!
>   She went away with song,
> With Music waiting on her steps,
>   And shoutings of the throng;
> But some were sad and felt no mirth,
>   But only Music's wrong,
> In sounds that sang Farewell, Farewell,
>   To her you've loved so long.

[8] Thomas Hood (1799–1845), English romantic poet.

"Farewell, farewell, fair Ines!
    That vessel never bore
So fair a lady on its deck,
    Nor danced so light before.
Alas for pleasure on the sea,
    And sorrow on the shore!
The smile that blessed one lover's heart
    Has broken many more."

"The Haunted House," by the same author, is one of the truest poems
ever written; one of the *truest*, one of the most unexceptionable, one of the
most thoroughly artistic both in its theme and in its execution. It is, moreover, powerfully ideal, imaginative. I regret that its length renders it un-
suitable for the purposes of this Lecture. In place of it, permit me to offer
the universally appreciated "Bridge of Sighs."

"One more unfortunate,
    Weary of breath,
Rashly importunate,
    Gone to her death!

"Take her up tenderly,
    Lift her with care;
Fashioned so slenderly,
    Young, and so fair!

"Look at her garments
    Clinging like cerements;
Whilst the wave constantly
    Drips from her clothing;
Take her up instantly,
    Loving, not loathing.

"Touch her not scornfully;
    Think of her mournfully,
Gently and humanly;
    Not of the stains of her,—
All that remains of her
    Now is pure womanly.

"Make no deep scrutiny
    Into her mutiny
Rash and undutiful:
    Past all dishonor,
Death has left on her
    Only the beautiful.

"Still, for all slips of hers,
    One of Eve's family—
Wipe those poor lips of hers
    Oozing so clammily,

"Loop up her tresses
Escaped from the comb,
Her fair auburn tresses;
Whilst wonderment guesses
Where was her home?

"Who was her father?
Who was her mother?
Had she a sister?
Had she a brother?
Or was there a dearer one
Still, and a nearer one
Yet, than all other?

"Alas! for the rarity
Of Christian charity
Under the sun!
Oh, it was pitiful!
Near a whole city full,
Home she had none.

"Sisterly, brotherly,
Fatherly, motherly
Feelings had changed;
Love, by harsh evidence
Thrown from its eminence;
Even God's providence
Seeming estranged.

"Where the lamps quiver
So far in the river,
With many a light
From window and casement,
From garret to basement,
She stood, with amazement,
Houseless by night.

"The bleak wind of March
Made her tremble and shiver,
But not the dark arch,
Or the black flowing river:
Mad from life's history,
Glad to death's mystery,
Swift to be hurled—
Anywhere, anywhere
Out of the world!

"In she plunged boldly,
No matter how coldly
The rough river ran,—
Over the brink of it,
Picture it—think of it,

Dissolute man!
Lave in it, drink of it,
Then, if you can!

"Take her up tenderly,
Lift her with care;
Fashioned so slenderly,
Young, and so fair!

"Ere her limbs frigidly
Stiffen too rigidly,
Decently—kindly—
Smoothe and compose them;
And her eyes, close them,
Staring so blindly!

"Dreadfully staring
Through muddy impurity,
As when with the daring
Last look of despairing
Fixed on futurity.

"Perishing gloomily,
Spurred by contumely,
Cold inhumanity,
Burning insanity,
Into her rest.—
Cross her hands humbly,
As if praying dumbly,
Over her breast!

"Owning her weakness,
Her evil behavior,
And leaving, with meekness,
Her sins to her Saviour!"

The vigor of this poem is no less remarkable than its pathos. The versification, although carrying the fanciful to the very verge of the fantastic,
is nevertheless admirably adapted to the wild insanity which is the thesis
of the poem.

Among the minor poems of Lord Byron, is one which has never received
from the critics the praise which it undoubtedly deserves:—

"Though the day of my destiny's over,
    And the star of my fate hath declined,
Thy soft heart refused to discover
    The faults which so many could find;
Though thy soul with my grief was acquainted,
    It shrunk not to share it with me,
And the love which my spirit hath painted
    It never hath found but in *thee*.

"Then when nature around me is smiling,
    The last smile which answers to mine,
I do not believe it beguiling,
    Because it reminds me of thine;
And when winds are at war with the ocean,
    As the breasts I believed in with me,
If their billows excite an emotion,
    It is that they bear me from *thee*.

"Though the rock of my last hope is shivered,
    And its fragments are sunk in the wave,
Though I feel that my soul is delivered
    To pain—it shall not be its slave.
There is many a pang to pursue me;
    They may crush, but they shall not contemn;
They may torture, but shall not subdue me;
    'T is of *thee* that I think—not of them.

"Though human, thou didst not deceive me;
    Though woman, thou didst not forsake;
Though loved, thou forborest to grieve me;
    Though slandered, thou never couldst shake;
Though trusted, thou didst not disclaim me;
    Though parted, it was not to fly;
Though watchful, 't was not to defame me;
    Nor mute, that the world might belie.

"Yet I blame not the world, nor despise it,
    Nor the war of the many with one—
If my soul was not fitted to prize it,
    'T was folly not sooner to shun;
And if dearly that error hath cost me,
    And more than I once could foresee,
I have found that, whatever it lost me,
    It could not deprive me of *thee*.

"From the wreck of the past, which hath perished,
    Thus much I at least may recall:
It hath taught me that what I most cherished
    Deserved to be dearest of all.
In the desert a fountain is springing,
    In the wide waste there still is a tree,
And a bird in the solitude singing,
    Which speaks to my spirit of *thee*."

Although the rhythm here is one of the most difficult, the versification could scarcely be improved. No nobler *theme* ever engaged the pen of poet. It is the soul-elevating idea, that no man can consider himself entitled to complain of Fate while, in his adversity, he still retains the unwavering love of woman.

From Alfred Tennyson—although in perfect sincerity I regard him as the noblest poet that ever lived—I have left myself time to cite only a very brief specimen. I call him, and *think* him, the noblest of poets, *not* because the impressions he produces are, at *all* times, the most profound, *not* because the poetical excitement which he induces is, at *all* times, the most intense, but because it *is*, at all times, the most ethereal,—in other words, the most elevating and the most pure. No poet is so little of the earth, earthy. What I am about to read is from his last long poem, "The Princess":—

"Tears, idle tears, I know not what they mean,
Tears from the depth of some divine despair
Rise in the heart, and gather to the eyes,
In looking on the happy autumn fields,
And thinking of the days that are no more.

"Fresh as the first beam glittering on a sail
That brings our friends up from the underworld;
Sad as the last which reddens over one
That sinks with all we love below the verge;
So sad, so fresh, the days that are no more.

"Ah, sad and strange as in dark summer dawns
The earliest pipe of half-awakened birds
To dying ears, when unto dying eyes
The casement slowly grows a glimmering square;
So sad, so strange, the days that are no more.

"Dear as remembered kisses after death,
And sweet as those by hopeless fancy feigned
On lips that are for others; deep as love,
Deep as first love, and wild with all regret;
O Death in Life, the days that are no more!"

Thus, although in a very cursory and imperfect manner, I have endeavored to convey to you my conception of the Poetic Principle. It has been my purpose to suggest that, while this Principle itself is, strictly and simply, the Human Aspiration for Supernal Beauty, the manifestation of the Principle is always found in *an elevating excitement of the Soul,* quite independent of that passion which is the intoxication of the Heart, or of that Truth which is the satisfaction of the Reason. For, in regard to Passion, alas! its tendency is to degrade rather than elevate the Soul. Love, on the contrary—Love, the true, the divine Eros, the Uranian as distinguished from the Dionaean Venus [9]—is unquestionably the purest and truest of all poetical themes. And in regard to Truth—if, to be sure, through the attainment of a truth we are led to perceive a harmony where none was apparent before, we experience at once the true poetical effect; but this effect is referable to the harmony alone, and not in the least degree to the truth which merely served to render the harmony manifest.

[9] The "Dionaean," or sensual aspect, as opposed to the Uranian, or heavenly aspect, of Venus, the goddess of love.

We shall reach, however, more immediately a distinct conception of what the true Poetry is, by mere reference to a few of the simple elements which induce in the Poet himself the true poetical effect. He recognizes the ambrosia, which nourishes his soul, in the bright orbs that shine in Heaven, in the volutes of the flower, in the clustering of low shrubberies, in the waving of the grain-fields, in the slanting of the tall, Eastern trees, in the blue distance of mountains, in the grouping of clouds, in the twinkling of half-hidden brooks, in the gleaming of silver rivers, in the repose of sequestered lakes, in the star-mirroring depths of lonely wells. He perceives it in the songs of birds, in the harp of Æolus, in the sighing of the night-wind, in the repining voice of the forest, in the surf that complains to the shore, in the fresh breath of the woods, in the scent of the violet, in the voluptuous perfume of the hyacinth, in the suggestive odor that comes to him at eventide from far-distant, undiscovered islands, over dim oceans, illimitable and unexplored. He owns it in all noble thoughts, in all unworldly motives, in all holy impulses, in all chivalrous, generous, and self-sacrificing deeds. He feels it in the beauty of woman, in the grace of her step, in the lustre of her eye, in the melody of her voice, in her soft laughter, in her sigh, in the harmony of the rustling of her robes. He deeply feels it in her winning endearments, in her burning enthusiasms, in her gentle charities, in her meek and devotional endurances; but above all—ah! far above all—he kneels to it, he worships it in the faith, in the purity, in the strength, in the altogether divine majesty of her *love*.

Let me conclude by the recitation of yet another brief poem—one very different in character from any that I have before quoted. It is by Motherwell,[10] and is called "The Song of the Cavalier." With our modern and altogether rational ideas of the absurdity and impiety of warfare, we are not precisely in that frame of mind best adapted to sympathize with the sentiments, and thus to appreciate the real excellence, of the poem. To do this fully, we must identify ourselves, in fancy, with the soul of the old cavalier.

> "Then mounte! then mounte, brave gallants, all
>   And don your helmes amaine:
> Deathe's couriers, Fame and Honor, call
>   Us to the field againe.
> No shrewish teares shall fill our eye
>   When the sword-hilt's in our hand;
> Heart-whole we'll part and no whit sighe
>   For the fayrest of the land;
> Let piping swaine, and craven wight,
>   Thus weepe and puling crye,
> Our business is like men to fight,
>   And hero-like to die!"

[10] William Motherwell (1797–1835), Scottish poet and writer of ballads.

EDGAR ALLAN POE

MARGINALIA [1]
(1844–1849)

NATIONALITY IN AMERICAN LITERATURE

MUCH HAS been said, of late, about the necessity of maintaining a proper *nationality* in American Letters; but what this nationality *is*, or what is to be gained by it, has never been distinctly understood. That an American should confine himself to American themes, or even prefer them, is rather a political than a literary idea—and at best is a questionable point. We would do well to bear in mind that "distance lends enchantment to the view." *Ceteris paribus*, a foreign theme is, in a strictly literary sense, to be preferred. After all, the world at large is the only legitimate stage for the autorial *histrio*.

But of the need of *that* nationality which defends our own literature, sustains our own men of letters, upholds our own dignity, and depends upon our own resources, there cannot be the shadow of a doubt. Yet here is the very point at which we are most supine. We complain of our want of an International Copyright, on the ground that this want justifies our publishers in inundating us with British opinion in British books; and yet when these very publishers at their own obvious risk, and even obvious loss, do publish an American book, we turn up our noses at it with supreme contempt (this is a general thing) until it (the American book) has been dubbed "readable" by some illiterate Cockney critic. Is it too much to say that, with us, the opinion of Washington Irving—of Prescott—of Bryant— is a mere nullity in comparison with that of any anonymous sub-sub-editor of the Spectator, the Athenaeum, or the "London Punch"? It is *not* saying too much, to say this. It is a solemn—an absolutely awful act. Every publisher in the country will admit it to be a fact. There is not a more disgusting spectacle under the sun than our subserviency to British criticism. It is disgusting, first, because it is truckling, servile, pusillanimous—secondly, because of its gross irrationality. We *know* the British to bear us little but ill will—we know that, in no case, do they utter unbiased opinions of American books—we know that in the few instances in which our writers have been treated with common decency in England, these writers have either openly paid homage to English institutions, or have had lurking

[1] The "Marginalia" were a series of articles published by Poe from 1844 to 1849 in the *Democratic Review*, *Godey's Lady's Book*, *Graham's Magazine*, and the *Southern Literary Messenger*. These articles were short, often of only a single paragraph. A collection of the "Marginalia" may be found in volume seven of the *Works*, ed. by Stedman and Woodberry (New York, 1914).

at the bottom of their hearts a secret principle at war with Democracy:—
we *know* all this, and yet, day after day, submit our necks to the degrading
yoke of the crudest opinion that emanates from the fatherland. Now if we
must have nationality, let it be a nationality that will throw off this yoke.

The chief of the rhapsodists who have ridden us to death like the Old
Man of the Mountain, is the ignorant and egotistical Wilson. We use the
term rhapsodists with perfect deliberation; for, Macaulay, and Dilke,[2]
and one or two others excepted, there is not in Great Britain a critic who
can be fairly considered worthy the name. The Germans, and even the
French, are infinitely superior. As regards Wilson,[3] no man ever penned
worse criticism or better rhodomontade. That he is "egotistical" his works
show to all men, running as they read. That he is "ignorant" let his absurd
and continuous schoolboy blunders about Homer bear witness. Not long
ago we ourselves pointed out a series of similar inanities in his review of
Miss Barrett's poems—a series, we say, of gross blunders, arising from sheer
ignorance—and we defy him or any one to answer a single syllable of what
we then advanced.

And yet this is the man whose simple *dictum* (to our shame be it
spoken) has the power to make or to mar any American reputation! In
the last number of Blackwood, he has a continuation of the dull "Specimens
of the British Critics," and makes occasion wantonly to insult one of the
noblest of our poets, Mr. Lowell. The point of the whole attack consists
in the use of slang epithets and phrases of the most ineffably vulgar
description. "Squabashes" is a pet term. "Faugh!" is another. "We are
Scotsmen to *the spine!*" says Sawney—as if the thing were not more than
self-evident. Mr. Lowell is called "a magpie," an "ape," a "Yankee cockney," and his name is intentionally miswritten *John* Russell Lowell. Now
were these indecencies perpetrated by an American critic, that critic would
be sent to Coventry by the whole press of the country, but since it is
Wilson who insults us, we, as in duty bound, not only submit to the insult,
but echo it, as an excellent jest, throughout the length and breadth of the
land. *Quamdiu Catilina?* [How long, O Cataline?] We do indeed demand
the nationality of self-respect. In Letters as in Government we require a
Declaration of Independence. A better thing still would be a Declaration
of War—and that war should be carried forthwith "into Africa."

The Effect of Rhyme

The effect derivable from well-managed rhyme is very imperfectly understood. Conventionally "rhyme" implies merely close similarity of sound at
the ends of verse, and it is really curious to observe how long mankind
have been content with their limitation of the idea. What, in rhyme, first
and principally pleases, may be referred to the human sense or apprecia-

[2] Charles W. Dilke (1789-1864), English critic, contributor to the *Athenaeum*.
[3] John Wilson (1785-1854), Scottish critic; made voluminous contributions to
Blackwood's Magazine (in 1834 over fifty articles) under the name of Christopher
North.

tion of *equality*—the common element, as might be easily shown, of all the gratification we derive from music in its most extended sense—very especially in its modifications of metre and rhythm. We see, for example, a crystal, and are immediately interested by the equality between the sides and angles of one of its faces—but, on bringing to view a second face, in all respects similar to the first, our pleasure seems to be *squared*—on bringing to view a third, it appears to be *cubed*, and so on: I have no doubt, indeed, that the delight experienced, if measurable, would be found to have exact mathematical relations, such, or nearly such as I suggest—that is to say, as far as a certain point, beyond which there would be a decrease, in similar relations. Now here, as the ultimate result of analysis, we reach the sense of mere *equality,* or rather the human delight in this sense; and it was an instinct, rather than a clear comprehension of this delight as a principle, which, in the first instance, led the poet to attempt an increase of the effect arising from the mere similarity (that is to say equality) between two sounds—led him, I say, to attempt increasing this effect by making a secondary equalization, in placing the rhymes at equal distances —that is, at the ends of lines of equal length. In this manner, rhyme and the termination of the line grew connected in men's thoughts—grew into a conventionalism—the principle being lost sight of altogether. And it was simply because Pindaric verses had, before this epoch, existed—*i.e.,* verses of unequal length—that rhymes were subsequently found at unequal distances. It was for this reason solely, I say—for none more profound—rhyme had come to be regarded as of right appertaining to the *end* of verse—and here we complain that the matter has finally rested.

But it is clear that there was much more to be considered. So far, the sense of *equality* alone, entered the effect; or, if this equality was slightly varied, it was varied only through an accident—the accident of the existence of Pindaric metres. It will be seen that the rhymes were always *anticipated.* The eye, catching the end of a verse, whether long or short, expected, for the ear, a rhyme. The great element of unexpectedness was not dreamed of—that is to say, of novelty—of originality. "But," says Lord Bacon, (how justly!) "there is no exquisite beauty without some *strangeness* in the proportions." Take away this element of strangeness—of unexpectedness—of novelty—of originality—call it what we will—and all that is *ethereal* in loveliness is lost at once. We lose—we miss the *unknown*—the vague—the uncomprehended, because offered before we have time to examine and comprehend. We lose, in short, all that assimilates the beauty of earth with what we dream of the beauty of Heaven.

Perfection of rhyme is attainable only in the combination of the two elements, Equality and Unexpectedness. But as evil cannot exist without good, so unexpectedness must arise from expectedness. We do not contend for mere *arbitrariness* of rhyme. In the first place, we must have equidistant or regularly recurring rhymes, to form the basis, expectedness, out of which arises the element, unexpectedness, by the introduction of rhymes, not arbitrarily, but with an eye to the greatest amount of unexpectedness. We should not introduce them, for example, at such points that the entire line is a multiple of the syllables preceding the points. When, for instance, I write—

>   And the silken, sad, uncertain rustling of each purple curtain,

I produce more, to be sure, but not remarkably more than the ordinary effect of rhymes regularly recurring at the ends of lines; for the number of syllables in the whole verse is merely a multiple of the number of syllables preceding the rhyme introduced at the middle, and there is still left, therefore, a certain degree of expectedness. What there is of the element, unexpectedness, is addressed, in fact, to the eye only—for the ear divides the verse into two ordinary lines thus:

>   And the silken, sad, uncertain
>   Rustling of each purple curtain.

I obtain, however, the whole effect of unexpectedness, when I write—

>   *Thrilled* me, *filled* me with fantastic terrors never felt before.

N.B. It is very commonly supposed that rhyme, as it now ordinarily exists, is of modern invention—but see the "Clouds" of Aristophanes. Hebrew verse, however, did *not* include it—the termination of the lines, where most distinct, never showing anything of the kind.

TENNYSON'S MUSIC

I am not sure that Tennyson is not the greatest of poets. The uncertainty attending the public conception of the term "poet" alone prevents me from demonstrating that he *is*. Other bards produce effects which are, now and then, otherwise produced than by what we call poems; but Tennyson an effect which only a poem does. His alone are idiosyncratic poems. By the enjoyment or non-enjoyment of the "Morte D'Arthur," or of the "Aenone," I would test any one's ideal sense.

There are passages in his works which rivet a conviction I had long entertained, that the *indefinite* is an element in the true ποίησις [work of poetry]. Why do some persons fatigue themselves in attempts to unravel such fantasy-pieces as the "Lady of Shalott"? As well unweave the *"ventum textilem"* [fabric of the winds]. If the author did not deliberately propose himself a suggestive indefinitiveness of meaning, with the view of bringing about a definitiveness of vague and therefore of spiritual *effect*—this, at least, arose from the silent analytical promptings of that poetic genius which, in its supreme development, embodies all orders of intellectual capacity.

I *know* that indefinitiveness is an element of the true music—I mean of the true musical expression. Give to it any undue decision—imbue it with any very determinate tone—and you deprive it, at once, of its ethereal, its ideal, its intrinsic and essential character. You dispel its luxury of dream.

You dissolve the atmosphere of the mystic upon which it floats. You exhaust it of its breath of faëry. It now becomes a tangible and easily appreciable idea—a thing of the earth, earthy. It has not, indeed, lost its power to please, but all which I consider the distinctiveness of that power. And to the uncultivated talent, or to the unimaginative apprehension, this deprivation of its most delicate grace will be, not unfrequently, a recommendation. A determinateness of expression is sought—and often by composers who should know better—is sought as a beauty rather than rejected as a blemish. Thus we have, even from high authorities, attempts at absolute *imitation* in music. Who can forget the silliness of the "Battle of Prague"? What man of taste but must laugh at the interminable drums, trumpets, blunderbusses, and thunder? *"Vocal* music," says L'Abbate Gravina, who would have said the same thing of instrumental, "ought to imitate the natural language of the human feelings and passions, rather than the warbling of Canary birds, which our singers, now-a-days, affect so vastly to mimic with their quaverings and boasted cadences." This is true only so far as the "rather" is concerned. If any music must imitate anything, it were assuredly better to limit the imitation as Gravina suggests.

Tennyson's shorter pieces abound in minute rhythmical lapses sufficient to assure me that—in common with all poets living or dead—he has neglected to make precise investigation of the principles of metre; but, on the other hand, so perfect is his rhythmical instinct in general, that, like the present Viscount Canterbury, he seems *to see with his ear.*

HENRY WADSWORTH LONGFELLOW

From THE DEFENCE OF POETRY [1]
(1832)

. . . As no 'Apologie for Poetrie' has appeared among us, we hope that
Sir Philip Sidney's Defence will be widely read and long remembered.
O that in our country, it might be the harbinger of as bright an intellectual
day as it was in his own!—With us, the spirit of the age is clamorous for
utility—for visible, tangible utility,—for bare, brawny, muscular utility. We
would be roused to action by the voice of the populace, and the sounds of
the crowded mart, and not 'lulled asleep in shady idleness with poet's
pastimes.' We are swallowed up in schemes for gain, and engrossed with
contrivances for bodily enjoyments, as if this particle of dust were immortal,—as if the soul needed no aliment, and the mind no raiment. We
glory in the extent of our territory, in our rapidly increasing population, in
our agricultural privileges, and our commercial advantages. We boast of
the magnificence and beauty of our natural scenery,—of the various climates of our sky,—the summers of our Northern regions,—the salubrious
winters of the South, and of the various products of our soil, from the
pines of our Northern highlands to the palm-tree and aloes of our Southern
frontier. We boast of the increase and extent of our physical strength, the
sound of populous cities, breaking the silence and solitude of our Western
territories,—plantations conquered from the forest, and gardens springing
up in the wilderness. Yet the true glory of a nation consists not in the
extent of its territory, the pomp of its forests, the majesty of its rivers, the
height of its mountains, and the beauty of its sky; but in the extent of its
mental power,—the majesty of its intellect,—the height and depth and
purity of its moral nature. It consists not in what nature has given to the
body, but in what nature and education have given to the mind:—not in
the world around us, but in the world within us:—not in the circumstances of fortune, but in the attributes of the soul:—not in the corruptible,
transitory, and perishable forms of matter, but in the incorruptible, the
permanent, the imperishable mind. True greatness is the greatness of
the mind;—the true glory of a nation is moral and intellectual pre-eminence.

But still the main current of education runs in the wide and not well
defined channel of immediate and practical utility. The main point is,
how to make the greatest progress in worldly prosperity,—how to advance

---

[1] A review of Sir Philip Sidney's *The Defence of Poesy*. From the *North American
Review*, XXXIV (1832).

most rapidly in the career of gain. This, perhaps, is necessarily the case to a certain extent in a country, where every man is taught to rely upon his own exertions for a livelihood, and is the artificer of his own fortune and estate. But it ought not to be exclusively so. We ought not, in the pursuit of wealth and worldly honor, to forget those embellishments of the mind and the heart, which sweeten social intercourse and improve the condition of society. And yet, in the language of Dr. Paley,[2] 'Many of us are brought up with this world set before us, and nothing else. Whatever promotes this world's prosperity is praised; whatever hurts and obstructs this world's prosperity is blamed; and there all praise and censure end. We see mankind about us in motion and action, but all these motions and actions directed to worldly objects. We hear their conversation, but it is all the same way. And this is what we see and hear from the first. The views, which are continually placed before our eyes, regard this life alone and its interests. Can it then be wondered at, that an early worldly-mindedness is bred in our hearts so strong, as to shut out heavenly-mindedness entirely!'—And this, though not in so many words, yet in fact and in its practical tendency, is the popular doctrine of utility.

Now, under correction be it said, we are much led astray by this word utility. There is hardly a word in our language whose meaning is so vague, and so often misunderstood and misapplied. We too often limit its application to those acquisitions and pursuits, which are of immediate and visible profit to ourselves and the community; regarding as comparatively or utterly useless many others, which, though more remote in their effects and more imperceptible in their operation, are, notwithstanding, higher in their aim, wider in their influence, more certain in their results, and more intimately connected with the common weal. We are too apt to think that nothing can be useful, but what is done with a noise, at noon-day, and at the corners of the streets; as if action and utility were synonymous, and it were not as useless to act without thinking, as it is to think without acting. But the truth is, the word utility has a wider signification than this. It embraces in its proper definition whatever contributes to our happiness; and thus includes many of those arts and sciences, many of those secret studies and solitary avocations, which are generally regarded either as useless, or as absolutely injurious to society. Not he alone does service to the State, whose wisdom guides her councils at home, nor he whose voice asserts her dignity abroad. A thousand little rills, springing up in the retired walks of life, go to swell the rushing tide of national glory and prosperity; and whoever in the solitude of his chamber, and by even a single effort of his mind, has added to the intellectual pre-eminence of his country, has not lived in vain, nor to himself alone. Does not the pen of the historian perpetuate the fame of the hero and the statesman? Do not their names live in the song of the bard? Do not the pencil and the chisel touch the soul while they delight the eye? Does not the spirit of the patriot and the sage, looking from the painted canvass, or eloquent from the marble lip, fill our hearts with the veneration for all that is great in intellect, and godlike in virtue?

[2] William Paley (1743–1805), British philosopher and theologian.

If this be true, then are the ornamental arts of life not merely ornamental, but at the same time highly useful; and Poetry and the Fine Arts become the instruction, as well as the amusement of mankind. They will not till our lands, nor freight our ships, nor fill our granaries and our coffers; but they will enrich the heart, freight the understanding, and make up the garnered fulness of the mind. And this we hold to be the true use of the subject.

Among the barbarous nations, which, in the early centuries of our era, overran the South of Europe, the most contumelious epithet which could be applied to a man, was to call him a Roman. All the corruption and degeneracy of the Western Empire were associated, in the minds of the Gothic tribes, with a love of letters and the fine arts. So far did this belief influence their practices, that they would not suffer their children to be instructed in the learning of the South. 'Instruction in the sciences,' said they, 'tends to corrupt, enervate, and depress the mind; and he who has been accustomed to tremble under the rod of a pedagogue, will never look on a sword or a spear with an undaunted eye.' * We apprehend that there are some, and indeed not a few in our active community, who hold the appellation of scholar and man of leters in as little repute, as did our Gothic ancestors that of Roman; associating with it about the same ideas of effeminacy and inefficiency. They think, that the learning of books is not wisdom; that study unfits a man for action; that poetry and nonsense are convertible terms; that literature begets an effeminate and craven spirit; in a word, that the dust and cobwebs of a library are a kind of armor, which will not stand long against the hard knocks of 'the bone and muscle of the State,' and the 'huge two-fisted sway' of the stump orator. Whenever intellect is called into action, they would have the mind display a rough and natural energy,—strength, straight-forward strength, untutored in the rules of art, and unadorned by elegant and courtly erudition. They want the stirring voice of Demosthenes, accustomed to the roar of the tempest, and the dashing of the sea upon its hollow-sounding shore; rather than the winning eloquence of Phalereus, coming into the sun and dust of the battle, not from the martial tent of the soldier, but from the philosophic shades of Theophrastus.[3]

But against no branch of scholarship is the cry so loud as against poetry, 'the quintessence, or rather the luxury of all learning.' Its enemies pretend, that it is injurious both to the mind and the heart; that it incapacitates us for the severer discipline of professional study; and that, by exciting the feelings and misdirecting the imagination, it unfits us for the common duties of life, and the intercourse of this matter-of-fact world. And yet such men have lived, as Homer, and Dante, and Milton;—poets and scholars, whose minds were bathed in song, and yet not weakened; men who severally carried forward the spirit of their age, who soared upward on the wings of poetry, and yet were not unfitted to penetrate the deepest recesses of

* Procop. de bello Gothor. ap. Robertson, Hist. Charles V. Vol. I, p. 234 [Longfellow's note].

[3] Greek philosopher, ca. 372–287 B.C.

the human soul, and search out the hidden treasures of wisdom, and the secret springs of thought, feeling, and action. None fought more bravely at Marathon, Salamis, and Plataea, than did the poet Æschylus.[4] Richard Coeur-de-Lion was a poet; but his boast was in his very song:

> 'Bon guerrier à l'estendart
> Trouvaretz le Roi Richard.'

Ercilla and Garcilasso were poets,[5] but the great epic of Spain was written in the soldier's tent and on the field of battle, and the descendant of the Incas was slain in the assault of a castle in the South of France. Cervantes lost an arm at the battle of Lepanto, and Sir Philip Sidney was the breathing reality of the poet's dream, a living and glorious proof, that poetry neither enervates the mind nor unfits us for the practical duties of life.

Nor is it less true, that the legitimate tendency of poetry is to exalt, rather than to debase,—to purify, rather than to corrupt. Read the inspired pages of the Hebrew prophets; the eloquent aspirations of the Psalmist! Where did ever the spirit of devotion bear up the soul more steadily and loftily, than in the language of their poetry? And where has poetry been more exalted, more spirit-stirring, more admirable, or more beautiful, than when thus soaring upward on the wings of sublime devotion, the darkness and shadows of earth beneath it, and from above the brightness of an opened heaven pouring around it? It is true, the poetic talent may be, for it has been, most lamentably perverted. But when poetry is thus perverted,—when it thus forgets its native sky to grovel in what is base, sensual, and depraved,—though it may not have lost all its original brightness, nor appear less than 'the excess of glory obscured,' yet its birth-right has been sold, its strength has been blasted, and its spirit wears 'deep scars of thunder.'

It does not, then, appear to be the necessary nor the natural tendency of poetry to enervate the mind, corrupt the heart, or incapacitate us for performing the private and public duties of life. On the contrary, it may be made, and should be made, an instrument for improving the condition of society, and advancing the great purpose of human happiness. Man must have his hours of meditation as well as of action. The unities of time are not so well preserved in the great drama, but that moments will occur, when the stage must be left vacant, and even the busiest actors pass behind the scenes. There will be eddies in the stream of life, though the main current sweeps steadily onward, till 'it pours in full cataract over the grave.' There are times, when both mind and body are worn down by the severity of daily toil; when the grasshopper is a burden; and thirsty with the heat of labor, the spirit longs for the waters of Shiloah, that go softly. At such seasons, both mind and body should unbend themselves; they should be set free from the yoke of their customary service, and thought take some other

[4] Greek tragic poet and dramatist, 525–456 B.C.
[5] Alonso De Ercilla Y Zúniga (1533–1594), Spanish soldier and poet. Garcilasso De La Vega (1503–1536), Spanish soldier and poet.

direction, than that of the beaten, dusty thoroughfare of business. And there are times, too, when the divinity stirs within us; when the soul abstracts herself from the world, and the slow and regular motions of earthly business do not keep pace with the Heaven-directed mind. Then earth lets go her hold; the soul feels herself more akin to Heaven; and soaring upward, the denizen of her native sky, she 'begins to reason like herself, and to discourse in a strain above mortality.' Call, if you will, such thoughts and feelings the dreams of the imagination; yet they are no unprofitable dreams. Such moments of silence and meditation are often those of the greatest utility to ourselves and others. Yes, we would dream awhile, that the spirit is not always the bondman of the flesh; that there is something immortal in us, something, which amid the din of life, urges us to aspire after the attributes of a more spiritual nature. Let the cares and business of the world sometimes sleep, for this sleep is the awakening of the soul.

To fill up these interludes of life with a song, that shall soothe our worldly passions and inspire us with a love of Heaven and virtue, seems to be the peculiar province of poetry.

. . . In fine, we think that all the popular objections against poetry may be, not only satisfactorily, but triumphantly answered. They are all founded upon its abuse, and not upon its natural and legitimate tendencies. Indeed, popular judgment has seldom fallen into a greater error, than that of supposing that poetry must necessarily, and from its very nature, convey false and therefore injurious impressions. The error lies in not discriminating between what is true to nature, and what is true to fact. From the very nature of things, neither poetry nor any one of the imitative arts, can in itself be false. They can be false no farther than, by the imperfection of human skill, they convey to our minds imperfect and garbled views of what they represent. Hence a painting, or poetical description, may be true to nature, and yet false in point of fact. The canvass before you may represent a scene, in which every individual feature of the landscape shall be true to nature;—the tree, the water-fall, the distant mountain,—every object there shall be an exact copy of an original, that has a real existence, and yet the scene itself may be absolutely false in point of fact. Such a scene, with the features of the landscape combined precisely in the way represented, may exist nowhere but in the imagination of the artist. The statue of the Venus de' Medici is the perfection of female beauty; and every individual feature had its living original. Still the statue itself had no living archetype. It is true to nature, but it is not true to fact. So with the stage. The scene represented, the characters introduced, the plot of the piece, and the action of the performers may all be conformable to nature, and yet not be conformable to any pre-existing reality. The characters there personified may never have existed; the events represented may never have transpired. And so, too, with poetry. The scenes and events it describes; the characters and passions it portrays, may all be natural though not real. Thus, in a certain sense, fiction itself may be true,—true to the nature of things, and consequently true in the impressions it conveys. And hence the reason, why fiction has always been made so subservient to the cause of truth.

Allowing, then, that poetry is nothing but fiction; that all it describes is false in point of fact; still its elements have a real existence, and the impressions we receive can be erroneous so far only, as the views presented to the mind are garbled and false to nature. And this is a fault incident to the artist, and not inherent in the art itself. So that we may fairly conclude, from these considerations, that the natural tendency of poetry is to give us correct moral impressions, and thereby advance the cause of truth and the improvement of society.

There is another very important view of the subject, arising out of the origin and nature of poetry, and its intimate connexion with individual character and the character of society.

The origin of poetry loses itself in the shades of a remote and fabulous age, of which we have only vague and uncertain traditions. Its fountain, like that of the river of the desert, springs up in a distant and unknown region, the theme of visionary story, and the subject of curious speculation. Doubtless, however, it originated amid the scenes of pastoral life, and in the quiet and repose of a golden age. There is something in the soft melancholy of the groves, which pervades the heart, and kindles the imagination. Their retirement is favorable to the musings of the poetic mind. The trees that waved their leafy branches to the summer wind, or heaved and groaned beneath the passing storm,—the shadow moving on the grass,— the bubbling brook,—the insect skimming on its surface,—the receding valley and the distant mountain,—these would be some of the elements of pastoral song. Its subject would naturally be the complaint of a shepherd and the charms of some gentle shepherdess,

'A happy soul, that all the way
To Heaven, hath a summer's day.'

It is natural, too, that the imagination, familiar with the outward world, and connecting the idea of the changing seasons and the spontaneous fruits of the earth with the agency of some unknown power, that regulated and produced them, should suggest the thought of presiding deities, propitious in the smiling sky, and adverse in the storm. The fountain that gushed up as if to meet the thirsty lip, was made the dwelling of a nymph; the grove that lent its shelter and repose from the heat of noon, became the abode of dryads; a god presided over shepherds and their flocks, and a goddess shook the yellow harvest from her lap. These deities were propitiated by songs and festive rites. And thus poetry added new charms to the simplicity and repose of bucolic life, and the poet mingled in his verse the delights of rural ease, and the praise of the rural deities which bestowed them.

Such was poetry in those happy ages, when, camps and courts unknown, life was itself an eclogue. But in later days it sang the achievements of Grecian and Roman heroes, and pealed in the war-song of the Gothic

Scald. These early essays were rude and unpolished. As nations advanced in civilization and refinement, poetry advanced with them. In each successive age, it became the image of their thoughts and feelings, of their manners, customs, and characters; for poetry is but the warm expression of the thoughts and feelings of a people, and we speak of it as being national, when the character of a nation shines visibly and distinctly through it.

Thus, for example, Castilian poetry is characterized by sounding expressions, and that pomp and majesty, so peculiar to Spanish manners and character. On the other hand, English poetry possesses in a high degree the charms of rural and moral feeling; it flows onward like a woodland stream, in which we see the reflection of the sylvan landscape and of the heaven above us.

It is from this intimate connexion of poetry with the manners, customs, and characters of nations, that one of its highest uses is drawn. The impressions produced by poetry upon national character at any period, are again re-produced, and give a more pronounced and individual character to the poetry of a subsequent period. And hence it is, that the poetry of a nation sometimes throws so strong a light upon the page of its history, and renders luminous those obscure passages, which often baffle the long-searching eye of studious erudition. In this view, poetry assumes new importance with all who search for historic truth. Besides, the view of the various fluctuations of the human mind, as exhibited, not in history, but in the poetry of successive epochs, is more interesting, and less liable to convey erroneous impressions, than any record of mere events. The great advantage drawn from the study of history is not to treasure up in the mind a multitude of disconnected facts, but from these facts to derive some conclusions, tending to illustrate the movements of the general mind, the progress of society, the manners, customs, and institutions, the moral and intellectual character of mankind in different nations, at different times, and under the operation of different circumstances. Historic facts are chiefly valuable, as exhibiting intellectual phenomena. And so far as poetry exhibits these phenomena more perfectly and distinctly than history does, so far is it superior to history. The history of a nation is the external symbol of its character; from it, we reason back to the spirit of the age that fashioned its shadowy outline. But poetry is the spirit of the age itself,—embodied in the forms of language, and speaking in a voice that is audible to the external as well as the internal sense. The one makes known the impulses of the popular mind, through certain events resulting from them; the other displays the more immediate presence of that mind, visible in its action, and presaging those events. The one is like the marks left by the thunder-storm,—the blasted tree,—the purified atmosphere; the other like the flash from the bosom of the cloud, or the voice of the tempest, announcing its approach. The one is the track of the ocean on its shore; the other the continual movement and murmur of the sea.

Besides, there are epochs, which have no contemporaneous history; but have left in their popular poetry pretty ample materials for estimating the character of the times. The events, indeed, therein recorded, may be exaggerated facts, or vague traditions, or inventions entirely apocryphal; yet they faithfully represent the spirit of the ages which produced them; they contain indirect allusions and incidental circumstances, too insignificant in themselves to have been fictitious, and yet on that very account the most important parts of the poem, in a historical point of view. Such, for example, are the *Nibelungen Lied* in Germany; the *Poema del Cid* in Spain; and the *Songs of the Troubadours* in France. Hence poetry comes in for a large share in that high eulogy, which, in the true spirit of the scholar, a celebrated German critic has bestowed upon letters: 'If we consider literature in its widest sense, as the voice which gives expression to human intellect,—as the aggregate mass of symbols, in which the spirit of an age or the character of a nation is shadowed forth, then indeed a great and various literature is, without doubt, the most valuable possession of which any nation can boast'.*

From all these considerations, we are forced to the conclusion, that poetry is a subject of far greater importance in itself, and in its bearing upon the condition of society, than the majority of mankind would be willing to allow. We heartily regret, that this opinion is not a more prevailing one in our land. We give too little encouragement to works of imagination and taste. The vocation of the poet does not stand high enough in our esteem; we are too cold in admiration, too timid in praise. The poetic lute and the high-sounding lyre are much too often and too generally looked upon as the baubles of effeminate minds, or bells and rattles to please the ears of children. The prospect, however, brightens. But a short time ago, not a poet 'moved the wing, or opened the mouth, or peeped;' and now we have a host of them,—three or four good ones, and three or four hundred poor ones. This, however, we will not stop to cavil about at present. To those of them, who may honor us by reading our article, we would whisper this request,—that they should be more original, and withal more national. It seems every way important, that now, whilst we are forming our literature, we should make it as original, characteristic, and national as possible. To effect this, it is not necessary that the war-whoop should ring in every line, and every page be rife with scalps, tomahawks and wampum. Shade of Tecumseh forbid!—The whole secret lies in Sidney's maxim,—'Look in thy heart and write.' For

> 'Cantars non pot gaire valer,
> Si d'inz del cor no mov lo chang.' †

Of this anon. We will first make a few remarks upon the word *national*, as applied to the literature of a country; for when we speak of a national poetry, we do not employ the term in that vague and indefinite way, in which many writers use it.

---

* Schlegel. Lectures on the History of Literature, Vol. I. Lec. VII [Longfellow's note].
  † 'The poet's song is little worth,
     If it moveth not from within the heart.' [Longfellow's note]

A national literature, then, in the widest signification of the words, embraces every mental effort made by the inhabitants of a country, through the medium of the press. Every book written by a citizen of a country belongs to its national literature. But the term has also a more peculiar and appropriate definition; for when we say that the literature of a country is *national*, we mean that it bears upon it the stamp of national character. We refer to those distinguishing features, which literature receives from the spirit of a nation,—from its scenery and climate, its historic recollections, its Government, its various institutions,—from all those national peculiarities, which are the result of no positive institutions, and, in a word, from the thousand external circumstances, which either directly or indirectly exert an influence upon the literature of a nation, and give it a marked and individual character, distinct from that of the literature of other nations.

In order to be more definite and more easily understood in these remarks, we will here offer a few illustrations of the influence of external causes upon the character of the mind, the peculiar habits of thought and feeling, and, consequently, the general complexion of literary performances. From the causes enumerated above, we select natural scenery and climate, as being among the most obvious, in their influence upon the prevailing tenor of poetic composition. Every one who is acquainted with the works of the English Poets, must have noted, that a moral feeling and a certain rural quiet and repose are among their most prominent characteristics. The features of their native landscape are transferred to the printed page, and as we read we hear the warble of the sky-lark,—the 'hollow murmuring wind, or silver rain.' The shadow of the woodland scene lends a pensive shadow to the ideal world of poetry.

> 'Why lure me from these pale retreats?
> Why rob me of these pensive sweets?
> Can Music's voice, can Beauty's eye,
> Can Painting's glowing hand supply,
> A charm so suited to my mind,
> As blows this hollow gust of wind,
> As drops this little weeping rill
> Soft tinkling down the moss-grown hill,
> While through the west, where sinks the crimson day,
> Meek twilight slowly sails, and waves her banners grey? *

In the same richly poetic vein are the following lines from Collins's Ode to Evening.

> 'Or if chill blustering winds, or driving rain,
> Prevent my willing feet, be mine the hut,
> That from the mountain's side,
> Views wilds and swelling floods,

* Mason's Ode to a Friend [Longfellow's note].

'And hamlets brown, and dim-discover'd spires,
And hears their simple bell, and marks o'er all
        Thy dewy fingers draw
        The gradual dusky veil.'

In connexion with the concluding lines of these two extracts, and as an illustration of the influence of climate on the character of poetry, it is worthy of remark, that the English Poets excel those of the South of Europe in their descriptions of morning and evening. They dwell with long delight and frequent repetition upon the brightening glory of the hour, when 'the northern wagoner has set his sevenfold teme behind the stedfast starre;' and upon the milder beauty of departing day, when 'the bright-hair'd sun sits in yon western tent.' What, for example, can be more descriptive of the vernal freshness of a morning in May, than the often quoted song in Cymbeline?

'Hark! hark! the lark at heaven's gate sings,
        And Phoebus 'gins arise
His steeds to water at those springs
        On chalic'd flowers that *lies*:
And winking Mary-buds begin
        To ope their golden eyes;
With every thing that pretty bin;
        My lady sweet, arise;
                Arise, arise!'

How full of poetic feeling and imagery is the following description of the dawn of day, taken from Fletcher's Faithful Shepherdess! [6]

'See, the day begins to break,
And the light shoots like a streak
Of subtle fire, the wind blows cold,
While the morning doth unfold;
Now the birds begin to rouse,
And the squirrel from the boughs
Leaps, to get him nuts and fruit;
The early lark, that erst was mute,
Carols to the rising day
Many a note and many a lay.'

Still more remarkable than either of these extracts, as a graphic description of morning, is the following from Beattie's Minstrel.[7]

'But who the melodies of morn can tell?
The wild brook babbling down the mountain's side;
The lowing herd; the sheepfold's simple bell;

[6] John Fletcher (1579–1625), English dramatist of the Renaissance; his *Faithful Shepherdess* appeared in 1608.
[7] James Beattie (1735–1803), Scottish poet, wrote *The Minstrel* (1771, 74) which was regarded as one of the longest and one of the best poems of the century in the Spenserian stanza.

The pipe of early shepherd dim descried
In the lone valley; echoing far and wide
The clamorous horn along the cliffs above;
The hollow murmur of the ocean tide;
The hum of bees, and linnet's lay of love,
And the full choir that wakes the universal grove.

'The cottage curs at early pilgrim bark;
Crown'd with her pail, the tripping milk-maid sings;
The whistling ploughman stalks afield; and hark!
Down the rough slope the ponderous wagon rings;
Through rustling corn the hare astonish'd springs;
Slow tolls the village clock the drowsy hour;
The partridge bursts away on whirring wings;
Deep mourns the turtle in sequester'd bower;
And shrill lark carols clear from her aerial tower.'

Extracts of this kind we might multiply almost without number. The same may be said of similar ones, descriptive of the gradual approach of evening and the close of day. But we have already quoted enough for our present purpose. Now, to what peculiarities of natural scenery and climate may we trace these manifold and beautiful descriptions, which in their truth, delicacy and poetic coloring, surpass all the pictures of the kind in Tasso, Guarini, Boscan,[8] Garcilasso, and, in a word, all the most celebrated poets of the South of Europe? Doubtless, to the rural beauty which pervades the English landscape, and to the long morning and evening twilight of a northern climate.

Still, with all this taste for the charms of rural description and sylvan song, pastoral poetry has never been much cultivated, nor much admired in England. The Arcadia of Sir Philip Sidney, it is true, enjoyed a temporary celebrity, but this was, doubtless, owing in a great measure to the rank of its author; and though the pastorals of Pope are still read and praised, their reputation belongs in part to their author's youth at the time of their composition. Nor is this remarkable. For though the love of rural ease is characteristic of the English, yet the rigors of their climate render their habits of pastoral life any thing but delightful. In the mind of an Englishman, the snowy fleece is more intimately associated with the weaver's shuttle, than with the shepherd's crook. Horace Walpole has a humorous passage in one of his letters, on the affectation of pastoral habits in England. 'In short,' says he, 'every summer one lives in a state of mutiny and murmur, and I have found the reason; it is because we will affect to have a summer, and we have no title to any such thing. Our poets learnt their trade of the Romans, and so adopted the terms of their masters. They talk of shady groves, purling streams, and cooling breezes, and we get sore throats and agues by attempting to realize these visions. Master Damon writes a song, and invites Miss Chloe to enjoy the cool

---

[8] Torquato Tasso (1544–1595), Italian epic poet; Giovanni Battista Guarini (1538–1612), Italian poet; Juan Boscan (1490?–1542), Spanish poet and soldier.

of the evening, and the deuce a bit have we of any such thing as a *cool* evening. Zephyr is a north-east wind, that makes Damon button up to the chin, and pinches Chloe's nose till it is red and blue; and they cry, *This is a bad Summer*; as if we ever had any other. The best sun we have is made of Newcastle coal, and I am determined never to reckon upon any other.' On the contrary, the poetry of the Italians, the Spanish, and the Portuguese, is redolent of the charms of pastoral indolence and enjoyment; for they inhabit countries in which pastoral life is a reality and not a fiction, where the winter's sun will almost make you seek the shade, and the summer nights are mild and beautiful in the open air. The babbling brook and cooling breeze are luxuries in a Southern clime, where you

> 'See the sun set, sure he'll rise tomorrow,
> Not through a misty morning twinkling, weak as
>   A drunken man's dead eye, in maudlin sorrow,
> But with all heaven t' himself.'

A love of indolence and a warm imagination are characteristic of the inhabitants of the South. These are natural effects of a soft voluptuous climate. It is there a luxury to let the body lie at ease, stretched by a fountain in the lazy stillness of a summer noon, and suffer the dreamy fancy to lose itself in idle reverie, and give a form to the wind, and a spirit to the shadow and the leaf. Hence the prevalence of personification and the exaggerations of figurative language, so characteristic of the poetry of Southern nations. As an illustration, take the following beautiful sonnet from the Spanish. It is addressed to a mountain brook.

> 'Laugh of the mountain!—lyre of bird and tree!
>   Mirror of morn, and garniture of fields!
>   The soul of April, that so gently yields
> The rose and jasmin bloom, leaps wild in thee!
>
> 'Although, where'er thy devious current strays,
>   The lap of earth with gold and silver teems,
>   To me thy clear proceeding brighter seems
> Than golden sands, that charm each shepherd's gaze.
>
> 'How without guile thy bosom all transparent
>   As the pure crystal, lets the curious eye
>   Thy secrets scan, thy smooth round pebbles count!
> How, without malice murmuring, glides thy current!
> O sweet simplicity of days gone by!
> Thou shunnest the haunts of man, to dwell in limpid fount!'

We will pursue these considerations no longer, for fear of digressing too far. What we have already said will illustrate, perhaps superficially, but sufficiently for our present purpose, the influence of natural scenery and climate upon the character of poetical composition. It will at least show, that in speaking of this influence, we did not speak at random and without a distinct meaning. Similar, and much more copious illustrations of the influence of various other external circumstances on national literature, might here be given. But it is not our intention to go into details. They will naturally suggest themselves to the mind of every reflecting reader.

We repeat, then, that we wish our native poets would give a more national character to their writings. In order to effect this, they have only to write more naturally, to write from their own feelings and impressions, from the influence of what they see around them, and not from any preconceived notions of what poetry ought to be, caught by reading many books, and imitating many models. This is peculiarly true in descriptions of natural scenery. In these, let us have no more sky-larks and nightingales. For us they only warble in books. A painter might as well introduce an elephant or a rhinoceros into a New England landscape. We would not restrict our poets in the choice of their subjects, or the scenes of their story; but when they sing under an American sky, and describe a native landscape, let the description be graphic, as if it had been seen and not imagined. We wish too, to see the figures and imagery of poetry a little more characteristic, as if drawn from nature and not from books. Of this we have constantly recurring examples in the language of our North American Indians. Our readers will all recollect the last words of Pushmataha, the Choctaw Chief, who died at Washington in the year 1824. 'I shall die, but you will return to your brethren. As you go along the paths, you will see the flowers, and hear the birds; but Pushmataha will see them and hear them no more. When you come to your home, they will ask you, where is Pushmataha? and you will say to them, He is no more. They will hear the tidings *like the sound of the fall of a mighty oak in the stillness of the wood.*' More attention on the part of our writers, to these particulars, would give a new and delightful expression to the face of our poetry. But the difficulty is, that instead of coming forward as bold, original thinkers, they have imbibed the degenerate spirit of modern English poetry. They have hitherto been imitators either of decidedly bad, or of, at best, very indifferent models. It has been the fashion to write strong lines,—to aim at point and antithesis. This has made writers turgid and extravagant. Instead of ideas, they give us merely the signs of ideas. They erect a great bridge of words, pompous and imposing, where there is hardly a drop of thought to trickle beneath. Is not he, who thus apostrophizes the clouds, 'Ye posters of the wakeless air!'—quite as extravagant as the Spanish poet, who calls a star, a 'burning doublon of the celestial bank?' *Doblon ardiente del celeste banco!*

This spirit of imitation has spread far and wide. But a few years ago, what an aping of Lord Byron exhibited itself throughout the country! It was not an imitation of the brighter characteristics of his intellect, but a mimicry of his sullen misanthropy and irreligious gloom. We do not wish to make a bugbear of Lord Byron's name, nor figuratively to disturb his bones; still we cannot but express our belief, that no writer has done half so much to corrupt the literary taste as well as the moral principle of our

country, as the author of Childe Harold.* Minds that could not understand his beauties, could imitate his great and glaring defects. Souls that
could not fathom his depths, could grasp the straw and bubbles that floated
upon the agitated surface, until at length every city, town, and village
had its little Byron, its self-tormenting scoffer at morality, its gloomy mis-
anthropist in song. Happily, this noxious influence has been in some
measure checked and counteracted by the writings of Wordsworth, whose
pure and gentle philosophy has been gradually gaining the ascendency
over the bold and visionary speculations of an unhealthy imagination.
The sobriety, and, if we may use the expression, the republican simplicity of his poetry, are in unison with our moral and political doctrines.
But even Wordsworth, with all his simplicity of diction and exquisite
moral feeling, is a very unsafe model for imitation; and it is worth while
to observe, how invariably those who have imitated him have fallen into
tedious mannerism. As the human mind is so constituted, that all men
receive to a greater or less degree a complexion from those with whom
they are conversant, the writer who means to school himself to poetic
composition,—we mean so far as regards style and diction,—should be very
careful what authors he studies. He should leave the present age, and go
back to the olden time. He should make, not the writings of an individual, but the whole body of English classical literature, his study. There is
a strength of expression, a clearness, and force and raciness of thought
in the elder English poets, which we may look for in vain among those
who flourish in these days of verbiage. Truly the degeneracy of modern
poetry is no school-boy declamation! The stream, whose fabled fountain
gushes from the Grecian mount, flowed brightly though those ages, when
the souls of men stood forth in the rugged freedom of nature, and gave a
wild and romantic character to the ideal landscape. But in these practical days, whose spirit has so unsparingly levelled to the even surface of
utility the bold irregularities of human genius, and lopped off the luxuriance of poetic feeling, which once lent its grateful shade to the haunts
of song, that stream has spread itself into stagnant pools, which exhale
an unhealthy atmosphere, whilst the parti-colored bubbles that glitter on
its surface, show the corruption from which they spring.

Another circumstance which tends to give an effeminate and unmanly
character to our literature, is the precocity of our writers. Premature ex-

* We here subjoin Lord Byron's own opinion of the poetical taste of the present
age. It is from a letter in the second volume of Moore's Life of Byron. 'With regard to poetry in general, I am convinced, the more I think of it, that he and all of
us,—Scott, Southey, Wordsworth, Moore, Campbell, I,—are all in the wrong, one as
much as another; that we are upon a wrong revolutionary poetical system, or systems, and from which none but Rogers and Crabbe are free; and that the present and
next generations will finally be of this opinion. I am the more confirmed in this, by
having lately gone over some of our classics, particularly Pope, whom I tried in this
way;—I took Moore's poems and my own and some others, and went over them side
by side with Pope's, and I was really astonished (I ought not to have been so) and
mortified at the ineffable distance in point of sense, learning, effect, and even
imagination, passion and invention, between the Queen Anne's man, and us of
the Lower Empire. Depend upon it, it is all Horace then, and Claudian now, among
us; and if I had to begin again, I would mould myself accordingly' [Longfellow's
note].

hibitions of talent are an unstable foundation to build a national literature upon. Roger Ascham, the school-master of princes,[9] and for the sake of antithesis, we suppose, called the Prince of School-masters, has well said of precocious minds; 'They be like trees that showe forth faire blossoms and broad leaves in spring-time, but bring out small and not long-lasting fruit in harvest-time; and that only such as fall and rott before they be ripe, and so never, or seldome, come to any good at all.' It is natural that the young should be enticed by the wreaths of literary fame, whose hues are so passing beautiful even to the more sober-sighted, and whose flowers breathe around them such exquisite perfumes. Many are deceived into a misconception of their talents by the indiscreet and indiscriminate praise of friends. They think themselves destined to redeem the glory of their age and country; to shine as 'bright particular stars;' but in reality their genius

> 'Is like the glow-worm's light the apes so wonder'd at,
> Which, when they gather'd sticks and laid upon 't,
> And blew,—and blew,—turn'd tail and went out presently.'

We have set forth the portrait of modern poetry in rather gloomy colors; for we really think, that the greater part of what is published in this book-writing age, ought in justice to suffer the fate of the children of Thetis, whose immortality was tried by fire. We hope, however, that ere long, some one of our most gifted bards will throw his fetters off, and relying on himself alone, fathom the recesses of his own mind, and bring up rich pearls from the secret depths of thought.

[9] Roger Ascham (1515–1568), English Renaissance humanist and author of the *Scholemaster* (1570).

JAMES FENIMORE COOPER

PREFACE TO
HOME AS FOUND [1]
(1838)

THOSE WHO have done us the favor to read *Homeward Bound* will at once perceive that the incidents of this book commence at the point where those of the work just mentioned ceased.[2] We are fully aware of the disadvantage of dividing the interest of a tale in this manner; but in the present instance, the separation has been produced by circumstances over which the writer had very little control. As any one who may happen to take up this volume will very soon discover that there is other matter which it is necessary to know, it may be as well to tell all such persons, in commencement, therefore, that their reading will be bootless, unless they have leisure to turn to the pages of *Homeward Bound* for their cue.

We remember the despair with which that admirable observer of men, Mr. Mathews the comedian, confessed the hopelessness of success, in his endeavors to obtain a sufficiency of prominent and distinctive features to compose an entertainment founded on American character. The whole nation struck him as being destitute of salient points, and as characterized by a respectable mediocrity, that, however useful it might be in its way, was utterly without poetry, humor, or interest to the observer. For one who dealt principally with the more conspicuous absurdities of his fellow-creatures, Mr. Mathews was certainly right; we also believe him to have been right in the main, in the general tenor of his opinion; for this country, in its ordinary aspects, probably presents as barren a field to the writer of fiction, and to the dramatist, as any other on earth; we are not certain that we might not say the most barren. We believe that no attempt to delineate ordinary American life, either on the stage or in the pages of a novel, has been rewarded with success. Even those works in which the desire to illustrate a principle has been the aim, when the picture has been brought within this homely frame, have had to contend with disadvantages that have been commonly found insurmountable. The latter being the intention of this book, the task has been undertaken with a perfect consciousness of all its difficulties, and with scarcely a hope of success. It would be indeed a desperate undertaking, to think of making anything interesting in the way of a *Roman de Société* in this country; still, useful glances may possibly be made even in that direction, and we trust that the fidelity of one or two of our portraits will be recognized by

[1] London, 1838.
[2] Cooper's *Homeward Bound* appeared earlier in the same year as *Home as Found.*

234

the looker-on, although they will very likely be denied by the sitters themselves.

There seems to be a pervading principle in things, which gives an accumulating energy to any active property that may happen to be in the ascendant at the time being: money produces money; knowledge is the parent of knowledge; and ignorance fortifies ignorance. In a word, like begets like. The governing social evil of America is provincialism; a misfortune that is perhaps inseparable from her situation. Without a social capital, with twenty or more communities divided by distance and political barriers, her people, who are really more homogeneous than any other of the same numbers in the world perhaps, possess no standard for opinion, manners, social maxims, or even language. Every man, as a matter of course, refers to his own particular experience, and praises or condemns agreeably to notions contracted in the circle of his own habits, however narrow, provincial, or erroneous they may happen to be. As a consequence, no useful stage can exist; for the dramatist who should endeavor to delineate the faults of society, would find a formidable party arrayed against him, in a moment, with no party to defend. As another consequence, we see individuals constantly assailed with a wolf-like ferocity, while society is everywhere permitted to pass unscathed.

That the American nation is a great nation, in some particulars the greatest the world ever saw, we hold to be true, and are as ready to maintain as any one can be; but we are also equally ready to concede, that it is very far behind most polished nations in various essentials, and chiefly that it is lamentably in arrears to its own avowed principles. Perhaps this truth will be found to be the predominant thought, throughout the pages of "Home as Found."

JAMES FENIMORE COOPER

PREFACE TO
AFLOAT AND ASHORE [1]
(1844)

THE WRITER has published so much truth which the world has insisted was fiction, and so much fiction which has been received as truth, that, in the present instance, he is resolved to say nothing on the subject. Each of his readers is at liberty to believe just as much, or as little, of the matter here laid before him, or her, as may suit his or her notions, prejudices, knowledge of the world, or ignorance. If anybody is disposed to swear he knows precisely where Clawbonny is, that he was well acquainted with old Mr. Hardinge, nay, has often heard him preach—let him make his affidavit, in welcome. Should he get a little wide of the mark, it will not be the first document of that nature which has possessed the same weakness.

It is possible that certain captious persons may be disposed to inquire into the *cui bono?* of such a book. The answer is this. Every thing which can convey to the human mind distinct and accurate impressions of events, social facts, professional peculiarities, or past history, whether of the higher or more familiar character, is of use. All that is necessary is, that the pictures should be true to nature, if not absolutely drawn from living sitters. The knowledge we gain by our looser reading often becomes serviceable in modes and manners little anticipated in the moments when it is acquired.

Perhaps the greater portion of all our peculiar opinions have their foundation in prejudices. These prejudices are produced in consequence of its being out of the power of any one man to see, or know, every thing. The most favored mortal must receive far more than half of all that he learns on his faith in others; and it may aid those who can never be placed in positions to judge for themselves of certain phases of men and things, to get pictures of the same, drawn in a way to give them nearer views than they might otherwise obtain. This is the greatest benefit of all light literature in general, it being possible to render that which is purely fictitious even more useful than that which is strictly true, by avoiding extravagances, by portraying with fidelity, and, as our friend Marble might say, by "generalizing" with discretion.

This country has undergone many important changes since the commencement of the present century. Some of these changes have been for the better; others, we think out of all question, for the worse. The last

[1] London, 1844.

is a fact that can be known to the generation which is coming into life by report only, and these pages may possibly throw some little light on both points, in representing things as they were. The population of the republic is probably something more than eighteen millions and a half to-day; in the year of our Lord one thousand eight hundred, it was but a little more than five millions. In 1800, the population of New York was somewhat less than six hundred thousand souls; to-day it is probably a little less than two millions seven hundred thousand souls. In 1800, the town of New York had sixty thousand inhabitants; whereas, including Brooklyn and Williamsburg, which then virtually had no existence, it must have at this moment quite four hundred thousand. These are prodigious numerical changes, that have produced changes of another sort. Although an increase of numbers does not necessarily infer an increase of high civilization, it reasonably leads to the expectation of great melioration in the commoner comforts. Such has been the result, and to those familiar with facts as they now exist, the difference will probably be apparent in these pages.

Although the moral changes in American society have not kept pace with those that are purely physical, many that are essential have nevertheless occurred. Of all the British possessions on this continent, New York, after its conquest from the Dutch, received most of the social organization of the mother country. Under the Dutch, even, it had some of these characteristic peculiarities in its patroons; the lords of the manor of the New Netherlands. Some of the southern colonies, it is true, had their caciques and other semi-feudal and semi-savage noblesse, but the system was of short continuance; the peculiarities of that section of the country arising principally from the existence of domestic slavery on an extended scale. With New York it was different. A conquered colony, the mother country left the impression of its own institutions more deeply engraved than on any of the settlements that were commenced by grants to proprietors, or under charters from the crown. It was strictly a royal colony, and so continued to be, down to the hour of separation. The social consequences of this state of things were to be traced in her habits until the current of immigration became so strong as to bring with it those that were conflicting, if not absolutely antagonist. The influence of these two sources of thought is still obvious to the reflecting, giving rise to a double set of social opinions; one of which bears all the characteristics of its New England and puritanical origin, while the other may be said to come of the usages and notions of the middle states, proper.

This is said in anticipation of certain strictures that will be likely to follow some of the incidents of our story, it not being always deemed an essential in an American critic that he should understand his subject. Too many of them, indeed, justify the retort of the man who derided the claims to knowledge of life set up by a neighbor, that "had been to meetin' and had been to mill." We can all obtain some notions of the portion of a subject that is placed immediately before our eyes; the difficulty is to understand that which we have no means of studying.

On the subject of the nautical incidents of this book, we have endeavored to be as exact as our authorities will allow. We are fully aware of the importance of writing what the world thinks, rather than what is true, and are not conscious of any very palpable errors of this nature.

It is no more than fair to apprise the reader that our tale is not completed in the first part, or the volumes that are now published. This the plan of the book would not permit; but we can promise those who may feel any interest in the subject, that the season shall not pass away, so far as it may depend on ourselves, without bringing the narrative to a close. Poor Captain Wallingford is now in his sixty-fifth year, and is naturally desirous of not being hung up long on the tenter-hooks of expectation so near the close of life. The old gentleman having seen much and suffered much, is entitled to end his days in peace. In this mutual frame of mind between the principal and his editors, the public shall have no cause to complain of unnecessary delay, whatever may be its rights of the same nature on other subjects.

The author—perhaps editor would be the better word—does not feel himself responsible for all the notions advanced by the hero of this tale, and it may be as well to say as much. That one born in the Revolution should think differently from the men of the present day, in a hundred things, is to be expected. It is in just this difference of opinion that the lessons of the book are to be found.

JAMES FENIMORE COOPER

THE DEERSLAYER

PREFACE TO THE LEATHER-STOCKING TALES [1]

(1850)

THIS SERIES of Stories, which has obtained the name of "The Leather-Stocking Tales," has been written in a very desultory and inartificial manner. The order in which the several books appeared was essentially different from that in which they would have been presented to the world, had the regular course of their incidents been consulted. In the Pioneers, the first of the series written, the Leather-Stocking is represented as already old, and driven from his early haunts in the forest, by the sound of the axe, and the smoke of the settler. "The Last of the Mohicans," the next book in the order of publication, carried the readers back to a much earlier period in the history of our hero, representing him as middle-aged, and in the fullest vigor of manhood. In the Prairie, his career terminates, and he is laid in his grave. There, it was originally the intention to leave him, in the expectation that, as in the case of the human mass, he would soon be forgotten. But a latent regard for this character induced the author to resuscitate him in "The Pathfinder," a book that was not long after succeeded by "The Deerslayer," thus completing the series as it now exists.

While the five books that have been written were originally published in the order just mentioned, that of the incidents, insomuch as they are connected with the career of their principal character, is, as has been stated, very different. Taking the life of the Leather-Stocking as a guide, "The Deerslayer" should have been the opening book, for in that work he is seen just emerging into manhood; to be succeeded by "The Last of the Mohicans," "The Pathfinder," "The Pioneers," and "The Prairie." This arrangement embraces the order of events, though far from being that in which the books at first appeared. "The Pioneers" was published in 1822; "The Deerslayer" in 1841; making the interval between them nineteen years. Whether these progressive years have had a tendency to lessen the value of the last-named book by lessening the native fire of its author, or of adding somewhat in the way of improved taste and a more matured judgment, is for others to decide.

If anything from the pen of the writer of these romances is at all to outlive himself, it is, unquestionably, the series of "The Leather-Stocking

[1] In preparation for the Putnam edition of his novels, Cooper arranged those in which Natty Bumppo (Leather-Stocking) appeared according to the sequence of events in Natty's life, and this special preface was written for the series. *The Deerslayer* was published in New York in 1850.

239

Tales." To say this, is not to predict a very lasting reputation for the series itself, but simply to express the belief it will outlast any, or all, of the works from the same hand.

It is undeniable that the desultory manner in which "The Leather-Stocking Tales" were written, has, in a measure, impaired their harmony, and otherwise lessened their interest. This is proved by the fate of the two books last published, though probably the two most worthy an enlightened and cultivated reader's notice. If the facts could be ascertained, it is probable the result would show that of all those (in America, in particular) who have read the three first books of the series, not one in ten has a knowledge of the existence even of the two last. Several causes have tended to produce this result. The long interval of time between the appearance of "The Prairie" and that of "The Pathfinder," was itself a reason why the later books of the series should be overlooked. There was no longer novelty to attract attention, and the interest was materially impaired by the manner in which events were necessarily anticipated, in laying the last of the series first before the world. With the generation that is now coming on the stage this fault will be partially removed by the edition contained in the present work, in which the several tales will be arranged solely in reference to their connexion with each other.

The author has often been asked if he had any original in his mind, for the character of Leather-Stocking. In a physical sense, different individuals known to the writer in early life, certainly presented themselves as models, through his recollections; but in a moral sense this man of the forest is purely a creation. The idea of delineating a character that possessed little of civilization but its highest principles as they are exhibited in the uneducated, and all of savage life that is not incompatible with these great rules of conduct, is perhaps natural to the situation in which Natty was placed. He is too proud of his origin to sink into the condition of the wild Indian, and too much a man of the woods not to imbibe as much as was at all desirable, from his friends and companions. In a moral point of view it was the intention to illustrate the effect of seed scattered by the way side. To use his own language, his "gifts" were "white gifts," and he was not disposed to bring on them discredit. On the other hand, removed from nearly all the temptations of civilized life, placed in the best associations of that which is deemed savage, and favorably disposed by nature to improve such advantages, it appeared to the writer that his hero was a fit subject to represent the better qualities of both conditions, without pushing either to extremes.

There was no violent stretch of the imagination, perhaps, in supposing one of civilized associations in childhood, retaining many of his earliest lessons amid the scenes of the forest. Had these early impressions, however, not been sustained by continued, though casual connexion with men of his own color, if not of his own caste, all our information goes to show he would soon have lost every trace of his origin. It is believed that sufficient attention was paid to the particular circumstances in which this individual was placed to justify the picture of his qualities that has been drawn. The Delawares early attracted the attention of missionaries, and were a tribe unusually influenced by their precepts and example. In many instances they became Christians, and cases occurred in which their subsequent lives gave proof of the efficacy of the great moral changes that had taken place within them.

A leading character in a work of fiction has a fair right to the aid which can be obtained from a poetical view of the subject. It is in this view, rather than in one more strictly circumstantial, that Leather-Stocking has been drawn. The imagination has no great task in portraying to itself a being removed from the every-day inducements to err, which abound in civilized life, while he retains the best and simplest of his early impressions; who sees God in the forest; hears him in the winds; bows to him in the firmament that o'ercanopies all; submits to his sway in a humble belief of his justice and mercy; in a word, a being who finds the impress of the Deity in all the works of nature, without any of the blots produced by the expedients, and passion, and mistakes of man. This is the most that has been attempted in the character of Leather-Stocking. Had this been done without any of the drawbacks of humanity, the picture would have been, in all probability, more pleasing than just. In order to preserve the *vrai-semblable*, therefore, traits derived from the prejudices, tastes, and even the weaknesses of his youth, have been mixed up with these higher qualities and longings, in a way, it is hoped, to represent a reasonable picture of human nature, without offering to the spectator a "monster of goodness."

It has been objected to these books that they give a more favorable picture of the red man than he deserves. The writer apprehends that much of this objection arises from the habits of those who have made it. One of his critics, on the appearance of the first work in which Indian character was portrayed, objected that its "characters were Indians of the school of Heckewelder,[2] rather than the school of nature." These words quite probably contain the substance of the true answer to the objection. Heckewelder was an ardent, benevolent missionary, bent on the good of the red man, and seeing in him one who had the soul, reason, and characteristics of a fellow-being. The critic is understood to have been a very distinguished agent of the government, one very familiar with Indians, as they are seen at the councils to treat for the sale of their lands, where little or none of their domestic qualities come in play, and where, indeed, their evil passions are known to have the fullest scope. As just would it be to draw conclusions of the general state of American society from the scenes of the capital, as to suppose that the negotiating of one of these treaties is a fair picture of Indian life.

[2] Cooper's chief source of information concerning the Indians apparently was *An Account of the History, Manners, and Customs of the Indian Nations who once Inhabited Pennsylvania and the Neighboring States* by the Rev. John Heckewelder, a Moravian missionary, which was published in 1819.

It is the privilege of all writers of fiction, more particularly when their works aspire to the elevation of romances, to present the *beau-idéal* of their characters to the reader. This it is which constitutes poetry, and to suppose that the red man is to be represented only in the squalid misery or in the degraded moral state that certainly more or less belongs to his condition, is, we apprehend, taking a very narrow view of an author's privileges. Such criticism would have deprived the world of even Homer.

RALPH WALDO EMERSON

THE POET [1]
(1844)

THOSE WHO are esteemed umpires of taste are often persons who have acquired some knowledge of admired pictures or sculptures, and have an inclination for whatever is elegant; but if you inquire whether they are beautiful souls, and whether their own acts are like fair pictures, you learn that they are selfish and sensual. Their cultivation is local, as if you should rub a log of dry wood in one spot to produce fire, all the rest remaining cold. Their knowledge of the fine arts is some study of rules and particulars, or some limited judgment of color or form, which is exercised for amusement or for show. It is a proof of the shallowness of the doctrine of beauty as it lies in the minds of our amateurs, that men seem to have lost the perception of the instant dependence of form upon soul. There is no doctrine of forms in our philosophy. We were put into our bodies, as fire is put into a pan to be carried about; but there is no accurate adjustment between the spirit and the organ, much less is the latter the germination of the former. So in regard to other forms, the intellectual men do not believe in any essential dependence of the material world on thought and volition. Theologians think it a pretty air-castle to talk of the spiritual meaning of a ship or a cloud, of a city or a contract, but they prefer to come again to the solid ground of historical evidence; and even the poets are contented with a civil and conformed manner of living, and to write poems from the fancy, at a safe distance from their own experience. But the highest minds of the world have never ceased to explore the double meaning, or shall I say the quadruple or the centuple or much more manifold meaning, of every sensuous fact; Orpheus, Empedocles, Heraclitus, Plato, Plutarch, Dante, Swedenborg,[2] and the masters of sculpture, picture and poetry. For we are not pans and barrows, nor even porters of the fire and torch-bearers, but children of the fire, made of it, and only the same divinity transmuted and at two or three removes, when we know least about it. And this hidden truth, that the fountains whence all this river of Time and its creatures floweth are intrinsically ideal and beautiful, draws us to the consideration of the nature

[1] "The Poet" was the first essay in *Essays, Second Series* which was published in Boston, 1844.
[2] Orpheus, a Thracian poet and musician of Greek mythology; Empedocles and Heraclitus were Greek philosophers of the fifth century B.C.; Plutarch was a Greek biographer of the first century A.D., author of the famous *Lives*; Emanuel Swedenborg (1688-1772) was a Swedish scientist, philosopher, theologian, and mystic. Swedenborg and Plato are subjects of essays in Emerson's *Representative Men*.

and functions of the Poet, or the man of Beauty; to the means and materials he uses, and to the general aspect of the art in the present time.

The breadth of the problem is great, for the poet is representative. He stands among partial men for the complete man, and apprises us not of his wealth, but of the common wealth. The young man reveres men of genius, because, to speak truly, they are more himself than he is. They receive of the soul as he also receives, but they more. Nature enhances her beauty, to the eye of loving men, from their belief that the poet is beholding her shows at the same time. He is isolated among his contemporaries by truth and by his art, but with this consolation in his pursuits, that they will draw all men sooner or later. For all men live by truth and stand in need of expression. In love, in art, in avarice, in politics, in labor, in games, we study to utter our painful secret. The man is only half himself, the other half is his expression.

Notwithstanding this necessity to be published, adequate expression is rare. I know not how it is that we need an interpreter, but the great majority of men seem to be minors, who have not yet come into possession of their own, or mutes, who cannot report the conversation they have had with nature. There is no man who does not anticipate a supersensual utility in the sun and stars, earth and water. These stand and wait to render him a peculiar service. But there is some obstruction or some excess of phlegm in our constitution, which does not suffer them to yield the due effect. Too feeble fall the impressions of nature on us to make us artists. Every touch should thrill. Every man should be so much an artist that he could report in conversation what had befallen him. Yet, in our experience, the rays or appulses have sufficient force to arrive at the senses, but not enough to reach the quick and compel the reproduction of themselves in speech. The poet is the person in whom these powers are in balance, the man without impediment, who sees and handles that which others dream of, traverses the whole scale of experience, and is representative of man, in virtue of being the largest power to receive and to impart.

For the Universe has three children, born at one time, which reappear under different names in every system of thought, whether they be called cause, operation and effect; or, more poetically, Jove, Pluto, Neptune; or, theologically, the Father, the Spirit and the Son; but which we will call here the Knower, the Doer and the Sayer. These stand respectively for the love of truth, for the love of good, and for the love of beauty. These three are equal. Each is that which he is, essentially, so that he cannot be surmounted or analyzed, and each of these three has the power of the others latent in him and his own, patent.

The poet is the sayer, the namer, and represents beauty. He is a sovereign, and stands on the centre. For the world is not painted or adorned, but is from the beginning beautiful; and God has not made some beautiful things, but Beauty is the creator of the universe. Therefore the poet is not any permissive potentate, but is emperor in his own right. Criticism is infested with a cant of materialism, which assumes that manual skill and activity is the first merit of all men, and disparages such as say and do not, overlooking the fact that some men, namely poets, are natural sayers, sent into the world to the end of expression, and confounds them with those whose province is action but who quit it to imitate the sayers. But Homer's words are as costly and admirable to Homer as Agamemnon's victories are to Agamemnon. The poet does not wait for the hero or the sage, but, as they act and think primarily, so he writes primarily what will and must be spoken, reckoning the others, though primaries also, yet, in respect to him, secondaries and servants; as sitters or models in the studio of a painter, or as assistants who bring building-materials to an architect.

For poetry was all written before time was, and whenever we are so finely organized that we can penetrate into that region where the air is music, we hear those primal warblings and attempt to write them down, but we lose ever and anon a word or a verse and substitute something of our own, and thus miswrite the poem. The men of more delicate ear write down these cadences more faithfully, and these transcripts, though imperfect, become the songs of the nations. For nature is as truly beautiful as it is good, or as it is reasonable, and must as much appear as it must be done, or be known. Words and deeds are quite indifferent modes of the divine energy. Words are also actions, and actions are a kind of words.

The sign and credentials of the poet are that he announces that which no man foretold. He is the true and only doctor; he knows and tells; he is the only teller of news, for he was present and privy to the appearance which he describes. He is a beholder of ideas and an utterer of the necessary and causal. For we do not speak now of men of poetical talents, or of industry and skill in metre, but of the true poet. I took part in a conversation the other day concerning a recent writer of lyrics, a man of subtle mind, whose head appeared to be a music-box of delicate tunes and rhythms, and whose skill and command of language we could not sufficiently praise.[3] But when the question arose whether he was not only a lyrist but a poet, we were obliged to confess that he is plainly a contemporary, not an eternal man. He does not stand out of our low limitations, like a Chimborazo under the line,[4] running up from a torrid base through all the climates of the globe, with belts of the herbage of every latitude on its high and mottled sides; but this genius is the landscape-garden of a modern house, adorned with fountains and statues, with well-bred men and women standing and sitting in the walks and terraces. We hear, through all the varied music, the ground-tone of conventional life. Our poets are men of talents who sing, and not the children of music. The argument is secondary, the finish of the verses is primary.

For it is not metres, but a metre-making argument that makes a poem,— a thought so passionate and alive that like the spirit of a plant or an animal it has an architecture of its own, and adorns nature with a new thing. The thought and the form are equal in the order of time, but in the order of genesis the thought is prior to the form. The poet has a new

[3] Probably Tennyson.
[4] A mountain in Ecuador near the equator.

thought; he has a whole new experience to unfold; he will tell us how it was with him, and all men will be the richer in his fortune. For the experience of each new age requires a new confession, and the world seems always waiting for its poet. I remember when I was young how much I was moved one morning by tidings that genius had appeared in a youth who sat near me at table. He had left his work and gone rambling none knew whither, and had written hundreds of lines, but could not tell whether that which was in him was therein told; he could tell nothing but that all was changed,—man, beast, heaven, earth and sea. How gladly we listened! how credulous! Society seemed to be compromised. We sat in the aurora of a sunrise which was to put out all the stars. Boston seemed to be at twice the distance it had the night before, or was much farther than that. Rome,—what was Rome? Plutarch and Shakspeare were in the yellow leaf, and Homer no more should be heard of. It is much to know that poetry has been written this very day, under this very roof, by your side. What! that wonderful spirit has not expired! These stony moments are still sparkling and animated! I had fancied that the oracles were all silent, and nature had spent her fires; and behold! all night, from every pore, these fine auroras have been streaming. Every one has some interest in the advent of the poet, and no one knows how much it may concern him. We know that the secret of the world is profound, but who or what shall be our interpreter, we know not. A mountain ramble, a new style of face, a new person, may put the key into our hands. Of course the value of genius to us is in the veracity of its report. Talent may frolic and juggle; genius realizes and adds. Mankind in good earnest have availed so far in understanding themselves and their work, that the foremost watchman on the peak announces his news. It is the truest word ever spoken, and the phrase will be the fittest, most musical, and the unerring voice of the world for that time.

All that we call sacred history attests that the birth of a poet is the principal event in chronology. Man, never so often deceived, still watches for the arrival of a brother who can hold him steady to a truth until he has made it his own. With what joy I begin to read a poem which I confide in as an inspiration! And now my chains are to be broken; I shall mount above these clouds and opaque airs in which I live,—opaque, though they seem transparent,—and from the heaven of truth I shall see and comprehend my relations. That will reconcile me to life and renovate nature, to see trifles animated by a tendency, and to know what I am doing. Life will no more be a noise; now I shall see men and women, and know the signs by which they may be discerned from fools and satans. This day shall be better than my birthday: then I became an animal; now I am invited into the science of the real. Such is the hope, but the fruition is postponed. Oftener it falls that this winged man, who will carry me into the heaven, whirls me into mists, then leaps and frisks about with me as it were from cloud to cloud, still affirming that he is bound heavenward; and I, being myself a novice, am slow in perceiving that he does not know the way into the heavens, and is merely bent that I should admire his skill to rise like a fowl or a flying fish, a little way from the ground or the water; but the all-piercing, all-feeding and ocular air of heaven that man shall never inhabit. I tumble down again soon into my old nooks, and lead the life of exaggerations as before, and have lost my faith in the possibility of any guide who can lead me thither where I would be.

But, leaving these victims of vanity, let us, with new hope, observe how nature, by worthier impulses, has insured the poet's fidelity to his office of announcement and affirming, namely by the beauty of things, which becomes a new and higher beauty when expressed. Nature offers all her creatures to him as a picture-language. Being used as a type, a second wonderful value appears in the object, far better than its old value; as the carpenter's stretched cord, if you hold your ear close enough, is musical in the breeze. "Things more excellent than every image," says Jamblichus,[5] "are expressed through images." Things admit of being used as symbols because nature is a symbol, in the whole, and in every part. Every line we can draw in the sand has expression; and there is no body without its spirit or genius. All form is an effect of character; all condition, of the quality of the life; all harmony, of health; and for this reason a perception of beauty should be sympathetic, or proper only to the good. The beautiful rests on the foundations of the necessary. The soul makes the body, as the wise Spenser teaches:—

> "So every spirit, as it is more pure,
> And hath in it the more of heavenly light,
> So it the fairer body doth procure
> To habit in, and it more fairly dight,
> With cheerful grace and amiable sight.
> For, of the soul, the body form doth take,
> For soul is form, and doth the body make."

Here we find ourselves suddenly not in a critical speculation but in a holy place, and should go very warily and reverently. We stand before the secret of the world, there where Being passes into Appearance and Unity into Variety.

The Universe is the externization of the soul. Wherever the life is, that bursts into appearance around it. Our science is sensual, and therefore superficial. The earth and the heavenly bodies, physics and chemistry, we sensually treat, as if they were self-existent; but these are the retinue of that Being we have. "The mighty heaven," said Proclus,[6] "exhibits, in its transfigurations, clear images of the splendor of intellectual perceptions; being moved in conjunction with the unapparent periods of intellectual natures." Therefore science always goes abreast with the just elevation of

[5] Iamblichus (d. ca. 330 A.D.), one of the most important of the Alexandrian Neo-Platonic philosophers.

[6] Proclus (410–485 A.D.), one of the Alexandrian Neo-Platonists. The Neo-Platonists (Plotinus, Proclus, Iamblichus, and Porphyry) were one of the major influences on the thought of Emerson.

the man, keeping step with religion and metaphysics; or the state of science is an index of our self-knowledge. Since every thing in nature answers to a moral power, if any phenomenon remains brute and dark it is because the corresponding faculty in the observer is not yet active.

No wonder then, if these waters be so deep, that we hover over them with a religious regard. The beauty of the fable proves the importance of the sense; to the poet, and to all others; or, if you please, every man is so far a poet as to be susceptible of these enchantments of nature; for all men have the thoughts whereof the universe is the celebration. I find that the fascination resides in the symbol. Who loves nature? Who does not? Is it only poets, and men of leisure and cultivation, who live with her? No; but also hunters, farmers, grooms and butchers, though they express their affection in their choice of life and not in their choice of words. The writer wonders what the coachman or the hunter values in riding, in horses and dogs. It is not superficial qualities. When you talk with him he holds these at as slight a rate as you. His worship is sympathetic; he has no definitions, but he is commanded in nature by the living power which he feels to be there present. No imitation or playing of these things would content him; he loves the earnest of the north wind, of rain, of stone and wood and iron. A beauty not explicable is dearer than a beauty which we can see to the end of. It is nature the symbol, nature certifying the supernatural, body overflowed by life which he worships with coarse but sincere rites.

The inwardness and mystery of this attachment drive men of every class to the use of emblems. The schools of poets and philosophers are not more intoxicated with their symbols than the populace with theirs. In our political parties, compute the power of badges and emblems. See the great ball which they roll from Baltimore to Bunker Hill! [7] In the political processions, Lowell goes in a loom, and Lynn in a shoe, and Salem in a ship. Witness the cider-barrel, the log-cabin, the hickory-stick, the palmetto, and all the cognizances of party. See the power of national emblems. Some stars, lilies, leopards, a crescent, a lion, an eagle, or other figure which came into credit God knows how, on an old rag of bunting, blowing in the wind on a fort at the ends of the earth, shall make the blood tingle under the rudest or the most conventional exterior. The people fancy they hate poetry, and they are all poets and mystics!

Beyond this universality of the symbolic language, we are apprised of the divineness of this superior use of things, whereby the world is a temple whose walls are covered with emblems, pictures and commandments of the Deity,—in this, that there is no fact in nature which does not carry the whole sense of nature; and the distinctions which we make in events and in affairs, of low and high, honest and base, disappear when nature is used as a symbol. Thought makes everything fit for use. The vocabulary of an omniscient man would embrace words and images excluded from polite conversation. What would be base, or even obscene,

[7] This reference and those immediately following is to the presidential election of 1840, in which Harrison defeated Van Buren.

to the obscene, becomes illustrious, spoken in a new connection of thought. The piety of the Hebrew prophets purges their grossness. The circumcision is an example of the power of poetry to raise the low and offensive. Small and mean things serve as well as great symbols. The meaner the type by which a law is expressed, the more pungent it is, and the more lasting in the memories of men; just as we choose the smallest box or case in which any needful utensil can be carried. Bare lists of words are found suggestive to an imaginative and excited mind: as it is related of Lord Chatham that he was accustomed to read in Bailey's Dictionary when he was preparing to speak in Parliament. The poorest experience is rich enough for all the purposes of expressing thought. Why covet a knowledge of new facts? Day and night, house and garden, a few books, a few actions, serve us as well as would all trades and all spectacles. We are far from having exhausted the significance of the few symbols we use. We can come to use them yet with a terrible simplicity. It does not need that a poem should be long. Every word was once a poem. Every new relation is a new word. Also we use defects and deformities to a sacred purpose, so expressing our sense that the evils of the world are such only to the evil eye. In the old mythology, mythologists observe, defects are ascribed to divine natures, as lameness to Vulcan, blindness to Cupid, and the like,— to signify exuberances.

For as it is dislocation and detachment from the life of God that makes things ugly, the poet, who re-attaches things to nature and the Whole,— re-attaching even artificial things and violation of nature, to nature, by a deeper insight,—disposes very easily of the most disagreeable facts. Readers of poetry see the factory-village and the railway, and fancy that the poetry of the landscape is broken up by these; for these works of art are not yet consecrated in their reading; but the poet sees them fall within the great Order not less than the beehive or the spider's geometrical web. Nature adopts them very fast into her vital circles, and the gliding train of cars she loves like her own. Besides, in a centred mind, it signifies nothing how many mechanical inventions you exhibit. Though you add millions, and never so surprising, the fact of mechanics has not gained a grain's weight. The spiritual fact remains unalterable, by many or by few particulars; as no mountain is of any appreciable height to break the curve of the sphere. A shrewd country-boy goes to the city for the first time, and the complacent citizen is not satisfied with his little wonder. It is not that he does not see all the fine houses and know that he never saw such before, but he disposes of them as easily as the poet finds place for the railway. The chief value of the new fact is to enhance the great and constant fact of Life, which can dwarf any and every circumstance, and to which the belt of wampum and the commerce of America are alike.

The world being thus put under the mind for verb and noun, the poet is he who can articulate it. For though life is great, and fascinates and absorbs; and though all men are intelligent of the symbols through which it is named; yet they cannot originally use them. We are symbols and inhabit symbols; workmen, work, and tools, words and things, birth and death, all are emblems; but we sympathize with the symbols, and being infatuated with the economical uses of things, we do not know that they are thoughts. The poet, by an ulterior intellectual perception, gives them a power which makes their old use forgotten, and puts eyes and a tongue into every dumb and inanimate object. He perceives the independence of the thought on the symbol, the stability of the thought, the accidency and fugacity of the symbol. As the eyes of Lyncaeus [8] were said to see through the earth, so the poet turns the world to glass, and shows us all things in their right series and procession. For through that better perception he stands one step nearer to things, and sees the flowing or metamorphosis; perceives that thought is multiform; that within the form of every creature is a force impelling it to ascend into a higher form; and following with his eyes the life, uses the forms which express that life, and so his speech flows with the flowing of nature. All the facts of the animal economy, sex, nutriment, gestation, birth, growth, are symbols of the passage of the world into the soul of man, to suffer there a change and reappear a new and higher fact. He uses forms according to the life, and not according to the form. This is true science. The poet alone knows astronomy, chemistry, vegetation and animation, for he does not stop at these facts, but employs them as signs. He knows why the plain or meadow of space was strown with these flowers we call suns and moons and stars; why the great deep is adorned with animals, with men, and gods; for in every word he speaks he rides on them as the horses of thought.

By virtue of this science the poet is the Namer or Language-maker, naming things sometimes after their appearance, sometimes after their essence, and giving to every one its own name and not another's, thereby rejoicing the intellect, which delights in detachment or boundary. The poets made all the words, and therefore language is the archives of history, and, if we must say it, a sort of tomb of the muses. For though the origin of most of our words is forgotten, each word was at first a stroke of genius, and obtained currency because for the moment it symbolized the world to the first speaker and to the hearer. The etymologist finds the deadest word to have been once a brilliant picture. Language is fossil poetry. As the limestone of the continent consists of infinite masses of the shells of animalcules, so language is made up of images or tropes, which now, in their secondary use, have long ceased to remind us of their poetic origin. But the poet names the thing because he sees it, or comes one step nearer to it than any other. This expression or naming is not art, but a second nature, grown out of the first, as a leaf out of a tree. What we call nature is a certain self-regulated motion or change; and nature does all things by her own hands, and does not leave another to baptize her but baptizes herself; and this through the metamorphosis again. I remember that a certain poet described it to me thus:—

Genius is the activity which repairs the decays of things, whether wholly or partly of a material and finite kind. Nature, through all her kingdoms, insures herself. Nobody cares for planting the poor fungus; so she shakes

---

[8] Member of the mythological band who sailed in search of the Golden Fleece.

down from the gills of one agaric countless spores, any one of which, being preserved, transmits new billions of spores to-morrow or next day. The new agaric of this hour has a chance which the old one had not. This atom of seed is thrown into a new place, not subject to the accidents which destroyed its parent two rods off. She makes a man; and having brought him to ripe age, she will no longer run the risk of losing this wonder at a blow, but she detaches from him a new self, that the kind may be safe from accidents to which the individual is exposed. So when the soul of the poet has come to ripeness of thought, she detaches and sends away from it its poems or songs,—a fearless, sleepless, deathless progeny, which is not exposed to the accidents of the weary kingdom of time; a fearless, vivacious offspring, clad with wings (such was the virtue of the soul out of which they came) which carry them fast and far, and infix them irrecoverably into the hearts of men. These wings are the beauty of the poet's soul. The songs, thus flying immortal from their mortal parent, are pursued by clamorous flights of censures, which swarm in far greater numbers and threaten to devour them; but these last are not winged. At the end of a very short leap they fall plump down and rot, having received from the souls out of which they came no beautiful wings. But the melodies of the poet ascend and leap and pierce into the deeps of infinite time.

So far the bard taught me, using his freer speech. But nature has a higher end, in the production of new individuals, than security, namely *ascension*, or the passage of the soul into higher forms. I knew in my younger days the sculptor who made the statue of the youth which stands in the public garden. He was, as I remember, unable to tell directly what made him happy or unhappy, but by wonderful indirections he could tell. He rose one day, according to his habit, before the dawn, and saw the morning break, grand as the eternity out of which it came, and for many days after, he strove to express this tranquillity, and lo! his chisel had fashioned out of marble the form of a beautiful youth, Phosphorus, whose aspect is such that it is said all persons who look on it become silent. The poet also resigns himself to his mood, and that thought which agitated him is expressed, but *alter idem*, in a manner totally new. The expression is organic, or the new type which things themselves take when liberated. As, in the sun, objects paint their images on the retina of the eye, so they, sharing the aspiration of the whole universe, tend to paint a far more delicate copy of their essence in his mind. Like the metamorphosis of things into higher organic forms is their change into melodies. Over everything stands its daemon or soul, and, as the form of the thing is reflected by the eye, so the soul of the thing is reflected by a melody. The sea, the mountain-ridge, Niagara, and every flower-bed, pre-exist, or super-exist, in pre-cantations, which sail like odors in the air, and when any man goes by with an ear sufficiently fine, he overhears them and endeavors to write down the notes without diluting or depraving them. And herein is the legitimation of criticism, in the mind's faith that the poems are a corrupt version of some text in nature with which they ought to be made to tally. A rhyme in one of our sonnets should not be less pleasing than the iterated nodes of a seashell, or the resembling difference of a group of flowers. The pairing of the birds is an idyl, not tedious as our idyls are; a tempest is a rough ode, without falsehood or rant; a summer, with its harvest sown, reaped and stored, is an epic song, subordinating how many admirably executed parts. Why should not the symmetry and truth that modulate these, glide into our spirits, and we participate the invention of nature?

This insight, which expresses itself by what is called Imagination, is a very high sort of seeing, which does not come by study, but by the intellect being where and what it sees; by sharing the path or circuit of things through forms, and so making them translucid to others. The path of things is silent. Will they suffer a speaker to go with them? A spy they will not suffer; a lover, a poet, is the transcendency of their own nature,—him they will suffer. The condition of true naming, on the poet's part, is his resigning himself to the divine *aura* which breathes through forms, and accompanying that.

It is a secret which every intellectual man quickly learns, that beyond the energy of his possessed and conscious intellect he is capable of a new energy (as of an intellect doubled on itself), by abandonment to the nature of things; that beside his privacy of power as an individual man, there is a great public power on which he can draw, by unlocking, at all risks, his human doors, and suffering the ethereal tides to roll and circulate through him; then he is caught up into the life of the Universe, his speech is thunder, his thought is law, and his words are universally intelligible as the plants and animals. The poet knows that he speaks adequately then only when he speaks somewhat wildly, or "with the flower of the mind;" not with the intellect used as an organ, but with the intellect released from all service and suffered to take its direction from its celestial life; or as the ancients were wont to express themselves, not with intellect alone but with the intellect inebriated by nectar. As the traveller who has lost his way throws his reins on his horse's neck and trusts to the instinct of the animal to find his road, so must we do with the divine animal who carries us through this world. For if in any manner we can stimulate this instinct, new passages are opened for us into nature; the mind flows into and through things hardest and highest, and the metamorphosis is possible.

This is the reason why bards love wine, mead, narcotics, coffee, tea, opium, the fumes of sandalwood and tobacco, or whatever other procurers of animal exhilaration. All men avail themselves of such means as they can, to add this extraordinary power to their normal powers; and to this end they prize conversation, music, pictures, sculpture, dancing, theatres, travelling, war, mobs, fires, gaming, politics, or love, or science, or animal intoxication,—which are several coarser or finer *quasi*-mechanical substitutes for the true nectar, which is the ravishment of the intellect by coming nearer to the fact. These are auxiliaries to the centrifugal tendency of a man, to his passage out into free space, and they help him to escape the custody of that body in which he is pent up, and of that jail-yard of individual relations in which he is enclosed. Hence a great number of such as were professionally expressers of Beauty, as painters, poets, musicians and actors, have been more than others wont to lead a life of pleasure and indulgence; all but the few who received the true nectar; and, as it was a spurious mode of attaining freedom, as it was an emancipation not into the heavens but into the freedom of baser places, they were punished for that advantage they won, by a dissipation and deterioration. But never can any advantage be taken of nature by a trick. The spirit of the world, the great calm presence of the Creator, comes not forth to the sorceries of opium or of wine. The sublime vision comes to the pure and simple soul in a clean and chaste body. That is not an inspiration, which we owe to narcotics, but some counterfeit excitement and fury. Milton says that the lyric poet may drink wine and live generously, but the epic poet, he who shall sing of the gods and their descent unto men, must drink water out of a wooden bowl.[9] For poetry is not 'Devil's wine,' but God's wine. It is with this as it is with toys. We fill the hands and nurseries of our children with all manner of dolls, drums and horses; withdrawing their eyes from the plain face and sufficing objects of nature, the sun and moon, the animals, the water and stones, which should be their toys. So the poet's habit of living should be set on a key so low that the common influences should delight him. His cheerfulness should be the gift of the sunlight; the air should suffice for his inspiration, and he should be tipsy with water. That spirit which suffices quiet hearts, which seems to come forth to such from every dry knoll of sere grass, from every pine stump and half-imbedded stone on which the dull March sun shines, comes forth to the poor and hungry, and such as are of simple taste. If thou fill thy brain with Boston and New York, with fashion and covetousness, and wilt stimulate thy jaded senses with wine and French coffee, thou shalt find no radiance of wisdom in the lonely waste of the pine woods.

If the imagination intoxicates the poet, it is not inactive in other men. The metamorphosis excites in the beholder an emotion of joy. The use of symbols has a certain power of emancipation and exhilaration for all men. We seem to be touched by a wand which makes us dance and run about happily, like children. We are like persons who come out of a cave or cellar into the open air. This is the effect on us of tropes, fables, oracles and all poetic forms. Poets are thus liberating gods. Men have really got a new sense, and found within their world another world, or nest of worlds; for, the metamorphosis once seen, we divine that it does not stop. I will not now consider how much this makes the charm of algebra and the mathematics, which also have their tropes, but it is felt in every definition; as when Aristotle defines *space* to be an immovable vessel in which things are contained;—or when Plato defines a *line* to be a flowing point; or *figure* to be a bound of solid; and many the like. What a joyful sense of freedom we have when Vitruvius announces the old opinion of artists that no architect can build any house well who does not know something

[9] See Milton's "Sixth Latin Elegy," ll. 55-78.

of anatomy.[10] When Socrates, in Charmides,[11] tells us that the soul is cured of its maladies by certain incantations, and that these incantations are beautiful reasons, from which temperance is generated in souls; when Plato calls the world an animal, and Timaeus affirms that the plants also are animals; [12] or affirms a man to be a heavenly tree, growing with his root, which is his head, upward; and, as George Chapman, following him writes,

> "So in our tree of man, whose nervie root
> Springs in his top;"—

when Orpheus speaks of hoariness as "that white flower which marks extreme old age;" when Proclus calls the universe the statue of the intellect; when Chaucer, in his praise of 'Gentilesse,' compares good blood in mean condition to fire, which, though carried to the darkest house betwixt this and the mount of Caucasus, will yet hold its natural office and burn as bright as if twenty thousand men did it behold; when John saw, in the Apocalypse, the ruin of the world through evil, and the stars fall from heaven as the fig tree casteth her untimely fruit; when Aesop reports the whole catalogue of common daily relations through the masquerade of birds and beasts;—we take the cheerful hint of the immortality of our essence and its versatile habit and escapes, as when the gypsies say of themselves "it is in vain to hang them, they cannot die."

The poets are thus liberating gods. The ancient British bards had for the title of their order, "Those who are free throughout the world." They are free, and they make free. An imaginative book renders us much more service at first, by stimulating us through its tropes, than afterward when we arrive at the precise sense of the author. I think nothing is of any value in books excepting the transcendental and extraordinary. If a man is inflamed and carried away by his thought, to that degree that he forgets the authors and the public and heeds only this one dream which holds him like an insanity, let me read his paper, and you may have all the arguments and histories and criticism. All the value which attaches to Pythagoras, Paracelsus, Cornelius Agrippa, Cardan, Kepler, Swedenborg, Schelling, Oken,[13] or any other who introduces questionable facts into his cosmogony, as angels, devils, magic, astrology, palmistry, mesmerism, and so on, is the certificate we have of departure from routine, and that here is a new witness. That also is the best success in conversation, the

[10] First century B.C., author of the only surviving Roman treatise on architecture.
[11] One of the Platonic dialogues.
[12] One of the Platonic dialogues.
[13] Pythagoras (ca. 582–ca. 500 B.C.), Greek philosopher and mathematician; Paracelsus (Theophrastus Bombastus von Hohenheim) (1493?–1541), Swiss-German alchemist and metaphysician; Cornelius Agrippa (1486–1535), German writer, soldier, physician, and by common reputation a magician; Girolamo Cardano (1501–1576), Italian mathematician and astrologer; Johann Kepler (1571–1630), German astronomer; Friedrich Wilhelm Schelling (1775–1854), German philosopher; Lorenz Oken (1779–1851), German naturalist and philosopher of the transcendental school.

magic of liberty, which puts the world like a ball in our hands. How cheap even the liberty then seems; how mean to study, when an emotion communicates to the intellect the power to sap and upheave nature; how great the perspective! nations, times, systems, enter and disappear like threads in tapestry of large figure and many colors; dream delivers us to dream, and while the drunkenness lasts we will sell our bed, our philosophy, our religion, in our opulence.

There is good reason why we should prize this liberation. The fate of the poor shepherd, who, blinded and lost in the snowstorm, perishes in a drift within a few feet of his cottage door, is an emblem of the state of man. On the brink of the waters of life and truth, we are miserably dying. The inaccessibleness of every thought but that we are in, is wonderful. What if you come near to it; you are as remote when you are nearest as when you are farthest. Every thought is also a prison; every heaven is also a prison. Therefore we love the poet, the inventor, who in any form, whether in an ode or in an action or in looks and behavior, has yielded us a new thought. He unlocks our chains and admits us to a new scene.

This emancipation is dear to all men, and the power to impart it, as it must come from greater depth and scope of thought, is a measure of intellect. Therefore all books of the imagination endure, all which ascend to that truth that the writer sees nature beneath him, and uses it as his exponent. Every verse or sentence possessing this virtue will take care of its own immortality. The religions of the world are the ejaculations of a few imaginative men.

But the quality of the imagination is to flow, and not to freeze. The poet did not stop at the color or the form, but read their meaning; neither may he rest in this meaning, but he makes the same objects exponents of his new thought. Here is the difference betwixt the poet and the mystic, that the last nails a symbol to one sense, which was a true sense for a moment, but soon becomes old and false. For all symbols are fluxional; all language is vehicular and transitive, and is good, as ferries and horses are, for conveyance, not as farms and houses are, for homestead. Mysticism consists in the mistake of an accidental and individual symbol for an universal one. The morning-redness happens to be the favorite meteor to the eyes of Jacob Behmen,[14] and comes to stand to him for truth and faith; and, he believes, should stand for the same realities to every reader. But the first reader prefers as naturally the symbol of a mother and child, or a gardener and his bulb, or a jeweller polishing a gem. Either of these, or of a myriad more, are equally good to the person to whom they are significant. Only they must be held lightly, and be very willingly translated into the equivalent terms which others use. And the mystic must be steadily told,—All that you say is just as true without the tedious use of that symbol as with it. Let us have a little algebra, instead of this trite rhetoric,—universal signs, instead of these village symbols,—and we shall

[14] Jakob Behmen (Boehme) (1575–1624), German mystic.

both be gainers. The history of hierarchies seems to show that all religious error consisted in making the symbol too stark and solid, and was at last nothing but an excess of the organ of language.

Swedenborg, of all men in the recent ages, stands eminently for the translator of nature into thought. I do not know the man in history to whom things stood so uniformly for words. Before him the metamorphosis continually plays. Everything on which his eye rests, obeys the impulses of moral nature. The figs become grapes whilst he eats them. When some of his angels affirmed a truth, the laurel twig which they held blossomed in their hands. The noise which at a distance appeared like gnashing and thumping, on coming nearer was found to be the voice of disputants. The men in one of his visions, seen in heavenly light, appeared like dragons, and seemed in darkness; but to each other they appeared as men, and when the light from heaven shone into their cabin, they complained of the darkness, and were compelled to shut the window that they might see.

There was this perception in him which makes the poet or seer an object of awe and terror, namely that the same man or society of men may wear one aspect to themselves and their companions, and a different aspect to higher intelligences. Certain priests, whom he describes as conversing very learnedly together, appeared to the children who were at some distance, like dead horses; and many the like misappearances. And instantly the mind inquires whether these fishes under the bridge, yonder oxen in the pasture, those dogs in the yard, are immutably fishes, oxen and dogs, or only so appear to me, and perchance to themselves appear upright men; and whether I appear as a man to all eyes. The Brahmins and Pythagoras propounded the same question, and if any poet has witnessed the transformation he doubtless found it in harmony with various experiences. We have all seen changes as considerable in wheat and caterpillars. He is the poet and shall draw us with love and terror, who sees through the flowing vest the firm nature, and can declare it.

I look in vain for the poet whom I describe. We do not with sufficient plainness or sufficient profoundness address ourselves to life, nor dare we chaunt our own times and social circumstance. If we filled the day with bravery, we should not shrink from celebrating it. Time and nature yield us many gifts, but not yet the timely man, the new religion, the reconciler, whom all things await. Dante's praise is that he dared to write his autobiography in colossal cipher, or into universality. We have yet had no genius in America, with tyrannous eye, which knew the value of our incomparable materials, and saw, in the barbarism and materialism of the times, another carnival of the same gods whose picture he so much admires in Homer; then in the Middle Age; then in Calvinism. Banks and tariffs, the newspaper and caucus, Methodism and Unitarianism, are flat and dull to dull people, but rest on the same foundations of wonder as the town of Troy and temple of Delphi, and are as swiftly passing away. Our log-rolling, our stumps and their politics, our fisheries, our Negroes and Indians, our boats and our repudiations, the wrath of rogues and the pusillanimity of honest men, the northern trade, the southern planting, the western clearing, Oregon and Texas, are yet unsung. Yet America is a poem in our eyes; its ample geography dazzles the imagination, and it will not wait long for metres. If I have not found that excellent combination of gifts in my countrymen which I seek, neither could I aid myself to fix the idea of the poet by reading now and then in Chalmers's collection of five centuries of English poets. These are wits more than poets, though there have been poets among them. But when we adhere to the ideal of the poet, we have our difficulties even with Milton and Homer. Milton is too literary, and Homer too literal and historical.

But I am not wise enough for a national criticism, and must use the old largeness a little longer, to discharge my errand from the muse to the poet concerning his art.

Art is the path of the creator to his work. The paths or methods are ideal and eternal, though few men ever see them; not the artist himself for years, or for a lifetime, unless he come into the conditions. The painter, the sculptor, the composer, the epic rhapsodist, the orator, all partake one desire, namely to express themselves symmetrically and abundantly, not dwarfishly and fragmentarily. They found or put themselves in certain conditions, as, the painter and sculptor before some impressive human figures; the orator into the assembly of the people; and the others in such scenes as each has found exciting to his intellect; and each presently feels the new desire. He hears a voice, he sees a beckoning. Then he is apprised, with wonder, what herds of daemons hem him in. He can no more rest; he says, with the old painter, "By God it is in me and must go forth of me." He pursues a beauty, half seen, which flies before him. The poet pours out verses in every solitude. Most of the things he says are conventional, no doubt; but by and by he says something which is original and beautiful. That charms him. He would say nothing else but such things. In our way of talking we say 'That is yours, this is mine;' but the poet knows well that it is not his; that it is as strange and beautiful to him as to you; he would fain hear the like eloquence at length. Once having tasted this immortal ichor, he cannot have enough of it, and as an admirable creative power exists in these intellections, it is of the last importance that these things get spoken. What a little of all we know is said! What drops of all the sea of our science are baled up! and by what accident it is that these are exposed, when so many secrets sleep in nature! Hence the necessity of speech and song; hence these throbs and heart-beatings in the orator, at the door of the assembly, to the end namely that thought may be ejaculated as Logos, or Word.

Doubt not, O poet, but persist. Say 'It is in me, and shall out.' Stand there, balked and dumb, stuttering and stammering, hissed and hooted, stand and strive, until at last rage draw out of thee that *dream*-power which every night shows thee is thine own; a power transcending all limit and privacy, and by virtue of which a man is the conductor of the whole river of electricity. Nothing walks, or creeps, or grows, or exists, which must not in turn arise and walk before him as exponent of his meaning.

Comes he to that power, his genius is no longer exhaustible. All the creatures by pairs and by tribes pour into his mind as into a Noah's ark, to come forth again to people a new world. This is like the stock of air for our respiration or for the combustion of our fireplace; not a measure of gallons, but the entire atmosphere if wanted. And therefore the rich poets, as Homer, Chaucer, Shakspeare, and Raphael, have obviously no limits to their works except the limits of their lifetime, and resemble a mirror carried through the street, ready to render an image of every created thing.

O poet! a new nobility is conferred in groves and pastures, and not in castles or by the sword-blade any longer. The conditions are hard, but equal. Thou shalt leave the world, and know the muse only. Thou shalt not know any longer the times, customs, graces, politics, or opinions of men, but shalt take all from the muse. For the time of towns is tolled from the world by funereal chimes, but in nature the universal hours are counted by succeeding tribes of animals and plants, and by growth of joy on joy. God wills also that thou abdicate a manifold and duplex life, and that thou be content that others speak for thee. Others shall be thy gentlemen and shall represent all courtesy and worldly life for thee; others shall do the great and resounding actions also. Thou shalt lie close hid with nature, and canst not be afforded to the Capitol or the Exchange. The world is full of renunciations and apprenticeships, and this is thine; thou must pass for a fool and a churl for a long season. This is the screen and sheath in which Pan has protected his well-beloved flower, and thou shalt be known only to thine own, and they shall console thee with tenderest love. And thou shalt not be able to rehearse the names of thy friends in thy verse, for an old shame before the holy ideal. And this is the reward; that the ideal shall be real to thee, and the impressions of the actual world shall fall like summer rain, copious, but not troublesome to thy invulnerable essence. Thou shalt have the whole land for thy park and manor, the sea for thy bath and navigation, without tax and without envy; the woods and the rivers thou shalt own, and thou shalt possess that wherein others are only tenants and boarders. Thou true land-lord! sea-lord! air-lord! Wherever snow falls or water flows or birds fly, wherever day and night meet in twilight, the blue heaven is hung by clouds or sown with stars, wherever are forms with transparent boundaries, wherever are outlets into celestial space, wherever is danger, and awe, and love,—there is Beauty, plenteous as rain, shed for thee, and though thou shouldst walk the world over, thou shalt not be able to find a condition inopportune or ignoble.

HENRY DAVID THOREAU

THOMAS CARLYLE AND HIS WORKS [1]
(1847)

WHEN WE remember how these volumes came over to us, with their encouragement and provocation from mouth to mouth, and what commotion they created in many private breasts, we wonder that the country did not ring, from shore to shore, from the Atlantic to the Pacific, with its greeting; and the Boons and Crockets of the West make haste to hail him, whose wide humanity embraces them too. Of all that the packets have brought over to us, has there been any richer cargo than this? What else has been English news for so long a season? What else, of late years, has been England to us—to us who read books, we mean? Unless we remembered it as the scene where the age of Wordsworth was spending itself, and a few younger muses were trying their wings, and from time to time, as the residence of Landon,[2] Carlyle alone, since the death of Coleridge, has kept the promise of England. It is the best apology for all the bustle and the sin of commerce, that it has made us acquainted with the thoughts of this man. Commerce would not concern us much if it were not for such results as this. New England owes him a debt which she will be slow to recognize. His earlier essays reached us at a time when Coleridge's were the only recent words which had made any notable impression so far, and they found a field unoccupied by him, before yet any words of moment had been uttered in our midst. He had this advantage, too, in a teacher, that he stood near to his pupils; and he has no doubt afforded reasonable encouragement and sympathy to many an independent but solitary thinker. Through him, as usher, we have been latterly, in a great measure, made acquainted with what philosophy and criticism the nineteenth century had to offer—admitted, so to speak, to the privileges of the century; and what he may yet have to say, is still expected here with more interest than any thing else from that quarter.

It is not in man to determine what his style shall be. He might as well determine what his thoughts shall be. We would not have had him write always as in the chapter on Burns, and the Life of Schiller, and elsewhere. No; his thoughts were ever irregular and impetuous. Perhaps as he grows older and writes more he acquires a truer expression; it is in some respects manlier, freer, struggling up to a level with its fountain-head. We think it is the richest prose style we know of.

---

[1] First printed in *Graham's Magazine*, XXX (1847), 145, 238.
[2] This should read Landor (Walter Savage Landor). There are numerous typographical errors in this article which is here reprinted from the text of the magazine.

Who cares what a man's style is, so it is intelligible—as intelligible as his thought. Literally and really, the style is no more than the *stylus*, the pen he writes with—and it is not worth scraping and polishing, and gilding, unless it will write his thoughts the better for it. It is something for use, and not to look at. The question for us is not whether Pope had a fine style, wrote with a peacock's feather, but whether he uttered useful thoughts. Translate a book a dozen times from one language to another, and what becomes of its style? Most books would be worn out and disappear in this ordeal. The pen which wrote it is soon destroyed, but the poem survives. We believe that Carlyle has, after all, more readers, and is better known today for this very originality of style, and that posterity will have reason to thank him for emancipating the language, in some measure, from the fetters which a merely conservative, aimless, and pedantic literary class had imposed upon it, and setting an example of greater freedom and naturalness. No man's thoughts are new, but the style of their expression is the never failing novelty which cheers and refreshes men. If we were to answer the question, whether the mass of men, as we know them, talk as the standard authors and reviewers write, or rather as this man writes, we should say that he alone begins to write their language at all, and that the former is, for the most part, the mere effigies of a language, not the best method of concealing one's thoughts even, but frequently a method of doing without thoughts at all.

In his graphic description of Richter's style,[3] Carlyle describes his own pretty nearly; and no doubt he first got his own tongue loosened at that fountain, and was inspired by it to equal freedom and originality. "The language," as he says of Richter, "groans with indescribable metaphors and allusions to all things, human and divine, flowing onward, not like a river, but like an inundation; circling in complex eddies, chafing and gurgling, now this way, now that;" but in Carlyle, "the proper current" never "sinks out of sight amid the boundless uproar." Again: "His very language is Titanian—deep, strong, tumultuous, shining with a thousand hues, fused from a thousand elements, and winding in labyrinthic mazes."

In short, if it is desirable that a man be eloquent, that he talk much, and address himself to his own age mainly, then this is not a bad style of doing it. But if it is desired rather that he pioneer into unexplored regions of thought, and speak to silent centuries to come, then, indeed, we could wish that he had cultivated the style of Goethe more, that of Richter less; not that Goethe's is the kind of utterance most to be prized by mankind, but it will serve for a model of the best that can be successfully cultivated.

But for style, and fine writing, and Augustan ages—that is but a poor style, and vulgar writing, and a degenerate age, which allows us to remember these things. This man has something to communicate. Carlyle's are not, in the common sense, works of art in their origin and aim; and yet, perhaps, no living English writer evinces an equal literary talent. They are such works of art only as the plough, and corn-mill, and steam-

[3] Jean Paul (Johann Paul) Richter (1763–1825), noted German author and stylist.

engine—not as pictures and statues. Others speak with greater emphasis to scholars, as such, but none so earnestly and effectually to all who can read. Others give their advice, he gives his sympathy also. It is no small praise that he does not take upon himself the airs, has none of the whims, none of the pride, the nice vulgarities, the starched, impoverished isolation, and cold glitter of the spoiled children of genius. He does not need to husband his pearl, but excels by a greater humanity and sincerity.

He is singularly serious and untrivial. We are every where impressed by the rugged, unwearied, and rich sincerity of the man. We are sure that he never sacrificed one jot of his honest thought to art or whim, but to utter himself in the most direct and effectual way, that is the endeavor. These are merits which will wear well. When time has worn deeper into the substance of these books, this grain will appear. No such sermons have come to us here out of England, in late years, as those of this preacher; sermons to kings, and sermons to peasants, and sermons to all intermediate classes. It is in vain that John Bull, or any of his cousins, turns a deaf ear, and pretends not to hear them, nature will not soon be weary of repeating them. There are words less obviously true, more for the ages to hear, perhaps, but none so impossible for this age not to hear. What a cutting cimitar was that "past and present," going through heaps of silken stuffs, and glibly through the necks of men, too, without their knowing it, leaving no trace. He has the earnestness of a prophet. In an age of pedantry and dilettantism, he has no grain of these in his composition. There is no where else, surely, in recent readable English, or other books, such direct and effectual teaching, reproving, encouraging, stimulating, earnestly, vehemently, almost like Mahomet, like Luther; not looking behind him to see how his *Opera Omnia* will look, but forward to other work to be done. His writings are a gospel to the young of this generation; they will hear his manly, brotherly speech with responsive joy, and press forward to older or newer gospels.

We should omit a main attraction in these books, if we said nothing of their humor. Of this indispensable pledge of sanity, without some leaven of which the abstruse thinker may justly be suspected of mysticism, fanaticism, or insanity, there is a superabundance in Carlyle. Especially the transcendental philosophy needs the leaven of humor to render it light and digestible. In his later and longer works it is an unfailing accompaniment, reverberating through pages and chapters, long sustained without effort. The very punctuation, the italics, the quotation marks, the blank spaces and dashes, and the capitals, each and all are pressed into its service.

Every man, of course, has his fane, from which even the most innocent conscious humor is excluded; but in proportion as the writer's position is high above his fellows, the range of his humor is extended. To the thinker, all the institutions of men, as all imperfection, viewed from the point of equanimity, are legitimate subjects of humor. Whatever is not necessary, no matter how sad or personal, or universal a grievance, is, indeed, a jest more or less sublime.

Carlyle's humor is vigorous and Titanic, and has more sense in it than the sober philosophy of many another. It is not to be disposed of by laughter and smiles merely; it gets to be too serious for that—only they may laugh who are not hit by it. For those who love a merry jest, this is a strange kind of fun—rather too practical joking, if they understand it. The pleasant humor which the public loves, is but the innocent pranks of the ballroom, harmless flow of animal spirits, the light plushy pressure of dandy pumps, in comparison. But when an elephant takes to treading on your corns, why then you are lucky if you sit high, or wear cowhide. His humor is always subordinate to a serious purpose, though often the real charm for the reader, is not so much in the essential progress and final upshot of the chapter, as in this indirect side-light illustration of every hue. He sketches first with strong, practical English pencil, the essential features in outline, black on white, more faithfully than Dryasdust would have done, telling us wisely whom and what to mark, to save time, and then with brush of camel's hair, or sometimes with more expeditious swab, he lays on the bright and fast colors of his humor everywhere. One piece of solid work, be it known, we have determined to do, about which let there be no jesting, but all things else under the heavens, to the right and left of that, are for the time fair game. To us this humor is not wearisome, as almost every other is. Rabelais, for instance, is intolerable; one chapter is better than a volume—it may be sport to him, but it is death to us. A mere humorist, indeed, is a most unhappy man; and his readers are most unhappy also.

Humor is not so distinct a quality as, for the purposes of criticism, it is commonly regarded, but allied to every, even the divinest faculty. The familiar and cheerful conversation about every hearth-side, if it be analyzed, will be found to be sweetened by this principle. There is not only a never-failing, pleasant, and earnest humor kept up there, embracing the domestic affairs, the dinner, and the scolding, but there is also a constant run upon the neighbors, and upon church and state, and to cherish and maintain this, in a great measure, the fire is kept burning, and the dinner provided. There will be neighbors, parties to a very genuine, even romantic friendship, whose whole audible salutation and intercourse, abstaining from the usual cordial expressions, grasping of hands, or affectionate farewells, consists in the mutual play and interchange of a genial and healthy humor, which excepts nothing, not even themselves, in its lawless range. The child plays continually, if you will let it, and all its life is a sort of practical humor of a very pure kind, often of so fine and ethereal a nature, that its parents, its uncles and cousins, can in no wise participate in it, but must stand aloof in silent admiration, and reverence even. The more quiet the more profound it is. Even nature is observed to have her playful moods or aspects, of which man seems sometimes to be the sport.

But, after all, we could sometimes dispense with the humor, though unquestionably incorporated in the blood, if it were replaced by this author's gravity. We should not apply to himself, without qualification, his remarks on the humor of Richter. With more repose in his inmost being, his humor would become more thoroughly genial and placid. Humor is apt to imply but a half satisfaction at best. In his pleasantest and most genial hour, man smiles but as the globe smiles, and the works of nature. The fruits *dry* ripe, and much as we relish some of them, in their green and pulpy state, we lay up for our winter store, not out of these, but the rustling autumnal harvests. Though we never weary of this vivacious wit, while we are perusing its work, yet when we remember it from afar, we sometimes feel balked and disappointed, missing the security, the simplicity, and frankness, even the occasional magnanimity of acknowledged dullness and bungling. This never-failing success and brilliant talent become a reproach. To the most practical reader the humor is certainly too obvious and constant a quality. When we are to have dealings with a man, we prize the good faith and valor of soberness and gravity. There is always a more impressive statement than consists with these victorious comparisons. Besides, humor does not wear well. It is commonly enough said, that a joke will not bear repeating. The deepest humor will not keep. Humors do not circulate but stagnate, or circulate partially. In the oldest literature, in the Hebrew, the Hindoo, the Persian, the Chinese, it is rarely humor, even the most divine, which still survives, but the most sober and private, painful or joyous thoughts, maxims of duty, to which the life of all men may be referred. After time has sifted the literature of a people, there is left only their SCRIPTURE, for that is WRITING, *par excellence.* This is as true of the poets, as of the philosophers and moralists by profession; for what subsides in any of these is the moral only, to re-appear as dry land at some remote epoch.

We confess that Carlyle's humor is rich, deep, and variegated, in direct communication with the back bone and risible muscles of the globe—and there is nothing like it; but much as we relish this jovial, this rapid and delugeous way of conveying one's views and impressions, when we would not converse but meditate, we pray for a man's diamond edition of his thought, without the colored illuminations in the margin—the fishes and dragons, and unicorns, the red or the blue ink, but its initial letter in distinct skeleton type, and the whole so clipped and condensed down to the very essence of it, that time will have little to do. We know not but we shall immigrate soon, and would fain take with us all the treasures of the east, and all kinds of *dry*, portable soups, in small tin canisters, which contain whole herds of English beeves, boiled down, will be acceptable.

The difference between this flashing, fitful writing and pure philosophy, is the difference between flame and light. The flame, indeed, yields light, but when we are so near as to observe the flame, we are apt to be incommoded by the heat and smoke. But the sun, that old Platonist, is set so far off in the heavens, that only a genial summer-heat and ineffable day-light can reach us. But many a time, we confess, in wintery weather, we have been glad to forsake the sun-light, and warm us by these Promethean flames.

Carlyle must undoubtedly plead guilty to the charge of mannerism. He not only has his vein, but his peculiar manner of working it. He has a style which can be imitated, and sometimes is an imitator of himself. Every man, though born and bred in the metropolis of the world, will still have some provincialism adhering to him; but in proportion as his aim is simple and earnest, he approaches at once the most ancient and the most modern men. There is no mannerism in the Scriptures. The style of proverbs, and indeed of all *maxims*, whether measured by sentences or by chapters, if they may be said to have any style, is one, and as the expression of one voice, merely an account of the matter by the latest witness. It is one advantage enjoyed by men of science, that they use only formulas which are universal. The common language and the common sense of mankind, it is most uncommon to meet with in the individual. Yet liberty of thought and speech is only liberty to think the universal thought, and speak the universal language of men, instead of being enslaved to a particular mode. Of this universal speech there is very little. It is equable and sure; from a depth within man which is beyond education and prejudice.

Certainly, no critic has anywhere said what is more to the purpose, than this which Carlyle's own writings furnish, which we quote, as well for its intrinsic merit as for its pertinence here. "It is true," says he, thinking of Richter, "the beaten paths of literature lead the safeliest to the goal; and the talent pleases us most, which submits to shine with new gracefulness through old forms. Nor is the noblest and most peculiar mind too noble or peculiar for working by prescribed laws; Sophocles, Shakspeare, Cervantes, and in Richter's own age, Goethe, how little did they innovate on the given forms of composition, how much in the spirit they breathed into them! All this is true; and Richter must lose of our esteem in proportion." And again, in the chapter on Goethe, "We read Goethe for years before we come to see wherein the distinguishing peculiarity of his understanding, of his disposition, even of his way of writing, consists! It seems quite a simple style, [that of his?] remarkable chiefly for its calmness, its perspicuity, in short, its commonness; and yet it is the most uncommon of all styles." And this, too, translated for us by the same pen from Schiller,[4] which we will apply not merely to the outward form of his works, but to their inner form and substance. He is speaking of the artist. "Let some beneficent divinity snatch him, when a suckling, from the breast of his mother, and nurse him with the milk of a better time, that he may ripen to his full stature beneath a distant Grecian sky. And having grown to manhood, let him return, a foreign shape, into his century; not, however, to delight it by his presence, but, dreadful, like the son of Agamemnon, to purify it. The matter of his works he will take from the present, but their form he will derive from a nobler time; nay, from beyond all time, from the absolute unchanging unity of his own nature."

But enough of this. Our complaint is already out of all proportion to our discontent.

[4] Johann Schiller (1759-1805), German poet, dramatist, and philosopher.

Carlyle's works, it is true, have not the stereotyped success which we call classic. They are a rich but inexpensive entertainment, at which we are not concerned lest the host has strained or impoverished himself to feed his guests. It is not the most lasting word, nor the loftiest wisdom, but rather the word which comes last. For his genius it was reserved to give expression to the thoughts which were throbbing in a million breasts. He has plucked the ripest fruit in the public garden; but this fruit already least concerned the tree that bore it, which was rather perfecting the bud at the foot of the leaf stalk. His works are not to be studied, but read with a swift satisfaction. Their flavor and gust is like what poets tell of the froth of wine, which can only be tasted once and hastily. On a review we can never find the pages we had read. The first impression is the truest and the deepest, and there is no reprint, no *double entendre*, so to speak, for the alert reader. Yet they are in some degree true natural products in this respect. All things are but once, and never repeated. The first faint blushes of the morning, gilding the mountain tops, the pale phosphor and saffron-colored clouds do verily transport us to the morning of creation; but what avails it to travel eastward, or look again there an hour hence? We should be as far in the day ourselves, mounting toward our meridian. These works were designed for such complete success that they serve but for a single occasion. It is the luxury of art, when its own instrument is manufactured for each particular and present use. The knife which slices the bread of Jove ceases to be a knife when this service is rendered.

But he is wilfully and pertinaciously unjust, even scurrilous, impolite, ungentlemanly; calls us "Imbeciles," "Dilettants," "Philistines," implying sometimes what would not sound well expressed. If he would adopt the newspaper style, and take back these hard names—but where is the reader who does not derive some benefit from these epithets, applying them to himself? Think not that with each repetition of them there is a fresh overflowing of bile; oh no! Perhaps none at all after the first time, only a faithfulness, the right name being found, to apply it—"They are the same ones we meant before"—and ofttimes with a genuine sympathy and encouragement expressed. Indeed, there appears in all his writings a hearty and manly sympathy with all misfortune and wretchedness, and not a weak and sniveling one. They who suspect a Mephistopheles, or sneering, satirical devil, under all, have not learned the secret of true humor, which sympathizes with the gods themselves, in view of their grotesque, half-finished creatures.

He is, in fact, the best tempered, and not the least impartial of reviewers. He goes out of his way to do justice to profligates and quacks. There is somewhat even Christian, in the rarest and most peculiar sense, in his universal brotherliness, his simple, child-like endurance, and earnest, honest endeavor, with sympathy for the like. And this fact is not insignificant, that he is almost the only writer of biography, of the lives of men, in modern times. So kind and generous a tribute to the genius of Burns cannot be expected again, and is not needed. We honor him for his noble reverence for Luther, and his patient, almost reverent study of Goethe's genius, anxious that no shadow of his author's meaning escape him for want of trustful attention. There is nowhere else, surely, such determined and generous love of whatever is manly in history. His just appreciation of any, even inferior talent, especially of all sincerity, under whatever guise, and all true men of endeavor, must have impressed every reader. Witness the chapters on Werner, Heyne, even Cagliostro,[5] and others. He is not likely to underrate his man. We are surprised to meet with such a discriminator of kingly qualities in these republican and democratic days, such genuine loyalty all thrown away upon the world.

Carlyle, to adopt his own classification, is himself the hero, as literary man. There is no more notable workingman in England, in Manchester or Birmingham, or the mines round about. We know not how many hours a-day he toils nor for what wages, exactly, we only know the results for us. We hear through the London fog and smoke the steady systole, diastole, and vibratory hum, from "Somebody's Works" there; the "Print Works," say some; the "Chemicals," say others; where something, at any rate, is manufactured which we remember to have seen in the market. This is the place, then. Literature has come to mean, to the ears of laboring men, something idle, something cunning and pretty merely, because the nine hundred and ninety-nine really write for fame or for amusement. But as the laborer works, and soberly by the sweat of his brow earns bread for his body, so this man *works* anxiously and *sadly*, to get bread of life, and dispense it. We cannot do better than quote his own estimate of labor from Sartor Resartus.

"Two men I honor, and no third. First; the toil-worn craftsman that with earth-made implement laboriously conquers the earth, and makes her man's. Venerable to me is the hard hand; crooked, coarse, wherein, notwithstanding, lies a cunning virtue, indefeasibly royal, as of the sceptre of this planet. Venerable, too, is the rugged face, all weather-tanned, besoiled, with its rude intelligence; for it is the face of a man living manlike. Oh, but the more venerable for thy rudeness, and even because we must pity as well as love thee. Hardly-entreated brother! For us was thy back so bent, for us were thy straight limbs and fingers so deformed; thou wert our conscript, on whom the lot fell, and fighting our battles wert so marred. For in thee, too, lay a god-created form, but it was not to be unfolded; encrusted must it stand with the thick adhesions and defacements of labor; and thy body, like thy soul, was not to know freedom. Yet toil on, toil on; *thou* art in thy duty, be out of it who may; thou toilest for the altogether indispensable, for daily bread."

"A second man I honor, and still more highly; him who is seen toiling for the spiritually indispensable; not daily bread, but the bread of life. Is not he, too, in his duty, endeavoring toward inward harmony, revealing

---

[5] Abraham Werner (1750–1817), German scientist; Christian Heyne (1729–1812), German classical scholar; Alessandro Cagliostro (Giuseppe Balsamo) (1743–1795), Italian alchemist and impostor.

this, by act or by word, through all his outward endeavors, be they high or low? Highest of all, when his outward and his inward endeavor are one; when we can name him Artist; not earthly craftsman only, but inspired thinker, that with heaven-made implement conquers heaven for us. If the poor and humble toil that we have food, must not the high and glorious toil for him in return, that he have light, have guidance, freedom, immortality? These two in all their degrees, I honor; all else is chaff and dust, which let the wind blow whither it listeth."

"Unspeakably touching is it, however, when I find both dignities united; and he that must toil outwardly for the lowest of man's wants, is also toiling inwardly for the highest. Sublimer in this world know I nothing than a peasant saint, could such now anywhere be met with. Such a one will take thee back to Nazareth itself; thou wilt see the splendor of heaven spring forth from the humblest depths of earth, like a light shining in great darkness."

Notwithstanding the very genuine, admirable, and loyal tributes to Burns, Schiller, Goethe, and others, Carlyle is not a critic of poetry. In the book of heroes, Shakspeare, the hero, as poet, comes off rather slimly. His sympathy, as we said, is with the men of endeavor; not using the life got, but still bravely getting their life. "In fact," as he says of Cromwell, "every where we have to notice the decisive, practical *eye* of this man; how he drives toward the practical and practicable; has a genuine insight into what *is* fact." You must have very stout legs to get noticed at all by him. He is thoroughly English in his love of practical men, and dislike for cant, and ardent enthusiastic heads that are not supported by any legs. He would kindly knock them down that they may regain some vigor by touching their mother earth. We have often wondered how he ever found out Burns, and must still refer a good share of his delight in him to neighborhood and early association. The Lycidas and Comus appearing in Blackwood's Magazine, would probably go unread by him, nor lead him to expect a Paradise Lost. The condition of England question is a practical one. The condition of England demands a hero, not a poet. Other things demand a poet; the poet answers other demands. Carlyle in London, with this question pressing on him so urgently, sees no occasion for minstrels and rhapsodists there. Kings may have their bards when there are any kings. Homer would *certainly* go a begging there. He lives in Chelsea, not on the plains of Hindostan, nor on the prairies of the West, where settlers are scarce, and a man must at least go *whistling* to himself.

What he says of poetry is rapidly uttered, and suggestive of a thought, rather than the deliberate development of any. He answers your question, What is poetry? by writing a special poem, as that Norse one, for instance, in the Book of Heroes, altogether wild and original—answers your question, What is light? by kindling a blaze which dazzles you, and pales sun and moon, and not as a peasant might, by opening a shutter. And, certainly, you would say that this question never could be answered but by the grandest of poems; yet he has not dull breath and stupidity enough, perhaps, to give the most deliberate and universal answer, such as the fates wring from illiterate and unthinking men. He answers like Thor, with a stroke of his hammer, whose dint makes a valley in the earth's surface.

Carlyle is not a *seer*, but a brave looker-on and *reviewer*; not the most free and catholic observer of men and events, for they are likely to find him preoccupied, but unexpectedly free and catholic when they fall within the focus of his lens. He does not live in the present hour, and read men and books as they occur for his theme, but having chosen this, he directs his studies to this end.

But if he supplies us with arguments and illustrations against himself, we will remember that we may perhaps be convicted of error from the same source—stalking on these lofty reviewer's stilts so far from the green pasturage around. If we look again at his page, we are apt to retract somewhat that we have said. Often a genuine poetic feeling dawns through it, like the texture of the earth seen through the dead grass and leaves in the spring. There is indeed more poetry in this author than criticism on poetry. He often reminds us of the ancient Scald,[6] inspired by the grimmer features of life, dwelling longer on Dante than on Shakspeare. We have not recently met with a more solid and unquestionable piece of poetic work than that episode of "The Ancient Monk," in Past and Present, at once idyllic, narrative, heroic; a beautiful restoration of a past age. There is nothing like it elsewehere that we know of. The History of the French Revolution is a poem, at length got translated into prose; an Iliad, indeed, as he himself has it—"The destructive wrath of Sansculotism: this is what we speak, having unhappily no voice for singing."

One improvement we could suggest in this last, as indeed in most epics, that he should let in the sun oftener upon his picture. It does not often enough appear, but it is all revolution, the old way of human life turned simply bottom upward, so that when at length we are inadvertently reminded of the "Brest Shipping," a St. Domingo colony, and that anybody thinks of owning plantations, and simply turning up the soil there, and that now at length, after some years of this revolution, there is a falling off in the importation of sugar, we feel a queer surprise. Had they not sweetened their water with Revolution then? It would be well if there were several chapters headed "Work for the Mouth"—Revolution-work inclusive, of course—"Altitude of the Sun," "State of the Crops and Markets," "Meteorological Observations," "Attractive Industry," "Day Labor," &c., just to remind the reader that the French peasantry did something beside go without breeches, burn châteaus, get ready knotted cords, and embrace and throttle one another by turns. These things are sometimes hinted at, but they deserve a notice more in proportion to their importance. We want not only a background to the picture, but a ground under the feet also. We remark, too, occasionally, an unphilosophical habit, common enough elsewhere, in Alison's History of Modern Europe, for instance, of saying, undoubtedly with effect, that if a straw had not fallen

⁶ Skald, an ancient Scandinavian poet.

this way or that, why then—but, of course, it is as easy in philosophy to make kingdoms rise and fall as straws. The old adage is as true for our purpose, which says that a miss is as good as a mile. Who shall say how near the man came to being killed who was not killed? If an apple had not fallen then we had never heard of Newton and the law of gravitation; as if they could not have contrived to let fall a pear as well.

The poet is blithe and cheery ever, and as well as nature. Carlyle has not the simple Homeric health of Wordsworth, nor the deliberate philosophic turn of Coleridge, nor the scholastic taste of Landor, but, though sick and under restraint, the constitutional vigor of one of his old Norse heroes, struggling in a lurid light, with Iötuns still, striving to throw the old woman, and "she was Time"—striving to lift the big cat—and that was "The Great World-Serpent, which, tail in mouth, girds and keeps up the whole created world." The smith, though so brawny and tough, I should not call the healthiest man. There is too much shop-work, too great extremes of heat and cold, and incessant ten-pound-ten and thrashing of the anvil, in his life. But the haymaker's is a true sunny perspiration, produced by the extreme of summer heat only, and conversant with the blast of the zephyr, not of the forge-bellows. We know very well the nature of this man's sadness, but we do not know the nature of his gladness. There sits Bull in the court all the year round, with his hoarse bark and discontented growl—not a cross dog, only a canine habit, verging to madness some think—now separated from the shuddering travelers only by the paling, now heard afar in the horizon, even melodious there; baying the moon o' nights, *baying the sun by day*, with his mastiff mouth. He never goes after the cows, nor stretches in the sun, nor plays with the children. Pray give him a longer rope, ye gods, or let him go at large, and never taste raw meat more.

The poet will maintain serenity in spite of all disappointments. He is expected to preserve an unconcerned and healthy outlook over the world while he lives. *Philosophia practica est eruditionis meta*, philosophy practiced is the good of learning; and for that other, *Oratoris est celare artem*,[7] we might read, *Herois est celare pugnam*,[8] the hero will conceal his struggles. Poetry is the only life got, the only work done, the only pure product and free labor of man, performed only when he has put all the world under his feet, and conquered the last of his foes.

Carlyle speaks of Nature with a certain unconscious pathos for the most part. She is to him a receded but ever memorable splendor, casting still a reflected light over all his scenery. As we read his books here in New England, where there are potatoes enough, and every man can get his living peacefully and sportively as the birds and bees, and need think no more of that, it seems to us as if by the world he often meant London, at the head of the tide upon the Thames, the sorest place on the face of the earth, the very citadel of conservatism. Possibly a South African village might have furnished a more hopeful, and more exacting audience, or

---

[7] "The art of the orator is to hide art."
[8] "The art of the hero is to conceal his struggles."

in the silence of the wilderness and the desert, he might have addressed himself more entirely to his true audience, posterity.

In his writings, we should say that he, as conspicuously as any, though with little enough expressed or even conscious sympathy, represents the Reformer class, and all the better for not being the acknowledged leader of any. In him the universal plaint is most settled, unappeasable and serious. Until a thousand named and nameless grievances are righted, there will be no repose for him in the lap of nature, or the seclusion of science and literature. By foreseeing it he hastens the crisis in the affairs of England, and is as good as many years added to her history.

As we said, we have no adequate word from him concerning poets— Homer, Shakspeare; nor more, we might add, of Saints—Jesus; nor philosophers—Socrates, Plato; nor mystics—Swedenborg. He has no articulate sympathy at least with such as these as yet. Odin, Mahomet; Cromwell, will have justice at his hands, and we would leave him to write the eulogies of all the giants of the will, but the kings of men, whose kingdoms are wholly in the hearts of their subjects, strictly transcendent and moral greatness, which is highest and worthiest in character, he is not inclined to dwell upon or point to. To do himself justice, and set some of his readers right, he should give us some transcendent hero at length, to rule his demigods and Titans; develop, perhaps, his reserved and dumb reverence for Christ, not speaking to a London or Church of England audience merely. Let *not* "sacred silence meditate that sacred matter" forever, but let us have sacred speech and sacred scripture thereon. True reverence is not necessarily dumb, but ofttimes prattling and hilarious as children in the spring.

Every man will include in his list of worthies those whom he himself best represents. Carlyle, and our countryman Emerson, whose place and influence must ere long obtain a more distinct recognition, are, to a certain extent, the complement of each other. The age could not do with one of them, it cannot do with both. To make a broad and rude distinction, to suit our present purpose, the former, as critic, deals with the men of action—Mahomet, Luther, Cromwell; the latter with the thinkers— Plato, Shakspeare, Goethe, for though both have written upon Goethe, they do not meet in him. The one has more sympathy with the heroes, or practical reformers, the other with the observers, or philosophers. Put these worthies together, and you will have a pretty fair representation of mankind; yet with one or more memorable exceptions. To say nothing of Christ, who yet awaits a just appreciation from literature, the peacefully practical hero, whom Columbus may represent, is obviously slighted; but above and after all, the Man of the Age, come to be called workingman, it is obvious that none yet speaks to his condition, for the speaker is not yet in his condition. There is poetry and prophecy to cheer him, and advice of the head and heart to the hands; but no very memorable coöperation, it must be confessed, since the Christian era, or rather since Prometheus tried it. It is even a note-worthy fact, that a man addresses effectually in another only himself still, and what he himself does and is, alone can he prompt the other to do and to become. Like speaks to like only; labor to labor, philosophy to philosophy, criticism to criticism, poetry to poetry, &c. Literature speaks how much still to the past, how little to the future, how much to the east, how little to the west—

> In the East fames are won,
> In the West deeds are done.

One more merit in Carlyle, let the subject be what it may, is the freedom of prospect he allows, the entire absence of cant and dogma. He removes many cart-loads of rubbish, and leaves open a broad highway. His writings are all enfenced on the side of the future and the possible. He does not place himself across the passage out of his books, so that none may go freely out, but rather by the entrance, inviting all to come in and go through. No gins, no network, no pickets here, to restrain the free thinking reader. In many books called philosophical, we find ourselves running hither and thither, under and through, and sometimes quite unconsciously straddling some imaginary fence-work, which in our clairvoyance we had not noticed, but fortunately, not with such fatal consequences as happen to those birds which fly against a white-washed wall, mistaking it for fluid air. As we proceed the wreck of this dogmatic tissue collects about the organs of our perception, like cobwebs about the muzzles of hunting dogs in dewy mornings. If we look up with such eyes as these authors furnish, we see no heavens, but a low pent-roof of straw or tiles, as if we stood under a shed, with no sky-light through which to glimpse the blue.

Carlyle, though he does but inadvertently direct our eyes to the open heavens, nevertheless, lets us wander broadly underneath, and shows them to us reflected in innumerable pools and lakes. We have from him, occasionally, some hints of a possible science of astronomy even, and revelation of heavenly arcana, but nothing definite hitherto.

These volumes contain not the highest, but a very practicable wisdom, which startles and provokes, rather than informs us. Carlyle does not oblige us to think; we have thought enough for him already, but he compels us to act. We accompany him rapidly through an endless gallery of pictures, and glorious reminiscences of experiences unimproved. "Have you not had Moses and the prophets? Neither will ye be persuaded if one should rise from the dead." There is no calm philosophy of life here, such as you might put at the end of the Almanac, to hang over the farmer's hearth, how men shall live in these winter, in these summer days. No philosophy, properly speaking, of love, or friendship, or religion, or politics, or education, or nature, or spirit; perhaps a nearer approach to a philosophy of kingship, and of the place of the literary man, than of any thing else. A rare preacher, with prayer, and psalm, and sermon, and benediction, but no contemplation of man's life from serene oriental ground, nor yet from the stirring occidental. No thanksgiving sermon for the holydays, or the Easter vacations, when all men submit to float on the full currents of life.

When we see with what spirits, though with little heroism enough, wood-choppers, drovers, and apprentices, take and spend life, playing all day long, sunning themselves, shading themselves, eating, drinking, sleeping, we think that the philosophy of their life written would be such a level natural history as the Gardener's Calendar, and the works of the early botanists, inconceivably slow to come to practical conclusions; its premises away off before the first morning light, ere the heather was introduced into the British isles, and no inferences to be drawn during this noon of the day, not till after the remote evening shadows have begun to fall around.

There is no philosophy here for philosophers, only as every man is said to have his philosophy. No system but such as is the man himself; and, indeed, he stands compactly enough. No progress beyond the first assertion and challenge, as it were, with trumpet blast. One thing is certain, that we had best be doing something in good earnest, henceforth forever; that's an indispensable philosophy. The before impossible precept *"know thyself,"* he translates into the partially possible one, *"know what thou canst work at."* Sartor Resartus is, perhaps the sunniest and most philosophical, as it is the most autobiographical of his works, in which he drew most largely on the experience of his youth. But we miss everywhere a calm depth, like a lake, even stagnant, and must submit to rapidity and whirl, as on skates, with all kinds of skillful and antic motions, sculling, sliding, cutting punch-bowls and rings, forward and backward. The talent is very nearly equal to the genius. Sometimes it would be preferable to wade slowly through a Serbonian bog, and feel the juices of the meadow. We should say that he had not speculated far, but faithfully, living up to it. He lays all the stress still on the most elementary and initiatory maxims, introductory to philosophy. It is the experience of the religionist. He pauses at such a quotation as, "It is only with renunciation that life, properly speaking, can be said to begin;" or, "Doubt of any sort cannot be removed except by action;" or, "Do the duty which lies nearest thee." The chapters entitled, "The Everlasting No," and "The Everlasting Yea," contain what you might call the religious experience of his hero. In the latter, he assigns to him these words, brief, but as significant as any we remember in this author:—"One BIBLE I know, of whose plenary inspiration doubt is not so much as possible; nay, with my own eyes I saw the God's-hand writing it: thereof all other Bibles are but leaves." This belongs to "The Everlasting Yea;" yet he lingers unaccountably in "The Everlasting No," under the negative pole. "Truth!" he still cries with Teufelsdröckh, "though the heavens crush me for following her: no falsehood! though a whole celestial Lubberland were the price of apostacy." Again, "Living without God in the world, of God's light I was not utterly bereft; if my as yet sealed eyes, with their unspeakable longing, could nowhere see Him, nevertheless, in my heart He was present, and his heaven-written law still stood legible and sacred there." Again, "Ever from that time, [*the era of his Protest,*] the temper of my misery was changed: not fear or whining sorrow was it, but indignation and grim, fire-eyed defiance." And in the "Centre of Indifference," as editor, he observes, that "it was no longer a quite hopeless unrest," and then proceeds, not in his best style, "For the fire-baptized soul, long so scathed and thunder-riven, here feels its own freedom, which feeling is its Baphometic Baptism: the citadel of its whole kingdom it has thus gained by assault, and will keep inexpungable; outward from which the remaining dominions, not, indeed, without hard battling, will doubtless by degrees be conquered and pacificated."

Besides some philosophers of larger vision, Carlyle stands like an honest, half-despairing boy, grasping at some details only of their world systems. Philosophy, certainly, is some account of truths, the fragments and very insignificant parts of which man will practice in this work-shop; truths infinite and in harmony with infinity; in respect to which the very objects and ends of the so-called practical philosopher, will be mere propositions, like the rest. It would be no reproach to a philosopher, that he knew the future better than the past, or even than the present. It is better worth knowing. He will prophecy, tell what is to be, or in other words, what alone is, under appearances, laying little stress on the boiling of the pot, or the Condition of England question. He has no more to do with the condition of England than with her national debt, which a vigorous generation would not inherit. The philosopher's conception of things will, above all, be truer than other men's, and his philosophy will subordinate all the circumstances of life. To live like a philosopher, is to live, not foolishly, like other men, but wisely, and according to universal laws. In this, which was the ancient sense, we think there has been no philosopher in modern times. The wisest and most practical men of recent history, to whom this epithet has been hastily applied, have lived comparatively meagre lives, of conformity and tradition, such as their fathers transmitted to them. But a man may live in what style he can. Between earth and heaven, there is room for all kinds. If he take counsel of fear and prudence, he has already failed. One who believed, by his very constitution, some truth which a few words express, would make a revolution never to be forgotten in this world; for it needs but a fraction of truth to found houses and empires on.

However, such distinctions as poet and philosopher, do not much assist our final estimate of a man; we do not lay much stress on them. "A man's a man for a' that." If Carlyle does not take two steps in philosophy, are there any who take three? Philosophy having crept clinging to the rocks, so far, puts out its feelers many ways in vain. It would be hard to surprise him by the relation of any important human experience, but in some nook or corner of his works, you will find that this, too, was sometimes dreamed of in his philosophy.

To sum up our most serious objections, in a few words, we should say that Carlyle indicates a depth,—and we mean not impliedly, but distinctly, —which he neglects to fathom. We want to know more about that which he wants to know as well. If any luminous star, or undissolvable nebula, is visible from his station, which is not visible from ours, the interests of science require that the fact be communicated to us. The universe expects every man to do his duty in his parallel of latitude. We want to hear more of his inmost life; his hymn and prayer, more; his elegy and eulogy, less; that he should speak more from his character, and less from his talent; communicate centrally with his readers, and not by a side; that he should say what he believes, without suspecting that men disbelieve it, out of his never-misunderstood nature. Homer and Shakspeare speak directly and confidently to us. The confidence implied in the unsuspicious tone of the world's worthies, is a great and encouraging fact. Dig up some of the earth you stand on, and show that. If he gave us religiously the meagre results of his experience, his style would be less picturesque and diversified, but more attractive and impressive. His genius can cover all the land with gorgeous palaces, but the reader does not abide in them, but pitches his tent rather in the desert and on the mountain peak.

When we look about for something to quote, as the fairest specimen of the man, we confess that we labor under an unusual difficulty; for his philosophy is so little of the proverbial or sentential kind, and opens so gradually, rising insensibly from the reviewer's level, and developing its thought completely and in detail, that we look in vain for the brilliant passages, for point and antithesis, and must end by quoting his works entire. What in a writer of less breadth would have been the proposition which would have bounded his discourse, his column of victory, his Pillar of Hercules, and *ne plus ultra*, is in Carlyle frequently the same thought unfolded; no Pillar of Hercules, but a considerable prospect, north and south, along the Atlantic coast. There are other pillars of Hercules, like beacons and light-houses, still further in the horizon, toward Atlantis, set up by a few ancient and modern travelers; but, so far as this traveler goes, he clears and colonizes, and all the surplus population of London is bound thither at once. What we would quote is, in fact, his vivacity, and not any particular wisdom or sense, which last is ever synonymous with sentence, [*sententia,*] as in his contemporaries, Coleridge, Landor and Wordsworth.

We have not attempted to discriminate between his works, but have rather regarded them all as one work, as is the man himself. We have not examined so much as remembered them. To do otherwise, would have required a more indifferent, and perhaps even less just review, than the present. The several chapters were thankfully received, as they came out, and now we find it impossible to say which was best; perhaps each was best in its turn. They do not require to be remembered by chapters—that is a merit—but are rather remembered as a well-known strain, reviving from time to time, when it had nearly died away, and always inspiring us to worthier and more persistent endeavors.

In his last work, "The Letters and Speeches of Oliver Cromwell," Carlyle has added a chapter to the history of England; has actually written a chapter of her history, and, in comparison with this, there seems to be no other,—this, and the thirty thousand or three hundred thousand pamphlets in the British Museum, and that is all. This book is a practical comment on Universal History. What if there were a British Museum in Athens and Babylon, and nameless cities! It throws light on the history of the Iliad and the labors of Pisistratus.[9] History is, then, an account of memorable events that have sometime transpired, and not an incredible and confused fable, quarters for scholars merely, or a gymnasium for poets and orators. We may say that he has dug up a hero, who was buried alive in his battle-field, hauled him out of his cairn, on which every passer had cast a pamphlet. We had heard of their digging up Arthurs before to be sure they were there; and, to be sure they were there, their bones, seven feet of them; but they had to bury them again. Others have helped to make known Shakspeare, Milton, Herbert, to give a name to such treasures as we all possessed; but, in this instance, not only a lost character has been restored to our imaginations, but palpably a living body, as it were, to our senses, to wear and sustain the former. His Cromwell's restoration, if England will read it faithfully, and addressed to New England too. Every reader will make his own application.

To speak deliberately, we think that in this instance, vague rumor and a vague history have for the first time been subjected to a rigid scrutiny, and the wheat, with at least novel fidelity, sifted from the chaff; so that there remain for result,—First, Letters and Speeches of Oliver Cromwell, now for the first time read or readable, and well nigh as complete as the fates will permit; secondly, Deeds, making an imperfect and fragmentary life, which may, with probability, be fathered upon him; thirdly, this wreck of an ancient picture, the present editor has, to the best of his ability, restored, sedulously scraping away the daubings of successive bunglers, and endeavoring to catch the spirit of the artist himself. Not the worst, nor a barely possible, but for once the most favorable construction has been put upon this evidence of the life of a man, and the result is a picture of the ideal Cromwell, the perfection of the painter's art. Possibly this was the actual man. At any rate, this only can contain the actual hero. We confess that when we read these Letters and Speeches, unquestionably Cromwell's, with open and confident mind, we get glimpses occasionally of a grandeur and heroism, which even this editor has not proclaimed. His "Speeches" make us forget modern orators, and might go right into the next edition of the Old Testament, without alteration. Cromwell *was* another sort of man than *we* had taken him to be. These Letters and Speeches have supplied the lost key to his character. Verily another soldier than Bonaparte; rejoicing in the triumph of a psalm; to whom psalms were for Magna Charta and Heralds' Book, and whose victories were "crowning mercies." For stern, antique, and practical religion, a man unparalleled, since the Jewish dispensation, in the line of kings. An old Hebrew warrior, indeed, and last right-hand man of the Lord of Hosts, that has blown his ram's horn about Jericho. Yet, with a remarkable common sense and unexpected liberality, there was joined in him, too, such a divine madness, though with large and sublime features, as that of those dibblers of beans on St. George's Hill, whom Carlyle tells of. He still listened to ancient and decaying oracles. If his actions were not

[9] ca. 605–527 B.C. Tyrant of Athens, patron of literature. Tradition ascribes to him the first written text of the whole of the poems of Homer.

always what Christianity or the truest philosophy teaches, still they never fail to impress us as noble, and however violent, will always be pardoned to the great purpose and sincerity of the man. His unquestionable hardness, not to say willfulness, not prevailing by absolute truth and greatness of character, but honestly striving to bend things to his will, is yet grateful to consider in this or any age. As John Maidstone said, "He was a strong man in the dark perils of war; in the high places of the field, hope shone in him like a pillar of fire, when it had gone out in the others." And as Milton sang, whose least testimony cannot be spared—

"Our chief of men,
Guided by faith and matchless fortitude."

None ever spake to Cromwell before, sending a word of cheer across the centuries—not the "hear!" "hear!" of modern parliaments, but the congratulation and sympathy of a brother soul. The Letters and Speeches owe not a little to the "Intercalations" and "Annotations" of the "latest of the Commentators." The reader will not soon forget how like a happy merchant in the crowd, listening to his favorite speaker, he is all on the alert, and sympathetic, nudging his neighbors from time to time, and throwing in his responsive or interrogatory word. All is good, both that which he didn't hear, and that which he did. He not only makes him speak audibly, but he makes all parties listen to him, all England sitting round, and give in their comments, "groans," or "blushes," or "assent;" indulging sometimes in triumphant malicious applications to the present day, when there is a palpable hit; supplying the look and attitude of the speaker, and the tone of his voice, and even rescuing his unutterable, wrecked and submerged thought,—for this orator begins speaking anywhere within sight of the beginning, and leaves off when the conclusion is visible. Our merchant listens, restless, meanwhile, encouraging his fellow-auditors, when the speech grows dim and involved, and pleasantly congratulating them, when it runs smoothly; or, in touching soliloquy, he exclaims, "Poor Oliver, noble Oliver"—"Courage, my brave one!"

And all along, between the Letters and Speeches, as readers well remember, he has ready such a fresh top-of-the-morning salutation as conjures up the spirits of those days, and men go marching over English sward, not wired skeletons, but with firm, elastic muscles, and clang of armor on their thighs, if they wore swords, or the twang of psalms and canticles on their lips. His blunt, "Who are you?" put to the shadowy ghosts of history, they vanish into deeper obscurity than ever. Vivid phantasmagorian pictures of what is transpiring in England in the meanwhile, there are, not a few, better than if you had been there to see.

All of Carlyle's works might well enough be embraced under the title of one of them, a good specimen brick, "On Heroes, Hero-worship, and the Heroic in History." Of this department, he is the Chief Professor in the World's university, and even leaves Plutarch behind. Such intimate and living, such loyal and generous sympathy with the heroes of history, not one in one age only, but forty in forty ages, such an unparalleled reviewing and greeting of all past worth, with exceptions, to be sure,—but exceptions were the rule, before,—it was, indeed, to make this the age of review writing, as if now one period of the human story were completing itself, and getting its accounts settled. This soldier has told the stories with new emphasis, and will be a memorable hander-down of fame to posterity. And with what wise discrimination he has selected his men, with reference both to his own genius and to theirs: Mahomet,—Dante,—Cromwell,—Voltaire,—Johnson,—Burns,—Goethe,—Richter,—Schiller,—Mirabeau; could any of these have been spared? These we wanted to hear about. We have not as commonly the cold and refined judgment of the scholar and critic merely, but something more human and affecting. These eulogies have the glow and warmth of friendship. There is sympathy not with mere fames, and formless, incredible things, but with kindred men,—not transiently, but life-long he has walked with them.

The attitude of some, in relation to Carlyle's love of heroes, and men of the sword, reminds us of the procedure at the anti-slavery meetings, when some member, being warmed, begins to speak with more latitude than usual of the Bible or the Church, for a few prudent and devout ones to spring a prayer upon him, as the saying is; that is, propose suddenly to unite in prayer, and so solemnize the minds of the audience, or dismiss them at once; which may oftener be to interrupt a true prayer by most gratuitous profanity. But the spring of this trap, we are glad to learn, has grown somewhat rusty, and is not so sure of late.

No doubt, some of Carlyle's worthies, should they ever return to earth, would find themselves unpleasantly put upon their good behavior, to sustain their characters; but if he can return a man's life more perfect to our hands, than it was left at his death, following out the design of its author, we shall have no great cause to complain. We do not want a Daguerreotype likeness. All biography is the life of Adam,—a much-experienced man,—and time withdraws something partial from the story of every individual, that the historian may supply something general. If these virtues were not in this man, perhaps they are in his biographer,—no fatal mistake. Really, in any other sense, we never do, nor desire to, come at the historical man,—unless we rob his grave, that is the nearest approach. Why did he die, then? *He* is with his bones, surely.

No doubt, Carlyle has a propensity to *exaggerate* the heroic in history, that is, he creates you an ideal hero rather than another thing, he has most of that material. This we allow in all its senses, and in one narrower sense it is not so convenient. Yet what were history if he did not exaggerate it? How comes it that history never has to wait for facts, but for a man to write it? The ages may go on forgetting the facts never so long, he can remember two for every one forgotten. The musty records of history, like the catacombs, contain the perishable remains, but only in the breast of genius are embalmed the souls of heroes. There is very little of what is called criticism here; it is love and reverence, rather, which deal with qualities not relatively, but absolutely great; for whatever is admirable in a man is something infinite, to which we cannot set bounds. These sentiments allow the mortal to die, the immortal and divine to survive. There is something antique, even in his style of treating his subject, reminding us that Heroes and Demigods, Fates and Furies, still exist, the common man is nothing to him, but after death the hero is apotheosized and has a place in heaven, as in the religion of the Greeks.

Exaggeration! was ever any virtue attributed to a man without exaggeration? was ever any vice, without infinite exaggeration? Do we not exaggerate ourselves to ourselves, or do we recognize ourselves for the actual men we are? Are we not all great men? Yet what are we actually to speak of? We live by exaggeration, what else is it to anticipate more than we enjoy? The lightning is an exaggeration of the light. Exaggerated history is poetry, and truth referred to a new standard. To a small man every greater is an exaggeration. He who cannot exaggerate is not qualified to utter truth. No truth we think was ever expressed but with this sort of emphasis, so that for the time there seemed to be no other. Moreover, you must speak loud to those who are hard of hearing, and so you acquire a habit of shouting to those who are not. By an immense exaggeration we appreciate our Greek poetry and philosophy, and Egyptian ruins; our Shakspeares and Miltons, our Liberty and Christianity. We give importance to this hour over all other hours. We do not live by justice, but by grace. As the sort of justice which concerns us in our daily intercourse is not that administered by the judge, so the historical justice which we prize is not arrived at by nicely balancing the evidence. In order to appreciate any, even the humblest man, you must first, by some good fortune, have acquired a sentiment of admiration, even of reverence, for him, and there never were such exaggerators as these. Simple admiration for a hero renders a juster verdict than the wisest criticism, which necessarily degrades what is high to its own level. There is no danger in short of saying too much in praise of one man, provided you can say more in praise of a better man. If by exaggeration a man can create for us a hero, where there was nothing but dry bones before, we will thank him, and let Dryasdust administer historical justice. This is where a true history properly begins, when some genius arises, who can turn the dry and musty records into poetry. As we say, looking to the future, that what is best is truest, so, in one sense, we may say looking into the past, for the only past that we are to look at, must also be future to us. The great danger is not of excessive partiality or sympathy with one, but of a shallow justice to many, in which, after all, none gets his deserts. Who has not experienced that praise is truer than naked justice? As if man were to be the judge of his fellows, and should repress his rising sympathy with the prisoner at the bar, considering the many honest men abroad, whom he had never countenanced.

To try him by the German rule of referring an author to his own standard, we will quote the following from Carlyle's remarks on history, and leave the reader to consider how far his practice has been consistent with his theory. "Truly, if History is Philosophy teaching by experience, the writer fitted to compose history, is hitherto an unknown man. The experience itself would require all knowledge to record it, were the All-wisdom needful for such Philosophy as would interpret it, to be had for asking. Better were it that mere earthly historians should lower such pretensions, more suitable for omniscience than for human science; and aiming only at some picture of the things acted, which picture itself, will at best be a poor approximation, leave the inscrutable purport of them an acknowledged secret; or, at most, in reverent Faith, far different from that teaching of Philosophy, pause over the mysterious vestiges of Him, whose path is in the great deep of Time, whom history indeed reveals, but only all History and in Eternity, will clearly reveal."

Who lives in London to tell this generation who have been the great men of our race? We have read that on some exposed place in the City of Geneva, they have fixed a brazen indicator for the use of travelers, with the names of the mountain summits in the horizon marked upon it, "so that by taking sight across the index you can distinguish them at once. You will not mistake Mont Blanc, if you see him, but until you get accustomed to the panorama, you may easily mistake one of his court for the king." It stands there a piece of mute brass, that seems nevertheless to know in what vicinity it is: and there perchance it will stand, when the nation that placed it there has passed away, still in sympathy with the mountains, forever discriminating in the desert.

So, we may say, stands this man, pointing as long as he lives, in obedience to some spiritual magnetism, to the summits in the historical horizon, for the guidance of his fellows.

Truly, our greatest blessings are very cheap. To have our sunlight without paying for it, without any duty levied,—to have our poet there in England, to furnish us entertainment, and what is better provocation, from year to year, all our lives long, to make the world seem richer for us, the age more respectable, and life better worth the living,—all without expense of acknowledgment even, but silently accepted out of the east, like morning light as a matter of course.

JOHN GREENLEAF WHITTIER

EVANGELINE [1]
(1848)

EUREKA! HERE, then, we have it at last,—an American poem, with the lack of which British reviewers have so long reproached us. Selecting the subject of all others best calculated for his purpose,—the expulsion of the French settlers of Acadie from their quiet and pleasant homes around the Basin of Minas, one of the most sadly romantic passages in the history of the Colonies of the North,—the author has succeeded in presenting a series of exquisite pictures of the striking and peculiar features of life and nature in the New World. The range of these delineations extends from Nova Scotia on the northeast to the spurs of the Rocky Mountains on the west and the Gulf of Mexico on the south. Nothing can be added to his pictures of quiet farm-life in Acadie, the Indian summer of our northern latitudes, the scenery of the Ohio and Mississippi Rivers, the bayous and cypress forests of the South, the mocking-bird, the prairie, the Ozark hills, the Catholic missions, and the wild Arabs of the West, roaming with the buffalo along the banks of the Nebraska. The hexameter measure he has chosen has the advantage of a prosaic freedom of expression, exceedingly well adapted to a descriptive and narrative poem; yet we are constrained to think that the story of *Evangeline* would have been quite as acceptable to the public taste had it been told in the poetic prose of the author's *Hyperion*.

In reading it and admiring its strange melody we were not without fears that the success of Professor Longfellow in this novel experiment might prove the occasion of calling out a host of awkward imitators, leading us over weary wastes of hexameters, enlivened neither by dew, rain, nor fields of offering.

Apart from its Americanism, the poem has merits of a higher and universal character. It is not merely a work of art; the pulse of humanity throbs warmly through it. The portraits of Basil the blacksmith, the old notary, Benedict Bellefontaine, and good Father Felician, fairly glow with life. The beautiful Evangeline, loving and faithful unto death, is a heroine worthy of any poet of the present century.

The editor of the Boston *Chronotype*, in the course of an appreciative review of this poem, urges with some force a single objection, which we are induced to notice, as it is one not unlikely to present itself to the minds of other readers:—

"We think Mr. Longfellow ought to have expressed a much deeper indignation at the base, knavish, and heartless conduct of the English and

[1] Published Jan. 27, 1848, in *The National Era*, Washington.

Colonial persecutors than he has done. He should have put far bolder and deeper tints in the picture of suffering. One great, if not the greatest, end of poetry is rhadamanthine justice. The poet should mete out their deserts to all his heroes; honor to whom honor, and infamy to whom infamy, is due.

"It is true that the wrong in this case is in a great degree fathered upon our own Massachusetts; and it may be said that it is a foul bird that pollutes its own nest. We deny the applicability of the rather musty proverb. All the worse. Of not a more contemptible vice is what is called American literature guilty than this of unmitigated self-laudation. If we persevere in it, the stock will become altogether too small for the business. It seems that no period of our history has been exempt from materials for patriotic humiliation and national self-reproach; and surely the present epoch is laying in a large store of that sort. Had our poets always told us the truth of ourselves, perhaps it would now be otherwise. National self-flattery and concealment of faults must of course have their natural results."

We must confess that we read the first part of *Evangeline* with something of the feeling so forcibly expressed by Professor Wright. The natural and honest indignation with which, many years ago, we read for the first time that dark page of our Colonial history—the expulsion of the French neutrals—was reawakened by the simple pathos of the poem; and we longed to find an adequate expression of it in the burning language of the poet. We marvelled that he who could so touch the heart by his description of the sad suffering of the Acadian peasants should have permitted the authors of that suffering to escape without censure. The outburst of the stout Basil, in the church of Grand Pré, was, we are fain to acknowledge, a great relief to us. But, before reaching the close of the volume, we were quite reconciled to the author's forbearance. The design of the poem is manifestly incompatible with stern "rhadamanthine justice" and indignant denunciation of wrong. It is a simple story of quiet pastoral happiness, of great sorrow and painful bereavement, and of the endurance of a love which, hoping and seeking always, wanders evermore up and down the wilderness of the world, baffled at every turn, yet still retaining faith in God and in the object of its lifelong quest. It was no part of the writer's object to investigate the merits of the question at issue between the poor Acadians and their Puritan neighbors. Looking at the materials before him with the eye of an artist simply, he has arranged them to suit his idea of the beautiful and pathetic, leaving to some future historian the duty of sitting in judgment upon the actors in the atrocious outrage which furnished them. With this we are content. The poem now has unity and sweetness which might have been destroyed by attempting to avenge the wrongs it so vividly depicts. It is a psalm of love and forgiveness: the gentleness and peace of Christian meekness and forbearance breathe through it. Not a word of censure is directly applied to the marauding workers of the mighty sorrow which it describes just as it would a calamity from the elements,—a visitation of God. The reader, however, cannot fail

to award justice to the wrong-doers. The unresisting acquiescence of the
Acadians only deepens his detestation of the cupidity and religious bigotry
of their spoilers. Even in the language of the good Father Felician, be-
seeching his flock to submit to the strong hand which had been laid upon
them, we see and feel the magnitude of the crime to be forgiven:—

> "Lo, where the crucified Christ from his cross is gazing
>   upon you!
> See in those sorrowful eyes what meekness and holy com-
>   passion!
> Hark! how those lips still repeat the prayer, O Father,
>   forgive them!
> Let us repeat that prayer in the hour when the wicked
>   assail us;
> Let us repeat it now, and say, O Father, forgive them!"

How does this simple prayer of the Acadians contrast with the "deep
damnation of their taking off!"

The true history of the Puritans of New England is yet to be written.
Somewhere midway between the caricatures of the Church party and the
self-laudations of their own writers the point may doubtless be found from
whence an impartial estimate of their character may be formed. They had
noble qualities: the firmness and energy which they displayed in the
colonization of New England must always command admiration. We
would not rob them, were it in our power to do so, of one jot or tittle of
their rightful honor. But, with all the lights which we at present possess,
we cannot allow their claim of saintship without some degree of qualification. How they seemed to their Dutch neighbors at New Netherlands, and
their French ones at Nova Scotia, and to the poor Indians, hunted from
their fisheries and game-grounds, we can very well conjecture. It may be
safely taken for granted that their gospel claim to the inheritance of the
earth was not a little questionable to the Catholic fleeing for his life from
their jurisdiction, to the banished Baptist shaking off the dust of his feet
against them, and to the martyred Quaker denouncing woe and judgment
upon them from the steps of the gallows. Most of them were, beyond a
doubt, pious and sincere; but we are constrained to believe that among
them were those who wore the livery of heaven from purely selfish motives,
in a community where church-membership was an indispensable requisite,
the only *open sesame* before which the doors of honor and distinction
swung wide to needy or ambitious aspirants. Mere adventurers, men of
desperate fortune, bankrupts in character and purse, contrived to make
gain of godliness under the church and state government of New England,
put on the austere exterior of sanctity, quoted Scripture, anathematized
heretics, whipped Quakers, exterminated Indians, burned and spoiled the
villages of their Catholic neighbors, and hewed down their graven images
and "houses of Rimmon." It is curious to observe how a fierce religious
zeal against heathen and idolaters went hand in hand with the old Anglo-
Saxon love of land and plunder. Every crusade undertaken against the

Papists of the French colonies had its Puritan Peter the Hermit to summon the saints to the wars of the Lord. At the siege of Louisburg, ten years before the onslaught upon the Acadian settlers, one minister marched with the Colonial troops, axe in hand, to hew down the images in the French churches; while another officiated in the double capacity of drummer and chaplain,—a "drum ecclesiastic," as Hudibras has it.

At the late celebration of the landing of the Pilgrims in New York, the orator of the day labored at great length to show that the charge of intolerance, as urged against the colonists of New England, is unfounded in fact. The banishment of the Catholics was very sagaciously passed over in silence, inasmuch as the Catholic Bishop of New York was one of the invited guests, and (hear it, shade of Cotton Mather!) one of the regular toasts was a compliment to the Pope. The expulsion of Roger Williams was excused and partially justified; while the whipping, ear-cropping, tongue-boring, and hanging of the Quakers was defended, as the only effectual method of dealing with such devil-driven heretics, as Mather calls them. The orator, in the new-born zeal of his amateur Puritanism, stigmatizes the persecuted class as "fanatics and ranters, foaming forth their mad opinions;" compares them to the Mormons and the crazy followers of Mathias; and cites an instance of a poor enthusiast, named Eccles, who, far gone in the "tailor's melancholy," took it into his head that he must enter into a steeple-house pulpit and stitch breeches "in singing time,"— a circumstance, by the way, which took place in Old England,—as a justification of the atrocious laws of the Massachusetts Colony. We have not the slightest disposition to deny the fanaticism and folly of some few professed Quakers in that day; and had the Puritans treated them as the Pope did one of their number whom he found crazily holding forth in the church of St. Peter, and consigned them to the care of physicians as religious monomaniacs, no sane man could have blamed them. Every sect, in its origin, and especially in its time of persecution, has had its fanatics. The early Christians, if we may credit the admissions of their own writers or attach the slightest credence to the statements of pagan authors, were by no means exempt from reproach and scandal in this respect. Were the Puritans themselves the men to cast stones at the Quakers and Baptists? Had they not, in the view at least of the Established Church, turned all England upside down with their fanaticisms and extravagances of doctrine and conduct? How look they as depicted in the sermons of Dr. South, in the sarcastic pages of Hudibras,[2] and the coarse caricatures of the clerical wits of the times of the second Charles? With their own backs scored and their ears cropped for the crime of denying the divine authority of church and state in England, were they the men to whip Baptists and hang Quakers for doing the same thing in Massachusetts?

Of all that is noble and true in the Puritan character we are sincere admirers. The generous and self-denying apostleship of Eliot[3] is, of itself,

[2] A mock-heroic poem satirizing the Puritans which was published in 1663-64 by the English author, Samuel Butler (1612-1680).

[3] John Eliot (1604-1690), American colonial clergyman known as the "Apostle to the Indians."

a beautiful page in their history. The physical daring and hardihood with which, amidst the times of savage warfare, they laid the foundations of mighty states, and subdued the rugged soil, and made the wilderness blossom; their steadfast adherence to their religious principles, even when the Restoration had made apostasy easy and profitable; and the vigilance and firmness with which, under all circumstances, they held fast their chartered liberties and extorted new rights and privileges from the reluctant home government,—justly entitle them to the grateful remembrance of a generation now reaping the fruits of their toils and sacrifices. But, in expressing our gratitude to the founders of New England, we should not forget what is due to truth and justice; nor, for the sake of vindicating them from the charge of that religious intolerance which, at the time, they shared with nearly all Christendom, undertake to defend, in the light of the nineteenth century, opinions and practices hostile to the benignant spirit of the gospel and subversive of the inherent rights of man.

JOHN GREENLEAF WHITTIER

PREFACE TO
SONGS OF THREE CENTURIES [1]
(1875)

IT WOULD be doing injustice to the compiler of this volume to suppose that his work implied any lack of appreciation of the excellent anthologies already published in this country. Dana's "Household book of Poetry" is no misnomer; and the honored names of Bryant and Emerson are a sufficient guaranty for "Parnassus" and the "Library of Song." With no thought of superseding or even of entering into direct competition with these large and valuable collections, it has been my design to gather up in a comparatively small volume, easily accessible to all classes of readers, the wisest thoughts, rarest fancies, and devoutest hymns of the metrical authors of the last three centuries. To use Shelley's definition of poetry, I have endeavored to give something like "a record of the best thoughts and happiest moments of the best and happiest minds." The plan of my work has compelled me to confine myself, in a great measure, to the lyrical productions of the authors quoted, and to use only the briefer poems of the old dramatists and such voluminous writers as Spenser, Milton, Dryden, Cowper, Pope, Byron, Scott, Wordsworth, and the Brownings. Of course, no anthology, however ample its extracts, could do justice to the illimitable genius of Shakespeare.

It is possible that it may be thought an undue prominence has been given to the poetry of the period beginning with Cowper and reaching down to Tennyson and his living contemporaries. But it must be considered that the last century has been prolific in song; and, if Shakespeare and Milton still keep their unapproachable position, "souls like stars that dwell apart," there can be little doubt that the critical essayist of the twentieth century will make a large advance upon the present estimate, not only of Cowper and Burns, but of Wordsworth, Coleridge, Shelley, Keats, Browning, Tennyson, and Emerson.

It will be seen that the middle of the sixteenth century is the earliest date of my citations. The great name of Chaucer does not appear; and some of the best of the early ballad poetry of England and Scotland has been reluctantly omitted. James I.,[2] whose Queen's Quhair, has hidden his kingly crown under the poet's garland, William Dunbar,[3] and Sack-

---

[1] Boston, 1875.
[2] King James I of England (1566–1625) wrote a considerable amount of verse in his native Scottish dialect.
[3] William Dunbar (ca. 1460–ca. 1520), one of the Scottish Chaucerians.

ville, Earl of Dorset,[4] may well be thought worthy of a place in any collection of English verse, but the language and rhythm of these writers render them well-nigh unintelligible to the ordinary reader.

The selections I have made indicate, in a general way, my preferences; but I have not felt at liberty to oppose my own judgment or prejudice to the best critical authorities, or to attempt a reversal of the verdicts of Time. It would be too much to hope that I have, in all cases, made the best possible exposition of an author's productions. Judging from my own experience in looking over selected poems, I cannot doubt that my readers will often have occasion to question the wisdom of my choice, and regret the omission of favorite pieces. It is rarely that persons of equal capacity for right judging can be found to coincide entirely in regard to the merits of a particular poem. The canons of criticism are by no means fixed and infallible; and the fashion of poetry, like that of the world, "passeth away." Not only every age, but every reader, holds the right of private judgment. It would be difficult for any literary inquisitor-general to render a good reason for condemning as a heretic the man who finds the "Castle of Indolence" pleasanter reading than the "Faerie Queene," who prefers Cowper to Dryden, Scott to Byron, and Shelley to Scott, who passes by Moore's "Lalla Rookh"[5] to take up Clough's "Bothie of Tober-na Vuolich,"[6] who thinks Emerson's "Threnody" better than Milton's "Lycidas," and who would not exchange a good old ballad or song of Burns for the stateliest of epics.

The considerable space which I have given to American authors will, I trust, find its justification in the citations from their writings. The poetical literature of our country can scarcely be said to have a longer date than that of a single generation. As a matter of fact, the very fathers of it are still living. It really commenced with Bryant's "Thanatopsis" and Dana's[7] "Buccaneer." The grave, philosophic tone, chaste simplicity of language, freedom of versification, and freshness and truth of illustration, which marked the former poem, and the terse realism of the "Buccaneer," with its stern pictures of life and nature drawn with few strokes sharp and vigorous as those of Retzsch's outlines,[8] left the weak imitators of an artificial school without an audience. All further attempts to colonize the hills and pastures of New England from old mythologies were abandoned; our boys and girls no longer figured in impossible pastorals. If we have no longer ambitious Columbiads and Conquests of Canaan,[9] we have at least truth and nature, wit and wisdom, in Bryant's "Robert of Lincoln,"

---

[4] Thomas Sackville (1536–1608), English poet and contributor to the *Mirror for Magistrates*.
[5] An Oriental poem by Thomas Moore (1779–1852), published in 1817.
[6] Written in 1848 by the British poet Arthur Hugh Clough (1819–1861).
[7] Richard Henry Dana, Jr. (1815–1882), American novelist and literary critic.
[8] Moritz Retzsch (1779–1857) was a German painter whose work was distinguished by and much admired for its exquisite delicacy and refinement of form and expression.
[9] *The Columbiad* (1807) is by Joel Barlow (1754–1812); *The Conquest of Canaan* (1785) is by Timothy Dwight (1752–1817). Both are epics.

Emerson's "Humblebee," Lowell's "Courtin'," and "The One-Hoss Shay" of Holmes.

In dealing with contemporary writers I have found myself embarrassed by the very large number of really noticeable poems, many of which, although in my own estimation vastly better than those of some of the old versifiers whose age and general reputation have secured them a place in this volume, I have been compelled to omit solely from lack of space. The future gleaner in the fields over which I have passed will doubtless find many an ungarnered sheaf quite as well worth preserving as these I have gathered within the scanty limits of my compendium. The rare humorists of our time, especially such poets as Holmes and Lowell, can be only partially represented in these necessarily brief selections.

It may be observed that the three divisions of the book do not strictly correspond to the headings which indicate them,—the first, for instance, beginning before Shakespeare and ending somewhat after Milton. It is difficult to be quite exact in such classifications; and as it seemed desirable to make their number as small as possible. I trust the few leading names mentioned may serve to characterize the periods they accompany with a sufficient degree of accuracy. Pope was doubtless the great master of what is sometimes spoken of as artificial verse, shaping the mould of poetic thought for his own and the succeeding generation; but as Dryden stands in point of time nearer to the colossal name which closes the first period of English song, he has been chosen as a representative of the second, in connection and contrast with Burns, who, in his vigorous rebound from the measured pomp of rhymed heroics to the sturdiest and homeliest Scottish simplicity, gave to the modern lyric its inspiration, striking for the age the musical pitch of true and tender emotion, as decidedly as Wordsworth has touched for it the keynote of the thoughtful harmonies of natural and intellectual beauty. Tennyson undoubtedly stands at the head of all living singers, and his name might well serve as the high-water mark of modern verse; but, as our volume gives a liberal space to American authorship, I have ventured to let the name of the author of "Evangeline," represent, as it well may, the present poetic culture of our English-speaking people at home and abroad.

While by no means holding myself to a strict responsibility as regards the sentiment and language of the poems which make up this volume, and while I must confess to a large tolerance of personal individuality manifesting itself in widely varying forms of expression, I have still somewhat scrupulously endeavored to avoid in my selections everything which seemed liable to the charge of irreverence or questionable morality. In this respect the poetry of the last quarter of a century, with a few exceptions, has been noteworthy for purity of thought and language, as well as for earnestness and religious feeling. The Muse of our time is a free but profoundly reverent inquirer; it is rarely found in "the seat of the scorner." If it does not always speak in the prescribed language of creed and formula, its utterances often give evidence of fresh communion with that Eternal Spirit whose responses are never in any age or clime withheld from the devout questioner.

My great effort has been to make a thoroughly readable book. With this in view I have not given tedious extracts from dull plays and weary epics, but have gathered up the best of the old ballads and short, time-approved poems, and drawn largely from contemporary writers and the waifs and estrays of unknown authors. I have also, as a specialty of the work, made a careful selection of the best hymns in our language. I am prepared to find my method open to criticism from some quarters, but I have catered not so much for the scholarly few as for the great mass of readers to whose "snatched leisure" my brief lyrical selections would seem to have a special adaptation.

It only remains for me to acknowledge the valuable suggestions and aid I have received from various sources during the preparation of this volume, and especially the essential assistance I have had from Lucy Larcom of Beverly Farms, to whose services I have before been indebted in the compilation of "Child Life."

HERMAN MELVILLE

HAWTHORNE AND HIS MOSSES [1]
(1850)

A PAPER chamber in a fine old farmhouse, a mile from any other dwelling, and dipped to the eaves in foliage—surrounded by mountains, old woods, and Indian pools,—this, surely, is the place to write of Hawthorne. Some charm is in this northern air, for love and duty seem both impelling to the task. A man of a deep and noble nature has seized me in this seclusion. His wild witch voice rings through me; or, in softer cadences, I seem to hear it in the songs of the hillside birds that sing in the larch trees at my window.

Would that all excellent books were foundlings, without father or mother, that so it might be we could glorify them, without including their ostensible authors! Nor would any true man take exception to this; least of all, he who writes, "When the artist rises high enough to achieve the beautiful, the symbol by which he makes it perceptible to mortal senses becomes of little value in his eyes, while his spirit possesses itself in the enjoyment of the reality."

But more than this. I know not what would be the right name to put on the title page of an excellent book; but this I feel, that the names of all fine authors are fictitious ones, far more so than that of Junius; simply standing, as they do, for the mystical, ever-eluding spirit of all beauty, which ubiquitously possesses men of genius. Purely imaginative as this fancy may appear, it nevertheless seems to receive some warranty from the fact that on a personal interview no great author has ever come up to the idea of his reader. But that dust of which our bodies are composed, how can it fitly express the nobler intelligences among us? With reverence be it spoken, that not even in the case of one deemed more than man, not even in our Savior, did his visible frame betoken anything of the augustness of the nature within. Else, how could those Jewish eyewitnesses fail to see heaven in his glance!

It is curious how a man may travel along a country road, and yet miss the grandest or sweetest of prospects by reason of an intervening hedge, so like all other hedges, as in no way to hint of the wide landscape beyond. So has it been with me concerning the enchanting landscape in the soul of this Hawthorne, this most excellent Man of Mosses. His *Old Manse* has been written now four years, but I never read it till a day or two since. I had seen it in the bookstores—heard of it often—even had it recommended to me by a tasteful friend, as a rare, quiet book, perhaps too deserving of popularity to be popular. But there are so many books

[1] Published in *The Literary World*, VII (1850), 125–26; 186–87.

called "excellent," and so much unpopular merit, that amid the thick stir of other things, the hint of my tasteful friend was disregarded, and for four years the *Mosses on the Old Manse* never refreshed me with their perennial green. It may be, however, that all this while the book, likewise, was only improving in flavor and body. At any rate, it so chanced that this long procrastination eventuated in a happy result. At breakfast the other day, a mountain girl, a cousin of mine, who for the last two weeks has every morning helped me to strawberries and raspberries, which, like the roses and pearls in the fairy tale, seemed to fall into the saucer from those strawberry beds, her cheeks—this delightful creature, this charming Cherry says to me—"I see you spend your mornings in the hay-mow; and yesterday I found there Dwight's *Travels in New England*.[2] Now I have something far better than that, something more congenial to our summer on these hills. Take these raspberries, and then I will give you some moss." "Moss!" said I. "Yes, and you must take it to the barn with you, and good-by to Dwight."

With that she left me, and soon returned with a volume, verdantly bound, and garnished with a curious frontispiece in green; nothing less than a fragment of real moss, cunningly pressed to a fly-leaf. "Why, this," said I, spilling my raspberries, "this is the *Mosses from an Old Manse*." "Yes," said Cousin Cherry, "Yes, it is that flowery Hawthorne." "Hawthorne and Mosses," said I, "no more it is morning: it is July in the country: and I am off for the barn."

Stretched on that new-mown clover, the hillside breeze blowing over me through the wide barn door, and soothed by the hum of the bees in the meadows around, how magically stole over me this Mossy Man! and how amply, how bountifully, did he redeem that delicious promise to his guests in the Old Manse, of whom it is written: "Others could give them pleasure, or amusement, or instruction—these could be picked up anywhere; but it was for me to give them rest—rest, in a life of trouble! What better could be done for those weary and world-worn spirits? . . . what better could be done for anybody who came within our magic circle than to throw the spell of a tranquil spirit over him?" So all that day, half buried in the new clover, I watched this Hawthorne's "Assyrian dawn, and Paphian sunset and moonrise from the summit of our eastern hill."

The soft ravishments of the man spun me round about in a web of dreams, and when the book was closed, when the spell was over, this wizard "dismissed me with but misty reminiscences, as if I had been dreaming of him."

What a wild moonlight of contemplative humor bathes that Old Manse!—the rich and rare distilment of a spicy and slowly-oozing heart. No rollicking rudeness, no gross fun fed on fat dinners, and bred in the lees of wine,—but a humor so spiritually gentle, so high, so deep, and yet so richly relishable, that it were hardly inappropriate in an angel. It is the very religion of mirth; for nothing so human but it may be advanced to that. The orchard of the Old Manse seems the visible type of the fine

[2] Timothy Dwight's *Travels in New-England and New-York* (1821–22).

mind that has described it—those twisted and contorted old trees, "they stretch out their crooked branches, and take such hold of the imagination that we remember them as humorists and odd-fellows." And then, as surrounded by these grotesque forms, and hushed in the noonday repose of this Hawthorne's spell, how aptly might the still fall of his ruddy thoughts into your soul be symbolized by: "In the stillest afternoon, if I listened, the thump of a great apple was audible, falling without a breath of wind, from the mere necessity of perfect ripeness." For no less ripe than ruddy are the apples of the thoughts and fancies in this sweet Man of Mosses.

Buds and Bird Voices. What a delicious thing is that! "Will the world ever be so decayed, that spring may not renew its greenness?" And the *Fire Worship.* Was ever the hearth so glorified into an altar before? The mere title of that piece is better than any common work in fifty folio volumes. How exquisite is this: "Nor did it lessen the charm of his soft, familiar courtesy and helpfulness that the mighty spirit, were opportunity offered him, would run riot through the peaceful house, wrap its inmates in his terrible embrace, and leave nothing of them save their whitened bones. This possibility of mad destruction only made his domestic kindness the more beautiful and touching. It was so sweet of him, being endowed with such power, to dwell day after day, and one long lonesome night after another, on the dusky hearth, only now and then betraying his wild nature by thrusting his red tongue out of the chimney top! True, he had done much mischief in the world, and was pretty certain to do more; but his warm heart atoned for all. He was kindly to the race of man; and they pardoned his characteristic imperfections."

But he has still other apples, not quite so ruddy, though full as ripe: apples that have been left to wither on the tree, after the pleasant autumn gathering is past. The sketch of *The Old Apple Dealer* is conceived in the subtlest spirit of sadness; he whose "subdued and nerveless boyhood prefigured his abortive prime, which likewise contained within itself the prophecy and image of his lean and torpid age." Such touches as are in this piece cannot proceed from any common heart. They argue such a depth of tenderness, such a boundless sympathy with all forms of being, such an omnipresent love, that we must needs say that this Hawthorne is here almost alone in his generation—at least, in the artistic manifestation of these things. Still more. Such touches as these—and many, very many similar ones, all through his chapters—furnish clues whereby we enter a little way into the intricate, profound heart where they originated. And we see that suffering, sometime or other, and in some shape or other—this only can enable any man to depict it in others. All over him, Hawthorne's melancholy rests like an Indian summer, which, though bathing a whole country in one softness, still reveals the distinctive hue of every towering hill and each far-winding vale.

But it is the least part of genius that attracts admiration. Where Hawthorne is known, he seems to be deemed a pleasant writer, with a pleasant style,—a sequestered, harmless man, from whom any deep and weighty thing would hardly be anticipated—a man who means no meanings. But there is no man in whom humor and love, like mountain peaks, soar to such a rapt height as to receive the irradiations of the upper skies; there is no man in whom humor and love are developed in that high form called genius; no such man can exist without also possessing, as the indispensable complement of these, a great, deep intellect, which drops down into the universe like a plummet. Or, love and humor are only the eyes through which such an intellect views this world. The great beauty in such a mind is but the product of its strength. What, to all readers, can be more charming than the piece entitled *Monsieur du Miroir*; and to a reader at all capable of fully fathoming it, what, at the same time, can possess more mystical depth of meaning?—yes, there he sits and looks at me—this "shape of mystery," this "identical MONSIEUR DU MIROIR!" "Methinks I should tremble now were his wizard power of gliding through all impediments in search of me to place him suddenly before my eyes."

How profound, nay, appalling, is the moral evolved by the *Earth's Holocaust*; where—beginning with the hollow follies and affectations of the world—all vanities and empty theories and forms are, one after another, and by an admirably graduated, growing comprehensiveness, thrown into the allegorical fire, till, at length, nothing is left but the all-engendering heart of man; which remaining still unconsumed, the great conflagration is naught.

Of a piece with this is the *Intelligence Office*, a wondrous symbolizing of the secret workings in men's souls. There are other sketches still more charged with ponderous import.

The Christmas Banquet and *The Bosom Serpent* would be fine subjects for a curious and elaborate analysis, touching the conjectural parts of the mind that produced them. For spite of all the Indian-summer sunlight on the hither side of Hawthorne's soul, the other side—like the dark half of the physical sphere—is shrouded in a blackness, ten times black. But this darkness but gives more effect to the ever-moving dawn, that forever advances through it, and circumnavigates his world. Whether Hawthorne has simply availed himself of this mystical blackness as a means to the wondrous effects he makes it to produce in his lights and shades; or whether there really lurks in him, perhaps unknown to himself, a touch of Puritanic gloom,—this, I cannot altogether tell. Certain it is, however, that this great power of blackness in him derives its force from its appeals to that Calvinistic sense of Innate Depravity and Original Sin, from whose visitations, in some shape or other, no deeply thinking mind is always and wholly free. For, in certain moods, no man can weigh this world without throwing in something, somehow like Original Sin, to strike the uneven balance. At all events, perhaps no writer has ever wielded this terrific thought with greater terror than this same harmless Hawthorne. Still more: this black conceit pervades him through and through. You may be witched by his sunlight—transported by the bright gildings in the skies he builds over you; but there is the blackness of darkness beyond; and even his bright gildings but fringe and play upon the edges of thunder-clouds. In one word, the world is mistaken in this Nathaniel Hawthorne. He himself must often have smiled at its absurd misconception of him. He is immeasurably deeper than the plummet of the mere critic. For it is not the brain that can test such a man; it is only the heart. You cannot come to know greatness by inspecting it; there is no glimpse to be caught of it, except by intuition; you need not ring it, you but touch it, and you find it is gold.

Now, it is that blackness in Hawthorne, of which I have spoken, that so fixes and fascinates me. It may be, nevertheless, that it is too largely developed in him. Perhaps he does not give us a ray of light for every shade of his dark. But however this may be, this blackness it is that furnishes the infinite obscure of his background—that background against which Shakespeare plays his grandest conceits, the things that have made for Shakespeare his loftiest but most circumscribed renown, as the profoundest of thinkers. For by philosophers Shakespeare is not adored, as the great man of tragedy and comedy: "Off with his head; so much for Buckingham!" This sort of rant, interlined by another hand, brings down the house—those mistaken souls, who dream of Shakespeare as a mere man of Richard the Third humps and Macbeth daggers. But it is those deep, far-away things in him; those occasional flashings-forth of the intuitive Truth in him; those short, quick probings at the very axis of reality,— these are the things that make Shakespeare, Shakespeare. Through the mouths of the dark characters of Hamlet, Timon, Lear, and Iago, he craftily says, or sometimes insinuates the things which we feel to be so terrifically true that it were all but madness for any good man, in his own proper character, to utter, or even hint of them. Tormented into desperation, Lear, the frantic king, tears off the mask, and speaks the same madness of vital truth. But, as I before said, it is the least part of genius that attracts admiration. And so, much of the blind, unbridled admiration that has been heaped upon Shakespeare has been lavished upon the least part of him. And few of his endless commentators and critics seem to have remembered, or even perceived, that the immediate products of a great mind are not so great as that undeveloped and sometimes undevelopable yet dimly-discernible greatness to which those immediate products are but the infallible indices. In Shakespeare's tomb lies infinitely more than Shakespeare ever wrote. And if I magnify Shakespeare, it is not so much for what he did do as for what he did not do, or refrained from doing. For in this world of lies, Truth is forced to fly like a sacred white doe in the woodlands; and only by cunning glimpses will she reveal herself, as in Shakespeare and other masters of the great Art of Telling the Truth, even though it be covertly and by snatches.

But if this view of the all-popular Shakespeare be seldom taken by his readers, and if very few who extol him have ever read him deeply, or, perhaps, only have seen him on the tricky stage (which alone made, and is still making him, his mere mob renown)—if few men have time, or patience, or palate, for the spiritual truth as it is in that great genius—it is then no matter of surprise that in a contemporaneous age Nathaniel Hawthorne is a man as yet almost utterly mistaken among men. Here and there, in some quiet armchair in the noisy town, or some deep nook among the noiseless mountains, he may be appreciated for something of what he is. But unlike Shakespeare, who was forced to the contrary course by circumstances, Hawthorne (either from simple disinclination, or else from inaptitude) refrains from all the popularizing noise and show of broad farce and blood-besmeared tragedy; content with the still, rich utterance of a great intellect in repose, and which sends few thoughts into circulation, except they be arterialized at his large warm lungs, and expanded in his honest heart.

Nor need you fix upon that blackness in him, if it suit you not. Nor, indeed, will all readers discern it; for it is, mostly, insinuated to those who may best understand it, and account for it; it is not obtruded upon everyone alike.

Some may start to read of Shakespeare and Hawthorne on the same page. They may say that if an illustration were needed, a lesser light might have sufficed to elucidate this Hawthorne, this small man of yesterday. But I am not willingly one of those who, as touching Shakespeare at least, exemplify the maxim of Rochefoucauld,[3] that "we exalt the reputation of some, in order to depress that of others"—who, to teach all noble-souled aspirants that there is no hope for them, pronounce Shakespeare absolutely unapproachable. But Shakespeare has been approached. There are minds that have gone as far as Shakespeare into the universe. And hardly a mortal man, who, at some time or other, has not felt as great thoughts in him as any you will find in Hamlet. We must not inferentially malign mankind for the sake of any one man, whoever he may be. This is too cheap a purchase of contentment for conscious mediocrity to make. Besides, this absolute and unconditional adoration of Shakespeare has grown to be a part of our Anglo-Saxon superstitions. The Thirty-Nine Articles are now forty. Intolerance has come to exist in this matter. You must believe in Shakespeare's unapproachability, or quit the country. But what sort of a belief is this for an American, a man who is bound to carry republican progressiveness into Literature as well as into Life? Believe me, my friends, that men not very much inferior to Shakespeare are this day being born on the banks of the Ohio. And the day will come when you shall say, Who reads a book by an Englishman that is a modern? The great mistake seems to be, that even with those Americans who look forward to the coming of a great literary genius among us, they somehow fancy he will come in the costume of Queen Elizabeth's day; be a writer of dramas founded upon old English history or the tales of Boccaccio.[4] Whereas, great geniuses are parts of the times, they themselves are the times, and possess a corresponding coloring. It is of a piece with the Jews,

[3] François Duc de La Rochefoucauld (1613–1680), French courtier and moralist. His *Maximes* were published in 1665.
[4] Giovanni Boccaccio (1313–1375), Italian writer and poet. Several of Shakespeare's plays were based upon his tales.

who, while their Shiloh was meekly walking in their streets, were still praying for his magnificent coming; looking for him in a chariot, who was already among them on an ass. Nor must we forget that, in his own lifetime, Shakespeare was not Shakespeare, but only Master William Shakespeare of the shrewd, thriving business firm of Condell, Shakespeare and Co., proprietors of the Globe Theater in London; and by a courtly author, of the name of Chettle, was looked at as an "upstart crow," beautified "with other birds' feathers." [5] For, mark it well, imitation is often the first charge brought against originality. Why this is so, there is not space to set forth here. You must have plenty of sea-room to tell the Truth in; especially when it seems to have an aspect of newness, as America did in 1492, though it was then just as old, and perhaps older than Asia, only those sagacious philosophers, the common sailors, had never seen it before, swearing it was all water and moonshine there.

Now I do not say that Nathaniel of Salem is a greater man than William of Avon, or as great. But the difference between the two men is by no means immeasurable. Not a very great deal more, and Nathaniel were verily William.

This, too, I mean: that if Shakespeare has not been equaled, give the world time, and he is sure to be surpassed in one hemisphere or the other. Nor will it at all do to say that the world is getting gray and grizzled now, and has lost that fresh charm which she wore of old, and by virtue of which the great poets of past times made themselves what we esteem them to be. Not so. The world is as young today as when it was created; and this Vermont morning dew is as wet to my feet as Eden's dew to Adam's. Nor has nature been all over ransacked by our progenitors, so that no new charms and mysteries remain for this latter generation to find. Far from it. The trillionth part has not yet been said; and all that has been said but multiplies the avenues to what remains to be said. It is not so much paucity as superabundance of material that seems to incapacitate modern authors.

Let America, then, prize and cherish her writers; yea, let her glorify them. They are not so many in number as to exhaust her goodwill. And while she has good kith and kin of her own to take to her bosom, let her not lavish her embraces upon the household of an alien. For believe it or not, England, after all, is in many things an alien to us. China has more bonds of real love for us than she. But even were there no strong literary individualities among us, as there are some dozens at least, nevertheless, let America first praise mediocrity even, in her children, before she praises (for everywhere, merit demands acknowledgment from everyone) the best excellence in the children of any other land. Let her own authors, I say, have the priority of appreciation. I was much pleased with

[5] Henry Chettle (ca. 1560–ca. 1607), English printer and playwright. Melville unknowingly is unfair to Chettle, who was merely the publisher of Robert Greene's (1560–1592) *Groatsworth of Wit* (1592) in which the statement concerning Shakespeare is found.

a hot-headed Carolina cousin of mine, who once said, "If there were no other American to stand by, in literature, why, then, I would stand by Pop Emmons and his *Fredoniad*,[6] and till a better epic came along, swear it was not very far behind the Iliad." Take away the words, and in spirit he was sound.

Not that American genius needs patronage in order to expand. For that explosive sort of stuff will expand though screwed up in a vise, and burst it, though it were triple steel. It is for the nation's sake, and not for her authors' sake, that I would have America be heedful of the increasing greatness among her writers. For how great the shame, if other nations should be before her, in crowning her heroes of the pen! But this is almost the case now. American authors have received more just and discriminating praise (however loftily and ridiculously given, in certain cases) even from some Englishmen, than from their own countrymen. There are hardly five critics in America; and several of them are asleep. As for patronage, it is the American author who now patronizes his country, and not his country him. And if at times some among them appeal to the people for more recognition, it is not always with selfish motives, but patriotic ones.

It is true that but few of them as yet have evinced that decided originality which merits great praise. But that graceful writer who perhaps of all Americans has received the most plaudits from his own country for his productions—that very popular and amiable writer, however good and self-reliant in many things, perhaps owes his chief reputation to the self-acknowledged imitation of a foreign model, and to the studied avoidance of all topics but smooth ones.[7] But it is better to fail in originality than to succeed in imitation. He who has never failed somewhere, that man cannot be great. Failure is the true test of greatness. And if it be said that continual success is a proof that a man wisely knows his powers, it is only to be added that, in that case, he knows them to be small. Let us believe it, then, once for all, that there is no hope for us in these smooth, pleasing writers that know their powers. Without malice, but to speak the plain fact, they but furnish an appendix to Goldsmith and other English authors. And we want no American Goldsmiths, nay, we want no American Miltons. It were the vilest thing you could say of a true American author that he were an American Tompkins. Call him an American and have done, for you cannot say a nobler thing of him. But it is not meant that all American writers should studiously cleave to nationality in their writings; only this, no American writer should write like an Englishman or a Frenchman; let him write like a man, for then he will be sure to write like an American. Let us away with this leaven of literary flunkeyism toward England. If either must play the flunkey in this thing, let England do it, not us. While we are rapidly preparing for that political supremacy among the nations which prophetically awaits us at the close of

[6] The *Fredoniad; or Independence Preserved—an Epic Poem of the War of 1812* was written by Richard Emmons, M.D., and is notorious for its bathos.
[7] Probably Washington Irving.

the present century, in a literary point of view, we are deplorably unpre-
pared for it; and we seem studious to remain so. Hitherto, reasons might
have existed why this should be; but no good reason exists now. And all
that is requisite to amendment in this matter is simply this: that while
fully acknowledging all excellence everywhere, we should refrain from
unduly lauding foreign writers, and, at the same time, duly recognize the
meritorious writers, that are our own; those writers who breathe that
unshackled, democratic spirit of Christianity in all things, which now
takes the practical lead in this world, though at the same time led by
ourselves—us Americans. Let us boldly condemn all imitation, though it
comes to us graceful and fragrant as the morning; and foster all originality,
though at first it be crabbed and ugly as our own pine knots. And if any
of our authors fail, or seem to fail, then, in the words of my Carolina
cousin, let us clap him on the shoulder and back him against all Europe
for his second round. The truth is, that in one point of view this matter of
a national literature has come to such a pass with us, that in some sense
we must turn bullies, else the day is lost, or superiority so far beyond us,
that we can hardly say it will ever be ours.

  And now, my countrymen, as an excellent author of your own flesh and
blood—an unimitating, and, perhaps, in his way, an inimitable man—
whom better can I commend to you, in the first place, than Nathaniel
Hawthorne? He is one of the new, and far better generation of your
writers. The smell of your beeches and hemlocks is upon him; your own
broad prairies are in his soul; and if you travel away inland into his deep
and noble nature, you will hear the far roar of his Niagara. Give not over
to future generations the glad duty of acknowledging him for what he is.
Take that joy to yourself, in your own generation; and so shall he feel
those grateful impulses on him, that may possibly prompt him to the full
flower of some still greater achievement in your eyes. And by confessing
him you thereby confess others; you brace the whole brotherhood. For
genius, all over the world, stands hand in hand, and one shock of recognition runs the whole circle round.

  In treating of Hawthorne, or rather of Hawthorne in his writings (for I
never saw the man; and in the chances of a quiet plantation life, remote
from his haunts, perhaps never shall); in treating of his works, I say, I
have thus far omitted all mention of his *Twice-Told Tales* and *Scarlet
Letter*. Both are excellent, but full of such manifold, strange, and diffusive
beauties, that time would all but fail me to point the half of them out.
But there are things in those two books which, had they been written
in England a century ago, Nathaniel Hawthorne had utterly displaced
many of the bright names we now revere on authority. But I am content
to leave Hawthorne to himself, and to the infallible finding of posterity;
and however great may be the praise I have bestowed upon him, I feel
that in so doing I have served and honored myself, rather than him. For,
at bottom, great excellence is praise enough to itself; but the feeling of a
sincere and appreciative love and admiration toward it, this is relieved by
utterance, and warm, honest praise ever leaves a pleasant flavor in the

mouth; and it is an honorable thing to confess to what is honorable in others.

But I cannot leave my subject yet. No man can read a fine author, and relish him to his very bones while he reads, without subsequently fancying to himself some ideal image of the man and his mind. And if you rightly look for it, you will almost always find that the author himself has somewhere furnished you with his own picture. For poets (whether in prose or verse), being painters by nature, are like their brethren of the pencil, the true portrait-painters, who, in the multitude of likenesses to be sketched, do not invariably omit their own; and in all high instances, they paint them without any vanity, though at times with a lurking something that would take several pages to properly define.

I submit it, then, to those best acquainted with the man personally, whether the following is not Nathaniel Hawthorne; and to himself, whether something involved in it does not express the temper of his mind —that lasting temper of all true, candid men—a seeker, not a finder yet:

> A man now entered, in neglected attire, with the aspect of a thinker, but somewhat too roughhewn and brawny for a scholar. His face was full of sturdy vigor, with some finer and keener attribute beneath; though harsh at first, it was tempered with the glow of a large, warm heart, which had force enough to heat his powerful intellect through and through. He advanced to the Intelligencer, and looked at him with a glance of such stern sincerity, that perhaps few secrets were beyond its scope.
> "I seek for Truth," said he.

Twenty-four hours have elapsed since writing the foregoing. I have just returned from the haymow, charged more and more with love and admiration of Hawthorne. For I have just been gleaning through the *Mosses*, picking up many things here and there that had previously escaped me. And I found that but to glean after this man is better than to be in at the harvest of others. To be frank (though, perhaps, rather foolish), notwithstanding what I wrote yesterday of these *Mosses*, I had not then culled them all; but had, nevertheless, been sufficiently sensible of the subtle essence in them as to write as I did. To what infinite height of loving wonder and admiration I may yet be borne, when by repeatedly banqueting on these *Mosses* I shall have thoroughly incorporated their whole stuff into my being—that, I cannot tell. But already I feel that this Hawthorne has dropped germinous seeds into my soul. He expands and deepens down, the more I contemplate him; and further and further, shoots his strong New England roots into the hot soil in my Southern soul.

By careful reference to the table of contents, I now find that I have gone through all the sketches; but that when I yesterday wrote, I had not at all read two particular pieces, to which I now desire to call special attention—*A Select Party* and *Young Goodman Brown*. Here, be it said to all those whom this poor fugitive scrawl of mine may tempt to the perusal of the *Mosses*, that they must on no account suffer themselves to be trifled with, disappointed, or deceived by the triviality of many of the titles to these sketches. For in more than one instance the title utterly belies the piece. It is as if rustic demijohns containing the very best and costliest of Falernian and Tokay were labeled "Cider," "Perry," and "Elderberry wine." The truth seems to be, that like many other geniuses, this Man of Mosses takes great delight in hoodwinking the world—at least, with respect to himself. Personally, I doubt not that he rather prefers to be generally esteemed but a so-so sort of author; being willing to reserve the thorough and acute appreciation of what he is, to that party most qualified to judge—that is, to himself. Besides, at the bottom of their natures, men like Hawthorne, in many things, deem the plaudits of the public such strong presumptive evidence of mediocrity in the object of them, that it would in some degree render them doubtful of their own powers did they hear much and vociferous braying concerning them in the public pastures. True, I have been braying myself (if you please to be witty enough to have it so), but then I claim to be the first that has so brayed in this particular matter; and, therefore, while pleading guilty to the charge, still claim all the merit due to originality.

But with whatever motive, playful or profound, Nathaniel Hawthorne has chosen to entitle his pieces in the manner he has, it is certain that some of them are directly calculated to deceive—egregiously deceive, the superficial skimmer of pages. To be downright and candid once more, let me cheerfully say that two of these titles did dolefully dupe no less an eager-eyed reader than myself; and that, too, after I had been impressed with a sense of the great depth and breadth of this American man. "Who in the name of thunder" (as the country people say in this neighborhood), "who in the name of thunder would anticipate any marvel in a piece entitled *Young Goodman Brown?*" You would, of course, suppose that it was a simple little tale, intended as a supplement to *Goody Two Shoes*. Whereas, it is deep as Dante; nor can you finish it without addressing the author in his own words—"It shall be yours to penetrate, in every bosom, the deep mystery of sin." . . . And with Young Goodman, too, in allegorical pursuit of his Puritan wife, you cry out in your anguish:

> "Faith!" shouted Goodman Brown, in a voice of agony and desperation; and the echoes of the forest mocked him, crying, "Faith! Faith!" as if bewildered wretches were seeking her all through the wilderness.

Now this same piece entitled *Young Goodman Brown* is one of the two that I had not all read yesterday; and I allude to it now, because it is, in itself, such a strong, positive illustration of the blackness in Hawthorne which I had assumed from the mere occasional shadows of it, as revealed in several of the other sketches. But had I previously perused *Young Goodman Brown*, I should have been at no pains to draw the conclusion, which I came to at a time when I was ignorant that the book contained one such direct and unqualified manifestation of it.

The other piece of the two referred to is entitled *A Select Party*, which, in my first simplicity upon originally taking hold of the book, I fancied must treat of some pumpkin-pie party in old Salem; or some chowder party on Cape Cod. Whereas, by all the gods of Peedee, it is the sweetest and sublimest thing that has been written since Spenser wrote. Nay, there is nothing in Spenser that surpasses it, perhaps nothing that equals it. And the test is this. Read any canto in *The Faerie Queene* and then read *A Select Party*, and decide which pleases you most, that is, if you are qualified to judge. Do not be frightened at this; for when Spenser was alive, he was thought of very much as Hawthorne is now—was generally accounted just such a "gentle," harmless man. It may be that to common eyes the sublimity of Hawthorne seems lost in his sweetness,—as perhaps in that same *Select Party* of his; for whom he has builded so august a dome of sunset clouds, and served them on richer plate than Belshazzar when he banqueted his lords in Babylon.

But my chief business now is to point out a particular page in this piece, having reference to an honored guest, who under the name of the Master Genius but in the guise "of a young man of poor attire, with no insignia of rank or acknowledged eminence," is introduced to the Man of Fancy, who is the giver of the feast. Now, the page having reference to this Master Genius so happily expresses much of what I yesterday wrote, touching the coming of the literary Shiloh of America, that I cannot but be charmed by the coincidence; especially when it shows such a parity of ideas, at least in this one point, between a man like Hawthorne and a man like me.

And here let me throw out another conceit of mine touching this American Shiloh, or Master Genius, as Hawthorne calls him. May it not be that this commanding mind has not been, is not, and never will be, individually developed in any one man? And would it, indeed, appear so unreasonable to suppose that this great fullness and overflowing may be, or may be destined to be, shared by a plurality of men of genius? Surely, to take the very greatest example on record, Shakespeare cannot be regarded as in himself the concretion of all the genius of his time; nor as so immeasurably beyond Marlowe, Webster, Ford, Beaumont, Jonson, that these great men can be said to share none of his power? For one, I conceive that there were dramatists in Elizabeth's day, between whom and Shakespeare the distance was by no means great. Let anyone, hereto little acquainted with those neglected old authors, for the first time read them thoroughly, or even read Charles Lamb's *Specimens* of them, and he will be amazed at the wondrous ability of those Anaks of men, and shocked at this renewed example of the fact that Fortune has more to do with fame than merit,—though without merit, lasting fame there can be none.

Nevertheless, it would argue too ill of my country were this maxim to hold good concerning Nathaniel Hawthorne, a man who already in some few minds has shed "such a light as never illuminates the earth save when a great heart burns as the household fire of a grand intellect."

The words are his—in the *Select Party*; and they are a magnificent setting to a coincident sentiment of my own, but ramblingly expressed yesterday, in reference to himself. Gainsay it who will, as I now write, I am

Posterity speaking by proxy—and after-times will make it more than good, when I declare that the American who up to the present day has evinced, in literature, the largest brain with the largest heart, that man is Nathaniel Hawthorne. Moreover, that whatever Nathaniel Hawthorne may here-after write, *Mosses from an Old Manse* will be ultimately accounted his masterpiece. For there is a sure, though secret sign in some works which proves the culmination of the powers (only the developable ones, how-ever) that produced them. But I am by no means desirous of the glory of a prophet. I pray Heaven that Hawthorne may yet prove me an im-postor in this prediction. Especially, as I somehow cling to the strange fancy that, in all men, hiddenly reside certain wondrous, occult properties —as in some plants and minerals—which by some happy but very rare accident (as bronze was discovered by the melting of the iron and brass at the burning of Corinth) may chance to be called forth here on earth; not entirely waiting for their better discovery in the more congenial, blessed atmosphere of heaven.

Once more—for it is hard to be finite upon an infinite subject, and all subjects are infinite. By some people this entire scrawl of mine may be esteemed altogether unnecessary, inasmuch "as years ago" (they may say) "we found out the rich and rare stuff in this Hawthorne, whom you now parade forth, as if only you *yourself* were the discoverer of this Portuguese diamond in your literature." But even granting all this—and adding to it the assumption that the books of Hawthorne have sold by the five thou-sand—what does that signify? They should be sold by the hundred thou-sand; and read by the million; and admired by every one who is capable of admiration.

HERMAN MELVILLE

From THE CONFIDENCE MAN [1]
(1857)

CHAPTER XIV

As THE last chapter was begun with a reminder looking forward, so the present must consist of one glancing backward.

To some, it may raise a degree of surprise that one so full of confidence, as the merchant has throughout shown himself, up to the moment of his late sudden impulsiveness, should, in that instance, have betrayed such a depth of discontent. He may be thought inconsistent, and even so he is. But for this, is the author to be blamed? True, it may be urged that there is nothing a writer of fiction should more carefully see to, as there is nothing a sensible reader will more carefully look for, than that, in the depiction of any character, its consistency should be preserved. But this, though at first blush seeming reasonable enough, may, upon a closer view, prove not so much so. For how does it couple with another requirement—equally insisted upon, perhaps—that, while to all fiction is allowed some play of invention, yet, fiction based on fact should never be contradictory to it; and is it not a fact that, in real life, a consistent character is a *rara avis?* [2] Which being so, the distaste of readers to the contrary sort in books, can hardly arise from any sense of their untrueness. It may rather be from perplexity as to understanding them. But if the acutest sage be often at his wits' ends to understand living character, shall those who are not sages expect to run and read character in those mere phantoms which flit along a page, like shadows along a wall? That fiction, where every character can, by reason of its consistency, be comprehended at a glance, either exhibits but sections of character, making them appear for wholes, or else is very untrue to reality; while, on the other hand, that author who draws a character, even though to common view incongruous in its parts, as the flying-squirrel, and, at different periods, as much at variance with itself as the butterfly is with the caterpillar into which it changes, may yet, in so doing, be not false but faithful to facts.

If reason be judge, no writer has produced such inconsistent characters as nature herself has. It must call for no small sagacity in a reader unerringly to discriminate in a novel between the inconsistencies of conception and those of life as elsewhere. Experience is the only guide here; but as no one man can be coextensive with *what is,* it may be unwise in every case to rest upon it. When the duck-billed beaver of Australia was first

[1] New York, 1857.
[2] Literally, a "rare bird."

brought stuffed to England, the naturalists, appealing to their classifications, maintained that there was, in reality, no such creature; the bill in
the specimen must needs be, in some way, artificially stuck on.

But let nature, to the perplexity of the naturalists, produce her duck-
billed beavers as she may, lesser authors, some may hold, have no business
to be perplexing readers with duck-billed characters. Always, they should
represent human nature not in obscurity, but transparency, which, indeed,
is the practice with most novelists, and is, perhaps, in certain cases, some
way felt to be a kind of honour rendered by them to their kind. But
whether it involve honour or otherwise might be mooted, considering that,
if these waters of human nature can be so readily seen through, it may be
either that they are very pure or very shallow. Upon the whole, it might
rather be thought, that he, who, in view of its inconsistencies, says of human nature the same that, in view of its contrasts, is said of the divine
nature, that it is past finding out, thereby evinces a better appreciation of
it than he who, by always representing it in a clear light, leaves it to be
inferred that he clearly knows all about it.

But though there is a prejudice against inconsistent characters in books,
yet the prejudice bears the other way, when what seemed at first their
inconsistency, afterward, by the skill of the writer, turns out to be their
good keeping. The great masters excel in nothing so much as in this very
particular. They challenge astonishment at the tangled web of some character, and then raise admiration still greater at their satisfactory unravel-
ling of it; in this way throwing open, sometimes to the understanding even
of school misses, the last complications of that spirit which is affirmed by
its Creator to be fearfully and wonderfully made.

At least, something like this is claimed for certain psychological novelists; nor will the claim be here disputed. Yet, as touching this point, it
may prove suggestive, that all those sallies of ingenuity, having for their
end the revelation of human nature on fixed principles, have, by the best
judges, been excluded with contempt from the ranks of the sciences—palmistry, physiognomy, phrenology, psychology. Likewise, the fact, that in
all ages such conflicting views have, by the most eminent minds, been
taken of mankind, would, as with other topics, seem some presumption
of a pretty general and pretty thorough ignorance of it. Which may appear the less improbable if it be considered that, after poring over the
best novels professing to portray human nature, the studious youth will
still run risk of being too often at fault upon actually entering the world;
whereas, had he been furnished with a true delineation, it ought to fare
with him something as with a stranger entering, map in hand, Boston
town; the streets may be very crooked, he may often pause; but, thanks
to his true map, he does not hopelessly lose his way. Nor, to this comparison, can it be an adequate objection, that the twistings of the town are
always the same, and those of human nature subject to variation. The
grand points of human nature are the same to-day as they were a thousand years ago. The only variability in them is in expression, not in feature.

But as, in spite of seeming discouragement, some mathematicians are yet in hopes of hitting upon an exact method of determining the longitude, the more earnest psychologists may, in the face of previous failures, still cherish expectations with regard to some mode of infallibly discovering the heart of man.

But enough has been said by way of apology for whatever may have seemed amiss or obscure in the character of the merchant; so nothing remains but to turn to our comedy, or, rather, to pass from the comedy of thought to that of action.

Chapter XXXIII

But ere be given the rather grave story of Charlemont, a reply must in civility be made to a certain voice which methinks I hear, that, in view of past chapters, and more particularly the last, where certain antics appear, exclaims: How unreal all this is! Who did ever dress or act like your cosmopolitan? And who, it might be returned, did ever dress or act like harlequin?

Strange, that in a work of amusement, this severe fidelity to real life should be exacted by anyone, who, by taking up such a work, sufficiently shows that he is not unwilling to drop real life, and turn, for a time, to something different. Yes, it is, indeed, strange that anyone should clamour for the thing he is weary of; that anyone, who, for any cause, finds real life dull, should yet demand of him who is to divert his attention from it, that he should be true to that dullness.

There is another class, and with this class we side, who sit down to a work of amusement tolerantly as they sit at a play, and with much the same expectations and feelings. They look that fancy shall evoke scenes different from those of the same old crowd round the custom-house counter, and same old dishes on the boarding-house table, with characters unlike those of the same old acquaintances they meet in the same old way every day in the same old street. And as, in real life, the proprieties will not allow people to act out themselves with that unreserve permitted to the stage; so, in books of fiction, they look not only for more entertainment, but, at bottom, even for more reality, than real life itself can show. Thus, though they want novelty, they want nature, too; but nature unfettered, exhilarated, in effect transformed. In this way of thinking, the people in a fiction, like the people in a play, must dress as nobody exactly dresses, talk as nobody exactly talks, act as nobody exactly acts. It is with fiction as with religion: it should present another world, and yet one to which we feel the tie.

If, then, something is to be pardoned to well-meant endeavour, surely a little is to be allowed to that writer who, in all his scenes, does but seek to minister to what, as he understands it, is the implied wish of the more indulgent lovers of entertainment, before whom harlequin can never appear in a coat too parti-coloured, or cut capers too fantastic.

One word more. Though everyone knows how bootless it is to be in all cases vindicating one's self, never mind how convinced one may be that he is never in the wrong; yet, so precious to man is the approbation of his kind, that to rest, though but under an imaginary censure applied to but a work of imagination, is no easy thing. The mention of this weakness will explain why all such readers as may think they perceive something inharmonious between the boisterous hilarity of the cosmopolitan with the bristling cynic, and his restrained good-nature with the boon companion, are now referred to that chapter where some similar apparent inconsistency in another character is, on general principles, modestly endeavoured to be apologised for.

CHAPTER XLIV

'Quite an Original': a phrase, we fancy, rather oftener used by the young, or the unlearned, or the untravelled, than by the old, or the well-read, or the man who has made the grand tour. Certainly, the sense of originality exists at its highest in an infant, and probably at its lowest in him who has completed the circle of the sciences.

As for original characters in fiction, a grateful reader will, on meeting with one, keep the anniversary of that day. True, we sometimes hear of an author who, at one creation, produces some two or three score such characters; it may be possible. But they can hardly be original in the sense that Hamlet is, or Don Quixote, or Milton's Satan. That is to say, they are not, in a thorough sense, original at all. They are novel, or singular, or striking, or captivating, or all four at once.

More likely, they are what are called odd characters; but for that, are no more original, than what is called an odd genius, in his way, is. But, if original, whence came they? Or where did the novelist pick them up?

Where does any novelist pick up any character? For the most part, in town, to be sure. Every great town is a kind of man-show, where the novelist goes for his stock, just as the agriculturist goes to the cattle-show for his. But in the one fair, new species of quadrupeds are hardly more rare, than in the other are new species of characters—that is, original ones. Their rarity may still the more appear from this, that, while characters, merely singular, imply but singular forms, so to speak, original ones, truly so, imply original instincts.

In short, a due conception of what is to be held for this sort of personage in fiction would make him almost as much of a prodigy there, as in real history is a new law-giver, a revolutionising philosopher, or the founder of a new religion.

In nearly all the original characters, loosely accounted such in works of invention, there is discernible something prevailingly local, or of the age; which circumstance, of itself, would seem to invalidate the claim, judged by the principles here suggested.

Furthermore, if we consider, what is popularly held to entitle characters in fiction to being deemed original, is but something personal—confined to itself. The character sheds not its characteristic on its surroundings, whereas, the original character, essentially such, is like a revolving

Drummond light, raying away from itself all round it—everything is lit by it, everything starts up to it (mark how it is with Hamlet), so that, in certain minds, there follows upon the adequate conception of such a character, an effect, in its way, akin to that which in Genesis attends upon the beginning of things.

For much the same reason that there is but one planet to one orbit, so can there be but one such original character to one work of invention. Two would conflict to chaos. In this view, to say that there are more than one to a book, is good presumption there is none at all. But for new, singular, striking, odd, eccentric, and all sorts of entertaining and instructive characters, a good fiction may be full of them. To produce such characters, an author, beside other things, must have seen much, and seen through much: to produce but one original character, he must have had much luck.

There would seem but one point in common between this sort of phenomenon in fiction and all other sorts: it cannot be born in the author's imagination—it being as true in literature as in zoology, that all life is from the egg.

In the endeavour to show, if possible, the impropriety of the phrase, *Quite an Original*, as applied by the barber's friends, we have, at unawares, been led into a dissertation bordering upon the prosy, perhaps upon the smoky. If so, the best use the smoke can be turned to, will be, by retiring under cover of it, in good trim as may be, to the story.

NATHANIEL HAWTHORNE

PREFACE TO
THE HOUSE OF THE SEVEN GABLES [1]
(1851)

WHEN A writer calls his work a Romance, it need hardly be observed that he wishes to claim a certain latitude, both as to its fashion and material, which he would not have felt himself entitled to assume had he professed to be writing a Novel. The latter form of composition is presumed to aim at a very minute fidelity, not merely to the possible, but to the probable and ordinary course of man's experience. The former—while, as a work of art, it must rigidly subject itself to laws, and while it sins unpardonably so far as it may swerve aside from the truth of the human heart—has fairly a right to present that truth under circumstances, to a great extent, of the writer's own choosing or creation. If he think fit, also, he may so manage his atmospherical medium as to bring out or mellow the lights and deepen and enrich the shadows of the picture. He will be wise, no doubt, to make a very moderate use of the privileges here stated, and, especially, to mingle the Marvellous rather as a slight, delicate, and evanescent flavor, than as any portion of the actual substance of the dish offered to the public. He can hardly be said, however, to commit a literary crime even if he disregard this caution.

In the present work, the author has proposed to himself—but with what success, fortunately, it is not for him to judge—to keep undeviatingly within his immunities. The point of view in which this tale comes under the Romantic definition lies in the attempt to connect a bygone time with the very present that is flitting away from us. It is a legend prolonging itself, from an epoch now gray in the distance, down into our own broad daylight, and bringing along with it some of its legendary mist, which the reader, according to his pleasure, may either disregard, or allow it to float almost imperceptibly about the characters and events for the sake of a picturesque effect. The narrative, it may be, is woven of so humble a texture as to require this advantage, and, at the same time, to render it the more difficult of attainment.

Many writers lay very great stress upon some definite moral purpose, at which they profess to aim their works. Not to be deficient in this particular, the author has provided himself with a moral,—the truth, namely, that the wrong-doing of one generation lives into the successive ones, and, divesting itself of every temporary advantage, becomes a pure and uncontrollable mischief; and he would feel it a singular gratification if this

[1] Boston, 1851.

307

romance might effectually convince mankind,—or, indeed, any one man,— of the folly of tumbling down an avalanche of ill-gotten gold, or real estate, on the heads of an unfortunate posterity, thereby to maim and crush them, until the accumulated mass shall be scattered abroad in its original atoms. In good faith, however, he is not sufficiently imaginative to flatter himself with the slightest hope of this kind. When romances do really teach anything, or produce any effective operation, it is usually through a far more subtile process than the ostensible one. The author has considered it hardly worth his while, therefore, relentlessly to impale the story with its moral as with an iron rod,—or, rather, as by sticking a pin through a butterfly,—thus at once depriving it of life, and causing it to stiffen in an ungainly and unnatural attitude. A high truth, indeed, fairly, finely, and skilfully wrought out, brightening at every step, and crowning the final development of a work of fiction, may add an artistic glory, but it is never any truer, and seldom any more evident, at the last page than at the first.

The reader may perhaps choose to assign an actual locality to the imaginary events of this narrative. If permitted by the historical connection,— which, though slight, was essential to his plan,—the author would very willingly have avoided anything of this nature. Not to speak of other objections, it exposes the romance to an inflexible and exceedingly dangerous species of criticism, by bringing his fancy-pictures almost into positive contact with the realities of the moment. It has been no part of his object, however, to describe local manners, nor in any way to meddle with the characteristics of a community for whom he cherishes a proper respect and natural regard. He trusts not to be considered as unpardonably offending by laying out a street that infringes upon nobody's private rights, and appropriating a lot of land which had no visible owner, and building a house of materials long in use for constructing castles in the air. The personages of the tale—though they give themselves out to be of ancient stability and considerable prominence—are really of the author's own making, or, at all events, of his own mixing; their virtues can shed no lustre, nor their defects redound, in the remotest degree, to the discredit of the venerable town of which they profess to be inhabitants. He would be glad, therefore, if—especially in the quarter to which he alludes—the book may be read strictly as a Romance, having a great deal more to do with the clouds overhead than with any portion of the actual soil of the County of Essex.

NATHANIEL HAWTHORNE

PREFACE TO
THE BLITHEDALE ROMANCE [1]
(1852)

IN THE "Blithedale" of this volume many readers will, probably, suspect a faint and not very faithful shadowing of Brook Farm,[2] in Roxbury, which (now a little more than ten years ago) was occupied and cultivated by a company of socialists. The author does not wish to deny that he had this community in his mind, and that (having had the good fortune, for a time, to be personally connected with it) he has occasionally availed himself of his actual reminiscences, in the hope of giving a more life-like tint to the fancy-sketch in the following pages. He begs it to be understood, however, that he has considered the institution itself as not less fairly the subject of fictitious handling than the imaginary personages whom he has introduced there. His whole treatment of the affair is altogether incidental to the main purpose of the romance; nor does he put forward the slightest pretensions to illustrate a theory, or elicit a conclusion, favorable or otherwise, in respect to socialism.

In short, his present concern with the socialist community is merely to establish a theatre, a little removed from the highway of ordinary travel, where the creatures of his brain may play their phantasmagorical antics, without exposing them to too close a comparison with the actual events of real lives. In the old countries, with which fiction has long been conversant, a certain conventional privilege seems to be awarded to the romancer; his work is not put exactly side by side with nature; and he is allowed a license with regard to every-day probability, in view of the improved effects which he is bound to produce thereby. Among ourselves, on the contrary, there is as yet no such Faery Land, so like the real world, that, in a suitable remoteness, one cannot well tell the difference, but with an atmosphere of strange enchantment, beheld through which the inhabitants have a propriety of their own. This atmosphere is what the American romancer needs. In its absence, the beings of imagination are compelled to show themselves in the same category as actually living mortals; a necessity that generally renders the paint and pasteboard of their composition but too painfully discernible. With the idea of partially obviating this difficulty (the sense of which has always pressed very

---

[1] Boston, 1852.

[2] One of the most notable ventures in community living in America was Brook Farm (1841–1847), a cooperative community near West Roxbury, Mass., under the leadership of George Ripley. At one time or another during its short existence most of the chief figures of the transcendentalist movement were associated with it. Hawthorne joined the community for a short time in 1841.

heavily upon him), the author has ventured to make free with his old and affectionately remembered home at Brook Farm, as being certainly the most romantic episode of his own life,—essentially a day-dream, and yet a fact,—and thus offering an available foothold between fiction and reality. Furthermore, the scene was in good keeping with the personages whom he desired to introduce.

These characters, he feels it right to say, are entirely fictitious. It would, indeed (considering how few amiable qualities he distributes among his imaginary progeny), be a most grievous wrong to his former excellent associates, were the author to allow it to be supposed that he has been sketching any of their likenesses. Had he attempted it, they would at least have recognized the touches of a friendly pencil. But he has done nothing of the kind. The self-concentrated Philanthropist; the high-spirited Woman, bruising herself against the narrow limitations of her sex; the weakly Maiden, whose tremulous nerves endow her with Sibylline attributes; the Minor Poet, beginning life with strenuous aspirations, which die out with his youthful fervor,—all these might have been looked for at Brook Farm, but, by some accident, never made their appearance there.

The author cannot close his reference to this subject, without expressing a most earnest wish that some one of the many cultivated and philosophic minds, which took an interest in that enterprise, might now give the world its history. Ripley, with whom rests the honorable paternity of the institution, Dana, Dwight, Channing, Burton, Parker, for instance,—with others, whom he dares not name, because they veil themselves from the public eye,—among these is the ability to convey both the outward narrative and the inner truth and spirit of the whole affair, together with the lessons which those years of thought and toil must have elaborated, for the behoof of future experimentalists. Even the brilliant Howadji might find as rich a theme in his youthful reminiscences of Brook Farm, and a more novel one,—close at hand as it lies,—than those which he has since made so distant a pilgrimage to seek, in Syria and along the current of the Nile.[3]

[3] *Nile Notes of a Howadji* (1851) and *The Howadji in Syria* (1852) were published by George William Curtis, who, like Hawthorne, was once a member of Brook Farm.

JAMES RUSSELL LOWELL

THE FUNCTION OF THE POET [1]
(1855)

WHETHER, AS some philosophers assume, we possess only the fragments of a great cycle of knowledge in whose centre stood the primeval man in friendly relations with the powers of the universe, and build our hovels out of the ruins of our ancestral palace; or whether, according to the development theory of others, we are rising gradually, and have come up out of an atom instead of descending from an Adam, so that the proudest pedigree might run up to a barnacle or a zoöphyte at last, are questions that will keep for a good many centuries yet. Confining myself to what little we can learn from history, we find tribes rising slowly out of barbarism to a higher or lower point of culture and civility, and everywhere the poet also is found, under one name or other, changing in certain outward respects, but essentially the same.

And however far we go back, we shall find this also—that the poet and the priest were united originally in the same person; which means that the poet was he who was conscious of the world of spirit as well as that of sense, and was the ambassador of the gods to men. This was his highest function, and hence his name of "seer." He was the discoverer and declarer of the perennial beneath the deciduous. His were the *epea pteroenta*, the true "winged words" that could fly down the unexplored future and carry the names of ancestral heroes, of the brave and wise and good. It was thus that the poet could reward virtue, and, by and by, as society grew more complex, could burn in the brand of shame. This is Homer's character of Demodocus, in the eighth book of the "Odyssey," "whom the Muse loved and gave the good and ill"—the gift of conferring good or evil immortality. The first histories were in verse; and sung as they were at feasts and gatherings of the people, they awoke in men the desire of fame, which is the first promoter of courage and self-trust, because it teaches men by degrees to appeal from the present to the future. We may fancy what the influence of the early epics was when they were recited to men who claimed the heroes celebrated in them for their ancestors, by what Bouchardon,[2] the sculptor, said, only two centuries ago: "When I read Homer, I feel as if I were twenty feet high." Nor have poets lost their power over the future in modern times. Dante lifts up by the hair the face of some petty traitor, the Smith or Brown of some provin-

---

[1] This was the concluding lecture in the course which Lowell read before the Lowell Institute in the winter of 1855. First published in *Century*, XXV (1894), 432.
[2] Edme Bouchardon (1698–1762), French sculptor.

cial Italian town, lets the fire of his Inferno glare upon it for a moment, and it is printed forever on the memory of mankind. The historians may iron out the shoulders of Richard the Third as smooth as they can, they will never get over the wrench that Shakespeare gave them.

The peculiarity of almost all early literature is that it seems to have a double meaning, that, underneath its natural, we find ourselves continually seeing or suspecting a supernatural meaning. In the older epics the characters seem to be half typical and only half historical. Thus did the early poets endeavor to make realities out of appearances; for, except a few typical men in whom certain ideas get embodied, the generations of mankind are mere apparitions who come out of the dark for a purposeless moment, and reënter the dark again after they have performed the nothing they came for.

Gradually, however, the poet as the "seer" became secondary to the "maker." His office became that of entertainer rather than teacher. But always something of the old tradition was kept alive. And if he has now come to be looked upon merely as the best expresser, the gift of seeing is implied as necessarily antecedent to that, and of seeing very deep, too. If any man would seem to have written without any conscious moral, that man is Shakespeare. But that must be a dull sense, indeed, which does not see through his tragic—yes, and his comic—masks awful eyes that flame with something intenser and deeper than a mere scenic meaning—a meaning out of the great deep that is behind and beyond all human and merely personal character. Nor was Shakespeare himself unconscious of his place as a teacher and profound moralist: witness that sonnet in which he bewails his having neglected sometimes the errand that was laid upon him:

> Alas, 't is true I have gone here and there,
> And made myself a motley to the view,
> Gored mine own thoughts, sold cheap what is most dear,
> Made old offences of affections new;
> Most true it is that I have look'd on truth
> Askance and strangely;

the application of which is made clear by the next sonnet, in which he distinctly alludes to his profession.

There is this unmistakable stamp on all the great poets—that, however in little things they may fall below themselves, whenever there comes a great and noble thing to say, they say it greatly and nobly, and bear themselves most easily in the royalties of thought and language. There is not a mature play of Shakespeare's in which great ideas do not jut up in mountainous permanence, marking forever the boundary of provinces of thought, and known afar to many kindreds of men.

And it is for this kind of sight, which we call insight, and not for any faculty of observation and description, that we value the poet. It is in proportion as he has this that he is an adequate expresser, and not a juggler with words. It is by means of this that for every generation of man he plays the part of "namer." Before him, as before Adam, the creation passes to be named anew: first the material world; then the world of passions and emotions; then the world of ideas. But whenever a great imagination comes, however it may delight itself with imaging the outward beauty of things, however it may seem to flow thoughtlessly away in music like a brook, yet the shadow of heaven lies also in its depth beneath the shadow of earth. Continually the visible universe suggests the invisible. We are forever feeling this in Shakespeare. His imagination went down to the very bases of things, and while his characters are the most natural that poet ever created, they are also perfectly ideal, and are more truly the personifications of abstract thoughts and passions than those of any allegorical writer whatever.

Even in what seems so purely a picturesque poem as the "Iliad," we feel something of this. Beholding as Homer did, from the tower of contemplation, the eternal mutability and nothing permanent but change, he must look underneath the show for the reality. Great captains and conquerors came forth out of the eternal silence, entered it again with their trampling hosts, and shoutings, and trumpet-blasts, and were as utterly gone as those echoes of their deeds which he sang, and which faded with the last sound of his voice and the last tremble of his lyre. History relating outward events alone was an unmeaning gossip, with the world for a village. This life could only become other than phantasmagoric, could only become real, as it stood related to something that was higher and permanent. Hence the idea of Fate, of a higher power unseen—that shadow, as of an eagle circling to its swoop, which flits stealthily and swiftly across the windy plains of Troy. In the "Odyssey" we find pure allegory.

Now, under all these names—praiser, seer, soothsayer—we find the same idea lurking. The poet is he who can best see and best say what is ideal—what belongs to the world of soul and of beauty. Whether he celebrate the brave and good man, or the gods, or the beautiful as it appears in man or nature, something of a religious character still clings to him; he is the revealer of Deity. He may be unconscious of his mission; he may be false to it; but in proportion as he is a great poet, he rises to the level of it the more often. He does not always directly rebuke what is bad and base, but indirectly by making us feel what delight there is in the good and fair. If he besiege evil, it is with such beautiful engines of war (as Plutarch tells us of Demetrius) that the besieged themselves are charmed with them. Whoever reads the great poets cannot but be made better by it, for they always introduce him to a higher society, to a greater style of manners and of thinking. Whoever learns to love what is beautiful is made incapable of the low and mean and bad. If Plato excludes the poets from his Republic, it is expressly on the ground that they speak unworthy things of the gods; that is, that they have lost the secret of their art, and use artificial types instead of speaking the true universal language of imagination.[3] He who translates the divine into the vulgar, the spiritual into the sensual, is the reverse of a poet.

[3] See especially Books II and X of Plato's *Republic*.

The poet, under whatever name, always stands for the same thing—imagination. And imagination in its highest form gives him the power, as it were, of assuming the consciousness of whatever he speaks about, whether man or beast, or rock or tree. It is the ring of Canace,[4] which whoso has on understands the language of all created things. And as regards expression, it seems to enable the poet to condense the whole of himself into a single word. Therefore, when a great poet has said a thing, it is finally and utterly expressed, and has as many meanings as there are men who read his verse. A great poet is something more than an interpreter between man and nature; he is also an interpreter between man and his own nature. It is he who gives us those key-words, the possession of which makes us masters of all the unspected treasure-caverns of thought, and feeling, and beauty which open under the dusty path of our daily life.

And it is not merely a dry lexicon that he compiles,—a thing which enables us to translate from one dead dialect into another as dead,—but all his verse is instinct with music, and his words open windows on every side to pictures of scenery and life. The difference between the dry fact and the poem is as great as that between reading the shipping news and seeing the actual coming and going of the crowd of stately ships,—"the city on the inconstant billows dancing,"—as there is between ten minutes of happiness and ten minutes by the clock. Everybody remembers the story of the little Montague who was stolen and sold to the chimney-sweep: how he could dimly remember lying in a beautiful chamber; how he carried with him in all his drudgery the vision of a fair, sad mother's face that sought him everywhere in vain; how he threw himself one day, all sooty as he was from his toil, on a rich bed and fell asleep, and how a kind person woke him, questioned him, pieced together his broken recollections for him, and so at last made the visions of the beautiful chamber and the fair, sad countenance real to him again. It seems to me that the offices that the poet does for us are typified in this nursery-tale. We all of us have our vague reminiscences of the stately home of our childhood,—for we are all of us poets and geniuses in our youth, while earth is all new to us, and the chalice of every buttercup is brimming with the wine of poesy,—and we all remember the beautiful, motherly countenance which nature bent over us there. But somehow we all get stolen away thence; life becomes to us a sooty taskmaster, and we crawl through dark passages without end—till suddenly the word of some poet redeems us, makes us know who we are, and of helpless orphans makes us the heir to a great estate. It is to our true relations with the two great worlds of outward and inward nature that the poet reintroduces us.

But the imagination has a deeper use than merely to give poets a power of expression. It is the everlasting preserver of the world from blank materialism. It forever puts matter in the wrong, and compels it to show its title to existence. Wordsworth tells us that in his youth he was some-

---

[4] In Chaucer's "Squire's Tale," Canace, daughter of King Cambuscan, possesses a magic ring by means of which she can understand the love plaint of a female hawk.

times obliged to touch the walls to find if they were visionary or no, and such experiences are not uncommon with persons who converse much with their own thoughts. Dr. Johnson said that to kick one's foot against a stone was a sufficient confutation of Berkeley,[5] and poor old Pyrrho[6] has passed into a proverb because, denying the objectivity of matter, he was run over by a cart and killed. But all that he affirmed was that to the soul the cart was no more real than its own imaginative reproduction of it, and perhaps the shade of the philosopher ran up to the first of his deriders who crossed the Styx with a triumphant "I told you so! The cart did not run over *me*, for here I am without a bone broken."

And, in another sense also, do those poets who deal with human character, as all the greater do, continually suggest to us the purely phantasmal nature of life except as it is related to the world of ideas. For are not their personages more real than most of those in history? Is not Lear more authentic and permanent than Lord Raglan? Their realm is a purely spiritual one in which space and time and costume are nothing. What matters it that Shakespeare puts a seaport in Bohemia, and knew less geography than Tommy who goes to the district school? He understood eternal boundaries, such as are laid down on no chart, and are not defined by such transitory affairs as mountain chains, rivers, and seas.

No great movement of the human mind takes place without the concurrent beat of those two wings, the imagination and the understanding. It is by the understanding that we are enabled to make the most of this world, and to use the collected material of experience in its condensed form of practical wisdom; and it is the imagination which forever beckons toward that other world which is always future, and makes us discontented with this. The one rests upon experience; the other leans forward and listens after the *in*experienced, and shapes the features of that future with which it is forever in travail. The imagination might be defined as the common sense of the invisible world, as the understanding is of the visible; and as those are the finest individual characters in which the two moderate and rectify each other, so those are the finest eras where the same may be said of society. In the voyage of life, not only do we depend on the needle, true to its earthly instincts, but upon observation of the fixed stars, those beacons lighted upon the eternal promontories of heaven above the stirs and shiftings of our lower system.

But it seems to be thought that we have come upon the earth too late, that there has been a feast of imagination formerly, and all that is left for us is to steal the scraps. We hear that there is no poetry in railroads and steamboats and telegraphs, and especially none in Brother Jonathan. If this be true, so much the worse for him. But because *he* is a materialist, shall there be no more poets? When we have said that we live in a materialistic age we have said something which meant more than we intended. If we say it in the way of blame, we have said a foolish thing, for probably one age is as good as another, and, at any rate, the worst is good

---

[5] George Berkeley (1685-1753), British idealistic philosopher.
[6] Pyrrho (ca. 365-ca. 275 B.C.), Greek skeptic philosopher.

enough company for us. The age of Shakespeare was richer than our own, only because it was lucky enough to have such a pair of eyes as his to see it, and such a gift of speech as his to report it. And so there is always room and occasion for the poet, who continues to be, just as he was in the early time, nothing more nor less than a "seer." He is always the man who is willing to take the age he lives in on trust, as the very best that ever was. Shakespeare did not sit down and cry for the water of Helicon to turn the wheels of his little private mill at the Bankside. He appears to have gone more quietly about his business than any other playwright in London, to have drawn off what water-power he needed from the great prosy current of affairs that flows alike for all and in spite of all, to have ground for the public what grist they wanted, coarse or fine, and it seems a mere piece of luck that the smooth stream of his activity reflected with such ravishing clearness every changing mood of heaven and earth, every stick and stone, every dog and clown and courtier that stood upon its brink. It is a curious illustration of the friendly manner in which Shakespeare received everything that came along,—of what a *present* man he was,—that in the very same year that the mulberry-tree was brought into England, he got one and planted it in his garden at Stratford.

It is perfectly true that this is a materialistic age, and for that very reason we want our poets all the more. We find that every generation contrives to catch its singing larks without the sky's falling. When the poet comes, he always turns out to be the man who discovers that the passing moment is the inspired one, and that the secret of poetry is not to have lived in Homer's day, or Dante's, but to be alive now. To be alive now, that is the great art and mystery. They are dead men who live in the past, and men yet unborn that live in the future. We are like Hans in Luck, forever exchanging the burdensome good we have for something else, till at last we come home empty-handed.

That pale-faced drudge of Time opposite me there, that weariless sexton whose callous hands bury our rosy hours in the irrevocable past, is even now reaching forward to a moment as rich in life, in character, and thought, as full of opportunity, as any since Adam. This little isthmus that we are now standing on is the point to which martyrs in their triumphant pain, prophets in their fervor, and poets in their ecstasy, looked forward as the golden future, as the land too good for them to behold with mortal eyes; it is the point toward which the faint-hearted and desponding hereafter will look back as the priceless past when there was still some good and virtue and opportunity left in the world.

The people who feel their own age prosaic are those who see only its costume. And that is what makes it prosaic—that we have not faith enough in ourselves to think our own clothes good enough to be presented to posterity in. The artists fancy that the court dress of posterity is that of Van Dyck's time, or Caesar's. I have seen the model of a statue of Sir Robert Peel,[7]—a statesman whose merit consisted in yielding gracefully to the present,—in which the sculptor had done his best to travesty the

[7] Sir Robert Peel (1788–1850), British prime minister 1834–35 and 1841–46.

real man into a make-believe Roman. At the period when England produced its greatest poets, we find exactly the reverse of this, and we are thankful that the man who made the monument of Lord Bacon had genius to copy every button of his dress, everything down to the rosettes on his shoes, and then to write under his statue, "Thus sat Francis Bacon"—not "Cneius Pompeius"—"Viscount Verulam." Those men had faith even in their own shoe-strings.

After all, how is our poor scapegoat of a nineteenth century to blame? Why, for not being the seventeenth, to be sure! It is always raining opportunity, but it seems it was only the men two hundred years ago who were intelligent enough not to hold their cups bottom-up. We are like beggars who think if a piece of gold drop into their palm it must be counterfeit, and would rather change it for the smooth-worn piece of familiar copper. And so, as we stand in our mendicancy by the wayside, Time tosses carefully the great golden to-day into our hats, and we turn it over grumblingly and suspiciously, and are pleasantly surprised at finding that we can exchange it for beef and potatoes. Till Dante's time the Italian poets thought no language good enough to put their nothings into but Latin,—and indeed a dead tongue was the best for dead thoughts,—but Dante found the common speech of Florence, in which men bargained and scolded and made love, good enough for him, and out of the world around him made a poem such as no Roman ever sang.

In our day, it is said despairingly, the understanding reigns triumphant: it is the age of common sense. If this be so, the wisest way would be to accept it manfully. But, after all, what is the meaning of it? Looking at the matter superficially, one would say that a striking difference between our science and that of the world's gray fathers is that there is every day less and less of the element of wonder in it. What they saw written in light upon the great arch of heaven, and, by a magnificent reach of sympathy, of which we are incapable, associated with the fall of monarchs and the fate of man, is for us only a professor, a piece of chalk, and a blackboard. The solemn and unapproachable skies we have vulgarized; we have peeped and botanized among the flowers of light, pulled off every petal, fumbled in every calyx, and reduced them to the bare stem of order and class. The stars can no longer maintain their divine reserves, but whenever there is a conjunction and congress of planets, every enterprising newspaper sends thither its special reporter with his telescope. Over those arcana of life where once a mysterious presence brooded, we behold scientific explorers skipping like so many incarnate notes of interrogation. We pry into the counsels of the great powers of nature, we keep our ears at the keyhole, and know everything that is going to happen. There is no longer any sacred inaccessibility, no longer any enchanting unexpectedness, and life turns to prose the moment there is nothing unattainable. It needs no more a voice out of the unknown proclaiming "Great Pan is dead!" We have found his tombstone, deciphered the arrowheaded inscription upon it, know his age to a day, and that he died universally regretted.

Formerly science was poetry. A mythology which broods over us in our cradle, which mingles with the lullaby of the nurse, which peoples the day with the possibility of divine encounters, and night with intimation of demonic ambushes, is something quite other, as the material for thought and poetry, from one that we take down from our bookshelves, as sapless as the shelf it stood on, as remote from all present sympathy with man or nature as a town history with its genealogies of Mr. Nobody's great-grandparents.

We have utilized everything. The Egyptians found a hint of the solar system in the concentric circles of the onion, and revered it as a symbol, while we respect it as a condiment in cookery, and can pass through all Weathersfield without a thought of the stars. Our world is a museum of natural history; that of our forefathers was a museum of supernatural history. And the rapidity with which the change has been going on is almost startling, when we consider that so modern and historical a personage as Queen Elizabeth was reigning at the time of the death of Dr. John Faustus,[8] out of whose story the Teutonic imagination built up a mythus that may be set beside that of Prometheus.[9]

Science, looked at scientifically, is bare and bleak enough. On those sublime heights the air is too thin for the lungs, and blinds the eyes. It is much better living down in the valleys, where one cannot see farther than the next farmhouse. Faith was never found in the bottom of a crucible, nor peace arrived at by analysis or synthesis. But all this is because science has become too grimly intellectual, has divorced itself from the moral and imaginative part of man. Our results are not arrived at in that spirit which led Kepler [10] (who had his theory-traps set all along the tracks of the stars to catch a discovery) to say, "In my opinion the occasions of new discoveries have been no less wonderful than the discoveries themselves."

But we are led back continually to the fact that science cannot, if it would, disengage itself from human nature and from imagination. No two men have ever argued together without at least agreeing in this, that something more than proof is required to produce conviction, and that a logic which is capable of grinding the stubbornest facts to powder (as every man's *own* logic always is) is powerless against so delicate a structure as the brain. Do what we will, we cannot contrive to bring together the yawning edges of proof and belief, to weld them into one. When Thor strikes Skrymir [11] with his terrible hammer, the giant asks if a leaf has fallen. I need not appeal to the Thors of argument in the pulpit, the senate, and the mass-meeting, if they have not sometimes found the popular giant as provokingly insensible. The $\sqrt{-x}$ is nothing in comparison with the chance-caught smell of a single flower which by the magic of association recreates for us the unquestioning day of childhood. Demon-

[8] Legendary magician and charlatan of the sixteenth century.
[9] Greek mythological character. A Titan fabled to have made men out of clay, to have stolen fire for them from Olympus, and to have taught them various arts.
[10] Johann Kepler (1571–1630), famous German astronomer.
[11] Figures of Scandinavian mythology. Thor was the god of thunder.

stration may lead to the very gate of heaven, but there she makes us a civil bow, and leaves us to make our way back again to Faith, who has the key. That science which is of the intellect alone steps with indifferent foot upon the dead body of Belief, if only she may reach higher or see farther.

But we cannot get rid of our wonder—we who have brought down the wild lightning, from writing fiery doom upon the walls of heaven, to be our errand-boy and penny-postman. Wonder is crude imagination; and it is necessary to us, for man shall not live by bread alone, and exact knowledge is not enough. Do we get nearer the truth or farther from it that we have got a gas or an imponderable fluid instead of a spirit? We go on exorcising one thing after another, but what boots it? The evasive genius flits into something else, and defies us. The powers of the outer and inner world form hand in hand a magnetic circle for whose connection man is necessary. It is the imagination that takes his hand and clasps it with that other stretched to him in the dark, and for which he was vainly groping. It is that which renews the mystery in nature, makes it wonderful and beautiful again, and out of the gases of the man of science remakes the old spirit. But we seem to have created too many wonders to be capable of wondering any longer; as Coleridge said, when asked if he believed in ghosts, that he had seen too many of them. But nature all the more imperatively demands it, and science can at best but scotch it, not kill it. In this day of newspapers and electric telegraphs, in which common sense and ridicule can magnetize a whole continent between dinner and tea, we say that such a phenomenon as Mahomet were impossible, and behold Joe Smith and the State of Deseret! Turning over the yellow leaves of the same copy of "Webster on Witchcraft" which Cotton Mather studied, I thought, "Well, that goblin is laid at last!"—and while I mused the tables were turning, and the chairs beating the devil's tattoo all over Christendom. I have a neighbor who dug down through tough strata of clay to a spring pointed out by a witch-hazel rod in the hands of a seventh son's seventh son, and the water is the sweeter to him for the wonder that is mixed with it. After all, it seems that our scientific gas, be it never so brilliant, is not equal to the dingy old Aladdin's lamp.

It is impossible for men to live in the world without poetry of some sort or other. If they cannot get the best they will get some substitute for it, and thus seem to verify Saint Augustine's [12] slur that it is wine of devils. The mind bound down too closely to what is practical either becomes inert, or revenges itself by rushing into the savage wilderness of "isms." The insincerity of our civilization has disgusted some persons so much that they have sought refuge in Indian wigwams and found refreshment in taking a scalp now and then. Nature insists above all things upon balance. She contrives to maintain a harmony between the material and spiritual, nor allows the cerebrum an expansion at the cost of the cerebellum. If the character, for example, run on one side into religious enthusiasm, it is not

[12] Saint Augustine (354–430), Bishop of Hippo, one of the most famous of the early Church fathers, author of *City of God* and the *Confessions*.

unlikely to develop on the other a counterpoise of worldly prudence. Thus the Shaker and the Moravian [13] are noted for thrift, and mystics are not always the worst managers. Through all changes of condition and experience man continues to be a citizen of the world of idea as well as the world of fact, and the tax-gatherers of both are punctual.

And these antitheses which we meet with in individual character we cannot help seeing on the larger stage of the world also, a moral accompanying a material development. History, the great satirist, brings together Alexander and the blower of peas to hint to us that the tube of the one and the sword of the other were equally transitory; but meanwhile Aristotle was conquering kingdoms out of the unknown, and establishing a dynasty of thought from whose hand the sceptre has not yet passed. So there are Charles V, and Luther; the expansion of trade resulting from the Spanish and Portuguese discoveries, and the Elizabethan literature; the Puritans seeking spiritual El Dorados while so much valor and thought were spent in finding mineral ones. It seems to be the purpose of God that a certain amount of genius shall go to each generation, particular quantities being represented by individuals, and while no *one* is complete in himself, all collectively make up a whole ideal figure of a man. Nature is not like certain varieties of the apple that cannot bear two years in succession. It is only that her expansions are uniform in all directions, that in every age she completes her circle, and like a tree adds a ring to her growth be it thinner or thicker.

Every man is conscious that he leads two lives, the one trivial and ordinary, the other sacred and recluse; the one which he carries to the dinner-table and to his daily work, which grows old with his body and dies with it, the other that which is made up of the few inspiring moments of his higher aspiration and attainment, and in which his youth survives for him, his dreams, his unquenchable longings for something nobler than success. It is this life which the poets nourish for him, and sustain with their immortalizing nectar. Through them he feels once more the white innocence of his youth. His faith in something nobler than gold and iron and cotton comes back to him, not as an upbraiding ghost that wrings its pale hands and is gone, but beautiful and inspiring as a first love that recognizes nothing in him that is not high and noble. The poets are nature's perpetual pleaders, and protest with us against what is worldly. Out of their own undying youth they speak to ours. "Wretched is the man," says Goethe, "who has learned to despise the dreams of his youth!" It is from this misery that the imagination and the poets, who are its spokesmen, rescue us. The world goes to church, kneels to the eternal Purity, and then contrives to sneer at innocence and ignorance of evil by calling it green. Let every man thank God for what little there may be left in him of his vernal sweetness. Let him thank God if he have still the capacity for feeling an unmarketable enthusiasm, for that will make

---

[12] American religious sects. The Moravians trace their origin to John Huss (1369?–1415), Bohemian religious reformer and martyr. The Shakers derived their name from movements of the body which form part of their ceremonial.

him worthy of the society of the noble dead, of the companionship of the poets. And let him love the poets for keeping youth young, woman womanly, and beauty beautiful.

There is as much poetry as ever in the world if we only knew how to find it out; and as much imagination, perhaps, only that it takes a more prosaic direction. Every man who meets with misfortune, who is stripped of material prosperity, finds that he has a little outlying mountain-farm of imagination, which did not appear in the schedule of his effects, on which his spirit is able to keep itself alive, though he never thought of it while he was fortunate. Job turns out to be a great poet as soon as his flocks and herds are taken away from him.

There is no reason why our continent should not sing as well as the rest. We have had the practical forced upon us by our position. We have had a whole hemisphere to clear up and put to rights. And we are descended from men who were hardened and stiffened by a downright wrestle with necessity. There was no chance for poetry among the Puritans. And yet if any people have a right to imagination, it should be the descendants of these very Puritans. They had enough of it, or they could never have conceived the great epic they did, whose books are States, and which is written on this continent from Maine to California.

But there seems to be another reason why we should not become a poetical people. Formerly the poet embodied the hopes and desires of men in visible types. He gave them the shoes of swiftness, the cap of invisibility and the purse of Fortunatus. These were once stories for grown men, and not for the nursery as now. We are apt ignorantly to wonder how our forefathers could find satisfaction in fiction the absurdity of which any of our primary-school children could demonstrate. But we forget that the world's gray fathers were children themselves, and that in their little world, with its circle of the black unknown all about it, the imagination was as active as it is with people in the dark. Look at a child's toys, and we shall understand the matter well enough. Imagination is the fairy godmother (every child has one still), at the wave of whose wand sticks become heroes, the closet in which she has been shut fifty times for being naughty is turned into a palace, and a bit of lath acquires all the potency of Excalibur.

But nowadays it is the understanding itself that has turned poet. In her railroads she has given us the shoes of swiftness. Fine-Ear herself could not hear so far as she, who in her magnetic telegraph can listen in Boston and hear what is going on in New Orleans. And what need of Aladdin's lamp when a man can build a palace with a patent pill? The office of the poet seems to be reversed, and he must give back these miracles of the understanding to poetry again, and find out what there is imaginative in steam and iron and telegraph-wires. After all, there is as much poetry in the iron horses that eat fire as in those of Diomed that fed on men. If you cut an apple across you may trace in it the lines of the blossom that the bee hummed around in May, and so the soul of poetry survives in things prosaic. Borrowing money on a bond does not seem the most promising subject in the world, but Shakespeare found the "Merchant of Venice" in it. Themes of song are waiting everywhere for the right man to sing them, like those enchanted swords which no one can pull out of the rock till the hero comes, and he finds no more trouble than in plucking a violet.

John Quincy Adams, making a speech at New Bedford, many years ago, reckoned the number of whaleships (if I remember rightly) that sailed out of that port, and, comparing it with some former period, took it as a type of American success. But, alas! it is with quite other oil that those far-shining lamps of a nation's true glory which burn forever must be filled. It is not by any amount of material splendor or prosperity, but only by moral greatness, by ideas, by works of imagination, that a race can conquer the future. No voice comes to us from the once mighty Assyria but the hoot of the owl that nests amid her crumbling palaces. Of Carthage, whose merchant-fleets once furled their sails in every port of the known world, nothing is left but the deeds of Hannibal. She lies dead on the shore of her once subject sea, and the wind of the desert only flings its handfuls of burial-sand upon her corpse. A fog can blot Holland or Switzerland out of existence. But how large is the space occupied in the maps of the soul by little Athens and powerless Italy! They were great by the soul, and their vital force is as indestructible as the soul.

Till America has learned to love art, not as an amusement, not as the mere ornament of her cities, not as a superstition of what is *comme il faut* for a great nation, but for its humanizing and ennobling energy, for its power of making men better by arousing in them a perception of their own instincts for what is beautiful, and therefore sacred and religious, and an eternal rebuke of the base and worldly, she will not have succeeded in that high sense which alone makes a nation out of a people, and raises it from a dead name to a living power. Were our little mother-island sunk beneath the sea, or, worse, were she conquered by Scythian barbarians, yet Shakespeare would be an immortal England, and would conquer countries, when the bones of her last sailor had kept their ghastly watch for ages in unhallowed ooze beside the quenched thunders of her navy.

Old Purchas in his "Pilgrims" [14] tells of a sacred caste in India who, when they go out into the street, cry out, "Poo! Poo!" to warn all the world out of their way lest they should be defiled by something unclean. And it is just so that the understanding in its pride of success thinks to pooh-pooh all that it considers impractical and visionary. But whatever of life there is in man, except what comes of beef and pudding, is in the visionary and unpractical, and if it be not encouraged to find its activity or its solace in the production or enjoyment of art and beauty, if it be bewildered or thwarted by an outward profession of faith covering up a practical unbelief in anything higher and holier than the world of sense, it will find vent in such wretched holes and corners as table-tippings and

[14] Samuel Purchas (1577?-1626) continued the work of Richard Hakluyt, compiling from materials in manuscript or already published separately, his huge *Hakluytus Posthumus or Purchas His Pilgrims* (1625).

mediums who sell news from heaven at a quarter of a dollar the item. Imagination cannot be banished out of the world. She may be made a kitchen-drudge, a Cinderella, but there are powers that watch over her. When her two proud sisters, the intellect and understanding, think her crouching over her ashes, she startles and charms by her splendid apparition, and Prince Soul will put up with no other bride.

The practical is a very good thing in its way—if it only be not another name for the worldly. To be absorbed in it is to eat of that insane root which the soldiers of Antonius found in their retreat from Parthia—which whoso tasted kept gathering sticks and stones as if they were some great matter till he died.

One is forced to listen, now and then, to a kind of talk which makes him feel as if this were the after-dinner time of the world, and mankind were doomed hereafter forever to that kind of contented materialism which comes to good stomachs with the nuts and raisins. The dozy old world has nothing to do now but stretch its legs under the mahogany, talk about stocks, and get rid of the hours as well as it can till bedtime. The centuries before us have drained the goblet of wisdom and beauty, and all we have left is to cast horoscopes in the dregs. But divine beauty, and the love of it, will never be without apostles and messengers on earth, till Time flings his hour-glass into the abyss as having no need to turn it longer to number the indistinguishable ages of Annihilation. It was a favorite speculation with the learned men of the sixteenth century that they had come upon the old age and decrepit second childhood of creation, and while they maundered, the soul of Shakespeare was just coming out of the eternal freshness of Deity, "trailing" such "clouds of Glory" as would beggar a Platonic year of sunsets.

No; morning and the dewy prime are born into the earth again with every child. It is our fault if drought and dust usurp the noon. Every age says to her poets, like the mistress to her lover, "Tell me what I am like"; and, in proportion as it brings forth anything worth seeing, has need of seers and will have them. Our time is not an unpoetical one. We are in our heroic age, still face to face with the shaggy forces of unsubdued Nature, and we have our Theseuses and Perseuses, though they may be named Israel Putnam and Daniel Boone.[15] It is nothing against us that we are a commercial people. Athens was a trading community; Dante and Titian were the growth of great marts, and England was already commercial when she produced Shakespeare.

This lesson I learn from the past: that grace and goodness, the fair, the noble, and the true, will never cease out of the world till the God from whom they emanate ceases out of it; that they manifest themselves in an eternal continuity of change to every generation of men, as new duties and occasions arise; that the sacred duty and noble office of the poet is to reveal and justify them to men; that so long as the soul endures, endures

[15] Theseus and Perseus were both heroes of Greek mythology. Israel Putnam (1718–1790) was a famous general of the Revolutionary war. Daniel Boone (1734–1820) was the famous American frontiersman.

also the theme of new and unexampled song; that while there is grace in grace, love in love, and beauty in beauty, God will still send poets to find them and bear witness of them, and to hang their ideal portraitures in the gallery of memory. God with us is forever the mystical name of the hour that is passing. The lives of the great poets teach us that they were the men of their generation who felt most deeply the meaning of the present.

JAMES RUSSELL LOWELL

THE IMAGINATION [1]
(1855)

IMAGINATION IS the wings of the mind; the understanding, its feet. With these it may climb high, but can never soar into that ampler ether and diviner air whence the eye dominates so uncontrolled a prospect on every hand. Through imagination alone is something like a creative power possible to man. It is the same in Æschylus as in Shakespeare, though the form of its manifestation varies in some outward respects from age to age. Being the faculty of vision, it is the essential part of expression also, which is the office of all art.

But in comparing ancient with modern imaginative literature, certain changes especially strike us, and chief among them a stronger infusion of sentiment and what we call the picturesque. I shall endeavor to illustrate this by a few examples. But first let us discuss imagination itself, and give some instances of its working.

"Art," says Lord Verulam, "is man added to Nature" (*homo additus naturae*); and we may modernize his statement, and adapt it to the demands of aesthetics, if we define art to be Nature infused with and shaped by the imaginative faculty of man; thus, as Bacon says elsewhere, "conforming the shows of things to the desires of the mind." Art always platonizes: it results from a certain finer instinct for form, order, proportion, a certain keener sense of the rhythm there is in the eternal flow of the world about us, and its products take shape around some idea preëxistent in the mind, are quickened into life by it, and strive always (cramped and hampered as they are by the limitations and conditions of human nature, of individual temperament, and outward circumstances) toward ideal perfection—toward what Michelangelo called

Ideal form, the universal mould.

Shakespeare, whose careless generalizations have often the exactness of scientific definitions, tells us that

The lunatic, the lover, and the poet,
Are of imagination all compact;

[1] A small portion of this lecture appeared at the time of its delivery, in January, 1855, in a report printed in the *Boston Daily Advertiser*. First published in *Century*, XXV (1894), 716.

that

> as imagination bodies forth
> The forms of things unknown, the poet's pen
> Turns them to shapes, and gives to airy nothing
> A local habitation and a name.

And a little before he had told us that

> Lovers and madmen have such seething brains,
> Such shaping fantasies, that apprehend
> More than cool reason ever comprehends.

Plato had said before him (in his "Ion") that the poet is possessed by a spirit not his own, and that he cannot poetize while he has a particle of understanding left. Again he says that the bacchantes, possessed by the god, drink milk and honey from the rivers, and cannot believe, *till they recover their senses,* that they have been drinking mere water. Empedocles [2] said that "the mind could only conceive of fire by being fire."

All these definitions imply in the imaginative faculty the capabilities of ecstasy and possession, that is, of projecting itself into the very consciousness of its object, and again of being so wholly possessed by the emotion of its object that in expression it takes unconsciously the tone, the color, and the temperature thereof. Shakespeare is the highest example of this—for example, the parting of Romeo and Juliet. There the poet is so possessed by the situation, has so mingled his own consciousness with that of the lovers, that all nature is infected too, and is full of partings:

> Look, love, what envious streaks
> Do lace the *severing* clouds in yonder east.

In Shelley's "Cenci," on the other hand, we have an instance of the poet's imagination giving away its own consciousness to the object contemplated, in this case an inanimate one.

> Two miles on this side of the fort, the road
> Crosses a deep ravine; 't is rough and narrow,
> And winds with short turns down the precipice;
> And in its depth there is a mighty rock
> Which has, from unimaginable years,
> Sustained itself with terror and with toil
> Over a gulf, and with the agony
> With which it clings seems slowly coming down;
> Even as a wretched soul hour after hour
> Clings to the mass of life; yet clinging, leans;
> And leaning, makes more dark the dread abyss
> In which it fears to fall: beneath this crag,
> Huge as despair, as if in weariness,
> The melancholy mountain yawns.

[2] Greek philosopher of the fifth century B.C.

The hint of this Shelley took from a passage in the second act of Calderon's [3] "Purgatorio de San Patricio."

> No ves ese peñasco que parece
> Que se esta sustentando con trabajo,
> Y con el ansia misma que padece
> Ha tantos siglos que se viene abajo?

which, retaining the measure of the original, may be thus paraphrased:

> Do you not see that rock there which appeareth
> To hold itself up with a throe appalling,
> And, through the very pang of what it feareth,
> So many ages hath been falling, falling?

You will observe that in the last instance quoted the poet substitutes his own *impression* of the thing for the thing itself; he forces his own consciousness upon it, and herein is the very root of all sentimentalism. Herein lies the fault of that subjective tendency whose excess is so lamented by Goethe and Schiller, and which is one of the main distinctions between ancient and modern poetry. I say in its excess, for there are moods of mind of which it is the natural and healthy expression. Thus Shakespeare in his ninety-seventh sonnet:

> How like a winter hath my absence been
> From thee, the pleasure of the fleeting year!
> What freezings have I felt, what dark days seen,
> What old December's bareness everywhere!
> And yet this time remov'd was summer's time.

It is only when it becomes a habit, instead of a mood of the mind, that it is a token of disease. Then it is properly dyspepsia, liver-complaint—what you will, but certainly not imagination as the handmaid of art. In that service she has two duties laid upon her: one as the *plastic* or *shaping* faculty, which gives form and proportion, and reduces the several parts of any work to an organic unity foreordained in that idea which is its germ of life; and the other as the *realizing* energy of thought which conceives clearly all the parts, not only in relation to the whole, but each in its several integrity and coherence.

We call the imagination the creative faculty. Assuming it to be so, in the one case it acts by deliberate forethought, in the other by intense sympathy—a sympathy which enables it to realize an Iago as happily as a Cordelia, a Caliban as a Prospero. There is a passage in Chaucer's "House of Fame" which very prettily illustrates this latter function:

> Whan any speche ycomen ys
> Up to the paleys, anon ryght
> Hyt wexeth lyke the same wight,

[3] Pedro Calderón de la Barca (1600–1681), Spanish dramatist and poet.

Which that the worde in erthe spak,
Be hyt clothed red or blak;
And so were hys lykenesse,
And spake the word, that thou wilt gesse
That it the same body be,
Man or woman, he or she.

We have the highest, and indeed an almost unique, example of this kind of sympathetic imagination in Shakespeare, who becomes so sensitive, sometimes, to the thought, the feeling, nay, the mere whim or habit of body of his characters, that we feel, to use his own words, as if "the dull substance of his flesh were thought." It is not in mere intensity of phrase, but in the fitness of it to the feeling, the character, or the situation, that this phase of the imaginative faculty gives witness of itself in expression. I know nothing more profoundly imaginative therefore in its bald simplicity than a line in Webster's "Duchess of Malfy." Ferdinand has procured the murder of his sister the duchess. When her dead body is shown to him he stammers out:

Cover her face; mine eyes dazzle; she died young.

The difference between subjective and objective in poetry would seem to be that the aim of the former is to express a mood of the mind, often something in itself accidental and transitory, while that of the latter is to convey the impression made upon the mind by something outside of it, but taken up into the mind and idealized (that is, stripped of all unessential particulars) by it. The one would fain set forth your view of the thing (modified, perhaps, by your breakfast), the other would set forth the very thing itself in its most concise individuality. Subjective poetry may be profound and imaginative if it deal with the primary emotions of our nature, with the soul's inquiries into its own being and doing, as was true of Wordsworth; but in the very proportion that it is profound, its range is limited. Great poetry should have breadth as well as height and depth; it should meet men everywhere on the open levels of their common humanity, and not merely on their occasional excursions to the heights of speculation or their exploring expeditions among the crypts of metaphysics.

But however we divide poetry, the office of imagination is to disengage what is essential from the crowd of accessories which is apt to confuse the vision of ordinary minds. For our perceptions of things are gregarious, and are wont to huddle together and jostle one another. It is only those who have been long trained to shepherd their thoughts that can at once single out each member of the flock by something peculiar to itself. That the power of abstraction has something to do with the imagination is clear, I think, from the fact that everybody is a dramatic poet (so far as the conception of character goes) in his sleep. His acquaintances walk and talk before him on the stage of dream precisely as in life. When he wakes, his genius has flown away with his sleep. It was indeed nothing more than that his mind was not distracted by the multiplicity of details which the senses force upon it by day. He thinks of Smith, and it is no longer a mere name on a door-plate or in a directory; but Smith himself is there, with those marvellous commonplaces of his which, could you only hit them off when you were awake, you would have created Justice Shallow. Nay, is not there, too, that offensively supercilious creak of the boots with which he enforced his remarks on the war in Europe, when he last caught you at the corner of the street and decanted into your ears the stale settlings of a week of newspapers? Now, did not Shakespeare tell us that the imagination *bodies forth*? It is indeed the *verbum caro factum*—the word made flesh and blood.

I said that the imagination always idealizes, that in its highest exercise, for example, as in the representation of character, it goes behind the species to the genus, presenting us with everlasting types of human nature, as in Don Quixote and Hamlet, Antigone and Cordelia, Alcestis and Amelia. By this I mean that those features are most constantly insisted upon, not in which they differ from other men, but from other kinds of men. For example, Don Quixote is never set before us as a mere madman, but as the victim of a monomania, and that, when you analyze it, of a very noble kind—nothing less, indeed, than devotion to an unattainable ideal, to an anachronism, as the ideals of imaginative men for the most part are. Amid all his ludicrous defeats and disillusions, this poetical side of him is brought to our notice at intervals, just as a certain theme recurs again and again in one of Beethoven's symphonies, a kind of clue to guide us through those intricacies of harmony. So in Lear, one of Shakespeare's profoundest psychological studies, the weakness of the man is emphasized, as it were, and forced upon our attention by his outbreaks of impotent violence; so in Macbeth, that imaginative bias which lays him open to the temptation of the weird sisters is suggested from time to time through the whole tragedy, and at last unmans him, and brings about his catastrophe in his combat with Macduff. This is what I call ideal and imaginative representation, which marks the outlines and boundaries of character, not by arbitrary lines drawn at this angle or that, according to the whim of the tracer, but by those mountain-ranges of human nature which divide man from man and temperament from temperament. And as the imagination of the reader must reinforce that of the poet, reducing the generic again to the specific, and defining it into sharper individuality by a comparison with the experiences of actual life, so, on the other hand, the popular imagination is always poetic, investing each new figure that comes before it with all the qualities that belong to the genus. Thus Hamlet, in some one or other of his characteristics has been the familiar of us all, and so from an ideal and remote figure is reduced to the standard of real and contemporary existence; while Bismarck,[4] who, if we knew him, would probably turn out to be a comparatively simple character, is invested with all the qualities which have ever been attributed to the typical statesman, and is clearly as imaginative a personage as the Marquis of Posa, in Schil-

[4] Otto von Bismarck (1815–1898), first chancellor of the modern German empire, 1871–1890.

ler's [5] "Don Carlos." We are ready to accept any *coup de théâtre* of him. Now, this prepossession is precisely that for which the imagination of the poet makes us ready by working on our own.

But there are also lower levels on which this idéalization plays its tricks upon our fancy. The Greek, who had studied profoundly what may be called the machinery of art, made use even of mechanical contrivances to delude the imagination of the spectator, and to entice him away from the associations of everyday life. The cothurnus lifted the actor to heroic stature, the mask prevented the ludicrous recognition of a familiar face in "Œdipus" and "Agamemnon"; it precluded grimace, and left the countenance as passionless as that of a god; it gave a more awful reverberation to the voice, and it was by the voice, that most penetrating and sympathetic, one might almost say incorporeal, organ of expression, that the great effects of the poet and tragic actor were wrought. Everything, you will observe, was, if not lifted above, at any rate removed, however much or little, from the plane of the actual and trivial. Their stage showed nothing that could be met in the streets. We barbarians, on the other hand, take delight precisely in that. We admire the novels of Trollope and the groups of Rogers [6] because, as we say, they are so *real*, while it is only because they are so matter-of-fact, so exactly on the level with our own trivial and prosaic apprehensions. When Dante lingers to hear the dispute between Sinon and Master Adam, Virgil, type of the higher reason and the ideal poet, rebukes him, and even angrily.

> E fa ragion ch'io ti sia sempre allato
> Si più avvien che fortuna t' accoglia
> Ove sien genti in simigliante piato;
> Chè voler ciò udire è bassa voglia.

> Remember, I am always at thy side,
> If ever fortune bring thee once again
> Where there are people in dispute like this,
> For wishing to hear that is vulgar wish.

Verse is another of these expedients for producing that frame of mind, that prepossession, on the part of hearer or reader which is essential to the purpose of the poet, who has lost much of his advantage by the invention of printing, which obliges him to appeal to the eye rather than the ear. The rhythm is no arbitrary and artificial contrivance. It was suggested by an instinct natural to man. It is taught him by the beating of his heart, by his breathing, hastened or retarded by the emotion of the moment. Nay, it may be detected by what seems the most monotonous of motions, the flow of water, in which, if you listen intently, you will discover a beat as regular as that of the metronome. With the natural presumption of all self-taught men, I thought I had made a discovery in this secret confided

---

[5] Friedrich Schiller (1759–1805), German poet and dramatist.
[6] John Rogers (1829–1904), American sculptor—famous for his enormously popular small groups of figures, known as "Rogers Groups."

to me by Beaver Brook, till Professor Peirce told me it was always allowed for in the building of dams. Nay, for my own part, I would venture to affirm that not only metre but even rhyme itself was not without suggestion in outward nature. Look at the pine, how its branches balancing each other, ray out from the tapering stem in stanza after stanza, how spray answers to spray in order, strophe, and antistrophe, till the perfect tree stands an embodied ode, Nature's triumphant vindication of proportion, number, and harmony. Who can doubt the innate charm of rhyme who has seen the blue river repeat the blue o'erhead; who has been ravished by the visible consonance of the tree growing at once toward an upward and downward heaven on the edge of the twilight cove; or who has watched how, as the kingfisher flitted from shore to shore, his visible echo flies under him, and completes the fleeting couplet in the visionary vault below? At least there can be no doubt that metre, by its systematic and regular occurrence, gradually subjugates and tunes the senses of the hearer, as the wood of the violin arranges itself in sympathy with the vibration of the strings, and thus that predisposition to the proper emotion is accomplished which is essential to the purpose of the poet. You must not only expect, but you must expect in the right way; you must be magnetized beforehand in every fibre by your own sensibility in order that you may feel what and how you ought. The right reception of whatever is ideally represented demands as a preliminary condition an exalted, or, if not that, then an excited, frame of mind both in poet and hearer. The imagination must be sensitized ere it will take the impression of those airy nothings whose image is traced and fixed by appliances as delicate as the golden pencils of the sun. Then that becomes a visible reality which before was but a phantom of the brain. Your own passion must penetrate and mingle with that of the artist that you may interpret him aright. You must, I say, be prepossessed, for it is the mind which shapes and colors the reports of the senses. Suppose you were expecting the bell to toll for the burial of some beloved person and the church-clock should begin to strike. The first lingering blow of the hammer would beat upon your very heart, and thence the shock would run to all the senses at once; but after a few strokes you would be undeceived, and the sound would become commonplace again. On the other hand, suppose that at a certain hour you knew that a criminal was to be executed; then the ordinary striking of the clock would have the sullen clang of a funeral bell. So in Shakespeare's instance of the lover, does he not suddenly find himself sensible of a beauty in the world about him before undreamed of, because his passion has somehow got into whatever he sees and hears? Will not the rustle of silk across a counter stop his pulse because it brings back to his sense the odorous whisper of Parthenissa's robe? Is not the beat of the horse's hoofs as rapid to Angelica pursued as the throbs of her own heart huddling upon one another in terror, while it is slow to Sister Anne, as the pulse that pauses between hope and fear, as she listens on the tower for rescue, and would have the rider "spur, though mounted on the wind"?

Dr. Johnson tells us that that only is good poetry which may be translated into sensible prose. I greatly doubt whether any very profound emotion can be so rendered. Man is a metrical animal, and it is not in prose but in nonsense verses that the young mother croons her joy over the new centre of hope and terror that is sucking life from her breast. Translate passion into sensible prose and it becomes absurd, because subdued to workaday associations, to that level of common sense and convention where to betray intense feeling is ridiculous and unmannerly. Shall I ask Shakespeare to translate me his love "still climbing trees in the Hesperides"? Shall I ask Marlowe how Helen could "make him immortal with a kiss," or how, in the name of all the Monsieur Jourdains, at once her face could "launch a thousand ships and burn the topless towers of Ilion"? Could Æschylus, if put upon the stand, defend his making Prometheus cry out,

> O divine ether and swift-winged winds,
> Ye springs of rivers, and of ocean waves
> The innumerable smile, all mother Earth,
> And Helios' all-beholding round, I call:
> Behold what I, a god, from gods endure!

Or could Lear justify his

> I tax not you, you elements, with unkindness;
> I never gave you kingdoms, call'd you children!

No; precisely what makes the charm of poetry is what we cannot explain any more than we can describe a perfume. There is a little quatrain of Gongora's quoted by Calderon in his "Alcalde of Zalamea" which has an inexplicable charm for me:

> Las flores del romero,
>   Niña Isabel,
> Hoy son flores azules,
>   Y mañana serán miel.[7]

If I translate it, 't is nonsense, yet I understand it perfectly, and it will, I dare say, outlive much wiser things in my memory. It is the very function of poetry to free us from that witch's circle of common sense which holds us fast in its narrow enchantment. In this disenthralment, language and verse have their share, and we may say that language also is capable of a certain idealization. Here is a passage from the XXXth song of Drayton's "Poly-Olbion":

---

[7] The quatrain is by Luis de Gongora y Argote (1561–1627), Spanish poet. Following is a literal translation of the stanza:
> The flowers of the rosemary,
>   Child Isabel,
> Today are blue flowers,
>   And tomorrow shall be honey.

> Which Copland scarce had spoke, but quickly every Hill
> Upon her verge that stands, the neighbouring valleys fill;
> Helvillon from his height, it through the mountains threw,
> From whom as soon again, the sound Dunbalrase drew,
> From whose stone-trophied head, it on to Wendrosse went,
> Which tow'rds the sea again, resounded it to Dent,
> That Broadwater therewith within her banks astound,
> In sailing to the sea, told it in Egremound.

This gave a hint to Wordsworth, who, in one of his "Poems on the Naming of Places," thus prolongs the echo of it:

> Joanna, looking in my eyes, beheld
> That ravishment of mine, and laughed aloud,
> The Rock, like something starting from a sleep,
> Took up the Lady's voice, and laughed again;
> The ancient Woman seated on Helm-crag
> Was ready with her cavern; Hammer-scar,
> And the tall steep of Silver-how, sent forth
> A noise of laughter; southern Loughrigg heard,
> And Fairfield answered with a mountain tone;
> Helvellyn far into the clear blue sky
> Carried the Lady's voice,—old Skiddaw blew
> His speaking-trumpet;—back out of the clouds
> Of Glaramara southward came the voice;
> And Kirkstone tossed it from his misty head.

Now, this passage of Wordsworth I should call the idealization of that of Drayton, who becomes poetical only in the "stone-trophied head of Dunbalrase"; and yet the thought of both poets is the same.

Even what is essentially vulgar may be idealized by seizing and dwelling on the generic characteristics. In "Antony and Cleopatra" Shakespeare makes Lepidus tipsy, and nothing can be droller than the drunken gravity with which he persists in proving himself capable of bearing his part in the conversation. We seem to feel the whirl in his head when we find his mind revolving round a certain fixed point to which he clings as to a post. Antony is telling stories of Egypt to Octavius, and Lepidus, drawn into an eddy of the talk, interrupts him:

> *Lepidus:* You gave strange serpents there.
> *Antony (trying to shake him off):* Ay, Lepidus.
> *Lepidus:* Your serpent of Egypt is bred now of your mud by the operation of your sun: so is your crocodile.
> *Antony (thinking to get rid of him):* They are so.

Presently Lepidus has revolved again, and continues, as if he had been contradicted:

> Nay, certainly, I have heard the Ptolemies' pyramises are very goodly things; without contradiction, I have heard that.

And then, after another pause, still intent on proving himself sober, he asks, coming round to the crocodile again:

> What manner o' thing is your crocodile?

Antony answers gravely:

> It is shaped, sir, like itself, and it is as broad as it hath breadth; it is just so high as it is, and moves with its own organs; it lives by that which nourisheth it; and the elements once out of it, it transmigrates.
> *Lepidus:* What color is it of?
> *Antony:* Of its own color, too.
> *Ledipus (meditatively):* 'T is a strange serpent.

The ideal in expression, then, deals also with the generic, and evades embarrassing particulars in a generalization. We say Tragedy with the dagger and bowl, and it means something very different to the aesthetic sense from Tragedy with the case-knife and the phial of laudanum, though these would be as effectual for murder. It was a misconception of this that led poetry into that slough of poetic diction where everything was supposed to be made poetical by being called something else, and something longer. A boot became "the shining leather that the leg encased"; coffee, "the fragrant juice of Mocha's berry brown," whereas the imaginative way is the most condensed and shortest, conveying to the mind a feeling of the thing, and not a paraphrase of it. Akin to this was a confounding of the pictorial with the imaginative, and personification with that typical expression which is the true function of poetry. Compare, for example, Collins's Revenge with Chaucer's.

> Revenge impatient rose;
> He threw his blood-stained sword in thunder down,
> And, with a withering look,
> The war-denouncing trumpet took,
> And blew a blast so loud and dread,
> Were ne'er prophetic sound so full of woe!
> And ever and anon he beat
> The doubling drum with furious heat.

"Words, words, Horatio!" Now let us hear Chaucer with his single stealthy line that makes us glance over our shoulder as if we heard the murderous tread behind us:

> The smiler with the knife hid under the cloak.

Which is the more terrible? Which has more danger in it—Collins's noise or Chaucer's silence? Here is not the mere difference, you will perceive, between ornament and simplicity, but between a diffuseness which distracts, and a condensation which concentres the attention. Chaucer has chosen out of all the rest the treachery and the secrecy as the two points most apt to impress the imagination.

The imagination, as concerns expression, condenses; the fancy, on the other hand, adorns, illustrates, and commonly amplifies. The one is suggestive, the other picturesque. In Chapman's "Hero and Leander," I read—

> Her fresh-heat blood cast figures in her eyes,
> And she supposed she saw in Neptune's skies
> How her star wonder'd, wash'd in smarting brine,
> For her love's sake, that with immortal wine
> Should be embathed, and swim in more heart's-ease
> Than there was water in the Sestian seas.

In the epithet "star," Hero's thought implies the beauty and brightness of her lover and his being the lord of her destiny, while in "Neptune's skies" we have not only the simple fact that the waters are the atmosphere of the sea-god's realm, but are reminded of that reflected heaven which Hero must have so often watched as it deepened below her tower in the smooth Hellespont. I call this as high an example of fancy as could well be found; it is picture and sentiment combined—the very essence of the picturesque.

But when Keats calls Mercury "the star of Lethe," the word "star" makes us see him as the poor ghosts do who are awaiting his convoy, while the word "Lethe" intensifies our sympathy by making us feel his coming as they do who are longing to drink of forgetfulness. And this again reacts upon the word "star," which, as it before expressed only the shining of the god, acquires a metaphysical significance from our habitual association of star with the notions of hope and promise. Again nothing can be more fanciful than this bit of Henry More the Platonist:[8]

> What doth move
> The nightingale to sing so fresh and clear?
> The thrush or lark that, mounting high above,
> Chants her shrill notes to heedless ears of corn
> Heavily hanging in the dewy morn?

But compare this with Keats again:

> The voice I hear this passing night was heard
> In ancient days by emperor and clown;
> Perhaps the self-same song that found a path
> Through the sad heart of Ruth when, sick for home,
> She stood in tears amid the alien corn.

The imagination has touched that word "alien," and we see the field through Ruth's eyes, as she looked round on the hostile spikes, not merely through those of the poet.

[8] One of the Cambridge (England) Platonists (1614–1687).

WALT WHITMAN

PREFACE TO LEAVES OF GRASS [1]
(1855)

AMERICA DOES not repel the past or what it has produced under its forms or amid other politics or the idea of castes or the old religions . . . accepts the lesson with calmness . . . is not so impatient as has been supposed that the slough still sticks to opinions and manners and literature while the life which served its requirements has passed into the new life of the new forms . . . perceives that the corpse is slowly borne from the eating and sleeping rooms of the house . . . perceives that it waits a little while in the door . . . that it was fittest for its days . . . that its action has descended to the stalwart and well-shaped heir who approaches . . . and that he shall be fittest for his days.

The Americans of all nations at any time upon the earth have probably the fullest poetical nature. The United States themselves are essentially the greatest poem. In the history of the earth hitherto the largest and most stirring appear tame and orderly to their ampler largeness and stir. Here at last is something in the doings of man that corresponds with the broadcast doings of the day and night. Here is not merely a nation but a teeming nation of nations. Here is action untied from strings necessarily blind to particulars and details magnificently moving in vast masses. Here is the hospitality which forever indicates heroes. . . . Here are the roughs and beards and space and ruggedness and nonchalance that the soul loves. Here the performance disdaining the trivial unapproached in the tremendous audacity of its crowds and groupings and the push of its perspective spreads with crampless and flowing breadth and showers its prolific and splendid extravagance. One sees it must indeed own the riches of the summer and winter, and need never be bankrupt while corn grows from the ground or the orchards drop apples or the bays contain fish or men beget children upon women.

Other states indicate themselves in their deputies . . . but the genius of the United States is not best or most in its executives or legislatures, nor in its ambassadors or authors or colleges or churches or parlors, nor even in its newspapers or inventors . . . but always most in the common people. Their manners speech dress friendships—the freshness and candor of their physiognomy—the picturesque looseness of their carriage . . . their deathless attachment to freedom—their aversion to anything indecorous or soft or mean—the practical acknowledgment of the citizens of one

[1] The text is that of the original edition published in Brooklyn, 1855. When the preface was revised and reprinted in 1882, it was changed considerably, losing much of the vigorous style characteristic of Whitman's early expression.

state by the citizens of all other states—the fierceness of their roused re-sentment—their curiosity and welcome of novelty—their self-esteem and wonderful sympathy—their susceptibility to a slight—the air they have of persons who never knew how it felt to stand in the presence of superiors—the fluency of their speech—their delight in music, the sure symptom of manly tenderness and native elegance of soul . . . their good temper and openhandedness—the terrible significance of their elections—the President's taking off his hat to them not they to him—these too are unrhymed poetry. It awaits the gigantic and generous treatment worthy of it.

The largeness of nature or the nation were monstrous without a corre-sponding largeness and generosity of the spirit of the citizen. Not nature nor swarming states nor streets and steamships nor prosperous business nor farms nor capital nor learning may suffice for the ideal of man . . . nor suffice the poet. No reminiscences may suffice either. A live nation can always cut a deep mark and can have the best authority the cheapest . . . namely from its own soul. This is the sum of the profitable uses of individuals or states and of present action and grandeur and of the subjects of poets.—As if it were necessary to trot back generation after generation to the eastern records! As if the beauty and sacredness of the demonstrable must fall behind that of the mythical! As if men do not make their mark out of any times! As if the opening of the western continent by discovery and what has transpired since in North and South America were less than the small theatre of the antique or the aimless sleep-walking of the middle ages! The pride of the United States leaves the wealth and finesse of the cities and all returns of commerce and agriculture and all the magnitude of geography or shows of exterior victory to enjoy the breed of full-sized men or one full-sized man unconquerable and simple.

The American poets are to enclose old and new for America is the race of races. Of them a bard is to be commensurate with a people. To him the other continents arrive as contributions . . . he gives them reception for their sake and his own sake. His spirit responds to his country's spirit . . . he incarnates its geography and natural life and rivers and lakes. Missis-sippi with annual freshets and changing chutes, Missouri and Columbia and Ohio and Saint Lawrence with the falls and beautiful masculine Hudson, do not embouchure where they spend themselves more than they embouchure into him. The blue breadth over the inland sea of Vir-ginia and Maryland and the sea off Massachusetts and Maine and over Manhattan Bay and over Champlain and Erie and over Ontario and Huron and Michigan and Superior, and over the Texan and Mexican and Flo-ridian and Cuban seas and over the seas off California and Oregon, is not tallied by the blue breadth of the waters below more than the breadth of above and below is tallied by him. When the long Atlantic coast stretches longer and the Pacific coast stretches longer he easily stretches with them north or south. He spans between them also from east to west and reflects what is between them. On him rise solid growths that offset the growths of pine and cedar and hemlock and live oak and locust and chestnut and cypress and hickory and lime tree and cottonwood and tulip tree and cactus and wild vine and tamarind and persimmon . . . and tangles as tangled as any cane brake or swamp . . . and forests coated with transparent ice and icicles hanging from the boughs and crackling in the wind . . . and sides and peaks of mountains . . . and pasturage sweet and free as savannah or upland or prairie . . . with flights and songs and screams that answer those of the wild pigeon and highhole and orchard oriole and coot and surf duck and red-shouldered hawk and fish hawk and white ibis and Indian hen and cat owl and water pheasant and qua-bird and pied sheldrake and blackbird and mockingbird and buzzard and condor and night heron and eagle. To him the hereditary countenance descends both mother's and father's. To him enter the essences of the real things and past and present events—of the enormous diversity of tempera-ture and agriculture and mines—the tribes of red aborigines—the weather-beaten vessels entering new ports or making landings on rocky coasts—the first settlements north or south—the rapid stature and muscle—the haughty defiance of '76, and the war and peace and formation of the con-stitution . . . the union always surrounded by blatherers and always calm and impregnable—the perpetual coming of immigrants—the wharf-hem'd cities and superior marine—the unsurveyed interior—the loghouses and clearings and wild animals and hunters and trappers . . . the free com-merce—the fisheries and whaling and golddigging—the endless gestation of new states—the convening of Congress every December, the members duly coming up from all climates and the uttermost parts . . . the noble char-acter of the young mechanics and of all free American workmen and work-women . . . the general ardor and friendliness and enterprise—the perfect equality of the female with the male . . . the large amativeness—the fluid movement of the population—the factories and mercantile life and labor-saving machinery—the Yankee swap—the New York firemen and the target excursion—the southern plantation life—the character of the north-east and of the northwest and southwest—slavery and the tremulous spreading of hands to protect it, and the stern opposition to it which shall never cease till it ceases or the speaking of tongues and the moving of lips cease. For such the expression of the American poet is to be transcendant and new. It is to be indirect and not direct or descriptive or epic. Its quality goes through these to much more. Let the age and wars of other nations be chanted and let their eras and characters be illustrated and that finish the verse. Not so the great psalm of the republic. Here the theme is creative and has vista. Here comes one among the well-beloved stone-cutters and plans with decision and science and sees the solid and beautiful forms of the future where there are now no solid forms.

Of all nations the United States with veins full of poetical stuff most need poets and will doubtless have the greatest and use them the greatest. Their Presidents shall not be their common referee so much as their poets shall. Of all mankind the great poet is the equable man. Not in him but off from him things are grotesque or eccentric or fail of their sanity. Nothing out of its place is good and nothing in its place is bad. He bestows on every object or quality its fit proportions neither more nor less. He is the arbiter of the diverse and he is the key. He is the equalizer of his age and land . . . he supplies what wants supplying and checks what wants checking. If peace is the routine out of him speaks the spirit of peace, large, rich, thrifty, building vast and populous cities, encouraging agriculture and the arts and commerce—lighting the study of man, the soul, immortality—federal, state or municipal government, marriage, health, free trade, intertravel by land and sea . . . nothing too close, nothing too far off . . . the stars not too far off. In war he is the most deadly force of the war. Who recruits him recruits horse and foot . . . he fetches parks of artillery the best that engineer ever knew. If the time becomes slothful and heavy he knows how to arouse it . . . he can make every word he speaks draw blood. Whatever stagnates in the flat of custom or obedience or legislation he never stagnates. Obedience does not master him, he masters it. High up out of reach he stands turning a concentrated light . . . he turns the pivot with his finger . . . he baffles the swiftest runners as he stands and easily overtakes and envelops them. The time straying toward infidelity and confections and persiflage he withholds by his steady faith . . . he spreads out his dishes . . . he offers the sweet firm-fibered meat that grows men and women. His brain is the ultimate brain. He is no arguer . . . he is judgment. He judges not as the judge judges but as the sun falling around a helpless thing. As he sees the farthest he has the most faith. His thoughts are the hymns of the praise of things. In the talk on the soul and eternity and God off of his equal plane he is silent. He sees eternity less like a play with a prologue and denouement . . . he sees eternity in men and women . . . he does not see men and women as dreams or dots. Faith is the antiseptic of the soul . . . it pervades the common people and preserves them . . . they never give up believing and expecting and trusting. There is that indescribable freshness and unconsciousness about an illiterate person that humbles and mocks the power of the noblest expressive genius. The poet sees for a certainty how one not a great artist may be just as sacred and perfect as the greatest artist. . . . The power to destroy or remold is freely used by him but never the power of attack. What is past is past. If he does not expose superior models and prove himself by every step he takes he is not what is wanted. The presence of the greatest poet conquers . . . not parleying or struggling or any prepared attempts. Now he has passed that way see after him! there is not left any vestige of despair or misanthropy or cunning or exclusiveness or the ignominy of a nativity or color or delusion of hell or the necessity of hell . . . and no man thenceforward shall be degraded for ignorance or weakness or sin.

The greatest poet hardly knows pettiness or triviality. If he breathes into any thing that was before thought small it dilates with the grandeur and life of the universe. He is a seer . . . he is individual . . . he is complete in himself . . . the others are as good as he, only he sees it and they do not. He is not one of the chorus . . . he does not stop for any regulations . . . he is the president of regulation. What the eyesight does to the rest he does to the rest. Who knows the curious mystery of the eyesight? The other senses corroborate themselves, but this is removed from any proof but its own and foreruns the identities of the spiritual world. A single glance of it mocks all the investigations of man and all the instruments and books of the earth and all reasoning. What is marvelous? what is unlikely? what is impossible or baseless or vague? after you have once just opened the space of a peach pit and given audience to far and near and to the sunset and had all things enter with electric swiftness softly and duly without confusion or jostling or jam.

The land and sea, the animals fishes and birds, the sky of heaven and the orbs, the forests mountains and rivers, are not small themes . . . but folks expect of the poet to indicate more than the beauty and dignity which always attach to dumb real objects . . . they expect him to indicate the path between reality and their souls. Men and women perceive the beauty well enough . . . probably as well as he. The passionate tenacity of hunters, woodmen, early risers, cultivators of gardens and orchards and fields, the love of healthy women for the manly form, seafaring persons, drivers of horses, the passion for light and the open air, all is an old varied sign of the unfailing perception of beauty and of a residence of the poetic in outdoor people. They can never be assisted by poets to perceive . . . some may but they never can. The poetic quality is not marshalled in rhyme or uniformity or abstract addresses to things nor in melancholy complaints or good precepts, but is the life of these and much else and is in the soul. The profit of rhyme is that it drops seeds of a sweeter and more luxuriant rhyme, and of uniformity that it conveys itself into its own roots in the ground out of sight. The rhyme and uniformity of perfect poems show the free growth of metrical laws and bud from them as unerringly and loosely as lilacs or roses on a bush, and take shapes as compact as the shapes of chestnuts and oranges and melons and pears, and shed the perfume impalpable to form. The fluency and ornaments of the finest poems or music or orations or recitations are not independent but dependent. All beauty comes from beautiful blood and a beautiful brain. If the greatnesses are in conjunction in a man or woman it is enough . . . the fact will prevail through the universe . . . but the gaggery and gilt of a million years will not prevail. Who troubles himself about his ornaments or fluency is lost. This is what you shall do: Love the earth and sun and the animals, despise riches, give alms to everyone that asks, stand up for the stupid and crazy, devote your income and labor to others, hate tyrants, argue not concerning God, have patience and indulgence toward the people, take off your hat to nothing known or unknown or to any man or number of men, go freely with powerful uneducated persons and with the young and with the mothers of families, read these leaves in the open air every season of every year of your life, re-examine all you have been told at school or church or in any book, dismiss whatever insults your own soul, and your very flesh shall be a great poem and have the richest fluency not only in its words but in the silent lines of its lips and face and between the lashes of your eyes and in every motion and joint of your body. . . . The poet shall not spend his time in unneeded work. He shall know that the ground is always ready plowed and manured . . . others may not know it but he shall. He shall go directly to the creation. His trust shall master the trust of everything he touches . . . and shall master all attachment.

The known universe has one complete lover and that is the greatest poet. He consumes an eternal passion and is indifferent which chance happens and which possible contingency of fortune or misfortune and persuades daily and hourly his delicious pay. What balks or breaks others is fuel for his burning progress to contact and amorous joy. Others proportions of the reception of pleasure dwindle to nothing to his proportions. All expected from heaven or from the highest he is rapport with in the sight of the daybreak or a scene of the winter woods or the presence of children playing or with his arm round the neck of a man or woman. His love above all love has leisure and expanse . . . he leaves room ahead of himself. He is no irresolute or suspicious lover . . . he is sure . . . he scorns intervals. His experience and the showers and thrills are not for nothing. Nothing can jar him . . . suffering and darkness cannot—death and fear cannot. To him complaint and jealously and envy are corpses buried and rotten in the earth . . . he saw them buried. The sea is not surer of the shore or the shore of the sea than he is of the fruition of his love and of all perfection and beauty.

The fruition of beauty is no chance of hit or miss . . . it is inevitable as life . . . it is exact and plumb as gravitation. From the eyesight proceeds another eyesight and from the hearing proceeds another hearing and from the voice proceeds another voice eternally curious of the harmony of things with man. To these respond perfections not only in the committees that were supposed to stand for the rest but in the rest themselves just the same. These understand the law of perfection in masses and floods . . . that its finish is to each for itself and onward from itself . . . that it is profuse and impartial . . . that there is not a minute of the light or dark nor an acre of the earth or sea without it—nor any direction of the sky nor any trade or employment nor any turn of events. This is the reason that about the proper expression of beauty there is precision and balance . . . one part does not need to be thrust above another. The best singer is not the one who has the most lithe and powerful organ . . . the pleasure of poems is not in them that take the handsomest measure and similes and sound.

Without effort and without exposing in the least how it is done the greatest poet brings the spirit of any or all events and passions and scenes and persons some more and some less to bear on your individual character as you hear or read. To do this well is to compete with the laws that pursue and follow time. What is the purpose must surely be there and the clue of it must be there . . . and the faintest indication is the indication of the best and then becomes the clearest indication. Past and present and future are not disjoined but joined. The greatest poet forms the consistence of what is to be from what has been and is. He drags the dead out of their coffins and stands them again on their feet . . . he says to the past, Rise and walk before me that I may realize you. He learns the lesson . . . he places himself where the future becomes present. The greatest poet does not only dazzle his rays over character and scenes and passions . . . he finally ascends and finishes all . . . he exhibits the pinnacles that no man can tell what they are for or what is beyond . . . he glows a moment on the extremest verge. He is most wonderful in his last half-hidden smile or frown . . . by that flash of the moment of parting the one that sees it shall be encouraged or terrified afterwards for many years. The greatest poet does not moralize or make applications of morals . . . he knows the soul. The soul has that measureless pride which consists in never acknowledging any lessons but its own. But it has sympathy as measureless as its pride and the one balances the other and neither can stretch too far while it stretches in company with the other. The inmost secrets of art sleep with the twain. The greatest poet has lain close betwixt both and they are vital in his style and thoughts.

The art of art, the glory of expression and the sunshine of the light of letters is simplicity. Nothing is better than simplicity . . . nothing can make up for excess or for the lack of definiteness. To carry on the heave of impulse and pierce intellectual depths and give all subjects their articulations are powers neither common nor very uncommon. But to speak in literature with the perfect rectitude and insouciance of the movements of animals and the unimpeachableness of the sentiment of trees in the woods and grass by the roadside is the flawless triumph of art. If you have looked on him who has achieved it you have looked on one of the masters of the artists of all nations and times. You shall not contemplate the flight of the graygull over the bay or the mettlesome action of the blood horse or the tall leaning of sunflowers on their stalk or the appearance of the sun journeying through heaven or the appearance of the moon afterward with any more satisfaction than you shall contemplate him. The greatest poet has less a marked style and is more the channel of thoughts and things without increase or diminution, and is the free channel of himself. He swears to his art, I will not be meddlesome, I will not have in my writing any elegance or effect or originality to hang in the way between me and the rest like curtains. I will have nothing hang in the way, not the richest curtains. What I tell I tell for precisely what it is. Let who may exalt or startle or fascinate or sooth I will have purposes health or heat or snow has and be as regardless of observation. What I experience or portray shall go from my composition without a shred of my composition. You shall stand by my side and look in the mirror with me.

The old red blood and stainless gentility of great poets will be proved by their unconstraint. A heroic person walks at his ease through and out of that custom or precedent or authority that suits him not. Of the traits of the brotherhood of writers savants musicians inventors and artists nothing is finer than silent defiance advancing from new free forms. In the need of poems philosophy politics mechanism science behavior, the craft of art, an appropriate native grand opera, shipcraft, or any craft, he is greatest forever and forever who contributes the greatest original practical example.

The cleanest expression is that which finds no sphere worthy of itself and makes one.

The messages of great poets to each man and woman are, Come to us on equal terms, Only then can you understand us, We are no better than you, What we enclose you enclose, What we enjoy you may enjoy. Did you suppose there could be only one Supreme? We affirm there can be unnumbered Supremes, and that one does not countervail another any more than one eyesight countervails another . . . and that men can be good or grand only of the consciousness of their supremacy within them. What do you think is the grandeur of storms and dismemberments and the deadliest battles and wrecks and the wildest fury of the elements and the power of the sea and the motion of nature and of the throes of human desires and dignity and hate and love? It is that something in the soul which says, Rage on, Whirl on, I tread master here and everywhere, Master of the spasms of the sky and of the shatter of the sea, Master of nature and passion and death, And of all terror and all pain.

The American bards shall be marked for generosity and affection and for encouraging competitors. . . . They shall be kosmos . . . without monopoly or secrecy . . . glad to pass any thing to any one . . . hungry for equals night and day. They shall not be careful of riches and privilege they shall be riches and privilege . . . they shall perceive who the most affluent man is. The most affluent man is he that confronts all the shows he sees by equivalents out of the stronger wealth of himself. The American bard shall delineate no class of persons nor one or two out of the strata of interests nor love most nor truth most nor the soul most nor the body most . . . and not be for the eastern states more than the western or the northern states more than the southern.

Exact science and its practical movements are no checks on the greatest poet but always his encouragement and support. The outset and remembrance are there . . . there are the arms that lifted him first and brace him best . . . there he returns after all his goings and comings. The sailor and traveler . . . the anatomist chemist astronomer geologist phrenologist spiritualist mathematician historian and lexicographer are not poets, but they are the lawgivers of poets and their construction underlies the structure of every perfect poem. No matter what rises or is uttered they sent the seed of the conception of it . . . of them and by them stand the visible proofs of souls . . . always of their father-stuff must be begotten the sinewy races of bards. If there shall be love and content between the father and the son and if the greatness of the son is the exuding of the greatness of the father there shall be love between the poet and the man of demonstrable science. In the beauty of poems are the tuft and final applause of science.

Great is the faith of the flush of knowledge and of the investigation of the depths of qualities and things. Cleaving and circling here swells the soul of the poet yet is president of itself always. The depths are fathomless and therefore calm. The innocence and nakedness are resumed . . . they are neither modest nor immodest. The whole theory of the

special and supernatural and all that was twined with it or educed out of
it departs as a dream. What has ever happened . . . what happens and
whatever may or shall happen, the vital laws enclose all . . . they are
sufficient for any case and for all cases . . . none to be hurried or retarded . . . any miracle of affairs or persons inadmissible in the vast
clear scheme where every motion and every spear of grass and the frames
and spirits of men and women and all that concerns them are unspeakably perfect miracles all referring to all and each distinct and in its place.
It is also not consistent with the reality of the soul to admit that there is
anything in the known universe more divine than men and women.

Men and women and the earth and all upon it are simply to be taken
as they are, and the investigation of their past and present and future
shall be unintermitted and shall be done with perfect candor. Upon this
basis philosophy speculates ever looking toward the poet, ever regarding
the eternal tendencies of all toward happiness never inconsistent with what
is clear to the senses and to the soul. For the eternal tendencies of all
toward happiness make the only point of sane philosophy. Whatever
comprehends less than that . . . Whatever is less than the laws of light
and of astronomical motion . . . or less than the laws that follow the
thief the liar the glutton and the drunkard through this life and doubtless
afterward . . . or less than vast stretches of time or the slow formation of
density or the patient upheaving of strata—is of no account. Whatever
would put God in a poem or system of philosophy as contending against
some being or influence, is also of no account. Sanity and ensemble characterize the great master . . . spoilt in one principle all is spoilt. The
great master has nothing to do with miracles. He sees health for himself
in being one of the mass . . . he sees the hiatus in singular eminence.
To the perfect shape comes common ground. To be under the general
law is great for that is to correspond with it. The master knows that he
is unspeakably great and that all are unspeakably great . . . that nothing
for instance is greater than to conceive children and bring them up well
. . . that to be is just as great as to perceive or tell.

In the make of the great masters the idea of political liberty is indispensable. Liberty takes the adherence of heroes wherever men and women
exist . . . but never takes any adherence or welcome from the rest more
than from poets. They are the voice and exposition of liberty. They out
of ages are worthy the grand idea . . . to them it is confided and they
must sustain it. Nothing has precedence of it and nothing can warp or
degrade it. The attitude of great poets is to cheer up slaves and horrify
despots. The turn of their necks, the sound of their feet, the motions of
their wrists, are full of hazard to the one and hope to the other. Come nigh
them awhile and though they neither speak or advise you shall learn the
faithful American lesson. Liberty is poorly served by men whose good
intent is quelled from one failure or two failures or any number of
failures, or from the casual indifference or ingratitude of the people, or
from the sharp show of the tushes of power, or the bringing to bear soldiers and cannon or any penal statutes. Liberty relies upon itself, invites

no one, promises nothing, sits in calmness and light, is positive and composed, and knows no discouragement. The battle rages with many a loud
alarm and frequent advance and retreat . . . the enemy triumphs . . .
the prison, the handcuffs, the iron necklace and anklet, the scaffold, gar-
rote and lead balls do their work . . . the cause is asleep . . . the strong
throats are choked with their own blood . . . the young men drop their
eyelashes toward the ground when they pass each other . . . and is
liberty gone out of that place? No never. When liberty goes it is not the
first to go nor the second nor third to go . . . it waits for all the rest to
go . . . it is the last. . . . When the memories of the old martyrs are
faded utterly away . . . when the large names of patriots are laughed at
in the public halls from the lips of the orators . . . when the boys are no
more christened after the same but christened after tyrants and traitors
instead . . . when the laws of the free are grudgingly permitted and
laws for informers and blood money are sweet to the taste of the people
. . . when I and you walk abroad upon the earth stung with compassion at the sight of numberless brothers answering our equal friendship and calling no man master—and when we are elated with noble
joy at the sight of slaves . . . when the soul retires in the cool communion of the night and surveys its experience and has much extasy over
the word and deed that put back a helpless innocent person into the gripe
of the gripers or into any cruel inferiority . . . when those in all parts of
these states who could easier realize the true American character but do
not yet—when the swarms of cringers, suckers, doughfaces, lice of politics,
planners of sly involutions for their own preferment to city offices or state
legislatures or the judiciary or congress or the presidency, obtain a response
of love and natural deference from the people whether they get the
offices or no . . . when it is better to be a bound booby and rogue in
office at a high salary than the poorest free mechanic or farmer with his
hat unmoved from his head and firm eyes and a candid and generous
heart . . . and when servility by town or state or the federal government
or any oppression on a large scale or small scale can be tried on without
its own punishment following duly after in exact proportion against the
smallest chance of escape . . . or rather when all life and all the souls
of men and women are discharged from any part of the earth—then only
shall the instinct of liberty be discharged from that part of the earth.

As the attributes of the poets of the kosmos concenter in the real body
and soul and in the pleasure of things they possess the superiority of
genuineness over all fiction and romance. As they emit themselves facts
are showered over with light . . . the daylight is lit with more volatile
light . . . also the deep between the setting and rising sun goes deeper
many fold. Each precise object or condition or combination or process
exhibits a beauty . . . the multiplication table its—old age its—the carpenter's trade its—the grand opera its . . . the huge hulled clean-shaped
New York clipper at sea under steam or full sail gleams with unmatched
beauty . . . the American circles and large harmonies of government
gleam with theirs . . . and the commonest definite intentions and actions

with theirs. The poets of the kosmos advance through all interpositions and coverings and turmoils and stratagems to first principles. They are of use . . . they dissolve poverty from its need and riches from its conceit. You large proprietor they say shall not realize or perceive more than anyone else. The owner of the library is not he who holds a legal title to it having bought and paid for it. Anyone and everyone is owner of the library who can read the same through all the varieties of tongues and subjects and styles, and in whom they enter with ease and take residence and force toward paternity and maternity, and make supple and powerful and rich and large. . . . These American states strong and healthy and accomplished shall receive no pleasure from violations of natural models and must not permit them. In paintings or moldings or carvings in mineral or wood, or in the illustrations of books or newspapers, or in any comic or tragic prints, or in the patterns of woven stuffs or anything to beautify rooms or furniture or costumes, or to put upon cornices or monuments or on the prows or sterns of ships, or to put anywhere before the human eye indoors or out, that which distorts honest shapes or which creates unearthly beings or places or contingencies is a nuisance and revolt. Of the human form especially it is so great it must never be made ridiculous. Of ornaments to a work nothing outre can be allowed . . . but those ornaments can be allowed that conform to the perfect facts of the open air and that flow out of the nature of the work and come irrepressibly from it and are necessary to the completion of the work. Most works are most beautiful without ornament. . . . Exaggerations will be revenged in human physiology. Clean and vigorous children are jetted and conceived only in those communities where the models of natural forms are public every day. . . . Great genius and the people of these states must never be demeaned to romances. As soon as histories are properly told there is no more need of romances.

The great poets are also to be known by the absence in them of tricks and by the justification of perfect personal candor. Then folks echo a new cheap joy and a divine voice leaping from their brains: How beautiful is candor! All faults may be forgiven of him who has perfect candor. Henceforth let no man of us lie, for we have seen that openness wins the inner and outer world and that there is no single exception, and that never since our earth gathered itself in a mass have deceit or subterfuge or prevarication attracted its smallest particle or the faintest tinge of a shade—and that through the enveloping wealth and rank of a state or the whole republic of states a sneak or sly person shall be discovered and despised . . . and that the soul has never been once fooled and never can be fooled . . . and thrift without the loving nod of the soul is only a fetid puff . . . and there never grew up in any of the continents of the globe nor upon any planet or satellite or star, nor upon the asteroids, nor in any part of ethereal space, nor in the midst of density, nor under the fluid wet of the sea, nor in that condition which precedes the birth of babes, nor at any time during the changes of life, nor in that condition that follows what we term death, nor in any stretch of abeyance or action afterward of vitality, nor in any process of formation or reformation anywhere, a being whose instinct hated the truth.

Extreme caution or prudence, the soundest organic health, large hope and comparison and fondness for women and children, large alimentiveness and destructiveness and causality, with a perfect sense of the oneness of nature and the propriety of the same spirit applied to human affairs . . . these are called up of the float of the brain of the world to be parts of the greatest poet from his birth out of his mother's womb and from her birth out of her mother's. Caution seldom goes far enough. It has been thought that the prudent citizen was the citizen who applied himself to solid gains and did well for himself and his family and completed a lawful life without debt or crime. The greatest poet sees and admits these economies as he sees the economies of food and sleep, but has higher notions of prudence than to think he gives much when he gives a few slight attentions at the latch of the gate. The premises of the prudence of life are not the hospitality of it or the ripeness and harvest of it. Beyond the independence of a little sum laid aside for burial money, and of a few clapboards around and shingles overhead on a lot of American soil owned, and the easy dollars that supply the year's plain clothing and meals, the melancholy prudence of the abandonment of such a great being as a man is to the toss and pallor of years of moneymaking with all their scorching days and icy nights and all their stifling deceits and underhanded dodgings, or infinitesimals of parlors, or shameless stuffing while others starve . . . and all the loss of the bloom and odor of the earth and of the flowers and atmosphere and of the sea and of the true taste of the women and men you pass or have to do with in youth or middle age, and the issuing sickness and desperate revolt at the close of a life without elevation or naivete, and the ghastly chatter of a death without serenity or majesty, is the great fraud upon modern civilization and forethought, blotching the surface and system which civilization undeniably drafts, and moistening with tears the immense features it spreads and spreads with such velocity before the reached kisses of the soul. . . . Still the right explanation remains to be made about prudence. The prudence of the mere wealth and respectability of the most esteemed life appears too faint for the eye to observe at all when little and large alike drop quietly aside at the thought of the prudence suitable for immortality. What is wisdom that fills the thinness of a year or seventy or eighty years to wisdom spaced out by ages and coming back at a certain time with strong reinforcements and rich presents and the clear faces of wedding guests as far as you can look in every direction running gaily toward you? Only the soul is of itself . . . all else has reference to what ensues. All that a person does or thinks is of consequence. Not a move can a man or woman make that affects him or her in a day or a month or any part of the direct lifetime or the hour of death but the same affects him or her onward afterward through the indirect lifetime. The indirect is always as great and real as the direct. The spirit received from the body just as much as it gives to the body. Not one name of word or deed . . . not of venereal sores or discolorations . . . not the privacy of the onanist . . . not of the putrid veins of gluttons or rum drinkers . . . not peculation or cunning or betrayal or murder . . . no serpentine poison of those that seduce women . . . not the foolish yielding of women . . . not prostitution . . . not of any depravity of young men . . . not of the attainment of gain by discreditable means . . . not any nastiness of appetite . . . not any harshness of officers to men or judges to prisoners or fathers to sons or sons to fathers or husbands to wives or bosses to their boys . . . not of greedy looks or malignant wishes . . . nor any of the wiles practiced by people upon themselves . . . ever is or ever can be stamped on the program but it is duly realized and returned, and that returned in further performances . . . and they returned again. Nor can the push of charity or personal force ever be anything else than the profoundest reason, whether it brings arguments to hand or no. No specification is necessary . . . to add or subtract or divide is in vain. Little or big, learned or unlearned, white or black, legal or illegal, sick or well, from the first inspiration down the windpipe to the last expiration out of it, all that a male or female does that is vigorous and benevolent and clean is so much sure profit to him or her in the unshakable order of the universe and through the whole scope of it forever. If the savage or felon is wise it is well . . . if the greatest poet or savant is wise it is simply the same . . . if the President or chief justice is wise it is the same . . . if the young mechanic or farmer is wise it is no more or less . . . if the prostitute is wise it is no more or less. The interest will come round . . . all will come round. All the best actions of war and peace . . . all help given to relatives and strangers and the poor and old and sorrowful and young children and widows and the sick, and to all shunned persons . . . all furtherance of fugitives and of the escape of slaves . . . all the self-denial that stood steady and aloof on wrecks and saw others take the seats of the boats . . . all offering of substance or life for the good old cause, or for a friend's sake or opinion's sake . . . all pains of enthusiasts scoffed at by their neighbors . . . all the vast sweet love and precious suffering of mothers . . . all honest men baffled in strifes recorded or unrecorded . . . all the grandeur and good of the few ancient nations whose fragments of annals we inherit . . . and all the good of the hundreds of far mightier and more ancient nations unknown to us by name or date or location . . . all that was ever manfully begun, whether it succeeded or not . . . all that has at any time been well suggested out of the divine heart of man or by the divinity of his mouth or by the shaping of his great hands . . . and all that is well thought or done this day on any part of the surface of the globe . . . or on any of the wandering stars or fixed stars by those there as we are here . . . or that is henceforth to be well thought or done by you whoever you are, or by anyone—these singly and wholly inured at their time and inure now and will inure always to the identities from which they sprung or shall spring. . . . Did you guess any of them lived only its moment? The world does not so exist . . . no parts palpable or impalpable so exist . . . no result exists now without being from its long antecedent result, and that from its antecedent, and so backward without the farthest mentionable spot coming a bit nearer to the beginning than any other spot. . . . Whatever satisfies the soul is truth. The prudence of the greatest poet answers at last the craving and glut of the soul, is not contemptuous of less ways of prudence if they conform to its ways, puts off nothing, permits no let-up for its own case or any case, has no particular sabbath or judgment day, divides not the living from the dead or the righteous from the unrighteous, is satisfied with the present, matches every thought or act by its correlative, knows no possible forgiveness or deputed atonement . . . knows that the young man who composedly periled his life and lost it has done exceeding well for himself, while the man who has not periled his life and retains it to old age in riches and ease has perhaps achieved nothing for himself worth mentioning . . . and that only that person has no great prudence to learn who has learnt to prefer real long-lived things, and favors body and soul the same, and perceives the indirect assuredly following the direct, and what evil or good he does leaping onward and waiting to meet him again—and who in his spirit in any emergency whatever neither hurries or avoids death.

The direct trial of him who would be the greatest poet is today. If he does not flood himself with the immediate age as with vast oceanic tides . . . and if he does not attract his own land body and soul to himself and hang on its neck with incomparable love and plunge his semitic muscle into its merits and demerits . . . and if he be not himself the age transfigured . . . and if to him is not opened the eternity which gives similitude to all periods and locations and processes and animate and inanimate forms, and which is the bond of time, and rises up from its inconceivable vagueness and infiniteness in the swimming shape of today, and is held by the ductile anchors of life, and makes the present spot the passage from what was to what shall be, and commits itself to the representation of this wave of an hour and this one of the sixty beautiful children of the wave— let him merge in the general run and wait his development. . . . Still the final test of poems or any character or work remains. The prescient poet projects himself centuries ahead and judges performer or performance after the changes of time. Does it live through them? Does it still hold on untired? Will the same style and the direction of genius to similar points be satisfactory now? Has no new discovery in science or arrival at superior planes of thought and judgment and behavior fixed him or his so that either can be looked down upon? Have the marches of tens and hundreds and thousands of years made willing detours to the right hand and the left hand for his sake? Is he beloved long and long after he is buried? Does the young man think often of him? and the young woman think often of him? and do the middle-aged and the old think of him?

A great poem is for ages and ages in common and for all degrees and complexions and all departments and sects and for a woman as much as a man and a man as much as a woman. A great poem is no finish to a man or woman but rather a beginning. Has anyone fancied he could sit at last under some due authority and rest satisfied with explanations and realize and be content and full? To no such terminus does the greatest poet bring . . . he brings neither cessation or sheltered fatness and ease. The touch of him tells in action. Whom he takes he takes with firm sure grasp into live regions previously unattained . . . thenceforward is no rest . . . they see the space and ineffable sheen that turn the old spots and lights into dead vacuums. The companion of him beholds the birth and progress of stars and learns one of the meanings. Now there shall be a man cohered out of tumult and chaos . . . the elder encourages the younger and shows him how . . . they two shall launch off fearlessly together till the new world fits an orbit for itself and looks unabashed on the lesser orbits of the stars and sweeps through the ceaseless rings and shall never be quiet again.

There will soon be no more priests. Their work is done. They may wait awhile . . . perhaps a generation or two . . . dropping off by degrees. A superior breed shall take their place . . . the gangs of kosmos and prophets en masse shall take their place. A new order shall arise and they shall be the priests of man, and every man shall be his own priest. The churches built under their umbrage shall be the churches of men and women. Through the divinity of themselves shall the kosmos and the new breed of poets be interpreters of men and women and of all events and things. They shall find their inspiration in real objects today, symptoms of the past and future. . . . They shall not deign to defend immortality or God or the perfection of things or liberty or the exquisite beauty and reality of the soul. They shall arise in America and be responded to from the remainder of the earth.

The English language befriends the grand American expression . . . it is brawny enough and limber and full enough. On the tough stock of a race who through all change of circumstances was never without the idea of political liberty, which is the animus of all liberty, it has attracted the terms of daintier and gayer and subtler and more elegant tongues. It is the powerful language of resistance . . . it is the dialect of common sense. It is the speech of the proud and melancholy races and of all who aspire. It is the chosen tongue to express growth faith self-esteem freedom justice equality friendliness amplitude prudence decision and courage. It is the medium that shall well nigh express the inexpressible.   •

No great literature nor any like style of behavior or oratory or social intercourse or household arrangements or public institutions or the treatment by bosses of employed people, nor executive detail or detail of the army or navy, nor spirit of legislation or courts or police or tuition or architecture or songs or amusements or the costumes of young men, can long elude the jealous and passionate instinct of American standards. Whether or no the sign appears from the mouths of the people, it throbs a live interrogation in every freeman's and freewoman's heart after that which passes by or this built to remain. Is it uniform with my country? Are its disposals without ignominious distinctions? Is it for the evergrowing communes of brothers and lovers, large, well united, proud beyond the old models, generous beyond all models? Is it something grown fresh out of the fields or drawn from the sea for use to me today here? I know that what answers for me an American must answer for any individual or nation that serves for a part of my materials. Does this answer? or is it without reference to universal needs? or sprung of the needs of the less developed society of special ranks? or old needs of pleasure overlaid by modern science and forms? Does this acknowledge liberty with audible and absolute acknowledgment, and set slavery at naught for life and death? Will it help breed one good shaped and well hung man, and a woman to be his perfect and independent mate? Does it improve manners? Is it for the nursing of the young of the republic? Does it solve readily with the sweet milk of the nipples of the breasts of the mother of many children? Has it too the old ever-fresh forbearance and impartiality? Does it look with the same love on the last born and those hardening toward stature, and on the errant, and on those who disdain all strength of assault outside of their own.

The poems distilled from other poems will probably pass away. The coward will surely pass away. The expectation of the vital and great can only be satisfied by the demeanor of the vital and great. The swarms of the polished deprecating and reflectors and the polite float off and leave no remembrance. America prepares with composure and good will for the visitors that have sent word. It is not intellect that is to be their warrant and welcome. The talented, the artist, the ingenious, the editor, the statesman, the erudite . . . they are not unappreciated . . . they fall in their place and do their work. The soul of the nation also does its work. No disguise can pass on it . . . no disguise can conceal from it. It rejects none, it permits all. Only toward as good as itself and toward the like of itself will it advance half-way. An individual is as superb as a nation when he has the qualities which make a superb nation. The soul of the largest and wealthiest and proudest nation may well go half-way to meet that of its poets. The signs are effectual. There is no fear of mistake. If the one is true the other is true. The proof of a poet is that his country absorbs him as affectionately as he has absorbed it.

WALT WHITMAN

A BACKWARD GLANCE O'ER TRAVEL'D ROADS [1]
(1888)

PERHAPS THE best of songs heard, or of any and all true love, or life's fairest episodes or sailors', soldiers' trying scenes on land or sea, is the *résumé* of them, or any of them, long afterwards, looking at the actualities away back past, with all their practical excitations gone. How the soul loves to float amid such reminiscences!

So here I sit gossiping in the early candlelight of old age—I and my book—casting backward glances over our travel'd road. After completing, as it were, the journey—(a varied jaunt of years, with many halts and gaps of intervals—or some lengthen'd ship-voyage, wherein more than once the last hour had apparently arrived, and we seem'd certainly going down— yet reaching port in a sufficient way through all discomfitures at last)— After completing my poems, I am curious to review them in the light of their own (at the time unconscious, or mostly unconscious) intentions, with certain unfoldings of the thirty years they seek to embody. These lines, therefore, will probably blend the weft of first purposes and speculations, with the warp of that experience afterwards, always bringing strange developments.

Result of seven or eight stages and struggles extending through nearly thirty years, (as I nigh my three-score-and-ten I live largely on memory,) I look upon *Leaves of Grass*, now finish'd to the end of its opportunities and powers, as my definitive *carte visite* to the coming generations of the New World,[*] if I may assume to say so. That I have not gain'd the acceptance of my own time, but have fallen back on fond dreams of the future—anticipations—("still lives the song, though Regnar dies")—That from a worldly and business point of view *Leaves of Grass* has been worse than a failure—that public criticism on the book and myself as author of it yet shows mark'd anger and contempt more than anything else—("I find a solid line of enemies to you everywhere,"—letter from W. S. K., Boston, May 28, 1884)—And that solely for publishing it I have been the object of two or three pretty serious special official buffetings—is all probably no more than I ought to have expected. I had my choice when I commenc'd. I bid neither for soft eulogies, big money returns, nor the approbation of existing schools and conventions. As fulfill'd or partially fulfill'd, the best comfort of the whole business (after a small band of the dearest

---

[1] Published as a Preface to *November Boughs* (Philadelphia, 1888).

[*] When Champollion, on his deathbed, handed to the printer the revised proof of his Egyptian Grammar, he said gayly, "Be careful of this—it is my carte de visite to posterity." [Whitman's note]

friends and upholders ever vouchsafed to man or cause—doubtless all the
more faithful and uncompromising—this little phalanx!—for being so few)
is that, unstopp'd and unwarp'd by any influence outside the soul within
me, I have had my say entirely my own way, and put it unerringly on
record—the value thereof to be decided by time.

In calculating that decision, William O'Connor and Dr. Bucke [2] are
far more peremptory than I am. Behind all else that can be said, I consider *Leaves of Grass* and its theory experimental—as, in the deepest sense,
I consider our American republic itself to be, with its theory. (I think I
have at least enough philosophy not to be too absolutely certain of anything, or any results.) In the second place, the volume is a *sortie*—whether
to prove triumphant, and conquer its field of aim and escape and construction, nothing less than a hundred years from now can fully answer.
I consider the point that I have positively gain'd a hearing, to far more
than make up for any and all other lacks and withholdings. Essentially,
that was from the first, and has remain'd throughout, the main object.
Now it seems to be achiev'd, I am certainly contented to waive any otherwise momentous drawbacks, as of little account. Candidly and dispassion-
ately reviewing all my intentions, I feel that they were creditable—and I
accept the result, whatever it may be.

After continued personal ambition and effort, as a young fellow, to
enter with the rest into competition for the usual rewards, business, political, literary, etc.—to take part in the great *mêlée*, both for victory's prize
itself and to do some good—After years of those aims and pursuits, I found
myself remaining possess'd, at the age of thirty-one to thirty-three, with a
special desire and conviction. Or rather, to be quite exact, a desire that
had been flitting through my previous life, or hovering on the flanks,
mostly indefinite hitherto, had steadily advanced to the front, defined
itself, and finally dominated everything else. This was a feeling or ambition to articulate and faithfully express in literary or poetic form, and
uncompromisingly, my own physical, emotional, moral, intellectual, and
esthetic Personality, in the midst of, and tallying, the momentous spirit
and facts of its immediate days, and of current America—and to exploit
that Personality, identified with place and date, in a far more candid and
comprehensive sense than any hitherto poem or book.

Perhaps this is in brief, or suggests, all I have sought to do. Given the
Nineteenth Century, with the United States, and what they furnish as
area and points of view, *Leaves of Grass* is, or seeks to be, simply a faithful
and doubtless self-will'd record. In the midst of all, it gives one man's—the
author's—identity, ardors, observations, faiths, and thoughts, color'd hardly
at all with any decided coloring from other faiths or other identities.
Plenty of songs had been sung—beautiful, matchless songs—adjusted to
other lands than these—another spirit and stage of evolution; but I would

[2] William O'Connor was a devoted friend of Whitman who published in 1866 a
pamphlet in defense of the poet, *The Good Gray Poet: A Vindication*. Dr. Richard
Maurice Bucke, a Canadian physician of London, Ontario, was likewise a close personal friend of the poet and published in 1883 the first complete life of Whitman,
Walt Whitman.

sing, and leave out or put in, quite solely with reference to America and today. Modern science and democracy seem'd to be throwing out their challenge to poetry to put them in its statements in contradistinction to the songs and myths of the past. As I see it now (perhaps too late,) I have unwittingly taken up that challenge and made an attempt at such statements—which I certainly would not assume to do now, knowing more clearly what it means.

For grounds for *Leaves of Grass*, as a poem, I abandon'd the conventional themes, which do not appear in it: none of the stock ornamentation, or choice plots of love or war, or high, exceptional personages of Old-World song; nothing, as I may say, for beauty's sake—no legend, or myth, or romance, nor euphemism, nor rhyme. But the broadest average of humanity and its identities in the now ripening Nineteenth Century, and especially in each of their countless examples and practical occupations in the United States today.

One main contrast of the ideas behind every page of my verses, compared with establish'd poems, is their different relative attitude toward God, toward the objective universe, and still more (by reflection, confession, assumption, &c.) the quite changed attitude of the ego, the one chanting or talking, toward himself and toward his fellow-humanity. It is certainly time for America, above all, to begin this readjustment in the scope and basic point of view of verse; for everything else has changed. As I write, I see in an article on Wordsworth, in one of the current English magazines, the lines, "A few weeks ago an eminent French critic said that, owing to the special tendency to science and to its all-devouring force, poetry would cease to be read in fifty years." But I anticipate the very contrary. Only a firmer, vastly broader, new area begins to exist—nay, is already form'd—to which the poetic genius must emigrate. Whatever may have been the case in years gone by, the true use for the imaginative faculty of modern times is to give ultimate vivification to facts, to science, and to common lives, endowing them with glows and glories and final illustriousness which belong to every real thing, and to real things only. Without that ultimate vivification—which the poet or other artist alone can give—reality would seem incomplete, and science, democracy, and life itself, finally in vain.

Few appreciate the moral revolutions of our age, which have been profounder far than the material or inventive or war-produced ones. The Nineteenth Century, now well toward its close (and ripening into fruit the seeds of the two preceding centuries *)—the uprisings of national masses and shiftings of boundary lines—the historical and other prominent facts of the United States—the war of attempted Secession—the stormy rush and haste of nebulous forces—never can future years witness more excitement and din of action—never completer change of army front along

---

* The ferment and germination even of the United States today, dating back to, and in my opinion mainly founded on, the Elizabethan age in English history, the age of Francis Bacon and Shakespeare. Indeed, when we pursue it, what growth or advent is there that does not date back, back, until lost—perhaps its most tantalizing clues lost—in the receded horizons of the past? [Whitman's note]

the whole line, the whole civilized world. For all these new and evolutionary facts, meanings, purposes, new poetic messages, new forms and expressions, are inevitable.

My Book and I—what a period we have presumed to span! those thirty years from 1850 to '80—and America in them! Proud, proud indeed may we be, if we have cull'd enough of that period in its own spirit to worthily waft a few live breaths of it to the future!

Let me not dare, here or anywhere, for my own purposes, or any purposes, to attempt the definition of Poetry, nor answer the question what it is. Like Religion, Love, Nature, while those terms are indispensable, and we all give a sufficiently accurate meaning to them, in my opinion no definition that has ever been made sufficiently encloses the name Poetry; nor can any rule or convention ever so absolutely obtain but some great exception may arise and disregard and overturn it.

Also it must be carefully remember'd that first-class literature does not shine by any luminosity of its own; nor do its poems. They grow of circumstances, and are evolutionary. The actual living light is always curiously from elsewhere—follows unaccountable sources, and is lunar and relative at the best. There are, I know, certain controlling themes that seem endlessly appropriated to the poets—as war, in the past—in the Bible, religious rapture and adoration—always love, beauty, some fine plot, or pensive or other emotion. But, strange as it may sound at first, I will say there is something striking far deeper and towering far higher than those themes for the best elements of modern song.

Just as all the old imaginative works rest, after their kind, on long trains of presuppositions, often entirely unmention'd by themselves, yet supplying the most important bases of them, and without which they could have had no reason for being, so *Leaves of Grass*, before a line was written, presupposed something different from any other, and, as it stands, is the result of such presupposition. I should say, indeed, it were useless to attempt reading the book without first carefully tallying that preparatory background and quality in the mind. Think of the United States today—the facts of these thirty-eight or forty empires solder'd in one—sixty or seventy millions of equals with their lives, their passions, their future—these incalculable, modern, American, seething multitudes around us, of which we are inseparable parts! Think, in comparison, of the petty environage and limited area of the poets of past or present Europe, no matter how great their genius. Think of the absence and ignorance in all cases hitherto, of the multitudinousness, vitality, and the unprecedented stimulants of today and here. It almost seems as if a poetry with cosmic and dynamic features of magnitude and limitlessness suitable to the human soul were never possible before. It is certain that a poetry of absolute faith and equality for the use of the democratic masses never was.

In estimating first-class song, a sufficient Nationality, or, on the other hand, what may be call'd the negative and lack of it, (as in Goethe's case, it sometimes seems to me,) is often, if not always, the first element. One needs only a little penetration to see, at more or less removes, the ma-

terial facts of their country and radius, with the coloring of the moods of
humanity at the time, and its gloomy or hopeful prospects, behind all
poets and each poet, and forming their birthmarks. I know very well that
my *Leaves* could not possibly have emerged or been fashion'd or completed, from any other era than the latter half of the Nineteenth Century,
nor any other land than democratic America, and from the absolute triumph of the National Union arms.

And whether my friends claim it for me or not, I know well enough,
too, that in respect to pictorial talent, dramatic situations, and especially
in verbal melody and all the conventional technique of poetry, not only
the divine works that today stand ahead in the world's reading but dozens
more, transcend (some of them immeasurably transcend) all I have done,
or could do. But it seem'd to me, as the objects in Nature, the themes of
estheticism, and all special exploitations of the mind and soul, involve
not only their own inherent quality, but the quality, just as inherent and
important, of *their point of view,** the time had come to reflect all themes
and things, old and new, in the lights thrown on them by the advent of
America and democracy—to chant those themes through the utterance of
one, not only the grateful and reverent legatee of the past, but the born
child of the New World—to illustrate all through the genesis and ensemble of today; and that such illustration and ensemble are the chief
demands of America's prospective imaginative literature. Not to carry out,
in the approved style, some choice plot of fortune or misfortune, or fancy,
or fine thoughts, or incidents, or courtesies—all of which has been done
overwhelmingly and well, probably never to be excell'd—but that while in
such aesthetic presentation of objects, passions, plots, thoughts, etc., our
lands and days do not want, and probably will never have, anything better than they already possess from the bequests of the past, it still remains
to be said that there is even toward all those a subjective and contemporary point of view appropriate to ourselves alone, and to our new genius
and environments, different from anything hitherto; and that such conception of current or gone-by life and art is for us the only means of
their assimilation consistent with the Western world.

Indeed, and anyhow, to put it specifically, has not the time arrived when,
(if it must be plainly said, for democratic America's sake, if for no other)
there must imperatively come a readjustment of the whole theory and
nature of Poetry? The question is important, and I may turn the argument over and repeat it: Does not the best thought of our day and Republic conceive of a birth and spirit of song superior to anything past or present? To the effectual and moral consolidation of our lands (already, as
materially establish'd, the greatest factors in known history, and far, far
greater through what they prelude and necessitate, and are to be in future)—to conform with and build on the concrete realities and theories of
the universe furnish'd by science, and henceforth the only irrefragable
basis for anything, verse included—to root both influences in the emo-

* According to Immanuel Kant, the last essential reality, giving shape and significance to all the rest. [Whitman's note]

tional and imaginative action of the modern time, and dominate all that precedes or opposes them—is not either a radical advance and step forward, or a new verteber of the best song indispensable?

The New World receives with joy the poems of the antique, with European feudalism's rich fund of epics, plays, ballads—seeks not in the least to deaden or displace those voices from our ear and area—holds them indeed as indispensable studies, influences, records, comparisons. But though the dawn-dazzle of the sun of literature is in those poems for us of today—though perhaps the best parts of current character in nations, social groups, or any man's or woman's individuality, Old World or New, are from them—and though if I were ask'd to name the most precious bequest to current American civilization from all the hitherto ages, I am not sure but I would name those old and less old songs ferried hither from east and west—some serious words and debits remain; some acrid considerations demand a hearing. Of the great poems receiv'd from abroad and from the ages, and today enveloping and penetrating America, is there one that is consistent with these United States, or essentially applicable to them as they are and are to be? Is there one whose underlying basis is not a denial and insult to democracy? What a comment it forms, anyhow, on this era of literary fulfillment, with the splendid day-rise of science and resuscitation of history, that our chief religious and poetical works are not our own, nor adapted to our light, but have been furnish'd by far-back ages out of their arriere and darkness, or, at most, twilight dimness! What is there in those works that so imperiously and scornfully dominates all our advanced civilization, and culture?

Even Shakespeare, who so suffuses current letters and art (which indeed have in most degrees grown out of him,) belongs essentially to the buried past. Only he holds the proud distinction for certain important phases of that past, of being the loftiest of the singers life has yet given voice to. All, however, relate to and rest upon conditions, standards, politics, sociologies, ranges of belief, that have been quite eliminated from the Eastern hemisphere, and never existed at all in the Western. As authoritative types of song they belong in America just about as much as the persons and institutions they depict. True, it may be said, the emotional, moral, and aesthetic natures of humanity have not radically changed —that in these the old poems apply to our times and all times, irrespective of date; and that they are of incalculable value as pictures of the past. I willingly make those admissions and to their fullest extent; then advance the points herewith as of serious, even paramount importance.

I have indeed put on record elsewhere my reverence and eulogy for those never-to-be-excell'd poetic bequests, and their indescribable preciousness as heirlooms for America. Another and separate point must now be candidly stated. If I had not stood before those poems with uncover'd head, fully aware of their colossal grandeur and beauty of form and spirit, I could not have written *Leaves of Grass*. My verdict and conclusions as illustrated in its pages are arrived at through the temper and inculcation of the old works as much as through anything else—perhaps more than through anything else. As America fully and fairly construed is the legitimate result and evolutionary outcome of the past, so I would dare to claim for my verse. Without stopping to qualify the averment, the Old World has had the poems of myths, fictions, feudalism, conquest, caste, dynastic wars, and splendid exceptional characters and affairs, which have been great; but the New World needs the poems of realities and science and of the democratic average and basic equality, which shall be greater. In the center of all, and object of all, stands the Human Being, toward whose heroic and spiritual evolution poems and everything directly or indirectly tend, Old World or New.

Continuing the subject, my friends have more than once suggested—or may be the garrulity of advancing age is possessing me—some further embryonic facts of *Leaves of Grass*, and especially how I enter'd upon them. Dr. Bucke has, in his volume, already fully and fairly described the preparation of my poetic field, with the particular and general plowing, planting, seeding, and occupation of the ground, till everything was fertilized, rooted, and ready to start its own way for good or bad. Not till after this, did I attempt any serious acquaintance with poetic literature. Along in my sixteenth year I had become the possessor of a stout, well-cramm'd one-thousand-page octavo volume (I have it yet,) containing Walter Scott's poetry entire—an inexhaustible mine and treasury of poetic forage (especially the endless forests and jungles of notes)—has been so to me for fifty years, and remains so to this day.*

Later, at intervals, summers and falls, I used to go off, sometimes for a week at a stretch, down in the country, or to Long Island's seashores—there, in the presence of outdoor influences, I went over thoroughly the Old and New Testaments, and absorb'd (probably to better advantage for me than in any library or indoor room—it makes such difference *where* you read,) Shakespeare, Ossian,[3] the best translated versions I could get of Homer, Aeschylus, Sophocles, the old German Nibelungen,[4] the ancient Hindu poems,[5] and one or two other masterpieces, Dante's among them. As it happen'd, I read the latter mostly in an old wood. The *Iliad* (Buckley's prose version) I read first thoroughly on the peninsula of Orient, northeast end of Long Island, in a shelter'd hollow of rocks and sand, with the sea on each side. (I have wonder'd since why I was not overwhelm'd by those mighty masters. Likely because I read them, as described, in the

---

* Sir Walter Scott's *Complete Poems*; especially including Border Minstrelsy; then Sir Tristrem; Lay of the Last Minstrel; Ballads from the German; Marmion; Lady of the Lake; Vision of Don Roderick; Lord of the Isles; Rokeby; Bridal of Triermain; Field of Waterloo; Harold the Dauntless; all the Dramas; various Introductions, endless interesting Notes and Essays on Poetry, Romance, etc.

Lockhart's 1833 (or '34) edition with Scott's latest and copious revisions and annotations. (All the poems were thoroughly read by me, but the ballads of the Border Minstrelsy over and over again.) [Whitman's note]

[3] James Macpherson (1736–1796), Scotch poet, collected and published the supposed versions of the Ossianic poems.

[4] Middle High German epic of the thirteenth century.

[5] There is some evidence that Whitman was familiar with the *Vedas*, sacred scriptures of Hinduism, and with *The Bhagavad Gita* which offers many interesting parallels with Whitman's own work.

full presence of Nature, under the sun, with the far-spreading landscape and vistas, or the sea rolling in.)

Toward the last I had among much else look'd over Edgar Poe's poems—of which I was not an admirer, tho' I always saw that beyond their limited range of melody (like perpetual chimes of music bells, ringing from lower *b* flat up to *g*) they were melodious expressions, and perhaps never-excell'd ones, for certain pronounc'd phases of human morbidity. (The Poetic area is very spacious—has room for all—has so many mansions!) But I was repaid in Poe's prose by the idea that (at any rate for our occasions, our day) there can be no such thing as a long poem.[6] The same thought had been haunting my mind before, but Poe's argument, though short, work'd the sum and proved it to me.

Another point had an early settlement, clearing the ground greatly. I saw, from the time my enterprise and questionings positively shaped themselves (how best can I express my own distinctive era and surroundings, America, Democracy?) that the trunk and center whence the answer was to radiate, and to which all should return from straying however far a distance, must be an identical body and soul, a personality—which personality, after many considerations and ponderings I deliberately settled should be myself—indeed could not be any other. I also felt strongly (whether I have shown it or not) that to the true and full estimate of the Present both the Past and the Future are main considerations.

These, however, and much more might have gone on and come to naught (almost positively would have come to naught,) if a sudden, vast, terrible, direct and indirect stimulus for new and national declamatory expression had not been given to me. It is certain, I say, that, although I had made a start before, only from the occurrence of the Secession War, and what it show'd me as by flashes of lightning, with the emotional depths it sounded and arous'd (of course, I don't mean in my own heart only, I saw it just as plainly in others, in millions)—that only from the strong flare and provocation of that war's sights and scenes the final reasons-for-being of an autochthonic and passionate song definitely came forth.

I went down to the war fields in Virginia (end of 1862), lived thenceforward in camp—saw great battles and the days and nights afterward—partook of all the fluctuation, gloom, despair, hopes again arous'd, courage evoked—death readily risk'd—*the cause*, too—along and filling those agonistic and lurid following years, 1863-'64-'65—the real parturition years (more than 1776-'83) of this henceforth homogeneous Union. Without those three or four years and the experiences they gave, *Leaves of Grass* would not now be existing.

But I set out with the intention also of indicating or hinting some point-characteristics which I since see (though I did not then, at least not definitely) were bases and object-urgings toward those *Leaves* from the first. The word I myself put primarily for the description of them as they stand

[6] Poe develops this idea in "The Poetic Principle" (1850).

at last is the word Suggestiveness. I round and finish little, if anything; and could not, consistently with my scheme. The reader will always have his or her part to do, just as much as I have had mine. I seek less to state or display any theme or thought, and more to bring you, reader, into the atmosphere of the theme or thought—there to pursue your own flight. Another impetus-word is Comradeship as for all lands, and in a more commanding and acknowledg'd sense than hitherto. Other word signs would be Good Cheer, Content, and Hope.

The chief trait of any given poet is always the spirit he brings to the observation of Humanity and Nature—the mood out of which he contemplates his subjects. What kind of temper and what amount of faith report these things? Up to how recent a date is the song carried? What the equipment, and special raciness of the singer—what his tinge of coloring? The last value of artistic expressers, past and present—Greek aesthetes, Shakespeare—or in our own day Tennyson, Victor Hugo, Carlyle, Emerson—is certainly involv'd in such questions. I say the profoundest service that poems or any other writings can do for their reader is not merely to satisfy the intellect, or supply something polish'd and interesting, nor even to depict great passions, or persons or events, but to fill him with vigorous and clean manliness, religiousness, and give him *good heart* as a radical possession and habit. The educated world seems to have been growing more and more ennuyed for ages, leaving to our time the inheritance of it all. Fortunately there is the original inexhaustible fund of buoyancy, normally resident in the race, forever eligible to be appeal'd to and relied on.

As for native American individuality, though certain to come, and on a large scale, the distinctive and ideal type of Western character (as consistent with the operative political and even moneymaking features of United States' humanity in the Nineteenth Century as chosen knights, gentlemen and warriors were the ideals of the centuries of European feudalism) it has not yet appear'd. I have allow'd the stress of my poems from beginning to end to bear upon American individuality and assist it—not only because that is a great lesson in Nature, amid all her generalizing laws, but as counterpoise to the leveling tendencies of Democracy—and for other reasons. Defiant of ostensible literary and other conventions, I avowedly chant "the great pride of man in himself," and permit it to be more or less a *motif* of nearly all my verse. I think this pride indispensable to an American. I think it not inconsistent with obedience, humility, deference, and self-questioning.

Democracy has been so retarded and jeopardized by powerful personalities, that its first instincts are fain to clip, conform, bring in stragglers, and reduce everything to a dead level. While the ambitious thought of my song is to help the forming of a great aggregate Nation, it is, perhaps, altogether through the forming of myriads of fully develop'd and enclosing individuals. Welcome as are equality's and fraternity's doctrines and popular education, a certain liability accompanies them all, as we see.

That primal and interior something in man, in his soul's abysms, coloring all, and, by exceptional fruitions, giving the last majesty to him—something continually touch'd upon and attain'd by the old poems and ballads of feudalism, and often the principal foundation of them—modern science and democracy appear to be endangering, perhaps eliminating. But that forms an appearance only; the reality is quite different. The new influences, upon the whole, are surely preparing the way for grander individualities than ever. Today and here personal force is behind everything, just the same. The times and depictions from the *Iliad* to Shakespeare inclusive can happily never again be realized—but the elements of courageous and lofty manhood are unchanged.

Without yielding an inch the workingman and workingwoman were to be in my pages from first to last. The ranges of heroism and loftiness with which Greek and feudal poets endow'd their god-like or lordly born characters—indeed prouder and better based and with fuller ranges than those —I was to endow the democratic averages of America. I was to show that we, here and today, are eligible to the grandest and the best—more eligible now than any times of old were. I will also want my utterances (I said to myself before beginning) to be in spirit the poems of the morning. (They have been founded and mainly written in the sunny forenoon and early midday of my life.) I will want them to be the poems of women entirely as much as men. I have wish'd to put the complete Union of the States in my songs without any preference or partiality whatever. Henceforth, if they live and are read, it must be just as much South as North—just as much along the Pacific as Atlantic—in the valley of the Mississippi, in Canada, up in Maine, down in Texas, and on the shores of Puget Sound.

From another point of view *Leaves of Grass* is avowedly the song of Sex and Amativeness, and even Animality—though meanings that do not usually go along with those words are behind all, and will duly emerge; and all are sought to be lifted into a different light and atmosphere. Of this feature, intentionally palpable in a few lines, I shall only say the espousing principle of those lines so gives breath of life to my whole scheme that the bulk of the pieces might as well have been left unwritten were those lines omitted. Difficult as it will be, it has become, in my opinion, imperative to achieve a shifted attitude from superior men and women toward the thought and fact of sexuality, as an element in character, personality, the emotions, and a theme in literature. I am not going to argue the question by itself; it does not stand by itself. The vitality of it is altogether in its relations, bearings, significance—like the clef of a symphony. At last analogy the lines I allude to, and the spirit in which they are spoken, permeate all *Leaves of Grass*, and the work must stand or fall with them, as the human body and soul must remain as an entirety.

Universal as are certain facts and symptoms of communities or individuals all times, there is nothing so rare in modern conventions and poetry as their normal recognizance. Literature is always calling in the doctor for consultation and confession, and always giving evasions and swathing suppressions in place of that "heroic nudity" * on which only a genuine diagnosis of serious cases can be built. And in respect to editions of *Leaves of Grass* in time to come (if there should be such) I take occasion now to confirm those lines with the settled convictions and deliberate renewals of thirty years, and to hereby prohibit, as far as word of mine can do so, any elision of them.

Then still a purpose enclosing all, and over and beneath all. Ever since what might be call'd thought, or the budding of thought, fairly began in my youthful mind, I had had a desire to attempt some worthy record of that entire faith and acceptance ("to justify the ways of God to man" is Milton's well-known and ambitious phrase) which is the foundation of moral America. I felt it all as positively then in my young days as I do now in my old ones; to formulate a poem whose every thought or fact should directly or indirectly be or connive at an implicit belief in the wisdom, health, mystery, beauty of every process, every concrete object, every human or other existence, not only consider'd from the point of view of all, but of each.

While I cannot understand it or argue it out, I fully believe in a clue and purpose in Nature, entire and several; and that invisible spiritual results, just as real and definite as the visible, eventuate all concrete life and all materialism, through Time. My book ought to emanate buoyancy and gladness legitimately enough, for it was grown out of those elements, and has been the comfort of my life since it was originally commenced.

One main genesis-motive of the *Leaves* was my conviction (just as strong today as ever) that the crowning growth of the United States is to be spiritual and heroic. To help start and favor that growth—or even to call attention to it, or the need of it—is the beginning, middle and final purpose of the poems. (In fact, when really cipher'd out and summ'd to the last, plowing up in earnest the interminable average fallows of humanity—not "good government" merely, in the common sense—is the justification and main purpose of these United States.)

Isolated advantages in any rank or grace or fortune—the direct or indirect threads of all the poetry of the past—are in my opinion distasteful to the republican genius, and offer no foundation for its fitting verse. Establish'd poems, I know, have the very great advantage of chanting the already perform'd, so full of glories, reminiscences dear to the minds of men. But my volume is a candidate for the future. "All original art," says Taine,[7] anyhow, "is self-regulated, and no original art can be regulated from without; it carries its own counterpoise, and does not receive it from elsewhere—lives on its own blood"—a solace to my frequent bruises and sulky vanity.

As the present is perhaps mainly an attempt at personal statement or illustration, I will allow myself as further help to extract the following anecdote from a book, *Annals of Old Painters*, conn'd by me in youth.

* *Nineteenth Century*, July 1883. [Whitman's note]
[7] Hippolyte Taine (1828–1893), French philosopher, historian, and literary critic.

Reubens, the Flemish painter, in one of his wanderings through the galleries of old convents, came across a singular work. After looking at it thoughtfully for a good while, and listening to the criticisms of his suite of students, he said to the latter, in answer to their questions, (as to what school the work implied or belong'd,) "I do not believe the artist, unknown and perhaps no longer living, who has given the world this legacy, ever belong'd to any school, or ever painted anything but this one picture, which is a personal affair—a piece out of a man's life."

Leaves of Grass indeed (I cannot too often reiterate) has mainly been the outcropping of my own emotional and other personal nature—an attempt, from first to last, to put a *Person*, a human being (myself, in the latter half of the Nineteenth Century, in America,) freely, fully and truly on record. I could not find any similar personal record in current literature that satisfied me. But it is not on *Leaves of Grass* distinctively as *literature*, or a specimen thereof, that I feel to dwell, or advance claims. No one will get at my verses who insists upon viewing them as a literary performance, or attempt at such performance, or as aiming mainly toward art or aestheticism.

I say no land or people or circumstances ever exisited so needing a race of singers and poems differing from all others, and rigidly their own, as the land and people and circumstances of our United States need such singers and poems today, and for the future. Still further, as long as the States continue to absorb and be dominated by the poetry of the Old World, and remain unsupplied with autochthonous song, to express, vitalize and give color to and define their material and political success, and minister to them distinctively, so long will they stop short of first-class Nationality and remain defective.

In the free evening of my day I give to you, reader, the foregoing garrulous talk, thoughts, reminiscences,

> As idly drifting down the ebb,
> Such ripples, half-caught voices, echo from the shore.

Concluding with two items for the imaginative genius of the West, when it worthily rises—First, what Herder taught to the young Goethe, that really great poetry is always (like the Homeric or Biblical canticles) the result of a national spirit,[8] and not the privilege of a polish'd and select few; Second, that the strongest and sweetest songs yet remain to be sung.

[8] Johann Herder (1744–1803), German poet and philosopher, whose *Spirit of Hebrew Poetry* (1782–83) develops the idea that poetry is the result of a national spirit. Whitman could have found the same idea developed in Taine's *History of English Literature* (1863).

OLIVER WENDELL HOLMES

From OVER THE TEACUPS [1]
(1891)

[REALISM IN LITERATURE]

WE GOT talking on the subject of *realism*, of which so much has been said of late.

It seems to me, I said, that the great additions which have been made by realism to the territory of literature consist largely in swampy, malarious, ill-smelling patches of soil which had previously been left to reptiles and vermin. It is perfectly easy to be original by violating the laws of decency and the canons of good taste. The general consent of civilized people was supposed to have banished certain subjects from the conversation of well bred people and the pages of respectable literature. There is no subject, or hardly any, which may not be treated of at the proper time, in the proper place, by the fitting person, for the right kind of listener or reader. But when the poet or the story-teller invades the province of the man of science, he is on dangerous ground. I need say nothing of the blunders he is pretty sure to make. The imaginative writer is after effects. The scientific man is after truth. Science is decent, modest; does not try to startle, but to instruct. The same scenes and objects which outrage every sense of delicacy in the story-teller's highly colored paragraphs can be read without giving offence in the chaste language of the physiologist or the physician.

There is a very celebrated novel, "Madame Bovary," the work of M. Flaubert,[2] which is noted for having been the subject of prosecution as an immoral work. That it has a serious lesson there is no doubt, if one will drink down to the bottom of the cup. But the honey of sensuous description is spread so deeply over the surface of the goblet that a large proportion of its readers never think of its holding anything else. All the phases of unhallowed passion are described in full detail. That is what the book is bought and read for, by the great majority of its purchasers, as all but simpletons very well know. That is what makes it sell and brought it into the courts of justice. This book is famous for its realism; in fact, it is recognized as one of the earliest and most brilliant examples of that modern style of novel which, beginning where Balzac [3] left off, attempted to do for literature what the photograph has done for art. For those who take the trouble to drink out of the cup below the rim of honey, there is a

---

[1] Boston, 1891.
[2] Gustave Flaubert (1821–1880), French realistic novelist, whose *Madame Bovary* (1857) is a scrupulously truthful portrayal of life.
[3] Honoré de Balzac (1799–1850), French realistic novelist.

scene where realism is carried to its extreme,—surpassed in horror by no
writer, unless it be the one whose name must be looked for at the bottom
of the alphabet, as if its natural place were as low down in the dregs of
realism as it could find itself. This is the death-bed scene, where Madame
Bovary expires in convulsions. The author must have visited the hospitals for the purpose of watching the terrible agonies he was to depict,
tramping from one bed to another until he reached the one where the
cries and contortions were the most frightful. Such a scene he has reproduced. No hospital physician would have pictured the struggle in such
colors. In the same way, that other realist, M. Zola,[4] has painted a patient
suffering from delirium tremens, the disease known to common speech as
"the horrors." In describing this case he does all that language can do to
make it more horrible than the reality. He gives us, not realism, but super-
realism, if such a term does not contradict itself.

In this matter of the literal reproduction of sights and scenes which
our natural instinct and our better informed taste and judgment teach us
to avoid, art has been far in advance of literature. It is three hundred
years since Joseph Ribera, more commonly known as Spagnoletto, was
born in the province of Valencia, in Spain. We had the misfortune of
seeing a painting of his in a collection belonging to one of the French
princes, and exhibited at the Art Museum. It was that of a man performing upon himself the operation known to the Japanese as hara-kiri. Many
persons who looked upon this revolting picture will never get rid of its
remembrance, and will regret the day when their eyes fell upon it. I
should share the offence of the painter if I ventured to describe it. Ribera
was fond of depicting just such odious and frightful subjects. "Saint
Lawrence writhing on his gridiron, Saint Sebastian full of arrows, were
equally a source of delight to him. Even in subjects which had no such
elements of horror he finds the materials for the delectation of his fero-
cious pencil; he makes up for the defect by rendering with a brutal realism deformity and ugliness."

The first great mistake made by the ultra-realists, like Flaubert and
Zola, is, as I have said, their ignoring the line of distinction between
imaginative art and science. We can find realism enough in books of
anatomy, surgery, and medicine. In studying the human figure, we want
to see it clothed with its natural integuments. It is well for the artist to
study the écorché in the dissecting-room, but we do not want the Apollo
or the Venus to leave their skins behind them when they go into the
gallery for exhibition. Lancisi's[5] figures show us how the great statues
look when divested of their natural covering. It is instructive, but useful
chiefly as a means to aid in the true artistic reproduction of nature. When
the hospitals are invaded by the novelist, he should learn something from
the physician as well as from the patients. Science delineates in mono-

---

[4] Émile Zola (1840–1902), recognized head of the French naturalistic school of
fiction. His theories, and those of the naturalists, can be found in his *Le Roman
expérimental* (The Experimental Novel) which appeared in 1880.
[5] Giovanni Lancisi (1654–1720), Italian physician and writer.

chrome. She never uses high tints and strontian lights to astonish lookers-on. Such scenes as Flaubert and Zola describe would be reproduced in their essential characters, but not dressed up in picturesque phrases. That is the first stumbling-block in the way of the reader of such realistic stories as those to which I have referred. There are subjects which must be investigated by scientific men which most educated persons would be glad to know nothing about. When a realistic writer like Zola surprises his reader into a kind of knowledge he never thought of wishing for, he sometimes harms him more than he has any idea of doing. He wants to produce a sensation, and he leaves a permanent disgust not to be got rid of. Who does not remember odious images that can never be washed out from the consciousness which they have stained? A man's vocabulary is terribly retentive of evil words, and the images they present cling to his memory and will not loose their hold. One who has had the mischance to soil his mind by reading certain poems of Swift will never cleanse it to its original whiteness. Expressions and thoughts of a certain character stain the fibre of the thinking organ, and in some degree affect the hue of every idea that passes through the discolored tissues.

This is the gravest accusation to bring against realism, old or recent, whether in the brutal paintings of Spagnoletto or in the unclean revelations of Zola. Leave the description of the drains and cesspools to the hygienic specialist, the painful facts of disease to the physician, the details of the laundry to the washer-woman. If we are to have realism in its tedious descriptions of unimportant particulars, let it be of particulars which do not excite disgust. Such is the description of the vegetables in Zola's "Ventre de Paris," where, if one wishes to see the apotheosis of turnips, beets, and cabbages, he can find them glorified as supremely as if they had been symbols of so many deities; their forms, their colors, their expression, worked upon until they seem as if they were made to be looked at and worshipped rather than to be boiled and eaten.

I am pleased to find a French critic of M. Flaubert expressing ideas with which many of my own entirely coincide. "The great mistake of the realists," he says, "is that they profess to tell the truth because they tell everything. This puerile hunting after details, this cold and cynical inventory of all the wretched conditions in the midst of which poor humanity vegetates, not only do not help us to understand it better, but, on the contrary, the effect on the spectators is a kind of dazzled confusion mingled with fatigue and disgust. The material truthfulness to which the school of M. Flaubert more especially pretends misses its aim in going beyond it. Truth is lost in its own excess."

I return to my thoughts on the relations of imaginative art in all its forms with science. The subject which in the hands of the scientific student is handled decorously,—reverently, we might almost say,—becomes repulsive, shameful, and debasing in the unscrupulous manipulations of the low-bred man of letters.

I confess that I am a little jealous of certain tendencies in our own American literature, which led one of the severest and most outspoken of our satirical fellow-countrymen, no longer living to be called to account for it, to say, in a moment of bitterness, that the mission of America was to vulgarize mankind. I myself have sometimes wondered at the pleasure some Old World critics have professed to find in the most lawless freaks of New World literature. I have questioned whether their delight was not like that of the Spartans in the drunken antics of their Helots. But I suppose I belong to another age, and must not attempt to judge the present by my old-fashioned standards.

[On Whitman]

Thomas Jefferson is commonly recognized as the first to proclaim before the world the political independence of America. It is not so generally agreed upon as to who was the first to announce the literary emancipation of our country.

One of Mr. Emerson's biographers has claimed that his Phi Beta Kappa Oration was our Declaration of Literary Independence.[6] But Mr. Emerson did not cut himself loose from all the traditions of Old World scholarship. He spelled his words correctly, he constructed his sentences grammatically. He adhered to the slavish rules of propriety, and observed the reticences which a traditional delicacy has considered inviolable in decent society. . . . He was not always so careful as he might have been in the rhythm and rhyme of his verse, but in the main he recognized the old established laws which have been accepted as regulating both. . . .

A stronger claim might be urged for Mr. Whitman. He takes into his hospitable vocabulary words which no English dictionary recognizes as belonging to the language,—words which will be looked for in vain outside of his own pages. He accepts as poetical subjects all things alike, common and unclean, without discrimination, miscellaneous as the contents of the great sheet which Peter saw let down from heaven. He carries the principle of republicanism through the whole world of created objects. He will "thread a thread through [his] poems," he tells us, "that no one thing in the universe is inferior to another thing." No man has ever asserted the surpassing dignity and importance of the American citizen so boldly and freely as Mr. Whitman. He calls himself "teacher of the unquenchable creed, namely, egotism." He begins one of his chants, "I celebrate myself," but he takes us all in as partners in his self-glorification. He believes in America as the new Eden.

> "A world primal again,—vistas of glory incessant and
>   branching,
> A new race dominating previous ones and grander far,
> New politics—new literature and religions—new inven-
>   tions and arts."

[6] Holmes himself made this statement concerning Emerson's "The American Scholar" in his *Ralph Waldo Emerson* (1885), p. 88. Emerson delivered the oration at Harvard in 1837.

Of the new literature he himself has furnished specimens which certainly have all the originality he can claim for them. . . .

. . . So far as concerns literary independence, if we understand by that term the getting rid of our subjection to British criticism, such as it was in the days when the question was asked, "Who reads an American book?" we may consider it pretty well established. If it means dispensing with punctuation, coining words at will, self-revelation unrestrained by a sense of what is decorous, declamations in which everything is glorified without being idealized, "poetry" in which the reader must make the rhythms which the poet has not made for him, then I think we had better continue literary colonists. I shrink from a lawless independence to which all the virile energy and trampling audacity of Mr. Whitman fail to reconcile me. But there is room for everybody and everything in our huge hemisphere. Young America is like a three-year-old colt with his saddle and bridle just taken off. The first thing he wants to do is to *roll*. He is a droll object, sprawling in the grass with his four hoofs in the air; but he likes it, and it won't harm us. So let him roll,—let him roll!

PART III

REALISM AND AESTHETICISM

REALISM AND AESTHETICISM

W HEN ONE TURNS to the books and periodicals of those divided years of the Reconstruction Era, it becomes apparent that the older and simpler designation, "the Age of Realism," has tended to obscure the complexity of American criticism in what has been termed "the Gilded Age." [1] The rise of realism during this period has been viewed by some literary historians as having taken place out of the ashes of a dead romantic idealism. To some extent the reading of the literary history of the period as being principally a manifestation of the progress of realism has some validity. Yet a survey of the criticism of the period reveals that romanticism continued as a not negligible factor in literary theory.[2]

Many of the great romantics, Whitman, Emerson, Lowell, Whittier, Longfellow, among others, were active throughout much of the period and maintained the aesthetics and ideals of the older tradition. Strongly influenced by the tradition of romanticism were such prominent critics of the period as T. S. Perry, E. C. Stedman, George E. Woodberry, Thomas Bailey Aldrich, and Hamilton Wright Mabie, representatives of what George Santayana called "the Genteel tradition." Thus the literary activity of the period might more accurately be described as a constant action and reaction between the two fundamental attitudes toward life and art represented by realism and romanticism.

During the post-Civil War years, when intellectual America under the impact of new ideas and forces was seeking a new orientation, the younger generation of writers turned to realism hoping to find an aesthetics more suitable than the declining principles of romanticism to express an age which was becoming increasingly more scientific and empirical. By the 1870's the lines of controversy were forming in the periodicals between the new writers who were interested in a more scientific and a more truthful treatment of life in literature and those who, fearful of scientific determinism and of a concern with a too literal interpretation of the

[1] For more detailed studies of the decline of romanticism and the transition to realism, see Floyd Stovall, "Why Idealism Declined," in *Transitions in American Literary History*, edited by Harry H. Clark (Durham, N. C., 1954); Robert Falk, "Why Realism Arose," *ibid.*; Frank L. Lucas, *The Decline and Fall of the Romantic Ideal* (New York, 1936); Sten Liljegren, *The Revolt Against Romanticism in American Literature* (Upsala, 1945). General studies dealing with the development of American thought during the period include Merle Curti, *The Growth of American Thought* (New York, 1943), and Henry Steele Commager, *The American Mind: An Interpretation of American Thought and Character since the 1880's* (New Haven, 1950). For a concise survey of the literary criticism of the period, see Harry H. Clark, "American Literary Criticism to 1919," in Joseph Shipley, editor, *Dictionary of World Literature* (New York, 1943), pp. 23-24.

[2] See Leonard I. Lutwack, *The Dynamics of Conservative Criticism: Literary Criticism in American Magazines, 1880-1900.* Unpublished dissertation (Ohio State, 1950).

surface aspects of life, sought to prolong a more conservative and a more idealistic philosophy of letters.

In spite of the growing influence and popularity during the 1870's of realism in fiction as evidenced by the work of Mark Twain, Bret Harte, and other regional writers, the chief outlets for literary expression at the opening of the decade of the eighties still remained under the control of a conservative tradition. Thomas Bailey Aldrich had become editor of the *Atlantic Monthly* while Edmund Clarence Stedman was editor of the *Century Magazine*. Between them, the *Century* and the *Atlantic* constituted what was generally assumed to be the intellectual voice of America.[3] Actually it was the voice of conservatism, of "gentility," of a tradition that looked back upon the gentlemanliness, the idealism, of the great New Englanders with a kind of reverential esteem. The traditionalists were opposed to the growing materialism of the nation, and they sadly noted that idealism no longer had the field to itself.

Among the writers and critics usually grouped together as members of the "genteel tradition" were Edmund Clarence Stedman, Bayard Taylor, George Boker, Richard Henry Stoddard, Thomas Bailey Aldrich, Hamilton Wright Mabie, George E. Woodberry, and Brander Matthews.[4] Of these Bayard Taylor was its most noted literary figure, Stedman its most distinguished critic. They did not congregate in the same area—many even forsook America for the older culture of Europe—but they were all united with the common bond of idealism.

Edmund Clarence Stedman, New York stock broker and literary critic, was among the first and the most capable spokesmen of the "genteel" in American criticism.[5] Holding that criticism should be "gentle" and appreciative rather than judicial, Stedman, in his own criticism, tends to be diffuse and to lack that sharpness of definition which is associated with a great critic. Concerning the highly judicial criticism of Poe, Stedman wrote that "I hold it a sign of progress that criticism by force of arms would now be less effective." That this emphasis upon gentleness at times caused him to abdicate his function as a critic can be seen in the comment he made concerning *Evangeline*: ". . . this one poem, thus far the flower of American idylls, known in all lands, I will not approach in a critical spirit. There are rooms in every house where one treads with softened footfall."

[3] See George E. De Mille, "Stedman, Arbiter of the Eighties," *Publications Modern Language Association*, XLI (1926), 756–66.

[4] See "Defenders of Ideality," in *Literary History of the United States*, edited by Robert Spiller, *et al.* (New York, 1948). For a recent reinterpretation, see F. I. Carpenter, "The Genteel Tradition: A Reinterpretation," *New England Quarterly*, XV (1942), 427–43.

[5] The fullest life of Stedman is Laura Stedman and George M. Gould, *Life and Letters of Edmund Clarence Stedman*, 2 vols. (New York, 1910), with a full bibliography compiled by Alice Marsland, II, 613–54. For a study of Stedman as a literary critic, see George E. De Mille, *Literary Criticism in America* (New York, 1931), pp. 133–57. For a study of classical influences, see John P. Pritchard, "Edmund Clarence Stedman," in *Return to the Fountains* (Durham, N. C., 1942), pp. 119–34.

The earliest critical volume, *Victorian Poets*, which Stedman published in 1875, remains as one of his most valuable studies. Applying in part the method of Taine, Stedman attempts to approach the literature of the period as a manifestation of certain scientific, economic, social, and intellectual tendencies of the times. While the book contains some excellent criticism, particularly the essay on Landor, and while Stedman was the first American critic to concern himself with the influence of science on thought, whenever Stedman leaves the realm of the purely appreciative it becomes for the most part inadequate.

Ten years later, in 1885, Stedman published his *Poets of America*, a volume which reveals his same propensity for gentleness and appreciation in criticism. The book is notable principally for its discerning essay on Whitman, one of the first to be written by a critic generally accepted by the American public. While as an idealist Stedman objects at times to Whitman's sensuality, the essay hails his work as possessing the best hope for the future. The critical insights of the essay remain surprisingly valid, particularly Stedman's perceptiveness in relating Whitman's style to the King James version of the Bible and in apprehending that, rather than being formless, Whitman's work actually demonstrated a distinctive form and a definite technique.

After surveying nineteenth-century literature in England and America, Stedman turned to what he intended to be his major work, the construction of a theory of poetry. Bringing to this task a sense of beauty, form, and finish disciplined by a wide acquaintance with and a love for the Greek and Latin classics, Stedman published in 1892 his *The Nature and Elements of Poetry*.[6] Early in his career, he had collaborated with George Woodberry on a life of Poe with the result that one finds certain of Poe's critical theories concerning poetry appearing in this volume. Like Poe, Stedman's basic thesis is that poetry is the creation of beauty. Poe had said "Poetry is the rhythmical creation of beauty." In the chapter, "What is Poetry?" Stedman elaborates: "Poetry is rhythmical, imaginative, language, expressing the invention, taste, thought, passion, and insight of the human soul." Stedman, however, would not maintain, as Poe had, that beauty stemmed largely from the manner, form, or technique:

> No work of art has real import, none endures, unless the maker has something to say—some thought which he must express imaginatively, whether to the eye in stone or on canvas, or to the ear in music or artistic speech; this thought, the imaginative conception moving him to utterance, being his creative idea—his art-ideal.

The one point that Stedman repeats often in his criticism is that poetry, to achieve beauty, must first of all be passionate. Without passion there remains only the exclusive presentation of thought and truth, two ele-

[6] For an analysis of the classical elements in *The Nature and Elements of Poetry*, see Pritchard, *Return to the Fountains*.

ments that by themselves make poetry didactic and hence untrue in the artistic sense. A just balance is necessary: "Feeling is the excitant of genuine poetry. The Miltonic canon, requiring the sensuous beauty which taste alone insures, demands, last of all, as if laying stress upon its indispensability, that poetry should be passionate."

With Poe, Stedman admits the superiority of music over the other arts to capture the soul of man and transport him to another world; and, like Poe, Stedman feels that music and poetry at their highest must join because "in music the soul most nearly attains the great end for which it struggles—supernal beauty." There is also the suggestion in the critical theory of Stedman that, again like Poe, he valued words to a great extent for their rhythmical quality; for he says of poetry: "Its vibrations excite the reflex action that creates in the mind of the receiver a vision corresponding to the imagination of the poet."

The signal concept of beauty about which Stedman's criticism revolves is significant only when beauty is faithful to supreme ideals. And for beauty to achieve this aim, the elements of truth and ethics must be an integral part. Transcendental beauty necessarily embodies an idealization of the selective processes of the artist; it is this which enables Stedman to dismiss morality as an element of criticism, for an art work which suggests the fitness and perfection of the universe is both beautiful and true: "If all natural things make for beauty,—if the statement is well founded that they are as beautiful as they can be under their conditions,—then truth and beauty, in the last reduction, are equivalent terms, and beauty is the unveiled shining countenance of truth." But this truth is not didacticism:

> A certain kind of preachment, antipathetic to the spirit of poetry, has received the name of didacticism. Instinct tells us that it is a heresy in any form of art.
>
> . . . pedagogic formulas of truth . . . preach, as I have said elsewhere, the gospel of half-truths, uttered by those who have not the insight to perceive the soul of truth, the expression of which is always beauty.

While Stedman admires Whitman's freedom and inclusiveness, his taste is repulsed by the poet's unvarying realism. Like all good critics, Stedman's appeal is to reality, but his realism does not apprehend drawing things so much as they are as what they should be at their best. "This," he says, "lifts them out of the common, or, rather, it is thus we get at the power and mystery of common things . . . there is nothing more lifeless, because nothing is more devoid of feeling and suggested movement, than servilely accurate imitation of nature."

It cannot be denied that Stedman formulated a quite thorough critical position. It gave both design and method for literary production, a philosophical attitude resembling in all of its essentials that of other members of the tradition. But it failed to take notice of the far-reaching changes occurring in the life about him, and failed to adapt itself sufficiently to assure a greater measure of permanence.

As the 1880's progressed, the transition to a more pragmatic fidelity to life became even more conspicuously evident. The history of the growth of American realistic critical principles and their application to practice differs in a very fundamental aspect from that of European realism.[7] American culture was heterogeneous; it did not have the benefit of a great literary tradition except in so far as it patterned itself on its European ancestry. The country was still young and enthusiastic; the frontier which was just coming to an end was still a force in the consciousness of the people. A native literature peculiarly American still seemed in the future, and men set themselves to the task of discovering what its essential features should be.[8]

The emphasis was now to be on the characteristic, the local, as a faithful and perspicuous artist would see it and set it down for all posterity,[9] a tendency, it should be noted, which had its origins in romanticism and which can be seen in the criticism of such writers as Bryant and Whittier. Only then could Americans claim to have a distinctly American literature. Whereas realism in Europe was a concerted action and reaction based upon scientific findings and having a definite philosophy, American realism stemmed, at least until the literary advent of Howells and James, in large measure from the attempt to record the folkways of the nation. The rise of historical criticism and the more recent influence of Taine[10] had contributed to the conception of literature as the product of a certain time, place, and race, and had tended to reinforce the incipient localism of many romantic writers.

The literary artists who answered the call for local color were numerous. Harriet Beecher Stowe, Edward Eggleston, Joel Chandler Harris, George Washington Cable, Sarah Orne Jewett, Bret Harte, Mark Twain, Hamlin Garland, and others were all familiar to the readers of the period. Their attitude could be expressed by what Mrs. Stowe had to say of her work:

> My object is to interpret to the world the New England life and character in that particular time of its history which may be called the seminal period. . . . In doing this work, I have tried to make my mind

[7] There is an unpublished dissertation by Henry J. Runyan on *The Backgrounds and Origins of Realism in the American Novel, 1850–1880* (Wisconsin, 1949). Also see Harry W. Reninger, *The Theory and Practice of the American Novel, 1867–1903,* unpublished dissertation (Michigan, 1938).

[8] See Benjamin T. Spencer, "The New Realism and a National Literature," *Publications Modern Language Association,* LVI (1941), 1116-32.

[9] For a study of regionalism, see Cary McWilliams, *The New Regionalism in American Literature* (Seattle, Wash., 1930), and "Localism in American Criticism," *Southwest Review,* XIX (1934), 410-28.

[10] The most incisive statement of Taine's method may be found in his Introduction to *The History of English Literature* (1863-67). The best essay on Taine is in Irving Babbitt, *Masters of Modern French Criticism* (Boston, 1912), 218-56.

as still and passive as a looking-glass, or a mountain lake, and then to give you merely the images reflected there. I desire that you should see the characteristic persons of those times, and hear them talk. . . . My studies for this object have been . . . taken from real characters, real scenes, and real incidents.

Bret Harte, born an Easterner, achieved fame as a local color writer in the West, bringing to that region a sense of form in art that until then had been the sole preoccupation of the East.[11] From 1864 to 1871 Harte worked in turn as editor of the *Californian* and then the *Overland Monthly* before he gave up the West and returned to the East.

Harte's critical work is relatively small in quantity and for the most part written early in his literary career, but placed in perspective yields a surprisingly consistent theory.[12] The greater part of Harte's critical writing concerns itself with the common, the local, the humorous, and the representative. Of these he apparently valued most of all the principle of humor, suspecting it lay at the base of all good writing. In discussing Artemus Ward in 1863, he finds the national characteristic of "audacious exaggeration—of perfect lawlessness," and attributes it to an instinctive sympathy with the "boundless prairies, limitless rivers, and stupendous cataracts" that make the West. One should judge, Harte implies, by what the author intended and how well he achieved that intention. If Ward's humor is "fun without application," nevertheless:

> . . . Mr. Ward is the American humorist, *par excellence*, and "his book" is the essence of that fun which overlies the surface of our national life . . . a humor that has more or less local coloring, that takes kindly to, and half elevates, slang, that is of to-day and full of present application.

What began as a suspicion in the criticism of Harte—that humor is fundamental and engrained in the truly American artist—is fully accepted and delineated in "The Rise of the Short Story," which appeared in the *Cornhill Magazine* in 1899. When humor is missing, something "distinctly American" is missing also. Americans like Poe, Longfellow, and Hawthorne constructed their stories from the driftwood of Europe and

[11] The authoritative life of Harte is George R. Stewart, Jr., *Bret Harte: Argonaut and Exile* (Boston, 1931). Also see Henry Childs Merwin, *The Life of Bret Harte, with Some Account of the California Pioneers* (Boston and New York, 1911). Critical estimates of Harte in relation to American humor and regionalism include Walter Blair, *Native American Humor* (New York, 1937); Fred Lewis Pattee, "Bret Harte," in *The Development of the American Short Story* (New York, 1923); and "Bret Harte," in *A History of American Literature Since 1870* (New York, 1922); Arthur Hobson Quinn, *American Fiction* (New York, 1936); Constance Rourke, *American Humor: A Study of the National Character* (New York, 1931); and Walter Taylor, "The Fiction of Regionalism," in *A History of American Literature* (New York, 1936). A valuable study of the California scene of Harte's time is Franklin D. Walker, *San Francisco's Literary Frontier* (New York, 1939).

[12] A brief but valuable study of Harte's literary criticism is in Joseph B. Harrison, introduction to *Bret Harte: Representative Selections* (New York, 1941).

consequently "even when graced by the style of the best masters . . . were distinctly provincial." The European influence had been long and lasting, and had resulted in a complete separation of the American artist from his fellow men so far as art was concerned. Then a profound and subtle virtue began to pervade American writing:

> . . . while the American literary imagination was still under the influ-
> ence of English tradition, an unexpected factor was developing to
> diminish its power. It was *Humour*—of a quality as distinct and original
> as the country and civilization in which it was developed. . . . It was
> concise and condensed, yet suggestive. . . . It voiced not only the
> dialect, but the habits of thought of a people or locality. . . . It was a
> foe to prolixity of any kind, it admitted no fine writing nor affectation
> of style. . . . By degrees it developed character with its incident, often,
> in a few lines, gave a striking photograph of a community or a section,
> but always reached its conclusion without an unnecessary word.

The repeated emphasis of Harte upon humor and the art of story-telling suggests that he prized highest of all the ability of an artist to captivate the reader and keep him absorbed. In an essay on "My Favorite Novelist and His Best Work," Harte writes that "the primary function of the novel is to interest the reader in its *story*—in the progress of some well-developed plot to a well-defined climax, which may be either expected or unexpected by him. After this it may have a purpose or moral; may be pathetic, humorous, or felicitous in language; but it must first interest as a story." Harte's favorite novelist is Alexandre Dumas and the best work is *The Count of Monte Cristo*.

When Harte believed that a writer violated his craft, his criticism was quick and scathing. Writing of Benjamin Disraeli's *Lothair* in the *Overland* in 1870, he says that it belongs to "the Post-pliocene period of novel-writing—a kind of Paleozoic era, when the lack of human life was made up by a vast deal of rank and sloppy vegetation." He conceives the novel to be artificial and stilted in diction, its style insincere and undramatic. The characters are "generally vapid, and when the reader does not find them so he may be pretty sure they are unreal. . . . The dialogue bears the same relation to the characters, being either flat and ungrammatical, or extravagant and incomprehensible." Disraeli vitiated whatever power he might have had, and the result is a work neither honest, faithful, nor sincere.

With Charles Reade, on the other hand, Harte recognizes qualities with which he is in sympathy. Chiefly there is the sincere attempt to simulate nature. Reade has a moral to his novel, and has a tendency to exaggeration, but it is confined to incident and not logic, style, or his conclusions. "We can stand much," writes Harte, "that is extravagant and marvelous in the action of our heroes, but we challenge at once any high-flown sentiment, or specious moralizing." Harte emphasizes that so long as the writer confines himself to the story without superimposing a moral, and so long as he remains faithful and logical to his premises, he remains in the main-stream of honest literature be he realist or romanticist.

In "A Few Words about Mr. Lowell," which first appeared in the *New Review* in 1891, Harte praises Lowell for having portrayed the real Yankee and for having demonstrated such a "keen instinctive insight into the personal character of the New Englander." It is Lowell's perception of the concrete and the local which lends integrity to his work and gives it that form which comes as a result of fidelity to subject.

In his "Condensed Novels," First Series, most of which appeared in 1865–1866, Harte ingeniously parodies those qualities in such writers as Cooper, Dumas, Dickens, and others which he regards as defects in their work: Cooper's exaggerated heroisms, sentimentality, and lack of consistency; Dumas's excesses of fellowship and prodigious feats in the three musketeers; and Dickens' excessive sentimentalism. All of the parodies in "Condensed Novels" involve violation of what Harte considers to be the standards of good writing: common sense, fidelity to life, economy, and above all the logical consistency of the work of art itself.

While Harte never developed his critical theories into a systematic doctrine as Poe had, there are implied in his critical work certain standards from which he never deviated. He always scored the "indigestible moral pie, sensational hot coffee, sentimental tea, and emotional soda water" served to an unwary public. One criticized a writer by first ascertaining what that writer had attempted and then by whether he had succeeded. Consequently, it came down ultimately to how much the form, the technique, was adapted to the conditions the author had set. An obtruding moral, didacticism, excessive sentimentality, snobbery, and excessive stylistic finery were the hobgoblins of his critical mind. His personal interest lay in the local color school and its fidelity to American life, but he did not deny that there were other methods of writing. And regarding American literature, he phrased it most concisely when he said:

> It would seem evident, therefore, that the secret of the American short story was the treatment of characteristic American life, with absolute knowledge of its peculiarities and sympathy with its methods; with no fastidious ignoring of its habitual expression, or the inchoate poetry that may be found even hidden in its slang; with no moral determination except that which may be the legitimate outcome of the story itself; with no more elimination than may be necessary for the artistic conception, and never from the fear of the "fetish" of conventionalism. Of such is the American short story to-day—the germ of American literature to come.

If Bret Harte had cast about for a writer who exemplified the relation between humor and the typical American short story, his most logical choice would have been Mark Twain. For Twain had steeped himself in the stories of the frontier; his first efforts were attempts to duplicate the extravagant and grotesque humor heard about him; his rise to fame was precipitated by the general acclaim which considered him to be a literary comedian; and his final, polished work was grounded in the local color tradition.[13] He admirably lived his own critical dictum that "almost the whole capital of the novelist is the slow accumulation of *un*conscious observation—absorption."

Twain arrived at the high tide of the local color movement and in a sense marks its apogee. Like the local colorists, he did not believe in the existence of general human characteristics that could be called "American," but conceived of the nation in terms of its representative regions. In 1895, in "What Paul Bourget Thinks of Us," he wrote: "Does the native novelist try to generalize the nation? No, he lays plainly before you the ways and speech and life of a few people grouped in a certain place—his own place— and that is one book." The ideal of "the great American novel" is impossible of achievement; the nation is a composite and can be only known as a collective knowledge of its authors.[14]

Like Harte, Twain insisted on the critic first ascertaining what the author intended and how well that intention was achieved. The unfavorable reception of his *A Connecticut Yankee in King Arthur's Court* was quick to elicit a response from him:

> . . . a man who is white-washing a fence is doing a useful thing, so also is the man who is adorning a rich man's house with costly frescoes; and all of us are sane enough to judge these performances by standards proper to each. Now, then, to be fair an author ought to be allowed to put upon his book an explanatory line: "This is written for the Head; This is written for the Belly and the Members." And the critic ought to hold himself honor bound to put away from him his ancient habit of judging all books by one standard, and thenceforth follow a fairer course.[15]

The ultimate standard is the inner consistency of the work of art itself. Hence, to a great extent, the critic concerns himself with the form and the techniques that move the story along. Running throughout his essays and letters are such remarks as:

[13] The authorized biography of Twain is Albert B. Paine, *Mark Twain, A Biography*, 3 vols. (New York, 1912). Paine's edition of *Mark Twain's Letters, Arranged with Comment*, 2 vols. (New York, 1917) and of *Mark Twain's Notebook* (New York, 1935) contain fundamental sources. Two recent studies by Bernard De Voto are *Mark Twain's America* (Boston, 1932) and *Mark Twain at Work* (Cambridge, 1942). Other general studies include Edward C. Wagenknecht, *Mark Twain: The Man and His Work* (New Haven, 1935); William Dean Howells, *My Mark Twain: Reminiscences and Criticisms* (New York, 1910); Minnie M. Brashear, *Mark Twain: Son of Missouri* (Chapel Hill, N. C., 1934); Henry S. Canby, *Turn West Turn East: Mark Twain and Henry James* (Boston, 1951); and Dixon Wecter, *Sam Clemens of Hannibal* (Boston, 1952). Special studies of Mark Twain's literary theory are Brander Matthews, "Mark Twain and the Art of Writing," in *Essays on English* (New York, 1921); George W. Feinstein, "Mark Twain's Idea of Story Structure," *American Literature*, XVIII (1946), 160–63, and his unpublished dissertation, *Mark Twain's Literary Opinions* (Iowa, 1946).

[14] For Twain's relation to the local color movement and to American humor, see Walter Blair, *Native American Humor* (New York, 1937).

[15] *Letters*, II, pp. 526–28.

Say what the author proposes to say, not merely come near it.
Use the right word, not its second cousin.
Eschew surplusage.
Do not omit necessary details.
Avoid slovenliness of form.
Use good grammar.
Employ a simple and straightforward style.

These assertions are plainly matters of technique, and in most instances are the points Twain chooses to criticize when reviewing an author.

What Twain had to say of James Fenimore Cooper and Sir Walter Scott clearly indicates his literary standards. He accused both of being imperfect observers and using stage properties when the inventive faculty flagged. He imprecated Scott's characters as "bloodless shams, these milk-and-water humbugs," whose author is significantly lacking in all the qualities that make an artist. Of *Ivanhoe* he wrote: "Lord, it's all so juvenile! so artificial, so shoddy; and such wax figures and skeletons and spectres." [16] Personages in a tale, he thought, should exhibit sufficient excuse for being there and should be alive, except in the case of corpses, and the reader should be able to tell the corpses from the others. Twain was not sure that either was true for Scott and Cooper. In writing of Cooper, in "Fenimore Cooper's Literary Offences" (1895),[17] he thought that when a person talks like an "illustrated, gilt-edged, tree-calf, hand-tooled, seven-dollar Friendship offering in the beginning of a paragraph, he shall not talk like a negro minstrel in the end of it." Further, "the personages of a tale, when conversing, shall sound like human talk, and be talk such as human beings would be likely to talk in the given circumstances, and have a discoverable meaning, also a discoverable purpose, and a show of relevancy, and remain in the neighborhood of the subject in hand, and be interesting to the reader, and help out the talk, and stop when people cannot think of anything more to say." What Twain wants, above all, then, is consistency, both of plot and character, and when these are missing the form fails and the work is not art.

Twain's criticisms of specific writers are, for the most part, scattered throughout his works and letters, and do not reveal an entirely systematic critical theory. While his criticism of George Eliot, Hawthorne, and Henry James for their tendency to overanalyze is understandable in view of Twain's theories of fiction, his violent dislike for Jane Austen, which prompted him to comment that any library is a good library that does not include her books, is difficult to comprehend particularly in view of the adulation of her by his close friend Howells. His most unstinted praise was reserved for Howells although it may have been biased by the close friendship that existed between them. In an essay on Howells, Twain referred to him as "my only author," and praised him for his ability to make motives and feelings clear "without analyzing the guts out of them,

---

[16] *Letters*, II, p. 737.
[17] See S. L. Clemens, "Fenimore Cooper's Further Literary Offences," *New England Quarterly*, XIX (1946), 291–301.

the way George Eliot does." He also praised the consistency of Howells' work: "The creatures of God do not act out their natures more unerringly than yours do." And he praised Howells' style because "For forty years his English has been to me a continual delight and astonishment."

Again, in praising Zangwill, the same standards of style and the inner consistency of the work are applied:

> Zangwill's "Master" is done in good English—what a rare thing good English is! and the grammar is good, too—and what a very, very rare thing that is! The characters are real, they are flesh and blood, they are definite; one knows what they will do in nearly any given set of circumstances. And when there is an incident, an episode, it comes about in a natural way, and happens just as it would happen in actual life.

The invention that Twain demanded of an author he did not consider an excessive demand. He considered an author not so much a creator as a machine which took the material of reality, worked it, and spewed out the product. If the product was inferior, it was because the machine was not working with the precision of which it was theoretically capable:

> Man's mind is a clever machine, and can work up materials into ingenious fancies and ideas, but it can't create the material; none but the gods can do that. In Sweden I saw a vast machine receive a block of wood, and turn it into marketable matches in two minutes. It could do everything but make the wood. That is the kind of machine the human mind is. Maybe this is not a large compliment, but it is all I can afford.

A writer is no better than his mind-machine, a limitation from which there is no appeal. All depended, for Twain, upon the inner coherency, consistency, and simplicity of the art work itself; and if such a problem as morality arose, as when he worried three weeks whether or not to expel the word "hell" in *Huckleberry Finn*, it was because of the immensely practical concern over the public's anticipated reception. He thought a tale should accomplish something and arrive somewhere, and in his own work that is what he strove to effect.

The man who had done most to bring Mark Twain before the eastern public and to bring his literary efforts up to the norm befitting Twain's genius was William Dean Howells. For thirty-four years, from the time of his occupancy of "The Editor's Study" in *Harper's Magazine* in 1886 until his death in 1920, he was easily one of the most potent voices in American criticism and one of the most influential forces in the rise of realism.[18]

[18] The most satisfactory study of Howells is Delmar G. Cooke, *William Dean Howells: A Critical Study* (New York, 1922). Also see Oscar W. Firkins, *William Dean Howells, A Study* (Cambridge, 1924). Recent studies of Howells' criticism include Herbert Edwards, "Howells and the Controversy over Realism in American Fiction," *American Literature*, III (1931), 237–48; Carl Van Doren, "Howells and Realism," in *The American Novel* (New York, revised edition, 1940); Arthur Hobson Quinn, "William Dean Howells and the Establishment of Realism," in *American Fiction* (New York, 1936); Lionel Trilling, "William Dean Howells and the Roots

Howells was fortunate in espousing a cause which for us today, with the advantage of hindsight, seemed destined for success; but we must not forget that literary movements are born and die amongst men, and that in the final analysis it is men who champion them and give them their impetus. If realism won a victory, Howells is entitled to a large share of the glory.

The striking factor in Howells' intellectual and critical character is his completely unswerving devotion to truth. His truth is "the irreducible and stubborn facts" of everyday experience, the concrete expression of a concrete world. "Realism," he constantly proclaimed, "is nothing more and nothing less than the truthful treatment of material." He could not conceive the necessity for an author's perversion of reality: "If I were authorized to address any words directly to our novelists I should say, Do not trouble yourselves about standards or ideals; but try to be faithful and natural; remember that there is no greatness, no beauty, which does not come from truth to your own knowledge of things."

Before this destroyer of images and tradition even the classics of fiction fared poorly. He never deviated from his norm. One after another, writers passed before his judicial bench and few came through unscathed. The "divine Jane" Austen reaped her reward, but Scott and Bulwer, Dickens, Charlotte Brontë, Thackeray, even George Eliot, and Balzac in part, were damned. In judging artistic work "We must ask ourselves before we ask anything else, Is it true?—true to the motives, the impulses, the principles that shape life of actual men and women? This truth, which necessarily includes the highest morality and the highest artistry—this truth given, the book cannot be wicked and cannot be weak. . . ." The book may be technically perfect, may have the highest form and the choicest style, but if it is not faithful to life, it is not art. The "simple, the natural, and the honest" were the instruments with which he judged a work's fidelity to reality—moreover, they were criteria which were within reach of all.

Giving expression to the mood of revolt against all things "Victorian" which had reached its peak in the 1920's, Sinclair Lewis, on accepting the Nobel Prize in Stockholm in 1930, spoke of the false and life-denying standards of Howells, who had "the code of a pious old maid." That Howells cannot be considered "Victorian" or "genteel" in any narrow understanding of those terms is evidenced by even a superficial and unbiased examination of his criticism.

---

of Modern Taste," *Partisan Review*, XVIII (1951), 516–36; Leonard Lutwack, "William Dean Howells and the 'Editor's Study'," *American Literature*, XXIV (1952), 195–207; Everett Carter, "William Dean Howells' Theory of Critical Realism," *English Literary History*, XVI (1949), 151–66; Harry H. Clark, "Howells," in *Literary Criticism, Pope to Croce*, ed. by Gay Wilson Allen and Harry H. Clark (New York, 1941); Clara Kirk and Rudolph Kirk, introduction to *William Dean Howells: Representative Selections* (New York, 1950). Unpublished dissertations include Charles T. Miller, *Howells's Theory of the Novel* (Chicago, 1947); Clifton Malone, *The Hitherto Uncollected Critical Opinions of William Dean Howells* (Oklahoma, 1947); and Everett Carter, *William Dean Howells' Theory of Realism in Fiction* (Los Angeles, 1947).

In 1893, when Howells enthusiastically greeted H. B. Fuller's *The Cliff-Dwellers,* American naturalism was dawning.[19] In a perceptive review of Fuller's work,[20] Howells called the roll of the book's virtues; and those virtues of a work lighted by the "intense electric glare of the realism" sound like naturalism now. The technique and the method, he said, are those of Zola. The characters are as "odious" as people can be; "they are such as human nature abandoned to mere business, and having no ideal but commercial success and social success, must be." The relation of the characters to one another is mainly through accident, Howells noted, but "accident in our economic life . . . more than will or conscience, is the determining force," and "the conception of the story fully justifies itself to the reader's intelligence." The situation abounds "in what is crude, brute, ugly." And finally, though "the artist who deals with this material does not pretend to like it,"

> he is too much of an artist to let you see that he dislikes it. He knows it is simply his affair to let you see it as he sees it; then, if you are not like it and of it, you will find it moralizing itself to you.

Since Frank Norris's *McTeague* has been called "the most consistently naturalistic work of the period," Howells' reaction to that novel might be expected to indicate what he thought of naturalistic technique. For here, if anywhere, he should have recognized the influence of a form other than the realism he had been championing for so long. Recognizing that *McTeague* was different from "the old-fashioned American novel," Howells' conclusion was that the difference is due to Zola, although Norris, he said, "does not go to Zola's lengths, breadths, and depths." [21] Although pointing out that the inevitable result of "expansion in fiction" is to render it unfit for living-rooms, "where the ladies of the family sit and the children go in and out," Howells did not find any fault with the subject matter.

That Howells regarded *McTeague* as an important landmark in American fiction is evident from his wondering whether the time had come to abandon "the old fashioned American ideal of a novel as something which may be read by all ages and sexes." But the decision of whether the old ideals should be abandoned rested with society and not with the author. Just as in *Criticism and Fiction* (1891) he had insisted on the greater truth of a fiction which pictures the conventions that are a part of real life, so now he was concerned lest in throwing over the proprieties fiction should sacrifice realism. If the old-fashioned ideal of the novel had involved hypocrisy, so had life. If fiction now was to ignore the conventions, society should make sure it was ready to get along without them too. The principal criticism which Howells had to make of *McTeague* had to do precisely

---

[19] See Alexander Cowie, *The Rise of the American Novel* (New York, 1948), who dates the beginning of naturalism from the publication of this novel. Theodore Dreiser remarked that this book and Fuller's *With the Procession* (1895) were "the birth cries of naturalism in this country."
[20] "The Cliff-Dwellers," *Harper's Bazaar,* XXVI (1893).
[21] "A Case in Point," *Literature,* n.s. I (1899).

with this point of the novel reflecting life realistically. "His true picture of life is not true," he said, "because it leaves beauty out." He explained: "Life is squalid and cruel and vile and hateful, but it is noble and tender and pure and lovely too. By and by he will put these traits in and then his powerful scene will be a reflection of reality . . ." [22]

In his *North American Review* article on Hamlin Garland in 1912, he brought up the question of Garland's frankness, which he assumed others had questioned besides himself; he pointed out that Garland's refusal "to ignore what cannot be denied" was different from "that bad allure of so much modern fiction in its dances of the seven veils," because the former "puts the gross passions . . . to shame, rather than flatters or entices them." Howells' high opinion of Garland had not changed since his early welcoming of that forerunner of naturalism to the ranks of the realists in 1891. Then he had seen fit to point out a certain rudeness in style, but he had not objected to Garland's material or his approach to it. Indeed, he had been Garland's champion against the attackers of realism. He had praised his "fine courage" in leaving facts with the reader "ungarnished and unvarnished" and had commented on the rareness of this trait in Anglo-Saxon writers, "so infantile and feeble is the custom of our art." [23]

A common opinion is that Howells was violently opposed to the inclusion of coarse subject matter in fiction; so common is this opinion that Howells has come to be considered a bulwark against the invasion of the American novel by aspects of life other than the smiling ones. Complaints against his genteelness date back at least as far as Gertrude Atherton's famous attack in 1904.[24] Such a picture of Howells can hardly be reconciled with his reviews of writers who were naturalists, or who had strong tendencies in that direction. In spite of what his attackers have called his "irrational moral inhibitions" and the "Boston-spinster sentences in his essays," Howells championed Crane, Norris, Twain, Garland, Fuller, Herrick, to mention only a few, a list which sounds like a roll-call of America's more radical realists.

Nor can this interpretation be reconciled with Howells' appraisal of Zola after the French naturalist's death. He insisted that Zola was one of the most moral of authors, and he credited the "French realists" with breaking "the tradition of the French romanticists that vice was or might be something graceful, something poetic, something gay, brilliant, something superior almost." [25] Zola's books, Howells said, are "most pitilessly moral," and yet he did not deny Zola's indecency: "His books may be, and I suppose they often are, indecent, but they are not immoral; they may disgust, but they will not deprave; only those rotten can scent corruption in them . . ." And, he continued, we must realize "that anxiety for sincerity

---

[22] For additional criticism by Howells of Norris, see "Frank Norris," *North American Review*, CLXXV (1902).

[23] See "Editor's Study," *Harper's*, LXXXIII (1891), p. 640.

[24] "Why is American Literature Bourgeois?" *North American Review*, CLXXVII (1904), 771–81.

[25] See "Émile Zola," *North American Review*, CLXXV (1902), 587–96.

and truth, springing from the sense of pity and justice, makes indecency a condition of portraying human nature so that it may look upon its image and be ashamed." When the rebels of the 1920's made fun of Howells, as one critic has recently pointed out, they forgot that "in case of a conflict," between honesty and decency, Howells "had been quick to put honesty first." [26]

Concerning technique in fiction, Howells seemed to be opposed to too many details, too much literalism, too much analysis. To him, going too far in any of these directions resulted in a distortion of reality, hence in romanticism. The reason for his reluctance to reread the works of Edgar Allan Poe illustrates this point: "That unsparing detail, that analysis, that series of characterless events deter me, repel me . . . Poe's method is always mechanical, his material is mostly unimportant." By Howells' standards, both art and reality demand that selection be made of details which will present the truth as the author sees it. Mere accumulation of detail cannot give a true picture of life because the mind of the reader cannot always grasp the significance of massed facts; insight into reality is gained by suggestion or by details selected not to color the picture but to clarify it. The true artist works by "seizing every suggestion of experience and observation, turning it to the utmost account, piecing it out by his invention, building it up into a structure of fiction where its origin was lost to all but himself, and often even to himself."

Howells' insistence on the artistic nature of fiction led him to disapprove of the technique of the naturalists when it became too documentary in its effort to be scientific. When he praised any particular novels—whether naturalistic, near-naturalistic, realistic, or romantic—he praised them for the same qualities, the faithfulness and power with which they represented real life. When he condemned any tendency in fiction, it was one that he thought resulted in a distortion of reality.

Howells lived up to his own ideal of a critic who judged each work by its trueness to life and not by a model; one who knew that his office was to discover principles of literature, not to establish them—"to report, not to create"; who understood how to reduce his work "to the business of observing, recording, and comparing . . . analyzing the material . . . and then synthetizing"; who went about his task humbly because he realized that creative writers might have something to teach him about life.

The atmosphere that Howells found so conducive to his temperament proved an unsatisfactory one for Henry James. James needed the congenial air of culture which perhaps he might have found at a somewhat earlier date in his quiet New England heritage, but that way of life was already, in his time, being disturbed by the tumult rising in the West and the rapid growth of industrialization in the East. Travelling in Europe at an early age, he acquired then the lifelong appreciation of European

[26] Granville Hicks, "A Grasping Imagination," *Sewanee Review*, LIX (1951), 505–17.

culture that would later alienate him from America and cause him to establish residence in England.[27]

Henry James's literary criticism contrasts rather sharply with that of his contemporaries, such as Howells or the local color writers. Beginning with his earliest reviews there is indication of an emphasis upon the artistic, upon problems of technique, which becomes more pronounced as his work progresses through "The Art of Fiction" to the prefaces which he wrote for the New York edition of his works.

James's career as a literary critic began in 1864 when his first review was published in the New York *Nation*. [28] During this first period of his career, he wrote many reviews for such magazines as the *Nation* and the *North American Review*, which reveal him basing his judgments on preconceived principles, interested mainly in "ideas," and evaluating works of art largely in the light of stiff moral standards. He perceived the function of the critic to be somewhat that of a judge handing down decisions based on a rigidly codified law, embellishing these, as do most respectable judges, with enlightening advice. The critic is also the custodian of public taste.[29]

The early critical principles of James are evident in his comment that Sainte-Beuve, the great French critic, was "little of a moralist" and not "overmuch of a thinker." Swinburne also lacked thought as he was overbalanced by an "inordinate sense of the picturesque." As for Whitman, James wrote that "We look in vain . . . through your book for a single idea." Criticizing the poet for his lack of taste and lack of poetic discipline, James concluded with this bit of advice: "It is not enough to be rude, lugubrious, and grim. You must also be serious. You must forget yourself in your ideas."

James even as a young critic, however, showed the sensitivity to method and form that was to characterize his entire critical career. While admiring

[27] Biographical studies of James and his work include Pelham Edgar, *Henry James: Man and Author* (London, 1927); F. W. Dupee, *Henry James* (New York, 1951); F. O. Matthiessen, *Henry James: The Major Phase* (New York, 1944) and *The James Family* (New York, 1947); Elizabeth Stevens, *The Crooked Corridor; A Study of Henry James* (New York, 1949); Michael Swan, *Henry James* (London, New York, 1950); and Van Wyck Brooks, *The Pilgrimage of Henry James* (New York, 1925). Much valuable information is contained in *The Letters of Henry James*. edited by Percy Lubbock, 2 vols. (New York, 1920), and in *The Notebooks of Henry James*, edited by F. O. Matthiessen and Kenneth Murdock (New York, 1947). Studies of James's technique and development include Joseph W. Beach, *The Method of Henry James* (New Haven, 1918); Cornelia Kelley, *The Early Development of Henry James* (Urbana, Ill., 1930); and Robert P. Warren, editor, the Henry James Number, *Kenyon Review*, V (1943), 481–617. Studies of James's criticism include Morris Roberts, *Henry James's Criticism* (Cambridge, 1929); R. P. Blackmur, "Introduction" to *The Art of the Novel: Critical Prefaces, by Henry James* (New York, 1934); Léon Edel, *The Prefaces of Henry James* (Paris, 1931); Lyon N. Richardson, introduction, *Henry James: Representative Selections* (New York, 1941); and F. R. Leavis, "Henry James and the Function of Criticism," *Scrutiny*, XV (1948), 98–104.

[28] See Laurence Barrett, "Young Henry James, Critic," *American Literature*, XX (1949), 385–400; and Van Wyck Brooks, "Henry James as a Reviewer," in *Sketches in Criticism* (New York, 1932). Morris Roberts, *Henry James's Criticism*, presents a good analysis of James's early criticism.

[29] Many of the early reviews of James are collected in *Notes and Reviews* (Cambridge, 1921) and *Views and Reviews* (Boston, 1908).

George Eliot's "English decorum and moral interest," he nevertheless censured her lack of selectivity in the use of commonplace detail pointing out that the story, not local color embellishments, is the soul of a novel. Similarly his review of *Les Travailleurs de la Mer* reprimanded Victor Hugo for lack of selectivity in his characterization: "But when M. Victor Hugo picks up a supernumerary he is not wont to set him down until he has bedecked him with more epigrams, anecdotes, formulas, and similes than would furnish forth a dozen ordinary heroes."

French Poets and Novelists, which appeared in London in 1878, revealed a more mature James, one who had become more sympathetic and who exhibited a greater perceptiveness of form and less reliance on "principles." James, while still harshly judicial concerning the French lack of morality and grace, nevertheless demonstrated an increased admiration for their technical curiosity, their explorations, and their constant critical discussions. His hostility revealed itself in his reference to the fiction of Balzac, whom he was later to admire, as the "dreams of an ambitious hair dresser," and in his criticism of Flaubert for sacrificing charm, good taste, and morality to a "treacherous ideal" which was nothing more than "to begin on the outside and end there." Gautier and Baudelaire likewise received unfavorable criticism. His essay on Alfred de Musset, however, revealed a more sympathetic attitude and a greater degree of perceptiveness. He admired in de Musset the frankness, grace, and harmony with which emotions are expressed: "What makes him valuable is just this gift for the expression of that sort of emotion which the conventions and proprieties of life, the dryness of ordinary utterances, the stiffness of most imaginations, leave quite in the vague, and yet which forms a part of human nature important enough to have its exponent."

The volume on Hawthorne which James wrote for the English Men of Letters series in 1879 is on the whole a sympathetic and perceptive piece of criticism. Tracing most of what he considers Hawthorne's faults, his thinness and over-fancifulness, to the provincialism of his New England background, James expressed regret that Hawthorne could not have lived in the more congenial English atmosphere. James's realism is evident in his criticism of the lack of realistic detail, the extreme ingenuity, and the "insistence" upon symbolism in Hawthorne's fiction. In spite of such specific criticisms, the tone of the book is one of admiration. James praised the depth and moral quality of Hawthorne's imagination and the grace and purity of his style. In comparison with the grossness and moral indifference of such French writers as Balzac, Gautier, and Flaubert, the English spiritual and moral richness of Hawthorne is to be preferred even though his fiction lacks to a degree the artistry of the French. His reference to *The Scarlet Letter* as "the finest piece of imaginative writing yet put forth in the country" reveals the perceptiveness of James's criticism.

It is by a shift in his attitude toward Sainte-Beuve that we are made aware of the rapidly developing maturity of James. In an article written in 1880, James referred to Sainte-Beuve as the "genius of observation, discretion, and taste." In him, James saw both "masculine" and "feminine" qualities: solid sense, exactness, observation, psychology in addition to delicate taste, subtility, and penetration. He now saw clearly that the critic was not the lawgiver but the "student, inquirer, observer, interpreter, commentator whose aim was to arrive at justness of characterization."

In "The Art of Fiction," which was published in 1884, James says, "A novel is in its broadest definition a personal, a direct impression of life . . ." In spite of the fact that he demanded that fiction be true to life, be typical, James recognized that in the great writer realism and romance are mixed: "He commits himself in both directions, not quite at the same time nor to the same effect, of course, but by some need of performing his whole possible revolution, by the law of some rich passion in him for extremes. . . . His current remains therefore extraordinarily rich and mixed, washing us successively with the warm wave of the near and familiar and the tonic shock, as may be, of the far and strange." In either case, fiction is not a literal transcript of life but, at its best, "the state of private intercourse with things, the kind of current that in a given personal experience flows to and fro between the imagination and the world."

For James, in fiction, "It is the special picture that must stand or fall, according as it seems to possess truth or to lack it." What the artist must do is produce "the illusion of life. The cultivation of this success, the study of this exquisite process, form, to my taste, the beginning and the end of the art of the novelist." There are no other obligations for the novelist, no other purposes he must have or causes he must preach. He points out that "The only obligation to which in advance we may hold the novel, without incurring the accusation of being arbitrary, is that it be interesting," meaning that there must be no other *a priori* rules set up about what the novelist should write or how he should write.

The basic difference between the views of James and those of many other theorists of fiction of his day lies in an attitude toward the subject matter of fiction. For most others, the greater value of fiction lay in subject. For James, on the other hand, the emphasis lay, not precisely on technique, but on the organic relationship of technique to subject. "We must grant the artist his subject, his idea . . .: our criticism is applied only to what he makes of it." James wants to know what the artist "makes of" his matter—that is, how he renders it, how interesting he makes it, how successfully he manages to make it look like life, and how well he informs it with meaning.

What Howells had continually propounded, the intimate relation between concrete fact and aesthetic beauty, James separates, and, while still emphasizing the close relation between art and reality, therefore places most emphasis upon problems of form and technique. He did not share Howells' enthusiasm for the plain, unvarnished facts of life. Rather, he was interested in the skill, the art, the execution of the artist in giving a "feeling" or "spirit" of reality to the whole work.

While denying that a work of art should have "a conscious moral purpose," James was at all times keenly aware of the organic relationship between the work of art and its creator, of the fact that the literary creator's moral character automatically determines the moral quality of his creation. With this principle, he combined his interest in the mechanical aspects of art, or the technique, to arrive at a complete conception of the art work itself.

For James "It is art that *makes* life, makes interest, makes importance." While actual life is "all inclusion and confusion," James would use art to bring pattern and meaning out of life by pointing out that art is "all discrimination and selection" of what is centrally revelatory and "typical." Literal transcription is not enough, for art requires the focused ordering of reality by the shaping imagination to bring out its deeper or symbolic meaning. Hence, while a defender of realism, James was not, himself, in sympathy with the more extreme aspects of that movement such as the naturalism of Zola or the "veritism" of Garland. Primarily interested in a realism conveyed through psychological analysis and speculation, James showed little interest in a reportorial realism, or a realism which concerned itself primarily with social problems.

As a critic, James's perceptions continually deepened and grew more refined. He became increasingly concerned with the technique, or what he would call the "art" of fiction; and his prefaces, which he began to write in 1907, for the New York edition of his works reveal a preoccupation with form, prose style, and structural problems, as well as with increasingly complex aspects of moral and psychological experience.

Defining the novel, as he had earlier, as the "most magnificent form of art" and one beyond escapism, didacticism, and "rigid formalism," and as primarily having a "large, free, character of an immense and exquisite *correspondence with life*," James sought to avoid some of the more artificial devices of story-telling. One of the main principles which he developed in the prefaces is that which is concerned with the use of what James calls "compositional centres" or "reflectors." James saw that such a correspondence with life as the novel aims at involved avoiding "omniscience" on the author's part and adopting a point of view consistently maintained by which the story unfolds dramatically from scene to scene as an observer comes to assemble knowledge from episode to episode in real life. The novelist's first care is to provide himself with such a "centre" or "reflector":

> To lift our subject out of the sphere of anecdote and place it in the sphere of drama, liberally considered, to give it dignity by extracting its finest importance, causing its parts to flower together into some splendid special sense, we supply it with a large lucid reflector, which we find only, as I have already noted, in that mind and soul concerned in the business that have at once the highest sensibility and the highest capacity, or that are, as we may call it, most admirably agitated.

It is only through such a "large lucid reflector" as the "acute central consciousness" of the novel that the values of the story can be given full meaning and expression, and the unity of the subject can be secured. This

plea for the use of such a central intelligence in fiction is frequent throughout the prefaces, and this technique lies at the very heart of James's work.[30]
It is also related to his conception of fiction as an organic form, one which
will possess no life of its own and will not be able to move of itself unless
it is possessed of such a "centre."

Another artistic principle which is stressed throughout the prefaces is
that of "fore-shortening," which is related to James's lifelong concern that
neither plot nor "huge amounts of life" be equated with the story, the
objective reality. Foreshortening conduced, he said, "to the only compactness that has charm, to the only spareness that has a force, to the only
simplicity that has a grace—those, in each order, that produced the *rich*
effect." Obviously foreshortening implies, for James, an act of intelligence
on the part of the novelist, a control of the story by heightening the
quality of the representation and quickening the intensity and realization
of the theme.[31]

Henry James thought of true criticism as an art, "one of the most difficult, the most delicate." In the essay on "Criticism," he wrote that the
critical sense "is absolutely rare, and the possession of the cluster of
qualities that minister to it is one of the highest distinctions." Concerning
the prefaces to the New York edition, he wrote to William Dean Howells
in 1908 that "They are, in general, a sort of plea for Criticism, for Discrimination, for Appreciation on other than infantile lines—as against the
so almost universal Anglo-Saxon absence of these things; which tends so,
in our general trade, it seems to me, to break the heart. . . . They ought,
collected together, none the less, to form a sort of comprehensive manual
or *vade mecum* for aspirants in our arduous profession."

A voluminous and discriminating critic, James developed gradually from
evaluation in the light of rigid moral standards to inductive inquiry and a
subtle perception of aesthetic nuances, with Sainte-Beuve as his master:
"Just in proportion as he reacts and reciprocates and penetrates, is the critic
a valuable instrument." Sympathetically "aware" and "indefatigably supple," he must be sensitive to the extent to which the author carries out his
own distinctive intentions. Both technical and devoted to humane values,
the criticism of Henry James has done more than that of any other critic
to raise fiction to a fine art and to endow criticism itself with more perceptive principles of form, taste, and method.

The waning years of the nineteenth century saw a modification of earlier
theories of realism by conditions of social unrest within the country and
by the impact of new scientific and literary ideas from Europe. Among the
most influential factors in this period was naturalism, particularly as

[30] Cf. *The Ambassadors* which is unified by being seen entirely through the con-
sciousness of Strether, the "reflector." See Joseph W. Beach, *The Method of Henry
James*; Léon Edel, *The Prefaces of Henry James*; R. P. Blackmur, "Introduction" to
The Art of the Novel; and R. W. Short, "Some Critical Terms of Henry James,"
Publications Modern Language Association, LXV (1950), 667–80.
[31] See Morris Roberts, "Henry James and the Art of Foreshortening," *Review of
English Studies*, XXII (1946), 207–14.

developed by Émile Zola in *The Experimental Novel*.[32] Naturalism is akin to realism in its emphasis upon fidelity to life, but it went much further in its exaggerated insistence upon completely scientific observation. Man could be considered in no other way but as a natural being. The special fact of reality, not James's illusion of reality created by the artist, governed the attitude toward fiction. As Zola said, determinism dominates everything. Man is not a creature controlling his own destiny, but rather a helpless victim of forces within himself and of environment without himself which determine his life and his fate.

Social and economic changes within the United States were influential in creating a climate of opinion that was receptive to naturalism. The rapid change from an agrarian to an industrial economy, with a consequent mushrooming of cities, brought in its wake numerous social and economic problems. Trusts, corruption in officialdom, exploitation of labor: these brought an organized revolt through congressional act, labor organization, and popular uprising. The railroad strikes of 1886 and the Chicago Haymarket riot of the same year did much to buttress the already deep-seated antagonism between capital and labor. By 1887 the western boom had ground to a standstill, mortgages were foreclosed by the thousands, and the farmers, for their own protection, formed active alliances that eventually became identified with the Populist party. The culminating crisis was the major panic of 1893. For four long years the country sat out a depression that all but wiped out the economy.

Already Europe had quickened to the new concepts of biological evolution and economic, psychological, and physical determinism.[33] Soon these new ideas spread to America and, strengthened by such accounts as Jacob

[32] Special studies dealing with naturalism in American literature and criticism include Lars Ahnebrink, *The Beginnings of Naturalism in American Fiction* (Cambridge, 1950); Alfred Kazin, *On Native Grounds* (New York, 1942); C. C. Walcutt, "The Naturalism of Vandover and the Brute," in *Forms of Modern Fiction*, edited by William Van O'Connor (Minneapolis, Minn., 1948); Robert Spiller, "Toward Naturalism in Fiction," *Literary History of the United States*; Malcolm Cowley, "'Not Men': A Natural History of American Naturalism," *Kenyon Review*, IX (1947), 414–35; "Naturalism in American Literature," in *Evolutionary Thought in America*, edited by Stow Persons (New Haven, 1950); William C. Frierson and Herbert Edwards, "Impact of French Naturalism on American Critical Opinion, 1877–1892," *Publications Modern Language Association*, LXIII (1948), 1007–16; John R. Dunbar, *The Reception of European Literary Naturalism in the United States, 1870–1900*, unpublished dissertation (Harvard, 1948); and Harry Hartwick, *The Foreground of American Fiction* (New York, 1934). For the influence of Zola, see Matthew Josephson, *Zola and His Time* (New York, 1928); Herbert Edwards, "Zola and American Critics," *American Literature*, IV (1932), 114–29; A. J. Salvan, *Zola aux Etats Unis* (Providence, R.I., 1943); and Everett T. Lloyd, *The Evolution of the Attitude in the United States Toward Émile Zola*, unpublished dissertation (New York, 1949).

[33] For more detailed studies of the new ideas on American thought, see Richard Hofstadter, *Social Darwinism in American Thought, 1860–1915* (Philadelphia, 1944); Stow Persons, editor, *Evolutionary Thought in America* (New Haven, 1950); Arthur E. Jones, *Darwinism and Its Relationship to Realism and Naturalism in American Fiction, 1860–1900* (Madison, N. J., 1950); Oscar Cargill, *Intellectual America: Ideas on the March* (New York, 1941); W. M. Payne, "American Literary Criticism and the Doctrine of Evolution," *International Monthly*, II (1900), 26–46; 127–53. For a more general study of the period, see Thomas Beer, *The Mauve Decade: American Life at the End of the Nineteenth Century* (New York, 1926).

Riis's *How the Other Half Lives*, found a receptive audience. From this dark time the bleak pessimism and protestations of men like Stephen Crane, Jack London, and Theodore Dreiser were to come like ominous thunder.

From this time of unrest also came the militantly realistic early writings of Hamlin Garland. Garland, a son of the Middle Border, managed to recapture much of the harshness of life in that pioneer environment, its social injustice, and its social decay. This life was life without glamour or romance, and in his early years, before good fortune had mellowed him, Garland spoke frankly and honestly. Henry George had trained him in economics, Taine in historical criticism, Darwin and Spencer in philosophy, and Walt Whitman, Émile Zola, Ibsen, Turgenev, and Tolstoy in literature.[34]

Garland followed Howells and James in insisting upon a truthful fidelity to reality, but he went much further in his uncompromising attitude toward reality than did either Howells or James. Science had shown what could be done with facts. Writers noted this, and, imbued with scientific enthusiasm, looked to the society about them for the facts of fiction. Thus the process was more or less inductive; one saw first the subtle and social contrasts lying about him and from them theory was developed. As Garland wrote in *Crumbling Idols* (1894): "This *theory* of the veritist is, after all, a statement of his passion for truth and for individual expression. The passion does not spring from theory; the theory rises from the love of verities, which seems to increase day by day all over the western world."

Garland insisted upon a literature at once individual and true to one's experience. The writer, so far as past literature is concerned, is alone in a sort of primitive isolation. There is only the self and the locality, and from the interplay great literature develops. Reflecting Taine's concept of the organic relationship between literature and its time, place, and race, Garland wrote: "It is a settled conviction with me that each locality must produce its own literary record, each special phase of life utter its own voice." "Veritism," he continued, "as I understand it, puts aside all models, even living writers. Whatever he may do unconsciously the artist must consciously stand alone before nature and before life."

The concept of evolution as developed by Darwin and Spencer also reinforced his thinking along these lines. Times change, and the change is measured in terms of progress. What was good for one's ancestors can-

---

[34] No adequate study of Garland has yet been published. A thorough analysis of his thought and reading may be found in the unpublished dissertation of Benjamin F. Gronewold, *The Social Criticism of Hamlin Garland* (New York, 1943). Another unpublished dissertation dealing with the important early period of his life is Eldon C. Hill, *A Biographical Study of Hamlin Garland from 1860–1895* (Ohio State, 1940). Brief critical studies include Carl Van Doren, *Contemporary American Novelists* (New York, 1922), pp. 38–47; Fred L. Pattee, *The Development of the American Short Story* (New York, 1923), pp. 313–17; Vernon L. Parrington, *Main Currents in American Thought* (New York, 1930), III, 288–300; Walter F. Taylor, *The Economic Novel in America* (Chapel Hill, N. C., 1942), pp. 148–83; Robert Spiller, introduction to *Crumbling Idols* (Gainesville, Fla., 1952); and Lucy L. Hazard, *The Frontier in American Literature* (New York, 1927), pp. 261–67.

not suffice for the present. The demand is always for freshness, for new ideas, for complete change. "The splendid light of the development theory, uttered by Spencer and Darwin," had made Garland's period one of the most conclusively analytical in all history. He saw the "development theory" equally as applicable to literature as to social environment: "Once prove literature and art subject to social conditions, to environment and social conformation, and the dominance of the epic in one age, and of the drama in another, became as easy to understand and to infer as any other fact of a people's history."

That Garland was not a naturalist in the sense of Zola is evident when Garland implies that Zola was wrong in practice if not in theory when his art concerned itself with the obscene. For Garland, reality is varied, and the characteristic cannot be discerned as indecent or impure: "This literature will not deal with crime and abnormities nor with deceased persons. It will deal, I believe, with the wholesome love of honest men for honest women, with the heroism of labor, the comradeship of men,—a drama of average types of character, infinitely varied, but always characteristic." Garland's debt here is rather obviously to Whitman and to Howells.

With Garland's realism there are blended strong romantic tendencies stemming from the belief that evolution meant progress. One of the reasons for portraying the evils of the present is to hasten that age of peace and beauty assured in the future by the process of evolution:

> The realist or veritist is really an optimist, a dreamer. He sees life in terms of what it might be, as well as in terms of what it is; but he writes of what is, and, at his best, suggests what is to be, by contrast. He aims to be perfectly truthful in his delineation of his relation to life, but there is a tone . . . of sorrow that the good time moves so slowly in its approach.[35]

For Garland difference, the plastic and vital quality of all life, is the significant factor in great literature, and this factor can best be observed in the local color movement. Thus the new literature is to be a combination of the old-world concept of beauty and the purely American concept of significance; it is to be the ". . . most human and humane literature ever seen." And, in addition, he continues: "What we should stand for is not universality of theme, but beauty and strength of treatment, leaving the writer to choose his theme because he loves it."

The literary theory of Garland also reflected some of the theories of the French Impressionistic movement. The Impressionists too appealed to nature, which was to be the artist's only model. Fidelity to past masters was inimical to freshness and individuality. The Impressionists sought to heighten the sense of reality in art by capturing the effect of a single, momentary instance of the world's impression upon sight, the particular colorful interval which stimulated and activated the senses. It was a

[35] Cf. Ruth Raw, "Hamlin Garland, the Romanticist," *Sewanee Review*, XXXVI (1928), 202–10.

unified impression gained through the painting of masses for effect and not in order to create a mosaic.[36] Impressionism tended to favor the use of the local as subject and to place greater emphasis upon technique rather than universality of theme: "This brings me to my settled conviction that art, to be vital, must be local in its subject; its universal appeal must be in its working out,—in the way it is done."

Garland's basic view of literature, however, is that it is sociologic. The writer is an integrated member of a certain society, and his product is directed to that public to digest as best it can. As the society changes and gives way to the new, so must the work of art. But this evolutionary destructive force is countered by a conservative force which attempts to stop the process, or, at least, to establish an equilibrium:

> In evolution there are always two vast fundamental forces: one, the inner, which propels; the other, the outer, which adapts and checks. One forever thrusts toward new forms, the other forever moulds, conserves, adapts, reproduces. Progress is the resultant of these forces. . . . The force that flowers is the individual, that which checks and moulds is environment. Impulse is the stronger to-day, tomorrow conformity chills and benumbs. Of such cycles is the history of art.

A blending of realism and romanticism, strongly influenced by Taine, Darwin, and Spencer, Garland's literary criticism is representative of the direction American literary thought was taking at the end of the nineteenth century.[37]

An omnivorous reader of Zola, Frank Norris is typical not only of the influence of Zola upon American literary thought but also of the frequent modification of Zola's principles by American writers and critics.[38] Like Zola, Norris was at his best in painting the vast canvases where human experiences take place before a panorama of epic proportion. The novelist must deal, he wrote, "with elemental forces, motives that stir whole nations."

Norris thought that the twentieth century's mode of expression was the novel, just as in previous ages it had been successively the epic, the paint-

---

[36] See *Crumbling Idols*, p. 124.

[37] Further examples of Garland's application to literature of the concept of evolution and the theory of Taine can be found in his "The West in Literature," *Arena*, VI (1892), 669–76; "The Future of Fiction," *ibid.*, VII (1893), 513–24; and "Productive Conditions of American Literature," *Forum*, VII (1894), 690–98.

[38] Biographical studies of Norris include Franklin Walker, *Frank Norris: A Biography* (New York, 1932) and Ernest Marchand, *Frank Norris: A Study* (Stanford, 1942). Critical studies of Norris are Vernon L. Parrington, *Main Currents in American Thought* (New York, 1930), III, 329–34; Harry Hartwick, *The Foreground of American Fiction* (New York, 1934), 45–66; Walter F. Taylor, *The Economic Novel in America* (Chapel Hill, N. C., 1942), 282–306; Herbert Edwards, "Zola and the American Critics," *American Literature*, IV (1932), 114–29; Charles C. Walcutt, "Frank Norris on Realism and Naturalism," *American Literature*, XIII (1941), 61–63; Alfred Kazin, "Three Pioneer Realists," *Saturday Review of Literature*, VI (Jan. 11, 1930), p. 3; and Fred L. Pattee, *The New American Literature* (New York, 1930). Special studies of the French influence on Norris are L. Ahnebrink, *The Influence of Émile Zola on Frank Norris* (Cambridge, 1947), and Marius Biencourt, *Une Influence du Naturalisme Français en Amérique: Frank Norris* (Paris, 1933).

ing, the Cathedral, the satirical poem. In this light the work of the novelist takes on new meaning. No longer is he concerned merely with the thought of provoking interest and pleasure. The people look to him for truth, and it is his responsibility to provide it. Writing in *The Responsibilities of the Novelist* (1903), Norris stated:

> The People have a right to the Truth as they have a right to life, liberty and the pursuit of happiness. It is *not* right that they be exploited and deceived with false views of life, false characters, false sentiment, false morality, false history, false philosophy, false emotions, false heroism, false notions of self-sacrifice, false views of religion, of duty, of conduct and of manners.

Thus the writer who addresses himself to the reading public has a heavy duty to tell the truth. It is an ethical problem and the writer should approach it with soberness, earnestness, and with an abiding consciousness of his own limitations.

In contrast with Zola's ideal of the novelist not being selective but rather being an objective, scientific, recorder of facts, Norris felt that the high ideal of disinterestedness, of remaining utterly still and reflecting reality to the reader much as a mirror does, was in point of fact impossible so long as men are men. Every writer, in so far as he prepares to write, has an end, a purpose. And this end, as brought forth in the novel, may be of three orders: to tell something, to show something, or to prove something. The first concerns itself merely with things or with an elaboration of complication, as for instance *The Three Musketeers*. The second, of a higher order, concerns itself with character, such as *Romola* does. The third, that which proves something, Norris thought to be of the highest order:

> The third, and what we hold to be the best class, proves something, draws conclusions from a whole congeries of forces, social tendencies, race impulses, devotes itself not to a study of men but of man. In this class falls the novel with the purpose, such as "Les Miserables."

The third class Norris conceived to embody all of the best of the previous two. In order to accomplish its aim it must first of all tell something, then analyze and penetrate to the innermost nature of its subject in a thoroughly concrete manner. The writer must never forget the nature of his vehicle. His intention is to preach, but fiction is the concrete expression of men and women in concrete situations and cannot be handled as a sociological or polemical tract. "The preaching, the moralizing," Norris maintained, "is the result not of direct appeal by the writer, but is made—should be made—to the reader by the very incidents of the story." Thus the novel as an art form is upheld at the same time as its purpose is the edification of the reader.

If Norris deviated from the realistic position of impersonal reporting, the deviation was a conscious one. He had already enunciated his theory that the great novel must have a higher purpose than merely telling something. He specifically criticized realism for too often skimming the surface of things, whereas romanticism, he felt, penetrated deeper into true reality and was of infinitely sterner stuff. "Realism," he wrote, "is the kind of fiction that confines itself to the type of normal life." On the other hand, "Romance, I take it, is the kind of fiction that takes cognizance of variations from the type of normal life." While failing to distinguish clearly between realism and romanticism, his definition of the romance offers an interesting parallel to the naturalistic principle of not dealing with the typical but with, as Zola stated it, "a slice of life." [39]

Norris recognized at least another kind of realism than that which confined itself to the universal. In the following statement he is obviously thinking of realism in the sense of the local color tradition:

> But in the fictitious presentation of an epoch of a people, the writer must search for the idiosyncrasy, the characteristic . . . that distinguishes the times or place treated from all other times and all other places. He must address himself to the task of picturing the peculiarity . . . that obtains in that locality and nowhere else. [40]

In general, however, Norris felt realism, as he understood it, to be cramping; it prevented stretching one's legs and engaging in a little bit of teaching or moralizing. There was more to life than talking over teacups and meeting probable people in probable situations as he interpreted the interests of realism. And so he turned to what he called "romance": ". . . to Romance belongs the wide world for range, and the unplumbed depths of the human heart, and the mystery of sex, and the problems of life, and the black, unsearched penetralia of the soul of man."

Concerned with the increasing lack of interest in aesthetic and artistic considerations, which had been hastened by the materialism of middleclass taste and by the emphasis of naturalism upon the "scientific" method in literature, Lewis E. Gates felt that impressionism could be of service. Popularized in Europe by Walter Pater and Anatole France, America had been slow in adopting this seemingly iconoclastic doctrine. Gates was not, however, a "pure" impressionist in the sense that Pater and France were. In addition to calling for a new study of aesthetics and for the intellectual reawakening of the reader of literature, Gates also demanded a firm sense of both the milieu of the work of art itself and of the contemporary milieu. Thus the new study of aesthetics, the psychological criticism of Sainte-Beuve, and the three cardinal principles of Taine's criticism all find a satisfactory point of rest in the criticism of the appreciative and open-minded Gates. [41]

Gates pointed out that impressionism requires delicacy of perception, sympathetic and mobile mood: in short, a constant awareness of the aesthetics of art. When these are lost, as Matthew Arnold lost his in the

[39] Howells termed naturalism "romanticism" because it dealt with the abnormal. There is considerable evidence that Norris did likewise.

[40] See "Two Uncollected Essays of Frank Norris," *American Literature*, VIII (1936), 193.

[41] There are no satisfactory studies of Gates. Some information is available in the *Literary History of the United States* and other reference works of a similar nature.

heat of an embattled campaign for the moral regeneration of his country-men, critical acumen is lost also.[42] Pater retained his artistic sincerity and came to be one of the greatest critics of an era; his faculty of disinterested-ness, and flexibility of temperament, is the goal for which all good critics must aim, according to Gates.

In an essay, "Impressionism and Appreciation," reprinted in *Studies and Appreciations* (1900), Gates pointed out that it was neither Arnold nor Pater who was responsible for the introduction of impressionism. Rather, they were only the culminating points in a long, historical progression of the human spirit. The period of the last two hundred years, from Thom-son's *Seasons,* say, to our own era, had been a period of increasing sensi-tivity to nature in art, and to art in criticism. In criticism the time lapse can be measured from Addison's work on the imagination and *Paradise Lost;* and while Addison was primitive in his constant generalizing and use of abstract terms, he was the beginning of a long growth in the culti-vation of the critic's sensory apparatus, a growth whose end was impres-sionism:

> In short, what has occurred is this: a poem in its relation to the critic has been gradually carried over from the outside world and made an inti-mate part of the critic's personality; it has been transformed from an ex-ternal object, loosely related to universal mind and generalized emotion of which the critic stands as type, into a series of thought-waves and nerve-vibrations that run at a special moment through an active brain and a sensitive temperament.

Thus, according to Gates, impressionism justifies itself historically. But there is also a psychological justification. More and more the realization has grown that art is inspiring and stimulating to the reader and that its consequence is creative energy. Part of a work's power stems from the intellectual and emotional propensity of the reader; the reader in a sense fills in and adds to the value. It was this that led Anatole France to deny such a thing as a criticism of literature; what was called criticism was little more than the recitation of one's personal adventures with a book. For Gates, however, France went too far. In literature there is also the original pleasure-value the author intended, and that too must be sympa-thetically considered. It is objective as well as a source for potential stimula-tion. A work of art is many things. First of all the writer has perceived some aspect of personal experience. This stirs his emotion; images rise following the laws of association which serve to heighten the intellectual thought at the same time as they are providing for sensory vitality. Finally, the work is bodied forth in an intimate sound pattern and recorded.

But beyond this personal artistic energy there is the milieu, the spirit of the age, and it too plays its role. An artist, according to Gates, is in part a product of his time. If the work is concerned with life, the mould-ing force of his day and generation adds its color, determines much of the intellectual tone, and even the instinctive selection of incidents which the

[42] See his essay on Arnold in *Three Studies in Literature* (New York, 1899), 124–211.

work contains. Try as one may, he cannot escape the moral, the social, the ideal considerations that characterize the period.

Gates parted company with the pure impressionist when he stated that criticism should be more than the registering of one's personal delight. The central, objective core of the work always remains an expression of both the artist and of his milieu; and this, in addition to confiding the pleasure of a happy moment, is a legitimate province of criticism. Hence a new critic is required, and Gates found him in the "appreciator": a man of universal and discerning taste, devoted to the historical, psychological, and impressionistic methods of criticism.

But the appreciative critic's duty does not end there. For a work of art is historical in so far as there is a time-lapse between its publication and its reading by the critic. During that period new concepts, new knowledge, new experiences have been constantly impressing themselves upon the critic, which in their rich and varied complexity in a sense reinforce the original expression of the work and enhance its meaning: "Always, then, in the complete appreciation of a work of art there is this superimposition of other moods upon the mood of the creative artist—there is a reinforcement of the original effect by the delicate interfusion of new tones and strains of feeling."

Thus the appreciative study of Fra Lippo Lippi's Madonnas is aided by not only a recognition of the artist's own religious and tender wistfulness, of the difficulties under which he labored in a yet primitive craft, of the contrast between Lippo Lippi and his contemporaries, but also by our own modern mood of half-credulous insight gained through the acquisition of knowledge from the years lying between.

As a final consideration, "the critic must bear in mind that it is distinctly for the men of his own day that he is revitalizing art; that it is for them that his specialized temperament is to use its resources." Matthew Arnold's dictum of detachment still holds true; something of the dilettante must be in every critic, he must hold to no one program, whether it be in the fields of morals or of politics or of literature. Above all, the retention of open-minded curiosity and variety of vision are the trademarks of the appreciative critic. All contemporary movements must interest him, but none may claim him. ". . . he will become," exclaimed Gates, "in very truth, the specialized temperament of the moment, interpreting the past to the present."

Gates, a professor of English at Harvard, died too soon to realize his full critical development; but his two small volumes of critical theory culled from his Harvard lectures did much to popularize his modified form of impressionism and to add to the growing demand for a greater aesthetic appreciation of art.[43]

[43] Other impressionists in the criticism of the period include Edgar Saltus and Vance Thompson. The principal works of Saltus are *Balzac* (1884) which contains some interesting comment on realism in ficton; *Love and Lore* (1890) which in the section on "Morality and Fiction" contains one of the first attacks on Puritanism in fiction; and *Oscar Wilde* (1917). The principal work of Thompson is *French Portraits* (1899).

By 1900 the force of the "Genteel Tradition" had largely spent itself and the voice of realism was being superseded by that of naturalism. Another element in American criticism, often called "the Aesthetic Revolt," began to take shape, largely influenced by impressionism and by the continental writings of Lemaître, Croce, and Remy de Gourmont, that insisted upon the study of a work of art in terms of that work itself. The term aesthetics took on new meaning and new vitality under the impetus of the work of men like James Huneker, George Santayana, and J. E. Spingarn, a richness that was to eventuate in the "New Criticism" of the twentieth century. Essentially, it was a criticism concerned largely with expression, with problems of art and execution. No longer was the critic to dabble in terms of conduct, value, or cause-and-effect relationships.

James Gibbons Huneker, whose principal contributions to criticism were written between 1899 and 1921, asserted with force and clarity the utter subjectivity of criticism: "Neither praise nor blame should be the goal of the critic. To spill his own soul, that should be his aim." And again, "Humbly to follow and register his emotions aroused by a masterpiece is his function." This is, in contrast with Gates, "pure" impressionism, and it was, almost invariably, the method of Huneker.[44]

To criticism, Huneker brought an intense, enthusiastic appreciation that was at once versatile and usually unerring. He styled himself "Jack of the Seven Arts," and in three of them—music, painting, and literature—he attained a catholic knowledge that enabled him to pass from one to the other for suitable analogies to the work under discussion. Enthusiastic and always voluble, he brought, through the medium of his newspaper columns, to provincial America names that many American critics had not dared to touch—Baudelaire, Nietzsche, Ibsen, Hauptmann, and others. His master in criticism is Remy de Gourmont to whom he dedicated one of his books and about whom he wrote one of his best critical essays. Cosmopolitan in the sense that few American critics have been, widely travelled and widely acquainted in Europe, Huneker, nevertheless, unlike Henry James, always remained an American at heart.

To Huneker, the great critical bugaboo is always certitude. What matters above all is the expression of a work of art. All else is by the way. The great artist is primarily concerned with the mastery of his material; the matter of originality dominates and guides him, the personal expression of a personal motivation. It can be no other way, for beauty is relative: "There is no absolute in beauty; expression, not beauty, is the aim of art."

[44] No authoritative study of Huneker has been made. A brief sketch is Benjamin De Casseres, *James Gibbons Huneker* (New York, 1925). Two early critical estimates are by H. L. Mencken: "James Huneker," in *A Book of Prefaces* (New York, 1917), pp. 151–94, and "James Huneker," in *Prejudices*, 3rd series (New York, 1922), pp. 65–83. The major analysis of Huneker's criticism is George E. De Mille, *Literary Criticism in America* (New York, 1931), 206–45. Other studies include E. C. Fay, "Huneker's Criticism of French Literature," *French Review*, XIV (1940), 130–37; John P. Pritchard and John M. Raines, "James Gibbons Huneker, Critic of the Seven Arts," *American Quarterly*, II (1950), 53–61; Van Wyck Brooks, *Sketches in Criticism* (New York, 1932), 230–35; and Alfred Kazin, *On Native Grounds* (New York, 1942), 62–66.

All his force, clearness, and cleverness was directed to the problems of form, expression, and experiment. And so the one attitude most important to the critic is that of sympathy. Only then can the "academic" be fought. Better by far to extoll the new even at the expense of one's private distaste than to fall into a stultifying conservatism. Thus he can say of Picasso: "It's anarchic, certainly; that's why we tolerate it despite its appalling ugliness; anything is better than the parrot-like repetitions of the academic." The right of the artist to do as he pleases is peculiarly his. Like Henry James, Huneker believed that subject is a matter of the artist's concern, not that of the critics. He visualized art as a triumphant synthesis of the artistic mind with the artistic material:

> The majority of persons do not go to the theatre for the sheer joy of the acting, do not read books because they are well written, or look at pictures because they are painted artistically. The subject, the story, the anecdote, the "human interest," "little touches," all the various traps that snare the attention from poor and mediocre workmanship—the traps of sentimentalism, of false feeling, of cheap pathos, and of the cheap moral, these the greater public willingly embraces, and hates to be reminded of its lack of taste, of its ignorance.

He respected Baudelaire's criticism because his judgment concerned itself more with form than subject. All the imagination in the world cannot compensate if the technique is bad. The true artistic temperament, then, "is the perception and appreciation of beauty in pigment, form, tone, words, or in nature."

His argument with subject Huneker also extended to apply to reformers and moral task-masters, an extension quite in keeping with a critic who extolled form and technique above all else to catch the peculiar quality that differentiated an artist from all others and made his work original and artistically satisfying. Shaw—"preacher George," Huneker labeled him—sermonized, and missed a healthy virility in his drama. Huneker denied the position taken by Frank Norris that the work of art is greatest when it attempts to prove something. To this, Huneker impatiently pointed out that "Your reformer who puts plays on the stage to prove something is only half an artist, no matter what his wit or the justice of his cause." The true critical position is Spingarn's: "As Professor Spingarn would say, the province of the critic is to ask: 'What has the poet to express, and how has he expressed it?' . . . The critical rule of thumb has with the dealer in moral platitudes forever disappeared from the scene."

An intense individualist himself, he was likewise interested in the personality of the artist. He could think of nothing more interesting than "a peep in the laboratory of a great artist's mind." To offset this interest in personality, there is always in Huneker's criticism the interest in questions of form and style. His one, constant demand was that art should be consciously artistic, which is well illustrated in his criticism of Zola whom he condemned not on moral grounds, as had most of the critics of the day, but rather on the grounds that "he lacked finish."

Huneker's own statement that "I don't believe in movements or schematologies, or any one method of seeing or writing," applies above all else to his own criticism. He never developed a systematic critical doctrine. Speaking of his book *Iconoclasts* (1905), he himself summed up his position in relation to criticism:

> That book contained no preface which might have helped the reader across arid and thorny definitions; no friendly footnotes; not even a postlude instead of a preface, in which would be found a neat little theory of a school or a "stream of tendencies"; no special application of the art of plumbing to doctrines held by various dramatists. I confess I am still a skeptic as to the value of "general ideas," believing more in their dissociation, as practiced by Remy de Gourmont.

George Santayana's *The Sense of Beauty* (1896) was his first contribution to American letters, and it at once aligned him with those who were primarily interested in the aesthetics of art; they in turn welcomed his contribution to the revolt against the realists and moralists. A man of almost ascetic life, his work in philosophy, poetry, and literary criticism is of lasting value. He was born in Spain, came to America early and received his Ph.D. from Harvard where he remained as an instructor in philosophy. His style is urbane, the sentences beautifully turned and richly illustrated.[45]

There is a quiet epicureanism in his demeanor which shows in his work an acceptance of life as it is, not as it should be. Very early he had arrived at his naturalistic philosophy, but here one finds not the despair and pessimism usually associated with that attitude. Instead, there is an aesthetic appreciation of life, a sense of beauty that draws one in even when in heartiest disagreement.

In *The Sense of Beauty* Santayana states that the science which pretends to understand and estimate the meaning of beauty is aesthetics, a word that signifies no more than the perception of values. Yet in a natural universe devoid of reason, it is folly to speak of values. Values are attached to objects in so far as we appreciate them, so that Santayana, with Spinoza, can say we desire "nothing because it is good, but it is good only because we desire it." There are no absolutes to measure the worth of things; the imparting of values is finally personal and subjective.

Santayana's rationale of poetry is found in his essay on "The Elements and Function of Poetry," which appeared in his *Interpretations of Poetry and Religion* (1900). For him the vehicle of poetry is its own excuse for being in so far as it subserves the sense of beauty. Its matter is words, and

[45] The best source material is to be found in Santayana's autobiography, *Persons and Places* (New York, 1944–1945). Studies of Santayana's philosophy include George W. Howgate, *George Santayana* (Philadelphia, 1938); Van Meter Ames, *Proust and Santayana: The Aesthetic Way of Life* (Chicago, 1937); and Paul A. Schilpp, *The Philosophy of George Santayana* (Chicago, 1940). Studies of Santayana as a critic and man of letters include Katherine Gilbert, "Santayana's Doctrine of Aesthetic Expression," *Philosophical Review*, XXV (1926), 221–35; John Crowe Ransom, "Art and Mr. Santayana," *Virginia Quarterly Review*, XIII (1937), 420–36; and George W. Howgate, "Santayana and Humanism," *Sewanee Review*, XLIII (1935), 49–57.

words have an intellectual content, but the instrument has significance for its own sake and for its own sweetness. The distinguishing element in poetry compared to prose lies in the philosophical superiority of poetry. Just as poetry is more philosophical than history because it presents memorable types of men and things apart from the irrelevance of particular circumstances, so in terms of substance and texture, poetry is more philosophical than prose because it is more akin to our immediate experience. But what Santayana wishes to make clear is that poetry intensifies experience and perceives analogies not noted by the mass of mankind: "The poet's art is to a great extent the art of intensifying emotions by assembling the scattered objects that naturally arouse them."

Like Stedman, he believes that poetry is an idealizing art. It reverts to experience to gain material for the imagination to knead into an art form more befitting the aesthetic appetite of man. But Stedman's failing, and that of the group about him, was the continued reliance upon traditional conventions. Creative poetry, according to Santayana, destroys conventions:

> The great function of poetry . . . is precisely this: to repair to the material for experience, seizing hold of the reality of sensation and fancy beneath the surface of conventional ideas, and then out of that living but indefinite material to build new structures, richer, finer, fitter to the primary tendencies of our nature, truer to the ultimate possibilities of the soul.

Santayana finds that the one great controlling principle in all works of art is beauty: "But one principle is present throughout—the principle of beauty,—the art of assimilating phenomena, whether words, images, emotions, or systems of ideas, to the deeper innate cravings of the mind." He had previously observed that poetry of this sort is not the poetry of Pope, for instance. Pope, though he is not inharmonious, is too intellectual, has too little aesthetic appeal. There is too much thought plainly given without euphuism. The glow of sense must be an integral part of poetry, else the chilly thought destroys our aesthetic sense in regarding the expression. And so Santayana arrives at his definition: ". . . we may say that poetry is metrical and euphuistic discourse, expressing thought which is both sensuous and ideal."

Emphasizing an appreciative grasp of the work of art itself, Santayana set aside the historical approach to literature and offered instead one that was primarily psychological: "aesthetic judgments as phenomena of mind." A great renewal of interest in aesthetics came as the result of the publication in 1896 of *The Sense of Beauty,* in which he offered his definition of the three orders of beauty as residing in form, expression, and material. In *Three Philosophical Poets,* published in 1910, he demonstrated how this theory of beauty might be applied to the work of three such poets as Dante, Lucretius, and Goethe, and how philosophical and literary criticism might combine to render a total evaluation which would at the same time concern itself with both the aesthetic and ideological aspects of the work of art. Much of the renewed interest around the turn of the century in the aesthetic judgment of art can be attributed to the work of Santayana, and no judicious account of the development of contemporary critical theory could be made without recognizing his contribution.

Another movement which was significant during this period as a force in what has been called the "aesthetic revolt" was that which has been termed "expressionism." The movement stemmed largely from Benedetto Croce, the Italian philosopher, whose greatest disciple in American criticism was Joel E. Spingarn, a professor of comparative literature at Columbia University, who had studied under Croce in Italy and had returned to teach in the United States.[46]

Croce's principal work is his *Esthetic*, published in 1902, in which he attempts to answer the age-old question, What is beauty? His response is that beauty is essentially an inward thing; it is the mental formation in the beholder of a series of images that captures the essence of a work of art. It is the intuitive imagination which is responsible for the process; imagination neither classifies nor defines; it perceives and presents images to the mind—nothing more. Thus in the logical order imagination precedes thought, indeed is necessary for thought. Man is first of all an artist and only secondly a thinker. The greatest power of which man is capable is the correct and competent ability to intuit and imagine the expressive image. This is the aesthetic secret,—beauty is adequate expression.

Spingarn primarily was interested in the theory of criticism rather than in the practice of it. According to Spingarn, criticism is an attempt to answer these questions: "What has the poet tried to do, and how has he fulfilled his intention?" In his famous lecture on "The New Criticism," which he gave in 1910 and which is an excellent exposition of the Crocean aesthetic, he expanded and discussed this approach to literary criticism. The primary aim of Spingarn's theory was to reduce criticism to purely aesthetic principles and to eliminate moral, social, and psychological inquiries and confine it to an apprehension of the artist's intention and a study of his expression. The secret, according to Spingarn, lies in exposing the vital and essential spirit which informs a work of art, in determining how it is true to itself:

> . . . the poet's aim must be judged at the moment of the creative act, that is to say, by the art of the poem itself, and not by the vague ambitions which he imagines to be his real intentions before or after the creative act is achieved. For to create a work of art is the goal of every artist; and all questions in regard to his achievement are merely different ways of helping to answer the one supreme question: Has he or has he not created a work of art?

Acting on the basis of this theory, Spingarn throws out the "dead lumber" of literary criticism:

> In the first place, we have done with all the old Rules.
> We have done with the genres, or literary kinds.

[46] There is no authoritative work on Spingarn. A brief analysis of his work and its significance can be found in the *Literary History of the United States*.

> We have done with the theory of style, with metaphor,
> simile, and all the paraphernalia of Graeco-Roman
> rhetoric.
> We have done with all moral judgment of art as art.
> We have done with technique as separate from art.
> We have done with the race, the time, the environment of
> a poet's work as an element in Criticism.

After this disposal of "outworn" critical theories, what is left? Spingarn would answer the art work and the critic in a sort of union whose result is a further creative act: ". . . taste must reproduce the work of art within itself in order to understand and to judge it; and at that moment aesthetic judgment becomes nothing more nor less than creative art itself."

Constantly it is Spingarn's emphasis on art as an organic whole that confronts the reader. Completeness and perfection are the art work's characteristics. "The poet's only moral duty, as a poet," he says, "is to be true to his art, and to express his vision of reality as well as he can." In poetry, discussion of rhythm, metre, and other poetic devices in the abstract is meaningless. Such an art work is above all individual, filled with life, organic: "They have made it clear, in a word, that rhythm and metre must be regarded as aesthetically identical with style, as style is identical with artistic form, and form in its turn is the work of art in its spiritual and indivisible self."

Like Huneker, Spingarn's sympathies are entirely on the side of the artist. It is the artist who creates, who brings forth a vision of life that is intimately his. "The virtue of all art is that it is always more or less mad," Spingarn claims, adding that this cardinal nobility is the distinguishing mark of all great poetry. And again, Spingarn, like Huneker, directs his barbed shaft at the academies: "Some . . . may have forgotten that the imagination is governed by an inner logic of its own, and not by caprice; but even caprice is better than stagnation, even caprice is better than the lifeless logic of the schools."

Spingarn, with the classical tradition for support, asserts it is the artistic "divine madness" that is forever inimical to the academic. It is unhampered freedom of self-expression, not mental unbalance, that is the result of this "madness"—a freedom which the inhibited man must always view with something akin to amazement. But it is not anarchic freedom: ". . . the Greeks, on the whole, realized that the poet has to be able to do two things, to let himself go and to master himself, and that the second is artistically impotent without the first."

Because of his sneers at pedantry and the nonsensical adoration of formal rules, Spingarn was often dubbed an impressionist. But, unlike the impressionists, he did value learning, although for him it was not analogous to academic scholarship. According to Spingarn, scholarship is only part of the critic's learning; the greater part is knowledge of the spirit of art and experience in discerning the aesthetic aims of great artists. In his essay on "Criticism in the United States" (1924), he further clarified his concept of criticism:

> Criticism is essentially an expression of taste, or that faculty of imaginative sympathy by which the reader or spectator is able to re-live the vision created by the artist . . . but it attains its end and becomes criticism in the highest sense only when taste is guided by knowledge and rises to the level of thought, for then, and only then, does the critic give us something that the artist as artist cannot give.

Three things are necessary for the critic: "education in aesthetic thinking"; "scholarship—that discipline of knowledge which will give us at one and the same time a wider international outlook and a deeper national insight"; and, above all, "a deeper sensibility, a more complete submission to the imaginative will of the artist."

It is more than likely that one phase of the Crocean aesthetic as expressed by Spingarn did much to influence subsequently a number of American critics—the method by which criticism, discarding the problem of value, is limited to formal analysis, to a consideration of aesthetic phenomena. This critical approach, which is the logical end of Poe's and James's theory of the critic's function, was encouraging to the development of a school of criticism which was to emphasize sensitiveness to form and language. By objectifying the work of art for the analytical examination of the critic, the Crocean aesthetic in many respects made possible the literary criticism of such men as T. S. Eliot, John Crowe Ransom, Allen Tate, and R. P. Blackmur.

The placing of arbitrary limits on any literary movement or period is at best an artificial measure, since the continuity of American literary history does not countenance such compartmentalization. Nevertheless practical purposes are served. It allows the isolation of general currents flowing through a period, the placement of them within their historical context, and the observation of their relations.

Such a study of American criticism from the Civil War to 1910 reveals a great diversity within the critical theory of the period. This is in marked contrast to the preceding period of American criticism, from, say, the late 1820's to the Civil War, which presents a much more effective unifying principle in romanticism.

The "Genteel Tradition," a term apparently coined by Santayana and quickly taken up and made a term of opprobrium, supported throughout the period the older New England tradition which had in it the idealism of Emerson and his followers. Exhibiting a strong moral sense, they almost always saw intellectual, political, economic, and aesthetic considerations in the light of ethical significance. As late as 1904 such a tone pervades the introduction and almost all of the essays in William Morton Payne's anthology *American Literary Criticism*. While it is true that specific differences exist between the critics ordinarily grouped in this tradition, "genteel" critics for the most part all ignored the American environment, particularly the grosser and more vulgar aspects of it, tended to abstract literature from life, and to associate it with traditional forms of idealism.

Howells, James, and many other critics in the period who were interested in the aesthetics of realism, had a common principle that literature should tell the truth, but each critic was apt to define reality in a slightly different way and to search for truth in diverse sources. Many critics believed that by adopting the methods and the findings of science, the artist and critic could learn how reality could be apprehended. Whereas Zola in 1880 had been called obscene, by the time of his death in 1902 he had been given a large measure of respect as a scientific writer. This effort to adapt the methods of science to literature and to criticism led to a respect for carefully accumulated detail, for hereditary influences, to a preoccupation with disease and brutal and violent scenes, and to a conception of character as being determined by environment, all of which led Frank Norris to the conclusion that naturalism "is a form of romanticism, not an inner circle of realism."

The influence of Taine was one of the most significant forces in the criticism of the period. C. M. Gayley and F. N. Scott in *An Introduction to the Methods and Materials of Literary Criticism* (1899) reported that Taine's criticism was "better known in this country" than that "of any other foreign writer." Even the "genteel" critic, William Morton Payne, believed Taine's theories to be the best example of "the scientific method in historical criticism." And he wrote that "the tendency of modern criticism is unquestionably towards a scientific method." It seems evident that much of Taine's popularity at this time was due to the broad and deep influence on earlier American criticism of Herder, Schlegel, and Madame de Staël; and it is difficult to determine to just what extent Taine himself can be regarded as simply a product of these earlier critics. Not all American critics, however, were unperceptive of Taine's limitations. Henry James, in his *Atlantic Monthly* review of Van Laun's translation of Taine's *History of English Literature* (1871), pointed out that Taine oversimplified and that "there is a constantly visible hiatus between his formula and his application of it." Irving Babbitt in *The Masters of Modern French Criticism* (1912) likewise saw Taine's shortcomings.

While many critics were seeking reality through the methods and findings of science and through such concepts as environment, heredity, determinism, and evolution, still others were seeking it in terms of the life of the common man and of society. Although in some respects influenced by the science of the day, perhaps Howells's criticism and his concept of realism is best illuminated by this approach.

One of the most heated arguments in American criticism of the period was that concerning the supremacy of beauty of form in a work of art as opposed to the moral and philosophical truth of its content. This, more than any other factor, offers evidence of the growing aesthetic emphasis in critical theory at the end of the century. Garland's statement in *Crumbling Idols* that "truth is a higher quality than beauty" represents one side of the argument. Santayana, however, in the influential *The Sense of Beauty*, made a sharp distinction between the sphere of aesthetics and that of ethics. The artist Whistler in *The Gentle Art of Making Enemies* (1890) took great pleasure in baiting those who found art "moral and useful." Impressionistic theories of criticism tended greatly to reinforce the aesthetic position. Particularly influential in the attack on American provincialism was the cosmopolitan and impressionistic Huneker, around whom there gradually formed an influential group of critics, including H. L. Mencken, George Jean Nathan, Carl Van Vechten, and Paul Rosenfeld. Spingarn's exposition of Croce's expressionistic theories is the logical culmination, within the limits of the period, of the aesthetic "revolt" in criticism. Of all the critics, only Henry James seems to have made a satisfactory reconciliation between fact and mind—reality and imagination.[47]

Continuing the rapid growth toward the achievement of a more fully comprehensive body of literary criticism which had its inception in the period of romanticism, within less than thirty-five years after the Civil War, American criticism had matured and had become a subject for serious study.

[47] An interesting contemporary treatment of this same problem may be found in Lionel Trilling's *The Liberal Imagination* (New York, 1950).

Critical Essays of Realism and Aestheticism

HENRY JAMES

THE ART OF FICTION [1]
(1888)

I SHOULD not have have affixed so comprehensive a title to these few remarks, necessarily wanting in any completeness upon a subject the full consideration of which would carry us far, did I not seem to discover a pretext for my temerity in the interesting pamphlet lately published under this name by Mr. Walter Besant.[2] Mr. Besant's lecture at the Royal Institution—the original form of his pamphlet—appears to indicate that many persons are interested in the art of fiction, and are not indifferent to such remarks, as those who practise it may attempt to make about it. I am therefore anxious not to lose the benefit of this favourable association, and to edge in a few words under cover of the attention which Mr. Besant is sure to have excited. There is something very encouraging in his having put into form certain of his ideas on the mystery of story-telling.

It is a proof of life and curiosity—curiosity on the part of the brotherhood of novelists as well as on the part of their readers. Only a short time ago it might have been supposed that the English novel was not what the French call *discutable*.[3] It had no air of having a theory, a conviction, a consciousness of itself behind it—of being the expression of an artistic faith, the result of choice and comparison. I do not say it was necessarily the worse for that: it would take much more courage than I possess to intimate that the form of the novel as Dickens and Thackeray (for instance) saw it had any taint of incompleteness. It was, however, *naïf* (if I may help myself out with another French word); and evidently if it be destined to suffer in any way for having lost its *naïveté* it has now an idea of making sure of the corresponding advantages. During the period I have alluded to there was a comfortable, good-humored feeling abroad that a novel is a novel, as a pudding is a pudding, and that our only business with it could be to swallow it. But within a year or two, for some reason or other, there have been signs of returning animation—the era of discussion would appear to have been to a certain extent opened. Art lives upon discussion, upon experiment, upon curiosity, upon variety of attempt, upon the exchange of views and the comparison of stand-points; and there is a presumption that those times when no one has anything particular to say about it, and has no reason to give for practice or preference, though they may be times of honour, are not times of development—are times, possibly

[1] First published in *Longman's Magazine*, September, 1884. The text reprinted here is from *Partial Portraits* (New York, 1888).
[2] Sir Walter Besant (1836-1901), English novelist and critic.
[3] "debatable."

even, a little of dulness. The successful application of any art is a delightful spectacle, but the theory too is interesting; and though there is a great deal of the latter without the former I suspect there has never been a genuine success that has not had a latent core of conviction. Discussion, suggestion, formulation, these things are fertilizing when they are frank and sincere. Mr. Besant has set an excellent example in saying what he thinks, for his part, about the way in which fiction should be written, as well as about the way in which it should be published; for his view of the 'art,' carried on into an appendix, covers that too. Other labourers in the same field will doubtless take up the argument, they will give it the light of their experience, and the effect will surely be to make our interest in the novel a little more what it had for some time threatened to fail to be—a serious, active, inquiring interest, under protection of which this delightful study may, in moments of confidence, venture to say a little more what it thinks of itself.

It must take itself seriously for the public to take it so. The old superstition about fiction being 'wicked' has doubtless died out in England; but the spirit of it lingers in a certain oblique regard directed toward any story which does not more or less admit that it is only a joke. Even the most jocular novel feels in some degree the weight of the proscription that was formerly directed against literary levity: the jocularity does not always succeed in passing for orthodoxy. It is still expected, though perhaps people are ashamed to say it, that a production which is after all only a 'make-believe' (for what else is a 'story'?) shall be in some degree apologetic—shall renounce the pretension of attempting really to represent life. This, of course, any sensible, wide-awake story declines to do, for it quickly perceives that the tolerance granted to it on such a condition is only an attempt to stifle it disguised in the form of generosity. The old evangelical hostility to the novel, which was as explicit as it was narrow, and which regarded it as little less favourable to our immortal part than a stage-play, was in reality far less insulting. The only reason for the existence of a novel is that it does attempt to represent life. When it relinquishes this attempt, the same attempt that we see on the canvas of the painter, it will have arrived at a very strange pass. It is not expected of the picture that it will make itself humble in order to be forgiven; and the analogy between the art of the painter and the art of the novelist is, so far as I am able to see, complete. Their inspiration is the same, their process (allowing for the different quality of the vehicle) is the same, their success is the same. They may learn from each other, they may explain and sustain each other. Their cause is the same, and the honour of one is the honour of another. The Mahometans think a picture an unholy thing, but it is a long time since any Christian did, and it is therefore the more odd that in the Christian mind the traces (dissimulated though they may be) of a suspicion of the sister art should linger to this day. The only effectual way to lay it to rest is to emphasize the analogy to which I just alluded—to insist on the fact that as the picture is reality, so the novel is history. That is the only general description (which does it justice) that we may give of the novel. But history also is allowed to represent life; it is not, any more than painting, expected to apologize. The subject-matter of fiction is stored up likewise in documents and records, and if it will not give itself away, as they say in California, it must speak with assurance, with the tone of the historian. Certain accomplished novelists have a habit of giving themselves away which must often bring tears to the eyes of people who take their fiction seriously. I was lately struck, in reading over many pages of Anthony Trollope, with his want of discretion in this particular. In a digression, a parenthesis or an aside, he concedes to the reader that he and this trusting friend are only 'making believe.' He admits that the events he narrates have not really happened, and that he can give his narrative any turn the reader may like best. Such a betrayal of a sacred office seems to me, I confess, a terrible crime; it is what I mean by the attitude of apology, and it shocks me every whit as much in Trollope as it would have shocked me in Gibbon or Macaulay. It implies that the novelist is less occupied in looking for the truth (the truth, of course I mean, that he assumes, the premises that we must grant him, whatever they may be) than the historian, and in doing so it deprives him at a stroke of all his standing-room. To represent and illustrate the past, the actions of men, is the task of either writer, and the only difference that I can see is, in proportion as he succeeds, to the honour of the novelist, consisting as it does in his having more difficulty in collecting his evidence, which is so far from being purely literary. It seems to me to give him a great character, the fact that he has at once so much in common with the philosopher and the painter; this double analogy is a magnificent heritage.

It is of all this evidently that Mr. Besant is full when he insists upon the fact that fiction is one of the *fine* arts, deserving in its turn of all the honours and emoluments that have hitherto been reserved for the successful profession of music, poetry, painting, architecture. It is impossible to insist too much on so important a truth, and the place that Mr. Besant demands for the work of the novelist may be represented, a trifle less abstractly, by saying that he demands not only that it shall be reputed artistic, but that it shall be reputed very artistic indeed. It is excellent that he should have struck this note, for his doing so indicates that there was need of it, that his proposition may be to many people a novelty. One rubs one's eyes at the thought; but the rest of Mr. Besant's essay confirms the revelation. I suspect in truth that it would be possible to confirm it still further, and that one would not be far wrong in saying that in addition to the people to whom it has never occurred that a novel ought to be artistic, there are a great many others who, if this principle were urged upon them, would be filled with an indefinable mistrust. They would find it difficult to explain their repugnance, but it would operate strongly to put them on their guard. 'Art,' in our Protestant communities, where so many things have got so strangely twisted about, is supposed in certain circles to have some vaguely injurious effect upon those who make it an important consideration, who let it weigh in the balance. It is assumed to be opposed in some mysterious manner to morality, to amusement, to instruction.

When it is embodied in the work of the painter (the sculptor is another affair!) you know what it is: it stands there before you, in the honesty of pink and green and a gilt frame; you can see the worst of it at a glance, and you can be on your guard. But when it is introduced into literature it becomes more insidious—there is danger of its hurting you before you know it. Literature should be either instructive or amusing, and there is in many minds an impression that these artistic preoccupations, the search for form, contribute to neither end, interfere indeed with both. They are too frivolous to be edifying, and too serious to be diverting; and they are moreover priggish and paradoxical and superfluous. That, I think, represents the manner in which the latent thought of many people who read novels as an exercise in skipping would explain itself if it were to become articulate. They would argue, of course, that a novel ought to be 'good,' but they would interpret this term in a fashion of their own, which indeed would vary considerably from one critic to another. One would say that being good means representing virtuous and aspiring characters, placed in prominent positions; another would say that it depends on a 'happy ending,' on a distribution at the last of prizes, pensions, husbands, wives, babies, millions, appended paragraphs, and cheerful remarks. Another still would say that it means being full of incident and movement, so that we shall wish to jump ahead, to see who was the mysterious stranger, and if the stolen will was ever found, and shall not be distracted from this pleasure by any tiresome analysis or 'description.' But they would all agree that the 'artistic' idea would spoil some of their fun. One would hold it accountable for all the description, another would see it revealed in the absence of sympathy. Its hostility to a happy ending would be evident, and it might even in some cases render any ending at all impossible. The 'ending' of a novel is, for many persons, like that of a good dinner, a course of dessert and ices, and the artist in fiction is regarded as a sort of meddlesome doctor who forbids agreeable aftertastes. It is therefore true that this conception of Mr. Besant's of the novel as a superior form encounters not only a negative but a positive indifference. It matters little that as a work of art it should really be as little or as much of its essence to supply happy endings, sympathetic characters, and an objective tone, as if it were a work of mechanics: the association of ideas, however incongruous, might easily be too much for it if an eloquent voice were not sometimes raised to call attention to the fact that it is at once as free and as serious a branch of literature as any other.

Certainly this might sometimes be doubted in presence of the enormous number of works of fiction that appeal to the credulity of our generation, for it might easily seem that there could be no great character in a commodity so quickly and easily produced. It must be admitted that good novels are much compromised by bad ones, and that the field at large suffers discredit from overcrowding. I think, however, that this injury is only superficial, and that the superabundance of written fiction proves nothing against the principle itself. It has been vulgarized, like all other kinds of literature, like everything else to-day, and it has proved more

than some kinds accessible to vulgarization. But there is as much difference
as there ever was between a good novel and a bad one: the bad is swept
with all the daubed canvases and spoiled marble into some unvisited limbo,
or infinite rubbish-yard beneath the back-windows of the world, and the
good subsists and emits its light and stimulates our desire for perfection.
As I shall take the liberty of making but a single criticism of Mr. Besant,
whose tone is so full of the love of his art, I may as well have done with
it at once. He seems to me to mistake in attempting to say so definitely
beforehand what sort of an affair the good novel will be. To indicate the
danger of such an error as that has been the purpose of these few pages;
to suggest that certain traditions on the subject, applied *a priori,* have
already had much to answer for, and that the good health of an art which
undertakes so immediately to reproduce life must demand that it be perfectly free. It lives upon exercise, and the very meaning of exercise is freedom. The only obligation to which in advance we may hold a novel,
without incurring the accusation of being arbitrary, is that it be interesting. That general responsibility rests upon it, but it is the only one I can
think of. The ways in which it is at liberty to accomplish this result (of
interesting us) strike me as innumerable, and such as can only suffer
from being marked out or fenced in by prescription. They are as various
as the temperament of man, and they are successful in proportion as they
reveal a particular mind, different from others. A novel is in its broadest
definition a personal, a direct impression of life: that, to begin with, constitutes its value, which is greater or less according to the intensity of the
impression. But there will be no intensity at all, and therefore no value,
unless there is freedom to feel and say. The tracing of a line to be followed,
of a tone to be taken, of a form to be filled out, is a limitation of that
freedom and a suppression of the very thing that we are most curious
about. The form, it seems to me, is to be appreciated after the fact: then
the author's choice has been made, his standard has been indicated; then
we can follow lines and directions and compare tones and resemblances.
Then in a word we can enjoy one of the most charming of pleasures, we
can estimate quality, we can apply the test of execution. The execution
belongs to the author alone; it is what is most personal to him, and we
measure him by that. The advantage, the luxury, as well as the torment
and responsibility of the novelist, is that there is no limit to what he may
attempt as an executant—no limit to his possible experiments, efforts, discoveries, successes. Here it is especially that he works, step by step, like
his brother of the brush, of whom we may always say that he has painted
his picture in a manner best known to himself. His manner is his secret,
not necessarily a jealous one. He cannot disclose it as a general thing if he
would; he would be at a loss to teach it to others. I say this with a due
recollection of having insisted on the community of method of the artist
who paints a picture and the artist who writes a novel. The painter *is* able
to teach the rudiments of his practice, and it is possible, from the study
of good work (granted the aptitude), both to learn how to paint and to
learn how to write. Yet it remains true, without injury to the *rapproche-*

ment, that the literary artist would be obliged to say to his pupil much more than the other, 'Ah, well, you must do it as you can!' It is a question of degree, a matter of delicacy. If there are exact sciences, there are also exact arts, and the grammar of painting is so much more definite that it makes the difference.

I ought to add, however, that if Mr. Besant says at the beginning of his essay that the 'laws of fiction may be laid down and taught with as much precision and exactness as the laws of harmony, perspective, and proportion,' he mitigates what might appear to be an extravagance by applying his remark to 'general' laws, and by expressing most of these rules in a manner with which it would certainly be unaccommodating to disagree. That the novelist must write from his experience, that his 'characters must be real and such as might be met with in actual life'; that 'a young lady brought up in a quiet country village should avoid descriptions of garrison life,' and 'a writer whose friends and personal experiences belong to the lower middle-class should carefully avoid introducing his characters into society'; that one should enter one's notes in a commonplace book; that one's figures should be clear in outline; that making them clear by some trick of speech or of carriage is a bad method, and 'describing them at length' is a worse one; that English Fiction should have a 'conscious moral purpose'; that 'it is almost impossible to estimate too highly the value of careful workmanship—that is, of style'; that 'the most important point of all is the story,' that 'the story is everything': these are principles with most of which it is surely impossible not to sympathize. That remark about the lower middle-class writer and his knowing his place is perhaps rather chilling; but for the rest I should find it difficult to dissent from any one of these recommendations. At the same time, I should find it difficult positively to assent to them, with the exception, perhaps, of the injunction as to entering one's notes in a common-place book. They scarcely seem to me to have the quality that Mr. Besant attributes to the rules of the novelist—the 'precision and exactness' of 'the laws of harmony, perspective, and proportion.' They are suggestive, they are even inspiring, but they are not exact, though they are doubtless as much so as the case admits of: which is a proof of that liberty of interpretation for which I just contended. For the value of these different injunctions—so beautiful and so vague—is wholly in the meaning one attaches to them. The characters, the situation, which strike one as real will be those that touch and interest one most, but the measure of reality is very difficult to fix. The reality of Don Quixote or of Mr. Micawber is a very delicate shade; it is a reality so coloured by the author's vision that, vivid as it may be, one would hesitate to propose it as a model: one would expose one's self to some very embarrassing questions on the part of a pupil. It goes without saying that you will not write a good novel unless you possess the sense of reality; but it will be difficult to give you a recipe for calling that sense into being. Humanity is immense, and reality has a myriad forms; the most one can affirm is that some of the flowers of fiction have the odour of it, and others have not; as for telling you in advance how your nosegay should be composed, that is another affair. It is equally excellent and inconclusive to say that one must write from experience; to our suppositious aspirant such a declaration might savour of mockery. What kind of experience is intended, and where does it begin and end? Experience is never limited, and it is never complete; it is an immense sensibility, a kind of huge spider-web of the finest silken threads suspended in the chamber of consciousness, and catching every air-borne particle in its tissue. It is the very atmosphere of the mind; and when the mind is imaginative—much more when it happens to be that of a man of genius—it takes to itself the faintest hints of life, it converts the very pulses of the air into revelations. The young lady living in a village has only to be a damsel upon whom nothing is lost to make it quite unfair (as it seems to me) to declare to her that she shall have nothing to say about the military. Greater miracles have been seen than that, imagination assisting, she should speak the truth about some of these gentlemen. I remember an English novelist, a woman of genius, telling me that she was much commended for the impression she had managed to give in one of her tales of the nature and way of life of the French Protestant youth. She had been asked where she learned so much about this recondite being, she had been congratulated on her peculiar opportunities. These opportunities consisted in her having once, in Paris, as she ascended a staircase, passed an open door where, in the household of a *pasteur*,[4] some of the young Protestants were seated at table around a finished meal. The glimpse made a picture; it lasted only a moment, but that moment was experience. She had got her direct personal impression, and she turned out her type. She knew what youth was, and what Protestantism; she also had the advantage of having seen what it was to be French, so that she converted these ideas into a concrete image and produced a reality. Above all, however, she was blessed with the faculty which when you give it an inch takes an ell, and which for the artist is a much greater source of strength than any accident of residence or of place in the social scale. The power to guess the unseen from the seen, to trace the implication of things, to judge the whole piece by the pattern, the condition of feeling life in general so completely that you are well on your way to knowing any particular corner of it—this cluster of gifts may almost be said to constitute experience, and they occur in country and in town, and in the most differing stages of education. If experience consists of impressions, it may be said that impressions *are* experience, just as (have we not seen it?) they are the very air we breathe. Therefore, if I should certainly say to a novice, 'Write from experience and experience only,' I should feel that this was rather a tantalizing monition if I were not careful immediately to add, 'Try to be one of the people on whom nothing is lost!'

I am far from intending by this to minimize the importance of exactness—of truth of detail. One can speak best from one's own taste, and I may therefore venture to say that the air of reality (solidity of specification) seems to me to be the supreme virtue of a novel—the merit on which all its other merits (including that conscious moral purpose of which Mr.

4 "pastor."

Besant speaks) helplessly and submissively depend. If it be not there they are all as nothing, and if these be there, they owe their effect to the success with which the author has produced the illusion of life. The cultivation of this success, the study of this exquisite process, form, to my taste, the beginning and the end of the art of the novelist. They are his inspiration, his despair, his reward, his torment, his delight. It is here in very truth that he competes with life; it is here that he competes with his brother the painter in *his* attempt to render the look of things, the look that conveys their meaning, to catch the colour, the relief, the expression, the surface, the substance of the human spectacle. It is in regard to this that Mr. Besant is well inspired when he bids him take notes. He cannot possibly take too many, he cannot possibly take enough. All life solicits him, and to 'render' the simplest surface, to produce the most momentary illusion, is a very complicated business. His case would be easier, and the rule would be more exact, if Mr. Besant had been able to tell him what notes to take. But this, I fear, he can never learn in any manual; it is the business of his life. He has to take a great many in order to select a few, he has to work them up as he can, and even the guides and philosophers who might have most to say to him must leave him alone when it comes to the application of precepts, as we leave the painter in communion with his palette. That his characters 'must be clear in outline,' as Mr. Besant says—he feels that down to his boots; but how he shall make them so is a secret between his good angel and himself. It would be absurdly simple if he could be taught that a great deal of 'description' would make them so, or that on the contrary the absence of description and the cultivation of dialogue, or the absence of dialogue and the multiplication of 'incident,' would rescue him from his difficulties. Nothing, for instance, is more possible than that he be of a turn of mind for which this odd, literal opposition of description and dialogue, incident and description, has little meaning and light. People often talk of these things as if they had a kind of internecine distinctness, instead of melting into each other at every breath, and being intimately associated parts of one general effort of expression. I cannot imagine composition existing in a series of blocks, nor conceive, in any novel worth discussing at all, of a passage of description that is not in its intention narrative, a passage of dialogue that is not in its intention descriptive, a touch of truth of any sort that does not partake of the nature of incident, or an incident that derives its interest from any other source than the general and only source of the success of a work of art—that of being illustrative. A novel is a living thing, all one and continuous, like any other organism, and in proportion as it lives will it be found, I think, that in each of the parts there is something of each of the other parts. The critic who over the close texture of a finished work shall pretend to trace a geography of items will mark some frontiers as artificial, I fear, as any that have been known to history. There is an old-fashioned distinction between the novel of character and the novel of incident which must have cost many a smile to the intending fabulist who was keen about his work. It appears to me as little to the point as the equally celebrated distinction between the novel and the romance—to answer as little to any reality. There are bad novels and good novels, as there are bad pictures and good pictures; but that is the only distinction in which I see any meaning, and I can as little imagine speaking of a novel of character as I can imagine speaking of a picture of character. When one says picture one says of character, when one says novel one says of incident, and the terms may be transposed at will. What is character but the determination of incident? What is incident but the illustration of character? What is either a picture or a novel that is *not* of character? What else do we seek in it and find in it? It is an incident for a woman to stand up with her hand resting on a table and look out at you in a certain way; or if it be not an incident I think it will be hard to say what it is. At the same time it is an expression of character. If you say you don't see it (character in *that—allons donc!*),[5] this is exactly what the artist who has reasons of his own for thinking he *does* see it undertakes to show you. When a young man makes up his mind that he has not faith enough after all to enter the church as he intended, that is an incident, though you may not hurry to the end of the chapter to see whether perhaps he doesn't change once more. I do not say that these are extraordinary or startling incidents. I do not pretend to estimate the degree of interest proceeding from them, for this will depend upon the skill of the painter. It sounds almost puerile to say that some incidents are intrinsically much more important than others, and I need not take this precaution after having professed my sympathy for the major ones in remarking that the only classification of the novel that I can understand is into that which has life and that which has it not.

The novel and the romance, the novel of incident and that of character—these clumsy separations appear to me to have been made by critics and readers for their own convenience, and to help them out of some of their occasional queer predicaments, but to have little reality or interest for the producer, from whose point of view it is of course that we are attempting to consider the art of fiction. The case is the same with another shadowy category which Mr. Besant apparently is disposed to set up—that of the 'modern English novel'; unless indeed it be that in this matter he has fallen into an accidental confusion of standpoints. It is not quite clear whether he intends the remarks in which he alludes to it to be didactic or historical. It is as difficult to suppose a person intending to write a modern English as to suppose him writing an ancient English novel: that is a label which begs the question. One writes the novel, one paints the picture, of one's language and of one's time, and calling it modern English will not, alas! make the difficult task any easier. No more, unfortunately, will calling this or that work of one's fellow-artist a romance—unless it be, of course, simply for the pleasantness of the thing, as for instance when Hawthorne gave this heading to his story of *Blithedale*. The French, who have brought the theory of fiction to remarkable completeness, have but one name for the novel, and have not attempted smaller

[5] "come now!"

things in it, that I can see, for that. I can think of no obligation to which the 'romancer' would not be held equally with the novelist; the standard of execution is equally high for each. Of course it is of execution that we are talking—that being the only point of a novel that is open to contention. This is perhaps too often lost sight of, only to produce interminable confusions and cross-purposes. We must grant the artist his subject, his idea, his *donnée*: our criticism is applied only to what he makes of it. Naturally I do not mean that we are bound to like it or find it interesting: in case we do not our course is perfectly simple—to let it alone. We may believe that of a certain idea even the most sincere novelist can make nothing at all, and the event may perfectly justify our belief; but the failure will have been a failure to execute, and it is in the execution that the fatal weakness is recorded. If we pretend to respect the artist at all, we must allow him his freedom of choice, in the face, in particular cases, of innumerable presumptions that the choice will not fructify. Art derives a considerable part of its beneficial exercise from flying in the face of presumptions, and some of the most interesting experiments of which it is capable are hidden in the bosom of common things. Gustave Flaubert [6] has written a story about the devotion of a servant-girl to a parrot, and the production, highly finished as it is, cannot on the whole be called a success. We are perfectly free to find it flat, but I think it might have been interesting; and I, for my part, am extremely glad he should have written it; it is a contribution to our knowledge of what can be done—or what cannot. Ivan Turgénieff [7] has written a tale about a deaf and dumb serf and a lap-dog, and the thing is touching, loving, a little masterpiece. He struck the note of life where Gustave Flaubert missed it—he flew in the face of a presumption and achieved a victory.

Nothing, of course, will ever take the place of the good old fashion of 'liking' a work of art or not liking it: the most improved criticism will not abolish that primitive, that ultimate test. I mention this to guard myself from the accusation of intimating that the idea, the subject, of a novel or a picture, does not matter. It matters, to my sense, in the highest degree, and if I might put up a prayer it would be that artists should select none but the richest. Some, as I have already hastened to admit, are much more remunerative than others, and it would be a world happily arranged in which persons intending to treat them should be exempt from confusions and mistakes. This fortunate condition will arrive only, I fear, on the same day that critics become purged from error. Meanwhile, I repeat, we do not judge the artist with fairness unless we say to him, 'Oh, I grant you your starting-point, because if I did not I should seem to prescribe to you, and heaven forbid I should take that responsibility. If I pretend to tell you what you must not take, you will call upon me to tell you then what you must take; in which case I shall be prettily caught. Moreover, it isn't till I have accepted your data that I can begin to measure you. I have the standard, the pitch; I have no right to tamper with

---

[6] French realistic novelist (1821–1880).
[7] Russian realistic novelist (1818–1883).

your flute and then criticize your music. Of course I may not care for your idea at all; I may think it silly, or stale, or unclean; in which case I wash my hands of you altogether. I may content myself with believing that you will not have succeeded in being interesting, but I shall, of course, not attempt to demonstrate it, and you will be as indifferent to me as I am to you. I needn't remind you that there are all sorts of tastes: who can know it better? Some people, for excellent reasons, don't like to read about carpenters; others, for reasons even better, don't like to read about courtesans. Many object to Americans. Others (I believe they are mainly editors and publishers) won't look at Italians. Some readers don't like quiet subjects; others don't like bustling ones. Some enjoy a complete illusion, others the consciousness of large concessions. They choose their novels accordingly, and if they don't care about your idea they won't, *a fortiori*, care about your treatment.'

So that it comes back very quickly, as I have said, to the liking: in spite of M. Zola,[8] who reasons less powerfully than he represents, and who will not reconcile himself to this absoluteness of taste, thinking that there are certain things that people ought to like, and that they can be made to like. I am quite at a loss to imagine anything (at any rate in this matter of fiction) that people *ought* to like or to dislike. Selection will be sure to take care of itself, for it has a constant motive behind it. That motive is simply experience. As people feel life, so they will feel the art that is most closely related to it. This closeness of relation is what we should never forget in talking of the effort of the novel. Many people speak of it as a factitious, artificial form, a product of ingenuity, the business of which is to alter and arrange the things that surround us, to translate them into conventional, traditional moulds. This, however, is a view of the matter which carries us but a very short way, condemns the art to an eternal repetition of a few familiar *clichés*, cuts short its development, and leads us straight up to a dead wall. Catching the very note and trick, the strange irregular rhythm of life, that is the attempt whose strenuous force keeps Fiction upon her feet. In proportion as in what she offers us we see life *without* rearrangement do we feel that we are touching the truth; in proportion as we see it *with* rearrangement do we feel that we are being put off with a substitute, a compromise and convention. It is not uncommon to hear an extraordinary assurance of remark in regard to this matter of rearranging, which is often spoken of as if it were the last word of art. Mr. Besant seems to me in danger of falling into the great error with his rather unguarded talk about 'selection.' Art is essentially selection, but it is a selection whose main care is to be typical, to be inclusive. For many people art means rose-coloured window-panes, and selection means picking a bouquet for Mrs. Grundy. They will tell you glibly that artistic considerations have nothing to do with the disagreeable, with the ugly; they will rattle off shallow commonplaces about the province of art and the limits of art till you are moved to some wonder in return as to the province and the limits of ignorance. It appears to me that no one can ever have made a seriously artistic at-

[8] French naturalistic novelist (1840-1902).

tempt without becoming conscious of an immense increase—a kind of revelation—of freedom. One perceives in that case—by the light of a heavenly ray—that the province of art is all life, all feeling, all observation, all vision. As Mr. Besant so justly intimates, it is all experience. That is a sufficient answer to those who maintain that it must not touch the sad things of life, who stick into its divine unconscious bosom little prohibitory inscriptions on the end of sticks, such as we see in public gardens— 'It is forbidden to walk on the grass; it is forbidden to touch the flowers; it is not allowed to introduce dogs or to remain after dark; it is requested to keep to the right.' The young aspirant in the line of fiction whom we continue to imagine will do nothing without taste, for in that case his freedom would be of little use to him; but the first advantage of his taste will be to reveal to him the absurdity of the little sticks and tickets. If he have taste, I must add, of course he will have ingenuity, and my disrespectful reference to that quality just now was not meant to imply that it is useless in fiction. But it is only a secondary aid; the first is a capacity for receiving straight impressions.

Mr. Besant has some remarks on the question of 'the story' which I shall not attempt to criticize, though they seem to me to contain a singular ambiguity, because I do not think I understand them. I cannot see what is meant by talking as if there were a part of a novel which is the story and part of it which for mystical reasons is not—unless indeed the distinction be made in a sense in which it is difficult to suppose that any one should attempt to convey anything. 'The story,' if it represents anything, represents the subject, the idea, the *donnée* of the novel; and there is surely no 'school'—Mr. Besant speaks of a school—which urges that a novel should be all treatment and no subject. There must assuredly be something to treat; every school is intimately conscious of that. This sense of the story being the idea, the starting-point, of the novel, is the only one that I see in which it can be spoken of as something different from its organic whole; and since in proportion as the work is successful the idea permeates and penetrates it, informs and animates it, so that every word and every punctuation-point contribute directly to the expression, in that proportion do we lose our sense of the story being a blade which may be drawn more or less out of its sheath. The story and the novel, the idea and the form, are the needle and thread, and I never heard of a guild of tailors who recommended the use of the thread without the needle, or the needle without the thread. Mr. Besant is not the only critic who may be observed to have spoken as if there were certain things in life which constitute stories, and certain others which do not. I find the same odd implication in an entertaining article in the *Pall Mall Gazette*, devoted, as it happens, to Mr. Besant's lecture. 'The story is the thing' says this graceful writer, as if with a tone of opposition to some other idea. I should think it was, as every painter who, as the time for 'sending in' his picture looms in the distance, finds himself still in quest of a subject—as every belated artist not fixed about his theme will heartily agree. There are some subjects which speak to us and others which do not, but he would be a clever man who should undertake to give a rule—an *index expurga-torius*—by which the story and the no-story should be known apart. It is impossible (to me at least) to imagine any such rule which shall not be altogether arbitrary. The writer in the *Pall Mall* opposes the delightful (as I suppose) novel of *Margot la Balafrée* to certain tales in which 'Bostonian nymphs' appear to have 'rejected English dukes for psychological reasons.' I am not acquainted with the romance just designated, and can scarcely forgive the *Pall Mall* critic for not mentioning the name of the author, but the title appears to refer to a lady who may have received a scar in some heroic adventure. I am inconsolable at not being acquainted with this episode, but am utterly at a loss to see why it is a story when the rejection (or acceptance) of a duke is not, and why a reason, psychological or other, is not a subject when a cicatrix is. They are all particles of the multitudinous life with which the novel deals, and surely no dogma which pretends to make it lawful to touch the one and unlawful to touch the other will stand for a moment on its feet. It is the special picture that must stand or fall, according as it seems to possess truth or to lack it. Mr. Besant does not, to my sense, light up the subject by intimating that a story must, under penalty of not being a story, consist of 'adventures.' Why of adventures more than of green spectacles? He mentions a category of impossible things, and among them he places 'fiction without adventure.' Why without adventure, more than without matrimony, or celibacy, or parturition, or cholera, or hydropathy, or Jansenism? This seems to me to bring the novel back to the hapless little *rôle* of being an artificial, ingenious thing—bring it down from its large, free character of an immense and exquisite correspondence with life. And what *is* adventure, when it comes to that, and by what sign is the listening pupil to recognize it? It is an adventure—an immense one—for me to write this little article; and for a Bostonian nymph to reject an English duke is an adventure only less stirring, I should say, than for an English duke to be rejected by a Bostonian nymph. I see dramas within dramas in that, and innumerable points of view. A psychological reason is, to my imagination, an object adorably pictorial; to catch the tint of its complexion—I feel as if that idea might inspire one to Titianesque efforts. There are few things more exciting to me, in short, than a psychological reason, and yet, I protest, the novel seems to me the most magnificent form of art. I have just been reading, at the same time, the delightful story of *Treasure Island*, by Mr. Robert Louis Stevenson and, in a manner less consecutive, the last tale from M. Edmond de Goncourt,[9] which is entitled *Chérie*. One of these works treats of murders, mysteries, islands of dreadful renown, hairbreadth escapes, miraculous coincidences and buried doubloons. The other treats of a little French girl who lived in a fine house in Paris, and died of wounded sensibility because no one would marry her. I call *Treasure Island* delightful, because it appears to me to have succeeded wonderfully in what it attempts; and I venture to bestow no epithet upon *Chérie*, which strikes me as having failed deplorably in what it attempts—that

[9] French artist and novelist (1822–1896).

is in tracing the development of the moral consciousness of a child. But one of these productions strikes me as exactly as much of a novel as the other, and as having a 'story' quite as much. The moral consciousness of a child is as much a part of life as the islands of the Spanish Main, and the one sort of geography seems to me to have those 'surprises' of which Mr. Besant speaks quite as much as the other. For myself (since it comes back in the last resort, as I say, to the preference of the individual), the picture of the child's experience has the advantage that I can at successive steps (an immense luxury, near to the 'sensual pleasure' of which Mr. Besant's critic in the *Pal Mall* speaks) say Yes or No, as it may be, to what the artist puts before me. I have been a child in fact, but I have been on a quest for a buried treasure only in supposition, and it is a simple accident that with M. de Goncourt I should have for the most part to say No. With George Eliot, when she painted that country with a far other intelligence, I always said Yes.[10]

The most interesting part of Mr. Besant's lecture is unfortunately the briefest passage—his very cursory allusion to the 'conscious moral purpose' of the novel. Here again it is not very clear whether he be recording a fact or laying down a principle; it is a great pity that in the latter case he should not have developed his idea. This branch of the subject is of immense importance, and Mr. Besant's few words point to considerations of the widest reach, not to be lightly disposed of. He will have treated the art of fiction but superficially who is not prepared to go every inch of the way that these considerations will carry him. It is for this reason that at the beginning of these remarks I was careful to notify the reader that my reflections on so large a theme have no pretension to be exhaustive. Like Mr. Besant, I have left the question of the morality of the novel till the last, and at the last I find I have used up my space. It is a question surrounded with difficulties, as witness the very first that meets us, in the form of a definite question, on the threshold. Vagueness, in such a discussion, is fatal, and what is the meaning of your morality and your conscious moral purpose? Will you not define your terms and explain how (a novel being a picture) a picture can be either moral or immoral? You wish to paint a moral picture or carve a moral statue: will you not tell us how you would set about it? We are discussing the Art of Fiction; questions of art are questions (in the widest sense) of execution; questions of morality are quite another affair, and will you not let us see how it is that you find it so easy to mix them up? These things are so clear to Mr. Besant that he has deduced from them a law which he sees embodied in English Fiction, and which is 'a truly admirable thing and a great cause for congratulation.' It is a great cause for congratulation indeed when such thorny problems become as smooth as silk. I may add that in so far as Mr. Besant perceives that in point of fact English Fiction has addressed itself preponderantly to these delicate questions he will appear to many people to have made a vain discovery. They will have been positively struck, on the contrary, with the moral timidity of the usual English

[10] The refrence is to *Silas Marner* by George Eliot (1819–1880).

novelist; with his (or with her) aversion to face the difficulties with which on every side the treatment of reality bristles. He is apt to be extremely shy (whereas the picture that Mr. Besant draws is a picture of boldness), and the sign of his work, for the most part, is a cautious silence on certain subjects. In the English novel (by which of course I mean the American as well), more than in any other, there is a traditional difference between that which people know and that which they agree to admit that they know, that which they see and that which they speak of, that which they feel to be a part of life and that which they allow to enter into literature. There is a great difference, in short, between what they talk of in conversation and what they talk of in print. The essence of moral energy is to survey the whole field, and I should directly reverse Mr. Besant's remark and say not that the English novel has a purpose, but that it has a diffidence. To what degree a purpose in a work of art is a source of corruption I shall not attempt to inquire; the one that seems to me least dangerous is the purpose of making a perfect work. As for our novel, I may say lastly on this score that as we find it in England to-day, it strikes me as addressed in a large degree to 'young people,' and that this in itself constitutes a presumption that it will be rather shy. There are certain things which it is generally agreed not to discuss, not even to mention, before young people. That is very well, but the absence of discussion is not a symptom of the moral passion. The purpose of the English novel— 'a truly admirable thing, and a great cause for congratulation'—strikes me therefore as rather negative.

There is one point at which the moral sense and the artistic sense lie very near together; that is in the light of the very obvious truth that the deepest quality of a work of art will always be the quality of the mind of the producer. In proportion as that intelligence is fine will the novel, the picture, the statue partake of the substance of beauty and truth. To be constituted of such elements is, to my vision, to have purpose enough. No good novel will ever proceed from a superficial mind; that seems to me an axiom which, for the artist in fiction, will cover all needful moral ground: if the youthful aspirant take it to heart it will illuminate for him many of the mysteries of 'purpose.' There are many other useful things that might be said to him, but I have come to the end of my article, and can only touch them as I pass. The critic in the *Pall Mall Gazette*, whom I have already quoted, draws attention to the danger, in speaking of the art of fiction, of generalizing. The danger that he has in mind is rather, I imagine, that of particularizing, for there are some comprehensive remarks which, in addition to those embodied in Mr. Besant's suggestive lecture, might without fear of misleading him be addressed to the ingenuous student. I should remind him first of the magnificence of the form that is open to him, which offers to sight so few restrictions and such innumerable opportunities. The other arts, in comparison, appear confined and hampered; the various conditions under which they are exercised are so rigid and definite. But the only condition that I can think of attaching to the composition of the novel is, as I have already said, that it be sincere.

This freedom is a splendid privilege, and the first lesson of the young novelist is to learn to be worthy of it.

'Enjoy it as it deserves (I should say to him); take possession of it, explore it to its utmost extent, publish it, rejoice in it. All life belongs to you, and do not listen either to those who would shut you up into corners of it and tell you that it is only here and there that art inhabits, or to those who would persuade you that this heavenly messenger wings her way outside of life altogether, breathing a superfine air, and turning away her head from the truth of things. There is no impression of life, no manner of seeing it and feeling it, to which the plan of the novelist may not offer a place; you have only to remember that talents so dissimilar as those of Alexandre Dumas and Jane Austen, Charles Dickens and Gustave Flaubert have worked in this field with equal glory. Do not think too much about optimism and pessimism; try and catch the colour of life itself. In France to-day we see a prodigious effort (that of Emile Zola, to whose solid and serious work no explorer of the capacity of the novel can allude without respect), we see an extraordinary effort vitiated by a spirit of pessimism on a narrow basis. M. Zola is magnificent, but he strikes an English reader as ignorant; he has an air of working in the dark; if he had as much light as energy, his results would be of the highest value.[11] As for the aberrations of a shallow optimism, the ground (of English fiction especially) is strewn with their brittle particles as with broken glass. If you must indulge in conclusions, let them have the taste of a wide knowledge. Remember that your first duty is to be as complete as possible—to make as perfect a work. Be generous and delicate and pursue the prize.'

[11] For a later and more complete estimate of Zola by James, see his essay on Zola in *Notes on Novelists* (1914).

HENRY JAMES

PREFACE TO
THE AMBASSADORS [1]
(1909)

NOTHING IS more easy than to state the subject of "The Ambassadors,"
which first appeared in twelve numbers of "The North American Review"
(1903) and was published as a whole the same year. The situation involved is gathered up betimes, that is in the second chapter of Book Fifth,
for the reader's benefit, into as few words as possible—planted or "sunk,"
stiffly and saliently, in the centre of the current, almost perhaps to the
obstruction of traffic. Never can a composition of this sort have sprung
straighter from a dropped grain of suggestion, and never can that grain,
developed, overgrown and smothered, have yet lurked more in the mass as
an independent particle. The whole case, in fine, is in Lambert Strether's
irrepressible outbreak to little Bilham on the Sunday afternoon in Glo-
riani's garden, the candour with which he yields, for his young friend's
enlightenment, to the charming admonition of that crisis. The idea of
the tale resides indeed in the very fact that an hour of such unprecedented
ease should have been felt by him *as* a crisis, and he is at pains to express it for us as neatly as we could desire. The remarks to which he thus
gives utterance contain the essence of "The Ambassadors," his fingers
close, before he has done, round the stem of the full-blown flower; which,
after that fashion, he continues officiously to present to us. "Live all you
can; it's a mistake not to. It does n't so much matter what you do in particular so long as you have your life. If you have n't had that what *have*
you had? I'm too old—too old at any rate for what I see. What one loses
one loses; make no mistake about that. Still, we have the illusion of freedom; therefore don't, like me to-day, be without the memory of that illusion. I was either, at the right time, too stupid or too intelligent to have
it, and now I'm a case of reaction against the mistake. Do what you like
so long as you don't make it. For it *was* a mistake. Live, live!" Such is the
gist of Strether's appeal to the impressed youth, whom he likes and whom
he desires to befriend; the word "mistake" occurs several times, it will be
seen, in the course of his remarks—which gives the measure of the signal
warning he feels attached to his case. He has accordingly missed too much,
though perhaps after all constitutionally qualified for a better part, and
he wakes up to it in conditions that press the spring of a terrible question.
Would there yet perhaps be time for reparation?—reparation, that is, for
the injury done his character; for the affront, he is quite ready to say, so

[1] From *The Novels and Tales of Henry James* (New York, 1909), Vol. XXI.

stupidly put upon it and in which he has even himself had so clumsy a hand? The answer to which is that he now at all events *sees*; so that the business of my tale and the march of my action, not to say the precious moral of everything, is just my demonstration of this process of vision.

Nothing can exceed the closeness with which the whole fits again into its germ. That had been given me bodily, as usual, by the spoken word, for I was to take the image over exactly as I happened to have met it. A friend had repeated to me, with great appreciation, a thing or two said to him by a man of distinction, much his senior, and to which a sense akin to that of Strether's melancholy eloquence might be imputed—said as chance would have, and so easily might, in Paris, and in a charming old garden attached to a house of art, and on a Sunday afternoon of summer, many persons of great interest being present. The observation there listened to and gathered up had contained part of the "note" that I was to recognise on the spot as to my purpose—had contained in fact the greater part; the rest was in the place and the time and the scene they sketched: these constituents clustered and combined to give me further support, to give me what I may call the note absolute. There it stands, accordingly, full in the tideway; driven in, with hard taps, like some strong stake for the noose of a cable, the swirl of the current roundabout it. What amplified the hint to more than the bulk of hints in general was the gift with it of the old Paris garden, for in that token were sealed up values infinitely precious. There was of course the seal to break and each item of the packet to count over and handle and estimate; but somehow, in the light of the hint, all the elements of a situation of the sort most to my taste were there. I could even remember no occasion on which, so confronted, I had found it of a livelier interest to take stock, in this fashion, of suggested wealth. For I think, verily, that there are degrees of merit in subjects—in spite of the fact that to treat even one of the most ambiguous with due decency we must for the time, for the feverish and prejudiced hour, at least figure its merit and its dignity as *possibly* absolute. What it comes to, doubtless, is that even among the supremely good—since with such alone is it one's theory of one's honour to be concerned—there is an ideal *beauty* of goodness the invoked action of which is to raise the artistic faith to its maximum. Then truly, I hold, one's theme may be said to shine, and that of "The Ambassadors," I confess, wore this glow for me from beginning to end. Fortunately thus I am able to estimate this as, frankly, quite the best, "all round," of my productions; any failure of that justification would have made such an extreme of complacency publicly fatuous.

I recall then in this connexion no moment of subjective intermittence, never one of those alarms as for a suspected hollow beneath one's feet, a felt ingratitude in the scheme adopted, under which confidence fails and opportunity seems but to mock. If the motive of "The Wings of the Dove," as I have noted, was to worry me at moments by a sealing-up of its face—though without prejudice to its again, of a sudden, fairly grimacing with expression—so in this other business I had absolute conviction and constant clearness to deal with; it had been a frank proposition, the whole bunch of data, installed on my premises like a monotony of fine weather. (The order of composition, in these things, I may mention, was reversed by the order of publication; the earlier written of the two books having appeared as the later.) Even under the weight of my hero's years I could feel my postulate firm; even under the strain of the difference between those of Madame de Vionnet and those of Chad Newsome, a difference liable to be denounced as shocking, I could still feel it serene. Nothing resisted, nothing betrayed, I seem to make out, in this full and sound sense of the matter; it shed from any side I could turn it to the same golden glow. I rejoiced in the promise of a hero so mature, who would give me thereby the more to bite into—since it's only into thickened motive and accumulated character, I think, that the painter of life bites more than a little. My poor friend should have accumulated character, certainly; or rather would be quite naturally and handsomely possessed of it, in the sense that he would have, and would always have felt he had, imagination galore, and that this yet would n't have wrecked him. It was immeasurable, the opportunity to "do" a man of imagination, for if *there* might n't be a chance to "bite," where in the world might it be? This personage of course, so enriched, would n't give me, for his type, imagination in *predominance* or as his prime faculty, nor should I, in view of other matters, have found that convenient. So particular a luxury—some occasion, that is, for study of the high gift in *supreme* command of a case or of a career—would still doubtless come on the day I should be ready to pay for it; and till then might, as from far back, remain hung up well in view and just out of reach. The comparative case meanwhile would serve —it was only on the minor scale that I had treated myself even to comparative cases.

I was to hasten to add however that, happy stopgaps as the minor scale had thus yielded, the instance in hand should enjoy the advantage of the full range of the major; since most immediately to the point was the question of that *supplement* of situation logically involved in our gentleman's impulse to deliver himself in the Paris garden on the Sunday afternoon— or if not involved by strict logic then all ideally and enchantingly implied in it. (I say "ideally," because I need scarce mention that for development, for expression of its maximum, my glimmering story was, at the earliest stage, to have nipped the thread of connexion with the possibilities of the actual reported speaker. *He* remains but the happiest of accidents; his actualities, all too definite, precluded any range of possibilities; it had only been his charming office to project upon that wide field of the artist's vision—which hangs there ever in place like the white sheet suspended for the figures of a child's magic-lantern—a more fantastic and more moveable shadow.) No privilege of the teller of tales and the handler of puppets is more delightful, or has more of the suspense and the thrill of a game of difficulty breathlessly played, than just this business of looking for the unseen and the occult, in a scheme half-grasped, by the light or, so to speak, by the clinging scent, of the gage already in hand. No dreadful old pursuit of the hidden slave with bloodhounds and the rag of association can ever, for "excitement," I judge, have bettered it at its best. For the dramatist always, by the very law of his genius, believes not only in a possible right issue from the rightly-conceived tight place; he does much more than this—he believes, irresistibly, in the necessary, the precious "tightness" of the place (whatever the issue) on the strength of any respectable hint. It being thus the respectable hint that I had with such avidity picked up, what would be the story to which it would most inevitably form the centre? It is part of the charm attendant on such questions that the "story," with the omens true, as I say, puts on from this stage the authenticity of concrete existence. It then *is*, essentially—it begins to be, though it may more or less obscurely lurk; so that the point is not in the least what to make of it, but only, very delightfully and very damnably, where to put one's hand on it.

In which truth resides surely much of the interest of that admirable mixture for salutary application which we know as art. Art deals with what we see, it must first contribute full-handed that ingredient; it plucks its material, otherwise expressed, in the garden of life—which material elsewhere grown is stale and uneatable. But it has no sooner done this than it has to take account of a *process*—from which only when it's the basest of the servants of man, incurring ignominious dismissal with no "character," does it, and whether under some muddled pretext of morality or on any other, pusillanimously edge away. The process, that of the expression, the literal squeezing-out, of value is another affair—with which the happy luck of mere finding has little to do. The joys of finding, at this stage, are pretty well over; that quest of the subject as a whole by "matching," as the ladies say at the shops, the big piece with the snippet, having ended, we assume, with a capture. The subject is found, and if the problem is then transferred to the ground of what to do with it the field opens out for any amount of doing. This is precisely the infusion that, as I submit, completes the strong mixture. It is on the other hand the part of the business that can least be likened to the chase with horn and hound. It's all a sedentary part—involves as much ciphering, of sorts, as would merit the highest salary paid to a chief accountant. Not, however, that the chief accountant has n't *his* gleams of bliss; for the felicity, or at least the equilibrium, of the artist's state dwells less, surely in the further delightful complications he can smuggle in than in those he succeeds in keeping out. He sows his seed at the risk of too thick a crop; wherefore yet again, like the gentlemen who audit ledgers, he must keep his head at any price. In consequence of all which, for the interest of the matter, I might seem here to have my choice of narrating my "hunt" for Lambert Strether, of describing the capture of the shadow projected by my friend's anecdote, or of reporting on the occurrences subsequent to that triumph. But I had probably best attempt a little to glance in each direction; since it comes to me again and again, over this licentious record, that one's bag of adventures, conceived or conceivable, has been only half-emptied by the mere telling of one's story. It depends so on what one means by that equivocal quantity. There is the story of one's hero, and then, thanks to the intimate connexion of things, the story of one's story itself. I blush to confess it, but if one's a dramatist one's a dramatist, and the latter imbroglio is liable on occasion to strike me as really the more objective of the two.

The philosophy imputed to him in that beautiful outbreak, the hour there, amid such happy provision, striking for him, would have been then, on behalf of my man of imagination, to be logically and, as the artless craft of comedy has it, "led up" to; the probable course to such a goal, the goal of so conscious a predicament, would have in short to be finely calculated. Where has he come from and why has he come, what is he doing (as we Anglo-Saxons, and we only, say in our foredoomed clutch of exotic aids to expression) in that *galère*? [2] To answer these questions plausibly, to answer them as under cross-examination in the witness-box by counsel for the prosecution, in other words satisfactorily to account for Strether and for his "peculiar tone," was to possess myself of the entire fabric. At the same time the clue to its whereabouts would lie in a certain *principle* of probability: he would n't have indulged in his peculiar tone without a reason; it would take a felt predicament or a false position to give him so ironic an accent. One had n't been noting "tones" all one's life without recognising when one heard it the voice of the false position. The dear man in the Paris garden was then admirably and unmistakeably *in* one— which was no small point gained; what next accordingly concerned us was the determination of *this* identity. One could only go by probabilities, but there was the advantage that the most general of the probabilities were virtual certainties. Possessed of our friend's nationality, to start with, there was a general probability in his narrower localism; which, for that matter, one had really but to keep under the lens for an hour to see it give up its secrets. He would have issued, our rueful worthy, from the very heart of New England—at the heels of which matter of course a perfect train of secrets tumbled for me into the light. They had to be sifted and sorted, and I shall not reproduce the detail of that process; but unmistakeably they were all there, and it was but a question, auspiciously, of picking among them. What the "position" would infallibly be, and why, on his hands, it had turned "false"—these inductive steps could only be as rapid as they were distinct. I accounted for everything—and "everything" had by this time become the most promising quantity—by the view that he had come to Paris in some state of mind which was literally undergoing, as a result of new and unexpected assaults and infusions, a change almost from hour to hour. He had come with a view that might have been figured by a clear green liquid, say, in a neat glass phial; and the liquid, once poured into the open cup of *application*, once exposed to the action of another air, had begun to turn from green to red, or whatever, and might, for all he knew, be on its way to purple, to black, to yellow. At the still wilder extremes represented perhaps, for all he could say to the contrary, by a variability so violent, he would at first, naturally, but have gazed in surprise and alarm; whereby the *situation* clearly would spring from the play of wildness and the development of extremes. I saw in a moment that,

[2] Literally "galley"; hence, drudgery or slavery.

should this development proceed both with force and logic, my "story" would leave nothing to be desired. There is always, of course, for the story-teller, the irresistible determinant and the incalculable advantage of his interest in the story *as such*; it is ever, obviously, overwhelmingly, the prime and precious thing (as other than this I have never been able to see it); as to which what makes for it, with whatever headlong energy, may be said to pale before the energy with which it simply makes for itself. It rejoices, none the less, at its best, to seem to offer itself in a light, to seem to know, and with the very last knowledge, what it's about—liable as it yet is at moments to be caught by us with its tongue in its cheek and absolutely no warrant but its splendid impudence. Let us grant then that the impudence is always there—there, so to speak, for grace and effect and *allure*; there, above all, because the Story is just the spoiled child of art, and because, as we are always disappointed when the pampered don't "play up," we like it, to that extent, to look all its character. It probably does so, in truth, even when we most flatter ourselves that we negotiate with it by treaty.

All of which, again, is but to say that the *steps*, for my fable, placed themselves with a prompt and, as it were, functional assurance—an air quite as of readiness to have dispensed with logic had I been in fact too stupid for my clue. Never, positively, none the less, as the links multiplied, had I felt less stupid than for the determination of poor Strether's errand and for the apprehension of his issue. These things continued to fall together, as by the neat action of their own weight and form, even while their commentator scratched his head about them; he easily sees now that they were always well in advance of him. As the case completed itself he had in fact, from a good way behind, to catch up with them, breathless and a little flurried, as he best could. *The* false position, for our belated man of the world—belated because he had endeavoured so long to escape being one, and now at last had really to face his doom—the false position for him, I say, was obviously to have presented himself at the gate of that boundless menagerie primed with a moral scheme of the most approved pattern which was yet framed to break down on any approach to vivid facts; that is to any at all liberal appreciation of them. There would have been of course the case of the Strether prepared, wherever presenting himself, only to judge and to feel meanly; but *he* would have moved for me, I confess, enveloped in no legend whatever. The actual man's note, from the first of our seeing it struck, is the note of discrimination, just as his drama is to become, under stress, the drama of discrimination. It would have been his blest imagination, we have seen, that had already helped him to discriminate; the element that was for so much of the pleasure of my cutting thick, as I have intimated, into his intellectual, into his moral substance. Yet here it was, at the same time, just here, that a shade for a moment fell across the scene.

There was the dreadful little old tradition, one of the platitudes of the human comedy, that people's moral scheme *does* break down in Paris; that nothing is more frequently observed; that hundreds of thousands of

more or less hypocritical or more or less cynical persons annually visit
the place for the sake of the probable catastrophe, and that I came late
in the day to work myself up about it. There was in fine the *trivial*
association, one of the vulgarest in the world; but which gave me pause
no longer, I think, simply because its vulgarity is so advertised. The
revolution performed by Strether under the influence of the most interesting of great cities was to have nothing to do with any *bêtise* [3] of the
imputably "tempted" state; he was to be thrown forward, rather, thrown
quite with violence, upon his lifelong trick of intense reflexion: which
friendly test indeed was to bring him out, through winding passages,
through alternations of darkness and light, very much *in* Paris, but with
the surrounding scene itself a minor matter, a mere symbol for more things
than had been dreamt of in the philosophy of Woollett. Another surrounding scene would have done as well for our show could it have represented a place in which Strether's errand was likely to lie and his crisis to
await him. The *likely* place had the great merit of sparing me preparations; there would have been too many involved—not at all impossibilities,
only rather worrying and delaying difficulties—in positing elsewhere Chad
Newsome's interesting relation, his so interesting complexity of relations.
Strether's appointed stage, in fine, could be but Chad's most luckily selected one. The young man had gone in, as they say, for circumjacent
charm; and where he would have found it, by the turn of his mind, most
"authentic," was where his earnest friend's analysis would most find *him*;
as well as where, for that matter, the former's whole analytic faculty would
be led such a wonderful dance.

"The Ambassadors" had been, all conveniently, "arranged for"; its first
appearance was from month to month, in "The North American Review"
during 1903, and I had been open from far back to any pleasant provocation for ingenuity that might reside in one's actively adopting—so as to
make it, in its way, a small compositional law—recurrent breaks and re-
sumptions. I had made up my mind here regularly to exploit and enjoy
these often rather rude jolts—having found, as I believed, an admirable
way to it; yet every question of form and pressure, I easily remember,
paled in the light of the major propriety, recognised as soon as really
weighed; that of employing but one centre and keeping it all within my
hero's compass. The thing was to be so much this worthy's intimate adventure that even the projection of his consciousness upon it from beginning to end without intermission or deviation would probably still leave
a part of its value for him, and *a fortiori* for ourselves, unexpressed. I
might, however, express every grain of it that there would be room for—on
condition of contriving a splendid particular economy. Other persons in
no small number were to people the scene, and each with his or her
axe to grind, his or her situation to treat, his or her coherency not to fail
of, his or her relation to my leading motive, in a word, to establish and
carry on. But Strether's sense of these things, and Strether's only, should
avail me for showing them; I should know them but through his more or

[3] "silliness," "stupidity."

less groping knowledge of them, since his very gropings would figure among his most interesting motions, and a full observance of the rich rigour I speak of would give me more of the effect I should be most "after" than all other possible observances together. It would give me a large unity, and that in turn would crown me with the grace to which the enlightened story-teller will at any time, for his interest, sacrifice if need be all other graces whatever. I refer of course to the grace of intensity, which there are ways of signally achieving and ways of signally missing—as we see it, all round us, helplessly and woefully missed. Not that it is n't, on the other hand, a virtue eminently subject to appreciation—there being no strict, no absolute measure of it; so that one may hear it acclaimed where it has quite escaped one's perception, and see it unnoticed where one has gratefully hailed it. After all of which I am not sure, either, that the immense amusement of the whole cluster of difficulties so arrayed may not operate, for the fond fabulist, when judicious not less than fond, as his best of determinants. That charming principle is always there, at all events, to keep interest fresh: it is a principle, we remember, essentially ravenous, without scruple and without mercy, appeased with no cheap nor easy nourishment. It enjoys the costly sacrifice and rejoices thereby in the very odour of difficulty—even as ogres, with their "Fee-faw-fum!" rejoice in the smell of the blood of Englishmen.

Thus it was, at all events, that the ultimate, though after all so speedy, definition of my gentleman's job—his coming out, all solemnly appointed and deputed, to "save" Chad, and his then finding the young man so disobligingly and, at first, so bewilderingly not lost that a new issue altogether, in the connexion, prodigiously faces them, which has to be dealt with in a new light—promised as many calls on ingenuity and on the higher branches of the compositional art as one could possibly desire. Again and yet again, as, from book to book, I proceed with my survey, I find no source of interest equal to this verification after the fact, as I may call it, and the more in detail the better, of the scheme of consistency "gone in" for. As always—since the charm never fails—the retracing of the process from point to point brings back the old illusion. The old intentions bloom again and flower—in spite of all the blossoms they were to have dropped by the way. This is the charm, as I say, of adventure transposed—the thrilling ups and downs, the intricate ins and outs of the compositional problem, made after such a fashion admirably objective, becoming the question at issue and keeping the author's heart in his mouth. Such an element, for instance, as his intention that Mrs. Newsome, away off with her finger on the pulse of Massachusetts, should yet be no less intensely than circuitously present through the whole thing, should be no less felt as to be reckoned with than the most direct exhibition, the finest portrayal at first hand could make her, such a sign of artistic good faith, I say, once it's unmistakeably there, takes on again an actuality not too much impaired by the comparative dimness of the particular success. Cherished intention too inevitably acts and operates, in the book, about fifty times as little as I had fondly dreamt it might; but that scarce spoils for me the pleasure of recognising the fifty ways in which I had sought to provide for it. The mere charm of seeing such an idea constituent, in its degree; the fineness of the measures taken—a real extension, if successful, of the very terms and possibilities of representation and figuration—such things alone were, after this fashion, inspiring, such things alone were a gage of the probable success of that dissimulated calculation with which the whole effort was to square. But oh the cares begotten, none the less, of that same "judicious" sacrifice to a particular form of interest! One's work should have composition, because composition alone is positive beauty; but all the while—apart from one's inevitable consciousness too of the dire paucity of readers ever recognising or ever missing positive beauty—how, as to the cheap and easy, at every turn, how, as to immediacy and facility, and even as to the commoner vivacity, positive beauty might have to be sweated for and paid for! Once achieved and installed it may always be trusted to make the poor seeker feel he would have blushed to the roots of his hair for failing of it; yet, how, as its virtue can be essentially but the virtue of the whole, the wayside traps set in the interest of muddlement and pleading but the cause of the moment, of the particular bit in itself, have to be kicked out of the path! All the sophistications in life, for example, might have appeared to muster on behalf of the menace—the menace to a bright variety—involved in Strether's having all the subjective "say," as it were, to himself.

Had I, meanwhile, made him at once hero and historian, endowed him with the romantic privilege of the "first person"—the darkest abyss of romance this, inveterately, when enjoyed on the grand scale—variety, and many other queer matters as well, might have been smuggled in by a back door. Suffice it, to be brief, that the first person, in the long piece, is a form foredoomed to looseness, and that looseness, never much my affair, had never been so little so as on this particular occasion. All of which reflexions flocked to the standard from the moment—a very early one—the question of how to keep my form amusing while sticking so close to my central figure and constantly taking its pattern from him had to be faced. He arrives (arrives at Chester) as for the dreadful purpose of giving his creator "no end" to tell about him—before which rigorous mission the serenest of creators might well have quailed. I was far from the serenest; I was more than agitated enough to reflect that, grimly deprived of one alternative or one substitute for "telling," I must address myself tooth and nail to another. I could n't, save by implication, make other persons tell *each other* about him—blest resource, blest necessity, of the drama, which reaches its effects of unity, all remarkably, by paths absolutely opposite to the paths of the novel: with other persons, save as they were primarily *his* persons (not he primarily but one of theirs), I had simply nothing to do. I had relations for him none the less, by the mercy of Providence, quite as much as if my exhibition *was* to be a muddle; if I could only by implication and a show of consequence make other persons tell each other about him, I could at least make him tell *them* whatever in the world he must; and could so, by the same token—which was a further luxury thrown in—see straight into the deep differences between what that could do for me, or at all events for *him*, and the large ease of "autobiography." It may be asked why, if one so keeps to one's hero, one should n't make a single mouthful of "method," should n't throw the reins on his neck and, letting them flap there as free as in "Gil Blas" [4] or in "David Copperfield," equip him with the double privilege of subject and object—a course that has at least the merit of brushing away questions at a sweep. The answer to which is, I think, that one makes that surrender only if one is prepared *not* to make certain precious discriminations.

The "first person" then, so employed, is addressed by the author directly to ourselves, his possible readers, whom he has to reckon with, at the best, by our English tradition, so loosely and vaguely after all, so little respectfully, on so scant a presumption of exposure to criticism. Strether, on the other hand, encaged and provided for as "The Ambassadors" encages and provides, has to keep in view proprieties much stiffer and more salutary than any our straight and credulous gape are likely to bring home to him, has exhibitional conditions to meet, in a word, that forbid the terrible *fluidity* of self-revelation. I may seem not to better the case for my discrimination if I say that, for my first care, I had thus inevitably to set him up a confidant or two, to wave away with energy the custom of the seated mass of explanation after the fact, the inserted block of merely referential narrative, which flourishes so, to the shame of the modern impatience, on the serried page of Balzac, but which seems simply to appal our actual, our general weaker, digestion. "Harking back to make up" took at any rate more doing, as the phrase is, not only than the reader of to-day demands, but than he will tolerate at any price any call upon him either to understand or remotely to measure; and for the beauty of the thing when done the current editorial mind in particular appears wholly without sense. It is not, however, primarily for either of these reasons, whatever their weight, that Strether's friend Waymarsh is so keenly clutched at, on the threshold of the book, or that no less a pounce is made on Maria Gostrey—without even the pretext, either, of *her* being, in essence, Strether's friend. She is the reader's friend much rather—in consequence of dispositions that make him so eminently require one; and she acts in that capacity, and *really* in that capacity alone, with exemplary devotion, from beginning to end of the book. She is an enrolled, a direct, aid to lucidity; she is in fine, to tear off her mask, the most unmitigated and abandoned of *ficelles*.[5] Half the dramatist's art, as we well know—since if we don't it's not the fault of the proofs that lie scattered about us—is in the use of *ficelles*; by which I mean in a deep dissimulation of his dependence on them. Waymarsh only to a slighter degree belongs, in the whole business, less to my subject than to my treatment of it; the interesting proof, in these connexions, being that one has but to take one's subject for the stuff of drama to interweave with enthusiasm as many Gostreys as need be.

---

[4] A picaresque novel, very loose in structure, by Alain Lesage. The first six books were published in 1715, the next three in 1724, and the final three in 1735.
[5] "stage-trick" or "trick of the trade."

The material of "The Ambassadors," conforming in this respect exactly to that of "The Wings of the Dove," published just before it, is taken absolutely for the stuff of drama; so that, availing myself of the opportunity given me by this edition for some prefatory remarks on the latter work, I had mainly to make on its behalf the point of its scenic consistency. It disguises that virtue, in the oddest way in the world, by just *looking*, as we turn its pages, as little scenic as possible; but it sharply divides itself, just as the composition before us does, into the parts that prepare, that tend in fact to over-prepare, for scenes, and the parts, or otherwise into the scenes, that justify and crown the preparation. It may definitely be said, I think, that everything in it that is not scene (not, I of course mean, complete and functional scene, treating *all* the submitted matter, as by logical start, logical turn, and logical finish) is discriminated preparation, is the fusion and synthesis of picture. These alternations propose themselves all recogniseably, I think, from an early stage, as the very form and figure of "The Ambassadors"; so that, to repeat, such an agent as Miss Gostrey, pre-engaged at a high salary, but waits in the draughty wing with her shawl and her smelling-salts. Her function speaks at once for itself, and by the time she has dined with Strether in London and gone to a play with him her intervention as a *ficelle* is, I hold, expertly justified. Thanks to it we have treated scenically, and scenically alone, the whole lumpish question of Strether's "past," which has seen us more happily on the way than anything else could have done; we have strained to a high lucidity and vivacity (or at least we hope we have) certain indispensable facts; we have seen our two or three immediate friends all conveniently and profitably in "action"; to say nothing of our beginning to descry others, of a remoter intensity, getting into motion, even if a bit vaguely as yet, for our further enrichment. Let my first point be here that the scene in question, that in which the whole situation at Woollett and the complex forces that have propelled my hero to where this lively extractor of his value and distiller of his essence awaits him, is normal and entire, is really an excellent *standard* scene; copious, comprehensive, and accordingly never short, but with its office as definite as that of the hammer on the gong of the clock, the office of expressing *all that is in* the hour.

The *"ficelle"* character of the subordinate party is as artfully dissimulated, throughout, as may be, and to that extent that, with the seams or joints of Maria Gostrey's ostensible connectedness taken particular care of, duly smoothed over, that is, and anxiously kept from showing as "pieced on," this figure doubtless achieves, after a fashion, something of the dignity of a prime idea: which circumstance but shows us afresh how many quite incalculable but none the less clear sources of enjoyment for the infatuated artist, how many copious springs of our never-to-be-slighted "fun" for the reader and critic susceptible of contagion, may sound their incidental plash as soon as an artistic process begins to enjoy free development. Exquisite—in illustration of this—the mere interest and amusement of such at once "creative" and critical questions as how and where and why to make Miss Gostrey's false connexion carry itself, under a due high polish, as a real one. Nowhere is it more of an artful expedient for mere consistency of form, to mention a case, than in the last "scene" of the book, where its function is to give or to add nothing whatever, but only to express as vividly as possible certain things quite other than itself and that are of the already fixed and appointed measure. Since, however, all art is *expression,* and is thereby vividness, one was to find the door open here to any amount of delightful dissimulation. These verily are the refinements and ecstasies of method—amid which, or certainly under the influence of any exhilarated demonstration of which, one must keep one's head and not lose one's way. To cultivate an adequate intelligence for them and to make that sense operative is positively to find a charm in any produced ambiguity of appearance that is not by the same stroke, and all helplessly, an ambiguity of sense. To project imaginatively, for my hero, a relation that has nothing to do with the matter (the matter of my subject) but has everything to do with the manner (the manner of my presentation of the same) and yet to treat it, at close quarters and for fully economic expression's possible sake, as if it were important and essential—to do that sort of thing and yet muddle nothing may easily become, as one goes, a signally attaching proposition; even though it all remains but part and parcel, I hasten to recognise, of the merely general and related question of expressional curiosity and expressional decency.

I am moved to add after so much insistence on the scenic side of my labour that I have found the steps of re-perusal almost as much waylaid here by quite another style of effort in the same signal interest—or have in other words not failed to note how, even so associated and so discriminated, the finest proprieties and charms of the non-scenic may, under the right hand for them, still keep their intelligibility and assert their office. Infinitely suggestive such an observation as this last on the whole delightful head, where representation is concerned, of possible variety, of effective expressional change and contrast. One would like, at such an hour as this, for critical license, to go into the matter of the noted inevitable deviation (from too fond an original vision) that the exquisite treachery even of the straightest execution may ever be trusted to inflict even on the most mature plan—the case being that, though one's last reconsidered production always seems to bristle with that particular evidence, "The Ambassadors," would place a flood of such light at my service. I must attach to my final remark here a different import; noting in the other connexion I just glanced at that such passages as that of my hero's first encounter with Chad Newsome, absolute attestations of the non-scenic form though they be, yet lay the firmest hand too—so far at least as intention goes—on representational effect. To report at all closely and completely of what "passes" on a given occasion is inevitably to become more or less scenic; and yet in the instance I allude to, *with* the conveyance, expressional curiosity and expressional decency are sought and arrived at under quite another law. The true inwardness of this may be at bottom but that one of the suffered treacheries has consisted precisely, for Chad's whole figure and presence, of a direct presentability diminished and compromised—despoiled, that is, of its *proportional* advantage; so that, in a word, the whole economy of his author's relation to him has at important points to be redetermined. The book, however, critically viewed, is touchingly full of these disguised and repaired losses, these insidious recoveries, these intensely redemptive consistencies. The pages in which Mamie Pocock gives her appointed and, I can't but think, duly felt lift to the whole action by the so inscrutably-applied side-stroke or short-cut of our just watching, and as quite at an angle of vision as yet untried, her single hour of suspense in the hotel salon, in our partaking of her concentrated study of the sense of matters bearing on her own case, all the bright warm Paris afternoon, from the balcony that overlooks the Tuileries garden— these are as marked an example of the representational virtue that insists here and there on being, for the charm of opposition and renewal, other than the scenic. It would n't take much to make me further argue that from an equal play of such oppositions the book gathers an intensity that fairly adds to the dramatic—though the latter is supposed to be the sum of all intensities; or that has at any rate nothing to fear from juxtaposition with it. I consciously fail to shrink in fact from that extravagance—I risk it, rather, for the sake of the moral involved; which is not that the particular production before us exhausts the interesting questions it raises, but that the Novel remains still, under the right persuasion, the most independent, most elastic, most prodigious of literary forms.

WILLIAM DEAN HOWELLS

From CRITICISM AND FICTION [1]

(1891)

II

[REALISM AND CRITICISM]

I SHOULD, indeed, prefer another line of Keats's, if I were to profess any formulated creed, and should feel much safer with his "Beauty is Truth, Truth Beauty," than even with my friend's reformation of the more quoted verse. It brings us back to the solid ground taken by Mr. Symonds,[2] which is not essentially different from that taken in the great Mr. Burke's *Essay on the Sublime and the Beautiful*[3]—a singularly mod-'ern book, considering how long ago it was wrote (as the great Mr. Steele [4] would have written the participle a little longer ago), and full of a certain well-mannered and agreeable instruction. In some things it is of that droll little eighteenth-century world, when philosophy had got the neat little universe into the hollow of its hand, and knew just what it was, and what it was for; but it is quite without arrogance. "As for those called critics," the author says,[5] "they have generally sought the rule of the arts in the wrong place; they have sought among poems, pictures, engravings, statues, and buildings; but art can never give the rules that make an art. This is, I believe, the reason why artists in general, and poets principally, have been confined in so narrow a circle; they have been rather imitators of one another than of nature. Critics follow them, and therefore can do little as guides. I can judge but poorly of anything while I measure it by no other standard than itself. The true standard of the arts is in every man's power; and an easy observation of the most common, sometimes of the meanest things, in nature will give the truest lights, where the greatest sagacity and industry that slights such observation must leave us in the dark, or, what is worse, amuse and mislead us by false lights."

If this should happen to be true—and it certainly commends itself to acceptance—it might portend an immediate danger to the vested interests of criticism, only that it was written a hundred years ago; and we shall probably have the "sagacity and industry that slights the observation" of nature long enough yet to allow most critics the time to learn some more useful trade than criticism as they pursue it. Nevertheless, I am in hopes

[1] New York, 1891.
[2] John Addington Symonds (1840–1893), English scholar and poet.
[3] Edmund Burke's (1729–1797) essay, *Philosophical Inquiry into the Origin of Our Ideas on the Sublime and Beautiful*, was published in 1756.
[4] Richard Steele (1672–1729), English periodical essayist.
[5] Howells is here quoting from Burke's essay.

that the communistic era in taste foreshadowed by Burke is approaching, and that it will occur within the lives of men now overawed by the foolish old superstition that literature and art are anything but the expression of life, and are to be judged by any other test than that of their fidelity to it. The time is coming, I hope, when each new author, each new artist, will be considered, not in his proportion to any other author or artist, but in his relation to the human nature, known to us all, which it is his privilege, his high duty, to interpret. "The true standard of the artist is in every man's power" already, as Burke says; Michelangelo's "light of the piazza," the glance of the common eye, is and always was the best light on a statue; Goethe's "boys and blackbirds" have in all ages been the real connoisseurs of berries; but hitherto the mass of common men have been afraid to apply their own simplicity, naturalness, and honesty to the appreciation of the beautiful. They have always cast about for the instruction of some one who professed to know better, and who browbeat wholesome common-sense into the self-distrust that ends in sophistication. They have fallen generally to the worst of this bad species, and have been "amused and misled" (how pretty that quaint old use of amuse is!) "by the false lights" of critical vanity and self-righteousness. They have been taught to compare what they see and what they read, not with the things that they have observed and known, but with the things that some other artist or writer has done. Especially if they have themselves the artistic impulse in any direction they are taught to form themselves, not upon life, but upon the masters who became masters only by forming themselves upon life. The seeds of death are planted in them, and they can produce only the still-born, the academic. They are not told to take their work into the public square and see if it seems true to the chance passer, but to test it by the work of the very men who refused and decried any other test of their own work. The young writer who attempts to report the phrase and carriage of everyday life, who tries to tell just how he has heard men talk and seen them look, is made to feel guilty of something low and unworthy by people who would like to have him show how Shakespeare's men talked and looked, or Scott's, or Thackeray's, or Balzac's, or Hawthorne's, or Dickens's; he is instructed to idealize his personages, that is, to take the life-likeness out of them, and put the book-likeness into them. He is approached in the spirit of the pedantry into which learning, much or little, always decays when it withdraws itself and stands apart from experience in an attitude of imagined superiority, and which would say with the same confidence to the scientist: "I see that you are looking at a grasshopper there which you have found in the grass, and I suppose you intend to describe it. Now don't waste your time and sin against culture in that way. I've got a grasshopper here, which has been evolved at considerable pains and expense out of the grasshopper in general; in fact, it's a type. It's made up of wire and card-board, very prettily painted in a conventional tint, and it's perfectly indestructible. It isn't very much like a real grasshopper, but it's a great deal nicer, and it's served to represent the notion of a grasshopper ever since man emerged from barbarism. You may say that it's artificial. Well, it is artificial; but then it's ideal too; and what you want to do is to cultivate the ideal. You'll find the books full of my kind of grasshopper, and scarcely a trace of yours in any of them. The thing that you are proposing to do is commonplace; but if you say that it isn't commonplace, for the very reason that it hasn't been done before, you'll have to admit that it's photographic."

As I said, I hope the time is coming when not only the artist, but the common, average man, who always "has the standard of the arts in his power," will have also the courage to apply it, and will reject the ideal grasshopper wherever he finds it, in science, in literature, in art, because it is not "simple, natural, and honest," because it is not like a real grasshopper. But I will own that I think the time is yet far off, and that the people who have been brought up on the ideal grasshopper, the heroic grasshopper, the impassioned grasshopper, the self-devoted, adventureful, good old romantic card-board grasshopper, must die out before the simple, honest, and natural grasshopper can have a fair field. I am in no haste to compass the end of these good people, whom I find in the mean time very amusing. It is delightful to meet one of them, either in print or out of it—some sweet elderly lady or excellent gentleman whose youth was pastured on the literature of thirty or forty years ago—and to witness the confidence with which they preach their favorite authors as all the law and the prophets. They have commonly read little or nothing since, or, if they have, they have judged it by a standard taken from these authors, and never dreamed of judging it by nature; they are destitute of the documents in the case of the later writers; they suppose that Balzac was the beginning of realism, and that Zola is its wicked end; they are quite ignorant, but they are ready to talk you down, if you differ from them, with an assumption of knowledge sufficient for any occasion. The horror, the resentment, with which they receive any question of their literary saints is genuine; you descend at once very far in the moral and social scale, and anything short of offensive personality is too good for you; it is expressed to you that you are one to be avoided, and put down even a little lower than you have naturally fallen.

These worthy persons are not to blame; it is part of their intellectual mission to represent the petrifaction of taste, and to preserve an image of a smaller and cruder and emptier world than we now live in, a world which was feeling its way toward the simple, the natural, the honest, but was a good deal "amused and misled" by lights now no longer mistakable for heavenly luminaries. They belong to a time, just passing away, when certain authors were considered authorities in certain kinds, when they must be accepted entire and not questioned in any particular. Now we are beginning to see and to say that no author is an authority except in those moments when he held his ear close to Nature's lips and caught her very accent. These moments are not continuous with any authors in the past, and they are rare with all. Therefore I am not afraid to say now that the greatest classics are sometimes not at all great, and that we can profit by them only when we hold them, like our meanest contemporaries, to a

strict accounting, and verify their work by the standard of the arts which
we all have in our power, the simple, the natural, and the honest.

Those good people must always have a hero, an idol of some sort, and
it is droll to find Balzac, who suffered from their sort such bitter scorn and
hate for his realism while he was alive, now become a fetich in his turn, to
be shaken in the faces of those who will not blindly worship him. But it
is no new thing in the history of literature: whatever is established is
sacred with those who do not think. At the beginning of the century,
when romance was making the same fight against effete classicism which
realism is making to-day against effete romanticism, the Italian poet
Monti [6] declared that "the romantic was the cold grave of the Beautiful,"
just as the realistic is now supposed to be. The romantic of that day and
the real of this are in certain degree the same. Romanticism then sought,
as realism seeks now, to widen the bounds of sympathy, to level every
barrier against aesthetic freedom, to escape from the paralysis of tradition.
It exhausted itself in this impulse; and it remained for realism to assert
that fidelity to experience and probability of motive are essential conditions
of a great imaginative literature. It is not a new theory, but it has never
before universally characterized literary endeavor. When realism becomes
false to itself, when it heaps up facts merely, and maps life instead of
picturing it, realism will perish too. Every true realist instinctively knows
this, and it is perhaps the reason why he is careful of every fact, and feels
himself bound to express or to indicate its meaning at the risk of over-
moralizing. In life he finds nothing insignificant; all tells for destiny and
character; nothing that God has made is contemptible. He cannot look
upon human life and declare this thing or that thing unworthy of notice,
any more than the scientist can declare a fact of the material world beneath
the dignity of his inquiry. He feels in every nerve the equality of things
and the unity of men; his soul is exalted, not by vain shows and shadows
and ideals, but by realities, in which alone the truth lives. In criticism it is
his business to break the images of false gods and misshapen heroes, to
take away the poor silly toys that many grown people would still like to
play with. He cannot keep terms with "Jack the Giant-killer" or "Puss-in-
Boots," under any name or in any place, even when they reappear as the
convict Vautrec, or the Marquis de Montrivaut, or the Sworn Thirteen
Noblemen. He must say to himself that Balzac, when he imagined these
monsters, was not Balzac, he was Dumas; he was not realistic, he was
romanticistic.

XV
[REALISM AND THE ENGLISH NOVEL]

Which brings us again, after this long way about, to Jane Austen and
her novels, and that troublesome question about them. She was great and
they were beautiful, because she and they were honest, and dealt with
nature nearly a hundred years ago as realism deals with it to-day. Realism

[6] Vincenzo Monti (1754-1828), Italian poet.

is nothing more and nothing less than the truthful treatment of material, and Jane Austen was the first and the last of the English novelists to treat material with entire truthfulness. Because she did this, she remains the most artistic of the English novelists, and alone worthy to be matched with the great Scandinavian and Slavic and Latin artists. It is not a question of intellect, or not wholly that. The English have mind enough; but they have not taste enough; or, rather, their taste has been perverted by their false criticism, which is based upon personal preference, and not upon principle; which instructs a man to think that what he likes is good, instead of teaching him first to distinguish what is good before he likes it. The art of fiction, as Jane Austen knew it, declined from her through Scott, and Bulwer,[7] and Dickens, and Charlotte Brontë, and Thackeray, and even George Eliot, because the mania of romanticism had seized upon all Europe, and these great writers could not escape the taint of their time; but it has shown few signs of recovery in England, because English criticism, in the presence of the Continental masterpieces, has continued provincial and special and personal, and has expressed a love and a hate which had to do with the quality of the artist rather than the character of his work. It was inevitable that in their time the English romanticists should treat, as Señor Valdés[8] says, "the barbarous customs of the Middle Ages, softening and distorting them, as Walter Scott and his kind did;" that they should "devote themselves to falsifying nature, refining and subtilizing sentiment, and modifying psychology after their own fancy," like Bulwer and Dickens, as well as like Rousseau and Madame de Staël,[9] not to mention Balzac, the worst of all that sort at his worst. This was the natural course of the disease; but it really seems as if it were their criticism that was to blame for the rest: not, indeed, for the performance of this writer or that, for criticism can never affect the actual doing of a thing; but for the esteem in which this writer or that is held through the perpetuation of false ideals. The only observer of English middle-class life since Jane Austen worthy to be named with her was not George Eliot, who was first ethical and then artistic, who transcended her in everything but the form and method most essential to art, and there fell hopelessly below her. It was Anthony Trollope who was most like her in simple honesty and instinctive truth, as unphilosophized as the light of common day; but he was so warped from a wholesome ideal as to wish at times to be like Thackeray, and to stand about in his scene, talking it over with his hands in his pockets, interrupting the action, and spoiling the illusion in which alone the truth of art resides. Mainly, his instinct was too much for his ideal, and with a low view of life in its civic relations and a thoroughly bourgeois soul, he yet produced works whose beauty is surpassed only by the effect of a more poetic writer in the novels of Thomas Hardy. Yet if a vote of English criticism even at this late day, when all Continental Europe has the light of aesthetic truth, could be taken, the majority against

[7] Edward Lytton Bulwer (1803–1873), English novelist.
[8] Armando Valdés (1853–1938), Spanish novelist.
[9] Madame de Staël (1766–1817), French novelist and critic.

these artists would be overwhelmingly in favor of a writer who had so little artistic sensibility, that he never hesitated on any occasion, great or small, to make a foray among his characters, and catch them up to show them to the reader and tell him how beautiful or ugly they were; and cry out over their amazing properties.

XXI
[ART AND DEMOCRACY]

. . . In fine, I would have our American novelists be as American as they unconsciously can. Matthew Arnold complained that he found no "distinction" in our life, and I would gladly persuade all artists intending greatness in any kind among us that the recognition of the fact pointed out by Mr. Arnold ought to be a source of inspiration to them, and not discouragement. We have been now some hundred years building up a state on the affirmation of the essential equality of men in their rights and duties, and whether we have been right or been wrong the gods have taken us at our word, and have responded to us with a civilization in which there is no "distinction" perceptible to the eye that loves and values it. Such beauty and such grandeur as we have is common beauty, common grandeur, or the beauty and grandeur in which the quality of solidarity so prevails that neither distinguishes itself to the disadvantage of anything else. It seems to me that these conditions invite the artist to the study and the appreciation of the common, and to the portrayal in every art of those finer and higher aspects which unite rather than sever humanity, if he would thrive in our new order of things. The talent that is robust enough to front the every-day world and catch the charm of its work-worn, care-worn, brave, kindly face, need not fear the encounter, though it seems terrible to the sort nurtured in the superstition of the romantic, the bizarre, the heroic, the distinguished, as the things alone worthy of painting or carving or writing. The arts must become democratic, and then we shall have the expression of America in art; and the reproach which Arnold was half right in making us shall have no justice in it any longer; we shall be "distinguished."

XXIII
[ART AND MORALITY]

One of the great newspapers the other day invited the prominent American authors to speak their minds upon a point in the theory and practice of fiction which had already vexed some of them. It was the question of how much or how little the American novel ought to deal with certain facts of life which are not usually talked of before young people, and especially young ladies. Of course the question was not decided, and I forget just how far the balance inclined in favor of a larger freedom in the matter. But it certainly inclined that way; one or two writers of the sex which is somehow supposed to have purity in its keeping (as if purity were a thing that did not practically concern the other sex, preoccupied with serious affairs) gave it a rather vigorous tilt to that side. In view of this fact it would not be the part of prudence to make an effort to dress the balance; and indeed I do not know that I was going to make any such effort. But there are some things to say, around and about the subject, which I should like to have some one else say, and which I may myself possibly be safe in suggesting.

One of the first of these is the fact, generally lost sight of by those who censure the Anglo-Saxon novel for its prudishness, that it is really not such a prude after all; and that if it is sometimes apparently anxious to avoid those experiences of life not spoken of before young people, this may be an appearance only. Sometimes a novel which has this shuffling air, this effect of truckling to propriety, might defend itself, if it could speak for itself, by saying that such experiences happened not to come within its scheme, and that, so far from maiming or mutilating itself in ignoring them, it was all the more faithfully representative of the tone of modern life in dealing with love that was chaste, and with passion so honest that it could be openly spoken of before the tenderest society bud at dinner. It might say that the guilty intrigue, the betrayal, the extreme flirtation even, was the exceptional thing in life, and unless the scheme of the story necessarily involved it, that it would be bad art to lug it in, and as bad taste as to introduce such topics in a mixed company. It could say very justly that the novel in our civilization now always addresses a mixed company, and that the vast majority of the company are ladies, and that very many, if not most, of these ladies are young girls. If the novel were written for men and for married women alone, as in continental Europe, it might be altogether different. But the simple fact is that it is not written for them alone among us, and it is a question of writing, under cover of our universal acceptance, things for young girls to read which you would be put out-of-doors for saying to them, or of frankly giving notice of your intention, and so cutting yourself off from the pleasure—and it is a very high and sweet one—of appealing to these vivid, responsive intelligences, which are none the less brilliant and admirable because they are innocent.

One day a novelist who liked, after the manner of other men, to repine at his hard fate, complained to his friend, a critic, that he was tired of the restriction he had put upon himself in this regard; for it is a mistake, as can be readily shown, to suppose that others impose it. "See how free those French fellows are!" he rebelled. "Shall we always be shut up to our tradition of decency?"

"Do you think it's much worse than being shut up to their tradition of indecency?" said his friend.

Then that novelist began to reflect, and he remembered how sick the invariable motive of the French novel made him. He perceived finally that, convention for convention, ours was not only more tolerable, but on the whole was truer to life, not only to its complexion, but also to its texture. No one will pretend that there is not vicious love beneath the surface of our society; if he did, the fetid explosions of the divorce trials

would refute him; but if he pretended that it was in any just sense characteristic of our society, he could be still more easily refuted. Yet it exists,
and it is unquestionably the material of tragedy, the stuff from which
intense effects are wrought. The question, after owning this fact, is
whether these intense effects are not rather cheap effects. I incline to think
they are, and I will try to say why I think so, if I may do so without
offence. The material itself, the mere mention of it, has an instant fascination; it arrests, it detains, till the last word is said, and while there is anything to be hinted. This is what makes a love intrigue of some sort all but
essential to the popularity of any fiction. Without such an intrigue the
intellectual equipment of the author must be of the highest, and then he
will succeed only with the highest class of readers. But any author who
will deal with a guilty love intrigue holds all readers in his hand, the
highest with the lowest, as long as he hints the slightest hope of the
smallest potential naughtiness. He need not at all be a great author; he
may be a very shabby wretch, if he has but the courage or the trick of
that sort of thing. The critics will call him "virile" and "passionate"; decent
people will be ashamed to have been limed by him; but the low average
will only ask another chance of flocking into his net. If he happens to be
an able writer, his really fine and costly work will be unheeded, and the
lure to the appetite will be chiefly remembered. There may be other qualities which make reputations for other men, but in his case they will count
for nothing. He pays this penalty for his success in that kind; and every
one pays some such penalty who deals with some such material.

But I do not mean to imply that his case covers the whole ground. So
far as it goes, though, it ought to stop the mouths of those who complain
that fiction is enslaved to propriety among us. It appears that of a certain
kind of impropriety it is free to give us all it will, and more. But this is not
what serious men and women writing fiction mean when they rebel against
the limitations of their art in our civilization. They have no desire to deal
with nakedness, as painters and sculptors freely do in the worship of
beauty; or with certain facts of life, as the stage does, in the service of
sensation. But they ask why, when the conventions of the plastic and
histrionic arts liberate their followers to the portrayal of almost any phase
of the physical or of the emotional nature, an American novelist may not
write a story on the lines of *Anna Karénina* or *Madame Bovary*. They wish
to touch one of the most serious and sorrowful problems of life in the spirit
of Tolstoy and Flaubert,[10] and they ask why they may not. At one time,
they remind us, the Anglo-Saxon novelist did deal with such problems—
De Foe in his spirit, Richardson in his, Goldsmith in his. At what moment
did our fiction lose this privilege? In what fatal hour did the Young Girl
arise and seal the lips of Fiction, with a touch of her finger, to some of the
most vital interests of life?

Whether I wished to oppose them in their aspiration for greater freedom,
or whether I wished to encourage them, I should begin to answer them by

[10] Count Lyof Tolstoy (1828–1910), Russian realistic novelist, wrote *Anna Karenina* in 1877. Gustave Flaubert (1821–1880) wrote *Madame Bovary* in 1857.

saying that the Young Girl has never done anything of the kind. The manners of the novel have been improving with those of its readers; that is all. Gentlemen no longer swear or fall drunk under the table, or abduct young ladies and shut them up in lonely country-houses, or so habitually set about the ruin of their neighbors' wives, as they once did. Generally, people now call a spade an agricultural implement; they have not grown decent without having also grown a little squeamish, but they have grown comparatively decent; there is no doubt about that. They require of a novelist whom they respect unquestionable proof of his seriousness, if he proposes to deal with certain phases of life; they require a sort of scientific decorum. He can no longer expect to be received on the ground of enter-tainment only; he assumes a higher function, something like that of a physician or a priest, and they expect him to be bound by laws as sacred as those of such professions; they hold him solemnly pledged not to betray them or abuse their confidence. If he will accept the conditions, they give him their confidence, and he may then treat to his greater honor, and not at all to his disadvantage, of such experiences, such relations of men and women as George Eliot treats in *Adam Bede,* in *Daniel Deronda,* in *Romola,* in almost all her books; such as Hawthorne treats in *The Scarlet Letter;* such as Dickens treats in *David Copperfield;* such as Thackeray treats in *Pendennis,* and glances at in every one of his fictions; such as most of the masters of English fiction have at some time treated more or less openly. It is quite false or quite mistaken to suppose that our novels have left untouched these most important realities of life. They have only not made them their stock in trade; they have kept a true perspective in regard to them; they have relegated them in their pictures of life to the space and place they occupy in life itself, as we know it in England and America. They have kept a correct proportion, knowing perfectly well that unless the novel is to be a map, with everything scrupulously laid down in it, a faithful record of life in far the greater extent could be made to the exclu-sion of guilty love and all its circumstances and consequences.

I justify them in this view not only because I hate what is cheap and meretricious, and hold in peculiar loathing the cant of the critics who require "passion" as something in itself admirable and desirable in a novel, but because I prize fidelity in the historian of feeling and character. Most of these critics who demand "passion" would seem to have no conception of any passion but one. Yet there are several other passions: the passion of grief, the passion of avarice, the passion of pity, the passion of ambition, the passion of hate, the passion of envy, the passion of devotion, the passion of friendship; and all these have a greater part in the drama of life than the passion of love, and infinitely greater than the passion of guilty love. Wit-tingly or unwittingly, English fiction and American fiction have recognized this truth, not fully, not in the measure it merits, but in greater degree than most other fiction.

EDMUND CLARENCE STEDMAN

WHAT IS POETRY? [1]
(1892)

THESE LECTURES, as I have intimated, are purposely direct of statement, and even elementary. From my point of view this does not of itself imply a lack of respect for the intelligence of the listener. The most advanced star-gazer holds to his mathematics; while, as to poetry, enthusiasts find it easier to build fine sentences than to make clear to others, if to themselves, the nature of that which affects them so inspiringly. I trust that you are willing, in place of the charm of style and the jest and epigram of discourses for entertainment, to accept a search for the very stuff whereof the Muse fashions her transubstantial garments—to discover what plant or moth supplies the sheeny fibre; in what heat, what light, the iridescent fabric is dyed and spun and woven.

It has occurred to me—I think it may not seem amiss to you—that this eager modern time, when the world has turned critic, this curious evening of the century, when the hum of readers and the mists of thought go up from every village; when poetry is both read and written, whether well or ill, more generally than ever before; and when clubs are formed for its study and enjoyment, where commentators urban or provincial, masters and mistresses of analytics, devote nights to the elucidation of a single verse or phrase—it has occurred to me that this is an opportune time for the old questions, so often received as if it were a jet of cold water upon steam or the stroke of midnight at a masquerade—an apt time to ask ourselves, What, then, is poetry, after all? What are the elements beneath its emotion and intellectual delight? Let us have the primer itself. For, if such a primer be not constructible, if it be wholly missing or disdained, you may feel and enjoy a poem, but you will hardly be consistent in your discourse upon it, and this whether you concern yourself with Browning, or Meredith, or Ibsen,—as is now the mode,—or with the masterworks of any period.

Nevertheless, we too must begin our answer to the question, What is poetry? by declaring that the essential *spirit* of poetry is indefinable. It is something which is perceived and felt through a reciprocal faculty shared by human beings in various degrees. The range of these degrees is as wide as that between the boor and the sensitive adept—between the racial Calibans and Prosperos. The poetic spirit is absolute and primal, acknowledged but not reducible, and therefore we postulate it as an axiom of nature and sensation.

[1] From *The Nature and Elements of Poetry* (Boston, 1892). First given as a lecture at Johns Hopkins University in 1891.

To state this otherwise: it is true that the poetic essence always has been a force, an energy, both subtile and compulsive; a primal force, like that energy the discovery of whose unities is the grand physical achievement of this century. The shapes which it informs are Protean, and have a seeming elusiveness. Still, even Proteus, as Vergil tells us, is capturable. Force, through its vehicle of light, becomes fixed within the substance of our planet; in the carbon of the fern, the tree, the lump of coal, the diamond. The poetic spirit becomes concrete through utterance, in that poetry which enters literature; that is, in the concrete utterances of age after age. Nothing of this is durably preserved but that which possesses the crystalline gift of receiving and giving out light indefinitely, yet losing naught from its reservoir. Poetry is the diamond of these concretions. It gives out light of its own, but anticipates also the light of after-times, and refracts it with sympathetic splendors.

With this uttered poetry, then, we are at present concerned. Whether sung, spoken, or written, it is still the most vital form of human expression. One who essays to analyze its constituents is an explorer undertaking a quest in which many have failed. Doubtless he too may fail, but he sets forth in the simplicity of a good knight who does not fear his fate too much, whether his desert be great or small.

In this mood seeking a definition of that poetic utterance which is or may become of record,—a definition both defensible and inclusive, yet compressed into a single phrase,—I have put together the following statement:

Poetry is rhythmical, imaginative language, expressing the invention, taste, thought, passion, and insight, of the human soul.

First of all, and as a corollary,—a resultant from the factors of imaginative invention and expression,—we infer that poetry is, in common with the other art products, a creation, of which the poet is the creator, the maker. *Expression* is the avowed function of all the arts, their excuse for being; out of the need for it, art in the rude and primitive forms has ever sprung. No work of art has real import, none endures, unless the maker has something to say—some thought which he must express imaginatively, whether to the eye in stone or on canvas, or to the ear in music or artistic speech; this thought, the imaginative conception moving him to utterance, being his creative idea—his art-ideal. This simple truth, persistently befogged by the rhetoric of those who do not "see clear and think straight," and who always underrate the strength and beauty of an elementary fact, is the last to be realized by commonplace mechanicians. They go through the process of making pictures or verses without the slightest mission— really with nothing to say or reveal. They mistake the desire to beget for the begetting power. Their mimes and puppets have everything but souls. Now, the imaginative work of a true artist, conveying his own ideal, is creative because it is the expression, the new embodiment, of his particular nature, the materialization of something which renders him a congener, even a part, of the universal soul—that divinity whose eternal function it is to create. The expressive artist is to this extent indeed fashioned after his Maker. He can even declare, in the words of Beddoes,[2] who used them, however, to reveal his surprising glimpses of evolution:—

> "I have a bit of *Fiat* in my soul,
> And can myself create my little world."

At the same time, the quality of the poet's creation, be it lyrical, narrative, or dramatic, is in a sense that of revelation. He cannot invent forms and methods and symbols out of keeping with what we term the nature of things; such inventions, if possible, would be monstrous, baleful, not to be endured. But he utters, reveals, and interprets what he sees with that inward vision, that second sight, the prophetic gift of certain personages,—that which I mean by "insight," and through which the poet is thought to be inspired. This vision penetrates what Plato conceived to be the quintessence of nature, what Wordsworth, in his very highest mood, declares that we perceive only when

> "we are laid asleep
> In body, and become a living soul:
> While with an eye made quiet by the power
> Of harmony, and the deep power of joy,
> We see into the life of things."

The creative insight, according to its degree, is allied with, if not the source of, the mysterious endowment named genius, which humdrum intellects have sought to disallow, claiming that it lies chiefly in one of its frequent attributes,—industry,—but which the wisdom of generations has indubitably recognized. The antique and idealistic notion of this gift is given in "Ion":[3] "A poet . . . is unable to compose poetry until he becomes inspired and is out of his sober senses, and his imagination is no longer under his control; for he does not compose by art, but through a divine power." The modern and scientific rendering is that of the exact investigator, Hartmann,[4] who traces this power of genius to its inmost cell, and classifies it as the spontaneous, involuntary force of the untrammelled soul,—in precise terms, "the activity and efflux of the Intellect freed from the domination of the Conscious Will." Whichever statement you accept,—and I see no reason why the two are not perfectly concordant,—here is the apparently superhuman gift which drew from Sophocles that cry of wonder, "Aeschylus does what is right without knowing it."

As an outcome of genius producing the semblance of what its insight discovers, poetry aims to convey beauty and truth in their absolute simplicity of kind, but limitless variety of guise and adaptation. The poet's vision of these is shared to some extent by all of us, else his appeal would not be universal. But to *his* inborn taste and wisdom is given the power of coadequate expression. Taste has been vilely mistaken for a sentiment,

---

[2] Thomas Lovell Beddoes (1803–1849), English dramatist.
[3] One of the Platonic dialogues.
[4] Karl Hartmann (1842–1906), German philosopher.

and disgust with its abuse may have incited the Wordsworthians and others to disqualify it. They limited their own range by so doing. The world forgives most sins more readily than those against beauty. There was something ridiculous, if heroic, in the supercilious attitude of our transcendentalists, not only putting themselves against the laity, but opposing the whole body of their fellow seers and artists, whose solace for all labors ever has been the favor of their beloved mistress Beauty,—the inspirer of creative taste.

The truth is that taste, however responsive to cultivation, is inborn,—as spontaneous as insight, and, indeed, with an insight of its own. Schlegel's [5] alertness with respect to the aesthetic moved him to define even genius as "the almost unconscious choice of the highest degree of excellence, and, consequently," he added, "it is taste in its highest activity." Profound thinkers, lofty and unselfish natures, may flourish without taste: if so, they miss a sense, nor only one that is physical,—something else is lacking, if the body be the symbol of the soul. I would not go so far as to say of one born, for instance, without ear for melody, that there will be "no music in his soul" when that is disembodied. It is finer to believe that

> "whilst this muddy vesture of decay
> Doth grossly close it in"

such a one cannot hear it; that

> "The soul, with nobler resolutions deck'd,
> The body stooping, does herself erect."

But taste, whether in or out of the body, is a faculty for want of which many ambitious thinkers have in the end failed as poets. It is a sense, however, the functions of which are very readily assumed and mechanically imitated. At periods when what are called false and artificial standards have prevailed, as in French and English letters from 1675 to 1790, the word "taste" has been on every one's lips, and the true discernment of beauty has been supposed to be supreme, when in fact merely the crown and sceptre of taste have been set up and its mantle stuffed with straw. At this very time art is suffering everywhere from an immense variety of standards and models, and our taste, in spite of the diverse and soulless yet attractive productions of the studio and the closet, is that of an interregnum.

Assuming that the artist's conceptions are spontaneous and imaginative, their working out brings into play the conscious intellect. He gives us thought, building up masterpieces from the germinal hint or motive: his wisdom is of so pure a type that through it the poet and the philosopher, in their ultimate and possible development, seem united. It is the exclusive presentation of thought and truth that makes poetry didactical, and hence untrue in the artistic sense. For taste has been finely declared to be "the artistic ethics of the soul," and it is only through a just balance of

[5] Friedrich von Schlegel (1772-1829), German poet and critic.

all the elements in question that poetry rises above ordinary and universal human speech and becomes a veritable art.

Under the conditions of these reciprocal elements, the poet's nature, "all touch, all eye, all ear," exalted to a creative pitch, becomes *emotional*. Feeling is the excitant of genuine poetry. The Miltonic canon, requiring the sensuous beauty which taste alone insures, demands, last of all, as if laying stress upon its indispensability, that poetry should be passionate. It is the impassioned spirit that awakes the imagination, whose taste becomes alert, that hears whisperings which others do not hear,—which it does not itself hear in calmer periods,—that breaks into lyric fervor and melody, and that arouses kindred spirits with recital of its brave imaginings. Feeling of any kind is the touch upon the poet's electric keyboard; the *passio vera*[6] of his more intense moods furnishes the impulse and the power for effective speech. His emotion instinctively acquires the tone and diction fitted to its best expression. Even the passion of a hateful nature is not without a certain distinction. Flame is magnificent, though it feed upon the homes of men.

Right here we stop to consider that thus far our discussion of the poetic elements applies with almost equal significance to all the fine arts; each of them, in fact, being a means of expressing the taste, thought, passion, imagination, and insight, of its devotee. The generic principles of one are those of all. Analysis of one is to this extent that of art as art: a remark illustrated by the talk of every noteworthy virtuoso, from Angelo[7] to Reynolds and Ruskin and Taine. Reflect for an instant upon the simultaneous appearance of a certain phase, such as Preraphaelitism,[8] in the plastic, structural, and decorative arts, in imaginative literature, and on the stage itself, and you see that the Muses are indeed sisters, and have the same food and garments,—often the same diseases. But take for granted the "consensus of the arts." What is it, then, that differentiates them? Nothing so much as their respective vehicles of expression. The key-stone of our definition is the statement that poetry, in the concrete and as under consideration, is *language*. Words are its specific implements and substance. And art must be distinguished, whatsoever its spirit, by its concrete form. A picture of the mind is not a painting. There is a statue in every stone; but what matters it, if only the brooding sculptor sees it? A cataract, a sunset, a triumph, a poetic atmosphere, or mood, or effect,—none of these is a poem. When Emerson and Miss Fuller went together to see Fanny Elssler dance, and the philosopher whispered to the sibyl, "Margaret, this is poetry!" and the sibyl rejoined, "Waldo, it is religion!" they both, I take it, would have confessed with Hosea that they had used similitudes. We are now considering the palpable results of inspiration. Poetry houses it-

---

[6] "true passion."

[7] Michelangelo (1475-1564), Italian sculptor, painter, architect, and poet.

[8] The Pre-Raphaelite group was formed in 1848 and consisted of D. G. Rossetti, W. Holman Hunt, John Millais, Thomas Woolner, Walter Deverell, James Collinson, and W. M. Rossetti. Characteristics of Pre-Raphaelitism were a devotion to religious, medieval, and romantic themes, a painstaking representationalism, and the use of vivid color. The movement was most influential in painting and poetry.

self in *words*, sung, spoken, or inscribed, though there is a fine discrimination in the opening sentence of Ben Jonson's Grammar, which declares of language that "the writing [of it] is but an accident."

Language is colloquial and declarative in our ordinary speech, and on its legs for common use and movement. Only when it takes wings does it become poetry. As the poet, touched by emotion, rises to enthusiasm and imaginative power or skill, his speech grows *rhythmic*, and thus puts on the attribute that distinguishes it from every other mode of artistic expression—the guild-mark which, rightly considered, establishes the nature of the thing itself. At this date there is small need to descant upon the universality of rhythm in all relations of force and matter, nor upon its inherent consonance with the lightest, the profoundest, sensations of the living soul. Let us accept the wisdom of our speculative age, which scrutinizes all phenomena and reaches the scientific bases of experience, and, looking from nadir to zenith, acknowledges a psychological impulse behind every physical function. The earliest observers saw that life was rhythmical, that man and brute are the subjects of recurrent touch, sensation, order, and are alike responsive to measured sound, the form of rhythm most obvious and recognizable; that music, for instance, affects the most diverse animate genera, from the voiceless insect and serpent to the bird with its semi-vocal melody, and the man whom it incites to speech and song. The ancients no less comprehended the rhythm of air and water, the multitudinous harmonies, complex and blended, of ocean surges and wind-swept pines. But our new empiricism, following where intuition leads the way, comprehends the function of *vibrations*: it perceives that every movement of matter, seized upon by universal force, is *vibratory*; that vibrations, and nothing else, convey through the body the look and voice of nature to the soul; that thus alone can one incarnate individuality address its fellow; that, to use old Bunyan's imagery, these vibrations knock at the ear-gate, and are visible to the eye-gate, and are sentient at the gates of touch of the living temple. The word describing their action is in evidence: they "thrill" the body, they thrill the soul, both of which respond with subjective, interblending vibrations, according to the keys, the wave-lengths, of their excitants.

Thus it is absolutely true that what Buxton Forman calls "idealized language," that is, speech which is imaginative and rhythmical, goes with emotional thought; and that words exert a mysterious and potent influence, thus chosen and assorted, beyond their normal meanings. Equally true it is that natural poets in sensitive moods have this gift of choice and rhythmic assortment, just as a singer is born with voice and ear, or a painter with a knack of drawing likenesses before he can read or write. It is not too much to say that if not born with this endowment he is not a poet: a poetic nature, if you choose,—indeed, often more good, pure, intellectual, even more sensitive, than another with the "gift,"—and, again, one who in time by practice may excel in rhythmical mechanism him that has the gift but slights it; nevertheless, over and over again, not a born poet, not of the royal breed that by warrant roam the sacred groves.

I lay stress upon this, because, in an age of economics and physics and prose fiction, the fashion is to slight the special distinction of poetry and to deprecate its supremacy by divine right, and to do this as our democracy reduces kingcraft—through extending its legitimate range. You cannot force artists, architects, musicians, to submit to such a process, for material dividing lines are too obvious. Otherwise, some would undoubtedly make the attempt. But poetic vibrations are impalpable to the carnal touch, and unseen by the bodily eye, so that every realist, according to his kind, either discredits them or lays claim to them. All the same, nothing ever has outrivaled or ever will outrival, as a declaration of the specific quality of poetry, the assertion that its makers do

> "feed on thoughts, that *voluntary* move
> Harmonious numbers;"

and the minstrel poet, of my acceptation, "lisped in numbers" as an infant —and well does the hackneyed verse reiterate, "for the numbers came."

Aside from the vibratory mission of rhythm, its little staff of adjuvants, by the very discipline and limitations which they impose, take poetry out of the place of common speech, and make it an art which lifts the hearer to its own unusual key. Schiller[9] writes to Goethe that "rhythm, in a dramatic work, treats all characters and all situations according to one law. . . . In this manner it forms the atmosphere for the poetic creation. The more material part is left out, for only what is spiritual can be borne by this thin element." In real, that is, spontaneous minstrelsy, the fittest assonance, consonance, time, even rhyme,—if rhyme be invoked, and rhyme has been aptly called "both a memory and a hope,"—come of themselves with the imaginative thought. The soul may conceive unconsciously, and, as I believe in spite of certain metaphysicians, without the use of language; but when the wire is put up, the true and only words—just so far as the conception is true and clear and the minstrel's gift coequal—are flashed along it. Such is the test of genuineness, the underlying principle being that the masterful words of all poetic tongues are for the most part in both their open and consonantal sounds related to their meanings, so that with the inarticulate rhythm of impassioned thought we have a correspondent verbal rhythm for its vehicle. The whole range of poetry which is vital, from the Hebrew psalms and prophecies, in their original text and in our great English version, to the Georgian lyrics and romances and the Victorian idyls, confirms the statement of Mill[10] that "the deeper the feeling, the more characteristic and decided the rhythm." The rapture of the poet governs the tone and accent of his

> "high and passionate thoughts
> To their own music chanted."

Whoever, then, chooses to exempt poetry from this affinity with rhythm is not considering the subject-matter of these discourses. Not that I would

[9] Johann Schiller (1759–1805), German poet and dramatist.
[10] James Mill (1773–1836), British critic and philosopher.

magnify its office, or lessen the claims of other forms of imaginative and emotional expression. "The glory of the celestial is one, and the glory of the terrestrial is another. . . . There is one glory of the sun, and another glory of the moon." Nor do I ask you, with the Scripture, to set one above the other: count them of equal rank, if you like,—as in truth they seem to be in a time which has produced not only "In Memoriam," "Pippa Passes," "The Problem," but also "A Tale of Two Cities," "Henry Esmond," ".The Scarlet Letter,"—but count them as *different*. Of one thing I am assured, that every recognized poet will claim the vitality of this difference—a professional claim, without doubt, but not as though made by a lawyer or a divine, since their professions are more arbitrary and acquired. I confess that natural aptitude justifies in a measure the expressions "a born lawyer," "a born doctor," etc.; still, more of what we call professional skill is obtained by training than by derivation. The reverse of this is true of minstrelsy, and thus it chances that for a thousand excellent lawyers you shall not discover one superior poet.

It is not essential now, when the trick of making clever verse is practised, like all the minor technics of decoration, music, and so on, by many more or less cultured persons with a talent for mimicry, to discuss historic forms of measure, and to show why rhythm is not confined to any formal measures rhymed or unrhymed. Yet even rhyme, in our tongue, has advantages apart from its sound, when so affluent and strong a workman as Browning uses it in some of his most extended poems as a brake on the whirl and rush of an over-productive genius. All the varied potencies of rhythm,—its trinity of time-beat, consonance, and assonance, its repetends and refrains and accidental wandering melodies and surprises,—are the vibrations of the poetic fervor made manifest, and the poet's conveyance of it to his listeners.

Now, we have seen that the term poetry was long applied to all imaginative literature. I recognize the fact that the portion of it which was only germinal with the ancients, but is the chief characteristic of our modern age, the prose tale or romance,—that this, our prose fiction, is equally a part of the feigned history celebrated by Plato and Bacon and Sidney,[11] of the thing creatively invented rather than of things debated or recorded. It is often imbued with the true spirit of poesy, and is almost always more original in plot, narrative, structure, than its sister art. It well may supply the topic for a series of discourses. Among the brilliant romancers and novelists are not a few who, were not fiction the dominant mode of our time, would possibly have wreaked their thoughts upon expression in rhythmical form. But to see how distinct a thing it is, and also to illustrate my belief that a dramatic poet may as well not originate his own narrative or plot, read a story of Boccaccio[12] or a chronicle by Holinshead,[13] and then the play of

[11] Cf. Plato's *Ion* and *Republic*, X; Bacon's *Advancement of Learning*; Sidney's *Defence of Poesy.*

[12] Giovanni Boccaccio (1313-1375), Italian writer and poet, some of whose tales were used by Shakespeare as a basis for some of his plays.

[13] English chronicler (d. about 1580). His *Chronicles* were the source of Shakespeare's history plays.

Shakespeare's moulded upon it. The masterly novelist, the better to control his plot and to reflect life as it is, keeps his personal emotion within such command that it fails to become rhythmical. Where it gets the better of him, and he breaks into blank verse or singsong, his work is infallibly weakened; it may catch the vulgar ear, but is distinctly less enduring. Who now can abide the tricky metrical flow of certain sentimental passages in Dickens? And Dickens, by the way,—nature's own child and marvellous, as in truth he was,—occasionally set himself to write poetic verse, but he knew no trick of it, and could acquire none. His lyrics were mostly commonplace. This was to be expected, for a real poet usually writes good prose, and rarely rhythmical prose as prose, though he may elect, with Macpherson,[14] Blake, Tourgenieff,[15] Emerson, and Whitman, to cast his poetry in rhythmical prose form. Thackeray, who was a charming poet, of a light but distinct quality above which he was too genuine to venture, put no metrics into his novels. See how definite the line between the prose and the verse of Milton, Goethe, Landor, Coleridge, or Bryon. Of Emerson I have said elsewhere that his prose was poetry, and his poetry light and air. There is a class of writers, of much account in their day, whose native or purposed confusion between rhythmical and true prose attracts by its glamour, and whom their own generation, at least, can ill spare. Of such was Richter,[16] and such in a measure have been De Quincey, Wilson,[17] Carlyle, and even Ruskin, each after his kind. The strong personality of a writer forces its way. But it is to be noted that these after a time fall into distrust, as if the lasting element of true art had somehow escaped them. Certain latter-day lights well might take a lesson from the past. These illuminati leave firm ground, but do they rise to the upper air? There is something eerie and unsubstantial about them as they flit in a moonlit limbo between earth and sky. Howbeit, they are what they are, and may safely plead that it is more to be what they can be than not to be at all. The difference betwixt poetical prose and the prose of a poet is exemplified by Mark Pattison's [18] citation of the two at their best—the prose of Jeremy Taylor [19] and that of Milton, the former "loaded with imagery on the outside," but the latter "colored by imagination from within."

In short, although throughout our survey, and especially in the Orient, the most imaginative poetry often chants itself in rhythmic prose, the less rhythm there is in the prose of an essayist or novelist the better, even though it characterizes an interlude. As a drop of prosaic feeling is said to precipitate a whole poem, so a drop of sentimental rhythm will bring a limpid tale or essay to cloudy effervescence. As for eloquence, which also

---

[14] James Macpherson (1736–1796), Scottish poet, collector of the supposed Ossianic poems.

[15] Ivan Turgenev (1818–1883), Russian novelist.

[16] Jean Paul Richter (1763–1825), German author.

[17] John Wilson (1785–1854), British critic, contributor to *Blackwood's Magazine* under the name of Christopher North.

[18] Mark Pattison (1813–1884), English scholar and clergyman, author of the *Life of John Milton* (1879).

[19] Jeremy Taylor (1613–1667), English theologian and preacher, noted for his fine baroque style.

was classed with poetry by our ancestors, and which is subjective and passionate, I do not say that it may not rise by borrowing wings; but in a
poem the force and eloquence pure and simple cannot be prolonged without lessening ideality and the subtlest quality of all,—suggestiveness,—and
rhetoric is as false a note as didacticism in the poet's fantasia.

It is worth while to observe, in passing, that there never was a time
before our own in literary history when more apparent successes, more
curious and entertaining works, were achieved by determined and sincere
aspirants who enter, not through original bent, but under gradual training
and "of malice aforethought," fields to which they are not born inheritors,—the joint domains of poetry and prose fiction. Their output deceives
even the critic, because it does serve a purpose, until he reflects that none
of it is really a force,—really something new, originative, enduring. Such
a force was that of Fielding, of Byron, of Scott, of Keats, of Wordsworth,
of Browning; and many lesser but fresh and natural poets and novelists are
forces in their several degrees. What they produce, from its individual,
often revolutionary, quality, is an actual addition to literature. But we see
natural critics and moralists, persons of learning, of high cultivation in
the focal centres of literary activity, who develop what *is* inborn with
them—an exquisite gift of appreciation, and in time a stalwart purpose to
rival the poets and novelists on their own ground. This they undertake at
that mature age when the taste and judgment are fully ripe, and after admirable service as scholars, essayists, and the like. Now, there scarcely is
an instance, in the past, of a notable poet or romancer who did not begin,
however late, by producing poetry or fiction, however crude, and this
whether or not he afterward made excursions into the fields of analysis
or history or aesthetics. Mr. Howells is a living illustration of this natural
process. He began as a poet, and then, after excursions into several literary
fields that displayed his humor, taste, and picturesqueness, he caught the
temper of his period as a novelist, and helped to lead it. The cleverness
and occasional "hits" of various self-elected poets and tale-writers are,
however, noteworthy, even bewildering. At this moment many who command public attention and what is called the professional market have
previously demonstrated that their natural bent was that of didactic and
analytic, rather than of emotional and creative writers. Their success has
been a triumph of culture, intellect, and will power. These instances, as I
have said of an eminent poet and essayist now no more, almost falsify the
adage that a poet is born, not made. Still, we bear in mind that precisely
analogous conditions obtain in the cognate artistic professions,—in painting, music, architecture. The poets and novelists by cultivation, despite
their apparent vogue in the most extended literary market the world
has ever seen, and ambitious as their work may be, lack, in my opinion, the
one thing needed to create a permanent force in the arts, and that is the
predestined call by nature and certain particles of her "sacred fire."

We need not enter the poet's workshop and analyze the physics and philosophy controlling the strings of his lyre. That a philosophical law underlies each cadence, every structural arrangement, should be known in this

very spot, if anywhere, where not alone the metrics and phonetics, and what has been called the rationale, of verse, but therewithal the spirit of the poetry of the East, of our classical antiquity, of the Romance tongues, of the Norse, and of our own composite era, are in the air, one may say, and are debated with a learning and enthusiasm for which a few of us, in my own academic days, hungered in vain. Here, too, it was that the most analytic treatise ever conceived, upon the technics of rhythmical effect, was written by your own poet, Lanier,[20] for whom the sister-spirits of Music and Poesy contended with a rivalry as strong as that between "twin daughters of one race," both loving, and both worshipped by, one whom death too soon removed while he strove to perfect their reconciliation. Though poetry must come by the first intention, if at all, and inspiration laughs at technical processes, even the unlettered minstrel conforms to law, as little conscious of it as some vireo in the bush is conscious of the score by which a Burroughs or an Olive Miller transfers the songster's tirra-lirra to the written page.[21] The point remains that poetry is ideal expression through words, and that words are not poetry unless they reach a stress that is *rythmical*. Painting is a mode of expression, being visible color and shadow distributed upon a material surface; the language of poetry is another mode, because it is *articulate* thought and feeling. Sidney pointed merely to the fact that rhythm is not confined to verse, when he spoke of "apparelled verse" as "an ornament, and no cause to poetry, since there have been many most excellent poets that never have versified"; and he added that "now swarm many versifiers that need never answer to the name of poet." Wordsworth's familiar recognition of "the poets that ne'er have penned their inspiration" was a just surmise; but such a poet is one *in posse*,[22] assuredly not *in esse*,[23] not a maker. Swinburne traverses the passage with a bit of common sense—"There is no such thing as a dumb poet or a handless painter. The essence of an artist is that he should be articulate."

Submitting these views with respect to a scientific definition of poetry, I ask your attention to a brief consideration of its bounds and liberties, as compared with those of music and the respective arts of design.

The specific province, by limitation, of Sculpture, the art consecrated to the antique precision of repose, is to express ideals of form *arrested as to movement and time*. Its beauteous or heroic attitudes are caught at the one fit moment, and forever transfixed in rigid stone or wood or metal. Painting has an additional limitation; it gives only the *similitude* of form in all its dimensions, and only from one point of a beholder's view. To offset this, the range of the painter is marvellously broadened by the truth of perspective, the magic and vital potency of color, the tremulous life of atmosphere, and the infinite gradations and contrasts of light and shade.

---

[20] The reference is to Sidney Lanier's (1842–1881) *The Science of English Verse* (1880).
[21] John Burroughs (1837–1921) and Olive Miller (1831–1918) were American naturalists and authors of books on birds.
[22] "in potentiality"
[23] "in being"

The mystical warmth and force of the Christian humanities are radiant in this enrapturing art. Yet its office is to capture the one ideal moment, the lifelong desire of Faust, and to force it to obey the mandate:—

"Ah, still delay—thou art so fair!"

Such are the arts addressed to the eye alone, both of them lending their service to the earliest, the latest, the most various, of all material constructions—Architecture, whose pediments and roofs and walls originate in our bodily necessities, whose pinnacles typify our worship and aspiration, and which so soon becomes the beneficiary and the incasement of its decorative allies. None of the three can directly express time or movement, but there is practically no limit to their voiceless representation of space and multitude.

But movement in time is a special function of Music, that heavenly maid, never so young as now, and still the sovereign of the passions, reaching and rousing the soul through sound-vibrations perpetually changing as they flow. To this it adds the sympathetic force of harmonic counterpoint. Its range, then, is freer than that of the plastic and structural arts, by this element of progressive change. Under its spell, thrilling with the sensations which it can excite, and which really are immanent in our own nature, considering moreover the superb mathematics of its harmony, and again that it has been the last in development of all these arts, we question whether it is not only superior to them but even to that one to which these lectures are devoted. All feel, at least, the force of Poe's avowal that music and poetry at their highest must go together, because "in music the soul most nearly attains the great end for which it struggles,—supernal beauty." And so old John Davies,[24] in praise of music,—

"The motion which the ninefold sacred quire
Of angels make: the bliss of all the blest,
Which (next the Highest) most fills the highest desire."

Schopenhauer[25] thought that the musician, because there is no sound in nature fit to give him more than a suggestion for a model, "approaches the original sources of existence more closely than all other artists, nay, even than Nature herself." Herbert Spencer[26] has suggested that music may take rank as the highest of the fine arts, as the chief medium of sympathy, enabling us to partake the feeling which excites it, and "as an aid to the achievement of that higher happiness which it indistinctly shadows forth." And in truth, if the intercourse of a higher existence is to be effected through sound-vibrations rather than through the swifter light-waves, or by means of aught save the absolute celestial insight, one may fondly conceive music to be the language of the earth-freed, as of those imagined seraphim with whom feeling is "deeper than all thought."

[24] English poet (1569-1626).
[25] Arthur Schopenhauer (1788-1860), German philosopher and man of letters.
[26] English philosopher (1820-1903).

Consider, on the other hand, how feeling governs the simple child, "that lightly draws its breath," while thought begins its office as the child grows in strength and knowledge, and it is a fair inference that thought is the higher attribute, and that the suggestion of emotion by music is a less vital art than that of intellectual speech. The dumb brutes partake far more of man's emotion than of his mental intelligence. Neither is music— despite our latter-day theorists who defy the argument of Lessing's[27] Laocoön and would make one art usurp the province of another, and despite its power as an indirect incentive to thought by rousing the emotions —a vehicle for the conveyance of precise and varied ideas. The clearer the idea, the more exact the language which utters and interprets it. This, then, is the obvious limitation of music: it can traverse a range of feeling that may govern the tone of the hearer's contemplations, it can "fill all the stops of life with tuneful breath" and prolong their harmonic intervals indefinitely, but the domain of absolute *thought*, while richer and more imperial for its excitation, is not mastered by it. Of that realm music can make no exact chart.

Thus far, we have no art without its special office, and none that is not wanting in some capacity displayed by one or more of the rest. Each goes upon its appointed way. Now comes poetry,—rhythmical, creative language, compact of beauty, imagination, passion, truth,—in no wise related, like the plastic arts, to material substance; less able than its associate, music, to move the soul with those dying falls of sound that increase and lessen thought and the power to harbor it; almost a voiceless spirit of invention, working without hands, yet the more subtile, potent, inclusive, for this evasive ideality, and for creations that are impalpable except through the arbitrary and non-essential symbols by which it now addresses itself to the educated eye.

Permit me to select, almost at random, from Keats and Tennyson, ready illustrations of the bounds and capabilities of the various arts—passages necessarily familiar, since they *are* from Keats and Tennyson, but chosen from those masters because, of all English poets since Spenser, they are most given to picture-making, to the craft that is, as we say, artistic, picturesque. A stanza from the "Ode on a Grecian Urn" describes, and rivals in verse, the ravishing power of a bit of sculpture to perpetuate arrested form and attitude—yes, even the suggestion of arrested music:—

> "Heard melodies are sweet, but those unheard
>   Are sweeter; therefore, ye soft pipes, play on—
> Not to the sensual ear, but, more endear'd,
>   Pipe to the spirit ditties of no tone.
> Fair youth, beneath the trees, thou canst not leave
>   Thy song, nor ever can those trees be bare;
> Bold lover, never, never canst thou kiss,
>   Though winning near the goal; yet, do not grieve—
> She cannot fade, though thou hast not thy bliss;
>   Forever wilt thou love, and she be fair."

[27] Gotthold Lessing (1729-1781), German dramatist and critic. The *Laocoön* was published in 1766.

These undying lines not only define by words the power and limits of the sculptor, but are almost a matchless example of the farthest encroachment poetry can make upon sculpture's own province.* What it cannot do is to combine the details of the carving so as to produce them to the mind, as sculpture does to the eye, at a single instant of time. It lingers exquisitely upon each in succession. Progressive time is required for its inclusion of the effects of a Grecian frieze or scroll. Now, take from Tennyson's lovely but lighter poem, "The Day-Dream,"—a lyrical idyl at the acme of melodious and fanciful picture-making,—a stanza which seems to match with a certain roundness and color the transfixing effect of the painter's handiwork. It portrays a group entranced by the spell that has doomed to a hundred years of abeyance and motionlessness the life of the king's palace and the Sleeping Beauty. In the poems of Keats and Tennyson, as I say, artists find their sculptures and paintings already designed for them, so that these poets are the easiest of all to illustrate with some measure of adequacy. The theme of the following lines, rendered by a painter, would show the whole group and scene at a flash of the eye; poetry cannot do this, yet, aided by its moving panorama, the listener has painted all in his mind when the last word is uttered:—

"More like a picture seemeth all
Than those old portraits of old kings,
That watch the sleepers from the wall.

"Here sits the butler with a flask
Between his knees, half-drain'd; and there
The wrinkled steward at his task,
The maid-of-honor blooming fair;
The page has caught her hand in his:
Her lips are sever'd as to speak:
His own are pouted to a kiss:
The blush is fix'd upon her cheek."

It is to be noted, as we read, that Tennyson's personages, and those of Keats as well, are mostly conventional figures, as characterless as those on a piece of tapestry. The genius of neither poet is preferably dramatic: they do not get at individuality by dramatic insight like Shakespeare, nor by monodramatic soliloquy and analysis, like the strenuous Browning. Their dramas are for the most part masques containing *eidullia* (little pictures); though who can doubt that Keats, had he lived, would have developed the highest dramatic power? Remember what the less sensuous, more lyrical Shelley achieved in "The Cenci," when only four years beyond the age at which Keats imagined his "gold Hyperion, lovelorn Porphyro." But, to resume, see what poetry, in addition to the foregoing

* Since the first appearance of this lecture I have seen a finely penetrative essay by Mr. J. W. Comyns Carr (*The new Quarterly Magazine*, October, 1875), in which this same Ode is quoted to illustrate the ideal calm sought for by "The Artistic Spirit in Modern Poetry." As no better example can be found, in conveyance of the poetic and the plastic methods respectively, I do not hesitate to retain it. [Stedman's note]

counterfeit of the painter's ocular presentment, can bring about in its own field through its faculty of *movement in time*—a power entirely wanting to the arts which it has just mimicked. Note how it breaks the spell of transfixed attitude, of breathless color and suspended action; how it lets loose the torrents of Life at the instant of the "fated fairy prince's" experimental kiss:—

> "A touch, a kiss! the charm was snapt.
>   There rose a noise of striking clocks,
> And feet that ran, and doors that clapt,
>   And barking dogs, and crowing cocks;
>
> A fuller light illumined all,
>   A breeze thro' all the garden swept,
> A sudden hubbub shook the hall,
>   And sixty feet the fountain leapt.
>
> .   .   .   .
>
> The maid and page renew'd their strife,
>   The palace bang'd, and buzz'd, and clackt,
> And all the long-pent stream of life
>   Dash'd downward in a cataract.

That is the stream which the painter has no art to undam. Only by a succession of pictures can he suggest its motion or follow the romance to its sequel; and that he can do even this with some fitness in the case of a Tennysonian ballad is because the laureate, as we see, counterfeits the painter's own method more artistically than other idyllists of rank in our time. If art is the fit and beautiful conformation of matter infused with the spirit of man, it must indeed have life. The most nimble, ardent, varied transfer of the vital spirit is by means of language, and of all language that of the poet is the most alive and expressive. Observe, again, that in what are called art circles—Arcadian groups of those devoted to art and letters— the imaginative writers are apt to interest themselves far more with respect to the plastic arts than the sculptors and painters with respect to poetry and romance; and well they may, since the poet enriches his work by using all artistic effects, while nothing is more dangerous to a painter, for example, than that he should give his picture a literary cast, as the phrase is, and make it too closely tell a story or rehearse a poem. This of itself tends to confirm Lessing's apothegm that "the poet is as far beyond the painter as life is better than a picture."

The conquests of poetry, in fine, are those of pure intelligence, and of emotion that is unfettered. Like the higher mathematics, it is not dependent on diagrams, for the mind to which it appeals is a responsive draughtsman of lines finer and more complex than any known to brush or graver. It creates no beauty of form beyond the accidental symbols grouped in script and print, none of light and color, while the ear is less touched by it than by the melodies or harmonies of music; for its melody is that of flexible speech, and it knows not counterpoint, but must resort to the value of successive strains. Yet we say that it has form and outline of its own, an architecture of its own, its own warmth and color, and, like music, life, and withal no little of music's vocal charm, in that through words it idealizes these "sweet influences," and is chartered to convey them all to the inward sight, the spiritual hearing, of the citadeled soul, with so apt suggestion that the poet's fellow-mortals, of like passions and perceptions with himself, see and hear and feel with much of his distinct individuality. Its vibrations excite the reflex action that creates in the mind of the receiver a vision corresponding to the imagination of the poet. Here is its specific eminence: it enables common mortals to think as the poet thinks, to use his wings, move through space and time, and out of space and time, untrammelled as the soul itself; it can feel, moan, weep, laugh, be eloquent, love, hate, aspire, for all—and with its maker; can reflect, and know, and ever seek for knowledge; can portray all times and seasons, and describe, express, interpret, the hiddenmost nature of man. Through poetry soul addresses soul without hindrance, by the direct medium of speech. Words are its atmosphere and very being: language, which raises man above the speechless intelligences; which, with resources of pitch, cadence, time, tone, and universal rhythm, is in a sense a more advanced and complex music than music itself—that idealized language which, as it ever has been the earliest form of emotional expression, appears almost a gift captured in man's infancy from some "imperial palace whence he came." To the true poet, then, we say, like the bard to Israfel:—

> "The ecstasies above
>   With thy burning measures suit—
> Thy grief, thy joy, thy hate, thy love,
>   With the fervor of thy lute—
>   Well may the stars be mute."

HAMLIN GARLAND

From CRUMBLING IDOLS [1]

(1894)

LOCAL COLOR IN ART

LOCAL COLOR in fiction is demonstrably the life of fiction. It is the native element, the differentiating element. It corresponds to the endless and vital charm of individual peculiarity. It is the differences which interest us; the similarities do not please, do not forever stimulate and feed as do the differences. Literature would die of dry rot if it chronicled the similarities only, or even largely.

Historically, the local color of a poet or dramatist is of the greatest value. The charm of Horace is the side light he throws on the manners and customs of his time. The vital in Homer lies, after all, in his local color, not in his abstractions. Because the sagas of the North delineate more exactly how men and women lived and wrought in those days, therefore they have always appealed to me with infinitely greater power than Homer.

Similarly, it is the local color of Chaucer that interests us to-day. We yawn over his tales of chivalry which were in the manner of his contemporaries, but the Miller and the Priest interest us. Wherever the man of the past in literature showed us what he really lived and loved, he moves us. We understand him, and we really feel an interest in him.

Historically, local color has gained in beauty and suggestiveness and humanity from Chaucer down to the present day. Each age has embodied more and more of its actual life and social conformation until the differentiating qualities of modern art make the best paintings of Norway as distinct in local color as its fiction is vital and indigenous.

Every great moving literature to-day is full of local color. It is this element which puts the Norwegian and Russian almost at the very summit of modern novel writing,[2] and it is the comparative lack of this distinctive flavor which makes the English and French take a lower place in truth and sincerity.

Everywhere all over the modern European world, men are writing novels and dramas as naturally as the grass or corn or flax grows. The Provençal, the Hun, the Catalonian, the Norwegian, is getting a hearing.[3] This literature is not the literature of scholars; it is the literature of lovers and

[1] Chicago, 1894.
[2] It is probable that Garland is referring to the work of the Norwegian Björnstjerne Björnson (1832–1910) and the Russian Ivan Turgenev (1818–1883), two of the best-known novelists of the latter part of the nineteenth century.
[3] Rather widespread regionalism in Europe preceded and paralleled that in America. Representative of this movement would be the poetry of the Provençal Frédéric Mistral (1830–1914), of the Hungarian János Arany (1817–1882), and the plays of the Catalonian Ángel Guimerá (1847–1924).

doers; of men who love the modern and who have not been educated to despise common things.

These men are speaking a new word. They are not hunting themes, they are struggling to express.

Conventional criticism does not hamper or confine them. They are rooted in the soil. They stand among the corn-fields and they dig in the peat-bogs. They concern themselves with modern and very present words and themes, and they have brought a new word which is to divide in half the domain of beauty.

They have made art the re-creation of the beautiful *and the significant*. Mere beauty no longer suffices. Beauty is the world-old aristocrat who has taken for mate this mighty young plebeian Significance. Their child is to be the most human and humane literature ever seen.

It has taken the United States longer to achieve independence of English critics than it took to free itself from old-world political and economic rule. Its political freedom was won, not by its gentlemen and scholars, but by its yeomanry; and in the same way our national literature will come in its fulness when the common American rises spontaneously to the expression of his concept of life.

The fatal blight upon most American art has been, and is to-day, its imitative quality, which has kept it characterless and factitious,—as forced rose-culture rather than the free flowering of native plants.

Our writers despised or feared the home market. They rested their immortality upon the "universal theme," which was a theme of no interest to the public and of small interest to themselves.

During the first century and a half, our literature had very little national color. It was quite like the utterance of corresponding classes in England. But at length Bryant and Cooper felt the influence of our mighty forests and prairies. Whittier uttered something of New England boy-life, and Thoreau prodded about among newly discovered wonders, and the American literature got its first start.

Under the influence of Cooper came the stories of wild life from Texas, from Ohio, and from Illinois. The wild, rough settlements could not produce smooth and cultured poems or stories; they only furnished forth rough-and-ready anecdotes, but in these stories there were hints of something fine and strong and native.

As the settlements increased in size, as the pressure of the forest and the wild beast grew less, expression rose to a higher plane; men softened in speech and manner. All preparations were being made for a local literature raised to the level of art.

The Pacific slope was first in the line. By the exceptional interest which the world took in the life of the gold fields, and by the forward urge which seems always to surprise the pessimist and the scholiast, two young men were plunged into that wild life, led across the plains set in the shadow of Mount Shasta, and local literature received its first great marked, decided impetus.[4]

[4] It would seem that Garland is referring to Bret Harte (1836–1902) and Joaquin Miller (1841?–1913).

To-day we have in America, at last, a group of writers who have no suspicion of imitation laid upon them. Whatever faults they may be supposed to have, they are at any rate, themselves. American critics can depend upon a characteristic American literature of fiction and the drama from these people.

The corn has flowered, and the cotton-boll has broken into speech.

Local color—what is it? It means that the writer spontaneously reflects the life which goes on around him. It is natural and unstrained art.

It is, in a sense, unnatural and artificial to find an American writing novels of Russia or Spain or the Holy Land. He cannot hope to do it so well as the native. The best he can look for is that poor word of praise, "He does it very well, considering he is an alien."

If a young writer complain that there are no themes at home, that he is forced to go abroad for prospective and romance, I answer there is something wrong in his education or his perceptive faculty. Often he is more anxious to win a money success than to be patiently one of art's unhurried devotees.

I can sympathize with him, however, for criticism has not helped him to be true. Criticism of the formal kind and spontaneous expression are always at war, like the old man and the youth. They may politely conceal it, but they are mutually destructive.

Old men naturally love the past; the books they read are the masterpieces; the great men are all dying off, they say; the young man should treat lofty and universal themes, as they used to do. These localisms are petty. These truths are disturbing. Youth annoys them. Spontaneousness is formlessness, and the criticism that does not call for the abstract and the ideal and the beautiful is leading to destruction, these critics say.

And yet there is a criticism which helps, which tends to keep a writer at his best; but such criticism recognizes the dynamic force of a literature, and tries to spy out tendencies. This criticism to-day sees that local color means national character, and is aiding the young writer to treat his themes in the best art.

I assert it is the most natural thing in the world for a man to love his native land and his native, intimate surroundings. Born into a web of circumstances, enmeshed in common life, the youthful artist begins to think. All the associations of that childhood and the love-life of youth combine to make that web of common affairs, threads of silver and beads of gold; the near-at-hand things are the dearest and sweetest after all.

As the reader will see, I am using local color to mean something more than a forced study of the picturesque scenery of a State.

Local color in a novel means that it has such quality of texture and back-ground that it could not have been written in any other place or by any one else than a native.

It means a statement of life as indigenous as the plant-growth. It means that the picturesque shall not be seen by the author,—that every tree and bird and mountain shall be dear and companionable and necessary, not picturesque; the tourist cannot write the local novel.

From this it follows that local color must not be put in for the sake of local color. It must go in, it *will* go in, because the writer naturally carries it with him half unconsciously, or conscious only of its significance, its interest to him.

He must not stop to think whether it will interest the reader or not. He must be loyal to himself, and put it in because he loves it. If he is an artist, he will make his reader feel it through his own emotion.

What we should stand for is not universality of theme, but beauty and strength of treatment, leaving the writer to choose his theme because he loves it.

Here is the work of the critic. Recognizing that the theme is beyond his control, let him aid the young writer to delineate simply and with unwavering strokes. Even here the critic can do little, if he is possessed of the idea that the young writer of to-day should model upon Addison or Macaulay or Swift.

There are new criterions to-day in writing as in painting, and individual expression is the aim. The critic can do much to aid a young writer to *not* copy an old master or any other master. Good criticism can aid him to be vivid and simple and unhackneyed in his technique, the subject is his own affair.

I agree with him who says, Local art must be raised to the highest levels in its expression; but in aiding this perfection of technique we must be careful not to cut into the artist's spontaneity. To apply ancient dogmas of criticism to our life and literature would be benumbing to artist and fatal to his art.

The Local Novel

The local novel seems to be the heir-apparent to the kingdom of poesy. It is already the most promising of all literary attempts to-day; certainly it is the most sincere. It seems but beginning its work. It is "hopelessly contemporaneous;" that is its strength. It is (at its best) unaffected, natural, emotional. It is sure to become all-powerful. It will redeem American literature, as it has already redeemed the South from its conventional and highly wrought romanticism.

By reason of growing truth and sincerity the fiction of the South has risen from the dead. It is now in the spring season of shooting wilding plants and timorous blades of sown grains. Its future is assured. Its soil is fertilized with the blood of true men. Its women are the repositories of great, vital, sincere, emotional experiences which will inevitably appear in their children, and at last in art, and especially in fiction. The Southern people are in the midst of a battle more momentous than the Rebellion, because it is the result of the Rebellion; that is, the battle of intrenched privilege against the swiftly-spreading democratic idea of equality before the law and in the face of nature.

They have a terribly, mightily dramatic race-problem on their hands. The South is the meeting-place of winds. It is the seat of swift and almost incalculable change; and this change, this battle, this strife of invisible powers, is about to enter their fiction.

The negro has already entered it. He has brought a musical speech to his masters, and to the new fiction. He has brought a strange and pleading song into music. The finest writers of the New South already find him a never-failing source of interest. He is not, of course, the only subject of Southern fiction, nor even the principal figure; but he is a necessary part, and a most absorbingly interesting part.

The future of fiction in the South will also depict the unreconstructed rebel unreservedly, and the race-problem without hate or contempt or anger; for the highest art will be the most catholic in its sympathy. It will delineate vast contending forces, and it will be a great literature.

The negro will enter the fiction of the South, first, as subject; second, as artist in his own right. His first attempts will be imitative, but he will yet utter himself, as surely as he lives. He will contribute a poetry and a novel as peculiarly his own as the songs he sings. He may appear, also, in a strange half-song, half-chant, and possibly in a drama peculiar to himself; but in some form of fiction he will surely utter the sombre and darkly-florid genius for emotional utterance which characterizes him.

In the North the novel will continue local for some time to come. It will delineate the intimate life and speech of every section of our enormous and widely scattered republic. It will catch and fix in charcoal the changing, assimilating races, delineating the pathos and humor and the infinite drama of their swift adjustment to new conditions. California, New Mexico, Idaho, Utah, Oregon, each wonderful locality in our Nation of Nations will yet find its native utterance. The superficial work of the tourist and outsider will not do. The real novelist of these sections is walking behind the plow or trudging to school in these splendid potential environments.

This local movement will include the cities as well, and St. Louis, Chicago, San Francisco, will be delineated by artists born of each city, whose work will be so true that it could not have been written by any one from the outside. The real utterance of a city or a locality can only come when a writer is born out of its intimate heart. To such an one, nothing will be "strange" or "picturesque;" all will be familiar, and full of significance or beauty. The novel of the slums must be written by one who has played there as a child, and taken part in all its amusements; not out of curiosity, but out of pleasure seeking. It cannot be done from above nor from the outside. It must be done out of a full heart and without seeking for effect.

The artist should not look abroad to see how others are succeeding. Success does not always measure merit. It took nearly a third of a century for Whitman and Monet[5] to be recognized. The great artist never conforms. He does not trail after some other man's success. He works out his individual perception of things.

The contrast of city and country, everywhere growing sharper, will find its reflection in this local novel of the immediate future,—the same trag-

[5] Claude Monet (1840-1926), French painter and leader of the Impressionists.

edies and comedies, with the essential difference called local color, and taking place all over the land, wherever cities arise like fungi, unhealthy, yet absorbing as subjects of fictional art.

As I have elsewhere pointed out, the drama will join the novel in this study of local conditions. It will be derived from fiction, and in many cases the dramatist and novelist will be the same person. In all cases the sincerity of the author's love for his scenes and characters will find expression in tender care for truth, and there will be made to pass before our eyes wonderfully suggestive pictures of other lives and landscapes. The drama will grow in dignity and importance along these lines.

Both drama and novel will be colloquial. This does not mean that they will be exclusively in the dialects, but the actual speech of the people of each locality will unquestionably be studied more closely than ever before. Dialect is the life of a language, precisely as the common people of the nation form the sustaining power of its social life and art.

And so in the novel, in the short story, and in the drama—by the work of a multitude of loving artists, not by the work of an over-topping personality —will the intimate social, individual life of the nation be depicted. Before this localism shall pass away, such a study will have been made of this land and people as has never been made by any other age or social group,—a literature from the plain people, reflecting their unrestrained outlook on life, subtle in speech and color, humane beyond precedent, humorous, varied, simple in means, lucid as water, searching as sunlight.

To one who believes each age to be its own best interpreter, the idea of "decay of fiction" never comes. That which the absolutist takes for decay is merely change. The conservative fears change; the radical welcomes it. The conservative tries to argue that fundamentals cannot change; that they are the same yesterday, to-day, and tomorrow. If that were true, then a sorrowful outlook on the future would be natural. Such permanency would be death. Life means change.

As a matter of fact, the minute differentiations of literature which the conservative calls its non-essentials, are really its essentials. Vitality and growth are in these "non-essentials." It is the difference in characters, not their similarity, which is forever interesting. It is the subtle coloring individuality gives which vitalizes landscape art, and so it is the subtle differences in the interpretation of life which each age gives that vitalizes its literature and makes it its own.

The individuality of the artist is the saving grace of art; and landscape painting will not be fantastic so long as men study nature. It will never be mere reproduction so long as the artist represents it as he sees it. The fact will correct the fantasy. The artist will color the fact.

The business of the present is not to express fundamentals, but to sincerely present its own minute and characteristic interpretation of life. This point cannot be too often insisted upon. Unless a writer add something to the literature of his race, has he justification? Is there glory in imitation? Is the painter greatest who copies old masters, or is it more praiseworthy to embody an original conception? These are very important questions for the young artist.

To perceive the hopelessness of absolutism in literature, you have but to stop a moment to think. Admit that there are perfect models to which must be referred all subsequent writing, and we are committed to a barren round of hopeless imitations. The young writer is disheartened or drawn off into imitations, and ruined for any real expression. This way of looking at literature produced our Barlows and Coltons and Hillhouses,[6] with their "colossi of cotton-batting," and it produces blank-verse dramas to-day.

But the relativists in art are full of hope. They see that life is the model, —or, rather, that each man stands accountable to himself first, and to the perceived fact of life second. Life is always changing, and literature changes with it. It never decays; it changes. Poetry—that is to say *impassioned personal outlook on life*—is in no more danger of extinction to-day than in the days of Edmund Spenser. The American novel will continue to grow in truth to American life without regard to the form and spirit of the novel or drama of the past. Consciously or unconsciously, the point of view of the modern writer is that of the veritist, or truth stater.

Once out of the period of tutelage, it is natural for youth to overleap barriers. He naturally discards the wig and cloak of his grandfathers. He comes at last to reject, perhaps a little too brusquely, the models which conservatism regards with awe. He respects them as history, but he has life, abounding, fresh, contiguous life; life that stings and smothers and overwhelms and exalts, like the salt, green, snow-tipped ocean surf; life, with its terrors and triumphs, right here and now; its infinite drama, its allurement, its battle, and its victories. Life is the model, truth is the master, the heart of the man himself his motive power. The pleasure of re-creating in the image of nature is the artist's unfailing reward.

To him who sees that difference, not similarity, is the vitalizing quality, there is no sorrow at change. The future will take care of itself. In the space of that word "difference" lies all the infinite range of future art. Some elements are comparatively unchanging. The snow will fall, spring will come, men and women love, the stars will rise and set, and grass return again and again in vast rhythms of green, but society will not be the same.

The physical conformation of our nation will change. It will lose its wildness, its austerity. Its unpeopled plains will pass away, and gardens will bloom where the hot sand now drifts. Cities will rise where now the elk and the mountain lions are. Swifter means of transportation will bring the lives of different sections into closer relationship. It will tend to equalize intellectual opportunities. The physical and mental life of men and women will be changed, the relation of man to man, and man to woman, will change in detail, and the fiction of the future will express these changes.

To the veritist, therefore, the present is the vital theme. The past is dead, and the future can be trusted to look after itself. The young men and maidens of that time will find the stars of their present brighter than the

[6] Joel Barlow's (1754–1812) *The Columbiad* (1807), James A. Hillhouse's (1789–1841) *Hadad* (1825), and George Colton's (1818–1847) *Tecumseh* (1842) were all long, overambitious poems.

stars of '92, the people around them more absorbing than books, and their own outlook on life more reasonable than that of dead men. Their writing and painting, in proportion to its vitality and importance, will reflect this, their natural attitude, toward life and history.

MARK TWAIN

FENIMORE COOPER'S LITERARY OFFENSES [1]
(1895)

The Pathfinder and *The Deerslayer* stand at the head of Cooper's novels as artistic creations. There are others of his works which contain parts as perfect as are to be found in these, and scenes even more thrilling. Not one can be compared with either of them as a finished whole.

The defects in both of these tales are comparatively slight. They were pure works of art.—*Prof. Lounsbury.*

The five tales reveal an extraordinary fullness of invention.

. . . One of the very greatest characters in fiction, Natty Bumppo. . . .

The craft of the woodsman, the tricks of the trapper, all the delicate art of the forest, were familiar to Cooper from his youth up.—*Prof. Brander Matthews.*

Cooper is the greatest artist in the domain of romantic fiction yet produced by America.—*Wilkie Collins.*

It seems to me that it was far from right for the Professor of English Literature in Yale, the Professor of English Literature in Columbia, and Wilkie Collins to deliver opinions on Cooper's literature without having read some of it. It would have been much more decorous to keep silent and let persons talk who have read Cooper.

Cooper's art has some defects. In one place in *Deerslayer,* and in the restricted space of two-thirds of a page, Cooper has scored 114 offenses against literary art out of a possible 115. It breaks the record. There are nineteen rules governing literary art in the domain of romantic fiction—some say twenty-two. In *Deerslayer* Cooper violated eighteen of them. These eighteen require:

1. That a tale shall accomplish something and arrive somewhere. But the *Deerslayer* tale accomplishes nothing and arrives in the air.

2. They require that the episodes of a tale shall be necessary parts of the tale, and shall help to develop it. But as the *Deerslayer* tale is not a tale, and accomplishes nothing and arrives nowhere, the episodes have no rightful place in the work, since there was nothing for them to develop.

3. They require that the personages in a tale shall be alive, except in the case of corpses, and that always the reader shall be able to tell the corpses from the others. But this detail has often been overlooked in the *Deerslayer* tale.

[1] Published originally in the *North American Review,* CLXI (1895), 1-12.

4. They require that the personages in a tale, both dead and alive, shall exhibit a sufficient excuse for being there. But this detail also has been overlooked in the *Deerslayer* tale.

5. They require that when the personages of a tale deal in conversation, the talk shall sound like human talk, and be talk such as human beings would be likely to talk in the given circumstances, and have a discoverable meaning, also a discoverable purpose, and a show of relevancy, and remain in the neighborhood of the subject in hand, and be interesting to the reader, and help out the tale, and stop when the people cannot think of anything more to say. But this requirement has been ignored from the beginning of the *Deerslayer* tale to the end of it.

6. They require that when the author describes the character of a personage in his tale, the conduct and conversation of that personage shall justify said description. But this law gets little or no attention in the *Deerslayer* tale, as Natty Bumppo's case will amply prove.

7. They require that when a personage talks like an illustrated, gilt-edged, tree-calf, hand-tooled, seven-dollar Friendship Offering in the beginning of a paragraph, he shall not talk like a negro minstrel in the end of it. But this rule is flung down and danced upon in the *Deerslayer* tale.

8. They require that crass stupidities shall not be played upon the reader as "the craft of the woodsman, the delicate art of the forest," by either the author or the people in the tale. But this rule is persistently violated in the *Deerslayer* tale.

9. They require that the personages of a tale shall confine themselves to possibilities and let miracles alone; or, if they venture a miracle, the author must so plausibly set it forth as to make it look possible and reasonable. But these rules are not respected in the *Deerslayer* tale.

10. They require that the author shall make the reader feel a deep interest in the personages of his tale and in their fate; and that he shall make the reader love the good people in the tale and hate the bad ones. But the reader of the *Deerslayer* tale dislikes the good people in it, is indifferent to the others, and wishes they would all get drowned together.

11. They require that the characters in a tale shall be so clearly defined that the reader can tell beforehand what each will do in a given emergency. But in the *Deerslayer* tale this rule is vacated.

In addition to these large rules there are some little ones. These require that the author shall

12. *Say* what he is proposing to say, not merely come near it.

13. Use the right word, not its second cousin.

14. Eschew surplusage.

15. Not omit necessary details.

16. Avoid slovenliness of form.

17. Use good grammar.

18. Employ a simple and straightforward style.

Even these seven are coldly and persistently violated in the *Deerslayer* tale.

Cooper's gift in the way of invention was not a rich endowment; but such as it was he liked to work it, he was pleased with the effects, and indeed he did some quite sweet things with it. In his little box of stage-properties he kept six or eight cunning devices, tricks, artifices for his savages and woodsmen to deceive and circumvent each other with, and he was never so happy as when he was working these innocent things and seeing them go. A favorite one was to make a moccasined person tread in the tracks of the moccasined enemy, and thus hide his own trail. Cooper wore out barrels and barrels of moccasins in working that trick. Another stage-property that he pulled out of his box pretty frequently was his broken twig. He prized his broken twig above all the rest of his effects, and worked it the hardest. It is a restful chapter in any book of his when somebody doesn't step on a dry twig and alarm all the reds and whites for two hundred yards around. Every time a Cooper person is in peril, and absolute silence is worth four dollars a minute, he is sure to step on a dry twig. There may be a hundred handier things to step on, but that wouldn't satisfy Cooper. Cooper requires him to turn out and find a dry twig; and if he can't do it, go and borrow one. In fact, the Leatherstocking Series ought to have been called the Broken Twig Series.

I am sorry there is not room to put in a few dozen instances of the delicate art of the forest, as practised by Natty Bumppo and some of the other Cooperian experts. Perhaps we may venture two or three samples. Cooper was a sailor—a naval officer; yet he gravely tells us how a vessel, driving toward a lee shore in a gale, is steered for a particular spot by her skipper because he knows of an *undertow* there which will hold her back against the gale and save her. For just pure woodcraft, or sailorcraft, or whatever it is, isn't that neat? For several years Cooper was daily in the society of artillery, and he ought to have noticed that when a cannon-ball strikes the ground it either buries itself or skips a hundred feet or so; skips again a hundred feet or so—and so on, till finally it gets tired and rolls. Now in one place he loses some "females"—as he always calls women—in the edge of a wood near a plain at night in a fog, on purpose to give Bumppo a chance to show off the delicate art of the forest before the reader. These mislaid people are hunting for a fort. They hear a cannon-blast, and a cannon-ball presently comes rolling into the wood and stops at their feet. To the females this suggests nothing. The case is very different with the admirable Bumppo. I wish I may never know peace again if he doesn't strike out promptly and *follow the track* of that cannon-ball across the plain through the dense fog and find the fort. Isn't it a daisy? If Cooper had any real knowledge of Nature's ways of doing things, he had a most delicate art in concealing the fact. For instance: one of his acute Indian experts, Chingachgook (pronounced Chicago, I think), has lost the trail of a person he is tracking through the forest. Apparently that trail is hopelessly lost. Neither you nor I could ever have guessed out the way to find it. It was very different with Chicago. Chicago was not stumped for long. He turned a running stream out of its course, and there, in the slush in its old bed, were that person's moccasin tracks. The current did not wash them away, as it would have done in all other like cases—no, even the eternal laws of Nature have to vacate when Cooper wants to put up a delicate job of woodcraft on the reader.

We must be a little wary when Brander Matthews tells us that Cooper's books "reveal an extraordinary fullness of invention." As a rule, I am quite willing to accept Brander Matthews's literary judgments and applaud his lucid and graceful phrasing of them; but that particular statement needs to be taken with a few tons of salt. Bless your heart, Cooper hadn't any more invention than a horse; and I don't mean a high-class horse, either; I mean a clothes-horse. It would be very difficult to find a really clever "situation" in Cooper's books, and still more difficult to find one of any kind which he has failed to render absurd by his handling of it. Look at the episodes of "the caves"; and at the celebrated scuffle between Maqua and those others on the table-land a few days later; and at Hurry Harry's queer water-transit from the castle to the ark; and at Deerslayer's half-hour with his first corpse; and at the quarrel between Hurry Harry and Deerslayer later; and at—but choose for yourself; you can't go amiss.

If Cooper had been an observer his inventive faculty would have worked better; not more interestingly, but more rationally, more plausibly. Cooper's proudest creations in the way of "situations" suffer noticeably from the absence of the observer's protecting gift. Cooper's eye was splendidly inaccurate. Cooper seldom saw anything correctly. He saw nearly all things as through a glass eye, darkly. Of course a man who cannot see the commonest little every-day matters accurately is working at a disadvantage when he is constructing a "situation." In the *Deerslayer* tale Cooper has a stream which is fifty feet wide where it flows out of a lake; it presently narrows to twenty as it meanders along for no given reason, and yet when a stream acts like that it ought to be required to explain itself. Fourteen pages later the width of the brook's outlet from the lake has suddenly shrunk thirty feet, and become "the narrowest part of the stream." This shrinkage is not accounted for. The stream has bends in it, a sure indication that it has alluvial banks and cuts them; yet these bends are only thirty and fifty feet long. If Cooper had been a nice and punctilious observer he would have noticed that the bends were oftener nine hundred feet long than short of it.

Cooper made the exit of that stream fifty feet wide, in the first place, for no particular reason; in the second place, he narrowed it to less than twenty to accommodate some Indians. He bends a "sapling" to the form of an arch over this narrow passage, and conceals six Indians in its foliage. They are "laying" for a settler's scow or ark which is coming up the stream on its way to the lake; it is being hauled against the stiff current by a rope whose stationary end is anchored in the lake; its rate of progress cannot be more than a mile an hour. Cooper describes the ark, but pretty obscurely. In the matter of dimensions "it was little more than a modern canal-boat." Let us guess, then, that it was about one hundred and forty feet long. It was of "greater breadth than common." Let us guess, then, that it was about sixteen feet wide. This leviathan had been prowling down bends which were but a third as long as itself, and scraping between banks where it had only two feet of space to spare on each side. We cannot too much admire this miracle. A low-roofed log dwelling occupies "two-thirds of the ark's length,"—a dwelling ninety feet long and sixteen feet wide, let us say—a kind of vestibule train. The dwelling has two rooms—each forty-five feet long and sixteen feet wide, let us guess. One of them is the bedroom of the Hutter girls, Judith and Hetty; the other is the parlor in the day-time, at night it is papa's bedchamber. The ark is arriving at the stream's exit now, whose width has been reduced to less than twenty feet to accommodate the Indians—say to eighteen. There is a foot to spare on each side of the boat. Did the Indians notice that there was going to be a tight squeeze there? Did they notice that they could make money by climbing down out of that arched sapling and just stepping aboard when the ark scraped by? No, other Indians would have noticed these things, but Cooper's Indians never notice anything. Cooper thinks they are marvelous creatures for noticing, but he was almost always in error about his Indians. There was seldom a sane one among them.

The ark is one hundred and forty feet long; the dwelling is ninety feet long. The idea of the Indians is to drop softly and secretly from the arched sapling to the dwelling as the ark creeps along under it at the rate of a mile an hour, and butcher the family. It will take the ark a minute and a half to pass under. It will take the ninety-foot dwelling a minute to pass under. Now, then, what did the six Indians do? It would take you thirty years to guess, and even then you would have to give it up, I believe. Therefore, I will tell you what the Indians did. Their chief, a person of quite extraordinary intellect for a Cooper Indian, warily watched the canal-boat as it squeezed along under him, and when he had got his calculations fined down to exactly the right shade, as he judged, he let go and dropped. And *missed the house!* That is actually what he did. He missed the house, and landed in the stern of the scow. It was not much of a fall, yet it knocked him silly. He lay there unconscious. If the house had been ninety-seven feet long he would have made the trip. The fault was Cooper's, not his. The error lay in the construction of the house. Cooper was no architect.

There still remained in the roost five Indians. The boat has passed under and is now out of their reach. Let me explain what the five did—you would not be able to reason it out for yourself. No. 1 jumped for the boat, but fell in the water astern of it. Then No. 2 jumped for the boat, but fell in the water still farther astern of it. Then No. 3 jumped for the boat, and fell a good way astern of it. Then No. 4 jumped for the boat, and fell in the water *away* astern. Then even No. 5 made a jump for the boat—for he was a Cooper Indian. In the matter of intellect, the difference between a Cooper Indian and the Indian that stands in front of the cigar-shop is not spacious. The scow episode is really a sublime burst of invention; but it does not thrill, because the inaccuracy of the details throws a sort of air of fictitiousness and general improbability over it. This comes of Cooper's inadequacy as an observer.

The reader will find some examples of Cooper's high talent for inaccurate observation in the account of the shooting-match in *The Pathfinder.*

A common wrought nail was driven lightly into the target, its head having been first touched with paint.

The color of the paint is not stated—an important omission, but Cooper deals freely in important omissions. No, after all, it was not an important omission; for this nail-head is *a hundred yards from* the marksmen, and could not be seen by them at that distance, no matter what its color might be. How far can the best eyes see a common house-fly? A hundred yards? It is quite impossible. Very well; eyes that cannot see a house-fly that is a hundred yards away cannot see an ordinary nail-head at that distance, for the size of the two objects is the same. It takes a keen eye to see a fly or a nail-head at fifty yards—one hundred and fifty feet. Can the reader do it?

The nail was lightly driven, its head painted, and game called. Then the Cooper miracles began. The bullet of the first marksman chipped an edge of the nail-head; the next man's bullet drove the nail a little way into the target—and removed all the paint. Haven't the miracles gone far enough now? Not to suit Cooper; for the purpose of this whole scheme is to show off his prodigy, Deerslayer-Hawkeye-Long-Rifle-Leatherstocking-Pathfinder-Bumppo before the ladies.

"Be all ready to clench it, boys!" cried out Pathfinder, stepping into his friend's tracks the instant they were vacant. "Never mind a new nail; I can see that, though the paint is gone, and what I can see I can hit at a hundred yards, though it were only a mosquito's eye. Be ready to clench!"

The rifle cracked, the bullet sped its way, and the head of the nail was buried in the wood, covered by the piece of flattened lead.

There, you see, is a man who could hunt flies with a rifle, and command a ducal salary in a Wild West show to-day, if we had him back with us.

The recorded feat is certainly surprising just as it stands; but it is not surprising enough for Cooper. Cooper adds a touch. He has made Pathfinder do this miracle with another man's rifle; and not only that, but Pathfinder did not have even the advantage of loading it himself. He had everything against him, and yet he made that impossible shot; and not only made it, but did it with absolute confidence, saying, "Be ready to clench." Now a person like that would have undertaken that same feat with a brickbat, and with Cooper to help he would have achieved it, too.

Pathfinder showed off handsomely that day before the ladies. His very first feat was a thing which no Wild West show can touch. He was standing with the group of marksmen, observing—a hundred yards from the target, mind; one Jasper raised his rifle and drove the center of the bull's-eye. Then the Quartermaster fired. The target exhibited no result this time. There was a laugh. "It's a dead miss," said Major Lundie. Pathfinder waited an impressive moment or two; then said, in that calm, indifferent, know-it-all way of his, "No, Major, he has covered Jasper's bullet, as will be seen if any one will take the trouble to examine the target."

Wasn't it remarkable! How *could* he see that little pellet fly through the air and enter that distant bullet-hole? Yet that is what he did; for nothing is impossible to a Cooper person. Did any of those people have any deep-seated doubts about this thing? No; for that would imply sanity, and these were all Cooper people.

The respect for Pathfinder's skill and for his *quickness and accuracy of sight* [the italics are mine] was so profound and general, that the instant he made this declaration the spectators began to distrust their own opinions, and a dozen rushed to the target in order to ascertain the fact. There, sure enough, it was found that the Quartermaster's bullet had gone through the hole made by Jasper's, and that, too, so accurately as to require a minute examination to be certain of the circumstance, which, however, was soon clearly established by discovering one bullet over the other in the stump against which the target was placed.

They made a "minute" examination; but never mind, how could they know that there were two bullets in that hole without digging the latest one out? for neither probe nor eyesight could prove the presence of any more than one bullet. Did they dig? No; as we shall see. It is the Pathfinder's turn now; he steps out before the ladies, takes aim, and fires.

But, alas! here is a disappointment; an incredible, an unimaginable disappointment—for the target's aspect is unchanged; there is nothing there but that same old bullet-hole!

"If one dared to hint at such a thing," cried Major Duncan, "I should say that the Pathfinder has also missed the target!"

As nobody had missed it yet, the "also" was not necessary; but never mind about that, for the Pathfinder is going to speak.

"No, no, Major," said he, confidently, "that *would* be a risky declaration. I didn't load the piece, and can't say what was in it; but if it was lead, you will find the bullet driving down those of the Quartermaster and Jasper, else is not my name Pathfinder."

A shout from the target announced the truth of this assertion.
Is the miracle sufficient as it stands? Not for Cooper. The Pathfinder speaks again, as he "now slowly advances toward the stage occupied by the females":

"That's not all, boys, that's not all; if you find the target touched at all, I'll own to a miss. The Quartermaster cut the wood, but you'll find no wood cut by that last messenger."

The miracle is at last complete. He knew—doubtless *saw*—at the distance of a hundred yards—that his bullet had passed into the hole *without fraying the edges*. There were now three bullets in that one hole—three bullets embedded processionally in the body of the stump back of the target. Everybody knew this—somehow or other—and yet nobody had dug any of them out to make sure. Cooper is not a close observer, but he is interesting. He is certainly always that, no matter what happens. And he is more interesting when he is not noticing what he is about than when he is. This is a considerable merit.

The conversations in the Cooper books have a curious sound in our modern ears. To believe that such talk really ever came out of people's mouths would be to believe that there was a time when time was of no value to a person who thought he had something to say; when it was the custom to spread a two-minute remark out to ten; when a man's mouth was a rolling-mill, and busied itself all day long in turning four-foot pigs of thought into thirty-foot bars of conversational railroad iron by attenuation; when subjets were seldom faithfully stuck to, but the talk wandered all around and arrived nowhere; when conversations consisted mainly of irrelevancies, with here and there a relevancy, a relevancy with an embarrassed look, as not being able to explain how it got there.

Cooper was certainly not a master in the construction of dialogue. Inaccurate observation defeated him here as it defeated him in so many other enterprises of his. He even failed to notice that the man who talks corrupt English six days in the week must and will talk it on the seventh, and can't help himself. In the *Deerslayer* story he lets Deerslayer talk the showiest kind of book-talk sometimes, and at other times the basest of base dialects. For instance, when some one asks him if he has a sweetheart, and if so, where she abides, this is his majestic answer:

> "She's in the forest—hanging from the boughs of the trees, in a soft rain—in the dew on the open grass—the clouds that float about in the blue heavens—the birds that sing in the woods—the sweet springs where I slake my thirst—and in all the other glorious gifts that come from God's Providence!"

And he preceded that, a little before, with this:

> "It consarns me as all things that touches a fri'nd consarns a fri'nd."

And this is another of his remarks:

> "If I was Injin born, now, I might tell of this, or carry in the scalp and boast of the expl'ite afore the whole tribe; or if my inimy had only been a bear"—[and so on].

We cannot imagine such a thing as a veteran Scotch Commander-in-Chief comporting himself in the field like a windy melodramatic actor, but Cooper could. On one occasion Alice and Cora were being chased by the French through a fog in the neighborhood of their father's fort:

> *"Point de quartier aux coquins!"* cried an eager pursuer, who seemed to direct the operations of the enemy.

> "Stand firm and be ready, my gallant 60ths!" suddenly exclaimed a voice above them; "wait to see the enemy; fire low, and sweep the glacis."

> "Father! father," exclaimed a piercing cry from out the mist; "it is I! Alice! thy own Elsie! spare, O! save your daughters!"

> "Hold!" shouted the former speaker, in the awful tones of parental agony, the sound reaching even to the woods, and rolling back in sol-

emn echo. " 'Tis she! God has restored me my children! Throw open the sally-port; to the field, 60ths, to the field! pull not a trigger, lest ye kill my lambs! Drive off these dogs of France with your steel!"

Cooper's word-sense was singularly dull. When a person has a poor ear for music he will flat and sharp right along without knowing it. He keeps near the tune, but it is *not* the tune. When a person has a poor ear for words, the result is a literary flatting and sharping; you perceive what he is intending to say, but you also perceive that he doesn't *say* it. This is Cooper. He was not a word-musician. His ear was satisfied with the *approximate* word. I will furnish some circumstantial evidence in support of this charge. My instances are gathered from half a dozen pages of the tale called *Deerslayer*. He uses "verbal" for "oral"; "precision" for "facility"; "phenomena" for "marvels"; "necessary" for "predetermined"; "unsophisticated" for "primitive"; "preparation" for "expectancy"; "rebuked" for "subdued"; "dependent on" for "resulting from"; "fact" for "condition"; "fact" for "conjecture"; "precaution" for "caution"; "explain" for "determine"; "mortified" for "disappointed"; "meretricious" for "factitious"; "materially" for "considerably"; "decreasing" for "deepening"; "increasing" for "disappearing"; "embedded" for "inclosed"; "treacherous" for "hostile"; "stood" for "stooped"; "softened" for "replaced"; "rejoined" for "remarked"; "situation" for "condition"; "different" for "differing"; "insensible" for "unsentient"; "brevity" for "celerity"; "distrusted" for "suspicious"; "mental imbecility" for "imbecility"; "eyes" for "sight"; "counteracting" for "opposing"; "funeral obsequies" for "obsequies."

There have been daring people in the world who claimed that Cooper could write English, but they are all dead now—all dead but Lounsbury. I don't remember that Lounsbury makes the claim in so many words, still he makes it, for he says that *Deerslayer* is a "pure work of art." Pure, in that connection, means faultless—faultless in all details—and language is a detail. If Mr. Lounsbury had only compared Cooper's English with the English which he writes himself—but it is plain that he didn't; and so it is likely that he imagines until this day that Cooper's is as clean and compact as his own. Now I feel sure, deep down in my heart, that Cooper wrote about the poorest English that exists in our language, and that the English of *Deerslayer* is the very worst that even Cooper ever wrote.

I may be mistaken, but it does seem to me that *Deerslayer* is not a work of art in any sense; it does seem to me that it is destitute of every detail that goes to the making of a work of art; in truth, it seems to me that *Deerslayer* is just simply a literary *delirium tremens*.

A work of art? It has no invention; it has no order, system, sequence, or result; it has no life-likeness, no thrill, no stir, no seeming of reality; its characters are confusedly drawn, and by their acts and words they prove that they are not the sort of people the author claims that they are; its humor is pathetic; its pathos is funny; its conversations are—oh! indescribable; its love-scenes odious; its English a crime against the language.

Counting these out, what is left is Art. I think we must all admit that.

MARK TWAIN

From WHAT PAUL BOURGET THINKS OF US [1]
(1895)

... A FOREIGNER can photograph the exteriors of a nation, but I think
that that is as far as he can get. I think that no foreigner can report its
interior—its soul, its life, its speech, its thought. I think that a knowledge
of these things is acquirable in only one way—not two or four or six—*absorption*; years and years of unconscious absorption; years and years of intercourse with the life concerned; of living it, indeed; sharing personally in
its shames and prides, its joys and griefs, its loves and hates, its prosperi-
ties and reverses, its shows and shabbinesses, its deep patriotisms, its whirlwinds of political passion, its adorations—of flag, and heroic dead, and the
glory of the national name. Observation? Of what real value is it? One
learns peoples through the heart, not the eyes or the intellect.

There is only one expert who is qualified to examine the souls and the
life of a people and make a valuable report—the native novelist. This expert is so rare that the most populous country can never have fifteen conspicuously and confessedly competent ones in stock at one time. This native
specialist is not qualified to begin work until he has been absorbing during
twenty-five years. How much of his competency is derived from conscious
"observation"? The amount is so slight that it counts for next to nothing
in the equipment. Almost the whole capital of the novelist is the slow
accumulation of *un*conscious observation—absorption. The native expert's
intentional observation of manners, speech, character, and ways of life can
have value, for the native knows what they mean without having to cipher
out the meaning. But I should be astonished to see a foreigner get at the
right meanings, catch the elusive shades of these subtle things. Even the
native novelist becomes a foreigner, with a foreigner's limitations, when
he steps from the state whose life is familiar to him into a state whose life
he has not lived. Bert Harte got his California and his Californians by unconscious absorption, and put both of them into his tales alive. But when
he came from the Pacific to the Atlantic and tried to do Newport life from
study—conscious observation—his failure was absolutely monumental. Newport is a disastrous place for the unacclimated observer, evidently.

To return to novel-building. Does the native novelist try to generalize
the nation? No, he lays plainly before you the ways and speech and life
of a few people grouped in a certain place—his own place—and that is one
book. In time he and his brethren will report to you the life and the people

[1] Published originally in the *North American Review*, CLX (1895), 48–62. Paul
Bourget (1852–1935) was a French novelist who in 1894 recorded his impressions of
his visit to the United States.

of the whole nation—the life of a group in a New England village; in a New York village; in a Texan village; in an Oregon village; in villages in fifty states and territories; then the farm-life in fifty states and territories; a hundred patches of life and groups of people in a dozen widely separated cities. And the Indians will be attended to; and the cowboys; and the gold and silver miners; and the negroes; and the Idiots and Congressmen; and the Irish, the Germans, the Italians, the Swedes, the French, the Chinamen, the Greasers; and the Catholics, the Methodists, the Presbyterians, the Congregationalists, the Baptists, the Spiritualists, the Mormons, the Shakers, the Quakers, the Jews, the Campbellites, the infidels, the Christian Scientists, the Mind-Curists, the Faith-Curists, the Train-robbers, the White Caps, the Moonshiners. And when a thousand able novels have been written, *there* you have the soul of the people, the life of the people, the speech of the people; and not anywhere else can these be had. And the shadings of character, manners, feelings, ambitions, will be infinite.

> *The nature of a people* is always of a similar shade in its vices and its virtues, in its frivolities and in its labor. *It is this physiognomy which it is necessary to discover*, and every document is good, from the hall of a casino to the church, from the foibles of a fashionable woman to the suggestions of a revolutionary leader. I am therefore quite sure that this *American soul*, the principal interest and the great object of my voyage, appears behind the records of Newport for those who choose to see it.
> —M. Paul Bourget.

[The italics are mine.] It is a large contract which he has undertaken. "Records" is a pretty poor word there, but I think the use of it is due to hasty translation. In the original the word is *fastes*. I think M. Bourget meant to suggest that he expected to find the great "American soul" secreted behind the *ostentations* of Newport; and that he was going to get it out and examine it, and generalize it, and psychologize it, and make it reveal to him its hidden vast mystery: "the nature of the people" of the United States of America. We have been accused of being a nation addicted to inventing wild schemes. I trust that we shall be allowed to retire to second place now.

There isn't a single human characteristic that can be safely labeled "American." There isn't a single human ambition, or religious trend, or drift of thought, or peculiarity of education, or code of principles, or breed of folly, or style of conversation, or preference for a particular subject for discussion, or form of legs or trunk or head or face or expression or complexion, or gait, or dress, or manners, or disposition, or any other human detail, inside or outside, that can rationally be generalized as "American."

Whenever you have found what seems to be an "American" peculiarity, you have only to cross a frontier or two, or go down or up in the social scale, and you perceive that it has disappeared. And you can cross the Atlantic and find it again. There may be a Newport religious drift, or sporting drift, or conversational style or complexion, or cut of face, but there are entire empires in America, north, south, east, and west, where you could not find your duplicates. It is the same with everything else which one might propose to call "American." M. Bourget thinks he has found the American Coquette. If he had really found her he would also have found, I am sure, that she was not new, that she exists in other lands in the same forms, and with the same frivolous heart and the same ways and impulses. I think this because I have seen our coquette; I have seen her in life; better still, I have seen her in our novels, and seen her twin in foreign novels. I wish M. Bourget had seen ours. He thought he saw her. And so he applied his System to her. She was a Species. So he gathered a number of samples of what seemed to be her, and put them under his glass, and divided them into groups which he calls "types," and labeled them in his usual scientific way with "formulas"—brief, sharp descriptive flashes that make a person blink, sometimes, they are so sudden and vivid. As a rule they are pretty far-fetched, but that is not an important matter; they surprise, they compel admiration, and I notice by some of the comments which his efforts have called forth that they deceive the unwary. Here are a few of the coquette variants which he has grouped and labeled:

THE COLLECTOR.
THE EQUILIBREE.
THE PROFESSIONAL BEAUTY.
THE BLUFFER.
THE GIRL-BOY.

If he had stopped with describing these characters we should have been obliged to believe that they exist; that they exist, and that he has seen them and spoken with them. But he did not stop there; he went further and furnished to us light-throwing samples of their behavior, and also light-throwing samples of their speeches. He entered those things in his note-book without suspicion, he takes them out and delivers them to the world with a candor and simplicity which show that he believed them genuine. They throw altogether too much light. They reveal to the native the origin of his find. I suppose he knows how he came to make that novel and captivating discovery, by this time. If he does not, any American can tell him—any American to whom he will show his anecdotes. It was "put up" on him, as we say. It was a jest—to be plain, it was a series of frauds. To my mind it was a poor sort of jest, witless and contemptible. The players of it have their reward, such as it is; they have exhibited the fact that whatever they may be they are not ladies. M. Bourget did not discover a type of coquette; he merely discovered a type of practical joker. One may say *the* type of practical joker, for these people are exactly alike all over the world. Their equipment is always the same: a vulgar mind, a puerile wit, a cruel disposition as a rule, and always the spirit of treachery. . . .

BRET HARTE

THE RISE OF THE 'SHORT STORY'[1]
(1899)

As it has been the custom of good-natured reviewers to associate the present writer with the origin of the American 'short story,' he may have a reasonable excuse for offering the following reflections—partly the result of his own observations during the last thirty years, and partly from his experience in the introduction of this form of literature to the pages of the 'Western Magazine,' of which he was editor at the beginning of that period. But he is far from claiming the invention, or of even attributing its genesis to that particular occasion. The short story was familiar enough in form in America during the early half of the century; perhaps the proverbial haste of American life was some inducement to its brevity. It had been the medium through which some of the most characteristic work of the best American writers had won the approbation of the public. Poe— a master of the art, as yet unsurpassed—had written; Longfellow and Hawthorne had lent it the graces of the English classics. But it was not the American short story of to-day. It was not characteristic of American life, American habits nor American thought. It was not vital and instinct with the experience and observation of the average American; it made no attempt to follow his reasoning or to understand his peculiar form of expression— which it was apt to consider vulgar; it had no sympathy with those dramatic contrasts and surprises which are the wonders of American civilisation; it took no account of the modifications of environment and of geographical limitations; indeed, it knew little of American geography. Of all that was distinctly American it was evasive—when it was not apologetic. And even when graced by the style of the best masters, it was distinctly provincial.

It would be easier to trace the causes which produced this than to assign any distinct occasion or period for the change. What was called American literature was still limited to English methods and upon English models. The best writers either wandered far afield for their inspiration, or, restricted to home material, were historical or legendary; artistically contemplative of their own country, but seldom observant. Literature abode on a scant fringe of the Atlantic seaboard, gathering the drift from other shores, and hearing the murmur of other lands rather than the voices of its own; it was either expressed in an artificial treatment of life in the cities, or, as with Irving, was frankly satirical of provincial social ambition. There was much 'fine' writing; there were American Addisons, Steeles, and Lambs—

[1] Published in the *Cornhill Magazine*, VII (1899).

485

there were provincial 'Spectators' and 'Tatlers.'[2] The sentiment was English. Even Irving in the pathetic sketch of 'The Wife' echoed the style of 'Rosamund Grey.' There were sketches of American life in the form of the English Essayists, with no attempt to understand the American character. The literary man had little sympathy with the rough and half-civilised masses who were making his country's history; if he used them at all it was as a foil to bring into greater relief his hero of the unmistakable English pattern. In his slavish imitation of the foreigner, he did not, however, succeed in retaining the foreigner's quick appreciation of novelty. It took an Englishman to first develop the humour and picturesqueness of American or 'Yankee' dialect, but Judge Haliburton[3] succeeded better in reproducing 'Sam Slick's' speech than his character. Dr. Judd's 'Margaret'[4]—one of the earlier American stories—although a vivid picture of New England farm life and strongly marked with local colour, was in incident and treatment a mere imitation of English rural tragedy. It would, indeed, seem that while the American people had shaken off the English yoke in Government, politics, and national progression, while they had already startled the old world with invention and originality in practical ideas, they had never freed themselves from the trammels of English literary precedent. The old sneer 'Who reads an American book?' might have been answered by another: 'There are no *American* books.'

But while the American literary imagination was still under the influence of English tradition, an unexpected factor was developing to diminish its power. It was *Humour*—of a quality as distinct and original as the country and civilisation in which it was developed. It was at first noticeable in the anecdote or 'story,' and, after the fashion of such beginnings, was orally transmitted. It was common in the bar-rooms, the gatherings in the 'country store,' and finally at public meetings in the mouths of 'stump orators.' Arguments were clinched, and political principles illustrated, by 'a funny story.' It invaded even the camp meeting and pulpit. It at last received the currency of the public press. But wherever met it was so distinctly original and novel, so individual and characteristic, that it was at once known and appreciated abroad as 'an American story.' Crude at first, it received a literary polish in the press, but its dominant quality remained. It was concise and condense, yet suggestive. It was delightfully extravagant —or a miracle of understatement. It voiced not only the dialect, but the habits of thought of a people or locality. It gave a new interest to slang. From a paragraph of a dozen lines it grew into a half column, but always retaining its conciseness and felicity of statement. It was a foe to prolixity of any kind, it admitted no fine writing nor affectation of style. It went directly to the point. It was burdened by no conscientiousness; it was often irreverent; it was devoid of all moral responsibility—but it was original!

[2] Eighteenth-century English periodicals edited by Addison and Steele.

[3] Thomas Haliburton (1796–1865), Canadian judge, historian, and humorist. In 1835 he contributed a series of letters to a Halifax newspaper under the pseudonym of "Sam Slick," clock-peddler. These were collected and published in 1837; a series of books followed, many written after he had gone to England.

[4] Sylvester Judd (1813–1853), Unitarian clergyman, published *Margaret* in 1845.

By degrees it developed character with its incident, often, in a few lines, gave a striking photograph of a community or a section, but always reached its conclusion without an unnecessary word. It became—and still exists— as an essential feature of newspaper literature. It was the parent of the American 'short story.'

But although these beginnings assumed more of a national character than American serious or polite literature, they were still purely comic, and their only immediate result was the development of a number of humourists in the columns of the daily press—all possessing the dominant national quality with a certain individuality of their own. For a while it seemed as if they were losing the faculty of story-telling in the elaboration of eccentric character—chiefly used as a vehicle for smart sayings, extravagant incident, or political satire. They were eagerly received by the public and, in their day, were immensely popular, and probably were better known at home and abroad than the more academic but less national humourists of New York or Boston. The national note was always struck even in their individual variations, and the admirable portraiture of the shrewd and humorous showman in 'Artemus Ward'[5] survived his more mechanical bad spelling. Yet they did not invade the current narrative fiction; the short and long story-tellers went with their old-fashioned methods, their admirable morals, their well-worn sentiments, their colourless heroes and heroines of the first ranks of provincial society. Neither did social and political convulsions bring anything new in the way of Romance. The Mexican war gave us the delightful satires of Hosea Biglow,[6] but no dramatic narrative. The anti-slavery struggle before the War of the Rebellion produced a successful partisan political novel—on the old lines—with only the purely American characters of the negro 'Topsy,' and the New England 'Miss Ophelia.' The War itself, prolific as it was of poetry and eloquence—was barren of romance, except for Edward Everett Hale's artistic and sympathetic *The Man without a Country*.[7] The tragedies enacted, the sacrifices offered, not only on the battle-field but in the division of families and households; the conflict of superb Quixotism and reckless gallantry against Reason and Duty fought out in quiet border farmhouses and plantations; the reincarnation of Puritan and Cavalier in a wild environment of trackless wastes, pestilential swamps and rugged mountains; the patient endurance of both the conqueror and the conquered: all these found no echo in the romance of the period. Out of the battle smoke that covered half a continent drifted into the pages of magazines shadowy but correct figures of blameless virgins of the North—heroines or fashionable belles—habited as hospital nurses, bearing away the deeply wounded but more deeply misunderstood Harvard or Yale graduate lover who had rushed to bury his broken heart in the conflict. It seems almost incredible that, until the last few years, nothing worthy of that tremendous episode has been preserved by the pen of the romancer.

[5] Charles Farrar Browne ("Artemus Ward") (1834–1867), American humorist.
[6] Character in James Russell Lowell's satiric *The Biglow Papers* (1848).
[7] Edward Everett Hale's (1822–1909) "The Man without a Country," appeared in the *Atlantic Monthly* in 1863.

But if the war produced no characteristic American story it brought the literary man nearer his work. It opened to him distinct conditions of life in his own country, of which he had no previous conceptions; it revealed communities governed by customs and morals unlike his own, yet intensely human and American. The lighter side of some of these he had learned from the humourists before alluded to; the grim realities of war and the stress of circumstances had suddenly given them a pathetic or dramatic reality. Whether he had acquired this knowledge of them with a musket or a gilded strap on his shoulder, or whether he was later a peaceful 'carpet-bagger' into the desolate homes of the south and south-west, he knew something personally of their romantic and picturesque value in story. Many cultivated aspirants for literature, as well as many seasoned writers for the press, were among the volunteer soldiery. Again, the composition of the army was heterogeneous: regiments from the West rubbed shoulders with regiments from the East; spruce city clerks hobnobbed with backwoodsmen, and the student fresh from college shared his rations with the half-educated western farmer. The Union, for the first time, recognised its component parts; the natives knew each other. The literary man must have seen heroes and heroines where he had never looked for them, situations that he had never dreamt of. Yet it is a mortifying proof of the strength of inherited literary traditions, that he never dared until quite recently to make a test of them. It is still more strange that he should have waited for the initiative to be taken by a still more crude, wild, and more western civilisation—that of California!

The gold discovery had drawn to the Pacific slope of the continent a still more heterogeneous and remarkable population. The immigration of 1849 and 1850 had taken farmers from the plough, merchants from their desks, and students from their books, while every profession was represented in the motley crowd of gold-seekers. Europe and her colonies had contributed to swell these adventurers—for adventurers they were whatever their purpose; the risks were great, the journey long and difficult—the nearest came from a distance of over a thousand miles; that the men were necessarily pre-equipped with courage, faith and endurance was a foregone conclusion. They were mainly young; a grey-haired man was a curiosity in the mines in the early days, and an object of rude respect and reverence. They were consequently free from the trammels of precedent or tradition in arranging their lives and making their rude homes. There was a singular fraternity in this ideal republic into which all men entered free and equal. Distinction of previous position or advantages were unknown, even record and reputation for ill or good were of little benefit or embarrassment to the possessor; men were accepted for what they actually were, and what they could do in taking their part in the camp or settlement. The severest economy, the direst poverty, the most menial labour carried no shame nor disgrace with it; individual success brought neither envy nor jealousy. What was one man's fortune to-day might be the luck of another to-morrow. Add to this Utopian simplicity of the people, the environment of magnificent scenery, a unique climate, and a vegetation that was marvellous in its proportions and spontaneity of growth; let it be further considered that the strongest relief was given to this picture by its setting among the crumbling ruins of early Spanish possession—whose monuments still existed in Mission and Presidio, and whose legitimate Castilian descendants still lived and moved in picturesque and dignified contrast to their energetic invaders—and it must be admitted that a condition of romantic and dramatic possibilities was created unrivalled in history.

But the earlier literature of the Pacific slope was, like that of the Atlantic seaboard, national and characteristic only in its humour. The local press sparkled with wit and satire, and, as in the East, developed its usual individual humourists. Of these should be mentioned the earliest pioneers of Californian humour—Lieut. Derby,[8] a U.S. army engineer officer, author of a series of delightful extravagances known as the 'Squibob Papers,' and the later and universally known 'Mark Twain,' who contributed 'The Jumping Frog of Calaveras' to the columns of the weekly press. 'The San Francisco News Letter,' whose whilom contributor, Major Bierce,[9] has since written some of the most graphic romances of the Civil War; 'The Golden Era,' in which the present writer published his earlier sketches, and 'The Californian,' to which, as editor, in burlesque imitation of the enterprise of his journalistic betters, he contributed 'The Condensed Novels,' were the foremost literary weeklies. These were all more or less characteristically American, but it was again remarkable that the more literary, romantic, and imaginative romances had no national flavour. The better remembered serious work in the pages of the only literary magazine 'The Pioneer,' was a romance of spiritualism and psychological study, and a poem on the Chandos picture of Shakespeare!

With this singular experience before him, the present writer was called upon to take the editorial control of the 'Overland Monthly,' a much more ambitious magazine venture than had yet appeared in California. The best writers had been invited to contribute to its pages. But in looking over his materials on preparing the first number, he was discouraged to find the same notable lack of characteristic fiction. There were good literary articles, sketches of foreign travel, and some essays in description of the natural resources of California—excellent from a commercial and advertising viewpoint. But he failed to discover anything of that wild and picturesque life which had impressed him, first as a truant schoolboy, and afterwards as a youthful schoolmaster among the mining population. In this perplexity he determined to attempt to make good the deficiency himself. He wrote 'The Luck of Roaring Camp.' However far short it fell of his ideal and his purpose, he conscientiously believed that he had painted much that 'he saw, and part of which he was,' that his subject and characters were distinctly Californian, as was equally his treatment of them. But an unexpected circumstance here intervened. The publication of the story was objected to by both printer and publisher, virtually for not being in the con-

[8] George Horatio Derby (1823-1861), American humorist, wrote the *Squibob Papers* in 1859.
[9] Ambrose Bierce (1842-1914?), American writer of fiction.

ventional line of subject, treatment, and morals! The introduction of the abandoned outcast mother of the foundling 'Luck,' and the language used by the characters, received a serious warning and protest. The writer was obliged to use his right as editor to save his unfortunate contribution from oblivion. When it appeared at last, he saw with consternation that the printer and publisher had really voiced the local opinion; that the press of California was still strongly dominated by the old conservatism and conventionalism of the East, and that when 'The Luck of Roaring Camp' was not denounced as 'improper' and 'corrupting,' it was coldly received as being 'singular' and 'strange.' A still more extraordinary instance of the 'provincial note' was struck in the criticism of a religious paper that the story was strongly 'unfavourable to immigration' and decidedly unprovocative of the 'investment of foreign capital.' However, its instantaneous and cordial acceptance as a new departure by the critics of the Eastern States and Europe, enabled the writer to follow it with other stories of a like character. More than that, he was gratified to find a disposition on the part of his contributors to shake off their conservative trammels, and in an admirable and original sketch of a wandering circus attendant called 'Centrepole Bill,' he was delighted to recognise and welcome a convert. The term 'imitators,' often used by the critics who, as previously stated, had claimed for the present writer the *invention* of this kind of literature, could not fairly apply to those who had cut loose from conventional methods, and sought to honestly describe the life around them, and he can only claim to have shown them that it could be done. How well it has since been done, what charm of individual flavour and style has been brought to it by such writers as Harris, Cable, Page, Mark Twain in 'Huckleberry Finn,' the author of the 'Prophet of the Great Smoky Mountains,' and Miss Wilkins,[10] the average reader need not be told. It would seem evident, therefore, that the secret of the American short story was the treatment of characteristic American life, with absolute knowledge of its peculiarities and sympathy with its methods; with no fastidious ignoring of its habitual expression, or the inchoate poetry that may be found even hidden in its slang; with no moral determination except that which may be the legitimate outcome of the story itself; with no more elimination than may be necessary for the artistic conception, and never from the fear of the 'fetish' of conventionalism. Of such is the American short story of to-day—the germ of American literature to come.

[10] Harte is here calling the roll of American local color writers. Joel Chandler Harris (1848–1908) in Georgia; George Washington Cable (1844–1925) in Louisiana; Thomas Nelson Page (1853–1922) in Virginia; "Charles Egbert Craddock" (Mary Noailles Murfree) (1850–1922), author of *The Prophet of the Great Smoky Mountains* (1885) in Tennessee; and Mary E. Wilkins Freeman (1852–1930) in New England were among the leading writers of regional fiction.

GEORGE SANTAYANA

THE ELEMENTS AND FUNCTION OF POETRY [1]
(1900)

IF A critic, in despair of giving a serious definition of poetry, should be satisfied with saying that poetry is metrical discourse, he would no doubt be giving an inadequate account of the matter, yet not one of which he need be ashamed or which he should regard as superficial. Although a poem be not made by counting of syllables upon the fingers, yet "numbers" is the most poetical synonym we have for verse, and "measure" the most significant equivalent for beauty, for goodness, and perhaps even for truth. Those early and profound philosophers, the followers of Pythagoras,[2] saw the essence of all things in number, and it was by weight, measure, and number, as we read in the Bible, that the Creator first brought Nature out of the void. Every human architect must do likewise with his edifice; he must mould his bricks or hew his stones into symmetrical solids and lay them over one another in regular strata, like a poet's lines.

Measure is a condition of perfection, for perfection requires that order should be pervasive, that not only the whole before us should have a form, but that every part in turn should have a form of its own, and that those parts should be coördinated among themselves as the whole is coördinated with the other parts of some greater cosmos. Leibnitz[3] lighted in his speculations upon a conception of organic nature which may be false as a fact, but which is excellent as an ideal; he tells us that the difference between living and dead matter, between animals and machines, is that the former are composed of parts that are themselves organic, every portion of the body being itself a machine, and every portion of that machine still a machine, and so *ad infinitum;* whereas, in artificial bodies the organization is not in this manner infinitely deep. Fine Art, in this as in all things, imitates the method of Nature and makes its most beautiful works out of materials that are themselves beautiful. So that even if the difference between verse and prose consisted only in measure, that difference would already be analogous to that between jewels and clay.

The stuff of language is words, and the sensuous material of words is sound; if language therefore is to be made perfect, its materials must be made beautiful by being themselves subjected to a measure, and endowed with a form. It is true that language is a symbol for intelligence rather than a stimulus to sense, and accordingly the beauties of discourse which commonly attract attention are merely the beauties of the objects and ideas

[1] From *Interpretations of Poetry and Religion* (New York, 1900).
[2] Greek philosopher, mathematician, and religious reformer (ca. 582–ca. 500 B.C.).
[3] Gottfried von Leibnitz (1646–1716), German philosopher and scientific genius.

signified; yet the symbols have a sensible reality of their own, a euphony which appeals to our senses if we keep them open. The tongue will choose those forms of utterance which have a natural grace as mere sound and sensation; the memory will retain these catches, and they will pass and repass through the mind until they become types of instinctive speech and standards of pleasing expression.

The highest form of such euphony is song; the singing voice gives to the sounds it utters the thrill of tonality,—a thrill itself dependent, as we know, on the numerical proportions of the vibrations that it includes. But this kind of euphony and sensuous beauty, the deepest that sounds can have, we have almost wholly surrendered in our speech. Our intelligence has become complex, and language, to express our thoughts, must commonly be more rapid, copious, and abstract than is compatible with singing. Music at the same time has become complex also, and when united with words, at one time disfigures them in the elaboration of its melody, and at another overpowers them in the volume of its sound. So that the art of singing is now in the same plight as that of sculpture,—an abstract and conventional thing surviving by force of tradition and of an innate but now impotent impulse, which under simpler conditions would work itself out into the proper forms of those arts. The truest kind of euphony is thus denied to our poetry. If any verses are still set to music, they are commonly the worst only, chosen for the purpose by musicians of specialized sensibility and inferior intelligence, who seem to be attracted only by tawdry effects of rhetoric and sentiment.

When song is given up, there still remains in speech a certain sensuous quality, due to the nature and order of the vowels and consonants that compose the sounds. This kind of euphony is not neglected by the more dulcet poets, and is now so studied in some quarters that I have heard it maintained by a critic of relative authority that the beauty of poetry consists entirely in the frequent utterance of the sound of "j" and "sh," and the consequent copious flow of saliva in the mouth. But even if saliva is not the whole essence of poetry, there is an unmistakable and fundamental diversity of effect in the various vocalization of different poets, which becomes all the more evident when we compare those who use different languages. One man's speech, or one nation's, is compact, crowded with consonants, rugged, broken with emphatic beats; another man's, or nation's, is open, tripping, rapid, and even. So Byron, mingling in his boyish fashion burlesque with exquisite sentiment, contrasts English with Italian speech:—

> I love the language, that soft bastard Latin
> Which melts like kisses from a female mouth
> And sounds as if it should be writ on satin
> With syllables which breathe of the sweet South,
> And gentle liquids gliding all so pat in
> That not a single accent seems uncouth,
> Like our harsh Northern whistling, grunting guttural
> Which we're obliged to hiss and spit and sputter all."

And yet these contrasts, strong when we compare extreme cases, fade from our consciousness in the actual use of a mother-tongue. The function makes us unconscious of the instrument, all the more as it is an indispensable and almost invariable one. The sense of euphony accordingly attaches itself rather to another and more variable quality; the tune, or measure, or rhythm of speech. The elementary sounds are prescribed by the language we use, and the selection we may make among those sounds is limited; but the arrangement of words is still undetermined, and by casting our speech into the moulds of metre and rhyme we can give it a heightened power, apart from its significance. A tolerable definition of poetry, on its formal side, might be found in this: that poetry is speech in which the instrument counts as well as the meaning—poetry is speech for its own sake and for its own sweetness. As common windows are intended only to admit the light, but painted windows also to dye it, and to be an object of attention in themselves as well as a cause of visibility in other things, so, while the purest prose is a mere vehicle of thought, verse, like stained glass, arrests attention in its own intricacies, confuses it in its own glories, and is even at times allowed to darken and puzzle in the hope of casting over us a supernatural spell.

Long passages in Shelley's "Revolt of Islam" and Keats' "Endymion" are poetical in this sense; the reader gathers, probably, no definite meaning, but is conscious of a poetic medium, of speech euphonious and measured, and redolent of a kind of objectless passion which is little more than the sensation of the movement and sensuous richness of the lines. Such poetry is not great; it has, in fact, a tedious vacuity, and is unworthy of a mature mind; but it is poetical, and could be produced only by a legitimate child of the Muse. It belongs to an apprenticeship, but in this case the apprenticeship of genius. It bears that relation to great poems which scales and aimless warblings bear to great singing—they test the essential endowment and fineness of the organ which is to be employed in the art. Without this sensuous background and ingrained predisposition to beauty, no art can reach the deepest and most exquisite effects; and even without an intelligible superstructure these sensuous qualities suffice to give that thrill of exaltation, that suggestion of an ideal world, which we feel in the presence of any true beauty.

The sensuous beauty of words and their utterance in measure suffice, therefore, for poetry of one sort—where these are, there is something unmistakably poetical, although the whole of poetry, or the best of poetry, be not yet there. Indeed, in such works as "The Revolt of Islam" or "Endymion" there is already more than mere metre and sound; there is the colour and choice of words, the fanciful, rich, or exquisite juxtaposition of phrases. The vocabulary and the texture of the style are precious; affected, perhaps, but at any rate refined.

This quality, which is that almost exclusively exploited by the Symbolist, we may call euphuism—the choice of coloured words and rare and elliptical phrases. If great poets are like architects and sculptors, the euphuists are like goldsmiths and jewellers; their work is filigree in precious metals, encrusted with glowing stones. Now euphuism contributes not a little to the poetic effect of the tirades of Keats and Shelley; if we wish to see the power of versification without euphuism we may turn to the tirades of Pope, where metre and euphony are displayed alone, and we have the outline or skeleton of poetry without the filling

> "In spite of pride, in erring reason's spite,
> One truth is clear, Whatever is, is right."

We should hesitate to say that such writing was truly poetical; so that some euphuism would seem to be necessary as well as metre, to the formal essence of poetry.

An example of this sort, however, takes us out of the merely verbal into the imaginative region; the reason that Pope is hardly poetical to us is not that he is inharmonious,—not a defect of euphony,—but that he is too intellectual and has an excess of mentality. It is easier for words to be poetical without any thought, when they are felt merely as sensuous and musical, than for them to remain so when they convey an abstract notion,—especially if that notion be a tart and frigid sophism, like that of the couplet just quoted. The pyrotechnics of the intellect then take the place of the glow of sense, and the artifice of thought chills the pleasure we might have taken in the grace of expression.

If poetry in its higher reaches is more philosophical than history, because it presents the memorable types of men and things apart from unmeaning circumstances, so in its primary substance and texture poetry is more philosophical than prose because it is nearer to our immediate experience. Poetry breaks up the trite conceptions designated by current words into the sensuous qualities out of which those conceptions were originally put together. We name what we conceive and believe in, not what we see; things, not images; souls, not voices and silhouettes. This naming, with the whole education of the senses which it accompanies, subserves the uses of life; in order to thread our way through the labyrinth of objects which assault us, we must make a great selection in our sensuous experience; half of what we see and hear we must pass over as insignificant, while we piece out the other half with such an ideal complement as is necessary to turn it into a fixed and well-ordered world. This labour of perception and understanding, this spelling of the material meaning of experience is enshrined in our work-a-day language and ideas; ideas which are literally poetic in the sense that they are "made" (for every conception in an adult mind is a fiction), but which are at the same time prosaic because they are made economically, by abstraction, and for use.

When the child of poetic genius, who has learned this intellectual and utilitarian language in the cradle, goes afield and gathers for himself the aspects of Nature, he begins to encumber his mind with the many living impressions which the intellect rejected, and which the language of the intellect can hardly convey; he labours with his nameless burden of perception, and wastes himself in aimless impulses of emotion and revery, until finally the method of some art offers a vent to his inspiration, or to such part of it as can survive the test of time and the discipline of expression.

The poet retains by nature the innocence of the eye, or recovers it easily; he disintegrates the fictions of common perception into their sensuous elements, gathers these together again into chance groups as the accidents of his environment or the affinities of his temperament may conjoin them; and this wealth of sensation and this freedom of fancy, which make an extraordinary ferment in his ignorant heart, presently bubble over into some kind of utterance.

The fulness and sensuousness of such effusions bring them nearer to our actual perceptions than common discourse could come; yet they may easily seem remote, overloaded, and obscure to those accustomed to think entirely in symbols, and never to be interrupted in the algebraic rapidity of their thinking by a moment's pause and examination of heart, nor ever to plunge for a moment into that torrent of sensation and imagery over which the bridge of prosaic associations habitually carries us safe and dry to some conventional act. How slight that bridge commonly is, how much an affair of trestles and wire, we can hardly conceive until we have trained ourselves to an extreme sharpness of introspection. But psychologists have discovered, what laymen generally will confess, that we hurry by the procession of our mental images as we do by the traffic of the street, intent on business, gladly forgetting the noise and movement of the scene, and looking only for the corner we would turn or the door we would enter. Yet in our alertest moment the depths of the soul are still dreaming; the real world stands drawn in bare outline against a background of chaos and unrest. Our logical thoughts dominate experience only as the parallels and meridians make a checkerboard of the sea. They guide our voyage without controlling the waves, which toss for ever in spite of our ability to ride over them to our chosen ends. Sanity is a madness put to good uses; waking life is a dream controlled.

Out of the neglected riches of this dream the poet fetches his wares. He dips into the chaos that underlies the rational shell of the world and brings up some superfluous image, some emotion dropped by the way, and re-attaches it to the present object; he reinstates things unnecessary, he emphasizes things ignored, he paints in again into the landscape the tints which the intellect has allowed to fade from it. If he seems sometimes to obscure a fact, it is only because he is restoring an experience. We may observe this process in the simplest cases. When Ossian,[4] mentioning the sun, says it is round as the shield of his fathers, the expression is poetical. Why? Because he has added to the word sun, in itself sufficient and unequivocal, other words, unnecessary for practical clearness, but serving to restore the individuality of his perception and its associations in his mind. There is no square sun with which the sun he is speaking of could be confused; to stop and call it round is a luxury, a halting in the sensation for

[4] James Macpherson (1736–1796), Scottish poet, published in 1760 supposed versions of poems written by Ossian, legendary Gaelic poet of the third century.

the love of its form. And to go on to tell us, what is wholly impertinent, that the shield of his fathers was round also, is to invite us to follow the chance wanderings of his fancy, to give us a little glimpse of the stuffing of his own brain, or, we might almost say, to turn over the pattern of his embroidery and show us the loose threads hanging out on the wrong side. Such an escapade disturbs and interrupts the true vision of the object, and a great poet, rising to a perfect conception of the sun and forgetting himself, would have disdained to make it; but it has a romantic and pathological interest, it restores an experience, and is in that measure poetical. We have been made to halt at the sensation, and to penetrate for a moment into its background of dream.

But it is not only thoughts or images that the poet draws in this way from the store of his experience, to clothe the bare form of conventional objects: he often adds to these objects a more subtle ornament, drawn from the same source. For the first element which the intellect rejects in forming its ideas of things is the emotion which accompanies the perception; and this emotion is the first thing the poet restores. He stops at the image, because he stops to enjoy. He wanders into the by-paths of association because the by-paths are delightful. The love of beauty which made him give measure and cadence to his words, the love of harmony which made him rhyme them, reappear in his imagination and make him select there also the material that is itself beautiful, or capable of assuming beautiful forms. The link that binds together the ideas, sometimes so wide apart, which his wit assimilates, is most often the link of emotion; they have in common some element of beauty or of horror.

The poet's art is to a great extent the art of intensifying emotions by assembling the scattered objects that naturally arouse them. He sees the affinities of things by seeing their common affinities with passion. As the guiding principle of practical thinking is some interest, so that only what is pertinent to that interest is selected by the attention; as the guiding principle of scientific thinking is some connection of things in time or space, or some identity of law; so in poetic thinking the guiding principle is often a mood or a quality of sentiment. By this union of disparate things having a common overtone of feeling, the feeling is itself evoked in all its strength; nay, it is often created for the first time, much as by a new mixture of old pigments Perugino [5] could produce the unprecedented limpidity of his colour, or Titian [6] the unprecedented glow of his. Poets can thus arouse sentiments finer than any which they have known, and in the act of composition become discoverers of new realms of delightfulness and grief. Expression is a misleading term which suggests that something previously known is rendered or imitated; whereas the expression is itself an original fact, the values of which are then referred to the thing expressed, much as the honours of a Chinese mandarin are attributed retroactively to his parents. So the charm which a poet, by his art of combining images and shades of emotion, casts over a scene or an action, is attached to the prin-

[5] Italian painter (1446–1524).
[6] One of the most famous Italian painters of the Venetian school (1477–1576).

cipal actor in it, who gets the benefit of the setting furnished him by a well-stocked mind.

The poet is himself subject to this illusion, and a great part of what is called poetry, although by no means the best part of it, consists in this sort of idealization by proxy. We dye the world of our own colour; by a pathetic fallacy, by a false projection of sentiment, we soak Nature with our own feeling, and then celebrate her tender sympathy with our moral being. This aberration, as we see in the case of Wordsworth, is not inconsistent with a high development of both the faculties which it confuses,—I mean vision and feeling. On the contrary, vision and feeling, when most abundant and original, most easily present themselves in this undivided form. There would be need of a force of intellect which poets rarely possess to rationalize their inspiration without diminishing its volume: and if, as is commonly the case, the energy of the dream and the passion in them is greater than that of the reason, and they cannot attain true propriety and supreme beauty in their works, they can, nevertheless, fill them with lovely images and a fine moral spirit.

The pouring forth of both perceptive and emotional elements in their mixed and indiscriminate form gives to this kind of imagination the directness and truth which sensuous poetry possesses on a lower level. The outer world bathed in the hues of human feeling, the inner world expressed in the forms of things,—that is the primitive condition of both before intelligence and the prosaic classification of objects have abstracted them and assigned them to their respective spheres. Such identifications, on which a certain kind of metaphysics prides itself also, are not discoveries of profound genius; they are exactly like the observation of Ossian that the sun is round and that the shield of his fathers was round too; they are disintegrations of conventional objects, so that the original associates of our perceptions reappear; then the thing and the emotion which chanced to be simultaneous are said to be one, and we return, unless a better principle of organization is substituted for the principle abandoned, to the chaos of a passive animal consciousness, where all is mixed together, projected together, and felt as an unutterable whole.

The pathetic fallacy is a return to that early habit of thought by which our ancestors peopled the world with benevolent and malevolent spirits; what they felt in the presence of objects they took to be a part of the objects themselves. In returning to this natural confusion, poetry does us a service in that she recalls and consecrates those phases of our experience which, as useless to the understanding of material reality, we are in danger of forgetting altogether. Therein is her vitality, for she pierces to the quick and shakes us out of our servile speech and imaginative poverty; she reminds us of all we have felt, she invites us even to dream a little, to nurse the wonderful spontaneous creations which at every waking moment we are snuffing out in our brain. And the indulgence is no mere momentary pleasure; much of its exuberance clings afterward to our ideas; we see the more and feel the more for that exercise; we are capable of finding greater entertainment in the common aspects of Nature and life.

When the veil of convention is once removed from our eyes by the poet, we are better able to dominate any particular experience and, as it were, to change its scale, now losing ourselves in its infinitesimal texture, now in its infinite ramifications.

If the function of poetry, however, did not go beyond this recovery of sensuous and imaginative freedom, at the expense of disrupting our useful habits of thought, we might be grateful to it for occasionally relieving our numbness, but we should have to admit that it was nothing but a relaxation; that spiritual discipline was not to be gained from it in any degree, but must be sought wholly in that intellectual system that builds the science of Nature with the categories of prose. So conceived, poetry would deserve the judgment passed by Plato on all the arts of flattery and entertainment; it might be crowned as delightful, but must be either banished altogether as meretricious or at least confined to a few forms and occasions where it might do little harm. The judgment of Plato has been generally condemned by philosophers, although it is eminently rational, and justified by the simplest principles of morals. It has been adopted instead, although unwittingly, by the practical and secular part of mankind, who look upon artists and poets as inefficient and brain-sick people under whose spell it would be a serious calamity to fall, although they may be called in on feast days as an ornament and luxury together with the cooks, hairdressers, and florists.

Several circumstances, however, might suggest to us the possibility that the greatest function of poetry may be still to find. Plato, while condemning Homer, was a kind of poet himself; his quarrel with the followers of the Muse was not a quarrel with the goddess; and the good people of Philistia, distrustful as they may be of profane art, pay undoubting honour to religion, which is a kind of poetry as much removed from their sphere as the midnight revels upon Mount Citheron, which, to be sure, were also religious in their inspiration. Why, we may ask, these apparent inconsistencies? Why do our practical men make room for religion in the background of their world? Why did Plato, after banishing the poets,[7] poetize the universe in his prose? Because the abstraction by which the world of science and of practice is drawn out of our experience is too violent to satisfy even the thoughtless and vulgar; the ideality of the machine we call Nature, the conventionality of the drama we call the world, are too glaring not to be somehow perceived by all. Each must sometimes fall back upon the soul; he must challenge this apparition with the thought of death; he must ask himself for the mainspring and value of his life. He will then remember his stifled loves; he will feel that only his illusions have ever given him a sense of reality, only his passions the hope and the vision of peace. He will read himself through and almost gather a meaning from his experience; at least he will half believe that all he has been dealing with was a dream and a symbol, and raise his eyes toward the truth beyond.

This plastic moment of the mind, when we become aware of the artificiality and inadequacy of what common sense perceives, is the true moment

[7] The reference is to Plato's *Republic;* see Books II and X.

of poetic opportunity,—an opportunity, we may hasten to confess, which is generally missed. The strain of attention, the concentration and focussing of thought on the unfamiliar immediacy of things, usually brings about nothing but confusion. We are dazed, we are filled with a sense of unutterable things, luminous yet indistinguishable, many yet one. Instead of rising to imagination, we sink into mysticism.

To accomplish a mystical disintegration is not the function of any art; if any art seems to accomplish it, the effect is only incidental, being involved, perhaps, in the process of constructing the proper object of that art, as we might cut down trees and dig them up by the roots to lay the foundations of a temple. For every art looks to the building up of something. And just because the world built up by common sense and natural science is an inadequate world (a skeleton which needs the filling of sensation before it can live), therefore the moment when we realize its inadequacy is the moment when the higher arts find their opportunity. When the world is shattered to bits they can come and "build it nearer to the heart's desire."

The great function of poetry, which we have not yet directly mentioned, is precisely this: to repair to the material of experience, seizing hold of the reality of sensation and fancy beneath the surface of conventional ideas, and then out of that living but indefinite material to build new structures, richer, finer, fitter to the primary tendencies of our nature, truer to the ultimate possibilities of the soul. Our descent into the elements of our being is then justified by our subsequent freer ascent toward its goal; we revert to sense only to find food for reason; we destroy conventions only to construct ideals.

Such analysis for the sake of creation is the essence of all great poetry. Science and common sense are themselves in their way poets of no mean order, since they take the material of experience and make out of it a clear, symmetrical, and beautiful world; the very propriety of this art, however, has made it common. Its figures have become mere rhetoric and its metaphors prose. Yet, even as it is, a scientific and mathematical vision has a higher beauty than the irrational poetry of sensation and impulse, which merely tickles the brain, like liquor, and plays upon our random, imaginative lusts. The imagination of a great poet, on the contrary, is as orderly as that of an astronomer, and as large; he has the naturalist's patience, the naturalist's love of detail and eye trained to see fine gradations and essential lines; he knows no hurry; he has no pose, no sense of originality; he finds his effects in his subject, and his subject in his inevitable world. Resembling the naturalist in all this, he differs from him in the balance of his interests; the poet has the concreter mind; his visible world wears all its colours and retains its indwelling passion and life. Instead of studying in experience its calculable elements, he studies its moral values, its beauty, the openings it offers to the soul: and the cosmos he constructs is accordingly an ideal theatre for the spirit in which its noblest potential drama is enacted and its destiny resolved.

This supreme function of poetry is only the consummation of the method by which words and imagery are transformed into verse. As verse breaks up the prosaic order of syllables and subjects them to a recognizable and pleasing measure, so poetry breaks up the whole prosaic picture of experience to introduce into it a rhythm more congenial and intelligible to the mind. And in both these cases the operation is essentially the same as that by which, in an intermediate sphere, the images rejected by practical thought, and the emotions ignored by it, are so marshalled as to fill the mind with a truer and intenser consciousness of its memorable experience. The poetry of fancy, of observation, and of passion moves on this intermediate level; the poetry of mere sound and virtuosity is confined to the lower sphere; and the highest is reserved for the poetry of the creative reason. But one principle is present throughout,—the principle of Beauty,— the art of assimilating phenomena, whether words, images, emotions, or systems of ideas, to the deeper innate cravings of the mind.

Let us now dwell a little on this higher function of poetry and try to distinguish some of its phases.

The creation of characters is what many of us might at first be tempted to regard as the supreme triumph of the imagination. If we abstract, however, from our personal tastes and look at the matter in its human and logical relations, we shall see, I think, that the construction of characters is not the ultimate task of poetic fiction. A character can never be exhaustive of our materials: for it exists by its idiosyncrasy, by its contrast with other natures, by its development of one side, and one side only, of our native capacities. It is, therefore, not by characterization as such that the ultimate message can be rendered. The poet can put only a part of himself into any of his heroes, but he must put the whole into his noblest work. A character is accordingly only a fragmentary unity; fragmentary in respect to its origin,—since it is conceived by enlargement, so to speak, of a part of our own being to the exclusion of the rest,—and fragmentary in respect to the object it presents, since a character must live in an environment and be appreciated by contrast and by the sense of derivation. Not the character, but its effects and causes, is the truly interesting thing. Thus in master poets, like Homer and Dante, the characters, although well drawn, are subordinate to the total movement and meaning of the scene. There is indeed something pitiful, something comic, in any comprehended soul; souls, like other things, are only definable by their limitations. We feel instinctively that it would be insulting to speak of any man to his face as we should speak of him in his absence, even if what we say is in the way of praise: for absent he is a character understood, but present he is a force respected.

In the construction of ideal characters, then, the imagination is busy with material,—particular actions and thoughts,—which suggest their unification in persons; but the characters thus conceived can hardly be adequate to the profusion of our observations, nor exhaustive, when all personalities are taken together, of the interest of our lives. Characters are initially imbedded in life, as the gods themselves are originally imbedded in Nature. Poetry must, therefore, to render all reality, render also the background of its figures, and the events that condition their acts. We must place them in that indispensable environment which the landscape furnishes to the eye and the social medium to the emotions.

The visible landscape is not a proper object for poetry. Its elements, and especially the emotional stimulation which it gives, may be suggested or expressed in verse; but landscape is not thereby represented in its proper form; it appears only as an element and associate of moral unities. Painting, architecture, and gardening, with the art of stage setting, have the visible landscape for their object, and to those arts we may leave it. But there is a sort of landscape larger than the visible, which escapes the synthesis of the eye; it is present to that topographical sense by which we always live in the consciousness that there is a sea, that there are mountains, that the sky is above us, even when we do not see it, and that the tribes of men, with their different degrees of blamelessness, are scattered over the broad-backed earth. This cosmic landscape poetry alone can render, and it is no small part of the art to awaken the sense of it at the right moment, so that the object that occupies the centre of vision may be seen in its true lights, coloured by its wider associations, and dignified by its felt affinities to things permanent and great. As the Italian masters were wont not to paint their groups of saints about the Virgin without enlarging the canvas, so as to render a broad piece of sky, some mountains and rivers, and nearer, perhaps, some decorative pile; so the poet of larger mind envelops his characters in the atmosphere of Nature and history, and keeps us constantly aware of the world in which they move.

The distinction of a poet—the dignity and humanity of his thought— can be measured by nothing, perhaps, so well as by the diameter of the world in which he lives; if he is supreme, his vision, like Dante's, always stretches to the stars. And Virgil, a supreme poet sometimes unjustly be- littled, shows us the same thing in another form; his landscape is the Roman universe, his theme the sacred springs of Roman greatness in piety, constancy, and law. He has not written a line in forgetfulness that he was a Roman; he loves country life and its labours because he sees in it the origin and bulwark of civic greatness; he honours tradition because it gives perspective and momentum to the history that ensues; he invokes the gods, because they are symbols of the physical and moral forces by which Rome struggled to dominion.

Almost every classic poet has the topographical sense; he swarms with proper names and allusions to history and fable; if an epithet is to be thrown in anywhere to fill up the measure of a line, he chooses instinc- tively an appellation of place or family; his wine is not red, but Samian; his gorges are not deep, but are the gorges of Haemus; his songs are not sweet, but Pierian. We may deride their practice as conventional, but they could far more justly deride ours as insignificant. Conventions do not arise without some reason, and genius will know how to rise above them by a fresh appreciation of their rightness, and will feel no temptation to overturn them in favour of personal whimsies. The ancients found poetry not so much in sensible accidents as in essential forms and noble associa- tions; and this fact marks very clearly their superior education. They dominated the world as we no longer dominate it, and lived, as we are too distracted to live, in the presence of the rational and the important.

A physical and historical background, however, is of little moment to the poet in comparison with that other environment of his characters,—the dramatic situations in which they are involved. The substance of poetry is, after all, emotion; and if the intellectual emotion of comprehension and the mimetic one of impersonation are massive, they are not so intense as the appetites and other transitive emotions of life; the passions are the chief basis of all interests, even the most ideal, and the passions are seldom brought into play except by the contact of man with man. The various forms of love and hate are only possible in society, and to imagine occasions in which these feelings may manifest all their inward vitality is the poet's function,—one in which he follows the fancy of every child, who puffs himself out in his day-dreams into an endless variety of heroes and lovers. The thrilling adventures which he craves demand an appropriate theatre; the glorious emotions with which he bubbles over must at all hazards find or feign their correlative objects.

But the passions are naturally blind, and the poverty of the imagination, when left alone, is absolute. The passions may ferment as they will, they never can breed an idea out of their own energy. This idea must be furnished by the senses, by outward experience, else the hunger of the soul will gnaw its own emptiness for ever. Where the seed of sensation has once fallen, however, the growth, variations, and exuberance of fancy may be unlimited. Only we still observe (as in the child, in dreams, and in the poetry of ignorant or mystical poets) that the intensity of inwardly generated visions does not involve any real increase in their scope or dignity. The inexperienced mind remains a thin mind, no matter how much its vapours may be heated and blown about by natural passion. It was a capital error in Fichte and Schopenhauer [8] to assign essential fertility to the will in the creation of ideas. They mistook, as human nature will do, even when at times it professes pessimism, an ideal for a reality: and because they saw how much the will clings to its objects, how it selects and magnifies them, they imagined that it could breed them out of itself. A man who thinks clearly will see that such self-determination of a will is inconceivable, since what has no external relation and no diversity of structure cannot of itself acquire diversity of functions. Such inconceivability, of course, need not seem a great objection to a man of impassioned inspiration; he may even claim a certain consistency in positing, on the strength of his preference, the inconceivable to be a truth.

The alleged fertility of the will is, however, disproved by experience, from which metaphysics must in the end draw its analogies and plausibility. The passions discover, they do not create, their occasions; a fact which is patent when we observe how they seize upon what objects they find, and how reversible, contingent, and transferable the emotions are in respect to their objects. A doll will be loved instead of a child, a child

[8] Johann Fichte (1762–1814) and Arthur Schopenhauer (1788–1860) were German philosophers.

instead of a lover, God instead of everything. The differentiation of the passions, as far as consciousness is concerned, depends on the variety of the objects of experience,—that is, on the differentiation of the senses and of the environment which stimulates them.

When the "infinite" spirit enters the human body, it is determined to certain limited forms of life by the organs which it wears; and its blank potentiality becomes actual in thought and deed, according to the fortunes and relations of its organism. The ripeness of the passions may thus precede the information of the mind and lead to groping in by-paths without issue; a phenomenon which appears not only in the obscure individual whose abnormalities the world ignores, but also in the starved, half-educated genius that pours the whole fire of his soul into trivial arts or grotesque superstitions. The hysterical forms of music and religion are the refuge of an idealism that has lost its way; the waste and failures of life flow largely in those channels. The carnal temptations of youth are incidents of the same maladaptation, when passions assert themselves before the conventional order of society can allow them physical satisfaction, and long before philosophy or religion can hope to transform them into fuel for its own sacrificial flames.

Hence flows the greatest opportunity of fiction. We have, in a sense, an infinite will; but we have a limited experience, an experience sadly inadequate to exercise that will either in its purity or its strength. To give form to our capacities nothing is required but the appropriate occasion; this the poet, studying the world, will construct for us out of the materials of his observations. He will involve us in scenes which lie beyond the narrow lane of our daily ploddings; he will place us in the presence of important events, that we may feel our spirit rise momentarily to the height of his great argument. The possibilities of love or glory, of intrigue and perplexity, will be opened up before us; if he gives us a good plot, we can readily furnish the characters, because each of them will be the realization of some stunted potential self of our own. It is by the plot, then, that the characters will be vivified, because it is by the plot that our own character will be expanded into its latent possibilities.

The description of an alien character can serve this purpose only very imperfectly; but the presentation of the circumstances in which that character manifests itself will make description unnecessary, since our instinct will supply all that is requisite for the impersonation. Thus it seems that Aristotle was justified in making the plot the chief element in fiction: for it is by virtue of the plot that the characters live, or, rather, that we live in them, and by virtue of the plot accordingly that our soul rises to that imaginative activity by which we tend at once to escape from the personal life and to realize its ideal. This idealization is, of course, partial and merely relative to the particular adventure in which we imagine ourselves engaged. But in some single direction our will finds self-expression, and understands itself; runs through the career which it ignorantly coveted, and gathers the fruits and the lesson of that enterprise.

This is the essence of tragedy: the sense of the finished life, of the will fulfilled and enlightened: that purging of the mind so much debated upon, which relieves us of pent-up energies, transfers our feelings to a greater object, and thus justifies and entertains our dumb passions, detaching them at the same time for a moment from their accidental occasions in our earthly life. An episode, however lurid, is not a tragedy in this nobler sense, because it does not work itself out to the end; it pleases without satisfying, or shocks without enlightening. This enlightenment, I need hardly say, is not a matter of theory or of moral maxims; the enlightenment by which tragedy is made sublime is a glimpse into the ultimate destinies of our will. This discovery need not be an ethical gain—Macbeth and Othello attain it as much as Brutus and Hamlet—it may serve to accentuate despair, or cruelty, or indifference, or merely to fill the imagination for a moment without much affecting the permanent tone of the mind. But without such a glimpse of the goal of a passion the passion has not been adequately read, and the fiction has served to amuse us without really enlarging the frontiers of our ideal experience. Memory and emotion have been played upon, but imagination has not brought anything new to the light.

The dramatic situation, however, gives us the environment of a single passion, of life in one of its particular phases; and although a passion, like Romeo's love, may seem to devour the whole soul, and its fortunes may seem to be identical with those of the man, yet much of the man, and the best part of him, goes by the board in such a simplification. If Leonardo da Vinci, for example, had met in his youth with Romeo's fate, his end would have been no more ideally tragic than if he had died at eighteen of a fever; we should be touched rather by the pathos of what he had missed, than by the sublimity of what he had experienced. A passion like Romeo's, compared with the ideal scope of human thought and emotion, is a thin dream, a pathological crisis.

Accordingly Aristophanes, remembering the original religious and political functions of tragedy, blushes to see upon the boards a woman in love. And we should readily agree with him, but for two reasons,—one, that we abstract too much, in our demands upon art, from nobility of mind, and from the thought of totality and proportion; the other, that we have learned to look for a symbolic meaning in detached episodes, and to accept the incidental emotions they cause, because of their violence and our absorption in them, as in some sense sacramental and representative of the whole. Thus the picture of an unmeaning passion, of a crime without an issue, does not appear to our romantic apprehension as the sorry farce it is, but rather as a true tragedy. Some have lost even the capacity to conceive of a true tragedy, because they have no idea of a cosmic order, of general laws of life, or of an impersonal religion. They measure the profundity of feeling by its intensity, not by its justifying relations; and in the radical disintegration of their spirit, the more they are devoured the more they fancy themselves fed. But the majority of us retain some sense of a meaning in our joys and sorrows, and even if we cannot pierce to their ultimate object, we feel that what absorbs us here and now has a merely borrowed or deputed power; that it is a symbol and foretaste of all reality speaking to the whole soul. At the same time our intelligence is too confused to give us any picture of that reality, and our will too feeble to marshal our disorganized loves into a religion consistent with itself and harmonious with the comprehended universe. A rational ideal eludes us, and we are the more inclined to plunge into mysticism.

Nevertheless, the function of poetry, like that of science, can only be fulfilled by the conception of harmonies that become clearer as they grow richer. As the chance note that comes to be supported by a melody becomes in that melody determinate and necessary, and as the melody, when woven into a harmony, is explicated in that harmony and fixed beyond recall, so the single emotion, the fortuitous dream, launched by the poet into the world of recognizable and immortal forms, looks in that world for its ideal supports and affinities. It must find them or else be blown back among the ghosts. The highest ideality is the comprehension of the real. Poetry is not at its best when it depicts a further possible experience, but when it initiates us, by feigning something which as an experience is impossible, into the meaning of the experience which we have actually had.

The highest example of this kind of poetry is religion; and although disfigured and misunderstood by the simplicity of men who believe in it without being capable of that imaginative interpretation of life in which its truth consists, yet this religion is even then often beneficent, because it colours life harmoniously with the ideal. Religion may falsely represent the ideal as a reality, but we must remember that the ideal, if not so represented, would be despised by the majority of men, who cannot understand that the value of things is moral, and who therefore attribute to what is moral a natural existence, thinking thus to vindicate its importance and value. But value lies in meaning, not in substance; in the ideal which things approach, not in the energy which they embody.

The highest poetry, then, is not that of the versifiers, but that of the prophets, or of such poets as interpret verbally the visions which the prophets have rendered in action and sentiment rather than in adequate words. That the intuitions of religion are poetical, and that in such intuitions poetry has its ultimate function, are truths of which both religion and poetry become more conscious the more they advance in refinement and profundity. A crude and superficial theology may confuse God with the thunder, the mountains, the heavenly bodies, or the whole universe; but when we pass from these easy identifications to a religion that has taken root in history and in the hearts of men, and has come to flower, we find its objects and its dogmas purely ideal, transparent expressions of moral experience and perfect counterparts of human needs. The evidence of history or of the senses is left far behind and never thought of; the evidence of the heart, the value of the idea, are alone regarded.

Take, for instance, the doctrine of transubstantiation. A metaphor here is the basis of a dogma, because the dogma rises to the same subtle region as the metaphor, and gathers its sap from the same soil of emotion. Religion has here rediscovered its affinity with poetry, and in insisting on the truth of its mystery it unconsciously vindicates the ideality of its truth.

Under the accidents of bread and wine lies, says the dogma, the substance of Christ's body, blood, and divinity. What is that but to treat facts as an appearance, and their ideal import as a reality? And to do this is the very essence of poetry, for which everything visible is a sacrament—an outward sign of that inward grace for which the soul is thirsting.

In this same manner, where poetry rises from its elementary and detached expressions in rhythm, euphuism, characterization, and story-telling, and comes to the consciousness of its highest function, that of portraying the ideals of experience and destiny, then the poet becomes aware that he is essentially a prophet, and either devotes himself, like Homer or Dante, to the loving expression of the religion that exists, or like Lucretius [9] or Wordsworth, to the heralding of one which he believes to be possible. Such poets are aware of their highest mission; others, whatever the energy of their genius, have not conceived their ultimate function as poets. They have been willing to leave their world ugly as a whole, after stuffing it with a sufficient profusion of beauties. Their contemporaries, their fellow-countrymen for many generations, may not perceive this defect, because they are naturally even less able than the poet himself to understand the necessity of so large a harmony. If he is short-sighted, they are blind, and his poetic world may seem to them sublime in its significance, because it may suggest some partial lifting of their daily burdens and some partial idealization of their incoherent thoughts.

Such insensibility to the highest poetry is no more extraordinary than the corresponding indifference to the highest religion; nobility and excellence, however, are not dependent on the suffrage of half-baked men, but on the original disposition of the clay and the potter; I mean on the conditions of the art and the ideal capacities of human nature. Just as a note is better than a noise because, its beats being regular, the ear and brain can react with pleasure on that regularity, so all the stages of harmony are better than the confusion out of which they come, because the soul that perceives that harmony welcomes it as the fulfilment of her natural ends. The Pythagoreans were therefore right when they made number the essence of the knowable world, and Plato was right when he said harmony was the first condition of the highest good. The good man is a poet whose syllables are deeds and make a harmony in Nature. The poet is a rebuilder of the imagination, to make a harmony in that. And he is not a complete poet if his whole imagination is not attuned and his whole experience composed into a single symphony.

For his complete equipment, then, it is necessary, in the first place, that he sing; that his voice be pure and well pitched, and that his numbers flow; then, at a higher stage, his images must fit with one another; he must be euphuistic, colouring his thoughts with many reflected lights of memory and suggestion, so that their harmony may be rich and profound; again, at a higher stage, he must be sensuous and free, that is, he must build up his world with the primary elements of experience, not with the conventions of common sense or intelligence; he must draw the whole soul into his harmonies, even if in doing so he disintegrates the

[9] Roman poet (97?–53 B.C.), author of *De Rerum Natura.*

partial systematizations of experience made by abstract science in the categories of prose. But finally, this disintegration must not leave the poet weltering in a chaos of sense and passion; it must be merely the ploughing of the ground before a new harvest, the kneading of the clay before the modelling of a more perfect form. The expression of emotion should be rationalized by derivation from character and by reference to the real objects that arouse it—to Nature, to history, and to the universe of truth; the experience imagined should be conceived as a destiny, governed by principles, and issuing in the discipline and enlightenment of the will. In this way alone can poetry become an interpretation of life and not merely an irrelevant excursion into the realm of fancy, multiplying our images without purpose, and distracting us from our business without spiritual gain.

If we may then define poetry, not in the formal sense of giving the minimum of what may be called by that name, but in the ideal sense of determining the goal which it approaches and the achievement in which all its principles would be fulfilled, we may say that poetry is metrical and euphuistic discourse, expressing thought which is both sensuous and ideal.

Such is poetry as a literary form; but if we drop the limitation to verbal expression, and think of poetry as that subtle fire and inward light which seems at times to shine through the world and to touch the images in our minds with ineffable beauty, then poetry is a momentary harmony in the soul amid stagnation or conflict,—a glimpse of the divine and an incitation to a religious life.

Religion is poetry become the guide of life, poetry substituted for science or supervening upon it as an approach to the highest reality. Poetry is religion allowed to drift, left without points of application in conduct and without an expression in worship and dogma; it is religion without practical efficacy and without metaphysical illusion. The ground of this abstractness of poetry, however, is usually only its narrow scope; a poet who plays with an idea for half an hour, or constructs a character to which he gives no profound moral significance, forgets his own thought, or remembers it only as a fiction of his leisure, because he has not dug his well deep enough to tap the subterraneous springs of his own life. But when the poet enlarges his theatre and puts into his rhapsodies the true visions of his people and of his soul, his poetry is the consecration of his deepest convictions, and contains the whole truth of his religion. What the religion of the vulgar adds to the poet's is simply the inertia of their limited apprehension, which takes literally what he meant ideally, and degrades into a false extension of this world on its own level what in his mind was a true interpretation of it upon a moral plane.

This higher plane is the sphere of significant imagination, of relevant fiction, of idealism become the interpretation of the reality it leaves behind. Poetry raised to its highest power is then identical with religion grasped in its inmost truth; at their point of union both reach their utmost purity and beneficence, for then poetry loses its frivolity and ceases to demoralize, while religion surrenders its illusions and ceases to deceive.

LEWIS E. GATES

IMPRESSIONISM AND APPRECIATION [1]
(1900)

PURE IMPRESSIONISM in literary criticism has of late years grown into great favour, both among critics themselves and with the public. The essentials of a good critic—so the rubric has come to run—are sensitiveness to the varying appeal of art, and the ability to translate this appeal into images and phrases. The impressionist must have delicacy of perception, mobility of mood, reverence for the shade, and a sure instinct for the specific integrating phrase, and for the image tinged with feeling.

The popular legend that places Matthew Arnold at the head of this critical tradition in England is at least partly true; he certainly cared more for the shade and sought more patiently to define it, than any earlier English critic. The cult of the shade was one of the many good things that came to him from France. But Arnold the critic was no match for Arnold the foe of Philistinism. Though he had early insisted on the need of detachment in literary criticism, Arnold suffered his moods to be perturbed and his temperament to be blurred by worry over practical and public questions of the hour; and in later years he grew so intent on coaching his fellow-countrymen in morals and religion as to lose in some degree his critical zest for refinements that had no direct ethical value. It is rather to Walter Pater among English essayists that the modern impressionist looks for precept and example in his search for disinterestedness, for artistic sincerity, and for flexibleness of temperament; and it is Pater who, more than all other English critics, has illustrated what appreciative criticism may accomplish.

Yet if we consider the matter more carefully, impressionism is neither Arnold's nor Pater's importation or invention. It is the result of far deeper influences than any one man could have put in play. It is indeed the expression in literature of certain spiritual tendencies that have long been developing,—tendencies the growth of which may be traced in man's relation to nature as well as to art. And it is because the moods and the in-instincts and the methods of impressionism may thus be discovered working themselves out connectedly and progressively in the history of the human spirit, that they must be regarded as justifying themselves, and as deserving from even the most conservative judges some degree of recognition and acceptance. Little by little, during the last two centuries, the human spirit has gained a finer and closer sense of the worth and meaning of every individual moment of pleasure in the presence alike of nature

[1] From *Studies and Appreciations* (New York, 1900).

and of art. The record of this increase of sensitiveness toward nature is to be found in poetry, and toward art in criticism.

Thomson's *Seasons* may be taken as representing the utmost sensitiveness to nature of which the early eighteenth century was capable. Even for a modern reader, Thomson's descriptions still have considerable charm; but what such a reader soon notes is that the effects Thomson portrays are all generalized effects, grouped significantly under the names of the four seasons. Typical spring, typical summer, and so on—these Thomson portrays, and of these he feels what may be called the generalized emotional value. Beyond this typical treatment of nature and these generalized emotions he does not pass. As we go on, however, through the poetry of the century, nature becomes gradually more localized; poets dare to mark with specific detail—to picture vividly—individual objects, and they feel, and set down in their verse, the general charm that *this* landscape, *this* smiling valley, or *this* brimming river, has for an impressionable observer. Cowper has thus recorded much of the beauty of the valley of the Ouse, with delicate truth and finished art. Yet, be it noted, he has included in his record little or no suggestion of his own peculiar momentary moods. In Wordsworth and the Romantic poets, the impressions of nature are still further defined—are individualized both in place and in time; at last we have "the time and the place and the loved one all together." Continually, in Romantic poetry, a special bit of nature, tinged with the colour of a fleeting mood, is enshrined in verse; the fusion of nature with man's spirit is relatively complete.

In criticism, too,—that is, in man's conscious relation to *art,*—a similar growth in sensitiveness and in concreteness of matter and mood may be traced. Addison was the first to try to work out, in his *Pleasures of the Imagination,* the psychology of artistic enjoyment; and his papers on *Paradise Lost* come nearer being patient and vital appreciation of literature than any earlier English criticism comes. Yet, after all, they get little beyond a conventional and general classification of impressions. Addison's words of praise and blame are few, literal, abstract, colourless. "Just," "natural," "elegant," "beautiful," "wonderfully beautiful and poetical"— these words and phrases, and others like them, are used again and again; and rarely indeed does Addison escape from such tagging generalities, and define a personal impression vividly and imaginatively. The history of literary criticism from Addison's day to our own is, if viewed in one way, the history of the ever-increasing refinement of the critic's sensorium; it is the history of the critic's increasing sensitiveness to delicate shades of spiritual experience in his reaction on literature; and finally, it is the history of a growing tendency on the part of the critic to value, above all else, his own intimate personal relation to this or that piece of literature—a tendency that more and more takes the form of prizing the fleeting mood, the passing poignant moment of enjoyment in the presence of art, until at last certain modern critics refuse, on principle, to feel twice alike about the same poem. In short, what has occurred is this: a poem in its relation to the critic has been gradually carried over from the outside world and made an intimate part of the critic's personality; it has been transformed from an external object, loosely related to universal mind and generalized emotion of which the critic stands as type, into a series of thought-waves and nerve-vibrations that run at a special moment through an active brain and a sensitive temperament. For the pre-Addisonian critic, a poem was something to be scanned and handled, like an exquisite casket, and to be praised in general terms for its conventional design, its ingenious setting of jewel-like ornaments, and its sure and skilful execution; for the modern impressionistic critic, it is like the tone of a dear voice, like the breath of early morning, like any intangible greeting that steals across the nerves and cherishes them with an intimately personal appeal.

Impressionism, then, justifies itself historically. But more than this, it justifies itself psychologically; for it recognizes with peculiar completeness the vitalizing power of literature—its fashion of putting into play the whole nature of each reader it addresses and its consequent, unlimited, *creative* energy. A piece of scientific writing offers to every man the same studiously unequivocal message; as far as the writer is consistently scientific, his terms have only an intellectual value, put only the mind into play, and guide all minds through the same routine of syllogism and inference to an inevitable conclusion. In contrast with this uniformity in the appeal of science is the infinite variableness and adaptability of literature. Every piece of literature is a mimic piece of life that tempts the reader to capture from it, with mind and heart and imagination, an individual bliss; he may, in some measure, shape it as he will—work out his own destiny with it. A theorem from Euclid once mastered is one and the same thing to every man—perennially monotonous. A play of Shakespeare's (or, for that matter, a sonnet of Rossetti's) speaks a language that varies in its power and suggestion according to the personality of the hearer, and even according to his mood; the poem gets its value, as life gets its value, from the temperament that confronts it; and it is this enchanting fickleness in literature that of late years impressionism has been more and more noting and illustrating, until some critics, like M. Anatole France,[2] assure us that literary criticism is nothing, and should be nothing, but the recital of one's personal adventures with a book.

It is a mistake, then, to protest against the growth of impressionism, as some nervous guardians of the public literary conscience are inclined to protest, as if a parasitic form of literature were creeping into undue importance. Regarded as literature about literature, impressionism may seem an overrefined product—two degrees removed from actual life, fantastically unreal; but regarded as the intimate record of what a few happy moments have meant to an alert mind and heart, impressionism is transcendently close to fact. The popularity of impressionism is only one sign more that we are learning to prize, above most things else, richness of spiritual experience. The sincere and significant mood—this is what we have come to care for, whether the mood be suggested by life, by nature, or by art and literature. False moods expressed maladroitly will doubtless

[2] French impressionistic literary critic and novelist (1844–1924).

try to get themselves accepted, just as artificial poems about nature have multiplied endlessly since Wordsworth's day. The counterfeit merely proves the worth of the original. In an age that has learned to look on art with conscious sincerity, and to recognize that the experience offered in art rivals religious experience in renovating and stimulating power, there must more and more come to be an imaginative literature that takes its inspiration direct from art; of such imaginative literature critical impressionistic writing is one of the most vital forms.

But though impressionistic writing may, as literature, not only justify itself, but prove to be sincerely expressive of some of the most original tendencies of the modern mind, the case is somewhat different when such writing is considered as literary criticism pure and simple, and is cross-questioned as to whether or no it can do the work that has hitherto been exacted of literary criticism. Some French critic, perhaps M. Jules Lemaître,[3] has been accused of turning an essay on a volume of Renan's *Histoire des origines du christianisme* into a lyrical recital of his own boyish delights with a Noah's ark. Instances enough of such critical waywardness must have fallen under every one's eye who keeps the run of current essay-work. Sainte-Beuve [4] long ago said of Taine [5] that in criticising an author he was apt to pull all the blankets to his own side of the bed. And what was true of Taine, because of his devotion to theory, is true of many modern critics, because of their wilfulness and caprice—or, to put the matter more sympathetically, because of their over-ruling delight in their own sensibility and impressionableness; they care for themselves more than for their author. When such egoism goes with genius and with artistic resource, the resulting essays justify themselves, because they reveal in fascinating wise new phases of the ever-varying spiritual consciousness of the age. But even in such cases, where a really original personality, under the chance stimulus of literature, flashes out at us winning and imaginatively suggestive glimpses of itself, it may be doubted whether the essay that results is, properly speaking, criticism. Nor is this doubt a mere quibble over terms. The doubt involves several serious questions as regards the nature of a work of art and the critic's proper mode of approach to art. Paradoxical folk have sometimes asserted that what is best worth while in a work of art is what the author never meant to put in it, and that the superlative act of the critic is to find in a work of art for the delight of modern temperaments some previously unsuspected implication of beauty. Paradoxes aside, how much truth is there in this conception of the critic's task? and how much truth in the conception that goes with it of the essentially relative and variable character of art? We may grant that a piece of writing is *literature*, providing it is a beautiful and significant revelation of personality, whether the nerve-vibrations that it utters take their start from life or nature or art. But is such a piece of writing *criticism* if in commenting on a work of art it wilfully neglects its in-

[3] French impressionistic literary critic and poet (1853–1914).
[4] Charles Augustin Sainte-Beuve (1804–1869), French critic.
[5] Hippolyte Taine (1828–1893), French historian and literary critic.

tended value as conceived in the mind of the original artist and as expressing, at least in part, the genius of the age whose life he shared? Can *criticism* properly neglect this original pleasure-value in a work of art? Can it furthermore neglect that permanent and deeply enwrought pleasure, involved in a work of art, through which it has always ministered and will always minister to normal human nature? Can *criticism* properly confine itself to the record of a momentary shiver across a single set of possibly degenerate nerves?

Surely, there is something objective in a work of art even when the work of art is regarded simply and solely as potential pleasure; and surely it is part of the task of the critic to take this objective character into full consideration. Unless he does so, his appreciation of the work will not be properly critical; nor indeed, for that matter, will his appreciation gather the full measure of personal delight that the work of art offers him. Just here lies the distinction between whimsical impressionism—which may be literature, very delightful literature, but lacks the perspective essential to criticism—and vital appreciation, which is indeed criticism in its purest and most suggestive form.

A work of art is a permanent incarnation of spiritual energy waiting for release. Milton long ago called a good book "the precious life-blood of a master-spirit stored up on purpose to a life beyond life." We nowadays may go even farther than this, and find treasured up in a piece of literature certain definite blisses and woes and flashes of insight that once went thrilling through a special temperament and mind. The most recent psychological explanations of artistic creation * concern themselves continually with the feelings of the artist; they trace out minutely the ways in which through the play of the artist's feelings a work of art is instinctively and surely generated. The poet concentrates his thought on some concrete piece of life, on some incident, character, or bit of personal experience; because of his emotional temperament, this concentration of interest stirs in him a quick play of feeling and prompts the swift concurrence of many images. Under the incitement of these feelings, and in accordance with laws of association that may at least in part be described, these images grow bright and clear, take definite shapes, fall into significant groupings, branch and ramify, and break into sparkling mimicry of the actual world of the senses—all the time delicately controlled by the poet's conscious purpose and so growing intellectually significant, but all the time, if the work of art is to be vital, impelled also in their alert weaving of patterns by the moods of the poet, by his fine instinctive sense of the emotional expressiveness of this or that image that lurks in the background of his consciousness. For this intricate web of images, tinged with his most intimate moods, the poet through his intuitive command of words finds an apt series of sound-symbols and records them with written characters. And so a poem arises through an exquisite distillation of personal moods into imagery and into language, and is ready to offer to all future generations its undiminishing store of spiritual joy and strength.

* See, for example, Professor Dilthey's *Die Einbildungskraft des Dichters*. [Gates's note]

But it is not merely the poet's own spiritual energy that goes into his poem. The spirit of the age—if the poem include much of life in its scope, if it be more than a lyric—enters also into the poem, and moulds it and shapes it, and gives it in part its colour and emotional cast and intellectual quality. In every artist there is a definite mental bias, a definite spiritual organization and play of instincts, which results in large measure from the common life of his day and generation, and which represents this life— makes it potent—within the individuality of the artist. This so-called "acquired constitution of the life of the soul"—it has been described by Professor Dilthey [6] with noteworthy acuteness and thoroughness—determines in some measure the contents of the artist's mind, for it determines his interests, and therefore the sensations and perceptions that he captures and automatically stores up. It guides him in his judgments of worth, in his instinctive likes and dislikes as regards conduct and character, and controls in large measure the play of his imagination as he shapes the action of his drama or epic and the destinies of his heroes. Its prejudices interfiltrate throughout the molecules of his entire moral and mental life, and give to each image and idea some slight shade of attractiveness or repulsiveness, so that when the artist's spirit is at work under the stress of feeling, weaving into the fabric of a poem the competing images and ideas in his consciousness, certain ideas and images come more readily and others lag behind, and the resulting work of art gets a colour and an emotional tone and suggestions of value that subtly reflect the genius of the age. Thus it is that into a work of art there creeps a prevailing sort of spiritual energy that may be identified as also operating throughout the social life of the time, and as finding its further expressions in the precepts and the parables of the moralist, in the statecraft of the political leader, in the visionary dreams of the prophet and priest, and, in short, in all the various ideals, mental, moral, and social, that rule the age.

Now, as for the impressionistic writer about literature—he is apt to concern himself very little with this historical origin of a work of art. In dealing with the poetry of a long past age, he will very likely refuse the hard task of "trundling back his soul" two hundred or two thousand years and putting himself in close sympathy with the people of an earlier period. He is apt to take a poem very much as he would take a bit of nature—as a pretty play of sound or imagery upon the senses; and he may, indeed, capture through this half-sensuous treatment of art, a peculiar, though wayward, delight. But the appreciative critic is not content with this. He is, to be sure, well aware that his final enjoyment of a poem of some earlier age will be a far subtler and richer experience than would be the mere repetition of the pleasures that the poem gave its writer; that his enjoyment will have countless overtones and undertones that could not have existed for the producer of the poem or for its original hearers. But he also believes that the generating pleasures that produced the work of art, and that once

[6] Wilhelm Dilthey (1834–1911), German philosopher, best known for his attempt to set psychology as the basis for scientific research in history and sociology, and ignoring metaphysics.

thrilled in a single human spirit, in response to the play and counter-play upon him of the life of his time, must remain permanently the central core of energy in the work of art; and that only as he comes to know those pleasures with fine intimacy, can he conjure out of the work of art its perfect acclaim of delight for now and here.

Therefore the appreciative critic makes use of the historical method in his study of literature. He does not use this method as the man of science uses it, for the final purpose of understanding and explaining literature as a mass of sociological facts governed by fixed laws. This rationalization of literature is not his chief concern, though he may pass this way on his journey to his special goal. But he is persuaded that in all the art and all the literature that reach the present out of the past, spirit speaks to spirit across a vast gulf of time; that he can catch the precise quality of one of these voices that come down the years only through the aid of delicate imaginative sympathy with the life of an elder generation; and that he can develop to certainty of response this divining sympathy only through patient and loyal study of the peculiar play of the powers that built up in the minds and the imaginations of those earlier men their special vision of earth and heaven.

Difficult and elusive indeed are the questions he must ask himself about the art from a distant age, if he is to be sure of just the quality of the pleasure that went into its creation. If it be Greek art that he seeks to appreciate, he will study and interpret it as the expression of the spirit of Greek life, of a spirit that lived along the nerves and fibres of an entire social organism, of a spirit that sprung from the unconscious depths of instinct, out of which slowly bodied themselves forth conscious purposes and clear ideals, and that penetrated and animated all fashions and forms of belief and behaviour, and gave them their colour and shape and rhythm. He will trace out and capture the quality of this spirit as it expressed itself in the physical life of the Greeks, in their social customs, in their weaving of scientific systems, in their worship of nature, and in the splendid intricacies of their religious ritual and mysteries. And so he will hope to gain at last a sure sense of the peculiar play of energy that found release in some one of their poems, or in the marble or bronze of a hero or a god.

But the universal element in the poetry of an age by no means completes the objective character of the feeling the poetry has treasured for the delight of later times. In the case of all poetry not communal in its origin, the pleasure involved in a poem was generated in the consciousness of a single artist, and had a definite quality that partook of his individuality. Therefore the appreciative critic has a further nice series of identifications before him in his ideal search for the delight that inheres in a poem. Just what was the innermost nature of the poet who appeals to us in it, often so pathetically, down through the perilous ways of time? What was the special vision of life that he saw and felt the thrill of? What were the actual rhythms of the quicksilver passion in his veins? What was the honeydew on which he fed? What was the quintessential pleasure that he, among all men of his day, distilled into his verse?

Fantastic or insoluble these questions may seem unless with regard to poets about whom we have the closest personal memoranda. Yet critics have now and then answered such questions with surprising insight, even in the case of poets the gossip of whose lives is wholly unknown to us, and whose form of art was least personal in its revelations. Professor Dowden's [7] grouping of Shakespeare's plays in accordance with the prevailing spiritual tone-colour of each and the moods toward life that are imaginatively uttered —moods of debonair light-heartedness, of rollicking jollity, of despairing pessimism, or of luminous golden-tempered comprehension—is an admirable example of the possible intimate interpretation of a poet's varying emotions as treasured in his art.

Here, then, are suggested two ways in which the appreciative critic who would make his impression of a work of art something more than a superficial momentary irritation of pleasure and pain will contrive to direct the play of his spiritual energy. He will realize, as far as he can, the primal vital impulse that wrought out the work of art; he will, in appreciating a poem, discover and recreate in his own soul the rhythms of delight with which the poem vibrated for the men of the age whose life the poem uttered; and he will also discern and realize those actual moods, those swift counter-changes of feeling, which once, in a definite place and at a definite moment, within the consciousness of a single artist evoked images and guided them into union, charged them with spiritual power, and called into rhythmical order sound-symbols to represent them thenceforth for ever.

But it must at once be noted that this mimetic enjoyment is after all only the beginning of that process of vitalization by which an appreciative critic wins from a work of art its entire store of delight. The mood of the modern critic is something far subtler than any mere repetition of the mood of the original creative artist; it contains in itself a complexity and a richness of suggestion and *motifs* that correspond to all the gains the human spirit has made since the earlier age. Indeed, these subtle spiritual differences begin to declare themselves the moment the critic tries to describe the earlier enjoyment enshrined in a work of art. Walter Pater, for example, in noting in his essay on Winckelmann, the serene equipoise in Greek art between man's spirit and his body, at once involuntarily sets over against this mood the later mood in which spirit usurps and so tyrannizes over matter in its exaction of expression as to distort the forms of art, and render them "pathetic." No such contrast as this was present in the mind of the Greek as he enjoyed his own art; nor any contrast with a hungry, over-subtle intellectualism, such as nowadays makes the modern consciousness anxious for the individualizing accurate detail and the motley effects of realism. Yet these contrasts and others like them are part of the very essence of our modern delight in the freedom and largeness and calm strength of Greek art. Perhaps the Greek had more zest in his art than we have in it; but his enjoyment certainly had not the luxurious intricacy and the manifold implications of our enjoyment.

Always, then, in the complete appreciation of a work of art there is this superimposition of other moods upon the mood of the creative artist—

[7] Edward Dowden (1843–1913), Irish literary critic and historian.

there is a reinforcement of the original effect by the delicate interfusion of new tones and strains of feeling. Often this is as if harmonies once written for a harpsichord were played upon a modern piano whose "temperament" has been made rich and expressive through the artful use and adjustment of all possible overtones. We shall be able to draw from the music new shades of meaning and of beauty. But the original chords—those we should scrupulously repeat; and the original tone-colour, too, it were well to have at least in memory. If a critic will win from early Florentine painting— from the work, for example, of Fra Lippo Lippi [8]—its innermost value for the modern temperament, he will first recover imaginatively the sincere religious impulse and the naïve religious faith, as well as the dawning delight in the opening possibilities of a new art, which animated those early painters. He will try to catch the very mood that underlies the tender mystic wistfulness of Lippo Lippi's Madonnas, and that gives them their soft and luminous constraint in the midst of the eager adoration of shepherd boys and attending angels. He will recognize this mood as perhaps all the more appealing because of the quaint incompleteness of the artist's technique, his loyal archaic awkwardness, his religious formalism and symbolism, his unsure perspective, all the tantalizing difficulties of execution through which his vision of beauty made its way into colour and form. This mood will define itself for the critic through the aid of many nicely modulated contrasts—through contrast, it may be, with the more shadowed and poignantly mysterious Madonnas of Botticelli,[9] and with the splendid and victorious womanhood of Titian's Madonnas,[10] with the gentle and terrestrial grace of motherhood in those of Andrea del Sarto,[11] and with the sweetly ordered comeliness of Van Dyck's Madonnas.[12] But above all, it will define itself through contrast with our modern mood toward the Madonna and the religious ideas she symbolizes—through contrast with our sophisticated reverie, our hardly won half-credence, and our wise, pathetic insight. And through this contrast the earlier mood will gain for us a certain poignancy of delight; for the mood will come to us as something restored as by miracle out of the otherwise irrecoverable past of the spirit— out of the past of that spirit whose wayfaring through passions of aspiration and joy, and through drear times of sadness and desolation, was *our* wayfaring, since we have gathered into ourselves all the usufruct of it:—

> "Oh! what is this that knows the road I came,
> The flame turned cloud, the cloud returned to flame,
> The lifted, shifted steeps and all the way?"

The appreciative critic, then, should know the characteristic joy of every generation of men, and the special joy of each individual artist. He is to be a specialist in historic delight, as the poet is a specialist in the joys of

---

[8] Fra Filippo Lippi (1406–1469).
[9] Sandro Botticelli (1444?–1510), Italian painter.
[10] Vecelli Titian (ca. 1477–1576), Italian painter.
[11] Andrea Del Sarto (1486–1531), Italian painter.
[12] Sir Anthony Van Dyck (1599–1641), Flemish painter.

his own day and generation. And therefore in trying to make real to the men of his own time the special bliss that an older work of art contains for them, the appreciative critic will not be content, as is the impressionistic critic, with interpreting it in terms of some chance wayward mood. He will wish to relumine and make potent all that is emotionally vital in the work of art; he will capture again its original quality; he will revive imaginatively those moments of bliss in the history of the human spirit which are closely akin to this bliss and which yet vary from it finely, and moments, too, that contrast broadly and picturesquely with it, all the moments, indeed, which his divining instinct directs him toward, as fit to throw into relief by contrast what is quintessential in this one moment of spiritual ardour. Thus he will try to offer to the men of his own day a just appreciation of the peculiar joy that, in the passage of years, the human spirit has stored up for itself in this record of one of its earlier phases of experience.

Throughout all his patient search for the precise quality of a work of art, the critic will, of course, make wise use of the science of aesthetics. Its analyses and principles are supposed to reveal and sum up in terse formulas the mystery of beauty, and they should therefore offer the critic a means of steadying himself into a sincerely sympathetic and uneccentric report of the special charm that lurks in a work of art. Yet it must at once be noted that for the appreciative critic the whole region of aesthetics is full of danger. Aesthetic theorizing has been the pet pastime of many callous and horny-eyed philosophers, whose only knowledge of beauty has come by hearsay. Nothing worse can happen to a critic than to be caught in the meshes of such thinkers' *a priori* theories, so much depends on the critic's keeping an intimately vital relation to the art of which he will interpret the peculiar power. Of recent years, however, the science of aesthetics has been rescued from the region of metaphysics, and has been brought very close to fact and made very real and suggestive through the use of psychological methods of study. The peculiar genius of the artist has been analyzed and described; the characteristics of his temperament have been noted with the nicest loyalty; and particularly the play of his special faculty, the imagination, as this faculty through the use of sensations and images and moods and ideas creates a work of art, has been followed out with the utmost delicacy of observation by such acute and sensitive analysts as M. Gabriel Séailles, M. Michaut,[13] and Professor Dilthey. The behaviour, too, of the mind that is enjoying a work of art—this has been minutely studied and described; the "effects" and the "impressions" have been recorded by such masters of silvery instruments for weighing a fancy and measuring a motive as Fechner. The relations between all these impressions and effects and the form and content of a work of art have been tabulated. And so the science of aesthetics has become a really vital record of what may be called the mind's normal behaviour both in the creation and in the enjoyment of art.

[13] M. Gabriel Séailles (1852–1922), French philosopher and critic. Gustave Michaut (1870–   ), French literary critic.

The expert critic must some time or other have followed out all these devious analyses and tracked out the intricate workings both of the typical artist's and of the typical appreciator's mind. Such an abstract initiation will have quickened his powers of perception in numberless ways, will have made him alive to countless signs and suggestions in a work of art that might otherwise have appealed to him in vain, and above all will serve to steady him against extravagance and grotesque caprice in appreciation. In these analyses and principles he has the sensitive record of a consensus of expert opinion on the nature of artistic enjoyment—its causes and varieties. Through the help of these canons he may guard against meaningless egoism; he may manoeuvre wisely within the region of the normal; he may keep within measurable distance of the tastes and the temperaments of his fellows. He will be able to test his impressions, to judge of their relative importance, to restrain personal whim within bounds, and to remain sanely true to the predominating interests of the normal human mind.

Not that the critic will let his use of aesthetic formulas and points of view conventionalize or stereotype his treatment of art. If he be happily individual and alert, he will refuse to have forced upon him a system, a method, unalterable preconceptions, or habitual modes of approach to art. He will keep in his repeated encounters with a work of art much of the dilettante's bright wilfulness and fickleness. He will go to it in all moods and all weathers, will wait upon its good pleasure, and will note delightedly all its fleeting aspects. But these stray impressions will not content him, nor will he care to report them as of themselves forming a valid and final appreciation. He will play the pedant with himself; he will, in sober moments of wise hypocrisy, test the worth of his impressions by approved and academic standards; and he will scrutinize them in the light of those canons which the best modern theorizers in things aesthetic have worked out psychologically. He will select and arrange and make significant and unify. And so, while approaching a work of art unconventionally and communing with it intimately, he will, in commenting on it, keep his casual and personal sense of its charm within limits, and be intent on doing full justice to what the work of art may well mean to the normal man in normal moods.

Moreover, this aesthetic initiation will reveal to the critic one special sort of pleasure stored in a work of art that the layman is peculiarly apt to miss —the pleasure that may be won from tracing out the artist's mastery of technique and the secrets of his victorious execution. Here, again, the critic, if he is to make the work of art give up its quintessential quality, must call the historical method to his aid. An artist who, at any moment in the history of art, wishes to express his vision of beauty through the medium and the technique of his special art, whether it be painting, or music, or poetry, always confronts a definite set of limiting conditions. He finds certain fashions prevailing in his art; he finds in vogue certain conventional ways of treating material; he finds certain fixed forms offering themselves for his use—forms like the sonata and the concerto in music, or like the sonnet and the drama in poetry. These forms are traditional, have various laws and regulations attached to their handling, and in a sense limit the freedom of the artist, require him to make certain concessions, force him to conceive his material in stereotyped ways, and to cast it in pre-determined moulds. An artist has always to find out for himself how far he can use these old forms; how far he can limit himself advantageously through accepting old conventions, whether his peculiar vision of beauty can be fully realized within the limits of the established technique, or whether he must be an innovator.

There is a curious and exquisite pleasure to be won from watching artists at close quarters with technical problems of this sort, and from observing the fine certainty with which genius gets the better of technical difficulties, through accepting a convention here, through following a fashion there, through slightly or even audaciously altering received forms or modes to secure scope for novel moods or hitherto unattained effects. An artist's vital relation to the past of his art—this is something that as it shows itself here and there in his work, the sensitive and alert critic finds keen pleasure in detecting. Here, again, the critic's specialized temperament and knowledge mediate between the art of earlier times and the men of his own day, and reveal through the help of aesthetics and history the peculiar pleasure with which art has, consciously or unconsciously, been charged.

Finally, the critic must bear in mind that it is distinctly for the men of his own day that he is revitalizing art; that it is for them that his specialized temperament is to use its resources. Every age, some one has said, must write its own literary criticism; and this holds specially true of appreciative criticism. The value of a work of art depends on what it finds in the consciousness to which it appeals; and because individuality is deeper and richer now than it has ever been before, and because the men of to-day are "the heirs of the ages," and have "ransacked the ages and spoiled the climes," a great traditional work of art ought to have a richer, more various, more poignant value for modern men than it had for their predecessors. Even in the matter of sense-perceptions this progress is noticeable. "Our forefathers," says a recent essayist on M. Claude Monet, "saw fewer tones and colours than we; they had, in fact, a simpler and more naïve vision; the modern eye is being educated to distinguish a complexity of shades and varieties of colour before unknown." If there has been this increase of delicate power even in a slowly changing physical organ, far greater have been the increase and diversification of sensitiveness in the region of spiritual perception. New facts and ideas have been pouring into the national consciousness from the physical sciences during the last half-century, tending to transform in countless subtle ways man's sense of his own place in the universe, his ideals of brotherhood, of justice, of happiness, and his orientation toward the Unseen. The half-mystical control that has of late years been won over physical forces, the increased speed with which news flies from country to country, the cheap and swift modes of travel from land to land which break down the barriers between the most widely divergent civilizations—all these influences are reacting continually on the life of the spirit, are stirring men's minds to new thoughts and new moods, and developing in them new aptitudes and new powers. For minds thus changed and thus touched into new alertness and sensitiveness, past art must take on new phases, reveal in itself new suggestions, and acquire or lose stimulating power in manifold ways. These alterations of value the appreciative critic ought to feel and transcribe.

And therefore the critic's must not be a "cloistered virtue"; at least imaginatively, he must be in sympathy with the whole life of his time. He must be intimately aware of its practical aims and preoccupations, of its material strivings, of all the busy play of its social activities, of its moral and religious perturbations, even of its political intrigues. Doubtless Matthew Arnold was right when he insisted on "detachment" as the first requisite of good criticism. But in urging detachment, Arnold meant simply that the critic must not let himself become the victim of practical problems or party organizations; that he must not let his imagination be seized upon by a set of definite ideas that are at once to be realized in fact; that he must not become an intellectual or moral or political bigot or a mere Tory or Radical advocate—the one-idea'd champion of a programme. The critic must have much of the dilettante's fine irresponsibility, perhaps even something of the cynic's amused aloofness from the keen competitions of daily life. But he must also have the dilettante's infinite variety, his intense dramatic curiosity, and his alert, wide-ranging vision. He should know the men of his own day through and through in all their tastes and tempers, and should be even more sensitively aware than they are themselves of their collective prejudices. So he should deepen his personality and as far as possible include within it whatever is most characteristic of his age. In the terms of all this, as well as of his own fleeting moods, he will try to appreciate past art. And so he will become, in very truth, the specialized temperament of the moment, interpreting the past to the present.

Continually, then, in his search for the pleasure involved in a work of art, the critic finds that he must go outside the work of art and go beyond his own momentary state of consciousness; he must see the work of art in its relations to larger and larger groups of facts; and he can charm out of it its true quality only by interpreting its sensations and images and rhythms as expressing something far greater than themselves, and as appealing to something far more permanent than his own fleeting moods. He must put the work of art in its historical setting; he must realize it in its psychological origin; he must conceive of it as one characteristic moment in the development of the human spirit, and in order thus to vitalize it he must be aware of it in its contrasting relations with other characteristic moments and phases of this development; and, finally, he must be alive to its worth as a delicately transparent illustration of aesthetic law. In regarding the work of art under all these aspects, his aim is primarily not to explain and not to judge or dogmatize, but to enjoy; to realize the manifold charm the work of art has gathered into itself from all sources, and to interpret this charm imaginatively to the men of his own day and generation.

FRANK NORRIS

From THE RESPONSIBILITIES OF THE NOVELIST [1]
(1903)

The Novel With a "Purpose"

AFTER YEARS of indoctrination and expostulation on the part of the artists, the people who read appear at last to have grasped this one precept—"the novel must not preach," but "the purpose of the story must be subordinate to the story itself." It took a very long time for them to understand this, but once it became apparent they fastened upon it with a tenacity comparable only to the tenacity of the American schoolboy to the date "1492." "The novel must not preach," you hear them say.

As though it were possible to write a novel without a purpose, even if it is only the purpose to amuse. One is willing to admit that this savours a little of quibbling, for "purpose" and purpose to amuse are two different purposes. But every novel, even the most frivolous, must have some reason for the writing of it, and in that sense must have a "purpose."

Every novel must do one of three things—it must (1) tell something, (2) show something, or (3) prove something. Some novels do all three of these; some do only two; all must do at least one.

The ordinary novel merely tells something, elaborates a complication, devotes itself primarily to *things*. In this class comes the novel of adventure, such as "The Three Musketeers."

The second and better class of novel shows something, exposes the workings of a temperament, devotes itself primarily to the minds of human beings. In this class falls the novel of character, such as "Romola."

The third, and what we hold to be the best class, proves something, draws conclusions from a whole congeries of forces, social tendencies, race impulses, devotes itself not to a study of men but of man. In this class falls the novel with the purpose, such as "Les Miserables."

And the reason we decide upon this last as the highest form of the novel is because that, though setting a great purpose before it as its task, it nevertheless includes, and is forced to include, both the other classes. It must tell something, must narrate vigorous incidents and must show something, must penetrate deep into the motives and character of type-men, men who are composite pictures of a multitude of men. It must do this because of the nature of its subject, for it deals with elemental forces, motives that stir whole nations. These cannot be handled as abstractions in fiction. Fiction can find expression only in the concrete. The elemental

---

[1] New York, 1903.

forces, then, contribute to the novel with a purpose to provide it with vigorous action. In the novel, force can be expressed in no other way. The social tendencies must be expressed by means of analysis of the characters of the men and women who compose that society, and the two must be combined and manipulated to evolve the purpose—to find the value of x.

The production of such a novel is probably the most arduous task that the writer of fiction can undertake. Nowhere else is success more difficult; nowhere else is failure so easy. Unskilfully treated, the story may dwindle down and degenerate into mere special pleading, and the novelist become a polemicist, a pamphleteer, forgetting that, although his first consideration is to prove his case, his *means* must be living human beings, not statistics, and that his tools are not figures, but pictures from life as he sees it. The novel with a purpose *is,* one contends, a preaching novel. But it preaches by telling things and showing things. Only, the author selects from the great storehouse of actual life the things to be told and the things to be shown, which shall bear upon his problem, his purpose. The preaching, the moralizing, is the result not of direct appeal by the writer, but is made—should be made—to the reader by the very incidents of the story.

But here is presented a strange anomaly, a distinction as subtle as it is vital. Just now one has said that in the composition of the kind of novel under consideration the *purpose* is for the novelist the all-important thing, and yet it is impossible to deny that the *story,* as a mere story, is to the story-writer the one great object of attention. How reconcile then these two apparent contradictions?

For the novelist, the purpose of his novel, the problem he is to solve, is to his story what the keynote is to the sonata. Though the musician cannot exaggerate the importance of the keynote, yet the thing that interests him is the sonata itself. The keynote simply coördinates the music, systematizes it, brings all the myriad little rebellious notes under a single harmonious code.

Thus, too, the purpose in the novel. It is important as an end and also as an ever-present guide. For the writer it is as important only as a note to which his work must be attuned. The moment, however, that the writer becomes really and vitally interested in his purpose his novel fails.

Here is the strange anomaly. Let us suppose that Hardy, say, should be engaged upon a story which had for purpose to show the injustices under which the miners of Wales were suffering. It is conceivable that he could write a story that would make the blood boil with indignation. But he himself, if he is to remain an artist, if he is to write his novel successfully, will, as a novelist, care very little about the iniquitous labour system of the Welsh coal-mines. It will be to him as impersonal a thing as the key is to the composer of a sonata. As a man Hardy may or may not be vitally concerned in the Welsh coal-miner. That is quite unessential. But as a novelist, as an artist, his sufferings must be for him a matter of the mildest interest. They are important, for they constitute his keynote. They are *not* interesting for the reason that the working out of his *story,* its people, episodes, scenes and pictures, is for the moment the most interesting thing in all the world to him, exclusive of everything else. Do you think that Mrs. Stowe was more interested in the slave question than she was in the writing of "Uncle Tom's Cabin"? Her book, her manuscript, the page-to-page progress of the narrative, were more absorbing to her than all the Negroes that were ever whipped or sold. Had it not been so, that great purpose novel never would have succeeded.

Consider the reverse—"Fecondité," for instance. The purpose for which Zola wrote the book ran away with him. He really did care more for the depopulation of France than he did for his novel. Result—sermons on the fruitfulness of women, special pleading, a farrago of dry, dull incidents, overburdened and collapsing under the weight of a theme that should have intruded only indirectly.

This is preëminently a selfish view of the question, but it is assuredly the only correct one. It must be remembered that the artist has a double personality, himself as a man and himself as an artist. But, it will be urged, how account for the artist's sympathy in his fictitious characters, his emotion, the actual tears he sheds in telling of their griefs, their deaths, and the like?

The answer is obvious. As an artist his sensitiveness is quickened because they are characters in his novel. It does not at all follow that the same artist would be moved to tears over the report of parallel catastrophes in real life. As an artist, there is every reason to suppose he would welcome the news with downright pleasure. It would be for him "good material." He would see a story in it, a good scene, a great character. Thus the artist. What he would do, how he would feel as a man is quite a different matter.

To conclude, let us consider one objection urged against the novel with a purpose by the plain people who read. For certain reasons, difficult to explain, the purpose novel always ends unhappily. It is usually a record of suffering, a relation of tragedy. And the plain people say, "Ah, we see so much suffering in the world, why put it into novels? We do not want it in novels."

One confesses to very little patience with this sort. "We see so much suffering in the world already!" Do they? Is this really true? The people who buy novels are the well-to-do people. They belong to a class whose whole scheme of life is concerned solely with an aim to avoid the unpleasant. Suffering, the great catastrophes, the social throes, that annihilate whole communities, or that crush even isolated individuals—all these are as far removed from them as earthquakes and tidal-waves. Or, even if it were so, suppose that by some miracle these blind eyes were opened and the sufferings of the poor, the tragedies of the house around the corner, really were laid bare. If there is much pain in life, all the more reason that it should appear in a class of literature which, in its highest form, is a sincere transcription of life.

It is the complaint of the coward, this cry against the novel with a purpose, because it brings the tragedies and griefs of others to notice. Take this element from fiction, take from it the power and opportunity to prove that injustice, crime and inequality do exist, and what is left? Just the amusing novels, the novels that entertain. The juggler in spangles, with his balancing-pole and gilt ball, does this. You may consider the modern novel from this point of view. It may be a flippant paper-covered thing of swords and cloaks, to be carried on a railway journey and to be thrown out the window when read, together with the sucked oranges and peanut shells. Or it may be a great force, that works together with the pulpit and the universities for the good of the people, fearlessly proving that power is abused, that the strong grind the faces of the weak, that an evil tree is still growing in the midst of the garden, that undoing follows hard upon unrighteousness, that the course of Empire is not yet finished, and that the races of men have yet to work out their destiny in those great and terrible movements that crush and grind and rend asunder the pillars of the houses of the nations.

Fiction may keep pace with the Great March, but it will not be by dint of amusing the people. The muse is a teacher, not a trickster. Her rightful place is with the leaders, but in the last analysis that place is to be attained and maintained not by cap-and-bells, but because of a serious and sincere interest, such as inspires the great teachers, the great divines, the great philosophers, a well-defined, well-seen, courageously sought-for purpose.

J. E. SPINGARN

THE NEW CRITICISM [1]
(1910)

"WHAT DROLL creatures these college professors are whenever they talk about art," wrote Flaubert [2] in one of his letters, and voiced the world's opinion of academic criticism. For the world shares the view of the Italian poet that "monks and professors cannot write the lives of poets," and looks only to those rich in literary experience for its opinions on literature. But the poets themselves have had no special grudge against academic criticism that they have not felt equally for every other kind. For the most part, they have objected to all criticism, since what each mainly seeks in his own case is not criticism, but uncritical praise. "Kill the dog, he is a reviewer," cried the young Goethe; and in an age nearer our own William Morris expressed his contempt for those who earn a livelihood by writing their opinions of the works of others. Fortunately for Criticism, it does not live by the grace of poets, to whom it can be of small service at its best, but by the grace of others who have neither the poet's genius nor the critic's insight. I hope to persuade you this evening that the poets have been mistaken in their very conception of the critic's craft, which lives by a power that poets and critics share together. The secret of this power has come to men slowly, and the knowledge they have gained by it has transformed their idea of Criticism. What this secret is, and into what new paths Criticism is being led by it, is the subject of my lecture to-night.

I

At the end of the last century, France once more occupied the center of that stage whose auditors are the inheritors of European civilization. Once more all the world listened while she talked and played, and some of the most brilliant of her talk was now on the question of the authority of Criticism. It is not my purpose to tell you (what you know already) with what sober and vigorous learning the official critics of the *Revue des deux Mondes* [3] espoused the cause of old gods with the new weapons of science, and with what charm and tact, with what grace and suppleness of thought, Jules Lemaître and Anatole France, [4] to mention no others, defended the free play of the appreciative mind. Some of the sparks that were beaten out on the anvil of controversy have become fixed stars, the

---

[1] Delivered as a lecture in 1910; first published in New York, 1911.
[2] Gustave Flaubert (1821–1880), French novelist.
[3] One of the most prominent French literary journals, founded in 1829.
[4] Jules Lemaître (1853–1915), French impressionistic literary critic and poet. Anatole France (1844–1924), French impressionistic literary critic and novelist.

classical utterances of Criticism, as when Anatole France described the critic not as a judge imposing sentence, but as a sensitive soul detailing his "adventures among masterpieces."

To have sensations in the presence of a work of art and to express them, that is the function of Criticism for the impressionistic critic. His attitude he would express somewhat in this fashion: "Here is a beautiful poem, let us say Shelley's *Prometheus Unbound*. To read it is for me to experience a thrill of pleasure. My delight in it is itself a judgment, and what better judgment is it possible for me to give? All that I can do is to tell how it affects me, what sensations it gives me. Other men will derive other sensations from it, and express them differently; they too have the same right as I. Each of us, if we are sensitive to impressions and express ourselves well, will produce a new work of art to replace the work which gave us our sensations. That is the art of Criticism, and beyond that Criticism can not go."

We shall not begrudge this exquisite soul the pleasure of his sensations or his cult of them, nor would he be disconcerted if we were to point out that the interest has been shifted from the work of art to his own impressions. Let us suppose that you say to him: "We are not interested in you, but in *Prometheus Unbound*. To describe the state of your health is not to help us to understand or to enjoy the poem. Your criticism constantly tends to get away from the work of art, and to center attention on yourself and your feelings."

But his answer would not be difficult to find: "What you say is true enough. My criticism tends to get farther and farther from the work of art and to cast a light upon myself; but all criticism tends to get away from the work of art and to substitute something in its place. The impressionist substitutes himself, but what other form of criticism gets closer to *Prometheus Unbound*? Historical criticism takes us away from it in a search of the environment, the age, the race, the poetic school of the artist; it tells us to read the history of the French Revolution, Godwin's [5] *Political Justice*, the *Prometheus Bound* of Aeschylus,[6] and Calderón's[7] *Mágico Prodigioso*. Psychological criticism takes me away from the poem, and sets me to work on the biography of the poet; I wish to enjoy *Prometheus Unbound*, and instead I am asked to become acquainted with Shelley the man. Dogmatic criticism does not get any closer to the work of art by testing it according to rules and standards; it sends me to the Greek dramatists, to Shakespeare, to Aristotle's *Poetics*, possibly to Darwin's *Origin of Species*, in order that I may see how far Shelley has failed to give dramatic reality to his poem, or has failed to observe the rules of his *genre;* but that means the study of other works, and not of *Prometheus Unbound*. Aesthetics takes me still farther afield into speculations on art and beauty. And so it is with every form of Criticism. Do not deceive yourself. All criticism tends to shift the interest from the work of art to something else. The other critics

---

[5] William Godwin (1756–1836), English political writer, novelist, and historian.
[6] First Greek tragic dramatist (525–456 B.C.).
[7] Pedro Calderón de La Barca (1600–1681), Spanish poet and dramatist.

give us history, politics, biography, erudition, metaphysics. As for me, I re-dream the poet's dream, and if I seem to write lightly, it is because I have awakened, and smile to think I have mistaken a dream for reality. I at least strive to replace one work of art by another, and art can only find its *alter ego* in art."

It would be idle to detail the arguments with which the advocates of the opposing forms of Criticism answered these questionings. Literary eru-dition and evolutionary science were the chief weapons used to fight this modern heresy, but the one is an unwieldy and the other a useless weapon in the field of aesthetic thought. On some sides, at least, the position of the impressionists was impregnable; but two points of attack were open to their opponents. They could combat the notion that taste is a substitute for learning, or learning a substitute for taste, since both are vital to Criticism; and they could maintain that the relativity of taste does not in any sense affect its authority. In this sense impressionistic Criticism erred only less grievously than the "judicial" Criticism which opposed it.

But these arguments are not my present concern; what I wish to point out is that the objective and dogmatic forms of Criticism were fighting no new battle against impressionistic Criticism in that decade of controversy. It was a battle as old as the earliest reflection on the subject of poetry, if not as old as the sensitiveness of poets. Modern literature begins with the same doubts, with the same quarrel. In the sixteenth century the Italians were formulating that classical code which imposed itself on Europe for two centuries, and which, even in our generation, Brunetière [8] has merely disguised under the trappings of natural science. They evolved the dramatic unities, and all those rules which the poet Pope imagined to be "Nature still but Nature methodized." But at the very moment when their spokes-man Scaliger [9] was saying that "Aristotle is our emperor, the perpetual dic-tator of all the fine arts," another Italian, Pietro Aretino,[10] was insisting that there is no rule except the whim of genius and no standard of judg-ment beyond individual taste.

The Italians passed on the torch to the French of the seventeenth cen-tury, and from that day to this the struggle between the two schools has never ceased to agitate the progress of Criticism in France. Boileau [11] against Saint-Évremond,[12] Classicists against Romanticists, dogmatists against impressionists,—the antinomy is deep in the French nature, indeed in the nature of Criticism itself. Listen to this: "It is not for the purpose of deciding on the merit of this noble poet [Virgil], nor of harming his reputation, that I have spoken so freely concerning him. The world will continue to think what it does of his beautiful verses; and as for me, I judge nothing, I only say what I think, and what effect each of these things produces on my heart and mind." Surely these words are from the lips of Lemaître himself! "I judge nothing; I only say what I feel." But no,

[8] Ferdinand Brunetière (1849–1906), French literary critic.
[9] Julius Caesar Scaliger (1484–1558), Italian classical scholar and literary critic.
[10] Italian writer and poet (1492–1556).
[11] Nicolas Boileau (1636–1711), French poet and literary critic.
[12] French writer and critic (1610–1703).

these are the utterances of the Chevalier de Méré, a wit of the age of Louis XIV, and he is writing to the secretary of that stronghold of authority, the French Academy. For some men, even in the age of Boileau, criticism was nothing but an "adventure among masterpieces."

No, it is no new battle; it is the perpetual conflict of Criticism. In every age Impressionism (or enjoyment) and dogmatism (or judgment) have grappled with one another. They are the two sexes of Criticism; and to say that they flourish in every age is to say that every age has its masculine as well as its feminine criticism,—the masculine criticism that may or may not force its own standards on literature, but that never at all events is dominated by the object of its studies; and the feminine criticism that responds to the lure of art with a kind of passive ecstasy. In the age of Boileau it was the masculine type which gave the tone to Criticism; in our own, outside of the unversities, it has certainly been the feminine. But they continue to exist side by side, ever falling short of their highest powers, unless mystically mated,—judgment erecting its edicts into arbitrary standards and conventions, enjoyment lost in the mazes of its sensuous indecision.

Yet if we examine these opposing forms of Criticism in our own age, we shall find, I think, that they are not wholly without a common ground to meet on; that, in fact, they are united in at least one prepossession which they do not share with the varying forms of Criticism in any of the earlier periods of its history. The Greeks conceived of literature, not as an inevitable expression of creative power, but as a reasoned "imitation" or reshaping of the materials of life; for Aristotle, poetry is the result of man's imitative instinct, and differs from history and science in that it deals with the probable or possible rather than with the real. The Romans conceived of literature as a noble art, intended (though under the guise of pleasure) to inspire men with high ideals of life. The classicists of the sixteenth and seventeenth centuries accepted this view in the main; for them, literature was a kind of exercise,—a craft acquired by study of the classics, and guided in the interpretation of nature by the traditions of Greek and Roman art. For these men literature was as much a product of reason as science or history. The eighteenth century complicated the course of Criticism by the introduction of vague and novel criteria, such as "imagination," "sentiment," and "taste," yet it was only in part able to liberate itself from the older tradition.

But with the Romantic Movement there developed the new idea which coördinates all Criticism in the nineteenth century. Very early in the century, Mme de Staël [13] and others formulated the idea that literature is an "expression of society." Victor Cousin [14] founded the school of art for art's sake, enunciating "the fundamental rule, that expression is the supreme law of art." Later, Sainte-Beuve [15] developed and illustrated his theory that literature is an expression of personality. Still later, under the influence of

---

[13] French novelist and critic (1766–1817).
[14] French philosopher (1792–1867).
[15] Charles Augustin Sainte-Beuve (1804–1869), French literary critic.

natural science, Taine took a hint from Hegel and elaborated the idea that literature is an expression of race, age, and environment. The extreme impressionists prefer to think of art as the exquisite expression of delicate and fluctuating sensations or impressions of life. But for all these critics and theorists, literature is an expression of something, of experience or emotion, of the external or internal, of the man himself or something outside the man; yet it is always conceived of as an art of expression.

The objective, the dogmatic, the impressionistic critics of our day may set for themselves very different tasks, but the idea of expression is implicit in all they write. They have, as it were, this bond of blood: they are not merely man and woman, but brother and sister; and their father, or grandfather, was Sainte-Beuve. The bitter but acute analysis of his talent which Nietzsche [16] has given us in the *Twilight of the Idols* brings out very clearly this dual side of his seminal power, the feminine sensitiveness and the masculine detachment. For Nietzsche, he is "nothing of a man; he wanders about, delicate, curious, tired, pumping people, a female after all, with a woman's revengefulness and a woman's sensuousness, a critic without a standard, without firmness, and without backbone." Here it is the impressionist in Sainte-Beuve that arouses the German's wrath. But in the same breath we find Nietzsche blaming him for "holding up objectivity as a mask;" and it is on this objective side that Sainte-Beuve becomes the source of all those historical and psychological forms of critical study which have influenced the academic thought of our day, leading insensibly, but inevitably, from empirical investigation to empirical law. The pedigree of the two schools thereafter is not difficult to trace: on the one side, from Sainte-Beuve through *l'art pour l'art* to impressionism, and on the other, from Sainte-Beuve through Taine to Brunetière and his egregious kin.

French criticism has been leaning heavily on the idea of expression for a century or more, but no attempt has been made in France to understand its aesthetic content, except for a few vague echoes of German thought. For the first to give philosophic precision to the theory of expression, and to found a method of Criticism based upon it, were the Germans of the age that stretches from Herder to Hegel. All the forces of philosophical thought were focused on this central concept, while the critics enriched themselves from out this golden store. I suppose you all remember the famous passage in which Carlyle describes the achievement of German criticism in that age. "Criticism," says Carlyle, "has assumed a new form in Germany. It proceeds on other principles and proposes to itself a higher aim. The main question is not now a question concerning the qualities of diction, the coherence of metaphors, the fitness of sentiments, the general logical truth in a work of art, as it was some half century ago among most critics, neither is it a question mainly of a psychological sort to be answered by discovering and delineating the peculiar nature of the poet from his poetry, as is usual with the best of our own critics at present; but it is, not indeed exclusively, but inclusively, of its two other questions, properly and ultimately a question of the essence and peculiar life of the poetry itself.

[16] Friedrich Nietzsche (1844–1900), German philosopher.

. . . The problem is not now to determine by what mechanism Addison composed sentences and struck out similitudes, but by what far finer and more mysterious mechanism Shakespeare organized his dramas and gave life and individuality to his Ariel and his Hamlet. Wherein lies that life; how have they attained that shape and individuality? Whence comes that empyrean fire which irradiates their whole being, and pierces, at least in starry gleams, like a diviner thing, into all hearts? Are these dramas of his not veri-similar only, but true; nay, truer than reality itself, since the essence of unmixed reality is bodied forth in them under more expressive similes? What is this unity of pleasures; and can our deeper inspection discern it to be indivisible and existing by necessity because each work springs as it were from the general elements of thought and grows up therefrom into form and expansion by its own growth? Not only who was the poet and how did he compose, but what and how was the poem, and why was it a poem and not rhymed eloquence, creation and not figured passion? These are the questions for the critic. Criticism stands like an interpreter between the inspired and the uninspired; between the prophet and those who hear the melody of his words, and catch some glimpse of their material meaning, but understand not their deeper import."

I am afraid that no German critic wholly realized this ideal; but it was at least the achievement of the Germans that they enunciated the doctrine, even if they did not always adequately illustrate it in practice. It was they who first realized that art has performed its function when it has expressed itself; it was they who first conceived of Criticism as the study of expression. "There is a destructive and a creative or constructive criticism," said Goethe; the first measures and tests literature according to mechanical standards, the second answers the fundamental questions: "What has the writer proposed to himself to do? and how far has he succeeded in carrying out his own plan?" Carlyle, in his essay on Goethe, almost uses Goethe's own words, when he says that the critic's first and foremost duty is to make plain to himself "what the poet's aim really and truly was, how the task he had to do stood before his eye, and how far, with such materials as were afforded him, he has fulfilled it."

This has been the central problem, the guiding star, of all modern criticism. From Coleridge to Pater, from Sainte-Beuve to Lamaître, this is what critics have been striving for, even when they have not succeeded; yes, even when they have been deceiving themselves into thinking that they were striving for something else. This was not the ideal of the critics of Aristotle's day, who, like so many of their successors, censured a work of art as "irrational, impossible, morally hurtful, self-contradictory, or contrary to technical correctness." This was not Boileau's standard when he blamed Tasso for the introduction of Christian rather than pagan mythology into epic poetry; [17] nor Addison's, when he tested *Paradise Lost* according to the rules of Le Bossu; [18] nor Dr. Johnson's, when he lamented

[17] Torquato Tasso (1544–1595) published his great epic poem, the *Gerusalemme Liberata* (Jerusalem Delivered), in 1574.
[18] French writer and literary critic (1631–1680).

the absence of poetic justice in *King Lear*, or pronounced dogmatically that the poet should not "number the streaks of the tulip." What has the poet tried to do, and how has he fulfilled his intention? What is he striving to express and how has he expressed it? What impression does his work make on me, and how can I best express this impression? These are the questions that modern critics have been taught to ask when face to face with the work of a poet. Only one *caveat* must be borne in mind when attempting to answer them: the poet's intentions must be judged at the moment of the creative act, as mirrored in the work of art itself, and not by the vague ambitions which he imagines to be his real intentions before or after the creative act is achieved.

II

The theory of expression, the concept of literature as an art of expression, is the common ground on which critics have met for a century or more. Yet how many absurdities, how many complicated systems, how many confusions have been superimposed on this fundamental idea; and how slowly has its full significance become the possession of critics! To accept the naked principle is to play havoc with these confusions and complications; and no one has seen this more clearly, or driven home its inevitable consequences with more intelligence and vigor, than an Italian thinker and critic of our own day, Benedetto Croce,[19] who has been gaining ground in the English-speaking world from the day when Mr. Balfour,[20] seven or eight years ago, gave him a kind of official introduction in his Romanes Lecture. But I for one needed no introduction to his work; under his banner I enrolled myself long ago, and here re-enroll myself in what I now say. He has led aesthetic thought inevitably from the concept that art is expression to the conclusion that all expression is art. Time does not permit, nor reason ask, that we should follow this argument through all its *pros* and *cons*. If this theory of expression be once and for all accepted, as indeed it has been partly though confusedly accepted by all modern critics, the ground of Criticism is cleared of its dead lumber and its weeds. I propose now merely to point out this dead lumber and these weeds. In other words, we shall see to what conclusions the critical thought and practice of a century have been inevitably converging, and what elements of the old Criticism and the old literary history are disappearing from the new.

In the first place, we have done with all the old Rules. The very conception of "rules" harks back to an age of magic, and reminds the modern of those mysterious words which the heroes of the fairy-tales are without reason forbidden to utter; the rules are a survival of the savage *taboo*. We find few arbitrary rules in Aristotle, who limited himself to empirical inductions from the experience of literature; but they appear in the later Greek rhetoricians; and in the Romans, empirical induction has been hardened

[19] Italian philosopher and critic (1866–1952).
[20] Arthur James, 1st Earl of Balfour (1848–1930), British statesman, philosopher, and critic.

into dogma. Horace lays down the law to the prospective playwright in this manner: "You must never have more than three actors on the stage at any one time; you must never let your drama exceed five acts." It is unnecessary to trace the history of these rules, or to indicate how they increased in number, how they were arranged into a system by the classicists of the sixteenth and seventeenth centuries, and how they burdened the creative art of that period. They were never without their enemies. We have seen how Aretino was pitted against Scaliger, Saint-Évremond against Boileau; and in every age the poets have astounded the critics by transgressing rules without the sacrifice of beauty; but it was not until the end of the eighteenth century that the Romanticists banished them from the province of Criticism. The pedantry of our own day has borrowed "conventions" from history and "technique" from science as substitutes for the outworn formulae of the past; but these are merely new names for the old mechanical rules; and they too will go, when Criticism clearly recognizes in every work of art a spiritual creation governed by its own law.

We have done with the *genres* or literary kinds. Their history is inseparably bound up with that of the classical rules. Certain works of literature have a general resemblance and are loosely classed together (for the sake of convenience) as lyric, comedy, tragedy, epic, pastoral, and the like; the classicists made of each of these divisions a fixed norm governed by inviolable laws. The separation of the *genres* was a consequence of this law of classicism: comedy should not be mingled with tragedy, nor epic with lyric. But no sooner was the law enunciated than it was broken by an artist impatient or ignorant of its restraints, and the critics have been obliged to explain away these violations of their laws, or gradually to change the laws themselves. But if art is organic expression, and every work of art is to be interrogated with the question, "What has it expressed, and how completely?" there is no place for the question whether it has conformed to some convenient classification of critics or to some law derived from this classification. The lyric, the pastoral, the epic, are abstractions without concrete reality in the world of art. Poets do not really write epics, pastorals, lyrics, however much they may be deceived by these false abstractions; they express themselves, and this expression is their only form. There are not, therefore, only three, or ten, or a hundred literary kinds; there are as many kinds as there are individual poets. But it is in the field of literary history that this error is most obvious. Shakespeare wrote *King Lear, Venus and Adonis,* and a sequence of sonnets. What becomes of Shakespeare, the creative artist, when these three works are separated from one another by the historian of poetry; when they lose their connection with his single creative soul, and are classified with other works with which they have only a loose and vague relation? To slice up the history of English literature into compartments marked comedy, tragedy, lyric, and the like, is to be guilty of a complete misunderstanding of the meaning of Criticism; and literary history becomes a logical absurdity when its data are not organically related but cut up into sections, and placed in such compartments as these. Only in one sense has any of these terms any profound significance, and that is the use of the word "lyric" to represent the free expressiveness of art. All art is lyrical,—the *Divine Comedy*, *King Lear*, Rodin's "Thinker," the Parthenon, a Corot landscape, a Bach fugue, or Isadora Duncan's dancing, as much as the songs of Heine or Shelley.

We have done with the comic, the tragic, the sublime, and an army of vague abstractions of their kind. These have grown out of the generalizations of the Alexandrian critics,[21] acquiring a new lease of life in the eighteenth century. Gray and his friend West corresponded with each other on the subject of the sublime; later, Schiller[22] distinguished between the naïve and the sentimental; Jean Paul[23] defined humor, and Hegel[24] defined the tragic. If these terms represent the content of art, they may be relegated to the same category as joy, hate, sorrow, enthusiasm; and we should speak of the comic in the same general way in which we might speak of the expression of joy in a poem. If, on the other hand, these terms represent abstract classifications of poetry, their use in criticism sins against the very nature of art. Every poet re-expresses the universe in his own way, and every poem is a new and independent expression. The tragic does not exist for Criticism, but only Aeschylus and Calderón, Shakespeare and Racine.[25] There is no objection to the use of the word tragic as a convenient label for somewhat similar poems, but to find laws for the tragic and to test creative artists by such laws as these is simply to give a more abstract form to the outworn classical conception of dramatic rules.

We have done with the theory of style, with metaphor, simile, and all the paraphernalia of Graeco-Roman rhetoric. These owe their existence to the assumption that style is separate from expression, that it is something which may be added or subtracted at will from the work of art, a flourish of the pen, an external embellishment, instead of the poet's individual vision of reality, "the music of his whole manner of being." But we know that art *is* expression, that it is complete in itself, that to alter it is to create another expression and therefore to create another work of art. If the poet, for example, says of springtime that " 'Tis now the blood runs gold," he has not employed a substitute for something else, such as "the blood tingles in our veins;" he has expressed his thought in its completeness, and there is no equivalent for his expression except itself.

> "Each perfect in its place; and each content
> With that perfection which its being meant."

---

[21] School of criticism in Alexandria which flourished between 306 B.C. and 642 A.D. They were concerned with the study of the classics and the criticism of prosody and metre. Some were interested primarily in grammar. Their works were written by and for the learned and appealed to a very small public. Their main concern was for the technical aspects of literary expression. Leading critics included Aristarchus, Zenodotus, Apolonius Rhodius, and Callimachus.

[22] Johann Schiller (1759–1805), German poet, dramatist, and critic.

[23] Jean Paul Richter (1763–1825), German author.

[24] Friedrich Hegel (1770–1831), German philosopher.

[25] Jean Racine (1639–1669), French tragic dramatist.

Such expressions are still called metaphors in the text-books; but metaphor, simile, and all the old terms of classical rhetoric are signs of the zodiac, magical incantations, astrological formulae, interesting only to antiquarian curiosity. To Montaigne [26] they suggested "the prattle of chambermaids;" to me they suggest rather the drone and singsong of many schoolmistresses. We still hear talk of the "grand style," and essays on style continue to be written, like the old "arts of poetry" of two centuries ago. But the theory of styles has no longer a real place in modern thought; we have learned that it is no less impossible to study style as separate from the work of art than to study the comic as separate from the work of the comic artist.

We have done with all moral judgment of literature. Horace said that pleasure and profit are the end of art, and for many centuries the critics quarreled over the terms "pleasure" and "profit." Some said that poetry was meant to instruct; some, merely to please; some, to do both. Romantic criticism first enunciated the principle that art has no aim except expression; that its aim is complete when expression is complete; that "beauty is its own excuse for being." It is not the function of poetry to further any moral or social cause, any more than it is the function of bridge-building to further the cause of Esperanto. If the achievement of the poet be to express any material he may select, and to express it with a completeness that we recognize as perfection, obviously morals can play no part in the judgment which Criticism may form of his work. To say that poetry is moral or immoral is as meaningless as to say that an equilateral triangle is moral and an isosceles triangle immoral, or to speak of the immorality of a musical chord or a Gothic arch. It is only conceivable in a world in which dinner table conversation runs after this fashion: "This cauliflower would be good if it had only been prepared in accordance with international law." "Do you know why my cook's pastry is so good? Because he has never told a lie or seduced a woman." We do not concern ourselves with morals when we test the engineer's bridge or the scientist's researches; indeed we go farther, and say that it is the moral duty of the scientist to disregard any theory of morals in his search for truth. Beauty's world is remote from both these standards; she aims neither at morals nor at truth. Her imaginary creations, by definition, make no pretence to reality, and cannot be judged by reality's tests. The poet's only moral duty, as a poet, is to be true to his art, and to express his vision of reality as well as he can. If the ideals enunciated by poets are not those which we admire most, we must blame not the poets but ourselves: in the world where morals count we have failed to give them the proper material out of which to rear a nobler edifice. No critic of authority now tests literature by the standards of ethics.

We have done with the confusion between the drama and the theatre which has permeated dramatic criticism for over half a century. The theory that the drama is not a creative art, but a mere product of the physical exigencies of the theatre, is as old as the sixteenth century. An Italian scholar of that age was the first to maintain that plays are intended to be acted on

[26] Michel de Montaigne (1533–1592), French essayist.

a stage, under certain restricted physical conditions, and before a large
and heterogeneous crowd; dramatic performance has developed out of these
conditions, and the test of its excellence is therefore the pleasure it gives
to the mixed audience that supports it. This idea was taken hold of by some
of the German romanticists, for the purpose of justifying the Shakespearean drama in its apparent divergence from the classical "rules." Shakespeare cannot be judged by the rules of the Greek theatre (so ran their
argument), for the drama is an inevitable product of theatrical conditions;
these conditions in Elizabethan England were not the same as those of Per-
iclean Athens; and it is therefore absurd to judge Shakespeare's practice
by that of Sophocles. Here at least the idea helped to bring Shakespeare
home to many new hearts by ridding the age of mistaken prejudices, and
served a useful purpose, as a specious argument may persuade men to
contribute to a noble work, or a mad fanatic may rid the world of a tyrant.
But with this achievement its usefulness but not its life was ended. It has
been developed into a system, and become a dogma of dramatic critics; it
is our contemporary equivalent for the "rules" of seventeenth-century pedantry. As a matter of fact, the dramatic artist is to be judged by no other
standard than that applied to any other creative artist: what has he tried to
express, and how has he expressed it? It is true that the theatre is not only
an art but a business, and the so-called "success" of a play is of vital interest to the theatre in so far as it is a commercial undertaking. "The success
may justify the playwright," said an old French critic, "but it may not be so
easy to justify the success." The test of "success" is an economic test, and
concerns not art or the criticism of art, but political economy. Valuable contributions to economic and social history have been made by students who
have investigated the changing conditions of the theatre and the vicissitudes of taste on the part of theatrical audiences; but these have the same
relation to Criticism, and to the drama as an art, that a history of the publisher's trade and its influence on the personal fortunes of poets would bear
to the history of poetry.

We have done with technique as separate from art. It has been pointed
out that style cannot be disassociated from art; and the false air of science
which the term "technique" seems to possess should not blind us to the
fact that it too involves the same error. "Technique is really personality;
that is the reason why the artist cannot teach it, why the pupil cannot learn
it, and why the aesthetic critic can understand it," says Oscar Wilde, in a
dialogue on "The Critic as Artist," which, amid much perversity and paradox, is illumined by many flashes of strange insight. The technique of
poetry cannot be separated from its inner nature. Versification cannot be
studied by itself, except loosely and for convenience; it remains always an
inherent quality of the single poem. No two poets ever write in the same
metre. Milton's line:—

"These my sky-robes spun out of Iris' woof"

is called an iambic pentameter; but it is not true that artistically it has
something in common with every other line possessing the same succession

of syllables and accents; in this sense it is not an iambic pentameter; it is only one thing; it is the line:—

"These my sky-robes spun out of Iris' woof."

We have done with the history and criticism of poetic themes. It is possible to speak loosely of the handling of such a theme as Prometheus by Aeschylus and by Shelley, of the story of Francesca da Rimini, by Dante, Stephen Phillips,[27] and D'Annunzio,[28] or the story of King Arthur by Malory and Tennyson; but strictly speaking, they are not employing the same theme at all. Each artist is expressing a certain material and labeling it with an historic name. For Shelley Prometheus is only a label; he is expressing his artistic conception of life, not the history of a Greek Titan. It is the vital flame he has breathed into his work that makes it what it is, and with this vital flame (and not with labels) the critic should concern himself in the works of poets. The same answer must be given to those critics who insist on the use of contemporary material in poetry, and praise the poets whose subjects are drawn from the life of our own time. But even if it were possible for critics to determine in advance the subject-matter of poetry or to impose subjects on poets, how can a poet deal with anything but contemporary material? How can a twentieth-century poet, even when he imagines that he is concerned with Greek or Egyptian life, deal with any subject but the life of his own time, except in the most external and superficial detail? Cynics have said since the first outpourings of men's hearts, "There is nothing new in art; there are no new subjects." But the very reverse is true. There are no old subjects; every subject is new as soon as it has been transformed by the imagination of the poet.

We have done with the race, the time, the environment of a poet's work as an element in Criticism. To study these phases of a work of art is to treat it as an historic or social document, and the result is a contribution to the history of culture or civilization, with only a subsidiary interest for the history of art. "Granted the times, the environment, the race, the passions of the poet, what has he done with his materials, how has he converted poetry out of reality?" To answer this question of the Italian De Sanctis[29] as it refers to each single work of art is to perform what is truly the critic's vital function; this is to interpret "expression" in its rightful sense, and to liberate aesthetic Criticism from the vassalage to *Kulturgeschichte*[30] imposed on it by the school of Taine.

We have done with the "evolution" of literature. The concept of progress was first applied to literature in the seventeenth century, but at the very outset Pascal[31] pointed out that a distinction must here be made between science and art; that science advances by accumulation of knowledge, while the changes of art cannot be reduced to any theory of prog-

[27] English poet (1868–1915).
[28] Gabriele D'Annunzio (1863–1938), Italian poet.
[29] Francesco De Sanctis (1817–1883), Italian scholar and critic.
[30] "study of culture."
[31] Blaise Pascal (1623–1662), French religious philosopher and mathematician.

ress. As a matter of fact, the theory involves the ranking of poets according to some arbitrary conception of their value; and the ranking of writers in order of merit has become obsolete, except in the "hundred best books" of the last decade and the "five-foot shelves" of yesterday. The later nineteenth century gave a new air of verisimilitude to this old theory by borrowing the term "evolution" from science; but this too involves a fundamental misconception of the free and original movement of art. A similar misconception is involved in the study of the "origins" of art; for art has no origin separate from man's life.

> "In climes beyond the solar road,
>   Where shaggy forms o'er ice-built mountains roam,
>   The Muse has broke the twilight-gloom";

but though she wore savage raiment, she was no less the Muse. Art is simple at times, complex at others, but it is always art. The simple art of early times may be studied with profit; but the researches of anthropology have no vital significance for Criticism, unless the anthropologist studies the simplest forms of art in the same spirit as its highest; that is, unless the anthropologist is an aesthetic critic.

Finally, we have done with the old rupture between genius and taste. When Criticism first propounded as its real concern the oft-repeated question: "What has the poet tried to express and how has he expressed it?" Criticism prescribed for itself the only possible method. How can the critic answer this question without becoming (if only for a moment of supreme power) at one with the creator? That is to say, taste must reproduce the work of art within itself in order to understand and judge it; and at that moment aesthetic judgment becomes nothing more nor less than creative art itself. The identity of genius and taste is the final achievement of modern thought on the subject of art, and it means that fundamentally, in their most significant moments, the creative and the critical instincts are one and the same. From Goethe to Carlyle, from Carlyle to Arnold, from Arnold to Symons,[32] there has been much talk of the "creative function" of Criticism. For each of these men the phrase held a different content; for Arnold it meant merely that Criticism creates the intellectual atmosphere of the age,—a social function of high importance, perhaps, yet wholly independent of aesthetic significance. But the ultimate truth toward which these men were tending was more radical than that, and plays havoc with all the old platitudes about the sterility of taste. Criticism at last can free itself of its age-long self-contempt, now that it may realize that aesthetic judgment and artistic creation are instinct with the same vital life. This identity does not sum up the whole life of the complex and difficult art of Criticism, but without it, Criticism would really be impossible. "Genius is to aesthetics what the ego is to philosophy, the only supreme and absolute reality," said Schelling;[33] and without subduing the mind to this tran-

[32] Arthur Symons (1865–1945), English poet and critic.
[33] Friedrich Schelling (1775–1854), German philosopher.

scendental system, it remains true that what must always be inexplicable to mere reflection is just what gives power to poetry; that intellectual curiosity may amuse itself by asking its little questions of the silent sons of light, but they vouchsafe no answer to art's pale shadow, thought; the gods are kind if they give up their secret in another work of art, the art of Criticism, that serves as some sort of mirror to the art of literature, only because in their flashes of insight taste and genius are one.

JAMES HUNEKER

REMY DE GOURMONT [1]
(1917)

I

THOSE WERE days marked by a white stone when arrived in the familiar yellow cover a new book, with card enclosed from "Remy de Gourmont, 71, rue des Saints-Pères, Paris." Sometimes I received as many as two in a year. But they always found me eager and grateful, did those precious little volumes bearing the imprint of the *Mercure de France*, with whose history the name of De Gourmont is so happily linked. And there were post-cards too in his delicate handwriting on which were traced sense and sentiment; yes, this man of genius possessed sentiment, but abhorred sentimentality. His personal charm transpired in a friendly salutation hastily pencilled. He played exquisitely upon his intellectual instrument, and knew the value of time and space. So his post-cards are souvenirs of his courtesy, and it was through one, which unexpectedly fell from the sky in 1897, I began my friendship with this distinguished French critic. His sudden death in 1915 at Paris (he was born 1858), caused by apoplexy, was the heroic ending of a man of letters. Like Flaubert he was stricken while at his desk. I can conceive no more fitting end for a valiant soldier of literature. He was a moral hero and the victim of his prolonged technical heroism.

De Gourmont was incomparable. Thought, not action, was his chosen sphere, but ranging up and down the vague and vast territory of ideas he encountered countless cerebral adventures; the most dangerous of all. An aristocrat born, he was, nevertheless, a convinced democrat. The latch was always lifted on the front door of his ivory tower. He did live in a certain sense a cloistered existence, a Benedictine of arts and letters; but he was not, as has been said, a sour hermit nursing morose fancies in solitude. De Gourmont, true pagan, enjoyed the gifts the gods provide, and had, despite the dualism of his nature, an epicurean soul. But of a complexity. He never sympathised with the disproportionate fuss raised by the metaphysicians about Instinct and Intelligence, yet his own magnificent cerebral apparatus was a battle-field over which swept the opposing hosts of Instinct and Intelligence, and in a half-hundred volumes the history of this conflict is faithfully set down. As personal as Maurice Barrès,[2] without his egoism, as subtle as Anatole France,[3] De Gourmont saw life steadier

[1] From *Unicorns* (New York, 1917).
[2] French novelist and politician (1862–1923).
[3] French novelist and essayist (1844–1924).

and broader than either of these two contemporaries. He was one who said "vast things simply." He was the profoundest philosopher of the three, and never, after his beginnings, exhibited a trace of the dilettante. Life soon became something more than a mere spectacle for him. He was a meliorist in theory and practice, though he asserted that Christianity, an Oriental-born religion, has not become spiritually acclimated among Occidental peoples. But he missed its consoling function; religion, the poetry of the poor, never had for him the prime significance that it had for William James; [4] a legend, vague, vast, and delicious.

Old frontiers have disappeared in science and art and literature. We have Maeterlinck,[5] a poet writing of bees, Poincaré,[6] a mathematician opening our eyes to the mystic gulfs of space; solid matters resolved into mist, and the law of gravitation questioned. The new horizons beckon ardent youth bent on conquering the secrets of life. And there are more false beacon-lights than true. But if this is an age of specialists a man occasionally emerges who contradicts the formula. De Gourmont was at base a poet; also a dramatist, novelist, raconteur, man of science, critic, moralist of erudition, and, lastly, a philosopher. Both formidable and bewildering were his accomplishments. He is a poet in his Hieroglyphes, Oraisons mauvaises, Le Livre des Litanies, Les Saintes du Paradis, Simone, Divertissements—his last appearance in singing robes (1914); he is a raconteur—and such tales—in Histoires magiques, Prose moroses, Le Pèlerin du silence, D'un Pays lointain, Couleurs; a novelist in Merlette—his first book—Sixtine, Le Fantôme, les Chevaux de Diomède, Le Songe d'une Femme, Une Nuit au Luxembourg, Un Coeur virginal; dramatist in Théodat, Phénissa, Le vieux Roi, Lilith; as master critic of the aesthetics of the French language his supremacy is indisputable; it is hardly necessary to refer here to Le Livre des Masques, in two volumes, the five volumes of Promenades littéraires, the three of Promenades philosophiques; as moralist he has signed such works as l'Idealisme, La Culture des Idées, Le Chemin de Velours; historian and humanist, he has given us Le Latin mystique; grammarian and philologist, he displays his learning in Le Problème du Style, and Esthétique de la Langue française, and incidentally flays an unhappy pedagogue who proposed to impart the secret of style in twenty lessons. He edited many classics of French literature.

His chief contribution to science, apart from his botanical and entomological researches, is Physique de l'Amour, in which he reveals himself as a patient, thorough observer in an almost new country. And what shall we say to his incursions into the actual, into the field of politics, sociology and hourly happenings of Paris life; his Epilogues (three volumes), Dialogues des Amateurs, the collected pages from his monthly contributions to Mercure de France? Nothing human was alien to him, nor inhuman, for he rejected as quite meaningless the latter vocable, as he rejected such clichés as "organic and inorganic." Years before we heard of a pluralistic

---

[4] American psychologist and pragmatic philosopher (1842–1910).
[5] Maurice Maeterlinck (1862–1949), Belgian-French dramatist and poet.
[6] Jules Henri Poincaré (1854–1912), French mathematician.

universe De Gourmont was a pragmatist, though an idealist in his conception of the world as a personal picture. Intensely interested in ideas, as he was in words, he might have fulfilled Lord Acton's [7] wish that some one would write a History of Ideas. At the time of his death the French thinker was composing a work entitled La Physique des Moeurs, in which he contemplated a demonstration of his law of intellectual constancy.

A spiritual cosmopolitan, he was like most Frenchmen, an ardent patriot. The little squabble in the early eighties over a skit of his, Le Joujou—patriotisme (1883), cost him his post at the National Library in Paris. As a philosopher he deprecated war; as a man, though too old to fight, he urged his countrymen to victory, as may be noted in his last book, Pendant l'Orage (1916). But the philosopher persists in such a sorrowful sentence as: "In the tragedy of man peace is but an entr'acte." To show his mental balance at a time when literary men, artists, and even philosophers, indulged in unseemly abuse, we read in Jugements his calm admission that the war has not destroyed for him the intellectual values of Goethe, Schopenhauer, or Nietzsche.[8] He owes much to their thought as they owed much to French thought; Goethe has said as much; and of Voltaire and Chamfort,[9] Schopenhauer was a disciple. Without being a practical musician, De Gourmont was a lover of Beethoven and Wagner. He paid his compliments to Romain Rolland,[10] whose style, both chalky and mucilaginous, he dislikes in that overrated and spun-out series Jean-Christophe. Another little volume, La Belgique littéraire, was published in 1915, which, while it contains nothing particularly new about Georges Rodenbach, Emile Verhaeren, Van Lerberghe, Camille Lemonnier,[11] and Maurice Maeterlinck, is excellent reading. The French critic was also editor of the Revue des Idées, and judging from the bibliography compiled by Pierre de Querlon as long ago as 1903, he was a collaborator of numerous magazines. He wrote on Emerson, English humour, or Thomas à Kempis [12] with the same facility as he dissected the mystic Latin writers of the early centuries after Christ. Indeed, such versatility was viewed askance by the plodding crowd of college professors, his general adversaries. But his erudition could not be challenged; only two other men matched his scholarship, Anatole France and the late Marcel Schwob.[13] And we have only skimmed the surface of his accomplishments. Remy de Gourmont is the Admirable Crichton [14] of French letters.

[7] English historian (1834–1902).
[8] Arthur Schopenhauer (1788–1860) and Friedrich Nietzsche (1844–1900) were German philosophers.
[9] Nicolas Chamfort (1741–1794), French revolutionist and poet.
[10] French author (1866–1944).
[11] Rodenbach (1786–1869), Belgian writer; Verhaeren (1855–1916), Belgian poet; Van Lerberghe (1861–1907), Belgian poet and dramatist; Lemonnier (1844–1913), Belgian novelist and critic.
[12] Augustinian canon and writer (ca. 1380–1471).
[13] French writer and critic (1867–1905).
[14] James Crichton (1560?–1582), Scottish scholar, poet, and adventurer who spoke many languages.

II

Prodigious incoherence might be reasonably expected from this diversity of interests, yet the result is quite the reverse. The artist in this complicated man banished confusion. He has told us that because of the diversity of his aptitudes man is distinguished from his fellow animals, and the variety in his labours is a proof positive of his superiority to such fellow critics as the mentally constipated Brunetière,[15] the impressionistic Anatole France, the agile and graceful Lemaître, and the pedantic philistine Faguet.[16] But if De Gourmont always attains clarity with no loss of depth, he sometimes mixes his genres; that is, the poet peeps out in his reports of the psychic life of insects, as the philosopher lords it over the pages of his fiction. A mystic betimes, he is a crystal-clear thinker. And consider the catholicity evinced in Le Livre des Masques. He wrote of such widely diverging talents as Maeterlinck, Mallarmé, Villiers de l'Isle Adam, and Paul Adam;[17] of Henri de Regnier and Jules Renard;[18] of Huysmans and Jules Laforgue;[19] the mysticism of Francis Poictevin's[20] style and the imagery of Saint-Pol-Roux[21] he defined, and he displays an understanding of the first symbolist poet, Arthur Rimbaud,[22] while disliking the personality of that abnormal youth. But why recite this litany of new talent literally made visible and vocal by our critic? It is a pleasure to record the fact that most of his swans remained swans and did not degenerate into tame geese. In this book he shows himself a profound psychologist.

Insatiably curious, he yet contrived to drive his chimeras in double harness and safely. His best fiction is Sixtine and Une Nuit au Luxembourg, if fiction they may be called. Never will their author be registered among best-sellers. Sixtine deals with the adventures of a masculine brain. Ideas are the hero. In Un Coeur virginal we touch earth, fleshly and spiritually. This story shocked its readers. It may be considered as a sequel to Physique de l'Amour. It shows mankind as a gigantic insect indulging in the same apparently blind pursuit of sex sensation as a beetle, and also shows us the "female of our species" endowed with less capacity for modesty than the lady mole, the most chaste of all animals. Disconcerting, too, is the psychology of the heroine's virginal soul, not, however, cynical; cynicism is the irony of vice, and De Gourmont is never cynical. But a master of irony.

[15] Ferdinand Brunetière (1849–1906), French literary critic.
[16] Emile Faguet (1847–1916), French writer and scholar.
[17] Stéphane Mallarmé (1842–1898), French poet; Villiers de l'Isle Adam (1840–1889), French poet, novelist, and dramatist; Paul Adam (1862–1920), French symbolist novelist.
[18] Henri de Regnier (1864–   ), French poet; Jules Renard (1864–1910), French poet, novelist, dramatist.
[19] J. K. Huysmans (1848–1907), French novelist and critic; Jules Laforgue (1860–1887), French symbolist poet.
[20] French poet (1854–1904).
[21] French romantic poet (1861–   ).
[22] French symbolist poet (1854–1891).

Une Nuit au Luxembourg has been done into English. It handles with delicacy and frankness themes that in the hands of a lesser artist would be banished as brutal and blasphemous. The author knows that all our felicity is founded on a compromise between the dream and reality, and for that reason while he signals the illusion he never mocks it; he is too much an idealist. In the elaborately carved cups of his tales, foaming over with exquisite perfumes and nectar, there lurks the bitter drop of truth. He could never have said with Proudhon [23] that woman is the desolation of the just; for him woman is often an obsession. Yet, captain of his instincts, he sees her justly; he is not subdued by sex. With a gesture he destroys the sentimental scaffolding of the sensualist and marches on to new intellectual conquests.

In Lilith, an Adamitic Morality, he reveals his Talmudic lore. The first wife of our common ancestor is a beautiful hell-hag, the accomplice of Satan in the corruption of the human race. This mediaeval play is epical in its Rabelaisian plainness of speech. Perhaps the Manichean in De Gourmont fabricated its revolting images. He had traversed the Baudelairian steppes of blasphemy and black pessimism; Baudelaire,[24] a poet who was a great critic. Odi profanum vulgus! [25] was De Gourmont's motto, but his soul was responsive to so many contacts that he emerged, as Barrès emerged, a citizen of the world. Anarchy as a working philosophy did not long content him, although he never relinquished his detached attitude of proud individualism. He saw through the sentimental equality of J.-J. Rousseau. Rousseau it was who said that thinking man was a depraved animal. Perhaps he was not far from the truth. Man is an affective animal more interested in the immediate testimony of his senses than in his intellectual processes. His metaphysic may be but the reverberation of his sensations on the shore of his subliminal self, the echo of the sounding shell he calls his soul. And our critic had his scientific studies to console him for the inevitable sterility of soul that follows egoism and a barren debauch of the sensations. He did not tarry long in the valley of excess. His artistic sensibility was his saviour.

Without being a dogmatist, De Gourmont was an antagonist of absolutism. A determinist, (which may be dogmatism à rebours), a relativist, he holds that mankind is not a specially favoured species of the animal scale; thought is only an accident, possibly the result of rich nutrition. An automaton, man has no free will, but it is better for him to imagine that he has; it is a sounder working hypothesis for the average human. The universe had no beginning, it will have no end. There is no first link or last in the chain of causality. Everything must submit to the law of causality; to explain a blade of grass we must dismount the stars. Nevertheless, De Gourmont no more than Renan, had the mania of certitude. Humbly he interrogates the sphinx. There are no isolated phenomena in time or space. The mass of matter is eternal. Man is an animal submitting to the

[23] Pierre-Joseph Proudhon (1809–1865), French philosophical anarchist.
[24] Charles Pierre Baudelaire (1821–1867), French poet.
[25] "Hate the commonplace."

same laws that govern crystals or brutes. He is the expression of matter in physique and chemistry. Repetition is the law of life. Thought is a physiological product; intelligence the secretion of matter and is amenable to the law of causality. (This sounds like Taine's famous definition of virtue and vice.) And who shall deny it all in the psychochemical laboratories? It is not the rigid old-fashioned materialism, but a return to the more plastic theories of Lamarck [26] and the transformism of the Dutch botanist, Hugo de Vries.[27] For De Gourmont the Darwinian notion that man is at the topmost notch of creation is as antique and absurd as most cosmogonies; indeed, it is the Asiatic egocentric idea of creation. Jacob's ladder repainted in Darwinian symbols. Voilà l'ennemi! said De Gourmont and put on his controversial armour. What blows, what sudden deadly attacks were his!

Quinton [28] has demonstrated to the satisfaction of many scientists that bird life came later on our globe than the primates from whom we stem. The law of thermal constancy proves it by the interior temperature of birds. Man preceded the carnivorous and ruminating animals, of whom the bodily temperature is lower than that of birds. The ants and bees and beavers are not a whit more automatic than mankind. Automatism, says Ribot,[29] is the rule. Thought is not free, wrote William James, when to it an affirmation is added; then it is but the affirmation of a preference. "L'homme," asserts De Gourmont, "varie à l'infini sa mimique. Sa supériorité, c'est la diversité immense de ses aptitudes." [30] He welcomed Jules de Gaultier and his theory of Bovaryisme; [31] of the vital lie, because of which we pretend to be what we are not. That way spells security, if not progress. The idea of progress is another necessary illusion, for it provokes a multiplicity of activities. Our so-called free will is naught but the faculty of making a decision determined by a great and varied number of motives. As for morality, it is the outcome of tribal taboos; the insect and animal world shows deepest-dyed immorality, revolting cruelty, and sex perversity. Rabbits and earthworms through no fault of their own suffer from horrible maladies. From all of which our critic deduces his law of intellectual constancy. The human brain since prehistoric times has been neither diminished nor augmented; it has remained like a sponge, which can be dry or saturated, but still remains itself. It is a constant. In a favourable environment it is enriched. The greatest moment in the history of the human family was the discovery of fire by an anthropoid of genius. Prometheus then should be our god. Without him we should have remained more or less simian, and probably of arboreal habits.

[26] Jean Baptiste Lamarck (1744–1829), French pre-Darwinian evolutionist.
[27] Dutch botanist (1848–1935).
[28] René Quinton (1867–1925), French naturalist.
[29] Théodule-Armand Ribot (1839–1916), French philosopher.
[30] "Man infinitely varies his imitation. His superiority is the immense diversity of his aptitudes."
[31] Jules de Gaultier (1858–), French philosopher. His theory of "Bovaryisme" concerns the disposition which man has of conceiving himself to be other than what he is and of lying to himself.

III

·A synthetic brain is De Gourmont's, a sower of doubts, though not a
No-Sayer to the universe. He delights in challenging accepted "truths."
Of all modern thinkers a master of Vues d'ensembles,[32] he smiles at the
pretensions, usually a mask for poverty of ideas, of so-called "general ideas."
He dissociates such conventional grouping of ideas as Glory, Justice, Decadence. The shining ribs of disillusion shine through his psychology; a
psychology of nuance and finesse. Disillusioning reflections, these. Not to
be put in any philosophical pigeonhole, he is as far removed from the
eclecticism of Victor Cousin [33] as from the verbal jugglery and metaphysical murmurings of Henri Bergson.[34] The world is his dream; but it is a
tangible dream, charged with meaning, order, logic. The truest reality is
thought. Action spoils. (Goethe said: "Thought expands, action narrows.")
Our abstract ideas are metaphysical idols, says Jules de Gaultier. The
image of the concrete is De Gourmont's touch-stone. Théophile Gautier [35]
declared that he was a man for whom the visible world existed. He mis-
judged his capacity for apprehending reality. The human brain, excellent instrument in a priori combinations is inept at perceiving realities.
The "Sultan of the Epithet," as De Goncourt [36] nicknamed "le bon Théo,"
was ·not the "Emperor of Thought," according to Henry James, and for
him it was a romantic fiction spun in the rich web of his fancy. A vaster,
greyer world is adumbrated in the books of De Gourmont. He never allowed symbolism to deform his representation of sober, every-day life.
He pictured the future domain of art and ideas as a fair and shining landscape no longer a series of little gardens with high walls. A hater of formulas, sects, schools, he teaches that the capital crime of the artist, the
writer, the thinker, is conformity. (Yet how serenely this critic swims in
classic currents!) The artist's work should reflect his personality, a magnified reflection. He must create his own aesthetic. There are no schools,
only individuals. And of consistency he might have said that it is oftener
a mule than a jewel.

Sceptical in all matters, though never the fascinating sophist that is
Anatole France, De Gourmont criticised the thirty-six dramatic situations,
reducing the number to four. Man as centre in relation to himself; in relation to other men; in relation to the other sex; in relation to God, or
Nature. His ecclesiastical *fond* may be recognised in Le Chemin de Velours with its sympathetic exposition of Jesuit doctrine, and the acuity
of its judgments on Pascal and the Jansenists.[37] The latter section is an
illuminating foot-note to the history of Port-Royal by Sainte-Beuve. The

[32] "views of all the parts of a thing taken together."
[33] French philosopher (1792–1867).
[34] French philosopher (1859–1941).
[35] French poet (1811–1872).
[36] Edmond de Goncourt (1822–1896), French art critic, historian, and novelist.
[37] Seventeenth-century followers of the doctrinal system of Cornelis Jansen, Roman
Catholic bishop of Ypres, which maintained the radical corruption of human nature
and the inability of the will to do good, and that Christ died for the predestined and
not for all men.

younger critic has the supple intellect of the supplest-minded Jesuit. His bias toward the order is unmistakable. There are few books I reread with more pleasure than this Path of Velvet. Certain passages in it are as silky and sonorous as the sound of Eugène Ysaye's violin.

The colour of De Gourmont's mind is stained by his artistic sensibility. A maker of images, his vocabulary astounding as befits both a poet and philologist, one avid of beautiful words, has variety. The temper of his mind is tolerant, a quality that has informed the finer intellects of France since Montaigne. His literary equipment is unusual. A style as brilliant, sinuous, and personal as his thought; flexible or massive, continent or coloured, he discourses at ease in all the gamuts and modes major, minor, and mixed. A swift, weighty style, the style of a Latinist; a classic, not a romantic style. His formal sense is admirable. The tenderness of Anatole France is absent, except in his verse, which is less spontaneous than volitional. A pioneer in new aesthetic pastures, De Gourmont is a poet for poets. He has virtuosity, though the gift of tears nature—possibly jealous because of her prodigality—has denied him. But in the curves of his over-arching intellect there may be found wit, gaiety, humour, the Gallic attributes, allied with poetic fancy, profundity of thought, and a many-sided comprehension of life, art, and letters. He is in the best tradition of French criticism only more versatile than either Sainte-Beuve or Taine; as versatile as Doctor Brandes[38] or Arthur Symons,[39] and that is saying much. With Anatole France he could have exclaimed: "The longer I contemplate human life, the more I believe that we must give it, for witnesses and judges, Irony and Pity. . . ."

[38] Georg Brandes (1842–1947), Danish literary critic.
[39] English poet and critic (1865–1945).

PART IV

TRENDS IN MODERN LITERARY CRITICISM

TRENDS IN MODERN LITERARY CRITICISM[1]

As the nineteenth century had drawn to a close, American criticism had witnessed the death of Walt Whitman, the last of the great romantic critics, and the rise of a realism in literary criticism which was hostile to the romantic creed. Realism had first asserted itself significantly in the criticism of William Dean Howells and Henry James; and what has been called the "Revolt of the Nineties" saw the full expression of realism and naturalism through the work of writers like Hamlin Garland, Frank Norris, and Stephen Crane.

With the exception of the "aesthetic revolt," American criticism had continued pretty much along two divergent ways, the idealistic and the realistic. But just as naturalism represented a rather pronounced change in the realistic tradition, there began during the early years of the twentieth century to be significant changes in the ranks of idealism. The result was a movement more or less foreshadowed by William Crary Brownell [2] which was to become known, under the leadership of Irving Babbitt and Paul Elmer More, as humanism and which was to be one of the most influential forces in modern criticism.[3] There was to be no longer an unques-

[1] General studies dealing with the development of American thought during the period include Merle Curti, *The Growth of American Thought* (New York, 1943); and Henry Steele Commager, *The American Mind: An Interpretation of American Thought and Character since the 1880's* (New Haven, 1950). The only book-length study of criticism in the period is William Van O'Connor, *An Age of Criticism: 1900-1950* (Chicago, 1952). The best brief analyses are in the *Literary History of the United States*, and Morton D. Zabel, introduction to *Literary Opinion in America* (New York, rev. ed., 1951). Bernard Smith's *Forces in American Criticism* (New York, 1939) contains an analysis of the criticism of the period to the date of its publication, but is strongly biased by the author's Marxism. A brief survey of the period is Clarence D. Thorpe and Norman E. Nelson, "Criticism in the Twentieth Century: A Bird's Eye View," *English Journal*, XXXVI (1947), 165-73. A partial study is Charles I. Glicksberg's "Two Decades of American Criticism," *Dalhousie Review*, XVI (1936), 229-42. There is an unpublished dissertation by Barbara Woodward on *Theories of Meaning in Poetry, 1915-1940: A Critical History* (Michigan, 1946). Included among the best anthologies of the criticism of the period are Joel E. Spingarn, editor, *Criticism in America: Its Function and Status* (New York, 1924), which covers the years 1910-1923; Robert W. Stallman, editor, *Critiques and Essays in Criticism: 1920-1948* (New York, 1949); John W. Aldridge, editor, *Critiques and Essays on Modern Fiction, 1920-1951* (New York, 1952); Morton D. Zabel, editor, *Literary Opinion in America* (New York, rev. ed., 1951); and Charles I. Glicksberg, editor, *American Literary Criticism, 1900-1950* (New York, 1951).

[2] For critical estimates of W. C. Brownell, see Louis J. A. Mercier, "W. C. Brownell and our Neo-Barbarism," *Forum*, LXXXI (1929), 376-81, and *Le Mouvement Humaniste aux Etats Unis* (Paris, 1928); Bernard Bandler II, "The Humanism of W. C. Brownell," *Hound & Horn*, II (1929), 205-22; and Harry M. Campbell, unpublished dissertation, *A Critical Study of W. C. Brownell* (Vanderbilt, 1942). Brownell's principal works are *French Traits* (Meadville, Pa., 1896), *Victorian Prose Masters* (New York, 1901), *American Prose Masters* (New York, 1909), *Criticism* (New York, 1914), and *Standards* (New York, 1917).

[3] The best studies of humanism as a literary movement are Louis J. A. Mercier, *Le Mouvement Humaniste aux Etats Unis* (Paris, 1928), **and in Robert Shafer,**

tioning acceptance of tradition. Instead, tradition was re-examined and revaluated, and the base poured for an enduring structure that would withstand the carping criticism of the "barbarians," as the humanists conceived younger critics like Van Wyck Brooks, H. L. Mencken, Lewis Mumford, and Randolph Bourne to be.[4]

The battle resolved itself into a long and continuous argument whether man is totally the product of natural and social forces or whether he does not have some inner guiding principle, some rule of measure, that gives both direction and standards. The humanists held the latter, and while they rejected the genteel tradition's unquestioning allegiance to the New England heritage, they conceived of literature as having an essentially moral purpose which an analytic judgment could search out. Thus humanism could find no more in Dreiser than the crude excitement of novelty, intensity, and strangeness. The instabilities, the modern emphasis on the psychic and irrational elements of the mind, seemed to them to have replaced the expression of the universal personality. And so they bent all their energies to the cause.

The reaction of humanism was directly counter to romanticism and naturalism as they had appeared in American literature and criticism, calling as it did for a return to the concepts of the dignity of man, of the *via media* of classical Greek culture, of the older humanism over the newer humanitàrianism, and of the transcendence of hope and tradition over the prevailing attitudes of doubt and pessimism. Men like Irving Babbitt and Paul Elmer More believed romanticism and naturalism had degraded man; their call was for a rich and positive affirmation of the best that man had produced in the course of centuries. Permanent values were seen to have after all a meaning and inescapable bearing upon the conduct of man. These values were regarded, not as rigid and fast rules abstractly accessible to reason, but as elastic and adaptable keystones gathered from the wealth of the ages. In the application to criticism, humanism was to concern itself with a selection of subjects intrinsically proper to man, subjects that have a definite basis of values. Its twin ends were proper judgment and proper evaluation.

The central assumption of humanism is that of a dualism of man and nature, and that man's primary concern is his own world of ethical values and qualities which sets him apart from the merely quantitative order of nature. Opposing the monism assumed by both romanticism and naturalism, humanism holds that no principles of rational or spiritual guidance, no ethical values, can be supplied by a naturalistic philosophy which holds that man is merely a creature motivated by purely natural instincts. Both the Greek and Christian traditions, which have been the guiding tradi-

---

Paul Elmer More and American Criticism (New Haven, 1935). Also see G. R. Elliott, *Humanism and Imagination* (Chapel Hill, N.C., 1938) and Norman Foerster, *Toward Standards: A Study of the Present Critical Movement in American Letters* (New York, 1930).

[4] See Stuart Sherman, Introduction to Brownell's *American Prose Masters* (New York, 1909, reprinted 1923).

tions in man's past experience, sharply differentiate between the human and the natural.

Unlike the anarchy of romanticism, humanism, true to its Hellenic origin, places faith in reason; unlike science and naturalism it recognizes a power above reason which is the human or ethical imagination. Man, through both his reason and ethical imagination, recognizes the ultimate principle of restraint and control—"that there is a law for man and a law for thing" which cannot be confused without falling into the anarchy of romanticism and naturalism which do not recognize the "inner check" of ethical principle. Avoiding the dogmatic and ascetic tendencies of religion as being provocative of a too harsh, or unnatural, dualism of the flesh and the spirit, and recognizing the importance of both science and art to man, nevertheless humanism agrees with both the religious and Greek traditions in its perception of "this ethical will as a power above that of the individual self."

The critical method of humanism consists essentially of three approaches to the judgment of a work of art. First, an attempt is made to understand the work in terms of its historical background. Second, the historical understanding of the work must be supplemented by a sympathetic attempt to understand, to re-create, the aesthetic experience, or intention, of the work. With all the knowledge which has been gained through the attempt to understand the work both historically and sympathetically at his disposal, the critic is ready to undertake the third step, the specific task of criticism, which is to judge the value of the work. Humanism recognizes two kinds of value, or beauty, the quantitative and the qualitative. The former raises the question of the *degree* in which the artist has succeeded in his intention; the latter raises the question of what *kind* of value, or beauty, does the work have. Here there can be no question that the value of one artist's work might be greater than that of another—no matter whether both have been equally successful in achieving their aesthetic intention. Here the criterion applied is that of truth, things as they really are, with reference to the perfection of the human type. Humanism views classicism, with its emphasis on reason and the ethical will, as opposed to romanticism with its emphasis on sense impressions and natural feeling, as being the nearest approach to an ideal art in the qualitative sense.

Irving Babbitt was a professor of comparative literature at Harvard when his crusading and embattled nature first attracted notice.[5] To many it was

---

[5] There is no biography of Babbitt. But see the memoirs by thirty-nine contributors brought together by Frederick Manchester and Odell Shepard in *Irving Babbitt: Man and Teacher* (New York, 1941). Critical studies include Edmund Wilson, "Notes on Babbitt and More," *New Republic*, LXII (1930), 115–20; G. R. Elliott, "T. S. Eliot and Irving Babbitt," *American Review*, VII (1936), 442–54; Paul Elmer More, "Irving Babbitt," *ibid.*, III (1934), 23–40; T. S. Eliot, "The Humanism of Irving Babbitt," *Forum*, LXXX (1928), 37–44; and R. P. Blackmur, "Humanism and Symbolic Imagination: Notes on Rereading Irving Babbitt," *Southern Review*, VII (1941), 309–25. For a study of classical influences on Babbitt's thinking, see John P. Pritchard, *Return to the Fountains: Some Classical Sources of American Criticism* (Durham, N.C., 1942), pp. 170–79. Babbitt's place in the humanist movement is discussed by Louis J. A. Mercier, *Le Mouvement Humaniste* (Paris, 1928).

refreshing to hear it emphatically stated that the course of literature was following a tributary and not the main stream, that the aesthetes and Menckenians were perverting a tradition originated by the Greeks which man had slowly and laboriously pursued through the centuries. Literature's salvation lay only in returning to the well springs of Greek classicism with its restraint, moderation, and middle way, Babbitt wrote in *Literature and the American College* (1908).

As revealed in his book *Rousseau and Romanticism* (1919), Babbitt's quarrel is particularly with the romanticists and their insistence on throwing off restraint altogether. These eulogize freedom, love, and liberty to such an extent that the terms become remindful of vices, and not of the highest virtuous connotations they once had. The highest law of all, the law of measure, has been discarded, and an anarchy substituted which Babbitt terms "eleutheromania," the shedding of all limitations. Tolstoy is eleutheromaniac in his notion of sympathy, Nietzsche in his notion of liberty. And the two together point out the opposite poles of Rousseauism.

Babbitt was not attempting to give a rounded estimate of Rousseau, but, as he stated in the introduction to *Rousseau and Romanticism*, he was tracing main currents of romanticism as a part of his search for a set of principles to oppose naturalism. Knowing that there is a healthy romanticism in even the greatest of poets when they are inspired to express truth with piercing insight or startling beauty, what Babbitt objected to was that in pursuing the vital in life and art, Rousseau went wrong, intellectually and morally. He agreed with and enjoyed Dr. Johnson's remark that "Rousseau is a rascal who ought to be hunted out of society." "The Rousseauist," Babbitt said, "lives according to nature, completely extinguishes that portion of himself which sets him apart from nature—his reason and will. The real danger of the nature cult is its effeminacy, its enervating, relaxing, pantheistic revery. It is the abdication of the higher part of man."

The chief point for man to remember is that there are two laws, law for man and law for thing. The two should not be confused. Man as thing grows by expansion, but man as man grows by a deepening and concentrating within himself by which he discovers his essential dignity and the laws of unity, measure, and purpose:

> This true nature, the point of pause and perfection, can be judged only with reference to the human law and its demands for unity, measure, and purpose, and not with reference to the physical law which in itself can give only an endless flux and relativity. Nature is the region of the Many. If art is to be humanized, it must not simply flow with nature but be checked and tempered by some perception of the One.

In the application of humanism to form and expression, Babbitt perceived the same anarchy in literature as he had observed in humanity at large. The neo-classicists had exalted form into a mechanical, inert formality, while the romantics, lately exemplified by Croce, had raised expression to an intuitive, sensory plane whose form evolved in a sort of divine emanation. Babbitt saw the need for reconciling the two: "Any sound analysis of beauty will always recognize two elements,—an element that is expansive and vital and may be summed up by the term expression, and in contrast to this an element of form that is felt rather as limiting and circumscribing law."

The limiting law is of course held flexibly, aided by those intuitions higher than sense. He conceded intellectualism in art may result from an intuitive personal approach, but the intuition itself is based upon the moderation and restraint, the law of measure, first given currency by the Greeks. Above all, no longer can the arts be indeterminate, absorbed in the phenomena of flux and change at the expense of the enduring:

> . . . if emotion is to be humanized it must become selective, and in direct proportion as it becomes selective it ceases to be indeterminate: it acquires aim and purpose, form and proportion. The mere outward push of expression does not by itself suffice. The object on which expression expends itself must be intrinsically worth while, and this is a point that must be determined on other and higher grounds than individual feeling.

Likewise, in literary criticism Babbitt attempted to supply an element of discipline in the disordered world of romanticism and naturalism. He made it clear that there could be no criticism without judgment of values and that the critic must "rate creation with reference to some standard set above both his own temperament and that of the creator. . . . He will begin to have taste only when he refers the creative expression and his impression of it to some standard that is set above both." The critic must bring to his task not only a sensitive taste but one that has been disciplined by an acquaintance with world literature, particularly the classics of the Greek tradition, which will enable him to know the enduring common denominators of art.

The critic must perceive that there are different levels of value in literature and that these levels of value depend on the quality of the insight into human nature displayed by the literary artist, and his interpretation of life:

> Of course the "Ancient Mariner" has merit. It is sheer magic! But the adventures of the Mariner are not a part of universal human experience. Do not misunderstand me. I demand merely that we recognize in literature different levels of value. And works like the "Ancient Mariner" or Keats's "Ode to a Nightingale," while excellent in their way, do not approach the highest level. It is precisely in this, the failure to admit such gradations, that the expressionist critics err most flagrantly.

The highest values of literature, Babbitt perceived, were those which reflected standards of wholeness, measure, proportion, and the human norm—standards which were constant in the human tradition and which were not subject to the flux and change of the time-spirit. A great work of art should reveal the discipline of reason and the ethical imagination, and should give evidence of the ethical dignity of man through the ideals of humility and restraint.

Like Irving Babbitt, Paul Elmer More thought that criticism was largely valueless if there were not a point of focus, a center from which the critic may render his judgment.[6] In an essay on "Criticism," published in the first book of the Shelburne Essays (1904), he criticized nineteenth-century critics, like Arnold, because "they missed a philosophy which could bind together their moral and their aesthetic sense, a positive principle besides the negative force of ridicule and irony; and missing this, they left criticism more easily subject to a one-sided and dangerous development." He felt that literary criticism was "the specific exercise of a faculty which works in many directions. All scholars, whether they deal with history or sociology or philosophy or language or, in the narrower use of the word, literature, are servants of the critical spirit, in so far as they transmit and interpret and mold the sum of experience from man to man and generation to generation."

More's "positive principle" of criticism was dualism, an affirmation of the similar realities of the many and the one as exhibited in the human consciousness and in nature. It is Babbitt's humanism with a new name, perhaps a better philosophical grasp of the issues involved, and certainly more penetrating than Babbitt's theory in its strict adherence to the field where every criticism must ultimately seek its justification: its application to individual works. More's best known collection is the *Shelburne Essays* (11 vols., 1904–1921) in which the philosophical implications of dualism were applied to literature and literature weighed in the balance. More than Babbitt he was a critic of individual writers.

More agrees with William James that the phenomena most near at hand, the guise in which nature appears to us most clearly, is one of flux and change. But there is, against James, the human consciousness of something changeless, steadfast, and immutable about which the flux of the world is constantly moving:

> How can one recall the innumerable witnesses of religion, or hearken to the self-revelation of the poets, how can one look into the mirror of one's own life, and not perceive that the sense of something immutable and unmoved exists in some way side by side with the sense of everlasting flux, that there is within us some
> "central peace subsisting at the heart of endless agitation"?

Psychologically, this immutability appears in man as an "inner check" against the passing activities and impulses:

[6] The most important study of More as a critic is Robert Shafer, *Paul Elmer More and American Criticism* (New Haven, 1935). There is an unpublished dissertation by William Zoller on *Paul Elmer More's Literary Criticism* (California, 1946). Other critical studies include S. G. Brown, "Paul Elmer More as Critic," *Sewanee Review*, XLVII (1939), 476–97; and Horace Gregory, "On Paul Elmer More and His Shelburne Essays," *Accent*, IV (1944), 140–49. A study of classical influences on More's thought is in John P. Pritchard, *Return to the Fountains*, pp. 180–90. There is a discussion of More's place in the humanist movement in Louis J. A. Mercier, *Le Mouvement Humaniste*.

Beside the flux of life there is also that within man which displays itself intermittently as an inhibition upon this or that impulse, prevent-
ing its prolongation in activity, and making a pause or eddy, so to speak,
in the stream. This negation of the flux we call the inner check. It is
not the mere blocking of one impulse by another, which is a quality of
the confusion of the flux itself, but a restraint upon the flux exercised
by a force contrary to it.

As Babbitt had said, to seek the source and meaning of this check is beyond the intellectual ken of man. Its ultimate source is unfathomable, can
never be expressed in rational terms:

> This dualism of consciousness, it seems, is the last irrational fact, the
> report behind which we cannot go, the decision against which there is
> no appeal, the reality which only stands out the more clearly the more
> it is questioned. If a man denies this dualism of consciousness there is
> no argument with him, but a fundamental difference of intuition which
> will follow into every view of philosophy and criticism.

It is this peculiar manifestation of the One in the manyness of nature
that breeds in us a sense of beauty. The beautiful conforms to the "inner
check," finding its expression in terms of design, harmony, relations, form,
all that formative purity that communicates the permanence of masterly
order: "The consolation of nature is an impersonal emotion arising from
the confirmation of our inner consciousness of dualism; for beauty is, as it
were, a visible image of the possible happiness of the soul."

This dualism of consciousness is the safeguard by means of which literature is prevented from being only the esoteric, individual expression
of impulse and begins taking on meaning for mankind as a whole. The
universality of human experience is embodied in the art work. Individuality in art, in so far as it partakes of art, stems from the personal temperament, impulses, and egotism of the artistic creator; universality in art
stems from the temperament when united to the inner check of the soul,
partakes of the character of the artist, and is the expression of a unique
and yet universal personality. Here, maintains More, is the secret to the
great art of the ages, its universal appeal to all men regardless of climes
and cultures. Great art is essentially homogeneity derived from heterogeneity, the shaped and molded product drawn from the constant flow of
things:

> Works of art are varied in so far as they are created by the imagination
> out of the material of the flux, and substantially they depend on the
> richness of the artist's experience. Formally they rise to a common stand-
> ard of excellence in so far as the imagination of the artist is subject to the
> control of the unvaried inner check. So, too, taste, or the appreciation of
> art, passes from the impressionistic whim of the individual and from
> the larger convention of an age or a people to a universal canon just to
> the degree that it is regulated by the inner check. Criticism is thus not
> left to waver without a fixed criterion; and in the understanding of

dualism it possesses further a key to the main divergences of thought and action, and a constant norm of classification.

It was because of his recognition of this dualism that More, in his literary criticism, never deviated from the principle that what must be judged carefully in literature is the insight into human nature of the artist. This led him to disagree with any theory of art for art's sake which held that literature can be judged without regard to that which it expresses, and it led him to insist that criticism of literature is inseparable from the criticism of life. It did not follow, for More, that literature should be asked to preach moral lessons but that it be a faithful reflection of life —and one which reflects that constancy as well as change characterizes the world and that it is the constant which is universal to man and in terms of which alone can order be brought out of the chaos of flux and change.

Criticism must recognize this constant element in life and that at least it is presumed that the work of Homer and other literary pieces similarly sanctioned by tradition "embody qualities which it is very much our concern to appreciate, and which we have every reason to use as a criterion." It is only as the individual accepts the authority of the conserved experiences of the race, that he can become fully human and fully disciplined. However, the aim of culture, of tradition, according to More, "is not to merge the present in a sterile dream of the past, but to hold the past as a living force in the present."

As More grew older, his attention was given increasingly to the historical background of humanism, to an attempt to integrate the Christian idea with Platonism and the Greek tradition. This represents a development from the position which More earlier held in the *Shelburne Essays*. Whereas the work of Babbitt and the earlier criticism of More sought to find a philosophic substitute, in the form of modern humanism, not only for Christianity, but for religion, More's later criticism, unlike that of Babbitt, led him to realize the validity and force of religious faith. In the Preface to the third edition of *Platonism*, More writes:

> I can foresee no restoration of humane studies to their lost position of leadership until they are felt once more to radiate from some central spiritual truth. I do not believe that the aesthetic charms of literature can supply this want, nor is it clear to me that a purely scientific analysis of the facts of moral experience can furnish the needed motive; the former is too apt to run into dillettantism, and the latter appeals too little to the imagination and the springs of enthusiasm. Only through the centralizing force of religious faith or through its equivalent in philosophy can the intellectual life regain its meaning and authority for earnest men.

More brought to the criticism of literature a learning and a taste which had been disciplined by a long, thorough, and comprehensive study of both ancient and modern literatures and thought—an erudition and a high seriousness which admitted of no suspicion. Like Babbitt, he has been accused of "Puritan" and "genteel" tendencies, of confining art in the restricted circle of his own moral prejudices. So recent has been the conflict between humanism and the forces of the realistic and aesthetic traditions of literary criticism that no accurate or unbiased recognition has been made of the contributions of More and Babbitt to modern American criticism.

A new revival of literary activity began around 1912, with the "new poetry" of Amy Lowell and the Imagists, Robert Frost, Carl Sandburg, and others; and with the work of a large number of writers of fiction, including Theodore Dreiser, Sherwood Anderson, and Sinclair Lewis. This renewed creative activity was accompanied by a realistic revival in literary criticism which was not only antagonistic to nineteenth-century romanticism but also to some of the earlier realistic critics such as Howells and James who had, the new generation thought, been too much influenced by the genteel tradition and by the academies.

Attacking the genteel tradition, the academic in literary criticism, and the aesthetes, the critical revolt aimed at a rediscovery of the American spirit and plainly declared itself in 1913 with the appearance of John Macy's *Spirit of American Literature*. Sympathetic with the aims of realism, particularly as it had been stated by Hamlin Garland and Frank Norris, life as it actually existed in the United States was to be the primary standard of value in the judgment of literature. Considering earlier realists, like Howells and James, over-refined and tame, Macy declared that most American writers were too "idealistic, sweet, delicate," and they "turn their backs on life, miss its intensities, its significance."

Following the lead established by Macy, Van Wyck Brooks in a book published in 1915, *America's Coming of Age*, gave further impetus to the direction that this new movement in critical realism was to take.[7] Before either American literature or criticism could realize their full potentialities, there must be a new and more realistic understanding of America itself. *Letters and Leadership* (1918) continued this revision of the view of American society. He saw the utilitarian and materialistic preoccupations of American society as the limiting and frustrating influences in American life, which have prevented the growth of a literature that in scope and maturity could challenge the literature of Europe. It was almost as if American life itself had reached "A state of arrested development"; "Such, in fact, is the deficiency of personal impulse, of the creative will, in America, so overwhelming is the demand laid upon Americans to serve ulterior and impersonal ends, that it is as if the springs of spiritual action had altogether evaporated."

[7] For more complete studies of Van Wyck Brooks as a critic, see Stanley Hyman, "Van Wyck Brooks and Biographical Criticism," in *The Armed Vision* (New York, 1948), pp. 106–26; Charles I. Glicksberg, "Van Wyck Brooks," *Sewanee Review*, XLIII (1935), 175–86; René Wellek, "Van Wyck Brooks and a National Literature," *American Prefaces*, VII (1942), 292–306; Oscar Cargill, "The Ordeal of Van Wyck Brooks," *College English*, VIII (1946), 55–61; Howard Mumford Jones, "The Pilgrimage of Van Wyck Brooks," *Virginia Quarterly Review*, VIII (1932), 439–42; and Seward Collins, "Criticism in America; The Origins of a Myth," *Bookman*, LXXI (1930), 241–56, 353–64. There is an unpublished dissertation by Leo J. Steinlein on *The Critical Theories of Van Wyck Brooks* (New York, 1948).

America after the Civil War had seen the growth of a cultural environment which had served only to cripple and to retard American writers:

> "How can one explain why, at a time when America, in every other department of life, was more distinctly colonial than it is now, American literature commanded the full respect of Americans, while today, when the colonial tradition is vanishing all about us, it so little commands their respect that they go after any strange god from England."

The full flowering of the radicalism of the revolt in American criticism, which had been begun by Macy and contributed to by writers like Brooks and Randolph Bourne,[8] was reached in the work of H. L. Mencken, who developed from a purely literary critic into a sort of universal iconoclast, attacking the orthodox in religion, politics, in morals, as well as in literature.[9] Edmund Wilson has expressed the significance of Mencken and his contribution to American criticism in this way:

> Brooks exposed the negative aspects of our literary tradition and urged us to get away from our governesses, Mencken showed the positive value of our vulgar heritage; and he did more than anyone else in his field to bring about that "coming-of-age" for which Brooks sounded the hour. The publication of Mencken's Book of Prefaces in 1917, with its remarkable essay on Dreiser and its assault on "Puritanism as a Literary Force," was a cardinal event for the new American literature. Mencken did not precisely discover Dreiser, but he was able to focus him clearly for the first time as a figure of dignity and distinction, because he appreciated and made us taste the Americanism of Dreiser as Americanism, without attempting to write him down for not being something other than American.

Mencken himself saw the function of the critic "to provoke the reaction between the work of art and the spectator. The spectator, untutored, stands unmoved; he sees the work of art, but it fails to make any intel-

---

[8] For Bourne's criticism, see Untimely Papers (New York, 1919) edited by James Oppenheim; and History of a Literary Radical, and Other Essays (New York, 1920) edited with an introduction by Van Wyck Brooks. The best critical study is Louis Filler, Randolph Bourne (Washington, 1943).

[9] Recent book-length studies of Mencken are William Manchester, Disturber of the Peace: The Life of H. L. Mencken (New York, 1951), and Edgar Kemler, The Irreverent Mr. Mencken (Boston, 1950). Also see Ernest A. Boyd, H. L. Mencken (New York, 1925), and Isaac Goldberg, The Man Mencken: A Biographical and Critical Survey (New York, 1925). Briefer critical estimates are Edmund Wilson, "H. L. Mencken," New Republic, XXVII (1921), 10-13; Fred L. Pattee, "A Critic in C Major," in Side-Lights on American Literature (New York, 1922), 56-97; Stuart P. Sherman, "Mr. Mencken, the Jeune Fille, and the New Spirit in Letters," in Americans (New York, 1922), 1-12; Carl Van Doren, "Smartness and Light: H. L. Mencken," in Many Minds (New York, 1924), 120-35; Joseph W. Beach, "Mr. Mencken," in The Outlook for American Prose (Chicago, 1926), 81-92; Irving Babbitt, "The Critic and American Life," Forum, LXXIX (1928), 161-76; Henry S. Canby, American Estimates (New York, 1929), 58-61; Benjamin De Casseres, Mencken and Shaw (New York, 1930), 3-103; and Van Wyck Brooks, "Mr. Mencken and the Prophets," in Sketches in Criticism (New York, 1932), 26-33. Studies of Mencken prior to 1929 are usually inclined to be biased. More recent works are somewhat more objective.

ligible impression on him; if he were spontaneously sensitive to it, there would be no need for criticism."

In his essay on "Puritanism as a Literary Force," [10] he revealed his antipathy toward any and all ethical or ideal concepts of art which he broadened into a revolt against any tradition which smacked of the intellectual or the dogmatic, whether moral or aesthetic. Continuing the reinterpretation of American literature which had characterized the critical revolt set off by Macy, Mencken, through his praise and evaluation of such writers as Dreiser, Sandburg, and Lewis pointed out what values were to be found in a new realistic and critical appraisal of the common and the "vulgar" in American life.[11]

Like Huneker, he was basically an impressionistic interpreter of literature and life; like Huneker he waged a relentless warfare with all that was academic and authoritarian. Possessed of a sensibility that was primarily pragmatic and unrefined, Mencken was least successful in dealing with the subtlety of writers like Henry James.

With the work of men like Mencken, Brooks, Randolph Bourne, and Lewis Mumford,[12] realism made significant gains in American criticism in the period 1915 to 1925. While it is probably true that little "great" criticism was produced by the realists in this period, the value of their work in the reinterpretation of the American past and of American literature should not be underestimated. At a time when there was danger of literature being widely separated from life, the criticism of the realists and the iconoclasts brought it closer to the simple facts of ordinary experience and did much to strip it of the over-refinement of the aesthetic and academic approach, at the same time widening the artistic horizons for writers by attacking the narrow prejudices of the genteel tradition. With these values came, of course, the corresponding weakness of the realists in their attitudes toward the intellectual, the aesthetic, and the experimental in art, which was reflected in the production of a criticism sorely in need of social and artistic disciplines.

The weakness of specific critical judgment and the lack of an artistic discipline which characterized the criticism of the realists was soon to be corrected by the work of an American expatriate in England, T. S. Eliot, who began by pointing out the defects in modern criticism and by reexamining the basis of the European traditions of literature. Little interested in the reinterpretation of America or in the creation of new standards of social realism, Eliot was primarily concerned with the aesthetic and the technical in the criticism of literature—with purely artistic considerations.[13]

[10] Published in *A Book of Prefaces* (New York, 1917).
[11] Also see "The American Tradition," *Literary Review*, IV (1923), 277–78.
[12] See *The Golden Day* (New York, 1926), *Herman Melville* (New York, 1929), and *The Brown Decades* (1931).
[13] A major study of Eliot is F. O. Matthiessen, *The Achievement of T. S. Eliot* (New York, 1948). The most extensive treatment of Eliot as a critic is Victor H. Brombert, *The Criticism of T. S. Eliot* (New Haven, 1949). Other valuable studies include Yvor Winters, "T. S. Eliot: or, The Illusion of Reaction," in *The Anatomy of Nonsense* (Norfolk, Conn., 1943), pp. 120–67; Stanley E. Hyman, "T. S. Eliot

Poe had been the first American critic to attempt to bring to American literary criticism the discipline of a critical method based primarily on an aesthetic and technical approach to literature. Later in the nineteenth century, Henry James's criticism was written from the same point of view. In the first decade of the twentieth century, critics like Huneker, Gates, and Spingarn were instrumental in promoting an aesthetic criticism by their attack on the academic in criticism and by their defense of purely aesthetic standards. Unlike Henry James, however, the particular weakness of these immediate predecessors of Eliot in aesthetic criticism lay in their deficiency in the detailed, specific analysis of the literary work itself.

To bring criticism into active collaboration with traditional values, to assert the necessity of technical and aesthetic evidences as the basis of genuine critical judgment, have been paramount in Eliot's critical work and have made him, above any other, the dominating influence in aesthetic analysis after 1920—a major force among critics as diverse as Edmund Wilson, Kenneth Burke, John Crowe Ransom, Allen Tate, and R. P. Blackmur.

Eliot believes that the function of criticism is "the elucidation of art and the correction of taste," and "to bring the poet back to life." The "tools" of the critic, with which he performs this function, are "comparison and analysis," and the end of criticism is to establish "a tradition," a sense of the continuity between present literature and the past. As he wrote in "Tradition and the Individual Talent" (1917):

> Tradition involves, in the first place, the historical sense . . . and the historical sense involves a perception, not only of the pastness of the past, but of its presence; the historical sense compels a man to write not merely with his own generation in his bones, but with a feeling that the whole of the literature of Europe from Homer and within it the whole of the literature of his own country has a simultaneous existence and composes a simultaneous order. . . .

In the introduction to his first collection of essays, *The Sacred Wood* (1920), Eliot wrote that "It is part of the business of the critic to preserve tradition—where a good tradition exists," and in the book Eliot makes it clear that what he considered to be a "good tradition" was that of "the

and Tradition in Criticism," in *The Armed Vision* (New York, 1948), pp. 73–105; Edmund Wilson, "T. S. Eliot," in *Axel's Castle* (New York, 1931), pp. 93–131; Leonard Unger, editor, *T. S. Eliot: A Selected Critique* (New York, 1948); R. P. Blackmur, "In the Hope of Straightening Things Out," *Kenyon Review*, XIII (1951), 303–14, a study of Eliot's critical doctrines; Harry M. Campbell, "An Examination of Modern Critics: T. S. Eliot," *Rocky Mountain Review*, VIII (1944), 128–38; Ruth C. Child, "The Early Critical Work of T. S. Eliot: An Assessment," *College English*, XII (1951), 269–75; Charles I. Glicksberg, "T. S. Eliot as Critic," *Arizona Quarterly*, IV (1948), 225–36; Michael F. Moloney, "Mr. Eliot and Critical Tradition," *Thought*, XXI (1946), 455–74; John Crowe Ransom, "T. S. Eliot: The Historical Critic," in *The New Criticism* (Norfolk, Conn., 1941), pp. 135–208; "Eliot and the Metaphysicals," *Accent*, I (1941), 148–56; David Daiches, "T. E. Hulme and T. S. Eliot," in *Poetry and the Modern World* (Chicago, 1940); and J. R. Daniells, "T. S. Eliot and His Relation to T. E. Hulme," *University Toronto Quarterly*, II (1933), 380–96.

literature of the great ages, the sixteenth and seventeenth centuries." This was further developed in his essay on "The Metaphysical Poets" published a year later.

A key concept in the criticism of Eliot is that he constantly emphasizes "using" tradition as a basis for the comparison and analysis of literature. When Eliot, for example, wrote his essay on "Henry James" he analyzed James against the background of Hawthorne, seeing both of them as in the same "tradition" of fiction. This comparison served to illuminate the work of both James and Hawthorne and also served to illuminate the nature of the literary tradition itself—its continuity over a period of time.

Eliot's "tradition" has perhaps one fault—that it is exclusive rather than inclusive, since no attempt is made to include all of the great literary figures of the past but rather only those who seem to fit into Eliot's own concept of the "tradition." In general, by using the term "tradition" Eliot means "classic" as opposed to "romantic," since the classic is "complete" and "orderly" while the romantic he sees as "fragmentary" and "chaotic."

Pointing out the defects of criticism which showed historical, deterministic, ethical, or impressionistic biases, Eliot saw in Remy de Gourmont a model critic: "He combined to a remarkable degree sensitiveness, erudition, sense of fact and sense of history, and generalizing power." Eliot's ideal critic, then, is a kind of scholar-critic, much the same as the one envisioned by Ezra Pound, one whose sensibility has been disciplined and conditioned by formal principles of art and one who can bring to criticism of literature a comparative technique combined with the ability to analyze closely and to elucidate texts.

Another of Eliot's critical principles is that of the impersonal nature of art: "Poetry is not a turning loose of emotion; but an escape from personality," and "The progress of an artist is a continual self-sacrifice, a continual extinction of personality." The theory of the "objective correlative," which Eliot developed in his essay on "Hamlet and His Problems" (1919), is a way of barring emotion from poetry, of rendering it "objective," in accordance with his belief that poetry should be impersonal and "traditional." [14]

Since his renouncing of "poetry as poetry" in a new preface to *The Sacred Wood* written in 1928, and following his conversion to Anglo-Catholicism, Eliot's criticism has been more concerned with metaphysical and somewhat less with purely aesthetic problems. A steadily decreasing proportion of his work deals with literature as literature; rather, there is an attempt to deal with it in terms of its broader moral, traditional, and human conditions. While this represents a development from Eliot's earlier, purely aesthetic, criticism, it does not represent a repudiation of the critical principles which he had formulated; while "The 'greatness' of literature cannot be determined solely by literary standards; . . . we must remember that whether it is literature or not can be determined only by literary standards."

[14] See Eliseo Vivas, "The Objective Correlative of T. S. Eliot," *American Bookman*, I (1944), 7–18.

Around the example of Eliot, the "younger generation" of critics rallied, in opposition to the school of Van Wyck Brooks and Mencken.[15] These younger men felt that their interests could not be represented in the established journals, and following the first World War they associated themselves with the "little magazines" and some of the "unpopular" journals: *The Little Review, Secession, The Dial* (which was the chief organ of the Eliot influence, 1921–1928), *Hound & Horn, The Southern Review, Partisan Review,* and the *Kenyon Review.* Only the last two of these publications have survived. While not in agreement from the point of view of political bias, they nevertheless expressed a single literary tradition: all assumed the value and even the autonomy of works of the imagination.[16]

The years from 1915 to 1925 had been devoted to an attack on conservatism, on the "vested interests" of literature and criticism—call them idealism, Puritanism, the genteel tradition, the academic—which had represented the forces of reaction to the younger critics. It had been a decade not only of a new poetry, a new fiction, but of a new criticism whose exponents had fallen generally into two groups: the "historical-patriotic" and the realists and iconoclasts led by Brooks, Bourne, Mencken, Lewis Mumford, and others—and the aesthetic "rebels" led by Ezra Pound[17] and T. S. Eliot.[18]

While these two forces were struggling for supremacy, an older school of critics, the Humanists, headed by Paul Elmer More and Irving Babbitt, had, at the end of the twenties, a brief resurgence. They opposed, in principle, both of the new critical groups. Recognition of the common enemy of reaction, in the form of the Humanists, led to an alliance on the part of the realists and aesthetes although the two groups differed in their artistic and technical principles.

The controversy between the Humanists and the realists and aesthetes culminated in 1930 with the appearance of a Humanist symposium, *Humanism and America,* in which Babbitt and More accompanied by such followers as Norman Foerster, Robert Shafer, and Prosser Hall Frye led the defense of the Humanist position. It was immediately attacked by a counter-symposium, edited by Hartley Grattan, *The Critique of Humanism* (1930), in which the younger critics, including Edmund Wilson, Malcolm Cowley, Kenneth Burke, Allen Tate, R. P. Blackmur, and others, defended the "rebels."

In these two books, the two main trends in American criticism that had descended from the nineteenth century were fully displayed: on one side, the reaffirmation of classical critical standards combined with the union

[15] See Gorham B. Munson, "The Young Critics of the Nineteen-Twenties," *Bookman,* LXX (1929), 369–73.

[16] For a detailed study of the little magazines, see Frederick J. Hoffman, Charles Allen, and Carolyn F. Ulrich, *The Little Magazine: A History and a Bibliography* (Princeton, 1946).

[17] For Pound's critical work see *Instigations* (New York, 1920), particularly the essay on Henry James; and *Make It New: Essays by Ezra Pound* (New Haven, 1935).

[18] For a general study of the 1920's, see Howard Mumford Jones, *The Bright Medusa* (Urbana, Ill., 1952).

of ethical and aesthetic judgment; on the other, the social realism and the liberal emancipation of Emerson's and Whitman's lineage, combined now with the aesthetic which had its antecedents in the criticism of Poe and Henry James. No controversy in American criticism has ever more pointedly shown the divided inheritance of American literature. While a violent controversy ensued, it had subsided within a year. Not only were no significant issues decided but the issues themselves were poorly defined by both sides and tended, amidst the confusion, to be reduced merely to attacks on the "genteel" and the "Puritan" in Humanist criticism. The extent of the confusion of issues involved is clearly shown by the appearance of Eliot in the Humanist volume, whereas most of his "school" were in the opposition. While the defects of More and Babbitt as literary critics were exposed, in the heat of the controversy their significance to American criticism was ignorantly dismissed. Completely ignored was the fact that Eliot and most of the modern critical tradition learned from More and Babbitt certain of their basic critical principles: that no artist can be isolated, and none can hope to comprehend the present except in the light of the past; and that violence, chaos, and the presentation of unanalyzed emotion are poor artistic technique.

The collapse of the stock market in 1929 and the Humanist controversy marked the end of an era in twentieth-century criticism and the rise in the thirties of the "Marxist school" of critics,[19] of whom Kenneth Burke,[20] James T. Farrell,[21] Granville Hicks,[22] and Edmund Wilson were among the most conspicuous. Wilson's *Axel's Castle* (1934) and Burke's *Counter-*

---

[19] While Marxist criticism first rose to prominence in the 1930's the plea for a sociological literature and criticism is much older than that. John Curtis Underwood in *Literature and Insurgency* (New York, 1914) praised the reforming novelists Frank Norris and David Graham Phillips whom he considered our greatest writers and who, he felt, would restore individuality, realism, and honesty to American literature. Concerned primarily with the sociological function of literature rather than with any consideration of artistic competence, he thought Howells and James too "genteel" while Twain was the great "democrat." The relationship between Underwood's views and those of the muckraking movement are clear. In 1924, Upton Sinclair in *Mammonart* stated the case for literature as class propaganda. Victor F. Calverton as editor of the *Modern Quarterly* and in *The Newer Spirit: A Sociological Criticism of Literature* (New York, 1925) likewise made a plea for literature that serves a social function. For studies of Marxist criticism, see Ernest Boyd, "Marxian Literary Critics," *Scribner's*, XCVIII (1935), 342–46; and Stanley Hyman, "Marxist Literary Criticism," *Antioch Review*, VII (1947), 541–68.

[20] For studies of Burke's criticism, see Stanley Hyman, "Kenneth Burke and the Criticism of Symbolic Action," in *The Armed Vision* (New York, 1948), pp. 347–94; Austin Warren, "Kenneth Burke: His Mind and Art," *Sewanee Review*, XLI (1933), 344–63; Charles I. Glicksberg, "Kenneth Burke: The Critics' Critic," *South Atlantic Quarterly*, XXXVI (1937), 74–84; and Marius Bewley, "Kenneth Burke as Literary Critic," *Scrutiny*, XV (1948), 254–77.

[21] For discussions of James T. Farrell as a literary critic, see Irving Howe, "James T. Farrell as Critic," *Partisan Review*, XIV (1947); and Charles I. Glicksberg, "The Criticism of James T. Farrell," *Southwest Review*, XXXV (1950), 189–96.

[22] For Hicks's criticism see particularly *The Great Tradition* (1933) in which he equates literary tradition with Marxist political and social views. See also his "The Crisis in Criticism," *New Masses* (1933) in which he gives the rules for the "perfect Marxian novel." Later work includes *Figures of Transition* (1939); "The Failure of 'Left' Criticism," *New Republic*, CIII (1940), 345–47; and "The Intransigence of Edmund Wilson," *Antioch Review*, VI (1946), 550–62.

Statement (1931) and *Permanence and Change* (1936) represent some of the ablest literary criticism from the Marxist point of view in this period. *A Note on Literary Criticism*, published by James T. Farrell in 1936, attempted to correct some of the more obvious errors inherent in Marxist criticism which supposed that "proletarian" literature could be something entirely different from other literature.

While some of the Marxists tended to become fanatics, like Bernard Smith in *Forces in American Criticism* (1934), and to be as dogmatic as the Humanists, and even narrower in their insistence upon the social principle in criticism and the attack on capitalistic monopoly and competitive license, what is sound in the best Marxist writers, the principle that literature must come out of life, is in agreement with traditional literary theory in all times. By 1940, the Marxist school had begun to break up; the work of such critics as Burke in *The Philosophy of Literary Form* (1941) and the later writings of Wilson show an obvious expansion of interests and a much greater objectivity.[23]

Edmund Wilson, as he gradually became disillusioned with Russian Communism, rejected Marxism in favor of a more general and more objective social and historical approach to the criticism of literature.[24] Concerned primarily with the interpretation of the content of literature, in a sense probably that much of contemporary criticism is not, he seems to regard himself as primarily a historical critic. In the dedication to his book, *Axel's Castle* (1934), he describes literary criticism as "a history of man's ideas and imaginings in the setting of the conditions which shaped them."[25] The historical method, according to Wilson, not only embraces the general social and historical background of the work of art, but also concerns itself with biography and hence with the findings of psychology and psychoanalysis. The three historical critics Wilson names as his "chief ancestors" are Vico, Herder, and Taine, although when consideration is given to the strong biographical and psychological element in his criticism, it is obvious that he also has fallen heir to the method of Sainte-Beuve as well.

While the earlier work of Wilson shows both a sociological and psychological approach to criticism, greater emphasis is placed on the sociological; his later criticism has shifted in its approach to place more emphasis on the psychological although still retaining the social principle as

---

[23] For studies of the decline of literary Marxism, see Philip Rahv, "Proletarian Literature: An Autopsy," *Southern Review*, IV (1939); and Charles I. Glicksberg, "The Decline of Literary Marxism," *Antioch Review*, I (1941), 452–62.

[24] Among the best studies of Wilson's criticism are Stanley Hyman, "Edmund Wilson and Translation in Criticism," in *The Armed Vision* (New York, 1948), pp. 19–48; E. K. Brown, "The Method of Edmund Wilson," *University Toronto Quarterly*, XI (1941), 105–11; Delmore Schwartz, "The Writing of Edmund Wilson," *Accent*, II (1942), 177–86; George Snell, "An Examination of Modern Critics: Edmund Wilson. The Historical Critic," *Rocky Mountain Review*, VIII (1944), 36–44; F. W. Dupee, "Edmund Wilson's Criticism," *Partisan Review*, IV (1938), 48–51; R. Adams, "Masks and Delays: Edmund Wilson as Critic," *Sewanee Review*, LVI (1948), 272–86; and Theodore B. Dolmatch, "Edmund Wilson as Literary Critic," *University Kansas City Review*, XVII (1951), 213–19.

[25] Cf. his "The Historical Interpretation of Literature," in *The Triple Thinkers* (New York, rev. ed., 1948).

an important factor in the method. His analysis of Proust from the psycho-logical point of view, in terms of Proust's "abnormal dependence on his mother," and the resulting "impulses toward a sterile and infantile per-versity," and his discussion of Proust's novel as the "Heart-break House of capitalist culture," illustrate how well he could employ both the sociological and psychological criteria simultaneously.

In addition to the employment of the historical method, in Wilson's un-derstanding of the term, his literary criticism reveals his ability through a highly sensitive reading of the text to consider the aesthetic elements of literature as something not completely determined by social conditions. His *The Triple Thinkers* (1938—revised 1948) and *The Wound and the Bow* (1941—revised 1947) illustrate his ability to coordinate social, aesthetic, and psychological analysis in the interpretation of literature from a broadly human and cultural point of view.

The sweeping transformation in literary criticism which has occurred during the last ten years can scarcely be exaggerated. This has taken place, for the most part, under the leadership of the group known as the "New Critics."[26] Cleanth Brooks, John Crowe Ransom, and others held that if literature has any value beyond the historical, that value must be located in the area of art and philosophy. This is the point of view, in general, of the New Criticism. It is a reaction against the historical criti-cism of the academicians, the too little attention given by the Humanists to the study of literature as an art, and against the humanitarianism of the Marxist critics. It bears in some respects a resemblance to the position held earlier by Spingarn and other expressionistic critics who were likewise in their time reacting against the purely historical approach to literature.

The phrase, "The New Criticism," is not itself new. It was used as early as 1910 by Spingarn as the title of a lecture given at Columbia Uni-versity, which was later published as a chapter in *Creative Criticism* (1917). It first appeared in its present meaning as the title of a book pub-lished by John Crowe Ransom in 1941, a book which heralded a new ap-proach to criticism.[27]

[26] Much has been written on the "New Criticism." Among the most valuable and most representative commentaries are the following: Robert W. Stallman, "The New Critics," in *Critiques and Essays in Criticism*, edited by Robert W. Stallman (New York, 1941), and "The New Criticism and the Southern Critics," in *A South-ern Vanguard* edited by Allen Tate (New York, 1947); William Van O'Connor, "This Alexandrian Criticism," *American Scholar*, XIV (1945), 357–61, and "A Short View of the New Criticism," *College English*, XXXVIII (1949), 489–97; Elder Olson, "Recent Literary Criticism," *Modern Philology*, XL (1943), 275–83; Herbert J. Muller, "The New Criticism in Poetry," *Southern Review*, VI (1941), 811–39; David Daiches, "The New Criticism: Some Qualifications," *English Jour-nal*, XXXIX (1950), 64–72; *College English*, XI (1950), 242–50; W. J. Ong, "The Meaning of the 'New Criticism,'" in *Twentieth Century English*, edited by W. S. Knickerbocker (New York, 1946), pp. 344–83; Douglas Bush, "The New Criti-cism: Some Old-Fashioned Queries," *Publications Modern Language Association*, LXIV (1949), 13–21; Cleanth Brooks, "The New Criticism: A Brief for the De-fense," *American Scholar*, XIII (1944), 435–49; H. Trowbridge, "Aristotle and the 'New Criticism,'" *Sewanee Review*, LII (1944), 537–55; and Robert G. Davis, "The New Criticism and the Democratic Tradition," *American Scholar*, XIX (1949–50), 9–19.
[27] Edwin B. Burgum's *The New Criticism* (1930), a collection of essays chiefly aesthetic, may perhaps be considered an immediate predecessor of Ransom's book.

I. A. Richards' *Principles of Criticism* (1924) and *Practical Criticism* (1929) had pointed to a more subtle and a more philosophical approach to literature as an art. Much emphasis was placed upon the language of poetry, its structure and texture. It was in some respects a return to the Aristotelian method and to the late medieval and Renaissance approach to literary study with the technical equipment of rhetoric and poetic theory— a tradition which had given way before the textual and documentary criticism of the eighteenth- and nineteenth-century German scholars.

The New Critics are for the most part in agreement in subordinating all other considerations to a concern for literature as a work of art. They are likewise for the most part at one in their Aristotelian principles: "that art is a making, that literature is the art of making structures of sound and meaning, that such structures are ultimately ontological, matter and form being fused in a literary work as in any other being, that the end of literature is delight in perception and contemplation." The delight of a work of art is refined by an understanding of the complexities of its structure and texture. As the title of Cleanth Brooks's book implies, a poem is seen as being similar to a "well wrought urn" in its quality as a work of art which is to be enjoyed and understood. It is thus the burden of the critic to "elucidate" as thoroughly as possible, and with full recognition of the complexities involved, all of the elements of metre, sound patterns, imagery, and sense which unite to make up the complete work of art. With the New Criticism, the study of literature has once again become an artistic and a human discipline rather than a vague appreciation or a merely factual job of research.

One of the members of this group who has most consistently applied its ideas to literature is Cleanth Brooks.[28] Like Eliot, Brooks in his first book of criticism, *Modern Poetry and the Tradition* (1939), returns to the tradition of the metaphysical poetry and "wit" embracing principally the seventeenth century: Donne and the Metaphysical Poets, Jonson, Herrick, and others; and in the twentieth century: Hardy, Yeats, Eliot, among others. With the exception of isolated figures like Swift, Gay, Blake, Emily Dickinson, and Hopkins, Brooks skips from the late seventeenth century to the twentieth.

In addition to *The New Criticism* (1941), see also Ransom's *The World's Body* (1938) and *The Intent of the Critic* (1941). Also important for a study of Ransom's criticism are the essays: "The Bases of Criticism," *Sewanee Review*, LII (1944), 556–71; "Poetry: The Formal Analysis," *Kenyon Review*, IX (1947), 436–56; "The Literary Criticism of Aristotle," *Kenyon Review*, X (1948), 382–402; and "The Understanding of Fiction," *Kenyon Review*, XII (1950), 189–218. Studies of Ransom's criticism include E. B. Burgum, "An Examination of Modern Critics: John Crowe Ransom," *Rocky Mountain Review*, VIII (1944), 87–93; and Morgan Blum, "John Crowe Ransom, Critic," *Western Review*, XIV (1950), 85–102. There are two unpublished dissertations on Ransom's criticism: Fred H. Stocking, *Poetry as Knowledge: The Critical Theory of John Crowe Ransom and Allen Tate* (Michigan, 1946), and Gordon H. Mills, *Ontology and Myth in the Criticism of John Crowe Ransom* (Iowa, 1943).

[28] For studies of Brooks's criticism, see Albrecht B. Strauss, "The Poetic Theory of Cleanth Brooks," *Centenary Review*, I (1949), 10–22; and R. S. Crane, "Cleanth Brooks; or, The Bankruptcy of Critical Monism," *Modern Philology*, XLV (1948), 226–45.

He accepts the difficulty presented by the imagery of modern poetry to those readers who are used to nineteenth-century poetry. Modern poets and the Metaphysicals are united in their stand on metaphor as opposed to the poets of the two intervening centuries. Much metaphysical poetry attains seriousness, not despite the use of wit, but by means of it. Brooks sees wit as "not merely an acute perception of analogies; it is a lively awareness of the fact that the obvious attitude toward a given situation is not the only possible attitude." The book illustrates the method of the New Criticism by its close textual analysis of the poems considered as being in the "tradition."

Brooks's second book, *The Well Wrought Urn* (1947), bears the subtitle *Studies in the Structure of Poetry*, which is revealing of the concentration of the book on a technical explanation of poetic structure, and on the elaborate reading of texts.[29] He points out that the entire poem itself is the only proper explanation of what it says. Poems speak indirectly, using words in no dictionary sense, but giving a meaning not otherwise expressible except in a particular context. The methods characteristic of poetry are symbol rather than abstraction, suggestion rather than pronouncement, metaphor rather than direct statement.

Brooks maintains that a poem must be read and understood through "structure." "Structure" is not subject matter, form, literary type, or any other constituent element of poetry, but rather the meanings, evaluations, and interpretations of the poem in its various parts. In dealing with "structure" in this sense, he speaks of "ambiguity," "paradox," "irony," and "complex of attitudes." By thinking of a poem as a combination of statement and decoration, a false dichotomy is created between form and matter that is, at best, a logical distinction alone.

Brooks does not agree with those critics who hold that "rational meaning" is the primary virtue of poetry. He says that such a distinction forces poetry to invade the areas of science or philosophy or theology. Poetry expresses ideas, but expressed outside the poem these ideas are abstractions and lose much of their meaning. He points out that to say a poem is not paraphrasable is not to say that it is without coherence:

> The poem does not merely eventuate in a logical conclusion. The conclusion of the poem is the working out of the various tensions—set up by whatever means—by proposition, metaphors, symbols. The unity is achieved by a dramatic process, not a logical; it represents an equilibrium of forces, not a formula. It is "proved" as a dramatic conclusion is proved: by its ability to resolve the conflicts which have been accepted as the donées of the drama.

Brooks in "The Language of Paradox" (1942) holds that paradox is the special, and exclusive, language of poetry. The scientist is alone in desiring a language free of connotation. Poets use no notation. Poetic language possesses meaning only in the unique relationships of the in-

---

[29] Cf. Brooks's "My Credo: The Formalist Critic," *Kenyon Review*, XIII (1951) and "A Note on 'History' and 'Criticism,'" *Sewanee Review*, LXI (1953).

dividual poems. In analyzing Donne's "The Canonization," Brooks demonstrates how paradox informs the poem: gives it dignity, expresses what cannot be stated in simple, scientific terms. Paradox is defined as a device for contrasting the conventional views of a situation with a more inclusive view so that a fuller insight and texture of meaning may be obtained and the whole presented with greater dramatic force.

One of the features of modern criticism has been the emphasis placed on the close technical reading of texts as a method of critical analysis. Various critics who represent the attitudes of the New Criticism have written much suggesting not only that the close reading of texts is an important function of criticism, but that it is its only legitimate function.

Another contemporary critic who is in the same tradition of criticism is R. P. Blackmur, who conceives the "common labour of literary criticism" to be: "the collection of facts about literary works, and comment on the management, the craft, the technique, of these works; and this labour, in so far as it leaves the reader in the works themselves, is the only one in itself worth doing."[30]

Like Brooks and the New Critics in general, and like Henry James, Blackmur insists on the importance of technique: "in craft, all values lie." He sees that perhaps one of the greatest weaknesses of American culture is in never having produced "a dominant class in our society which has set a high value on the aesthetic mode of understanding or expressing human life," which has resulted in a corresponding lack of understanding and sympathy for art. This point of view is in keeping with Blackmur's insistence upon the reader of poetry "reading with his mind, not his eye," and upon his experiencing the form, or art, of the poem as well as the content, and that he like poetry *as* poetry.

He sees criticism as performing two functions: "to promote intimacy with particulars," and "to judge the standard of achievement." He insists that criticism "elucidate" the work by close textual analysis and that it must always lead the reader to the work itself:

> A good critic keeps his criticism from becoming either instinctive or vicarious, and the labour of his understanding is always specific, like the art which he examines; and he knows that the sum of his best work comes only to the pedagogy of elucidation and appreciation. He observes facts and delights in discriminations. The object remains, and should remain, itself, only made more available and seen in a clearer light.

Blackmur's *The Double Agent* (1935) bears the revealing subtitle *Essays in Craft and Elucidation*, and its method is based on an extremely

---

[30] For discussions of Blackmur as a literary critic, see Stanley Hyman, "R. P. Blackmur and the Expense of Greatness," in *The Armed Vision* (New York, 1948), pp. 239–71; Delmore Schwartz, "The Critical Method of R. P. Blackmur," *Poetry*, LIII (1938), 28–39; Allen Tate, "R. P. Blackmur," *Southern Review*, III (1937), 183–98; Ray B. West, Jr., "An Examination of Modern Critics: R. P. Blackmur," *Rocky Mountain Review*, VIII (1945), 139–45; and R. W. B. Lewis, "Casella as Critic: A Note on R. P. Blackmur," *Kenyon Review*, XIII (1951), 458–74.

subtle and brilliant elucidation of texts. Repudiating sociological criticism, particularly when the criteria are misapplied by men like Granville Hicks, and making little use of psychoanalytical methods, he insists that criticism deal with literature as literature and that it deal centrally with the text itself. Using the comparative technique at times, as in the essays on Pound and Hart Crane, he nevertheless does not carry it as far as Eliot, where at times it seems to be a distraction from the work of art itself.

In keeping with his emphasis on the close scrutiny of the text itself, Blackmur attaches much importance to words. In *The Expense of Greatness* (1940), in the chapter on Melville, he writes: "Words, and their intimate arrangements, must be the ultimate as well as the immediate source of every effect in the written or spoken arts." Hence, in his critical essays, one finds a strong verbal emphasis, as in his study of the language of E. E. Cummings in order to determine "the quality of the meaning his use of these words permits." In his analysis of the poems of Wallace Stevens, he employs the same method of defining the nature of Stevens' art on the basis of a close study of his language. His approach to Emily Dickinson likewise is to be found "in the words she used and in the way she put them together."

Few contemporary critics have stressed as much as he has the difficulty of true criticism. When he speaks of criticism, it is most often in such terms as "job of work," "burden of the critic," "expense," which are revealing of his belief that the poet has a perfect right to make any demands he may wish on the critic's knowledge or sensibility: ". . . the writer must reflect that he is performing *the most arduous critical act of which he is capable*. . . . It is in this sense that the composition of a great poem is a labour of unrelenting criticism, and the full reading of it only less so. . . ."

Nowhere is the value of this willingness of Blackmur to assume "the burden of the critic" more evident than in his essays on "difficult" poets such as Ezra Pound or W. B. Yeats. No one has demonstrated a greater capacity for the painstaking investigation and analysis of the text that contemporary criticism considers so essential to the criticism of literature.

In another direction than the "New Criticism," the work of Lionel Trilling illustrates the continuing investigation in contemporary criticism of the social and cultural bases of literature, which had begun with the movement toward a more critical realism about 1912 and which continued to develop through the Marxist and sociological criticism of the thirties.

In 1950, Trilling published a collection of his essays in a book entitled *The Liberal Imagination*, which reflects "the liberal way of looking at life and letters" of which he is an accredited spokesman. It is a work in which he seeks to loosen up the thinking of liberal intellectuals and to recall them to a sense of the variety and possibility inherent in the idea of liberalism. The central problem with which the book concerns itself is the paradox that liberalism, in America, has been growing arid culturally. "The liberal ideology," he states, "has been at best a matter of indifference to the writers whom serious criticism has designated as the greatest figures of our time." Moreover, liberalism has of recent years "produced a literature of piety—commercially successful but having neither imagination nor mind."

A penetrating critique of contemporary liberalism, these essays point to the flaccidity and corruption in what Trilling calls "the liberal imagination," which has failed because it has not seen life whole; because it "has not seen that man lives by poetry as well as bread-and-realism." He accuses "liberal critics" of censoring the subtle and disturbing talent of Henry James while ignoring or "sentimentalizing" the clumsiness of a writer like Theodore Dreiser. He sees liberalism in literary criticism drifting toward "a denial of the emotions and the imagination; toward an unbridled and over-simplifying rationalism, hostile to complexity and suspicious of intellect"—viewing crude experience as somehow "virtuous" and the only reality.[31] In an essay on *The Princess Casamassima*, he offers convincing evidence that, compared to Henry James, Dreiser knew considerably less about social and political reality.

Urging liberal critics to "take hold of complexity," Trilling questions the modern conception of "reality" which is associated only with "the vigorous," "the actual," "real life," as opposed to other poorly defined terms like "idealistic," "romantic," or "genteel." In this respect it is the first duty of criticism today "to recall liberalism to its first essential imagination of variousness and possibility, which implies the awareness of complexity and difficulty."

In many respects unlike the theory of the New Criticism, Trilling holds that in fiction ideas count for more than technique or craft. With this principle in view, he analyzes the intellectual and literary stature of a number of writers. Among the writers discussed in the essays, Mark Twain, Henry James, and F. Scott Fitzgerald seem to embody, in varying degree, those qualities which, for him, produce the best kind of art: depth of vision, breadth of understanding, comprehension, and genius for expression. Dreiser, on the other hand, he sees as bumbling in thought and art; Sherwood Anderson is "nearly one-dimensional" in dealing with life.

In spite of his insistence upon the intimate relation of literature and politics, Trilling does not cut himself off dogmatically from works of art produced by writers with whom he disagrees politically. He does not reject Eliot, Yeats, or Joyce although he believes them to be "indifferent to, or even hostile to, the tradition of democratic liberalism as we know it." His freedom from pedantry, his awareness of the intimate relation between literature and life, his recognition that criticism must be re-established in a living context mark in general his contributions to contemporary criticism.

Contemporary criticism would seem to resolve itself into a few fairly distinct main trends. The work of aesthetic criticism, of formal textual analysis, deriving from Poe, Henry James, Ezra Pound, and T. S. Eliot, is being carried on by such critics as Cleanth Brooks, R. P. Blackmur, Allen

---

[31] Cf. Trilling's "Parrington, Mr. Smith, and Reality," *Partisan Review*, VII (1940), 24-40.

Tate,[32] John Crowe Ransom, and Kenneth Burke. The historical interpretation of literature in terms of its social and cultural relationships is represented by such writers as Edmund Wilson, Lionel Trilling, F. O. Matthiessen,[33] Alfred Kazin,[34] and David Daiches,[35] and Yvor Winters.[36] The interpretation of literature in terms of such related fields as psychology and semantics can be seen in the work of such critics as Wilson, Burke, Blackmur, Stanley Hyman,[37] and W. H. Auden.[38] Psychoanalytical criticism likewise has been popular.[39]

[32] For Tate's criticism, see his *Reactionary Essays on Poetry and Ideas* (1936), *Reason and Madness: Critical Essays* (1941), *On the Limits of Poetry: Selected Essays 1928-1948* (1948), *The Hovering Fly* (1949), and *Forlorn Demon* (1953). Studies of Tate as a critic include Clifford Amyx, "The Aesthetics of Allen Tate," *Western Review*, XIII (1949), 135-44; and Richmond C. Beatty, "Allen Tate as Man of Letters," *South Atlantic Quarterly*, XLVII (1948), 226-41. There is an unpublished dissertation by Fred H. Stocking on *Poetry as Knowledge: The Critical Theory of John Crowe Ransom and Allen Tate* (Michigan, 1946).

[33] Representative of Matthiessen's criticism are *The Achievement of T. S. Eliot* (1948), *American Renaissance* (1941), *Henry James, the Major Phase* (1944), *The James Family* (1947), and *Theodore Dreiser* (1951). For a study of his criticism, see John Crowe Ransom, "The Criticism of F. O. Matthiessen," *Sewanee Review*, LXI (1953).

[34] Kazin's most representative work is *On Native Grounds: An Interpretation of Modern American Prose Literature* (1942).

[35] Daiches' work includes *The Place of Meaning in Poetry* (1935), *Literature and Society* (1938), *The Novel and the Modern World* (1940), *Poetry and the Modern World* (1940), *Robert Louis Stevenson* (1947), and *A Study of Literature* (1948). Also see "The Principles of Literary Criticism," *New Republic*, XCVIII (1939), 95-98; and "The New Criticism: Some Qualifications," *College English*, XXXIX (1950), 64-72.

[36] Representative works of Winters include *Primitivism and Decadence: A Study of American Experimental Poetry* (1937), *Maule's Curse: Seven Studies in the History of American Obscurantism* (1938), *The Anatomy of Nonsense* (1943), and *In Defense of Reason* (1947). For studies of Winters' criticism, see Stanley Hyman, "Yvor Winters and Evaluation in Criticism," *The Armed Vision* (New York, 1948), pp. 49-72; R. P. Blackmur, "A Note on Yvor Winters," *Poetry*, LVII (1940), 144-52; and Ray B. West, Jr., "The Language of Criticism," *Rocky Mountain Review*, VIII (1943), 12-13, 15.

[37] Hyman's most representative work is *The Armed Vision: A Study in the Methods of Modern Literary Criticism* (1948). Also see "The Psychoanalytic Criticism of Literature," *Western Review*, XII (1948), 106-15; "The Critic as Narcissus," *Accent*, VIII (1948), 187-91; and "The Deflowering of New England," *Hudson Review*, II (1950), 600-12.

[38] See "Criticism in a Mass Society," in *The Intent of the Critic*, edited by Donald A. Stauffer (Princeton, N.J., 1941); "Henry James and the Artist in America," *Harper's*, CXCVII (1948), 36-40; "Yeats as an Example," *Kenyon Review*, X (1948), 163-81; and "Some Notes on D. H. Lawrence," *Nation*, CLXIV (1947), 482-84.

[39] Van Wyck Brooks's *The Ordeal of Mark Twain* (1920) is a psychoanalytic biography considering the repressions of Twain as being crucial in his formation as a writer and as prohibiting his true greatness. Raymond Weaver's *Herman Melville* (1920) is a consideration of the influence of sexual repression. Joseph Wood Krutch's *Edgar Allan Poe* (1926) deals with Poe's abnormalities and the unconscious. Most recently Roy Basler's *Sex, Psychology and Literature* (1948) advocates the psychoanalytical method and sees Freudian psychology as the key to a critical understanding of literature. The most detailed study is Frederick J. Hoffman, *Freudianism and the Literary Mind* (Baton Rouge, La., 1945). See also his "Psychoanalysis and Literary Criticism," *American Quarterly*, II (1950), 144-54. One of the best essays is Kenneth Burke, "Freud—and the Analysis of Poetry," in *The Philosophy of Literary Form* (New York, 1941). Also see Stanley E. Hyman, "The Psychoanalytic Criticism of Literature," *Western Review*, XII (1948), 106-15; and H. E. Cory, "Psychoanalysis and Literary Criticism," *University California Publications in Modern Philology*, XI (1928), 187-94.

Any interpretation of contemporary criticism on the basis of general trends or categories is apt to be not only arbitrary but also to a certain extent misleading. Most critics do not confine themselves to a single approach, such as the historical, the aesthetic, the psychological, but rather make use of various approaches in varying degrees. Even the use of a general term such as the "New Criticism" while it designates a certain method in literary criticism of some contemporary critics does not define the differences which exist between them. Within these limitations, however, there are obvious advantages in pointing out trends, since it is mainly through such general tendencies that the shifting attitudes and methods in literary criticism from one period of time to another may be distinguished and characterized.

The last fifty years have been the most active and the most comprehensive in the history of American literary criticism. While the "ideal critic" has probably not appeared, American criticism has for the first time developed a perceptiveness, a resourcefulness, and a diversity of critical methods which indicate that it has finally reached its maturity.

Trends in Modern Critical Essays

PAUL ELMER MORE

CRITICISM [1]
(1910)

OF ALL Matthew Arnold's books I sometimes think that not the least precious is the slender posthumous volume published by his daughter in 1902. It was long his habit to carry in his pocket a narrow diary in which he jotted down engagements for the day, mingled with short quotations from the books he was reading to serve as amulets, so to speak, against the importunities of business. The quotations for a selection of years printed by Mrs. Wodehouse from these *Notebooks* form what might be called the critic's breviary. Here, if anywhere, we seem to feel the very beating of the critic's heart, and to catch the inner voice of recollection and duty, corresponding to the poet's "gleam," which he followed so devoutly in his life. I do not know to what work in English to liken it unless it be the notebooks containing quotations from Marcus Aurelius [2] and Epictetus [3] written down by the author of the *Characteristics* with his comments, which Dr. Rand edited in 1900 as the *Philosophical Regimen of Anthony, Earl of Shaftesbury*. [4]

Nor is it mere chance that Matthew Arnold and Shaftesbury should have left for posthumous publication these private memoranda, which with all their differences of form and substance are in their final impression upon the mind so curiously alike; for the two men themselves, in their outlook on life and in their relation to their respective ages, had much in common, and there is perhaps no better way to reach a dispassionate understanding of the virtue and limitations of criticism than by comparing Arnold with his great forerunner of the early eighteenth century. Both men were essentially critical in their mental habit, and both magnified the critic's office. "I take upon me," said Shaftesbury, "absolutely to condemn the fashionable and prevailing custom of inveighing against critics as the common enemies, the pests and incendiaries of the commonwealth of Wit and Letters. I assert, on the contrary, that they are the props and pillars of this building; and that without the encouragement and propagation of such a race, we should remain as Gothic architects as ever." And the purpose of Shaftesbury in upholding the function of criticism was much the same as Arnold's; he too was offended by the Gothic and barbarous self-complacency of his contemporaries—the Philistines, as he might have called them. As Arnold protested that the

---

[1] This essay appeared in *Shelburne Essays, Seventh Series* (Boston, 1910).
[2] (A.D. 121–180), emperor of Rome, A.D. 161–180. Stoic philosopher and writer.
[3] Epictetus (A.D. 60?–120?), Stoic philosopher.
[4] Anthony Ashley Cooper, third Earl of Shaftesbury (1671–1713), English deist.

work of the English romantic revival was doomed "to prove hardly more lasting than the productions of far less splendid epochs"; that Byron was "empty of matter," Shelley "incoherent," and Wordsworth "wanting in completeness and variety," just because they lacked critical background; so his predecessor censured the literature of his day. "An English author would be all genius," says Shaftesbury. "He would reap the fruits of art, but without study, pains, or application. He thinks it necessary, indeed (lest his learning should be called in question), to show the world that he errs knowingly against the rules of art."

Against this presumption of genius on the one hand and the self-complacency of Philistinism on the other, both critics took up the same weapons—the barbs of ridicule and irony. With Shaftesbury this method was an avowed creed. His essays are no more than sermons on two texts: that of Horace, "*Ridiculum acri fortius et melius magnas plerumque secat res*—a jest often decides weighty matters better and more forcibly than can asperity"; and the saying of Gorgias Leontinus,[5] which he misinterprets and expands for his own purpose, "That humor was the only test of gravity; and gravity of humor. For a subject which would not bear raillery was suspicious; and a jest which would not bear a serious examination was certainly false wit." With this touchstone of truth he proceeds to test the one-sided enthusiasms of his day, the smirking conceits, the pedantic pretensions, and the narrow dogmatisms whether of science or religion. "There is a great difference," he says, "between seeking how to raise a laugh from everything, and seeking in everything what justly may be laughed at. For nothing is ridiculous except what is deformed; nor is anything proof against raillery except what is handsome and just." The comic spirit is thus a kind of purgation of taste, and a way or return to nature. How deliberately Matthew Arnold used this weapon of ridicule in the service of sweet reasonableness, which is only his modern phrase, a little sentimentalised, for eighteenth-century nature; how magisterially he raised the laugh against his enemies, the bishops and the great austere toilers of the press and the mighty men of political Philistia, no one needs be told who has enjoyed the elaborate irony of *Culture and Anarchy* or of *Friendship's Garland*.

Sweet reasonableness, or "sweetness and light," to use the phrase as Arnold took it from Swift's *Battle of the Books,* is, I have suggested, little more than the modern turn for the deist's nature and reason; how nearly the two ideals approach each other you may see by comparing the "good-breeding," which is the aim of Shaftesbury's philosophy, with the "culture" which is the end of Arnold's criticism. "To philosophize," said the former, "in a just signification, is but to carry good-breeding a step higher. For the accomplishment of breeding is, to learn whatever is decent in company or beautiful in arts, and the sum of philosophy is, to learn what is just in society and beautiful in Nature and the order of the world." I have wondered sometimes whether Matthew Arnold had these words in mind when

---

[5] Greek orator and sophist of the fifth century B.C. One of the earliest writers on rhetoric. One of the Platonic dialogues, the "Gorgias," is named for him.

he formulated his definition of culture; whether his famous command is really but another echo from the ancient quarrel of the deists.[6] The whole scope of the essay on *Sweetness and Light* is, he avows, "to recommend culture as the great help out of our present difficulties; culture being a pursuit of our total perfection by means of getting to know, on all the matters which most concern us, the best which has been thought and said in the world (Shaftesbury, too, like Arnold, is insistent on the *exemplaria Graeca*); and through this knowledge, turning a stream of fresh and free thought upon our stock notions and habits."

There is, I trust, something more than a pedantic curiosity in such a parallel, which might yet be much prolonged, between the author of *Culture and Anarchy* and the author of the *Characteristics*. It proves, if proof be necessary, more clearly than would any amount of direct exposition, that Matthew Arnold's method of criticism was not an isolated product of the nineteenth century, but that he belongs to one of the great families of human intelligence, which begins with Cicero, the father of them all, and passes through Erasmus and Boileau and Shaftesbury and Sainte-Beuve.[7] These are the exemplars—not complete individually, I need not say—of what may be called the critical spirit: discriminators between the false and the true, the deformed and the normal; preachers of harmony and proportion and order, prophets of the religion of taste. If they deal much with the criticism of literature, this is because in literature more manifestly than anywhere else life displays its infinitely varied motives and results; and their practice is always to render literature itself more consciously a criticism of life. The past is the field out of which they draw their examples of what is in conformity with nature and of what departs from that norm. In that field they balance and weigh and measure; they are by intellect hesitators, but at heart very much in earnest. They are sometimes contrasted to their detriment with the so-called creative writers, yet they themselves stood each among the first writers of his day, and it is not plain that, for instance, Tennyson, in any true estimation added more to the intellectual life of the world than Matthew Arnold, or Lucretius[8] than Cicero, though their method and aim may have been different. The more significant comparison at least is not with the so-called creative writers, but with the great fulminators of new creeds—between Matthew Arnold and the Carlyles and Ruskins and Huxleys of his day; between Shaftesbury and, let us say, Rousseau, Boileau and Descartes; Erasmus and Luther; Cicero and St. Paul. Such a contrast might seem at first to lie as much in efficiency as in quality. In the very nature of things the man who seizes on one deep-

---

[6] Deism flourished in eighteenth-century England. The deists believed in the existence of a God based solely on the evidence of reason and nature only, with rejection of supernatural revelation. The deists conceived of God as having remained indifferent to the world after having created it, permitting it to operate itself according to the laws of nature.

[7] Cicero (106–43 B.C.), Roman orator and writer. Desiderius Erasmus (1466?–1536), Dutch humanist, theologian, and satirist. Nicolas Boileau (1636–1711), French poet and literary critic. Charles-Augustin Sainte-Beuve (1804–1869), French critic.

[8] Lucretius (*ca.* 96–*ca.* 55 B.C.), Roman poet.

reaching idea, whether newly found or rediscovered, and with single-hearted fervor forces it upon the world, might appear to have the advantage in power over the man of critical temper, who weighs and refines; who is for ever checking the enthusiasm of the living by the authority of the dead; and whose doctrine, even though in the end he may assert it with sovereign contempt of doubters, is still the command to follow the well-tried path of common-sense. Better the half-truth that makes for action and jostles the world out of its ruts, men cry, than such a timid search for the whole truth as paralyzes the will, and may after all prove only an exchange of depth for breadth. That might appear to be the plain lesson of history; yet I am not so sure. Is there not a possibility that in our estimate of these powers we are a little betrayed by the tumult of the times, just as we are prone in other things to mistake bustle for movement? The critical spirit, as it has been exercised, may have its limitations and may justly be open to censure, but I doubt if its true reproach will turn out in the end to be a lack of efficiency in comparison with the more assertive force of the reformers. I am inclined to believe, for instance, that the balancing spirit of Erasmus is really more at work among us today than that of the dogmatic and reforming Luther; that Cicero's philosophy, though they would gape to hear it said, is really more in the hearts of the men you will meet in the street than is the theology of St. Paul. This may be in part because the representatives of the critical spirit, by their very lack of warping originality and by their endeavor to separate the true from the false, the complete from the one-sided, stand with the great conservative forces of human nature, having their fame certified by the things that endure amid all the betrayals of time and fashion. I know the deductions that must be made from that kind of fame. Cicero, it will be said, when in his *De Finibus* he brought together the various experiences of antiquity in regard to the meaning and values of life, weighing the claims of Stoic [9] and Epicurean [10] and the others, may have stood for something more comprehensive and balanced than did St. Paul with his new dogma of justification by faith. Yet St. Paul's theory of justification by faith, though it may be losing for us its cogent veracity, was the immediate driving force of history and a power that remade the world, while Cicero's nice discussions remained a luxury of the learned few. In one sense that is indisputably true; and yet, imprudent as it may sound, I question whether it is the whole truth. When I consider the part played by Stoic and Epicurean philosophies in the Renaissance and the transcendent influence of Cicero's dissertations upon the men of that day; when I consider that the impulse of Deism in the eighteenth century, as seen in Shaftesbury and his successors, was at bottom little more than a revival of this same Stoicism, as it had been subdued

[9] School of philosophy founded by Zeno, Greek philosopher of the fifth century B.C., who taught that men should be free from passion, unmoved by joy or grief, and submit without complaint to unavoidable necessity.

[10] Philosophical system established by Epicurus, Greek philosopher (342?–270 B.C.), who taught that the world resulted from a fortuitous concourse of atoms and that the highest good in life is pleasure, which consists in freedom from disturbance or pain.

to the emotions by Cicero and mixed with Epicureanism; that Shaftesbury was, in fact, despite his worship of Epictetus, almost a pure Ciceronian; and when I consider that out of Deism sprang the dominant religion and social philosophy of our present world—when I consider these and many other facts, I question whether Cicero, while he certainly represents what is more enduring, has not been also, actually and personally, as dynamic an influence in civilization as St. Paul, though the noise, no doubt, and the tumult have been around the latter. We are still too near Matthew Arnold's day to determine the resultant of all the forces then at work, yet it would not be very rash even now to assert that his critical essays will be found in the end a broader and more lasting, as they are a saner, influence than the exaggerated aestheticism of Ruskin or the shrill prophesying of Carlyle or the scientific dogmatism of Huxley. No, if there is any deduction to be made to the value of criticism, it is not on the side of efficiency. It is well to remember Matthew Arnold's own words. "Violent indignation with the past," he says, "abstract systems of renovation applied wholesale, a new doctrine drawn up in black and white for elaborating down to the very smallest details a rational society for the future—these are the ways of Jacobinism. . . . Culture (it is his word here for criticism) is always assigning to system-makers and systems a smaller share in the bent of human destiny than their friends like."

Perhaps it is a secret inkling of this vanity of the critic in its widest bearing, besides a natural antagonism of temper, that leads so many to carp against him and his trade. The inveterate hostility of "creative" writers to criticism is well known, and has been neatly summed up by E. S. Dallas [11] in *The Gay Science:*

> Ben Jonson spoke of critics as tinkers, who make more faults than they mend; Samuel Butler, as the fierce inquisitors of wit, and as butchers who have no right to sit on a jury; Sir Richard Steele, as of all mortals the silliest; Swift, as dogs, rats, wasps, or, at best, drones of the learned world; Shenstone, as asses, which by gnawing vines first taught the advantage of pruning them; Burns, as cutthroat bandits in the path of fame; Walter Scott, humorously reflecting the general sentiment, as caterpillars.

The droll thing about it is that every one of these critics of criticism was so ready to act himself as butcher or ass or caterpillar. It is a common trick of the guild. For a modern instance, turn to Mr. Horace Traubel, the shirt-sleeved Boswell of Walt Whitman,[12] and you will find pages of conversation recorded in which the seer of Camden belabors the professors of criticism and in almost the same breath exercises the art upon his brother poets with delightful frankness and at times rare penetration. But this ancient feud of the gentlemen of the pen is a special form, due in part to special causes, of the hostility that so often manifests itself against the

[11] American writer and critic of the late nineteenth and early twentieth centuries.
[12] Horace Traubel, close friend of Walt Whitman, published *With Walt Whitman in Camden,* a three-volume record of daily conversations with Whitman.

critical spirit in general. The man of system and the man of unhesitating action are likely to feel something like contempt for the mind that balances and waits. The imperial Mommsen [13] felt this contempt, and showed it, in his treatment of Cicero; it is rife even yet in the current tone of condescension toward Erasmus as compared with Luther, to which Matthew Arnold replied by calling Luther "a Philistine of genius"; Warburton [14] showed it in his sneers at Shaftesbury as the man of taste, and Cardinal Newman has, with splendid politeness, echoed them; Matthew Arnold was equally feared and despised in his own lifetime, and it is an odd fact that you will today scarcely pick up a piece of third-rate criticism (in which there is likely to be anything at work rather than the critical spirit), but you will come upon some gratuitous fling against him. Most bitter of all was Henry Sidgwick's [15] arraignment of "The Prophet of Culture" in *Macmillan's Magazine* for August, 1867. There if anywhere the critical spirit was stabbed with its own weapon. You will recall the image of the pouncet-box:

> Mr. Arnold may say that he does not discourage action, but only asks for delay, in order that we may act with sufficient knowledge. This is the eternal excuse of indolence—insufficient knowledge. . . . One cannot think on this subject without recalling the great man who recommended to philosophy a position very similar to that now claimed for culture. I wish to give Mr. Arnold the full benefit of his resemblance to Plato. But when we look closer at the two positions, the dissimilarity comes out: they have a very different effect on our feelings and imagination; and I confess I feel more sympathy with the melancholy philosopher looking out with hopeless placidity "from beneath the shelter of some wall" than with a cheerful modern liberal, tempered by renouncement, shuddering aloof from the rank exhalations of vulgar enthusiasm, and holding up the pouncet-box of culture betwixt the wind and his nobility.

Such an onslaught on our prophet of culture as a languid and shrinking dilettante was fair enough in the heat of controversy and was at least justified by its own art, if not by certain affectations of its victim's style; but I protest against accepting it as essentially true. Any one might perceive that Matthew Arnold had beneath the irony and suavity of his manner a temper of determined seriousness; that, like the bride of Giacopone di Todi in his sonnet, his Muse might be young, gay, and radiant outside, but had

> a hidden ground
> Of thought and of austerity within.

It would be interesting in this respect to continue the comparison of Arnold and Shaftesbury, and to show how near together they stood in their attitude toward nature and society and in their religion, and how pro-

[13] Theodor Mommsen (1817–1903), German classical scholar and historian.
[14] William Warburton (1698–1779), English critic and editor.
[15] Nineteenth-century American writer and critic.

found was their own enthusiasm beneath their hostility to the sham or undisciplined enthusiasms of the day. Lord Shaftesbury might say that we have "in the main a witty and good-humored religion," as Matthew Arnold might ridicule the sourness of the Nonconformists and the bleakness of the reformers in whose assemblies any child of nature, if he shall stray thither, is smitten with lamentation and mourning and woe; but there was solemnity enough, however we may rate their insight, in their own search for the God that sits concealed at the center. Shaftesbury's creed became the formula of the deists. "Still ardent in its pursuit," the soul, he says, "rests not here, nor satisfies itself with the beauty of a part, but, extending further its communicative bounty, seeks the good of all, and affects the interest and prosperity of the whole. True to its native world and higher country, 'tis here it seeks order and perfection; wishing the best, and hoping still to find a just and wise administration. And since all hope of this were vain and idle if no universal mind presided; since without such a supreme intelligence and providential care the distracted universe must be condemned to suffer infinite calamities; 'tis here the generous mind labors to discover that healing cause by which the interest of the whole is securely established, the beauty of things and the universal order happily sustained." Matthew Arnold condensed that rhetoric into a phrase: "The stream of tendency, not ourselves, which makes for righteousness."

But the strongest evidence of their austerity of purpose is seen in those private notebooks which led me to couple their names together in this study of the spirit of criticism. This is not the time to deal at length with that sober and anxious self-examination of the noble Lord, as Shaftesbury's enemies of the Church were so fond of calling him. It is one of the important documents to show how completely Deism was a revival of pagan morality. It is, in brief, no more than a translation of the great maxims of antiquity into modern purposes: the inner record of a man seeking character in the two elements of attention (προςοχή) and the harmony of life (verae numerosque modosque vitae), and of a man who thought that this pursuit must be maintained unrelentingly. Of the two books it may seem strange that Matthew Arnold's, which consists merely of brief quotations without comment, should really open to us more intimately the author's heart than does the direct self-questioning of Shaftesbury's. Yet a book more filled with sad sincerity, a more perfect confession of a life's purpose, will scarcely be found than these memoranda. "I am glad to find," he wrote once in a letter to his sister, "that in the past year I have at least accomplished more than usual in the way of reading the books which at the beginning of the year I had put down to be read. . . . The importance of reading, not slight stuff to get through the time, but the best that has been written, forces itself upon me more and more every year I live." Now the Notebooks not only preserve some of these annual lists of books to be read, but show, in quintessential phrase, just what the books actually read meant to him. Some of the quotations are repeated a number of times, and if frequency of repetition can be taken as a criterion the maxim closest to Arnold's heart was the sentence, from what source I do not know: "Semper *aliquid certi proponendum est*—always some certain end must be kept in view." It is but an expansion of the same idea that he expresses in the words set down more than once from some French author: "A working life, a succession of labors which fill and moralize the days!" and in the beloved command of the Imitation: *"Cum multa legeris et cognoveris, ad unum semper oportet redire principium*—when you have read and learned many things, it is necessary always to return to one principle." That principle he sets down in aphorisms and exhortations from a hundred diverse sources —nowhere, perhaps, more succinctly than in the broken phrases of the stoic Lucan: [16]

> servare modum, finemque tenere
> Naturamque sequi—
> Nec sibi, sed toti genitum se credere mundo—
> In commune bonus.
>
> (To preserve measure, to hold fast to the end,
> and follow nature—To believe oneself born not for one-
> self alone but for all the world—good for the community
> of mankind.)

He might well have applied to his own pursuit of culture the eulogy he quotes concerning another: "Study, which for most men is only a frivolous amusement and often dangerous, was for Dom Rivet a serious occupation consecrated by religion."

It was not a mere dilettante of sweetness and light who day by day laid such maxims as these upon his breast; it was not one who held up the pouncet-box of culture betwixt the wind and his nobility. Matthew Arnold, if any man in his generation, was by temperament a stoic for whom duty and submission and reverence made up the large part of life; and there is something of what we call the irony of fate in the thought that he who made σπουδαιότης, *high seriousness,* the test of great literature, should have suffered the reproach of levity. Yet, after all, fate is never quite blind in these things, and if criticism has thus drawn upon itself the censure of men like Sidgwick we may feel assured that in some way it has failed of the deeper truth. Those reproaches may in part be due to prejudice and revenge and the inevitable contrast of temperaments; they may err in ascribing to the critic a want of efficiency, as they may be wantonly perverse in denouncing him for frivolity; but they have a meaning and they cannot be overlooked. Now the future is often a strange revealer of secret things, and there is no surer way to detect the weak side of a leader than by studying the career of his disciples, or even of his successors.

You are familiar with the story of the concluding chapter of Pater's *Renaissance*—how it was withdrawn from the second edition of that book because the author "conceived it might possibly mislead some of those young men into whose hands it might fall"; and how it was restored, with some slight changes, to the later editions where it now stands. And you

---

[16] Roman poet (A.D. 39–65).

know the moral of that essay: that life is but an uncertain interval before the universal judgment of death, a brief illusion of stability in the eternal flux, and that "our one chance lies in expanding that interval, in getting as many pulsations as possible into the given time." And "of this wisdom," he concludes, "the poetic passion, the desire of beauty, the love of art for art's sake, has most; for art comes to you professing frankly to give nothing but the highest quality to your moments as they pass and simply for those moments' sake." That philosophy of the Oxonian Epicurus and its scandal in a very un-Epicurean land are familiar enough; but perhaps we do not always stop to think how plausibly this doctrine of crowning our moments with the highest sensations of art flows from Matthew Arnold's definition of criticism as the disinterested endeavor "to know the best that is known and thought in the world, irrespectively of practice, politics and everything of the kind."

The next step from Pater's Epicureanism, and so by a further remove from Arnold's criticism, brings us to one whose name, unfortunately, must always be mentioned with regret, but who is more significant in the development of English letters than is sometimes allowed. At the time when Paterism, as a recent writer has said, was "tripping indelicately along the Oxford High and by the banks of the Cherwell," a young votary of the Muses from Dublin came upon the scene, and began to push the doctrine of Pater as far beyond what the master intended as Pater had gone beyond Matthew Arnold. This is the young man who "would occasionally be seen walking the streets carrying a lily or a sunflower in his hand, at which he would gaze intently and admiringly." He had fashioned himself deliberately to pose as the head of a new sect of "aesthetes," as they styled themselves, who expanded Arnold's excluded tribe of Philistines to embrace all the sober citizens of the world. The fate of Oscar Wilde is still like a fresh wound in the public memory. What I wish to call to your mind is the direct connection (strengthened no doubt by influences from across the Channel) between Pater's philosophy of the sensation-crowded moment and such a poem as that in which Wilde attempted to concentrate all the passionate moments of the past in his gloating revery upon *The Sphinx*. He was himself not unaware of the treachery of the path he had chosen; the sonnet which he prefixed to his book of poems is sincere with the pathos of conscious insincerity, and is a memorable comment on one of the tragic ambitions of a century:

> To drift with every passion till my soul
> Is a stringed lute on which all winds can play,
> Is it for this that I have given away
> Mine ancient wisdom, and austere control?

> . . . .

> Surely there was a time I might have trod
> The sunlit heights, and from life's dissonance
> Struck one clear chord to reach the ears of God:

> Is that time dead? lo! with a little rod
> I did but touch the honey of romance—
> And must I lose a soul's inheritance?

The answer to the poet's query he was himself to write in *The Ballad of Reading Gaol:*

> Silently we went round and round,
>   And through each hollow mind
> The Memory of dreadful things
>   Rushed like a dreadful wind,
> And Horror stalked before each man,
>   And Terror crept behind.

This Memory of dreadful things is the too logical end, step by step, of the philosophy of the sensation-crowded moment; the concealed suspicion of it in Matthew Arnold's definition of criticism was the justification, if any there be, of the contempt hurled upon him by some of his contemporaries.

It is necessary to repeat that such a derivation from Matthew Arnold is essentially unfair because it leaves out of view the real purpose and heart of the man. If we could not read his great moral energy in his *Essays,* as I trust we all of us can, and if we did not know the profound influence of his critical philosophy upon the better life of our age, we could still dispel our doubts by looking into the *Notebooks,* in which memory is not turned to dreadful things for the soul's disgrace, but is the guide and impulse to strong resolution and beautiful forbearance. Yet withal it remains true that the Epicureanism of Pater and the hedonism of Oscar Wilde were able to connect themselves in a disquieting way with one side of Matthew Arnold's gospel of culture; and it behooves us who come upon the heels of this movement and who believe that the critical spirit is still to be one of the powers making in the world for right enjoyment, it behooves us to examine the first definition of culture or criticism—the words had about the same meaning as Arnold used them—and see whether something was not there forgotten. The fault lay not in any intrinsic want of efficiency in the critical spirit, nor in any want of moral earnestness in Matthew Arnold or Shaftesbury: that we have seen. But these men were lacking in another direction: they missed a philosophy which could bind together their moral and their aesthetic sense, a positive principle besides the negative force of ridicule and irony; and, missing this, they left criticism more easily subject to a one-sided and dangerous development.

To the nature of that omission, to the *porro unum necessarium,*[17] we may be directed, I think, by the critical theory of the one who carried the practice, in other respects, to its lowest degradation. In Oscar Wilde's dialogue on *The Critic as Artist,* one of the most extraordinary mixtures ever compounded of truth flaunting in the robes of error and error assuming the gravity of truth, you will remember that the advocate of criticism at the height of his argument proclaims the true man of culture to be him who

---

[17] "further necessary one."

has learned "the best that is known and thought in the world" (he uses Matthew Arnold's words), and who thus, as Matthew Arnold neglected to add, "bears within himself the dreams, and ideas, and feelings of myriad generations." The addition is important, how important, or at least how large, may be seen in the really splendid, if somewhat morbid, passage in which the idea is developed. Let me quote at some length:

> To know anything about oneself, one must know all about others. There must be no mood with which one cannot sympathise, no dead mode of life that one cannot make alive. Is this impossible? I think not. By revealing to us the absolute mechanism of all action, and so freeing us from the self-imposed and trammelling burden of moral responsibility, the scientific principle of Heredity has become, as it were, the warrant for the contemplative life. It has shown us that we are never less free than when we try to act. It has hemmed us round with the nets of the hunter, and written upon the wall the prophecy of our doom. We may not watch it, for it is within us. We may not see it, save in a mirror that mirrors the soul. It is Nemesis without her mask. It is the last of the Fates, and the most terrible. It is the only one of the Gods whose real name we know.

> And yet, while in the sphere of practical and external life it has robbed energy of its freedom and activity of its choice, in the subjective sphere, where the soul is at work, it comes to us, this terrible shadow, with many gifts in its hands, gifts of strange temperaments and subtle susceptibilities, gifts of wild ardors and chill moods of indifference, complex multiform gifts of thoughts that are at variance with each other, and passions that war against themselves. And so, it is not our own life that we live, but the lives of the dead, and the soul that dwells within us is no single spiritual entity, making us personal and individual, created for our service, and entering into us for our joy. . . . It can help us to leave the age in which we were born, and to pass into other ages, and find ourselves not exiled from their air. It can teach us how to escape from our experience and to realise the experiences of those who are greater than we are. The pain of Leopardi crying out against life becomes our pain. Theocritus blows on his pipe, and we laugh with the lips of nymph and shepherd. In the wolfskin of Pierre Vidal we flee before the hounds, and in the armor of Lancelot we ride from the bower of the Queen. We have whispered the secret of our love beneath the cowl of Abelard, and in the stained raiment of Villon have put our shame into song. We can see the dawn through Shelley's eyes, and when we wander with Endymion the Moon grows amorous of our youth. Ours is the anguish of Atys, and ours the weak rage and noble sorrows of the Dane. Do you think that it is the imagination that enables us to live these countless lives? Yes: it is the imagination; and the imagination is the result of heredity. It is simply concentrated race-experience.

Now, this theory of race-experience, as Oscar Wilde formulated it, lends itself, no doubt, to an easy fallacy. I am aware of the rebuke administered to one who was by the range of his knowledge and by his historic sense much more justified in such a presumption than was Oscar Wilde. "Is it not the strangest illusion," exclaimed the biographer of Renan, "to believe that the mere reading of the Acts of the martyrs is sufficient to give us their soul, to transfer to us in its real intensity the ardor which ravished them amidst their tortures? . . . Those who have lost all the energy of living and acting may, if they choose, shut themselves up in this kingdom of shadows; that is their affair. But that they should proclaim theirs as the true life, is not to be conceded to them." Séailles [18] was right. These men, whether it be a paradox-monger like Oscar Wilde or a great scholar like Renan, should have laid to heart the favorite maxim of Matthew Arnold, *semper aliquid certi proponendum est:* true culture has always before its eyes a definite end and is for self-discipline not for revery. Nor am I unaware that the theory as expressed by Oscar Wilde, is mixed up with his own personal taint of decadence. One thing at least is certain: that the way of the true critical spirit is not to free us, as he boasts, from "the self-imposed and trammelling burden of moral responsibility." His avowal in the same dialogue that the sole aim of art is to produce the "beautiful sterile emotions" so hateful to the world, his shameless vaunt that "there is nothing sane about the worship of beauty," his whole philosophy of the ego as above the laws of society, cannot be severed from the memory of dreadful things in which his own song ended: such a philosophy is in fact a denial of the validity of that very race-experience out of which he attempts to derive it. In this respect again he should have remembered the maxim of Matthew Arnold: "A working life, a succession of labors that fill and moralise the days." The aim of culture is not to merge the present in a sterile dream of the past, but to hold the past as a living force in the present. In omitting these aspects of criticism Pater and, to a greater extent, Oscar Wilde fell into extravagance far more deleterious to culture than was any omission or incompleteness on the part of Matthew Arnold.

Nevertheless, with all its false emphasis and its admixture of personal error, that positive and emotional reassumption of the past, that association of the contemplative life (the βιος θεωρητικός) with the rapture of memory, contains the hint of a great truth which must be grasped and properly exercised if criticism is to confirm itself against such hostility as has hereto kept it on the defensive. I would not say even that the mysticism, out of which Oscar Wilde's critical theory really springs, though expressed in the modish language of scientific evolution, is essentially perverse. For in a very true sense the past of mankind, by the larger race-memory and particularly by that form of it which we call literature, abides as a living reality in our present. We suffer not our individual destiny alone but the fates of humanity also. We are born into an inheritance of great emotions —into the unconquerable hopes and defeated fears of an immeasurable past, the tragedies and the comedies of love, the ardent aspirations of faith, the baffled questionings of evil, the huge laughter at facts, the deep-welling passion of peace. Without that common inheritance how inconceivably poor and shallow would be this life of the world and our life in it! These recorded emotions are, indeed, not for us what they were in actuality, nor

[18] Gabriel Séailles (1852–1922), French philosopher and author.

by sitting at our own ease with memory can we enter into the exact emotions of the martyr at the stake and the hero in his triumph. These things are now transmuted into something the same and different, something less and greater. The intensity of the actual moment they cannot possess, but on the other hand with this loss of separate reality they are associated with life as a whole, and in that unity of experience obtain, what they lacked before, a significance and design. They bear in a way the same relation to practical life as that life bore to the ideal world out of which it arose and into which it is continually passing. And thus this larger memory, in its transmuting and unifying power, may not unmeaningly be regarded as the purpose of activity, and literature may not too presumptuously be cherished as the final end of existence. Some such mystery as this was hinted in the Greek and Gnostic doctrine of the *logos*, the Word, and in the Hindu name for the creator as *vâcas pati*, Lord of the Word. And if such a theory sounds too absurdly metaphysical for the ears of prudent common-sense, consider that Homer, no philosopher of empty phrases surely, meant nothing very different when he judged of actions by their fame in future story. To him the warring of armies for ten long years and the desolation of Troy was for no other purpose than that the inner life of the race might be enriched by memory:

> Thus the gods fated, and such ruin wove
> That song might flourish for posterity.

And in this theory of memory criticism has an important office. We are beginning to hear a good deal these days about the French metaphysician, M. Henri Bergson,[19] of whom Prof. William James[20] has avowed himself a willing disciple, and whose disquisitions on *Matière et mémoire* and *L' Évolution créatrice* are perhaps more talked of than any other recent books of philosophy. I do not pretend to pronounce on the full scope of his theories, but his conception of the function of memory is rich with applications to the matter we have in hand. Our consciousness, that is to say our very self, is not, he says, a thing born new with each moment, not a *mens momentanea*,[21] but an uninterrupted stream of activity, and what we now feel is directly bound up with what we have felt before. Nor is this consciousness, on the other hand, a mere heaping together indiscriminately of perceptions and emotions, but it is an active faculty, or, I should prefer to say, the servant of some active faculty, that depresses this particular experience into the background and centers attention upon that other experience, thus by a process of criticism secreting the present, so to speak, out of the past. Such a philosophy finds a new and profound truth in the saying of Pascal:[22] *"Le mémoire est nécessaire à toutes les opérations de l'esprit—* memory is necessary to all the operations of the mind."

This notion of the active memory is, I am told by those who should know, mixed up in Bergson with a questionable metaphysic, yet in itself

---

[19] French philosopher and writer (1859–1941).
[20] American psychologist and philosopher (1842–1910).   [21] "mind in flux."
[22] Blaise Pascal (1623–1662), French philosopher and mathematician.

alone it should seem to be nothing more than the laborious expression of a very simple fact. We have all of us met now and then in our daily intercourse a man whose conversation impressed us immediately as possessing a certain ripeness of wisdom, a certain pertinency and depth of meaning. If we wished to characterize such a man in a single word, we should perhaps say that he was essentially educated. We feel that he has within him some central force which enables him to choose consistently amidst the innumerable conflicting impulses and attractions and dissipations of life, that he moves forward, not at haphazard, but by the direction of some principle of conduct, and that he can be depended upon for counsel and comfort. Well, if you stop to analyze this quality of mind, which we will call education, you will discover in every case, I believe, that the determining trait is just the force of a critical memory. I do not mean by this the mere facility of recalling the emotions and events and spectacles which have come to a man with the years; for such undisciplined reminiscence may be but a shabby wisdom to the man himself, as it may be the very contrary of joy to his hearer. I mean rather the faculty of selection as well as of retention, the weighing of cause and effect, the constant and active assumption of the past in the present, by which the events of life are no longer regarded as isolated and fortuitous moments, but are merged into a unity of experience. Those in whom this faculty rules are commonly the possessors of practical wisdom, but there are others, a few, who by its virtue are raised into another kind of wisdom. With these men the selective, reconciling memory is associated, more or less consciously, with the Platonic reminiscence [23] in such a manner that not only are the past and present of passing time made one but our ephemeral life is fitted into that great ring of eternity which Henry Vaughan saw as in a dream.[24] So it is that to them the things which others behold as sudden unrelated facts are made shadows and types of the everlasting ideas; and with the accumulation of knowledge they grow ripe in vision,

> Till old experience do attain
> To something like prophetic strain.

And as our private memory is not a merely passive retention of sensations, so in literature the critical spirit is at work as a conscious energy of selection. The function of criticism, as thus understood, is far removed from the surrender to luxurious revery which the impressionists believed it to be; nor is the good critic, as Anatole France said,[25] he who recounts the adventures of his soul amid masterpieces; he is rather one who has before him always the *aliquid certi,* the definite aim of a Matthew Arnold. He does not, like Oscar Wilde, seek by losing the present in the past to throw

[23] Plato believed that the soul brought with it into this world a memory of the world of ideas.

[24] The reference is to Henry Vaughan's (1622–1695) poem "The World," the first two lines of which are:

> I saw Eternity the other night,
> Like a great ring of pure and endless light.

[25] French novelist and literary critic (1844–1924), an impressionist.

off "the self-imposed and trammelling burden of moral responsibility"; he is rather one whose life is "a succession of labors that fill and moralise the days"—not in the narrow didactic sense, it need scarcely be said, but in so far as his task is a continual weighing of values. But the critical spirit is also something deeper than Matthew Arnold perceived, or, at least, clearly expressed. The error of criticism in his hands, as in the hands of his predecessors, was that in the exercise of judgment it used the past too much as a dead storehouse of precepts for school-mastering the present; it was not sufficiently aware of the relation of this faculty of judgment to the indwelling and ever-acting memory of things. Here is the one touch of insight needed, I think, to raise criticism, while not forgetting its special duty of discrimination and judgment, to a more independent and self-respecting *genre*. In its conscious creation of the field of the present out of the past it takes an honored, if not equal, place by the side of those impulses, more commonly recognized as creative, which are continually adding new material for its selective energy. "Valuing is creating," said Nietzsche; [26] "to value is the treasure and jewel among all things valued." The critical spirit is thus akin to that force of design or final cause in the Aristotelian sense, which we are beginning once more to divine as the guiding principle, itself unchanged, at work within the evolutionary changes of nature; and in so far as it becomes aware of this high office it introduces into our intellectual life an element outside of alteration and growth and decay, a principle to which time is the minister and not the master.

Literary criticism is, indeed, in this sense only the specific exercise of a faculty which works in many directions. All scholars, whether they deal with history or sociology or philosophy or language or, in the narrower use of the word, literature, are servants of the critical spirit, in so far as they transmit and interpret and mould the sum of experience from man to man and from generation to generation. Might not one even say that at a certain point criticism becomes almost identical with education, and that by this standard we may judge the value of any study as an instrument of education, and may estimate the merit of any special presentation of that study? It is at least, in the existing chaos of pedagogical theories, a question worthy of consideration.

[26] Freidrich Nietzsche (1844–1900), German philosopher.

IRVING BABBITT

From THE MASTERS OF
MODERN FRENCH CRITICISM [1]
(1912)

XI

[THE IDEAL CRITIC]

I

SAINTE-BEUVE [2] HIMSELF, as we saw, labored during the latter part of his life to correct, or one might more fairly say to complete, his earlier method and to assert once more the supremacy of judgment. It is curious to trace the transformation of the militant romanticist of 1830 into the conservative who finally extols as the true type of the critic Malherbe [3] and Boileau [4] and Dr. Johnson. He follows these men in founding his own judgments for the most part on the traditional standards of the classicist, yet no one knew better than Sainte-Beuve that these standards were doomed. "Let us be the last of our kind," he exclaims, "before the great confusion." *

The "great confusion" that Sainte-Beuve foresaw is now upon us. I pointed out that he himself has been correctly defined in his influence on his successors, not as a defender of standards and judgment, but as a great doctor of relativity. Now nearly all recent criticism, so far as it is anything more than a form of gossip and small talk, may be roughly classified as either impressionistic or scientific; and it is in this doctrine of relativity that both impressionistic and scientific critics unite. The impressionist is interested in a book only as it relates itself to his sensibility, and his manner of praising anything that makes this appeal to him is to say that it is "suggestive." The scientific critic for his part is interested solely in the way a book is related as a phenomenon to other phenomena, and when it is the culminating point or the point of departure of a large number of these relationships, he says that it is "significant" (the favorite word of Goethe). If the impressionist is asked to rise above his sensibility and judge by a more impersonal standard, he answers that there is no such impersonal element in art, but only "suggestiveness," and is almost ready to define art with a recent French writer as an "attenuated hypnosis." If the scientific

---

* *Portraits littéraires*, III, 550 [Babbitt's note].
[1] Boston, 1912.
[2] Charles-Augustin Sainte-Beuve (1804–1869), French literary critic.
[3] François de Malherbe (1555–1628), French poet and critic.
[4] Nicolas Boileau (1636–1711), French poet and critic.

critic in turn is urged to get behind the phenomena and rate a book with reference to a scale of absolute values, he absconds into his theory of the "unknowable."

We may illustrate by a familiar passage from Taine, who is easily the most eminent of those who have attempted to make criticism scientific.[5] "What do we see," he says in his English Literature, "under the fair glazed pages of a modern poem? A modern poet who has studied and travelled, a man like Alfred de Musset, Victor Hugo, Lamartine or Heine,[6] in a black coat and gloves, welcomed by the ladies, and making every evening his fifty bows and his score of *bons-mots* in society; reading the papers in the morning, lodging as a rule on a second floor; not over gay, because he has nerves, and especially because, in this dense democracy where we stifle one another, the discredit of official dignities has exaggerated his pretensions, while increasing his importance, and because the keenness of his feelings in general rather disposes him to think himself a god."

Now in the first place the results of this attempt to infer from a poem the life and personality of the poet are strangely uncertain. We read in the recently published letters of John Richard Green[7] that when Taine was in England getting information for the last volume of his "English Literature," he began talking about Tennyson with Palgrave,[8] a great friend of the laureate. "Wasn't he in early youth rich, luxurious, fond of pleasure, self-indulgent?" Taine asked. "I see it all in his early poems—his riot, his adoration of physical beauty, his delight in jewels, in the abandonment of all to pleasure, in wine, and . . ." "Stop! stop!" said Palgrave, out of all patience. "As a young man Tennyson was poor—he had little more than one hundred pounds a year, his habits were, as they still are, simple and reserved, he cared then as he cares now for little more than a chat and a pipe; he has never known luxury in your sense." Taine thanked Palgrave for his information—and when the book came out Tennyson was found still painted as the young voluptuary of the critic's fancy.*

Even assuming that Taine's inferences could be drawn correctly, he would have us fix our attention on precisely those features of a poem that are least poetical. The very prosaic facts he is looking for would be at least as visible in the writing of some mediocrity as in a work of the first order. It is, indeed, when Taine starts out to deal in this fashion with a poet of genius like Milton, to reduce "Paradise Lost" to a mere "sign," that the whole method is seen to be grotesquely inadequate. "Adam," says Taine in his critique of Milton, "is your true pater-familias with a vote, an M.P.,

---

* *Letters of John Richard Green*, 372. Green's anecdote is perhaps not entirely fair to Taine's account of Tennyson as it finally appeared. [Babbitt's note]

[5] Hippolyte Taine (1828–1893), French critic and historian, in his *History of English Literature* (1863) held the theory that literature was determined by and relative to its race, *milieu*, and time.

[6] Alfred de Musset (1810–1857), French poet and dramatist; Victor Hugo (1802–1885), French poet and novelist; Alphonse de Lamartine (1790–1869), French poet; Heinrich Heine (1797–1856), German poet.

[7] English historian (1837–1883).

[8] Francis Turner Palgrave (1824–1897), English poet and critic, whose *Golden Treasury of English Songs and Lyrics* (1861) is perhaps the most famous of all anthologies.

an old Oxford man," etc. He listens to the conversation of Adam and Eve, the first pair, only to hear "an English household, two reasoners of the period—Colonel Hutchinson and his wife. Good heavens! dress them at once"; and he continues in this vein for pages.

But, says M. Bourget,[9] speaking for the impressionists, there is another way of approaching the volume of verse that Taine would treat solely from the point of view of its "significance"; and in rendering the "suggestiveness" of the volume to the impressionist sensibility, M. Bourget proceeds to employ a luxuriance of epithet that lack of space forbids our quoting. He asks us to imagine a young woman alone in her boudoir on an overcast winter afternoon. A vague melancholy steals upon her as she reclines at ease in her long chair; all aquiver with ineffable longing, she turns to her favorite poet. She does not surmise behind the delicately tinted pages of the beloved book the prosaic facts of environment, the obscure animal origins of talent that are so visible to Taine. What she does perceive is the dream of the poet—"the inexpressible and mysterious beyond that he has succeeded in throwing like a halo round his verses." For Taine the stanzas are a result; for the young woman "who intoxicates her heart with them so deliciously," they are a cause. "She does not care for the alembic in which the magic philter has been distilled, provided only this magic is operative, provided her reading culminates in an exquisite and trembling exaltation," and "suggests to her dreams either sweet or sad, but always productive of ecstasy." Who does not see, concludes M. Bourget, that entirely different theories of art are implied in the two ways of approaching the volume of verse? *

The two theories are different, indeed; yet they are alike in this, that neither the "significance" of the volume to Taine nor its "suggestiveness" to M. Bourget affords any real means of escape from the quicksands of relativity to some firm ground of judgment. We may be sure that a third-rate bit of contemporary sentimentality will "suggest" more ineffable dreams to the young woman in the long chair than a play of Sophocles. To state the case more generally, how many books there are that were once infinitely suggestive and are still of the highest significance in literary history which yet intrinsically are now seen to be of very inferior value! This is eminently true of certain writings of Rousseau, to whom much of the peculiar exaggeration of the *sens propre*, or individual sense that one finds in the impressionists, can ultimately be traced.** If the special modes of sensibility that impressionism exhibits go back to Rousseau, its philosophical theory may best be considered as a reappearance in modern thought of

*Abridged from the chapter on Taine in *Essais de Psychologie contemporaine*. [Babbitt's note]

** "Voici enfin Jean-Jacques, précurseur du XIXe siècle, qui dans l'individu, c'est-à-dire dans le Moi affectif et passionnel, voit la mesure unique de toute chose." Pellissier, *Etudes de Littérature contemporaine*. Cf. Brunetière, *Nouvelles questions de critique*, 214. [Babbitt's note]

The quotation may be translated: "Here is finally Jean-Jacques, precursor of the nineteenth century, who in the individual, that is to say in the Self affective and under the influence of passions, sees the only measure of all things."

[9] Paul Bourget (1852–1935), French novelist and critic.

the ancient maxim that man is the measure of all things. This celebrated dictum became current at a decisive moment in Greek life and would indeed seem to sum up almost necessarily the point of view of any age that has cast off traditional standards. The all-important question is whether one interprets the maxim in the spirit of the sophists or in that of Socrates. The resemblance between the impressionistic and the sophistical understanding of the maxim is unmistakable; not only the individual man, but his present sensations and impressions are to be made the measure of all things. "All of us," says M. Anatole France, "judge everything by our own measure. How could we do otherwise, since to judge is to compare, and we have only one measure, which is ourselves; and this measure is constantly changing? We are all of us the sport and playthings of mobile appearances." * Perhaps no recent writer has shown more of the Socratic spirit in his use of the maxim than Emerson. "A true man," he says, "belongs to no other time and place, but is the centre of things. Where he is, there is nature. He measures you and all men and all events." Though Emerson thus asserts the maxim, he has not therefore succumbed, like M. France, to the doctrine of relativity and the feeling of universal illusion that accompanies it; on the contrary, he has attained to a new sense of the unity of human nature—a unity founded, not on tradition, but on insight. He says somewhere that he finds such an identity both of thought and sentiment in the best books of the world, that they seem to him to be the work of "one all-seeing, all-hearing gentleman." Now it is evidently this one all-seeing, all-hearing gentleman who is for Emerson the measure of all things. The individual man is the measure of all things only in so far as he has realized in himself this essential human nature. To be sure, the line is often hard to draw in practice between the two types of individualist. There were persons in ancient Athens—for example, Aristophanes in the "Clouds"—who treated Socrates as an ordinary sophist. In the same way, there are persons to-day who fail to see the difference between Emerson and an ordinary impressionist. "The source of Emerson's power," says Professor Santayana, "lay not in his doctrine but in his temperament." **

Emerson's language is often indistinguishable from that of the impressionist. "I would write on the lintels of my doorpost, *whim*." "Dream delivers us to dream, and there is no end to illusion." "Life is a flux of moods." But he is careful to add that "there is that in us which changes not and which ranks all sensations and states of mind." The impressionist denies this element of absolute judgment and so feels free to indulge his temperament with epicurean indolence; at the same time he has the contemptuous indulgence for others that befits beings who are the "sport and playthings of mobile appearances." M. France says that he "despises men tenderly." We would reply in the words of Burke that the "species of benevolence which arises from contempt is no true charity." Impressionism has led to a strange increase in the number of dilettantes and *jouisseurs lit-*

* *Vie lit.*, I, 318. [Babbitt's note]
** *Poetry and Religion*, 218. [Babbitt's note]

téraires,[10] who to the precept *de gustibus non* [11] have given developments that would certainly have surprised its author. The Horatian plea for an honest liberty of taste has its necessary corrective in the truth that is very bluntly stated in a Spanish proverb: "There are tastes that deserve the cudgel." * We are told that Sainte-Beuve was once so offended by an outrageous offence to good taste in a remark of Nicolardot's,[12] that, yielding to an irresistible impulse, he kicked him out of the room. Dante, in replying to a certain opponent, says, with the instinct of a true Italian, that he would like to answer such "bestiality not with words but with a knife." We must remember that "good taste" as formerly understood was made up of two distinct elements: first, one's individual sensibility, and secondly, a code of outer rules by which this sensibility was disciplined and held in check. The observance of these rules became for the community of well-bred people a sort of *noblesse oblige,* and taste in this sense has been rightly defined by Rivarol as a man's literary honor. Now that the outer code has been abrogated, taste is not therefore delivered over to the caprices of a vagrant sensibility; taste is attained only when this sensibility is rectified with reference to standards inwardly apprehended, and in this sense may be defined as a man's literary conscience; it is, in short, only one aspect of the struggle between our lower and higher selves. Some, indeed, would maintain that taste is not a thing thus to be won by any effort of the will, but is rather an inborn and incommunicable tact, a sort of mysterious election, a free gift of the muses to a predestined few; that in literature many are called and few are chosen. In the article "Goût" of the "Philosophical Dictionary," Voltaire discourses on the small number of the elect in matters of taste, and in almost the next article ("Grâce") turns all his powers of mockery on those who assert the same doctrine in religion. Not only individuals but whole nations were once held to be under the reprobation of the muses. As Voltaire says sadly, *presque tout l'univers est barbare.*[13] Perhaps even to-day persons might be found who would regard as legitimate the famous query of Father Bouhours [14] whether a German can have wit. There are only too many examples in Germany and elsewhere of how far infinite industry and good intentions are from sufficing for the attainment of taste. However it may be in theology, it remains true in literature, as Gautier [15] remarks, that works without grace are of no avail.

But one may recognize an element of predestination in the problem of taste and not therefore acquiesce in the impressionist's preaching of the fatality and finality of temperament. Every one, to be sure, has an initial or temperamental taste, but it is hard to say how far this taste may be transformed by subordinating it to the higher claims of our nature. Dr. Johnson says that if he had no duties and no reference to futurity he should spend

---

* "Hay gustos que merecen palos." [Babbitt's note]
[10] "literary dabblers."
[11] *de gustibus non est disputandum:* "there is no disputing tastes."
[12] Louis Nicolardot (1822–1888), French author and critic.
[13] "almost all the world is uncivilized."
[14] Father Dominique Bouhours (1628–1702), French Jesuit writer.
[15] Théophile Gautier (1811–1872), French poet and critic.

his life in driving briskly in a post-chaise with a pretty woman. Here then
is the temperamental taste of Dr. Johnson, and if he had been a disciple of
M. France, he might have accepted it as final. Boswell reports an outburst
of Johnson on this very subject: "Do not, Sir, accustom yourself to trust
to *impressions*. By trusting to impressions, a man may gradually come to
yield to them, and at length be subject to them, so as not to be a free agent,
or what is the same thing in effect, to *suppose* that he is not a free agent.
A man who is in that state should not be suffered to live; . . . there can be
no confidence in him, no more than in a tiger."

Johnson would evidently have agreed with the Buddhists in looking on
the indolent settling down of a man in his own temperament * as the chief
of all the deadly sins. A fulmination like the foregoing is good to clear the
air after the debilitating sophistries of M. France. Yet we feel that Johnson's point of view implies an undue denial of the individual's right to his
own impressions and that therefore it has become in some measure obsolete.
It is well for us, after all, to have fresh and vivid and personal impressions;
it is well for us, in short, to awaken our senses; but we should "awaken
our senses that we may the better judge"—and not simply that we may the
better enjoy. For instance, Walter Pater continually dwells on the need of
awakening our senses, but when he speaks of "living in the full stream of
refined sensation," when he urges us to gather ourselves together "into one
desperate effort to see and touch," there is a hedonistic flavor in these utterances that can escape no one. On the other hand, there should be no ascetic
denial of the value of the impression in itself. Brunetière is reported to
have said to another critic, whom he suspected of intellectual epicureanism,
"*You* always praise what pleases you, *I* never do." ** This is an asceticism of
taste worthy of the spectator of Racine's [16] comedy who wished to laugh
according to the rules. And so Brunetière was led naturally into his reactionary attitude; seeing only the evil possibilities of individualism, he would
have the modern man forego his claim to be the measure of all things, and
submit once more to outer authority. A certain type of seventeenth-century
critic attempted to establish a standard that was entirely outside the individual. The impressionist has gone to the opposite extreme and set up a
standard that is entirely within the individual. The problem is to find some
middle ground between Procrustes and Proteus; [17] and this right mean
would seem to lie in a standard that is in the individual and yet is felt by
him to transcend his personal self and lay hold of that part of his nature
that he possesses in common with other men.

* This is the full meaning of the Pâli term *pamâda*. The opposite quality, *appa-
mâda*, or strenuousness,—the unremitting exercise of the active will,—is the chief of
the Buddhist virtues; this Oriental strenuousness, one should hasten to add, is directed
towards self-conquest and not, like the Occidental variety, towards the conquest of
the outer world. [Babbitt's note]

** See Lemaître, *Contemporains*, VI, p. xi. Cf. Brunetière, *L'Evolution de la poésie
lyrique*, 25. [Babbitt's note]

[16] Jean Racine (1639–1699), French tragic dramatist.

[17] Procrustes was a legendary Greek robber who forced his guests to fit his bed,
cutting off their legs if they were too long or stretching them if they were too short.
Proteus was a Greek god who was able to change constantly into any form he might
wish.

The impressionist not only refuses the individual man any such principle of judgment to which he may appeal from his fleeting impressions;
he goes farther and refuses men collectively any avenue of escape from universal illusion and relativity; he denies in short the doctrine embodied in
the old church maxim, *Securus judicat orbis terrarum*,[18] a doctrine so
fundamental, we may note in passing, that in the form attributed to Lincoln it has become the cornerstone of democracy: "You cannot fool all the
people all the time." M. Anatole France is fond of insisting, like Sainte-
Beuve before him, that there inheres in mankind as a whole no such power
of righting itself and triumphing over its own errrors and illusions. A
whole chapter might be made up of passages from Sainte-Beuve on the
vanity of fame. "Posterity has allowed three fourths of the works of antiquity to perish," says M. France in turn; "it has allowed the rest to be
frightfully corrupted. . . . In the little that it has kept there are detestable
books which are none the less immortal. Varius,[19] we are told, was the
equal of Virgil. He has perished. Ælian [20] was an ass, and he survives.
There is posterity for you." † etc. Here again the contrast between the two
types of individualist is absolute. "There is no luck in literary reputation,"
says Emerson. "They who make up the final verdict for every book are not
the partial and noisy public of the hour, but a court as of angels; a public
not to be bribed, not to be entreated, and not to be overawed decides upon
every man's title to fame. Only those books come down which deserve to
last. Blackmore, Kotzebue, or Pollock [21] may endure for a night, but Moses
and Homer stand forever. The permanence of all books is fixed by no effort
friendly or hostile, but by their own specific gravity or the intrinsic importance of their contents to the constant mind of man."

We should add, then, in order to define our critical standard completely,
that the judgment of the keen-sighted few in the present needs to be rati-
fied by the verdict of posterity.**

III

What we are seeking is a critic who rests his discipline and selection
upon the past without being a mere traditionalist; whose holding of tradition involves a constant process of hard and clear thinking, a constant ad-

* *Vie littéraire*, I, 111. [Babbitt's note]
** The appeal to the judgment of the keen-sighted few, as opposed to that of the
many, appears in Aristotle, who always assumes an ideal reader, whom he refers to
variously as ὁ σπουδαῖος, ὁ φρόνιμος, ὁ εὐφυής.[22] The principle of universal consent
as applied to literature is first clearly stated by Longinus (περὶ ὕψους,[23] CAP. VII).
[Babbitt's note]
    [18] "the whole world forms its judgments without fear."
    [19] Roman elegiac, epic, and tragic poet of the first century B.C., friend of Virgil
and Horace.
    [20] Stoic philosopher and writer (*ca.* A.D. 170–235).
    [21] Richard Blackmore (1825–1900), English novelist; Ferdinand Kotzebue (1761–
1819), German dramatist; Walter Pollock (1850–1926), English scholar and critic.
    [22] "zealous, thoughtful (prudent), talented (clever, witty)."
    [23] "On the Sublime."

justment, in other words, of the experience of the past to the changing needs of the present.

Who are to be our models for this right critical interpretation of the past? They are curiously hard to find in the nineteenth century, in spite of the fact that it is commonly supposed to be the most historical of centuries. There prevailed during this period two main attitudes towards the past which may be defined, respectively, as the scientific and the romantic. The man with the scientific attitude is chiefly concerned with investigating and establishing the facts of the past. The romanticist, for his part, revels in the mere picturesqueness of the facts or else takes refuge in the past from the present, uses it, as Taine would say, to create for himself an alibi. But the past should be regarded primarily neither as a laboratory for research nor as a bower of dreams, but as a school of experience. Where, then, is the man who has been fully initiated into tradition, and at the same time knows how to bring it to bear upon the present? Even Sainte-Beuve does not fully satisfy us here. He was one of the victims of that naturalistic fatalism that has lain like a blight upon the human spirit for the past fifty years or more. "Man," he says, "has the *illusion* of liberty." What is the use of knowing the past if one is not free to profit by the knowledge? We think by contrast of Goethe (whom Sainte-Beuve himself calls the king of critics), and of Goethe's saying that the chief benefit one may derive from a total study of his work is a "certain inner freedom."

Goethe, indeed, comes nearer than any other modern to what we are seeking; not the romantic or scientific Goethe, it should be added, but the humanistic Goethe, who is revealed in the conversations with Eckermann and others, and in the critical utterances of his later years. As an actual practitioner of the art of criticism, he seems to me inferior to the best of the Frenchmen; but as an initiator into the critical habit of mind he is incomparable. He has, as Sainte-Beuve puts it, assimilated not merely tradition, but all traditions, and that without ceasing to be a modern of moderns; he keeps watch for every new sail on the horizon, but from the height of a Sunium. He would use the larger background and perspective to round out and support his individual insight and so make of the present what it should be—not the servile imitation, nor again the blank denial of the past, but its creative continuation. "To the errors and aberrations of the hour," he says, "we must oppose the masses of universal history." He would have us cease theorizing about the absolute and learn to recognize it in its actual manifestations. This particular form of the humanistic art of seeing the One in the Many would seem especially appropriate to an age like ours that differs above all from other ages, Greek and Roman antiquity, for example, in having at its command a vaster body of verified human experience.

I have said that the humanistic rather than the Rousseauistic Goethe is important for our purpose. But I should add that the process by which he passes from the Rousseauistic to the humanistic attitude is almost as instructive as the final result. The completeness of his reaction from the Rousseauistic theory of spontaneity or original genius, of which he was at the beginning the chief German exponent, may be inferred from a sentence I have already quoted. He did not go on, like Emerson, cultivating the delicious sense of indeterminate size, and feeling as elastic as the gas of gun-powder; he was not permanently satisfied, in short, with romantic megalomania; he discovered that man progresses by taking on limitations and not, as the Rousseauist would have us believe, by throwing them off. The lesson of "Wilhelm Meister," as of so much of his later writing, is that the individual must submit his temperament and impulses to something higher than themselves—in other words, he must renounce. The process of constant dying to one's self, that Goethe proclaims (stirb und werde), falls in, of course, with much that is most profound in religion; but Goethe's renunciation, it should be observed, is entirely unascetic. It seems the natural outgrowth of the experience of this life and not, as so often in religion, the violent contradiction of it.

What Goethe himself renounced was the world of Rousseauistic revery. He turned more and more from dreaming to doing. A man must, he says, combining the terminology of Leibnitz [24] with that of Aristotle, raise himself by constant striving from a mere monad to an entelechy. Only in this way may he hope for happiness in this world and continuance in the next. We may take, as best summing up the central thought of Goethe, the lines at the end of the Second Faust in which the angels proclaim salvation by works:—

> "Wer immer strebend sich bemüht,
> Den Können wir erlösen." [25]

Yet it is just here in connection with this doctrine of works, especially as exemplified in the Second Faust, that our first doubts about Goethe arise. I have quoted Goethe against Emerson. It is only fair to quote Emerson in return upon the limitations of Goethe. After praising Goethe heartily in his "Representative Men," he yet ends by saying that he did not worship the highest unity. So far as this judgment merely reflects the Rousseauistic side of Emerson, his suspicion of culture and his dislike of analysis, it is negligible. But Emerson was not only a Rousseauist but a seer, and his insight as well as his Rousseauism appears, as it seems to me, in the dictum that Goethe did not worship the highest unity.

Now to say of Goethe that he did not worshp the highest unity is simply another way of saying that he lacked religious elevation. In any case he is less open than most men of the last century to the charge of confusing the planes of being. He kept his outlook open and unobstructed by scientific or other dogmatism even on the religious plane. He purged and purified himself very completely of the pseudo-spirituality of the Rousseauist,— of that shrinking back from outer reality coupled with that giddy gazing into the bottomless pit of the "heart" against which he utters a warning in

[24] Gottfried Leibnitz (1646–1716), German philosopher, writer, and mathematician.

[25] "Who ever aspiring struggles on,
We know shall win salvation."

his "Tasso." * He escaped in short from the world of romantic dreaming that is within us. We have it, however, on rather high authority that the kingdom of heaven is also within. Even in the inner life itself, it would appear, there may be a choice of direction, a parting of the ways. Goethe would not have hesitated to reply that he had aimed to escape, not only from the romantic, but also from the Christian morbidness. I have quoted Sainte-Beuve's saying that Goethe had assimilated, not merely tradition, but all traditions. How about the tradition that goes back to Judaea? The reply is by no means simple. We remember the impressive tribute he paid to Christianity ** only a few weeks before his death, but then he also retained his early conviction that Pascal had done more harm to religion than all the deists and atheists of the eighteenth century. Now Pascal paints, though in somewhat less lurid hues, the same picture of human destiny as Jonathan Edwards: on the one hand, God in his absolute and arbitrary sovereignty; on the other, man weltering helplessly in his sin; the interval between only to be traversed by "thunderclaps and visible upsets of grace." This somewhat melodramatic form of Christianity, the tremendous spiritual romanticism of Saint Augustine, was undoubtedly distasteful to Goethe. As against this type of inwardness with its ascetic implications, he was for reconciling the flesh and the spirit, or as his detractors would say, for becoming a pagan. He had at least the advantages of being in accord in his attitude towards Augustinian Christianity with the main trend of the modern spirit. It would take almost unimaginable disasters to induce the world to give up its hard-won reconciliation of flesh and spirit, and once more go into sackcloth and ashes.

Goethe was, however, too great to deny entirely the truths of grace, or to lack the sense of man's helplessness in the hands of a higher power. He was capable of the obeisance of the spirit before this power and knew that if a man is not to remain a mere Titan his works must receive its blessing.† Yet he would have man dwell on works and the feasibility of works, and not on what is at bottom an insoluble mystery. No inconsiderable part of wisdom consists in just this: not to allow the mind to dwell on questions that are unprofitable in themselves or else entirely beyond its grasp.

* "Es liegt um uns herum
Gar mancher Abgrund, den das Schicksal grub;
Doch hier in unserm Herzen ist der tiefste,
Und reizend ist es, sich hinab zu stürzen." [Babbitt's note]

["There lie all about us
Many abysses that Fate has dug;
Yet here in our heart is the deepest,
And it is a temptation to plunge into it."]

** Conversation with Eckermann, 11 March, 1832. For the more important passages bearing on Goethe's religious opinions see Otto Harnack: *Goethe in der Epoche seiner Vollendung*, 50–90. [Babbitt's note]

† "Gross beginnet Ihr Titanen, aber leiten
Zu dem ewig Guten, ewig Schönen,
Ist der Götter Werk; die lasst gewähren!—" [Babbitt's note]
["The Titans begin greatly, but to guide
Eternal Good, eternal Beauty,
Is the work of Gods; remember this!"]

I may myself seem to be straying at present into regions rather remote from my topic and therefore unprofitable. My reply is that the chief problem of criticism, namely, the search for standards to oppose to individual caprice, is also the chief problem of contemporary thought in general: so that any solution which does not get back to first principles will be worthless. If in a book on French criticism, again, I am devoting so much space to Emerson and Goethe, my purpose is to emphasize in this way my belief that this problem of discipline and standards is not to be solved in terms of French life alone, as a whole school of contemporary French thinkers * incline to believe, but is international. Finally, if my discussion of grace and good works seems to some to have an old-fashioned flavor, I would reply with Sainte-Beuve that simple psychological analysis when carried to a certain point encounters in other terms the same questions as theology. Both in a man's native gift as well as in the use of this gift to some adequate end there is an element of grace. In enumerating the various explanations of this mystery that have been attempted, Sainte-Beuve neglected, as I pointed out, the very interesting explanation embodied in the Oriental doctrine of karma. According to karma all that large part of a man's life which is so plainly independent of his own will and works is simply the result of his previous works. This doctrine must affect its devotees very differently from Augustinian Christianity, substituting as it does a strict causal nexus for the somewhat melodramatic intervention of a divine *bon plaisir*. Yet it only puts the difficulty a few steps farther back; the doctrine itself, along with the belief in reincarnation it implies, is just as unthinkable from the platform of the ordinary intellect as the doctrine of grace. We have the testimony of Buddha, the chief exponent of karma, on this very point. He puts it down in his list of the four "unthinkables." ** In him who tries to grasp the workings of this law † directly, he says, grievous and vexatious mental habits will arise, which may even end in madness. The faith in karma is to remain in solution, as it were, in the background of our consciousness and from there to irradiate our action. Our actual attention should be fixed on the step in the "path" that is just ahead of us. We can infer what Buddha would have thought of the Augustinian †† Christians who would have man turn away from works and brood everlastingly on the mystery of grace. He would have agreed with Holmes that the only decent thing for a consistent Calvinist to do is to go mad.

Goethe, then, to return to him, may simply have showed his supreme good sense, his instinct for a sound spiritual hygiene, in turning away from grace to works. He established his own list of "unthinkables," which is not so different from that of Buddha as one might suppose. We may

* The so-called nationalists—Paul Bourget, Maurice Barrès, Charles Maurras, etc. [Babbitt's note]
** See *Anguttara Nikāya*, Part II, sect. 77. [Babbitt's note]
† The Pāli word is "kammavipāko." [Babbitt's note]
†† I do not mean to say that St. Augustine did not put great emphasis on works, but merely that the side of Christianity which shows most clearly his influence has put an even greater emphasis on grace. [Babbitt's note]

note, for example, that both men dismissed as unprofitable speculations about personal immortality.* How many other questions there are that professional philosophers are fond of discussing and that may be profitably dismissed either because they are insoluble in themselves or because they do not, in Buddha's phrase, "make for edification"! Men do not fail, Goethe insisted, so much from lack of light on ultimate problems as from neglect of the very obvious and often very humble duty which is immediately before them; from not having met, as he puts it, the demands of the day (*die Forderung des Tages*). In thus looking to immediate practice Goethe is at one with Dr. Johnson, the fit representative of a race that has shown a genius for conduct. All theory, says Johnson, makes against the freedom of the will and all experience in favor of it—the happiest utterance on this subject with which I am familiar. Like Goethe, Johnson simply refused, therefore, at the outset to enter into the metaphysical maze of either the dogmatic supernaturalist or the dogmatic naturalist. For the method of approach to the problem of a dogmatic naturalist like Taine involves, no less than that of the dogmatic supernaturalist, an attempt to think the unthinkable (as Buddha also pointed out).** Both the One and the Many as well as man's relation to them must forever elude final formulation.

Why, then, should we feel any doubt about Goethe's doctrine of work? The reply is that in his reaction from the romantic morbidness and what seemed to him the Christian morbidness he has transferred his work too much from the inner life of the individual to the outer world. This point may be made clear by comparing him with the great ancient of whom he is in some respects the disciple—Aristotle. For no one, I presume, would deny that Goethe is in his general temper far more Aristotelian than Platonic. Now if Plato anticipates on one side of his thinking the doctrine of grace, as when he says that virtue is "neither natural nor acquired but comes to the virtuous by the gift of God" ("Meno"), Aristotle goes steadily on the assumption that virtue can be acquired, and is therefore a thoroughgoing partisan of works. The works he would have us perform, however, are not primarily utilitarian. He would have us work to redeem our own lower self from evil habits, and not, like Faust, to reclaim marsh lands from the sea. Moreover, the purpose that is imposed on the lower self and by which it is disciplined is linked by a series of intermediary purposes to the supreme and perfect End itself; in other words, it rests ultimately on an intuition of what Emerson calls the highest unity. Aristotle is indeed less habitually conscious of this unity than Plato. Though even Plato seems terribly "at ease in Zion" to the austere Christian, he has more sense of man's helplessness before the infinite, more of that humility, in short, that the man whose attention is turned too exclusively to works is constantly in danger of losing.

* For Goethe's admirable utterances on this subject see Eckermann, 24 February, 1824. [Babbitt's note]
** In the passage I have already quoted. The Pāli word for the attempt to grasp the material world intellectually (which Buddha deems impossible) is "lokacintā." [Babbitt's note]

But though Aristotle is less preoccupied with the highest unity than
Plato, I believe that he is more pre-occupied with it than Goethe. Though
far more than a mere naturalist, as I have tried to show, Goethe, in the
last analysis, conceives of life more naturalistically, that is more expan-
sively, than Aristotle. He was born into an enormously expansive age and
was drawn into its main current. He found in the First Faust the happiest formulae for the two main forces that were to dominate this age—
scientific positivism (*Im Anfang war die Tat*) [26] and Rousseauistic romanticism (*Gefühl ist alles*).[27] The Aristotelian would object that the Deed
and the Emotion do not by themselves suffice, that some adequate purpose must intervene to direct the Deed and discipline the Emotion. And
Goethe himself became increasingly Aristotelian in this respect as he grew
older. Yet even so, he still conceives at the end of the Second Faust of
both the Deed and the Emotion too much in terms of expansion. I have
already criticised from the Aristotelian point of view his conception of the
Deed. Let us consider for a moment from the same point of view his conception of the Emotion. As is well known he praises as the most exalted
form of emotion the "eternal Feminine" which "draws us upward." We
are reminded here of Dante—a poet who will scarcely be accused of not
having worshipped the highest unity—and his proclamation of that "primal
love" that built the walls of hell.* Dante's conception implies a degree of
selectiveness that makes us shudder. But is it not evident that to conceive
of the highest love as Goethe did is to go to the opposite extreme, and
eliminate from it the element of judgment and selection entirely; to forget
that if the eternal Feminine draws us upward, only the eternal Masculine
can keep us up? The supreme love, we may surmise, is not exclusively
judicial or sympathetic, but a vital mediation between judgment and sympathy; it is selective love. It belongs to that superrational plane on which,
in Goethe's phrase, the indescribable is accomplished.**

We can now begin to see in what sense Emerson may have been right
in saying that Goethe did not worship the highest unity. His view of
life in the Second Faust evidently tends to fly apart into the two extremes
with which we have been so familiar during the past century—on the
one hand, the idea of work conceived primarily in a utilitarian spirit, and
on the other, diffusive, unselective sympathy. The supervention of the
highest unity would have restored the work from the outer world to the
breast of the individual and made the sympathy selective. We should
then have had a point of view more humanistic and less humanitarian. To
be sure, Goethe had no easy task in converting the mere romantic adventurer of the First Part (*der Unmensch ohne Zweck und Ruh*) [28] into a

---

* *Inf.*, III, v. 6. [Babbitt's note]
** "Das Unbeschreibliche,
     Hier ist es gethan." [Babbitt's note]
   [26] "In the beginning was the deed." The irony of the phrasing is obvious in its
reflection of the opening of the Gospel according to St. John: "In the beginning was
the Word . . ."
   [27] "feeling is all."
   [28] "the brute without purpose and without rest (peace)"

good humanist or even into a good humanitarian. If we wish to do full justice to Goethe as a humanist we should not therefore confine ourselves too strictly to Faust.

The true humanist, that is the man who is sympathetically selective, has his standard within him—living, flexible, intuitive. Aristotle would make such a man the arbiter of all questions of taste and conduct—they are to be as he would decide.* A man may thus belong to the keen-sighted few, Aristotle admits, simply because he is born such.** In not trying to get behind this fact, Aristotle showed his good sense, if to do so would have been to run into insoluble mysteries. As the Greek poet says, there are three classes of men, (1) those who have insight, (2) those who, lacking insight themselves, have yet the wit to recognize it in others, and (3) those who have neither insight nor the wit to recognize it (and these last, he adds, are the truly useless men). The uncomfortable fact about life is that so many men belong to the third class, that there are so many men whose heads, in Joubert's quaint phrase, have no skylights in them. Men may be very eminent in other ways and yet lack the skylights; Taine, it seems to me, lacked them. Nor do we escape from the difficulty by putting our main emphasis with M. Bergson, not on the spiritual but on the aesthetic intuitions. The ordinary man can no more by any effort of his own be as aesthetically perceptive as Keats, let us say, than he can be as spiritually perceptive as Emerson. The undertaking in either case is of the same order as that of adding a cubit to one's stature. To be completely equipped for criticism one should possess in some measure both kinds of perceptiveness.

We must not, however, bear down too heavily, as Voltaire does, for example, in matters of taste, on the evident element of grace and predestination, for this is to neglect the truth of works; still less must we see the measure of all things in the man in the street, for this is to neglect the truths of both grace and works; least of all must we, like Tolstoy,[31] seek our literary and artistic norm in the untutored peasant, for this is to set up a sort of inverted grace at the imminent risk of falling into bedlam delusion. The right use of grace and similar doctrines is to make us humble and not to make us morbid or discouraged. With due distrust of ourselves, a distrust that appears in our readiness to fortify our insight by tradition, with full admission that our works must be irradiated and guided from within and from above if they are not to prove vain, we must yet put our prime emphasis in literature, as elsewhere, on works. Now to perform works in the sense I have tried to define, that is, to feel in all one does the control of the highest unity, means in practice to select. All the knowledge and sympathy in the world can only prepare for the supreme, the distinctively human, act of selection. We must therefore train ourselves to

---

* The σπουδαῖος is ὥσπερ κανὼν καὶ μέτρον [29] *Eth. Nic.*, III, 4, 1133 a 33. [Babbitt's note]

** He is a εὐφυής[30] Cf. *Eth. Nic.*, III, 5, 1114 b 6. [Babbitt's note]

[29] "The zealous man is like a standard (canon) or norm."

[30] "well-endowed man."

[31] Lev Nikolaevich Tolstoy (1828–1910), Russian realistic novelist.

feel that outer objects are, in the phrase of Epictetus,[32] only the raw material for selection, and that it is possible to select. A great library, for example, is an infinite potentiality of selection, ranging from Zola [33] to Plato. In our attitude towards it, as in our other concerns, we are to appeal from our moods of lazy self-indulgence to our moods of strenuous endeavor, from Philip drunk to Philip sober. Our reading enters as one element into that sum of choices that determines at last our rank in the scale of being. Here as elsewhere, if we neglect the opportunities that the "hypocritic Days" bring with them as they pass in their endless file, we shall "too late under their solemn fillets see the scorn."

We must select constantly and resolutely, though without sourness or asceticism. The romanticists have been busy for a century or more instilling into our heads the notion that to be selective is to be narrow and probably ill-natured. We must not select but admire—admire like a brute, Hugo would add. When Gautier averred that if he thought even one of Hugo's verses bad, he would not confess the fact to himself at midnight in a dark cellar without a candle, he must have come near fulfilling the master's ideal. Many authors would no doubt like to see criticism reduced, as a romantic dilettante recently defined it, to the "art of praise." A cat may, however, according to the adage, be killed with cream; and it has become only too evident that criticism may be killed by an excess of the appreciative temper. The true mark of barbarism, according to Goethe, is to have no organ for discerning the excellent. One may show that he lacks this organ just as surely by overpraising as by overblaming. What we see in America to-day, for instance, is an endless procession of bad or mediocre books, each one saluted on its way to oblivion by epithets that would be deserved only by a masterpiece. We have, in fact, been having so many masterpieces of late that we have almost ceased to have any literature. The critic is anxious like everybody else to show that he is overflowing with the milk of human kindness, that he is, in short, a "beautiful soul." Moreover, in a country where the belief is held that all things will turn out fortunately if only we feel lovely enough about them, it is commercially profitable to have a beautiful soul. The Christian Scientists, indeed, may be said to have put the art of feeling lovely on a dividend-paying basis. On the other hand, the man who has too many exclusions and disapprovals will fall under the suspicion of not being an optimist, and not to pass as an optimist is in many parts of America to be discredited. It is of course better to be a eupeptic than a merely dyspeptic critic. From this point of view we are better off than New Zealand if we are to believe a recent New Zealand writer, who, after comparing American critics to a "community of monthly nurses cooing and cackling over a succession of incomparable literary births," says that in New Zealand the comparison suggested is that of a "pack of incorrigible terriers watching for so many rats or rabbits to leave their holes." But it is not a question of being either eupeptic or dyspeptic, but of having standards and the courage to apply

[32] Greek Stoic philosopher (A.D. 60?–120?).
[33] Émile Zola (1840–1902), French naturalistic novelist.

them. One may, as I have tried to show in the case of Joubert, be perfectly genial and good-natured, and at the same time extremely severe and selective.

The excess of the sympathetic and appreciative temper is of course nothing peculiar to America. As a matter of fact, Max Nordau [34] cites certain German critics as the worst examples of the disease he calls superlativism, by which he means the facile outpour of epithets pushed to the verge of hysteria. Modern criticism, in getting rid of formalism and in becoming comprehensive and sympathetic, has performed only half, and that the less difficult half, of its task. The time would seem especially ripe for taking up the second half of the task—that of finding some new principle of judgment and selection. Renan says that "Goethe embraced the universe in the vast affirmation of love," [*]—which is a somewhat hyperbolical way of saying that he is the worthy representative of a great era of expansion. But if Goethe were alive to-day, he might be less concerned with embracing the universe and more concerned with maintaining standards against the nightmare of an unselective democracy. We need not, again, admire Sainte-Beuve the less because we cannot admit, any more than in the case of Goethe, that the total emphasis of his criticism is just what we need at present. The *genre* in his hands, as I have tried to show, is expanding away from its centre. What seems desirable to-day is rather a movement that shall work in from the periphery of criticism in knowledge and sympathy to its heart and core in judgment. How peripheral criticism became during the nineteenth century may be inferred from the fact that Renan, for example, uses the word in a sense that is contrary to its very etymology.

What is most needed just now is not great doctors of relativity like Renan and Sainte-Beuve, but rather a critic who, without being at all rigid or reactionary, can yet carry into his work the sense of standards that are set above individual caprice and the flux of phenomena; who can, in short, oppose a genuine humanism to the pseudo-humanism of the pragmatists. A critic of this kind might be counted on to proclaim a philosophy, not of vital impulse, like M. Bergson, but of vital unity and vital restraint —restraint felt as an inner living law and not merely as a dead and mechanical outer rule. We may venture the paradox that criticism would derive less benefit at present from another Sainte-Beuve than from a second Boileau, that is, from a man who should work as effectively for the right kind of concentration in our own day as Boileau did in the seventeenth century. No sensible person would deny the narrowness of Boileau's range [**] or defend the formalism that appears so often in his theory. But his greatness, as Sainte-Beuve himself points out, lies elsewhere—in the native tact and almost infallible intuition he showed in his critical judgments.[†] All was not veto and restriction in his rôle, Sainte-Beuve goes on

[*] *Avenir de la science*, 448. [Babbitt's note]
[**] Sainte-Beuve enumerates Boileau's limitations in N. *Lundis*, I, 300–02. [Babbitt's note]
[†] See the important passage on the nature and rôle of the critic *Chateaubriand*, II, 114 ff. [Babbitt's note]
[34] German physican and writer (1849–1923).

to say, yet the restrictive element predominated. A modern Boileau, if he were to be effective, would have to take up in himself the main results of the great expansion of the last century, but he would be primarily concerned, not with embracing the universe in the vast affirmation of love, but with making keen and crisp discriminations between different degrees of merit or demerit. He would also feel in his own way that hatred with which Boileau said he had been inspired from the age of fifteen—the hatred of a stupid book; and he would not lack material on which to exercise it. In other words, the age offers an opening for satire; but it must be constructive satire, satire that implies standards and is "purified," as Boileau claims of his own, "by a ray of good sense." Nothing could be more inspiriting than some twentieth-century equivalent for those first satires * of Boileau when the bad authors went down before his epigrams like the suitors before the shafts of Odysseus.

IV

. . . Still a discipline in facts and in scientific and historic method is no equivalent for a true humanistic discipline. France in particular will suffer an irreparable loss if the new education results in a loosening or severing of the bond that connects it with its great humanistic past. A literal return to this past or to the past in general is, I have said, out of the question. We must have standards and select, but it must be on different principles. No poet, for example, has treated the problem of selection, which means in practice the problem of the freedom of the will, more profoundly than Dante. Yet Dante could scarcely have conceived of a selection entirely independent of two outer standards—the Pope in matters spiritual, the Emperor in matters temporal.** Nowadays if we have standards they must be inner standards, and therefore, as I have said, our problem has more in common with the problem as it presented itself to Socrates and the sophists. The great effort of Socrates, we are told, was to recover that firm foundation for human life which a misuse of the new intellectual spirit was rendering impossible.† To the excessive mental suppleness of the sophists there is often added to-day an undue emotional pliancy. If some remedy is not found the modern will, like the ancient Greek world, become the prey of its sophists. It will progress, not as our humanitarians would have us believe towards "some far-off divine event," but towards a decadent imperialism. What principle can set bounds to all this intellectual and emotional expansiveness? In the words of Cardinal Newman "What must be the face-to-face antagonist by which to withstand and baffle the fierce energy of passion and the all-corroding, all-dissolving energy of the intellect"—what he calls elsewhere "the wild living intellect of man"? The reply would seem to be that this face-to-face antagonist will be found, if at all, not in a form of authority which has become impos-

* Especially the ninth satire which has been termed "a martyrology of bad books and bad authors," and which M. Lanson calls a "terrible and admirable slaughter of reputations." [Babbitt's note]
** See especially his De Monarchia. [Babbitt's note]
† See Arnold's Speech at Eton in Mixed Essays. [Babbitt's note]

sible for so many moderns, but in the intuition of something at least as
living as the intellect, which, in exact proportion as it is perceived, imposes,
not merely on the intellect, but on man's whole being a controlling purpose. The world has been moving for some time past towards an entirely
different order of intuitions, and in a philosophy like that of M. Bergson
the pace has become headlong. I have, therefore, in my discussion of
critical standards put considerable emphasis on a thinker like Emerson,
who has a thoroughly modern view of authority, in some respects too
modern a view as I have tried to show, and is yet intuitive of the One
rather than of the Many.

In Emerson's study at Concord, which remains as at the time of his
death, almost the first object that meets one's eyes to the right on entering is a portrait of Sainte-Beuve. Emerson is said to have looked on this
portrait as a special treasure. There is scarcely a single mention of Sainte-
Beuve in Emerson's writings, and it is interesting to be able to connect
even thus superficially men so different as the great doctor of relativity and
the philosopher of the oversoul. The "Causeries du Lundi" and a book
like "Representative Men" are at the opposite poles of nineteenth-century
criticism; yet for this very reason and in spite of his humanitarian illusions,—in spite, we may add, of his curiously defective feeling for the formal side of art,—Emerson is the necessary corrective of Sainte-Beuve, who
has infinite breadth and flexibility, but is lacking in elevation. This lack
of elevation in Sainte-Beuve is not an accidental defect, but, as I have
tried to show, bears a direct relation to his naturalistic method. The inadequacy of naturalism has been even more manifest in recent criticism.
Sainte-Beuve himself maintained some balance between his regard for
traditional standards and his aspiration towards wider sympathy and knowledge. This balance has not been preserved by his successors. Knowledge
pursued as an end in itself and unsubordinated to any principle of judgment has degenerated into the narrowness of the specialist or into dillet-
tanteism. A too exclusive emphasis on breadth and keenness of sympathy
has led to the excesses of the impressionist. I have quoted Sainte-Beuve's
description of the critics of the First Empire as the "small change" of
Boileau. If the critics of to-day are to be anything more than the small
change of Sainte-Beuve—or rather of one side of Sainte-Beuve—they need
to cultivate, as a counterpoise to their use of the historical and biographical
method, a feeling for absolute values; in short, they need to supplement
Sainte-Beuve by what is best in a writer like Emerson. The point may
be illustrated by two passages, each impressive in its own way.

The first passage is from the end of "Port-Royal" where Sainte-Beuve
is commenting on his own efforts to attain the truth: "How little we can
do after all! How bounded is our gaze—how much it resembles a pale
torch lit up for a moment in the midst of a vast night! And how impotent
even he feels who has most at heart the knowing of his object, who has
made it his dearest ambition to grasp it, and his greatest pride to paint
it—how impotent he feels and how inferior to his task on the day when,
this task being almost terminated and the result obtained, the intoxication

of his strength dies away, when the final exhaustion and inevitable disgust seize upon him, and he perceives in his turn that he is only one of the most fugitive of illusions in the bosom of the infinite illusion!"

This sense of universal flux and relativity can by itself result only in what I have called elsewhere a false disillusion, the disillusion of decadence. But there is another type of disillusion: the perception of unity may become so intense that everything else seems unreal by comparison. To illustrate this, we may turn to Emerson. "There is," he says, "no chance and no anarchy in the universe. All is system and gradation. Every god is there sitting in his sphere. The young mortal enters the hall of the firmament; there he is alone with them alone, they pouring on him benedictions and gifts and beckoning him up to their thrones. On the instant and incessantly fall snowstorms of illusions. He fancies himself in a vast crowd which sways this way and that and whose movements and doings he must obey. . . . Every moment new changes and new showers of deceptions to baffle and distract him. And when by and by for an instant the air clears and the cloud lifts for a little, there are the gods still sitting around him on their thrones—they alone with him alone."

In passages like this Emerson furnishes some hint of how it is possible to accept the doctrine of relativity without loss of one's feeling for absolute values, and without allowing one's self to be devoured by the sense of illusion, as Amiel [35] was and Sainte-Beuve would have been if he had not found a sort of oblivion in unremitting toil. So far as Emerson does this, he aids criticism in its search for inner standards to take the place of the outer standards it has lost; he helps it to see in the present anarchy the potentialities of a higher order. What we need, he says, is a "coat woven of elastic steel," a critical canon, in short, that will restore to its rights the masculine judgment but without dogmatic narrowness. With such a canon, criticism might still cultivate the invaluable feminine virtues—it might be comprehensive and sympathetic without at the same time being invertebrate and gelatinous.

Our ideal critic, then, would need to combine the breadth and versatility and sense of differences of a Sainte-Beuve with the elevation and insight and sense of unity of an Emerson. It might be prudent to add of this critic in particular what Emerson has said of man in general, that he is a golden impossibility. But even though the full attainment of our standard should prove impossible, some progress might at least be made towards tempering with judgment the all-pervading impressionism of contemporary literature and life.

[35] Henri-Frédéric Amiel (1821–1881), French literary critic.

T. S. ELIOT

HAMLET AND HIS PROBLEMS [1]
(1919)

FEW CRITICS have even admitted that *Hamlet* the play is the primary problem, and Hamlet the character only secondary. And Hamlet the character has had an especial temptation for that most dangerous type of critic; the critic with a mind which is naturally of the creative order, but which through some weakness in creative power exercises itself in criticism instead. These minds often find in Hamlet a vicarious existence for their own artistic realization. Such a mind had Goethe, who made of Hamlet a Werther; and such had Coleridge, who made of Hamlet a Coleridge; and probably neither of these men in writing about Hamlet remembered that his first business was to study a work of art. The kind of criticism that Goethe and Coleridge produced, in writing of Hamlet, is the most misleading kind possible. For they both possessed unquestionable critical insight, and both make their critical aberrations the more plausible by the substitution—of their own Hamlet for Shakespeare's—which their creative gift effects. We should be thankful that Walter Pater did not fix his attention on this play.

Two writers of our own time, Mr. J. M. Robertson and Professor Stoll of the University of Minnesota, have issued small books which can be praised for moving in the other direction.[2] Mr. Stoll performs a service in recalling to our attention the labours of the critics of the seventeenth and eighteenth centuries,* observing that

> "they knew less about psychology than more recent Hamlet critics, but they were nearer in spirit to Shakespeare's art; and as they insisted on the importance of the effect of the whole rather than on the importance of the leading character, they were nearer, in their old-fashioned way, to the secret of dramatic art in general."

Qua work of art, the work of art cannot be interpreted; there is nothing to interpret; we can only criticise it according to standards, in comparison to other works of art; and for "interpretation" the chief task is the presentation of relevant historical facts which the reader is not assumed to know. Mr. Robertson points out, very pertinently, how critics have

---

* I have never, by the way, seen a cogent refutation of Thomas Rymer's objections to *Othello*. [Eliot's note]

[1] From *Selected Essays: 1917–1932* (New York, 1932; new edition with additional essays, 1950).

[2] John Mackinnon Robertson (1856–1933) published *Elizabethan Literature* in 1914 and *The Problem of Hamlet* in 1920. Elmer Edgar Stoll (1874–   ) published his *Hamlet, an Historical and Comparative Study* in 1919.

failed in their "interpretation" of *Hamlet* by ignoring what ought to be very obvious; that *Hamlet* is a stratification, that it represents the efforts of a series of men, each making what he could out of the work of his predecessors. The *Hamlet* of Shakespeare will appear to us very differently if, instead of treating the whole action of the play as due to Shakespeare's design, we perceive his *Hamlet* to be superposed upon much cruder material which persists even in the final form.

We know that there was an older play by Thomas Kyd,[3] that extraordinary dramatic (if not poetic) genius who was in all probability the author of two plays so dissimilar as *The Spanish Tragedy* and *Arden of Feversham*; and what this play was like we can guess from three clues: from *The Spanish Tragedy* itself, from the tale of Belleforest upon which Kyd's *Hamlet* must have been based, and from a version acted in Germany in Shakespeare's lifetime which bears strong evidence of having been adapted from the earlier, not from the later, play. From these three sources it is clear that in the earlier play the motive was a revenge-motive simply; that the action or delay is caused, as in *The Spanish Tragedy*, solely by the difficulty of assassinating a monarch surrounded by guards; and that the "madness" of Hamlet was feigned in order to escape suspicion, and successfully. In the final play of Shakespeare, on the other hand, there is a motive which is more important than that of revenge, and which explicitly "blunts" the latter; the delay in revenge is unexplained on grounds of necessity or expediency; and the effect of the "madness" is not to lull but to arouse the king's suspicion. The alteration is not complete enough, however, to be convincing. Furthermore, there are verbal parallels so close to *The Spanish Tragedy* as to leave no doubt that in places Shakespeare was merely *revising* the text of Kyd. And finally there are unexplained scenes—the Polonius-Laertes and the Polonius-Reynaldo scenes —for which there is little excuse; these scenes are not in the verse style of Kyd, and not beyond doubt in the style of Shakespeare. These Mr. Robertson believes to be scenes in the original play of Kyd reworked by a third hand, perhaps Chapman, before Shakespeare touched the play. And he concludes, with very strong show of reason, that the original play of Kyd was, like certain other revenge plays, in two parts of five acts each. The upshot of Mr. Robertson's examination is, we believe, irrefragable: that Shakespeare's *Hamlet*, so far as it is Shakespeare's, is a play dealing with the effect of a mother's guilt upon her son, and that Shakespeare was unable to impose this motive successfully upon the "intractable" material of the old play.

Of the intractability there can be no doubt. So far from being Shakespeare's masterpiece, the play is most certainly an artistic failure. In several ways the play is puzzling, and disquieting as is none of the others. Of all the plays it is the longest and is possibly the one on which Shakespeare spent most pains; and yet he has left in it superfluous and inconsistent scenes which even hasty revision should have noticed. The versification is variable. Lines like

[3] British dramatist (1558–1594).

> *Look, the morn, in russet mantle clad,*
> *Walks o'er the dew of yon high eastern hill,*

are of the Shakespeare of *Romeo and Juliet*. The lines in Act v, ch. ii,

> *Sir, in my heart there was a kind of fighting*
> *That would not let me sleep . . .*
> *Up from my cabin,*
> *My sea-gown scarf'd about me, in the dark*
> *Grop'd I to find out them: had my desire;*
> *Finger'd their packet;*

are of his mature period. Both workmanship and thought are in an unstable position. We are surely justified in attributing the play, with that
other profoundly interesting play of "intractable" material and astonishing
versification, *Measure for Measure*, to a period of crisis, after which follow the tragic successes which culminate in *Coriolanus*. *Coriolanus* may
be not as "interesting" as *Hamlet*, but it is, with *Antony and Cleopatra*,
Shakespeare's most assured artistic success. And probably more people have
thought *Hamlet* a work of art because they found it interesting, than
have found it interesting because it is a work of art. It is the "Mona Lisa"
of literature.

The grounds of *Hamlet's* failure are not immediately obvious. Mr.
Robertson is undoubtedly correct in concluding that the essential emotion
of the play is the feeling of a son towards a guilty mother:

> "[Hamlet's] tone is that of one who has suffered tortures on the score
> of his mother's degradation. . . . The guilt of a mother is an almost
> intolerable motive for drama, but it had to be maintained and empha-
> sized to supply a psychological solution, or rather a hint of one."

This, however, is by no means the whole story. It is not merely the
"guilt of a mother" that cannot be handled as Shakespeare handled the
suspicion of Othello, the infatuation of Antony, or the pride of Coriolanus. The subject might conceivably have expanded into a tragedy like
these, intelligible, self-complete, in the sunlight. *Hamlet*, like the sonnets,
is full of some stuff that the writer could not drag to light, contemplate,
or manipulate into art. And when we search for this feeling, we find it,
as in the sonnets, very difficult to localize. You cannot point to it in the
speeches; indeed, if you examine the two famous soliloquies you see the
versification of Shakespeare, but a content which might be claimed by
another, perhaps by the author of the *Revenge of Bussy d'Ambois*,[4] Act v,
sc. i. We find Shakespeare's Hamlet not in the action, not in any quotations that we might select, so much as in an unmistakable tone which is
unmistakably not in the earlier play.

The only way of expressing emotion in the form of art is by finding an
"objective correlative"; in other words, a set of objects, a situation, a chain

---

[4] By George Chapman. Published in 1607.

of events which shall be the formula of that *particular* emotion; such that
when the external facts, which must terminate in sensory experience, are
given, the emotion is immediately evoked. If you examine any of Shakespeare's more successful tragedies, you will find this exact equivalence;
you will find that the state of mind of Lady Macbeth walking in her
sleep has been communicated to you by a skilful accumulation of imagined sensory impressions; the words of Macbeth on hearing of his wife's
death strike us as if, given the sequence of events, these words were automatically released by the last event in the series. The artistic "inevitability"
lies in this complete adequacy of the external to the emotion; and this is
precisely what is deficient in *Hamlet*. Hamlet (the man) is dominated by
an emotion which is inexpressible, because it is in *excess* of the facts as
they appear. And the supposed identity of Hamlet with his author is
genuine to this point: that Hamlet's bafflement at the absence of objective equivalent to his feelings is a prolongation of the bafflement of his
creator in the face of his artistic problem. Hamlet is up against the difficulty that his disgust is occasioned by his mother, but that his mother is
not an adequate equivalent for it; his disgust envelops and exceeds her.
It is thus a feeling which he cannot understand; he cannot objectify it,
and it therefore remains to poison life and obstruct action. None of the
possible actions can satisfy it; and nothing that Shakespeare can do with
the plot can express Hamlet for him. And it must be noticed that the very
nature of the *données*[5] of the problem precludes objective equivalence. To
have heightened the criminality of Gertrude would have been to provide
the formula for a totally different emotion in Hamlet; it is just *because*
her character is so negative and insignificant that she arouses in Hamlet
the feeling which she is incapable of representing.

The "madness" of Hamlet lay to Shakespeare's hand; in the earlier play
a simple ruse, and to the end, we may presume, understood as a ruse by
the audience. For Shakespeare it is less than madness and more than
feigned. The levity of Hamlet, his repetition of phrase, his puns, are not
part of a deliberate plan of dissimulation, but a form of emotional relief.
In the character Hamlet it is the buffoonery of an emotion which can
find no outlet in action; in the dramatist it is the buffoonery of an emotion
which he cannot express in art. The intense feeling, ecstatic or terrible,
without an object or exceeding its object, is something which every person of sensibility has known; it is doubtless a subject of study for patholo-
gists. It often occurs in adolescence: the ordinary person puts these feelings to sleep, or trims down his feelings to fit the business world; the
artist keeps them alive by his ability to intensify the world to his emotions.
The Hamlet of Laforgue is an adolescent; the Hamlet of Shakespeare is
not, he has not that explanation and excuse. We must simply admit that
here Shakespeare tackled a problem which proved too much for him. Why
he attempted it at all is an insoluble puzzle; under compulsion of what
experience he attempted to express the inexpressibly horrible, we cannot
ever know. We need a great many facts in his biography; and we should

[5] "ideas" or "themes." Literally, "that which is given."

'like to know whether, and when, and after or at the same time as what personal experience, he read Montaigne, II. xii, *Apologie de Raimond Sebond*.[6] We should have, finally, to know something which is by hypothesis unknowable, for we assume it to be an experience which, in the manner indicated, exceeded the facts. We should have to understand things which Shakespeare did not understand himself.

[6] Michel de Montaigne (1533–1592), French essayist. The *Apologie* is to be found in the *Essais* of Montaigne.

T. S. ELIOT

THE METAPHYSICAL POETS [1]
(1921)

BY COLLECTING these poems * from the work of a generation more often named than read, and more often read than profitably studied, Professor Grierson has rendered a service of some importance. Certainly the reader will meet with many poems already preserved in other anthologies, at the same time that he discovers poems such as those of Aurelian Townshend [2] or Lord Herbert of Cherbury [3] here included. But the function of such an anthology as this is neither that of Professor Saintsbury's [4] admirable edition of Caroline poets nor that of the *Oxford Book of English Verse*. Mr. Grierson's book is in itself a piece of criticism and a provocation of criticism; and we think that he was right in including so many poems of Donne, elsewhere (though not in many editions) accessible, as documents in the case of "metaphysical poetry." The phrase has long done duty as a term of abuse or as the label of a quaint and pleasant taste. The question is to what extent the so-called metaphysicals formed a school (in our own time we should say a "movement"), and how far this so-called school or movement is a digression from the main current.

Not only is it extremely difficult to define metaphysical poetry, but difficult to decide what poets practise it and in which of their verses. The poetry of Donne (to whom Marvell and Bishop King are sometimes nearer than any of the other authors) is late Elizabethan, its feeling often very close to that of Chapman. The "courtly" poetry is derivative from Jonson, who borrowed liberally from the Latin; it expires in the next century with the sentiment and witticism of Prior. There is finally the devotional verse of Herbert, Vaughan, and Crashaw (echoed long after by Christina Rossetti and Francis Thompson); Crashaw, sometimes more profound and less sectarian than the others, has a quality which returns through the Elizabethan period to the early Italians. It is difficult to find any precise use of metaphor, simile, or other conceit, which is common to all the poets and at the same time important enough as an element of style to isolate these poets as a group. Donne, and often Cowley, employ a device which is sometimes considered characteristically "metaphysical"; the elaboration

---

* *Metaphysical Lyrics and Poems of the Seventeenth Century:* Donne to Butler. Selected and edited, with an Essay, by Herbert J. C. Grierson (Oxford: Clarendon Press. London: Milford). [Eliot's note]
[1] From *Selected Essays: 1917–1932* (New York, 1932; reprinted with additional essays in 1950).
[2] Seventeenth-century English poet.
[3] Edward, Baron Herbert of Cherbury (1583–1648), English poet and philosopher.
[4] George Saintsbury (1845–1933), English literary critic.

(contrasted with the condensation) of a figure of speech to the farthest stage to which ingenuity can carry it. Thus Cowley develops the commonplace comparison of the world to a chess-board through long stanzas (To Destiny), and Donne, with more grace, in *A Valediction*, the comparison of two lovers to a pair of compasses. But elsewhere we find, instead of the mere explication of the content of a comparison, a development by rapid association of thought which requires considerable agility on the part of the reader.

> *On a round ball*
> *A workman that hath copies by, can lay*
> *An Europe, Afrique, and an Asia*
> *And Quickly make that, which was nothing, All,*
>   *So doth each teare,*
>   *Which thee doth weare,*
> *A globe, yea, world by that impression grow,*
> *Till thy tears mixt with mine doe overflow*
> *This world, by waters sent from thee, my heaven dissolved so.*

Here we find at least two connexions which are not implicit in the first figure, but are forced upon it by the poet: from the geographer's globe to the tear, and the tear to the deluge. On the other hand, some of Donne's most successful and characteristic effects are secured by brief words and sudden contrasts:

> *A bracelet of bright hair about the bone,*

where the most powerful effect is produced by the sudden contrast of associations of "bright hair" and of "bone." This telescoping of images and multiplied associations is characteristic of the phrase of some of the dramatists of the period which Donne knew: not to mention Shakespeare, it is frequent in Middleton, Webster, and Tourneur, and is one of the sources of the vitality of their language.

Johnson, who employed the term "metaphysical poets," apparently having Donne, Cleveland, and Cowley chiefly in mind, remarks of them that "the most heterogeneous ideas are yoked by violence together." The force of this impeachment lies in the failure of the conjunction, the fact that often the ideas are yoked but not united; and if we are to judge of styles of poetry by their abuse, enough examples may be found in Cleveland to justify Johnson's condemnation. But a degree of heterogeneity of material compelled into unity by the operation of the poet's mind is omnipresent in poetry. We need not select for illustration such a line as:

> *Notre âme est un trois-mâts cherchant son Icarie;* [5]

we may find it in some of the best lines of Johnson himself (*The Vanity of Human Wishes*):

[5] "Our soul is a three-master seeking its Icarus."

> *His fate was destined to a barren strand,*
> *A petty fortress, and a dubious hand;*
> *He left a name at which the world grew pale,*
> *To point a moral, or adorn a tale.*

where the effect is due to a contrast of ideas, different in degree but the same in principle, as that which Johnson mildly reprehended. And in one of the finest poems of the age (a poem which could not have been written in any other age), the *Exequy* of Bishop King, the extended comparison is used with perfect success: the idea and the simile become one, in the passage in which the Bishop illustrates his impatience to see his dead wife, under the figure of a journey:

> *Stay for me there; I will not faile*
> *To meet thee in that hollow Vale.*
> *And think not much of my delay;*
> *I am already on the way,*
> *And follow thee with all the speed*
> *Desire can make, or sorrows breed.*
> *Each minute is a short degree,*
> *And ev'ry houre a step towards thee.*
> *At night when I betake to rest,*
> *Next morn I rise nearer my West*
> *Of life, almost by eight houres sail,*
> *Than when sleep breath'd his drowsy gale. . . .*
> *But heark! My Pulse, like a soft Drum*
> *Beats my approach, tells Thee I come;*
> *And slow howere my marches be,*
> *I shall at last sit down by Thee.*

(In the last few lines there is that effect of terror which is several times attained by one of Bishop King's admirers, Edgar Poe.) Again, we may justly take these quatrains from Lord Herbert's Ode, stanzas which would, we think, be immediately pronounced to be of the metaphysical school:

> *So when from hence we shall be gone,*
> *And be no more, nor you, nor I,*
> *As one another's mystery,*
> *Each shall be both, yet both but one.*
>
> *This said, in her up-lifted face,*
> *Her eyes, which did that beauty crown,*
> *Were like two starrs, that having faln down,*
> *Look up again to find their place:*
>
> *While such a moveless silent peace*
> *Did seize on their becalmed sense,*
> *One would have thought some influence*
> *Their ravished spirits did possess.*

There is nothing in these lines (with the possible exception of the stars, a simile not at once grasped, but lovely and justified) which fits Johnson's

general observations on the metaphysical poets in his essay on Cowley. A
good deal resides in the richness of association which is at the same time
borrowed from and given to the word "becalmed"; but the meaning is clear,
the language simple and elegant. It is to be observed that the language of
these poets is as a rule simple and pure; in the verse of George Herbert
this simplicity is carried as far as it can go—a simplicity emulated without
success by numerous modern poets. The *structure* of the sentences, on the
other hand, is sometimes far from simple, but this is not a vice; it is a
fidelity to thought and feeling. The effect, at its best, is far less artificial
than that of an ode by Gray. And as this fidelity induces variety of thought
and feeling, so it induces variety of music. We doubt whether, in the
eighteenth century, could be found two poems in nominally the same
metre, so dissimilar as Marvell's *Coy Mistress* and Crashaw's *Saint Teresa*;
the one producing an effect of great speed by the use of short syllables, and
the other an ecclesiastical solemnity by the use of long ones:

> *Love, thou art absolute sole lord*
> *Of life and death.*

If so shrewd and sensitive (though so limited) a critic as Johnson failed
to define metaphysical poetry by its faults, it is worth while to inquire
whether we may not have more success by adopting the opposite method:
by assuming that the poets of the seventeenth century (up to the Revolution) were the direct and normal development of the precedent age; and,
without prejudicing their case by the adjective "metaphysical," consider
whether their virtue was not something permanently valuable, which subsequently disappeared, but ought not to have disappeared. Johnson has
hit, perhaps by accident, on one of their peculiarities, when he observes
that "their attempts were always analytic"; he would not agree that, after
the dissociation, they put the material together again in a new unity.

It is certain that the dramatic verse of the later Elizabethan and early
Jacobean poets expresses a degree of development of sensibility which is
not found in any of the prose, good as it often is. If we except Marlowe, a
man of prodigious intelligence, these dramatists were directly or indirectly
(it is at least a tenable theory) affected by Montaigne. Even if we except
also Jonson and Chapman, these two were notably erudite, and were notably men who incorporated their erudition into their sensibility: their
mode of feeling was directly and freshly altered by their reading and
thought. In Chapman especially there is a direct sensuous apprehension of
thought, or a recreation of thought into feeling, which is exactly what we
find in Donne:

> *in this one thing, all the discipline*
> *Of manners and of manhood is contained;*
> *A man to join himself with th' Universe*
> *In his main sway, and make in all things fit*
> *One with that All, and go on, round as it;*
> *Not plucking from the whole his wretched part,*

> *And into straits, or into nought revert,*
> *Wishing the complete Universe might be*
> *Subject to such a rag of it as he;*
> *But to consider great Necessity.*

We compare this with some modern passage:

> *No, when the fight begins within himself,*
> *A man's worth something. God stoops o'er his head,*
> *Satan looks up between his feet—both tug—*
> *He's left, himself, i' the middle; the soul wakes*
> *And grows. Prolong that battle through his life!*

It is perhaps somewhat less fair, though very tempting (as both poets are concerned with the perpetuation of love by offspring), to compare with the stanzas already quoted from Lord Herbert's Ode the following from Tennyson:

> *One walked between his wife and child,*
> *With measured footfall firm and mild,*
> *And now and then he gravely smiled.*
> *The prudent partner of his blood*
> *Leaned on him, faithful, gentle, good,*
> *Wearing the rose of womanhood.*
> *And in their double love secure,*
> *The little maiden walked demure,*
> *Pacing with downward eyelids pure.*
> *These three made unity so sweet,*
> *My frozen heart began to beat,*
> *Remembering its ancient heat.*

The difference is not a simple difference of degree between poets. It is something which had happened to the mind of England between the time of Donne or Lord Herbert of Cherbury and the time of Tennyson and Browning; it is the difference between the intellectual poet and the reflective poet. Tennyson and Browning are poets, and they think; but they do not feel their thought as immediately as the odour of a rose. A thought to Donne was an experience; it modified his sensibility. When a poet's mind is perfectly equipped for its work, it is constantly amalgamating disparate experience; the ordinary man's experience is chaotic, irregular, fragmentary. The latter falls in love, or reads Spinoza, and these two experiences have nothing to do with each other, or with the noise of the typewriter or the smell of cooking; in the mind of the poet these experiences are always forming new wholes.

We may express the difference by the following theory: The poets of the seventeenth century, the successors of the dramatists of the sixteenth, possessed a mechanism of sensibility which could devour any kind of experience. They are simple, artificial, difficult, or fantastic, as their predecessors were; no less nor more than Dante, Guido Cavalcanti, Guinizelli, or

Cino.[6] In the seventeenth century a dissociation of sensibility set in, from which we have never recovered; and this dissociation, as is natural, was aggravated by the influence of the two most powerful poets of the century, Milton and Dryden. Each of these men performed certain poetic functions so magnificently well that the magnitude of the effect concealed the absence of others. The language went on and in some respects improved; the best verse of Collins, Gray, Johnson, and even Goldsmith satisfies some of our fastidious demands better than that of Donne or Marvell or King. But while the language became more refined, the feeling became more crude. The feeling, the sensibility, expressed in the *Country Church-yard* (to say nothing of Tennyson and Browning) is cruder than that in the *Coy Mistress.*

The second effect of the influence of Milton and Dryden followed from the first, and was therefore slow in manifestation. The sentimental age began early in the eighteenth century, and continued. The poets revolted against the ratiocinative, the descriptive; they thought and felt by fits, unbalanced; they reflected. In one or two passages of Shelley's *Triumph of Life,* in the second *Hyperion,* there are traces of a struggle toward unification of sensibility. But Keats and Shelley died, and Tennyson and Browning ruminated.

After this brief exposition of a theory—too brief, perhaps, to carry conviction—we may ask, what would have been the fate of the "metaphysical" had the current of poetry descended in a direct line from them, as it descended in a direct line to them? They would not, certainly, be classified as metaphysical. The possible interests of a poet are unlimited; the more intelligent he is the better; the more intelligent he is the more likely that he will have interests: our only condition is that he turn them into poetry, and not merely meditate on them poetically. A philosophical theory which has entered into poetry is established, for its truth or falsity in one sense ceases to matter, and its truth in another sense is proved. The poets in question have, like other poets, various faults. But they were, at best, engaged in the task of trying to find the verbal equivalent for states of mind and feeling. And this means both that they are more mature, and that they wear better, than later poets of certainly not less literary ability.

It is not a permanent necessity that poets should be interested in philosophy, or in any other subject. We can only say that it appears likely that poets in our civilization, as it exists at present, must be *difficult.* Our civilization comprehends great variety and complexity, and this variety and complexity, playing upon a refined sensibility, must produce various and complex results. The poet must become more and more comprehensive, more allusive, more indirect, in order to force, to dislocate if necessary, language into his meaning. (A brilliant and extreme statement of this view, with which it is not requisite to associate oneself, is that of M. Jean Epstein,[7] *La Poésie d'aujourd-hui.*) Hence we get something which looks

---

[6] Guido Cavalcanti (*ca.* 1252–1300), Guido Guinizelli (*ca.* 1240–1276), and Cino Da Pistoia (1270–1336) were among the very earliest Italian poets.
[7] Twentieth-century French poet and critic.

very much like the conceit—we get, in fact, a method curiously similar to that of the "metaphysical poets," similar also in its use of obscure words and of simple phrasing.

> O géraniums diaphanes, guerroyeurs sortilèges,
> Sacrilèges monomanes!
> Emballages, dévergondages, douches! O pressoirs
> Des vendanges des grands soirs!
> Layettes aux abois,
> Thyrses au fond des bois!
> Transfusions, représailles,
> Relevailles, compresses et l'éternal potion,
> Angélus! n'en pouvoir plus
> De débâcles nuptiales! de débâcles nuptiales! [8]

The same poet could write also simply:

> Elle est bien loin, elle pleure,
> Le grand vent se lamente aussi . . .[9]

Jules Laforgue,[10] and Tristan Corbière [11] in many of his poems, are nearer to the "school of Donne" than any modern English poet. But poets more classical than they have the same essential quality of transmuting ideas into sensations, of transforming an observation into a state of mind.

> Pour l'enfant, amoureux de cartes et d'estampes,
> L'univers et égal à son vaste appétit.
> Ah, que le monde est grand à la clarté des lampes!
> Aux yeux du souvenir que le monde est petit! [12]

In French literature the great master of the seventeenth century—Racine— and the great master of the nineteenth—Baudelaire—are in some ways more like each other than they are like any one else. The greatest two masters of diction are also the greatest two psychologists, the most curious explorers of the soul. It is interesting to speculate whether it is not a misfortune that two of the greatest masters of diction in our language, Milton and Dryden, triumph with a dazzling disregard of the soul. If we continued to produce Miltons and Drydens it might not so much matter, but as things are it is a pity that English poetry has remained so incomplete.

[8] "O translucent geraniums, magic warriors, crazed and sacrilegious! Packages, shameless acts, douches! O wine-presses of the grape-gathering of the majestic evenings! Layettes at bay, Thyrsus at the bottom of the wood! Transfusions, reprisals, elevating, compresses, and the eternal potion. Angelus! to be exhausted with nuptial disasters, with nuptial disasters!"
[9] "She is far away, she weeps,
The great wind laments also . . ."
[10] French symbolist poet (1860–1887).
[11] French symbolist poet (1845–1875).
[12] "For the child, lover of cards and stamps,
The universe is equal to his vast appetite.
Ah, how large the world is by the light of the lamps!
To the eyes of the memory, how small the world is!"

Those who object to the "artificiality" of Milton or Dryden sometimes tell us to "look into our hearts and write." But that is not looking deep enough; Racine or Donne looked into a good deal more than the heart. One must look into the cerebral cortex, the nervous system, and the digestive tracts.

May we not conclude, then, that Donne, Crashaw, Vaughan, Herbert and Lord Herbert, Marvell, King, Cowley at his best, are in the direct current of English poetry, and that their faults should be reprimanded by this standard rather than coddled by antiquarian affection? They have been enough praised in terms which are implicit limitations because they are "metaphysical" or "witty," "quaint" or "obscure," though at their best they have not these attributes more than other serious poets. On the other hand, we must not reject the criticism of Johnson (a dangerous person to disagree with) without having mastered it, without having assimilated the Johnsonian canons of taste. In reading the celebrated passage in his essay on Cowley we must remember that by wit he clearly means something more serious than we usually mean today; in his criticism of their versification we must remember in what a narrow discipline he was trained, but also how well trained; we must remember that Johnson tortures chiefly the chief offenders, Cowley and Cleveland. It would be a fruitful work, and one requiring a substantial book, to break up the classification of Johnson (for there has been none since) and exhibit these poets in all their difference of kind and of degree, from the massive music of Donne to the faint, pleasing tinkle of Aurelian Townshend—whose *Dialogue between a Pilgrim and Time* is one of the few regrettable omissions from the excellent anthology of Professor Grierson.

VAN WYCK BROOKS

From SKETCHES IN CRITICISM [1]

THE CRITICAL MOVEMENT IN AMERICA

(1921)

It was only the other day that America first came in for its effective share of self-criticism. The critical movement in America happened, as it were, overnight; and the critic in this country is still so new a type that we cannot be surprised if he is regarded as an undesirable alien, even a traitor. There is nothing else in all modern history like the unanimity of praise and confidence with which, by its passengers, the American Ship of State was launched and manned. In all our long nineteenth-century past, there was scarcely a breath of dissent, doubt, or censure: the semi-outlaw Whitman's *Democratic Vistas* was almost unique in this regard, for Emerson's and Lowell's strictures were lost in the flood of their social optimism. No wonder we became the most complacent of peoples. No wonder the tide of criticism rose at last.

One thinks of all this as one considers, for instance, such an alien point of reference as John Ruskin. To most of us, no doubt, Ruskin has always seemed a normal and familiar possession. Yet, as one reflects on his career, the thought comes to one's mind: How different this man was from anything the America of his day could have produced! Hear, for example, what Mr. Masefield recently said of him: "Ruskin, looking out upon his native land some eighty years ago, decided that he could not believe in it, that there was nothing spiritual there which he could trust, nor human work being done which he could share." Imagine a nineteenth-century American giving utterance to such a sentiment, the sentiment from which Ruskin's work sprang! Yet this was surely the animating sentiment of the greatest English literature of the century, even of Charles Dickens: who but Macaulay, of all the writers of England, was not filled, as regards the future of his people, with more or less fundamental doubts? And meanwhile the writers of America chanted a unanimous hymn to progress. They were happy, they were hopeful. They agreed, or seemed to agree, with the famous utterance of Edward Everett: [2] "Our government is in its theory perfect, and in its operation it is perfect also. Thus we have solved the great problem in human affairs." Was this because the American life of their epoch was finer and more wholesome than English life? Because it contained a greater spiritual promise? Few in our generation would affirm this. We know too well how fully justified were most of the Euro-

[1] New York, 1921.
[2] American political figure, orator, and literary critic, editor of the *North American Review* (1794–1865).

pean travelers' reflections on our old social life—which used to cause such resentment in American breasts: they were not malignant, those travelers' reflections, any more than the comments of the European critics and scholars—Ruskin himself, for instance—who looked upon "Americanism" as a poisonous growth that might well infect and destroy all civilization. And as we observe the complacency to which our national optimism gave birth, we ask ourselves whether this optimism was ever a symptom of health, whether it was not indeed the symptom of a great evil: the loss of a clear sense of the true values of life.

It is certain, in any case, that our criticism has suffered from the obvious necessity of making up for much lost time. We do not understand criticism, and this is because we have had so little of it. We have had no candid friends of our own race, no "national conscience," in short, such as every European people has had, for England is not unique in this respect: and, consequently, it was difficult a few years ago for most Americans to question the belief of Mr. Meredith Nicholson,[3] for instance, that "if there is any manifestation on earth of a divine ordering of things, it is here in America." This is the sort of belief the Philistine majority in every country cherishes in its heart; it is the sort of belief that Matthew Arnold so well described as "vulgar, and not only vulgar but retarding," for retarding it surely is if, in order to go somewhere, to get somewhere, to advance, to develop, we must first have an inner conviction that we have not already arrived. If American life as we know it is indeed a manifestation of a divine ordering of things, there is nothing for us to do but to continue to manifest our divinity. But is our life divine? Is it so much better than the life of England, France, Germany, Russia that the comments of a Ruskin, a Renan,[4] a Nietzsche[5] would have been sheer impertinences on our side of the Atlantic? The prosperous middle class the world over looks upon itself and its own fatness with an overkindly eye; but America is the only modern country where, until recent years, the prosperous middle class has gone unchallenged, where the Philistines have never been aroused to a sense of their limitations. Heine[6] never permitted the Germans to forget how much they had to learn; no one was ever more outspoken than Nietzsche in regard to "what the Germans lack." The French are complacent enough; but Renan never ceased to remind them of their "incurable religious mediocrity," of "the alternations of levity and dullness, of narrow timidity and foolish temerity" which are among the features of the French mind. Arnold, Ruskin, Carlyle, as we know, kept their guns steadily trained on the weaknesses of the English character; and while Ibsen lived how many illusions in regard to their peculiar superiority were the people of Norway suffered to cherish?

Merely to mention these names is to suggest how uniformly our American fur has been rubbed the right way. For while Emerson, Lowell, Whit-

---

[3] American poet, novelist, and essayist (1866–1947).
[4] Ernest Renan (1823–1892), French historian and literary critic.
[5] Friedrich Nietzsche (1844–1900), German philosopher.
[6] Heinrich Heine (1797–1856), German poet and critic.

man deplored the imperfections of our social life, their criticism was neither sustained nor drastic. Emerson was the incarnation of optimism and lived, besides, too much in a timeless world to concern himself with a single phase of history: this was not his rôle. Lowell was so conscious of that "certain condescension in foreigners" that he could not sufficiently draw the veil over the shortcomings of his countrymen. And there was Howells, with his rosy vision of the American scene, all the more delusive because he professed an intransigent realism. There was even Henry James, whom nothing could have induced to live in America: did he not apologize in one of his prefaces for having spoken in terms of disrespect of a certain small city in Massachusetts, adding so much thereby to the ultimate obloquy of those who have since reproached our Gopher Prairies? These men, of course, were not primarily critics, and that is just the point; Thoreau was not primarily a critic; in fact, before the war we had no critics. Those who could not put up with our life in the East quietly went West, and those who could not put up with our life at all quietly went to Europe. No one stood still and spoke out; and after the Civil War, even the voices of the traveling foreigners who told the truth about many of our ways were cloaked and muffled. Everyone waited, waited, by common consent, to see how the great experiment of democracy was going to work out. We had sixty years of grace while the oracles were dumb.

We were, in a word, singularly unconscious. America "just growed"— in the manner of the British Empire perhaps, but certainly in a very different manner from England itself, or France or Germany. It grew by sheer activity, expansion, immigration, without forethought, afterthought, reflection of any kind. That is to say, since no population is ever aware of itself as a population, save perhaps in times of war, it had no governing and directing minority more conscious than the multitude, more conscious of human values, no class of thinkers who, while having no administrative authority, might yet have exercised a real authority over popular opinion, interpreting the movements of society in the light of historical principles, and arousing in those who were intelligent and articulate a just sense of what was really happening. Who knew, for instance, that America was becoming an empire, apprehended this fact in all its implications? America never "meant" to become an empire, and few Americans know, even today, really know, I mean *apprehend*, that America is an empire, with all the paraphernalia of imperialism. This change came automatically, as it were, because, contrary as it plainly was to the professed genius of the Republic, no strong, articulate minority showed the people what was taking place before their eyes. One has only to compare the feeble protests that arose throughout this country over the annexation of the Philippines with the outburst of resentment and remonstrance, of satire and impassioned poetry, evoked in England by the Boer War, to perceive the difference between a conscious and an unconscious society; and the difference only widens when we remember that imperialism in the England of those days had been for generations a deliberate national policy.

So it was that after the Civil War our social history became an illustration of what might be called a policy of indifference. The individual stood aside and let things take their course. To a large extent, this has been true of our thought from the beginning: whether optimistic, as with Emerson and Whitman, or pessimistic, as with Henry Adams and Mark Twain, it has always tended to be fatalistic. It has assumed, or tended to assume, that things were "coming out all right," because Americans are Americans, or else that things were coming out all wrong, because nothing could stop them from doing so, because human life itself is a mistake, as Mark Twain thought, or because, as Henry Adams thought, evolution is merely a matter of thermodynamics. These attitudes are all fatalistic because they beg the question of human control or deny its possibility; and together they have formed the various strands of a national tradition in which the critical intellect has played scarcely any part whatever. That America must and will be perfect just by being itself, or that America is doomed and damned: these are the two poles between which, even to this day, our public opinion oscillates. The cultivated classes are too often convinced, although they keep their opinion to themselves, that the country is already doomed and damned. The rest are equally sure, not that the country will be, but that the country already is what Mr. Nicholson calls it; and they have plainly arrived at this opinion by lowering their human standards to a point where the great values of life do not exist. Mr. Nicholson, who speaks so complacently of the "divine ordering of things" in America, also says that a "town is better advertised by enlightened sanitary ordinances duly enforced than by the number of its citizens who are acquainted with the writings of Walter Pater. If Main Street knows," he adds, "what America is all about, and bathes itself and is kind and considerate of its neighbors, why not leave the rest on the knees of the gods?" Why, indeed, if we share Mr. Nicholson's indifference to the great human values? "We do not know," he says again, "we do not know but that in some far day a prowling New Zealander, turning up a banjo and a trap-drum amid the ruins of some American college, will account them nobler instruments than the lyre and lute." But why wait for the "ruins" of this American college? The ruins are with us already if we have lost a sense of the distinction between the trap-drum and the lyre and lute.

And the sense of this distinction has been lost, too largely lost, because criticism, in all these years, has failed to keep it alive. Mr. William Allen White [7] has observed that he would like to collect the junior pessimists who are raking America with their criticism and duck them in the town-pump. One readily understands Mr. White's resentment, for he has himself gone through life without once being held up, without once being checked in his rampant career of self-congratulation over the virtues of Kansas. And Mr. White's resentment is widely shared; one constantly hears of apostles of good-Americanism who have "had about enough" of these junior pessimists. And it cannot be denied that for this resentment there exists a certain reason, for few indeed of the pessimists in question are not open to the retort that they are themselves no more essentially

[7] Author, liberal, and well-known editor of the *Emporia Gazette* (Emporia, Kansas) (1868–1944).

civilized than the civilization they attack. We are always well aware of what they hate; we are seldom aware at all of what they love, and only what they love can civilize us. This is true; yet, save for these same vipers, whose critical equipment is, one admits, defective, where else in America can we turn for criticism? The "best" magazines freely open their columns to Mr. Nicholson's and Mr. White's opinions; the "best" people, as we are led to suppose, delight in these opinions. At every adverse comment on our civilization the cry still goes up: But there is so much to be said on the other side! And no one questions this; what one asserts, and asserts, and asserts again, is that there is so much to be said on *this* side. If it were not for these vipers who have risen among us, we should all find ourselves intellectually on the level of the "man in the street" for whom Messrs. Nicholson and White are so proud to speak. The conservative reviews, as one might think, exist for the purpose of combating the radical reviews, giving aid and comfort to that false Americanism, now dominant through the world, the rise and spread of which was the nightmare of those European critics of the nineteenth century whose standards they profess to uphold.

In short, before the emergence of our critical movement, the clear sense of the great values of life had long been submerged in America. For we are obliged to take Mr. White and Mr. Nicholson at their word and assume that they really do not know the difference between the trap-drum and the lyre and lute, or between the Valley of Democracy and the Kingdom of Heaven. We are even obliged to take at their word the defenders of some pseudo-American tradition who failed to challenge Edward Bok,[8] for instance, when he adopted the word "Americanization" to describe a career that was throughout devoted, with whatever good intentions, to the vulgarization of American life. And we cannot expect that those who are color-blind to the great values of life, in the name of which criticism speaks, will see anything but animus in this criticism, or regard it as anything but insulting. This indeed would be true if our criticism were ten times more certain of its values than it is: we know that Mr. White would as readily duck a Ruskin as a Mencken. For Americans are not accustomed to plain speaking. We cherish a romantic view of our activities, and an American spade, to most of us, is not a spade at all: it is a sword, an implement of knighthood, and to call it a spade is to challenge our fondest prepossessions. The romantic soul dwells in the region of hyperbole, and its virtues are not the virtues of understatement. This fact explains the apparent censoriousness of much of our recent social criticism. Some of this criticism has really been censorious, it has been so by reaction; but much of it has only appeared censorious. If we had been accustomed to a realistic view of affairs, and a true historic sense of human values, we should have accepted this criticism and even rejoiced in it.

For we know how America appears in the eyes of the world. The Japanese poet, Mr. Yone Noguchi,[9] is the spokesman of contemporary human-

---

[8] American editor and author (1863–1930). The reference is to Bok's use of the term in the title of his autobiography, *The Americanization of Edward Bok* (1920).
[9] Japanese poet (1875–   ).

ity when he describes our country as "floating comfortably on the ocean all by itself, as if a well-fed seal or lazy iceberg." And those who have an interest in America, its true life, its true historic rôle, are aware that such a posture is a perilous posture. No doubt, in the beginning, this uncritical attitude, this attitude of uncriticised faith and hope, contributed much to our dawning civilization. A new country is obliged to affirm its existence, to believe in itself against all comers. If the America of three generations ago had seen itself as Europeans saw it, as its own cultivated minds saw it in the privacy of their souls, it would have lost heart; for with nations as with individuals nothing is more paralyzing than a premature self-consciousness. Our old writers were surely aware of all that was imperfect in our society, but they were aware also that too much cannot be expected of a new country. They saw, moreover, that America was too deeply in the grip of unusual natural forces for criticism to have much effect upon it; for, as Frederick Turner pointed out in his study of *The Frontier in American History*,[10] the development of American civilization in the nineteenth century exhibited a constant return to primitive conditions on a continually advancing frontier-line. Our social development was always beginning again *de novo* on the frontier, and this largely prevented Americans even in the settled areas from retaining a firm hold upon civilized values. And so our old writers, convinced of the futility of criticism, turned their reluctant energies in other directions. Meanwhile, with few exceptions, the immigrants from the Old World belonged to the inarticulate classes; and for them it was enough or seemed enough, that the New World afforded them opportunities, of an economic sort, which they had not possessed in the Old. We know how these immigrants expressed themselves. Such works as *The Promised Land* and *The Making of an American* contributed immensely to our national self-esteem; and, what is more to the point, in the absence of native spokesmen who might have maintained the sense of human values, they served as the final proof in American eyes that our civilization was superior in all essentials to the civilization of Europe. In this realm, the realm of self-congratulation, it never rains but it pours.

Because of these peculiar circumstances, our social history differs from that of any of the European countries. We have never conceived it as possible to shape our social life. This social life has grown and changed so rapidly, so many racial strains have merged themselves in it, so many territories have opened before it, this life has indeed existed in such a flux that the idea of molding it has scarcely entered our calculations. It was this that prevented for so long the development of criticism in America. We know how quietistic Hawthorne was regarding every prospect of social change: we know his fear, embodied in the character of Hollingsworth,[11] of tampering with "the natural order of things." A similar diffidence inhibited Mark Twain, and surely this was one of the reasons that

---

[10] Turner (1861–1932), the famous American historian, published this influential work in 1920.

[11] One of the principal characters in Hawthorne's *The Scarlet Letter*.

led Henry Adams to hide his life and restrained him from coming forward as the critic he plainly wished to be. They felt, these gifted men, that the only course for them was to stand aside and watch the American process —some in faith, others in despair, and more and more in despair, as they saw how little the process contemplated of what to them was important for civilization. For they felt that they could never shape the process, or control it in any way. Yet the longer the process continued, the more it became apparent that Americans, in so far as they were Americans who piqued themselves on their "Americanism," were ceasing to desire, were ceasing even to be able to desire, consciously and with their minds and wills, any goals in life except the goals that were placed before them by the world of trade. Yes, even to the point where their perceptions had come to rest on a purely physical plane.

But *autres temps, autres moeurs*.[12] We have nourished ourselves on hope in America, where we should have nourished ourselves on desire. Many have hoped for America, few have desired for America. And desire is the mother of intention. And desire cannot come without criticism. "It is an *idea*," as John Eglinton says, for which we wait. "Without an idea man is frivolous, dissatisfied, despicable. With an idea the long-hoarded initiatives of his nature are liberated, he strains forward to new consummations." Criticism, so silent in the past, is vocal now in America; and why should it be vocal if there were not within it a sudden faith in the ability of Americans to shape their destiny, to mold it and give it form, to ride things as things have ridden them? The division between the two great camps of modern American writers is a division between those who are still satisfied with a national state of adolescence and those who exact of America the traits and responsibilities of maturity; and if the latter appear a little rough and importunate, it is because they are obliged to shake out of a deep sleep a population that should have been kept awake by an unbroken succession of gentle proddings. The recent damming-up of our social energies, through the closing of the frontier at the West and the slackening of immigration at the East, enables us really for the first time to submit to a candid scrutiny our prepossessions in regard to property and every other fundamental issue, to desire a great and beautiful corporate life. How scattered our forces have been! We have taken pleasure, it seems, in making machines of men; and repudiating the vision of a good society, we have not discouraged our finest intellects from giving up society as a bad job and devoting to the material periphery the passion they might have devoted to human beings. Our thought has been centrifugal instead of centripetal; it has gone out to the frame, it has never fixed itself upon the picture.

The great social thinkers, the great critics have given us a sense of society as a whole, and of man as a social animal, capable of molding his environment towards a humane ideal. And Ruskin, as Lawrence Binyon [13] says, might well have taken as his motto the lines of Blake:

[12] "other times, other customs."
[13] English poet and art historian (1869–1943).

> I will not cease from mental fight,
> Nor shall my sword sleep in my hand,
> Till we have built Jerusalem
> In England's green and pleasant land.

American criticism, too, is capable of such a vision. But this is certain, American criticism will never attain its object as long as it fails to conceive, as something ever-present in its purview, the "green and pleasant land" it contemplates. The great critics have always convinced the world in spite of the prepossessions of the world; it is their ability to do so that makes these critics great and worthy of attention, for unless they speak with reasonableness and human understanding they confess in their own words that they do not possess that in the name of which they pretend to speak. No doubt, for many years in this country the critics and the unconverted public are destined to wage the blindest kind of warfare; for the critical attitude in our general mind has perished from disuse. But as long as this continues let us remember that our work is only a kind of spadework, which antecedes the real task of criticism. To forget this is to have lost the battle. For Amiel [14] expressed the just motto of critics in those memorable words: "Truth should not merely conquer, it should win."

[14] Henri-Frédéric Amiel (1821–1881), French literary critic.

H. L. MENCKEN

From PREJUDICES: FOURTH SERIES [1]
(1924)

The American Novel

IT IS an ancient platitude of historical criticism that great wars and their sequelae are inimical to the fine arts, and particularly to the arts of letters. The kernel of truth in it lies in the obvious fact that a people engaged in a bitter struggle for existence have no time for such concerns, which demand not only leisure but also a certain assured feeling of security, well-being and self-sufficiency—in brief, the thing often called aristocratic (or sometimes intellectual) detachment. No man ever wrote good poetry with his wife in parturition in the next room, or the police preparing to raid his house, or his shirt-tail afire. He needs to be comfortable to do it, and if not actually comfortable, then at all events safe. Wars tend to make life uncomfortable and unsafe—but not, it must be observed, inevitably and necessarily, not always and invariably. A bitter and demoralizing struggle goes with wars that are lost, and the same struggle goes with wars that are won only by dint of stupendous and ruinous effort, but it certainly does not go with wars that are won easily. These last do not palsy and asphyxiate the artist, as he is palsied and asphyxiated by cholera morbus, suits for damages or marriage. On the contrary, they pump him full of ozone, and he is never more alive and lively than following them.

I point to a few familiar examples. The Civil War, as everyone knows, bankrupted the South and made life a harsh and bitter struggle for its people, and especially for the gentler and more civilized minority of its people. In consequence, the South became as sterile artistically, after Lee's surrender, as Mexico or Portugal, and even today it lags far behind the North in beautiful letters, and even further behind in music, painting and architecture. But the war, though it went on for four years, strained the resources of the North very little, either in men or in money, and so its conclusion found the Northerners very rich and cocky, and full of a yearning to astonish the world, and that yearning, in a few decades, set up a new and extremely vigorous American literature, created an American architecture of a revolutionary character, and even laid the first courses of American schools of music and painting. Mark Twain, Walt Whitman, Henry James, and William Dean Howells, all of them draft dodgers in the war itself, were in a very real sense products of the war, for they emerged as phenomena of the great outburst of creative energy that followed it, and all of them, including even James, were as thoroughly American as Jay Gould, P. T. Barnum, or Jim Fisk. The stars of the national

[1] New York, 1924.

letters in the years before the war had been Americans only by geographical accident. About Emerson there hung a smell of Königsberg and Weimar;[2] Irving was simply a New York Englishman; Poe was a citizen of No Man's Land; even Hawthorne and Cooper, despite their concern with American themes, showed not the slightest evidence of an American point of view. But Mark Twain, Howells and Whitman belonged to the Republic as palpably as Niagara Falls or Tammany Hall belonged to it, and so did James, though the thought horrified him and we must look at him through his brother William to get the proof. Turn now to Europe, France, harshly used in the war of 1870–71, was sterile for a decade, but the wounds were not deep, and recovery was in full swing by 1880. Germany, injured scarcely at all, produced Nietzsche almost before the troops got home, and was presently offering an asylum and an inspiration to Ibsen, preparing the way for the reform and modernization of the theatre, and making contributions of the utmost value to practically all of the arts and sciences. Spain, after the Armada, gave the world Cervantes and then expired; England produced Shakespeare and founded a literature that is not surpassed in history.

What has thus happened over and over again in the past—and I might pile up examples for pages—may be in process of repetition today, and under our very noses. All Europe, plainly enough, is in a state of exhaustion and depression, and in no department of human activity is the fact more visible than in that of the arts. Not only are the defeated nations, Russia, Germany, and Austria, producing nothing save a few extravagant eccentricities; there is also a great lowness of spirit in the so-called victorious nations, for their victory was almost as ruinous as defeat. France, as after 1870, is running to a pretentious and artificial morbidity in letters, and marking time in music and painting; Italy is producing little save psychopathological absurdities by such mountebanks as D'Annunzio and Papini,[3] even England shows all the signs of profound fatigue. The great English writers of the age before the war are passing. Meredith is gone; Hardy has put up his shutters; Kipling went to wreck in the war itself; Conrad is dead; Shaw, once so agile and diverting, becomes a seer and prophet. Nor is there any sign of sound progress among the younger men. Arnold Bennett, a star of brilliant promise in 1913, is today a smoking smudge. Wells has ceased to be an artist and become a prophet in the Sunday supplements. Masefield has got no further than he was on August 2, 1914. The rest of the novelists are simply chasing their own tails. The Georgian poets,[4] having emerged gloriously during the war, now disappear behind

[2] These towns were strongly associated with German romanticism. Königsberg was the birthplace of Kant; Weimar was a great center of literary activity, being especially associated with the work of Goethe, Schiller, Herder, and Wieland.

[3] Gabriele D'Annunzio (1863–1938), Italian poet, novelist, and dramatist. Giovanni Papini (1881–   ), Italian philosopher and writer.

[4] The Georgian poets were an ill-defined group whose poems appeared in an anthology, *Georgian Poetry*, edited by Edward Marsh, which appeared in 1912, 1915, 1917, 1919, and 1922. The name of the group was derived from the accession of George V in 1910. Such poets as Walter de la Mare (1873–   ), Wilfred Gibson (1878–   ), and William Davies (1871–1940) were representative of the group. G. K. Chesterton and D. H. Lawrence were infrequent contributors.

their manners. Only a few women, led by May Sinclair,[5] and a few iconoclastic young men, led by Aldous Huxley, are still indubitably alive.

It seems to me that, in the face of this dark depression across the water,
the literary spectacle on this side takes on an aspect that is extremely re-
assuring, and even a bit exhilarating. For the first time in history, there
begins to show itself the faint shadow of a hope that, if all goes well,
leadership in the arts, and especially in all the art of letters, may eventually transfer itself from the eastern shore of the Atlantic to the western
shore. Our literature, as I have more than once pointed out in the past,
is still oppressed by various heavy handicaps, chiefly resident in the failure
of the new aristocracy of money to function as an aristocracy of taste. The
artist among us is still a sort of pariah, beset by public contempt on the
one hand and by academic enmity on the other; he still lacks the public
position that his brothers enjoy in older and more civilized countries.
Nevertheless, it must be obvious to everyone that his condition tends to
improve materially—that, in our own time, it has improved materially—
that though his rewards remain meager, save in mere money, his freedom
grows steadily greater. And it must be obvious, too, that he begins to show
that that increasing freedom is not wholly wasted upon him—that he
knows how to use it, and is disposed to do so with some gusto. What all
the younger American writers have in common is a sort of new-found
elasticity or goatishness, a somewhat exaggerated sense of aliveness, a glowing delight in the spectacle before them, a vigorous and naïve self-consciousness. The schoolmaster critics belabor them for it, and call it a disrespect for tradition, and try to put it down by denouncing it as due to
corrupt foreign influences. But it is really a proof of the rise of nationalism
—perhaps of the first dawn of a genuine sense of nationality. No longer
imitative and timorous, as most of their predecessors were, these youngsters are attempting a first-hand examination of the national scene, and
making an effort to represent it in terms that are wholly American. They
are the pioneers of a literature that, whatever its defects in the abstract,
will at least be a faithful reflection of the national life, that will be more
faithful, indeed, in its defects than in its merits. In England the novel
subsides into formulae, the drama is submerged in artificialities, and even
poetry, despite occasional revolts, moves toward scholarliness and emptiness. But in America, since the war, all three show the artless and super-
abundant energy of little children. They lack, only too often, manner and
urbanity; it is no wonder that they are often shocking to pedants. But
there is the breath of life in them, and that life is far nearer its beginning
than its end.

The causes of all this are not far to seek. The American Legion is right:
we won the war. It cost us nothing in men; it brought us a huge profit in
money; as Europe has gone down, we have gone up. Moreover, it produced a vast discharge of spiritual electricity, otherwise and more injuri-
ously dissipated in the countries more harshly beset. The war was fought
ignobly; its first and most obvious effect was to raise up a horde of cads,

[5] English novelist (1879-1946).

and set them in authority as spokesmen of the nation. But out of that swinishness there was bound to come reaction, and out of the reaction there was bound to flow a desire to re-examine the whole national pretension—to turn on the light, to reject old formulae, to think things out anew and in terms of reality. Suddenly the old houses of cards came tumbling down, and the professors inhabiting them ran about in their nightshirts, bawling for the police. The war, first and last, produced a great deal more than John Dos Passos' *Three Soldiers*. It also produced Lewis' *Babbitt*, and Cabell's *Jurgen*, and Fergusson's *Capitol Hill* and O'Neill's *The Emperor Jones*. And, producing them, it ended an epoch of sweetness and light.

II

The young American literatus of today, with publishers ready and eager to give him a hearing, can scarcely imagine the difficulties which beset his predecessor of twenty years ago; he is, indeed, far too little appreciative of the freedom he has, and far too prone to flee from hard work to the solace of the martyr's shroud. When I first began practice as a critic, in 1908, there was yet plenty of excuse for putting it on. It was a time of almost inconceivable complacency and conformity. Hamilton Wright Mabie [6] was still alive and still taken seriously, and all the young pedagogues who aspired to the critical gown imitated him in his watchful stupidity. This camorra had delivered a violent wallop to Theodore Dreiser eight years before, and he was yet suffering from his bruises; it was not until 1911 that he printed *Jennie Gerhardt*. Miss Harriet Monroe [7] and her gang of new poets were still dispersed and inarticulate; Miss Amy Lowell, as yet unaware of Imagism, was writing polite doggerel in the manner of a New England schoolmarm; the reigning dramatists of the nation were Augustus Thomas, David Belasco, and Clyde Fitch; [8] Miss Cather was imitating Mrs. Wharton; Hergesheimer [9] had six years to go before he'd come to *The Lay Anthony*; Cabell [10] was known only as one who provided the text for illustrated gift-books; the American novelists most admired by most publishers, by most readers and by all practicing critics were Richard Harding Davis, Robert W. Chambers, and James Lane Allen.[11] It is hard indeed, in retrospect, to picture those remote days just as they were. They seem almost fabulous. The chief critical organ of the Republic was actually the Literary Supplement of the *New York Times*. *The Dial* was down with diabetes in Chicago; *The Nation* was made dreadful by the gloomy humors of Paul Elmer More; *The Bookman* was even more saccharine and sophomoric than it is today. When the

[6] American literary critic (1845–1916).
[7] American poet, founder of *Poetry: A Magazine of Verse* in Chicago in 1912, and the leader of the New Poetry movement.
[8] Augustus Thomas (1859–1934), David Belasco (1859–1931), and Clyde Fitch (1865–1909) were all American playwrights.
[9] Joseph Hergesheimer (1880–   ), American novelist.
[10] James Branch Cabell (1879–   ), American novelist.
[11] Richard Harding Davis (1864–1916); Robert William Chambers (1865–1933); James Lane Allen (1849–1925).

mild and pianissimo revolt of the middle 90's—a feeble echo of the English revolt—had spent itself, the Presbyterians marched in and took possession of the works. Most of the erstwhile revoltés boldly took the veil—notably Hamlin Garland.[12] No novel that told the truth about life as Americans were living it, no poem that departed from the old patterns, no play that had the merest ghost of an idea in it had a chance. When, in 1908, Mrs. Mary Roberts Rinehart printed a conventional mystery story which yet managed to have a trace of sense in it, it caused a sensation.[13] And when, two years later, Dr. William Lyon Phelps printed a book of criticism in which he actually ranked Mark Twain alongside Emerson and Haw-thorne,[14] there was as great a stirring beneath the college elms as if a naked fancy woman had run across the campus. If Hergesheimer had come into New York in 1908 with *Cytherea* under his arm, he would have worn out his pantaloons on publishers' benches without getting so much as a polite kick. If Eugene O'Neill had come to Broadway with *The Hairy Ape*, he would have been sent to Edward E. Rose [15] to learn the elements of his trade. The devilish and advanced thing, in those days, was for the fat lady star to give a couple of matinées of Ibsen's *A Doll's House*.

A great many men and a few women addressed themselves to the dispersal of this fog. Some of them were imaginative writers who found it simply impossible to bring themselves within the prevailing rules; some were critics; others were young publishers. As I look back, I can't find any sign of concerted effort; it was, in the main, a case of each on his own. The more contumacious of the younger critics, true enough, tended to rally 'round Huneker, who, as a matter of fact, was very little interested in American letters, and the young novelists had a leader in Dreiser, who, I suspect, was quite unaware of most of them. However, it was probably Dreiser who chiefly gave form to the movement, despite the fact that for eleven long years he was silent. Not only was there a useful rallying-point in the idiotic suppression of *Sister Carrie*; there was also the encouraging fact of the man's massive immovability. Physically and mentally he loomed up like a sort of headland—a great crag of basalt that no conceivable assault seemed able to touch. His predecessor, Frank Norris, was of much softer stuff. Norris, had he lived longer, would have been wooed and ruined, I fear, by the Mabies, Boyntons,[16] and other such Christian critics, as Garland had been wooed and ruined before him. Dreiser, fortunately for American letters, never had to face any such seduction. The critical schoolmarms, young and old, fell upon him with violence the moment he appeared above the horizon of his native steppe, and soon he was the

---

[12] The reference here is to the fact that while Garland's earlier fiction had been harshly realistic, his later fiction had turned to romance. Cf. the early *Main-Travelled Roads* (1891) with the later novel, *The Captain of the Gray Horse Troop* (1902).

[13] Mary Roberts Rinehart (1876–   ) published *The Circular Staircase* in 1908.

[14] William Lyon Phelps (1865–1943), American literary critic and educator, published his *Essays on Modern Novelists* in 1910.

[15] Twentieth-century dramatist and critic.

[16] Percy H. Boynton, twentieth-century American literary critic.

storm center of a battle-royal that lasted nearly twenty years. The man himself was solid, granitic, without nerves. Very little cunning was in him and not much bellicose enterprise, but he showed a truly appalling tenacity. The pedagogues tried to scare him to death, they tried to stampede his partisans and they tried to put him into Coventry and get him forgotten, but they failed every time. The more he was reviled, sneered at, neglected, the more resolutely he stuck to his formula. That formula is now every serious American novelist's formula. They all try to write better than Dreiser, and not a few of them succeed, but they all follow him in his fundamental purpose—to make the novel true. Dreiser added something, and here following him is harder: he tried to make the novel poignant—to add sympathy, feeling, imagination to understanding. It will be a long while before that enterprise is better managed than he managed it in *Jennie Gerhardt*.

Today, it seems to me, the American imaginative writer, whether he be novelist, poet or dramatist, is quite as free as he deserves to be. He is free to depict the life about him precisely as he sees it, and to interpret it in any manner he pleases. The publishers of the land, once so fearful of novelty, are now so hospitable to it that they constantly fail to distinguish the novelty that has hard thought behind it from that which has only some Village mountebank's desire to stagger the wives of Rotarians. Our stage is perhaps the freest in the world—not only to sensations, but also to ideas. Our poets get into print regularly with stuff so bizarre and unearthly that only Christian Scientists can understand it. The extent of this new freedom, indeed, is so great that large numbers of persons appear to be unable to believe in it; they are constantly getting into sweats about the taboos and inhibitions that remain, for example, those nourished by comstockery.[17] But the importance and puissance of comstockery, I believe, is quite as much overestimated as the importance and puissance of the objurgations still hurled at sense and honesty by the provincial professors of American Idealism, the Genius of America, and other such phantasms. The Comstocks, true enough, still raid an occasional book, particularly when their funds are running low and there is need to inflame Christian men, but that their monkeyshines ever actually suppress a book of any consequence I very much doubt. The flood is too vast for them. Chasing a minnow with desperate passion, they let a whole school of whales go by. In any case, they confine their operations to the single field of sex, and it must be plain that it is not in the field of sex that the hottest battles against the old American manner have been fought and won. *Three Soldiers* was far more subversive of that manner than all the stories of sex ever written in America—and yet *Three Soldiers* came out with the imprint of one of the most respectable American publishers, and was scarcely challenged. *Babbitt* scored a victory that was still easier, and yet more significant, for its target was the double one of American business and

---

[17] The term derives from Anthony Comstock (1844–1915), notorious American crusader against vice who at times was overzealous in his crusade against the fine arts and literature.

American Christianity; it set the whole world to laughing at two things that are far more venerated in the United States than the bodily chastity of women. Nevertheless, *Babbitt* went down so easily that even the alfalfa *Gelehrten* [18] joined in whooping for it, apparently on the theory that praising Lewis would make the young of the national species forget Dreiser. Victimized by their own craft, the *Gelehrten* thus made a foul attack upon their own principles, for if their principles did not stand against just such anarchistic and sacrilegious books, then they were without any sense whatever, as was and is, indeed, the case.

I shall not rehearse the steps in the advance from *Sister Carrie*, suppressed and proscribed, to *Babbitt*, swallowed and hailed. The important thing is that, despite the caterwauling of the Comstocks and the pedagogues, a reasonable freedom for the serious artist now prevails—that publishers stand ready to print him, that critics exist who are competent to recognize him and willing to do battle for him, and that there is a large public eager to read him. What use is he making of his opportunity? Certainly not the worst use possible, but also certainly not the best. He is free, but he is not yet, perhaps, worthy of freedom. He lets the popular magazine, the movie and the cheap-John publisher pull him too hard in one direction; he lets the vagaries of his politics pull him too hard in another. Back in 1908 I predicted the destruction of Upton Sinclair the artist by Upton Sinclair the visionary and reformer. Sinclair's bones now bleach upon the beach. Beside them repose those of many another man and woman of great promise—for example, Winston Churchill.[19] Floyd Dell is on his way—one novel and two doses of Greenwich Village psychology.[20] Hergesheimer writes novelettes for the *Saturday Evening Post*. Willa Cather has won the Pulitzer Prize—a transaction comparable to the election of Charles W. Eliot to the Elks.[21] Masters [22] turns to prose that somehow fails to come off. Dreiser, forgetting his trilogy,[23] experiments rather futilely with the drama, the essay, free verse. Fuller renounces the novel for book reviewing.[24] Tarkington is another Pulitzer prizeman, always on the verge of first-rate work but always falling short by an inch. Many of the White Hopes of ten or fifteen years ago perished in the war, as surely victims of its slaughter as Rupert Brooke or Otto Braun; it is, indeed, curious to note that practically every American author who moaned and sobbed for democracy between the years 1914 and 1919 is now extinct. The rest have gone down the chute of the movies.

[18] "scholars" or "academicians."

[19] American novelist (1871–1947).

[20] The reference is to Floyd Dell's (b. 1887) *Moon-Calf* which was published in 1920.

[21] Charles W. Eliot (1834–1926), American scholar, educator, and president of Harvard University.

[22] Edgar Lee Masters (1869–1950), American poet and writer.

[23] Of Dreiser's proposed trilogy, *The Financier* had appeared in 1912 and *The Titan* in 1914. The third novel, *The Stoic*, did not appear until 1947.

[24] Henry Blake Fuller (1857–1929), whose novels *The Cliff-Dwellers* ((1893), *Under the Skylights* (1901), and *On the Stairs* (1918) had received considerable contemporary praise for their realism.

But all this, after all, may signify little. The shock troops have been piled up in great masses, but the ground is cleared for those that follow. Well, then, what of the youngsters? Do they show any sign of seizing their chance? The answer is yes and no. On the one hand there is a group which, revolving 'round *The Bookman*, talks a great deal and accomplishes nothing. On the other hand there is a group which, revolving 'round *The Dial* and *The Little Review*, talks even more and does even less. But on the third hand, as it were, there is a group which says little and saws wood. There seems to be little in common between its members, no sign of a formal movement, with its blague and its bombast, but all of them have this in common: that they owe both their opportunity and their method to the revolution that followed *Sister Carrie*. Most of them are from the Middle West, but they are distinct from the Chicago crowd, now degenerated to posturing and worse. They are sophisticated, disillusioned, free from cant, and yet they have imagination. The raucous protests of the evangelists of American Idealism seem to have no more effect upon them than the advances of the Expressionists,[25] Dadaists,[26] and other such café-table prophets. Out of this dispersed and ill-defined group, I believe, something will come. Its members are those who are free from the two great delusions which, from the beginning, have always cursed American letters, the delusion that a work of art is primarily a moral document, that its purpose is to make men better Christians and more docile cannon-fodder, and the delusion that it is an exercise in logic, that its purpose is to prove something. These delusions, lingering beyond their time, are responsible for most of the disasters visible in the national literature today—the disasters of the radicals as well as those of the 100 per cent. dunderheads. The writers of the future, I hope and believe, will carefully avoid both of them.

[25] A group of artists whose theory of art, originating in Europe about the time of World War I, aimed at free expression of the artist's emotional reactions rather than the actual representation of objects as they actually exist.

[26] Members of an early nineteenth-century movement in art and literature which attempted to discredit all previous art by the use of the incongruous and the accidental. The movement took its name from the French review *Dada*, which was one of the leading periodicals of the movement.

R. P. BLACKMUR

THE CRAFT OF HERMAN MELVILLE:
A PUTATIVE STATEMENT [1]
From THE EXPENSE OF GREATNESS

(1938)

THIS ESSAY proposes to approach Herman Melville altogether gingerly and from behind the safe bulwark of his assured position—whatever that is—in American literature,—whatever *that* may be. The tacit assumption will be all along that Melville is a sufficiently great writer in a sufficiently interesting literature to make the sidelong look, the biased comment, and even a little boring-from-within, each valuable in itself, if perhaps only as characterising an inadequate response on the part of one reader. We need, of course, a preliminary assertion to get us under way; and the last thing we want is anything in the direction of reducing Melville's greatness to sub-human terms. What we want is an assertion that, pursued, will elucidate one aspect of the work actually performed, irrespective of its greatness.

If we assert that Melville was an imaginative artist in the realm of fiction, then it is legitimate to think of him as he was concerned with the craft of fiction in his two most interesting works, *Moby Dick* and *Pierre*. As a further limitation, let us think of the craft principally under two heads: dramatic form with its inspiriting conventions, and the treatment of language itself as a medium. Other matters may come in by the way, and further matters may suggest themselves in conclusion; but the mode of discovery will be everywhere at bottom in the consideration of the tools by which Melville himself secured his effects: the tools of craft.

It is of preliminary interest that Melville never influenced the direction of the art of fiction, though in *Pierre* he evidenced the direction, and it is astonishing, when you consider the magnitude of his sensibility, that he never affected the modes of apprehension, the sensibilities, of even the ablest of his admirers. He added nothing to the novel as a form, and his work nowhere showed conspicuous mastery of the formal devices of fiction which he used. Unlike most great writers of fiction, he left nothing to those who followed him except the general stimulus of high and devoted purpose and the occasional particular spur of an image or a rhythm. It is not that he is inimitable but that there was nothing formally organised enough in his work to imitate or modify or perfect. It is easy enough to say on this score that Melville was a sport, and unique, and perhaps that

[1] Originally published in the *Virginia Quarterly Review*, XIV (1938), 266–82. Reprinted in *The Expense of Greatness* (New York, 1940).

is the right thing to say; but it would be more useful if we were able to say that Melville's lack of influence at least partly arose from a series of technical defects in persuasive craft—from an inefficient relation between the writer and the formal elements of his medium. None of us would want to recommend his wares along the lines of Melville's strategy. To adumbrate such a statement is a part of this essay's purpose.

Of secondary, but deeply contributory interest is the fact that though a young man still as writers go, Melville wrote nothing of major significance in the forty years he lived after writing *Pierre*. (I mean that only a lesser case could be made out for *The Confidence Man* and *Billy Budd* than for *Pierre*, not that the later books were uninteresting; they could not fail of interest as forced through Melville's sensibility.) It was not that his mind rotted or that insight faltered. It was not, I think, that the poor reception of *Pierre*, nor the long aggravation of his private life, dried his desire as a novelist. It was, I think, partly bad luck—the luck of the age, if you like—though it was no worse than Dante's luck and not so bad as Villon's, as Melville himself knew; and it was partly that his work discovered for itself, if we may say so, and in the very process of writing, that it was not meant to be fiction. Melville was only a story teller betimes, for illustrative or apologetic or evangelical purposes, and when the *writing* of *Pierre* proved that the material of illustration had been exhausted in *Moby Dick*—which is one way of noting the break-down of *Pierre* as a story—there was no longer any need to tell a story. His means determined, as they always do, not the ends in view, but the ends achieved; and Melville had never predominantly relied upon the means of the novelist, had never attempted to use more than the overt form of the novel, until he attempted to compose *Pierre*.

What is really interesting, and what this essay intends to make most use of in this corner, is the light that *Pierre*, technically considered as a novel, casts upon the means, quite different from the means of fiction, which Melville actually employed both in *Moby Dick* and *Pierre* itself. For these books with their great effects, if they were not written out of the means of the novelist, were written out of great means of some other mode or modes of the imagination. It will most likely appear that there is an operative connection between Melville's lack of influence upon following writers and his forty years of comparative silence; and it is, again, a connection, as moral as may be, that can best be seen as a technical consideration. Similarly, the problem of the inarticulateness of *Hamlet* is better accounted for technically than philosophically. We shall see, or try to see, what modes determined what ends—but always provisionally within the modes of the rational imagination.

There is, again on this train, a dubious kind of consideration which in the very doubtfulness of its nature exerts its great attraction. In our literature we are accustomed to the question precisely because it gets itself asked at every turn. It is a coroner's question: what devilish thing did his age do to Melville? What malevolence was there in the current of American life that struck from the heights of possibility writer after writer, even those most satisfied with the American scene?—for the Longfellows, the Whittiers, the Holmeses were as fatally struck as Hawthorne and Melville and Mark Twain. But does an age act? Is not an age itself a long action, an unfolding, a display, a history, with limits set by the discernment and capacity of the observer, never by Clio [2] herself? And is not every age an enemy of every artist it cannot directly use, an enemy not out of antipathy but of inner necessity? An age moves; it is momentum felt. An artist expresses an arrested version of movement, expresses it at the level of actuality. But this is pushing consequence intolerably. We are all enemies of our age the moment we begin to tamper with it, whether we arrest it to take its picture, hasten it towards its end in the guise of leadership, or just consciously live in it our own lives. Consciousness is the agent, not the age.

It is the whole consciousness, not its mere miniscule conscience, that makes us cowards. Hence in all large doings we are adept at removing compassion from our experience by at once inserting it in the formula of a dead convention; and so are often enabled to skip consciousness, along with conscience, altogether. How otherwise could we attend the Christian service of Holy Communion, quite aside from the matter of faith and for the "poetry" in it merely, without terror and dismay and the conviction of inadequacy? How could we attend *King Lear* on the stage if we did not commonly channelise our attention upon the obscuring details of the performance, letting the actual play work in us, if at all, unawares? This is precisely what the artist cannot substantially do if his work is to live; and this is precisely what society compels him to seem to do if his work is to succeed in the open,—that is, be widely persuasive upon the consciousness of the great audience most artists aim at. Upon his skill and luck in performing this equivocal act depends all that part of an artist's achievement which rests on a firm relation with his age.

Here we have a crux in the deliberately maintained, wilfully heightened consciousness of the artist. It is the crux in which we see that the conceptual faculty of consciousness is honesty if we can manage it, but that the executive faculty of consciousness must be hypocrisy. I do not wish to strain or seem far-fetched, but I believe this to be a technical matter in so far as we think of the arts—whatever it may be in religion or politics, which are not always condemned to actuality but can often play free havoc with the ideal. What it comes to in practice is that the artist must dramatise his theme, his vision, his observation, his "mere" story, in terms of existing conventions however adverse those conventions may seem to his intentions, or however hollow or vain they ring when struck. The deadest convention was meant for life—to take its place, and if by putting life into it the artist does not always change it for the better, he at least shows it for what it is. Instinctive artists commonly resort to the nearest conventions susceptible of dramas. Consider the negro spirituals or the anonymous architecture of the twelfth century. Highly individualised artists have done the same. There is Dante who mastered the conventions of Tomistic Christianity to represent the actuality—far from Tomistic—of fourteenth century Italy;

[2] In mythology, the Muse of history.

and there is Henry James who resorted to the "social" conventions so well that many people for long believed he was taken in by them, when his predominant concern was to dramatise the actual good and evil of his time in terms of the conventions through which he most saw good and evil operating.

The point here is, for us, that Melville either refused or was unable to resort to the available conventions of his time as if they were real; he either preferred or was compelled to resort to most of the conventions he used for dramatic purposes not only as if they were unreal but also as if they were artificial. Artificial they surely were to the kind of philosopher Melville was—though they would not have seemed unreal to Montaigne or Plato; but to the dramatist of any description they would have glowed with the possibility of every reality. As for Melville's case we have his own words, put in extremity, for his attitude towards all conventions of the mind.

> For the more and the more that he wrote, and the deeper and deeper that he dived, Pierre saw the everlasting elusiveness of Truth; the universal lurking insincerity of even the greatest and purest written thoughts. Like knavish cards, the leaves of all great books were covertly packed. He was but packing one set the more; and that a very poor and jaded set and pack indeed.

Here we see the ineptitude, for the artist, of moral pre-occupation with what ought to be as compared with the equally moral obsession with what is. As thought, we can leave Melville's text alone, and insist merely that as an artist Melville misunderstood the import of his own words. The "universal lurking insincerity" he spoke of, is just the most fascinating aspect of the face of dramatic truth; and the conviction of it should liberate the artist's honesty among his material generally, as the preposterous fables of *Lear, Othello,* and the *Merchant of Venice* particularly liberated the profound honesty of Shakespeare, or as the *smallness* of life in Emma Bovary's town liberated Flaubert's honesty. Melville apparently felt that his insight condemned him to a species of dishonesty. Feeling the necessity—feeling the condemned state as unreprievable—he proceeded to employ conventions of character and form in which he obviously and almost avowedly did not believe. Had he been a convicted and not a condemned novelist he would have felt his insight of insincerity on the same level that he felt the convention in the following lines, in which he never detected the insincerity at all.

> It is a thing most sorrowful, nay shocking, to expose the fall of valor in the soul. Men may seem detestable as joint stock-companies and nations; knaves, fools, and murderers there may be; men may have mean and meagre faces; but man, in the ideal, is so noble and so sparkling, such a grand and glowing creature, that over any ignominious blemish in him all his fellows should run to throw their costliest robes. That immaculate manliness we feel within ourselves, so far within us, that it remains intact though all the outer character seem gone; bleeds with

the keenest anguish at the undraped spectacle of a valor-ruined man.
Nor can piety itself, at such a shameful sight, completely stifle her up-
braidings against the permitting stars.

At his best—his best as a novelist of character and aspiration—this sentiment controlled Melville's perception of dramatic fate. Had he felt the
immaculate manliness as Henry James, say, felt his perception of the
Sacred Fount, as a germinal, copulative, and plastic principle in every
human relation, and also as the very prod and forward stress towards form,
then his sentiment would not only have opened up inexhaustible subject-
matter, but would also have required of him that in his execution every
resource, every trick, every mediate insincerity, either of craft or of social
pattern, be used for the utmost there was in them. That would have been
to work on the representative, the dramatic level. What he did, as we shall
see more particularly below, was to work on the putative level. His work
constantly *said* what it was doing or going to do, and then, as a rule,
stopped short.

As it happens, Melville's is not a putative smallness but a putative immensity, and he puts it with such eloquence that the mere statement produces a lasting tone in the general atmosphere. He was without knowing
it in the habit of succumbing to the greatest insincerity of all, the intoxi-
cating insincerity of cadence and rhythm and apt image, or, to put it on
another plane, the insincerity of surrendering to the force of a single
insight, which sometimes amounts to a kind of self-violation. Who can
measure for example the effect of the preparatory statements about Ahab
upon our actual reception of him when he appears? For instance, in chapter XVI there is a paragraph about the greatness of some whaling men
rising from a combination of Quaker blood and the perils of the sea. "Nor
will it at all detract from him, dramatically regarded, if either by birth or
other circumstances, he have what seems a half wilful, over-ruling morbidness at the bottom of his nature. For all men tragically great are made so
through a certain morbidness. Be sure of this, O young ambition, all mortal greatness is but disease." . . . This is but one of the many preparatory, almost minatory statements that Melville made about Ahab. Many
directly named him; many more, like this one, were purely indirect and
putative in character. Ahab is not mentioned, but the reader who remembers the passage will know that it was he who was meant all the same;
and if the reader does remember it may well occur to him that Melville
meant his sentences about greatness and disease to spread throughout the
novel. They were planted of a purpose, whether by instinct or intention,
to prefigure in the general atmosphere the specific nature of the burden
Ahab wore.

The interesting thing is that Melville preferred to make his statement,
in which one version of the whole theme of the book is expressed, not
only baldly in isolation, but out of place and rootlessly; which is how the
reader will ultimately remember it. It worked, indeed; but it worked outside the story. A dramatist would have been compelled to find the senti-

ment of these sentences in a situation, an action, and they could have been used only as the situation called for them and the action carried them along; and a novelist when he can should follow the example of the dramatist. Melville, as we have said, preferred the non-dramatic mode. To put it sharply, he did not write of characters in action; he employed the shells of stock characters, heightened or resounding only by the eloquence of the author's voice, to witness, illustrate, decorate, and often as it happened to impede and stultify an idea in motion. This is, if you like, the mode of allegory—the highest form of the putative imagination, in which things are *said* but need not be *shown* to be other than they seem, and thus hardly require to *be* much of anything. But successful allegory—*La Vita Nuova* and *Pilgrim's Progress* [3]—requires the preliminary possession of a complete and stable body of belief appropriate to the theme in hand. Melville was not so equipped; neither was Hawthorne; neither was anyone in nineteenth-century America or since. That is why Melville's allegorical devices and patterns had to act *as if* they were agents in a novel; and that is why we are compelled to judge Melville at his most allegorical yet formally as a novelist.

Perhaps the point needs labouring. Many critics—many students of Melville—have done a good deal to make an allegorical interpretation of *Moby Dick*, and I am sure they are right and accurate in the form of what they say. Melville certainly had allegorical intentions. My argument—again it is technical—is that the elaboration of these intentions was among the causes that prevented him from the achievement of enacting composition and the creation of viable characters. He mistook allegory in *Moby Dick* as a sufficient enlivening agent for the form of the novel. Actually it was a chief defective element which, due to the peculiarly confused, inconsistent and incomplete state of belief he was in, he could not possibly have used to good advantage. In the craft of writing, in any form of expression, artificial allegory, like willed mysticism (of which Melville showed a trace), is a direct and easy mode only in that it puts so much in by intention as to leave nearly everything out in execution. Bad allegory, even to the allegorist, comes very soon to seem not worth doing; which is why charades and political parties break down. Melville's allegory in *Moby Dick* broke down again and again and with each resumption got more and more verbal, and more and more at the mercy of the encroaching event it was meant to transcend. It was an element in the putative mode in which, lofty as it was, Melville himself could not long deeply believe.

We have so far been concerned mostly with what Melville did not do as a practitioner in the novel and with certain possible causes which, technically, prevented him from doing what he wanted to do. Let us now examine particular instances of what he did do under the two heads first mentioned: dramatic form with its inspiriting conventions, and the treatment of language itself as medium. If anything so far said has made its point it will be in the degree that it certifies and illuminates what follows

[3] Dante's *La Vita Nuova* was published in about 1293; John Bunyan's *Pilgrim's Progress*, Part I in 1678 and Part II in 1684.

—in the degree, that is, that it makes it seem natural and just and necessary to find so much fault in a genius so great.

The dramatic form of a novel is what holds it together, makes it move, gives it a centre and establishes a direction; and it includes the agency of perception, the consciousness set up in the book upon which, or through which, the story is registered. Dramatic form cannot in practice be wholly isolated from other formal elements; form is the way things go together in their medium—and the medium itself, here language, may properly be considered the major element of form; but we may think of different ways in which things go together in a given work, and strangely, the labour of abstraction and violation will seem to deepen our intimacy with the substance of the work and, more valuable, to heighten our sense of how that substance is controlled. The sense of control is perhaps the highest form of apprehension; it is understanding without immersion.

The question we have here to ask then is how did Melville go about controlling his two novels, *Moby Dick* and *Pierre*? The general, strictly true, and mainly irrelevant answer would be: haphazardly—that is, through an attitude which varied from the arrogance of extreme carelessness to the humility of complete attention. It is not that he attended only to what seriously interested him, for he was as careless of what he thought important as of what he thought trivial, but that apparently he had no sure rule as to what required management and what would take care of itself. His rule was vagary, where consequential necessities did not determine otherwise. And even there, Melville's eye was not good; he did not always see that if you took one series of steps your choice of further directions was narrowed, and that you could not step in two directions at once without risk of crippling yourself. It is perhaps his intellectual consistency, which he felt putatively omniform, that made him incorrigibly inconsistent in the technical quarter. For example, in *Moby Dick*, after setting up a single consciousness to get inside of, he shifted from that consciousness at will without sense of inconsistency, and therefore, which is the important thing, without making any effort to warrant the shifts and make them credible. Ignorance could not have excused him, because he had the example of Hawthorne, who was adept at shifting his compositional centres without disturbing his gravity, plumb in front of him. Not ignorance, but ineptitude and failure to discriminate. For the contrary example, I can think of only three occasions of importance in *Pierre*, if we except the digressions of the author himself in his own voice, where the consciousness of the hero is not left the presumed sole register of the story. Of these occasions, two are unnecessary to the story, and the third, where in the very end the perceiving centre is turned over to the turnkey in the prison, funks its job. Yet in *Pierre* the theme cried out, one would think, for as many and as well chosen centres of consciousness as possible, all to be focussed on Pierre himself, the distraught and ambiguous, otherwise not measurable: the principle being that the abnormal can only be seen as viable, as really moving in response to the normal world, if seen through normal eyes.

Meanwhile we have approached a little nearer the composition of the two novels. Melville was right, granting the theme of *Moby Dick*, in choosing Ishmael the novice, to represent a story in which he had only a presumed and minor but omnipresent part; he was only wrong where he breached his choice without covering up. Ishmael, not otherwise ever named, is as mysterious as Ahab, but he is credible because he tells us not what he is but what he sees and what he sees other people see. The mere interposition of a participating consciousness between the story and its readers, once it has been made logical by tying the consciousness to the story, is a prime device of composition: it limits, compacts, and therefore controls what can be told and how. The only error Melville made is that he failed to distinguish between what Ishmael saw and what the author saw on his own account. If an author is to use digressions, which are confusing but legitimate by tradition, he ought to follow Fielding and put them in interchapters,[4] and especially where the narrative is technically in the first person. Otherwise, as with Ishmael, the narrator will seem to know too much at a given time for the story's good; it will tend to tell itself all at once, and the necessary modicum of stupidity in the operative consciousness will be blighted by excess intelligence. As Ahab said to the carpenter who handed him a lantern: "Thrusted light is worse than presented pistols." Ishmael of course is Melville's alter ego, which explains why so much is imputed to him, but does not condone the excess.

On the whole the mode of Ishmael is a success exactly where the mode of *Pierre* (another alter ego of Melville) is wrong. Ishmael is looking on, and able to see; Pierre is in the centre of his predicament, and lost in the action. Ishmael represents speech; Pierre represents rhetoric. Ishmael reports the abnormal, driven and demonic Ahab, either through his own normal sensibility or through the reported sensibilities of the mates and the crew. Pierre is seen principally without the intervening glass and focus of any sensibility whatever—so that he falls apart into a mere voice whenever he speaks, whereas the voice of Ahab, equally eloquent and rhetorical past belief, rings true in ears that have actually heard it.

It should be noted, curiously, that Ishmael is the only character in the book not "characterised" by Melville; he is merely situated in the centre, explained a little, and let speak his part of recording angel. The curiosity is that all the other characters except Ahab and Queequeg near the beginning (the night at the inn), although given set characterisations as they appear, are far less viable and are far less *present* in the book than Ishmael. The reason may be that the other characters are only pulled out at intervals and are usually given stock jobs to do, set speeches to make, whereas Ishmael, sacking his creative memory, is occupied all the time. Which suggests two or three things: that character requires the sense of continuous action to show continuously, that the mates and crew were not *in* the book substantially but that their real use was to divide up the representation of the image of Ahab. There is nothing illegitimate about

---

[4] Henry Fielding (1707–1754), English novelist, made extensive use of the interchapter particularly in *The History of Tom Jones, a Foundling* (1749).

such characters, but to be successful and maintain interest they must be given enough to do to seem everywhere natural, and never obviously used, as here, *only* to make the wheels go round. One suspects, therefore, that Ahab comes out a great figure more because of the eloquence of the author's putative conception of him, and Ishmael's feeling for him, than from any representational aids on the part of the crew. The result is a great figure, not a great character. Ahab is as solitary in the book as he was in his cabin.

Pierre was in his way as compositionally isolated as Ahab; he was so situated, and so equipped as a consciousness, that he recorded his own isolation to the point of solipsism. If Pierre was real, as he was asserted to be, then nothing else properly in the novel was real except in terms of his perception or through the direct and unwarrantable intervention of the author. That is the risk attached to making the protagonist record the action in which he participates to the exclusion of other agents and while the action is going on. Melville instinctively tried to get round the difficulty by resorting to a series of dramatic scenes in which Pierre was chief interlocutor. The device was the right one—or one of the right ones—but it failed to work for a number of reasons, of which the chief was that Melville had no talent for making his dramatic scenes objective except by aid of external and unrelated force—as in *Moby Dick* he was able to resort to the ordinary exigencies of life on a whaling ship. In *Pierre* the White Whale was entirely in the protagonist's own inadequate perception of it; and the real weight of the book—what it was really about: tragedy by unconsidered virtue—was left for the author's digressions and soliloquies to carry as it could; which is to say that the book had no compositional centre at all.

Something of the same sort may also be true of *Moby Dick*. Is it not possible to say that Ishmael, the narrator, provides only a false centre? Is it not true that a great part of the story's theme escapes him, is not recorded through his sensibility, either alone or in connection with others? Then the real centre would lie where? It would lie variously, I think, in the suspense attached to the character of Ahab and the half imputed, half demonstrated peril of the White Whale—the cold, live evil that is momently present. If we think of the book in that way, we may say that its compositional form is a long, constantly interrupted but as constantly maintained suspense, using as nexi or transitions the recurring verbal signs of Melville's allegory, Ahab's character, and the business of whaling. The business of whaling, including both the essays on anatomy and those on butchery, takes the most space and provides the most interest. All the reader has to do is to *feel* whaling as interest and he will recognise it as a compositional device mounting to the force of drama. Indeed we speak of the drama of whaling, or of cotton, or of gold without substantial injustice to the language; and I cannot for the life of me see why the drama of whaling should not be as efficient an agent of interest, if well felt, as the drama of who fired the second shot; and with Melville there is the additional advantage that the business of whaling points to the everlasting assassin instead of the casual and no doubt remorseful murderer. Interest is the thing of prime importance as any artist and any audience will tell you. If it takes up time and prepares for life, it does not matter how it is secured and does not fatally matter if it is overdone or vulgar in its appeal as it is in *Moby Dick*.

But is the real interest in the whaling or in the firing of the shot? Is it not always partly in the presentation, the feeling of detail and design, and partly in the image towards which the design points? Melville was lucky in *Oomoo* and *Typee*, to a less degree in *Mardi* and *White Jacket*, and most of all in *Moby Dick*; he was lucky or it was his genius that he had material in perfect factual control with which to take up time and point towards an image—in *Moby Dick* a profound and obsessive image of life. As it happened, it was in each case the material of a special and vanishing experience, dramatic enough in its own right to require very little fictionising—very little actualising—to exert the invaluable hold of natural interest over the average reader. If to interest, you add eloquence, you have all the essentials of the great novel below the first order. Many readers will be deceived and think the provision greater than it is. I have discovered a number of readers who on being asked reported enjoyment of a great story in a book of which Henry James would have said that it told no story to speak of; which indeed it does not.

In *Pierre* we are in a different box; a box quite empty of special material of objective interest to do for compositional strength otherwise lacking. There is no sea, or ship, or whale, or unique tradition of behaviour, no unusual daily life—most precious of all—to give atmosphere, and weight and movement to carry the book towards the image of its chosen end. Melville was required to depend more than ever before upon the actual technique of the craft, and nothing much else, to make the book hang together. What is most illuminating is most pitiful. The glaring weaknesses of *Pierre* show up the hidden weaknesses of *Moby Dick*, and each set of weaknesses shows the other as essential—at least in the critical context in which we here provisionally place both books.

That one novel may criticise another is a commonplace when we think of different authors, as when we say that the novels of Henry James form a criticism of the novels of Flaubert and Turgenev,[5] or that, in a way, the *Comedie Humaine* is a critique of the Waverley Novels.[6] I think it is equally true that a consideration of the failures of a single author will often form the severest criticism of his successes, and a consideration of his successes may relatively improve our estimation of his failures. A great author is of one substance and often of one theme, and the relation between his various creations is bound to be reciprocal, even mutual; each is the other in a different form. So with *Pierre* and *Moby Dick*. If we wish to take up thinking of the two novels together in this way—which is the

---

[5] Gustave Flaubert (1821–1880), French realistic novelist; Ivan Turgenev (1818–1883), Russian realistic novelist.

[6] The *Comedie Humaine* was written by Honoré de Balzac (1799–1850), French realistic novelist. The Waverley Novels were written by Sir Walter Scott.

purpose of this essay—the alert consciousness will be struck with the repetition of the vices of *Pierre* in *Moby Dick*, or struck the other way round with the fact that the tragedy of *Pierre* fails to come off as well as *Moby Dick* only because the later book lacked the demonstrable extraneous interest of whaling. The efforts at plot in the two books are as lame; narrative runs as often offside. Dramatic motive on the subordinate level is as weakly put; Starbuck's tentative rebellion against Ahab and the threatened revenge of Glendinning Stanly and Frederick Tartan upon Pierre are equally unconvincing. The dialogue is as by turns limp and stiff and flowery in one book as the other. The delineations of character are almost interchangeable examples of wooden caricature. And so on. More important, the force and nobility of conception, the profundity of theme, were as great in either book—not from the dramatic execution but in spite of it, in the simple strength of the putative statement, and in the digressions Melville made from the drama in front of him, which he could not manage, into apologues or sermons, which he superbly could.

The strength of the putative statement is only simple when thought of abstractly and as appealing to the intellect—to the putative element in appreciation: as if we read lyric poetry solely for the schematic paraphrase we make of it in popular discussion, or as if, in contemplating war, we thought only of political causes or in terms of the quartermaster's technique alone. What we want is to see what is the source of putative strength and how deeply its appeal is asserted; and in that pursuit we shall find ourselves instantly, I think, in the realm of language itself. Words, and their intimate arrangements, must be the ultimate as well as the immediate source of every effect in the written or spoken arts. Words bring meaning to birth and themselves contained the meaning as an imminent possibility before the pangs of junction. To the individual artist the use of words is an adventure in discovery; the imagination is heuristic among the words it manipulates. The reality you labour desperately or luckily to put into your words—and you may put it in consciously like Coleridge or by instinct as in the great ballads or from piety and passion like the translators of the Bible—you will actually have found there, deeply ready and innately formed to give objective being and specific idiom to what you knew and did not know that you knew. The excitement is past belief; as we know from the many myths of heavenly inspiration. And the routine of discovery is past teaching and past prediction; as we know from the vast reaches of writing, precious and viable to their authors, wholly without the conviction of being. Yet the adventure into the reality of words has a technique after the fact in the sense that we can disinguish its successful versions from those that failed, can measure provisionally the kinds and intensities of reality secured and attempted, and can even roughly guess at the conditions of convention and belief necessary for its emergence.

Melville is an excellent example for such an assay. We have only to relate the conception of the reality of language just adumbrated to the notion of the putative statement to see whence the strength of the latter comes; and we have only to relate the conception of language to its modifying context of conventions in order to understand the successes and at least excuse the many short-comings and over-leapings of Melville's attempts at the paramount and indefeasible reality that great words show. For Melville habitually used words greatly.

Let us take first an example not at all putative and with as little supporting context of convention as possible: an example of words composed entirely of feelings and the statement of sensuous facts, plus of course the usual situating and correlative elements which are the real syntax of imaginative language.

> To a landsman, no whale, nor any sign of a herring, would have been visible at that moment; nothing but a troubled bit of greenish white water, and thin scattered puffs of vapor hovering over it, and suffusingly blowing off to leeward, like the confused scud from white rolling billows. The air around suddenly vibrated and tingled, as it were, like the air over intensely heated plates of iron. Beneath this atmospheric waving and curling, and partially beneath a thin layer of water, also, the whales were swimming. Seen in advance of all the other indications, the puffs of vapor they spouted, seemed their forerunning couriers and detached flying outriders.

This is the bottom level of good writing, whether in prose or verse; and a style which was able to maintain the qualities of accurate objective feeling which it exemplifies at other levels and for other purposes could not help being a great style. The words have feelers of their own, and the author contributes nothing to the emotion they call forth except the final phrasing, which adds nothing but finish to the paragraph. It is an example of words doing their own work; and let no one think it is not imaginative work, or does not come to an emotion, because the mode is that of close description, and neither directly expressive nor enacting. Let us compare it, with achieved emotion in mind, with a deliberately "emotional" description taken from the chapter called Enceladus in *Pierre*.

> Cunningly masked hitherto, by the green tapestry of the interlacing leaves, a terrific towering palisade of dark mossy massiness confronted you; and, trickling with unevaporable moisture, distilled upon you from its beetling brow slow thunder-showers of water-drops, chill as the last dews of death. . . . All round and round, the grim scarred rocks rallied and re-rallied themselves; shot up, protruded, stretched, swelled, and eagerly reached forth; on every side bristlingly radiated with hideous repellingness. . . . 'Mid this spectacle of wide and wanton spoil, insular noises of falling rocks would boomingly explode upon the silence and fright all the echoes, which ran shrieking in and out among the caves, as wailing women and children in some assaulted town.

This is, if I may insist on the term, putative description. It asserts itself to be description and passes for description until it is looked into, when you see that it is primarily the *assertion* of an emotional relation to landscape, and through effects of which landscape is incapable. Its force de-

pends on the looseness, vagueness, and tumultuousness of the motion of
the words. As a matter of fact the words are so chosen and arranged that
they cannot contribute any material of emotion beyond that which may
be contained in a stock exclamation. The primary point of our comparison
is that the second passage dilutes and wastes an emotion assumed to have
existed prior to its expression, whereas the first passage built up and united
the elements of an emotion which exists only and actually in the words
employed. The first passage discovers its meaning in words, the second
never reached the condition of meaning. The first passage reminds you of
Gerard Hopkins, the second of Ann Radcliffe; [7] a contrast which brings
up the secondary point of our comparison.

The spirit of the gothic novel ran frothily through the popular literature
of America in the first half of the nineteenth century, ending possibly
with its own travesty in The Black Crook. Melville, faced with the bad
necessity, as it must have seemed to him, of popularising the material of
Pierre and Moby Dick, adopted outright the gothic convention of language
with all its archaisms and rhetorical inflations. The effect in the two books
was similar in fact though not quite the same in effect. Some of the soliloquies in Moby Dick seem more like tantrums than poetry, but they were
the tantrums of a great imagination fed with mastered material. In Pierre,
without any fund of nourishing material, the dialogues, soliloquies, and
meditations get lost in the flatulence of words.

Now, the gothic convention is not insusceptible of reality in itself, as
we see in Beckford and Peacock and Brontë [8]—perhaps in Poe and occasionally in Hawthorne—but it requires on the part of the author unconditional assent to it as a convention. This assent Melville could not give;
he used it, so far as I can see, as a solemn fraud and hoped for the best.
In Moby Dick the fraud passed preliminary muster because the lofty "unreal" terror that rode the Pequod made it seem at least plausible, even in
its greatest extravagance, as a vehicle of response. And there is the further
defence, often made, that the worst excesses of language and sentiment are
excusable because of the poetry they are supposed to hold. To which the
answer is that the poetry would have been better without the excess; when
Melville dropped the mode and wrote in language comparable to the passage first quoted above, as in Ahab's last soliloquy, better poetry was actually produced. But no one, so far as I know, unless it be Foster Damon
who writes con amore of anything both American and gothic,[9] has defended the excesses of Pierre, of which the passage quoted above is a tame
example.

It may be said in passing that what is often called the Elizabethan influence in Melville's prose might more accurately be called the gothic influence heightened by the greatness of Melville's intentions. If I may have

[7] Gerard Manley Hopkins (1844–1888), English poet; Ann Radcliffe (1764–
1823), English novelist, writer of Gothic romances.
[8] William Beckford (1759–1844), English novelist; Thomas Love Peacock (1785–
1866), English novelist; Charlotte Brontë (1816–1855), English novelist.
[9] S. Foster Damon is a contemporary literary critic. For his defense of Pierre, see
"Pierre the Ambiguous," Hound and Horn, II (1929), 107–18.

the notation for what it is worth, I suspect that in "the three boats swung over the sea like three samphire baskets over high cliffs," while the samphire baskets undoubtedly came from *King Lear*, still they had got well spattered with gothic mire on the long journey. Again, the sister-brother crux in *Pierre*, while it may be found in John Ford [10] has a very different reality of expression from that in Ford's verse.

> The menacings in thy eyes are dear delights to me; I grow up with thy own glorious stature; and in thee, my brother, I see God's indignant ambassador to me, saying—Up, up, Isabel, and take no terms from the common world, but do thou make terms to it, and grind thy fierce rights out of it! Thy catching nobleness unsexes me, my brother; and now I know that in her most exalted moment, then woman no more feels the twin-born softness of her breasts, but feels chain-armour palpitating there!

These lines, spoken by Isabel in response to similar declarations on the part of Pierre on the occasion of their second conversation, could not have been matched in Ford, but they could be matched a hundred times in the popular gothics. As for the minor effects of Elizabethan influence, where it has been said, by Mumford [11] among others, that Melville's prose is Websterian [12]—and perhaps it sometimes is—yet it far more often supplies us with Marlovian [13] tropes. For every phrase such as "the cheeks of his soul collapsed in him," there are a dozen on the tone of the following: "With a frigate's anchors for my bridle-bits and fasces of harpoons for spurs, would I could mount that whale and leap the topmast skies . . .!" This is the Marlowe of Tamerlane, and the unregenerate Marlowe letting himself go, not the Marlowe remodelled and compacted of *Faustus* and *The Jew*. Occasionally there is such a triumphant meeting of rhetoric and insight as the passage which contains the famous phrases: "To trail the genealogies of these high mortal miseries, carries us at last among the sourceless primogenitures of the gods,"—a passage more mindful of the *Urn Burial* than of anything in *The Duchess of Malfi*,[14] but which is mindful most of Melville himself.

If it was the gothic excess that gave occasional opportunity for magnificent flashes, we should be grateful to it that much: it is at least a delight by the way; but it far more often produced passages like the speech of Isabel, which are perhaps collector's items, but not delights. Besides, what is most and finally illuminating, when Melville really had something to say, and was not making a novel, he resorted to another mode, which was perhaps the major expressive mode of his day, the mode of the liberal

[10] English dramatist (1586–*ca.* 1655).

[11] Lewis Mumford, contemporary critic and biographer of Melville, published his *Herman Melville* in 1929.

[12] The reference is to the style of John Webster (*ca.* 1580–1638), English dramatist.

[13] Christoper Marlowe (1564–1593), English poet and dramatist.

[14] *Urn Burial* was published in 1658 by Sir Thomas Browne (1605–1682); *The Duchess of Malfi* appeared in 1613 and was written by John Webster.

Emersonian sermon, the moral apologue on the broad Christian basis. There Melville's natural aptitude lay; when he preaches he is released, and only then, of all weak specifications. That the sermon was to say the best of it an artificial mode in fiction mattered nothing, and emphasises the fact that Melville was only a novelist betimes. He made only the loosest efforts to tie his sermons into his novels, and was quite content if he could see that his novels illustrated his sermons and reasonably content if they did not; or so the books would show. He preached without scruple, and with full authority, because he felt in full command of the mode he used: he believed in its convention of structure and its deeper convention of its relation to society with all his heart. Father Mapple's sermon on Jonah and Plotinus Phinlimmon's lecture—it is really a sermon—on Chronometricals and Horologicals are the two sustained examples of self-complete form in his work. The doctrine might not have appealed to Channing or Parker,[15] but the form, the execution, the litheness and vigour and verve, the homely aptnesses, the startling comparisons, the lucidity of presentation of hard insights, the dramatic and pictorial quality of the illustrations, and above all the richness of impact and the weighted speed of the words, would have appealed as near perfection.

The curiosity—and Melville looked at is all curiosity—that needs emphasis here is that the vices of his style either disappeared or transpired only as virtues when he shifted his mode to the sermon, and this without any addition of insight or eloquence, but simply, I believe, because he had found a mode which suited the bent of his themes, which allowed the putative statement to reach its full glory without further backing, which made room for rhetoric and demanded digression, and which did not trouble him, so great was his faith in it, with its universal lurking insincerity. Consider the following lines, which form the counter sermon to Phinlimmon's lecture in *Pierre*.

> All profound things, and emotions of things are preceded and attended by Silence. What a silence is that with which the pale bride precedes the responsive *I will*, to the priest's solemn question, *Wilt thou have this man for thy husband?* In silence, too, the wedded hands are clasped. Yea, in silence the child Christ was born into the world. Silence is the general consecration of the universe. Silence is the invisible laying on of the Divine Pontiff's hands upon the world. Silence is at once the most harmless and the most awful thing in all nature. It speaks of the Reserved Forces of Fate. Silence is the only Voice of our God.

> Nor is this so august Silence confined to things simply touching or grand. Like the air, Silence permeates all things, and produces its magical power, as well during that peculiar mood which prevails at a solitary traveller's first setting forth on a journey, as at the unimaginable time when before the world was, Silence brooded on the face of the waters.

[15] William Ellery Channing (1780–1842) and Theodore Parker (1810–1860) were American transcendentalists.

The author of these paragraphs was at home in his words and completely mastered by them; and he had reached in that language, what Pierre never reached, the "sense of uncapitulatable security, which is only the possession of the furthest advanced and profoundest souls."

In our present context there seems little more to say. The consideration of Melville as a novelist should have shown, at least in the superficial aspects which this brief essay has been able to touch, that it was precisely the practice of that craft that put his books, and himself, at a loss, and left him silent, stultified, and, before the great face of possibility, impotent for forty years of mature life. I trust that it will have been shown as at least plausible that Melville suffered the exorbitant penalty of his great failure, not as a result of the injuries inflicted upon him by his age, but because of his radical inability to master a technique—that of the novel —radically foreign to his sensibility. The accidents of his career, the worse accidents of his needs, brought him to a wrong choice. Yet had he made a right choice, the accident of his state of beliefs might well have silenced him altogether. Judging by the reception of his two serious books, he would have been anathema as a preacher and unpublishable as an essayist. We should be grateful for his ill luck in only a lesser sense than we are for Dante's, or we should have lost the only great imagination in the middle period of the American nineteenth century: a putative statement to which all readers must assent.

EDMUND WILSON

THE HISTORICAL INTERPRETATION OF LITERATURE [1]

(1941)

I want to talk about the historical interpretation of literature—that is, about the interpretation of literature in its social, economic and political aspects.

To begin with, it will be worth while to say something about the kind of criticism which seems to be furthest removed from this. There is a kind of comparative criticism which tends to be non-historical. The essays of T. S. Eliot, which have had such an immense influence in our time, are, for example, fundamentally non-historical. Eliot sees, or tries to see, the whole of literature, so far as he is acquainted with it, spread out before him under the aspect of eternity. He then compares the work of different periods and countries, and tries to draw from it general conclusions about what literature ought to be. He understands, of course, that our point of view in connection with literature changes, and he has what seems to me a very sound conception of the whole body of writing of the past, as something to which new works are continually being added, and which is not thereby merely increased in bulk but modified as a whole—so that Sophocles is no longer precisely what he was for Aristotle, or Shakespeare what he was for Ben Jonson or for Dryden or for Dr. Johnson, on account of all the later literature that has intervened between them and us. Yet at every point of this continual accretion, the whole field may be surveyed, as it were, spread out before the critic. The critic tries to see it as God might; he calls the books to a Day of Judgment. And, looking at things in this way, he may arrive at interesting and valuable conclusions which could hardly be reached by approaching them in any other way. Eliot was able to see, for example—what I believe had never been noticed before—that the French Symbolist poetry of the nineteenth century had certain fundamental resemblances to the English poetry of the age of Donne. Another kind of critic would draw certain historical conclusions from these purely esthetic findings, as the Russian D. S. Mirsky [2] did; but Eliot does not draw them.

Another example of this kind of non-historical criticism, in a somewhat different way and on a somewhat different plane, is the work of the late George Saintsbury. Saintsbury was a connoisseur of wines; he wrote an

---

[1] Originally delivered as a lecture at Princeton in 1940, first published in *The Intent of the Critic*, ed. Donald A. Stauffer (New Haven, 1941). Reprinted in *The Triple Thinkers* (New York, revised edition, 1948).

[2] Contemporary historian of Russian literature (1890–   ).

entertaining book on the subject.[3] And his attitude toward literature, too, was that of the connoisseur. He tastes the authors and tells you about the vintages; he distinguishes the qualities of the various wines. His palate was as fine as could be, and he possessed the great qualification that he knew how to take each book on its own terms without expecting it to be some other book and was thus in a position to appreciate a great variety of kinds of writing. He was a man of strong social prejudices and peculiarly intransigent political views, but, so far as it is humanly possible, he kept them out of his literary criticism. The result is one of the most agreeable and most comprehensive commentaries on literature that have ever been written in English. Most scholars who have read as much as Saintsbury do not have Saintsbury's discriminating taste. Here is a critic who has covered the whole ground like any academic historian, yet whose account of it is not merely a chronology but a record of fastidious enjoyment. Since enjoyment is the only thing he is looking for, he does not need to know the causes of things, and the historical background of literature does not interest him very much.

There is, however, another tradition of criticism which dates from the beginning of the eighteenth century. In the year 1725, the Neapolitan philosopher Vico published *La Scienza Nuova*, a revolutionary work on the philosophy of history, in which he asserted for the first time that the social world was certainly the work of man, and attempted what is, so far as I know, the first social interpretation of a work of literature. This is what Vico says about Homer: 'Homer composed the *Iliad* when Greece was young and consequently burning with sublime passions such as pride, anger and vengeance—passions which cannot allow dissimulation and which consort with generosity; so that she then admired Achilles, the hero of force. But, grown old, he composed the *Odyssey*, at a time when the passions of Greece were already somewhat cooled by reflection, which is the mother of prudence—so that she now admired Ulysses, the hero of wisdom. Thus also, in Homer's youth, the Greek people liked cruelty, vituperation, savagery, fierceness, ferocity; whereas, when Homer was old, they were already enjoying the luxuries of Alcinoüs, the delights of Calypso, the pleasures of Circe, the songs of the sirens and the pastimes of the suitors, who went no further in aggression and combat than laying siege to the chaste Penelope—all of which practices would appear incompatible with the spirit of the earlier time. The divine Plato is so struck by this difficulty that, in order to solve it, he tells us that Homer had foreseen in inspired vision these dissolute, sickly and disgusting customs. But in this way he makes Homer out to have been but a foolish instructor for Greek civilization, since, however much he may condemn them, he is displaying for imitation these corrupt and decadent habits which were not to be adopted till long after the foundation of the nations of Greece, and accelerating the natural course which human events would take by spurring the Greeks on to corruption. Thus it is plain that the Homer of the

[3] *Notes in a Wine-Cellar* by George Edward Bateman Saintsbury (1845–1933), English literary critic and historian.

Iliad must have preceded by many years the Homer who wrote the *Odyssey*; and it is plain that the former must belong to the northeastern part of Greece, since he celebrates the Trojan War, which took place in his part of the country, whereas the latter belongs to the southeastern part, since he celebrates Ulysses, who reigned there.'

You see that Vico has here explained Homer in terms both of historical period and of geographical origin. The idea that human arts and institutions were to be studied and elucidated as the products of the geographical and climatic conditions in which the people who created them lived, and of the phase of their social development through which they were passing at the moment, made great progress during the eighteenth century. There are traces of it even in Dr. Johnson, that most orthodox and classical of critics—as, for example, when he accounts for certain characteristics of Shakespeare by the relative barbarity of the age in which he lived, pointing out, just as Vico had done, that 'nations, like individuals, have their infancy.' And by the eighties of the eighteenth century Herder,[4] in his *Ideas on the Philosophy of History*, was writing of poetry that it was a kind of 'Proteus among the people, which is always changing its form in response to the languages, manners, and habits, to the temperaments and climates, nay even to the accents of different nations.' He said—what could still seem startling even so late as that—that 'language was not a divine communication, but something men had produced themselves. In the lectures on the philosophy of history that Hegel delivered in Berlin in 1822–23, he discussed the national literatures as expressions of the societies which had produced them—societies which he conceived as great organisms continually transforming themselves under the influence of a succession of dominant ideas.

In the field of literary criticism, this historical point of view came to its first complete flower in the work of the French critic Taine, in the middle of the nineteenth century. The whole school of historian-critics to which Taine belonged—Michelet, Renan,[5] Sainte-Beuve—had been occupied in interpreting books in terms of their historical origins. But Taine was the first of these to attempt to apply such principles systematically and on a large scale in a work devoted exclusively to literature. In the Introduction to his *History of English Literature*, published in 1863, he made his famous pronouncement that works of literature were to be understood as the upshot of three interfusing factors: *the moment, the race and the milieu*. Taine thought he was a scientist and a mechanist, who was examining works of literature from the same point of view as the chemist's in experimenting with chemical compounds. But the difference between the critic and the chemist is that the critic cannot first combine his elements and then watch to see what they will do: he can only examine phenomena which have already taken place. The procedure that Taine actually fol-

---

[4] Johann Gottfried von Herder (1744–1803), German philosopher, poet, and critic. His *Ideas on the Philosophy of History* was published 1784–91.
[5] Jules Michelet (1798–1874) and Ernst Renan (1823–1892) were French historians and literary critics.

lows is to pretend to set the stage for the experiment by describing the moment, the race and the milieu, and then to say: 'Such a situation demands such and such a kind of writer.' He now goes on to describe the kind of writer that the situation demands, and the reader finds himself at the end confronted with Shakespeare or Milton or Byron or whoever the great figure is—who turns out to prove the accuracy of Taine's prognosis by precisely living up to this description.

There was thus a certain element of imposture in Taine; but it was the rabbits he pulled out that saved him. If he had really been the mechanist that he thought he was, his work on literature would have had little value. The truth was that Taine loved literature for its own sake—he was at his best himself a brilliant artist—and he had very strong moral convictions which give his writing emotional power. His mind, to be sure, was an analytic one, and his analysis, though terribly oversimplified, does have an explanatory value. Yet his work was what we call creative. Whatever he may say about chemical experiments, it is evident when he writes of a great writer that the moment, the race and the milieu have combined, like the three sounds of the chord in Browning's poem about Abt Vogler, to produce not a fourth sound but a star.

To Taine's set of elements was added, dating from the middle of the century, a new element, the economic, which was introduced into the discussion of historical phenomena mainly by Marx and Engels.[6] The non-Marxist critics themselves were at the time already taking into account the influence of the social classes. In his chapters on the Norman conquest of England, Taine shows that the difference between the literatures produced respectively by the Normans and by the Saxons was partly the difference between a ruling class, on the one hand, and a vanquished and repressed class, on the other. And Michelet, in his volume on the Regency, which was finished the same year that the *History of English Literature* appeared, studies the *Manon Lescaut* of the Abbé Prévost[7] as a document representing the point of view of the small gentry before the French Revolution. But Marx and Engels derived the social classes from the way that people made or got their livings—from what they called the *methods of production*; and they tended to regard these economic processes as fundamental to civilization.

The Dialectical Materialism of Marx and Engels was not really so materialistic as it sounds. There was in it a large element of the Hegelian idealism that Marx and Engels thought they had got rid of. At no time did these two famous materialists take so mechanistic a view of things as Taine began by professing; and their theory of the relation of works of literature to what they called the *economic base* was a good deal less simple than Taine's theory of the moment, the race and the milieu. They thought that art, politics, religion, philosophy and literature belonged to what

---

[6] Karl Marx (1818–1883) and Friedrich Engels (1820–1895) were German socialists. The first volume of Karl Marx' *Das Kapital* appeared in 1867; it was completed by Engels in 1885 and 1895.

[7] Antoine François Prévost D'Exiles (1697–1763) wrote *Manon* in 1731.

they called the *superstructure* of human activity; but they saw that the practitioners of these various professions tended also to constitute social groups, and that they were always pulling away from the kind of solidarity based on economic classes in order to establish a professional solidarity of their own. Furthermore, the activities of the superstructure could influence one another, and they could influence the economic base. It may be said of Marx and Engels in general that, contrary to the popular impression, they were tentative, confused and modest when it came down to philosophical first principles, where a materialist like Taine was cocksure. Marx once made an attempt to explain why the poems of Homer were so good when the society that produced them was from his point of view —that is, from the point of view of its industrial development—so primitive; and this gave him a good deal of trouble. If we compare his discussion of this problem with Vico's discussion of Homer, we see that the explanation of literature in terms of a philosophy of social history is becoming, instead of simpler and easier, more difficult and more complex.

Marx and Engels were deeply imbued, moreover, with the German admiration for literature, which they had learned from the age of Goethe. It would never have occurred to either of them that *der Dichter* [8] was not one of the noblest and most beneficent of humankind. When Engels writes about Goethe, he presents him as a man equipped for 'practical life,' whose career was frustrated by the 'misery' of the historical situation in Germany in his time, and reproaches him for allowing himself to lapse into the 'cautious, smug and narrow' philistinism of the class from which he came; but Engels regrets this, because it interfered with the development of the 'mocking, defiant, world-despising genius,' 'der geniale Dichter,' 'der gewaltige Poet,' [9] of whom Engels would not even, he says, have asked that he should have been a political liberal if Goethe had not sacrificed to his bourgeois shrinkings his truer esthetic sense. And the great critics who were trained on Marx—Franz Mehring [10] and Bernard Shaw —had all this reverence for the priesthood of literature. Shaw deplores the absence of political philosophy and what he regards as the middle-class snobbery in Shakespeare; but he celebrates Shakespeare's poetry and his dramatic imagination almost as enthusiastically as Swinburne does, describing even those potboiling comedies, *Twelfth Night* and *As You Like It*—the themes of which seem to him most trashy—as 'the Crown Jewels of English dramatic poetry.' Such a critic may do more for a writer by showing him as a real man dealing with a real world at a definite moment of time than the impressionist critic of Swinburne's type who flourished in the same period of the late nineteenth century. The purely impressionist critic approaches the whole of literature as an exhibit of belletristic jewels, and he can only write a rhapsodic catalogue. But when Shaw turned his spotlight on Shakespeare as a figure in the Shavian drama of history, he invested him with a new interest as no other English critic had done.

[8] "the poet."
[9] "the highly gifted poet," "the powerful poet."
[10] German critic (1846–1919), biographer and editor of Marx.

The insistence that the man of letters should play a political role, the disparagement of works of art in comparison with political action, were thus originally no part of Marxism. They only became associated with it later. This happened by way of Russia, and it was due to special tendencies in that country that date from long before the Revolution or the promulgation of Marxism itself. In Russia there have been very good reasons why the political implications of literature should particularly occupy the critics. The art of Pushkin itself,[11] with its marvelous power of implication, had certainly been partly created by the censorship of Nicholas I, and Pushkin set the tradition for most of the great Russian writers that followed him. Every play, every poem, every story, must be a parable of which the moral is *implied*. If it were stated, the censor would suppress the book as he tried to do with Pushkin's *Bronze Horseman*, where it was merely a question of the packed implications protruding a little too plainly. Right down through the writings of Chekhov and up almost to the Revolution, the imaginative literature of Russia presents the peculiar paradox of an art that is technically objective and yet charged with social messages. In Russia under the Tsar, it was inevitable that social criticism should lead to political conclusions, because the most urgent need from the point of view of any kind of improvement was to get rid of the tsarist regime. Even the neo-Christian moralist Tolstoy, who pretended to be non-political, was to exert a subversive influence, because his independent preaching was bound to embroil him with the Church, and the Church was an integral part of the tsardom. Tolstoy's pamphlet called *What Is Art?*, in which he throws overboard Shakespeare and a large part of modern literature, including his own novels, in the interest of his intransigent morality, is the example which is most familiar to us of the moralizing Russian criticism; but it was only the most sensational expression of a kind of approach which had been prevalent since Belinsky and Chernyshevsky[12] in the early part of the century. The critics, who were usually journalists writing in exile or in a contraband press, were always tending to demand of the imaginative writers that they should dramatize bolder morals.

Even after the Revolution had destroyed the tsarist government, this state of things did not change. The old habits of censorship persisted in the new socialist society of the Soviets, which was necessarily made up of people who had been stamped by the die of the despotism. We meet here the peculiar phenomenon of a series of literary groups that attempt, one after the other, to obtain official recognition or to make themselves sufficiently powerful to establish themselves as arbiters of literature. Lenin and Trotsky and Lunacharsky[13] had the sense to oppose these attempts: the comrade-dictators of Proletcult or Lev or Rapp[14] would certainly have been just as bad as the Count Benckendorff who made Pushkin miserable,

---

[11] Aleksander Pushkin (1799–1837), Russian poet and short-story writer.
[12] Vissarion Belinsky (1810–1848) and Nikolay Chernyshevsky (1828–1889) were Russian literary critics and arbiters of Russian literary taste.
[13] A. V. Lunacharsky (1876–1933), Russian revolutionary dramatist.
[14] Soviet writers' organizations.

and when the Stalin bureaucracy, after the death of Gorky, got control of this department as of everything else, they instituted a system of repression that made Benckendorff and Nicholas I look like Lorenzo de' Medici. In the meantime, Trotsky, who was Commissar of War but himself a great political writer with an interest in belles-lettres, attempted, in 1924, apropos of one of these movements, to clarify the situation. He wrote a brilliant and valuable book called *Literature and Revolution*, in which he explained the aims of the government, analyzed the work of the Russian writers, and praised or rebuked the latter as they seemed to him in harmony or at odds with the former. Trotsky is intelligent, sympathetic; it is evident that he is really fond of literature and that he knows that a work of art does not fulfill its function in terms of the formulas of party propaganda. But Mayakovsky,[15] the Soviet poet, whom Trotsky had praised with reservations, expressed himself in a famous joke when he was asked what he thought of Trotsky's book—a pun which implied that a Commissar turned critic was inevitably a Commissar still; and what a foreigner cannot accept in Trotsky is his assumption that it is the duty of the government to take a hand in the direction of literature.

This point of view, indigenous to Russia, has been imported to other countries through the permeation of Communist influence. The Communist press and its literary followers have reflected the control of the Kremlin in all the phases through which it has passed, down to the wholesale imprisonment of Soviet writers which has been taking place since 1935. But it has never been a part of the American system that our Republican or Democratic administration should lay down a political line for the guidance of the national literature. A recent gesture in this direction on the part of Archibald MacLeish, who seems a little carried away by his position as Librarian of Congress, was anything but cordially received by serious American writers. So long as the United States remains happily a non-totalitarian country, we can very well do without this aspect of the historical criticism of literature.

Another element of a different order has, however, since Marx's time been added to the historical study of the origins of works of literature. I mean the psychoanalysis of Freud. This appears as an extension of something which had already got well started before, which had figured even in Johnson's *Lives of the Poets*, and of which the great exponent had been Sainte-Beuve: the interpretation of works of literature in the light of the personalities behind them. But the Freudians made this interpretation more exact and more systematic. The great example of the psychoanalysis of an artist is Freud's own essay on Leonardo da Vinci; but this has little critical interest: it is an attempt to construct a case history. One of the best examples I know of the application of Freudian analysis to literature is in Van Wyck Brooks's book, *The Ordeal of Mark Twain*, in which Mr. Brooks uses an incident of Mark Twain's boyhood as a key to his whole career. Mr. Brooks has since repudiated the method he resorted to here, on the ground that no one but an analyst can ever know enough

[15] V. V. Mayakovsky (1894-1930).

about a writer to make a valid psychoanalytic diagnosis. This is true, and it is true of the method that it has led to bad results where the critic has built a Freudian mechanism out of very slender evidence, and then given us what is really merely a romance exploiting the supposed working of this mechanism, in place of an actual study that sticks close to the facts and the documents of the writer's life and work. But I believe that Van Wyck Brooks really had hold of something important when he fixed upon that childhood incident of which Mark Twain gave so vivid an account to his biographer—that scene at the deathbed of his father when his mother had made him promise that he would not break her heart. If it was not one of those crucial happenings that are supposed to determine the complexes of Freud, it has certainly a typical significance in relation to Mark Twain's whole psychology. The stories that people tell about their childhood are likely to be profoundly symbolic even when they have been partly or wholly made up in the light of later experience. And the attitudes, the compulsions, the emotional 'patterns' that recur in the work of a writer are of great interest to the historical critic.

These attitudes and patterns are embedded in the community and the historical moment, and they may indicate its ideals and its diseases as the cell shows the condition of the tissue. The recent scientific experimentation in the combining of Freudian with Marxist method, and of psychoanalysis with anthropology, has had its parallel development in criticism. And there is thus another element added to our equipment for analyzing literary works, and the problem grows still more complex.

The analyst, however, is of course not concerned with the comparative values of his patients any more than the surgeon is. He cannot tell you why the neurotic Dostoevsky produces work of immense value to his fellows while another man with the same neurotic pattern would become a public menace. Freud himself emphatically states in his study of Leonardo that his method can make no attempt to account for Leonardo's genius. The problems of comparative artistic value still remain after we have given attention to the Freudian psychological factor just as they do after we have given attention to the Marxist economic factor and to the racial and geographical factors. No matter how thoroughly and searchingly we may have scrutinized works of literature from the historical and biographical points of view, we must be ready to attempt to estimate, in some such way as Saintsbury and Eliot do, the relative degrees of success attained by the products of the various periods and the various personalities. We must be able to tell good from bad, the first-rate from the second-rate. We shall not otherwise write literary criticism at all, but merely social or political history as reflected in literary texts, or psychological case histories from past eras, or, to take the historical point of view in its simplest and most academic form, merely chronologies of books that have been published.

And now how, in these matters of literary art, do we tell the good art from the bad? Norman Kemp Smith, the Kantian philosopher, whose courses I was fortunate enough to take at Princeton twenty-five years ago, used to tell us that this recognition was based primarily on an emotional reaction. For purposes of practical criticism this is a safe assumption on which to proceed. It is possible to discriminate in a variety of ways the elements that in any given department go to make a successful work of literature. Different schools have at different times demanded different things of literature: *unity, symmetry, universality, originality, vision, inspiration, strangeness, suggestiveness, improving morality, socialist realism,* etc. But you could have any set of these qualities that any school of writing has called for and still not have a good play, a good novel, a good poem, a good history. If you identify the essence of good literature with any one of these elements or with any combination of them, you simply shift the emotional reaction to the recognition of the element or elements. Or if you add to your other demands the demand that the writer must have *talent,* you simply shift this recognition to the talent. Once people find some grounds of agreement in the coincidence of their emotional reactions to books, they may be able to discuss these elements profitably; but if they do not have this basic agreement, the discussion will make no sense.

But how, you may ask, can we identify this élite who know what they are talking about? Well, it can only be said of them that they are self-appointed and self-perpetuating, and that they will compel you to accept their authority. Impostors may try to put themselves over, but these quacks will not last. The implied position of the people who know about literature (as is also the case in every other art) is simply that they know what they know, and that they are determined to impose their opinions by main force of eloquence or assertion on the people who do not know. This is not a question, of course, of professional workers in literature—such as editors, professors and critics, who very often have no real understanding of the products with which they deal—but of readers of all kinds in all walks of life. There are moments when a first-rate writer, unrecognized or out of fashion with the official chalkers-up for the market, may find his support in the demand for his work of an appreciative cultivated public.

But what is the cause of this emotional reaction which is the critic's divining rod? This question has long been a subject of study by the branch of philosophy called esthetics, and it has recently been made a subject of scientific experimentation. Both these lines of inquiry are likely to be prejudiced in the eyes of the literary critic by the fact that the inquiries are sometimes conducted by persons who are obviously deficient in literary feeling or taste. Yet one should not deny the possibility that something of value might result from the speculations and explorations of men of acute minds who take as their given data the esthetic emotions of other men.

Almost everybody interested in literature has tried to explain to himself the nature of these emotions that register our approval of artistic works; and I of course have my own explanation.

In my view, all our intellectual activity, in whatever field it takes place, is an attempt to give a meaning to our experience—that is, to make life more practicable; for by understanding things we make it easier to survive and get around among them. The mathematician Euclid, working in a convention of abstractions, shows us relations between the distances of our unwieldy and cluttered-up environment upon which we are able to count. A drama of Sophocles also indicates relations between the various human impulses, which appear so confused and dangerous, and it brings out a certain justice of Fate—that is to say, of the way in which the interaction of these impulses is seen in the long run to work out—upon which we can also depend. The kinship, from this point of view, of the purposes of science and art appears very clearly in the case of the Greeks, because not only do both Euclid and Sophocles satisfy us by making patterns, but they make much the same kind of patterns. Euclid's *Elements* takes simple theorems and by a series of logical operations builds them up to a climax in the square on the hypotenuse. A typical drama of Sophocles develops in a similar way.

Some writers (as well as some scientists) have a different kind of explicit message beyond the reassurance implicit in the mere feat of understanding life or of molding the harmony of artistic form. Not content with such an achievement as that of Sophocles—who has one of his choruses tell us that it is better not to be born, but who, by representing life as noble and based on law, makes its tragedy easier to bear—such writers attempt, like Plato, to think out and recommend a procedure for turning it into something better. But other departments of literature—lyric poetry such as Sappho's,[16] for example—have *less* philosophical content than Sophocles. A lyric gives us nothing but a pattern imposed on the expression of a feeling; but this pattern of metrical quantities and of consonants and vowels that balance has the effect of reducing the feeling, however unruly or painful it may seem when we experience it in the course of our lives, to something orderly, symmetrical and pleasing; and it also relates this feeling to the more impressive scheme, works it into the larger texture, of the body of poetic art. The discord has been resolved, the anomaly subjected to discipline. And this control of his emotion by the poet has the effect at second-hand of making it easier for the reader to manage his own emotions. (Why certain sounds and rhythms gratify us more than others, and how they are connected with the themes and ideas that they are chosen as appropriate for conveying, are questions that may be passed on to the scientist.)

And this brings us back again to the historical point of view. The experience of mankind on the earth is always changing as man develops and has to deal with new combinations of elements; and the writer who is to be anything more than an echo of his predecessors must always find expression for something which has never yet been expressed, must master a new set of phenomena which has never yet been mastered. With each such victory of the human intellect, whether in history, in philosophy or in poetry, we experience a deep satisfaction: we have been cured of some ache of disorder, relieved of some oppressive burden of uncomprehended events.

This relief that brings the sense of power, and, with the sense of power, joy, is the positive emotion which tells us that we have encountered a

[16] Greek lyric poetess who lived about 600 B.C.

first-rate piece of literature. But stay! you may at this point warn: are not people often solaced and exhilarated by literature of the trashiest kind? They are: crude and limited people do certainly feel some such emotion in connection with work that is limited and crude. The man who is more highly organized and has a wider intellectual range will feel it in connection with work that is finer and more complex. The difference between the emotion of the more highly organized man and the emotion of the less highly organized one is a matter of mere gradation. You sometimes discover books—the novels of John Steinbeck, for example—that seem to mark precisely the borderline between work that is definitely superior and work that is definitely bad. When I was speaking a little while back of the genuine connoisseurs who establish the standards of taste, I meant, of course, the people who can distinguish Grade A and who prefer it to the other grades.

LIONEL TRILLING

REALITY IN AMERICA [1]
From THE LIBERAL IMAGINATION
(1940–1946)

i

IT IS possible to say of V. L. Parrington that with his *Main Currents in American Thought* he has had an influence on our conception of American culture which is not equaled by that of any other writer of the last two decades. His ideas are now the accepted ones wherever the college course in American literature is given by a teacher who conceives himself to be opposed to the genteel and the academic and in alliance with the vigorous and the actual. And whenever the liberal historian of America finds occasion to take account of the national literature, as nowadays he feels it proper to do, it is Parrington who is his standard and guide. Parrington's ideas are the more firmly established because they do not have to be imposed—the teacher or the critic who presents them is likely to find that his task is merely to make articulate for his audience what it has always believed, for Parrington formulated in a classic way the suppositions about our culture which are held by the American middle class so far as that class is at all liberal in its social thought and so far as it begins to understand that literature has anything to do with society.

Parrington was not a great mind; he was not a precise thinker or, except when measured by the low eminences that were about him, an impressive one. Separate Parrington from his informing idea of the economic and social determination of thought and what is left is a simple intelligence, notable for its generosity and enthusiasm but certainly not for its accuracy or originality. Take him even with his idea and he is, once its direction is established, rather too predictable to be continuously interesting; and, indeed, what we dignify with the name of economic and social determinism amounts in his use of it to not much more than the demonstration that most writers incline to stick to their own social class. But his best virtue was real and important—he had what we like to think of as the saving salt of the American mind, the lively sense of the practical, workaday world, of the welter of ordinary undistinguished things and people, of the tangible, quirky, unrefined elements of life. He knew what so many literary historians do not know, that emotions and ideas are the sparks that fly when the mind meets difficulties.

<hr>

[1] "Reality in America," part i, was first published in *Partisan Review*, VII (1940), 24–40; part ii was first published in *The Nation*, CLXII (1946), 466–72. The text is from *The Liberal Imagination* (New York, 1950).

Yet he had after all but a limited sense of what constitutes a difficulty. Whenever he was confronted with a work of art that was complex, personal and not liberal, that was not, as it were, a public document, Parrington was at a loss. Difficulties that were complicated by personality or that were expressed in the language of successful art did not seem quite real to him and he was inclined to treat them as aberrations, which is one way of saying what everybody admits, that the weakest part of Parrington's talent was his aesthetic judgment. His admirers and disciples like to imply that his errors of aesthetic judgment are merely lapses of taste, but this is not so. Despite such mistakes as his notorious praise of Cabell,[2] to whom in a remarkable passage he compares Melville, Parrington's taste was by no means bad. His errors are the errors of understanding which arise from his assumptions about the nature of reality.

Parrington does not often deal with abstract philosophical ideas, but whenever he approaches a work of art we are made aware of the metaphysics on which his aesthetics is based. There exists, he believes, a thing called *reality*; it is one and immutable, it is wholly external, it is irreducible. Men's minds may waver, but reality is always reliable, always the same, always easily to be known. And the artist's relation to reality he conceives as a simple one. Reality being fixed and given, the artist has but to let it pass through him, he is the lens in the first diagram of an elementary book on optics: Fig. 1, Reality: Fig. 2, Artist; Fig. 1', Work of Art. Figs. 1 and 1' are normally in virtual correspondence with each other. Sometimes the artist spoils this ideal relation by "turning away from" reality. This results in certain fantastic works, unreal and ultimately useless. It does not occur to Parrington that there is any other relation possible between the artist and reality than this passage of reality through the transparent artist; he meets evidence of imagination and creativeness with a settled hostility the expression of which suggests that he regards them as the natural enemies of democracy.

In this view of things, reality, although it is always reliable, is always rather sober-sided, even grim. Parrington, a genial and enthusiastic man, can understand how the generosity of man's hopes and desires may leap beyond reality; he admires will in the degree that he suspects mind. To an excess of desire and energy which blinds a man to the limitations of reality he can indeed be very tender. This is one of the many meanings he gives to *romance* or *romanticism*, and in spite of himself it appeals to something in his own nature. The praise of Cabell is Parrington's response not only to Cabell's elegance—for Parrington loved elegance—but also to Cabell's insistence on the part which a beneficent self-deception may and even should play in the disappointing fact-bound life of man, particularly in the private and erotic part of his life.*

The second volume of *Main Currents* is called *The Romantic Revolution in America* and it is natural to expect that the word romantic should

* See, for example, how Parrington accounts for the "idealizing mind"—Melville's—by the discrepancy between "a wife in her morning kimono" and "the Helen of his dreams." Vol. II, p. 259. [Trilling's note]
[2] James Branch Cabell (b. 1879), American novelist.

appear in it frequently. So it does, more frequently than one can count, and seldom with the same meaning, seldom with the sense that the word, although scandalously vague as it has been used by the literary historians, is still full of complicated but not wholly pointless ideas, that it involves many contrary but definable things; all too often Parrington uses the word romantic with the word romance close at hand, meaning *a* romance, in the sense that *Graustark*[3] or *Treasure Island* is a romance, as though it signified chiefly a gay disregard of the limitations of everyday fact. Romance is refusing to heed the counsels of experience (p. iii); it is ebullience (p. iv); it is utopianism (p. iv); it is individualism (p. vi); it is self-deception (p. 59)—"romantic faith . . . in the beneficent processes of trade and industry" (as held, we inevitably ask, by the romantic Adam Smith?); it is the love of the picturesque (p. 49); it is the dislike of innovation (p. 50) but also the love of change (p. iv); it is the sentimental (p. 192); it is patriotism, and then it is cheap (p. 235). It may be used to denote what is not classical, but chiefly it means that which ignores reality (pp. ix, 136, 143, 147, and *passim*); it is not critical (pp. 225, 235), although in speaking of Cooper and Melville, Parrington admits that criticism can sometimes spring from romanticism.

Whenever a man with whose ideas he disagrees wins from Parrington a reluctant measure of respect, the word romantic is likely to appear. He does not admire Henry Clay, yet something in Clay is not to be despised —his romanticism, although Clay's romanticism is made equivalent with his inability to "come to grips with reality." Romanticism is thus, in most of its significations, the venial sin of *Main Currents*; like carnal passion in the *Inferno*, it evokes not blame but tender sorrow. But it can also be the great and saving virtue which Parrington recognizes. It is ascribed to the transcendental reformers he so much admires; it is said to mark two of his most cherished heroes, Jefferson and Emerson: "they were both romantics and their idealism was only a different expression of a common spirit." Parrington held, we may say, at least two different views of romanticism which suggest two different views of reality. Sometimes he speaks of reality in an honorific way, meaning the substantial stuff of life, the ineluctable facts with which the mind must cope, but sometimes he speaks of it pejoratively and means the world of established social forms; and he speaks of realism in two ways: sometimes as the power of dealing intelligently with fact, sometimes as a cold and conservative resistance to idealism.

Just as for Parrington there is a saving grace and a venial sin, there is also a deadly sin, and this is turning away from reality, not in the excess of generous feeling, but in what he believes to be a deficiency of feeling, as with Hawthorne, or out of what amounts to sinful pride, as with Henry James. He tells us that there was too much realism in Hawthorne to allow him to give his faith to the transcendental reformers: "he was too much of a realist to change fashions in creeds"; "he remained cold to the revolutionary criticism that was eager to pull down the old temples

[3] Published in 1901 by George Barr McCutcheon (1866–1928), American novelist.

to make room for nobler." It is this cold realism, keeping Hawthorne apart from his enthusiastic contemporaries, that alienates Parrington's sympathy —"Eager souls, mystics and revolutionaries, may propose to refashion the world in accordance with their dreams; but evil remains, and so long as it lurks in the secret places of the heart, utopia is only the shadow of a dream. And so while the Concord thinkers were proclaiming man to be the indubitable child of God, Hawthorne was critically examining the question of evil as it appeared in the light of his own experience. It was the central fascinating problem of his intellectual life, and in pursuit of a solution he probed curiously into the hidden, furtive recesses of the soul." Parrington's disapproval of the enterprise is unmistakable.

Now we might wonder whether Hawthorne's questioning of the naïve and often eccentric faiths of the transcendental reformers was not, on the face of it, a public service. But Parrington implies that it contributes nothing to democracy, and even that it stands in the way of the realization of democracy. If democracy depends wholly on a fighting faith, I suppose he is right. Yet society is after all something that exists at the moment as well as in the future, and if one man wants to probe curiously into the hidden furtive recesses of the contemporary soul, a broad democracy and especially one devoted to reality should allow him to do so without despising him. If what Hawthorne did was certainly nothing to build a party on, we ought perhaps to forgive him when we remember that he was only one man and that the future of mankind did not depend upon him alone. But this very fact serves only to irritate Parrington; he is put out by Hawthorne's loneliness and believes that part of Hawthorne's insufficiency as a writer comes from his failure to get around and meet people. Hawthorne could not, he tells us, establish contact with the "Yankee reality," and was scarcely aware of the "substantial world of Puritan reality that Samuel Sewall [4] knew."

To turn from reality might mean to turn to romance, but Parrington tells us that Hawthorne was romantic "only in a narrow and very special sense." He was not interested in the world of, as it were, practical romance, in the Salem of the clipper ships; from this he turned away to create "a romance of ethics." This is not an illuminating phrase but it is a catching one, and it might be taken to mean that Hawthorne was in the tradition of, say, Shakespeare; but we quickly learn that, no, Hawthorne had entered a barren field, for although he himself lived in the present and had all the future to mold, he preferred to find many of his subjects in the past. We learn too that his romance of ethics is not admirable because it requires the hard, fine pressing of ideas, and we are told that "a romantic uninterested in adventure and afraid of sex is likely to become somewhat graveled for matter." In short, Hawthorne's mind was a thin one, and Parrington puts in evidence his use of allegory and symbol and the very severity and precision of his art to prove that he suffered from a sadly limited intellect, for so much fancy and so much art could scarcely be needed unless the writer were trying to exploit to the utmost the few poor ideas that he had.

[4] Puritan writer and diarist (1652-1730).

Hawthorne, then, was "forever dealing with shadows, and he knew that he was dealing with shadows." Perhaps so, but shadows are also part of reality and one would not want a world without shadows, it would not even be a "real" world. But we must get beyond Parrington's metaphor. The fact is that Hawthorne was dealing beautifully with realities, with substantial things. The man who could raise those brilliant and serious doubts about the nature and possibility of moral perfection, the man who could keep himself aloof from the "Yankee reality" and who could dissent from the orthodoxies of dissent and tell us so much about the nature of moral zeal, is of course dealing exactly with reality.

Parrington's characteristic weakness as a historian is suggested by his title, for the culture of a nation is not truly figured in the image of the current. A culture is not a flow, nor even a confluence; the form of its existence is struggle, or at least debate—it is nothing if not a dialectic. And in any culture there are likely to be certain artists who contain a large part of the dialectic within themselves, their meaning and power lying in their contradictions; they contain within themselves, it may be said, the very essence of the culture, and the sign of this is that they do not submit to serve the ends of any one ideological group or tendency. It is a significant circumstance of American culture, and one which is susceptible of explanation, that an unusually large proportion of its notable writers of the nineteenth century were such repositories of the dialectic of their times—they contained both the yes and the no of their culture, and by that token they were prophetic of the future. Parrington said that he had not set up shop as a literary critic; but if a literary critic is simply a reader who has the ability to understand literature and to convey to others what he understands, it is not exactly a matter of free choice whether or not a cultural historian shall be a literary critic, nor is it open to him to let his virtuous political and social opinions do duty for percipience. To throw out Poe because he cannot be conveniently fitted into a theory of American culture, to speak of him as a biological sport and as a mind apart from the main current, to find his gloom to be merely personal and eccentric, "only the atrabilious wretchedness of a dipsomaniac," as Hawthorne's was "no more than the skeptical questioning of life by a nature that knew no fierce storms," to judge Melville's response to American life to be less noble than that of Bryant or of Greeley,[5] to speak of Henry James as an escapist, as an artist similar to Whistler,[6] a man characteristically afraid of stress—this is not merely to be mistaken in aesthetic judgment; rather it is to examine without attention and from the point of view of a limited and essentially arrogant conception of reality the documents which are in some respects the most suggestive testimony to what America was and is, and of course to get no answer from them.

Parrington lies twenty years behind us, and in the intervening time there has developed a body of opinion which is aware of his inadequacies and of the inadequacies of his coadjutors and disciples, who make up what

[5] Horace Greeley (1811–1872), famous American journalist.
[6] James Abbott McNeill Whistler (1834–1903), American artist.

might be called the literary academicism of liberalism. Yet Parrington still stands at the center of American thought about American culture because, as I say, he expresses the chronic American belief that there exists an opposition between reality and mind and that one must enlist oneself in the party of reality.

ii

This belief in the incompatibility of mind and reality is exemplified by the doctrinaire indulgence which liberal intellectuals have always displayed toward Theodore Dreiser, an indulgence which becomes the worthier of remark when it is contrasted with the liberal severity toward Henry James. Dreiser and James: with that juxtaposition we are immediately at the dark and bloody crossroads where literature and politics meet. One does not go there gladly, but nowadays it is not exactly a matter of free choice whether one does or does not go. As for the particular juxtaposition itself, it is inevitable and it has at the present moment far more significance than the juxtaposition which once used to be made between James and Whitman. It is not hard to contrive factitious oppositions between James and Whitman, but the real difference between them is the difference between the moral mind, with its awareness of tragedy, irony, and multitudinous distinctions, and the transcendental mind, with its passionate sense of the oneness of multiplicity. James and Whitman are unlike not in quality but in kind, and in their very opposition they serve to complement each other. But the difference between James and Dreiser is not of kind, for both men addressed themselves to virtually the some social and moral fact. The difference here is one of quality, and perhaps nothing is more typical of American liberalism than the way it has responded to the respective qualities of the two men.

Few critics, I suppose, no matter what their political disposition, have ever been wholly blind to James's great gifts, or even to the grandiose moral intention of these gifts. And few critics have ever been wholly blind to Dreiser's great faults. But by liberal critics James is traditionally put to the ultimate question: of what use, of what actual political use, are his gifts and their intention? Granted that James was devoted to an extraordinary moral perceptiveness, granted too that moral perceptiveness has something to do with politics and the social life, of what possible practical value in our world of impending disaster can James's work be? And James's style, his characters, his subjects, and even his own social origin and the manner of his personal life are adduced to show that his work cannot endure the question. To James no quarter is given by American criticism in its political and liberal aspect. But in the same degree that liberal criticism is moved by political considerations to treat James with severity, it treats Dreiser with the most sympathetic indulgence. Dreiser's literary faults, it gives us to understand, are essentially social and political virtues. It was Parrington who established the formula for the liberal criticism of Dreiser by calling him a "peasant": when Dreiser thinks stupidly, it is because he has the slow stubbornness of a peasant; when he writes badly, it is because he is impatient of the sterile literary gentility of the bour-geoisie. It is as if wit, and flexibility of mind, and perception, and knowl-edge were to be equated with aristocracy and political reaction, while dullness and stupidity must naturally suggest a virtuous democracy, as in the old plays.

The liberal judgment of Dreiser and James goes back of politics, goes back to the cultural assumptions that make politics. We are still haunted by a kind of political fear of the intellect which Tocqueville observed in us more than a century ago.[7] American intellectuals, when they are being consciously American or political, are remarkably quick to suggest that an art which is marked by perception and knowledge, although all very well in its way, can never get us through gross dangers and difficulties. And their misgivings become the more intense when intellect works in art as it ideally should, when its processes are vivacious and interesting and brilliant. It is then that we like to confront it with the gross dangers and difficulties and to challenge it to save us at once from disaster. When intellect in art is awkward or dull we do not put it to the test of ultimate or immediate practicality. No liberal critic asks the question of Dreiser whether *his* moral preoccupations are going to be useful in confronting the disasters that threaten us. And it is a judgment on the proper nature of mind, rather than any actual political meaning that might be drawn from the works of the two men, which accounts for the unequal justice they have received from the progressive critics. If it could be conclusively demonstrated—by, say, documents in James's handwriting—that James ex-plicitly intended his books to be understood as pleas for co-operatives, labor unions, better housing, and more equitable taxation, the American critic in his liberal and progressive character would still be worried by James because his work shows so many of the electric qualities of mind. And if something like the opposite were proved of Dreiser, it would be brushed aside—as his doctrinaire anti-Semitism has in fact been brushed aside—because his books have the awkwardness, the chaos, the heaviness which we associate with "reality." In the American metaphysic, reality is always material reality, hard, resistant, unformed, impenetrable, and un-pleasant. And that mind is alone felt to be trustworthy which most re-sembles this reality by most nearly reproducing the sensations it affords.

In *The Rise of American Civilization*, Professor Beard[8] uses a signifi-cant phrase when, in the course of an ironic account of James's career, he implies that we have the clue to the irrelevance of that career when we know that James was "a whole generation removed from the odors of the shop." Of a piece with this, and in itself even more significant, is the com-ment which Granville Hicks makes in *The Great Tradition*[9] when he

[7] Count Alexis de Tocqueville (1805-1859), French statesman and author, pub-lished his *De la Démocratie en Amérique* in Paris in 1835. It still remains the classic account by a foreign observer of our manners and civilization. The latest edi-tion of the work, *Democracy in America*, edited by Phillips Bradley, appeared in two volumes, New York, 1945.

[8] Charles A. Beard (1874-1948), American historian, published *The Rise of American Civilization* in 1927-42.

[9] Granville Hicks (b. 1901) published his Marxist interpretation, *The Great Tradition*, in 1933 (rev. ed., 1935).

deals with James's stories about artists and remarks that such artists as James portrays, so concerned for their art and their integrity in art, do not really exist: "After all, who has ever known such artists? Where are the Hugh Verekers, the Mark Ambients, the Neil Paradays, the Overts, Limberts, Dencombes, Delavoys?" This question, as Mr. Hicks admits, had occurred to James himself, but what answer had James given to it? "If the life about us for the last thirty years refused warrant for these examples," he said in the preface to volume XII of the New York Edition, "then so much the worse for that life. . . . There are decencies that in the name of the general self-respect we must take for granted, there's a rudimentary intellectual honor to which we must, in the interest of civilization, at least pretend." And to this Mr. Hicks, shocked beyond argument, makes this reply, which would be astonishing had we not heard it before: "But this is the purest romanticism, this writing about what ought to be rather than what is!"

The "odors of the shop" are real, and to those who breathe them they guarantee a sense of vitality from which James is debarred. The idea of intellectual honor is not real, and to that chimera James was devoted. He betrayed the reality of what is in the interests of what ought to be. Dare we trust him? The question, we remember, is asked by men who themselves have elaborate transactions with what ought to be. Professor Beard spoke in the name of a growing, developing, and improving America. Mr. Hicks, when he wrote *The Great Tradition*, was in general sympathy with a nominally radical movement. But James's own transaction with what ought to be is suspect because it is carried on through what I have called the electrical qualities of mind, through a complex and rapid imagination and with a kind of authoritative immediacy. Mr. Hicks knows that Dreiser is "clumsy" and "stupid" and "bewildered" and "crude in his statement of materialistic monism"; he knows that Dreiser in his personal life—which is in point because James's personal life is always supposed to be so much in point—was not quite emancipated from "his boyhood longing for crass material success," showing "again and again a desire for the ostentatious luxury of the successful business man." But Dreiser is to be accepted and forgiven because his faults are the sad, lovable, honorable faults of reality itself, or of America itself—huge, inchoate, struggling toward expression, caught between the dream of raw power and the dream of morality.

"The liability in what Santayana called the genteel tradition was due to its being the product of mind apart from experience. Dreiser gave us the stuff of our common experience, not as it was hoped to be by any idealizing theorist, but as it actually was in its crudity." The author of this statement certainly cannot be accused of any lack of feeling for mind as Henry James represents it; nor can Mr. Matthiessen [10] be thought of as a follower of Parrington—indeed, in the preface to *American Renaissance* he has framed one of the sharpest and most cogent criticisms of Parrington's method. Yet Mr. Matthiessen, writing in the *New York Times Book*

[10] Francis Otto Matthiessen (1902–1950), American scholar and critic, published his *American Renaissance* in 1941.

Review about Dreiser's posthumous novel, *The Bulwark,* accepts the liberal cliché which opposes crude experience to mind and establishes Dreiser's value by implying that the mind which Dreiser's crude experience is presumed to confront and refute is the mind of gentility.

This implied amalgamation of mind with gentility is the rationale of the long indulgence of Dreiser, which is extended even to the style of his prose. Everyone is aware that Dreiser's prose style is full of roughness and ungainliness, and the critics who admire Dreiser tell us it does not matter. Of course it does not matter. No reader with a right sense of style would suppose that it does matter, and he might even find it a virtue. But it has been taken for granted that the ungainliness of Dreiser's style is the only possible objection to be made to it, and that whoever finds in it any fault at all wants a prettified genteel style (and is objecting to the ungainliness of reality itself). For instance, Edwin Berry Burgum,[11] in a leaflet on Dreiser put out by the Book Find Club, tells us that Dreiser was one of those who used—or, as Mr. Burgum says, utilized—"the diction of the Middle West, pretty much as it was spoken, rich in colloquialism and frank in the simplicity and directness of the pioneer tradition," and that this diction took the place of "the literary English, formal and bookish, of New England provincialism that was closer to the aristocratic spirit of the mother country than to the tang of everyday life in the new West." This is mere fantasy. Hawthorne, Thoreau, and Emerson were for the most part remarkably colloquial—they wrote, that is, much as they spoke; their prose was specifically American in quality, and, except for occasional lapses, quite direct and simple. It is Dreiser who lacks the sense of colloquial diction—that of the Middle West or any other. If we are to talk of bookishness, it is Dreiser who is bookish; he is precisely literary in the bad sense; he is full of flowers of rhetoric and shines with paste gems; at hundreds of points his diction is not only genteel but fancy. It is he who speaks of "a scene more distingué than this," or of a woman "artistic in form and feature," or of a man who, although "strong, reserved, aggressive, with an air of wealth and experience, was *soi-disant* and not particularly eager to stay at home." Colloquialism held no real charm for him and his natural tendency is always toward the "fine":

> . . . Moralists come and go; religionists fulminate and declare the pronouncements of God as to this; but Aphrodite still reigns. Embowered in the festal depths of the spring, set above her altars of porphyry, chalcedony, ivory and gold, see her smile the smile that is at once the texture and essence of delight, the glory and despair of the world! Dream on, oh Buddha, asleep on your lotus leaf, of an undisturbed Nirvana! Sweat, oh Jesus, your last agonizing drops over an unregenerate world! In the forests of Pan still ring the cries of the worshippers of Aphrodite! From her altars the incense of adoration ever rises! And see, the new red grapes dripping where votive hands new-press them!

Charles Jackson, the novelist, telling us in the same leaflet that Dreiser's style does not matter, remarks on how much still comes to us when we

[11] Contemporary American literary critic.

have lost by translation the stylistic brilliance of Thomas Mann or the Russians or Balzac. He is in part right. And he is right too when he says that a certain kind of conscious, supervised artistry is not appropriate to the novel of large dimensions. Yet the fact is that the great novelists have usually written very good prose, and what comes through even a bad translation is exactly the power of mind that made the well-hung sentence of the original text. In literature style is so little the mere clothing of thought—need it be insisted on at this late date?—that we may say that from the earth of the novelist's prose spring his characters, his ideas, and even his story itself.*

To the extent that Dreiser's style is defensible, his thought is also defensible. That is, when he thinks like a novelist, he is worth following—when by means of his rough and ungainly but no doubt cumulatively effective style he creates rough, ungainly, but effective characters and events. But when he thinks like, as we say, a philosopher, he is likely to be not only foolish but vulgar. He thinks as the modern crowd thinks when it decides to think: religion and morality are nonsense, "religionists" and moralists are fakes, tradition is a fraud, what is man but matter and impulses, mysterious "chemisms," what value has life anyway? "What, cooking, eating, coition, job holding, growing, aging, losing, winning, in so changeful and passing a scene as this, important? Bunk! It is some form of titillating illusion with about as much import to the superior forces that bring it all about as the functions and gyrations of a fly. No more. And maybe less." Thus Dreiser at sixty. And yet there is for him always the vulgarly saving suspicion that maybe, when all is said and done, there is Something Behind It All. It is much to the point of his intellectual vulgarity that Dreiser's anti-Semitism was not merely a social prejudice but an idea, a way of dealing with difficulties.

No one, I suppose, has ever represented Dreiser as a masterly intellect. It is even commonplace to say that his ideas are inconsistent or inadequate. But once that admission has been made, his ideas are hustled out of sight while his "reality" and great brooding pity are spoken of. (His pity is to be questioned: pity is to be judged by kind, not amount, and Dreiser's

---

* The latest defense of Dreiser's style, that in the chapter on Dreiser in the *Literary History of the United States,* is worth noting: "Forgetful of the integrity and power of Dreiser's whole work, many critics have been distracted into a condemnation of his style. He was, like Twain and Whitman, an organic artist; he wrote what he knew—what he was. His many colloquialisms were part of the coinage of his time, and his sentimental and romantic passages were written in the language of the educational system and the popular literature of his formative years. In his style, as in his material, he was a child of his time, of his class. Self-educated, a type or model of the artist of plebeian origin in America, his language, like his subject matter, is not marked by internal inconsistencies." No doubt Dreiser was an organic artist in the sense that he wrote what he knew and what he was, but so, I suppose, is every artist; the question for criticism comes down to *what* he knew and *what* he was. That he was a child of his time and class is also true, but this can be said of everyone without exception; the question for criticism is how he transcended the imposed limitations of his time and class. As for the defense made on the ground of his particular class, it can only be said that liberal thought has come to a strange pass when it assumes that a plebeian origin is accountable for a writer's faults through all his intellectual life. [Trilling's note]

pity—*Jennie Gerhardt* provides the only exception—is either destructive of its object or it is self-pity.) Why has no liberal critic ever brought Dreiser's ideas to the bar of political practicality, asking what use is to be made of Dreiser's dim, awkward speculation, of his self-justification, of his lust for "beauty" and "sex" and "living" and "life itself," and of the showy nihilism which always seems to him so grand a gesture in the direction of profundity? We live, understandably enough, with the sense of urgency; our clock, like Baudelaire's, has had the hands removed and bears the legend, "It is later than you think." But with us it is always a little too late for mind, yet never too late for honest stupidity; always a little too late for understanding, never too late for righteous, bewildered wrath; always too late for thought, never too late for naïve moralizing. We seem to like to condemn our finest but not our worst qualities by pitting them against the exigency of time.

But sometimes time is not quite so exigent as to justify all our own exigency, and in the case of Dreiser time has allowed his deficiencies to reach their logical, and fatal, conclusion. In *The Bulwark* Dreiser's characteristic ideas come full circle, and the simple, didactic life history of Solon Barnes, a Quaker business man, affirms a simple Christian faith, and a kind of practical mysticism, and the virtues of self-abnegation and self-restraint, and the belief in and submission to the hidden purposes of higher powers, those "superior forces that bring it all about"—once, in Dreiser's opinion, so brutally indifferent, now somehow benign. This is not the first occasion on which Dreiser has shown a tenderness toward religion and a responsiveness to mysticism. *Jennie Gerhardt* and the figure of the Reverend Duncan McMillan in *An American Tragedy* are forecasts of the avowals of *The Bulwark*, and Dreiser's lively interest in power of any sort led him to take account of the power implicit in the cruder forms of mystical performance. Yet these rifts in his nearly monolithic materialism cannot quite prepare us for the blank pietism of *The Bulwark*, not after we have remembered how salient in Dreiser's work has been the long surly rage against the "religionists" and the "moralists," the men who have presumed to believe that life can be given any law at all and who have dared to suppose that will or mind or faith can shape the savage and beautiful entity that Dreiser liked to call "life itself." Now for Dreiser the law may indeed be given, and it is wholly simple—the safe conduct of the personal life requires only that we follow the Inner Light according to the regimen of the Society of Friends,[12] or according to some other godly rule. And now the smiling Aphrodite set above her altars of porphyry, chalcedony, ivory, and gold is quite forgotten, and we are told that the sad joy of cosmic acceptance goes hand in hand with sexual abstinence.

Dreiser's mood of "acceptance" in the last years of his life is not, as a personal experience, to be submitted to the tests of intellectual validity. It consists of a sensation of cosmic understanding, of an overarching sense of

---

[12] The Quakers, a Christian sect founded by George Fox about 1650. They believed each individual possessed an "inner light" which was his guide in all matters in this world.

unity with the world in its apparent evil as well as in its obvious good. It is no more to be quarreled with, or reasoned with, than love itself—indeed, it is a kind of love, not so much of the world as of oneself in the world. Perhaps it is either the cessation of desire or the perfect balance of desires. It is what used often to be meant by "peace," and up through the nineteenth century a good many people understood its meaning. If it was Dreiser's own emotion at the end of his life, who would not be happy that he had achieved it? I am not even sure that our civilization would not be the better for more of us knowing and desiring this emotion of grave felicity. Yet granting the personal validity of the emotion, Dreiser's exposition of it fails, and is, moreover, offensive. Mr. Matthiessen has warned us of the attack that will be made on the doctrine of *The Bulwark* by "those who believe that any renewal of Christianity marks a new 'failure of nerve.'" But Dreiser's religious avowal is not a failure of nerve—it is a failure of mind and heart. We have only to set his book beside any work in which mind and heart are made to serve religion to know this at once. Ivan Karamazov's giving back his ticket of admission to the "harmony" of the universe suggests that *The Bulwark* is not morally adequate, for we dare not, as its hero does, blandly "accept" the suffering of others; and the Book of Job tells us that it does not include enough in its exploration of the problem of evil, and is not stern enough. I have said that Dreiser's religious affirmation was offensive; the offense lies in the vulgar ease of its formulation, as well as in the comfortable untroubled way in which Dreiser moved from nihilism to pietism.*

The Bulwark is the fruit of Dreiser's old age, but if we speak of it as a failure of thought and feeling, we cannot suppose that with age Dreiser weakened in mind and heart. The weakness was always there. And in a sense it is not Dreiser who failed but a whole way of dealing with ideas, a way in which we have all been in some degree involved. Our liberal, progressive culture tolerated Dreiser's vulgar materialism with its huge negation, its simple cry of "Bunk!," feeling that perhaps it was not quite intellectually adequate but certainly very *strong*, certainly very *real*. And now, almost as a natural consequence, it has been given, and is not unwilling to take, Dreiser's pietistic religion in all its inadequacy.

Dreiser, of course, was firmer than the intellectual culture that accepted him. He *meant* his ideas, at least so far as a man can mean ideas who is incapable of following them to their consequences. But we, when it came to his ideas, talked about his great brooding pity and shrugged the ideas off. We are still doing it. Robert Elias, the biographer of Dreiser, tells us that "it is part of the logic of [Dreiser's] life that he should have completed *The Bulwark* at the same time that he joined the Communists."

* This ease and comfortableness seem to mark contemporary religious conversions. Religion nowadays has the appearance of what the ideal modern house has been called, "a machine for living," and seemingly one makes up one's mind to acquire and use it not with spiritual struggle but only with a growing sense of its practicability and convenience. Compare *The Seven Storey Mountain*, which Monsignor Sheen calls "a twentieth-century form of the *Confessions* of St. Augustine," with the old, the as it were original, *Confessions* of St. Augustine. [Trilling's note]

Just what kind of logic this is we learn from Mr. Elias's further statement. "When he supported left-wing movements and finally, last year, joined the Communist Party, he did so not because he had examined the details of the party line and found them satisfactory, but because he agreed with a general program that represented a means for establishing his cherished goal of greater equality among men." Whether or not Dreiser was following the logic of his own life, he was certainly following the logic of the liberal criticism that accepted him so undiscriminatingly as one of the great, significant expressions of its spirit. This is the liberal criticism, in the direct line of Parrington, which establishes the social responsibility of the writer and then goes on to say that, apart from his duty of resembling reality as much as possible, he is not really responsible for anything, not even for his ideas. The scope of reality being what it is, ideas are held to be mere "details," and, what is more, to be details which, if attended to, have the effect of diminishing reality. But ideals are different from ideas; in the liberal criticism which descends from Parrington ideals consort happily with reality and they urge us to deal impatiently with ideas—a "cherished goal" forbids that we stop to consider how we reach it, or if we may not destroy it in trying to reach it the wrong way.

CLEANTH BROOKS

[MODERN CRITICISM] [1]
(1949)

"MODERN CRITICISM, through its exacting scrutiny of literary texts, has demonstrated with finality that in art beauty and truth are indivisible and one." So writes Mark Schorer in a recent essay on criticism, and he continues as follows: *

> The Keatsian overtones of these terms are mitigated and an old dilemma solved if for beauty we substitute form, and for truth, content. We may, without risk of loss, narrow them even more, and speak of technique and subject matter. Modern criticism has shown us that to speak of content as such is not to speak of art at all, but of experience, and that it is only when we speak of the *achieved* content, the form, the work of art as a work of art, that we speak as critics. The difference between content, or experience, and achieved content, or art, is technique.
>
> When we speak of technique, then, we speak of nearly everything. For technique is the means by which the writer's experience, which is his subject matter, compels him to attend to it; technique is the only means he has of discovering, exploring, developing his subject, of conveying its meaning, and, finally, of evaluating it.

I subscribe to all that is said here. It is an admirable summary of what modern criticism has achieved. But I envy Schorer his boldness of tone: "Modern criticism has demonstrated with finality," "Modern criticism has shown us," etc. For I am conscious that nearly every statement that he makes has been, and continues to be, challenged; and further, that some of those who would accept his summary as a statement of the accomplishment of modern criticism, place a very different value on the accomplishment. Modern criticism has been blamed for strangling the creative impulse, for producing an arid intellectualization of our poetry, for perverting literary studies. If one is to provide a really serviceable introduction to such a volume as this, he had better not leave such charges out of account. Ignored, such charges confuse the issues on every level.

There is something to be said, then, for a general stock-taking, and particularly at the present time. The recent publication of books like Stanley Hyman's *The Armed Vision*, and Eric Bentley's *The Importance of Scrutiny*, or of essays like R. P. Blackmur's *A Burden for Critics* and of Schorer's *Technique as Discovery*, already mentioned—all suggest the sense

* From *The Hudson Review*, 1 (Spring, 1948), 67. [Brooks's note]
[1] First published as a Foreword to *Critiques and Essays in Criticism 1920-1948*, selected by Robert Wooster Stallman. The Ronald Press, New York, 1949.

of a period's having been fulfilled. The criticism characteristic of our time has come to fruition, or has arrived at a turning point, or, as some writers hint, has now exhausted its energies. For those who would dwell upon this darker note there are further corroborative signs: the increasing tendency to talk about the "methods" of the "new" criticism; the growing academic respectability of the new criticism; the attempt to codify the new critics and to establish their sources and derivations. As it consolidates its gains, the new criticism ceases to be "new" and thus loses its romantic attractiveness, and with that, some of its more callow proponents. But, by the same token, it risks gaining the allegiance of another set of followers who hope to exploit it mechanically.

Yet, though a general stock-taking is in order, I shall not attempt it here. In the first place, it could hardly be done satisfactorily in a short introduction. In the second place, as a contributor to this volume, I do not wish to seem to sit in judgment upon my peers, defining what is central to the new criticism and what is peripheral. Suffice it to recognize that there is a large area of agreement among the critics represented in this volume. But they do not constitute a school—much less a guild. I have no wish to minimize their varying emphases and their active disagreements. It is even a question whether they are accurately described under a common name, and most of all under the name which has caught on—the "new criticism."

I suppose that when John Crowe Ransom chose the phrase a few years ago, he meant it to be a neutral and modest designation; i.e., the modern criticism, the contemporary criticism. Despite such intent, the name has hardly proved a happy choice. It has seemed to stress, perhaps arrogantly, the relative novelty of the criticism; and many popular reviewers and professors have been quick to sense in it a dangerous novelty. The typical professor of English is naturally and constitutionally opposed to change; the popular reviewer, in so far as his critical principles are concerned, only less so. Both have what amounts to a vested interest in a more desultory and less strenuous discussion of literature.

Yet much more than vested interests is of course involved. The misconceptions about modern criticism are too widespread and too persistent to be accounted for in such a fashion. They are very stubbornly rooted indeed. They are rooted, I believe, in an essentially romantic conception of poetry. This conception tends to take quite literally the view that poetry is the spontaneous overflow of emotion, and that its appreciation is best served by a corresponding overflow of emotion on the part of the reader. It conceives of the function of the intellect as only officious and meddling. The creation of poetry is magical, and if the intellect is brought into play at all in examining a poem, this is an attempt to expose the magic and thus do away with it.

Critical activity is therefore interpreted as somehow inimical to the creation of a robust poetry. Our own age, it is argued, is "Alexandrian," over-ingenious, self-conscious, and therefore cannot create anything but a kind of sophisticated intellectual poetry. The position is rarely argued: its strength is that it does not need to be argued. It is enough to catcall

"Alexandrian." But a little argument may serve to take some of the sting out of the epithet. If ours is a critical age, it is not because of this fact an uncreative age. Measured against the poetry of the Victorians, say, the poetry of the twentieth century compares very favorably indeed. That will be the consensus, I think, even of those who are worried about what they take to be the twentieth century's excessive interest in criticism. As for those who would dispute the achievement of the twentieth century in poetry, they might be reminded that they dispute it on the basis of a critical judgment of their own, and so are begging the very question which they are deciding.

In brief, what is important about a "critical" age is the soundness of its criticism—the matter of whether its criticism is good or bad—and not the mere fact that the age is interested in criticism. Everything else being equal, the production of a great deal of criticism probably argues for an intense interest in the arts, and normally goes hand in hand with creative activity. For criticism does not compete with creative activity. The critic is not in his arrogance offering a scheme which explains the construction of poetry, a formula by which poems are to be written. Nor is he, on the other hand, concerned with reducing the poem to an intellectual scheme in order to "explain" the poem—that is, to explain the poem away—expose the magic—kill the emotional response.

In referring such misconceptions of criticism to a naively romantic view of the arts, I have perhaps made them seem overnaive—too simple to be held by practising writers. In that case it may be well to illustrate from a recent review which appeared in one of our metropolitan bookpages. Alfred Kazin, the reviewer, is concerned about the impersonality and technicality of the sort of criticism contained in this volume. Its very "expertness," for him, is damning: *

> In our day the real princelings of criticism have been those who can manage, in some way or other, to sound like impersonal experts, and for whom the work before them is always an occasion for technical analysis or some sovereign redefinition of our lot. In one sense they have even set themselves up as the rivals to the works before them, and have sought by their expertness to replace them with their own. This is not . . . entirely due to the presumption of critics. We live in a time when an overwhelming sense of having come to the end of a period in man's total history has put a premium on intellectual revaluation rather than on the literature of "real" experience. But it certainly leads to arid intellectual pride, and even, as there is no lack of examples around us to prove, patronage of artists themselves.

Now the temptation of pride is a constant one, and in a fiercely competitive age like our own, men, including literary men, can never too often be warned against it. But to imply that the critics at whom Kazin points his finger are somehow especially susceptible as other critics (social, historical, etc.) are not, or, for that matter, as poets, novelists, and Saturday

* From Books (New York Herald Tribune), May 30, 1948, p. 5. [Brooks's note]

Reviewers of Literature are not, seems to me absurd. For the impersonality of the critic can just as fairly be interpreted as modesty rather than as arrogance—as an unwillingness to interpose his own personality between the reader and the work itself. Furthermore, the concern for technical analysis looks like a wholesome preoccupation with the work of art; that is, the critic is content to describe the work as sensitively as he can rather than to dilate upon his emotional response to it. Rivalry with the work of art is in fact more likely to be instituted by a critic who is anxious to stress his personal response or to use the work he discusses as a peg upon which to hang his own commentary on morals or politics.

I cannot therefore accept Kazin's suggestion that the new critics are on principle arrogant; but his other suggestion, namely, that the pressures of our age have something to do with the characteristic development of criticism in our time, seems to me quite true. I should prefer, however, to state the matter in somewhat different fashion—certainly not as the result of some "overwhelming sense of [our] having come to the end of a period in man's total history." I should prefer to put the case more modestly, and, I think, more specifically, thus: the raveling out of the Victorian poetic conventions coincided with the final breakdown of the current theory of poetic statement, itself some centuries old. It coincided also with the near collapse of linguistic training in our schools and colleges. All three are doubtless aspects of a general breakdown of the means of communication, but it may be serviceable to notice them separately.

The going to seed of a particular literary period may seem unimportant. But in this case it was special and significant, for the Victorian conventions represented what could be salvaged from a pre-scientific age, or represented compromises with the new scientific symbolism which had undercut the older poetic symbols. The Victorian conventions were thus the product of a poetics which had come dangerously close to relegating the specifically poetic uses of language to decoration and embellishment. This general impoverishment was, and is, abundantly reflected in the educational system—whether in the elementary grades or in the graduate school.

It would be unfair to say that the new poetry impinged upon an audience of illiterates. But the discovery that it lacked an audience that could read it soon raised a further and more fundamental question: whether that same audience could read any poetry, including the poetry of the past. The audience, of course, assumed that it could; but in that case, what did the typical reader derive from the poetry of the past—if he read it, and when he read it? Noble sentiments? Ethical doctrine? An escape from a dull and stale world? He read poetry for pleasure, to be sure. But pleasure becomes an even more ambiguous term in a day of mass-produced entertainment. If he answered "for truth," that term too, in an age overawed by the tremendous structure of science, called for elaborate definition and qualification. How could methods so notoriously unscientific as those of poetry yield anything resembling truth?

Questions of this sort are not, of course, new. But in our time it has become increasingly difficult to evade answering them. Partial solutions will no longer work. Compromises which apparently served the nineteenth century are no longer practical. This is not to say that the twentieth century has found the answers: it is to explain why it has had to canvass such questions thoroughly and *de novo*.

Thus far I have dealt with criticism as related to the impact of poetry on the modern world. But the problem has to be seen in broader terms. The rise of modern criticism is part of a general intensification of the study of language and symbolism. The development of semantics, symbolic logic, cultural anthropology, and the psychology of Jung and Freud may all be taken as responses to the same general situation. How they are specifically related to each other and what contributions these studies have made, or may make, to criticism are topics that I shall not attempt to discuss here. Suffice it that they all bear upon the problem of symbolism (logical and extra-logical) and represent attempts to recover symbolic "languages" whose real importance has become evident to us only as the supporting cultural pattern breaks down.

It is no accident, therefore, that a great deal of modern criticism has occupied itself with the problem of how language actually works and specifically how it works in a piece of literature. Because of this, there is a tendency to identify the new criticism with "close textual reading" and to assume that it is limited to problems of what used to be called "diction." The essays here collected should supply a corrective to such a view. Modern critics, it is perfectly true, tend to force attention back to the text of the work itself: that is, to look at the poem as a poem, not as an appendage to the poet's biography, nor as a reflection of his reading, nor as an illustration of the history of ideas. Such an emphasis naturally stresses a close reading of the text, and, since poems are written in words, careful attention to language. But, though the text must provide the ultimate sanction for the meaning of the work, that does not mean that close textual reading is to be conceived of as a sort of verbal piddling. Words open out into the larger symbolizations on all levels—for example, into archetypal symbol, ritual, and myth. The critic's concern for "language" need not be conceived narrowly, even if his concern leads to an intensive examination: it can be extended to the largest symbolizations possible. A renewed respect for words and a sense of their complexities are matters for congratulation. The alternative does not liberate: it leads away from literature altogether.

I have dealt with some of the honest and some of the willful misunderstandings of modern criticism. But these are probably calculated to do less damage than extravagant claims made for criticism. I shall cite only one example, though I think that it is a significant one. Stanley Hyman writes: * ". . . modern criticism for the most part no longer accepts its traditional status as an adjunct to 'creative' or 'imaginative' literature. . . ." " 'No exponent of criticism . . . has, I presume, ever made the preposterous assumption that criticism is an autotelic art,' T. S. Eliot wrote in 1923, in 'The Function of Criticism.' Whether or not anyone had made

* From *The Armed Vision* (New York: Alfred A. Knopf, 1948), p. 7. [Brooks's note]

that 'preposterous assumption' by 1923, modern criticism, which began more or less formally the following year with the publication of I. A. Richards's *Principles of Literary Criticism*, has been acting on it since."

I disagree. True, we can define art (Hyman suggests any "creation of meaningful patterns of experience") broadly enough to include criticism. But I think that we lose more than we gain. In any case, we risk confusing the issues, and, as has been pointed out, the issues are sufficiently confused as it is. Better to assign to literary criticism a more humble and a more specific function: let us say that the task of literary criticism is to put the reader in possession of the work of art.

To read a work of art successfully involves, of course, a process of imaginative reconstruction. The good reader thus necessarily makes use of a process related to that by which the author has constructed the work. If the poet is a maker, the critic is at least a remaker; and I suppose that the successful critic is entitled to claim that his work is imaginative in this sense. (He had certainly better not be lacking in imagination!) But I do not think that the critic is entitled to claim more, nor do I think that he wishes to claim more.

To put the reader into possession of the work of art. Is this a mere reading of the work or is it a judgment of it? Frankly, I do not see how the two activities can be separated. For to possess the work implies a knowledge of it as a work of art, not merely the knowledge of it as a document (political, philosophical, etc.), nor merely the knowledge of something abstracted from it (a logical scheme or paraphrase). The critic inevitably judges, but how explicit he is to make his judgment will obviously depend upon the circumstances. In some cases, and for some readers, he may think it enough to show the pattern of tensions in the work and the way in which they are resolved, or the failure to resolve them. In other cases, he may wish to make his judgment very explicit. But if a full reading of a work implies a judgment on it, a responsible judgment on it ought to imply that a full reading lies behind the judgment, and if called for, can be set forth. The attempt to drive a wedge between close reading of the text and evaluation of the work seems to me confused and confusing.

The essays collected in this volume provide more than a mere sampling of modern criticism. They have not been chosen at random. If they show a real diversity, they also suggest a unity, making as they do a collective comment on the central problems of criticism. They represent an achievement, and taken even at the lowest discount, a worthy achievement.

I have little to say about the future of criticism. I shall not say that the future of criticism is immense. But I think that I can point out something that needs to be done (and is in process of being done): that is, to discriminate more closely among the various problems with which criticism in the large is concerned. To give an example: Beardsley and Wimsatt have pointed out that the genesis of the work (how it was composed, what went into its making, etc.) constitutes a problem distinct from what may be called the analysis of the work in terms of its formal properties.[2] This lat-

---

[2] See "The Intentional Fallacy," *Sewanee Review*, LIV (1946), 468-88.

ter problem has in turn to be distinguished from the further problem which has to do with the actual effect of the work on various kinds of people and at various periods. All three problems are intimately related, and all may be worth discussion; but unless they are distinguished we shall get into trouble. For example, it is one thing to discuss *Uncle Tom's Cabin* in terms of its formal properties as a novel. It is a rather different thing to ask how Harriet Beecher Stowe came to write it, how it was shaped by the pressures of the time. It is still another thing to account for the way in which it affected men in the past, and to try to predict what further effects (if any) it may have in the future. Here the discriminations seem easy; but many who concede them here in this instance refuse to recognize them when we substitute for *Uncle Tom's Cabin, Paradise Lost,* or *Moby Dick,* or *The Four Quartets.*

To insist on a clearer marking of boundary lines, of course, may suggest more specialization, more technicalities, and the segregation of the critic into an even narrower compartment. But clearly marked boundary lines do not imply fences, barricades, or tariff walls. Nobody wants to restrict free trade—between scholarship and criticism, and least of all, between the various areas of criticism. But if the distinctions are real—if they actually exist—muddling of the boundary markers remedies nothing: it merely begets confusion. To indicate the boundaries clearly is actually to encourage free passage across them; for, as it is, we too often line up to defend them as national borders in the spirit of troops repelling an invasion. The critic occupied with the formal analysis of a work is damned for having offered an obviously inadequate account of the social pressures which played upon the author of the work, or for having left out of account the importance of the work as a political document, or he is reproached for having (or for not having) accounted for the composition of the work.

The ways in which we can view a poem or novel or drama are very nearly infinite. Some of them are of the highest importance. Some of them in our day have hardly got the attention which they deserve.

But instead of pining for the perfect critic who will do everything, it might be more sensible to see what the critics have actually done—to discriminate among the various "criticisms" in their proper relations to each other. Interrelated, they certainly are; but the ability to discriminate among them might allow us to make better use of the actual and limited, flesh-and-blood critics that we have.

SELECTED BIBLIOGRAPHY

A SELECTED BIBLIOGRAPHY OF AMERICAN CRITICISM

This selected bibliography is presented not as an exhaustive list but as an additional illustration of the major trends in American criticism throughout its development. It may suggest possibilities for further study in the work of major American critics.

Emphasis in selection has been placed upon the criticisms of American writers by American critics. The parts of the bibliography correspond to the major divisions of the book. Within each part the authors of the primary sources are listed alphabetically; the critical works of each author are listed chronologically. Secondary sources are divided into general works, those dealing with the background of the period or with movements in criticism within the period, and works on specific authors. Comments and criticism on a particular writer will frequently be found under a critic's name in a later part of the bibliography—e.g., Newton Arvin on Whitman in Part IV.

The titles of certain periodicals in the bibliography have been abbreviated as follows:

A:	Accent	MP:	Modern Philology
AL:	American Literature	N:	Nation
AM:	Atlantic Monthly	NAR:	North American Review
AP:	American Prefaces	NEQ:	New England Quarterly
AR:	American Review	NR:	New Republic
AS:	American Scholar	P:	Poetry
B:	Bookman	PR:	Partisan Review
CE:	College English	PMLA:	Publications of the Modern Language Association
D:	The Dial (1920–1929)		
ELH:	English Literary History	SeR:	Sewanee Review
F:	Forum	SR:	Southern Review
HH:	Hound and Horn	SRL:	Saturday Review of Literature
HR:	Hudson Review		
JEGP:	Journal English and Germanic Philology	SP:	Studies in Philology
		Sym:	Symposium
KR:	Kenyon Review	VQR:	Virginia Quarterly Review
MLN:	Modern Language Notes	WR:	Western Review
MLQ:	Modern Language Quarterly	YR:	Yale Review

GENERAL BIBLIOGRAPHIES

ALDRIDGE, JOHN W. *Critiques and Essays on Modern Fiction.* New York, 1952.
Cambridge History of American Literature. Edited by William P. Trent and others. New York, 1917–1921, 4 vols.; 1933, 3 vols.
CHARVAT, WILLIAM. *The Origins of American Critical Thought: 1810–1835.* Philadelphia, 1936.
CLARK, HARRY HAYDEN. "Literary Criticism in the *North American Review*, 1815–1835," *Transactions of the Wisconsin Academy of Sciences, Arts, and Letters,* XXXII (1940), 299–350.
HYMAN, STANLEY. *The Armed Vision.* New York, 1948.
LEARY, LEWIS. *Articles on American Literature, 1900–1950.* Durham, N.C., 1954.
Literary History of the United States. Edited by Robert E. Spiller and others. New York, 1948. 3 vols.
MILLER, PERRY, and JOHNSON, THOMAS H. *The Puritans.* New York, 1938.
PRITCHARD, JOHN P. *Return to the Fountains.* Durham, N.C., 1942.
Publications of the Modern Language Association, "Annual Bibliography for American Literature."
STAFFORD, JOHN. *The Literary Criticism of "Young America."* Berkeley, Calif., 1952.
STALLMAN, ROBERT W. *Critiques and Essays in Criticism.* New York, 1949.
———. *The Critic's Notebook.* Minneapolis, 1950.
WEST, RAY B., JR., *Essays in Modern Literary Criticism.* New York and Toronto, 1952.
ZABEL, MORTON D. *Literary Opinion in America.* New York, 1937; revised edition, 1951.

PART I. THE ORIGINS OF AMERICAN CRITICAL THEORY

THE PURITANS

PRIMARY SOURCES

ADAMS, JOHN. *Poems on Several Occasions.* Boston, 1745. "The Publisher to the Reader."
ALLEN, JAMES. *New-Englands Choicest Blessing.* Boston, 1679. "To the Reader."
BARNARD, JOHN. *Sermons on Several Subjects.* London, 1727. Dedication.
[Bay Psalm Book.] The Whole Book of Psalmes. Cambridge, 1640. Preface by Richard Mather.
BULKLEY, JOHN. Preface to Roger Wolcott, *Poetical Meditations.* New London, 1725.
BYLES, MATHER. An essay on style in *The American Magazine and Historical Chronicle.* Boston, January, 1745.
———. A Letter to Alexander Pope, October 7, 1727, in Arthur W. H. Eaton, *The Famous Mather Byles.* Boston, 1914. P. 233.
CHAPPELL, WILLIAM. *The Preacher, or The Art and Method of Preaching.* London, 1656.
EDWARDS, JONATHAN. *Five Discourses.* Boston, 1738. Preface.
ELIOT, JARED. *Essays upon Field-Husbandry.* New York, 1748. Preface.
FITCH, JAMES. *Peace the End of the Perfect and Upright.* Cambridge, 1672. Preface.
FOXCROFT, THOMAS. *A Practical Discourse.* Boston, 1718.

HOOKER, THOMAS. *A Survey of the Summe.* London, 1648. Preface.
MATHER, COTTON. *Manuductio ad Ministerium.* Boston, 1726. The section "Of Poetry and Style."
———. *Psalterium Americanum.* Boston, 1718. Introduction.
MATHER, INCREASE. *Some Important Truths.* London, 1674. "To the Reader."
MORRELL, WILLIAM. *New-England.* London, 1625. "To the Reader."
MORTON, WILLIAM. Preface to John Cotton, *The Way of Life.* London, 1641.
PRINCE, THOMAS. Preface to Thomas Hooker, *The Poor Doubting Christian.* Boston, 1743.
WALTER, THOMAS. *The Sweet Psalmist of Israel.* Boston, 1722. Dedication.
WIGGLESWORTH, MICHAEL. *The Day of Doom.* Boston, 1701. Invocation.
———. "The Prayse of Eloquence," in Samuel E. Morison, *Harvard College in the Seventeenth Century.* Cambridge, 1936. Pp. 180–83.

SECONDARY WORKS: GENERAL

Cambridge History of American Literature. Edited by William P. Trent and others. New York, 1917–1921, 4 vols.; 1933, 3 vols.
COOK, ELIZABETH G. *Literary Influences in Colonial Newspapers, 1704–1750.* New York, 1912.
GRIFFITHS, OLIVE M. *Religion and Learning.* Cambridge, Eng., 1935.
GUTHRIE, WARREN A. *The Development of Rhetorical Theory in America, 1635–1850.* Unpublished dissertation, Northwestern University, 1940.
JANTZ, H. S. "German Thought and Literature in New England, 1620–1820," *JEGP*, XLI (1942), 1–45.
MILLER, PERRY. *The New England Mind.* New York, 1939.
MILLER, PERRY, and JOHNSON, THOMAS H. *The Puritans.* New York, 1938.
MORISON, SAMUEL E. *Builders of the Bay Colony.* Boston, 1930.
———. *Harvard College in the Seventeenth Century.* Cambridge, 1936.
MURDOCK, KENNETH B. *Literature and Theology in Colonial New England.* Cambridge, 1949.
———. "The Puritan Tradition in American Literature," in *The Reinterpretation of American Literature.* New York, 1928.
PARRINGTON, VERNON L. *Main Currents in American Thought.* New York, 1930.
QUINN, ARTHUR H. "The Foundations of American Criticism," in *The Literature of the American People.* New York, 1951.
ROURKE, CONSTANCE. *The Roots of American Culture.* New York, 1942.
SPILLER, ROBERT, et al. *Literary History of the United States.* New York, 1948.
TYLER, MOSES C. *A History of American Literature During the Colonial Period, 1607–1765.* New York, 1878.
WRIGHT, THOMAS G. *Literary Culture in Early New England, 1620–1730.* New Haven, 1920.

SECONDARY WORKS: ON INDIVIDUAL AUTHORS

On Cotton Mather:
Murdock, Kenneth B. *Selections from Cotton Mather.* New York, 1926.
Wendell, Barrett. *Cotton Mather: The Puritan Priest.* New York, 1891, 1926.
On Wigglesworth:
Dean, John W. *Sketch of the Life of Rev. Michael Wigglesworth . . .* Albany, 1863.
Matthiessen, F. O. "Michael Wigglesworth, a Puritan Artist," *NEQ*, I (1928), 491–504.

NEOCLASSICISM

PRIMARY SOURCES

DENNIE, JOSEPH. "On Gothicism," *The Port Folio*, III (1803), 226.

———. "Freneau's Poems," *The Port Folio*, IV, Ser. 2 (1807), 251–53; 258–59; 313–15; 349–52.

DWIGHT, TIMOTHY. *A Dissertation on the History, Eloquence, and Poetry of the Bible*. New Haven, 1772.

———. *The Conquest of Canaan*. Hartford, 1785. Preface.

———. "The Friend, No. IV," *The American Museum*, V (1789), 564–67.

———. *Greenfield Hill*. New York, 1794. Preface.

———. *Remarks on the Review of Inchiquin's Letters*. Boston, 1815.

———. *Travels in New-England and New-York*. New Haven, 1821–1822. 4 vols.

FRANKLIN, BENJAMIN. "Dogood Papers, No. VII," *New England Courant*, June 18–June 25, 1722.

———. *Idea of the English School*. Philadelphia, 1751.

MILLER, SAMUEL. *A Brief Retrospect of the Eighteenth Century*. New York, 1803. 2 vols.

TRUMBULL, JOHN. *Essay on the Use and Advantages of the Fine Arts*. New Haven, 1770.

———. A treatise on versification in Noah Webster's *A Grammatical Institute of the English Language, Part II*. Hartford, 1785.

SECONDARY WORKS: GENERAL

BABCOCK, R. W. "The Idea of Taste in the Eighteenth Century," *PMLA*, L (1935), 922–26.

Cambridge History of American Literature. Edited by William P. Trent and others. New York, 1917–1921, 4 vols.; 1933, 3 vols.

CLARK, HARRY H. "The Influence of Science on American Ideas from 1775 to 1809," *Transactions of the Wisconsin Academy of Sciences, Arts, and Letters*, XXXV (1944), 305–49.

COLE, C. W. *The Beginnings of Literary Nationalism in America, 1775–1800*. Unpublished dissertation, George Washington University, 1935.

FAUST, CLARENCE H. "Why Puritanism Declined," in *Transitions in American Literary History*. Edited by Harry H. Clark. Durham, N.C., 1954.

FLEWELLING, HOWARD L. *Literary Criticism in American Periodicals, 1783–1820*. Unpublished dissertation, University of Michigan, 1931.

GALLAWAY, FRANCIS. *Reason, Rule, and Revolt in English Classicism*. New York, 1940.

GALLAWAY, W. F., JR. "The Conservative Attitude Toward Fiction, 1770–1830," *PMLA*, LV (1940), 1041–59.

GUTHRIE, WARREN A. *The Development of Rhetorical Theory in America, 1635–1850*. Unpublished dissertation, Northwestern University, 1940.

HOWARD, LEON. *The Connecticut Wits*. Chicago, 1943.

JANTZ, H. S. "German Thought and Literature in New England, 1620–1820," *JEGP*, XLI (1942), 1–45.

JONES, ARTHUR E. *A Study of Literary Criticism in America, 1742–1820*. Unpublished dissertation, Syracuse University, 1950.

Literary History of the United States. Edited by Robert Spiller and others. New York, 1948.

MOTT, FRANK L. *A History of American Magazines*. Cambridge, 1938. 3 vols.

OBERHOLTZER, ELLIS. *A Literary History of Philadelphia*. Philadelphia, 1906.

PARRINGTON, VERNON L. *The Connecticut Wits.* New York, 1926.
———. *Main Currents in American Thought.* New York, 1930.
RICHARDSON, LYON N. *A History of Early American Magazines 1741–1789.* New York, 1931.
ROURKE, CONSTANCE. *The Roots of American Culture.* New York, 1942.
SIBLEY, AGNES M. *Alexander Pope's Prestige in America, 1725–1835.* New York, 1949.
SMYTH, A. H. *Philadelphia Magazines.* Philadelphia, 1892.
TRACY, THOMAS J. *The American Attitude Toward American Literature During the Years 1800–1812.* Unpublished dissertation, St. John's University, Brooklyn, N. Y., 1941.
TYLER, MOSES C. *The Literary History of the American Revolution, 1763–1783.* New York, 1897. 2 vols.
WESTFALL, VAN R. *American Shakespearean Criticism, 1607–1865.* New York, 1939.

SECONDARY WORKS: ON INDIVIDUAL AUTHORS

On Charles Brockden Brown:
Marchand, Ernest. "The Literary Opinions of Charles Brockden Brown," *SP*, XXXI (1934), 541–66.

On Dennie:
Ellis, Milton. *Joseph Dennie and His Circle.* Austin, Texas, 1915.
Leary, Lewis. "Wordsworth in America: Addenda," *MLQ*, LVIII (1943), 391–93.
———. "Joseph Dennie on Benjamin Franklin: A Note on Early American Literary Criticism," *Pennsylvania Magazine of History and Biography*, LXXII (1948), 240–46.

On Dwight:
Buchanan, Lewis E. *Timothy Dwight, Man of Letters: His Ideas and Wit.* Unpublished dissertation, University of Wisconsin, 1940.
Cunningham, Charles E. *Timothy Dwight.* New York, 1942.
Howard, Leon. "Timothy Dwight," and "President Timothy Dwight," in *The Connecticut Wits.* Chicago, 1943.

On Franklin:
Ford, Paul L. *The Many-Sided Franklin.* New York, 1899.
McMaster, John B. *Benjamin Franklin as a Man of Letters.* Boston, 1887.
More, Paul Elmer. *Benjamin Franklin.* New York, 1900.
Van Doren, Carl. *Benjamin Franklin.* New York, 1938.

On Trumbull:
Cowie, Alexander. *John Trumbull: Connecticut Wit.* Chapel Hill, N.C., 1936.
———. "John Trumbull as a Critic of Poetry," *NEQ*, XI (1938), 773–93.
———. "John Trumbull Glances at Fiction," *AL*, XII (1940), 69–75.
Howard, Leon. "John Trumbull," in *The Connecticut Wits.* Chicago, 1943.

THE TRANSITION TO ROMANTICISM

PRIMARY SOURCES

BANCROFT, GEORGE. "The Value of Classical Learning," *NAR*, XIX (1824), 125–37.
———. "Life and Genius of Goethe," *NAR*, XIX (1824), 303–25.
———. "Herder's Writings," *NAR*, XX (1825), 138–47.
———. "Mrs. Hemans's Poems," *NAR*, XXIV (1827), 443–63.

———. *Literary and Historical Miscellanies.* New York, 1855.
BRYANT, WILLIAM CULLEN. "A Review of Solyman Brown's *An Essay on American Poetry*," *NAR*, VII (1818), 198–211.
———. "On the Use of Trisyllabic Feet in Iambic Verse," *NAR*, IX (1819), 426–31.
———. "Review of Catherine M. Sedgwick, *Redwood*," *NAR*, XX (1825), 245–72.
———. "Recent Poetry," *New York Review*, II (1826), 181–95.
———. "On Poetry in Its Relation to Our Age and Country" (lecture delivered in 1826), in *Prose Writings*, edited by Parke Godwin. New York, 1884. Vol. I.
———. "On Originality and Imitation" (lecture delivered in 1826), in *Prose Writings.* Vol. I.
———. "The Writings of Fitz-Greene Halleck," *New-York Mirror*, XIV (September 24, 1836).
———. "On the Life and Genius of Cooper" (1852), in *Prose Writings.* Vol. I.
———. "On the Life, Character, and Genius of Washington Irving" (1860), in *Prose Writings.* Vol. I.
———. "Franklin as a Poet" (1874), in *Prose Writings*, Vol. II.
———. "Abraham Cowley," *NAR*, CXXIV (1877), 368–82.
CHANNING, E. T. "On Models in Literature," *NAR*, III (1816), 202–9.
———. "Scott's Rob Roy," *NAR*, VII (1818), 149–84.
CHANNING, WILLIAM ELLERY. "Remarks on the Character and Writings of John Milton," *Christian Examiner*, III (1826), 29.
———. "The Importance and Means of a National Literature," *Christian Examiner*, VII (1830), 269–95.
———. *Works.* Boston, 1877.
———. *Notebook.* Boston, 1877.
DANA, RICHARD HENRY. "The Sylphs of the Seasons, by W. Allston," *NAR*, V (1817), 365–89.
———. "Old Times," *NAR*, V (1817), 4–11.
———. "Edgeworth's Readings on Poetry," *NAR*, VI (1818), 153–78.
———. "Hazlitt's English Poets," *NAR*, VIII (1819), 276–322.
———. *Poems and Prose Writings.* Boston, 1833.
DEXTER, FRANKLIN. "Fine Arts," *NAR*, XXVI (1828), 207–24.
EVERETT, A. H. "Geoffroy on Dramatic Literature," *NAR*, X (1820), 291–316.
———. "Lord Byron's Poems," *NAR*, XX (1825), 1–47.
———. "History of Intellectual Philosophy," *NAR*, XXIX (1829), 67–123.
———. "American Poets," *NAR*, XXXIII (1831), 297–324.
———. "Early Literature of Modern Europe," *NAR*, XXXVIII (1834), 158–77.
———. *Critical and Miscellaneous Essays.* Boston, 1845.
EVERETT, EDWARD. "Percival's Poems," *NAR*, XIV (1822), 1–15.
FELTON, CORNELIUS. "Greek Language and Literature," *NAR*, XLII (1836), 94–116.
GARDINER, W. H. "Cooper's *The Spy*," *NAR*, XV (1822), 250–82.
———. "Cooper's Novels," *NAR*, XXIII (1826), 150–97.
GILMAN, SAMUEL. "Brown's Philosophy of Mind," *NAR*, XIX (1824), 1–41.
GREENWOOD, F. W. P. "Wordsworth's Poems," *NAR*, XVIII (1824), 356–71.
HEDGE, F. H. "Coleridge," *Christian Examiner*, XIV (1833), 109–29.
IRVING, WASHINGTON. "Robert Treat Paine," *Analectic Magazine*, I (1813), 249–66.
———. "Edwin C. Holland," *Analectic Magazine*, III (1814), 242–52.
———. "Thomas Campbell," *Analectic Magazine*, V (1815), 234–50.
———. "A Royal Poet" and "Stratford-on-Avon," in *The Sketch Book.* New York, 1819–1820.
———. "Desultory Thoughts on Criticism," *Knickerbocker Magazine*, XIV (1839). 175–78.
KNAPP, JOHN. "National Poetry," *NAR*, VII (1818), 169–76.
KNAPP, SAMUEL L. *Lectures on American Literature.* New York, 1829.

Marsh, James (Ed.). Coleridge's *Aids to Reflection*. Burlington, Vt., 1829.
————. Coleridge's *The Friend*. Burlington, Vt., 1831.
————. (trans.) Herder's *Spirit of Hebrew Poetry*. Boston, 1833.
Montgomery, James. *Lectures on Poetry, Literature, etc*. New York, 1833.
Motley, John L. "Goethe's Works," *New York Review*, V (1839), 1–48.
————. "The Novels of Balzac," *NAR*, LXV (1847), 85–108.
Neal, John. "American Writers," *Blackwood's Magazine*, XVI (1824), 304–11, 415–28, 560–71, and XVII (1825), 48–69, 186–207.
————. *Randolph* [New York] 1823.
Peabody, W. B. O. "The Water-Witch," *NAR*, XXXII (1831), 508–23.
————. "Waverley Novels," *NAR*, XXXII (1831), 386–421.
Phillips, Willard. "Poems of Cowper," *NAR*, II (1816), 233–41.
————. "Godwin's Mandeville," *NAR*, VII (1818), 92–105.
————. "Bryant's Poems," *NAR*, XIII (1821), 380–84.
————. "Pelham," *NAR*, XXVIII (1829), 418–33.
Prescott, W. H. "Essay Writing," *NAR*, XIV (1822), 319–50.
————. "Italian Narrative Poetry," *NAR*, XIX (1824), 337–89.
————. "Novel Writing," *NAR*, XXV (1827), 183–203.
————. *Biographical and Critical Miscellanies*. New York, 1845.
Ripley, George. "The Spirit of Hebrew Poetry" (on Herder), *Christian Examiner*, XVIII (1835), 167–221.
Sparks, Jared. "Recent American Novels," *NAR*, XXI (1825), 79–104.
————. "John Brainard's Poems," *NAR*, XXI (1825), 217–24.
Tudor, William. "Guy Mannering," *NAR*, I (1815), 403–36.
————. "Miss Huntley's Poems," *NAR*, I (1815), 111–21.
————. "Hunt's *Rimini*," *NAR*, III (1816), 272–83.
Walsh, Robert. *Didactics, Social, Literary and Political*. Philadelphia, 1836.
Waterston, R. C. "Coleridge's Poems," *NAR*, XXXIX (1834), 437–58.
Winthrop, F. W. "On Beauty," *NAR*, VII (1818), 1–25.

Secondary Works: General

Bate, Walter Jackson. *From Classic to Romantic*. Cambridge, 1946.
Beatty, Arthur. *William Wordsworth, His Doctrine and Art in their Historical Relations*. Madison, Wis., revised edition, 1927.
Bowers, David (ed.). *Foreign Influences on American Life*. New Haven, 1944.
Brown, E. K. "The National Idea in American Criticism," *Dalhousie Review*, XIV (1934), 133–47.
Cairns, W. B. *On the Development of American Literature from 1815 to 1833*. Madison, Wis., 1898.
Cambridge History of American Literature. Edited by William P. Trent and others. New York, 1917–1921, 4 vols.; 1933, 3 vols.
Charvat, William. *The Origins of American Critical Thought: 1810–1835*. Philadelphia, 1936.
Clark, Harry H. "Literary Criticism in the North American Review, 1815–1835," *Transactions of the Wisconsin Academy of Sciences, Arts, and Letters*, XXXII (1940), 299–350.
————. "Nationalism in American Literature," *University of Toronto Quarterly*, II (1933), 492–519.
Foerster, Norman. "Wordsworth in America," *SP*, XXVI (1929), 85–95.
Goddard, H. C. "German Literature in New England in the Early 19th Century," in *Studies in New England Transcendentalism*. New York, 1908.
Goodnight, Scott H. *German Literature in American Magazines Prior to 1846*. Madison, Wis., 1907.
Heiser, Merrill. "Why Neo-classicism Declined," in *Transitions in American Literary History*, ed. by Harry H. Clark. Durham, N.C., 1954.

————. "Wordsworth in America," *MLN*, XLVIII (1933), 359–65.

————. "The American Revolt Against Pope," *SP*, XLIX (1952), 48–65.

HOWARD, LEON. "Changing Contradictions in the Late Eighteenth Century," in *Transitions in American Literary History*, ed. by Harry H. Clark, Durham, N.C., 1954.

JONES, HOWARD MUMFORD. *America and French Culture, 1750–1848*. Chapel Hill, N.C., 1927.

————. *Ideas in America*. Cambridge, 1944.

LELAND, L. P. *Theories of Fiction in America, 1789–1870*. Unpublished dissertation, The Ohio State University, 1940.

LEONARD, WILLIAM ELLERY. *Byron and Byronism in America*. Boston, 1905.

Literary History of the United States. Edited by Robert Spiller and others. New York, 1948.

LONG, ORIE W. *Literary Pioneers: Early American Explorers of European Culture*. Cambridge, 1935.

MARSH, G. L. "Early Reviews of Shelley," *MP*, XXVII (1929), 73.

McCLOSKEY, JOHN C. "The Campaign of Periodicals After the War of 1812 for National American Literature," *PMLA*, L (1935), 262–73.

McCOSH, JAMES. *The Scottish Philosophy*. New York, 1875.

McKENZIE, GORDON. *Critical Responsiveness: A Study of the Psychological Current in Later Eighteenth Century Criticism*. Berkeley, Calif., 1949.

MILLER, G. M. "The Historical Point of View in English Literary Criticism from 1570–1770," *Anglistische Forschungen*, Vol. 35, Heidelberg, 1913.

MOTT, FRANK L. *A History of American Magazines*. Cambridge, 1938. 3 vols.

NEWTON, ANNABEL. *Wordsworth in Early American Criticism*. Chicago, 1928.

ONG, WALTER J. "Psyche and the Geometers: Aspects of Associationist Critical Theory," *MP*, XLIX (1951), 16–27.

ORIANS, G. H. "Why Romanticism Arose," in *Transitions in American Literary History*, edited by Harry H. Clark. Durham, N.C., 1954.

PARRINGTON, VERNON L. *Main Currents in American Thought*. New York, 1930.

POWER, JULIA. *Shelley in America*. Lincoln, Neb., 1940.

RILEY, I. W. *American Philosophy—The Early Schools*. New York, 1907.

ROLLINS, HYDER E. *Keats' Reputation in America to 1848*. Cambridge, 1946.

SEDGWICK, W. E. "The Materials for American Literature: A Critical Problem of the Early Nineteenth Century," *Harvard Studies and Notes in Philosophy and Literature*, XVII (1935), 145–62.

SIBLEY, AGNES M. *Alexander Pope's Prestige in America, 1725–1835*. New York, 1949.

STREETER, ROBERT E. *Critical Ideas in the North American Review, 1815–1865*. Unpublished dissertation, Northwestern University, 1943.

————. "Association Psychology and Literary Nationalism in the *North American Review*," *AL*, XVII (1945), 243–54.

WARREN, HOWARD C. *A History of the Association Psychology*. New York, 1921.

WESTFALL, VAN R. *American Shakespearean Criticism, 1607–1865*. New York, 1939.

WHITFORD, R. C. "Mme de Staël's Literary Reputation in America," *MLN*, XXXIII (1918), 476–80.

WHITMER, ANNE B. *American Reaction to the Literary Criticism of Samuel Taylor Coleridge, 1830–1860*. Unpublished dissertation, The Ohio State University, 1939.

SECONDARY WORKS: ON INDIVIDUAL AUTHORS

On Bancroft:

Nye, Russel B. "George Bancroft, Early Critic of German Literature," *MLN*, LVIII (1943), 128–30.

OE, EDGAR ALLAN. "Tennyson's Poems," *Graham's Magazine*, XXI (1842), 152–53.
——. "Notes Upon English Verse," *Pioneer*, I (1843), 102–12.
——. "Our Magazine Literature," *New World*, VI (1843), 302–4.
——. "Continuation of the Voluminous History of the Little Longfellow War," *Broadway Journal*, II (1845), 161–63; 178–83; 194–98; 211–12.
——. "The Philosophy of Composition," *Graham's Magazine*, XXVIII (1846), 163–67.
——. "Nathaniel Hawthorne, Tale Writing," *Godey's Lady's Book*, XXXV (1847), 252–56.
——. "The Rationale of Verse," *Southern Literary Messenger*, XIV (1848), 577–85; 673–82.
——. "About Critics and Criticism," *Graham's Magazine*, XXXVI (1850), 49–

——. "The Poetic Principle," *Sartain's Union Magazine*, VII (1850), 231–39.
——. *The Complete Works of Edgar Allan Poe*. Edited by James A. Harrison. New York, 1902. "Literary Criticism," Vols. VIII–XIV; "Marginalia," Vol. XVI.
, WILLIAM GILMORE. *Views and Reviews in American Literature, History, and Fiction*. New York, 1845.
——. "Modern Prose Fiction," *Southern Quarterly*, XV (1849), 41–83.
——. "Recent American Poets," *Southern Quarterly*, XVI (1849), 224–32.
AU, HENRY DAVID. "Homer, Chaucer, Ossian," *The Dial*, IV (1844), 290.
——. "Thomas Carlyle and His Works," *Graham's Magazine*, XXX (1847), 145,

MAN, H. T. "James Fenimore Cooper," *NAR*, LXXXIX (1859), 289–316.
E, H. B. *Literary Criticism*. Philadelphia, 1856.
E, E. P. "Wordsworth's Poetical Works," *NAR*, LIX (1844), 352–84.
"The British Critics," *NAR*, LXI (1845), 468–97.
"Novels of the Season," *NAR*, LXVII (1848), 354–69.
Verplanck and Hudson: Shakespeare's Plays," *NAR*, LXVII (1848), 84–

The Life and Works of Henry Fielding," *NAR*, LXVIII (1849), 41–81.
merican Literature and Other Papers*. Boston, 1887.
, WALT. *Leaves of Grass*. Brooklyn, 1855. Preface.
emocratic Vistas*. Washington, 1871.
aves of Grass*. Fifth Edition. Washington, 1872. Preface.
aves of Grass*. Sixth Edition. Camden, 1876. Preface.
he Poetry of the Future," *NAR*, CXXXII (1881), 195–210.
lgar Poe's Significance," in *Specimen Days and Collect*. Philadelphia,

Tribute to Four Poets" (Emerson, Longfellow, Bryant, Whittier), in Days and Collect*.
Backward Glance O'er Travel'd Roads," in *November Boughs*. Phila- 888.
Bible as Poetry," in *November Boughs*.
ert Burns as Poet and Person," in *November Boughs*.
OHN GREENLEAF. "American Genius," *The Philadelphia Album*, III 54.
iterary Remains of John G. C. Brainard*. Hartford, 1832.
e to *Songs of Three Centuries*. Boston, 1875.
geline," in *Works*. Riverside Edition. Boston, 1888. Vol. VII.

SECONDARY WORKS: GENERAL

Romanticism and the American Renaissance," *AL*, XXIII (1952),

LSON. *American Prosody*. New York, 1935.

——. "George Bancroft's View of Shakespeare," *Shakespeare Association Bulletin*, XVIII (1943), 109–13.
——. *George Bancroft: Brahmin Rebel*. New York, 1944.

On Bryant:
Godwin, Parke. *A Biography of William Cullen Bryant with Extracts from His Private Correspondence*. New York, 1883. 2 vols.
Glicksberg, C. I. "Bryant and the United States Review," *NEQ*, VII (1934), 687–701.
Hudson, William P. "Archibald Alison and William Cullen Bryant," *AL*, XII (1940), 59–68.
McDowell, Tremaine. *William Cullen Bryant: Representative Selections*. New York, 1935. Introduction.

On William Ellery Channing:
Ladu, Arthur I. "Channing and Transcendentalism," *AL*, XI (1939), 129–37.
Peabody, Elizabeth. *Reminiscences of Rev. William Ellery Channing*. Boston, 1880.
Randel, William P. "Hawthorne, Channing, and Margaret Fuller," *AL*, X (1939), 472–76.
Spiller, Robert. "A Case for W. E. Channing," *NEQ*, III (1930), 55–81.

On Washington Irving:
Pochmann, Henry A. *Washington Irving: Representative Selections*. New York, 1934. Introduction.
Williams, Stanley T. *The Life of Washington Irving*. New York, 1935. 2 vols.

On James Marsh:
Nicolson, Marjorie. "James Marsh and the Vermont Transcendentalists," *Philosophical Review*, XXXIV (1925), 28–50.

On Motley:
Brooks, Van Wyck. *The Flowering of New England, 1815–1865*. New York, 1936. Pp. 334–42.
Holmes, Oliver Wendell. *John Lothrop Motley, A Memoir*. Boston, 1879.
Long, Orie W. *Literary Pioneers*. Cambridge, 1935. Pp. 199–224.
Schantz, B. T., and Higby, Chester P. *John Lothrop Motley: Representative Selections*. New York, 1939. Introduction.

On Neal:
Pattee, Fred L. (ed.). John Neal's *American Writers*. Durham, N.C., 1937. Introduction.
Rubin, Joseph. "John Neal's Poetics as an Influence on Whitman and Poe," *NEQ*, XIV (1941), 359–62.

On Prescott:
Charvat, William, and Kraus, Michael. *William Hickling Prescott: Representative Selections*. New York, 1943. Introduction.
Ticknor, George. *Life of William Hickling Prescott*. Boston, 1864.

PART II. THE AESTHETICS OF ROMANTICISM

PRIMARY SOURCES

ALLEN, GEORGE. "The Study of Works of Genius," *New York Review*, I (1837), 161–78.
——. "Reproductive Criticism," *New York Review*, II (1838), 49–75.
ALLSTON, WASHINGTON. *Lectures on Art, and Poems*. Edited by R. H. Dana, Jr. New York, 1850.

BOWEN, FRANCIS. "Nine New Poets," *NAR*, LXIV (1847), 402–34.
———. "Lowell's Poems," *NAR*, LXVI (1848), 458–82.
BRISTED, C. A. "The Scotch School of Philosophy and Criticism," *American Review*, II (1845), 386.
BROWNSON, ORESTES. "American Literature," *Boston Quarterly Review*, II (1839), 1–26.
———. "R. W. Emerson's Poems," *Brownson's Quarterly Review*, N.S. I (1847), 262–76.
———. "Wordsworth's Poetical Works," *Brownson's Quarterly Review*, III (1855), 525–38.
COOPER, JAMES FENIMORE. *Notions of the Americans*. Philadelphia, 1828.
———. *Gleanings in Europe: England*. Philadelphia, 1837.
———. *Precaution*. London, 1838. Preface.
———. *Home as Found*. London, 1838. Preface.
———. *Afloat and Ashore*. London, 1844. Preface.
———. *Satanstoe*. London, 1845. Preface.
———. *The Pioneers*. New York, 1850. Preface.
———. *The Deerslayer*. New York, 1850. Preface.
DUYCKINCK, E. A. "Crabbe," *New York Review*, I (1837), 96–109.
———. "Old English Literature—George Herbert," *New York Review*, II (1838), 111–33.
———. "Nationality in Literature," *Democratic Review*, XX (1847), 264–72.
———. "The Prose Writers of America," *Democratic Review*, XX (1847), 384–91.
EMERSON, RALPH WALDO. "Michael Angelo," *NAR*, XLIV (1837), 1–16.
———. *Literary Ethics*. Boston, 1838.
———. "Milton," *NAR*, XLVII (1838), 56–73.
———. "New Poetry," *The Dial*, I (1840), 220–32.
———. "Thoughts on Modern Literature," *The Dial*, I (1840), 137–58.
———. *Essays, First Series*. Boston, 1841.
———. "Thoughts on Art," *The Dial*, I (1841), 367–78.
———. "Transcendentalism," *The Dial*, II (1842), 382–84.
———. *Essays, Second Series*. Boston, 1844.
———. *Representative Men, Society and Solitude*. Boston, 1849.
———. "Thoreau," *AM*, X (1862), 239–49.
———. "Poetry and Imagination," in *Letters and Social Aims*. Boston, 1875. Pp. 3–67.
———. "Impressions of Thomas Carlyle in 1848," *Scribner's Magazine*, XXII (1881), 89–91.
———. *Art and Criticism, the Natural History of the Intellect and Other Papers*. Boston, 1904.
———. *The Journals of Ralph Waldo Emerson*. Edited by E. W. Emerson and W. E. Forbes. Boston, 1909–1914. 10 vols.
EVERETT, C. C. "Ruskin's Last Volume," *NAR*, LXXXIV (1857), 379–406.
———. "Elizabeth Barrett Browning," *NAR*, LXXXV (1857), 415–41.
———. "Tennyson," *NAR*, XC (1860), 1–21.
FISHER, S. G. "Art, Its Meaning and Method. Essays of Horace Binney Wallace," *NAR*, LXXXI (1855), 212–44.
FULLER, MARGARET. "A Short Essay on Critics," *The Dial*, I (1840), 5–11.
———. "Emerson's Essays," *New York Daily Tribune* (Dec. 7, 1844).
———. *Papers on Literature and Art*. New York, 1846. 2 vols.
GODWIN, PARKE. "Percy Bysshe Shelley," *Democratic Review*, XIII (1843), 603–23.
GRISWOLD, RUFUS W. *The Prose Writers of America*. Philadelphia, 1847.
HALE, E. E. "Leaves of Grass," *NAR*, LXXXII (1856), 275–77.
HAWTHORNE, NATHANIEL. "The Artist of the Beautiful," *Democratic Review*, XIV (1844), 605–17.
———. "Preface to Rappaccini's Daughter," *Democratic Review*, XV (1844), 545.
———. "P's Correspondence," *Democratic Review*, XVI (1845), 337–45.

HAWTHORNE, NATHANIEL. "Whittier's New England Super[...] World, I (1847), 247–48.
———. *The House of the Seven Gables*. Boston, 1851. Prefac[...]
———. *The Blithedale Romance*. Boston, 1852. Preface.
———. *The Marble Faun*. Boston, 1860. Preface.
———. *The American Notebooks*. Edited by Randall Stewar[...]
———. *The English Notebooks*. Edited by Randall Stewar[...]
HOLMES, OLIVER WENDELL. *The Autocrat of the Breakfa[...]
———. "Irving's Power of Idealization," *Critic*, III (1883[...]
———. *Ralph Waldo Emerson*. New York, 1885.
———. *Over the Teacups*. Boston, 1891.
———. Introduction to *Horatian Echoes* by John Osborn[...]
HUDSON, HENRY N. "Festus," *Whig Review*, V (1847), [...]
———. "Whipple's Essays and Reviews," *Whig Review* [...]
JONES, WILLIAM A. "Criticism in America," *Democrati[...] 49.
———. "Critics and Criticism of the Nineteenth Cent[...] (1844), 153–62.
———. "American Humor," *Democratic Review*, XV [...]
LONGFELLOW, HENRY WADSWORTH. "Anglo-Saxon L[...] XXXIII (1831), 325–50.
———. "Sidney's *Defense of Poesy*," *NAR*, XXXIV [...]
———. "The Spanish Language and Literature," [...]
———. "Old English Romances," *NAR*, XXXVII[...]
———. "Hawthorne's *Twice-Told Tales*," *NAR*, [...]
———. "German Writers: Heinrich Heine," [...] 134–37.
LOWELL, JAMES RUSSELL. "Edgar Allan Poe," [...] 49.
———. "The New Timon," *NAR*, LXIV (18[...]
———. "Disraeli's Tancred," *NAR*, LXV (18[...]
———. *A Fable for Critics*. Boston, 1848.
———. "Browning's Plays and Poems," *NA[...]
———. "Longfellow's Kavanagh: Nationalit[...] 196.
———. "Hawthorne's *The Marble Faun*," [...]
———. "Longfellow's *Tales of a Wayside* [...]
———. "Thoreau," *NAR*, CI (1865), 39[...]
———. "Whittier's 'Snow-Bound,'" *NAR* [...]
———. "Rousseau and the Sentimentalis[...]
———. *Among My Books, First Series*. [...]
———. *My Study Windows*. Boston, 18[...]
———. "The Shadow of Dante," *NAR* [...]
———. "James's Sketches," *N*, XX ([...]
———. *Among My Books, Second Se*[...]
———. *Latest Literary Essays and Ad*[...]
———. *The Old English Dramatists*. [...]
———. *Lectures on English Poets*. [...]
———. *The Function of the Poet* [...] Boston, 1920.
MELVILLE, HERMAN. "Hawthorn[...] (1850), 125–26; 186–87.
———. *The Confidence Man*. N[...]
PARKMAN, FRANCIS. "James Feni[...]
POE, EDGAR ALLAN. "William [...] senger, III (1835), 41–49.
———. "Exordium," *Graham's* [...]

N[...]
SIMM[...] an[...]

THORE[...]

238[...]
TUCKE[...]
WALLA[...]
WHIPPL[...]

119.

WHITMAN[...]
———. D[...]
———. Le[...]
———. Le[...]
———. "T[...]
———. "E[...]
1882–8[...]
———. "M[...]
Specimer[...]
———. "A[...]
delphia, [...]
———. "Th[...]
———. "Rob[...]
WHITTIER, J[...]
(1829), 3[...]
———. *The* [...]
———. Prefac[...]
———. "Evan[...]

ADAMS, R. P. [...]
419–32.
ALLEN, GAY W[...]

Bowers, David (ed.). *Foreign Influences on American Life*. New Haven, 1944.
Cambridge History of American Literature. Edited by William P. Trent and others. New York, 1917–1921, 4 vols.; 1933, 3 vols.
Clark, Harry H. "Nationalism in American Literature," *University of Toronto Quarterly*, II (1933), 492–519.
Clavel, Marcel. *Fenimore Cooper and His Critics*. Aix-en-Province, 1938.
Current-Garcia, Eugene. *Criticism and the Problem of Literary Expression in a Democratic Society: The Awakening of American Critical Thought, 1835–1850*. Unpublished dissertation, Harvard University, 1947.
Curti, Merle. *The Growth of American Thought*. New York, 1943.
Cushing, William. *Index to the North American Review (1815–1877)*. Cambridge, 1878.
De Mille, George E. "The Birth of the Brahmins," *SR*, XXXVII (1929), 172–88.
Drummond, Edward J. *A Critical History of Catholic Literary Criticism in America: Studies of Brownson, Azarias, and Egan, with an Essay for Catholic Critics*. Unpublished dissertation, University of Iowa, 1942.
Eby, Edwin H. *American Romantic Criticism, 1815–1860*. Unpublished dissertation, University of Washington, 1927.
Foerster, Norman. "Wordsworth in America," *SP*, XXVI (1929), 85–95.
Goddard, H. C. *Studies in New England Transcendentalism*. New York, 1908.
Gohdes, C. F. *The Periodicals of American Transcendentalism*. Durham, N.C., 1931.
Goodman, Paul. "Neo-Classicism, Platonism, and Romanticism," *Journal of Philosophy*, XXXI (1934), 148–63.
Graham, Walter. *Tory Criticism in the Quarterly Review, 1809–1853*. New York, 1921.
Howard, Leon. "Wordsworth in America," *MLN*, XLVIII (1933), 359–65.
Jackson, David K. *The Contributors and Contributions to the Southern Literary Messenger, 1834–1864*. Charlottesville, Va., 1936.
————. "An Estimate of the Influence of *The Southern Literary Messenger*, 1834–1864," *Southern Literary Messenger*, I (1939), 508–14.
Jones, Howard Mumford. *America and French Culture, 1750–1848*. Chapel Hill, N.C., 1927.
————. *Ideas in America*. Cambridge, 1944.
Leland, L. P. *Theories of Fiction in America, 1789–1870*. Unpublished dissertation, The Ohio State University, 1940.
Leonard, William Ellery. *Byron and Byronism in America*. Boston, 1905.
Long, Daniel P. *Dr. Johnson in America*. Unpublished dissertation, University of Illinois, 1939.
Matthiessen, F. O. *American Renaissance*. New York, 1941.
Miller, Perry. *The Transcendentalists: An Anthology*. Cambridge, 1950. Introduction.
Mott, Frank L. *A History of American Magazines*. Cambridge, 1938. 3 vols.
Newton, Annabel. *Wordsworth in Early American Criticism*. Chicago, 1928.
Parrington, Vernon L. *Main Currents in American Thought*. New York, 1930.
Pochmann, Henry. *New England Transcendentalism and St. Louis Hegelianism*. Philadelphia, 1948.
Power, Julia. *Shelley in America*. Lincoln, Neb., 1940.
Rabinovitz, A. L. "Criticism of French Novels in Boston Magazines, 1830–1860," *NEQ*, XIV (1941), 488–504.
Rollins, Hyder E. *Keats' Reputation in America to 1848*. Cambridge, 1946.
Schlesinger, Arthur M., Jr. *The Age of Jackson*. Boston, 1945.
Spencer, Benjamin T. "A National Literature, 1837–1855," *AL*, VIII (1936), 125–59.
Spiller, Robert E. "Critical Standards in the American Romantic Movement," *CE*, VIII (1947), 344–52.

STAFFORD, JOHN. *The Literary Criticism of "Young America,"* Berkeley, Calif., 1952.
STREETER, ROBERT E. *Critical Ideas in the North American Review, 1815–1865.* Unpublished dissertation, Northwestern University, 1943.
TAFT, KENDALL B. *The Minor Knickerbockers: Representative Selections.* New York, 1947. Introduction.
TOWNSEND, FRANCIS G. "The American Estimate of Ruskin, 1847–1860," *Philological Quarterly,* XXXII (1953), 69–82.
TRIMBLE, WILLIAM. "The Social Philosophy of the Loco-Foco Democracy," *American Journal of Sociology,* XXVI (1921), 709.
WAPLES, DOROTHY. *The Whig Myth of James Fenimore Cooper.* New Haven, 1938.
WELLEK, RENÉ. "The Minor Transcendentalists and the German Philosophers," *NEQ,* XV (1942), 669.
———. "The Concept of 'Romanticism' in Literary History," *Comparative Literature,* I (1949), 147–72.
WESTFALL, VAN R. *American Shakespearean Criticism, 1607–1865.* New York, 1939.
WHITMER, ANNE B. *American Reaction to the Literary Criticism of Samuel Taylor Coleridge, 1830–1860.* Unpublished dissertation, The Ohio State University, 1939.

SECONDARY WORKS: ON INDIVIDUAL AUTHORS

On Brownson:
Drummond, Edward J. *A Critical History of Catholic Literary Criticism in America.* Unpublished dissertation, University of Iowa, 1942.
Gohdes, C. F. "Orestes A. Brownson and *The Boston Quarterly Review,*" in *The Periodicals of Transcendentalism.* Durham, N.C., 1931.

On Cooper:
Grossman, James. *James Fenimore Cooper.* New York, 1949.
Lounsbury, T. R. *James Fenimore Cooper.* Boston, 1882.
Shulenberger, Arvid. *Cooper's Theory of Fiction: His Prefaces and Their Relation to His Novels.* Unpublished dissertation, University of Chicago, 1951.
Spiller, Robert E. *James Fenimore Cooper: Representative Selections.* New York, 1936. Introduction.
Waples, Dorothy. *The Novels of Cooper in Relation to American Criticism.* Unpublished dissertation, Yale, 1932.
———. *The Whig Myth of James Fenimore Cooper.* New Haven, 1938.

On Emerson:
Carpenter, F. I. *Ralph Waldo Emerson: Representative Selections.* New York, 1934. Introduction.
Falk, Robert P. "Emerson and Shakespeare," *PMLA,* LVI (1941), 523–43.
Flanagan, J. T. "Emerson as a Critic of Fiction," *Philological Quarterly,* XV (1936), 30–45.
Foerster, Norman. "Emerson on the Organic Principle in Art," *PMLA,* XLI (1926), 193–208.
———. "Emerson," in *American Criticism.* Boston, 1928.
Gorley, Jean. "Emerson's Theory of Poetry," *Poetry Review* (August, 1931), 263–73.
Hopkins, Vivian C. "The Influence of Goethe on Emerson's Aesthetic Theory," *Philological Quarterly,* XXVII (1948), 325–44.
———. *Spires of Form: A Study of Emerson's Aesthetic Theory.* Cambridge, 1951.
Jordan, Leah. *The Fundamentals of Emerson's Literary Criticism.* Unpublished dissertation, University of Pennsylvania, 1945.
Matthiessen, F. O. "From Emerson to Thoreau," in *American Renaissance.* New York, 1941.

Moore, J. B. "Emerson on Wordsworth," *PMLA*, XLI (1926), 179-92.

Pettigrew, R. C. "Emerson and Milton," *AL*, III (1931), 45-59.

Sutcliffe, E. G. "Emerson's Theories of Literary Expression," *University of Illinois Studies in Language and Literature*, VIII (1923), 9-143.

Thompson, Frank T. "Emerson's Indebtedness to Coleridge," *SP*, XXIII (1926), 55-76.

——. "Emerson and Carlyle," *SP*, XXIV (1927), 438-53.

——. "Emerson's Theory and Practice of Poetry," *PMLA*, XLIII (1928), 1170-84.

Woodberry, G. E. *Ralph Waldo Emerson*. New York, 1907.

On Margaret Fuller:

Burton, Roland. *Margaret Fuller's Criticism*. Unpublished dissertation, University of Iowa, 1941.

Ebbitt, Wilma R. *The Critical Essays of Margaret Fuller from the New York Tribune*. With Introduction and Notes. Unpublished dissertation, Brown University, 1943.

McMaster, H. N. "Margaret Fuller as a Literary Critic," *University of Buffalo Studies*, VII (1928), 35-100.

On Hawthorne:

Blodgett, Harold. "Hawthorne as Poetry Critic; Six Unpublished Letters to Lewis Mansfield," *AL*, XII (1940), 173-84.

Doubleday, Neal F. "Hawthorne and Literary Nationalism," *AL*, XII (1941), 447-53.

Foster, C. H. "Hawthorne's Literary Theory," *PMLA*, LVII (1942), 241-54.

Hoeltje, H. H. "Hawthorne's Review of *Evangeline*," *NEQ*, XXIII (1950), 232-35.

Howe, Irving. "Hawthorne on American Fiction," *American Mercury*, LXVIII (1949), 367-74.

James, Henry. *Hawthorne*. New York, 1879.

Matthiessen, F. O. "Hawthorne," in *American Renaissance*. New York, 1941.

Miller, H. P. "Hawthorne Surveys His Contemporaries," *AL*, XII (1940), 228-35.

Stewart, Randall. *Nathaniel Hawthorne*. New Haven, 1948.

Van Doren, Mark. *Nathaniel Hawthorne*. New York, 1949.

Warren, Austin. *Nathaniel Hawthorne: Representative Selections*. New York, 1934. Introduction.

On Holmes:

Clark, Harry H. "Dr. Holmes: A Re-interpretation," *NEQ*, XII (1939), 19-34.

Hayakawa, S. I., and Jones, Howard Mumford. *Oliver Wendell Holmes: Representative Selections*. New York, 1939. Introduction.

Howe, Mark A. De Wolfe. *Holmes of the Breakfast-Table*. New York, 1939.

Knickerbocker, W. S. "His Own Boswell: A Note on the Poetry of Oliver Wendell Holmes," *SeR*, XLI (1933), 454-66.

Morse, J. T. *Life and Letters of Oliver Wendell Holmes*. Boston, 1896, 2 vols.

Pritchard, John P. *Return to the Fountains*. Durham, N.C., 1942.

On Henry N. Hudson:

Stafford, John "Henry Norman Hudson and the Whig Use of Shakespeare," *PMLA*, LXVI (1951), 649-61.

On William A. Jones:

Stafford, John. "William A. Jones, Democratic Literary Critic," *Huntington Library Quarterly*, XII (1949), 289-302.

On Longfellow:

Hatfield, J. T. *New Light on Longfellow, with Special Reference to His Relations to Germany*. Boston, 1933.

Long, Orie W. *Literary Pioneers*. Cambridge, 1935.
Longfellow, Samuel. *The Life of Henry W. Longfellow*. Boston, 1886. 2 vols.
Shepard, Odell. *Henry Wadsworth Longfellow: Representative Selections*. New York, 1934. Introduction.

On Lowell:

Altick, R. D. "Was Lowell an Historical Critic?" *AL*, XIV (1942), 250–59.
Clark, Harry H. "Lowell's Criticism of Romantic Literature," *PMLA*, XLI (1926), 209–28.
———. "Lowell—Humanitarian, Nationalist, or Humanist?" *SP*, XXIII (1930), 411–41.
———, and Foerster, Norman. *James Russell Lowell: Representative Selections*. New York, 1947. Introduction.
De Mille, George E. "Lowell," in *Literary Criticism in America*. New York, 1931.
Foerster, Norman. "Lowell," in *American Criticism*. Boston, 1928.
Howard, Leon. *Victorian Knight Errant*. Berkeley, Calif., 1952.
James, Henry. "James Russell Lowell," *AM*, LXIX (1892), 35–50.
Lockwood, Ferris. "Mr. Lowell on Art-Principles," *Scribner's*, XV (1894), 186–89.
Miller, F. De Wolfe. "Twenty-eight Additions to the Canon of Lowell's Criticism," *Studies in Bibliography*, IV (1951), 205–10.
Murray, Byron D. *Lowell's Criticism of Dryden and Pope*. Unpublished dissertation, University of Iowa, 1946.
Pettigrew, R. C. "Lowell's Criticism of Milton," *AL*, III (1932), 457–64.
Pritchard, John P. "James Russell Lowell," in *Return to the Fountains*. Durham, N.C., 1942.
Reilly, J. J. *James Russell Lowell as a Critic*. New York, 1915.
Robertson, J. M. "Lowell as a Critic," *NAR*, CCIX (1919), 246–62.
Scudder, H. E. *James Russell Lowell*. Cambridge, 1901. 2 vols.
Warren, Austin. "Lowell on Thoreau," *SP*, XXVII (1930), 442–61.
White, W. "Two Versions of Lowell's 'Function of the Poet,'" *Philological Quarterly*, XX (1941), 587–96.
Wurfl, George. "Lowell's Debt to Goethe," *Pennsylvania State College Studies*, I, No. 2 (1936), 1–89.

On Melville:

Arvin, Newton. *Herman Melville*. New York, 1950.
Braswell, William. "Melville as a Critic of Emerson," *AL*, IX (1937), 317–34.
Chase, Richard, *Herman Melville*. New York, 1950.
Howard, Leon. *Herman Melville*. Berkeley, Calif., 1951.
Lewis, R. W. B. "Melville on Homer," *AL*, XXII (1950), 166–77.
Matthiessen, F. O. "Melville," in *American Renaissance*. New York, 1941.
Sedgwick, W. E. *Herman Melville*. Cambridge, 1945.
Thorp, Willard. *Herman Melville: Representative Selections*. New York, 1938. Introduction.

On Poe:

Alterton, Margaret. *Origins of Poe's Critical Theory*. Iowa City, Ia., 1925.
———, and Craig, Hardin. *Edgar Allan Poe: Representative Selections*. New York, 1935. Introduction.
Baldwin, Summerfield. "The Aesthetic Theory of Edgar Poe," *SeR*, XXVI (1918), 210–21.
Campbell, Killis. *The Mind of Poe, and Other Studies*. Cambridge, 1933.
Cooke, John E. *Poe as a Literary Critic*. Baltimore, 1946. Edited by N. Bryllin Fagin.
De Mille, George E. "Poe," in *Literary Criticism in America*. New York, 1931.
Foerster, Norman. "Quantity and Quality in Poe's Aesthetic," *SP*, XX (1923), 310–35.

FOERSTER, NORMAN. "Poe," in *American Criticism*. Boston, 1928.

Hull, William D. *A Canon of the Critical Work of Edgar Allan Poe, with a Study of Poe the Magazinist*. Unpublished dissertation, University of Virginia, 1941.

Jackson, David K. *Poe and the "Southern Literary Messenger."* Richmond, Va., 1934.

Lubell, Albert J. *Edgar Allan Poe, Critic and Reviewer*. Unpublished dissertation, New York University, 1951.

Pritchard, John P. "Edgar Allan Poe," in *Return to the Fountains*. Durham, N.C., 1942.

Quinn, Arthur Hobson. *Edgar Allan Poe*. New York, 1941.

Richardson, G. F. "Poe's Doctrine of Effect," *University of California Publications in Modern Philology*, XI (1928), 177–86.

Snell, George. "First of the New Critics," *Quarterly Review of Literature*, II (1946), 333–40.

Stedman, E. C. "Introduction to the Literary Criticism," in *The Works of Edgar Allan Poe*. Chicago, 1894–1895.

Stovall, Floyd. "Poe's Debt to Coleridge," *University of Texas Studies in English*, X (1930), 70–127.

Werner, W. L. "Poe's Theories and Practice in Poetic Technique," *AL*, II (1930), 157–65.

Wilson, Edmund. "Poe as a Literary Critic," N, CLV (1942), 452–53.

On Simms:

Palmer, Raymond C. *The Prose Fiction Theories of William Gilmore Simms*. Unpublished dissertation, University of Indiana, 1947.

Trent, William P. *William Gilmore Simms*. Boston, 1892.

On Thoreau:

Canby, Henry S. *Thoreau*. Boston, 1939.

Crawford, B. V. *Henry David Thoreau: Representative Selections*. New York, 1934. Introduction.

Krutch, Joseph Wood. *Henry David Thoreau*. New York, 1948.

Lorch, Fred W. "Thoreau and the Organic Principle of Poetry," *PMLA*, LIII (1938), 286–302.

Matthiessen, F. O. "From Emerson to Thoreau," in *American Renaissance*. New York, 1941.

Pritchard, John P. "Henry David Thoreau," in *Return to the Fountains*. Durham, N.C., 1942.

White, Viola C. "Thoreau's Opinion of Whitman," *NEQ*, VIII (1935), 262–64.

On Whitman:

Allen, Gay Wilson. *Walt Whitman Handbook*. Chicago, 1946.

Boatright, Mody C. "Whitman and Hegel," *University of Texas Studies in English*, IX (1929), 134–50.

Canby, Henry S. *Walt Whitman, an American*. Boston, 1943.

Foerster, Norman. "Whitman," in *American Criticism*. Boston, 1928.

Furness, C. J. "Walt Whitman's Estimate of Shakespeare," *Harvard Studies and Notes in Philology and Literature*, XIV (1932), 1–33.

Gummere, Francis B. "Whitman and Taine," in *Democracy and Poetry*. Boston, 1911.

Johnson, Maurice O. "Walt Whitman as a Critic of Literature," *Studies in Language, Literature, and Criticism*, University of Nebraska, No. 16 (1938). 73 pp.

Matthiessen, F. O. "Whitman," in *American Renaissance*. New York, 1941.

Pound, Louise. "Walt Whitman and the Classics," *Southwest Review*, X (1925), 75–83.

Schyberg, Frederik. *Walt Whitman.* Translated from the Danish by Evie Allison Allen. Introduction by Gay Wilson Allen. New York, 1951.

On Whittier:

Cady, E. H., and Clark, Harry H. *Whittier on Writers and Writing: The Uncollected Critical Writings of John Greenleaf Whittier.* Syracuse, N.Y., 1950.

Marcy, Clara P. *The Literary Criticism of John Greenleaf Whittier.* Unpublished dissertation, Boston University, 1946.

Mordell, Albert. *Quaker Militant: John Greenleaf Whittier.* Boston, 1933.

Pickard, Samuel T. *Life and Letters of John Greenleaf Whittier.* Boston, 1894, revised, 1907. 2 vols.

PART III. REALISM AND AESTHETICISM

PRIMARY SOURCES

BOYESEN, HJALMAR. *Essays on German Literature.* New York, 1892.

———. *Essays on Scandinavian Literature.* New York, 1895.

BURROUGHS, JOHN. *Whitman: A Study.* Boston, 1896.

———. *Literary Values.* Boston, 1902.

DE FOREST, JOHN W. "The Great American Novel," N, VI (1868), 27–29.

GARLAND, HAMLIN. "Mr. Howells's Latest Novels," *New England Magazine*, II (1890), 243–50.

———. "The West in Literature," *Arena*, VI (1892), 669–76.

———. "The Future of Fiction," *Arena*, VII (1893), 513–24.

———. *Crumbling Idols.* Chicago, 1894.

———. "Productive Conditions of American Literature," F, VII (1894), 690–98.

———. "Sanity in Fiction," NAR, CLXXVI (1903), 336–48.

———. "Stephen Crane as I knew him," YR, III (1914), 494–506.

———. "Limitations of Authorship in America," B, LIX (1924), 257–62.

GATES, LEWIS. "Taine and the Science of Criticism," N, LVI (1893), 193–94.

———. *Three Studies in Literature.* New York, 1899.

———. *Studies and Appreciations.* New York, 1900.

HARTE, BRET. "Railway Reading," *Californian*, V (1866), 9.

———. "Charles Dickens," *Overland*, V (1870), 90.

———. "English Notebooks of Nathaniel Hawthorne," *Overland*, V (1870), 289–91.

———. "A Few Words About Mr. Lowell," *New Review*, V (1891), 193.

———. "The Rise of the Short Story," *Cornhill Magazine*, VII (1899), 1–8.

———. *Stories and Poems and Other Uncollected Writings.* New York, 1914.

HEARN, LAFCADIO. *Interpretations of Literature.* Edited by John Erskine. New York, 1915.

———. *Appreciations of Poetry.* Edited by John Erskine. New York, 1916.

HOWELLS, WILLIAM DEAN. "James's Hawthorne," AM, XLV (1880), 282–85.

———. "Henry Wadsworth Longfellow," *Harvard Register*, III (1881), 1–2.

———. "Henry James," *Century*, XXV (1882), 25–29.

———. *Criticism and Fiction.* New York, 1891.

———. *My Literary Passions.* New York, 1895.

———. *Literary Friends and Acquaintances.* New York, 1900.

———. "A Possible Difference in English and American Fiction," NAR, CLXXIII (1901), 134–44.

———. "A Psychological Counter-Current in Recent Fiction," NAR, CLXXIII (1901), 872–88.

———. *Literature and Life.* New York, 1902.

———. "Puritanic Influences on American Literature," *Harper's Weekly*, XLVI (1902), 1110.

HOWELLS, WILLIAM DEAN. "Émile Zola," *NAR*, CLXXV (1902), 587–96.
———. "Frank Norris," *NAR*, CLXXV (1902), 769–78.
———. "Impressions of Emerson," *Harper's Weekly*, XLVII (1903), 916.
———. "The Art of Longfellow," *NAR*, CLXXXIV (1907), 472–85.
———. *My Mark Twain*. New York, 1910.
———. "Mr. Garland's Books," *NAR*, CXCVI (1912), 523–28.
———. "Mr. Henry James's Later Work," *NAR*, CCIII (1916), 572–84.
HUNEKER, JAMES. *Iconoclasts*. New York, 1905.
———. "Henrik Ibsen," *Scribner's*, XL (1906), 351–61.
———. "Anatole France," *NAR*, CLXXXIV (1907), 59–72.
———. "The Baudelaire Legend," *Scribner's*, XLV (1909), 240–49.
———. *Promenades of an Impressionist*. New York, 1910.
———. "The Genius of Joseph Conrad," *NAR*, CC (1914), 270–79.
———. *Ivory Apes and Peacocks*. New York, 1915.
———. *Unicorns*. New York, 1917.
———. *Bedouins*. New York, 1920.
———. *Variations*. New York, 1921.
JAMES, HENRY. "Novels of George Eliot," *AM*, XVIII (1866), 479.
———. "Taine's *English Literature*," *AM*, XXIX (1872), 469–72.
———. *French Poets and Novelists*. London, 1878.
———. *Hawthorne*. London, 1879.
———. *Partial Portraits*. New York and London, 1888.
———. "James Russell Lowell," *AM*, LXIX (1892), 35–50.
———. *Essays in London and Elsewhere*. New York, 1893.
———. "The Present Literary Situation in France," *NAR*, CLXIX (1899), 488–500.
———. "George Sand," *NAR*, CLXXIV (1902), 546–54.
———. "The Lesson of Balzac," *AM*, XCVI (1905), 166–80.
———. *Views and Reviews*. Boston, 1908.
———. "A Letter to Mr. Howells," *NAR*, CXCV (1912), 558–62.
———. *Notes on Novelists*. New York, 1914.
———. *The Letters*. Edited by Percy Lubbock. New York, 1920. 2 vols.
———. *Notes and Reviews*. Edited by Pierre de Chaignon la Rose. Cambridge, 1921.
———. *The Art of the Novel: Critical Prefaces of Henry James*. Edited by R. P. Blackmur. New York, 1934.
———. *The Notebooks of Henry James*. Edited by F. O. Matthiessen and Kenneth B. Murdock. New York, 1947.
LANIER, SIDNEY. *The Science of English Verse*. New York, 1880.
———. *The English Novel and the Principles of Its Development*. New York, 1883.
LONDON, JACK. "Phenomena of Literary Evolution," *B*, XII (1900), 148–51.
———. "The Terrible and Tragic in Fiction," *Critic*, XLII (1903), 539–43.
MABIE, HAMILTON WRIGHT. *Books and Culture*. New York, 1886.
———. *My Study Fire*. New York, 1901.
———. *Nature and Culture*. New York, 1904.
———. *Essays in Literary Interpretation*. New York, 1910.
MATTHEWS, BRANDER. *Literary Style*. 1882.
———. *An Introduction to the Study of American Literature*. New York, 1896.
———. *Aspects of Fiction and Other Ventures in Criticism*. New York, 1896.
———. *The American of the Future*. New York, 1909.
———. *Gateways to Literature*. New York, 1912.
NORRIS, FRANK. *Responsibilities of the Novelist*. New York, 1903.
———. "Two Uncollected Essays by Frank Norris," ed. by W. E. Martin. Jr., *AL*, VIII (1936), 190–98.
PAYNE, WILLIAM MORTON (ed.). *American Literary Criticism*. New York, 1904.
SALTUS, EDGAR. *Balzac*. New York, 1884.
———. *Love and Lore*. New York, 1890.

————. *Oscar Wilde*. New York, 1917.

SANTAYANA, GEORGE. *The Sense of Beauty*. New York, 1896.

————. *Interpretations of Poetry and Religion*. New York, 1900.

————. *Three Philosophical Poets*. New York, 1910.

————. *Character and Opinion in the United States*. New York, 1920.

————. "Dickens," *D*, LXXI (1921), 537–49.

————. "America's Young Radicals," *F*, LXVII (1922), 371–75.

————. *Obiter Scripta*. New York, 1936.

SPINGARN, J. E. *The New Criticism*. New York, 1911.

————. "Grocer-shop Critic and Real Critic," *D*, LVII (1914), 96–99.

————. *Creative Criticism and Other Essays*. New York, 1917; revised edition, 1931.

————. "American Criticism Today," *N*, XXVII (1920), 82–84.

————. *Scholarship and Criticism in the United States*. New York, 1922.

————. (ed.). *Criticism in America*. New York, 1924.

————. "Politics and the Poet," *AM*, CLXX (1942), 73–78.

STEDMAN, E. C. *Victorian Poets*. Boston, 1875.

————. *Poets of America*. Boston, 1885.

————. *The Nature and Elements of Poetry*. Boston, 1892.

————. *Genius and Other Essays*. New York, 1911.

TAYLOR, BAYARD. *Critical Essays and Literary Notes*. New York, 1880.

THOMPSON, VANCE. *French Portraits*. New York, 1899.

TWAIN, MARK. "Literary Nightmare," *AM*, XXXVII (1876), 167–69.

————. *Literary Essays*. New York, 1897.

————. "Howells," *Harper's*, CXIII (1906), 221–25.

————. *Mark Twain's Letters*. Edited by A. B. Paine. New York, 1917. 2 vols.

————. *In Defense of Harriet Shelley and Other Essays*. New York, 1918.

————. *Mark Twain's Autobiography*. Edited by A. B. Paine. New York, 1924. 2 vols.

————. *Mark Twain's Notebook*. Edited by A. B. Paine. New York, 1935.

————. *Mark Twain in Eruption*. Edited by Bernard De Voto, New York, 1940.

————. "Fenimore Cooper's Further Literary Offenses," edited by Bernard De Voto, *NEQ*, XIX (1946), 291–301.

WARNER, CHARLES DUDLEY. *The Relation of Literature to Life*. New York, 1897.

WOODBERRY, GEORGE E. *Studies in Letters and Life*. New York, 1890.

————. *America in Literature*. New York, 1903.

————. *The Torch*. New York, 1905.

————. *Two Phases of Criticism, Historical and Aesthetic*. New York, 1914.

————. *Literary Essays*. New York, 1920.

SECONDARY WORKS: GENERAL

AHNEBRINK, LARS. *The Beginnings of Naturalism in American Fiction*. Cambridge, 1950.

ALLEN, CHARLES. "Regionalism and the Little Magazines," *CE*, VII (1945), 10–16.

BEER, THOMAS. *The Mauve Decade: American Life at the End of the Nineteenth Century*. New York, 1926.

BROWN, HERBERT. "The Great American Novel," *AL*, VII (1935), 1–14.

Cambridge History of American Literature. Edited by William P. Trent and others. New York, 1917–1921, 4 vols.; 1933, 3 vols.

CARGILL, OSCAR. *Intellectual America*. New York, 1941.

CLARK, HARRY H. "American Literary Criticism to 1919," in *Dictionary of World Literature*. Edited by Joseph Shipley. New York, 1943.

COMMAGER, HENRY S. *The American Mind: An Interpretation of American Thought and Character Since the 1880's*. New Haven, 1950.

COWLEY, MALCOLM. " 'Not Men': A Natural History of American Naturalism," *KR*, IX (1947), 414–35.

CURTI, MERLE. *The Growth of American Thought.* New York, 1943.

DUNBAR, JOHN. *The Reception of European Literary Naturalism in the United States, 1870–1900.* Unpublished dissertation, Harvard University, 1948.

EDWARDS, HERBERT. "Zola and American Critics," *AL,* IV (1932), 114–29.

FALK, ROBERT P. *Representative American Criticism of Shakespeare, 1830–1885.* Unpublished dissertation, University of Wisconsin, 1940.

FARRELL, JAMES T. "Some Observations on Naturalism, So Called, in American Fiction," *Antioch Review,* X (1950), 247–64.

FOLEY, RICHARD. *Criticism in American Periodicals of the Works of Henry James from 1866–1916.* Washington, D.C., 1944.

FRIERSON, W. C., and EDWARDS, HERBERT, "Impact of French Naturalism on American Critical Opinion, 1877–1892," *PMLA,* LXIII (1948), 1007–16.

GRUENINGER, J. P. VON. "Goethe in American Periodicals, 1860–1900," *PMLA,* L (1935), 1155–64.

HARTWICK, HARRY. *The Foreground of American Fiction.* New York, 1934.

HOFSTADTER, RICHARD. *Social Darwinism in American Thought, 1860–1915.* Philadelphia, 1944.

JONES, ARTHUR E. *Darwinism and Its Relationship to Realism and Naturalism in American Fiction, 1860–1900.* Madison, N.J., 1950.

JONES, MALCOLM. *French Literature and American Criticism, 1870–1900: A Study in Periodical Literature.* Unpublished dissertation, Harvard University, 1936.

JOSEPHSON, MATTHEW. *Zola and His Time.* New York, 1928.

KAZIN, ALFRED. *On Native Grounds.* New York, 1942.

LILJEGREN, STEN. *The Revolt Against Romanticism in American Literature.* Upsala, Sweden, 1945.

LLOYD, EVERETT T. *The Evolution of the Attitude in the United States Toward Émile Zola.* Unpublished dissertation, New York University, 1949.

LUCAS, FRANK. *The Decline and Fall of the Romantic Ideal.* New York, 1936.

LUTWACK, LEONARD I. *The Dynamics of Conservative Criticism: Literary Criticism in American Magazines, 1880–1900.* Unpublished dissertation, The Ohio State University, 1950.

McWILLIAMS, CARY. "Localism in American Criticism," *Southwest Review,* XIX (1934), 410–28.

PAYNE, W. M. "American Literary Criticism and the Doctrine of Evolution," *International Monthly,* II (1900), 26–46; 127–53.

PECK, HARRY THURSTON. "Émile Zola," in *Studies in Several Literatures.* New York, 1909.

PERSONS, STOW (ed.). *Evolutionary Thought in America.* New Haven, 1950.

RENINGER, HARRY W. *The Theory and Practice of the American Novel, 1867–1903.* Unpublished dissertation, University of Michigan, 1938.

RUNYAN, HARRY J. *The Backgrounds and Origins of Realism in the American Novel, 1850–1880.* Unpublished dissertation, University of Wisconsin, 1949.

SALVAN, A. J. *Zola aux États Unis.* Providence, R.I., 1943.

SPEAKE, MARIAN R. *Contemporary American Criticism of Walt Whitman, 1855–1892.* Unpublished dissertation, University of Iowa, 1926.

SPENCER, BENJAMIN T. "The New Realism and a National Literature," *PMLA,* LVI (1941), 1116–32.

SPILLER, ROBERT. "Toward Naturalism in Fiction," in *Literary History of the United States.* New York, 1948.

TAYLOR, H. W. "Some Nineteenth Century Critics of Realism," *University of Texas Studies in English,* VIII (1928), 110–28.

TAYLOR, W. F. "That Gilded Age: Plain Talk About Some Recent Criticism and the National Tradition," *SeR,* XLV (1937), 41–54.

WALCUTT, C. C. "The Naturalism of Vandover and the Brute," in *Forms of Modern Fiction,* ed. by W. V. O'Connor. Minneapolis, 1948.

SECONDARY WORKS: ON INDIVIDUAL AUTHORS

On Garland:

Raw, Ruth M. "Hamlin Garland, the Romanticist," *SeR*, XXXVI (1928), 202-10.

Spiller, Robert (ed.). Garland's *Crumbling Idols*. Gainesville, Fla., 1952. Introduction.

Taylor, W. F. *The Economic Novel in America*. Chapel Hill, N.C., 1942. Pp. 148-82.

Van Doren, Carl. *Contemporary American Novelists*. New York, 1922. Pp. 38-47.

On Harte:

Harrison, Joseph B. *Bret Harte: Representative Selections*. New York, 1941. Introduction.

Quinn, Arthur Hobson. *American Fiction*. New York, 1936. Pp. 232-42.

Stewart, G. R., Jr. *Bret Harte*. Boston, 1931.

On Howells:

Budd, Louis J. "W. D. Howells' Defense of the Romance," *PMLA*, LXVII (1952), 32-42.

Carter, Everett. "William Dean Howells' Theory of Critical Realism," *ELH*, XVI (1949), 151-66.

Clark, Harry H. "Howells," in *Literary Criticism, Pope to Croce*, ed. by G. W. Allen and H. H. Clark. New York, 1941. Pp. 562-65.

———. "The Role of Science in the Thought of W. D. Howells," *Transactions of the Wisconsin Academy of Sciences, Arts, and Letters*, XLII (1953), 263-303.

Cooke, Delmar G. *William Dean Howells*. New York, 1922.

Edwards, Herbert. "Howells and the Controversy over Realism in American Fiction," *AL*, III (1931), 237-48.

James, Henry. "William Dean Howells," *Harper's Weekly*, XXX (1886), 394-95.

Kirk, Clara, and Kirk, Rudolph. *William Dean Howells: Representative Selections*. New York, 1950. Introduction.

Lutwack, Leonard. "William Dean Howells and the 'Editor's Study,'" *AL*, XXIV (1952), 195-207.

Malone, Clifton. *The Hitherto Uncollected Critical Opinions of William Dean Howells*. Unpublished dissertation, University of Oklahoma, 1947.

Matthews, Brander. "Mr. Howells as a Critic," *F*, XXXII (1902), 624-38.

Miller, Charles T. *Howells' Literary Criticism*. Unpublished dissertation, University of Chicago, 1947.

Scudder, H. E. "Mr. Howells' Literary Creed," *AM*, LXVIII (1891), 566-69.

Taylor, W. F. "William Dean Howells and the Economic Novel," *AL*, IV (1932), 113.

Trent, W. P. "Mr. Howells and Romanticism," in *The Authority of Criticism and Other Essays*. New York, 1899. Pp. 259-67.

Trilling, Lionel. "W. D. Howells and the Roots of Modern Taste," *PR*, XVIII (1951), 516-36.

Van Doren, Carl. "Howells and Realism," in *The American Novel*. New York, 1940.

On Huneker:

De Casseres, Benjamin. *James Gibbons Huneker*. New York, 1925.

De Mille, George E. "Huneker," in *Literary Criticism in America*. New York, 1931.

Fay, E. C. "Huneker's Criticism of French Literature," *French Review*, XIV (1940), 130-37.

Mencken, H. L. "James Huneker," *Century,* CII (1921), 191–97.

Pritchard, John P., and Raines, J. M. "James Gibbons Huneker, Critic of the Seven Arts," *American Quarterly,* II (1950), 53–61.

On James:

Barrett, Laurence. "Young Henry James, Critic," *AL,* XX (1949), 385–400.

Beach, Joseph Warren. *The Method of Henry James.* New Haven, 1918.

Blackmur, R. P. *The Art of the Novel: Critical Prefaces, by Henry James.* New York, 1934. Introduction.

Brooks, Van Wyck. *The Pilgrimage of Henry James.* New York, 1925.

———. "Henry James as a Reviewer," in *Sketches in Criticism.* New York, 1932.

Dupee, Frederick W. (ed.). *The Question of Henry James: A Collection of Critical Essays.* New York, 1945.

———. *Henry James.* New York, 1951.

Edel, Leon. *The Prefaces of Henry James.* Paris, 1931.

———. *Henry James: The Untried Years.* New York, 1953.

Edgar, Pelham. *Henry James: Man and Author.* New York, 1933.

Falk, Robert P. "Henry James's Romantic 'Vision of the Real' in the 1870's," *Essays Critical and Historical,* by members of the Departments of English, University of California. Berkeley, 1950.

Foley, Richard. *Criticism in American Periodicals of the Works of Henry James from 1866–1916.* Washington, 1944.

Hamilton, Eunice. "Biographical and Critical Studies of Henry James, 1941–1948," *AL,* XX (1949), 424–35.

Hughes, Hubert L. *Theory and Practice in Henry James.* Ann Arbor, 1926.

Kenyon Review. "The Henry James Number," V (1943).

Leavis, F. R. "Henry James and the Function of Criticism," *Scrutiny,* XV (1948), 98–104.

Littell, Philip. "Henry James as Critic," *NR,* I (1914), 26–28.

Little Review. "The Henry James Number," V (1918).

Matthiessen, F. O. *Henry James: The Major Phase.* New York, 1944.

———. *The James Family.* New York, 1947.

Raleigh, John H. "Henry James: The Poetics of Empiricism," *PMLA,* LXVI (1951), 107–23.

Richardson, Lyon. *Henry James: Representative Selections.* New York, 1941. Introduction.

Roberts, Morris. *Henry James's Criticism.* Cambridge, 1929.

———. "Henry James and the Art of Foreshortening," *Review of English Studies,* XXII (1946), 207–14.

Sherman, Stuart P. "The Aesthetic Idealism of Henry James," in *On Contemporary Literature.* New York, 1917.

Short, R. W. "Some Critical Terms of Henry James," *PMLA,* LXV (1950), 667–80.

Specker, Heidi. "The Change of Emphasis in the Criticism of Henry James," *English Studies,* XXIX (1948), 33–47.

Wade, Allen. "Henry James as Dramatic Critic," *Theatre Arts,* XXVII (1943), 735–40.

Zabel, Morton D. "The Poetics of Henry James," *Poetry,* XLV (1935), 270–76.

On Lanier:

Allen, Gay Wilson. "Sidney Lanier as a Literary Critic," *Philological Quarterly,* XVII (1938), 121–38.

On Norris:

Ahnebrink, L. *The Influence of Émile Zola on Frank Norris.* Cambridge, 1947.

Edwards, Herbert. "Zola and the American Critics," *AL,* IV (1932), 114–29.

Hartwick, Harry. *The Foreground of American Fiction.* New York, 1934. Pp. 45–66.

Marchand, Ernest. *Frank Norris: A Study.* Stanford University, Calif., 1942.

Walcutt, C. C. "Frank Norris on Realism and Naturalism," *AL*, XIII (1941), 61–63.

On Santayana:

Ames, Van Meter. *Proust and Santayana: The Aesthetic Way of Life.* Chicago, 1937.

Howgate, George. *George Santayana.* Philadelphia, 1938.

Gilbert, Katherine. "Santayana's Doctrine of Aesthetic Expression," *Philosophical Review*, XXV (1926), 221–35.

Ransom, John Crowe. "Art and Mr. Santayana," *Virginia Quarterly Review*, XIII (1937), 420–36.

On Stedman:

Carpenter, F. I. "The Genteel Tradition: A Reinterpretation," *NEQ*, XV (1942), 427–43.

De Mille, George E. "Stedman, Arbiter of the Eighties," *PMLA*, XLI (1926), 756–66.

———. "Stedman," in *Literary Criticism in America.* New York, 1931.

Pritchard, John P. "Edmund Clarence Stedman," in *Return to the Fountains.* Durham, N.C., 1942.

Stedman, Laura, and Gould, George M. *Life and Letters of Edmund Clarence Stedman.* New York, 1910. 2 vols.

Thorp, Willard, "Defenders of Ideality," in *Literary History of the United States,* ed. by Robert Spiller and others. New York, 1948.

On Taylor:

Beatty, Richmond C. *Bayard Taylor: Laureate of the Gilded Age.* Norman, Okla., 1936.

Frenz, Horst. "Bayard Taylor and the Reception of Goethe in America," *JEGP*, XLI (1942), 121–39.

On Twain:

Canby, Henry S. *Turn West Turn East: Mark Twain and Henry James.* Boston, 1951.

Feinstein, George. *Mark Twain's Literary Opinions.* Unpublished dissertation, University of Iowa, 1946.

———. "Mark Twain's Idea of Story Structure," *AL*, XVIII (1946), 160–63.

Howells, William Dean. *My Mark Twain.* New York, 1910.

Matthews, Brander. "Mark Twain, and the Art of Writing," in *Essays on English.* New York, 1921.

Paine, Albert B. *Mark Twain.* New York, 1912.

Wecter, Dixon. *Sam Clemens of Hannibal.* Boston, 1952.

On Woodberry:

Doyle, Joseph. *George E. Woodberry.* Unpublished dissertation, Columbia University, 1952.

Shackford, M. H. "George Edward Woodberry as Critic," *NEQ*, XXIV (1951), 510–27.

PART IV. TRENDS IN MODERN CRITICISM

PRIMARY SOURCES

AIKEN, CONRAD. *Scepticisms, Notes on Contemporary Poetry.* New York, 1919.

———. "The Novel as a Work of Art," *D*, LXXXIII (1927), 41–44.

———. "William Faulkner," *AM*, CLXIV (1939), 650–54.

———. "Poetry: What Direction?" *NR*, CIV (1941), 670–77.

———. "American Writers Come of Age," *AM*, CLXIX (1942), 476–81.

AIKEN, CONRAD. "The Novel as Form," *Harvard Advocate*, CXXXV (1951), 13, 24-26.

AMES, VAN METER. *Aesthetics of the Novel*. Berkeley, Calif., 1928.

ARVIN, NEWTON. "Whitman's Individualism," *NR*, LXXI (1932), 212-13.

———. "Henry James and the Almighty Dollar," *HH*, VII (1934), 434-43.

———. "The Usableness of Howells," *NR*, XCI (1937), 227-28.

———. *Whitman*. New York, 1938.

———. "Melville's Shorter Poems," *PR*, XVI (1949), 1034-46.

BABBITT, IRVING. *The New Laokoön*. Boston, 1910.

———. *The Masters of Modern French Criticism*. Boston, 1912.

———. "Bergson and Rousseau," *N*, XCV (1912), 452-55.

———. "Matthew Arnold," *N*, CV (1917), 117-21.

———. "Genius and Taste," *N*, CVI (1918), 138-41.

———. *Rousseau and Romanticism*. Boston, 1919.

———. "The Critic and American Life," *F*, LXXIX (1928), 161-76.

———. "Coleridge and Imagination," *B*, LXX (1929), 113-24.

———. "On 'Humanism': An Essay at Definition," in *Humanism and America*, ed. by Norman Foerster. New York, 1930.

———. *On Being Creative and Other Essays*. New York, 1932.

———. "Style in a Democracy," *SRL*, IX (1932), 325-26.

———. *Spanish Character and Other Essays*. Boston, 1940.

BARZUN, JACQUES. "To the Rescue of Romanticism," *AS*, IX (1940), 147-58.

———. "James the Melodramatist," *KR*, V (1943), 508-21.

———. "The Fetish of Form: An Example from Music," *KR*, XII (1950), 86-98.

BASLER, ROY. *Sex, Psychology and Literature*. New York, 1948.

BEACH, JOSEPH WARREN. *The Outlook for American Prose*. Chicago, 1926.

———. "The Novel from James to Joyce," *N*, CXXXII (1931), 634-36.

———. *The Twentieth Century Novel: Studies in Technique*. New York, 1932.

———. "Dos Passos: 1947," *SeR*, LV (1947), 406-18.

———. "The Sacred and Solitary Refuge" (On Henry James), *Furioso*, III (1947), 23-37.

BISHOP, JOHN PEALE. "Homage to Hemingway," *NR*, LXXXIX (1936), 39-42.

———. "The Discipline of Poetry," *VQR*, XIV (1938), 343-56.

———. "The Poems and Prose of E. E. Cummings," *SR*, IV (1938), 173-86.

———. "Myth and Modern Literature," *SRL*, XX (1939), 3-4.

———. "Poetry and Painting," *SeR*, LIII (1945), 247-58.

———. *Collected Essays of John Peale Bishop*. Edited by Edmund Wilson. New York, 1948.

BLACKMUR, R. P. "Wallace Stevens," *HH*, V (1932), 223-56.

———. "Masks of Ezra Pound," *HH*, VII (1934), 177-212.

———. *The Double Agent: Essays in Craft and Elucidation*. New York, 1935.

———. *The Expense of Greatness*. New York, 1940.

———. "Humanism and the Symbolic Imagination," *SR*, VII (1941), 309-25.

———. "The Enabling Act of Criticism," in *American Issues*, ed. by Willard Thorp. New York, 1941.

———. "The Sacred Fount" (On James), *KR*, IV (1942), 328-52.

———. "Between Myth and Philosophy," *SeR*, LIII (1942), 407-25.

———. "In the Country of the Blue" (On James), *KR*, V (1943), 595-617.

———. "Notes on Four Categories in Criticism," *SeR*, LIV (1946), 576-89.

———. "A Burden for Critics," *HR*, I (1948), 170-85.

———. "*Anna Karenina*: The Dialect of Incarnation," *KR*, XII (1950), 433-56.

———. "In the Hope of Straightening Things Out" (On Eliot), *KR*, XIII (1951), 303-14.

———. "The Loose and Baggy Monsters of Henry James," *A*, XI (1951), 129-46.

———. "The Harmony of True Liberalism: Henry Adams' *Mont-Saint-Michel and Chartres*," *SeR*, LX (1952), 1-27.

———. "Lord Tennyson's Scissors: 1912-1950," *KR*, XIV (1952), 1-20.

———. *Language as Gesture: Essays in Poetry*. New York, 1952.

BOGAN, LOUISE. *Achievement in American Poetry, 1900–1950.* Chicago, 1951.

BOURNE, RANDOLPH. "Theodore Dreiser," *NR*, II (1915), 7–8.

——. "The History of a Literary Radical," *YR*, VIII (1919), 468–84.

——. *The History of a Literary Radical and Other Essays.* Edited by Van Wyck Brooks. New York, 1920.

BROOKS, CLEANTH. "The Reading of Modern Poetry," *AR*, VIII (1937), 435–49.

——. "The Waste Land: An Analysis," *SR*, III (1937), 106–36.

——, and Warren, R. P. *Understanding Poetry.* New York, 1938; revised edition, 1951.

——. *Modern Poetry and the Tradition.* New York, 1939.

——. "The Poem as Organism," in *English Institute Annual: 1940.* New York, 1941.

——. "Literary History versus Criticism," *KR*, II (1940), 403–12.

——. "The Language of Paradox," in *The Language of Poetry,* ed. by Allen Tate. New York, 1942.

——. *The Well Wrought Urn: Studies in the Structure of Poetry.* New York, 1947.

——. "Milton and Critical Re-estimates," *PMLA*, LXVI (1951), 1045–54.

——. "Milton and the New Criticism," *SeR*, LIX (1951), 1–22.

——. "Absalom, Absalom: The Definition of Innocence," *SeR*, LIX (1951), 543–58.

——. "My Credo: The Formalist Critic," *KR*, XIII (1951), 72–81.

——. "A Note on 'History' and 'Criticism,'" *SeR*, LXI (1953), 129–35.

BROOKS, VAN WYCK. *America's Coming of Age.* New York, 1915.

——. "On Creating a Usable Past," *D*, LXIV (1918), 337–41.

——. *The Ordeal of Mark Twain.* New York, 1920; revised edition, 1932.

——. *Sketches in Criticism.* New York, 1921.

——. "Henry James: The First Phase," *D*, LXXIV (1923), 433–50.

——. *The Pilgrimage of Henry James.* New York, 1925.

——. "Emerson and the Reformers," *Harper's*, CLIV (1926), 114–19.

——. *Three Essays on America.* New York, 1934.

——. *The Flowering of New England.* New York, 1936.

——. *New England: Indian Summer.* New York, 1940.

——. *The World of Washington Irving.* New York, 1944.

——. *The Times of Melville and Whitman.* New York, 1947.

——. "Theodore Dreiser," *University Kansas City Review*, XVI (1950), 187–97.

——. *The Writer in America.* New York, 1952.

BROWNELL, WILLIAM C. *American Prose Masters.* New York, 1909.

——. *Criticism.* New York, 1914.

——. *Standards.* New York, 1917.

——. *The Genius of Style.* New York, 1925.

BUCK, PHILO, JR. *Literary Criticism.* New York, 1930.

——. *Directions in Contemporary Literature.* New York, 1942.

BURGUM, EDWIN B. (ed.). *The New Criticism.* New York, 1930.

BURKE, KENNETH. *Counter-Statement.* New York, 1931.

——. *Permanence and Change.* New York, 1935.

——. *The Philosophy of Literary Form.* New York, 1941.

——. "On Motivation in Yeats," *SR*, VII (1942), 547–61.

——. *A Grammar of Motives.* New York, 1945.

——. "Container and Thing Contained," *SeR*, LIII (1945), 56–78.

——. "The Temporizing of Essence," *KR*, VII (1945), 616–27.

——. *A Rhetoric of Motives.* New York, 1950.

——. "Ethan Brand: A Preparatory Investigation," *Hopkins Review*, V (1952), 45–65.

BUSH, DOUGLAS. "The Humanist Critic," *KR*, XIII (1951), 81–91.

CALVERTON, V. F. *The Newer Spirit: A Sociological Criticism of Literature.* New York, 1925.

CALVERTON, V. F. *The Liberation of American Literature.* New York, 1932.
———. "The American Revolutionary Tradition," *Scribner's*, XCV (1934), 352–57.
CANBY, HENRY S. *Definitions: Essays in Contemporary Criticism.* New York, 1922.
———. *American Estimates.* New York, 1929.
———. *Classic Americans.* New York, 1931.
———. *Thoreau.* New York, 1939.
———. *Walt Whitman, An American.* New York, 1943.
CARNS, HUNTINGTON (ed.). *Lectures in Criticism* (1949). A symposium of lectures on historical and modern theory in criticism, delivered at Johns Hopkins University in April, 1938, by R. P. Blackmur, Benedetto Croce, Henri Peyre, John Crowe Ransom, Herbert Read, and Allen Tate.
CATHER, WILLA. *On Writing: Critical Studies on Writing as an Art.* New York, 1949.
CHASE, RICHARD. "Notes on the Study of Myth," *PR*, XIII (1946), 338–46.
———. "The Progressive Hawthorne," *PR*, XVI (1949), 96–100.
———. *Quest for Myth.* New York, 1949.
———. *Herman Melville.* New York, 1949.
———. *Emily Dickinson.* New York, 1951.
COWLEY, MALCOLM. *Exile's Return.* New York, 1934.
———. "Robert Frost: A Dissenting Opinion," *NR*, CXI (1944), 312–13.
———. "William Faulkner's Legend of the South," *SeR*, LIII (1945), 343–61.
———. "Walt Whitman: The Miracle," *NR*, CXIV (1946), 385–88.
———. "Walt Whitman: The Secret," *NR*, CXIV (1946), 481–84.
———. "Hawthorne in the Looking Glass," *SeR*, LVI (1948), 545–63.
———. "The Scott Fitzgerald Story," *NR*, CXXIV (1951), 17–20.
CRANE, R. S. *Critics and Criticism, Ancient and Modern.* Chicago, 1952.
DAICHES, DAVID. *The Place of Meaning in Poetry.* New York, 1935.
———. *The Novel and the Modern World.* Chicago, 1939.
———. "The Principles of Literary Criticism," *NR*, XCVIII (1939), 95–98.
———. *Poetry and the Modern World.* Chicago, 1940.
———. "Sensibility and Technique: Preface to a Critique" (On James), *KR*, V (1943), 569–79.
———. *Study of Literature for Readers and Critics.* Ithaca, N.Y., 1948.
———. "T. S. Eliot," *YR*, XXXVIII (1949), 460–70.
———. *Willa Cather: A Critical Introduction.* Ithaca, N.Y., 1951.
DE VOTO, BERNARD. *Mark Twain's America.* New York, 1932.
———. *The Literary Fallacy.* New York, 1944.
———. *The World of Fiction.* Boston, 1950.
EASTMAN, MAX. *The Literary Mind: Its Place in an Age of Science.* New York, 1931.
———. *The Enjoyment of Poetry.* New York, 1939.
EDGAR, PELHAM. *The Art of the Novel.* New York, 1933.
———. *Henry James: Man and Author.* New York, 1935.
ELIOT, T. S. "The Possibility of a Poetic Drama," *D*, LXIX (1920), 441–47.
———. *The Sacred Wood.* New York, 1920.
———. "Ulysses, Order, and Myth," *D*, LXXV (1923), 480–83.
———. "Literature, Science, and Dogma," *D*, LXXXII (1927), 239–43.
———. *For Lancelot Andrewes.* New York, 1928.
———. "Isolated Superiority" (On Pound), *D*, LXXXIV (1928), 4–7.
———. *Selected Essays: 1917–1932.* New York, 1932. New edition with additional essays, 1950.
———. *The Use of Poetry and the Use of Criticism.* New York, 1933.
———. *After Strange Gods.* New York, 1934.
———. "Literature and the Modern World," *AP*, I (1935), 19–22.
———. "Notes Toward a Definition of Culture," *PR*, XI (1942), 145–57.
———. *The Music of Poetry.* New York, 1942.
———. *What Is a Classic?* New York, 1945.

ELIOT, T. S. "Ezra Pound," *P*, LXVIII (1946), 326-38.
———. "What Is Minor Poetry?" *SeR*, LIV (1946), 1-18.
———. "Milton," *SeR*, LVI (1948), 185-209.
———. *From Poe to Valéry*. New York, 1948.
———. *Poetry and Drama*. Cambridge, 1951.
———. "Vergil and the Christian World," *SeR*, LXI (1953), 1-14.
FARRELL, JAMES T. *A Note on Literary Criticism*. New York, 1936.
———. *Literature and Morality*. New York, 1947.
FOERSTER, NORMAN. *American Criticism*. Boston, 1928.
———. *Towards Standards*. New York, 1930.
———. (ed.). *American Critical Essays*. New York, 1930.
———. (ed.). *Humanism and America: Essays on the Outlook of Modern Civilization*. New York, 1930.
———. "The Esthetic Judgment and the Ethical Judgment," in *The Intent of the Critic*, ed. by Donald Stauffer. New York, 1941.
FOWLIE, WALLACE. *Rimbaud*. New York, 1946.
———. *Age of Surrealism*. New York, 1951.
FRANK, JOSEPH. "Spatial Form in Modern Literature," *SeR*, LIII (1945), 221-40, 433-56, 643-53.
———. "Romanticism and Reality in Robert Penn Warren," *HR*, IV (1951), 248-58.
FROST, ROBERT. "Education by Poetry," *AP*, VI (1940), 5-17.
———. "The Figure a Poem Makes," in *Collected Poems*. New York, 1942.
———. "The Constant Symbol," *AM*, CLXXVIII (1946), 50-52.
FRYE, PROSSER HALL. *Literary Reviews and Criticism*. New York, 1908.
———. *Romance and Tragedy*. New York, 1922.
———. *Visions and Chimeras*. New York, 1929.
GEISMAR, MAXWELL. *Writers in Crisis: The American Novel Between Two Wars*. New York, 1942.
———. *The Last of the Provincials: The American Novel 1915-1925*. New York, 1948.
GLASGOW, ELLEN. *A Certain Measure: An Interpretation of Prose Fiction*. New York, 1943.
GRATTAN, C. HARTLEY (ed.). *The Critique of Humanism: A Symposium*. New York, 1930.
GREENE, THEODORE M. *The Arts and the Art of Criticism*. Princeton, 1940.
HAMM, VICTOR M. *The Pattern of Criticism*. Milwaukee, 1951.
HARRIS, JULIAN (ed.). *The Humanities: An Appraisal*. Madison, Wis., 1950.
HICKS, GRANVILLE. *The Great Tradition*. New York, 1933; revised edition, 1935.
———. *Figures of Transition*. New York, 1939.
———. "The Failure of 'Left' Criticism," *NR*, CIII (1940), 345-47.
———. "Fiction and Social Criticism," *CE*, XIII (1952), 355-61; XLI (1952), 173-79.
HOFFMAN, FREDERICK J. *Freudianism and the Literary Mind*. Baton Rouge, La., 1946.
———. "Psychoanalysis and Literary Criticism," *American Quarterly*, II (1950), 144-54.
HYMAN, STANLEY E. "Henry Thoreau in Our Time," *AM*, CLXXVIII (1946), 137-38.
———. "The Critic as Narcissus," *A*, VIII (1948), 187-91.
———. "The Psychoanalytic Criticism of Literature," *WR*, XII (1948), 106-15.
———. "Modern Literary Criticism," *New Mexico Quarterly Review*, XVIII (1948).
———. "The Deflowering of New England," *HR*, II (1950), 600-12.
JARRELL, RANDALL. "The Obscurity of the Poet," *PR*, XVIII (1951), 66-81.
———. "Reflections on Wallace Stevens," *PR*, XVIII (1951), 335-44.

JONES, HOWARD MUMFORD. "Literary Scholarship and Contemporary Criticism," *English Journal*, XXIII (1934), 740–58.

———. "The Limits of Contemporary Criticism," *SRL*, XXIV (1941), 3–4, 17.

———. *The Theory of American Literature*. Ithaca, N.Y., 1949.

JORDAN, ELIJAH. *Essays in Criticism*. Chicago, 1952.

KAZIN, ALFRED. "Mr. Brooks's New England," *PR*, VII (1940), 402–5.

———. *On Native Grounds: An Interpretation of Modern Prose Literature*. New York, 1942.

———. "Faulkner: The Rhetoric and the Agony," *VQR*, XVIII (1942), 389–402.

———. "The Inmost Leaf" (Melville), *NR*, CXI (1944), 840–41.

———. *F. Scott Fitzgerald*. Cleveland, 1951.

KRUTCH, JOSEPH WOOD. *Edgar Allan Poe*. New York, 1926.

———. "Realism and Drama," *N*, CXXXIII (1931), 440–41.

———. "Philosophical Criticism," *N*, CXXXIV (1932), 407–8.

———. *Experience and Art: Some Aspects of the Esthetics of Literature*. New York, 1932.

———. "A Poem Is a Poem" (On Eliot), *N*, CXLII (1936), 679–80.

———. "On the Difficulty of Modern Poetry," *N*, CXLII (1936), 283–84.

———. "New, Newer, Newest" (Vogues in criticism), *N*, CLXXI (1950), 62–63.

LEWISOHN, LUDWIG. *Expression in America*. New York, 1932.

LEVIN, HARRY (ed.). *Perspectives of Criticism*. Cambridge, 1950.

———. "What Is Realism?" *Contemporary Literature*, III (1951), 193–99.

LOVEJOY, A. O. " 'Nature' as Aesthetic Norm," *MLN*, XLII (1927), 444–50.

LOWELL, AMY. *Six French Poets*. Boston, 1915.

———. *Tendencies in Modern American Poetry*. Boston, 1917.

———. "Walt Whitman and the New Poetry," *YR*, XVI (1927), 502–19.

———. *Poetry and Poets*. Boston, 1930.

LOWES, JOHN L. *Convention and Revolt in Poetry*. Boston, 1919, 1922.

———. *The Road to Xanadu*. London, 1927.

LUBBOCK, PERCY. *The Craft of Fiction*. New York, 1921.

MACLEISH, ARCHIBALD. "The Social Cant," *NR*, LXXIII (1932), 156–58.

———. "Poetry and the Public World," *AM*, CLXIII (1939), 823–31.

———. *The Irresponsibles*. New York, 1940.

———. *Poetry and Opinion*. Urbana, Ill., 1950.

MACY, JOHN. *The Spirit of American Literature*. New York, 1913.

———. *The Critical Game*. New York, 1922.

———. *American Writers on American Literature*. New York, 1931.

MATTHIESSEN, F. O. "Eliot's Quartets," *KR*, V (1943), 161–78.

———. "James and the Plastic Arts," *KR*, V (1943), 533–50.

———. "Henry James's Portrait of the Artist," *PR*, XI (1944), 71–87.

———. "The Problem of the Private Poet" (Emily Dickinson), *KR*, VII (1945), 584–97.

———. "Poe," *SeR*, LIV (1946), 175–205.

———. "American Poetry 1920–1940," *SeR*, LV (1947), 25–55.

———. *Theodore Dreiser*. New York, 1951.

———. *The Responsibilities of the Critic*. Selected by John Rackliffe. New York, 1952.

MCKEON, RICHARD. "The Philosophical Bases of Art and Criticism," *MP*, XLI (1943–1944), 65–87, 129–71.

MENCKEN, H. L. *A Book of Prefaces*. New York, 1917.

———. *Prejudices*. (Six series, 1919–1927)

———. "James Huneker," *Century*, CII (1921), 191–97

———. "The Motive of the Critic," *NR*, XXVIII (1921), 249–51.

———. "The American Tradition," *Literary Review*, IV (1923), 277–78.

———. *Selected Prejudices*. New York, 1927.

MONROE, HARRIET. *Poets and Their Art*. New York, 1926, 1932.

MOORE, MARIANNE. "The Cantos," *P*, XXXIX (1931), 37–50.

MOORE, MARIANNE. "Emily Dickinson," P, XLI (1933), 219–26.
———. "Henry James as a Characteristic American," HH, VII (1934), 363–72.
———. " 'It Is Not Forbidden to Think' " (On Eliot), N, CXLII (1935), 680–81.
———. "The Poetry of Wallace Stevens," P, XLIX (1937), 268–73.
———. "Feeling and Precision," SeR, LII (1944), 499–507.
MORE, PAUL ELMER. Shelburne Essays. (Eleven volumes, 1904–1921, of which the last four carried individual titles: The Drift of Romanticism (1913); Aristocracy and Justice (1915); With the Wits (1919); A New England Group and Others (1921).)
———. The New Shelburne Essays: The Demon of the Absolute. New York, 1928.
———. "The Modern Current in American Literature," F, LXXIX (1928), 127–36.
———. "The Revival of Humanism," B, LXXI (1930), 1–11.
———. "The Cleft Eliot," SRL, IX (1932), 233.
———. "Irving Babbitt," AR, III (1934), 23–40.
———. Selected Shelburne Essays. New York, 1935.
———. "The Modernism of French Poetry," AR, V (1935), 329–48.
———. On Being Human. Princeton, 1936.
MUMFORD, LEWIS. "The Emergence of a Past," NR, XLV (1925), 18–19.
———. Herman Melville. New York, 1929.
———. "The Image of Randolph Bourne," NR, LXIV (1930), 151–52.
O'CONNOR, WILLIAM VAN. "Shapiro on Rime," KR, VIII (1946), 113–22.
———. "The Little Magazine as a Cultural Journal," P, LXXII (1948), 339–42.
———. Sense and Sensibility in Modern Poetry. Chicago, 1948.
——— (ed.). Forms of Modern Fiction. Minneapolis, 1948.
———. The Shaping Spirit: A Study of Wallace Stevens. Chicago, 1950.
OLSON, ELDER. "The Argument of Longinus' On the Sublime," MP, XXXIX (1942), 225–58.
———. "Recent Literary Criticism," MP, XL (1943), 275–83.
———. "William Empson, Contemporary Criticism and Poetic Diction," MP, XLVII (1950), 222–52.
POUND, EZRA. The Spirit of Romance. London, 1910.
———. "In Explanation," "Brief Note," "A Shake Down," and "The Middle Years" (All on James), Little Review, V (1918), 5–41.
———. Instigations. New York, 1920.
———. "On Criticism in General," Criterion, I (1923), 143–56.
———. Make It New. New Haven, 1935.
———. The Letters of Ezra Pound. New York, 1946.
RAHV, PHILIP. "Proletarian Literature: A Political Autopsy," SR, IV (1939), 616–28.
———. Image and Idea. New York, 1949.
———. "Melville and His Critics," PR, XVII (1950), 732–35.
RANSOM, JOHN CROWE. God Without Thunder. New York, 1930.
———. "The Aesthetics of Regionalism," AR, II (1934), 290–310.
———. "The Tense of Poetry," SR, I (1935), 221–38.
———. The World's Body. New York, 1938.
———. "The Pragmatics of Art," KR, II (1940), 76–87.
———. The New Criticism. New York, 1941.
———. "The Bases of Criticism," SeR, LII (1944), 556–71.
———. "Poetry: The Formal Analysis," KR, IX (1947), 436–56.
———. "Poetry: The Final Cause," KR, IX (1947), 640–58.
———. "The Literary Criticism of Aristotle," KR, X (1948), 382–402.
———. "The Understanding of Fiction," KR, XII (1950), 189–218.
———. "William Wordsworth," KR, XII (1950), 498–519.
———. "The Poetry of 1900–1950," KR, XIII (1951), 445–54.
——— (ed.). The Kenyon Critics. New York, 1951.
———. "A Symposium: The Agrarians Today," Shenandoah, III (1952), 14–33.

SCHWARTZ, DELMORE. "Ernest Hemingway's Literary Situation," *SR*, III (1938), 769-89.

———. "John Dos Passos and the Whole Truth," *SR*, IV (1938), 351-67.

———. "*The Criterion*: 1922-1939," *KR*, I (1939), 437-50.

———. "The Poetry of Allen Tate," *SR*, V (1940), 419-38.

———. "The Isolation of Modern Poetry," *KR*, III (1941), 209-20.

———. "The Fiction of William Faulkner," *SR*, VII (1941), 145-60.

———. "T. S. Eliot as the International Hero," *PR*, XII (1945), 199-206.

———. "The Vocation of the Poet in the Modern World," *Poetry*, LXXVIII (1951), 223-32.

SHAPIRO, KARL. *Essay on Rime*. New York, 1947.

———. "English Prosody and Modern Poetry," *ELH*, XIV (1947), 77-92.

———. "A Farewell to Criticism," *P*, LXXI (1948), 196-217.

———. "Prosody as Meaning," *Poetry*, LXXIII (1949), 336-51.

SHERMAN, STUART P. *Americans*. New York, 1922.

———. *The Genius of America*. New York, 1923.

———. *The Main Stream*. New York, 1927.

SHIPLEY, JOSEPH T. *The Quest for Literature*. New York, 1931.

——— (ed.). *Dictionary of World Literature*. New York, 1943.

SINCLAIR, UPTON. *Mammonart*. New York, 1924.

SPENCER, THEODORE. "The Critic's Function," *SeR*, XLVII (1939), 552-58.

SPURGEON, CAROLINE. *Shakespeare's Imagery and What It Tells Us*. New York, 1935.

STALLMAN, ROBERT W. *Critiques and Essays in Criticism: 1920-1948*. New York, 1949.

———, and WEST, RAY B., JR. *The Art of Modern Fiction*. New York, 1949.

———. *The Critic's Notebook*. Minneapolis, 1950.

STAUFFER, DONALD (ed.). *The Intent of the Critic*. Princeton, 1941. (Four essays forming a symposium on the nature and motives of modern criticism, by Edmund Wilson, Norman Foerster, John Crowe Ransom, and W. H. Auden. The essays were given as lectures at Princeton in 1940-1941.)

———. *The Nature of Poetry*. New York, 1946.

———. "The Reading of a Lyric," *KR*, XI (1949), 426-40.

TATE, ALLEN. "Poetry and the Absolute," *SR*, XXXV (1927), 41-52.

———. "New England Culture and Emily Dickinson," *Sym*, III (1932), 206-26.

———. *Reactionary Essays on Poetry and Ideas*. New York, 1936.

———. "Tension in Poetry," *SR*, IV (1938), 101-15.

———. "Literature as Knowledge: Comment and Comparison," *SR*, VI (1941), 629-57.

———. *Reason in Madness: Critical Essays*. New York, 1941.

——— (ed.). *The Language of Poetry*. Princeton, 1942.

——— (ed.). *A Southern Vanguard*. New York, 1947.

———. *On the Limits of Poetry*. New York, 1948.

———. "Longinus," *HR*, I (1948), 344-61.

———. "Johnson on the Metaphysicals," *KR*, XI (1949), 377-94.

———. "Our Cousin, Mr. Poe," *PR*, XVI (1949), 1207-19.

———. *The Hovering Fly*. New York, 1949.

———. "Three Commentaries: Poe, James, Joyce," *SeR*, LVIII (1950), 1-15.

———. "Orthodoxy and the Standard of Literature," *NR* (Jan. 5, 1953), 24-25.

———. *Forlorn Demon*. Chicago, 1953.

TRILLING, LIONEL. *Matthew Arnold*. New York, 1939.

———. "Literary and Aesthetic," *KR*, II (1940), 152-73.

———. "Parrington, Mr. Smith and Reality," *PR*, VII (1940), 24-40.

———. "Sherwood Anderson," *KR*, III (1941), 293-302.

———. *E. M. Forster*. New York, 1943.

———. "Sermon on a Text from Whitman," *N*, CLX (1945), 215-16, 218-20.

———. "The Life of the Novel," *KR*, VIII (1946), 658-67.

TRILLING, LIONEL. "Manners, Morals and the Novel," *KR*, XII (1948), 477–97.
——. *The Liberal Imagination*. New York, 1950.
——. "W. D. Howells and the Roots of Modern Taste," *PR*, XVIII (1951), 516–36.
TUVE, ROSAMUND. *Elizabethan and Metaphysical Imagery*. Chicago, 1947.
UNDERWOOD, JOHN C. *Literature and Insurgency*. New York, 1914.
UNGER, LEONARD. *T. S. Eliot: A Selected Critique*. New York, 1948.
VAN DOREN, CARL. "The Flower of Puritanism," *N*, CXI (1920), 649–50.
——. *The American Novel*. New York, 1921; revised edition, 1940.
——. *Contemporary American Novelists*. New York, 1922.
——. "The Soil of the Puritans," *Century*, CV (1923), 629–36.
——. "American Realism," *NR*, XXXIV (1923), 107–9.
——. "Stephen Crane," *American Mercury*, I (1924), 11–14.
——. *American Literature: An Introduction*. New York, 1933.
——. *Benjamin Franklin*. New York, 1938. 3 vols.
VAN DOREN, MARK. "The Progress of Poetry," *N*, CXII (1921), 883–85.
——. *Edwin Arlington Robinson*. New York, 1927.
——. "What Is a Poet?" *N*, CXXXIV (1932), 624–25.
——. "The Art of American Fiction," *N*, CXXXVIII (1934), 471–73.
——. "Walt Whitman, Stranger," *American Mercury*, XXXV (1935), 277–85.
——. "The Achievements of Intellectualist Poetry," *AR*, VIII (1937), 449–56.
——. "The Happy Critic," *N*, CLXVIII (1949), 663.
——. *Nathaniel Hawthorne*. New York, 1949.
——. *Enjoying Poetry*. New York, 1951.
VIVAS, ELISEO. "The New Naturalism," *KR*, III (1941), 445–59.
——. "The Objective Correlative of T. S. Eliot," *American Bookman*, I (1944), 7–18.
——. "The Objective Basis of Criticism," *WR*, XII (1948), 197–210.
WARREN, AUSTIN. "The Criticism of Meaning," *SeR*, XLVI (1938), 213–22.
——. "Edward Taylor's Poetry: Colonial Baroque," *KR*, III (1941), 355–71.
——. "Literary Criticism," in *Literary Scholarship*. Chapel Hill, N.C., 1941.
——. "The Case of Vachel Lindsay," *A*, VI (1946), 320–39.
——. *Rage for Order: Essays in Criticism*. Chicago, 1948.
——, and WELLEK, RENÉ. *The Theory of Literature*. New York, 1949.
——. "My Credo: The Teacher as Critic," *KR*, XIII (1951), 225–30.
WARREN, ROBERT PENN. "The Reading of Modern Poetry" (with Cleanth Brooks), *AR*, VIII (1937), 435–49.
——, and BROOKS, CLEANTH. *Understanding Poetry*. New York, 1938; revised edition, 1951.
——. "Pure and Impure Poetry," *KR*, V (1943), 228–54.
——. "The Love and the Separateness in Miss Welty," *KR*, VI (1944), 246–59.
——. "Melville the Poet," *KR*, VIII (1946), 208–23.
——. *The Rime of the Ancient Mariner*. New York, 1946.
——. "Hemingway," *KR*, IX (1947), 1–28.
——. "A Note to *All the King's Men*," *SeR*, LXI (1953), 476–80.
WELLEK, RENÉ. "The Mode of Existence of a Literary Work of Art," *SR*, VII (1942), 735–54.
——, and AUSTIN, WARREN. *The Theory of Literature*. New York, 1949.
WHARTON, EDITH. *The Writing of Fiction*. New York, 1925.
WHITEHEAD, A. N. *Symbolism: Its Meaning and Effect*. New York, 1927, 1937.
WILLIAMS, WILLIAM CARLOS. "Marianne Moore," *D*, LXXVIII (1925), 393–401.
——. "An Approach to the Poem," in *English Institute Essays: 1947*. New York, 1948.
——. "Carl Sandburg's Complete Poems," *Poetry*, LXXVIII (1951), 345–51.
WILSON, EDMUND. *Axel's Castle: A Study of the Imaginative Literature of 1870–1930*. New York, 1931.

WILSON, EDMUND. "Art, the Proletariat, and Marx," *NR*, LXXVI (1933), 41–45.
———. "The Myth of the Marxist Dialectic," *PR*, VI (1938), 66–81.
———. *The Triple Thinkers*. New York, 1938; revised edition, 1948.
———. "Ernest Hemingway," *AM*, CLXIV (1939), 36–46.
———. "Literary Criticism and History," *AM*, CLXVIII (1941), 610–17.
———. *The Wound and the Bow*. New York, 1941.
———. "Poe as a Literary Critic," *N*, CLV (1942), 452–53.
——— (ed.). *The Shock of Recognition: The Development of Literature in the United States Recorded by the Men Who Made It*. New York, 1943.
———. *Classics and Commercials: A Literary Chronicle of the Forties*. New York, 1950.
———. "Edna St. Vincent Millay: A Memoir," *N*, CLXXIV (1952), 370–83.
———. *The Shores of Light*. New York, 1952.
WIMSATT, W. K., JR. "The Structure of the Concrete Universal," *PMLA*, LXII (1947), 262–80.
———. "The Affective Fallacy" (with M. C. Beardsley), *SeR*, LVII (1949), 31–55.
———. "History and Criticism, a Problematic Relationship," *PMLA*, LXVI (1951), 21–31.
WINTERS, YVOR. *Notes on the Mechanics of the Poetic Image*. New York, 1925.
———. "The Symbolist Influence," *HH*, IV (1931), 607–18.
———. *Primitivism and Decadence*. New York, 1937.
———. *Maule's Curse: Seven Studies in the History of American Obscurantism*. New York, 1938.
———. "T. S. Eliot: The Illusion of Reaction," *KR*, III (1941), 7–30, 221–39.
———. *The Anatomy of Nonsense*. New York, 1943.
———. *In Defense of Reason*. New York, 1947.
———. *Edwin Arlington Robinson*. New York, 1947.
———. "Robert Frost," *SeR*, LVI (1948), 568–70.
———. "The Audible Reading of Poetry," *HR*, IV (1951), 433–47.
ZABEL, MORTON D. "Towards Standards of Criticism," *P*, XLV (1934), 40–46.
———. "Rimbaud: Life and Legend," *PR*, VII (1940), 268–82.
———. "Joseph Conrad: Chance and Recognition," *SeR*, LIII (1945), 1–22.
———. "Willa Cather," *N*, CLXIV (1947), 713–16.

SECONDARY WORKS: GENERAL

ALDRIDGE, JOHN W. *After the Lost Generation*. New York, 1951.
BERNBAUM, ERNEST. "The Practical Results of the Humanistic Theories," *English Journal*, XX (1931), 103–9.
BOYD, ERNEST. "Marxian Literary Critics," *Scribner's*, XCVIII (1935), 342–46.
BROOKS, VAN WYCK. *The Confident Years, 1885–1915*. New York, 1951.
BUCK, GERTRUDE. *The Social Criticism of Literature*. New Haven, 1916.
CANBY, HENRY S. "The Expressionists," *Literary Review*, III (1922), 285–86.
———. "The New Humanists," *SRL*, VI (1930), 749–51.
COLLINS, SEWARD. "Criticism in America," *B*, LXXI (1930), 241–56, 353–64, 400–15; LXXII (1930), 145–64.
CORY, H. E. "Psychoanalysis and Literary Criticism," *University of California Publications in Modern Philology*, XI (1928), 187–94.
COWLEY, MALCOLM. " 'Not Men': A Natural History of American Naturalism," *KR*, IX (1947), 414–35.
———. "Naturalism in American Literature," in *Evolutionary Thought in America*, ed. by Stow Persons. New Haven, 1950.
CURTI, MERLE. *The Growth of American Thought*. New York, 1943.
DAICHES, DAVID. "The Scope of Sociological Criticism," *Epoch*, III (1950), 57–64.
DE MILLE, GEORGE E. *Literary Criticism in America*. New York, 1931.

DODDS, A. E., MRS. *The Romantic Theory of Poetry, an Examination in the Light of Croce's Aesthetic.* New York, 1926.

FARRELL, JAMES T. "Social Themes in American Realism," *English Journal,* XXXV (1946), 309–14.

——. "Some Observations on Naturalism, So Called, in American Fiction," *Antioch Review,* X (1950), 247–64.

FOERSTER, NORMAN. *Toward Standards: A Study of the Present Critical Movement in American Letters.* New York, 1930.

GLICKSBERG, C. I. "Two Decades of American Criticism," *Dalhousie Review,* XVI (1936), 229–42.

——. "The Decline of Literary Marxism," *Antioch Review,* I (1941), 452–62.

—— (ed.). *American Literary Criticism, 1900–1950.* New York, 1951.

GOHDES, C. F. "The Theme-Song of American Criticism," *University of Toronto Quarterly,* VI (1936), 49–65.

GRATTAN, C. HARTLEY. "The Present Situation in American Criticism," *SeR,* XL (1932), 11–23.

HEALY, J. V. "Contemporary Poetry Criticism," *Poetry,* LXI (1943), 672–80.

HOFFMAN, FREDERICK J., ALLEN, CHARLES, and ULRICH, CAROLYN. *The Little Magazine: A History and a Bibliography.* Princeton, 1946.

——, and VICKERY, OLGA. *William Faulkner: Two Decades of Criticism.* East Lansing, Mich., 1951.

——. *Freudianism and the Literary Mind.* Baton Rouge, La., 1945.

——. "Psychoanalysis and Literary Criticism," *American Quarterly,* II (1950), 144–54.

HYMAN, STANLEY E. "Marxist Literary Criticism," *Antioch Review,* VII (1947), 541–68.

——. "The Psychoanalytic Criticism of Literature," *WR,* XII (1948), 106–15.

——. *The Armed Vision: A Study in the Methods of Modern Literary Criticism.* New York, 1948.

JARRELL, RANDALL. "Contemporary Poetry Criticism," *NR,* CV (1941), 88–90.

JONES, HOWARD MUMFORD. *The Bright Medusa.* Urbana, Ill., 1952.

KAZIN, ALFRED. *On Native Grounds.* New York, 1942.

LOWELL, AMY. *Tendencies in Modern American Poetry.* Boston, 1917.

MERCIER, LOUIS J. A. *Le Mouvement Humaniste aux Etats-Unis.* Paris, 1928.

MULLER, HERBERT J. "Pathways in Recent Criticism," *SR,* IV (1939), 187–208.

——. *Science and Criticism.* New Haven, 1943.

MUNSON, G. B. "The Young Critics of the Nineteen-Twenties," *B,* LXX (1929), 369–73.

NOYES, ALFRED. "Longfellow and Modern Critics," in *Some Aspects of Modern Poetry.* New York, 1924.

O'CONNOR, WILLIAM VAN. "The Aesthetic Emphasis Before the Moderns," *New Mexico Quarterly Review,* XVII (1947), 5–16.

——. *An Age of Criticism 1900–1950.* Chicago, 1952.

RODNEY, W. J. *The Problem of 'Poetry and Belief' in Contemporary Criticism.* Washington, 1949.

SMITH, BERNARD. *Forces in American Criticism.* New York, 1939.

STEWART, RANDALL. "The Social School of American Criticism," *South Atlantic Quarterly,* XLIII (1944), 22–26.

THORPE, CLARENCE, and NORMAN, NELSON. "Criticism in the Twentieth Century: A Bird's Eye View," *English Journal,* XXXVI (1947), 165–73.

UNGER, LEONARD. *Donne's Poetry and Modern Criticism.* Chicago, 1950.

VIVAS, ELISEO. "Criticism and the Little Magazines," *WR,* XVI (1951), 9–18.

WARREN, AUSTIN. "The Achievement of Some Recent Critics," *Poetry,* LXXVII (1951).

WOODWARD, BARBARA. *Theories of Meaning in Poetry, 1915–1940: A Critical History.* Unpublished dissertation, University of Michigan, 1946.

ZABEL, MORTON D. *Literary Opinion in America.* New York, 1937; revised edition, 1951. Introduction.

ZABEL, MORTON D. "The Condition of American Criticism," *English Journal*, XVIII (1939), 417–28.

On the "New Criticism":

Baum, Bernard. "Corpus Delicti: Some Letters Mainly Concerned with the New Criticism," *South Atlantic Quarterly*, LI (1952), 261–75.

Brooks, Cleanth. "The New Criticism: A Brief for the Defense," *AS*, XIII (1944), 435–49.

Bush, Douglas. "The New Criticism: Some Old-Fashioned Queries," *PMLA*, LXIV (1949), 13–21.

Daiches, David. "The New Criticism: Some Qualifications," *English Journal*, XXXIX (1950), 64–72; *CE*, XI (1950), 242–50

Davis, Robert G. "The New Criticism and the Democratic Tradition," *AS*, XIX (1949–1950), 9–19.

Elton, William. *A Glossary of the New Criticism*. Chicago, 1948.

Muller, Herbert J. "The New Criticism in Poetry," *SR*, VI (1941), 811–39.

O'Connor, William Van. "This Alexandrian Criticism," *AS*, XIV (1945), 357–61.

———. "A Short View of the New Criticism," *CE*, XXXVIII (1949), 489–97.

Olson, Elder. "Recent Literary Criticism," *MP*, XL (1943), 275–83.

Ong, Walter J. "The Meaning of the 'New Criticism,'" in *Twentieth Century English*, ed. by W. S. Knickerbocker. New York, 1946.

Stallman, Robert W. "The New Criticism and the Southern Critics," in *A Southern Vanguard*, ed. by Allen Tate. New York, 1947.

———. "The New Critics," in *Critiques and Essays in Criticism: 1920–1948*, selected by Robert W. Stallman. New York, 1949.

Trowbridge, H. "Aristotle and the 'New Criticism,'" *SeR*, LII (1944), 537–55.

SECONDARY WORKS: ON INDIVIDUAL AUTHORS

On Babbitt:

Blackmur, R. P. "Humanism and Symbolic Imagination: Notes on Rereading Irving Babbitt," *SR*, VII (1941), 309–25.

Eliot, T. S. "The Humanism of Irving Babbitt," *F*, LXXX (1928), 37–44.

Elliott, G. R. "T. S. Eliot and Irving Babbitt," *AR*, VII (1936), 442–54.

Manchester, Frederick, and Shepard, Odell. *Irving Babbitt*. New York, 1941.

Mercier, Louis J. A. *Le Mouvement Humaniste aux Etats-Unis*. Paris, 1928.

More, Paul Elmer. "Irving Babbitt," *AR*, III (1934), 23–40.

Pritchard, John P. "Irving Babbitt," in *Return to the Fountains*. Durham, N.C., 1942.

Wilson, Edmund. "Notes on Babbitt and More," *NR*, LXII (1930), 115–20.

On Blackmur:

Hyman, Stanley E. "R. P. Blackmur and the Expense of Greatness," in *The Armed Vision*. New York, 1948.

Lewis, R. W. B. "Casella as Critic: A Note on R. P. Blackmur," *KR*, XIII (1951), 458–74.

Schwartz, Delmore. "The Critical Method of R. P. Blackmur," *Poetry*, LIII (1938), 28–39.

Tate, Allen. "R. P. Blackmur," *SR*, III (1937), 183–98.

West, Ray B., Jr. "An Examination of Modern Critics: R. P. Blackmur," *Rocky Mountain Review*, VIII (1945), 139–45.

On Brooks, Cleanth:

Crane, R. S. "Cleanth Brooks," *MP*, XLV (1948), 226–45.

Strauss, A. B. "The Poetic Theory of Cleanth Brooks," *Centenary Review*, I (1949), 10–22.

On Brooks, Van Wyck:
Cargill, Oscar. "The Ordeal of Van Wyck Brooks," *CE*, VIII (1946), 55–61.
Collins, Seward. "Criticism in America: The Origins of a Myth," *B*, LXXI (1930), 241–56, 353–64.
Glicksberg, C. I. "Van Wyck Brooks," *SeR*, XLIII (1935), 175–86.
Hyman, Stanley E. "Van Wyck Brooks and Biographical Criticism," in *The Armed Vision*. New York, 1948.
Jones, Howard Mumford. "The Pilgrimage of Van Wyck Brooks," *VQR*, VIII (1932), 439–42.
Steinlein, Leo J. *The Critical Theories of Van Wyck Brooks*. Unpublished dissertation, New York University, 1948.
Wellek, René. "Van Wyck Brooks and a National Literature," *AP*, VII (1942), 292–306.
Wilson, Edmund. "Imaginary Conversations: Mr. Van Wyck Brooks and Mr. Scott Fitzgerald," *NR*, XXXVIII (1924), 249–54.

On Brownell:
Bandler, Bernard, II. "The Humanism of W. C. Brownell," *HH*, II (1929), 205–22.
Campbell, Harry M. *A Critical Study of W. C. Brownell*. Unpublished dissertation, Vanderbilt University, 1942.
Mercier, Louis J. A. *Le Mouvement Humaniste aux Etats-Unis*. Paris, 1928.
———. "W. C. Brownell and Our Neo-Barbarism," *F*, LXXXI (1929), 376–81.
Wharton, Edith. "William C. Brownell," *Scribner's*, LXXXIV (1928), 596–602.

On Burke:
Bewley, Marius. "Kenneth Burke as Literary Critic," *Scrutiny*, XV (1948), 254–77.
Glicksberg, C. I. "Kenneth Burke: The Critics' Critic," *South Atlantic Quarterly*, XXXVI (1937), 74–84.
Hyman, Stanley E. "Kenneth Burke and the Criticism of Symbolic Action," in *The Armed Vision*. New York, 1948.
Nemerov, Howard. "A Note on the Terms of Kenneth Burke," *Furioso*, II (1947), 29–42.
Warren, Austin. "Kenneth Burke: His Mind and Art," *SeR*, XLI (1933), 344–63.

On Eliot:
Blackmur, R. P. "In the Hope of Straightening Things Out," *KR*, XIII (1951), 303–14.
Brombert, Victor. *The Criticism of T. S. Eliot*. New Haven, 1949.
Campbell, Harry M. "An Examination of Modern Critics: T. S. Eliot," *Rocky Mountain Review*, VIII (1944), 128–38.
Child, Ruth C. "The Early Critical Work of T. S. Eliot: An Assessment," *CE*, XII (1951), 269–75.
Daiches, David. "T. E. Hulme and T. S. Eliot," in *Poetry and the Modern World*. Chicago, 1940.
Daniells, J. R. "T. S. Eliot and His Relation to T. E. Hulme," *University of Toronto Quarterly*, II (1933), 380–96.
Elliott, G. R. "T. S. Eliot and Irving Babbitt," *AR*, VII (1936), 442–54.
Glicksberg, C. I. "T. S. Eliot as Critic," *Arizona Quarterly*, IV (1948), 225–36.
Hyman, Stanley E. "T. S. Eliot and Tradition in Criticism," in *The Armed Vision*. New York, 1948.
Kronenberger, Louis. "T. S. Eliot as Critic," *N*, CXL (1935), 452–53.
Matthiessen, F. O. *The Achievement of T. S. Eliot*. New York, 1948.
Maloney, Michael F. "Mr. Eliot and Critical Tradition," *Thought*, XXI (1946), 455–74.
Nicoll, Allardyce. "Mr. T. S. Eliot and the Revival of Classicism," *English Journal*, XXIII (1934), 269–78.

Ransom, John Crowe. "T. S. Eliot: The Historical Critic," in *The New Criticism*. New York, 1941.
Unger, Leonard (ed.). *T. S. Eliot: A Selected Critique*. New York, 1948.
Vivas, Eliseo. "The Objective Correlative of T. S. Eliot," *American Bookman*, I (1944), 7–18.
Wilson, Edmund. "T. S. Eliot," in *Axel's Castle*. New York, 1931.
Winters, Yvor. "T. S. Eliot: or, The Illusion of Reaction," in *The Anatomy of Nonsense*. Norfolk, Conn., 1943.

On Farrell:
Glicksberg, C. I. "The Criticism of James T. Farrell," *Southwest Review*, XXXV (1950), 189–96.
Howe, Irving. "James T. Farrell as Critic," *PR*, XIV (1947), 545–52.

On Hicks:
Farrell, James T. "Mr. Hicks: Critical Vulgarian," *American Spectator*, IV (1936), 21–26.
Glicksberg, C. I. "Granville Hicks and Marxist Criticism," *SeR*, XLV (1937), 129–40.

On Krutch:
Beach, Joseph Warren. "Mr. Krutch and Ideal Values in Literature," *International Journal of Ethics*, XLVIII (1938), 487–97.
Glicksberg, C. I. "Joseph Wood Krutch: Critic of Despair," *SeR*, XLIV (1936), 77–93.

On Matthiessen:
Ransom, John Crowe. "Responsible Criticism" (on Matthiessen), *SeR*, LXI (1953), 300–3.

On Mencken:
Babbitt, Irving. "The Critic and American Life," *F*, LXXIX (1928), 161–76.
Boyd, Ernest A. *H. L. Mencken*. New York, 1925.
Brooks, Van Wyck. "Mr. Mencken and the Prophets," in *Sketches in Criticism*. New York, 1932.
Kemler, Edgar. *The Irreverent Mr. Mencken*. Boston, 1950.
Manchester, William. *Disturber of the Peace: The Life of H. L. Mencken*. New York, 1951.
Pattee, Fred L. "A Critic in C Major," in *Side-Lights on American Literature*. New York, 1922.
Sherman, Stuart P. "Mr. Mencken, the Jeune Fille, and the New Spirit in Letters," in *Americans*. New York, 1922.
Van Doren, Carl. "Smartness and Light: H. L. Mencken," in *Many Minds*. New York, 1924.
Wilson, Edmund. "H. L. Mencken," *NR*, XXVII (1921), 10–13.

On More:
Brown, S. G. "Paul Elmer More as Critic," *SeR*, XLVII (1939), 476–97.
Gregory, Horace. "On Paul Elmer More and His Shelburne Essays," *A*, IV (1944), 140–49.
Pritchard, John P. "Paul Elmer More," in *Return to the Fountains*. Durham, N.C., 1942.
Shafer, Robert. *Paul Elmer More and American Criticism*. New Haven, 1935.
Wilson, Edmund. "Notes on Babbitt and More," *NR*, LXII (1930), 115–20.
Zoller, William. *Paul Elmer More's Literary Criticism*. Unpublished dissertation, University of California, 1946.

On Pound:
Russell, Peter (ed.). *An Examination of Ezra Pound*. New York, 1950.
West, Ray B., Jr. "Ezra Pound and Contemporary Criticism," *WR*, V (1949), 192–200.

On Ransom:

Blum, Morgan. "John Crowe Ransom, Critic," *WR*, XIV (1950), 85–102.

Burgum, Edwin B. "An Examination of Modern Critics: John Crowe Ransom," *Rocky Mountain Review*, VIII (1944), 87–93.

Mills, Gordon H. *Ontology and Myth in the Criticism of John Crowe Ransom.* Unpublished dissertation, University of Iowa, 1943.

Stocking, Fred H. *Poetry as Knowledge: The Critical Theory of John Crowe Ransom and Allen Tate.* Unpublished dissertation, University of Michigan, 1946.

On Tate:

Amyx, Clifford. "The Aesthetics of Allen Tate," *WR*, XIII (1949), 135–44.

Beatty, Richmond C. "Allen Tate as Man of Letters," *South Atlantic Quarterly*, XLVII (1948), 226–41.

Stocking, Fred H. *Poetry as Knowledge: The Critical Theory of John Crowe Ransom and Allen Tate.* Unpublished dissertation, University of Michigan, 1946.

On Wilson:

Adams, R. "Masks and Delays: Edmund Wilson as Critic," *SeR*, LVI (1948), 272–86.

Brown, E. K. "The Method of Edmund Wilson," *University of Toronto Quarterly*, XI (1941), 105–11.

Dolmatch, Theodore. "Edmund Wilson as Literary Critic," *University of Kansas City Review*, XVII (1951), 213–19.

Dupee, F. W. "Edmund Wilson's Criticism," *PR*, IV (1938), 48–51.

Hyman, Stanley E. "Edmund Wilson and Translation in Criticism," in *The Armed Vision.* New York, 1948.

Schwartz, Delmore. "The Writing of Edmund Wilson," *A*, II (1942), 177–86.

Snell, George. "An Examination of Modern Critics: Edmund Wilson," *Rocky Mountain Review*, VIII (1944), 36–44.

On Winters:

Blackmur, R. P. "A Note on Yvor Winters," *Poetry*, LVII (1940), 144–52.

Hyman, Stanley E. "Yvor Winters and Evaluation in Criticism," in *The Armed Vision.* New York, 1948.

Ransom, John Crowe. "Yvor Winters: The Logical Critic," *SR*, VI (1941), 558–83.

West, Ray B., Jr. "The Language of Criticism," *Rocky Mountain Review*, VIII (1943), 12–13, 15.